New York
New Jersey &
Pennsylvania

a Lonely Planet travel survival kit

Tom Smallman
Michael Clark
David Ellis
Eric Wakin

New York, New Jersey & Pennsylvania

1st edition

Published by
Lonely Planet Publications

Head Office:	PO Box 617, Hawthorn, Vic 3122, Australia
Branches:	155 Filbert St, Suite 251, Oakland, CA 94607, USA
	10 Barley Mow Passage, Chiswick, London W4 4PH, UK
	71 bis rue du Cardinal Lemoine, 75005 Paris, France

Printed by
Colorcraft Ltd, Hong Kong

Photographs by

Michael Clark	Kim Grant	Tom Smallman
David Ellis	Jane Leet	Tony Wheeler
Rick Gerharter		

(SLSDC) Photo courtesy of St Lawerence Seaway Development Corporation

Front cover: Hans Hansen, Image Bank, Philadelphia doors
Title page: Michael Clark, upstate New York chairs

Published
June 1997

Although the author and publisher have tried to make the information as accurate as possible, they accept no responsibility for any loss, injury or inconvenience sustained by any person using this book.

National Library of Australia Cataloguing in Publication Data

Smallman, Tom.
New York, New Jersey & Pennsylvania.

1st ed.
Includes index.
ISBN 0 86442 408 6.

1. New York (State) – Guidebooks. 2. New Jersey - Guidebooks.
3. Pennsylvania - Guidebooks I. Clark, Michael, 1944-. II. Ellis, David, 1962-.
III. Title. (Series: Lonely Planet travel survival kit).

917.40443

Tom Smallman

Tom was born and raised in the UK and now lives in Melbourne, Australia. He had a number of jobs before joining Lonely Planet as an editor and is now working full time as an author. He has worked as co-author on Lonely Planet's guides to Canada, Ireland and Dublin.

David Ellis

David was born in New York City and attended university in Boston and Dublin, Ireland, earning a degree in journalism and international affairs. After graduating he wrote news for an affiliate of National Public Radio and spent a year in London writing for the *Economist*. Over the past decade he's worked as a writer, editor and reviewer at *Time* and *People* magazines covering politics and culture from New York and Washington, DC. His work has appeared in many publications, including the *New Republic*, the *Australian*, the *Times* of London and *Who Weekly*. He has lived in three of New York's five boroughs (Brooklyn, Manhattan and the Bronx) and currently resides on New York's Roosevelt Island in the middle of the East River – a site described in detail inside this guidebook.

Michael S Clark

Michael Stamatios Clark was born in Ohio, raised in California and made his first trip to upstate New York in 1969 upon returning from Malawi, East Africa, where he taught science as a Peace Corps volunteer service. He attended University of California at Los Angeles, and between global travels taught in Riverside, CA, for 13 years. He later attended the University of Hawaii before embarking on teaching assignments in Malaysia and Japan. When not on the road, he teaches English as a Second Language at the University of California at Berkeley, and lives in Oakland, CA, with his wife Janet, daughter Melina and son Alexander.

Eric Wakin

Eric Wakin was born in New York City and grew up there and in Maryland. After completing a BA in English at Columbia University, he traveled in South and Southeast Asia. He has since studied at Chiang Mai University, earned MAs in Asian studies and political science at the University of Michigan, and written *Anthropology Goes to War: Professional Ethics and Counterinsurgency in Thailand* (University of Wisconsin/Center for Southeast Asian Studies). He is now back in New York working on a doctorate in American history.

From the Authors

Tom Smallman My thanks to Sue Graefe for her patience and support; Narelle Graefe for the background information she supplied me with; Ian 'Two Sheds' Denson and Nick for their encyclopedic knowledge; Lindy Mark for being so efficient; Heather and John for the loan of their books; the staff at the Free Library of Philadelphia; Bruce Boucek at Rand McNally in Philadelphia; Barbara Pope for her insights into Philly life; the staff at the HI-AYH office in Philadelphia; Anne-Marie Rodriguez of Greyhound International in New York City; the many people in the tourist offices who answered my queries; and finally, but by no means least, the hard-working Lonely Planet staff in the Oakland office.

David Ellis First and foremost, I must thank Jane Leet for her uncommon patience, unstinting energy, infectious enthusiasm and constant support throughout this project. I couldn't have dreamed for a better partner to join me in my exploration of the city.

Lisa and David Furrule were always there when I needed them, true friends whom I could count on.

Special thanks goes to a number of people for their assistance along the way, including Larry Mondi, Tom Gliatto, Bill McCauley, Richard Lacayo, Susan Reed, David Anderson, Mark Solomon, Peter Grossman and Howard Chua-Eoan for their companionship and help while researching this project. David Grogan, Joe Poindexter, Carrie Zimmerman and Lisa McLaughlin kindly shared their intimate knowledge of the city, while Tom Meltzer, Valerie Wares, Chris Songal and Paul Foglino provided libidinous companionship. Special thanks goes to fellow authors David Seideman and Lynn Schnurnberger and Daniel Levy.

Many, many people assisted me with information along the way, including Barry Popik, Theresa Osborne and Illana Harlow of the Queens Council on the Arts, Byron Saunders of the Queens Historical Society, Joy Farber of the New Jersey Division of Travel and Tourism, the Staten Island Borough President's Office, and the Fariel family of the Sea Breeze Inn in Amagansett, Long Island.

I'd also like to thank the Oakland staff of LP for their energy and enthusiasm.

Michael S Clark Special thanks to the many New Yorkers who guided, sheltered and sustained me throughout my travels there: Peter Davis, Bev Lazaar, Stanley McGaughey, Jeannine Laverty, Nan Miranda, Field Horne, Art and Donna, Spencer, Kate, Alan and Gabby for musical inspiration. Thanks also to the Lonely Planet staffers for their great encouragement and guidance, especially Caroline Liou, Carolyn Hubbard, Michelle Gagne, Alex Guilbert, Hugh D'Andrade and transplanted New Yorkers Don Waful and Dave Skibinski. And thanks to Janet, my loyal and loving reader.

Eric Wakin Thanks to Dave and Audrey Balog; the Catskills Center for Conservation & Development; Ethel Crystal, Valerie Driscoll, Elizabeth Forero, Tom Hartman, Michael Hughes; Cathy Ondrick; Elizabeth Priest; Sam Savitt; Jay Sedlack; Dan and Keungsuk Sexton; Andrea and Peggy and Ross Shiman; Ann Stavish Licciardello; and especially family members and best friends Daniel, Edward, Francesca, Jeanette and Lawrence Wakin.

This Book

Tom Smallman was coordinating author for this book, and provided winning coverage of Pennsylvania. Michael Clark covered New York state and David Ellis intrepidly covered New York City, Long Island and New Jersey. Eric Wakin provided manuscript from which portions of this first edition were written.

From the Publisher

Michelle Gagne was project editor for the book; Tom Downs edited New York City and proofed, Don Gates also proofed.

Special thanks to Caroline Liou and Carolyn Hubbard for their years of advance work in pulling all the strings together.

The cartographers in the trenches were Beca Lafore, Rini Keagy, Chris Salcedo, Hayden 'Mr New York' Foell with additional assistance from Blake Summers and Melissa J Webster. They were commanded by Alex Guilbert, who also did some maps.

Layout and design duties were performed by Scott Summers and Hugh D'Andrade. Illustrations are provided by Hugh D'Andrade, Rini Keagy, Hayden Foell and Mark Butler.

Thanks to Dan Hess and Michael Ballard who provided nuggets on a few features of the region.

Thanks also to Neil Tilbury for providing manuscript from which portions of this first edition were written.

Warning & Request

Things change – prices go up, schedules change, good places go bad and bad places go bankrupt – nothing stays the same. So, if you find things better or worse, recently opened or long since closed, please tell us and help make the next edition even more accurate and useful.

We value all of the feedback we receive from travelers. Julie Young coordinates a small team that reads and acknowledges every letter, postcard and e-mail, and ensures that every morsel of information finds its way to the appropriate authors, editors and publishers. Everyone who writes to us will find their name in the next edition of the appropriate guide and will also receive a free subscription to our quarterly newsletter, *Planet Talk*. The very best contributions will be rewarded with a free Lonely Planet guide.

Excerpts from your correspondence may appear in updates (found in the end pages of reprints); new editions of this guide; in our newsletter, *Planet Talk*; or in the Postcards section of our website – so please let us know if you don't want your letter published or your name acknowledged.

Contents

Map Legend

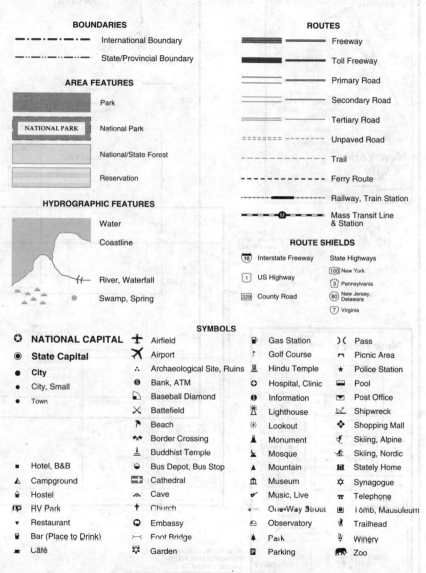

BOUNDARIES

— · — · — · — International Boundary

— · · — · · — · · State/Provincial Boundary

AREA FEATURES

Park

NATIONAL PARK National Park

National/State Forest

Reservation

HYDROGRAPHIC FEATURES

Water

Coastline

⊬⊬ River, Waterfall

◎ Swamp, Spring

ROUTES

Freeway

Toll Freeway

Primary Road

Secondary Road

Tertiary Road

===== ----- Unpaved Road

Trail

Ferry Route

Railway, Train Station

—M— Mass Transit Line & Station

ROUTE SHIELDS

⑩ Interstate Freeway

① US Highway

229 County Road

State Highways

100 New York

3 Pennsylvania

80 New Jersey, Delaware

7 Virginia

SYMBOLS

✪ **NATIONAL CAPITAL**
◉ **State Capital**
● **City**
● City, Small
● Town

■ Hotel, B&B
△ Campground
⌂ Hostel
🏕 RV Park
▼ Restaurant
🍷 Bar (Place to Drink)
☕ Café

✈ Airfield
✈ Airport
∴ Archaeological Site, Ruins
⑨ Bank, ATM
⚾ Baseball Diamond
✕ Battefield
⏹ Beach
✢ Border Crossing
⚊ Buddhist Temple
⊖ Bus Depot, Bus Stop
⊞ Cathedral
⌒ Cave
✝ Church
⊖ Embassy
⋈ Foot Bridge
❀ Garden

⛽ Gas Station
🏌 Golf Course
⚌ Hindu Temple
○ Hospital, Clinic
❶ Information
🏮 Lighthouse
✳ Lookout
▲ Monument
✦ Mosque
▲ Mountain
🏛 Museum
✔ Music, Live
◄ One-Way Street
⌂ Observatory
▲ Park
🅿 Parking

)(Pass
⋂ Picnic Area
★ Police Station
▭ Pool
✉ Post Office
⌔ Shipwreck
❖ Shopping Mall
⛷ Skiing, Alpine
⛷ Skiing, Nordic
🏛 Stately Home
✡ Synagogue
☎ Telephone
🏛 Tomb, Mausoleum
🏃 Trailhead
🍇 Winery
🐾 Zoo

Note: Not all symbols displayed above appear in this book.

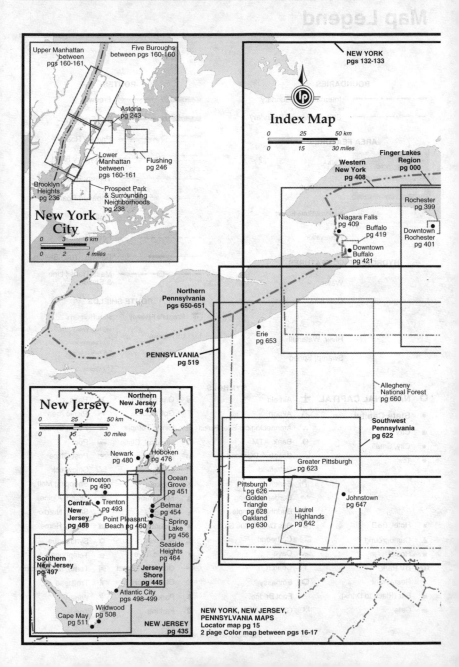

Map Legend

Index Map

NEW YORK
pgs 132-133

0   25   50 km
0   15   30 miles

Western
New York
pg 408

Finger Lakes
Region
pg 000

Rochester
pg 399

Niagara Falls
pg 409

Buffalo
pg 419

Downtown
Rochester
pg 401

Downtown
Buffalo
pg 421

Northern
Pennsylvania
pgs 650-651

Erie
pg 653

PENNSYLVANIA
pg 519

Allegheny
National Forest
pg 660

Southwest
Pennsylvania
pg 622

Greater Pittsburgh
pg 623

Pittsburgh
pg 626
Golden
Triangle
pg 628
Oakland
pg 630

Laurel
Highlands
pg 642

Johnstown
pg 647

Upper Manhattan
between
pgs 160-161

Five Buroughs
between pgs 160-160

Astoria
pg 243

Flushing
pg 246

Lower Manhattan
between pgs 160-161

Brooklyn
Heights
pg 236

Prospect Park
& Surrounding
Neighborhoods
pg 238

New York
City

0   3   6 km
0   2   4 miles

New Jersey

0   25   50 km
0   15   30 miles

Northern
New Jersey
pg 474

Newark
pg 480

Hoboken
pg 476

Princeton
pg 490

Ocean
Grove
pg 451

Central
New
Jersey
pg 488

Trenton
pg 493

Belmar
pg 454

Point Pleasant
Beach pg 460

Spring
Lake
pg 456

Seaside
Heights
pg 464

Southern
New Jersey
pg 497

Jersey
Shore
pg 445

Atlantic City
pgs 498-499

Cape May
pg 511

Wildwood
pg 508

NEW JERSEY
pg 435

NEW YORK, NEW JERSEY,
PENNSYLVANIA MAPS
Locator map pg 15
2 page Color map between pgs 16-17

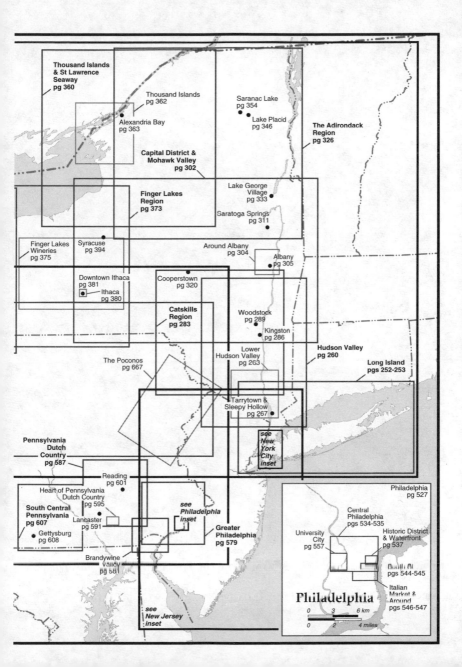

Thousand Islands & St Lawrence Seaway pg 360

Thousand Islands pg 362

Saranac Lake pg 354

Lake Placid pg 346

Alexandria Bay pg 363

The Adirondack Region pg 326

Capital District & Mohawk Valley pg 302

Lake George Village pg 333

Finger Lakes Region pg 373

Saratoga Springs pg 311

Finger Lakes Wineries pg 375

Syracuse pg 394

Around Albany pg 304

Albany pg 305

Downtown Ithaca pg 381

Cooperstown pg 320

Ithaca pg 380

Woodstock pg 289

Catskills Region pg 283

Kingston pg 286

Hudson Valley pg 260

The Poconos pg 667

Lower Hudson Valley pg 263

Long Island pgs 252-253

Tarrytown & Sleepy Hollow pg 267

see New York City inset

Pennsylvania Dutch Country pg 587

Reading pg 601

Heart of Pennsylvania Dutch Country pg 595

see Philadelphia inset

South Central Pennsylvania pg 607

Lancaster pg 591

Greater Philadelphia pg 579

Gettysburg pg 608

Brandywine Valley pg 581

see New Jersey inset

Philadelphia pg 527

Central Philadelphia pgs 534-535

University City pg 557

Historic District & Waterfront pg 537

Olula Ol pgs 544-545

Italian Market & Around pgs 546-547

Philadelphia

0   3   6 km

0   2   4 miles

Introduction

The states of New York, New Jersey and Pennsylvania – also collectively called the Mid-Atlantic States – occupy some of the most urbanized, industrialized and populated sections of the USA. And viewed from the New Jersey Turnpike, Pennsylvania Turnpike or any of the other main routes that traverse the region, this image of industrial sprawl and urban development can be readily reinforced. But it's only part of the picture. The states also encompass vast lakes, many rivers, huge forests, rolling green countryside, beautiful mountains, some expanses of wilderness and long stretches of natural coastline.

The many historical sites in the region reflect the three states' long history, while the major cities, particularly New York City and Philadelphia, are centers for world-class arts, entertainment and dining.

That New York City is one of the most visited cities in the world is no surprise. It has the US's largest collection of museums and galleries, and from thriving Broadway theater to Greenwich Village jazz clubs it's bustling with entertainment. It has some of the best and most ethnically diverse dining anywhere and the shopping possibilities are almost endless. It does have its urban problems, but this is still the world's most exhilarating city.

When many people think of New York they immediately think of the city, although the state of New York contains a whole lot more that stands in stark contrast to the skyscraper canyons of Manhattan. Nearby Long Island provides an escape from city life along its sandy beaches while upstate has plenty to offer the outdoor enthusiast. In the far northwest, on the Canadian border between Lake Erie and Lake Ontario, are the spectacular Niagara Falls. The Finger Lakes Region south of Lake Ontario has many dairy farms and vineyards producing some of the best wine in the country. The Hudson River cuts

through the forests of the Catskill Mountains and the Adirondack Mountains cover much of the northeast of the state.

Small in comparison with its neighbors and often dominated by them, New Jersey nevertheless has much to offer away from the industrialism with which most people associate it. Newark, the state's largest city, has many places of historic and cultural interest as do Princeton and

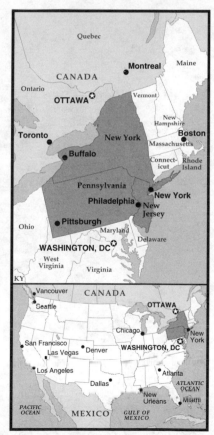

Morristown, towns closely associated with events in the Revolutionary War. In the northwest, New Jersey shares the Delaware Water Gap NRA with Pennsylvania while to the south there's the natural scenic beauty of the Pine Barrens. The Jersey Shore not only has the seaside resorts of Atlantic City and Cape May, but also miles of empty beaches.

Pennsylvania is rich in historical sites and beautiful scenery. Philadelphia and Pittsburgh, the state's two big cities, are both undergoing a revival and offer world-

class cultural attractions. To the west of Philadelphia, Pennsylvania Dutch Country is home to the Amish community, who reject many of the precepts and technologies of the modern world. Gettysburg National Military Park recalls the bloodiest battle in the Civil War. In the southwest the Laurel Highlands is a center for white-water rafting, while in the northwest you'll find the huge expanses of the Allegheny National Forest. In the northeast is the popular resort region and outdoor playground of the Pocono Mountains.

Winter in New York's Catskills

MICHAEL CLARK

TOM SMALLMAN

Allegheny River, near Tidioute,
Northern Pennsylvania

TONY WHEELER

Cascadilla Creek, Ithaca, NY

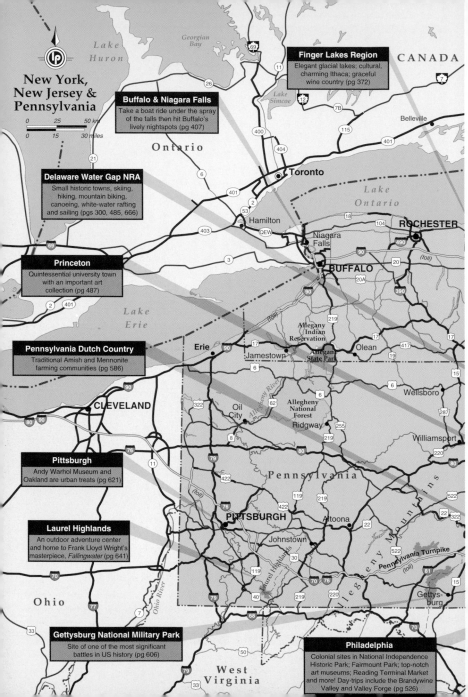

New York, New Jersey & Pennsylvania

Lake Huron

Georgian Bay

CANADA

0   25   50 km
0   15   30 miles

Ontario

Finger Lakes Region
Elegant glacial lakes; cultural, charming Ithaca; graceful wine country (pg 372)

Lake Simcoe

Belleville

Buffalo & Niagara Falls
Take a boat ride under the spray of the falls then hit Buffalo's lively nightspots (pg 407)

Toronto

Delaware Water Gap NRA
Small historic towns, skiing, hiking, mountain biking, canoeing, white-water rafting and sailing (pgs 300, 485, 666)

Hamilton

QEW

Lake Ontario

ROCHESTER

Niagara Falls

BUFFALO

(toll)

Princeton
Quintessential university town with an important art collection (pg 487)

Lake Erie

Pennsylvania Dutch Country
Traditional Amish and Mennonite farming communities (pg 586)

Erie

Allegany Indian Reservation

Jamestown

Allegany State Park

Olean

Wellsboro

CLEVELAND

Oil City

Allegheny National Forest

Ridgway

Williamsport

Pittsburgh
Andy Warhol Museum and Oakland are urban treats (pg 621)

Pennsylvania

PITTSBURGH

Altoona

Laurel Highlands
An outdoor adventure center and home to Frank Lloyd Wright's masterpiece, *Fallingwater* (pg 641)

Johnstown

Pennsylvania Turnpike

Ohio

Ohio River

Laurel Highlands

Allegheny Mountains

Gettysburg

Gettysburg National Military Park
Site of one of the most significant battles in US history (pg 606)

West Virginia

Philadelphia
Colonial sites in National Independence Historic Park; Fairmount Park; top-notch art museums; Reading Terminal Market and more! Day-trips include the Brandywine Valley and Valley Forge (pg 526)

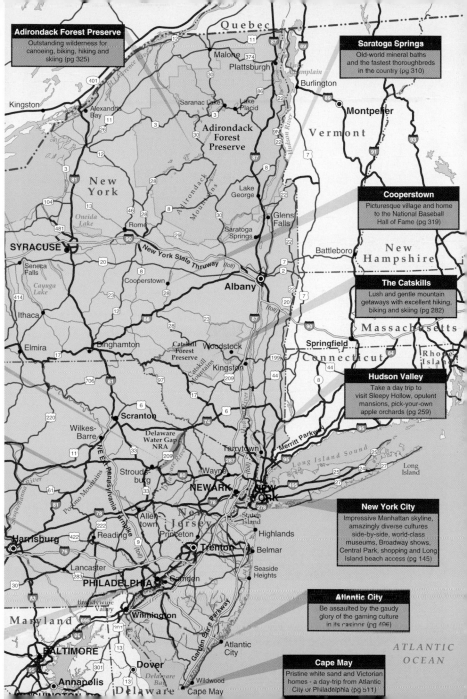

Adirondack Forest Preserve
Outstanding wilderness for canoeing, biking, hiking and skiing (pg 325)

Saratoga Springs
Old-world mineral baths and the fastest thoroughbreds in the country (pg 310)

Cooperstown
Picturesque village and home to the National Baseball Hall of Fame (pg 319)

The Catskills
Lush and gentle mountain getaways with excellent hiking, biking and skiing (pg 282)

Hudson Valley
Take a day trip to visit Sleepy Hollow, opulent mansions, pick-your-own apple orchards (pg 259)

New York City
Impressive Manhattan skyline, amazingly diverse cultures side-by-side, world-class museums, Broadway shows, Central Park, shopping and Long Island beach access (pg 145)

Atlantic City
Be assaulted by the gaudy glory of the gaming culture in its casinos (pg 496)

Cape May
Pristine white sand and Victorian homes - a day-trip from Atlantic City or Philadelphia (pg 511)

TOM SMALLMAN

Boathouse Row on the Schuylkill River in Fairmount Park, Philadelphia

MICHAEL CLARK

Lake Placid, Adirondack Forest Preserve, NY

Facts about the Region

HISTORY
Original Peoples
Scholars differ in their estimates, but somewhere between 15,000 and 35,000 years ago, during the last Ice Age, the first inhabitants of North America arrived from Asia. They traveled across the Bering Strait by way of a land bridge that formed when the accumulated ice of the polar glaciers lowered the world's sea levels. Over millennia, as the climate began to warm and the glaciers receded, subsequent migrations southward and eastward distributed the population throughout the Americas.

These first Americans were nomadic hunter-gatherers who lived in small bands, and this type of society existed on the continent until relatively recently. During the Ice Age they hunted mammoths, cave bears and giant sloths, but at the end of the Ice Age, when these animals became extinct, the people began to hunt for fish and the smaller animals we know today, such as deer. Success at hunting was often unpredictable, and wild-food crops (berries, fruits, roots and seeds), gathered mostly by women, were an important component of their diet. The hunter-gatherers' tools and weapons were made from stone, wood and bark, and their houses were made of bark or animal skins. They traveled on foot or by canoe and developed crafts in weaving and pottery.

There were two major groups of Native Americans in this region by the time Europeans began to arrive – the Algonquians and the Iroquois. The Algonquians occupied the Hudson Valley, Long Island, New Jersey, the Delaware River Valley and central Pennsylvania including part of the Susquehanna River. They were made up of the Lenni-Lanape (meaning 'original people' but called the Delaware by the British), Shawnee, Mohegan (or Mohican) and Munsee.

The Iroquois occupied central and western New York and parts of northwestern and central Pennsylvania. They included the Cayuga, Mohawk, Oneida, Onondaga and Seneca peoples who together formed the powerful Iroquois Confederacy in 1570. The Susquehannock people were also Iroquois and were named after the Susquehanna River where they lived.

European Arrival & Colonialism
The first European credited with visiting the region is the Italian navigator Giovanni da Verrazano, who sailed into New York Bay in 1524. In the early 17th century the English and French established trading relations with Native Americans, but Dutch and Swedish settlements initially expanded the European presence. In 1608 John Smith sailed up the Susquehanna River from Virginia into Pennsylvania.

The following year the English explorer Henry Hudson arrived in Delaware Bay and claimed the area for the Dutch East India Company, for whom he was working. (In 1609, it was the Dutch *East* India Company – which was formed in 1602. Even though Hudson didn't find the fabled Northwest Passage, the success of the new fur trading posts led to the formation in 1621 of the Dutch *West* India Company – with the aim of gaining dominance over the Atlantic trade. Why they changed names isn't clear; probably the accounting department's call.) Hudson was followed by Dutch explorers, and in 1624 settlements were established (in what was subsequently named New Netherland) by the Dutch West India Company at Fort Orange (present day Albany, NY) and Fort Nassau (present-day Gloucester City, NJ). Two years later a settlement was established at New Amsterdam at the southern end of Manhattan Island and in 1630 at Pavonia (in Jersey City, NJ).

Sweden established the permanent settlement of New Sweden at Wilmington (in Delaware), but Governor Johan Printz moved the capital, New Gothenburg, to Tinicum Island in the Delaware River near what would become Philadelphia. The brief Swedish presence in the New World ended in 1655 when the Dutch conquered New Sweden and annexed it to New Netherland. In 1664 the English, in turn, conquered the Dutch settlement (the Dutch were given modern-day Surinam in South America in exchange) and renamed it New York after the Duke of York (who became King James II of England in 1685). Parts of New Jersey were also acquired by the English, but differing proprietorial claims left it divided between East and West Jersey until 1702 at which time it became a royal province. New York and New Jersey shared the same royal governor until 1738.

In the meantime, on March 4, 1681, the Duke of York's brother, King Charles II, had given English Quaker William Penn a charter to own land west of the Delaware River in lieu of a £16,000 payment that was owed William's father, Admiral Penn. Charles II called the colony 'Penn' in honor of the admiral and William Penn added 'sylvania' (meaning 'woodlands'). Pennsylvania was to become the richest, most populous and most influential of Britain's colonies in 18th-century North America.

William Penn founded his colony as a 'holy experiment.' Although he only lived there briefly (from 1682 to 1684 and again from 1699 to 1701), as the governor and proprietor he ensured that, to a great degree, the colony respected religious freedom and liberal government. Rather optimistically, he named his capital Philadelphia (Greek for 'Brotherly Love'). He granted several fairly progressive 'frames of government' between himself and the colonists, establishing a code of laws and guaranteeing religious tolerance, trial by jury and protection of property. These were superseded by the 1701 Charter of Privilege, a constitution giving the Pennsylvania colonial assembly more power than any legislative body in Britain. Christian landholders were the only ones who could vote, but it was a start. The Charter of Privilege remained the colony's constitution until 1776.

During the first half of the 18th century there were conflicts in western Pennsylvania and western New York between the British colonists and the French and their Algonquian allies. These conflicts culminated in the French & Indian War from 1754-63. The Iroquois Confederacy allied itself with the British and this alliance was a significant factor in Britain's eventual defeat of the French.

Much of the earlier stages of the French & Indian War were fought in western Pennsylvania, where France and Britain clashed over trade and access to the Ohio River Valley. The French considered the Ohio River Valley an essential link between their colonies in Canada and Louisiana and were unhappy with merchants from Pennsylvania and Virginia trading with Native Americans in the area.

To protect their interests the French built a line of forts through western Pennsylvania. The British sent George Washington to warn off the French, but he was first ignored and then beaten at the Battle of Fort Necessity in Southwestern Pennsylvania in 1754. The French built Fort Duquesne at the confluence of the Ohio, Allegheny and Monongahela rivers (the site of present-day Pittsburgh), and in 1755 the British sent General Braddock to dislodge them, but he too was beaten.

In New York in 1758 the British were able to secure first the St Lawrence River when Lord Amherst captured Louisburg and then Lake Champlain in 1759 when he took Fort Carillon (renamed Fort Ticonderoga). General Wolfe's capture of Quebec in the same year meant that Britain's colonies in North America were safe, although peace wasn't signed for another four years.

Despite their alliance with the Iroquois, the British were less conciliatory than the

French in their relations with Native Indians. In 1763 an Ottawa Indian, Pontiac, emerged as a prophet and led attacks on British forts throughout western Pennsylvania and western New York in an attempt to drive the British out. Pontiac's fighters at first overwhelmed a number of forts, but by 1764 found that they couldn't succeed. With the defeat of Pontiac, the last impediments to westward colonial expansion in New York and Pennsylvania were swept away.

Some colonists, like William Penn, were fair in dealing with the original inhabitants and purchased land rather than taking it. Eventually, however, all the Native American groups were driven off the land, largely by the encroachment of European settlers.

The Break with Britain

The French & Indian War had increased Britain's costs in America tremendously. Britain in turn raised the taxes levied on the colonies and introduced stricter controls of colonial trade partly to protect its home industries. Many in the colonies opposed British policies and some merchants disliked what they saw as excessive British taxation. Philadelphians even turned away a British tea ship in 1773, though they didn't burn it as Bostonians did. A growing number of people began to consider separation from the mother country.

Not everyone was in favor of this course, however. The governor of New Jersey, William Franklin, the son of Benjamin Franklin, supported the British as did the wealthier merchants in New York. In Pennsylvania there were a good number of pacifist religious groups, like the Quakers, Mennonites and Amish. There was also a Church of England minority that supported Britain and a general disinterest in fighting among many German settlers.

In spite of this opposition and some apathy most people were in favor of separation, and the New York, New Jersey and Pennsylvania colonial governments voted to support the revolution. The First and Second Continental Congresses met in Philadelphia and the Declaration of Independence was adopted in the State House (now Independence Hall) in July 1776. At the same time the colonial governments of New York, New Jersey and Pennsylvania each approved a state constitution for themselves, but the former royal provinces still had to fight for recognition of their new status.

See the introductory chapter to each state for their individual history from this point.

GEOGRAPHY

New York, New Jersey and Pennsylvania occupy sections of a number of distinct physical regions. From west to east these are classified as: the Central Lowland, Appalachian Plateau, Appalachian Ridge & Valley, Blue Ridge Mountains, Piedmont Plateau, New England Upland and Atlantic Coastal Plain. The Appalachian Plateau, Appalachian Ridge & Valley and Blue Ridge Mountains are part of the geologically ancient, 1500 mile long Appalachian Mountains, which run from the Canadian border southwest into northern Alabama.

The narrow 30 mile wide northeastern strip of the Central Lowland follows the southern shores of Lake Erie and Lake Ontario and is known collectively as the Erie-Ontario Lowland. It consists of sedimentary rocks and its fertile clay soils are good for fruit-growing. Also consisting of sedimentary rocks, the Appalachian Plateau covers about half the area of Pennsylvania and New York and includes the Catskill, Pocono and Allegheny mountains. Its soils, however, are generally poor, except along the major river valleys where there are rich deposits of silt.

Consisting of limestone and sandstone, the Appalachian Ridge & Valley features a series of roughly 1000-foot-high ridges separated by wide, largely parallel valleys. The longest of these, and including a number of smaller valleys, is the 15 mile wide Great Valley, which stretches nearly the full length of the Appalachian Mountains. In New Jersey it's known as the Kittatinny Valley. Running northwest from

Georgia through Maryland, the Blue Ridge Mountains extend into southern Pennsylvania for about 50 miles. The eastern slopes of these mountains fall away sharply to the Piedmont Plateau, which also meets the Appalachian Ridge & Valley further north. The Piedmont Plateau is an area of low-lying land ranging in elevation from 100 feet to 500 feet and containing fertile limestone soils, underpinned by layers of red sandstone, shale and basalt rock.

North of the Piedmont Plateau the New England Upland stretches from Northern Pennsylvania and New Jersey through New York into Connecticut and Massachusetts. Largely made up of metamorphic rocks, its southern extension is known as the Reading Prong and includes the Taconic Mountains and Manhattan Island in New York and the New Jersey Highlands.

Stretching from Massachusetts to Mexico the Atlantic Coastal Plain is a mostly flat, raised, westward extension of the continental shelf. The plain only occupies relatively small sections of New York (Long Island and Staten Island) and Pennsylvania (the Philadelphia region) but covers 60% of New Jersey. Along New Jersey's Atlantic coast and along Delaware Bay are broad expanses of marshland; except in the state's southwest, most of the coastal plain's soil is poor.

The main river systems of the region are: the Delaware River, which borders eastern Pennsylvania, western New Jersey and southwestern New York and flows into Delaware Bay; the Susquehanna, which drains central Pennsylvania and parts of New York and flows south into Chesapeake Bay; the Ohio River and its tributaries the Allegheny and Monongahela rivers; and the Hudson River, an important transportation route that forms part of the border between New Jersey and New York.

The area boasts thousands of lakes created by receding glaciers at the end of the last Ice Age. New York has an extensive shoreline along Lake Ontario and Lake Erie, while northwestern Pennsylvania occupies a small section of the Lake Erie shore between New York and Ohio.

CLIMATE

Despite their proximity to the Atlantic Ocean, New York and Pennsylvania have continental climates, characterized by wide temperature differences between winter and summer. This is because the prevailing winds come from the western interior. New Jersey is classified as cool temperate.

Air-flows from the Atlantic Ocean and the Gulf of Mexico affect the climates of all three states, making temperature variations

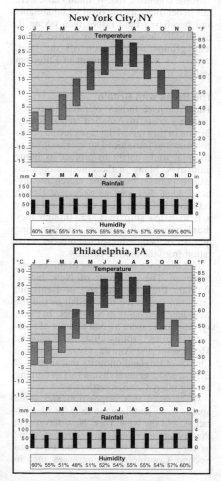

normally less extreme than states further inland. In New York City, for example, the average January temperature is 14°F, in July 77°F, though much greater extremes have been recorded. The warm moist air from the Gulf of Mexico in summer explains why places like Philadelphia and New York City often get so unbearably humid then. Spring and fall are generally mild with warm days and cool nights, although along the Atlantic coast the shift-

ing wind patterns during these seasons can cause very turbulent weather, including hurricanes.

Inland, the average temperatures for Pittsburgh are 38.9°F in January, 67.7°F in July.

Precipitation is fairly evenly distributed during the year, with annual falls generally between 32 and 48 inches. The highest snowfalls occur along the Erie-Ontario Lowland.

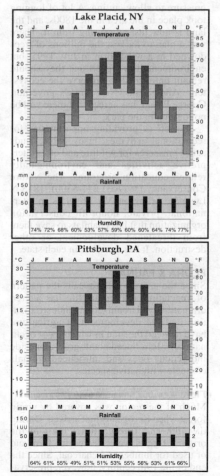

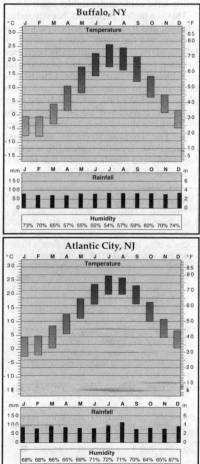

ECOLOGY & ENVIRONMENT

The growing level of awareness about ecology and the environment, plus the recognized value in 'green tourism' or 'eco-tourism' means that many natural areas increasingly enjoy varying degrees of protection and management from local, state and federal government agencies as well as from private ones. Since the 1970s lands have been acquired for important environmental and recreational purposes, and the emission of hazardous wastes and air pollution have come under tighter control.

This is a highly populated, heavily industrialized and intensively farmed part of the country, and the states' broad network of lakes and rivers have traditionally been used to dump large, toxic amounts of industrial, agricultural and human waste. Efforts have been made to clean them up, and some places, like Lake Erie, whose fish and plant life were considered all but dead in the 1970s, have shown considerable regeneration. The Hudson River is also much cleaner these days; the marine life is returning slowly and people actually fish for bass in season from New York City's piers.

New York was one of the first states in the country to adopt acid-rain controls, and air quality across the region has improved significantly since the federal government's 1990 Clean Air Act.

One of the biggest environmental issues in New York is the question of logging in Adirondack Park, which includes over 3900 sq miles of untouched forest located among 5470 sq miles of private land. Because there is so much private land in this wilderness area, there has long been pressure to allow cutting. A lot of logging took place in the area in the 1800s, and the land is now just recovering from it. There was a plan to harvest the millions of trees downed in a windstorm in July 1995, but environmentalists argued that they should remain untouched to preserve the ecosystem. And so far, New York's governor, George Pataki, has agreed that there will be no logging in the park.

As well as providing opportunities for recreational activities, many public lands act as preserves for wildlife and offer interpretive activities and environmentally related education programs. The Nature Conservancy (☎ (703) 841-5300), 1815 N Lynn St, Arlington, VA 22209, is an international, private, nonprofit conservation organization that buys habitats to save them from threatened development or other destruction. It has branches in each state.

FLORA & FAUNA

Since the arrival of Europeans the pattern of vegetation and animal life has altered dramatically. Urbanization, industrialization and the development of agriculture have reduced the area in which these occur naturally. Introduced plants grow alongside indigenous ones and introduced animals compete with native species.

Flora

Much of the region was covered by virgin forest when Europeans first arrived. During the 18th and 19th centuries most of the original forests were cleared for farmland or used for lumber and charcoal. Since the end of the 19th century, however, preserva-

---

New York City's Garbage

The five boroughs of New York City produce between 13,000 and 16,000 tons of trash daily, which is sent to the city's only garbage dump at Fresh Kills on Staten Island. The dump has been filling since 1948 and now, at nearly 3½ sq miles in area, is the world's largest. Understandably, for locals this is an unwanted claim to fame.

In 1996 the city's politicians, having vacillated for a long time, announced that the dump will close at the end of 2001. But the question remains of what to do with all that garbage after that date. Recycling at least some of it is one possibility and transporting it elsewhere is another. Some states, including Pennsylvania, have said that they're not prepared to have any of the city's trash dumped on them. At present it costs about $100 million each year to get rid of the garbage, but would cost almost double that if it were sent interstate. ∎

tion and reforestation has been successful. Over half of New York and Pennsylvania and more than 40% of New Jersey are covered by forest, the vast bulk of which is new-growth intermixed with a number of smaller areas of pristine, old-growth trees.

There are many different species, but most of the region's forests are dominated by northern broad-leaved hardwoods. Beech and sugar maple are the main ones, but others includes ash, basswood, birch, cherry, hickory, red maple, walnut and oak. Some forests, especially along the Atlantic coast, are made up chiefly of softwood conifers such as cedar, fir, hemlock, spruce and white and yellow pine.

Wildflowers common to the region include the azalea, black-eyed Susan, daisy, buttercup, dogwood, honeysuckle, mountain laurel, orchid and violet. In the Pine Barrens of southern New Jersey are some rare plant species including several insect-eating varieties.

Fauna

Before the arrival of Europeans, the region boasted many species, including black bear, Canada lynx, elk, bison, wolf and panther – some, like the panther, have disappeared and others exist in small numbers. Commonly seen among the region's smaller mammals are beaver, chipmunk, fox, opossum, rabbit, raccoon, squirrel, skunk and woodchuck. Of the larger mammals the white-tailed deer is widespread, but the black bear is largely restricted to the remote regions of the Appalachian Plateau and the Adirondack Mountains.

Two poisonous snakes are the timber rattlesnake found mostly on mountains and the copperhead common on rocky streambeds; nonpoisonous snakes are far more common.

New York, New Jersey and Pennsylvania are home to many species of year-round birds as well as temporary host to migratory ones. Birds that can be seen all year are the bluebird, bluejay, bobolink, eastern meadowlark, goldfinch, red-tailed hawk, owls and woodpeckers. Migratory birds include the hummingbird, hawk, falcon and bald eagle. Along the shores of lakes and the Atlantic coast are gulls, heron and osprey. Game birds include the wild duck, wild turkey (which Ben Franklin wanted to be the national bird), grouse, partridge, pheasant and quail.

Among the numerous varieties of fish found in the region's fresh waters are black bass, catfish, crappie, walleyed pike, pickerel, salmon, trout, muskellunge and whitefish; the salt waters contain bluefish, marlin, tuna and flounder as well as crabs, clams and oysters.

Endangered Species The reduction in wildlife habitats has meant that animals like the black bear and bobcat are restricted to small remote woodland areas. A small herd of wild elk, one of only two east of the Mississippi River, lives in Northern Pennsylvania.

At one time predatory birds like the hawk, falcon, osprey and bald eagle were threatened with extinction by hunters and the widespread use of chemicals (which become increasingly concentrated the further up the food chain). But their numbers have increased since they were protected by the federal Migratory Bird Treaty Act of 1972, the Endangered Species Act of 1978 and the 1973 ban on DDT. Nevertheless, some chemicals, though banned, persist in the environment, and natural habitats continue to be destroyed.

In the early 1970s New Jersey and Pennsylvania, together with Delaware, had only five nests of bald eagles, but now there are around 30. In 1993 the official status of the bald eagle in the US was upgraded from 'endangered' to 'threatened.' The bluebird has been close to extinction, but its numbers are gradually returning; it can be seen in Northern Pennsylvania.

The Massasauga is a rare and poisonous rattlesnake found in western Pennsylvania.

PARKS & FORESTS

The following are state- and federally maintained park and forest lands. For additional federal and national agencies, see the Outdoor Activities chapter.

National Park Service

There are no national parks in this region, but there are two national recreation areas (NRAs), one national reserve and a national seashore all administered by the National Park Service (NPS), an agent of the Department of the Interior. Unlike national parks, where development is severely restricted, NRAs usually have been substantially altered by human activity but retain some exceptional natural features. A national reserve and seashore are undeveloped tracts of land where natural ecosystems are maintained.

The Gateway NRA, at the entrance to the New York/New Jersey Estuary, is made up of Jamaica Bay (which includes a wildlife refuge), the Rockway Peninsula, Staten Island and Sandy Hook.

The Delaware Water Gap NRA straddles the Pennsylvania/New Jersey border along the winding Delaware River through the Kittatinny Ridge.

The Pinelands National Reserve, on the Atlantic Coastal Plain in southern New Jersey, is in a small region known as the Pine Barrens and consists of many bogs, marshes and dwarfed pines.

Fire Island National Seashore, off the southern shore of Long Island, is 1400 acres of wilderness.

The NPS also administers a number of national monuments, national memorials, national historic sites, national trails and national rivers throughout the region.

For more information write to the National Park Service, Mid-Atlantic Region, Customs House, Chestnut St, Philadelphia, PA 19106.

Golden Passports

Golden Age Passports are free and allow permanent US residents 62 years and older unlimited entry to all sites in the national park system and other federally operated facilities, with discounts on camping and other fees. Golden Access passports offer the same to US residents who are medically blind or permanently disabled.

Golden Eagle passports cost $50 annually and offer one-year entry into national parks to the holder and accompanying guests. You can apply in person for any of these at any NPS or USFS (see below) office or call Destinet (☎ (800) 635-2267) for information and ordering.

National Forests

National forests are operated by the United States Forest Service (USFS), a division of the United States Department of Agriculture (USDA). They are less protected and are managed under the principle of 'multiple use,' which includes timber cutting, watershed management, wildlife management and privately owned recreational facilities.

Allegheny National Forest in northwestern Pennsylvania is a huge tract of land (797 sq miles) incorporating reservoirs, lakes, rivers, towns and campgrounds and whose northern extension borders New York's Allegany State Forest. For information contact the Allegheny National Forest (☎ (814) 723-5150), PO Box 847, Warren, PA 16365; see the Northern Pennsylvania chapter. The smaller Finger Lakes National Forest (☎ (607) 594-5720), in southwest New York, is just over 20 sq miles in size; see New York's Finger Lakes chapter.

State Parks & Forests

New York, New Jersey and Pennsylvania each maintains its own system of state parks and state forests, many of which contain wildlife and wilderness areas as well as provide for recreational activities. For information, see the 'Facts about' chapter of each state, or contact one of the following organizations.

New York
    State Parks, Empire State Plaza,
    Albany, NY 12238 (☎ (518) 474-0456)

    Department of Environmental Conservation
    50 Wolf Rd, Room 11
    Albany, NY 12233-4255
    (☎ (518) 457-2500)

New Jersey
    Environmental Protection Department
    401 E State St, CN 402
    Trenton, NJ 08625-0402
    (☎ (609) 777-3373)

Pennsylvania
 Bureau of State Parks, PO Box 8551
 Harrisburg, PA 17105-8551
 (☎ (717) 675-1121, (800) 637-2757)

 Bureau of Forestry
 PO Box 8552
 Harrisburg, PA 17105-8552
 (☎ (717) 783-7941)

GOVERNMENT & POLITICS

The USA is a republic operating a federal system of government overseen by a president and a bicameral Congress, consisting of the 100 member Senate and the 435 member House of Representatives. New York, New Jersey and Pennsylvania send 31, 13 and 23 representatives to the US Congress; each elects two senators.

The president, whose term is for four years, is chosen by the Electoral College, which consists of electors (chosen by voters) from each state equivalent to its number of senators and representatives, who vote in accordance with the popular vote within their state. To be elected, the president must obtain a majority (270 – half plus one) of the total 538 electoral votes (the District of Columbia, which has three nonvoting representatives in Congress, nevertheless has three electoral votes). The President is elected for no more than two four-year terms.

The federal government has three branches: the legislature branch makes the laws, the executive branch carries them out and the judiciary branch studies and interprets both the Constitution and the laws.

The two main political parties are the Democrats and the Republicans; smaller parties include the Green party and Ross Perot's Reform party. Currently, the presidency is held by Bill Clinton, a Democrat, but both houses of Congress are headed by a Republican majority. The situation in both the House and Senate is subject to change following the congressional elections held every two years. By law, House members serve two-year terms and must run for office with every 'new congress;' Senators serve six year terms and approximately one-third of that body is elected in every congressional election.

The head of the state government is the governor, who presides over a bicameral legislature consisting of a senate and a house delegation. Smaller administrative districts within the states are divided into counties, cities, boroughs and townships. Each of the three states currently has a Republican governor. For more on each state's internal government, see its 'Facts about' chapter.

ECONOMY

In terms of gross national product (GNP), the USA is the richest country in the world. However, the trade deficit and the growing national debt are points of deep concern among citizens and economists alike.

While TV programs and Hollywood movies may show the flashier, richer side of the USA, the country is as diverse in its economic circumstances as it is in its cultures. The economies of New York, New Jersey and Pennsylvania have a number of features in common.

Pennsylvania and New York have small reserves of oil and larger amounts of natural gas; all three have deposits of salt, clay, sand, limestone and slate and small amounts of mineral ores such as copper, iron, silver, gold and zinc are mined. New York and New Jersey also supply gravel, and Pennsylvania has large amounts of coal (bituminous and anthracite). The timber industry has always been important, though less so in New Jersey and Pennsylvania today. Pennsylvania has a small fishing industry, but commercial fishing is important in New York and New Jersey, particularly the harvesting of saltwater fish and crustaceans.

Although manufacturing has diminished in importance relative to other parts of the US and to other industries, this remains one of the nation's leading industrial regions. The main type of manufactured goods are chemicals, electronic equipment, food products, industrial machinery, paper products, precision instruments and printed materials. Iron and steel production are also significant in New York and Pennsylvania.

Tourism continues to grow; the combined tourism income of the states is somewhere around $45 billion, and the industry employs about 1¼ million people. Visitors are attracted by the landscapes of all three states and the outdoor recreational activities they provide; New York and Pennsylvania also have many historical and cultural attractions, while New Jersey's gambling casinos average 30 million punters a year.

Each state has a diversified agricultural sector, but livestock and dairy farming earn the bulk of farming income for New York and Pennsylvania, while for New Jersey it's market gardening.

POPULATION & PEOPLE

The combined population of New York, New Jersey and Pennsylvania is over 37½ million and is steadily rising. New York has the highest population of the three, and New Jersey is one of the most densely populated states in the country.

Nearly half of New York's population lives in the New York City metropolitan area; in Pennsylvania it is concentrated in the southeast around Philadelphia and in the southwest around Pittsburgh; in New Jersey the highest concentration is in the Newark and Jersey City conurbation. See the introduction to each of these states, especially New York, for more on the racial diversity of the region.

Pennsylvania is the most rural of the states with just over 30% living in country areas. New York and New Jersey are two of the most urbanized states in the nation with respectively 84% and 89% of residents living in urban-designated areas.

Despite a common perception to the contrary, in terms of ethnicity the population of the region is still overwhelmingly white. According to the 1990 census they make up 74.4% in New York, 79.3% in New Jersey and 88.5% in Pennsylvania. Blacks make up the second largest ethnic group, comprising 15.9%, 13.1% and 9.2% respectively. These are followed by Asians, Hispanics and Native Americans. In New York and New Jersey many Hispanics are of Puerto Rican or Cuban origin. Native

Americans number about 90,000, of whom over two-thirds live in New York.

EDUCATION

School attendance is usually obligatory to the age of 16, and almost everyone graduates from high school. New York has the nation's largest public school system, which each year spends a multi-billion dollar budget. In all three states Catholic grammar schools are a prominent private choice.

New York, New Jersey and Pennsylvania have some of the most prestigious universities in the country, including Columbia, New York and Cornell universities in New York, Princeton in New Jersey and the University of Pennsylvania. Other important institutions are the US Military Academy at West Point, the State University system of New York, Rutgers University in New Jersey and Pennsylvania State University. Smaller colleges in New York include City College, Hunter, the New School, Parsons and the Fashion Institute of Technology in New York City, Ithaca College, and Skidmore College in Saratoga Springs. Smaller liberal arts colleges in Pennsylvania include Villanova University, the all-female Bryn Mawr College, Haverford College, Carnegie Mellon in Pittsburgh, Beaver College in Glenside (with an excellent exchange program), Swarthmore College, the Catholic Duquesne University in Pittsburgh, York College, Allentown College and Franklin & Marshall College (endowed by Benjamin Franklin).

ARTS

New York City is the arts capital of the world and has helped to shape much of the artistic and cultural life of the US. It's the nation's most important training and testing ground for painters, actors, dancers, musicians, writers, filmmakers and so on. That's why so many have spent at least part of their career here and why so many have incorporated aspects of the city into their work.

New York City has been the center of numerous artistic movements, many of which overlapped and influenced later developments. Ragtime musicians, for example, performed in vaudeville theaters and had their music published in Tin Pan Alley. The skills that actors and comics acquired in vaudeville they later used in movies and TV. The Jazz Age, which saw the flourishing of the arts in Harlem and of black music in general, was also reflected in the work of writers like F Scott Fitzgerald.

The country's main theatrical district is on Broadway and in the surrounding districts known as Off Broadway and Off-Off Broadway. Three major radio and TV networks – ABC, CBS and NBC – and several cable-TV channels are based in New York City. A number of TV programs are still produced here, and the city is used as the setting for many others. Movies also frequently use the city as a backdrop, and many of those working in films honed their skills in theater or TV. New York City is the magazine- and book-publishing center of the US, with a number of important publishing houses based here. It's also an important music publishing and recording center. These different cultural media feed off and into each other.

Helping to make sure that all this endeavor pays off are the Madison Ave advertising companies, the public-relations firms, impresarios, agents and other movers and shakers.

The variety and quantity of artistic pursuits also require financing, and the wealth that exists in New York City allows for both corporate and private sponsorship of the arts. In Philadelphia, sponsorship funds the same variety, but on a smaller scale. The benefit to tourism is recognized and helps ensure that public money is made available to promote the arts, and the whole region gains from the spill-over. The three states are home to a number of artists' colonies, while numerous arts and craft festivals take place throughout the year.

New York City, Philadelphia and the other major cities in the region have some of the foremost artistic institutions in the country. In addition, there are countless smaller theaters, galleries, orchestras, musical venues and museums, and outside the major cities almost every community of any size has its share of them.

Popular Music

Over the years, the region has produced a tremendous number of musicians who have had an enormous influence on popular music. New York City in particular attracts people from all over the country, and some of the most popular musical movements of the modern era have either begun or found their strongest expression there. Today, numerous clubs and bars exist in the major cities where the many forms of music from the past and present can be heard and often danced to.

Primarily thought of as piano music, ragtime (probably from 'ragged time' referring to its two-four rhythm base and syncopated melody) first became popular at the end of the 19th century, when it was performed in vaudeville theaters. One of its greatest exponents was Jelly Roll Morton, while Scott Joplin was one of its most important composers. A number of dances were identified with ragtime, including the fox trot, turkey trot and tango. Ragtime was popularized nationally through the sheet music published in Tin Pan Alley.

Tin Pan Alley was to dominate American popular music from the 1890s to the 1960s, when the factory approach to songwriting gave way to rock music's singer-songwriters. Tin Pan Alley originally referred to an area of New York City where music publishers and composers were centered, but it came to refer to popular music in general. Among its most influential composers were Irving Berlin, George and Ira Gershwin, Jerome Kern, Richard Rodgers, Oscar Hammerstein and Cole Porter. Later, writers like Gerry Goffin and Carole King and producer Phil Spector succeeded these masters, churning out 'girl group' hits in the Brill Building at 50th St and Broadway in New York City.

Strict enforcement of prohibition forced the closure of many clubs in Chicago, putting jazz musicians there out of work. New York City then became the center for

Frank Sinatra

Francis Albert Sinatra, Hoboken, New Jersey's most famous son was born of immigrant Italian parents on December 12, 1915.

In the 1930s he started his long career as an entertainer, singing in local venues around Hoboken. After winning an amateur talent competition he began singing on New Jersey radio then later joined the Harry James and Tommy Dorsey bands, before going solo in 1942. While he was with Tommy Dorsey, he had several hit songs and appeared in his first movie. By this time he had become a highly publicized teenage idol and in his public appearances was met by legions of screaming female fans – long before Elvis or the Beatles.

His first musical film was *Higher and Higher* (1943), but the best-remembered ones from this period are *Anchors Aweigh* (1945) and *On the Town* (1949), both of which also starred Pittsburgh's Gene Kelly.

In the early 1950s his popularity waned and his time in the entertainment industry seemed over after his vocal chords ruptured sending him off the performance stage. But he successfully revived his career when he won an Oscar for best supporting actor in *From Here to Eternity* (1953). It was a non-musical role and established Sinatra as a serious actor. He then went on to make a number of memorable films, some musical, others drama, including *High Society* (1956), with Grace Kelly and Bing Crosby, the spy thriller *The Manchurian Candidate* (1962) and *The Detective* (1968). Sinatra also broke ground by portraying a drug addict in the drama *The Man with the Golden Arm* (1955), the first major Hollywood film to realistically portray junkie life.

His return to success in films was matched by a revival in his musical career. His albums of the late '50s – recorded late at night, with an orchestra using Nelson Riddle's arrangements, were alternately moody (*In the Wee Small Hours*) or upbeat (*Sinatra's Swinging Session*) and introduced the idea of a 'concept album.' His singing had a new-found maturity and he garnered an international following as a cabaret performer. He appeared regularly at Caesar's Palace in Las Vegas and made numerous TV specials. The album *Come Fly With Me* (1959) proved hugely popular and his recordings of such

jazz during the 1920s and '30s. The city's preeminence in radio and recording was a significant factor in attracting musical artists, and they performed in venues like the Cotton Club in Harlem. The 1930s also saw the emergence of big-band jazz and swing orchestras led by such notables as Cab Calloway, Count Basie, Duke Ellington, Benny Goodman along with Jimmy and Tommy Dorsey. Many appeared regularly on broadcasts from famous hotels such as the old Hotel Pennsylvania, whose phone number 'Pennsylvania 6-5000' became the title of a hit song.

Jazz performances continued at small venues, and one of the greatest jazz singers of the age, Billie Holiday, learned her trade in the nightclubs of New York City. In the 1940s Dizzy Gillespie, a celebrated jazz trumpeter, helped create the bebop school of jazz improvisation with Charlie Parker and Thelonious Monk. Although the popularity of jazz declined, the music has survived and can still be heard at the Lincoln Center and numerous small clubs. Many of the best clubs were located in midtown Manhattan on 52nd St, but all were eradicated by the building boom of the '80s. Although the popularity of jazz declined, the music has survived and can still be heard at the Lincoln Center and numerous small clubs, including the Village Vanguard on Seventh Ave in Greenwich Village, perhaps the most famous jazz club on earth.

With rhythm and blues (R&B) in the 1950s, it was again New York City's role as a broadcasting and recording center that attracted performers like Fats Domino and Little Richard from other parts of the US. When white performers added bits of country music to R&B, it became known as songs as 'That's Life' and 'My Way' have become classics. He has had almost 100 hit singles during his long career.

Controversy always dogged Sinatra. His earlier marriages to Ava Gardner and Mia Farrow were turbulent, and there were constant stories of his Mafia connections. In the *Godfather*, the character of Johnny Fontaine, who approaches Don Corleone looking for a big movie role to boost his career, was widely assumed to be based on Sinatra. Those connections led to his inability to invest in the casinos that he helped popularize. When his home state of New Jersey opened casinos in Atlantic City, Sinatra was one of the first to embrace the woebegone resort community.

Sinatra is known for his arrogance and quick temper, but also for his generosity, and in 1971 he received the Jean Hersholt Humanitarian Award. He has been a strong supporter of the Democratic party and sang at John F Kennedy's inauguration, but after being frozen-out by the Kennedys due to his reputed underworld connections, he became more conservative. In 1985 it was Republican president Ronald Reagan who awarded him the Medal of Honor, the US's highest civilian accolade, in recognition of his contribution to American life. It was an honor criticized as inappropriate by some columnists. ∎

rock 'n' roll, a phrase first applied by Cleveland, OH, (later New York City) disc jockey Alan Freed, which in black slang was a euphemism for sex. The city's importance in music publishing meant that many of the great early rock 'n' roll songs were written by songwriters based here. Two of the most commercially successful were Jerry Leibler and Mike Stoller, who wrote such classics as 'Hound Dog' and 'Don't Be Cruel,' made famous by Elvis Presley. Other important songwriters included Burt Bacharach and Hal David.

In the 1950s black musicians combined rock 'n' roll, R&B and gospel music to produce soul and doo-wop music, the latter so-called because of the meaningless phrases sung in the harmony line. Like other black-music forms these too were copied by white musicians. The most enduring doo-wop band to come out of

New York was the Drifters, while Philadelphia produced so many soul musicians that the phenomenon was called 'Philadelphia Soul.' Frankie Valli and the Four Seasons, from Newark, NJ, were the most successful of the white doo-wop groups.

Folk music had been around since colonial times, but out of the difficult economic circumstances and political and social upheavals of the 1930s it developed into an important means of expression. Many folk musicians came to live in New York. Among the most influential were the left-wing singers Woody Guthrie and Pete Seeger, two of the foremost popularizers of American folk in the middle decades of this century. They inspired the Greenwich Village folk-rock scene of the 1960s, which was led by Bob Dylan – who had his first gigs at the club Folk City (now called the Kettle of Fish) – and also included Peter,

Paul & Mary, the most popular acoustic folk group of that decade. Simon & Garfunkel, who both grew up in the borough of Queens, also have roots in this music. Today, in the world of music recording, the picturesque town of Woodstock in the Catskills is second only to Nashville in the number of professional recording studios.

The influence of the Beatles led many musicians to develop their own material, and one of the most important, creative New York City bands to emerge in the 1960s was the Velvet Underground led by Lou Reed and John Cale, which also introduced the modern concept of self-promotion with their association to artist Andy Warhol. Their songs of alienation and violence presaged the music of punk rock, which emerged in the '70s as a reaction to the complex, self-important work of a number of rock bands. Punk artists sought to simplify music and make it more accessible; among them were the hugely influential Ramones, whose music helped to spur the British punk scene. CBGB, a club on the Bowery in the Lower East Side and a proving ground for bands like the Talking Heads, the Police and the Ramones, continues the alternative tradition today.

One of the greatest singer-songwriters to appear in the '70s was Bruce Springsteen, who, in recognition of his talent, was simply called 'The Boss.' He is most closely associated with the Jersey shore, particularly the hardscrabble town of Asbury Park, and his songs often deal with the toughness and disillusionment of working-class life in America.

Around the same time as punk's emergence, rap and hip-hop music and break dancing were developing in the discos and streets of New York's black neighborhoods. The two originators were Afrika Bambaataa and Grandmaster Flash. This style of music soon spread to other cities. By the early '80s it had moved into the mainstream with white performers either incorporating it into their music or doing straight rap themselves. Public Enemy was one of the most influential and controversial of black rap acts, while Salt 'n' Pepa have

been the most commercially successful female rap act. One of the country's most happening bands today is the Fugees, a hip-hop group from Newark who combine rap and rock in a commercial hybrid.

Acid jazz is a hybrid of jazz, soul, funk and hip-hop and has been promoted and performed by pioneer Miles Davis and the group Back 2 Basics. Of late, younger jazz artists have embraced more traditional strains in jazz – with trumpeter Wynton Marsalis and sax sensation Joshua Redman, often heard in New York clubs, leading the retro way.

Classical Music & Opera
The region has some of the foremost classical music and operatic institutions in the country, most of which undertake nation-wide tours. In New York City the Lincoln Center for the Performing Arts is the venue for such prestigious organizations as the New York Philharmonic Orchestra, the Metropolitan Opera Company and the New York City Opera. Carnegie Hall is the venue for solo to orchestral performances.

Though often overlooked, the New Jersey Symphony Orchestra, based at the Garden State Arts Center under the direction of young composer Hugh Wolff, travels the state and is worth a special mention.

Founded in 1924, the Curtis Institute of Music in Philadelphia is one of the world's leading centers for the advanced study of music. The Philadelphia Orchestra and the Pittsburgh Symphony Orchestra each have a world-class reputation. The Philadelphia Orchestra, like the New York City Ballet, makes its summer home in Saratoga Springs.

A student of the Curtis Institute of Music, Leonard Bernstein (1918-90) was the first major American-born classical conductor. He achieved fame in 1943 when he stepped in for an ailing conductor to lead the New York Philharmonic Orchestra, an event that wound up on the front page of the next day's *New York Times*. Later, Bernstein became musical director of the philharmonic while making frequent forays into popular music, most notably with the stage works *One The Town, Candide* and *West Side Story.*

Philadelphia's Marian Anderson (1902-93) was a noted contralto who broke racial barriers. She was the first permanent black member of the Metropolitan Opera Company, where she debuted in 1955.

Theater

In the three centuries since drama was first performed in New York City the theater has grown into one of its most noteworthy artistic institutions. After surviving periods of decline caused by the advent of talking pictures and then TV, Broadway and the surrounding district now have scores of theaters. They present a whole gamut of shows from experimental drama to big musical productions. At one time Philadelphia competed with New York City as the country's theatrical capital, but today it is mainly a testing ground for shows en route to Broadway.

At the end of the 19th century and for more than two decades into the 20th, vaudeville (light or comic theater interspersed with song-and-dance routines or other variety acts) was the most popular form of theater in the country and New York City was its center. The main venue was the Palace Theater in Times Square, although there were many other vaudeville theaters around town. The most famous vaudeville impresario was Florenz Ziegfeld (1867-1932) who was best known for his lavish revues, the Ziegfeld Follies, featuring female dancers. Vaudeville attracted performers from other forms of entertainment, including musicians from Tin Pan Alley, and when it finally died out in the 1930s, vaudeville performers like James Cagney and Groucho Marx were able to transfer their skills and experience to films, radio and TV.

Alternative, experimental drama arose in New York City in the 1950s and '60s, partly out of artistic rebellion and partly because of the prohibitive cost of performing on Broadway. New companies were formed, experimentation was encouraged

and young actors were urged to explore their skills and take risks. Alternative theater today can be found Off Broadway and Off-Off Broadway, terms which refer as much to the scale and cost of a production as to a theater's location. Recently, Off Broadway attitudes (or perhaps poses) have been embraced by the mainstream, as stripped down productions of *Chicago* and *Rent* have become major Broadway hits.

Broadway and Times Square are currently experiencing a renaissance, with big-dollar investment from companies like Disney inspiring a new generation of plays, which is trickling down to the Off Broadway and Off-Off Broadway scene. Mainstream theater relies mostly on big productions, as well as revivals and some imports from London's West End.

One of the great playwrights of the early 20th century was Eugene O'Neill (1888-1953), who was born in New York City and won three Pulitzer prizes for his plays in the 1920s. In 1936 he also won the Nobel prize for literature. *The Iceman Cometh* (1946) was his last Broadway play before he died, and *Long Day's Journey into Night* (1956) was produced posthumously.

Death of a Salesman (1949), for which he received the Pulitzer prize, is the most powerful play by Arthur Miller. A year later he wrote *The Crucible* about the Salem witch trials, which had contemporary parallels with McCarthyism. His most recent plays, *Broken Glass* (1994), about a middle-aged Jewish couple living in Brooklyn, and *The Ride Down Mount Morgan* (1995), about a man confronting his mortality, have debuted in London before coming the US stage. In his 80s, he continues to be a presence in American theater and on film with his recent screenplay for *The Crucible.*

Alternative theater has produced some of the most prestigious American playwrights of recent decades, some of whose works have also been shown on Broadway. Sam Shepherd (born 1943) received a Pulitzer prize for *Buried Child* (1979) and later did the screenplay for *Paris, Texas* (1984). Lanford Wilson (born 1937) wrote about the post-Vietnam War world of a Southern family in *Tally's Folly* (1979). In plays like *Speed the Plow* (1987) and *American Buffalo* (1974), David Mamet (born 1947) examined the psychological and ethical issues of modern urban society.

Neil Simon (born 1927), possibly the modern playwright most closely associated with New York, has written many comedies set in the city, most of which have been made into movies. He received a Tony award for *Biloxi Blues* (1985), then again for *Lost in Yonkers* (1990), for which he was also given the Pulitzer prize. He now has a Broadway theater named after him, though his most recent New York production, *London Suite* (1994), actually opened Off Broadway, downtown.

Musicals have always been a mainstay of New York theater, and the Tin Pan Alley composers (see Popular Music) wrote many of the most memorable. George and Ira Gershwin straddled classical and contemporary music in such works as the opera *Porgy & Bess* (1935). Cole Porter wrote the music and lyrics for numerous sophisticated Broadway musicals such as *Kiss Me Kate* (1948) and *Can Can* (1953). More recently, Stephen Sondheim (born 1930) has written varied and experimental popular Broadway fare including the lyrics for *West Side Story*, and music for *A Funny Thing Happened on the way to the Forum* (1962) and the Pulitzer-prize winning *Sunday in the Park with George* (1984).

Many famous performers had their career launched or achieved some of their greatest successes in New York City's theater. After their appearance together in *The Guardsman* (1924) the reputations of Alfred and Lynne Lunt were assured, and they went on to become the US's most successful acting partnership and now have a theater named after them. Carol Channing became a star after her appearance in the musical version of *Gentlemen Prefer Blondes* (1949) and has appeared in numerous revivals of her signature role in *Hello Dolly*. Dustin Hoffman first developed his talents in the avant-garde theater of the 1960s and returned in the '90s to play

Willy Loman in *Death of a Salesman*. Barbra Streisand's lead role in the Broadway musical *Funny Girl* (1964) brought her immediate stardom.

Dance

Modern dance, which challenged the strictures of classical ballet, was pioneered by Isadora Duncan (1877-1927), who spent four years in New York City before heading for Europe. Basing her ideas on ancient Greek concepts of beauty, she sought to make dance an intense form of self-expression.

In Los Angeles in 1915, Ted Shawn (1891-1972) and Ruth St Denis (1879-1968) formed Denishawn, a modern-dance company and school, which moved to New York in 1920 and remained the nation's leading company into the '30s.

Its most influential student was Pittsburgh's Martha Graham (1894-1991), who founded her Dance Repertory Theater in New York and a modern-dance school at Bennington College in Vermont. In her long career she choreographed over 140 dances and developed a new dance technique, now taught worldwide, aimed at expressing inner emotion and dramatic narrative. Her two most famous works were *Appalachian* (1944), dealing with frontier life, and *Clytemnestra* (1957), based on Greek myths.

Paul Taylor (born 1930) and Twyla Tharp (born 1942), two students of Martha Graham, succeeded her as the leading exponents of modern dance, but differed from her in that they borrowed themes from popular culture. Tharp danced with her own company till 1987, when she became artistic associate of the American Ballet Theater. Another student of Martha Graham, Alvin Ailey (1931-89) set up the Alvin Ailey American Dance Theater in 1958. His most famous work is *Revelations* (1960), a dance suite set to gospel music. Mark Morris (born 1956) is a celebrated dancer and choreographer who formed his own dance group in 1988, which performs at the Brooklyn Academy of Music.

City Center in New York City is the main

venue for the dance companies of Martha Graham, Paul Taylor and others, along with the Joyce Theater which is in the Chelsea neighborhood.

The School of American Ballet was founded in 1934 by Russian-born choreographer George Balanchine (1904-83). He then became artistic director of the New York City Ballet when it was founded in 1948 and turned it into one of the best ballet companies in the world. He adapted traditional ballet to modern influences and set new standards in performance. Jerome Robbins (born 1918), who took over from Balanchine in 1983, had previously collaborated with Leonard Bernstein on several of Broadway's biggest musicals, including *West Side Story* (1957).

The New York City Ballet delights upstate visitors every summer in Saratoga Springs, its summer home away from home. Saratoga Springs is also the home of the fine Museum of Dance.

The Pennsylvania Ballet, founded by Barbara Weisberger in 1964, and the Pittsburgh Ballet are also highly regarded.

Literature

New York City and Philadelphia were important literary centers as far back as colonial times, although the latter declined in relative importance during the 19th century. As New York City developed into the USA's publishing capital – a position it retains today – it attracted writers from all over the country. Many of them had their works first published in the city's newspapers and magazines.

Important early writers included John Woolman (1720-72), a Quaker and an abolitionist, whose *Some Considerations upon the Keeping of Negroes* (1756) was influential in the decades leading up to the Civil War. Some early writers focused on the American Revolution. *The Federalist*, the country's first literary classic, was a collection of essays by Alexander Hamilton, James Madison and others recommending endorsement of the new constitution. Philip Freneau (1752-1832) was an outstanding, patriotic lyrical poet whose satirical work bridged 18th-century traditionalism and 19th-century romanticism.

An essayist and short-story writer, Washington Irving (1783-1859) was the first American literary figure to receive international recognition. His country estate was called Sunnyside, on the Hudson River near Tarrytown, NY, and the area around it is described by him in the stories 'Sleepy Hollow' and 'The Legend of Sleepy Hollow.' He also wrote a widely praised satire, *History of New York* (1809), under the pen name of Dietrich Knickerbocker.

In tribute to the book a group of writers adopted the term 'Knickerbocker' for their movement to develop a recognizably American literature. Foremost among them was James Fenimore Cooper (1789-1851), who drew images of the landscape and pioneer life on the American frontier in his *Leatherstocking* stories and of Native Americans in such works as *The Last of the Mohicans* (1826).

The Knickerbockers were satirized by literary critic, poet and Gothic horror-story writer Edgar Allan Poe (1809-49), who lived for a time in Philadelphia before settling in New York City. Among his most famous works are 'The Pit and the Pendulum,' 'The Black Cat' and 'The Raven.' An earlier Gothic writer, Charles Brockden Brown (1771-1810) was reputedly the first person in the US to earn a living solely by writing.

A contemporary of Poe's and a fellow reviewer, Margaret Fuller's (1810-50) *Woman in the Nineteenth Century* (1845) disclosed conditions in prisons and hospitals and helped inspire the later feminist movement in the US.

Prior to the Civil War a group of writers became known as Pfaff's Cellar because they used to meet at a place by that name on Broadway. Its leading member was Long Island's Walt Whitman (1819-92), whose poetry celebrated the plurality of American democratic society. His life work is contained in *Leaves of Grass* (originally published in 1855 and enlarged in later editions), which is considered one of the masterpieces of world literature and, true to

The *New Yorker*

The *New Yorker* was founded in 1925 by Harold Ross and Jane Grant. It began life as a humor magazine directed at a cultured, literate, inquiring audience who were depicted on its first cover by a cartoon of a monocled dandy watching a butterfly. This cover illustration is reused every year on the anniversary of the first edition.

The magazine gradually became more literary and regularly featured poetry and fiction, articles on prominent figures and significant social and political issues, and reviews of art, novels, movies and theater.

By the middle of the century the magazine had become an institution, but declining readership and revenue forced it to make significant changes, including the addition of photographs and more coverage of popular culture. Despite the changes, the *New Yorker* retained its satirical style, sophisticated humor and interest in human foibles.

Over the years the magazine has published and brought to prominence numerous literary figures. Early contributors to the magazine were the members of the Algonquin Round Table, including Dorothy Parker. Other contributors have been JD Salinger, Rebecca West, Ogden Nash, John Cheever, EB White, Marianne Moore, Raymond Carver, Ann Beattie, Rita Dove, John Updike and others.

Illustrations have always been a signature of the magazine, which has included the work of Rea Irvin (who designed the illustration for the very first cover), Charles Addams and Peter Arno.

Recently, celebrity editor-in-chief Tina Brown took over the magazine and has tried to bring its stodgy old ways up to date – to the dismay of old-line New Yorkers. She introduced photographs to the magazine and hired Richard Avedon as the 'staff photographer.' Some writers – including Garrison Keillor and Jamaica Kincaid – quit the magazine in protest of her changes. Despite this, the magazine continues to be an excellent source for local commentary and theater and movie reviews, as well as the site of 'Goings on about Town,' one of the best events calendars. ∎

New York fashion, has earned him the distinction of having a mall named after him on Long Island.

As New York City's power in publishing grew during the second half of the century, it attracted more and more writers, some of whom lived in the districts around Gramercy Park and Madison Square. One of the most notable was Henry James (1843-1916), who, though he lived mostly in England, grew up in New York City and returned from time to time in later life. In *Washington Square* (1881) he described upper-class life in that area before the Civil War. The row houses that were occupied by New York society still line the northern edge of Washington Square Park today.

A close friend of James' was Edith Wharton (1862-1937), who chronicled the gilded-age of New York City in the Pulitzer-prize-winning *Age of Innocence* (1920) and other works. However, most of her old New York – the original Metropolitan Opera house, the Metropolitan Museum of Art and the mansions of Fifth Ave's 'Millionaire's Row' – have disappeared or been altered beyond recognition.

In the 1920s an influential, lively and witty group of literary figures who had gotten to know each other writing for the *New Yorker* magazine met regularly at the Algonquin Hotel. They were known as the Algonquin Round Table and often invited people from the theater and film world to their lunches. Perhaps the most gifted of them was Dorothy Parker (1893-1967), who wrote poetry, plays and short stories as well as reviews for magazines. Others were the essayist Robert Benchley, and commentators HL Mencken, Edna Ferber and James Thurber.

From the early 20th century onwards, Greenwich Village rose to prominence as an artistic and literary colony, and many writers achieved fame by contributing to its publications. Among these were the playwright Eugene O'Neill (see Theater earlier) and the poet ee cummings (1894-1962). Some of the early short stories of

F Scott Fitzgerald (1896-1940) were published here, too, and with the success of his first novel, *This Side of Paradise* (1920), he became the chronicler and self-styled representative of the Jazz Age. A later collection of his short stories was published under the title *Tales of the Jazz Age* (1922); many of his works feature upper-crust New York, and Long Island was the site for *The Great Gatsby* (1925).

By the end of WWI, Harlem had become a vibrant, predominantly black neighborhood with a growing self-assertiveness. The publication in 1917 by the short-lived Greenwich Village magazine *Seven Arts* of Claude McKay's story 'Harlem Dancer' is said to mark the start of the Harlem Renaissance. The renaissance reached its peak in the 1920s and '30s, and, as well as McKay, its leading authors included Wallace Thurman, Jean Toomer, Langston Hughes, Countée Cullen and Zora Neale Hurston. McKay's novel, *Home to Harlem* (1928), about a black army deserter, was a best seller. Hurston's *Their Eyes were Watching God* (1937), whose theme is female independence and male oppression, became an important feminist work.

The Beat movement of the 1950s had its origins in the previous decade when Alan Ginsberg and others were still students at Columbia University. Ginsberg moved to the East Village in 1953 and was soon joined by other members of the movement. Aided by drink and drugs, they rejected crass materialism and convention. One of the early important Beat novels was William S Burroughs' *Junkie* (1953), a stark account of his early life as a drug addict. In 1956, when Ginsberg published a collection of verse called *Howl and Other Poems*, the publisher was tried but acquitted for having put out an obscene work. The media attention made Ginsberg famous. When Jack Kerouac's *On the Road*, written in one sitting, it is said, on a large ream of typewriter paper in the Chelsea Hotel, hit the bookstores in 1957, it became the compulsory reading of a generation. Of course, JD Salinger's *Catcher in the Rye* (1951) has spoken to three generations of manic teenagers with its portrayal of the misadventures of Holden Caulfield.

By the mid-1960s the Beat era was over, but it did influence the hippie movement (it was Ginsberg who coined the term 'flower power') and today's spoken word performers. Spoken word is an attempt to bring poetry to an audience so it can hear the voice of the poets and the rhythm and music of their poetry.

Though not a beatnik, Thomas Pynchon portrayed the restlessness of younger New Yorkers in *V* (1963). Alternatively, a group of writers including John Cheever and John Updike set out to document northeastern life of the upper-middle class during this time.

EL Doctorow's works, including *Ragtime*, *The Book of Daniel* and *World's Fair*, are loftier ruminations on New York in its various eras, from turn-of-the-century boomtown to Cold War ideological battleground.

A newer, more energetic style of writing dominated the '70s and '80s, with some writers adopting phantasmagoric or gothic styles. Don DeLillo's *Great Jones Street* (1973) and Mark Helprin's *Winter's Tale* (1983) are prime examples this new disturbing view of society. Writer Paul Auster, who lives in the Park Slope section of Brooklyn, has won many followers abroad for his *New York Trilogy* and more recently wrote the screenplay for the Brooklyn-based movie *Smoke*.

Jay McInerney was first blessed, then cursed with association to the yuppified early '80s with his blockbuster first novel *Bright Lights, Big City* (1984). Tom Wolfe's *Bonfire of the Vanities* (1987) followed up with its comic canvass of a city out of control and split along racial lines. Tama Janowitz, author of *Slaves of New York*, covers much of the same ground and enjoys a life of literary celebrity, as has essayist Fran Liebowitz.

In recent years, many new writers and spoken-word performers have emerged in the East Village of New York City, debuting their work at various cafes, but for the most part the generation-X novelists have been based on the West Coast.

Film

History To name the people from this region who have contributed to American cinema is to give a roll-call of some of the country's greatest movie legends.

The pioneer of filmmaking in the US was Thomas Edison, who had studios in Orange, NJ, and in New York City. The first ever box-office smash, *The Great Train Robbery* (1903), was produced by Edwin S Porter, an employee of Edison's. The film's success led to the emergence of the first permanent cinemas, called nickelodeons. Most early production studios were based in New York City, the national center of the movie industry up to WWI. Thereafter, most production moved to Hollywood.

The decade following the war was the heyday of the silent era, and the soaring skyscrapers of Manhattan inspired movies like Fritz Lang's futuristic masterpiece *Metropolis* (1926).

Although the 1920s and '30s were a time when fewer mainstream films were being produced in New York City, the Harlem Renaissance made that neighborhood a dynamic focal point for black movies. The most prominent black filmmaker was Oscar Micheaux, who fashioned around 40 feature-length films, many of which he wrote, produced, directed and edited himself. Few of his movies have survived, but a notable exception is *Body and Soul* (1924) with Paul Robeson.

In New York City in 1926, *Don Juan*, starring John Barrymore, was the first film with synchronized sound to be shown in a commercial theater. A disc with sound effects and music – but no talking – was played at the same time as the film. The following year, the appearance and success of *The Jazz Singer* with Al Jolson ushered in the talkies. The rise of talking pictures took many Broadway actors to Hollywood. Yet some movies were still to be made in New York City, allowing actors to work on a film while continuing their Broadway commitments.

With the arrival of sound, screen musicals came into favor. A memorable early example, *42nd St* (1933) is about a chorus girl plucked from obscurity to become a star in a Broadway show. *On the Town* (1949), about three sailors on shore leave in New York City, stars Gene Kelly and Frank Sinatra. Sinatra sings 'New York, New York' in Rockefeller Center.

The greater realism that could be achieved through sound also boosted the popularity of gangster movies. One of the first was *Lights of New York* (1928), but the genre only really took off with the success of *Little Caesar* (1931). Three New York actors closely identified with the gangster movies of this period were Humphrey Bogart, James Cagney and Edward G Robinson, who forever created the tough-guy urban image portrayed to the rest of the world.

The search for realism also took filmmakers out onto the streets. Although the city had appeared in numerous films up to the 1940s, these had mostly been studio recreations. *Naked City* (1948), adapted from photographer Weegee's novel about New York police in pursuit of a murderer, was one of the first films to feature a substantial number of city locations.

After WWII, New York City became the center for avant garde, experimental films typified by the likes of Andy Warhol and William Klein. The commercial success of Warhol's *Chelsea Girls* (1966) paved the way for other underground films and inspired later independent filmmakers.

Although TV was seen as a big threat to Hollywood in the 1950s, in New York City the combined presence of the theater, the major TV broadcasters and Madison Ave advertisers promoted the resurgence of the local film industry. Elia Kazan started as an actor and director in theater and before making *On the Waterfront* (1954) about corruption on the city's docks.

Sidney Lumet got his start in live TV and directed his first film, the courtroom drama *12 Angry Men*, in 1957. He has made many movies in the city since, see New York films, below.

In the 1960s and '70s, Woody Allen (see the following page) and Martin Scorsese, born in Brooklyn and Queens, respectively,

Woody Allen

Allen Stewart Konigsberg was born in Brooklyn in 1935 and grew up in Flatbush; he changed his name to Woody Allen in 1952. While he was still at high school he began writing gags for newspaper columnists like Earl Wilson and for TV comedians such as Sid Caesar and Art Carney. He also wrote sketches for stage revues. He created an image for himself as an intellectual, sex-obsessed loser – his self-deprecating style of humor became popular, and in 1961 he began performing stand-up comedy using his own material at New York City nightclubs and cafes. He was soon appearing on TV chat shows as well.

During the 1960s he wrote comic essays for the *New Yorker*, several Broadway hits and three books, and began his regular Monday-night performances as a jazz clarinetist at Michael's Pub.

His first foray into the world of movies was *What's New Pussycat?* (1965), in which he acted and for which he wrote the screenplay. In the decades since, he has been involved in a succession of films as director, screenwriter, actor or combinations thereof. Most of the films have been set in New York City. Though they feature superb roles for women and lots of comedy, the one constant is Allen's same anxiety-ridden Jewish character.

His most critically and commercially successful film is *Annie Hall* (1975), which received three Oscars. One of the most autobiographical is *Manhattan* (1979), which deals with the sex life of a neurotic TV comedy writer obsessed with New York. He also won a best-screenplay Oscar for *Hannah & Her Sisters* (1986) and was nominated again for *Crimes & Misdemeanors* (1989). Allen never went to Hollywood to receive his awards (it's usually held on a Monday night when he is booked at Michael's).

In 1992 and '93, the spotlight was turned on him during the court battle with Mia Farrow for custody of their three children. He lost the battle when it was revealed that he was having an affair with her daughter Soon-Yi, who had been adopted during her earlier marriage to André Previn. It was made even worse when Farrow accused him of molesting one of their children, though no evidence of this was ever found.

Allen has always had a cult following and those events don't seem to have had a long-term affect on his audiences. He continues to make movies, including *Mighty Aphrodite* (1995), a parody of a Greek tragedy, again set in New York, and *Everyone Says I Love You* (1996), a quirky musical comedy featuring Goldie Hawn, Alan Alda and Allen himself crooning famous love songs in New York, Paris and Venice. ■

became strongly associated with the city. Martin Scorsese's films have usually shown the tougher, harder edge to life in the city. See New York films below for suggested features from these filmmakers.

In the 1980s and '90s a new generation of filmmakers emerged. Among them is Spike Lee, whose films depict the black urban experience of the Brooklyn he grew up in. *Do the Right Thing* (1989), a controversial film about black-white tensions, is his best known work.

The Region as a Backdrop Hundreds of feature films have been set in New York in particular, but also in New Jersey and Pennsylvania, while others have used the states as a backdrop. The following is just a sampling.

New York One of the most memorable films set in New York City is *King Kong*, (1933) in which a giant ape is brought back from Africa then terrorizes the city when it escapes. The Statue of Liberty features in the dramatic climax to Alfred Hitchcock's *Saboteur* (1942), when Norman Lloyd falls to his death.

Breakfast at Tiffany's (1961) stars Audrey Hepburn as Holly Golightly, a somewhat-crazy call girl. Produced in the same year, *West Side Story* is an Oscar-winning musical set in New York's West Side.

Midnight Cowboy (1969) is the story of a small-town hustler, played by Jon Voight, who teams up with the seedy, streetwise Ratso Rizzo, played by Dustin Hoffman.

In *Saturday Night Fever* (1977), John Travolta and the other boys from North Brooklyn live for their Saturday night disco dancing.

Most of Neil Simon's stage plays have been set in New York City and subsequently made into movies. These include *Barefoot in the Park* (1967), *The Odd Couple* (1968), *The Goodbye Girl* (1978) and *The Sunshine Boys* (1975). *Lost in Yonkers* (1991) isn't about the city, but growing up in the suburb.

One of Woody Allen's most autobiograph-ical films set in New York was *Manhattan* (1979), which deals with the sex life of a neurotic TV comedy writer obsessed with the city. His other New York films include *Annie Hall* (1977), *Bullets over Broadway* (1994) and *Mighty Aphrodite* (1995).

Martin Scorsese directed *Taxi Driver* (1975), which stars Robert de Niro as a psychotic ex-Marine who drives a New York City taxi at night. *Goodfellas* (1990) is a gangster movie about real-life hood Henry Hill. Scorsese also directed *New York, New York* (1977), a musical tribute to the city set in the Big-Band era of the late '40s.

Sidney Lumet's later films were mainly set in New York City. *Dog Day Afternoon* (1975) tells of two inept robbers trapped in a Brooklyn bank. *Serpico* (1974) is a true story about police corruption.

Even recently, Hollywood hasn't forgotten the exciting and diverse settings of New York City. Starring Michael Douglas and directed by Oliver Stone, *Wall Street* (1987) satirized the 'greed is good' belief of the 1980s' high-rolling money traders. In 1989, Katz's Deli on the Lower East Side was the setting for Meg Ryan's infamous 'orgasm' scene in *When Harry Met Sally*. Brian de Palma's *Carlito's Way* (1993), starring Al Pacino and Sean Penn, is about an ex-convict from the barrio who tries to go straight. Director Wayne Wang's *Smoke* (1995) and *Blue in the Face* (1996), written by Brooklyn-based author Paul Auster, both star Harvey Keitel as a cigar-store clerk in the borough of Brooklyn.

The list could possibly be endless.

New Jersey Hoboken's docks were the setting for Elia Kazan's intense thriller *On the Waterfront* (1954). It tells the story of stevedore Terry Malloy, who gets revenge on the dockland boss responsible for his brother's death. In *Return of the Secaucus Seven* (1979), directed by John Sayles, political activists from the 1960s get together for a reunion. *Atlantic City* (1981) with Burt Lancaster and Susan Sarandon is about some small-time crooks eager to cash in on the city's new casinos.

In *Jersey Girl* (1992), a romantic comedy about class differences, a New Jersey schoolteacher crashes her car into a Mercedes and falls in love with the wealthy, handsome male owner from Manhattan.

Pennsylvania *The Philadelphia Story* (1940) is a romantic comedy about a spoiled, wealthy Philadelphia socialite starring Katherine Hepburn, Cary Grant and Jimmy Stewart (who won an Oscar for his role). The film was later remade as the musical *High Society* (1956), with Bing Crosby, Frank Sinatra and Philadelphia's own Grace Kelly.

Adapted from Christopher Morley's popular novel, *Kitty Foyle* (1940) is a film about a working-class woman living in the Philadelphia suburb of Frankford and stars Ginger Rogers.

Cecil B de Mille's *The Unconquered* (1947) is about the pioneering days in America and was partly shot in Cook Forest State Park in Northern Pennsylvania.

Steve McQueen meets an alien in the 1958 sci-fi movie *The Blob*, set in the western Philadelphia suburb of Phoenix-ville. Paul Newman plays a lawyer in *The Young Philadelphians* (1959). *The Molly Maguires* (1969) with Richard Harris and Sean Connery tells the story of striking miners in 1870s Pennsylvania.

Sylvester Stallone's five-film Rocky series is about a Philadelphia boxer who makes the big time. Stallone won an Oscar for his portrayal of Rocky Balboa in the original *Rocky* (1976).

The Deer Hunter (1978) starring Robert de Niro and Meryl Streep is about a Pennsylvania steel worker who goes to Vietnam and returns home.

In *Blow Out* (1981) a presidential candidate dies in a car accident in Wissahickon Creek and a sound technician, played by John Travolta, suspects murder.

Eddie Murphy and Dan Ackroyd swap social positions in Philadelphia in *Trading Places* (1983). In *Witness* (1985) Harrison Ford plays a Philadelphia cop who hides out on an Amish farm in Pennsylvania Dutch Country to protect the young witness to a murder that took place in a restroom in Philadelphia's 30th St Station.

In *Philadelphia* (1993), Tom Hanks plays a young AIDS-afflicted lawyer battling the legal, physical and emotional ramifications of the disease and the prejudices surrounding it. *Gettysburg* (1993) tells the story of the three-day battle that altered the course of the Civil War; it stars Martin Sheen as General Lee.

Terry Gilliam's 1995 film *12 Monkeys* is a vision of the future after a virus has wiped out most of the human race; Bruce Willis' character travels back in time to present-day Philadelphia to trace the cause of the virus. There is an excellent opening scene featuring the elaborate John Wanamaker department store.

TV

Historically, New York City was the center of the TV industry, and the major networks still have their head offices there, but today most programs set in the city are taped in Los Angeles. Many of these programs are sold around the world and their images of New York City, with their unrealistically large apartments and equally unrealistically dangerous streets, are constantly transmitted into people's homes. TV series of recent decades with a New York City setting include *The Defenders*, *Kojak*, *McCloud*, *The Odd Couple*, *Cagney & Lacey*, *NYPD Blue*, *Seinfeld* and *Friends*.

The chat show *Late Night with David Letterman* and news program *60 Minutes* are two successful shows that are still produced in New York City.

Painting

Painting in the colonial period generally followed the portrait styles of the immigrant artists' parent countries. An important 18th-century figure was Pennsylvania-born portraitist Benjamin West (1738-1820). He went to Britain and helped found the Royal Academy in 1768 in London, of which he became the second president. Later, he introduced romantic art to America, but, drawing inspiration from the American

Revolution, he and others gave it a democratic flavor.

At the time of the separation from Britain, America's top portrait painter was Charles Willson Peale (1741-1827), whose subjects were among the most prominent political and social figures of the day.

As the 19th century wore on American artists became less influenced by British painting and turned more to the natural scenery for inspiration. These painters founded a tradition of landscape painting in the US and were collectively known as the Hudson River school because they often used the river valley as material for their compositions. Foremost among them was Thomas Cole (1801-48), whose paintings depicted the wonder and isolation of the countryside. The grandiose paintings of his protégé, Frederic Edwin Church (1826-1900), combined art with science and religion.

Thomas Eakins (1844-1916), who developed a realist style of painting, is generally considered one of the leading American artists of the 19th century. His paintings emphasized the human figure and perspective. His best known work is the realistic depiction of a surgical operation in *Clinic of Doctor Gross* (1875).

Impressionism in the US was best exemplified by the work of Childe Hassam (1859-1935), who explored revised forms of the style in his paintings of cityscapes and interiors. He was also a founding member of The Ten, a group of American impressionists who exhibited together up to WWI. Another impressionist painter, Mary Cassatt (1845-1926) was noted for her etchings and oil paintings of domestic scenes, though she spent most of her working life in Europe.

In the first decades of the 20th century several concurrent art forms appeared in New York City. Robert Henri (1865-1929) led a group of artists who came to be known as The Eight. They rejected impressionism, which they saw as too refined, and insisted on a realism that represented urban, working-class life. Largely in response to the age's increasing mechanization, a

semi-abstract style also developed; this was influenced by cubism, which was introduced to the city by the photographer Alfred Stieglitz.

In 1913, a young French painter, Marcel Duchamp (1887-1968), caused a sensation at the 1913 'Armory' show (officially called the International Exhibition of Modern Art) with his cubist *Nude Descending a Staircase*, which most critics noted didn't seem to portray a recognizable nude *or* a staircase. Duchamp told the newsman that was exactly the point, and thus the New York school of Dada was begun.

Taking its name from the French slang for hobbyhorse, the Dada movement was led by Duchamp, fellow countryman Francis Picabia and American Man Ray (1890-1976), who became known for their anti-war attitudes and deconstructive art that sought to shock and offend. By the '20s, most of the Dadaists had moved on – Ray to photography, Duchamp to full-time celebrity – but the movement remains influential.

Others practiced a hybrid form of expression, as in the paintings of Charles Demuth (1883-1935) and Charles Sheeler (1883-1965). Usually using urban and industrial America as their subject matter and identified by straight lines and geometric planes, their work was known as cubist realism or precisionism.

Painting flourished in Harlem during the Harlem Renaissance of the 1920s and '30s. One of the most prominent artists was Aaron Douglas (1899-1979), who did illustrations for such publications as Eugene O'Neill's *The Emperor Jones* (1926) as well as murals of black Americans and Africans.

American art flourished after WWII with the emergence of a new school of painting called abstract expressionism, which, because it centered on New York City, was also called the New York School. Simply defined, it combined spontaneity of expression with abstract forms composed haphazardly. Abstract expressionism dominated world art until the mid-1980s, and two of its most famous exponents were Jackson

Andy Warhol

Andy Warhol (1928-87), one of the most influential US artists of the 20th century, was born in Pittsburgh, PA, in the district of Oakland. His parents were Polish immigrants; it was his mother's encouragement that prompted him to attend art classes at the Carnegie Institute (now Carnegie Mellon University).

When he graduated in 1949 he moved to New York City, where he became one of the country's leading freelance commercial artists. He developed an interest in pop art and by the early '60s was exhibiting some of his now-famous works, including the innovative, multi-image silkscreen paintings of Marilyn Monroe and the Campbell's soup cans.

At this time he began making experimental, 'underground' 16 mm movies; one of his first was *Sleep* (1963), an eight-hour silent film of a man sleeping. Warhol also managed the rock group The Velvet Underground, which toured the country as part of his multimedia presentation 'The Exploding Plastic Inevitable.' In the early '60s he opened a new studio known as the Factory (because it produced so many works), which became a social and production center for avant-garde artists.

In 1968 he was near-fatally shot by Valerie Solanas who had been rejected as part of Warhol's artistic circle. The 1996 film *I Shot Andy Warhol* dramatizes her life, the times and the event. The following year he began publishing the magazine *Interview*, featuring articles on fashion, movies and glamorous people. During the 1970s and '80s he continued to make celebrity portraits as well as producing some of his greatest paintings.

After Warhol's death it was decided to devote a museum to the man and his work. He had lived most of his life and achieved his fame in New York City, but, despite some controversy, the museum was established in his home town of Pittsburgh. Other recent films to portray Warhol include *Basquiat* (1996), with Warhol played by his old friend David Bowie, about New York City's art-crazed '80s, and *The Doors* (1991), which gives a glimpse of Warhol and the Factory at work. ■

Pollock (1912-56) and William de Kooning (born 1904).

From the 1950s modern art began to borrow images, items and themes from popular culture in a new movement called pop art, whose aim was to bring art as close as possible to daily life. Roy Lichtenstein (born 1923) and Jasper Johns (born 1930) were important in its development, but the prolific and innovative Andy Warhol (1928-87) was the most influential and successful.

He worked in many different media – drawing, painting, sculpture, silk-screening, photography, film, video and music.

During the same period there appeared a school of minimalist art, which uses simple shapes and designs and little color. Frank Stella (born 1936) is among its leading exponents.

In the '80s Warhol's legacy of the artist-as-celebrity spawned a host of well-known painters and illustrators whose work, to many critics, is somewhat questionable. But several of the artists/hustlers have broken out from New York's SoHo gallery scene to become internationally known, among them Julian Schnabel, Kenny Scharf and the late Keith Haring, who began his career as an underground graffiti artist.

Photography

Photography developed as an art form at the end of the 19th century, especially under the guidance of Alfred Stieglitz (1864-1946), who produced a number images of New York City but also did portraits, including many of his wife, Georgia O'Keeffe. Alice Austen (1866-1952) took photographs of the city's middle class as well as of immigrants and street life.

The city's role as a publishing center provided work opportunities for photographers, particularly with the addition of advertising agencies, fashion companies and news-gathering organizations. *Life* magazine was influential in the development of photojournalism and kept a large staff of photographers. Among them was Margaret Bourke-White (1904-71), who covered WWII and the Korean war and was one of the first woman photographers assigned to cover the US armed forces. Another was Alfred Eisenstaedt (1898-1995), a portraitist and news photographer who took the famous image of a sailor kissing a nurse in Times Square at the end of WWII.

Weegee (1899-1968), whose real name was Arthur H Fellig, was a press photographer noted for his on-the-spot street photography, but who also did portraits of celebrities and world leaders. William Klein and Richard Avedon were fashion photographers who worked for magazines like *Vogue* and *Harper's Bazaar* in the 1950s and '60s. Avedon's work also included portraits and shots of Vietnam War protesters and the civil rights movement.

In more recent years, many photographers have become as famous for their commercial work as their more artistic endeavors. These include Stephen Meisel,

Herb Ritts and Annie Liebowitz. Others have forged careers that almost never reach the general public through advertising. Prominent in this latter group are a few who have documented a unique urban scene, including Nan Goldin, who charted the lives (and many deaths) of her transvestite and junkie friends from the '70s to the present day, and Cindy Sherman, who specializes in conceptual series (such as those inspired by movie stills and crime-scene photos).

Museums & Galleries

Important venues where American and international paintings and other artwork can be viewed include New York City's prestigious Metropolitan Museum of Art, the Museum of Modern Art, the Frick, especially for early American works; the Whitney Museum of American Art, especially for modern and contemporary art; the Brooklyn Art Museum, and the Guggenheim Museum. The Albany Institute of History and Art has an excellent collection of Hudson River school paintings.

New Jersey is home to the outstanding Art Museum at Princeton University, and the Newark Museum also houses a distinguished art collection.

In Philadelphia, the Philadelphia Museum of Art and the Rodin Museum are two of the world's finest art museums, while the Barnes Foundation Gallery contains one of the world's largest private collections. Also in Philadelphia, the Pennsylvania Academy of the Fine Arts is a noted teaching center and the Second Bank of the United States is home to the National Portrait Gallery. In Pittsburgh, the Carnegie Museum of Art houses many famous paintings and the Andy Warhol Museum is dedicated solely to his work.

Architecture

America's early architectural styles reflect the different origins of the European settlers. These styles, at first distinct, eventually began to merge. The two main early influences in this region were Dutch and British.

Dutch colonial style, which survived to the end of the 18th century, consisted of practical, simple, solid buildings of stone, brick and wood. A distinctive feature of the architecture was Dutch doors – an upper door to let air in and a lower door to keep animals out. It occurred mainly in the Hudson Valley, western Long Island and northern New Jersey. Examples of the style include the Vechte-Cortelyou House in Brooklyn, as well as the Van Riper-Hopper House in Wayne, NJ.

When the British took over, their styles – particularly Georgian, named after the British monarchs – began to dominate. In America this influence lasted roughly from the start of the 18th century until the American Revolution. The red-brick buildings are simple and symmetrical, with delicate glass fanlights over large, elegant doorways. Philadelphia's Independence Hall is a notable example. After the revolution the style was modified slightly and became known as federal.

From the end of the 18th century, neoclassical architecture based on Roman and Greek designs became popular, and many state houses and public buildings incorporating these designs were built well into the 20th century. Two early exponents of neoclassicism were William Strickland, who designed the Second Bank of the US (1824) in Philadelphia, and British-born architect Benjamin Latrobe (1764-1820). During the mid-19th century, architects Richard Morris Hunt (1827-95) and Henry Hobson Richardson (1838-86) studied in Paris and on their return incorporated renaissance and Romanesque styles into their designs.

These architects also designed Gothic Revival buildings, another popular architectural style of the 19th century. It was given expression in many churches, like Trinity Church in New York City (1846), but was also used in colleges and universities (where it was called 'collegiate Gothic') Examples include City College in upper Manhattan (at 138th St and St Nicholas Ave), and College Hall in the University of Pennsylvania. The most prominent exponent of Gothic Revival toward the end of the 19th century was Frank Furness (1839-1912) who designed numerous buildings in Philadelphia, including the Pennsylvania Academy of the Fine Arts. Gothic Revival was also used in the design of many early skyscrapers, like the Woolworth Building in New York City (1913).

Cass Gilbert (1859-1934) designed the Woolworth Building, but he was also one of the main proponents of the Beaux Arts style, a mixture of classical architecture and elaborate ornamentation, borrowed from Europe. He built New York City's Custom House (1907), now the Museum of the American Indian.

Stanford White (1853-1906), who designed the former Penn Station, was the most influential architect in New York at the turn of the century.

The prolific Frank Lloyd Wright (1869-1959), possibly the greatest architect of the 20th century, came to prominence in the Midwest about 1900 and went on to design such masterpieces as New York's Guggenheim Museum (1959) and Pennsylvania's Fallingwater (1939).

The most prominent architect in recent decades has been Philip Johnson (born 1906) who designed part of Lincoln Center (1964) and more than a dozen other buildings in New York City.

It is with the skyscraper that the modern American city is closely identified, and no city more so than New York. Once the initial engineering problems were overcome, high-rise buildings multiplied and grew ever higher. At 60 stories, the Woolworth Building had been the tallest in the world, but was then overtaken by the Art Deco Chrysler Building (1930) and the Empire State Building (1931). Ludwig Mies van der Rohe (1886-1969), a pioneer of glass skyscrapers, designed the exterior of the Seagram Building (1958), at Park Ave and East 53rd St, that signaled the birth of the modern office tower.

CULTURE & SOCIETY

It's difficult to identify specific characteristics of this region that separate it from the wider US culture, largely because as the arts and media capital of the US it has helped to shape so much of that culture. One chief feature of the region is its widespread urbanization (see Population & People). It can be also be said that the region's urban areas are perhaps the most ethnically diverse in the country, though throughout the region those of Germanic background have always had a strong influence. Successive waves of immigrants over the centuries have contributed to the broader culture, but many have retained or are rediscovering aspects of their original culture. Whole neighborhoods are occupied by specific ethnic groups; statewide, it might be entire towns.

The Amish (AH-mish) have kept their old customs and dress and often resist the use of machinery. They still farm with horses and oxen and their buggies are a familiar sight in Lancaster County, PA, which has the largest community. Their folk art and cooking are famous. They have attracted a lot of attention from inquisitive tourists but don't like having photographs taken where their faces can be seen, as these are viewed as graven images.

One generalization about the people of upstate New York might not apply to their neighbors in Pennsylvania or New Jersey. There is a distinctive New England feel about the region – from the self-reliant air of many locals to the occasional Quaker community.

Visitors should be cautious about commenting on local political issues – don't broadcast your animal rights convictions in a bar full of hunters or denounce clearcutting in a mill town, for example, without having some idea of your audience.

About the only bastion of fashion politesse are fancy restaurants and a few urban clubs, which still require jackets for men. In any other eatery you'll see everything from black T-shirts to $3000 suits.

The Automobile

Foreign visitors soon realize that, for better or worse, the automobile has a tremendous influence on the American way of life. The region has a reasonably broad public transportation network, but in many areas a car is a necessity, and the scaling down of rail and bus services in recent decades is part cause, part result of the rise in the use of the automobile. For many Americans though, a car is not only a means of transportation but also a symbol of independence, social class and economic success.

RELIGION

The US constitution mandates separation of church and state, yet issues like prayer in public schools and the teaching of creationism versus evolution continue to be the subject of political discourse. Nominal allegiance is more widespread than church attendance, but many churchgoers are extremely devout.

Largely because of the immigrant nature of American society, travelers can find members of just about every religion, faith or sect in the major cities and even smaller towns will have several religious groups.

The oldest religions in North America are Native American religions, greatly modified since contact with Europeans.

The USA is predominantly Christian, and Roman Catholics constitute the largest religious group in New York, New Jersey and Pennsylvania. Of the Protestant Christian groups the largest, in descending order, are Baptists, Methodists, Lutherans, Presbyterians and Episcopalians. Judaism is the largest non-Christian religion and Islam finds many adherents in the black community. Pennsylvania still has a number of Quakers, whose ancestors, most notably William Penn, founded the state on the principle of religious tolerance. That tolerance attracted religious refugees from Europe, including the Amish and Mennonites, who live mostly in the region known as Pennsylvania Dutch Country.

LANGUAGE

English is spoken throughout the USA, and American English is relatively uniform when compared to, say, the varieties of English spoken in Britain. Nevertheless, the US has regional differences in accent, idiom and use of vocabulary, and foreign visitors, even those fluent in English, may find it challenging when they come to this part of the country.

American English has borrowed words from the languages of successive waves of immigrants, and for many Philadelphia or New York City was their first point of arrival. From the Germans have come words like 'hoodlum,' from Yiddish-speaking Jews words like 'schmuck' (a 'fool'), from the Irish 'yous' for you, from Italian and Spanish many words relating to food and so on.

Visitors will hear, for example, the New Jersey accent where a word like 'heard' becomes 'hoid;' the distinctive vocabulary of blacks from Harlem or North Philadelphia; and the accent of the Amish in Pennsylvania who speak English when conducting business with outsiders but at home speak Pennsylvania Dutch (a corruption of 'Deutsch'), a German dialect.

In the 18th century, Ben Franklin, by trade a printer, sought to rationalize and standardize the disordered spelling of the English language. Although his plans weren't adopted at the time, he did influence Noah Webster, who published the *American Dictionary of the English Language* in 1828. It was Webster who popularized the change in spellings of such words as 'theater' for 'theatre,' 'color' for 'colour' and 'center' for 'centre,' though today people may still see both alternative spellings used.

English has never been made the country's official language, but there are calls by some to do so, fearing the encroachment of Spanish, the next most widely spoken language in the US.

In upstate New York near the border area with Canada some French is spoken and many of the inhabitants have surnames and traditions tied to French-Canadian life.

Facts for the Visitor

PLANNING

When to Go

When to visit the region largely depends on what you want to do when you get here. The months that are least hospitable to visitors are November to February, when it's cold, rainy and the daylight hours are short. But for skiers that's when many of the best snowfalls occur, and in the cities many cultural institutions like the symphony orchestras, opera and theater are most active. There are, in addition, festivals and sporting events throughout the year.

Late spring (late April to May) and fall are the best periods to visit, when most sights and tourist offices are open and the weather is generally mild and pleasant, though storms do occur especially along the coast. In the Adirondacks, 'mud season' arrives just after the first thaw. And, anywhere from late May to early July, the 'fifth season' arrives – with its prominent and hungry guest, the black fly. They bite.

Having a continental climate means the summers can get really hot, and warm air from the Gulf of Mexico can make the humidity stifling. 'Tourist season' throughout the region is summer – which begins on Memorial Day and ends on Labor Day. In many communities along the Jersey Shore, summer is the only time to go; many amusements and restaurants that can't survive on a local clientele are closed by mid-September, though some hotels remain open.

Mid-September through October is one of the busiest times, when people come to see the magnificent fall colors of the forests, but accommodations prices rise accordingly. And many visitors combine this with some early Christmas shopping in New York City's department stores or the factory outlets of New Jersey and Pennsylvania.

What Kind of Trip?

Your particular interests have a large bearing on the kind of trip it'll be, as will the amount of time and money at your disposal. The longer you stay, the more likely you'll step outside the often-superficial world of the tourist and the lower your relative daily expenses will be. If you're visiting from abroad and you're able to work or study in the US, make the most of the opportunity.

If your holiday is limited, try to leave enough time to do a walk or two through the countryside and spend a couple of days somewhere off the beaten track. New York City and Philadelphia are great cities, but can be expensive and only represent part of what there is to experience.

To many places outside the major cities there's no public transportation, so you may want to consider renting or buying a car. On the other hand, most attractions can be visited as part of a guided tour from the metropolitan centers. This is often a good way to get a quick overview of areas you're unfamiliar with and allows you to consider your options should you want to return and perhaps spend more time.

Traveling alone is fine, provided you follow the normal precautions, and is a great way to meet new people. Hostels and campgrounds are good places to meet fellow travelers and B&Bs are a good way to meet locals, who may offer insights unavailable at the nearby tourist office.

Maps

The maps in this book provide a useful first reference, and excellent maps are available throughout the USA. There are several different categories.

Street & Highway Maps Free state maps are available from state tourist offices and Welcome Centers (see Local Tourist Offices below), and city or town maps are available, free or low cost, from local tourist offices and/or chambers of commerce. These are usually adequate for most purposes. The Streetwise series of laminated fold-out maps are also quite good for major cities and significant neighborhoods within those cities.

The American Automobile Association (AAA) issues comprehensive and dependable highway maps, which are free with AAA membership or available to nonmembers for a few dollars. These maps range from national, regional and state maps to detailed maps of cities, counties and even relatively small towns.

Publishers that provide a similar range of maps are Hagstrom, Rand McNally and Gousha Travel Publications, and these can be bought at bookstores, convenience stores, gas stations etc.

Topographical Maps The US Geological Survey (USGS), an agency of the federal Department of the Interior, publishes detailed topographic maps of the country at different scales up to 1:250,000. Maps at 1:62,500, or approximately one inch to one mile, are ideal for backcountry hiking and backpacking.

A free catalog and a list of stores that sells its maps are available from USGS (☎ (303) 236-7477), Map & Book Sales, PO Box 25286, Denver, CO 80225. Many camping stores, NPS visitor centers and USFS ranger stations sell USGS maps of their immediate area.

The NPS provides maps of parks, NRAs, national reserves and national trails. USFS ranger stations sell maps of national forest areas for a few dollars.

The best commercially published hiking maps are from Jimapco (☎ (518) 899-5091). They make full color, topographic maps for every hiking region in New York state.

Atlases Visitors spending a significant amount of time in the region should try to acquire the appropriate state volume of the DeLorme Mapping series of atlases and gazeteers for New York and Pennsylvania. These contain detailed topographic and highway maps at a scale of 1:250,000 as well as helpful listings of campgrounds,

historic sites, parks, natural features and even scenic drives. They are especially useful off the main highways and cost about $20 each; they're readily available in good bookstores or you can contact DeLorme Mapping Company (☎ (207) 865-4171, (800) 335-6763), PO Box 298, Freeport, ME 04032.

Similar large-format city street atlases are produced by ADC The Map People (☎ (703) 750-0510; fax 750-3092), 6440 General Green Way, Alexandria, VA 22312.

What to Bring

Since you can buy just about anything along the way, it's better to pack light and pick up extras as you need them.

A travelpack – a combination of backpack and shoulder bag – is a good item for carrying gear. A travelpack's straps zip away inside the pack when not needed, making it easy to handle in airports and on crowded public transportation. It also looks reasonably smart and can be made reasonably thief-proof with small combination locks or even just a safety pin holding the zip tags together.

Your clothing will depend on the season. It's a good idea to bring a raincoat or an umbrella, and some warm clothes even in summer if you intend to visit areas of higher elevation. Insulation works on the principle of trapped air, so several layers of thin clothing are warmer than a single thick one (and will be easier to dry). Dress is usually casual.

A packing list might include a warm sweater, a solid and comfortable pair of shoes, shower shoes for shared bathrooms, waterproof jacket, combination padlock, neck pouch or money belt, small daypack and a toiletry bag stuffed with all the trimmings (toothpaste, shaving cream, band-aids etc).

A sleeping bag is useful in hostels and when visiting friends; get one that can be used as a quilt. A sleeping sheet with a pillow cover is necessary if you plan to stay in hostels, though you can buy or rent one if you don't bring your own.

Other possible items include a compass (to help orient yourself on walks), an alarm clock or watch with an alarm function and an adapter plug for electrical appliances and a small radio with an alarm and short-wave capability to tune-in to many of the region's hundreds of radio stations.

SUGGESTED ITINERARIES

There's no 'right' way to see this region, though it can help to have some sample itineraries that you can variously modify and combine to suit your interests and the time of year. In summer or in the autumn foliage season, try to visit cities on weekends and country towns and resorts on weekdays. This will help you find lower prices and fewer crowds.

One Week or Less

New York City is rightly the magnet that draws most visitors to the region, so if you only have a week or less, base yourself there. In the first two days you can visit the top attractions – the Statue of Liberty, Empire State Building, South Street Seaport, Rockefeller Center and Wall St, provided you map out a plan on getting to the paid-admission spots early in the morning.

Then take another day or two to explore the museums, like the Metropolitan Museum of Art, along Fifth Ave's Museum Mile, and stroll in Central Park. Exploring some well-known neighborhoods – SoHo, Chinatown and Greenwich Village – can be done in one (exhausting) day and might include a trip on the Staten Island Ferry. On any night, take in a famous bar, Broadway show or a club concert.

For excursions, you can easily plan a day trip to the lower Hudson Valley; an ideal destination offering an entertaining lesson in history. Tarrytown, on the east bank of the Hudson River, was the home of Washington Irving and his Ichabod Crane stories. Woodstock is in the Catskills, just west of the Hudson Valley and a two hour drive from Manhattan. This picturesque town has a thriving arts community and also offers one of the best views of the

Hudson Valley, below, from Overlook Mountain. Further north on the Hudson, between Hyde Park and Rhinebeck, the FDR Library & Museum and Eleanor Roosevelt's cottage of Val-kill are historical landmarks.

Or try to visit New Jersey's major northern cities of Hoboken, Newark or Jersey City. If you're too exhausted to travel to New York City's outer boroughs, all three of these New Jersey cities are readily accessible by public transportation (including ferries from Manhattan to Jersey City and Hoboken).

It's also possible (though a bit exhausting) to take a bus for a day trip to Atlantic City. The college towns of Princeton or the state capital of Trenton are also good day trips especially by car from Philadelphia. The activity-oriented visitor can head by car to the Poconos region of northern Pennsylvania, where winter skiing and summer amusements like hiking and horseback riding are popular in places such as the Delaware Water Gap.

From New York City, a day trip to Philadelphia to see its historic sites and perhaps one or two of its museums is also quite feasible by public transportation. If you're driving – and you leave early enough – you might take in some of the sights to the north of the city such as Washington Crossing Historic Park and the village of New Hope in Bucks County.

Two Weeks

In the second week you can explore further afield to get some taste of the variety of the region. Your itinerary will change depending on the season, but the following may be of some help.

Heading north to upstate New York, continue through the Hudson Valley, past Albany, to Saratoga Springs, home to culture, horses and bottled water. The town was famous in the 19th century for its European-like spas, the Lincoln and Roosevelt Baths. Saratoga is a small town with a lot to do. Take a short drive to see the ornate mansions on N Broadway, just south of Skidmore College. The nearby Saratoga

Battlefield offers a glimpse of the setting for the most pivotal battle of the War of Independence in 1777, when the British Crown forces surrendered to the colonies.

On the way back to New York City, Cooperstown can offer a day or two of touring. Besides the Baseball Hall of Fame, the James Fenimore Cooper Museum and the Farmers' Museum are both fascinating. Otsego Lake on the edge of town is a must stop, if for nothing else than to recover from trying to squeeze in too much of Cooperstown. The park by the lake is lovely and shaded.

If you head south from New York City along the coast you can spend a day or so at one or two of the New Jersey shore communities such as Ocean Grove, before heading west to Princeton, and another day to Camden to visit the New Jersey State Aquarium. From there it's just a short hop across the Delaware River into Philadelphia.

The center of Philadelphia is reasonably compact, so it's possible to see many of its major sights – Penn's Landing, Old Town, National Independence Historic Park, the Fairmount Parkway museums, South St, Society Hill, Italian Market – before heading to the nearby northwestern picturesque suburbs of Germantown, Manyunk or Chestnut Hill. If you still have time you might consider making a trip out to Valley Forge, the Brandywine Valley or Pennsylvania Dutch Country.

Three Weeks or More

With three weeks to spend, you'll have time to see New York City, Philadelphia and other major sights as well as venture to some of the more remote areas, many of which are of interest to outdoor enthusiasts. The region is small enough that you can combine many of these routes.

Upstate New York With more than seven days to spare outside of a major city, continue north in New York state past Saratoga Springs to Lake George and on to the Adirondack Mountains. Lake Placid is only the most famous name in the Adirondack

Park. Blue Mountain Lake, Saranac Lake and Long Lake are among the many small lakes that adorn this gentle rolling landscape. Hiking trails and canoe trails on chains of lakes and extensive rivers are common, and there are organizations and businesses there to help beginners and experts find their way, rent equipment and enjoy a safe adventure.

Exit the Adirondacks to the west through Watertown, then head south through Syracuse to Ithaca, on the southern tip of Cayuga Lake in the Finger Lakes region. Ithaca is a cultural gem, and a great place to begin a tour of the Finger Lakes. In fact, you can drive west in a zig-zag fashion through the lakes, often finding splendid towns at the top and bottom ends of each lake. Keuka Lake is famous for several wineries, and there's a self-guided winery tour that takes you around the lake. Further west is Canandaigua Lake, as beautiful as the others, but less frequented, with the charming town of Naples at its southern end.

Alternatively, you can miss the Adirondacks, to start upstate New York in the Finger Lakes region and continue north from Naples, and visit the George Eastman House in Rochester. This is the home of Kodak, and the lavish mansion is home to one of the best photography exhibits in the state.

Continue west to Buffalo. The Albright-Know Art Gallery is one of the largest museums in the northeast. Of course, Niagara Falls is the biggest attraction here, and you should time your visit to see the falls in the late afternoon light, from the Canadian side. Be sure to allow ample time to cross the international border, even though it's only a three minute drive.

Southwest New York is notable for the Chautauqua Institution, on the shore of Lake Chautauqua between Mayville and Jamestown. Chautauqua is an American classic, having served as a center for education and the arts since its founding in 1874.

From here you can venture into Northern Pennsylvania and the Allegheny National Forest and the Poconos. But to begin the return trip to New York City, take Route 17 east to Salamanca, just north of New York's Allegany State Park, and onto the junction with Route 417. This is one of the most scenic roads in all of the state, passing through Andover and on to Corning, home of the Corning Glass Center and Museum of Glass.

Continuing east, Ithaca, Cooperstown and the western Catskills are also on the way back to New York City.

New Jersey In New Jersey, seven spare days will provide you with enough time to visit the gambling tables of Atlantic City and, assuming you haven't lost all your money, a restful day or two in the charming town of Cape May at the state's southern tip; from there you can walk along New Jersey's whitest (and cleanest) beach or track migratory birds at Cape May Point State Park.

Pennsylvania In Pennsylvania, after visiting Pennsylvania Dutch Country head west to Gettysburg, where you can spend a full day touring the national military park with its Civil War sights and wandering around the historic town.

Pittsburgh is a few hours' drive west from Philadelphia and requires a couple of days to take in the views from Mt Washington, the Andy Warhol Museum and the Carnegie complex in Oakland. Southeast of the city are the Laurel Highlands where the main attractions are Frank Lloyd Wright's architectural gem, Fallingwater, and white-water rafting, canoeing and hiking. Rafting is at its best in spring when the rivers are at their highest and whitest. Allow at least a couple of days here.

Another four or five days would allow you to devote some time to outdoor recreational pursuits in the huge Allegheny National Forest, in Northern Pennsylvania, before heading east along scenic Route 6 to the Pocono Mountains with their natural beauty and wide range of outdoor activities. This trip is particularly worthwhile in autumn when the forest foliage changes color. From Northern Pennsylvania you can also head north to see the attractions of Western New York and from the Poconos it's only a few hours drive to New York City.

HIGHLIGHTS

Throughout the region, the forests' **fall foliage** is a huge attraction – even in New York City when the trees in Central Park lighten up. It's hard to believe the trees can produce so many shades of red. You can enjoy this in all three states with a few-hours' long drive through the countryside, or make a tour of it, staying at inns and B&Bs along the way.

New York

The extensive variety of New York's topography and cultures is stimulating, and often startling. Elements of the busy Big Apple, the agricultural Midwest and New England formality exist side by side. Ithaca and Saratoga Springs are two of the most culturally blessed towns in the state, and much more navigable than New York City. Saratoga Springs, in fact, has the best of both worlds in the summer: besides horse-racing, the city is the summer home to the New York City Ballet and the Philadelphia Philharmonic Orchestra.

New York City The view of **Manhattan's skyline** from the Staten Island or Statue of Liberty ferries is a familiar yet breathtaking sight that seems too spectacular to actually be real. You can visit many different cultures in the space of a single 90 minute walk – covering Lower Manhattan and the financial and courthouse district through to Chinatown, to Little Italy along Mulberry St; then to the funky downtown cafes in the East Village, where you'll also find Polish, Middle Eastern, Indian, Korean and Japanese restaurants and antique stores on E 9th St. (Not to mention the astounding number of different cultures found in the boroughs of Brooklyn and Queens.)

That, of course, is in addition to all the architectural and high-culture attractions of the city, including the **Metropolitan Museum of Art** and the **Museum of Modern Art**, two world-class institutions that should be on any art-lover's 'to-do' list.

Shopping in New York City To paraphrase the song, if you can't buy it here, you can't buy it anywhere. The city offers truc bargains (or the best selection at reasonable prices) in clothing, jewelry, electronics, antiquities, food and even just plain kitsch. You just need to know where to look and – most importantly – patronize reputable dealers in each category.

Long Island Summers Some of the country's prettiest beaches are accessible by public transportation from New York City. You can reach the egalitarian **Robert Moses State Park** in just about an hour by taking the train from Penn Station; ditto for the more exclusive **Hamptons** at the southern fork of Long Island as well as the wineries of the north fork, both about three hours by car or train.

The Catskills Lush and gentle mountain getaways exist alongside excellent hiking, biking and winter skiing among ridge-top views of the Hudson Valley below. Woodstock, home to a thriving arts and music community, still retains a convivial village atmosphere.

Hudson Valley This region, easily a day-trip from New York City, is home to Washington Irving's Sleepy Hollow legends, pick-your-own apple orchards, opulent mansions and riverside villages with funky bookstores and sidewalk bistros in the summertime.

Finger Lakes In this region you'll find elegant glacial lakes, charming Ithaca and the Cornell University Plantations, river gorges and Taughannock Falls, the highest in the state. Visit over 50 wineries between Canandaigua and Seneca lakes to sample the juice of the grape.

Cooperstown Many people pilgrimage to this picturesque, franchise free, lakeside village and home to the National Baseball Hall of Fame, always popular with children of all ages.

Adirondack Park This state park is an outstanding year-round wilderness region – a canoeing, biking and hiking mecca. It's home to Lake Placid, site of the 1932 and 1980 Winter Olympics. Don't miss the excellent collection of Indian lore at the Six Nations Museum, in Onchiota.

Saratoga Springs One of New York's loveliest towns, this is home to old-world mineral baths and to the fastest thoroughbred horses in the country at the Saratoga Race Track, where strolling minstrels delight summer crowds. Saratoga's Caffe Lena is the nation's oldest coffeehouse, and still hosts some of the country's best folk musicians.

Niagara Falls Seeing is believing. Take a boat ride under the spray of the falls or stand next to the roar of the water. In the evening, check out nearby Buffalo's lively theater and cafe scene.

New Jersey

Newark's Unknown Treasures Long overshadowed by New York City and beset by municipal corruption and urban decay, New Jersey's largest city is often ignored by travelers. But if you're in the area for a one-week stay or more, it's worth considering a quick day-trip via public transportation to visit the well-regarded **Newark Museum** along with the Ironbound district just east of the train/bus/subway station. There in the safe and friendly neighborhood of recent Portuguese immigrants you'll find a good selection of well-priced establishments offering delicious barbecue fare and wonderful baked goods.

Great Adventure If you're looking for a theme park, this is it. Great Adventure is the northeast's largest such park, larger in acreage than Disney World. Located in the middle of New Jersey, it features a drive-through safari park and more than 100 heart-stopping rides.

Princeton This is the quintessential university town and home to several famous

What New York, New Jersey & Pennsylvania Could Do Without:

- The entire region's seasonal weather extremes
- Attitude: In the region, there is a certain provincialism, perhaps common to places of international renown, among some people that can be bothersome. Their attitude seems to be: 'We're here, and there's no need to be anywhere else, or be too interested for that matter!' Most folks, of course, are quite helpful and curious.
- The high cost of accommodations and car rental in New York City. Both can be prohibitively expensive for residents and visitors alike.
- You can't buy liquor or wine from stores anywhere in New York state on Sunday. Barbaric.

- The hassle of getting to and from the NYC airports
- Getting around is a common gripe among New Yorkers, who are annoyed by such facts of life as tolls on the New York State Thruway.
- Mud and blackflies which drive people to the edge in May and June in the Adirondacks.
- New Jersey traffic cops
- New Jersey turnpike tolls and beach fees
- It's against the law to pump your own gas in New Jersey, so you have to wait a long time to fill up in summer weather.
- Hershey, PA's Hersheypark
- Some of Gettysburg's tacky museums ■

---

authors (Toni Morrison, Joyce Carol Oates), with a pleasant self-contained campus and an important art collection.

Cape May You can check out many perfectly maintained Victorian homes in this charming town, a short trip from either Atlantic City or Philadelphia. After a day of house-touring, you can sun yourself on the town's beach (featuring pristine white sand) or go birdwatching in the nearby observatory. There's also the free Cape May County Zoo, an impressive collection of animals.

New Jersey State Aquarium Though Camden is one of the most crime-ridden and depressed cities in the state, the new aquarium is an admirable and successful attempt to bring some life back to the waterfront. It's an easy day trip from Penn's Landing in Philadelphia.

Atlantic City This well-known beachfront community offers three reasons to visit: gambling, gambling and gambling. Be prepared to be assaulted by the gaudy glory of the gaming culture.

Pennsylvania

Philadelphia Many of Philadelphia's historical buildings have been restored since the 1976 bicentennial celebrations, and **National Independence Historic Park** with its Independence Hall and Liberty Bell serve as a reminder of the country's struggle for independence.

Take a scenic trip along Kelly Dr beside the Schuylkill River in **Fairmount Park**, the world's largest city park. At the southern end of the park is the **Philadelphia Museum of Art** one of the country's largest and best art museums; and from its steps there's a great view of the city back along the Benjamin Franklin Parkway. Philadelphia has many other interesting museums.

Another highlight is Philadelphia's food. It has some of the top restaurants in the country offering the best of haute cuisine, but quality and variety can be found at all budget levels.

Pennsylvania Dutch Country The commercialism notwithstanding, the area of Lancaster County east of the city of Lancaster is worth visiting to see how the

Amish retain their traditional way of life in the face of the pressures of modernity.

Gettysburg National Military Park The Battle of Gettysburg was one of the most significant in US history. Despite the many tourist traps, a visit to the town itself, with its historic buildings, the battlefield and the National Cemetery, where Lincoln gave his address, is well worth it.

Pittsburgh Take the Monongahela or Duquesne Incline up **Mt Washington** for a terrific view of the city's downtown, the Golden Triangle. The **Andy Warhol Museum**, dedicated entirely to the artist's work, stands as testimony to his importance in modern American and world art.

The **Cathedral of Learning** in the suburb of Oakland is an amazing example of Gothic architecture.

Laurel Highlands This popular recreational area in Southwestern Pennsylvania is most notable for its white-water rafting on the Youghiogheny River.

Allegheny National Forest This huge forest in Northern Pennsylvania is a great place to get away from it all. It has plenty of wildlife and provides opportunities for outdoor recreation including hiking, canoeing, cross-country skiing, birdwatching and fishing.

The Poconos The Pocono Mountains in northeastern Pennsylvania form a picturesque part of the state, and include scenic places like the **Delaware Water Gap National Recreation Area**. The small town of Jim Thorpe has retained its historic character. Skiing, hiking, mountain biking, canoeing and sailing are popular outdoor recreational activities.

Hershey The home of Hershey chocolate contains a heavily promoted but tacky theme park, with its mock chocolate factory, amusement park and nearby zoo. Kids probably love it.

TOURIST OFFICES
Local Tourist Offices
Each state is divided into tourism regions, each of which has a tourist bureau with information on the local area. The addresses for these regional tourist bureaus are given in each state's vacation guide, available from the state tourist office (see below). New Jersey and Pennsylvania also have a series of tourist offices called 'Welcome Centers' strategically positioned on the turnpikes and interstate highways.

Many towns don't have tourist offices as such; this function is often performed by the local chamber of commerce. They can provide information about what to see and where to stay, but often assume that tourists have unlimited budgets and travel by car; they're unlikely to refer visitors to budget accommodations and restaurants and may be unaware of transportation options. The address and phone number of tourist offices or chambers of commerce are given in the Information section for each town.

State Tourist Offices
State tourist offices supply free maps and colorful vacation guides with details of each state's main attractions. These brochures are updated annually and contain addresses and telephone numbers of local tourist offices, chambers of commerce, accommodations lists and other useful information. If you have a specific need or question, state tourist offices may be able to answer them directly or refer you to the appropriate office. The state authorities are:

New York
  Division of Tourism
  1 Commerce Plaza, Albany, NY 12245
  (☎ (800) 225-5697)

New Jersey
  Division of Travel & Tourism
  CN 826, 20 W State St, Trenton, NJ 08625
  (☎ (800) 537-7397)

Pennsylvania
  Office of Travel Marketing
  453 Forum Building, Harrisburg, PA 17120
  (☎ (717) 787-5453, (800) 237-4363)

EMBASSIES & CONSULATES

Foreign Embassies & Consulates in the USA

Most nations have an embassy or main consulate in Washington, DC. To find out the telephone number of your embassy or consulate call Washington, DC, information (☎ (202) 555-1212). Many also have a consulate in New York City and Philadelphia; see those chapters for a listing or check the local yellow pages of a telephone directory under 'Consulates.'

US Embassies & Consulates Abroad

US diplomatic offices abroad include the following:

Australia
US Embassy:
21 Moonah Place,
Yarralumla, ACT 2600
(☎ (2) 6270 5000)

US Consulate-General:
Level 59 MLC Center
19-29 Martin Place,
Sydney, NSW 2000
(☎ (2) 9373 9200)

There are also consulates in
Melbourne, Perth and Brisbane.

Austria
Boltzmanngasse 16, A-1091,
Vienna (☎ (1) 313-39)

Belgium
Blvd du Régent 27, B-1000,
Brussels (☎ (2) 513 38 30)

Canada
US Embassy:
100 Wellington St,
Ottawa, Ontario K1P 5T1
(☎ (613) 238-5335)

US Consulate-General:
1095 West Pender St,
Vancouver, BC V6E 2M6
(☎ (604) 685-1930)

US Consulate-General:
1155 rue St Alexandre,
Montreal, Quebec
(☎ (514) 398-9695)

There are also consulates in
Toronto, Calgary and Halifax.

Denmark
Dag Hammarskjolds Allé 24,
Copenhagen (☎ 31 42 31 44)

Finland
Itainen Puistotie 14A, Helsinki
(☎ (0) 171-931)

France
US Embassy:
2 rue St Florentin, 75001 Paris
(☎ (01) 42.96.12.02)

There are also consulates in
Bordeaux, Lyon, Marseilles,
Nice, Strasbourg and Toulouse.

Germany
Deichmanns Aue 29, 53179
Bonn (☎ (228) 33 91)

Greece
91 Vasilissis Sophias Blvd,
10160 Athens (☎ (1) 721-2951)

India
Shanti Path,
Chanakyapuri 110021,
New Delhi (☎ (11) 60-0651)

Indonesia
Medan Merdeka Selatan 5,
Jakarta (☎ (21) 360-360)

Ireland
42 Elgin Rd, Ballsbridge,
Dublin 4 (☎ (1) 687 122)

Israel
71 Hayarkon St, Tel Aviv
(☎ (3) 517-4338)

Italy
Via Vittorio Veneto 119a-121,
Rome (☎ (6) 46 741)

Japan
1-10-5 Akasaka Chome,
Minato-ku, Tokyo
(☎ (3) 224-5000)

Korea
82 Sejong-Ro, Chongro-ku,
Seoul (☎ (2) 397-4114)

Malaysia
376 Jalan Tun Razak, 50400
Kuala Lumpur (☎ (3) 248-9011)

Mexico
Paseo de la Reforma 305,
Cuauhtémoc,
06500 Mexico City
(☎ (5) 211-00-42)

Netherlands
US Embassy:
Lange Voorhout 102, 2514 EJ
The Hague (☎ (70) 310 92 09)

US Consulate:
Museumplein 19, 1071 DJ
Amsterdam (☎ (20) 310 9209)

New Zealand
29 Fitzherbert Terrace,
Thorndon, Wellington
(☎ (4) 722 068)

Norway
Drammensvein 18,
Oslo (☎ (22) 44 85 50)

Philippines
1201 Roxas Blvd, Ermita,
Manila 1000 (☎ (2) 521-7116)

Russia
Novinskiy Bul'var 19-23,
Moscow (☎ (095) 252-2451)

Singapore
30 Hill St, Singapore 0617
(☎ 338-0251)

South Africa
877 Pretorius St, Box 9536,
Pretoria 0001 (☎ (12) 342-1048)

Spain
Calle Serrano 75, 28006 Madrid
(☎ (1) 577 4000)

Sweden
Strandvagen 101,
S-115 89 Stockholm
(☎ (8) 783 5300)

Switzerland
Jubilaumsstrasse 93,
3005 Berne (☎ (31) 357 70 11)

Thailand
95 Wireless Rd, Bangkok
(☎ (2) 252-5040)

UK
US Embassy:
5 Upper Grosvenor St,
London W1A 1AE
(☎ (0171) 499 9000)

US Consulate-General:
3 Regent Terrace,
Edinburgh EH7 5BW
(☎ (131) 556 8315)

US Consulate-General:
Queens House,
Belfast BT1 6EQ
(☎ (1232) 328 239)

Tourist Offices Abroad

US consulates sometimes have tourist information to distribute. The United States Travel & Tourism Administration (USTTA) no longer has offices abroad.

A number of US cities, states and regions have tourism offices in the UK, but these can only be contacted by phone. A list of phone numbers is available from the US embassy or consulates in the UK. There's no number for New York state, but there are for the Port Authority of New York & New Jersey (☎ (0171) 439-0020), New Jersey (☎ (0171) 404-3703) and Pennsylvania (☎ (0171) 470-8801).

VISAS & DOCUMENTS

All foreign visitors (other than Canadians) must bring their passport. US citizens and Canadians may want a passport as well, in case they extend their travels into Mexico or beyond. Visitors should bring their driver's license and any health-insurance or travel-insurance cards.

You'll need a picture ID to show that you're over 21 to buy alcohol or gain admission to bars or clubs (make sure your driver's license has a photo on it, or else get some other form of ID). It's a good idea to make a couple photocopies of all your travel documents, including airline tickets, your passport and your international ID. Keep the copies separate from the originals.

Much of New York state's northwestern tier borders on Canada. In a few places, such as in the Thousand Islands and Niagara Falls, we even recommend crossing the border. See the sidebar in Niagara Falls in the Western New York chapter if you're considering such an excursion, as there are documents you may need.

Passport

Your most important travel document is a passport, which should remain valid for at least six months after your intended stay in the USA. If it's about to expire, renew it before you go. This may not be easy to do away from your home country.

Applying for or renewing a passport can take from a few days to several months, so don't leave it till the last minute. Things will probably happen faster if you do everything in person, but check first on what you need to take with you. Once you start traveling, carry your passport at all times and guard it carefully.

Visas

Canadians must have proof of Canadian citizenship, such as a citizenship card with photo ID or a passport. Visitors from other countries must have a valid passport and most visitors also require a US visa.

However, there is a reciprocal visa-waiver program in which citizens of certain countries may enter the USA for stays of 90 days or less without first obtaining a US visa. Currently these countries are the UK, New Zealand, Japan, Italy, Spain, Austria, the Netherlands, Belgium, Switzerland, France, Germany, Norway, Denmark, Sweden, Finland, Iceland, San Marino, Andorra, Luxembourg, Australia, Ireland, Argentina, Brunei, Liechtenstein and Monaco. Under this program you must have a roundtrip ticket that's nonrefundable in the USA and you won't be allowed to extend your stay beyond 90 days.

Other travelers need to obtain a visa from a US consulate or embassy. In most countries the process can be done by mail. You'll need to submit a recent photo (37 x 37 mm) with the application. Documents of financial stability and/or guarantees from a US resident are sometimes required, particularly for those from developing countries.

Visa applicants may be required to 'demonstrate binding obligations' that ensure their return home. Because of this requirement, those planning to travel through other countries before arriving in the USA are generally better off applying for their US visa while they're still in their home country, rather than while on the road.

The validity period for US visitor visas depends on which country you're from. The length of time you'll be allowed to stay in the USA is ultimately determined by US immigration authorities at the port of entry.

Incidentally, the infamous prohibition against issuing visas to people who 'have been members of communist organizations' has been dropped. An anachronism of the Cold War, it still appears on visa applications although most consular offices have penned a line through the item.

Visa Extensions If you want, need or hope to stay in the USA longer than the date stamped on your passport, go to the

HIV & Customs

Everyone entering the USA who isn't a US citizen is subject to the authority of the Immigration & Naturalization Service (INS), regardless of whether that person has legal immigration documents. The INS can keep someone from entering or staying in the USA by excluding or deporting them. This is especially relevant to travelers with the Human Immunodeficiency Virus (HIV). Though being HIV positive is not a ground for deportation, it is a 'ground of exclusion' and the INS can invoke it to refuse admission.

Although the INS doesn't test people for HIV at customs, it may try to exclude anyone who answers yes to this question on the non-immigrant visa application form: 'Have you ever been afflicted with a communicable disease of public health significance?' INS officials may also stop people if they seem sick, are carrying AIDS/HIV medicine or, sadly, if the officer happens to think the person looks gay, though sexual orientation is not legally a ground of exclusion.

It's imperative that visitors know and assert their rights. Immigrants and visitors should avoid contact with the INS until they discuss their rights and options with a trained immigration advocate. For legal immigration information and referrals to immigration advocates, contact The National Immigration Project of the National Lawyers Guild (☎ (617) 227-9727), 14 Beacon St, Suite 506, Boston, MA 02108; or Immigrant HIV Assistance Project, Bar Association of San Francisco (☎ (415) 267-0795), 685 Market St, Suite 700, San Francisco, CA 94105. ∎

local Immigration & Naturalization Service (INS) office (look in the local telephone directory's white pages under 'US Government') *before* the stamped date to apply for an extension. Anytime after that will usually lead to an unamusing conversation with an INS official who'll assume you want to work illegally. If you find yourself in that situation, it's a good idea to bring a US citizen with you to vouch for your character and to have some verification that you have enough currency to support yourself.

Travel Insurance

Make sure you take out travel insurance. This not only covers you for medical expenses (see Health, below) and luggage theft or loss, but also for cancellations or delays in your travel arrangements under certain circumstances (you might fall seriously ill two days before departure, for example) – and everyone should be covered for the worst possible case, such as an accident requiring hospital treatment and a flight home. Coverage depends on your insurance and type of ticket, so ask both your insurer and your ticket-issuing agency to explain where you stand. Ticket loss is also (usually) covered by travel insurance. Make sure you have a separate record of all your ticket details – or better still, a photocopy – in case the original is lost. Buy travel insurance as early as possible. If you buy it the week before you fly, you may find, for example, that you're not covered for delays to your flight caused by strikes or industrial action.

The insurance may seem expensive – but it's nowhere near as expensive as the enormous costs of a medical emergency in the USA.

Driver's License & Permits

Although many foreign nationals can drive in the US using their own driving license, either an International or Inter-American Driving Permit is useful. Local traffic police are more likely to accept it as valid identification than an unfamiliar document from another country. Your national automobile association can provide one for a nominal fee. They're usually valid for one year.

Automobile Association Membership
Cards If you plan on doing a lot of driving in the USA, it would be beneficial to join your national automobile association. Members of the American Automobile Association (AAA) or an affiliated automobile club can get car rental, accommodations and sightseeing admission discounts with membership cards. More importantly, it gives you access to AAA road service in case of an emergency.

Hostel Card
Most hostels in the USA are members of Hostelling International-American Youth Hostel (HI-AYH). HI was formerly the International Youth Hostel Federation (IYHF). You can purchase membership on the spot when checking in, although it's probably advisable to buy it before you leave home.

Student & Youth Cards
If you're a student, get an international student ID or bring along a school or university ID card to take advantage of the discounts available to students. The most useful of these is the International Student Identity Card (ISIC), which soon pays for itself; with it you get all sorts of discounts on transport, commercial goods and services and entry to museums and sights.

Seniors' Cards
See Senior Travelers, below.

CUSTOMS
US customs allows each person over the age of 21 to bring one liter of liquor and 200 cigarettes duty-free into the USA. US citizens are allowed to import, duty free, $400 worth of gifts from abroad, while non-US citizens are allowed to bring in $100 worth. If you're carrying more than $10,000 in US and foreign cash, traveler's checks, money orders and the like, you need to declare the excess amount. There

is no legal restriction on the amount that may be imported, but undeclared sums in excess of $10,000 may be subject to confiscation.

Certain items are either restricted or completely banned from entry. These include liquor-filled candies, fruits and plants, articles made from plants and animals in danger of extinction, firearms and munitions, fireworks, toxic substances, lottery tickets, meat, birds and their derivatives (like paté), dangerous or illegal drugs, domestic animals, pornographic articles, antiquities, switchblade knives and vehicles not in accordance with US pollution laws.

MONEY
Costs
Costs for accommodations vary seasonally, between cities and the countryside, and between resorts and motels etc. Generally, rates are higher in summer, between Memorial Day and Labor Day, but fall and Christmas are also busy times and winter ski resorts can be expensive. In Saratoga Springs, NY, for instance, during the summer racing season lodging is at such a premium that many locals rent out their homes for several weeks and finance their family vacations from the high rents they collect.

Camping is often the best option if you're on a limited budget and mainly interested in ex-urban adventure. You can camp for free in many places and cook for yourself in these campgrounds. Some full-service campgrounds charge up to about $22 a night for a site with recreational vehicle (RV) hookups, but most are cheaper.

Hostels exist, but they're relatively few, sometimes inconveniently located and charge around $10 per person. The cheapest motels, usually in commercial strips outside town, start around $35/45 a single/double. You can find satisfactory mid-range accommodations for $55 to $80 a double in most places, and some towns have luxury hotels with rooms from $100 to infinity. There are also world-class resorts where you can pay over $200 a day.

B&Bs start at about $40 for a double, but most are in the $60 to $100 range.

In hotels, beware of grossly inflated charges for some services, especially telephones and laundry. To avoid unpleasant surprises, ask about these before you incur any expenses. Many hotels have pay phones available, which are much cheaper than calling from your room, and cheap coin-operated laundries outside the hotel are an alternative to expensive hotel laundry charges.

Food is reasonably priced. Even the smallest town has a fast-food restaurant where you can get a large hamburger, soft drink and French fries for about $3 or $4. Good restaurant meals can be found for $10 or less. Many towns have all-you-can-eat restaurants where you can fill up for about $6. If you buy food at markets you may get by even more cheaply; in small corner stores food items tend to be 20¢ to 30¢ dearer. You can eat well any night in any town for under $25 per person. Interestingly, dining in a restaurant outside the major cities where the choices are limited can be more expensive.

A 12 ounce bottle of domestic beer can range from $1.50 to $5 in a bar or restaurant. A six-pack of domestic beers costs $6 to $8 in a supermarket or liquor store, while a six-pack of soft drinks is $1.50 to $3, depending on the brand. A cup of coffee is usually 50¢ to $1.

Inter-city public transportation is relatively expensive (and time consuming) compared to owning or renting a car and is less extensive than in other countries. In some areas a car is the only way of getting around.

Car rental is available in most towns of any size, and rates can be about $120 a week for the smallest (sub-compact) cars, but more often rentals begin around $150 for a week. In New York City, car rental can be very expensive at around $75 a day on weekends when demand is stronger. Insurance usually adds another $12 a day. Gasoline (petrol) ranges from about $1.15 to $1.75 for a US gallon, depending on the location and grade of fuel.

First-run movies are usually around $7,

but you can pay half price for matinees. Museums can range from free to as much as $10 to visit.

Carrying Money

Carry your money (and only the money you'll need for that day) somewhere inside your clothing (in a money belt, a bra or your socks) rather than in a handbag or an outside pocket. Put the money in several places. Most hotels and hostels provide safekeeping, so you can leave your money and other valuables with them. Hide or don't wear any valuable jewelry. A safety pin or key ring to hold the zipper tags of a daypack together can help deter theft.

Currency

The US dollar is divided into 100 cents (¢). Coins come in denominations of 1¢ (penny), 5¢ (nickel), 10¢ (dime), 25¢ (quarter) and the seldom seen 50¢ (half dollar). Notes come in $1, $2, $5, $10, $20, $50 and $100 denominations (you'll only occasionally come across $2 bills – they're perfectly legal). There's also a $1 coin that the government has tried unsuccessfully to bring into mass circulation; you may get them as change from ticket and stamp machines. Be aware that they look similar to quarters.

Cash & Traveler's Checks

Though carrying cash is more risky it's still a good idea to travel with some for the convenience; it's useful to help pay all those tips and some smaller, more remote places may not accept credit cards or traveler's checks. Traveler's checks offer greater protection from theft or loss and in many places can be used as cash. American Express and Thomas Cook are widely accepted and have efficient replacement policies.

Keeping a record of the check numbers and the checks you have used is vital when it comes to replacing lost traveler's checks. Keep this record separate from the checks themselves.

You'll save yourself trouble and expense if you buy traveler's checks in US dollars.

The savings you *might* make on exchange rates by carrying traveler's checks in a foreign currency don't make up for the hassle of exchanging them at banks and other facilities. Restaurants, hotels and most stores accept US-dollar traveler's checks as if they were cash, so if you're carrying traveler's checks in US dollars, the odds are you'll rarely have to use a bank or pay an exchange fee.

Take most of the checks in large denominations. It's only towards the end of a stay that you may want to change a small check to make sure you aren't left with too much local currency.

Automatic Teller Machines

Most banks have automatic teller machines (ATMs) that are usually open 24 hours a day. There are various ATM networks, and most banks are affiliated with several. Some of the most common are Cirrus, Plus, Star Systems and Interlink, which provide international links. For a nominal service charge, you can withdraw cash from an ATM using a credit card or a charge card. But beware – withdrawal charges have been exploding almost in direct proportion to the uses of ATMs. Credit cards usually have a 2% fee with a $2 minimum, but using bank cards linked to your personal checking account is usually far cheaper. Check with your bank or credit card company for exact information.

In addition to traditional bank locations, you can also find ATMs at most airports, large grocery stores, shopping malls and in a growing number of convenience stores.

In Pennsylvania ATMs are known as money access centers (MACs).

Credit & Debit Cards

Major credit and charge cards are widely accepted by car rental agencies and most hotels, restaurants, gas stations, shops and larger grocery stores. Many recreational and tourist activities can also be paid for by credit card. The most commonly accepted cards are Visa, MasterCard and American Express. However, Discover and Diners Club are also accepted by a fair number of

businesses. It's probably a good idea to have an American Express card and another credit card since a few places take one and not the other.

You'll find it hard to perform certain transactions without one. Ticket buying services, for instance, won't reserve tickets over the phone unless you offer a credit card number, and it's virtually impossible to rent a car without a credit card. Even if you loathe credit cards and prefer to rely on traveler's checks and ATMs, it's a good idea to carry one (best bets are Visa or MasterCard) for emergencies.

Places accepting Visa and MasterCard are also likely to accept debit cards. Unlike a credit card, a debit card deducts payment directly from the user's savings account. Instead of an interest rate, users are charged a minimal fee for the transaction. Check with your bank to confirm that your debit card is accepted in other states – debit cards from large commercial banks can often be used worldwide.

Lost or Stolen Cards

If you lose your credit cards or they get stolen, contact the company immediately; of course you should have your card numbers written down and kept separately from your wallet. Following are toll-free numbers for the main credit cards. Contact your bank if you lose your ATM card.

American Express	(800) 528-4800
Discover	(800) 347-2683
Diners Club	(800) 234-6377
MasterCard	(800) 826-2181
Visa	(800) 336-8472

International Transfers

You can instruct your bank back home to send you a draft. Specify the city, bank and branch to which you want your money directed, or ask your home bank to tell you where a suitable one is, and make sure you get the details right. The procedure is easier if you've authorized someone back home to access your account.

Money sent by telegraphic transfer should reach you within a week; by mail allow at least two weeks. When it arrives it will most likely be converted into local currency – you can take it as it is or purchase traveler's checks.

You can also transfer money through American Express, Thomas Cook or Western Union, though the latter has fewer international offices.

Changing Money

Branches of several regional banks exchange foreign currency or traveler's checks at regular teller windows. However, banks in outlying areas aren't asked to exchange money very often. You'll probably find it less of a hassle and waste of time if you change your money at larger cities. Nearly all banks buy and sell Canadian currency. It's best to change US to Canadian dollars at a Canadian bank. Relatively few places accept the Canadian dollar 'at par' any longer. Almost any business on either side of the US/Canadian border will honor a fair exchange rate so you should be aware of what it is. If you use a credit card you're guaranteed a good exchange rate.

At the main branch of banks money can be wired, currency purchased etc. Additionally, Thomas Cook, American Express and exchange windows in airports offer exchange (although you'll get a better rate at a bank, normally between 1% and 2%). Thomas Cook and American Express usually don't charge a fee for changing their traveler's checks into cash. In the main cities avoid cash-exchange kiosks, which charge a hefty fee for changing currencies.

At press time, exchange rates were:

A$1	=	$0.75
C$1	=	$0.74
DM1	=	$0.66
HK$10	=	$1.29
NZ$1	=	$0.68
UK£1	=	$1.51
Y100	=	$0.92

Tipping

Tipping is expected in restaurants, bars and better hotels, as well as by taxi drivers, hairdressers and baggage carriers. In restaurants, waitstaff are paid minimal wages and

rely upon tips to make a living. Tip 15% unless the service is terrible (in which case a complaint to the manager is warranted) or up to 20% if the service is great. Never tip in fast-food, take-out or buffet-style restaurants where you serve yourself.

Taxi drivers expect 10% and hairdressers get 15% if their service is satisfactory. Baggage carriers (skycaps in airports, bellboys in hotels) receive $1 for the first bag and 50¢ for each additional bag carried. In budget hotels (where there aren't bellboys anyway) tips aren't expected. In 1st class and luxury hotels, tipping can reach irritating proportions – doormen, bellboys, parking attendants, chambermaids are all tipped at least $1 for each service performed. However, simply saying 'thank you' to an attendant who merely opens the door when you could just as easily have done it yourself is OK.

Special Deals

The USA is probably the most promotion-oriented society on earth. Everything has an angle, and with a little detective work and a lot of gumption the traveler can find some worthwhile bargains. Off-season hotel prices, for example, are frequently negotiable. Be confident, but don't be rude.

Bulk warehouse stores and New York City discounters sell everything you could want at a discount. These are good places for items like batteries and film.

Sunday newspapers typically have discount coupons which can be used at supermarkets and department stores.

Supermarkets also run specials on tickets for local attractions, especially 'family' attractions, like amusement parks or professional sporting events (usually baseball). If there's downhill skiing within a two hour drive, cheap lift tickets are often available at supermarkets as well.

Often tourist offices and chambers of commerce put together free coupon books for local merchants – these include the state 'guidebook' publications available from their toll-free numbers. These typically offer discounts at local accommodations, attractions, business and restaurants.

Car rental agencies sometimes offer discounts in tandem with national motel chains. Since the deregulation of the US airline industry, airlines have been jockeying to provide the most appealing premiums for potential flyers. If you belong to any frequent-flyer programs, ask what discounts they entitle you to.

One general rule about promotions is that you should never pay for coupons: $40 for a coupon book that advertises $500 worth of discounts includes some snags. Often the coupons are for well-known places, but are valid during odd hours, for particular menus and other conditions apply that preclude true savings.

Taxes

Almost everything you buy in the USA is taxed. Occasionally, the tax is included in the advertised price (such as gas, drinks in a bar and entrance tickets for museums, theaters etc). Transport (taxi, bus, train and plane tickets) taxes are also usually included in the advertised price. Airport taxes of up to $3 per airport are added to the ticket price, not paid at the airport. Restaurant meals and drinks, motel rooms and most other purchases are taxed, and this is added to the advertised cost.

The tax rates are bewildering. For meals, rooms and other purchases, there are both state and local (city or county) taxes, as well as lodging, restaurant and car-rental taxes. This means that as you move around, you'll pay different taxes in every town. Basic state sales taxes are 5% in New York and New Jersey, and 6% in Pennsylvania, but most restaurants add 6% to 8% to the bill, most hotels add 8% to 13%, and most car rental companies add 7% to 13%.

Unless otherwise stated, the prices given in this book don't reflect the addition of local taxes.

POST & COMMUNICATIONS

Postal Rates

Postage rates increase every few years. Currently, rates for 1st class mail within the USA are 32¢ for letters up to one ounce

(23¢ for each additional ounce) and 20¢ for postcards.

International airmail rates (except Canada and Mexico) are 60¢ for a half ounce letter, $1 for a one ounce letter and 40¢ for each additional half ounce. International postcard rates are 40¢. Letters to Canada are 52¢ for a one ounce letter, and 40¢ for a postcard. Letters to Mexico are 40¢ for a half ounce letter, 45¢ for a one ounce letter and 35¢ for a postcard. Aerogrammes are 50¢.

The cost for parcels airmailed anywhere within the USA is $3 for two pounds or less, increasing by $1 per pound up to $6 for five pounds. For heavier items, rates differ according to the distance mailed. Books, periodicals and computer disks can be sent by a cheaper 4th class rate.

Sending Mail

If you have the correct postage, you can drop your mail (provided it is under one pound) into any blue mail box. These are found at many convenient locations including shopping centers, airports, street corners etc. The times of the next pickup are written inside the lid of the mail box. This sign also indicates the location of the nearest mail box with later or more frequent pickup.

If you need to buy stamps or weigh your mail, go to the nearest post office. Stores like Mail Boxes Etc will pack and send your items for additional charges. In addition, larger towns have branch post offices and post office centers in some shopping centers and drugstores. For the address of the nearest office, call the main post office listed under 'Postal Service' in the 'US Government' section in the local white pages telephone directory.

Usually post offices are open from 8 am to 5 pm Monday to Friday and 8 am to 3 pm on Saturday. Major cities like New York, Philadelphia and Pittsburgh have extremely convenient 24 hour service in a main branch.

Receiving Mail

You can have mail sent to you care of General Delivery at any post office that has its own zip (postal) code. It's best to have your intended date of arrival (if the sender knows it) clearly marked on the envelope. Mail is usually held for 10 days before it's returned to the sender. Alternatively, you can have mail sent to the local representative of American Express or Thomas Cook, which provide mail service for their clients.

Telephone

Phone numbers within the USA consist of a three digit area code followed by a seven digit local number. If you're calling locally, just dial the seven digit number. If you're calling long distance, dial 1 + the three digit area code + the seven digit number.

If you're calling from abroad, the international country code for the USA is '1.'

Most toll-free numbers (usually given an 800 or 888 area code) within the USA can be called from anywhere in the USA, others are only accessible regionally.

Local directory assistance can be reached by dialing ☎ 411. For directory assistance outside your area code, dial 1 + the three digit area code of the place you want to call + 555-1212. Regional and US area code maps are found in telephone directories.

Many businesses use letters instead of numbers for their telephone numbers in an attempt to make them snappy and memorable; for example, ☎ 800-USA-RAIL is Amtrak's national toll-free number. Sometimes it works, but sometimes it's difficult to read the letters on the dial pad. If you can't read the letters, here they are: 1 doesn't get any; 2 – ABC, 3 – DEF, 4 – GHI, 5 – JKL, 6 – MNO, 7 – PRS, 8 – TUV, 9 – WXY. Sorry, no Qs or Zs.

Rates Local calls usually cost 25¢ at pay phones, but some private phones may charge more. Many hotels (especially the more expensive ones) add a service charge of 50¢ to $1 for *every* call made from a room phone; they also have hefty surcharges for long-distance calls. Public pay phones, which can be found in most lobbies, are always cheaper. You can pump in quarters, use a phone or credit card or make collect calls from pay phones. An alternative is a phone debit card, which allows purchasers to pay in advance. These are available in convenience stores, airports, Western Union and some other sources.

When using phone cards, be aware of people watching you punch in your PIN, especially in public places like airports. New York airports and especially the Port Authority are notorious for this scam: Thieves memorize numbers and use them to make costly international calls. Shield the telephone with your body when punching in your credit card number.

Long-distance rates vary depending on the destination and which telephone company you use – call the operator (☎ 0) for rate information. Don't ask the operator to put your call through, however, because operator-assisted calls are much more expensive than direct-dial calls. Generally, nights (11 pm to 8 am), all day Saturday and from 8 am to 5 pm Sunday are the cheapest times to call (60% discount). A 35% discount applies in the evenings from 5 to 11 pm Sunday to Friday. Daytime calls (8 am to 5 pm Monday to Friday) are full-price calls within the USA.

International Calls To make an international call direct, dial 011 then the country code, followed by the area code and the phone number. You may need to wait as long as 45 seconds for the ringing to start. International rates vary depending on the time of day and the destination. For example, the cheapest rates to London are between 6 pm and 7 am, while when calling Sydney, the cheapest rates are 3 am to 2 pm. Again, rates vary depending on the telephone company used and the destination. Call the operator (☎ 0) for rates.

Fax, Telegraph & E-mail

Fax machines are easy to find in the USA at places like Kinko's (which has branches open 24 hours), Mail Boxes Etc and hotel business-service centers, but be prepared to pay over $1 a page. Telegraphs can be sent from Western Union (☎ (800) 325-6000).

E-mail and Internet browsing have

become a preferred method of communication and accessing information for many; however, unless you have a laptop and modem that can plug into a telephone socket, it's difficult to get on-line. Hotel business services may provide connections, and trendy cafes sometimes offer Internet access too. Quite a few attractions, hotels and other tourist-friendly places maintain e-mail addresses and websites posting current events, hours and admission or rate information.

BOOKS
Guidebooks
Most guidebooks focus on New York City or New York state, but there are a number of guides to other parts of the region as well.

The *Mid-Atlantic States* (Stewart, Chabori & Chang, 1989), part of the Smithsonian Guide to Historic America series, provides a glossy, beautifully photographed account of historically important places and buildings in New York, New Jersey and Pennsylvania.

The *Mobil Travel Guide – Mid-Atlantic*, published annually is aimed at the motorist and has listings of attractions, accommodations and eateries. It doesn't include New York, but it does include Delaware, Maryland, Virginia, West Virginia, North Carolina and South Carolina, as well as New Jersey and Pennsylvania.

Lonely Planet's *Washington, DC & the Capital Region* covers this region's neighboring states of Virginia, Maryland, Washington, DC and Delaware.

New York From a historical viewpoint the best are the Works Project Administration (WPA) guides to New York and to New Jersey, both published in 1939 as part of the WPA attempt to employ writers and artists. They're so wonderful they stand on their own today as good reading. For those interested in New York City's architecture, the American Institute of Architects' *Guide to New York City* (1988), edited by Norval White & Elliot Willinsky, is the classic text on the subject.

Ethnic New York (Passport Books, 1995)

by Mark Leeds is a good neighborhood-by-neighborhood guide. *Wonderful Weekends* (Frommers, 1994) by Marilyn Wood, has information on trips within a 200 mile radius of New York City; it's a good trip planner, but has little on public transportation – generally you'll need a car to use it. *Away for the Weekend* (Crown, 1995) by Eleanor Berman is similar.

The *Adventure Guide to the Catskills & Adirondacks* by WH Morrison (1995) is a small useful book with information on hiking and camping.

New Jersey Rutgers University Press has republished a series of guides by Henry Charleton Beck (1902-65), originally written in the 1930s and 40s. They include *Forgotten Towns of Southern New Jersey* as well as *Tales and Towns of Northern New Jersey*.

Guide to the Jersey Shore (Globe Pequot, 1995) by Robert Santelli describes the attractions, history and activities found there. *New Jersey Day Trips* (1995) by Barbara Hudgins lists things to see within the state as well as New York, Pennsylvania and Delaware.

Pennsylvania *The Pennsylvania One-Day Trip Book* (EPM Publications, 1995) by Jane Ockershausen describes 600 sites for the day-tripper.

There are several guides to Philadelphia. Insight Guides' *Philadelphia* (APA Publications, 1993) is a collection of essays and photographs on various aspects of the city. *Philadelphia Magazine* publishes an annual guide to the best things in town, called *Best of Philly – the Ultimate Guide* by Janet Bokovinsky Teacher.

Rich/Poor Man's Guide to Pittsburgh (New Pittsburgh Publications, 1994) by Dorothy A Miller concentrates mainly on entertainment and places to eat.

Travelogues
If you're interested in travelogues from a historical perspective, some literary luminaries of the past have left written records of their travels through this region as well as

other parts of the US. These include Charles Dickens, who wrote *American Notes* in 1842; William Russell, a journalist with the London *Times*, who described his visit in *My Diary North and South* (1850); Oscar Wilde, who wrote *Impressions of America* (1883); and GK Chesterton, who described his visit in *What I saw in America* (1923).

Poets have also written of their travel experiences, including Walt Whitman in *Specimen Days* (1882).

Beat author Jack Kerouac wrote about his journey across the country in *On The Road* (1957) and of his life in New York City in *Lonesome Traveler* (1960). In his last full-length book, *Travels with Charley* (1962), John Steinbeck describes his three month journey in a truck from New York to the West Coast with his wife's pet poodle. More recently, two chapters are devoted to the region in *Blue Highways* (1991) by William Least Heat-Moon, who traveled in his van called 'Ghost Dancing' through the back roads and small towns of America. Bill Bryson wrote humorously of his travels across 38 states in search of the perfect American small town in *The Lost Continent* (1989).

History

New York *The Epic of New York City* (1966) by Edward Robb Ellis is a massive (600 pages) sweeping, personality-based history of the city from Native Indian times to the mid-1960s.

Christopher Morley's New York City (Fordham University Press, 1988) contains accounts of his travels in and around the city in the 1930s and '40s. *The Lost World of the Fair* (1939) by David Gelernter is an engaging, well-written popular history of the 1939 World's Fair that captures the post-Depression, prewar prominence of New York. *Here is New York* (1949) is a classic novella-sized essay on New York by the elegant *New Yorker* writer EB White. His observations on the city remain insightful even today.

Manhattan '45 (1987) by Jan Morris is a quick look at New York City at its postwar heights, before the country fell in love with

suburban living and city centers began a two generation decline. *New York Days, New York Nights* (Atheneum, 1985) by Stephen Brook is a humorous account of aspects of life in the city.

New York Days (1993) by Willie Morris tells how he came as a young man from the South to New York City to seek his literary fortune and finds it to become editor of *Harper's Magazine* in its heyday. It's wonderfully descriptive of the 1960s literary era and new journalism, as well as the backstabbing in the profession.

The Power Broker (1974) by Robert Caro is an authoritative account of the life and times of town planner and public official Robert Moses (1888-1981), who largely created the modern New York City with all its flaws and glories. *New York When I Was Young* (1995) by Mary Cantwell is a sharply written memoir of life and love in the city during the '60s by a prominent *New York Times* editorial writer.

Among the many excellent histories of New York's cultural and political development, check the following: *The Common Landscape of America (1580-1845)* by John Stilgoe (Yale University Press) and *Wayne County: The Aesthetic Heritage of a Rural Area (A Catalog for the Environment)* by Steven Jacobs (Wayne County Historical Society).

Two smaller presses, both located in the Catskills, that publish works on the folklore and natural history of New York are Purple Mountain Press of Fleischmanns, NY, and Black Dome Press of Hansonville, NY.

New Jersey *This is New Jersey* (1978) by John Cunningham is a straightforward history of the state while *New Jersey: A History* (1984) by Thomas Fleming is the most recent historical overview of the state's development.

The Powerticians (1980), by Thomas FX Smith, a former mayor of Jersey City, is an entertaining, popular history of the Democratic Party's 'machine politics' that dominated the state's northern cities.

Patrimony: A True Story (1991) by

novelist Philip Roth deals with the life and death of the author's father and contains a good series of cameo images on growing up in Depression-era Newark. *Growing Up* (1982) by Russell Baker also deals with living in the state (and other locales) during the Depression and is one of the best childhood memoirs ever written.

Pennsylvania For colonial Pennsylvania, check out *William Penn's Holy Experiment: The Founding of Pennsylvania, 1681-1701* by Edwin Bronner (Greenwood Press, 1978) or JE Illick's *Colonial Pennsylvania* (Scribner, 1976). For the history of Pennsylvania during less-booming times, read *People, Property and Politics: Pennsylvania During the Great Depression* (Bucknell University Press, 1981) by Thomas Coode & Benjamin Bauman. *Philadelphia – a 300 year history* (WW Norton, 1982) is a series of essays on the city's history from 1681 to 1982 edited by Russell E Weigley.

Incidents in the Life of a Slave Girl by Harriet Jacobs tells her real-life story as she moved from Philadelphia to New York and New England. Originally published in 1862 it was republished by Harvard University Press in 1987.

The Battle of Gettysburg played a pivotal role in the Civil War and there are numerous books on the subject. Some of the best are Bruce Catton's *Gettysburg: The Final Fury* (Doubleday, 1974); Edward Stackpole's *They Met at Gettysburg* (Stackpole Books, 3rd edition, 1986); and George Rippey Stewart's *Pickett's Charge* (Houghton Mifflin, 1960).

Information on Pennsylvania's immigrants is found in John E Bodnar's *The Ethnic Experience in Pennsylvania* (Bucknell University Press, 1973).

For biographical information about Andrew Carnegie see James Howard Bridge's *The Inside Story of the Carnegie Steel Company*, a 1903 attack on Andrew Carnegie, reprinted by the University of Pittsburgh Press in 1991, or Harold C Livesay's *Andrew Carnegie and the Rise of Big Business* (1975).

The rise of Andrew Carnegie and the steel industry was not without incident, most notably the strike at Homestead in Pittsburgh in 1892. There are several books on the subject. *Homestead: The Glory & Tragedy of an American Steel Town* (Times Books, 1992) by William Sarrin and *The Battle for Homestead, 1880-1892, Politics, Culture, & Steel* (University of Pittsburgh Press, 1992) by Paul Krause are good histories. *The River Ran Red: Homestead 1892* (University of Pittsburgh Press, 1992) edited by David Demarest is a collection of excerpts from papers at the time. For a contemporary view see Arthur G Burgoyne's *The Homestead Strike of 1892*, published in 1893 and reprinted in 1979 by the University of Pittsburgh.

A detailed retelling of the Johnstown flood in Southwest Pennsylvania, the worst in US history, can be found in David McCullough's *The Johnstown Flood* (Simon & Schuster, 1968). *Christopher Morley's Philadelphia* (Fordham University Press, 1990), like his New York title, details his Philadelphia travels in the 1930s and '40s.

Route 40, once called the National Rd, was the main route west until the 1850s, and its story is told in *The National Road: Main Street of America* (Ohio Historical Society, 1975) and in *US 40* (Houghton Mifflin, 1953) by George Stewart.

General

The Encyclopedia of New York City (Yale University Press and New-York Historical Society, 1995) edited by Kenneth T Jackson is an excellent 1350 page record of the city. *Philadelphia Almanac* (Library Company of Philadelphia, 1995), edited by Kenneth Finkel, is a paperback replete with facts, figures and tales about the city. *Pittsburgh – An American City* (Urbina Publishing, 1990), with photos by Walt Urbina and text by Sally Webb, is a good photographic coffee-table record of Pittsburgh.

Marietta Holley: 'Life with Josiah Allen's Wife' by Kate Winter (1984) is a biography of the North Country (Adirondacks) humorist who wrote the *Samantha* books, which include the story 'Josiah Allen's Wife.'

Collected Poems (HarperCollins, 1981) by Edna St Vincent Millay is a collection of lyrical poetry by the 1923 Pulitzer Prize winner and Vassar graduate.

The Portable Dorothy Parker is a collection of Parker's sardonic writings. The book critic for the *New Yorker* from 1927 to 1933, Parker is often remembered for remarking that in an unsuccessful Broadway play Katharine Hepburn's acting 'ran the gamut of emotions from A to B.'

The House of Mirth by Edith Wharton is a satire about the turn-of-the-century aristocratic New York society, first published in 1905. *Fast Speaking Woman* (City Lights, 1996) by Anne Waldman is one of several titles by one of New York City's best-regarded poets.

For books on the Amish see Information in the introduction to the Pennsylvania Dutch Country chapter.

NEWSPAPERS & MAGAZINES

The USA supports a wide spectrum of newspapers and magazines, many of which are based in this region. New York City is the main magazine- and book-publishing center in the country and is a major proving ground for journalists and editors. It's the headquarters for such publishing giants as Condé Nast, Hachette Filippacci, Hearst, K-III, Time & Life, Time Warner etc. The city's multi-billion dollar industry produces more magazines per month than any other city in the nation.

Newspapers

Published in New York City, two of the highest circulating and most influential newspapers are the *Wall Street Journal* and *New York Times*; the latter is also published in several regional editions. The reliable *USA Today*, though not published in the city, is nationally distributed and has reasonable, but not comprehensive, political, sports and weather coverage. The loud, Rupert Murdoch-owned tabloid *New York Post* is *the* oldest newspaper in the US.

The *New Jersey Gazette* is the state's oldest newspaper, but the most influential paper is the *Newark Star Ledger*.

Important daily newspapers in Pennsylvania are the well-regarded *Philadelphia Inquirer*, plus the *Philadelphia Daily News*, *Pittsburgh Press* and *Pittsburgh Post-Gazette*.

All cities and larger towns have their local newspapers, and many ethnic newspapers are published throughout the region.

Magazines

Many nationally distributed magazines are published in New York City, including *Vanity Fair*, *Cosmopolitan*, *Esquire*, *GQ*, *Vogue* etc. These contain a significant amount of New York-centric information and often describe the latest trends as they emerge in the city. To a lot of people living even as close as Pittsburgh, these developments in chic clothing, food, music and design might often appear decidedly foreign.

As a major financial center, New York City also publishes the most prominent magazines relating to business and industry. If you're looking for employment, the end pages in these publications provide a glimpse of what's on offer. For the buzz on Wall St, pick up *Forbes*, *Money*, *Crain's New York Business* or *Fortune*. *Publishers Weekly* gives you the lowdown on book publishing in the city. *Advertising Age* is Madison Ave's tell-all for the advertising industry, while *Magazine Age* does the same for magazine publishing. *Women's Wear Daily* and *W* are New York City fashion-industry musts.

New York and the *New Yorker* magazines are distributed nationally and publish information on the goings on in the city. For more on New York City-related magazines, see that section under New York City's Information section. See also Facts about the Region for a sidebar on the history of the *New Yorker*.

Philadelphia Magazine is an influential monthly magazine and the *Farm Journal*, a Philadelphia publication, is one of the nation's leading farm magazines.

RADIO

Radio first appeared in the US when its inventor, Guglielmo Marconi, broadcasted a commentary on the America's Cup yachting race from New York Harbor in 1899. Then, in the early 20th century, two major advances occurred at New York's Columbia University. In 1913, Edwin H Armstrong, who was a student there, invented the speaker – up till that time a transmission could only be heard through earphones. By the end of the next two decades Armstrong had also successfully developed frequency modulation (FM), although it didn't become widely available until much later. Amplitude modulation (AM) was the most common form of transmission until the 1960s and 1970s.

In the meantime KDKA, the first permanent commercial broadcasting radio station in the world, opened in Pittsburgh in 1920. Soon after, companies like the Radio Corporation of America (RCA) set up a number of radio stations in the region. Several networks were founded in New York City, which remains the location of their headquarters today. The National Broadcasting Company (NBC) and the Columbia Broadcasting System (CBS) were formed in the 1920s, the American Broadcasting Company (ABC) in the 1940s.

The influence of radio around this time was graphically displayed when in 1938 Orson Welles broadcast a play about a Martian invasion of New Jersey. It was misinterpreted as a report on a real event and threw people into a panic.

From the 1960s onwards the number of radio stations proliferated and today most communities have their own local radio station. You can choose from literally hundreds of them. In and near major cities, there is a wide variety of music and entertainment, especially in New York City. The listening market there is so large, a radio station can maximize its profits by 'narrowcasting' – specializing in a particular type of music (rock, country & western etc) or news or talk radio.

There are numerous talk radio stations, especially on the AM dial, and they have gained much popularity. One manifestation of talk radio is 'shock' radio, which is typified by New York's Howard Stern, who is now heard nationally over hundreds of radio stations. National Public Radio (NPR) features a more level-headed approach to discussion, music and news. NPR's *Morning Edition* and its afternoon *All Things Considered* are the most worthwhile programs.

TV

New York City dominated TV during the first decades of the medium's development. The city pioneered a number of innovations, which included the introduction of the first mobile unit and the broadcasting of the first sporting fixture. WNBC-TV, which began operating in New York City in 1941, was the country's first commercial TV station. After WWII the popularity of TV mushroomed and network companies like ABC, CBS and NBC started broadcasting regularly.

New York wasn't the only city in the region where important changes occurred. In Pittsburgh, the TV station WQED pioneered community-sponsored educational TV when it began broadcasting in 1954.

Until the 1950s New York City also dominated much of the programming, most of which was broadcast live. But during that decade Hollywood movie studios began filming TV series and the production of most programs shifted to the West Coast, though news programming has remained in New York. Nevertheless, since that period some of the most successful programs in American TV have been produced in the city, including the *Ed Sullivan Show*, the *Cosby Show*, *60 Minutes* and the chat show *Late Night with Letterman*.

The main US TV networks have affiliated stations throughout the country. As well as the ABC, CBS and NBC networks in New York City there is also FOX and the Public Broadcasting Service (PBS). New York City is also an important center for network news and Cable News Network (CNN), a cable channel providing continuous news coverage. Cinemax, the Movie Channel and Viacom are three important cable-TV companies based in New York City.

PHOTOGRAPHY & VIDEO
Film & Equipment
Print film for all types of cameras is widely available at supermarkets and discount drugstores. 35 mm slide film is less available, though still carried at most places film is sold, and you will probably have to seek out a camera shop for black and white film.

Film can be bought at pharmacies and stores for about $8 for 36 exposures. Fuji and Kodak are the most widely available. Drugstores are good places to get your film processed cheaply. If it's dropped off by noon, you can usually pick it up the next day. A roll of 100 ASA 35 mm color film with 24 exposures will cost about $4.50 to $6 to process. If you want your pictures right away, you can find one hour processing services in the yellow pages under 'Photo Processing,' but they're more expensive. Many one hour photo finishers operate in the larger cities, and a few can be found near tourist attractions.

Film can be damaged by excessive heat, so don't leave your camera and film in the car on a hot summer day or place your camera on the dashboard while you're driving. The same goes for cold weather – be sure you don't leave it in your trunk on a freezing night.

It's worth carrying a spare battery for your camera to avoid disappointment when your camera dies in the middle of nowhere; even in suburban areas it may be difficult to replace. If you're buying a new camera for your trip, do so several weeks before leaving and practice using it.

Airport Security Passengers on flights have to pass their luggage through X-ray machines. Today's technology doesn't jeopardize lower-speed film, but it's best to carry film and cameras with you and ask the X-ray inspector to visually check your camera and film.

Photographing People
You can't generalize about how people will react to being photographed, but politeness and chatting beforehand will make things easier for you. The Amish in particular don't like having photographs taken of them. Many foreign-born street-stall owners and residents in ethnic neighborhoods resist being photographed by strangers. Sometimes it's for cultural reasons, but often it's because they're here illegally.

In cities, street performers enjoy being photographed provided you give them some money (it's their livelihood). Don't take photographs of any person acting crazily or suspiciously on the street.

Video Systems
Overseas visitors thinking of purchasing videos should remember that the USA uses the National Television System Committee (NTSC) color TV standard, which isn't compatible with other standards (Phase Alternative Line, or PAL; Systéme Electronique Couleur avec Mémoire, or SECAM) used in Africa, Europe, Asia and Australasia unless converted. It's best to keep those seemingly cheap movie purchases on hold until you get home.

TIME
New York, New Jersey and Pennsylvania are on Eastern Standard Time – five hours behind GMT/UTC, two hours ahead of Mountain Standard Time (Denver, CO) and three hours ahead of Pacific Standard Time (San Francisco and Los Angeles, CA, and Seattle, WA). Most of the US observes daylight-saving time: clocks go forward one hour from the last Sunday in April to the last Saturday in October, when the clocks are turned back one hour. It's easy to remember by the phrase 'spring ahead, fall back.'

In the US, dates are usually given with the month first, then the day, then the year.

ELECTRICITY
The USA uses 110 V and 60 cycles and plugs with two (flat) or three (two flat, one

round) pins. Plugs with three pins don't fit into a two-hole socket, but adapters are easy to buy. Two-pin plugs, especially ones with equal dimensions, can easily slip out of the socket. Should this happen a quick remedy is to stretch the prongs apart a bit for a tighter fit.

WEIGHTS & MEASURES

Although the metric system has made some inroads most Americans continue to resist its imposition.

Distances are in feet (ft), yards (yds) and miles (m). Three feet equal one yard, which is 0.914 meters; 1760 yards or 5280 feet equal one mile. Near the Canadian border you may see some distances marked in kilometers as well as miles.

Dry weights are measured by the ounce (oz), the pound (lb; 16 ounces are one pound) and ton (2000 pounds are one ton), but liquid measures differ from dry measures. One pint equals 16 fluid ounces. Two pints equal one quart, a common measure for liquids like milk, which is also sold in half gallons (two quarts) and gallons (four quarts). Gasoline is dispensed by the US gallon, which is about 20% less than the imperial gallon. US pints and quarts are also 20% less than imperial ones.

There is a conversion chart on the inside back cover of the book to make this all a bit easier.

LAUNDRY

Self-service, coin-operated laundry facilities are in most towns of any size, in hostels and in better campgrounds. Washing a load costs about $1.25 and drying it another $1.50 for 30 minutes. Coin-operated vending machines sell single-wash-size packages of detergent, but it's usually cheaper to pick up a small box at the supermarket. Some laundries have attendants who wash, dry and fold your clothes for an additional charge. To find a laundry, look under 'Laundries' or 'Laundries – Self-Service' in the yellow pages of the telephone directory. Dry cleaners are also listed under 'Laundries' or 'Cleaners.'

RECYCLING

Traveling by car seems to generate large numbers of cans and bottles. If you'd like to save these for recycling, you'll find recycling centers in the larger towns. Materials accepted are usually plastic and glass bottles, aluminum and tin cans and newspapers. Some campgrounds and a few roadside rest areas also have recycling bins next to the trash bins, so look out for those.

Perhaps better than recycling is to reduce your use of these products. Many gas stations and convenience stores sell large, inexpensive, plastic, insulated cups with lids which are ideal for hot and cold drinks. You can usually save a few cents by using your own cup to buy drinks.

Despite the appearance of many large cities, littering is frowned upon by most Americans. Travelers need to respect the places they're visiting even though some locals may not. Some states have anti-littering laws (which impose fines) to try to curb the problem. When you're hiking and camping in the wilderness, take out everything you bring in – including *any* garbage you create.

HEALTH

There are no prevalent diseases or risks associated with traveling in the USA or the region, and the country is well served by hospitals. However, because of the high cost of health care, international travelers should take out comprehensive travel insurance before they leave. If you're from a country with socialized medicine, find out what you'll need to do in order to be reimbursed for money you may spend on health care in the USA.

Also, if you fall ill in the USA, avoid going to emergency rooms. Although these are often the easiest places to get treatment, they're also incredibly expensive. Many city hospitals have 'urgent-care clinics,' designed to deal with walk-in clients with less-than-catastrophic injuries or illnesses.

You'll pay a lot less for treatment at these clinics. If you know someone in the area, consider asking them to phone their doctor; often private doctors are willing to examine foreign visitors as a courtesy to their regular patients, but a fee, often around $100, may still apply.

Predeparture Preparations

Health Insurance A travel-insurance policy to cover theft, loss and medical problems is a good idea, especially in the USA, where some hospitals refuse care without evidence of insurance. There's a wide variety of policies and your travel agent will have recommendations. International student travel policies handled by STA Travel or other student-travel organizations are usually a good value. Some policies offer lower and higher medical expenses options, but the higher one is chiefly for countries like the USA with extremely high medical costs. Check the small print.

Some policies specifically exclude 'dangerous activities' like scuba diving, motorcycling and even hiking. If these activities are on your agenda avoid this sort of policy.

You may prefer a policy that pays doctors or hospitals directly, rather than you paying first and claiming later. If you have to claim later, keep all documentation. Some policies ask you to call back ('collect' or 'reverse charge') to a center in your home country for an immediate assessment of your problem.

Check whether the policy covers ambulance fees or an emergency flight home. If you have to stretch out you'll need two seats and somebody has to pay for it!

Medical Kit Most medications are readily available and there's no need to pack extras. Hikers and backpackers should see the additional list in the Outdoor Activities chapter. A small, straightforward medical kit might include the following:

Aspirin, acetaminophen or Panadol
Antihistamine (such as Benadryl), which is useful as a decongestant for colds, to ease the itch from allergies, insect bites or stings and to help prevent motion sickness

Antibiotics, which are useful for traveling off the beaten track, but they must be prescribed and you should carry the prescription with you
Kaolin preparation (Pepto-Bismol), Immodium or Lomotil, for stomach upsets
Rehydration mixture, to treat severe diarrhea, particularly important if you're traveling with children
Antiseptic, mercurochrome and antibiotic powder or similar 'dry' spray, for cuts and grazes
Calamine lotion, to ease irritation from bites or stings
Bandages, for minor injuries
Scissors, tweezers and a thermometer (airlines prohibit mercury thermometers)
Insect repellent, sun-screen lotion and lip balm

Health Preparations If you're embarking on a long trip, make sure your teeth are in good shape. If you wear glasses, take a spare pair and your prescription. You can get a new pair made up quickly and competently for well under $100, depending on the prescription and frame you choose. If you require a particular medication, take an adequate supply and bring a prescription in case you lose your supply.

Immunizations Vaccinations aren't needed, but they may be necessary if you're stopping over on your way, and could be an entry requirement if you arrive from an infected area. If you're going to the US with stopovers in Asia, Africa or Latin America, check with your travel agent and doctor. Don't leave this till the last minute, as the vaccinations may have to be taken over several weeks.

All vaccinations should be recorded on an International Health Certificate, available from your physician or government health department.

Everyday Health

Care in what you eat and drink and maintenance of personal hygiene are the most important health rules, wherever you travel. Serious problems are unlikely in the US, but mild stomach upsets owing to a change in water and diet may occur. Water from a faucet is normally quite safe, and bottled drinking water is widely available.

If a restaurant or cafe looks clean and well run and if the vendor also looks clean and healthy, then the food is probably safe. In general, places that are packed with travelers or locals will be fine.

Food in the US is abundantly available no matter how small your budget. However, if you're traveling hard and fast and therefore missing meals, or if you simply lose your appetite, you can soon start to place your health at risk. Make sure your diet is well balanced.

In hot weather make sure you drink enough – don't rely on feeling thirsty to indicate when you should drink. Not needing to urinate or dark-yellow urine is a danger sign. Excessive sweating may lead to loss of salt and therefore muscle cramping. Adding salt to food will help.

Medical Problems & Treatment

Firstly, there are problems caused by extremes of temperature, altitude or motion. Then there are diseases and illnesses caused through poor environmental sanitation, insect bites or stings, and animal or human contact. Simple cuts, bites and scratches can also cause problems.

Wherever necessary seek qualified medical help for treatment and the administration of drugs. If you're from a foreign country, a consulate can usually recommend a good place.

Climatic & Geographical Ailments

Sunburn You can get sunburned quickly, even through cloud cover, especially if you're on water, snow or ice. Use a 15+ sunscreen lotion, wear a hat and cover up with a long-sleeved shirt and trousers. Calamine lotion is good for mild sunburn.

Heat Exhaustion Dehydration or salt deficiency can cause heat exhaustion. In hot conditions and if you're exerting yourself make sure you get sufficient non-alcoholic liquids. Salt deficiency is characterized by fatigue, lethargy, headaches, giddiness and muscle cramps. Vomiting or diarrhea can also deplete your liquid and salt levels.

Heat Stroke Long, continuous periods of exposure to high temperatures can leave you vulnerable to this serious, sometimes fatal, condition. It occurs when the body's heat-regulating mechanism breaks down and the body temperature rises to dangerous levels. Avoid excessive alcohol intake or strenuous activity.

Symptoms include feeling unwell, lack of perspiration and a high body temperature of 102 to 105° F (39 to 41°C). Hospitalization is essential for extreme cases, but meanwhile get out of the sun, remove clothing, cover with a wet sheet or towel and fan continually.

Fungal Infections Fungal infections like athlete's foot, jock itch or ringworm occur more often in hot weather. To prevent these, wear loose, comfortable clothes, avoid artificial fibers, wash frequently and dry carefully. If you do get an infection, wash the infected area daily with a disinfectant or medicated soap and water, and rinse and dry well. Apply an antifungal cream or powder and try to expose the infected area to air or sunlight as much as possible. Wash towels and underwear in hot water as well as changing them often.

Hypothermia This condition occurs when the body loses heat faster than it can produce it and the core temperature of the body falls. It's easy to progress from very cold to dangerously cold due to a combination of wind, wet clothing, fatigue and hunger, even if the air temperature is above freezing. If possible, avoid traveling alone; partners are more likely to avoid hypothermia successfully. If you must travel alone, especially when hiking, be sure someone knows your route and when you expect to return.

Seek shelter when bad weather is unavoidable. It's best to dress in layers, and a hat is important as a lot of heat is lost through the head. Woolen clothing and synthetics, which retain warmth even when wet, are superior to cottons. A quality sleeping bag is a worthwhile investment, although goose down loses much of its insulating qualities when wet. Carry high-energy, easily digestible snacks like chocolate or dried fruit.

To treat hypothermia, first get victims out of the wind or rain, remove their clothing if it's wet and replace it with dry, warm clothing. Give them hot liquids – not alcohol – and high-calorie, easily digestible food. In advanced stages it may be necessary to place victims in warm sleeping bags and get in with them. Don't rub victims – place them near a fire or, if possible, in a warm (not hot) bath.

Altitude Sickness Since most of this region is below 3500 feet it's unlikely that there'll be insufficient oxygen to cause altitude sickness except perhaps in a mild form – although there's no hard and fast rule about how high is too high. To prevent or minimize its impact it's wise to ascend slowly, sleep at a lower altitude than the greatest height reached during the day and take frequent rest days. Other measures include drinking extra fluids, eating light and avoiding smoking, alcohol or sedatives.

Symptoms include headaches, nausea, shortness of breath and physical weakness which may be exacerbated if combined with heat exhaustion, sunburn or hypothermia. Most people recover within a few hours or days. If the symptoms persist it's imperative to descend to lower elevations. For mild cases, everyday painkillers such as aspirin will relieve symptoms until the body adapts.

Motion Sickness Eating lightly before and during a trip reduces the chances of motion sickness. If you're prone to motion sickness, try to find a place that minimizes disturbance, for example, near the wing on aircraft, near the center on buses. Fresh air usually helps, while reading or cigarette smoke doesn't. Commercial anti-motion sickness preparations, which can cause drowsiness, have to be taken before the trip begins; when you're feeling sick it's too late. Ginger, a natural preventative, is available in capsule form.

Jet Lag Jet lag is experienced when a person travels by air across more than three time zones (each time zone usually represents a one hour time difference). It occurs because many functions of the human body (such as temperature, pulse rate and emptying of the bladder and bowels) are regulated by internal 24 hour cycles called circadian rhythms. When we travel long distances rapidly, our bodies take time to adjust to the 'new time' of our destination, and we may experience fatigue, disorientation, insomnia, anxiety, impaired concentration and loss of appetite. These effects are usually gone within three days of arrival, but there are ways of minimizing the impact of jet lag:

Rest for a couple of days prior to departure; try to avoid late nights and last-minute dashes for traveler's checks, passport etc.

Try to select flight schedules that minimize sleep deprivation; arriving late in the day means you can sleep soon after you arrive. For long flights, try to organize a stopover.

Avoid excessive eating (which bloats the stomach) and alcohol (which causes dehydration) during the flight. Instead, drink plenty of noncarbonated, nonalcoholic drinks such as fruit juice or water.

Avoid smoking, as this reduces the amount of oxygen in the airplane cabin even further and causes greater fatigue.

Make yourself comfortable by wearing loose-fitting clothes and perhaps bringing an eye mask and ear plugs to help you sleep.

Infectious Diseases

Diarrhea A change of water, food or climate can all cause the runs; diarrhea caused by contaminated food or water is more serious. Despite your precautions you may still have a mild bout of travelers' diarrhea, but a few rushed toilet trips with no other symptoms is not indicative of a serious problem. Moderate diarrhea, involving half a dozen loose movements in a day, is more of a nuisance.

Dehydration is the main danger, particularly for children, so fluid replacement is essential. Weak black tea with a little sugar, soda water, or soft drinks allowed to go flat and diluted 50% with water are all good.

With diarrhea more severe than this, go to the nearest hospital and have yourself checked. You may need a rehydrating solution to replace minerals and salts. Stick to a bland diet as you recover.

Giardiasis This disease is more commonly known as giardia, and sometimes 'beaver fever.' The intestinal parasite is present in contaminated water and has even contaminated apparently pristine streams in the backcountry, but is not common in urban areas.

Symptoms are stomach cramps, nausea, a bloated stomach, watery, foul-smelling diarrhea and frequent gas. Giardiasis can appear several weeks after exposure to the parasite; symptoms may disappear for a few days and then return, a pattern which may continue. If you feel you may have been exposed to the bacteria seek medical attention.

Rabies This isn't a major problem, but rabies is something to be aware of when spending time in the woods or undeveloped areas. Common animals most likely affected are the squirrel, skunk, raccoon and particularly the fox.

Any bite, scratch or even lick from a warm-blooded, furry animal should be cleaned immediately and thoroughly. Scrub with soap and running water, then clean with an alcohol solution. If there's any possibility that the animal is infected, medical help should be sought immediately. Even if the animal is not rabid, all bites should be treated seriously as they can become infected or result in tetanus. A rabies vaccination should be considered if you're in a high-risk category – eg if you intend to explore caves (bat bites can be dangerous) or work with animals.

Tetanus Tetanus, while difficult to treat, is preventable with immunization. To help prevent it, clean all cuts, punctures or animal bites. Tetanus is also known as lockjaw, and the first symptom may be discomfort in swallowing or stiffening of the jaw and neck; this is followed by painful convulsions of the jaw and whole body.

Sexually Transmitted Diseases (STDs)
Sexual contact with an infected sexual partner spreads these diseases. While abstinence is the only 100% preventative, using condoms is also effective. Gonorrhea and syphilis are the most common; sores, blisters or rashes around the genitals, discharges or pain when urinating are common symptoms. Symptoms may be less marked or not observed at all in women. Syphilis symptoms eventually disappear, but the disease continues and can cause severe problems in later years. The treatment of gonorrhea and syphilis is by antibiotics – seek medical attention if you think you might be infected.

There are numerous other STDs, for most of which effective treatment is available. However, there is no cure for herpes or HIV/AIDS.

HIV/AIDS The Human Immunodeficiency Virus (HIV) may develop into Acquired Immune Deficiency Syndrome (AIDS). Exposure to blood, blood products or bodily fluids may put the individual at risk. In industrialized countries like the US transmission is mostly through sexual contact between homosexual or bisexual males, or via contaminated needles shared by IV drug users. Apart from abstinence, the most effective preventative is always to practice safe sex using latex condoms. It's impossible to detect the HIV-positive status of an otherwise healthy-looking person without a blood test.

HIV/AIDS can also be spread through infected blood transfusions and by dirty needles – vaccinations, acupuncture, tattooing and ear or nose piercing can potentially be as dangerous as intravenous drug use if the equipment isn't clean. In the US, although there may be a risk of infection, it's very small. Fear of HIV infection should never preclude treatment for serious medical conditions. A good resource for help and information is the US Center of Disease Control AIDS Hotline (☎ (800) 342-2437).

Insect-Borne Diseases
Ticks Ticks are a parasitic arachnid often found in brush, forest and grasslands,

where hikers often get them on their legs or in their boots. The adults suck blood from hosts by burying their head into skin, but are often found unattached and can simply be brushed off. However, if one has attached itself to you, pulling it off and leaving the head in the skin increases the likelihood of infection or disease such as Lyme disease.

To avoid ticks on walks or hikes, wear long pants and use insect repellent; to induce ticks to let go, cover them in Vaseline, alcohol or oil. Always check your body for ticks after walking through a tick-infested area. If you get sick in the weeks following a bite, consult a doctor.

Bedbugs & Lice Bedbugs live in various places, but particularly in dirty mattresses and bedding. Spots of blood on bedclothes or on the wall around the bed suggest it's wise to find another hotel. Bedbugs leave itchy bites in neat rows. Calamine lotion may help.

Lice cause itching and discomfort. They make themselves at home in your hair (head lice), your clothing (body lice) or in your pubic hair (crabs). You catch lice through direct contact with infected people or by sharing combs, clothing and the like. Powder or shampoo treatment kills the lice; infected clothing should be washed in hot water.

TOILETS

New York City has been very slow in its promises to install public toilets – there's only one in City Hall park.

As a rule, there are no public toilets on the streets as in Europe, but bus, train and service stations, museums and larger stores have public bathrooms. Most facilities turn away nonpatrons from bathrooms, but it's possible to walk into many hotel lobbies, or into a crowded bar or restaurant if you're discreet and reasonably well dressed.

On a long drive in New York's Adirondacks, when each curve of the road promises hope for a rest stop, or at least a turn-out with a shade tree, remember Stewart's Convenience Stores. Toilets are free and clean.

WOMEN TRAVELERS

Women often face different situations from men when traveling and, especially if they're traveling alone, should maintain a little extra awareness of their surroundings. People in the region are generally friendly and happy to help travelers, but consider the following suggestions, which might help reduce or eliminate your chances of problems. The best advice is to trust your instincts.

Precautions

In general, exercise more vigilance in large cities than in rural areas. Try to avoid the 'bad' or unsafe neighborhoods or districts; if you go into or through these areas, it's best to go in a private vehicle (car or taxi). It's more dangerous at night, but in the worst areas crime can occur even in the daytime. If you're unsure which areas are considered unsafe, ask at your hotel or telephone the tourist office for advice. Tourist maps can sometimes be deceiving, compressing nontouristed areas and making distances seem shorter than they really are.

Even in rural areas, women may still be harassed by men unaccustomed to seeing women traveling solo. Try to avoid hiking or camping alone, especially in unfamiliar places. The 'buddy system' may not only help protect you from other humans, but may also help if you're injured or become ill.

The best way to deal with the threat of rape is to avoid putting yourself in vulnerable situations; using common sense will help avoid most problems. For example, you're more vulnerable if you've been drinking or using drugs than if you're sober; you're more vulnerable alone than with company; and you're more vulnerable in a high-crime urban neighborhood.

Some men may interpret a woman drinking alone in a bar as a bid for male company, whether it's intended that way or not. If you don't want the company, most men respect a firm but polite 'no thank you.' If you're the object of catcalls, don't engage the caller.

Hitchhiking isn't advisable; but if you

decide to hitch, do so with a companion. If you're driving alone, don't pick up hitch-hikers. If you get stuck on a road and need help, have a pre-made sign to signal for help. At night avoid getting out of your car to flag down help; turn on your hazard lights and wait for the police to arrive. Be extra careful at night on public transit, and remember to check the times of the last bus or train before you go out at night.

To deal with potential dangers, many women protect themselves with a whistle, mace (a chemical spray), cayenne pepper spray or some self-defense training. If you decide to purchase a spray, contact a police station to find out about regulations and training classes. Note that laws regarding sprays vary from state to state, though it is legal in New York. Because of its combustible nature it's a federal felony to carry a spray can on board an airplane.

If, despite all precautions, you are assaulted, call the police; in any emergency, telephoning '911' connects you with the emergency operator for police, fire and ambulance services. In some rural areas where 911 is not active, just dial 0 for the operator. Cities and larger towns have rape-crisis centers and women's shelters that provide help and support; these are usually listed in the telephone directory; if they're not, the police should be able to refer you to them.

Organizations

The headquarters for the National Organization for Women (NOW, ☎ (202) 331-0066), 1000 16th St NW, Suite 700, Washington, DC 20036, is a good resource for information and can refer you to state and local branches. Planned Parenthood (☎ (212) 541-7800), 810 Seventh Ave, New York, NY 10019, can refer you to clinics throughout the country and offer advice on health concerns and medical issues. Check the yellow pages under 'Women's Organizations & Services' for local resources.

GAY & LESBIAN TRAVELERS

Established gay communities exist in the major cities; in cities and on both coasts it's easier for gay men and women to live their lives with a certain amount of openness. San Francisco and New York City have the largest gay populations, but other larger cities have a gay neighborhood or area and even some smaller towns accept such alternative lifestyles. Outside the cities, gay or lesbian couples may encounter a double take at certain accommodations, but won't be turned away or overtly discriminated against.

In the middle of the country it's much harder to be open about your sexual preferences. The prevailing US attitude prefers that gay people are neither seen nor heard and gay travelers should be discreet (ie it's okay for same-sex couples to share a hotel room, not okay to hold hands in public), *especially* in predominantly rural areas.

Upstate New Yorkers seem to be a fairly accepting, if not approving, group. Like their nearby New England neighbors, they may be skeptical of noticeably different lifestyles, but not overtly critical.

Resources & Organizations

Two good national guidebooks are *The Women's Traveler*, providing listings for lesbians and *Damron's Address Book* for men, both published by the Damron Company (☎ (415) 255-0404, (800) 462-6654) PO Box 422458, San Francisco, CA 94142-2458. Ferrari's *Places for Women* and *Places for Men* are also useful, as are guides to specific cities (check out *Betty & Pansy's Severe Queer Reviews* to San Francisco, New York City and Washington, DC). Fodor's *Gay Guide to the USA* by Andrew Collins has coverage on Fire Island, New York City, New Hope (PA) and Philadelphia, as well as other major US cities. These are often found at any good bookstore.

Another good resource is the *Gay Yellow Pages* (☎ (212) 674-0120), PO Box 533, Village Station, NY 10014-0533, which has a national edition as well as numerous regional editions.

The club scene is ever changing, and most cities have a gay paper or alternative paper that lists what's happening or at least provides phone numbers of local organizations.

New York City's Lesbian and Gay Community Center (☎ (212) 620-7310), 208 W 13th St, New York, NY 10011, is open daily from 9 am to 11 pm, and provides services and assistance for travelers.

For people with on-line capabilities America Online hosts the Gay & Lesbian Community Forum. This is also the on-line home of National Gay/Lesbian Task Force (NGLTF), Gay & Lesbian Alliance Against Defamation (GLAAD), Parents-Friends of Lesbians & Gays (P-FLAG) and other regional, state and national organizations.

National resource numbers include the national AIDS/HIV hotline (☎ (800) 342-2437), the National Gay/Lesbian Task Force (☎ (202) 332-6483 in Washington, DC) and the Lambda Legal Defense Fund (☎ (212) 995-8585 in New York City, (213) 937-2727 in Los Angeles).

DISABLED TRAVELERS

Travel within the USA is becoming easier for people with disabilities. Public buildings (including hotels, restaurants, theaters and museums) are now required by law to be wheelchair accessible and to have available restroom facilities. Public transportation must be made accessible to all, including those in wheelchairs, and telephone companies are required to provide relay operators for the hearing impaired. Many banks now provide ATM instructions in Braille, and you'll find audible crossing signals as well as dropped curbs at busier roadway intersections.

Larger private and chain hotels have suites for disabled guests. Main car-rental agencies offer hand-controlled models at no extra charge. Major airlines, Greyhound buses and Amtrak trains allow service animals to accompany passengers and frequently sell two-for-one packages when attendants of seriously disabled passengers are required. Airlines also provide assistance for connecting, boarding and disembarking the flight – ask for assistance when making your reservation. (Note: airlines must accept wheelchairs as checked baggage and have an onboard chair available, though some advance notice may be required on smaller aircraft.) The more populous the area, the greater the likelihood of facilities for the disabled, so it's important to call ahead.

For New York state residents with permanent disabilities, the Access Pass provides free admission to all New York state parks and recreation areas.

Organizations

A number of organizations and tour providers specialize in the needs of disabled travelers:

Mobility International USA
  Mobility International, PO Box 3551, Eugene, OR 97403, advises disabled travelers on mobility issues and runs an exchange program (☎ (503) 343-1284)
Moss Rehabilitation Hospital's Travel Information Service
  1200 W Tabor Rd, Philadelphia, PA 19141-3099 (☎ (215) 456-9600, TTY 456-9602)
SATH
  Society for the Advancement of Travel for the Handicapped, 347 Fifth Ave, No 610, New York, NY 10016 (☎ (212) 447-7284)
Twin Peaks Press
  PO Box 129, Vancouver, WA 98666; publishes several handbooks for disabled travelers (☎ (360) 694-2462, (800) 637-2256)

SENIOR TRAVELERS

Though the age where senior discounts begin varies, travelers 50 years and up can receive cut rates on things like hotels, museums, restaurants and transportation, provided they show proof of their age. Sometimes these aren't publicized so don't be afraid to ask.

Visitors to national parks and campgrounds can cut costs greatly by using the Golden Age Passport (see National Park Service in the Facts about the Region chapter for information).

New York state residents score if they are 62 or older, with free access to all state parks, state historic sites and arboretums.

In the Adirondacks the Sagamore Institute (a national historic site) operates a fine

Elderhostel (see below) program for seniors. The program encourages continuing education for retired people in unusual settings; cultural and natural history is stressed. One popular program is the Grandparents' & Grandchildren's Summer Camp, a one week 'inter-generational' gathering. Reservations a year in advance recommended. For more information contact the Sagamore Institute (☎ (315) 354-5311), PO Box 146, Raquette Lake, NY 13436.

Organizations

National advocacy groups that can help in planning your travels include:

American Association of Retired Persons
  601 E St NW, Washington, DC 20049; advocacy group for Americans 50 years and older and a good resource for travel bargains and information; a one year membership for US residents costs $8; non-US residents are $10.
  (☎ (800) 424-3410)
Elderhostel
  75 Federal St, Boston, MA 02110-1941; nonprofit organization offering seniors the opportunity to attend academic college courses throughout the USA and Canada; programs last one to three weeks, include meals and accommodations and are open to people 55 years and older and their companions (☎ (617) 426-8056)
Grand Circle Travel
  347 Congress St, Boston, MA 02210; offers escorted tours and travel information in a variety of formats and distributes a free useful booklet, *Going Abroad: 101 Tips for Mature Travelers* (☎ (617) 350-7500, fax 350-6206)
National Council of Senior Citizens
  1331 F St NW, Washington DC, 20004; membership (you needn't be a US citizen to apply) gives access to added Medicare insurance, a mail-order prescription service and a variety of discount information and travel-related advice; fees are $13/30/150 for one year/three years/lifetime
  (☎ (202) 347-8800)

TRAVEL WITH CHILDREN

Successful travel with young children requires effort but can certainly be done.

Try not to overdo things and consider using some sort of self-catering accommodations as a base. Include children in the planning process; if they've helped to work out where you're going, they'll be more interested when they get there. Include a range of activities – balance a visit to the Metropolitan Museum of Art for example with one to the Liberty Science Center, where there are lots of hands-on exhibits. For more information see Lonely Planet's *Travel with Children* by Maureen Wheeler.

USEFUL ORGANIZATIONS
American Automobile Association

The AAA (check locally for telephone information), 1000 AAA Dr, Heathrow, FL 32746 has offices in all major cities and many smaller towns; it provides useful information, free maps and routine road services like tire repair and towing (free within a limited radius) to its members. Members of its foreign affiliates, like the Automobile Association in the UK, are entitled to the same services; for others, the basic membership fee is $39 per annum, plus a one time initiation fee of $17 (still an excellent investment for the maps alone, even for nonmotorists). Its nationwide toll-free roadside assistance number is ☎ (800) AAA-HELP, (800) 222-4357.

National Park Service (NPS) & US Forest Service (USFS)

For information on these see Parks & Forests in the Facts about the Region chapter, or the Outdoor Activities chapter.

DANGERS & ANNOYANCES
Crime

Crime is certainly present, especially in the larger cities like New York and Philadelphia, but isn't as prevalent as many visitors might fear. In New York City crime rates have fallen considerably since the 1970s and Philadelphia is ranked by the FBI as the safest of the nation's 12 largest metropolitan areas. Nevertheless, you should take the usual precautions.

Always lock cars and put *anything* out of sight, whether you're leaving the car for a few minutes or longer, and whether you're in a town or the remote backcountry. If your car is bumped from behind, don't stop – keep going to a well-lit area, service station or even a police station.

On foot, be aware of your surroundings and who may be watching you. Avoid walking dimly lit streets at night, particularly if you're alone. Walk purposefully. Exercise particular caution in large street-level parking lots or multistory parking structures at night. Avoid unnecessary displays of money or jewelry. Split up your money and credit cards to avoid losing everything, and try to use ATMs in well-trafficked areas.

In hotels, don't leave valuables lying around your room. Use safety-deposit boxes or at least place valuables in a locked bag. Don't open your door to strangers – check the peephole or call the front desk if unexpected people are trying to enter.

Street People & Begging
The USA has a lamentable record in dealing with its most unfortunate citizens. Street people and panhandlers may approach visitors in the larger cities and towns; most of them are harmless.

It's an individual judgment whether you believe their stories and offer them money or anything else, though it's immensely preferable to give to a recognized charity. If a stranger approaches you and doesn't ask for the time or directions and doesn't get to the point immediately, they will ask for money. It's a hard and fast rule. If it is a scam, they've probably had a lot of practice and will sound very convincing.

If you do give, don't wave a full wallet around – carry some change in a separate pocket. See also Dangers & Annoyances in New York City.

Guns
The USA has a widespread reputation, partly true but also exaggerated by the media, as a dangerous place because of the availability of firearms. Residents of rural areas often carry guns, but they usually use them against animals. Be careful in forests

during the fall hunting season when unsuccessful or drunken hunters may be less selective in their targets. Unregistered guns are banned in New York City and New Jersey.

Wildlife
If you're camping in the woods, beware of animals, mostly bears, looking for an easy snack. Keep your food in nylon bags; a sleeping-bag sack is good. Tie the sack to a rope and sling it high over a branch away from your tent and away from the trunk of the tree as some bears can climb. Don't leave food scraps around the site and never keep food in the tent. Don't try to get close-up photographs of bears and never come between a bear and its cubs. If you see a bear, try to get upwind so it can smell you and you won't startle it. When hiking in bear country, making a noise, talking or singing as you go warns them of your presence.

Drivers should watch for animals on highways. Hitting a deer at 55 mph will total your car, kill the animal and may kill you and/or other people.

Insects
In some rural areas you'll be plagued by mosquitoes, and if you're camping or hiking an insect repellent is a necessity. Lemon or orange peel rubbed on your skin helps if you have no repellent. As a rule, darker clothes are said to attract biting insects more than lighter ones. Try to minimize the amount of skin exposed by wearing a long-sleeved shirt, long pants and a close-fitting cap or hat.

Insects are at their worst deep in woods. In clearings, along shorelines or anywhere there's a breeze you'll be safer. Mosquitoes come out around sunset; building a fire, if it's allowed, will help keep them away.

EMERGENCY
If you need emergency assistance such as police, ambulance or fire department, call ☏ 911. This is free from any phone. A few rural phones might not have this service, in which case dial 0 for the operator and ask

for emergency assistance – it's still free. Travelers' Aid Society is an organization that will assist travelers in trouble. It has offices in large cities; local offices are listed in the phone book or you can dial ☎ 0 for the operator.

LEGAL MATTERS

Being pulled over for speeding is your most likely encounter with the law, but if you're stopped by the police for any reason, bear in mind that there's no system of paying on-the-spot fines. For traffic offenses, the police officer will explain your options to you. Attempting to pay the fine to the officer is frowned upon at best and may lead to a charge of bribery to compound your troubles. Should the officer decide that you should pay up front, they can exercise their authority and take you directly to the magistrate instead of allowing you the usual 30 day period to pay.

If you're arrested for more serious offenses, you're allowed to remain silent and are presumed innocent until proven guilty. There's no legal reason to speak to a police officer if you don't wish to. Any arrested person is legally allowed (and given) the right to make one phone call. If you don't have a lawyer or family member to help you, call your embassy or consulate. The police will give you the number if you ask for it.

Driving & Drinking Laws

Each state has its own laws so what may be legal in one state may be illegal in another. The drinking age is 21, and you need a photo ID to prove your age. Stiff fines, jail and other penalties could be incurred if you're caught driving under the influence of alcohol. During festive holidays and special events, road blocks are sometimes set up to deter drunk drivers. In resort communities, the police can pull you over late at night on suspicion of drinking alcohol. If this happens, you have the right to request an accurate blood test and to decline a breath test.

See also Car & Motorcycle in the Getting Around chapter.

BUSINESS HOURS

Generally speaking, business hours are from 9 am to 5 pm, but there are certainly no hard and fast rules. In any large city, a few supermarkets, restaurants and the lobby of the main post office are open 24 hours a day. Shops are often open until 9 pm in shopping malls, except on Sundays when hours are noon to 5 pm. Post offices generally open from 8 am to 4 or 5:30 pm Monday to Friday, and some open from 8 am to 3 pm on Saturday. Banks usually open from either 9 or 10 am to 3:30 or 4 pm Monday to Friday. A few banks open from 9 am to 2 or 4 pm on Saturdays. Basically, hours are decided by individual branches, so if you need specifics give the branch you want a call.

PUBLIC HOLIDAYS & SPECIAL EVENTS

On national public holidays banks, schools and government offices (including post offices) are closed and transportation, museums and other services are on a Sunday schedule. Public holidays falling on a Sunday are usually observed on the following Monday. Public holidays are denoted by an asterisk (*) in the month-by-month listing below.

Some national holidays are less official: these include things like Halloween and Mother's Day. In some cities with very ethnic cultures, traditional holidays of other countries are also celebrated with fanfare, such as St Patrick's Day in New York City. Some of these are local public holidays and therefore local banks, schools and government buildings are closed.

As well as the above national events, residents celebrate hundreds of regional special events, from highbrow arts festivals to down-home country fairs. Special event dates may vary from year to year; check with the state tourist boards or local tourist offices. For more details see state and geographical listings.

January

New Year's Day* – January 1

Martin Luther King Jr Day* – observed the third Monday of the month, it celebrates this civil rights leader's birthday (January 15, 1929).

Chinese New Year – begins at the end of January or beginning of February and lasts two weeks. The first day is celebrated with parades, firecrackers, fireworks and lots of food.

Winter Antiques Show, Manhattan, mid-January

Super Science Weekend, Trenton, second weekend in January

Mummers Parade, Philadelphia, January 1

February

Presidents' Day* – observed the third Monday of the month, it celebrates the birthdays of Abraham Lincoln (February 12, 1809) and George Washington (February 22, 1732).

Valentine's Day – February 14. No one knows why St Valentine is associated with romance in the USA, but this is the day of flowers and packed restaurants.

Black History Month, New York City, Newark, Philadelphia

Garden & Flower Show, Somerset, NJ

Philadelphia Flower Show, Philadelphia (February/March)

March

Easter* – observed the first Sunday after a full moon in March or April. Those who observe the holiday may go to church, paint eggs, eat chocolate or any mixture of the above. Travel during this weekend is usually expensive and crowded. Good Friday is not a public holiday and often goes unnoticed.

St Patrick's Day – March 17. The patron saint of Ireland is honored by all those who feel Irish in their blood, and by those who want to feel Irish beer in their blood. Many wear something green, stores sell green bread, bars serve green beer and towns and cities put on parades of marching bands and community groups. The region's premier parade is held in New York City.

The Cook & The Book, Philadelphia (March/April)

April

Passover – celebrated either in March or April, depending on the Jewish calendar. Families get together to honor their persecuted forebears, partake in the symbolic seder dinner and eat unleavened bread.

Avignon-New York Film Festival, Manhattan

Renaissance Festival, Brookville, Long Island

Niagara Spring Festival of Gold, Niagara Falls, Buffalo and several surrounding communities (mid-April to mid-May)

Cherry Blossom Festival, Newark

Philadelphia Antique Show & Sale, Philadelphia

Penn Relays, Philadelphia

May

Memorial Day* – observed the last Monday in the month, it honors the war dead (and is also the unofficial first day of the summer tourist season).

Cinco de Mayo – the day the Mexicans wiped out the French army in 1862. Americans now celebrate with Mexican food and margaritas.

Mother's Day – observed the second Sunday of the month, with lots of cards, flowers and busy restaurants.

Fleet Week, Manhattan, late May

Balloon Race, Wappingers Falls, NY

Shakespeare Festival, Madison, NJ

Arts & Music Festival, Hoboken

Memorial Day Parade, Atlantic City

Gettysburg Spring Bluegrass Festival, Gettysburg, first weekend of the month

Africamericas Festival, Philadelphia

Jambalaya Jam, Philadelphia

Philadelphia Festival of World Cinema, Philadelphia

Pittsburgh Folk Festival, Pittsburgh

Three Rivers Shakespeare Festival, Pittsburgh, May to July

Bach Festival, Bethlehem, PA, mid- to late May

June

Father's Day – third Sunday

JVC Jazz festival, Manhattan, June to July

Buskers' Fare Festival, Manhattan, June to July

Central Park Summerstage, Manhattan, June to August

Shakespeare in the Park, Manhattan, June to September

Welcome Back to Brooklyn Celebration, Brooklyn

Adirondack Festival of American Music, Saranac Lake, June to July

Jet Ski Races, Seaside Heights, NJ

Fresh Seafood Festival, Atlantic City

Waterloo Music Festival, Waterloo Village, NJ, June to August

Three Rivers Arts Festival, Pittsburgh

Civil War Heritage Days, Gettysburg, last weekend in June and first week of July

July

Independence Day* – July 4, more commonly called 4th of July, celebrates the adoption of the Declaration of Independence on that day in 1776; parades, fireworks displays and a huge variety of other events are held throughout the country. Notable fireworks demonstrations are held at New York Harbor, in the New Jersey shore towns, Philadelphia (see Philadelphia Freedom Festival)

Lincoln Center Festival, Manhattan, July to August

Mostly Mozart, Manhattan, July to August

Saratoga Jazz Festival, Saratoga

Black Arts and Cultural Festival, Albany

Chamber Music Festival, Lake Placid, July to September

Garden State Games, Edison

Pathmark Tennis Classic, Mahwah

New Jersey Festival of Ballooning, Readington

Philadelphia Freedom Festival, Philadelphia, first week of the month

South Side Summer Street Spectacular, Pittsburgh, mid-July

August

There are no public or national holidays in August.

Harlem Week, New York City

Hampton Classic Horse Show, Bridgehampton, NY

Summer Crafts Fair, Oneida Lake, NY

Baseball Hall of Fame Inductions, Cooperstown, NY

Bud at the Glen NASCAR Races, Watkins Glen, NY

New Jersey State Fair, Cherry Hill, first week in August

Philadelphia Folk Festival, Philadelphia

Gettysburg Fall Bluegrass Festival, Gettysburg, third weekend of the month

Pittsburgh Three Rivers Regatta, Pittsburgh

Harambee Black Arts Festival, Pittsburgh

Little League World Series, Williamsport, third week in August

September

Labor Day* – observed the first Monday of the month, it honors working people (and is also the unofficial end of the summer tourist season).

US Open Tennis Tournament, Queens

Queens Fall Festival, Queens, September to November

San Gennaro Festival, Manhattan, Little Italy, mid-month

New York is Book Country, Manhattan

New York Film Festival, Manhattan, late September to October

West Indian Festival, also known as Caribbean Day Parade, Brooklyn

State Apple Festival, New York statewide

Autumn Harvest Fair, Cooperstown, NY

Miss America Pageant, Atlantic City

Super Sunday, Philadelphia, second Sunday of the month

A Fair in the Park, Pittsburgh

October

Columbus Day* – observed the second Monday of the month, it commemorates the landing of Christopher Columbus in the Bahamas on October 12, 1492. Though it's a federal holiday, many Native Americans don't consider this day a cause for celebration.

Halloween – October 31. Kids and adults dress in costumes. In safer neighborhoods children go 'trick-or-treating' for candy.

New York City Marathon, last weekend in October or first weekend in November

Hampton's International Film Festival, Hampton NY

Octoberfest, Lake George, NY

Antique Car Show, Seaside Heights NJ

Indian Summer Weekend, Ocean City, NJ Columbus Day weekend

Victorian Week, Cape May, NJ mid-October

Columbus Day Parade, Philadelphia, New York City, second Monday of the month

Pennsylvania National Horse Show, Harrisburg, PA, mid-October

November

Election Day – held on the second Tuesday of the month. This is the chance for US citizens to perform their patriotic duty and vote.

Veterans' Day* – November 11, honors war veterans.

Thanksgiving* – observed the fourth Thursday of the month, it's a day of giving thanks and is traditionally celebrated with a big family dinner, usually turkey and fall harvest vegetables. The following day is declared by retailers as the biggest shopping day of the year.

Day of the Dead – observed in areas with Mexican communities on November 2. This is a day for families to honor dead relatives, and make breads and sweets resembling skeletons, skulls and such.

International Poster Fair, Manhattan

Edison Family Christmas, West Orange, NJ

Fairmount Park Marathon, Philadelphia, second
    or third Sunday of the month
Thanksgiving Day Parade, One in Manhattan and
    one in Philadelphia
Anniversary of Lincoln's Gettysburg Address,
    Gettysburg, November 19

December

Christmas* – December 25. Christmas Eve is as
    much of an event as the day itself, with
    church services, caroling in the streets and
    last-minute shopping.
Kwanzaa – held from December 26 to 31. This is
    a seven day African American celebration of
    cultural heritage. Families join together for a
    feast and practice seven different principles
    corresponding to the seven days of celebra-
    tion. A parade is held in Philadelphia.
New Year's Eve – December 31. Celebrated with
    dressing up and drinking champagne.
Rockefeller Center Christmas Tree Lighting,
    Manhattan, Tuesday after Thanksgiving
First Night, New York City, December 31
Christmas Candlelight Tour, Cape May, NJ
Christmas Tours of Historic Houses, Philadelphia
John Wanamaker's Light Show, Philadelphia
The Crossing, Washington Crossing Historic
    Park, December 25

WORK

Seasonal work is possible, in summer at
resorts, camps and on the Jersey Shore, in
winter at the ski areas; for information,
contact local chambers of commerce. It's
also possible to find year-round work in
city bars, restaurants, branches of fast-food
chains and local newspapers.

With some vocational skills, like excellent typing or computer applications
knowledge, temporary work in the cities
might pay fairly well (from $8 to $20 per
hour). Look up agencies in the Sunday
newspaper want-ads. If you want to work in
the USA and you're prepared to do anything and to work long hours for lousy pay,
you'll find something. Without skills
though, it's extremely difficult to find a job
that pays sufficiently well to enable you to
save much money.

You'll need to apply for a work visa
from the US embassy in your home
country before you leave. The type of visa
varies depending on how long you're

staying and the kind of work you plan to
do. Generally, you'll need either a J-1
visa, which you can obtain by joining a
visitor-exchange program, or a H-2B visa,
which you get when being sponsored by a
US employer. The latter is not easy to
obtain (since the employer has to prove
that no US citizen or permanent resident is
available to do the job); the former is
issued mostly to students for work in
summer camps.

ACCOMMODATIONS

This, along with transportation, will probably be your greatest expense. For budget
travel your options are camping, hostels,
some guesthouses and cheaper motels. In
general, budget to mid-range accommodations in the USA are fairly standardized and
undistinguished. There's often a vast difference between high- and low-season rates
and between weekend and weekday rates.
Prices in this book are generally high-
season prices and can only be a guideline.
Discounts are available at some motels for
senior citizens, commercial travelers and
members of AAA. Many hotels and motels
have smoking and nonsmoking rooms.

Reservations

Booking ahead gives you the peace of mind
of a guaranteed room when you arrive. The
cheapest bottom-end places may not accept
reservations, but you can call them and see
if they have a room – even if they don't take
reservations, they'll often hold a room for
you for an hour or two. It's possible to pull
into motels and hotels in New Jersey (even
Atlantic City) and find a place for $50 to
$75 a night. You simply can't do that in
New York, where it's a good idea to make a
reservation beforehand.

Chain hotels take reservations days or
months ahead. Normally, you have to give a
credit-card number to hold the room. If you
don't show and don't call to cancel, you'll
be charged the first night's rental. Cancellation policies vary – some let you cancel at
no charge 24 hours or 72 hours in advance;
others are less forgiving. Find out about
cancellation penalties when you book.

Also, let the hotel know if you plan to arrive late – many motels will rent your room if you haven't arrived or called by 6 pm. Chains often have a toll-free number (see below), but their central reservation system might not be aware of local availability and special discounts.

Some places, especially B&Bs and some cabins, won't accept credit cards and want a check as a deposit before they'll reserve you a room.

Camping

Public Campgrounds These are on public lands, such as national and state forests, NPS areas, state parks and US Army Corps of Engineers' land.

Free dispersed camping (meaning you can camp almost anywhere) is permitted in many public backcountry areas. Sometimes you can camp right from your car along a dirt road, and sometimes you can backpack your gear in. Information on where camping is permitted and detailed maps are available from many local ranger stations (addresses and telephone numbers are given in the text) and may be posted along the road. Sometimes a free camping permit is required. The less-developed sites are often on a first-come, first-served basis and can fill up on Friday nights. More-developed areas may accept or require reservations.

Camping in an undeveloped area, whether from your car or backpacking, entails basic responsibility. See the Outdoor Activities chapter for more on wilderness camping.

Developed areas usually have toilets, drinking water, fire pits (or charcoal grills) and picnic tables. Some don't have drinking water. At any rate, it's always a good idea to have a few gallons of water with you if you're going to be out in the boonies. These basic campgrounds usually cost about $7 to $10 a night. More-developed areas may have showers or recreational vehicle (RV) hookups These cost several dollars more.

A site is normally for up to six people (or two vehicles). If there are more of you,

Gas, Food, Lodging
When nearing a city on the highway you'll see signs saying 'Gas Food Lodging' followed by something like 'Next Three Exits.' Don't assume these exits lead directly into the city center – they don't. You'll end up traveling along commercial strips of chain motels, fast-food restaurants and gas stations. If you don't intend to stay in town, but would rather catch a few hours' sleep and head out early on the road, these establishments provide an alternative to downtown and – for better or worse – a bit of true Americana. ■

you'll need two sites. Public campgrounds often have seven- or 14-night limits.

Private Campgrounds These are on private property and are usually close to a lake or river region and/or in town. Most are designed with RVs in mind; tenters can camp, but fees are several dollars higher than in public campgrounds. Unless stated otherwise, fees given in the text are for two people per site. There's usually a charge of $1 to $3 per extra person; however, they may offer discounts for week or month stays. State and city taxes apply. Private campgrounds often have facilities lacking in many public ones. These include hot showers, coin laundry, swimming pool, full

RV hook-ups, games area, playground and convenience store.

Kampgrounds of America (KOA; ☎ (406) 248-7444), PO Box 30558, Billings, MT 59114-0558, a national network of private campgrounds, publishes an annual directory of its sites.

University Accommodations

Some universities and colleges offer their student accommodations to visitors during the holidays, usually from June to mid-August. Most rooms are comfortable and functional two-person dormitory or single rooms with shared bathroom. Prices start from $15 per person for a dormitory bed. For general information contact the Council on International Educational Exchange (CIEE; ☎ (212) 661-1414), 205 E 42nd St, New York, NY 10017.

Hostels

The US hostel network is less widespread than in Canada, the UK, Europe and Australia, and is predominantly in the north and coastal parts of the country. Not all hostels are affiliated with Hostelling International-American Youth Hostels (HI-AYH). Those that are offer discounts to HI-AYH members and usually allow nonmembers to stay for a few dollars more. Dormitory beds cost about $10 to $12 a night. Rooms are in the $20s for one or two people, sometimes more.

HI-AYH hostels expect you to rent or carry a sheet or sleeping bag to keep the beds clean. Dormitories are segregated by sex and curfews may exist. Kitchen and laundry privileges are usually available in return for light housekeeping duties. There are information and advertising boards, TV rooms and lounge areas. Alcohol may be banned. Reservations are advisable during the high season, when there may be a limit of a three night stay.

Reservations Reservations are accepted and advised during the high season – there may be a limit of a three night stay then. You can call HI-AYH's head office (☎ (202) 783-6161) to make reservations for any HI-AYH hostel, or use their code-based reservation service at ☎ (800) 909-4776. (You need the access code for the hostels to use this service, available from any HI-AYH office or their handbook.) For general information write or call HI-AYH at one of the following offices:

Head Office
    733 15th St, NW, Suite 840,
    Washington, DC 20005 (☎ (202) 783-6161)
Delaware Valley Council
    624 S 3rd St, Philadelphia, PA 19147
    (☎ (215) 925-6004)
Hudson Mohawk Council
    PO Box 6973, Albany, NY 12206
    (☎ (518) 472-1914)
New York City Hostel
    891 Amsterdam Ave, New York,
    NY 10025-4403 (☎ (212) 932-1860/2300)
Niagara Frontier Council
    PO Box 1110, Buffalo, NY 14209
    (☎ (716) 852-5222)
Pittsburgh Council
    Wightman School, Community Building,
    Room 204A, 5604 Solway St, Pittsburgh,
    PA 15217 (☎ (412) 422-2282)
Syracuse Council
    535 Oak St, Syracuse, NY 13203
    (☎ (315) 472-5788)

Independent hostels may offer a discount to HI-AYH members. They often have a few private single/double rooms available, although bathroom facilities are still usually shared. Kitchen, laundry, notice board and TV facilities are available, and rates are similar to HI-AYH.

Guesthouses

Another alternative is the simple guesthouse. These may be a spare room in someone's home, but are more commonly commercial lodging houses. They're normally found in places with a large tourist trade, such as Gettysburg. Rooms range in size with varying amenities and some include private bathrooms. Prices are from about $30 per person.

B&Bs

European visitors should be aware that North American B&Bs aren't the inexpensive accommodations found in Britain or Ireland. The cheapest establishments, with rooms in the $40s, may have clean but unexciting rooms with a shared bathroom and (usually) substantial breakfasts. Pricier places have rooms with private baths and, perhaps, amenities such as fireplaces, balconies and dining rooms with enticingly super breakfasts. Others may be in historical buildings, quaint country houses or luxurious urban homes.

Many require reservations and don't take walk-in customers. In fact, in larger urban centers, for security reasons there may be no external indication that a place is a B&B. Many B&Bs don't accept children or smokers; and pets are usually unwelcome; some prohibit alcohol or may have a curfew.

Most B&Bs fall in the $50 to $100 price range, but some go over $100 – especially in New York City. The best are distinguished by a friendly, personal attention to detail by owner/hosts who can provide you with local information, contacts and other amenities.

Lodges

Lodges are located throughout the region in the Poconos, Adirondacks and in the Catskills. They're often rustic-looking, but usually quite comfortable inside. Restaurants are on the premises and tour services are often available. They're not cheap, with most rooms going for close to $100 for a double during the high season, and many lodges are fully booked months in advance.

Hotels & Motels

Motel and hotel prices vary tremendously from season to season. A hotel charging $50 for a double in the high season may drop to $35 in the low and may raise its rates to $70 for a special event when the town is overflowing. A $200-a-night luxury resort may offer special weekend packages for $80 in the low season. Hotels may charge single and double rates during the week, but a flat cheaper room rate on weekends. At times, rates may depend on the size of the bed and/or the location of the room rather than the number of occupants. This guidebook gives rates for one or two people; extra people are charged between $3 and $10 per person. Be prepared to add room tax to prices.

Children are often allowed to stay free with their parents, but rules vary. Some hotels allow children under 18 to stay free with parents, others allow children under 12 and others may charge a few dollars per child. Call and inquire if you're traveling with a family.

The prices advertised by hotels are called 'rack rates' and aren't written in stone. If you ask about any specials that might apply you can often save a bit of money. Booking through a travel agent saves you some money as well. Members of the AARP and the AAA can qualify for a 'corporate' rate at several hotel chains.

Hotels and motels charge around 75¢ for local telephone calls versus 20¢ or 25¢ at a pay phone. Long-distance rates are inflated up 100% to 200%! It's best to use a pay phone.

Bottom-End Motels Motels with $35 rooms are found especially in small towns on major highways and the motel strips of larger towns. Popular towns won't have rock-bottom budget motels. Therefore, what may be a bottom-end motel in one town may pass for a mid-range hotel in another.

Rooms are usually small, beds may be soft or saggy, but the sheets should be clean. A minimal level of cleanliness is maintained, but expect scuffed walls, atrocious decor, old furniture, dim lighting and the smell of stale tobacco. Even these places, however, normally have a private shower, toilet and TV. Most have air-con and heat. Even the cheapest motels may advertise kitchenettes, which cost a few dollars more but give you the chance to cook a meal if you're tired of restaurants. Kitchenettes vary from a two-ring burner to a spiffy little mini-kitchen and may or may not have utensils. If you plan to do a lot of kitchenette cooking, carry your own set.

Motel & Hotel Chains The USA has many motel and hotel chains. These offer a standardized level of quality and style, but with some individual variations in facilities and prices depending on location. Travelers who like a particular chain and use it repeatedly – expecting and generally receiving the same level of comfort – should investigate the chain's frequent-guest program; discounts and guaranteed reservations are offered to faithful guests.

Several motel chains compete at the price level where rooms start in the $30s in the smaller towns or in the $40s in larger or more popular places. Beds are always reliably firm, decor fairly attractive and a 24 hour desk is often available; little extras like free coffee, cable or rental movies, or a bathtub with your shower may be offered. Chains in this range are Super 8 Motel, Days Inn or Econolodge. Some of these may have swimming pools.

Chains with rooms in the $45 to $80 range (depending on location) have noticeably nicer rooms. There may be a cafe, restaurant or bar on or adjacent to the premises; the swimming pool may be indoors and a spa or exercise room also available. Best Western has properties in most towns of any size and offers good rooms in this price range. Often they're the best available in a given town. Less widespread but also good are the Red Roof Inn and Comfort Inn.

Chains with widespread representation in the area are:

Best Western	(800) 528-1234
Comfort Inn, Sleep Inn	(800) 221-2222
Days Inn	(800) 329-7466
Econolodge, Rodeway Inn	(800) 424-4777
Red Roof Inns	(800) 843-7663
Super 8 Motel	(800) 800-8000
Travelodge	(800) 578-7878

Hotels There are, of course, nonchain establishments in these price ranges. A few of them are funky historical hotels, full of turn-of-the-century furniture. In New York City and Philadelphia there are many nonchain hotels, some on the pricier side, some on the lower end. Those that represent good value are listed in the text. They are less common outside of the major cities.

Cabins

In smaller towns, especially in the Adirondacks, Catskills, Poconos or along the Jersey Shore, cabins are available. These often come complete with fireplace, kitchen and an outdoor area with trees and maybe a stream a few steps away. They can be a bargain if you have three or more people. These are usually cheapest to rent by the week or month and are usually not 'winterized' – that is they are only available from May to November.

Resorts

Luxury resorts require a stay of several days to be appreciated and are often destinations in themselves. Some are devoted to skiing, while others include many recreational activities including golf, tennis, horseback riding and swimming. Lodging options usually include condominiums or hotel-like lodge rooms. Skiing resorts may charge $200 or so for a condo in midseason, then drop prices to less than half that in the snowless summer.

FOOD

The long Atlantic coastline, many lakes and fertile valleys with their orchards and farms provide a variety of high-quality, locally grown food. These range from the clams and oysters found on the coast, through the fruit and vegetables of the market gardens of New Jersey, to the meat and dairy products of Pennsylvania Dutch Country.

The different migrant groups that have helped make up the USA's cultural mosaic have contributed enormously to the diversity of ethnic cuisine. Chinese restaurants have been around a long time, but Thai,

Vietnamese, Indian and other Asian alternatives are more recent arrivals. Italian food is common, while French and other European cuisines are found in some areas. Mexican-style restaurants are also fairly common.

New York City and Philadelphia offer the widest variety of restaurants, including some of the best in the country.

Local Dishes

Many of the region's local dishes derive from those brought in or created by migrants. New York City is the pizza capital of the world, but initially the dish was a staple of some of Italy's poorer people. The average pizza slice is doughy and covered with sweet tomato sauce and gooey cheese. The city's Jewish community first introduced the immensely popular bagel to the nation. The best are water bagels, made of sweet dough and boiled before baking so that their crusty shells hide a springy center. Most New Yorkers have their bagels for breakfast with or without sweet butter or cream cheese.

The humble, ubiquitous hot dog was originally produced in Coney Island. Pastrami sandwiches are another quintessential New York item. Manhattan clam chowder is a local dish made with carrots, celery, green pepper and tomatoes.

Buffalo, NY, is the home, for better or worse, of 'buffalo wings,' or spicy chicken wings.

New York cheesecake is served plain or with pineapple and strawberry. The only way to combat a sweltering New York City summer day is to try an Italian ice, a rich creamy treat, halfway between an ice cream and a granita. At some of the better Italian ice places the ices come with chunks of real fruit. Another icy sweet is custard, a super rich ice cream that originated in the beach resort of Coney Island.

Submarine sandwiches are known as heroes in New York City and grinders in New Jersey. Philadelphia produces its own submarine sandwich called a hoagie, which is made with ham, provolone and salami and adorned with onions, lettuce, mayonnaise, pickle, tomato and olive oil.

Although imitated throughout the country, the best cheesesteak – a long sandwich roll filled with steak slices covered in cheese and onion – is found in Philadelphia. Philadelphia is sometimes jokingly called the Big Scrapple, because of another local dish, scrapple, made of cornmeal and ground meat fried together. You'll also find water ice, a mixture of crushed ice and fruit pulp and a variation on New York City's Italian ice.

Pennsylvania is famous for its pretzels, the best of which are reputedly made by the Amish of Pennsylvania Dutch Country. In addition, the region is noted for its baked fruit and fruit pies (such as shoo-fly pie, a tart filled with molasses and brown sugar) as well as cooked meats, especially Lebanon bologna.

Fast Food

Almost every settlement big enough to support a restaurant will have at least one of the many fast-food franchises McDonald's, Burger King, KFC, Pizza Hut etc – with their neon-lit logos visible from many blocks away. They're usually on or near the main drag downtown, close to major tourist attractions or along the highway commercial strips that inhabit the edges of so many towns. Since these eateries are so abundant and conspicuous they're rarely mentioned specifically in the text.

Vegetarian

While most Americans are carnivores, health concerns have largely been responsible for many to reduce their intake of meat, and vegetarianism is no longer the mark of an eccentric. Vegetarian restaurants can be found in the largest cities, like New York and Philadelphia, and many other restaurants including some chains have nonmeat dishes. Restaurants serving ethnic cuisine – Chinese, Mexican, Middle Eastern, Indian etc – usually have a vegetarian selection. Health-food stores and delis may be found in some small towns; in some areas you'll find meatless dishes are hard to come by, but most menus include egg dishes. Vegans, however, will find the going tough.

Markets & Roadside Stalls

Many cities have farmers' markets one or more days a week where fresh produce can be bought at reasonable prices. In the region's many rural areas, farmers' stalls sit beside highways and secondary roads, offering the crops of the season. Pumpkin, corn and fruit are items that are worth keeping an eye out for.

Most towns have a supermarket with a wide variety of fresh and prepared foods at reasonable prices. These are good for stocking up on supplies for camping trips or if you're staying in a summer resort rather than relying on outlying or local grocery stores which may inflate prices.

Mealtimes

Usually served between about 6 and 10 am, standard breakfasts are large and filling, often including eggs or an omelet, bacon or ham, fried potatoes, toast with butter and jam and coffee or tea. These cost from $3 to $5. Lunch is between 11 am and 2 pm. One strategy for enjoying good restaurants on a budget is to frequent them for lunch, when fixed-price specials are common.

Dinners, served between about 5 and 10 pm, are more expensive but often reasonably priced, and portions are usually large. Specials may also be available, but they're usually more expensive than lunch specials. Some of the better restaurants require reservations. Restaurants often close on Mondays.

DRINKS
Non-alcoholic Drinks

Most restaurants provide customers with free ice water – tap water is safe to drink. The usual soft drinks are available, although you may be asked if you drink Coke instead of Pepsi and vice-versa. Many restaurants offer milk or juices; a few have a wide variety of fruit juices. 'Lemonade' is a lemon-sugar-ice water

mix rather than the carbonated variety; if you want the fizzy kind, ask for a Sprite or Seven-Up.

Coffee is served more often than tea and is becoming more popular with the spread of coffee houses across the country. Espresso and cappuccino are widely available and specialty coffee bars and houses offer a host of different blends.

Drinkers of English-style tea will be disappointed. Tea is usually a cup of hot water with a tea bag next to it – milk isn't normally added but a slice of lemon often is. Iced lemon tea is popular and herbal teas are offered in better restaurants and coffee shops.

Alcoholic Drinks

Bland and boring 'name brand' domestic beers are available everywhere alcohol is sold. Most stores, restaurants and bars also offer much tastier but lesser-known local brews. These may cost a little more but are worth it. Imported beers are also easily available and, though more expensive, offer a wider choice of flavors than domestic brands.

Although not as common as on the West Coast there are some specialty beer-making operations known as microbreweries or brewpubs that echo British or German brewing styles. The beers are naturally brewed and sometimes cask conditioned. The beers are also available in bottles or on tap at bars and restaurants. There are a number of brewpubs like the Pennsylvania Brewing Company in Pittsburgh, Zip City in New York City or the Chapter House Brewpub in Ithaca.

Californian wines compete well with their European and Australian counterparts, but you'll also find local wines from places like the Finger Lakes region of New York and the Lake Erie region of both Pennsylvania and New York.

Some well-known cocktails first appeared in New York, the most famous of which is probably the Bloody Mary, a mixture of vodka and tomato juice. New Jersey bars tend to feature highly calorific (and sometimes highly alcoholic) specialty drinks such as Long Island Iced Tea, a potent dark-rum drink made without tea that you don't really see on Long Island, and Sea Breeze, a cranberry and vodka drink.

Alcohol is sold in liquor stores in New Jersey and Pennsylvania, but is available in food stores in New York. New York also has laws that prohibit the sale of package beer, wine and liquor on Sunday.

Alcohol & Drinking Age Persons under the age of 21 (minors) are prohibited from consuming alcohol. Carry a driver's license or passport as proof of age to enter a bar, order alcohol at a restaurant or buy alcohol. Servers have the right to ask to see your ID and may refuse service without it. Minors aren't allowed in bars and pubs, even to order nonalcoholic beverages. Unfortunately, this means that most dance clubs are also off-limits to minors, although a few clubs have solved the under-age problem with a segregated drinking area. More often than not minors are welcome in the dining areas of restaurants where alcohol may be served.

ENTERTAINMENT

The main centers for opera, theater, classical music and ballet are mentioned in the Arts section of the Facts about the Region chapter. In addition, many smaller towns have their own local amateur performance-art companies and venues.

Coffeehouses

The coffee craze that began in the northwest has swept across the USA. Coffeehouses serve Italian-style coffee drinks like cappuccino and caffe latte as well as wide varieties of brewed coffee blends with coffee from South America and Asia. Some coffeehouses offer book or poetry readings or live music on weekends; many are also found in larger bookstores like Barnes & Noble. Many people head to the sidewalk cafes to read their newspaper or people watch and aren't concerned too much about the subtlety of the coffee served.

Bars & Nightclubs

The distinction between bars and nightclubs can be academic. In general a bar is an establishment that serves alcohol and may offer live music on occasion, while a nightclub is a more formal venue that depends on live entertainment (usually but not always music) for its economic viability. In the big cities the distinction with restaurants can also be blurred, since most pubs and clubs offer food and some are worth going to just to eat; on the other hand some restaurants provide regular entertainment in order to attract customers.

In cities, bars and nightclubs present a variety of performances, ranging from rock, jazz, blues, folk and country & western (C&W) music to lounge singers and comedians. Some bars also have big TV screens showing major sporting events. In rural areas the regular attraction is a local dance band, playing a variety of styles, but usually C&W based. In small towns, a bar might be the best place in town to have a beer, shoot some pool and meet the locals.

Cinemas

While the video revolution drove some cinemas out of business many small towns have managed to keep theirs open. One of the responses to the video threat was to increase the number of screens, and today any reasonably sized town has a multi-screen cinema showing a variety of mainstream films on two to eight screens. Only the major cities have arthouse cinemas showing foreign, alternative or underground films. Entry prices are usually about $6 to $8.50, but matinees are often half price.

SPECTATOR SPORTS

Baseball (with its clone, softball), football and basketball are the cornerstone of spectator and recreational sports in the US. Football and basketball, in particular, are huge. See Spectator Sports under the destination headings for details on games or events.

Ticket Scalpers & Brokers

You can always find ticket scalpers hovering about at all major events – theaters, concerts, sports events, etc. This activity is legal in New Jersey and banned everywhere else, where transactions occur illegally, but are rarely busted. But let the buyer beware: the bigger the event, the larger the chance the scalper is selling a counterfeit ticket for five to 10 times face value (as happened in New York City during the 1996 World Series). If you're going to use a scalper, the best policy is to engage them only during regular season events, and offer money close to game time, when prices drop drastically.

You can also contact a 'ticket broker' – a licensed ticket retailer, and a safer bet – or a concierge in the major metropolitan hotels if you're desperate. Newspapers' sports pages are a good place to find brokers for major sporting events. In New York, they often take out small ads in the *New York Post* or *Daily News*. No matter how big the event, show or concert, great seats can be had right up to start time. Of course you'll pay more, and for some events prices can get into the hundreds of dollars. ∎

The major football teams are the New York Jets and New York Giants, although they actually play at the Meadowlands Sports Complex in East Rutherford, NJ, five miles west of New York City. The other main team in New York is the Buffalo Bills, although they don't get much spectator support, while in Pennsylvania the teams are the Philadelphia Eagles and Pittsburgh Steelers. The football season is from August through December, and the Superbowl is played on the third Sunday in January.

In basketball the region's major clubs are the New York Knickerbockers ('Knicks'), New Jersey Nets and Philadelphia '76ers (the 'Sixers'), and the season is October through July.

Two of the most famous baseball clubs in the US are the New York Yankees, 1996 World Champs who play at Yankee Stadium in the Bronx, and the New York Mets, who play at Shea Stadium in Queens; in Pennsylvania the major teams are the Philadelphia Phillies and Pittsburgh Pirates. The season is April through October, when the World Series is played. Minor league teams in the region include the Buffalo Bisons (NY), the Hudson Valley Renegades (NY), the Oneonta Yankees (NY), Rochester Red Wings (NY), Syracuse Chiefs (NY), Utica Blue Sox (NY), the New Jersey Cardinals (NJ), Princeton Reds (NJ), Trenton Thunder (NJ), the Erie Seawolves (PA), the Harrisburg Senators (PA), and the Reading Phillies (PA).

Ice hockey is also popular, and teams compete in the National Hockey League (NHL) for the Stanley Cup, which is awarded to the champions. The main clubs are the New York Rangers, New York Islanders, Buffalo Sabers, New Jersey Devils, Philadelphia Flyers and Pittsburgh Penguins. The NHL season is October through April.

Soccer hasn't enjoyed much success as a spectator sport, though the staging of the 1994 World Cup in the US revived interest and led to the creation of Major League Soccer in 1996. This region is represented by the New York/New Jersey Metrostars.

In New York City, Madison Square Garden is a world-famous sports venue; as well, Flushing Meadows in Queens is the site for pro tennis' US Open tournament in September.

Thoroughbred racing is rather popular and national events are held in summer at the Belmont Race Track on Long Island and in Saratoga Springs, NY, the home of the National Museum of Horseracing. Racing is also popular at well-kept Monmouth Park near the New Jersey shore.

THINGS TO BUY

The USA is the world's largest consumer society and New York City is its shopping capital. There, and in other big cities like Philadelphia, with their shopping malls, department stores, galleries, antique stores and markets, you'll be able to buy just about anything you could want or need.

There are many goods to be had in New York City – jewelry, inexpensive recorded music, sporting goods, shoes, leather, you name it. Check out the Things to Buy section in the New York City chapter. The information there might influence you to pack differently, budget differently and even reorganize your travel schedule differently to make a day for shopping!

New York City is the best place for cutting edge and traditional fashion. The stores on Madison Ave have the best in international designs, and there are signature shops from 30th St into the 70s. Saks Fifth Ave and Bloomingdale's have designer areas, and while Macy's sells designer clothes too, it's a little more downmarket. Hipper, 'chic'-er and antique clothes can be found in Greenwich Village, East Village and SoHo – in the summer check out the downtown street fairs, where clothing basics go for around $10 to $20. Designer discounters in the city include the retailers Daffy's, Century 21, Filene's Basement and Loehmann's. And don't forget to hang around the Fashion District (Seventh Ave and Broadway between 34th and 42nd) looking for 'sample sales' – designer clothing discounted directly from the manufacturer's offices. Sample sales

are often advertised by flyers handed out in the street or in building lobbies. One sale that has become quite well-advertised is '7th on Sale' – when designers sell clothes to raise money for AIDS causes.

New York City is also the best place to shop for professional-level photographic equipment; you can get good deals, but be sure to patronize a reputable dealer. A wide variety of ethnic food items, which are largely unavailable elsewhere in the country, can readily be found here.

New Jersey has numerous crafts fairs, and many people head to the state to buy clothes because the state levies no tax on clothing. Secaucus, a short ride from New York City, is noted for its discount factory outlets.

Philadelphia has centers for buying antiques, jewelry and commercial arts and crafts. In Pennsylvania Dutch Country you can buy hex signs and crafts made by the Amish, notably quilts, wooden furniture and faceless dolls. Pennsylvania also has no tax on clothing and there are numerous discount factory outlets, particularly in Reading. Civil War memorabilia is available in Gettysburg.

Also in Pennsylvania, farmers' markets, usually open one or two days a week, are good for buying cooked foods as well as fresh fruit and vegetables. Hershey is the place to fill up on chocolate.

Outdoor Activities

Although this region is heavily urbanized, the pursuit of many outdoor activities opens up some of its most beautiful and fascinating corners away from cities. Many activities are within the reach of the tightest budget, and a walk or cycle in the countryside will almost certainly be a highlight of your vacation. For those who have the money, activities like skiing, golf or fishing are available as part of holiday packages that include bed, board and transportation.

Most activities are well organized and have clubs and associations (some are listed here) that can give visitors invaluable information. Many have national or international affiliations, so check before leaving home.

The state and county tourist offices put out information covering many activities and these can be a starting point for further research.

New York and New Jersey Coastal Adventures (Country Roads Press, 1995) has information on activities along the shore, including sailing and whale watching. The *Pennsylvania Outdoor Activity Guide* (Country Roads Press, Castine, ME, 1995) by Sally Moore is a general overview of activities in the state. For New Jersey a similar book is *Enjoying New Jersey Outdoors* (Rutgers University Press, 1991) by Helen Lippman & Patricia Reardon. *New Jersey Outdoors* is a periodical produced by New Jersey's Department of Environmental Protection. See also Books, below under Hiking & Backpacking and Bicycling & Mountain Biking.

For physically disabled people New York's Department of Environmental Conservation (DEC) publishes *Opening the Outdoors to People with Disabilities*.

HIKING & BACKPACKING

On foot and on the trail is one of the best ways to appreciate the mountains, public forests, wildlife sanctuaries, wilderness areas and river and coastal areas of New York, New Jersey and Pennsylvania. Every weekend thousands of people take to the parks and countryside. Perhaps because the region is so crowded, a high premium is placed on open space and the chance to find some fresh air.

Planning

Information A variety of government and independent organizations provide information on all types of trails. For national and state government agencies see Parks & Forests in the Facts about the Region chapter.

Many abandoned former railroad lines that belonged both to railroad and mining companies are being converted to trails for public recreational use. There are now over 700 nationwide. These are managed nationally by the Rails-to-Trails Conservancy (☎ (202) 797-5400), 1400 16th St NW, Suite 300, Washington, DC 20036, a private nonprofit organization that has branches in individual states.

HI-AYH hostels are often in areas where hiking and other activities are available. For information see Hostels under Accommodations in the Facts for the Visitor chapter.

For further information contact:

Adirondack Mountain Club
    RR 3, Box 3055, Lake George, NY 12845
    (☎ (518) 668-4447)
Appalachian Mountain Club
    Manhattan Resource Center,
    5 Tudor City Place, New York, NY 10017
    (☎ (212) 986-1430)
Delaware Valley Orienteering Association
    212 Westover Dr, Cherry Hill, NJ 08034
Finger Lakes Trail Conference
    maintains an east-west trail from the
    Alleghenies to the Catskills.
    PO Box 18048, Rochester, NY 14618
    (FLTC; ☎ (716) 288-7191)
Keystone Trails Association
    PO Box 251, Cogan Station, PA 17728

Long Island Greenbelt Trail Conference
  maintains the Pine Barrens Trail and the
  Walt Whitman Trail, sells maps.
  23 Deer Path Rd, Central Islip, NY 11722
  (☎ (516) 360-0753)
New York-New Jersey Trail Conference
  maintains 800 miles of trails in
  southeastern New York and northern
  New Jersey; sells maps.
  232 Madison Ave, New York, NY 10016
  (☎ (212) 685-9699)
US Orienteering Federation
  PO Box 1444, Forest Park, GA 30051
Western Pennsylvania Conservancy
  Department OG, 316 4th Ave,
  Pittsburgh, PA 15222 (☎ (412) 288-2777)

Other organizations and outfitters can be great sources of information as well as providers of equipment, hiking partners and organized walks.

There's the Sierra Club Headquarters (☎ (415) 977-5500), 85 2nd St, 2nd Floor 2F, San Francisco, CA 94105, which publishes guides and has local clubs in the region: in New York, Sierra Club, Atlantic Chapter (☎ (518) 426-9144), 353 Hamilton St, Albany, NY 12210; in New Jersey, Sierra Club, NJ Chapter (☎ (609) 924-3141), 57 Mountain Ave, Princeton, NJ 08540; in Pennsylvania, Sierra Club, Pennsylvania Chapter (☎ (717) 232-0101), 600 N 2nd St, PO Box 606, Harrisburg, PA 17108.

Another organization with a good reputation is Earthwatch (☎ (617) 926-8200), 680 Mt Auburn St, Box 403, Watertown, MA 02272. They do national (and international) 'environmental science' working expeditions.

Eastern Mountain Sports has all-around outfitting stores in most major cities in the region, as does REI (☎ (800) 426-4840); check the yellow pages.

What to Bring The following equipment list is meant to be a general guideline for serious backcountry hiking of at least several days duration. Know yourself and what special things you may need on the trail, and consider the area and seasonal climatic conditions you'll be traveling in.

Useful Outdoor Organizations
Bureau of Land Management (BLM)
The BLM manages public use of federal lands, primarily concerning mineral and subsurface management. In addition, they offer no-frills camping, often in untouched settings. The regional office for the eastern US (☎ (703) 440-1713) can be contacted at 7450 Boston Blvd, Springfield, VA 22153.

US Fish & Wildlife Service (USFWS)
Each state has a few regional offices that provide information about viewing local wildlife. Their phone numbers can be found in the white pages phone directory under the 'US Government,' or you can call the Federal Information Center (☎ (800) 688-9889). See also Bird & Wildlife Watching, below.

US Army Corps of Engineers The northeast has lots of lakes and many of them with their surrounding land are operated by the US Army Corps of Engineers. The corps is responsible for flood control, hydropower production, shore protection and restoration, water supply and fish and wildlife management and outdoor recreation. For more information contact the following offices (there is no office in New Jersey):

New York
Mt Morris Dam, Mt Morris, NY 14510-9506 (☎ (716) 658-4220)

Pennsylvania
Wanamaker Building,
100 Penn Square East,
Philadelphia, PA 19107-3390
(☎ (215) 656-6515)

William S Moorhead Federal Building,
1000 Liberty Ave,
Pittsburgh, PA 15222-4186
(☎ (412) 644-6924)

This list is inadequate for snow country or backpacking in winter.

Boots – light to medium boots are recommended for day hikes, sturdy ones for extended trips with a heavy pack; most importantly, they should be well broken in and have a good heel.

Alternative footwear – flip-flops/mucklucks/sandals/running shoes for wearing around camp (optional) and canvas sneakers for crossing streams.

Socks – heavy polypropylene or wool stays warm even if wet; frequent changes during the day reduce the chance of blisters but are usually impractical.

Colors – subdued tones are recommended, though if you're hiking during hunting season, blaze orange is a necessity.

Shorts, light shirt – for everyday wear; remember that heavy cotton takes a long time to dry and is cold when wet.

Long-sleeve shirt – light cotton, wool or polypropylene; a button-down front makes layering easy and can be left open when the weather is hot and your arms need protection from the sun.

Long pants – heavy denim jeans take forever to dry; sturdy cotton or canvas pants are good trekking through brush, and cotton or nylon sweats are comfortable to wear around camp; long underwear with shorts over them is a good combination – warm but not cumbersome – for trail hiking where there isn't much brush.

Wool/ploypropylene/polar fleece sweater – essential in cold weather.

Rain gear – light, breathable and waterproof is the ideal combination.

Hat – wool or polypropylene is best for cold weather, a cotton hat with a brim is good for sun protection; about 80% of body heat escapes through the top of the head – keep your head (and neck) warm to reduce the chances of hypothermia.

Bandana/handkerchief – as well as its normal use, it's good for carrying a picnic lunch or as a flag (especially a red one).

Small towel – one that is indestructible and will dry quickly.

First-aid kit – should include self-adhesive bandages, disinfectant, antibiotic salve or cream, gauze, tape, small scissors and tweezers.

Knife, fork, spoon and mug – a double-layer plastic mug with a lid is best; a mug acts as an eating and drinking receptacle, mixing bowl and washbasin; the handle protects you from getting burned; bring an extra cup if you like to have a drink with your meal.

Pots and pans – aluminum cooking sets are best, but any sturdy one-quart pot is sufficient; a pot scrubber is helpful especially using cold water and no soap.

Stove – using butane or propane gas, should be lightweight and easy to operate; test the stove before you head out.

Water purifier – optional; water can be purified by boiling for at least 10 minutes.

Matches/lighter – waterproof matches and several lighters are useful.

Candle/lantern – candles are easy to operate, but hazardous in a tent; test the lantern before you hit the trail.

Flashlight – one per person; make sure to have fresh batteries and extra bulbs.

Sleeping bag – goosedown bags are warm and light, but useless when wet; outdoors stores rent synthetic bags.

Sleeping pad – optional; use a sweater or sleeping bag sack stuffed with clothes as a pillow.

Tent – should be waterproof or have waterproof cover; know how to put it up before you start out; remember your packs will be sharing the tent with you.

Camera/binoculars – bring extra film and waterproof film canisters (sealable plastic bags work well).

Compass and maps – each person should have their own.

Eyeglasses – contact-lens wearers should bring a back-up set.

Sundries – toilet paper, small sealable plastic bags, insect repellent, sun screen, lip balm, unscented moisturizing cream, moleskin for foot blisters, dental floss, sunglasses.

Food – Keeping your energy up is important, but so is keeping your pack light. Some staple foods are: oatmeal, bread (the denser the better), rice or pasta, instant soup or ramen noodles, dehydrated meat (jerky), dried fruit, energy bars, chocolate, trail mix (raisins and peanuts mixed with various other goodies), peanut butter and honey or jam.

Books Quite a few good how-to and where-to books exist. Chris Camden's *Backpacker's Handbook* (Ragged Mountain Press, 1992) is a collection of tips for life on the trail. More candid is *A Hiker's Companion* (The Mountaineers, 1992), written by Cindy Ross & Todd Gladfelter, who hiked 12,000 miles before sitting down to write. *How to Shit in the Woods* (Ten Speed Press, 1994) is Kathleen Meyer's explicit, comic and useful manual on toilet etiquette in the wilderness.

Countryman Press & Backcountry Publications publishes a series of individual books on hiking in New York, New Jersey and Pennsylvania; each contains 50 walks. They're available in bookstores or you can contact the publishers (☎ (800) 245 1451), PO Box 175AP, Woodstock, VT 05091-0175. *40 Great Rail-Trails in New York & New England* and *40 Great Rail-Trails in the Mid-Atlantic*, published by the Rails-to-Trails Conservancy, are directories of multi-use paths created from abandoned railroads.

In Pennsylvania the Keystone Trails Association publishes *Pennsylvania Hiking Trails*, which is updated regularly.

Maps A good map is essential for any hiking trip. NPS and USFS ranger stations usually stock topographical maps costing about $2 to $6. State park and forest bureaus also provide maps. Alternatively, try the local stationery or hardware store.

Longer hikes require two types of maps: USGS Quadrangles and USFS maps. To order a map index and price list, contact the USGS (☎ (303) 236-7477), Map & Book Sales, PO Box 25286, Denver, CO 80225. Excellent topographic maps of New York state are available from Jimapco. (See also Maps in the Facts for the Visitor chapter.)

Safety

The main things to reckon with are the changeable weather and your own frame of mind. Carry a rain jacket and light pair of long underwear at all times, even on shorter hikes. Backpackers should have a pack-liner (heavy-duty garbage bags work well), a full set of rain gear and food that doesn't need cooking. A positive attitude is helpful in any situation.

If possible never hike alone, but if you are traveling solo it's important to let someone know where you're going and how long you plan to be gone. Use sign-in boards at trailheads or ranger stations. Travelers seeking hiking companions can inquire or post notices at ranger stations, outdoors stores, campgrounds and hostels.

Forging rivers and streams is another potentially dangerous but often necessary part of hiking. On maintained trails bridges are usually available for crossing bodies of water, but not in wilderness areas where bridges are taboo.

If you have to cross a river in a wilderness area, on reaching it unclip all your pack straps – your pack is expendable, you are not. Avoid crossing barefoot – river cobblestones suck body heat out of your feet, numbing them and making it impossible to navigate. Bring a pair of lightweight canvas sneakers to avoid sloshing around in wet boots for the rest of your hike. Although cold water makes you want to cross as quickly as possible, don't rush things: take small steps, watch where you put your feet and keep your balance. Using a staff for balance is helpful, but don't rely on it to support all your weight. Don't enter water higher than mid-thigh; any higher and your body gives the current a large mass to work against.

If you get wet, wring out your clothes immediately, wipe off as much excess water from your body and hair as you can and put on some dry clothes. Synthetic fabrics and wool retain heat when they get wet, cotton doesn't.

People with little hiking or backpacking experience shouldn't attempt to do too much too soon. Know your limitations, know the route you're going to take and pace yourself accordingly. Remember, it's OK to turn back or not go as far as you originally intended. Plan your water supply and be careful with fires. Be very careful when walking during the hunting season (Thanksgiving to mid-December).

Contact with poisonous snakes is rare, but you should always check where you tread or place your hands.

Laws & Regulations

Most NPS areas, for instance the Delaware Water Gap NRA, require overnight hikers to carry backcountry permits, available from visitor centers or ranger stations. These must be obtained 24 hours in advance and require you to follow a specific itinerary. Most wilderness areas don't require permits for hiking and backpacking.

State game lands don't allow fires, and in

What is Wilderness?

The 1964 Wilderness Act, the first major act of Congress to set aside large road-less areas as federally administered wilderness, defined wilderness as:

. . . an area where the earth and its community of life are untrammeled by man, where man himself is a visitor who does not remain . . . It is a region which contains no permanent human inhabitants, no possibility for motorized travel, and is spacious enough so that a traveler crossing it by foot or horse must have the experience of sleeping out of doors. ■

other areas during periods of fire hazard (which is often summer and early fall) there are constraints on building open fires.

National Recreation Areas

There are no national parks in this region, but the NPS does administer the Gateway NRA, the Delaware Water Gap NRA, the Pinelands National Reserve and Fire Island National Seashore.

Collectively, the NPS, USFS, BLM and individual state park and state forest services manage roadless areas as wilderness, inaccessible to mechanized travel (see also Parks & Forests in the Facts about the Region chapter). Hikers seeking true wilderness should contact these organizations for information; see above.

For travelers with little hiking experience there are many short, well-marked, well-maintained trails which often have restroom facilities at either end and interpretive displays along the way. These trails give access to natural features and usually show up on maps as nature trails or self-guided interpretive trails.

Wilderness Camping

Camping in undeveloped areas is rewarding for its peacefulness, but it presents special concerns. Take care to ensure that the area you choose can comfortably support your presence, and leave the surroundings as you found them. Following are some guidelines:

Good campsites are found, not made; altering a site shouldn't be necessary.

Camp at least 200 feet (about 70 adult steps) from the nearest lake, river or stream.

Bury human waste in holes six to eight inches deep at least 200 feet from water, camp or trails; camouflage the hole when finished. Salt and minerals in urine attract deer; use a tent-bottle (funnel attachments are available for women) if you're prone to night calls from Mother Nature.

Use soaps and detergents sparingly or not at all; never allow these things to enter streams or lakes. When washing yourself (a backcountry luxury, not necessity), lather-up (with biodegradable soap) and rinse yourself with cans of water 200 feet from your water source. Scatter dishwater after removing all food particles.

Carry a lightweight stove for cooking and use a lantern instead of a fire.

If a fire is allowed and appropriate, dig out the topsoil and build a fire in the hole. Gather sticks no larger than an adult's wrist from the ground. Don't snap branches off live, dead or downed trees. Pour wastewater from meals around the perimeter of the campfire to prevent it from spreading, and thoroughly douse it before leaving or going to bed.

Establish a cooking area at least 100 yards from your tent and designate cooking clothes to leave in the food bag, away from your tent.

Burn cans to get rid of their odor, then remove the ashes and pack them out with you.

Pack out what you pack in, including all trash – yours *and* others.

Environmental Concerns

A code of backcountry ethics is evolving to deal with the growing numbers of people in the wilderness, which is composed of fragile environments that can't support a flood of human activity, especially insensitive and careless activity. Most conservation organizations and hikers' manuals have their own set of backcountry codes, which outline the same important principles: minimizing impact, leaving no trace and taking out only photographs and memories. Above all, even if it means walking through mud or crossing a patch of snow, hikers should stay on the main trail.

Routes

The states have many superb walks – long and short, rugged and gentle, mountain and coastal. Following are some of the major routes in the region, while others are mentioned in the body of the text.

The 2155 mile **Appalachian Trail** passes through 14 states, from Mt Katahdin in Maine to Springer Mountain in Georgia, following ridgetops ranging in height from about 500 feet to 1200 feet. To walk the full length takes about six months, though of course most people do shorter stretches. From Connecticut it enters New York State north of Pawling and heads southwest through the Taconic Mountains, Hudson Highlands, Ramapo Mountains and Hudson Valley. From there it passes through the Pocono Mountains and Delaware Water Gap NRA into central Pennsylvania then Maryland. For more information contact the Appalachian Trail Conference (☎ (304) 535-6331), PO Box 807, Harper's Ferry, WV 25425-0807.

The 3200 mile **North Country National Scenic Trail** is planned to run from Crown Point in New York to Lake Sakakawea, North Dakota, and will link the Appalachian Trail with the Lewis & Clark and Pacific Crest trails. It traverses Allegany State Park in New York and the Allegheny National Forest in Pennsylvania. For information contact the North Country Trail Association, PO Box 311, White Cloud, MI 49349.

New York offers an extensive and well-maintained trail system throughout the state. Volunteers in various hiking clubs do most of the work.

The **Canal Way Trail System** is being developed to follow the 338 miles of the Erie Canal, connecting such existing trails as the Erie Canal Trail, Old Erie Canal State Park Trail and the Mohawk-Hudson Bikeway. When the system is completed it will link the Hudson and Niagara rivers. For details contact the New York State Canal Corporation (☎ (518) 471-5011), PO Box 189, Albany, NY 12201.

The 350 mile **Finger Lakes Trail** runs east-west from the Catskill Mountains, through the state's southern tier into the Allegheny Mountains and connects with the North Country National Scenic Trail. For information contact the Finger Lakes Trail Conference (☎ (716) 288-7191), PO Box 18048, Rochester, NY 14618-0048.

In Adirondack Park one of the best known trails is the **Johns Brook Trail**, which covers 9.5 miles from Keene Valley to the summit of Mt Marcy, the highest of the 46 'High Peaks' in the region. Another well-known trail here is the 130 mile long **Northville-Placid Trail**. The trail that follows the **Ausable River** in the Adirondacks passes through some superb scenery.

The **Long Island Greenbelt** follows the Connetquot and Nissequoque rivers for 34 miles from Long Island Sound to Sunken Meadow State Park through wetlands and forest.

In Western New York, **Allegany State Park** has 80 miles of hiking trails. This connects with the **Allegheny National Forest** in Northern Pennsylvania.

In New Jersey the 50 mile **Batona Trail** starts at Lebanon State Forest and traverses Wharton State Forest to join Bass River State Forest. There are also good trails in High Point State Park, Swartswood State Park and Pinelands National Preserve.

As well as those mentioned above, important Pennsylvania walks include the **Susquehannock Trail System** in Northern Pennsylvania and the **Laurel Highlands Hiking Trail** in Southwestern Pennsylvania. The Poconos have hundreds of miles of trails.

BICYCLING & MOUNTAIN BIKING

Bicycling is an interesting, inexpensive, environmentally friendly and increasingly popular pastime and means of travel. Some cities have cycle lanes on some streets and cycle paths in larger parks, outside the cities, roads are good, shoulders are usually wide and there are many good routes for mountain bikes as well.

The many smaller highways criss-crossing the region (not interstates) offer cyclists access to an assortment of topographies from the steep river valleys and mountain ranges of the Adirondacks to the gently undulating farmland of Pennsylvania Dutch Country. In addition, there are several thousand miles of trails, either multi-use or for bicycling only, in NPS sites, the Allegheny National Forest, the various state parks, forests and game lands and those operated by the Rails-to-Trails Conservancy.

Planning

Information See Parks & Forests in the Facts about the Region chapter for addresses to write to for information on trails in NPS sites, state parks and national and state forests. (See also Planning under Hiking & Backpacking earlier.)

You can either bring your bike with you or there are many places where you can rent one from about $3 to $5 per hour, $20 to $25 per day. Spare parts are widely available and repair shops are numerous, but it's still important to be able to do basic mechanical work, like fixing a flat tire, yourself.

Members of the national League of American Bicyclists (LAB, ☎ (410) 539-3399, (800) 288-2453), 190 W Ostend St,

Suite 120, Baltimore, MD 21230, may transport their bikes for free on selected airlines. They also receive a list of hospitality homes in each state that offer simple accommodations to touring cyclists.

The Adventure Cycling Association (☎ (406) 721-1776), PO Box 8308, Missoula, MT 59807, formerly known as Bikecentennial, encourages cycle travel, publishes maps and helps develop bike trails.

For information about cycling in Pennsylvania contact the Bicycling Federation of Pennsylvania (☎ (717) 975-0888), PO Box 11625, Harrisburg, PA 17018. The Bicycle Touring Club of North Jersey (☎ (201) 284-0404), PO Box 839, Mahwah, NJ 07430, is one of the best resources for tours of the state and the northeast. The North Jersey Mountain Bike Club (☎ (201) 291-0690), 24 Central Ave, Rochelle Park, NJ 07662, specializes in more strenuous rides in the region.

Transportation Alternatives (☎ (212) 475-4600), 92 St Marks Place, NY 10003, offers weekend trips in and around New York City. For details on mountain biking tours, contact the New York International American Youth Hostels (☎ (212) 932-2300), 891 Amsterdam Ave, New York, NY 10025.

A number of other operators organize cycling vacations; state tourist offices can supply you with a list. HI-AYH and the Adventure Cycling Association are two national organizations that also offer cycling holidays.

What to Bring For any long-distance cycling your bike should be in good condition; make sure the brakes work properly. For night cycling it should be fitted with amber side reflectors, a rear reflector and a headlight visible from 500 feet. Other things to bring include a helmet, water bottles, panniers, tools, spare parts and maps. (See also What to Bring under Hiking & Backpacking earlier.)

Books The *Cyclist Yellow Pages* is an international directory of bicycling resources published by the Adventure Cycling Association. The League of American Bicyclists publishes an annual *Almanac*, listing contacts in each state along with information about bicycle routes and special events; it also publishes *The Tour Finder* with details of touring events in the US and abroad.

Countryman Press & Backcountry Publications (☎ (800) 245-1451), PO Box 175AP, Woodstock, VT 05091-0175, publishes books on cycling in the region, and the Rails-to-Trails Conservancy publishes directories of multi-use paths created from abandoned railroads (see Books under Hiking & Backpacking earlier).

Short Bike Rides in New Jersey (Globe Pequot, 1995) by Robert Santelli has descriptions of 30 bike tours of the state. Similar is *Short Bike Rides in New York City* (1995) by Phil & Wendy Harrington.

Maps The Adventure Cycling Association publishes trail maps with detailed information on topography, nature, history, lodging, food and bicycle stores. DeLorme's topographic *Atlas & Gazeteer* for each state is a good tool for planning trail rides. A map of the 35 mile Mohawk-Hudson Trail is available from the Schenectady County Department of Planning, 1 Broadway Center, Schenectady, NY 12305.

(See also Maps under Hiking & Backpacking earlier and in the Facts for the Visitor chapter.) Maps are also available from the following:

New York State Department of Transportation
WA Harriman Campus, Building 5, Albany, NY 12232 (☎ (518) 457-6400)
Pennsylvania Department of Transportation (PennDOT)
Pedestrian & Bicycle Coordinator, PO Box 2047, Harrisburg, PA 17105-2047 (☎ (717) 783-8444)
New Jersey Transportation Department
1035 Parkway Ave, CN 600, Trenton, NJ 08625 (☎ (609) 530-2000)

Transporting Your Bike Bicycles can be transported by air. You *can* disassemble them and put them in a bike bag or box, but it's much easier simply to wheel your bike to the check-in desk, where it should be treated as a piece of baggage, although airlines often charge an additional fee. You may have to remove the pedals and front tire so that it takes up less space in the aircraft's hold. Check any regulations or restrictions on the transportation of bicycles with the airline well in advance, preferably before you pay for your ticket. Remember that while some airlines welcome bicycles, others consider them a nuisance and do everything possible to discourage them.

You can also take bicycles on Greyhound buses and Amtrak trains, but again, check with them in advance. For full protection bicycles must be boxed.

Bikes are usually allowed on metropolitan public transportation, but are sometimes subject to byzantine restrictions that may be known only to the transit police who are empowered to write you a ticket. Call the local transit authority to determine whether you must avoid trains at rush hour or obtain a special pass.

Safety
On the road, bicyclists are generally treated courteously by motorists. You may, though, encounter the occasional careless one who passes too closely or too fast (or both). Helmets should always be worn to reduce the risk of head injury; in some states they are required by law. Always keep at least one hand on the handlebars. Stay close to the edge of roads and don't wear anything, such as headphones, that can reduce your ability to hear. Bicyclists should always lock their bicycles securely and be cautious about leaving bags on the bike, particularly in larger towns or more touristed locations.

Bicyclists should carry at least two full bottles of water and refill them at every opportunity.

Laws & Regulations
Cycling has increased in popularity so much in recent years that concerns have risen over damage to the environment,

especially from unchecked mountain biking. Know your environment and regulations before you ride.

Bikes are restricted from entering wilderness areas and some designated trails but may otherwise ride in NPS sites, state parks, national and state forests and BLM single-track trails. Trail etiquette requires that cyclists yield to other users. You need a permit to camp overnight along forest trails, but no camping is allowed on state game lands.

Bikes aren't allowed on interstate highways. In cities, obey traffic lights and signs and other road rules; yield to pedestrians; in downtown areas don't ride on the sidewalk unless there's a sign saying otherwise and don't ride two abreast unless in a cycle lane or path.

Routes

New York In Manhattan **Central Park** has lots of bike trails and **Battery Park** isn't a bad place for a ride on the weekend – otherwise leave the city-street cycling to the insane bike messengers. In the state, the Capital-Saratoga district's spectacular 35 mile **Mohawk-Hudson Bike-Hike Trail**, on former railroads and canal towpaths, is at the confluence of the Mohawk and Hudson rivers. For information contact the Albany County Planning Department (see above for maps; ☎ (518) 447-5660). Other popular cycling areas are the **Old Erie Canal State Park** (32 miles) and the 60 mile section of the **Barge Canal Recreationway** in Monroe and Orleans counties. It's possible to cycle long stretches of the **Seaway Trail**, the US's longest scenic byway, which runs parallel to the St Lawrence River, Lake Ontario, Niagara River and Lake Erie.

Several publications are available from New York state agencies. To receive 'Along the Bike Hike Trail,' contact the Environmental Clearinghouse of Schenectady, PO Box 113, Rexford, NY 12148.

New Jersey For the placid biker the best area to bicycle is the flat terrain around Cape May; you can pick up local maps and information from Shield's Bike Rentals (☎ (609) 884-1818), 11 Gurney St, in the town of Cape May. The back roads of northern New Jersey provide challenges for the more experienced rider. The Bicycle Touring Club of North Jersey and the North Jersey Mountain Bike Club (see above) can advise you on these.

Pennsylvania In Philadelphia the 25 mile **Fairmount Park Bikeway** heads northwest from the Philadelphia Museum of Art along the Schuylkill River and Wissahickon Creek to Pennypack Park. Contact the Fairmount Park Commission (☎ (215) 685-0000), Memorial Hall, Philadelphia, PA 19131. The southern section of the Fairmount Park Bikeway is also part of the **Schuylkill Trail**, which joins Philadelphia with Valley Forge National Historic Park via Manayunk and along the Schuylkill River and Route 422. For information contact Montgomery County City Planning Commission (☎ (610) 278-3736), Montgomery County Courthouse, Norristown, PA 19404.

The state parks have some great trails. **Moraine State Park**, in western Pennsylvania north of Pittsburgh, has a seven mile track beside Lake Arthur. Southeast of Pittsburgh in **Ohiopyle State Park** a 25 mile trail beside the Youghiogheny River connects Confluence and Wheeler Bottom via Ohiopyle village. In **Presque Isle State Park** on the shores of Lake Erie, a gentle 5.8 mile trail affords great views of Presque Isle Bay and the lake.

In the Pocono Mountains a 25 mile mountain-bike trail along a former railroad track through **Lehigh Gorge State Park** connects Jim Thorpe and White Haven. The rugged 15 mile **Switchback Gravity Railroad Trail** runs across the valley from Mauch Chunk Ridge to Pisgah Mountain via Jim Thorpe. For details write to Carbon County Park & Recreation Department (☎ (717) 325-3669), 625 Lentz Trail Rd, Jim Thorpe, PA 18229. The **North Country National Scenic Trail** is also popular for mountain biking.

DOWNHILL SKIING

The mountain ranges of the region have dozens of resorts offering great opportunities for skiing as well as other snow-related sports. Facilities range from day-only ski areas to resorts that are self-contained mini-cities, from gentle slopes for the learner to trails that challenge the most expert skier.

Planning

The skiing season lasts from about mid-December to early April, though it's sometimes possible to ski as early as November and as late as May. State tourist offices have information on resorts, and travel agents can arrange full-package tours that include transport and accommodations. Many of the resorts are close to towns so it's quite feasible to travel on your own to the slopes for the day and return to town at night. If you have travel insurance make sure that it covers you for winter sports.

Ski areas are often well equipped with accommodations, eateries, shops, entertainment venues, child-care facilities (both on and off the mountain) and transport. In fact, it's possible to stay a week at some of the bigger places without leaving the slopes. Ski areas have at least one comfortable base lodge with a rental office, ski shop and lockers. There are also cafeterias and lounges or bars where visitors can relax in warmth. You don't have to buy a lift ticket or pay to enjoy the base lodge.

At major ski areas, lift tickets usually cost $35 to $40 for a full day. Three-day or week-long lift passes are usually more economical, especially if they don't need to be used on consecutive days.

Equipment rentals are available at or near even the smallest ski areas, though renting equipment in a nearby town can be cheaper if you can transport it to the slopes.

For information on skiing nationally contact the US Recreational Ski Association (☎ (714) 634-1050), PO Box 25469, Anaheim, CA 92825 5469. Recreational programs for handicapped people are offered by National Handicapped Sports (☎ (916) 989-0402), 5932 Illinois Ave,

Orangeville, CA 95662. Skiers 70 years of age and over can contact the 70+ Ski Club (☎ (518) 399-5458), 104 East Side Dr, Ballston Lake, NY 12019.

In the book *Skiing America* (World Leisure Corporation, Hampstead, NH, 1994) Charles Leocha has compiled facts and figures about the USA's big ski resorts. *Ski* and *Skiing* are year-round magazines available in most newsstands, airports and sporting-goods stores. *Snow Country* magazine ranks ski resorts in the US using criteria that includes terrain, ski school, nightlife, lodging and dining.

Ski Schools

Visitors planning on taking lessons should rent equipment on the mountain since the price of a lesson, around $25 for a half a day, usually includes equipment rentals, with no discount for having your own gear. Children's ski schools are popular places to stash the kids for a day, offering lessons, day-care facilities and providing lunch for around $35 per child.

Ski Resorts

New York has numerous downhill ski resorts. Whiteface Mountain near Lake Placid in the Adirondack north country has hosted Winter Olympic alpine competitions. The Adirondacks have numerous other prime winter destinations, including Gore Mountain and Big Tupper. In the Catskills fairly close to New York City, Belleayre Mountain, Ski Windham and Hunter Mountain are the best known.

In New Jersey in the north of the state are Hidden Valley and Vernon Valley/Great Gorge, both near Vernon, and Craigmeur Ski Area near Ramsey township. Southwest of Mahwah near the New York border is Campgaw Mountain Ski Center. South of Lambertville close to the Delaware River is Belle Mountain.

Pennsylvania has 28 downhill ski areas with many of them in the northeast of the state in the Pocono Mountains. These include Camelback in Big Pocono State Park, Shawnee Mountain, Big Boulder Ski Area and Jack Frost Mountain Ski Area.

Further west along Route 6 near Coudersport is Denton Hill. Southeast of Pittsburgh in the Laurel Highlands, two popular ski areas with full amenities are Seven Springs Mountain Resort and Hidden Valley. In the southwest 20 miles east of Johnstown is Blue Knob Ski Resort.

Snowboarding

Snowboarding has swept the nation's ski culture and taken on a following of its own. Ski mountains are developing half-pipes and renting the necessary equipment in ski shops. Baggy pants, psychedelic jackets and funky hats have replaced more traditional ski garb. Snowboarders stand sideways, strapped to a board four or five feet long, to cruise down the mountains. The motion is comparable to surfing or skateboarding, rather than skiing; many resorts offer introductory lessons.

CROSS-COUNTRY SKIING

Cross-country skiing (also called ski touring or Nordic skiing) offers a chance to get some exercise, experience quiet, natural beauty at close quarters, escape the crowds at the ski resorts and save a few dollars by not buying a downhill lift ticket. The sport appeals to beginners in particular, because with a few lessons, you can be on your way.

NPS areas, USFS and US Army Corps of Engineers' lands, state parks and forests, the Rails-to-Trails Conservancy and private lands support hundreds of miles of cross-country trails, some operated under special-use permits by private industries. (For addresses see Parks & Forests in the

Facts about the Region chapter and Planning under Hiking & Backpacking earlier.) Rentals are available at outfitters like REI, Eastern Mountain Sports and other places near the trails.

Many ski resorts also provide groomed ski trails, but most cross-country skiers prefer to avoid the downhill crowds by visiting dedicated cross-country areas and backcountry trails. Most cross-country trails are described in kilometers rather than miles (see the conversion chart on the inside back cover).

The Cross-Country Ski Areas Association (☎ (603) 239-4341), 259 Bolton Rd, Winchester, NH 03460, is a national organization that publishes *The Best of Cross-Country Skiing*, a guide to the sport in North America.

Cross-country is popular around New York state, but the Finger Lakes region provides some of the best views while on skis. Near Ithaca, Buttermilk Falls State Park is popular, along with the nearby Finger Lakes National Forest area. Further west, Keuka Lake State Park is a fine and mostly flat ski area. Among the best places is Robert Moses State Park in the Thousand Islands region of the state.

The main spots for cross-country skiing in New Jersey are the parks and forests in the north of the state.

Some prime areas in Pennsylvania are the Allegheny National Forest in the northwest and the parks and forests in the Laurel Highlands in the southwest. In the Laurel Highlands, the Hidden Valley Nordic Center (☎ (814) 443-2600), 4 Craighead Dr, Hidden Valley, PA 15502, has rentals, instructors and child care. In the northeast the state parks in the Poconos have a variety of good trails as do the state forests in the northcentral region around Williamsport.

ROCK CLIMBING & MOUNTAINEERING

Rock climbing and mountaineering are demanding activities requiring top physical condition. They also require an understanding of the composition of various rock

types and their hazards as well as an understanding of other hazards of the high country and familiarity with a variety of equipment including ropes, chocks, bolts, carabiners and harnesses.

Rock climbers and mountaineers categorize routes on a scale of one to five. Class I is hiking, while Class II involves climbing on unstable materials like talus and may require use of the hands for keeping balance, especially with a heavy pack. Class III places the climber in dangerous situations, involving exposed terrain, with the likely consequences of a fall being a broken limb. Class IV involves steep rock, smaller holds and great exposure, with obligatory use of ropes and knowledge of knots and techniques like belaying and rappelling; the consequences of falling are death rather than injury. Class V divides into a dozen or more subcategories based on degree of difficulty and requires advanced techniques, including proficiency with rope.

The Access Fund, PO Box 67A25, Los Angeles, CA 90067, is a nonprofit organization working to keep climbing areas open to the public by purchasing or negotiating access to key sites.

Safety
Climbing is a potentially hazardous activity, though serious accidents are more spectacular than frequent; driving to the climbing site can be more dangerous than the climb itself. Nevertheless, climbers should be aware of hazards, which can contribute to falls and very serious injury or death. Weather is an important factor, as rain makes rock slippery and lightning can strike an exposed climber; hypothermia is an additional concern. In dry weather, lack of water can lead to dehydration.

Environmental Concerns
Many climbers follow guidelines similar to those established for hikers to preserve the resource on which their sport relies. These include concentrating impact in high-use areas by using established roads, trails and routes for access; dispersing use in pristine

areas and avoiding the creation of new trails; refraining from creating or enhancing handholds; and eschewing the placement of bolts wherever possible. Climbers should also take special caution to respect archaeological and cultural resources, such as rock art, and refrain from climbing in such areas.

Instruction
Travelers wishing to acquire climbing skills can do so at several schools and guide services. These include:

Mountain Skills Climbing School
    595 Peak Rd, New Paltz, NY 12484
    (☎ (914) 687-9643); it has another
    branch in Stone Ridge
Ascents of Adventure
    PO Box 6568, Albany, NY 12054
    (☎ (518) 459-4966)
Adirondack Alpine Adventures
    PO Box 179, Route 73, Keene, NY 12942
    (☎ (518) 576-9881)

Sites
The best climbing is in the Catskills, especially the Shawangunk Mountains, and in the Adirondack Mountains. Rock climbing near the town of New Paltz in the Shawangunk Mountains is becoming increasingly popular; parts of Minnewaska State Park (☎ (914) 255-0752) are now open to rock climbing. The park is surrounded by the Mohonk Preserve (☎ (914) 255-0919), which has been the prime rock climbing destination in the state.

In Pennsylvania some popular rock-climbing spots are Wissahickon Creek in Fairmount Park in northwest Philadelphia, Delaware Water Gap NRA, McConnell's Mill State Park north of Pittsburgh and Lehigh Gorge State Park in the Poconos.

Rock & Snow (☎ (914) 255-1311), 44 Main St, New Paltz, NY 12561 is an outfitter open daily year round, but hours vary by season.

WHITE WATER RAFTING & TUBING
The rivers of the region offer a number of opportunities for this most exhilarating of sports. Commercial outfitters provide

white-water experiences ranging from short, inexpensive morning or afternoon trips to overnight stays and three or four-day expeditions. Those outfitters on NPS, USFS, US Army Corps of Engineers, state park or state forest lands operate with permits from the appropriate agency. Individuals and groups with their own or rented equipment sometimes also need a permit.

White-water trips take place in either large rafts seating a dozen or more people, or smaller rafts seating half a dozen; the latter are more interesting and exciting because the ride over the rapids can be rougher and because everyone participates in rowing. Some trips may only be suitable for experienced rafters while some may have restrictions regarding age and/or weight.

Tubing is popular on smaller streams and rivers, but is often available when the spring runoff has quieted and the current isn't as rough. Often, one rents a 'tube' – or the inner tube of a tire – which may or may not be fitted with luxuries like handles or seats. Then, much like white-water rafting, tubers (people who tube and not the root vegetable) are 'put in' at the head of a river and they float downstream.

The American White-Water Affiliation (☎ (914) 688-5569), PO Box 85, Phoenicia, NY 12464, is a national organization that promotes white-water activity.

The Army Corps of Engineers manages many waterways; their contact information is at the front of this chapter.

Safety

While white-water trips aren't without danger and it's not unusual for participants to fall out of the raft in rough water, serious injuries are rare and the huge majority of trips are without incident. Outfitters usually give orientation and safety lectures before heading off. You don't have to be able to swim to participate, but you must wear a US Coast Guard-approved life jacket and should be in reasonably good

---

River Difficulty Rankings

River trips are classified on a scale of I to VI according to difficulty. On any river, classifications can vary over the course of the year, depending on the water level. Higher water levels, usually associated with spring runoff, can make a river trip either easier or more difficult by covering up hazards or increasing the velocity of the river, while lower water levels can expose hazards like rocks and whirlpools, making the river more exciting. Some rivers depend on water releases from upstream dams.

Class I – easy
Ranges from flatwater to occasional series of mild rapids.

Class II – medium
Frequent stretches of rapids with waves up to three feet high and easy chutes, ledges and falls. The best route is easy to identify and the entire river can be run in open canoes.

Class III – difficult
Features numerous rapids with high, irregular waves and difficult chutes and falls that often require scouting. They are for experienced paddlers who either use kayaks and rafts or have a spray cover for their canoe.

Class IV – very difficult
The river has long stretches of irregular waves, powerful back eddies and even constricted canyons. Scouting is mandatory and rescues can be difficult in many places. Suitable in rafts or white-water kayaks and paddlers equipped with helmets.

Class V – extremely difficult
The river has continuous violent rapids, powerful rollers and high unavoidable waves and haystacks. These rivers are only for white-water kayaks and paddlers who are proficient in the Eskimo roll.

Class VI – highest level of difficulty
Such a river is rarely run except by highly experienced kayakers under ideal conditions. ■

TOM SMALLMAN
Class II rafting on the Youghiogheny River, Ohiopyle State Park, Pennsylvania

physical condition. Keep your feet and arms inside the raft.

Trips have at least one river guide experienced in white-water rafting and trained in safety procedures and lifesaving techniques.

Sites
Between Hancock in New York and the Delaware Water Gap, the Delaware River, which connects all three states, is a popular National Wild & Scenic River. Other New York options include the Hudson River, where early spring rapids provide some of the most challenging opportunities; the Esopus River near Phoenicia; and the Black, Genesee, Moose and Sacandaga rivers.

In Pennsylvania's Laurel Highlands the Youghiogheny River has Class I to IV rapids. In the northeast in the Poconos white-water trips on the Lehigh River are best March through June and mid-September through mid-December; the Lackawaxen River, a tributary of the Delaware River, has Class I to III rapids in spring. Pine Creek, which flows through Pennsylvania's Grand Canyon in the northcentral mountains, has 20 miles of rapids.

CANOEING & KAYAKING
Many rafting rivers are just as good for canoeing or kayaking, and for those who prefer still water there are numerous lakes. Sea kayaking is also common along the coast and bays. Canoeing and kayaking offer travelers the chance to see things they

might otherwise miss – river gorges, lake edges, remote sections of wilderness and local wildlife.

If you don't have your own equipment it can often be rented from rafting outfitters or other small operations, which may double as campgrounds or summer resorts on the shore of a calm body of water. Wear woolen or polypropylene clothing or a wet suit; take spare paddles, a first-aid kit, a whistle and rescue line. State park-controlled waters usually require a permit to launch a boat.

Many maps and guides are available and you should study these to plan your route before setting off on any trip. As well as the American White-Water Affiliation (see above) organizations that can provide useful information are:

American Canoe Association
   7432 Alban Station Blvd, Suite B226,
   Springfield, VA 22150 (☎ (703) 451-0141)
US Canoe Association
   606 Ross St, Middletown, OH 45044
   (☎ (513) 422-3739)

The US Army Corps of Engineers, responsible for administering various lakes and rivers, produces brochures and navigational and nautical charts; for addresses see the Useful Organizations sidebar in this chapter.

Nautical charts can also be obtained from Distribution Branch (NCG33; ☎ (301) 436-6990), National Ocean Service, Riverdale, MD 20737.

Safety

Paddlers should be able to swim and all occupants should wear a life jacket. As in hiking try not to canoe/kayak alone and let someone know where you're heading and for how long. Keep a reasonable distance between your and other canoes.

If you do fall into the water stay upstream of the craft to avoid being hit by it and lay on your back with your feet facing downstream and up where you can see them. Hold on to your paddle as this will help make you more visible. Relax and breathe when you aren't going through waves. Turn over and swim when the water becomes calmer and don't try to stand in moving water in case your foot gets caught in a rock.

Sites

The following are in addition to the rivers mentioned under White-Water Rafting earlier.

The St Regis Canoe Area in New York's Adirondacks Forest Preserve is the best-known area in the state and is off limits to power boats. St Regis is a network of 58 interconnected lakes and ponds, connected primarily by the Raquette, St Regis and Saranac rivers. For more information, contact St Regis Canoe Outfitters (☎ (518) 891-1838). They can arrange canoe 'carries' for beginners and experts alike; they rent high quality, lightweight (40-pound) canoes and touring kayaks.

Also in the Adirondacks, the Ausable River carves its way through sandstone cliffs which rise several hundred feet high. The Genesee River in Letchworth State Park runs for 17 miles beneath a 600 foot gorge. The wetlands and wildlife around Oak Orchard on Lake Ontario attract canoeing enthusiasts.

In New Jersey canoeing/kayaking is a great way to explore Pinelands National Preserve, the Pine Barrens, Toms River and Barnegat Bay.

The 500 miles of the Susquehanna River and its tributaries begins at Otsego Lake in New York and flows south through central Pennsylvania into Chesapeake Bay in Maryland. In Philadelphia the Schuylkill River, a tributary of the Delaware River, flows through Fairmount Park. The Allegheny River (which heads north into New York) and its many branches offer opportunities to explore Allegheny National Forest. The Allegheny River also connects with the Ohio and Monongahela rivers in Pittsburgh.

FISHING

The Atlantic coastline, the thousands of lakes and ponds and the thousands of miles of rivers and streams make this a prime fishing region. Freshwater fish include varieties of trout, salmon, bass and pike, as well as muskellunge ('muskie'), sauger, shad and walleyed pike; in the Atlantic you'll find bluefish, flounder, giant tuna and even shark.

Anglers are required to have the appropriate state license and to abide by whatever seasonal or territorial regulations are in place. For instance, the same stream may have several sections with quite different restrictions on types of hooks, bait, seasons and what size and type of fish can be kept. It can be complicated so ask for current regulations at bait or sporting-goods stores or fish and wildlife offices, where you can often also buy a license.

Fishing licenses are issued to in-state and out-of-state anglers; the latter are more expensive. Both types of license can be bought for a year or shorter intervals. A license for fishing in the Delaware River is valid from any of the three states.

For information on fishing licenses, regulations and publications for each state contact:

New York
    Department of Environmental Conservation, 50 Wolf Rd, Albany, NY 12233-4255
    (☎ (518) 457-2500)
New Jersey
    Department of Environmental Protection, Division of Fish, Game & Wildlife, CN-400, Trenton, NJ 08625-0400
    (☎ (609) 292-2965)
Pennsylvania
    Fish & Boat Commission, PO Box 67000, Harrisburg, PA 17106 (☎ (717) 657-4518)

The streams of the Catskill Mountains are reputed to have some of the best trout fishing in the country, and the lakes of the Adirondacks, including the 469 sq miles of Lake Champlain, are home to bass, pike and salmon. Some of the best bass and muskellunge fishing is reputed to be found along the St Lawrence River in the northwest of New York. Chautauqua Lake in the far southwest corner of the state is noted for its giant muskellunge and Oneida Lake northeast of Syracuse for its walleyed pike.

In New Jersey fishing for sturgeon and salmon is popular in the Atlantic waters around Long Beach and Island Beach.

Yellow Breeches is a trout stream in Pennsylvania that attracts anglers from interstate and abroad. Lake Erie, once too polluted, is now visited by spawning salmon.

OTHER WATERSPORTS
The coastal waters and numerous lakes are havens for sailing, scuba diving, swimming and windsurfing; rentals and training can be found in many centers. In New York City, pool-based, scuba-diving orientation courses are offered at the Aqua Lung School of New York (☎ (212) 582-2800), 1089 Second Ave, NY, NY 10021, and at Pan Aqua (☎ (212) 496-2267), 101 W 75th St, NY, NY 10024. The New Jersey Department of Community Affairs (☎ (609) 984-6654), CN 814, Trenton, NJ 08625, provides the booklet *Scuba and Skin Diving in New Jersey* for anyone who sends in a $2 check or money order.

Popular sites for watersports are the Great Lakes of Erie and Ontario; the Finger Lakes region south of Rochester and Syracuse; Oneida Lake northeast of Syracuse; the lakes of the Adirondacks; the Atlantic waters around Long Beach, Island Beach, Point Pleasant and Cape May in New Jersey; and Lake Arthur in Moraine State Park north of Pittsburgh.

BIRD & WILDLIFE WATCHING
Despite the heavy urbanization of the region, the sanctuaries, preserves, wildlife management areas and vast number of state and federal public lands make bird and wildlife watching a rewarding pastime. Many species are protected by law. Several nationally based organizations are worth contacting for information. These are:

National Audubon Society
    700 Broadway, New York, NY 10003
    (☎ (212) 979-3000)
National Wildlife Federation
    1400 16th St NW,
    Washington, DC 20036-2266
    (☎ (202) 797-6800)
US Fish & Wildlife Service
    Region 5, 300 Westgate Center Dr,
    Hadley, MA 01035-9589
    (☎ (413) 253-8200)

The National Audubon Society has a regional office (☎ (717) 763-4985) at 1104 Fernwood Ave, No 300, Camp Hill, PA 17011, as well as local clubs and nature centers that often sponsor educational programs, hikes and trips to birdwatching areas. The society is interested in ecology, conservation and wildlife and publishes the magazine *Audubon*. The National Wildlife Federation publishes the magazine *National Wildlife*.

Pennsylvania Wildlife: A Viewer's Guide features 93 locations in the state notable for their wildlife and is available from the Pennsylvania Game Commission (☎ (717) 783-7507), Department MS, 2001 Elmerton Ave, Harrisburg, PA 17110-9797.

Both Orient Beach and Caleb Smith state parks on Long Island have many species of birds and mammals. The Gateway NRA contains the Jamaica Bay Wildlife Refuge plus Sandy Hook in New Jersey. Hollyhock Hollow Sanctuary in Selkirk has over 80 species of birds and other wildlife.

The Beaver Lake Nature Center in Baldwinsville in the Finger Lakes region, is an important stopover for migrating Canada geese. On the southern shore of Lake Ontario migrating and nesting waterfowl can be seen in the wetlands of the Oak Orchard and Tanawanda wildlife management areas and Iroquois National Wildlife Refuge.

The headlands and capes of New York and New Jersey also offer glimpses of sea turtles, dolphins and migrating gray whales. Favorite watching spots include Montauk on Long Island in New York and from Barnegat Inlet, Beach Haven, Wildwood and Cape May in New Jersey. You can also take boats out from Atlantic City.

In New Jersey important bird- and wildlife-watching sites include the Scherman-Hoffman Wildlife Sanctuary near Bernardsville; the Delaware & Raritan Canal State Park where the canal path has been designated a national recreation trail and you can see about 100 species of birds; Rancocal Nature Center at Mt Holly; the Brigantine National Wildlife Refuge at the southern tip of Long Beach; the Edwin B Forsythe National Wildlife Refuge north of Atlantic City; and Stone Harbor Bird Sanctuary.

In Pennsylvania some of the best spots for birdwatching are Hawk Mountain Sanctuary north of Reading, Presque Isle State Park on Lake Erie and Moraine State Park north of Pittsburgh. In the northwest, Pymatuning Wildlife Management Area houses the state's only nesting bald eagles. Allegheny National Forest is full of wildlife, including black bears, and nearby is a herd of wild elk. River otters can be seen in the Poconos.

HORSEBACK RIDING

There are scores of horseback riding ranches, stables, associations and clubs offering services from guided trips of a few hours to multi-day treks along mountain or forest trails. Many of them also offer lessons. Contact local tourist offices for information on these. Hundreds of miles of trails traverse the region on public lands; see Planning under Hiking & Backpacking earlier for addresses to contact for maps and details on these trails.

In New York City, Claremont Riding Academy (☎ (212) 724-5100), 175 W 89th St, NY 10024, arranges indoor lessons and rides in Central Park, as well as riding lessons and events in northern New Jersey. In upstate New York popular bridle trails

are found in the Catskill Mountains, Connetquot State Park Preserve, Allegany State Park, Rockefeller State Park Preserve and Highland Forest Park (in the Finger Lakes region).

In New Jersey, Bass River State Park has 100 miles of trails; other popular areas are Lockwood Gorge, Deer Path Park, Swartswood State Park, High Point State Park, Stokes State Forest, Washington Crossing State Park, Wharton State Forest and Island Beach State Park.

In Pennsylvania the 130 mile Horse-Shoe Trail leads from Valley Forge National Historic Park to join the Appalachian trail north-east of Harrisburg. There are many more trails in Pennsylvania's state parks and forests.

HANG GLIDING & PARAGLIDING

Hang-gliding and paragliding are great ways to experience the thrills of flight, and a number of schools cater for both novices and experienced fliers. The US Hang Gliding Association (USHGA; ☎ (719) 632-8300), PO Box 1330, Colorado Springs, CO 80901-1330, produces a directory of instructors and clubs nationwide. USHGA also publishes the monthly magazines *Hang Gliding* and *Paragliding* with news on current developments and events.

Some favorite spots are Ellenville in the Catskills, Hyner View in Pennsylvania's Hyner Run State Park and the Delaware Water Gap.

CAVING

Experienced spelunkers can explore caves in several areas and a number of caves are open to the casual visitor for guided interpretive tours.

Because of the delicate and tightly circumscribed subterranean environments, cavers must make special efforts to respect the ecosystem: leave no trace of human presence, avoid contact with sensitive formations and refrain from disturbing bats and other animals. Cavers should also travel in groups, with a minimum of three persons. Hazards associated with caving include poisonous gases and dangerous spores.

For general information enthusiasts can get in touch with the National Speleological Society (☎ (205) 852-1300), Cave Ave, Huntsville, AL 35810. Details about caving in Pennsylvania are available from the Pennsylvania Caves Association, RR 1, Box 280, Huntingdon, PA 16652.

Going Underground (Camino Books, 1991) by Sharon Hernes Silverman, is a guide to caves in New York and Pennsylvania, as well as Maryland, Virginia and West Virginia.

In New York, popular caving spots are Howe Caverns, with its underground lake, and Secret Caverns, both near Binghampton. Laurel Caverns in the Laurel Highlands is Pennsylvania's largest cave; also in the Laurel Highlands are Indian Caverns and Lincoln Caverns. Indian Echo Caverns is near Hershey and Crystal Cave is near Kutztown in Berks County.

GOLF

There are hundreds of public and private golf courses, often in beautiful settings, that range from the modest to the deluxe and expensive. The state tourist boards produce lists of many of them and have information on packaged golfing vacations that include food and accommodations.

It's advisable to book in advance, especially for public courses in the suburbs, which tend to be massively crowded on weekends and holidays. Most private clubs give members priority in booking tee-off times; it's usually easier to book a tee-off time on a public course, but on weekends, public holidays and days when the weather is good, it's often busy on all courses. You should also check whether there's a dress code and whether the course has golf clubs for rent if you don't have your own.

Getting There & Away

New York, New Jersey and Pennsylvania sit at the crossroads between the northeastern states of New England and the rest of the continenal USA. New York City is one of the country's major entry and exit points for international traffic.

Whether you're coming from another part of the country or from abroad, the easiest way to travel is by airplane. Within the USA you can also travel by bus, train or car, but that could take up much of your vacation time! This chapter focuses on getting to the main transportation hubs in the region from the major US ports of entry and other parts of the world.

Whichever way you're traveling, make sure you take out travel insurance (see Visas & Documents in the Facts for the Visitor chapter).

AIR
Airports & Airlines

Most air travelers to the region arrive at New York City's John F Kennedy (JFK) international airport (☎ (718) 656-4520) in Queens,

La Guardia airport (☎ (718) 533-3400) also in Queens, or at Newark international airport (☎ (201) 961-6000) in New Jersey across the Hudson River from New York City, which is the local hub for Continental Airlines. In Pennsylvania the major airports are in Philadelphia (☎ (215) 492-3181) and Pittsburgh (☎ (412) 472-3525/5525), which is also the home of USAir. For more airport information, see Getting There & Away in the destination chapters.

Smoking is prohibited on all domestic flights within the USA and on many international flights. Many airports in the USA also restrict smoking.

International airlines that fly to the region include the following (airlines serving domestic routes are asterisked).

Aer Lingus	(800) 223-6537
Aerolíneas Argentinas	(800) 333-0276
Air Canada	(800) 776-3000
Air France	(800) 237-2747
Air New Zealand	(800) 262-1234
Alaska Airlines*	(800) 426-0333
America West Airlines*	(800) 235-9292
American Airlines*	(800) 433-7300
British Airways	(800) 247-9297
Canadian Airlines	(800) 426-7000
China Airlines	(800) 227-5118
Continental Airlines*	(800) 525-0280
Delta Air Lines*	(800) 221-1212
Hawaiian Airlines*	(800) 367-5320
Japan Airlines	(800) 525-3663
KLM	(800) 374-7747
LANChile Airlines	(800) 488-0070
Lufthansa	(800) 645-3880
Midwest Express Airlines*	(800) 452-2022
Northwest Airlines	(800) 447-4747
Northwest (domestic)*	(800) 225-2525
Qantas Airways	(800) 227-4500
Scandinavian Airlines	(800) 221-2350
Singapore Airlines	(800) 742-3333
Southwest Airlines*	(800) 531-5601
Swissair	(800) 221-4750
TWA	(800) 892-4141
TWA (domestic)*	(800) 221-2000
United Airlines*	(800) 241-6522
USAir*	(800) 428-4322
Virgin Atlantic Airways	(800) 862-8621

Warning

The information in this chapter is particularly vulnerable to change: prices for international travel are volatile, routes are introduced and canceled, schedules change, special deals come and go, and rules and visa requirements are amended. Airlines and governments seem to take a perverse pleasure in making price structures and regulations as complicated as possible. Check directly with the airline or a travel agent to make sure you understand how a fare (and any ticket you may buy) works.

Get opinions, quotes and advice from as many airlines and travel agents as possible before you part with your hard-earned money. The details given in this chapter should be regarded as pointers and are no substitute for your own careful, up-to-date research. ∎

Arriving in the USA
Even if you're continuing immediately to another city, the first airport that you land at is where you must carry out immigration and customs formalities. If your luggage is checked from, say, London to Buffalo, you'll still have to take it through customs if you first land in New York City. Your connecting flight is classified as a domestic leg of the journey.

On the international leg, passengers aboard the airplane are given standard immigration and customs forms to fill out. The cabin crew will help you if you have any questions. After the plane lands, you first go through immigration. There are two lines: one for US citizens and residents, the other for nonresidents. Immigration formalities are usually straightforward if you have the necessary documents (passport and visa). Occasionally, you may be asked to show your ticket out of the US, but this doesn't happen often.

You then collect your baggage and pass through customs. If you don't have anything to declare, you'll probably clear customs quickly and without a luggage search, but you can't rely on it. (See also Customs in the Facts for the Visitor chapter.) Once you are through customs, you're officially in the country. If your flight is continuing to another city or you have a connecting flight, it's your responsibility to get your bags to the right place. Normally, there are airline counters or an airline official outside the customs area to help you.

Leaving the USA
You should check in for international flights two hours early. During check-in procedures, you'll be asked questions about whether you packed your own bags, whether anyone else has had access to them since you packed them and whether you've received any parcels to carry. These questions are for security reasons, and security measures have become even tighter following the crash of TWA flight 800 off the Long Island coast in 1996.

Baggage
On most domestic and international flights you're limited to two checked bags, or three if you don't have carry-on luggage. There could be a charge if you bring more or if the size of the bags exceeds the airline's limits. It's best to check with the individual airline if you're worried about this. On some international flights the luggage allowance is based on weight, not numbers; again, check with the airline.

If your luggage is delayed upon arrival (which is rare), some airlines give a cash advance to purchase necessities. If sporting equipment is misplaced, the airline may pay for rentals. Should the luggage be lost, it's important to submit a claim. The airline doesn't have to pay the full amount of the claim, but can estimate the value of your lost items. It may take them anywhere from six weeks to three months to process the claim and pay you.

Illegal Items Items that are illegal to take on a plane, either checked in with your baggage or as hand luggage, include aerosols of polishes, waxes etc; tear gas and pepper spray; camp stoves with fuel; and divers' tanks that are full. Matches shouldn't be checked in with your baggage.

Travelers with Special Needs
If you have a special need – a broken leg, dietary restrictions, dependence on a wheelchair, responsibility for a baby, fear of flying – let the airline know as soon as possible so that it can make arrangements accordingly. Remind them when you reconfirm your booking (at least 72 hours before departure) and again when you check in at the airport. It may also be worth phoning several airlines before you make your booking to find out how they handle your particular needs.

Airports and airlines can be surprisingly helpful, but they do need advance warning. Most international airports provide escorts from the check-in desk to the airplane where needed, and there should be ramps, accessible toilets and reachable phones.

Edible Airline Food
Many travelers complain about the 'snacks' and meals served on US domestic airlines. But you can increase your chances of getting something resembling real food if you request a 'low fat' meal when booking your flight.

Instead of being handed a prepackaged meal, you'll probably receive a sandwich prepared specifically before departure with real meat (usually turkey) unsoggy bread and a salad that doesn't resemble something flash frozen on Mars. Of course, you'll most likely forfeit any chance of getting your hands on that post-meal candy bar . . . ■

Aircraft toilets, on the other hand, are likely to present a problem; travelers should discuss this with the airline at an early stage and, if necessary, with their doctor.

Guide dogs for the blind often have to travel in a specially pressurized baggage compartment with other animals, away from their owner, though smaller guide dogs may be admitted to the cabin. Guide dogs are not subject to quarantine as long as they have proof of being vaccinated against rabies.

Deaf travelers can ask for airport and in-flight announcements to be written down for them.

Children under two travel for 10% of the standard fare (or free, on some airlines), as long as they don't occupy a seat. (They don't get a baggage allowance either.) 'Skycots' should be provided by the airline if requested in advance; these take a child weighing up to about 22 lbs. Children between two and 12 usually occupy a seat for half to two-thirds of the full fare, and do get a baggage allowance. Strollers can often be taken on as hand luggage.

Buying Tickets
The plane ticket will probably be the single most expensive item in your budget and buying it can be intimidating. Rather than just walking into the nearest travel agent or airline office, it pays to do some research of the current market. Start looking early – some of the cheapest tickets and best deals must be bought months in advance, some popular flights sell out early and special offers may be advertised.

Look at the travel sections of magazines like *Time Out* and *TNT* in the UK, or the Saturday editions of newspapers like the *New York Times*, *Los Angeles Times* in the US, or *Sydney Morning Herald* and *The Age* in Australia. Ads in these publications offer cheap fares, but don't be surprised if they're sold out when you contact the agents: they're usually low-season fares on obscure airlines with conditions attached. Talk to other recent travelers if possible – they may be able to stop you from making some of the same old mistakes.

Note High season in the USA is mid-June to mid-September (summer) and one week before and after Christmas. The best rates for travel to and in the USA are found November through March.

Call travel agents for bargains (airlines can supply information on routes and timetables; however, except at times of fare wars, they don't supply the cheapest tickets). Airlines often have competitive low-season, student and senior citizens' fares. Find out the fare, route, duration of the journey and any restrictions on the ticket. Fare levels change constantly and some fares which include accommodations may be as cheap as roundtrip fares.

Outside the US cheap tickets are available in two distinct categories: official and unofficial. Official ones have a variety of names, including budget, advance-purchase, Apex and super-Apex. Unofficial tickets are simply discounted tickets that the airlines release through selected travel agents (not through airline offices).

Wherever you buy your tickets, the cheapest are often nonrefundable and require an extra fee for changing your flight, if you're allowed to change your flight at all. Many insurance policies cover this loss if you have to change your flight for emergency reasons. Roundtrip (return) tickets often work out much cheaper than two one-way fares.

The fares quoted in this book should be used as a guide only and don't necessarily constitute a recommendation for the carrier.

If you're traveling from the UK, you'll probably find that the cheapest flights are advertised by obscure bucket shops. Many are honest and solvent, but there are a few rogues who'll take your money and disappear, to reopen elsewhere a month or two later under a new name. If you feel suspicious, don't give them all the money at once – leave a deposit of 20% or so and pay the balance on receiving the ticket. If they insist on cash in advance, go elsewhere. Once you have the ticket, phone the airline to confirm that you are booked on the flight.

You may decide to pay more than the rock-bottom fare by opting for the safety of a better-known travel agent. Established firms like Council Travel or STA Travel, which have offices internationally, or Travel CUTS in Canada, offer competitive prices to most destinations.

Once you have your ticket, write down its number, together with the flight number and other details, and keep the information somewhere separate. If the ticket is lost or stolen, this will help you get a replacement.

Remember to buy travel insurance as early as possible.

Visit USA Passes

Most domestic carriers offer Visit USA passes to non-US citizens. The passes are actually a book of coupons – each coupon equals a flight. Following are examples of the kinds of deals available, but it's a good idea to ask your travel agent about any others on offer.

You can buy Continental Airlines' Visit USA pass in conjunction with an international airline ticket anywhere outside the USA except Canada and Mexico. You must have your trip planned in advance and complete your travels within 60 days of your first flight within the USA or 81 days after arrival in the USA, whichever comes first.

If you decide to change destinations once you're in the USA, you'll be penalized at least $50. High-season prices are $379 for three coupons (minimum purchase) and $769 for eight (maximum purchase). The pass includes two free transits.

Northwest offers the same deal, but gives you the option of flying standby.

American Airlines uses the same coupon structure and also sells the passes outside the USA, excluding Canada and Mexico. You must reserve flights one day in advance, and if a coupon only takes you halfway to your destination, you'll have to buy the remaining ticket at full price.

Delta has two different systems for travelers coming from abroad. Visit USA gives travelers a discount, but you need to have your itinerary mapped out to take advantage of this. The other option is Discover America, in which a traveler buys up to 10 coupons good for standby travel anywhere in the continental USA, Canada and Mexico. One flight equals one coupon. Only two transcontinental flights are allowed – Delta prefers that your travels follow some sort of circular pattern. Four coupons cost $549, 10 cost $1249. Children's fares are $40 less. Coupons can only be purchased outside North America and Mexico in conjunction with an international flight.

When flying standby, call the airline a day or two before the flight and make a 'standby reservation.' This way you get priority over others who appear on the day and hope to get on the flight.

Getting Bumped

Airlines try to guarantee full planes by overbooking and relying on some passengers not to show up ('no shows'). This often means some passengers get 'bumped' off a flight, then have to wait for the next flight. This can be very frustrating, but if you have a day's leeway, you can take advantage of the system.

When you check in at the airline counter ask if they'll need volunteers to be bumped and what the compensation will be. Depending on the desirability of the flight, this can range from a $200 voucher toward your next flight to a fully paid roundtrip ticket. Try to confirm a later flight so you don't get stuck in the airport on standby. If you have to spend the night, airlines frequently foot the hotel bill for their 'bumpees.' It can be a great deal, and many people plan their trips with a day to spare in order to try for a free ticket that'll cover their next trip.

However, you should be aware that under this same system, being just a little late for boarding could get you bumped with none of the benefits.

Round-the-World Tickets

Round-the-World (RTW) tickets are popular and are often real bargains; they can work out to be no more expensive or even cheaper than an ordinary return ticket. Prices start at about UK£900, A$1800 or US$1300.

Official RTW tickets are usually put together by a combination of two airlines, and permit you to fly anywhere you want on their route systems as long as you do not backtrack. Other restrictions are that you must usually book the first sector in advance and cancelation penalties apply. There may be restrictions on the number of stops permitted and tickets are usually valid from 90 days up to a year. An alternative type of RTW ticket is one put together by a travel agent using a combination of discounted tickets.

Although most airlines restrict the number of sectors that can be flown within the USA and Canada to four, and some airlines black out a few heavily traveled routes (like Honolulu to Tokyo), stopovers are otherwise generally unlimited. In most cases a 14 day advance purchase is required. After the ticket is purchased, dates can be changed without penalty and tickets can be rewritten to add or delete stops for $50 each.

The majority of RTW tickets restrict you to just two airlines, British Airways and Qantas offer a RTW ticket called the Global Explorer that allows you to combine routes on both airlines to a total of 28,000 miles for US$2999 or A$3199 in the high season.

Qantas also flies in conjunction with American, Delta, Northwest, Canadian, Air France and KLM. Qantas RTW tickets, with any of the aforementioned partner airlines, cost US$3247 or A$3199.

Canadian Airlines offers numerous RTW combinations, such as with KLM that could include Cairo, Bombay, Delhi and Amsterdam for C$3648 and a third with South African Airways that could include Australia and Africa for C$3969.

Many other airlines also offer RTW tickets. TWA's lowest priced RTW, linking up with Korean Air, costs US$2087 and allows stops in Honolulu, Seoul, Tel Aviv, Amsterdam and Paris or London. (This one is not sold in Australia.)

Continental no longer offers RTW fares.

Circle-Pacific Tickets

Circle-Pacific tickets use a combination of airlines to circle the Pacific – combining Australia, New Zealand, North America and Asia. Rather than simply flying from point A to point B, these tickets allow you to swing through much of the Pacific Rim and eastern Asia taking in a variety of destinations – as long as you keep traveling in the same circular direction. As with RTW tickets there are advance-purchase restrictions and limits on how many stopovers you can take. These fares are likely to be around 15% cheaper than RTW tickets.

Circle-Pacific routes essentially have the same fares: A$3519 when purchased in Australia, US$2449 in the USA and C$2899 in Canada. Circle-Pacific fares include four stopovers with the option of adding additional stops at US$50 each. There's a 14 day advance-purchase requirement, a 25% cancelation penalty and a maximum stay of six months. There are also higher business-class and 1st class fares. Departure and airport-use taxes, which vary with the itinerary, are additional.

Qantas offers Circle Pacific routes in partnership with Delta, Japan Air Lines, Northwest or Continental. In the off-season, the Australian winter (June through

August), Qantas occasionally offers hefty discounts on tickets that use Qantas as the primary carrier.

United Airlines flies in conjunction with Cathay Pacific, Qantas, Ansett, Malaysia Airlines or British Airways. Canadian Airlines has Circle-Pacific fares from Vancouver that include, in one combination or another, virtually all Pacific Rim destinations. Canadian's partners include Qantas, Air New Zealand, Singapore, Garuda, Cathay Pacific or Malaysia airlines.

Within the USA

The *New York Times*, *Los Angeles Times*, *Chicago Tribune*, *San Francisco Examiner* and other major newspapers all produce weekly travel sections with numerous travel agents' ads. Council Travel (☎ (800) 226-8624) and STA Travel (☎ (800) 777-0112) have offices in major cities nationwide.

The magazine *Travel Unlimited*, PO Box 1058, Allston, MA 02134, publishes details of the cheapest air fares and courier possibilities.

Domestic airfares vary tremendously depending on the season you travel, the day of the week you fly, the length of your stay, how far in advance you pay and the flexibility of the ticket (in allowing for flight changes and refunds). There's also much competition and at any given time any one of the airlines could have the cheapest fare.

Domestic Airlines Major domestic airlines are asterisked in the toll-free phone list under Airports & Airlines earlier in this chapter. See also Getting There & Away in the Philadelphia and New York City chapters for airlines with offices in those cities.

Canada

Travel CUTS has offices in all major cities. The Toronto *Globe & Mail* and *Vancouver Sun* carry travel agents' ads; the magazine *Great Expeditions*, PO Box 8000-411, Abbotsford BC V2S 6H1, is also useful. Most connections between Canada and the region are through New York City. Roundtrip fares to/from Toronto with USAir and Delta Air Lines start from

around C$320 (US$237), to/from Montreal C$355 (US$263).

UK & Ireland

Check the ads in magazines like *Time Out* and *City Limits*, plus the Sunday papers and *Exchange & Mart*. Also check the free magazines widely available in London – start by looking outside the main railway stations.

Most British travel agents are registered with the Association of British Travel Agents (ABTA). If you've paid for your flight at an ABTA-registered agent who then goes out of business, ABTA will guarantee a refund or an alternative. Unregistered bucket shops are riskier but sometimes cheaper.

London is arguably the world's headquarters for bucket shops, which are well advertised and can usually beat published airline fares. Two good, reliable agents for cheap tickets in the UK are Trailfinders (☎ (171) 937-5400), 194 Kensington High St, London W8 7RG, and STA Travel (☎ (171) 937-9971), 86 Old Brompton Rd, London SW7 3LQ. Trailfinders produces a lavishly illustrated brochure including airfare details.

Virgin Atlantic has a standard, roundtrip, weekday, high-season fare from London to New York City for £663 (US$995); however cheaper advance-purchase ones are available. Aer Lingus has direct flights from Shannon and Dublin to New York City, but because competition on flights from London is fiercer, it's generally cheaper to fly to London first. Virgin Atlantic via London is often the cheapest option.

The Globetrotters Club, BCM Roving, London WC1N 3XX, publishes a newsletter called *Globe* that covers obscure destinations and can help you find travelling companions.

Continental Europe

Though London is the travel-discount capital of Europe, several other cities offer a range of good deals, especially Amsterdam and Athens. Many travel agents in

Europe have ties with STA Travel, where cheap tickets can be bought and STA Travel tickets can be altered free of charge (first change only).

In the Netherlands, NBBS Reizen is a popular nationwide travel agency; it has offices in Amsterdam at Roken 38 (☎ 624 09 89) and Leidestraat 53 (☎ 638 17 36). In Paris, Council Travel (☎ (1) 44 55 55 65) has its main office at 22 rue des Pyramides (1er). In Athens try International Student & Youth Travel Service (☎ (1) 323-3767), Nikis 11. The newsletter *Farang*, La Rue 8 á 4261 Braives, Belgium, deals with exotic destinations, as does the magazine *Aventure du Bout du Monde*, 116 rue de Javel, 75015 Paris, France.

On Virgin Atlantic flights from Paris to New York, a standard, roundtrip, weekday, high-season fare costs FF8040 (US$1545), but there's no doubt that cheaper advance-purchase fares are available.

Australia & New Zealand

In Australia and New Zealand, STA Travel and Flight Centres International are major dealers in cheap airfares; check the travel agents' ads in the yellow pages and call around. Qantas flies to Los Angeles from Sydney, Melbourne (via Sydney or Auckland) and Cairns with onward connections to Pittsburgh, Philadelphia and New York City on USAir. United Airlines flies to San Francisco and Los Angeles from Sydney.

The cheapest tickets have a 21 day advance-purchase requirement, a minimum stay of seven days and a maximum stay of 60 days.

Qantas flies from Melbourne or Sydney to New York for A$2582 (US$2013) in the high season. Flying with Air New Zealand is slightly cheaper, and both Qantas and Air New Zealand offer tickets with longer stays or stopovers, but you pay more. Full-time students can save A$80 (US$62) to A$140 (US$109) on roundtrip fares to the USA.

Roundtrip flights from Auckland to Los Angeles on Qantas cost NZ$1720 (US$1170) in the low season.

Asia

Hong Kong is the discount plane ticket capital of the region, but its bucket shops can be unreliable. Ask the advice of other travelers before buying a ticket. STA Travel has branches in Hong Kong, Tokyo, Singapore, Bangkok and Kuala Lumpur. Many, if not most flights to the USA are flown via Honolulu, HI.

Japan United Airlines has three flights a day to Honolulu from Tokyo with connections to West Coast cities like Los Angeles, San Francisco and Seattle. Northwest Airlines and Japan Air Lines also have daily flights to the West Coast from Tokyo; Japan Air Lines also flies to Honolulu from Osaka, Nagoya, Fukuoka and Sapporo.

Southeast Asia Numerous airlines fly to the USA from Southeast Asia; bucket shops in places like Bangkok and Singapore should be able to come up with the best deals. Tickets to the US West Coast often allow a free stopover in Honolulu.

Northwest Airlines flies to Honolulu from Hong Kong, Bangkok, Manila, Seoul and Singapore, with connections to the West Coast. Korean Air and Philippine Airlines also have flights from a number of Southeast Asian cities to Honolulu, with onward connections.

Central & South America

Most flights from Central and South America go via Miami, Houston or Los Angeles and some fly direct to New York City. Most countries' international flag carriers, like Aerolíneas Argentinas and LAN-Chile Airlines, as well as US airlines like United and American, serve these destinations. Continental has flights from about 20 cities in Mexico and Central America, including San Jose, Guatemala City, Cancún and Mérida.

LAND

Although major rail lines and interstate highways connect New York, New Jersey and Pennsylvania with the rest of the US, public transportation to remoter areas is limited.

Bus

Greyhound (☎ (800) 231-2222), the best-known nationwide bus company, runs cross-country buses from Los Angeles, San Francisco and Seattle on the West Coast and from southern cities like Atlanta and Miami to Philadelphia and New York City.

Because buses are so few, schedules are often inconvenient, fares are relatively high and bargain airfares can undercut buses on some long-distance routes. In some cases, on shorter routes, it can be cheaper to rent a car than ride the bus. However, long-distance bus trips are often available at bargain prices by purchasing or reserving tickets at least three days in advance.

Peter Pan Trailways (☎ (800) 343-9999) and Capitol Trailways (☎ (800) 444-2877) are two other major interstate bus lines serving the region.

These companies provide services to major cities and to minor towns that are on routes between major cities. They don't serve places off the main routes, so you won't find buses to most NPS areas for example or important tourist towns like Gettysburg.

See also Green Tortoise and East Coast Explorer under Organized Tours, below.

The one-way fare from New York City to Washington, DC, is only $26, which definitely beats air and train prices; the trip should take about 4½ hours though this depends on the volume of traffic. The fare from Philadelphia to San Francisco is $139 (27½ hours).

For more details on bus lines and fares, see Buses in the Getting Around chapter.

Canada If you're traveling from Canada, Greyhound connects most major Canadian centers with the main continental US cities, but often with a bus transfer at the border or the nearest town to it. Greyhound does, however, run directly from Toronto (via Niagara Falls and Buffalo) and Montreal to New York City.

Train

Amtrak (☎ (800) 872-7245), 60 Massachusetts Ave NE, Washington, DC 20002, operates the national passenger train system. Its routes and daily services have been scaled back over recent decades; yet this region features the most heavily traveled routes and service.

Long-distance travelers, say from the West Coast to the northeast, must make connections in Chicago. Nevertheless, train travel can be an experience in itself, offering meals on wheels, being rocked to sleep and splendid vistas from special carriages with large viewing windows.

Service In summer, extra trains are run to/from popular tourist destinations such as Rhode Island beaches or Cape Cod in Massachusetts. But throughout the year most service remains constant. See also the Getting There & Away section of the New York City chapter for information on Metro North trains which service many Connecticut towns.

The *Metroliner* (☎ (800) 523-8720) is a daily, fast-shuttle service between New York City and Washington, DC, via Newark, Trenton, Philadelphia, Wilmington and Baltimore. Seats on this service must be reserved. A cheaper, less-frequent, alternative express service – called Washington Express southbound, New York Express northbound – also runs between the two cities, but seats don't need to be reserved.

The *New England Express* (northbound) and *Tidewater Express* (southbound) trains operate daily between Boston, MA, and Richmond, VA, via Washington, DC, New York City, Newark and Philadelphia. These cities are connected with Toronto on the *Empire Service* and with Montreal on the *Adirondack*.

Finally, the *Vermonter* between Washington, DC, and Montreal, running via Connecticut and Vermont, stops daily at Newark, New York City and Philadelphia.

From Washington, DC, it's possible to connect with trains south to Miami and New Orleans.

In some areas, Amtrak operates a coordinated train/bus connecting service known as Amtrak Thruway. You must have an onward ticket before you can board the bus.

Tickets Tickets may be bought aboard the train without penalty if the station isn't open 30 minutes prior to boarding; otherwise there's a $7 penalty. Rail travel is generally cheaper by buying special fares in advance. Roundtrips are the best bargain, but even some of these may be as expensive as airfares.

Amtrak arranges a variety of tours and discounts. The best value is their All Aboard America fare which divides the country into eastern, central and western regions. If you want to travel in just one region the fare is $178, between two regions it's $228 and between three it's $278; these enable you to travel anywhere you want. Between mid-June and late August fares go up to $198, $278 and $338 respectively. There are limitations, however. Travel must be completed in 45 days, and you're only allowed up to three stopovers. Additional stopovers can be arranged at extra cost. Your entire trip must be reserved in advance, and the seats are limited so book as far ahead as possible. These tickets are for reclining seats; sleeping cars cost extra.

For further travel assistance, call Amtrak or ask your travel agent. Note that most small train stations don't sell tickets; you have to book them with Amtrak over the phone. Some small stations have no porters or other facilities, and trains may stop there only if you've bought a ticket in advance.

Car & Motorcycle

For information on buying or renting a car, or using a drive-away (driving a car for someone else), see the Getting Around chapter.

If you plan on driving from outside the region, I-95 is the major north-south route along the East Coast and stretches from the Canadian (Maine-New Brunswick) border to Miami, FL. The other main north-south route, I-81, runs from the New York-Ontario border through Pennsylvania to Maryland, Virginia and Tennessee. I-79 also heads north-south, off I-90 near Erie in

Pennsylvania to West Virginia. I-87 leads north from New York City to the Quebec border.

I-90 extends east-west from Boston in Massachusetts across New York State along the southern shore of Lake Erie through Pennsylvania to Ohio and onto Seattle in Washington State on the Pacific Northwest coast. I-80 runs from New York City through central Pennsylvania to San Francisco on the West Coast. Finally, I-70/76 stretches from Philadelphia through southern Pennsylvania to Ohio and meets I-15 in Utah.

If you're coming from Canada, automobile drivers and motorcyclists need the vehicle's registration papers and liability insurance. (See also Driver's License & Permits under Visas & Documents in the Facts for the Visitor chapter.) I-95 connects with the Trans-Canada Hwy at the Maine-New Brunswick border; at the New York-Quebec border I-87 meets Hwy 15 which leads north to Montreal. Near Kingston, Ontario, at the New York border northeast of Lake Ontario I-81 meets Hwy 401; southeast of Lake Ontario, I-90/I-190 connect with the Canadian highway system at Niagara Falls.

SEA

For those of you with plenty of time, cruise ships such as the *QE2* make transatlantic voyages, but the cruise itself is usually the vacation. Seaborne Cruise Line (☎ (800) 929-9595), 55 Francisco St, San Francisco, CA 94133, offers cruises from Montreal to New York City.

Some ocean-going freight lines also allow passengers on board. You can find out about these at a port city's docks or telephone directory. Two useful sources of information on freighters are Freighter World Cruises (☎ (818) 449-3106), 180 S Lake Ave No 335, Pasadena, CA 91101; and *Freighter Travel News*, 3524 Harts Lake Rd, Roy, WA 98580.

Several ferry services on the East Coast connect Canada with the USA. From Yarmouth, Nova Scotia, Marine Atlantic (☎ (800) 341-7981) operates a ferry service to Bar Harbor, ME, while Prince of Fundy Cruises (☎ (800) 341-7540) runs to Portland, ME. From Deer Island, New Brunswick, a ferry runs to Eastport, ME.

On the St Lawrence River, there is ferry service between Cape Vincent, NY, and Wolfe Island, Ontario (Canada), from mid-May to mid-October.

On Lake Champlain, there is daily ferry service between Port Kent, NY, and Burlington, Vermont, from May to mid-October; from Essex, NY, to Charlotte, VT, from April to January; from Fort Ticonderoga, NY, to Larrabees Point, VT, from May through October; and from Plattsburg, NY, in the Adirondacks to Grand Isle, VT, year round, depending on ice conditions.

A year-round ferry service across Delaware Bay connects Cape May in southern New Jersey with Lewes in Delaware. For information contact Cape May Terminal (☎ (609) 886-9699, (800) 643-3779), PO Box 827, North Cape May, NJ 08204.

ORGANIZED TOURS
For those with limited time, organized tours can be an efficient and relatively inexpensive way to go. Tours of the USA are so numerous that it's impossible to attempt a comprehensive listing. See your travel agent, check the small ads in newspaper travel pages or contact the American consulate in your country.

A number of companies offer standard guided tours of the region, usually by bus, and include accommodations. Any travel agent can tell you about these and arrange air, train or bus tickets to get you to the beginning of the tour.

Green Tortoise (☎ (415) 956-7500, (800) 867-8647), 494 Broadway, San Francisco, CA 94133, offers alternative bus transportation to New York with stops at places like hot springs and national parks. Meals are cooperatively cooked, and you sleep on bunks on the bus or camp. This isn't luxury travel, but it's fun.

East Coast Explorer (☎ (718) 694-9667, (800) 610-2680), based in the New York City borough of Queens, offers a similarly relaxing service. Once a week, following scenic back routes and using passenger vans carrying up to 14 people, it travels from Boston ($29 one way) or Washington, DC ($32 one way), stopping at places of interest on route to New York City. It picks up and drops off at convenient areas of cities and reservations are required one day to one month in advance. Contact Larry Lustig.

Trek America (☎ (908) 362-9198, (800) 221-0596; fax (908) 362-9313), PO Box 470, Blairstown, NJ 07825, offers roundtrip camping tours of the different areas of the country. In Britain contact them at Trek House (☎ (1869) 338777; fax (1869) 338846), The Bullring, Deddington, Banbury, Oxon OX15 0TT. These tours last from one to nine weeks and are designed for small, international groups (13 people maximum) of 18 to 38 year olds. Tour prices vary with the season, and July to September are the highest. Sample prices including food and occasional hotel nights are about $1000 for a 10 day tour to $3500 for a nine week tour of the entire country. Some side trips and cultural events are included in the price, and participants help with cooking and camp chores.

Similar deals are available from Suntreks (☎ (707) 523-1800, (800) 292-9696; fax (707) 523-1911), Sun Plaza, 77 W 3rd St, Santa Rosa, CA 95401. Suntreks also has offices in Australia (☎ (2) 9299-8844), 62 Mary St, Surry Hills, Sydney NSW 2010; Germany (☎ (89) 480-2831, fax (89) 480-2411), Swdanstrasse 21, D-81667 Munich; and Switzerland (☎ (1) 462-6161, fax (1) 462-6545), Birmensdorferstrasse 107, PO Box 8371, CH-8036, Zurich. Its tours attract predominantly young international travelers, although there is no age limit. Prices range from about $1600 for a three week trek to about $4500 for its 13 week around-America trek.

Road Runner USA/Canada (☎ (800) 873-5872), 6762A Centinela Ave, Culver City, CA 90230, organizes one and two week treks (or hikes) in conjunction with Hostelling International to different parts of the USA and across the country. It also has offices in Britain (☎ (1) 892 542010),

PO Box 105, Kelly House, Warwick Rd, Tunbridge Wells, Kent TN1 1ZN, and in Australia (☎ (2) 9299-8844), Wholesale Pty Ltd, 8th Floor, 350 Kent St, Sydney, NSW 2000.

AmeriCan Adventures (☎ (800) 864-0335), 6762A Centinela Ave, Culver City, CA 90230, offers seven to 21 day trips to different parts of the USA, usually following a theme. For worldwide sales contact its UK headquarters (☎ (1) 892 511894), 45 High St, Tunbridge Wells, Kent TN1 1XL.

Peter Pan Trailways (☎ (800) 237-8747), PO Box 1776, Springfield, MA 01102-1776, is one of the largest organized bus-tour operators in the northeast.

Getting Around

Airfares aren't cheap, but for those with a little extra money and not much time, the occasional flight may be useful. Land travel is generally less expensive and, of course, more interesting than flying. Buses provide the most extensive public transportation and are generally cheaper than the more-limited train service, though train travel can be quicker.

Public transportation doesn't reach many of the interesting more-isolated places, so having your own transport can be a major advantage. It's worth considering car rental for at least a part of your trip. You can use public transportation to towns and cities, then hire a car locally to get to places not served by public transportation. This option is usually more expensive than just renting a car and driving yourself everywhere, but it can cut down on long-distance driving trips.

AIR

The region is served by most domestic airlines (see the Getting There & Away chapter). Regular fares are expensive but you can save money if you have an advanced booking. Fares also drop considerably if you avoid peak times and fly early in the morning or late at night, or on specific flights. Ask about special fares when making reservations.

If you're arriving from abroad or another major US airport, it's usually much cheaper to buy a through ticket to small airports as part of your fare rather than separately.

Another alternative is an air pass, available from the major airlines flying between the USA and Europe, Asia and Australia. (See Visit USA Passes in the Getting There & Away chapter.)

Airports

The main airports in New York are John F Kennedy international (JFK, ☎ (718) 656 4520) and La Guardia (☎ (718) 533-3400) both in Queens, New York City. Greater

Buffalo international airport (☎ (716) 632-3115) is also busy serving upstate New York.

In New Jersey the main airport is Newark international (☎ (201) 961-2000) which also serves New York City and is the major hub of Continental Airlines. Other airports are Atlantic City international (☎ (609) 645-7895), Princeton (☎ (609) 921-3100) and Teterboro (☎ (201) 288-1775), one of the nation's leading hubs for private aircraft.

Philadelphia international (☎ (215) 492-3181) and Pittsburgh international (☎ (412) 472-3525/5525) are the two largest airports in Pennsylvania. Pittsburgh is the hub of USAir. Other airports serve Johnstown/Cambria County (☎ (814) 536-0002), Harrisburg (☎ (717) 948-3913), Lancaster (☎ (717) 569-1221) and Reading regional. (☎ (610) 372-4666).

Regional Airlines

The following list of airlines have service within the region:

America West Airlines	(800) 235-9292
American Eagle	(800) 433-7300
Continental Express	(800) 525-0280
Delta Connection	(800) 221-1212
Direct Air	(800) 428-0706
Midwest Express	(800) 452-2022
Northwest Airlink	(800) 225-2525
Spirit Airlines	(800) 772-7117
Trans World Express	(800) 221-2000
United Express	(800) 241-6522
USAir Express	(800) 428-4322
ValuJet Airlines	(800) 825-8538

BUS
Carriers

Greyhound (☎ (000) 231-2222), is the main long-distance carrier for the region. It has the most extensive routes and usually its own terminal, though these are sometimes in undesirable parts of town. However, the buses are reasonably comfortable and they usually run on time, and the company has a good safety record.

Greyhound connects large towns several times a day along major highways, stopping at smaller towns on the way. It has reduced or eliminated services to small rural communities that it once served efficiently. In many small towns, Greyhound no longer maintains terminals but merely stops at a given location such as a service station, grocery store or fast-food restaurant (which may be the only choice for a meal – bring your own food if burgers and fries are unappealing). At these 'terminals' passengers may be able to buy a ticket, but usually you pay the driver (with exact change) on boarding. Note that all buses are nonsmoking.

Other important bus lines operate in the region. Capitol Trailways (☎ (717) 233-7716, (800) 444-2877), runs between Washington, DC, and Baltimore, MD; it has many stops in central and eastern Pennsylvania as well as at Syracuse and Binghamton in New York. Peter Pan Trailways (☎ (800) 343-9999) operates between Washington, DC, and Boston, MA, via Philadelphia and New York City and also runs to Atlantic City.

Martz Trailways connects Philadelphia and other towns in eastern Pennsylvania with New York City and several towns in New Jersey. For information on Pennsylvania call ☎ (800) 432-8069, for New York and New Jersey call ☎ (800) 233-8604. Adirondack Trailways (☎ (518) 436-9651) runs to many major towns in New York State.

NJ Transit (☎ (215) 569-3752, (800) 228-8246 in the region) has a regular bus service from Atlantic City along the coast, extending north to New York City and south to Cape May.

Towns not on major routes are often served by local carriers. Greyhound and other bus lines often share the same terminal.

Fares
Tickets can be bought over the phone with a credit card (MasterCard or Visa) and mailed if bought 10 days in advance or

picked up at the terminal with proper identification. Greyhound terminals also accept American Express, travelers' checks, post office money orders and cash. Reservations are made with ticket purchases only. Fares can vary tremendously; it's best to call Greyhound for current details. The Ameripass (see below) is valid on other bus lines affiliated with Greyhound.

Special Fares Sometimes you can get discounted tickets if you buy them seven or 21 days in advance. Greyhound occasionally introduces a mileage-based discount-fare program that can be a bargain, especially for long distances, but it's a good idea to check the regular fare anyway. As with regular fares these promotional fares are subject to change.

Ameripass Greyhound's Ameripass is potentially useful if you're doing a lot of traveling, but the relatively high prices may impel you to travel more than you would normally simply to get your money's worth. Anyone can buy an Ameripass; it costs $179 for seven days of unlimited travel year round, $289 for 15 days and $399 for 30 days. Children under 11 travel for half price. You can get on and off at any Greyhound stop or terminal, and the Ameripass is available at every Greyhound terminal.

International Ameripass Only foreign tourists and foreign students and lecturers (with their families) staying less than a year can buy this pass. A four day pass with unlimited travel costs $99, but you can only travel on it Monday to Thursday. Higher rates don't have such time constraints and cost $159 for a seven day pass, $219 for a 15 day pass and $299 for a 30 day pass. The four day pass is non-refundable, but the others are, provided they haven't been used at all; you must claim the refund *before* you leave the US.

The pass is usually bought abroad at a travel agency. You can buy it in the USA but only through the Greyhound International office (☎ (212) 971-0492, fax (212) 967-2239), 625 8th Ave at the subway level of the Port Authority bus terminal in New York City. It's open Monday to Thursday from 8:30 am to 4:30 pm, Friday to 4 pm. Purchasers of an International Ameripass must complete an affidavit and present a passport or visa (or waiver) to the appropriate Greyhound officials. Purchases can also be made over the phone from anywhere in the US, but you'll need to give your passport number, your country and date of entry. These will be written on your International Ameripass when you receive it.

Costs

Generally, buses provide the cheapest form of public transportation. Peter Pan Trailways tends to be a shade cheaper than Greyhound. The one-way fare between New York City and Philadelphia is $13 (2½ hours). For specific fares check individual listings in the text.

TRAIN

Amtrak Amtrak (☎ (800) 872-7245), 60 Massachusetts Ave NE, Washington, DC 20002, connects the major cities in the region with stops at smaller towns along the routes. Amtrak fares vary, depending on different promotional fares and destinations. A reservation can be hard to get so plan ahead; the earlier it's made, the better the fare. A reservation can be held under your surname only. You can buy tickets by credit card over the phone, from a travel agent or at some (but not all) Amtrak stations.

Amtrak offers two main discount fare options: the All Aboard America fare (see Train in the Getting There & Away chapter) and the USA Rail Pass, which is only available to citizens of countries other than the US and Canada. A national pass costs $340 ($229 off peak) for 15 days, $425 ($339 off peak) for 30 days. A pass for the eastern region costs $200 ($179 off peak) for 15 days, $255 ($229 off peak) for 30 days. Peak season is from mid-June to late August.

The main Amtrak routes radiate from New York City: north to Albany, Schenectady and Rouses Point (near the Quebec border) and Montreal; northwest to Utica,

Syracuse, Buffalo and Niagara Falls; and southwest to Newark, Princeton, Trenton, Philadelphia, Harrisburg and Pittsburgh. From Harrisburg there are connections to Reading, Scranton and State College.

For more information on longer routes with service both inside and outside New York, New Jersey and Pennsylvania, see the Getting There & Away chapter.

Other Service New Jersey Transit (NJ Transit; ☎ (800) 228-8246) has a regular rail service from Atlantic City to Philadelphia, and also connects New York City with New Jersey's western suburbs and the Jersey Shore.

Philadelphia's Southern Pennsylvania Transportation Authority (SEPTA; ☎ (215) 580-7800) covers its suburbs extensively. The Long Island Rail Road (LIRR; ☎ (516) 822-5477, (718) 217-5477) connects New York City to Long Island; Metro North (☎ (212) 532-4900) trains connect New York City to its northern suburbs (Westchester) and Connecticut; Port Authority Trans-Hudson (PATH; ☎ (800) 234-7284) trains connect the city to New Jersey's northern cities, including Newark and Hoboken. For specifics on services and fares, check Getting There & Away under the destination headings in the text. See also Local Transport, below.

In some areas, privately owned tourist trains offer scenic day trips through the countryside. Some of them travel on narrow-gauge railroads built by former mining companies and are often powered by steam.

CAR & MOTORCYCLE

The US has an extensive highway system and since public transportation is limited it's worth considering traveling by car or motorcycle. Traveling with your own vehicle is the best, and often the only, way to get to remote places and it gives you the most flexibility.

Many US cities and towns owe their sprawl largely to the popularity of the automobile. Satellite communities – with their shopping malls, fast-food restaurants and

Pennsylvania Driving Problems

You can't talk about driving in Pennsylvania without mentioning the peculiarities of the state's highways and roads.

For some reason, on Pennsylvania highways the 'exit' sign with an arrow indicating a turnoff is often placed *after* the actual exit ramp. This is confusing if you're used to the final notice for a turn appearing before the exit ramp. Also there's often no sign indicating how much drivers should slow down or if the road is going to curve dangerously as you exit. Of course, you should always slow down, but the merge from highway to road may require slowing to any speed from 55 mph to 25 mph.

There are usually several signs for an exit before you get there, but they don't always correspond with each other. For example, an early sign might say the exit is for towns 'A and B' but when you come to the actual exit the sign will say something like 'Highway 1 east and west' rather than telling you whether the east or west direction of Highway 1 leads to town A or B, which were mentioned earlier. Before starting your journey it's a good idea to plan your route so that you know the exact sequence of highways to follow to get to your destination.

Approaches to bridges aren't always indicated. In Pittsburgh, for example, you may be traveling along a street then suddenly find yourself heading across a bridge out of town without any previous indication. ■

motels – have developed along highways and at the intersections of important routes. The attraction(s) you've come to see may be downtown, but the only affordable accommodations available may well be a number of miles away in one of these commercial strips, and the only means of access will be a car or motorcycle. Pittsburgh is a good example of this.

On the debit side, the independence you enjoy using your own vehicle tends to isolate you from the local people. The larger cities with their one-way traffic systems and complex network of highways into, through and around town can be confusing and wearing on the nerves. Also, finding somewhere convenient to park in unfamiliar city centers can be difficult and expensive.

You may want to consider getting an International or Inter-American Driving Permit to supplement your normal driver's license (see Visas & Documents in the Facts for the Visitor chapter).

Road Rules

You must be at least 16 years of age to drive; in New York City you *must* be 18 years of age, regardless of whether you are licensed to drive in other states. Speed limits are 65 mph on interstate highways and freeways unless otherwise posted. You can drive five mph over the limit without much likelihood of being pulled over, but if you're doing 10 mph over the limit, you'll be caught sooner or later. Speed limits on other highways are 55 mph or less, and in cities can vary from 25 to 45 mph. School zones can be as low as 15 mph during school hours – these limits are strictly enforced.

Seat belts are compulsory for drivers and front-seat passengers; children under four must use approved safety seats. Motorcyclists and their passengers must wear helmets.

See also Driving & Drinking Laws under Legal Matters in the Facts for the Visitor chapter.

Road Safety

To minimize the chance of theft, don't leave valuables (or anything) on view inside when the car is parked. Tuck items under the seat or, better still, put them in the trunk and make sure the car doesn't have trunk entry through the back seat; if it does, make sure it's locked. Don't leave valuables in the car overnight.

In more isolated areas, wild animals may

be seen foraging along the highways. Many, such as raccoons, are small, but a collision with a large animal like a deer can wreck a car. It may also severely injure or kill the occupants as well as the animal. Pay attention to the roadside, especially at night.

Road conditions are particularly difficult in winter. In an emergency dial ☎ 911. Tire chains are useful and sometimes required on snowy or icy roads. (Note that rental-car companies specifically prohibit the use of chains on their vehicles.) Other cold-weather precautions include keeping a woolen blanket, windshield ice-scraper, spade or snow shovel, flares and an extra pair of gloves and boots in the trunk for emergencies.

Car Rental

Major international rental agencies like Avis (☎ (800) 331-1212), Budget (☎ (800) 527-0700), Dollar (☎ (800) 800-4000), Hertz (☎ (800) 654-3131) and Thrifty (☎ (800) 367-2277) have offices throughout the region. To rent a car you must have a valid driver's license, be at least 25 years of age and present a major credit card or else a large cash deposit.

Many rental agencies have bargain rates for weekend or week-long rentals, especially outside the peak season or in conjunction with airline tickets. Prices vary greatly in relation to region, season and type or size of the car you'd like to rent. Generally, a subcompact costs about $50 per day. You're normally expected to return the car to where you picked it up; you can arrange to drop the car off elsewhere, but you'll have to pay a surcharge.

Basic liability insurance, which covers damage you may cause to another vehicle, is required by law and comes with the price of renting the car. Liability insurance is also called third-party coverage.

Collision Damage Waiver, also called Liability Damage Waiver, is optional; you don't need to buy this waiver to rent the car, but it does cover the full value of the vehicle in case of an accident, except when caused by acts of nature or fire. For a mid-sized car the cost for this extra coverage is around $15 per day. Agencies also add a daily fee for each additional driver in the car.

Some credit cards, such as the Master-Card Gold Card, cover collision insurance if you rent for 15 days or less and charge

---

Accidents Happen

It's important that a visitor knows the appropriate protocol when involved in a 'fender-bender.'

• Remain at the scene of the accident until you have exchanged information with the police or the other drivers involved, especially if there is substantial damage or personal injury – this is also important if you hit a large animal such as a deer. It may be necessary to move your car off the road for safety's sake, but leaving the scene of an accident is illegal. Get the other driver's name, address, driver's license number, license plate number and insurance information. Be prepared to provide any documentation you have, such as your passport, International Driving Permit and insurance documents. The only insurance information you need to reveal is the name of your insurance carrier and your policy number.

• Call the police (and an ambulance, if needed) immediately, and give the operator as much specific information as possible (your location, injuries etc). In cities, the emergency phone number is ☎ 911; in rural areas dial ☎ 0. If you're driving a rental car, call the rental company promptly.

• Tell your story to the police carefully. Refrain from answering any questions until you feel comfortable doing so (with a lawyer present, if need be). That's your right under the law.

• If a police officer suspects that you may have been driving under the influence of alcohol, he or she may ask you to take a breath-analysis test. If you refuse, your driving permit is suspended until a verdict is delivered in your court case. ■

the full cost of rental to your card. If you opt to do that, you'll need to sign the waiver, declining the coverage. If you already have collision insurance on your personal policy, the credit card covers the large deductible. To find out extents and details, contact the credit card company.

Some rental agencies no longer offer unlimited mileage in non-competitive markets – this greatly increases the cost of renting a car by adding a charge per mile.

Car Purchase

If you're spending several months in the USA, it's worth considering buying a car, which may work out cheaper than renting one. However, buying one can be complicated and requires plenty of research.

It's possible to buy a viable car for about $1500, but you can't expect to go too far before you'll need some repair work that could cost several hundred dollars. It doesn't hurt to spend more to get a quality vehicle. It's also worth spending $50 or so to have a mechanic check it for defects (some AAA offices have diagnostic centers where they do this on the spot for its members and those of foreign affiliates).

You can check out the official valuation of a used car by looking it up in the *Blue Book*, a listing of cars by make, model and year and the average resale price. Local public libraries have copies of the book as well as back issues of *Consumer Reports*, a magazine that annually tallies the repair records of common makes of cars.

If you want to buy a car, first contact AAA (☎ (800) 477-1222) for some general information (you need to be a member for this service). Then contact the Department of Motor Vehicles to find out about registration fees and insurance, which can be confusing and expensive. As an example, say you're a 30 year old, non-US citizen and you want to buy a 1986 Honda. If this is the first time you have registered a car in the USA, you'll have to pay about $300 first, then about $100 to $200 more for general registration.

Inspect the title carefully before buying the car; the owner's name on the title must match the identification of the person selling you the car. If you're a foreigner, you may find it useful to obtain a notarized document authorizing your use of the car, since the motor-vehicle bureau in the state where you buy the car may take several weeks or more to process the change in title.

Insurance While insurance isn't obligatory in every state, all states have financial-responsibility laws and insurance is highly desirable; otherwise, a serious accident could leave you a pauper. To grant insurance, some states request that you have a US driver's license and that you have been licensed for at least 18 months. If you meet these qualifications, you pay from $300 to $1200 a year for insurance, depending on where the car is registered and the state. Rates are generally lower if you register it at an address in the suburbs or in a rural area, rather than in a city center, and avoid registering in New Jersey, which has a notorious car theft problem.

Collision coverage is expensive, with high deductibles, and is generally not worthwhile unless the car is somewhat valuable. Regulations vary from state to state but are generally becoming more stringent throughout the USA.

Obtaining insurance, however, isn't as simple as walking into an agency, filling out a form and paying for it. Many agencies refuse to insure drivers who have no car insurance (a classic Catch 22!); those who do so often charge much higher rates because they presume a higher risk. Male drivers under the age of 25 pay astronomical rates. The minimum term for a policy is usually six months, but some insurance companies refund the difference on a pro-rated basis if the car is sold and the policy voluntarily terminated. It's advisable to shop around.

Drive-Aways

This is a cheap way to get around if you like long-distance driving and meet eligibility requirements. A drive-away is a car belonging to an owner who can't drive it to a specific destination but is willing to allow someone else to drive it for them. For example, if someone moves from Boston to Pittsburgh, they may elect to fly and leave the car with a drive-away agency. The agency will find a driver and take care of all the necessary insurance and permits. If you happen to want to drive from Boston to Pittsburgh, have a valid driver's license and a clean driving record, you can apply to drive the car. Normally, you have to pay a small refundable deposit. You pay for the gas (though sometimes a gas allowance is given).

You're allowed a set number of days to deliver the car – usually based on driving eight hours a day. You're also allowed a limited number of miles, based on the best route and allowing for reasonable side trips, so you can't just zigzag everywhere.

Drive-away companies often advertise in the classified sections of newspapers under 'Travel.' They're also listed in the yellow pages of the telephone directory under 'Automobile Transporters & Drive-Away Companies.' You need to be flexible about dates and destinations when you call. If you're going to a popular area, you may be able to leave within two days or less, or you may have to wait over a week before a car becomes available. The most readily available routes are coast to coast, though intermediate trips are certainly possible.

Shipping a Car or Motorcycle
In general, because good used cars are cheap in the USA, it's usually unnecessary to ship a car, but some people do take their own transport to the USA and beyond. Air-cargo planes have size limits, but a normal car or even a Land Rover can fit. For motorcyclists, air is probably the easiest option; you may be able to get a special rate for air cargo if you're flying with the same airline. Start by asking the cargo departments of the airlines that fly to your destination. Travel agents can sometimes help as well.

BICYCLE
See Bicycling & Mountain Biking in the Outdoor Activities chapter.

HITCHING
Travelers who hitch should understand that they are taking a serious risk. Many Americans think that it's crazy to hitch because of the potential dangers, and just don't do it; 'reasonable' people tend not to pick up hitchhikers, and almost nobody thinks it wise for a single woman to travel this way across the country.

If you do hitch, you should be extremely careful when accepting a lift – you may not be able to identify the local rapist/murderer before you get into the vehicle. If in doubt, don't. Ask the driver where they're going rather than telling them where you want to go. Hitching in pairs may be a little safer and you should let someone know where you're planning to go.

Hitching is illegal on the interstate highways, but you can stick out your thumb at the bottom of the on-ramp. Police routinely check hitchhikers' IDs, so be prepared for this. You may be asked to show them some money to prove you aren't destitute. (The police won't continue to hassle you if you have an ID and act reasonable.)

WALKING
Because of the great distances, only a handful of people use their feet as a primary means of transport. However, it's possible to traverse the region along sections of long-distance trails like the North Country National Scenic Trail and the Appalachian Trail, and to cover other interesting areas on foot. For more information see Hiking & Backpacking in the Outdoor Activities chapter.

BOAT
New York State has an extensive canal system, and you can hire canal boats to travel from Albany north along the Champlain Canal to Lake Champlain and west along the Erie Canal to Buffalo and the Great Lakes. For more information contact the New York State Canal Corporation, PO Box 189, Albany, NY 12201-0189. New York ferry service is detailed in the state information chapter.

From New Jersey, ferries connect Jersey

City and Hoboken with Manhattan across the Hudson River, and Camden with Philadelphia across the Delaware River.

LOCAL TRANSPORT

Comprehensive local bus networks exist in big cities and most larger towns, though some popular destinations, such as Gettysburg in Pennsylvania, have no public transportation. Other towns have bus systems with limited hours and routes, which make them unreliable as a primary means of local transport.

New York City, which has an extensive subway and bus system, and Metro North and the LIRR; and Philadelphia, which has SEPTA (see Train, above), have extensive urban and suburban transport systems. Also from Philadelphia, one subway line connects that city with Camden, NJ.

Most towns of any size have a taxi service. These can be expensive but aren't so outrageous if shared among two or three people. You can hail them on the street when their center roof-light is lit. Check the yellow pages under 'Taxi' for phone numbers and services. Drivers almost always expect a tip of about 10% of the fare.

New York City has the Staten Island ferry, but most ways of getting around a town by boat are as part of a guided tour.

ORGANIZED TOURS

If your time is limited, it might be worth considering an organized tour, which you can book through a travel agent, tourist office, sometimes through your hotel or directly through the tour companies themselves. The state tourist authorities have information on private tour companies.

Some of the larger bus companies like Gray Line or Peter Pan Trailways offer trips of varying lengths some of which include accommodations. Many small companies offer a variety of activity-based trips – you can hike, camp, bike, canoe or raft rivers, birdwatch etc. Many of these are listed in the text.

See Organized Tours in the Getting There & Away chapter.

Facts about New York

New York state is a world apart from its better known cousin, New York City. One of the original thirteen English colonies, upstate New York still retains some of the character associated with New England – its people are self-reliant, often stoic and proud of their close knit communities and relationship to the land.

Once a traveler manages to move beyond the gravitational pull of New York City, the state opens up in ways unimaginable from midtown Manhattan. An ongoing debate, of course, is what constitutes 'upstate' New York. Folks in the Adirondack's North Country refer casually to 'down-staters' as occupants of a different reality. On the other hand, it's not unusual to hear New York City dwellers discuss a trip 'upstate,' only to find out they went to Poughkeepsie, where commuter trains carry people in and out of the Big Apple every day of the week. A resident of Westchester County had the best definition I've heard of upstate: 'Any place north of where you are.' Indeed, the land and its recent history continually alter as you travel away from New York City's throbbing hub.

New York's early European history – much of it revealed through encounters with the indigenous Indian peoples – begins in the lower Hudson River Valley, along the banks of the river which Henry Hudson hoped was the long sought Northwest passage to the Pacific and storied lands beyond. He could hardly be blamed for his error in navigation; the Hudson estuary is one of the largest on the continent, with the salty waters of the Atlantic extending more than 50 miles upriver.

Navigation by water, in fact, shaped the state's evolution. The Hudson River, the Mohawk River, the canal system which connected Albany and Buffalo, Lake Ontario and Lake Erie, as well as the extensive network of rivers and ponds that cover much of the Adirondacks were all vital to the state's economic and social development. The state's four coastlines – Lake Erie, Ontario, the Atlantic and the St Lawrence Seaway – all contributed to a 19th century economic boom that saw New York ranked first in wealth and population well into the 20th century. From Buffalo to New York City, a series of industrial and manufacturing centers developed along the most navigable waterways.

In addition, the vast system of lakes, streams and falls confer impressive and fascinating physical beauty: from the roar of Niagara Falls in the northwest corner to the slender beauty of Taughannock Falls in the Finger Lakes region. Many of New York's waterways have also been fertile ground for the cultural, intellectual and artistic character of New York. Aside from the sparkle and international flavor of New York City, the upstate region has its own unique offerings, from the gorges of Ithaca and the Ivy League ambience of Cornell University to the charm of Saratoga Springs, where the New York City Ballet and the Philadelphia Philharmonic Orchestra make their summer home and strolling musicians entertain the winners and losers at the Saratoga racetrack.

Summer in the Adirondacks might put you in the middle of a storytelling festival, with musicians providing sweet accompaniment and local cooks providing sustenance. And for a bit of elegant nostalgia, New York is home of the National Baseball Hall of Fame in Cooperstown, positioned appropriately on Main St.

To the west, the 11 elegantly shaped Finger Lakes are home to a well-established wine region. Several of these are popular summer destinations for swimming, boating and fishing. The largest of the lakes are Cayuga, Seneca, Keuka, Canandaigua, Owasco and Skaneateles. In the southwest corner of the state, on the shore of Chautauqua Lake, the Chautauqua

Institution continues a 19th century tradition of enlightenment and entertainment in which enterprising speakers and performers once criss-crossed the country as part of the chautauqua circuit, now an indelible part of American, and New York, history.

But clearly the state – and, indeed, the entire Middle Atlantic region – is dominated by New York City, which will serve as the departure and entry point for most travelers who will use this volume. In a sense, Henry Hudson was but the first of many millions to build a future on the small island of Manhattan and its surrounding area. The city's reputation as an intellectual, economic and creative capital and place of opportunity for newcomers seems destined to continue to draw settlers and travelers alike in perpetuity.

HISTORY
Original Peoples
The history of New York begins with the influence that various Native American tribes held over the would-be colonial empires of France, Holland and England. A Native American confederacy known as the Five Nations and consisting of the Mohawk, Oneida, Onondaga, Cayuga and Seneca peoples controlled most of present-day New York from the Hudson River in the east to the Genessee River west of the Finger Lakes. This powerful tribal alliance was also known as the Iroquois Confederacy or Iroquois League and was joined in 1722 by the Tuscaroras to form the Six Nations. The less powerful Algonquians occupied the lower Hudson River area and parts of the seacoast. The power of the Iroquois peoples, their knowledge of the land and their propensity to trade with their early European counterparts, allowed them to leverage power among the quarreling Europeans.

European Arrival
Giovanni da Verrazano, representing France, was the first European to sail into New York's waters. Exploration and trade were sporadic until 1609, when Samuel de Champlain of France, fresh from founding

the colony of Quebec and naming a lake for himself, unwisely decided to fight the Iroquois, allying himself with the weaker Algonquians. The British were the eventual winners in managing to convince the Iroquois that protection and prosperity would result from an alliance with England. Of course, the Iroquois were the eventual losers.

That same year, 1609, Henry Hudson, in the employ of the Dutch East India Company, entered the bay of New York in his ship, *Half Moon*. Hudson first believed that he had found the fabled Northwest Passage leading to the Pacific. When the tidal river tapered to more modest proportions, Hudson was happy to report that Holland stood to reap the benefits of a vast trading enterprise with the Iroquois. A trading post and stockade was established at Fort Orange, near present-day Albany, and the strategic confluence of the Hudson and Mohawk rivers. (Today, many of the town names echo the early Dutch settlers: Voorheesville, Rensselaer, Rotterdam, Half Moon and Guilderland.)

The Dutch exploited the fur trade, but their attempts to settle the banks of the Hudson River never amounted to much, despite their offer of free land to 'all good inhabitants of the Netherlands.' Fort Amsterdam was replaced by New Amsterdam when the Dutch made their famous exchange for Manhattan with the local Algonquian Indians in 1626. But the Dutch territory, New Netherland, never surmounted the challenges it created; settlers were reluctant to inhabit the interior in great numbers. Conflicts with the 'River Indians' and Dutch colonial interests elsewhere finally gave way to an English takeover in 1664.

No one in New Amsterdam seemed to mind terribly, and no one asked the Algonquians, whose numbers and influence had been reduced greatly through conflict and disease. The takeover took only a few months, and the favorable terms of surrender offered by the British were readily accepted by the most prominent Dutch citizens, who were anxious to simply continue

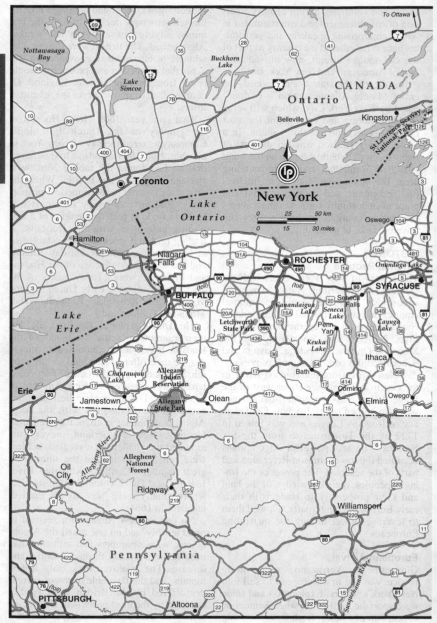

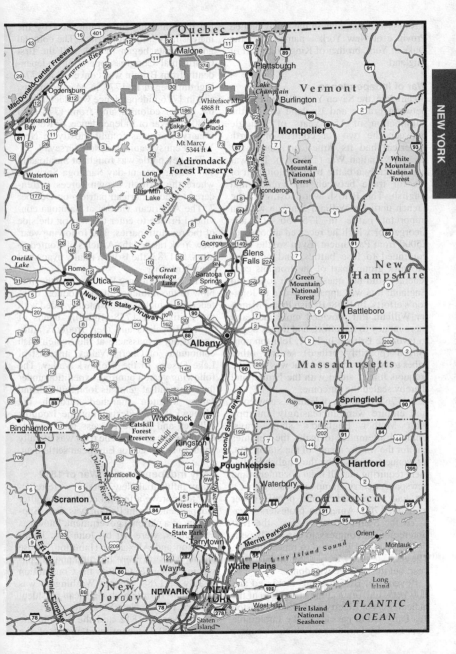

NEW YORK

business as usual, now in the newly named Province of New York – named after the Duke of York, brother of King Charles II of England.

War of Independence

Meanwhile, the Seven Years War in Europe between France and England (really the culmination of 150 years of struggle between the two for control of North America) had its American phase: the French & Indian War (1754-63). The war was basically a battle over exploitation of the fur trade between the French and English. The British were losing to the French until Sir William Johnson won an important battle in 1755-56 at Lake George, for which he received a bonus of £5000 from Parliament. Even so, the Brits continued to lose battles, and only the Mohawk group (part of the Iroquois confederacy) did not question their loyalty to England; this was apparently due to Johnson's efforts. In 1758, British Prime Minister William Pitt provided more men and more money to the effort, and things began to favor the British. In 1761, Johnson convinced (possibly bribed) several other tribes to switch sides, and that was that: the Iroquois finally sided with the British and thereby sealed the outcome.

By 1765, residents of Britain's new colonial empire were increasingly unhappy with Mother England's stern ways. England attempted to make the colonies pay for the war by means of the Stamp Act, a revenue tax passed by the English Parliament requiring that all legal documents and newspapers carry stamps indicating that a tax had been paid. Some people never learn. In 1766, American protesters organized the Stamp Act Congress, the first 'intercolonial' congress, to peacefully petition the King of England to repeal the act. The request was wisely granted that same year, but the damage was done.

Boycotts of British goods increased and riots occurred, often at the instigation of the radical Sons of Liberty. In 1773, the Boston Tea Party led to passage of the Intolerable Acts Law by Parliament, which of course led to numerous intolerable acts by the increasingly militant patriots. The colonial governments began to fail, and the first Continental Congress operating independently from Britain was convened in 1774. Fighting began in 1775 in Massachusetts, and in 1776 independence was declared by the former colonies, and from 1776 until 1780, the War of Independence, or Revolutionary War, was fought mostly in New York, Pennsylvania and New Jersey.

The key battle was fought at Saratoga in 1777 (near present-day Saratoga Springs), where the British Crown forces surrendered to the American patriots on October 7. The American victory at Saratoga convinced France to enter the war on the side of the revolutionaries. The following year, New York ratified the Articles of Confederation. In 1783, the British finally evacuated New York City.

The Revolutionary War was also the final blow to the influence of the Iroquois Confederacy, which had consistently sided with the British. In 1778, fighting bands of British Loyalists and their Iroquois allies carried out a massacre at the Scotch-Irish community of Cherry Valley, just east of Lake Otsego in the Mohawk Valley. The following year, a punitive expedition under the command of generals John Sullivan and James Clinton marched through the Mohawk Valley, destroying the Iroquois villages and in the process the Iroquois Confederacy as well. The road was literally about to be paved for European settlement.

Early Independence & War of 1812

Many influential New Yorkers were reluctant to approve a federal constitution after independence from Britain was won. Supporters of a national government, known as Federalists, were led by John Jay, James Madison and Alexander Hamilton, whose eloquent essays were instrumental in convincing delegates to ratify the Constitution in July of 1788. George Washington was inaugurated as the first American president in April 1789 in New York City.

The War of 1812 and the Napoleonic Wars (1800-15) continued many of the disputes of the major European powers and by definition added the newly independent Americans to the military scene. France was trying to maintain hegemony in Europe, and Britain began to interfere with US shipping, which was officially neutral. The US declared war on Britain, and much of the war was fought on the open sea. Other battles took place in Buffalo, NY, and Washington, DC, which the British succeeded in burning. The US victory established American naval power in the early 19th century, and soon the entire state of New York experienced a massive economic boom. Because of its strong transportation links, available labor and capital, New York quickly became the nation's center for trade, finance and manufacturing. The population soared, and factories and foundries sprang up across the state.

But the most dramatic economic development of the era was the completion in 1825 of the Erie Canal, an artificial waterway that connected Buffalo and Albany and, more significantly, the Hudson River to Lake Erie and the ports of the western Great Lakes. Its impact on the country was monumental at the time. It was not only an engineering marvel, but an economic one as well, which greatly accelerated the development of the country's expanding Northwest (now Midwest). With the expansion of the country's rail system later in the 19th century, the influence of the Erie Canal began to diminish.

The regions surrounding the canal were recently granted $160 million for renovation and revival for recreation, primarily boating.

Civil War

The debate over the nature of the new American government did not end with the celebration at Washington's 1789 inauguration. Longstanding social and economic differences between the North and the South led to inevitable economic conflicts, which finally escalated to military opposition. Both sides generally agreed that blacks were not the equal of whites, so the impetus of war wasn't really a civil rights

issue, but whether slave labor would be introduced in the territories, thus providing a cheap alternative to products produced by whites in the new factories of the northern states. Thus the territorial explosion of the early 19th century was the main reason slavery became an important issue in the 1850s. When Abraham Lincoln was elected president in 1860, South Carolina became the first of 11 southern states to secede from the Union.

The Civil War ended in 1865, partly due to the superior industrial resources of the Northern states, and of New York in particular. Over 500,000 troops came from New York to fight for the preservation of the Union. Of these, nearly 60,000 died on the battlefield – ironically about the same number of Americans who died a hundred years later in Vietnam. A controversy over the practice of drafting the poor (in this case, mostly poor Irish) to serve in the army, while the rich were able to buy their way out for $300, resulted in one of the country's most deadly riots ever, the Draft Riots of 1863 in New York City.

20th Century

Today, though much of New York's stormy past has dimmed, the state remains a vital region, full of contrasts. The prosperity that arose along the Erie Canal and made it a corridor of commerce eroded in this century, and the region became better known as 'the rust belt.' Today, many of the former industrial cities are working to revitalize themselves as cultural and economic centers.

The pristine beauty of the state's mountains and lakes is also being recaptured as civic groups from the Alleghenies to the Adirondacks work to maintain the land's splendid natural features.

GEOGRAPHY & GEOLOGY

New York's total land area comprises 47,939 sq miles, and its total inland water area is 1637 sq miles. The addition of New York's share of Lakes Erie and Ontario adds another 3140 sq miles to the total.

The most striking feature of New York's

waterways is their variety: the Atlantic sea-coast, two of the Great Lakes (Erie and Ontario), the Finger Lakes of central New York, Lake George and Lake Champlain, thousands of smaller lakes and ponds across the state, the St Lawrence Seaway and its 'Thousand Islands,' and an engineered canal system that connected many of the natural waterways and sustained much of New York's westward expansion.

The most striking topographical feature of the state is the Adirondack mountain range in the northeast. Though not particularly high in elevation, the Adirondacks are striking for their range, beauty and age. The ancient range was once covered by a continental glacier, resulting in a gently worn landscape of low relief highlighted by a number of dramatic peaks, known collectively as the High Peaks. The highest of the High Peaks is Mt Marcy (5344 feet), while the rest range in elevation from 4000 to 5000 feet. A group of mountain enthusiasts known as the '46ers' takes their name from the 46 highest of these. Much of the Adirondack range is covered by forests, and most areas are protected from extensive development.

As the continental glacier receded roughly 10,000 years ago, it left its dramatic legacy across the region. Valleys were carved and broadened, hills were rounded and gorges and waterfalls were created. Glaciers sculpted the Finger Lakes.

South of the Adirondacks, the Appalachian Plateau stretches from the Allegheny Mountains to the Catskills. The plateau extends to the shores of Lake Erie and Lake Ontario, where it forms a fertile plain that has been the basis of extensive agriculture.

The drainage of New York makes its way in several directions. Most of the Adirondack waterways drain into the St Lawrence system. Parts of the Catskills drain into the Delaware River and on to Delaware Bay. The source of the Hudson River is Lake Tear of the Clouds in the Adirondacks, the highest lake in the state. From there, the Hudson ranges over 306 miles until it reaches New York Bay.

CLIMATE

Like much of the northern US, New York state has a climate of extremes – hot and muggy in the summer, cold and wet in the winter. The Atlantic Ocean and the Great Lakes moderate the temperatures somewhat, but in the high Adirondacks severe winter storms and sub-zero temperatures are not unusual.

The phenomenon known as 'lake-effect snow' is famous from Syracuse to Buffalo, both for its quantity and its wet quality. Storms gain strength as they blow from the northwest to the southeast over the Great Lakes and tend to dump all the accumulated precipitation on the eastern shores.

Average mean temperatures in the state range from 21°F in January, 50°F in April, 70°F in July and 49°F in October.

ECOLOGY & ENVIRONMENT

Much of upstate New York's outdoor sparkle – from the high peaks of the Adirondacks to the shimmering Finger Lakes – dims a bit when the impact of a modern industrial society is taken into full account. The good news is that several organizations are working to check this impact, including efforts to bring environmentalists and commercial enterprises closer together; land use, wildlife preservation and agricultural practices are now topics for debate and compromise.

Water pollution impacts the health, vitality and spirit of the land and the people who live on it, prompting politicians of all parties to join with environmentalists in late 1996 to support a successful bond act that will provide billions of dollars for preservation and cleanup statewide.

Acid rain is a continuing problem in the industrial northeastern US and the Great Lakes region, as well as much of New York state. Airborne pollutants from as far away as Chicago, Detroit and Cleveland join the air stream, finding their way eventually to waterways. Most of the alpine areas in the Adirondacks are effected, and there are vigorous efforts to arrest erosion and to educate hikers and others who enjoy the land.

Newcomers to acid-rain impact need to know a deceptive fact: the acid affects all life forms, from plankton to minnows to dazzling brook trout – so much so that a small lake may look 'clearer' than ever. But clear does not mean clean, despite what the advertisers tell us; a little murky algae on the edges is what we want. (Algae is a living organism quite vulnerable to acid pollutants.) Many of the mountain lakes, in addition to the larger Finger Lakes, have increased acid levels, though acid rain isn't the only villain. In Lake Ontario, a combination of pollutants have led to contaminated fisheries; although locals continue to fish, ongoing studies suggest that nearly half of all the fish in the lake are unsafe to consume on a regular basis.

There are positive signs that environmental efforts are working. In the Adirondacks, moose are returning in greater numbers, mostly from Canada. The same is true for many birds of prey, including the bald eagle, peregrine falcon and osprey.

The ongoing efforts to preserve many of the wilderness areas of the Adirondacks and elsewhere calls to mind the definition of wilderness as stated in the National Wilderness Preservation Act (1964): 'A wilderness is hereby recognized as an area where the Earth and its community of life are untrammeled by man, where man himself is a visitor who does not remain.'

STATE PARKS & FORESTS

A too-common story by now, of course, is the impact that rapid industrialization has on the land, water and natural resources of any region on earth. In the late 1800s, when commerce and industry were in full swing in New York and much of America, the land was suffering. Destructive logging practices and the pollution of lakes and rivers by careless manufacturing interests were taking their toll on New York's abundant wildlife.

In the 1890s, the citizens of New York acted to make the Adirondacks and the Catskills part of a publicly owned forest preserve. The spirit of this effort is found in the 'Forever Wild' clause of the New York

state constitution, which proclaims: 'The land of the state, now owned or hereafter acquired, constituting the Forest Preserve as now fixed by law, shall be forever kept as wild forest lands. They shall not be leased, sold or exchanged, or be taken by any corporation, public or private, nor shall the timber thereon be sold, removed or destroyed.'

Briefly, more than half of New York state is covered in forests, with over 150 varieties of trees, including several types of pine, spruce, mountain ash, maple and oak. The alpine areas of the Adirondacks remain the most vulnerable to airborne pollutants and damage from hikers and others who visit the area. The Boots rattlesnake root and the alpine birch are two suffering species in particular that are drawing attention.

Much of the forest habitat of New York has improved quite a bit over the years, due mostly to the great efforts of volunteers and nature lovers of all kinds to treat the land with the respect it requires. The habitat is so improved, in fact, that the beaver, once trapped to near-extinction, is now returning in numbers great enough to allow it to be hunted. The same is true for wild turkeys and even Canada geese, whose steadily increasing population is unpopular with farmers who blame them for increasing crop damage.

According to the New York State Department of Environmental Conservation (DEC), other waterfowl, such as the mallard, are dwindling in number due to general environmental factors.

As more has been learned about the effects of acid rain, restocking efforts have grown. Pike, bass, perch and minnows are among those being restocked in great number. To help restore the plankton to the ponds and lakes of the Adirondacks, the DEC is liming these bodies of water. Plankton accumulates near the surface, and its absence in an otherwise clear pond is not a good sign; the sighting of a mallard on the pond is a much better sign.

Among New York state's extensive system of public lands, the Adirondack

Park is the largest (over 900 sq miles) and includes the Adirondack Forest Preserve (established a few years earlier in 1885). Roughly 40% of the park is designated public land, and much of that is pristine wilderness, protected by New York state's 'Forever Wild' clause.

The region is a year-round center for not only wilderness exploring, but also for hiking, canoeing, rock climbing and skiing. Lake Placid is in the heart of the Adirondack High Peaks region. Just northwest of the Adirondacks in the Thousand Islands region, Wellesley Island State Park is a wildlife sanctuary, popular camping area and home to an excellent nature center.

Closer to New York City, Bear Mountain State Park and Harriman State Park are popular hiking and mountain-biking destinations. Also close to New York City is the Rockefeller State Park Preserve, about three miles north of Tarrytown, a peaceful and secluded wooded area, great for walking and birdwatching.

Further north, but less than two hours by car from New York City, one of Washington Irving's favorite haunts, the Catskill Forest Preserve, is home to Kaaterskill Falls and the art and music lovers' town of Woodstock. Minnewaska State Park is nearby, near the town of New Paltz, and is a popular hiking and rock-climbing area.

Further west, in the Finger Lakes region, Taughannock Falls State Park is home to the highest waterfall in the state. Letchworth State Park, south of Rochester, is referred to as the 'Grand Canyon of the East' – rather unfair, because it is a stunning site on its own merits – and takes in the 600 foot deep Genesee River Gorge. Continuing west, Niagara Reservation State Park is home to the largest (not the highest) waterfall of all.

A free *Guide to New York State Operated Parks, Historic Sites and Their Programs* identifies hikes and other outdoor and cultural activities. Request it by writing to this simple address: State Parks, Albany, NY 12238.

GOVERNMENT & POLITICS

Just as it has long been prominent in the arts, culture and business, New York state has always played an outsized role in national politics. Six New Yorkers have been elected president, including two of the country's most important chief executives, Theodore Roosevelt and his cousin Franklin D Roosevelt. More recently, Democratic Governor Mario Cuomo was touted as a possible candidate for the Democratic party's presidential nomination. Though population shifts in the '70s led to the loss of several seats in the US House of Representatives, today the state has an impressive 33 electoral votes, with its congressional delegation of two senators and 31 representatives, the second largest voting block in the country behind California (though Texas is poised to displace New York as the second largest US state following the 2000 census).

New York is politically split between a heavily Democratic New York City and Republican-leaning voters in the rest of the state, and candidates of both parties can do well here in both national and local elections. As a consequence, New York has sent to the US Senate two men who could not be more dissimilar in style and political beliefs: Alfonse D'Amato and Daniel Patrick Moynihan. Known as 'Senator Pothole,' D'Amato is a partisan conservative Republican from the suburbs who has tirelessly pursued federal money for home state projects. The fussy, professorial Moynihan is a four-term liberal Democrat who uses his appearances on the senate floor as opportunities to deliver mini-lectures on government and history.

In the 1980s, formerly Democratic voters in the New York City suburbs became an increasingly unpredictable swing group. With the help of these voters, Bill Clinton beat George Bush in 1992 in New York by 15 percentage points, his largest margin anywhere. Yet Clinton bested that performance in 1996, when he out-polled challenger Bob Dole by 29 percentage points in the state.

But just two years later, suburbanites abandoned incumbent (and nationally popular) Democratic Governor Mario Cuomo following three lackluster terms, instead electing an obscure Republican legislator from Peekskill named George Pataki, a man hand-picked by Senator D'Amato for the nomination. See below for more on Pataki.

New York's governor serves a four-year term, as do the people elected to the three other state-wide offices: lieutenant governor, attorney general and comptroller (chief budget director). There is also a popularly elected legislature consisting of 61 state senators and 150 assembly members, each of whom serves two-year terms. In the state's 62 counties, local issues are decided by a governing board of supervisors, or 'county executive.' The exception to this rule are five counties – or boroughs – of New York City, which are each headed by powerless borough presidents.

For rural politicians who had long complained about being overshadowed by 'down-state interests' – a barely polite euphemism for New York City – Pataki's election heralded a new political climate. With Republicans controlling the senate and strong in the assembly, New York City finds itself with less clout in Albany, especially since its liberal Republican mayor, Rudolph Giuliani, crossed party lines to support Cuomo in the election campaign.

In 1995, Pataki began what promises to be four years of slashing social services and cutting taxes, little of which will help New York City solve its own massive budget problems. Yet both Pataki and Giuliani – in effect, rivals for the leadership of the state Republican party – have forged quiet accommodations on many major issues. Nevertheless, the political tensions between upstate and down-state have renewed the notion, first floated in the '30s, that New York City break away from upstate and declare itself the 51st state. That will never happen, if only because officeholders on both sides of the divide would then find themselves left with a greatly diminished political landscape.

ECONOMY

Though New York is still a national leader in agriculture, commerce and manufacturing, waves of layoffs and business retrenchments contributed to the loss of population and jobs from 1970 to '80. Cities largely dependent on one company for economic stability were particularly hard hit: there is Rochester, home of photographic giant Kodak, and the New York City suburb of Westchester County, where many IBM middle-managers and other 'downsized' workers resided. Even after the rest of the country recovered from the recession of early '90s, New York lagged behind economically and actually lost more than half a million jobs from 1989 to '93. There is a sense, however, that while the unemployment rate, taxes and cost of living in New York remain less favorable than the country as a whole, conditions seem to have stabilized.

Outside of the metropolitan areas, manufacturing is still the dominant concern. The state's production of printed reading materials (see below), precision electronics and heavy machinery contributes $80 billion to the economy and employs more than a million people.

Agriculture is also an important sector. There are more than 35,000 farms in the state producing diary products, apples and a variety of root vegetables. Many of these small farms have been able to supply the demand for organically-grown farm products. The Finger Lakes region and northeastern Long Island are known for wine grape production and their vineyards are tourist attractions.

Surprisingly, slightly more than half of New York's land mass is woodland, and forestry contributes $4 billion to the economy annually through the harvesting of timber for furniture and paper. The state is also country's leading producer of magazines and books, as well the most important market for literature (the majority of quality hardcover books sold in the US are bought in the metropolitan area). Mining of minerals such as salt, sand and gravel add to the economic picture.

NEW YORK

While New York City remains the nexus of world finance, computer technology has made 'Wall Street' more of an e-mail address than a physical location. Companies are increasingly moving their support operations out of expensive, crowded Manhattan to the suburbs and beyond. That has prompted the state to offer large tax incentives – some would say bribes – for corporations to remain.

One consistently bright spot is tourism, which has been a vitally important part of the local economy since with the introduction of the 'I Love New York' ad campaign in the mid-'70s. Visitors now spend more than $24 billion each year, and the travel industry already employs some 700,000 people – numbers that are sure to grow as long as the weak dollar keeps New York a cheap destination for visitors from Europe and Japan, where currencies remain strong against the US dollar.

POPULATION & PEOPLE

With 18 million residents, New York is the third most populous state in the nation, behind California and booming Texas. Three quarters of that total are white; 16% are black and 12% claim Hispanic background. Asians make up 4% of the population.

Approximately half of all state residents live in the New York City area, along with majority of those belonging to major ethnic groups. In fact, 28% of all city residents are foreign-born, buttressing its reputation as the nation's 'melting pot,' though that term seems somewhat quaint and misapplied in this era of enduring ethnic division.

Still, New York City is an example of racial diversity. The city is home to the largest Chinese population in the US, along with the country's largest bloc of Asian Indians. On Labor Day, the West Indian festival is attended by hundreds of thousands of Caribbean-born immigrants. New York City claims to have more Jews than anywhere outside of Israel, more native Greeks than anywhere outside of Athens, more native Russians than anywhere outside of Moscow, and perhaps more native Irish than anywhere outside of the British isles. Differences in culture and undocumented immigration may make some of these boasts statistically unprovable, but a walk through several of the city's neighborhoods leave the impression that the statement is probably not far off the mark.

Blacks

There are about three million blacks living in New York, more than in any other state. African slaves first arrived in New York in 1644, when it was still the Dutch colony of New Netherland. A few were able to obtain freedom. By the time the colonies went to war with Britain the African population numbered about two thousand, and slaves fought on both sides of the conflict in the hope of winning greater freedom. (After the war New York state freed those who fought in the local armed forces.) New York City and other towns around the state became station stops on the Underground Railroad. By the early 19th century, the abolitionist movement had been established in New York City, along with *Freedom's Journal*, the nation's first black newspaper. But voting rights were not bestowed on black males until well after the Civil War, in 1870. At the same time, blacks found themselves losing economic ground to growing numbers of immigrants from Ireland and Eastern Europe.

By the early 20th century, migrating African Americans from the South triggered the development of Harlem in northern Manhattan, helping to create a well-defined community with churches, black-owned businesses and nightclubs that welcomed whites from other neighborhoods. For the first time, a number of West Indian blacks became a significant part of the area's population. But the 'Harlem Renaissance' of the '20s ended abruptly with the Depression.

After WWII, it became clear that blacks were again economically lagging behind more entrenched second and third generation white ethnic groups. Not to mention that American white society was still barring them from schools and business. Yet city officials did little to address the situation until riots broke out in Harlem in 1964. By the 1970s, what was left of the black middle class had abandoned Harlem, following the path paved by white residents to the suburbs. Today recent black immigrants are again from Haiti and other Caribbean islands; 1.8 million African Americans live in New York City, about 27% of the city's total population.

Latin Americans

Hispanics make up 12% of the state's 18 million residents, about 2.1 million people.

About half of New York City's 1.8 million Latin American residents are of Puerto Rican descent, and began migrating from the island in significant numbers during the Depression. Throughout the '60s, political activism by 'Nuyoricans' (noor-EE-cans) led to increasing recognition of their contribution to city life, and the establishment of several important cultural institutions, including the Museo del Barrio near East Harlem, also known as Spanish Harlem.

Over the past 20 years there has been an influx Latinos from many other countries. Immigrants from Ecuador and Colombia have created new communities in Queens, and the Washington Heights section in Manhattan, even further north of Harlem, is home to many former citizens of the Dominican Republic and El Salvador. In fact, Washington Heights has seen the greatest influx of immigrants in the entire city.

Jews

The first Jews, a group of 24 refugees fleeing persecution in Brazil, came to New York in 1654, when it was still a Dutch colony. They have been an important part of the city's population and politics ever since. Until the early 20th century, most of this population lived in Manhattan's Lower East Side, and the neighborhood still retains its traditional character, even though most New Yorkers of Jewish background live elsewhere. In Brooklyn, the neighbor-hoods of Crown Heights and Williamsburg are still home to large numbers of Orthodox Jews, and an influx of immigrants from the former Soviet Union during the '80s added to their numbers. Today Jews comprise 15% of New York City's total population. They are the city's second-largest ethnic voting bloc, behind blacks. In some neighborhoods, most prominently the Crown Heights section of Brooklyn, there have been violent and long-standing tensions between local blacks and the growing community of Orthodox Jews, many of whom have emigrated from the former Soviet Union.

ARTS & EVENTS

New York City is without any doubt the nation's leader in almost every creative endeavor, but you can find art galleries, crafts and first-rate cultural institutions in almost every corner of the state. (See Arts in the Facts about the Region chapter which outlines New York's contributions to each of the categories below.)

Several hundred special events and festivals and take place each year, featuring everything from freshwater fishing in Chautauqua Lake near New York's western border to a marathon reading of *Moby-Dick* in the Long Island village of Sag Harbor. 'Going to the races' in New York can mean donning a jacket and tie to watch the August thoroughbred events held at the elegant Saratoga Springs track or showing up in a T-shirt to catch The Bud at the Glen NASCAR weekend in Watkins Glen.

Visual Arts

The most unique setting for sculpture in the state is the Storm King Art Center in Mountainville (see the Hudson Valley chapter), where more than 100 sculptures are on display in a 400 acre outdoor park that's open from April to November. More than 500,000 people travel annually to the industrial town of Corning to visit the Glass Center. The facility explains the science and art behind glass making and fiber optics, and allows visitors to watch factory workers in action. The nearby Rockwell

Museum houses the largest collection of Western art in the northeast, along with the world's largest collection of Steuben glass objects.

Native American crafts are sold in Salamanca on the Allegheny Reservation and by other tribes at roadside stands throughout the state. The town of Woodstock is host to a thriving group of painters and crafts folk. Columbia County, located on the Massachusetts border, is dotted with many museum-quality antiques galleries with prices to match the wares.

Music

Visitors familiar with Manhattan's abundance of musical styles will find the same range of choices available in the state's smaller cities. Rochester and Buffalo are home to well-regarded classical orchestras. Albany and Syracuse have a selection of venues catering to aficionados of jazz, rock and dance music. A thriving folk scene exists in the college towns of Schenectady, Poughkeepsie and Ithaca, and classical orchestras play in both Rochester and Buffalo. The free Syracuse Jazz Fest, held at the beginning of the summer season, is the largest event of its kind the northeast. The Performing Arts Center in Saratoga Springs is the site of annual visits by the Newport Jazz festival, Philadelphia Orchestra and New York City Opera.

Theater & Film

New York state is part of the 'Straw Hat Circuit' of summertime theatrical events. There's an outdoor Shakespeare festival in Albany's Washington Park, and the Empire State Institute for the Performing Arts stages dance events and plays at 'The Egg,' the capital's oddly shaped theater. Impressive student theatrical performances are regularly held in Troy's Schacht Fine Arts Center.

Many films and television series are shot at least partially in New York City. Recently films made on location are *City Hall*, *Die Hard with a Vengeance* and *Bullets Over Broadway*. The television

series *Law & Order* is one of the few network shows shot entirely in New York, though *NYPD Blue* visits several times a year for extensive location shots.

Movies shot elsewhere in the state include *Ironweed* (Albany), *Nobody's Fool* (the lower Hudson River Valley town of Cold Spring and surroundings) and *Hello Dolly* (Troy). *Niagara*, a steamy 1953 melodrama starring Joseph Cotten and Marilyn Monroe, features fabulous location shots of the famous falls. Independent director Hal Hartley, a Long Island native, returned there for *The Unbelievable Truth* and *Trust*.

RELIGION

Roman Catholics make up the largest single religious group in New York, at 44% of the population, followed by Baptists at 8%. Jews account for 7% of the population, with Methodists, Lutherans, Presbyterians and Episcopalians totaling a combined 13%.

Religious groups and fringe sects have found a home in Sullivan County, nestled among the Catskill Mountains, on the sites of several abandoned Jewish summer camps and resort hotels. The region is now home to Korean fundamentalist Christians, Zen Buddhists, Branch Davidians (followers of the late Texas cult leader David Koresh) and at least one ashram.

In New York City alone, often derided by outsiders as some sort of modern-day Sodom, there are over 6000 places of worship, including everything from Buddhist temples and kingdom halls used by Jehovah's Witnesses. Muslims have been part of the city's religious landscape since the late '50s, and now number more than 500,000. Most adherents follow the Sunni Islam tradition. In 1991, a huge new mosque opened at 96th St and Third Ave, a monument to the city's fastest growing religion.

LANGUAGE

New York is such a varied and large place that it is ludicrous to identify state-wide language patterns. In general, people who live in rural areas and fisherman on the eastern end of Long Island tend to speak in a clear but more deliberate manner. Terms of language tend to change as you move about the state – in New York City, if you want a soft drink, you ask for a 'soda,' but further north, the same thing is called a glass of 'pop.'

You will immediately recognize the elongated vowels of New York City dwellers, the reality sounds like a much milder version of the 'Noo Yawk Tawk' popularized in films and television. Older residents often have a strange cadence in their voices, pronouncing 'Broadway' and 'receipt' with a heavy emphasis on the *first* syllable. The New York accent grows stronger in the outer boroughs, provided the person you're speaking to wasn't born in another country! It's melting-pot history is partly the reason the city has such an interesting dialect – who knows whether Italian, Yiddish, Russian, French, Irish or whatever has had the most influence?

The city's huge Hispanic population has led to the emergence of Spanish as a semi-official second language. But so far, a Spanish-English hybrid has not developed for popular use, though everyone knows that a *bodega* is Spanish for a street corner convenience store.

It's easier to identify common phrases used or at least recognized by most New Yorkers, though even this is tricky because rap music is changing English in profound but as yet uncharted ways. But even the meaning of phrases changes from neighborhood to neighborhood: asking for a 'regular' coffee in Midtown means you'll get it with milk and a bit of sugar. The same request at a Wall Street area shop will lead the server to immediately throw three heaping spoonfuls of the sweet stuff in the cup, because that's the way the hyper stock brokers and lawyers like it served. A few sample words and phrases:

Big time – an all-out effort or massively good thing; eg 'I'm going to get a big time raise.'

Enough already – a less than polite request to stop; eg 'Enough already with your questions.'

Potholes – The ubiquitous craters in city streets that can mangle car tires or send in-line skaters flying.

Putz – an idiot

Schmuck – an idiot

Step lively – Subway conductor's command to commuters as he closes the doors on a train.

The whole nine yards – an all-out effort, no costs spared; construction worker lingo derived from the maximum capacity of a cement truck, which is nine cubic yards.

If all this is too confusing, then just remember the New Yorker's all-purpose phrase of general amazement and/or exasperation: 'You gotta be fuckin' kidding me.'

INFORMATION
Tourist Offices
See the Facts for the Visitor chapter for listings of New York state tourist offices. For a free copy of the *I Love New York* travel guide, call the Empire State Development office (☎ (800) 225-5697).

The Empire State Development office divides New York state into 11 tourist regions; the regions often subdivide themselves into sub-regions by county or geographical features such as islands (Long Island) or mountains (Adirondacks). See the regional chapter information headings and destination headings for chambers of commerce or convention and visitors bureaus.

Rural New York is well known for a variety of quality farms and orchards, roadside markets and stands and 'pick-your-own' farms. The New York State Department of Agriculture and Markets, 1 Winners Circle, Albany, NY 12235, issues a fruit and vegetable harvest calendar called the *New York State Guide to Farm Fresh Food* which is available by region.

Taxes
New York state imposes a sales tax of 7% on goods, most services and prepared foods. New York City imposes an additional 1.25% tax, bringing the total surcharge to 8.25%. Several categories of so-called

'luxury items' – including rental cars and dry cleaning – carry an additional city surcharge of 5%, so you wind up seeing 13.25% added to those bills.

Hotel rooms in New York City are subject 13.25% tax plus a flat $2 per night occupancy tax. Believe it or not, that reflects a reduction in the previous hotel tax.

Fishing

Anyone over the age of 16 needs a license to freshwater fish. The state Department of Conservation (DEC; ☎ 518-457-3521) in Albany establishes license fees and seasonal species regulations for each year (from October 1 to September 30). Non-resident adult license fees are $35 for the season, $20 for five days and $11 for one day, with discounts for students and seniors. Licenses are available at DEC regional offices, some state campgrounds, sporting goods stores and similar outfits. Mail order applications may be obtained in advance by writing to: DEC License Sales, 50 Wolf Rd, Room 111, Albany, NY 12233-4790.

New York City

Let other, more modest municipalities claim to be leading centers of manufacturing and agriculture, or serve as the capitals of their nations. New York City reserves for itself the only title that matters: 'The Capital of the World.' And the city has the arrogance to hang banners saying so along its avenues.

That boast has some validity: long after it ceased to be the geographic and political center of its nation, New York has continued to dominate the popular imagination. It has gained, then lost primacy in many different important endeavors, including politics, agriculture, manufacturing, shipping, as well as film and TV production. New Yorkers are thus conditioned by history to expect that their city will soon find a new activity to exploit, and remain ever-confident that no rival will ever equal it as a center for cultural and intellectual pursuits.

Numbers tell much of the story: with seven million residents, New York City has more than twice as many people as Los Angeles, the second largest US city. All these people are packed into 309 sq miles of space, just about 75% of Los Angeles County's total land mass. From this density comes New York's intensity.

Not that New Yorkers much notice it. Every day, they blithely stroll past – or live in – buildings that would dominate the skylines of almost any other major city. Yet this immensity of scale – and the crowding of so many colors and cultures within its borders – is what stuns people from more homogeneous locales. Many of the 27 million people who visit annually are conditioned by Hollywood (and lazy journalists) to assume that New York is a mayhem-ridden nightmare and often arrive gripped by a caution that borders on paranoia.

Yes, some of the clichés are true: a New Yorker talks faster and closer to your face – than just about anyone else. The European *pension* tradition never took hold

Tourists' Top 10
1 Broadway Theaters
   (9.5 million visitors)
2 Metropolitan Museum of Art
   (4.9 million)
3 Statue of Liberty/Ellis Island
   (4 million)
4 Empire State Building
   (3.1 million)
5 American Museum of
   Natural History
   (3 million)
6 Bronx Zoo
   (2 million)
7 World Trade Center/
   World Financial Center
   (1.8 million)
8 Museum of Modern Art
   (1.5 million)
9 Circle Line
   (1.2 million)
10 Guggenheim Museum/
   Guggenheim SoHo
   (1 million) ■

there, making it difficult, and at some times of the year nearly impossible, to find low cost accommodation. To survive in this crowded atmosphere, people close in on themselves. It could be argued that the city's reputation for rudeness – such as its citizens' habit of never standing to the right and walking to the left on escalators or thoughtlessly burying their faces in books – is simply the survival instinct carried to the *nth* degree. But contrary to New York's tough image, locals are regularly gracious and helpful to tourists, sometimes even

The Big Apple

It has long been thought that New York City was dubbed 'The Big Apple' by jazz musicians who regarded a gig in Harlem as a sure sign that they had made it to the top. But Barry Popik, a judge with the city's Parking Violations Bureau and an amateur historian, did extensive research into the phrase and came up with a surprising new answer. He discovered that the term first appeared in the 1920s when it was used by a writer named John FitzGerald who covered the horse races for the *Morning Telegraph*. Apparently stable hands in a New Orleans racetrack called a trip to a New York racecourse 'the Big Apple' – or greatest reward – for any talented thoroughbred. The slang passed into popular usage long after the newspaper – and FitzGerald – had disappeared. But to Popik's great annoyance, few city officials are eager to set the record straight, and so tourist literature still attributes the phrase to unnamed jazzmen. ∎

excuse themselves if they bump into you, and love to give directions, if only because visitor queries cater to their self-perceived expertise on the city.

Thanks to well-targeted community policing, along with a general decline in crime nationwide, New York is now one of the safest cities in the country. It is not even in the top 10 of the major US cities for violent crimes – in fact New York ranks about 130th among cities with populations of 100,000 people or more, with a crime rate lower than places like Washington, DC, Atlanta, St Petersburg and Birmingham. So the bottom line is that you should exercise sensible caution when visiting – just as you would in a city with a calmer reputation.

Being 'on' may be the New York style, but there isn't any particular look you can adopt to fit in here – practically anything goes. Yet even the most confident tourist can be marked as an outsider in dozens of tiny ways, such as actually looking up at the buildings you pass, crossing the street at a corner instead of jaywalking, or attempting to read the *New York Times* on a packed subway train without first folding it lengthwise and then in half.

All this required energy makes New York an exhausting holiday destination. This mega-city demands that you assault it with a game plan. Define your sightseeing priorities and get to them ahead of anyone else. Along the way, serendipitous occurrences will unfold, if only because some of the city's best entertainment can be found free on the streets.

That's why people feel a rush when they hit the streets from a hotel doorway or emerge from a subway station. They're about to experience something of a dysfunctional miracle.

HISTORY

The area now known as New York City had been occupied by Native Americans for more than 11,000 years before Giovanni da Verrazano, a Florentine hired by the French to explore the American northeastern coast, arrived in 1524. After his brief visit, no serious attempt was made to document the area or its peoples until 1609, when English explorer Henry Hudson, on a mission to find the Northwest Passage, anchored *Halve Maen (Half Moon)* in the harbor for 10 days before continuing up the river. 'It is as beautiful a land as one can hope to tread upon,' reported Hudson.

The local Munsee tribe had several names for the region, including *Manahatouh* ('place of gathering bow wood'), *Manahactanienk* ('place of general inebriation') and *Menatay* ('the island'). The name of Manhattan can be traced to any one of these words.

Colonial Era

By 1625, the first Dutch settlers were dispatched to establish a trading post they eventually called New Amsterdam, the seat of a much larger colony called New Netherland. Historians generally agree that the story behind the purchase of the island from local tribes for goods worth 60 guilders ($24), while sounding mythological, may actually be true (though a more accurate exchange rate for the goods would be about $600 – still a bargain).

In 1647, a new governor named Peter Stuyvesant arrived to impose order on what the Dutch government considered an unruly colony. His ban on alcohol and curtailment of religious freedoms caused unrest among the settlers, and few regretted the bloodless takeover of New Amsterdam by the British in 1664.

Renamed New York, in honor of King Charles II's brother the Duke of York, the port town retained much of its Dutch character well into the mid-18th century. By that time, opposition to the excesses of British colonial rule had developed and was given voice by John Peter Zenger's influential newspaper the *Weekly Journal*. Though many influential New Yorkers resisted a war for independence, New York's Commons – where City Hall stands today – was the center of many anti-British protests. King George III's troops controlled New York for most of the Revolutionary War and took their time going home, finally withdrawing in 1783, a full two years after the fighting stopped.

Boom Years

By the time George Washington was sworn in as president of the new republic on the balcony of Federal Hall on Wall St in 1789, New York was a bustling seaport of 33,000 people. The new congress abandoned the city after establishing the District of Columbia the following year. The move was probably driven by a dislike of the city by the founding fathers – Thomas Jefferson later said that he regarded New York to be a 'cloacina (sewer) of all the depravities of human nature.'

New York boomed in the early 19th century, and by 1830 its population approached 250,000. The $12 million Croton Aqueduct, completed in 1842, brought 72 million gallons of fresh water to the city each day, which not only improved public health conditions but finally allowed residents the opportunity to bathe regularly.

New York has always had wide gaps between the rich and poor and tensions between different racial groups. In the summer of 1863, poor Irish immigrants launched the 'draft riots,' in large part because of a provision that allowed wealthy men to pay $300 in order to avoid being conscripted to fight in the Civil War. Within days the rioters turned their anger on black citizens, who they considered the reason for the war and their main competition for work. More than 11 men were lynched in the streets and a black orphans' home was burned to the ground.

The years following the Union victory in the Civil War were a gilded age for both private and public figures. William Magear Tweed, notorious boss of the city's Tammany Hall Democratic organization, used public works projects to steal millions of dollars from the public treasury before being toppled from power. Meanwhile, robber barons like railroad speculator Jay Gould were able to amass tax-free fortunes that approached $100 million.

Growing Pains

As New York City's population more than doubled from 515,547 in 1850 to 1,164,673 in 1880, a tenement culture developed: the poorest New Yorkers invariably worked in dangerous factories and lived in squalid apartment blocks. The work of crusading journalist Jacob Riis, who chronicled how this 'other half' lived, shocked the city's middle class and led to the establishment of an independent health board as well as a series of workplace reforms. Meanwhile, millionaires like Andrew Carnegie (see biographical sidebar in Southwest Pennsylvania chapter), John D Rockefeller (see biographical sidebar in the Hudson Valley chapter) and John Jacob Astor began pouring money into public works, leading to the creation of institutions such as the New York Public Library in 1895.

The burgeoning of New York's population beyond the city's official borders led to the consolidation movement, as the city and its neighboring districts struggled to service the growing numbers. Residents of the independent districts of Queens, Staten Island, the Bronx and financially strapped Brooklyn voted to become 'boroughs' of New York City in 1898.

This new metropolis absorbed a second huge wave of European immigrants, and its population exploded once again, from just over three million in 1900 to seven million in 1930. During this period, horse-drawn trolleys were abandoned as a major network of underground subways and elevated trains ('els') made the city's outer reaches easily accessible.

During the Depression, a crusading mayor named Fiorello La Guardia fought municipal corruption and expanded the social service network, meanwhile civic planner Robert Moses used his politically appointed position as a parks commissioner to wield power without the obligation of answering to voters. He used that influence to remake the city's landscape through public works projects and highways that glorified the car culture and disdained public transportation. Unfortunately, Moses had the power of a modern-day Baron Haussmann but none of the master's aesthetic sense; his projects (which include the Triborough Bridge, Lincoln Center, several highways and Lower East Side projects) often destroyed entire neighborhoods and routed huge numbers of residents.

Tailspin & Renewal

While New York emerged from WWII proud and ready for business, the middle class began abandoning the city for its suburbs. Television production, manufacturing jobs and even the fabled Brooklyn Dodgers baseball team moved to the West Coast, along with the Dodgers' cross-town rivals the New York Giants.

By the '70s, the unreliable, graffiti-ridden subway system became an internationally recognized symbol of New York's psychic and economic tailspin. Only a massive federal loan program saved the city from bankruptcy.

During the anything-goes Reagan years, the city regained much of its swagger as billions were made on Wall St. Ed Koch,

the colorful and opinionated three term mayor, embodied a New Yorker's ability to charm and irritate at the same time. But in 1989, he was defeated in a Democratic primary election by David Dinkins, who went on the become the city's first black mayor. Dinkins, consistently criticized for merely presiding over a city government in need of reform, was narrowly defeated for a second term by moderate Republican Rudolph Giuliani. Because the current mayor conveys all the charm of a high school detention officer, his efforts to curtail excesses in city government and overhaul the troubled school system have stalled. Polls show that he is more respected than liked. But thanks to the big drop in crime and the weakness of his Democratic machine opponents (including Dinkins), Giuliani was widely regarded as unbeatable in the 1997 mayoral election. And for the first time in decades, the city is talking about starting huge (and necessary) projects to rebuild its infrastructure, such as a new rail tunnel under the Hudson River.

Strangely enough, New Yorkers head into the next millennium with the somewhat grudging feeling that, perhaps, the city has found a way to thrive as well as survive. But one thing seems certain: this is a very good time to visit New York.

ORIENTATION

Islands make up most of New York City's 309 sq mile land mass. Manhattan and Staten Island stand alone; Queens and Brooklyn comprise the western end of Long Island. Only the Bronx is connected to the US mainland.

The water gap between Brooklyn and Staten Island – the 'narrows' through which the first Europeans entered the area – serves as the entrance to New York Harbor, which is also accessible to ships from the north via Long Island Sound. Manhattan itself is bordered by two bodies of water, on the west by the Hudson River and on the east by the East River, both technically estuaries subject to tidal fluctuations.

Served by three major airports, two train terminals and a massive bus depot, New

York City is the most important transportation hub in the northeast. I-95, which runs from Maine to Florida, cuts through the city as the Cross Bronx Expressway. Via I-95, Boston is 194 miles to the north, Philadelphia 104 miles to the south and Washington, DC, is 235 miles south.

Manhattan

Most of Manhattan is extremely easy to navigate, thanks to a street plan imposed by a city planning commission in 1811 for the area north of Houston St. It created the current grid system of 14 named or numbered avenues running the north-south length of the island, crossed by east- west numbered streets. (If you intend to do a lot of walking, be aware that along the avenues 20 blocks is approximately one mile.)

Because the grid system was established long before the advent of the automobile, modern Manhattan suffers from tremendous traffic congestion, giving rise to the term 'gridlock.' This street plan had at least one other unintended consequence: the narrow streets precluded the creation of grand avenues in the European tradition, and discouraged the creation of buildings set back on large tracts of property. There was nowhere to go but up – and by the late 19th century Manhattan had a cluster of 'skyscrapers,' as prominent multistory office buildings were called.

Above Washington Square, Fifth Ave serves as the dividing line between the 'East Side' and the 'West Side.' Cross-street numbers begin there and grow higher toward each river, generally (but not exclusively) in 100-digit increments per block. Therefore, the Hard Rock Cafe, at 221 W 57th St, is slightly less than three blocks west of Fifth Ave.

Most New Yorkers give out addresses in shorthand by listing the cross street first and the avenue second, eg, 'we're at 33rd and Third.' If you are given an address on an avenue – such as '1271 Sixth Ave' – be sure to ask for the nearest cross street.

In the oldest part of New York City, from 14th St to the southern tip of Manhattan, travel becomes a bit trickier. Streets that

perhaps began as cow paths or merchants' byways snake along in a haphazard manner, which is why it is possible today to stand at the corner of W 4th St and W 10th St in Greenwich Village.

Broadway, the only avenue to cut diagonally across the island, was originally a woodland path used by Native Americans; it runs in some form from the tip of the island all the way to the state capital of Albany, 150 miles away. Today Wall St stands at the place where, in 1653, the Dutch residents of New Amsterdam constructed a wooden barrier at the town's northern border to ward off attacks from hostile natives.

Outer Boroughs

The grid plan is repeated in the other boroughs, with streets such as Northern Blvd in Queens laid over the old country pathways to the once-rural eastern areas of Long Island.

Neighborhoods

There's no method to the names that New Yorkers have given their neighborhoods. They can be purely geographical (the Lower East Side), ethnically descriptive (Chinatown) or just plain scary (Hell's Kitchen). Tribeca is the precious name given to the 'Triangle Below Canal St' that passed into popular use, as did SoHo, the square area south of Houston St.

Some have long outgrown their designations. Few residents of Chelsea know their area was named after an 18th century farm owned by a British army officer. Turtle Bay, a fashionable enclave surrounding the United Nations on the East Side of Manhattan, is named after a riverside cove that was drained in 1868.

The Upper East Side and Upper West Side include the areas above 59th St on either side of Central Park. Midtown generally refers to the largely commercial district from 59th St south to 34th St, an area which includes Rockefeller Center, Times Square, the Broadway theater district, major hotels, Grand Central Terminal and the Port Authority Bus Terminal.

Significant neighborhoods in the outer boroughs include Arthur Ave, Riverdale and City Island in the Bronx; Brooklyn Heights, Park Slope, Williamsburg and Brighton Beach in Brooklyn; and Astoria, Jackson Heights, Forest Hills and Flushing Meadows in Queens.

Maps

Good street plans are usually given away free in the lobby of any decent hotel. The *Streetwise* series of laminated, pocket-sized maps covers many specific neighborhoods and these maps are available at bookstores and better newsstands. If you want to explore the city at large, buy a five-borough street atlas. *Geographia* and *Hagstrom* both publish paperback-sized editions for under $10.

Most subway stations in Manhattan have 'Passenger Information Centers' next to the token booth with a wonderfully detailed map of the surrounding neighborhood, with all points of interests clearly marked. Taking a look before heading up the stairs may save you from getting lost.

You can get maps at the Hagstrom Map and Travel Center (☎ (212) 398-1222), 57 W 43rd St, and the Rand McNally Travel Store (☎ (212) 758-7488), 150 E 52nd St, which ships globes and atlases worldwide. Both stores sell colorful wall maps of Manhattan made by the Identity Map Company for about $25. Though not practical for walking the city, these wonderfully detailed maps make a great souvenir of your trip.

INFORMATION
Tourist Offices

The New York Convention and Visitors Bureau (☎ (800) 692-8474, fax (212) 245-5943; subway: 59th St–Columbus Circle) is located at Two Columbus Circle and is open from 9 am to 6 pm Monday to Friday and 10 am to 3 pm weekends and holidays. The 24 hour toll-free line offers information on special events and reservations. Callers from outside the US and Canada can access the service by dialing ☎ (212) 397-8222.

The Manhattan Borough President's office has established a Big Apple Greeters Program (☎ (212) 669-2896, fax (212) 669-4900), through which 500 volunteers welcome visitors to the city by offering free tours of lesser-known neighborhoods. Some greeters are multi-lingual and specialize in helping the disabled. Reservations must be made at least two days in advance.

The New York State tourist bureau (☎ (800) 225-5697) is located at 1515 Broadway at 45th St on the 52nd floor.

Foreign Consulates

The UN's presence in New York means that nearly every country in the world maintains diplomatic offices here. Check the Manhattan yellow pages under Consulates for a complete up-to-date listing. Some foreign consulates are:

Australia
    636 Fifth Ave, New York, NY 10011
    (☎ (212) 408-8400)
Canada
    1251 Sixth Ave, New York, NY 10020
    (☎ (212) 596-1700)
France
    934 Fifth Ave, New York, NY 10021
    (☎ (212) 606-3600)
Germany
    460 Park Ave, New York, NY 10022
    (☎ (212) 308-8700)
Ireland
    345 Park Ave, New York, NY 10154
    (☎ (212) 319-2555)
New Zealand
    780 Third Ave, Suite 1904, New York, NY
    10017 (☎ (212) 832-4038)
Spain
    150 E 58th St, New York, NY 10155
    (☎ (212) 355-4080)

Money

Given the prevalence of automated teller machines (ATMs) in New York City, you may draw cash directly from a home bank account, provided it is linked with the Cirrus or Plus networks. ATM fees are usually about $3; foreign-currency exchange commissions range from $3 to $5. Most New York banks are linked by the NYCE (New York Cash Exchange) system, and you can use local bank cards interchangeably at ATMs.

Chase Manhattan Bank's branch at the corner of Liberty and William Sts downtown offers a commission-free foreign-currency exchange service from 8 am to 3 pm Monday to Friday.

Thomas Cook Foreign Exchange has eight locations in the city. The Times Square office (☎ (212) 265-6049), 1590 Broadway at 48th St, is open Monday to Saturday from 9 am to 6 pm and Sunday from 9 am to 5 pm. American Express has an office in Bloomingdale's, 59th St and Lexington Ave (☎ (212) 705-3171), as well as offices at 374 Park Ave (☎ (212) 421-8240), 65 Broadway (☎ (212) 493-6500) and 150 E 42nd St (☎ (212) 687-3700).

Chequepoint (☎ (212) 750-2400) offers less-favorable rates at its office at 22 Central Park South and several other locations.

Banks are normally open Monday through Friday, usually from 9 am to 3 pm. The Chase Manhattan branch in Chinatown at the corner of Mott and Canal Sts is open seven days. Several other banks along Canal St also offer weekend hours.

Post

The main post office (☎ (212) 967-8585), 421 Eighth Ave at the corner of 33rd St (zip: 10001), is open 24 hours a day. The Rockefeller Center post office in the basement under 610 Fifth Ave is open Monday to Friday from 9:30 am to 5:30 pm.

The post office at Franklin D Roosevelt Station (☎ (212) 330-5549), 909 Third Ave at 55th St (zip: 10022), is open for most postal business from 9 am to 8 pm.

Poste restante mail is accepted at the main post office provided it is marked 'General Delivery.' This method is not recommended or reliable. The American Express office at 150 E 42nd St (zip: 10022) also offers a mail hold for cardholders.

Telephone & Fax

There are thousands of pay telephones on the streets, but those maintained by NYNEX, the local utility (soon to be called Bell Atlantic following a merger) are much more reliable than the others. Be particu-

KIM GRANT
Astounding! Three working phones!

larly careful about dialing long distance with a credit card on an unaffiliated phone; you may end up with a whopping bill from an unscrupulous long distance firm. It's much better to use the access lines of major carriers such as AT&T (☎ (800) 321-0288) or MCI (☎ (800) 888-8000).

Petty vandalism has led NYNEX to install dozens of telecard operated phones on subway platforms and near heavily trafficked street corners. Unfortunately, $5 and $10 telecards for these distinctive yellow phones are sold only at a relative handful of newsstands and pharmacies. Bodegas and many convenience stores sell pre-paid phone cards, but the key is to use these cards on a reliable public phone.

Directories are no longer provided at outdoor phone booths, so if you're unsure of a number dial ☎ 411 for information; it's a free call. However, NYNEX operators try to avoid providing addresses as a way to get you to spend a quarter on a call to the establishment you are looking for.

Kinko's (☎ (212) 308-2679), 16 E 52nd St, offers 24 hour fax service in addition to its computer and photocopying services at this office and nine other locations in Manhattan. Check the yellow pages under 'copying' for the closest location of a Kinko's or equivalent service.

Travel Agencies

Council Travel offers bookings at three sites: 148 W 4th St (☎ (212) 254-2525), 895 Amsterdam Ave (☎ (212) 666-4177) and at 205 E 42nd St (☎ (212) 661-1450).

STA Travel (☎ (212) 627-3111) is at 10 Downing St on Sixth Ave. The main American Express travel office (☎ (212) 421-8240), at 374 Park Ave, offers package deals. AAA (☎ (212) 757-2000), the 'auto club,' has offices at 1881 Broadway.

Bucket Shops Consolidators, or 'bucket shops,' are travel agencies that sell last-minute flights on scheduled carriers. They are located in Midtown office buildings and advertise weekly in the *Village Voice* and Sunday *New York Times*. Call around to get the best price, since some agencies have consolidator deals with only a handful of specific airlines. TFI Tours (☎ (212) 736-1140), 34 W 32nd St, is one of the few that accepts credit cards. Now Voyager (☎ (212) 431-1616) books courier flights and last-minute domestic specials. It's best to call their busy office after business hours to hear a voice menu of locations and conditions.

Bookstores

General There are several Barnes & Noble 'superstores': Union Square (☎ (212) 253-0810), Astor Place (☎ (212) 420-1322), 675 Sixth Ave at 22nd St (☎ (212) 727-1227), and 2289 Broadway at 82nd St (☎ (212) 362-8835). Each features over 200,000 titles, a music department, comfortable seating and a cafe where patrons can read magazines for free. The stores stay open from 9 am to 10 pm, seven days a week.

The Gotham Book Mart (☎ (212) 719-4448), 41 W 47th St, is one of the city's premier stand-alone shops; its trademark shingle declares that 'wise men fish here.' Coliseum Books (☎ (212) 757-8381), 1771 Broadway, has a huge selection of paperback fiction and out-of-print titles. Shakespeare and Co is a general interest shop with three locations: downtown at 716 Broadway (☎ (212) 529-1330), in the financial district at 1 Whitehall St (☎ (212) 742-7025) and on the Upper East Side at 939 Lexington Ave (☎ (212) 570-0201).

Three Lives (☎ (212) 741-2069), a Greenwich Village institution at 154 W 10th St, stocks a good number of biographies. Books and Co (☎ (212) 737-1450),

939 Madison Ave, is a distinguished store that has attracted dozens of major authors for readings; photos of their appearances line the walls. It's open from 10 am to 7 pm Monday to Saturday and 12 pm to 6 pm Sundays.

St Marks Book Shop (☎ (212) 260-7853), 31 Third Ave, specializes in political literature, poetry and academic journals.

The handsome Rizzoli store sells art books and general interest titles at two locations: 31 W 57th St (☎ (212) 759-2424) and 454 West Broadway (☎ (212) 674-1616).

Used The Strand (☎ (212) 473-1452), 828 Broadway, boasts of having eight miles of used books and review copies. The Argosy (☎ (212) 753-4455), 116 E 59th St, features estate sales and rare prints (it's closed Sundays). The dusty and colorful Chelsea Books and Records (☎ (212) 465-4340) can be found at 111 W 17th St.

Travel Travel titles and maps can be found at the Traveller's Bookstore (☎ (212) 664-0995) in the Time Warner building, 22 E 52nd St. The Complete Traveller (☎ (212) 685-9007), 199 Madison Ave (corner of 35th St), also offers an interesting selection of first editions and old Baedecker guides.

Civilized Traveler has two locations, on the Upper West Side at 2003 Broadway (☎ (212) 875-0306) and at 2 World Financial Center, 25 Liberty St (☎ (212) 786-3301).

Gay Every decent bookstore now includes a gay and lesbian department. A Different Light Bookstore (☎ (212) 989-4850), 151 W 19th St, has 15,000 titles on gay themes. It's open from 10 am to midnight and features a small cafe, several author readings a week and a free Sunday night movie series.

Gay Pleasures Books (☎ (212) 255-5756), 546-548 Hudson St, features gay titles and stocks magazines and all the entertainment weeklies.

Specialty Titles Applause Theater Books (☎ (212) 496-7511), 211 W 71 St, carries screenplays and film essays. The Drama

NEW YORK

Book Shop (☎ (212) 944-0595), in Times Square at 723 Seventh Ave, has the city's largest selection of plays.

Books of Wonder (☎ (212) 989-3270), at 16 W 18th St, carries children's titles and young adult fiction and is open from 10 am to 7 pm Monday to Saturday and 11 am to 6 pm Sunday.

East-West Books (☎ (212) 243-5994), 78 Fifth Ave, has a large stock of titles on Buddhism and Asian philosophies.

Whodunit lovers are served by the Mysterious Bookshop (☎ (212) 765-0900), 129 W 56th St, and Murder Ink (☎ (212) 362-8905), at 2486 Broadway.

Libraries

The main branch of the New York Public Library (☎ (212) 930-0800) on Fifth Ave at 42nd St is a significant architectural attraction and worth visiting if only to see the famous 3rd-floor reading room. Those looking for periodicals and book information will find fewer crowds at the Midtown Manhattan annex directly across Fifth Ave, or at the Jefferson Market branch (☎ (212) 243-4334), 425 Sixth Ave.

Media

Want a definition of 'information overload'? Walk into a well-stocked Manhattan newsstand. It's hard to determine a single best source for entertainment listings – each periodical tends to emphasize a particular type.

Newspapers & Magazines The *New York Times* (60¢, $2.50 Sunday) is still the nation's premier newspaper, with more foreign bureaus and reporters than any other publication in the world. Its Friday Weekend Section is an invaluable guide to cultural events. The *Wall Street Journal* is must reading for financial workers – though it has an excellent Washington bureau, the daily one column digest of world events won't be enough to satisfy news junkies. The *Daily News*, owned by real estate developer Mort Zuckerman, and *New York Post*, Rupert Murdoch's pale imitation of a London tabloid, are locked in permanent combat for readers. Each paper's business sections appear to exist solely to poke fun of the rival owner's financial interests.

The fabled *New Yorker* magazine (see sidebar in the Facts about the Region chapter) continues its 70 year tradition of publishing news, fiction and critical reviews, along with a new fixation on celebrity that has offended many older readers. The magazine's Goings on about Town section lists major art, cinema and music events. *New York* magazine does the same thing for its younger and more restaurant-oriented readers. The *Village Voice* (distributed free in Manhattan each Wednesday), is well known for its night life listings for the mainstream clubs and music venues. It's also the best-known source for fee-free rental apartments and roommate situations. The *New York Observer*, a weekly newspaper for people obsessed with the local media and politics, strives for quirkier listings of literary readings and parties in its 'Eight Day Week' column.

Into this fray comes *Time Out New York*, which is published Wednesdays and costs $1.95. It has the same format as its London cousin and has a very good section on gay and lesbian events. The magazine's features are unimpressive, but the comprehensive listings are the main selling point.

Where New York is the best free monthly guide to mainstream city events. Available at most hotels, it's more useful than two pocket-sized rivals, *The New York Quick Guide*, a monthly, and *City Guide*, published weekly.

Gay clubs and bars catering to every taste are listed in the free sheets *HX\Homo Xtra* and *Next*, which are given away free at most restaurants and bars. Other gay-oriented publications include the literary magazine *Christopher Street* ($3), and the weekly *New York Native*. The latter has a good bar directory and is widely distributed free in clubs, as is *Metrosource*, a lifestyle magazine.

Radio There are over 100 radio stations in the city, but most 'narrowcast' only one type of programming. This is particularly true on FM, where 'radio apartheid' exists and it's impossible to receive hip hop and rock on the same frequency.

On AM frequencies, WABC (770) is a talk radio station and home to conservative icon Rush Limbaugh. WOR (710), one of the nation's oldest stations, carries a calmer type of talk and WFAN (660) is a 24 hour sports station. WQEW (1560) broadcasts big band music and Sinatra standards. Spanish speakers listen to WKDM (1380) and WADO (1280). WWRL (1660) is a talk station aimed at the city's black community.

WCBS (880) and WINS (1010) carry news and weather updates every 10 minutes and WNYC-AM (820) broadcasts NPR.

On FM, classical music lovers turn to WNYC (93.9) and WQXR (96.3), which includes reviews and news reports from its owner, the *New York Times*. WBGO (88.3) carries National Public Radio in the morning and commercial-free jazz the rest of the day.

The best top-40/rock mixture can be found on WHTZ (100.3). WBLS (107.5) is a premier spot for soft black music, while WQHT (97.1) is known as 'Hot 97' for its hip hop and rap programming. At the moment, there are at least five stations broadcasting the tired format of 'classic rock.' Those seeking the widest musical variety should listen to WKCR (89.9) and WFMU (90.1), fringe stations with eclectic programming.

TV The comedian Fred Allen once said that TV was called a medium because 'nothing on it was either rare or well done.' A night watching the tube will prove the truth of his quip. The flagship stations of all four major networks – NBC, CBS, ABC and FOX – are located in New York City and carry familiar evening prime-time fare.

Cable carries well-known networks like CNN, MTV and HBO. Channels dedicated to sports, culture, history and old movies are available. News broadcasts from Britain, Ireland, France, Mexico, Greece, Korea, Japan and Germany also appear on

international channels each night between 7 and 11 pm. Manhattan cable also carries dozens of local amateur programs on the 'public access' channels. You can find everything from a strip show to a discussion of city real estate values on the air.

Campuses

New York is home to many world class private universities and fine public colleges, including Columbia, New York and Fordham universities, The New School for Social Research, the Cooper Union, and the various colleges of the City University of New York (CUNY). These urban educational centers are not physically separated from the city – in fact NYU's campus and dorm facilities are distributed throughout Greenwich Village. Columbia's main campus is set back from Broadway in Upper Manhattan and the City College campus of CUNY at St Nicholas Terrace is significant for its neo-Gothic design and worth a visit (subway: 137th St–City College).

Cultural Centers

New York City's major cultural centers include:

Alliance Française
　　22 E 60th St (☎ (212) 355-6100)
Asia Society
　　725 Park Ave (☎ (212) 288-6400)
Czech Center
　　1109 Madison Ave (☎ (212) 288-0830)
Goethe Institute
　　1014 Fifth Ave (☎ (212) 439-8700)
Hispanic Society of America
　　Broadway and 155th St (☎ (212) 690-0743)
Italian Cultural Institute
　　686 Park Ave (☎ (212) 879-4242)
Japan House
　　333 E 47th St (☎ (212) 832-1155)
Spanish Institute
　　684 Park Ave (☎ (212) 628-0420)
Swiss Institute
　　495 Broadway (☎ (212) 925-2035)

Laundry

Many New Yorkers live in apartments without laundry facilities, so most residential neighborhoods have an abundance of laundries. *Suds Cafe and Laundromat* (☎ (212) 741-2366), at 141 W 10th St, has a reputation as a social scene. It is open from 7 am to 10 pm daily.

Washing-machines generally cost $1.25 for a 25 minute cycle; dryers are $1.50 for 30 minutes. Many facilities offer pick-up laundry services at a rate of about $1 per pound of clothing.

Toilets
New York is not friendly to the weak of bladder. The explosion in the homeless population in the 1970s led to the closure of subway bathrooms and most facilities turn away non-patrons from bathrooms. However, it is possible to walk into a crowded bar or restaurant to use the bathroom if you are discreet and well dressed.

At the moment, there is just one modern public toilet, in the north end of City Hall Park, which is a model for an aborted series of public toilets. It costs 25¢ and almost no one knows about it.

Women Travelers
The subway should not be shunned by solo female travelers, though it's wise to ride in the conductor's car (in the middle of the train). If someone stares or acts in an annoying manner, simply move to another part of the car. Women are far more likely to encounter obnoxious behavior on the street, being greeted with whistles, muttered 'compliments' and even the occasional slurping sound. Any engagement amounts to encouragement – so simply walk on.

Medical Services
All hospital emergency rooms are obligated to receive sick visitors without regard to an ability to pay. However, showing up without insurance or money will virtually guarantee a long wait unless you are in extremis. The New York University Medical Center (☎ (212) 561-4347), 462 First Ave (at 32nd St), is easily reached by taxi.

There are several 24 hour Duane Reade pharmacy locations, including one on the corner of W 57th St and Broadway (☎ (212) 541-9708) and one on Sixth Ave and Waverly Place (☎ (212) 674-5357) near the W 8th St subway entrance. Kaufman's Pharmacy (☎ (212) 755-2266), 557 Lexington Ave at 50th St, is also always open and delivers medicine all hours.

Planned Parenthood (☎ (212) 677-6474) has its main clinic at 380 Second Ave.

Emergencies
For police, fire and ambulance calls, dial ☎ 911. The police department can be reached for non-emergencies at ☎ (212) 374-5000 from 7:30 am to 6 pm Monday to Friday. All federal, state and city government offices appear in a special section in the white pages; the front of every phone book also contains a complete list of community organizations. Here are some useful numbers:

Crime Victims Services	(212) 577-7777
Legal Aid Society	(212) 577-3300
Alcoholics Anonymous	(212) 647-1680
AIDS Hotline	(212) 447-8200
Gay and Lesbian Switchboard	(212) 777-1800
NYC Dept of Consumer Affairs	(212) 487-4398

Dangers & Annoyances
Beggars Criminal Willie Sutton, when asked why he robbed banks, replied 'that's where the money is!' The same philosophy prompts panhandlers to set up shop at subway entrances, landmarks and street corners heavily patronized by tourists. It's impossible to differentiate between those truly in need and someone on the hustle, and many tourists assuage their guilt by giving. But New Yorkers know that money handed out to beggars will probably go to support a drug or alcohol habit – and will certainly do nothing to change their condition.

If you wish to give to a legitimate organization helping people in need, contact Citymeals on Wheels (☎ (212) 687-1234), which reaches out to feed hundreds of hungry people each day.

Scams Requests for money come in dozens of forms, including appeals for a dubious support group ('I'm a member of the United Homeless Organization'), unsubtle appeals to tourist fear ('I don't want to hurt or rob anybody') or even guilt-trip opening lines ('I know you won't help me because I'm black/poor/homeless . . .'). Then there is the shoulder-shrugging appeal for help ('I just got locked out of my car and need money for a cab'). When approached by anyone with a sad story, remember that the person is asking a tourist for help because the police and most locals are wise to scams.

Finally, hustlers often set up three-card-monte games – where 'players' try to pick the red card out of three shuffled on the top of a cardboard box. This variation on the shell game is widely known to be a no-win scam. Yet enough tourists play along (or get their wallets lifted while watching the proceedings) to make it a common sight on downtown streets during the weekends.

The bottom line is to never, *ever* find yourself giving money to a stranger under any circumstances.

Drugs There is heavy drug activity in the far East Village in Alphabet City (Aves A, B, C and D), in Washington Square Park, along Amsterdam Ave above 100th St and especially in Washington Heights toward the northern tip of Manhattan. All three neighborhoods have the attendant dangers of such places. Expect to be approached by drug dealers if you wander into any of these places, and avoid walking through them at night.

GETTING THERE & AWAY
Air
New York is served by three major airports. John F Kennedy (JFK), 15 miles from Midtown Manhattan in southeastern Queens, is where most international flights land. La Guardia airport in northern Queens is eight miles away and services mostly domestic flights, including the air shuttles to Boston and Washington, DC. Newark international airport is in New Jersey, 10 miles directly to the west. It's the hub for Continental Airlines and is also used by international and domestic flights of all major carriers.

For information about getting to/from the airports see Getting Around, below.

The following airlines have offices downtown or at the airports:

Aer Lingus
    509 Madison Ave (☎ (212) 557-1110)
Aeromexico
    37 W 57th St (☎ (212) 754-2140)
Air Canada
    15 W 50th St (☎ (800) 776-3000)
Air France
    120 W 56th St (☎ (800) 321-4538)
American Airlines
    18 W 49th St (☎ (800) 433-7300)
British Airways
    530 Fifth Ave (☎ (800) 247-9297)
Continental Airlines
    100 E 42nd St (☎ (212) 319-9494)
Delta Airlines
    100 E 42nd St (☎ (212) 239-0700)
Finnair
    228 E 45th St (☎ (212) 499-9000)
Japan Air Lines
    JFK Airport (☎ (800) 525-3663)
Korean Air
    609 Fifth Ave (☎ (800) 438-5000)
Olympic
    647 Fifth Ave (☎ (800) 838-3825)
Philippine Airlines
    JFK Airport (☎ (800) 435-9725)
Qantas
    712 Fifth Ave (☎ (800) 227-4500)
Singapore Airlines
    55 E 59th St (☎ (212) 644-8801)
Swissair
    608 Fifth Ave (☎ (800) 842-2201)
Tower Air
    JFK Airport (☎ (718) 553-8500)
TWA
    1 E 59th St (☎ (800) 893-5436)
United Airlines
    100 E 42nd St (☎ (800) 241-6522)
USAir
    101 Park Ave (☎ (800) 428-4322)
Virgin Atlantic
    96 Morton St (☎ (212) 242-1330)

JFK This airport, which serves 30 million passengers a year, was voted the third worst airport facility in the world by business travelers, and it deserves the dishonor. US airlines used to build separate showcase terminals at JFK, and thus the airport grew to its current sprawling mess with no coherent plan to it as a whole. While some of the original airlines (Eastern, Pan Am) have disappeared, the terminals remain, linked by the JFK Expressway and a free shuttle bus. American Airlines, British Airways, Delta and TWA have their own terminals; most other airlines use the crowded International Arrivals Building. The airport information line (☎ (718) 244-4444) will tell you if the airport is closed in bad weather. The airlines themselves, however, are usually reluctant to give honest information about flight delays over the phone.

Until the airport undergoes a much needed multi-million dollar renovation, it's a place best avoided. JFK's Duty Free shops, like those in most US cities, are absolutely useless – you can get alcohol, electronics and clothes cheaper in town, so don't expect to embark on a last minute purchasing spree for anything other than cigarettes.

La Guardia If you're arriving or departing in the middle of the day, La Guardia (☎ (718) 533-3400) is a more convenient choice than JFK. USAir and the Delta shuttle each have dedicated terminals; all other airlines use the Central Terminal Building in front of the parking garage.

Newark Flights to/from Newark international airport (☎ (201) 961-6000) are sometimes a bit cheaper because of the erroneous perception that the airport is less accessible than JFK or La Guardia. In fact, Newark has a large and spanking-new international arrivals terminal. Plus, the airport's four terminals are now linked by a monorail system that will also be connected to the NJ Transit train system by the year 2000, offering a traffic-free trip to the airport from Manhattan.

Bus
All suburban and long-haul buses leave and depart from the Port Authority Bus Terminal (☎ (212) 564-8484), at 41st St and Eighth Ave. Greyhound (☎ (212) 971-6300, (800) 231-2222) links New York

with major cities across the country. Peter Pan Trailways (☎ (800) 343-9999) run buses to the nearest major cities, including a daily express to Boston for $24.95 one-way and $47.95 roundtrip.

Short Line (☎ (212) 736-4700) has numerous departures to towns in northern New Jersey and upstate New York. New Jersey Transit buses (☎ (201) 762-5100) serve the entire Garden State, with direct service to Atlantic City for $15 one way.

Port Authority has been modernized and is much improved in recent years. Though it's not as rough as its reputation, you can still be hassled by beggars asking for handouts or offering to carry bags for tips.

Short haul buses also leave for New Jersey from the terminal near the George Washington Bridge (☎ (212) 568-5323; subway: 175th St).

Train
Pennsylvania Station (Penn Station), 33rd St between Seventh and Eighth Aves, is the departure point for all Amtrak trains (☎ (212) 582-6875, (800) 872-7245), including the *Metroliner* service to Princeton, NJ, and Washington, DC. The Long Island Rail Road (LIRR; ☎ (718) 217-5477) serves several hundred thousand commuters each day from a newly renovated platform area to points in Brooklyn, Queens and the suburbs of Long Island, including the resort areas. New Jersey Transit (NJ Transit; ☎ (201) 763-5100) also operates trains from Penn Station to the suburbs and the Jersey Shore.

Only one company still departs from Grand Central Terminal, at Park Ave and 42nd St: the Metro North Rail Road (☎ (212) 532-4900) which serves the northern city suburbs and Connecticut.

GETTING AROUND
It's hard to exaggerate the problem of gridlock in Manhattan's streets. The entire center of the island's grid system is packed with cars during the day, and major avenues – primarily Lexington and Broadway, get tied up by double-parked trucks making deliveries to stores. The subway is

the fastest way to get between uptown and downtown points, and contrary to popular belief, taking it is statistically safer than walking the streets in broad daylight.

Like most New Yorkers, you should use the city buses exclusively to get to points located along the same avenue, when it's easy to calculate the amount of travel time by looking at the traffic.

The best overall plan is to use the subway all day until 10 pm, then use taxis at night. It's very important to note that taxis are obligated to take you anywhere you want to go within the five boroughs, as well as to Newark airport (though you must pay tolls each way). During rush hours, taxi drivers often brazenly refuse fares from airport-bound customers (particularly during bad weather) because they can pick up easier fares in town. *Do not* ask permission to get into the cab if you're going to the airports, and do not negotiate a higher price for the job above the metered fare. If the cabbie refuses your business, threaten to report his/her license number to the Taxi and Limousine Commission. Even if this is an empty threat, the cab driver will take it seriously enough to relent.

To/From the Airports

When departing for the airports in the middle of the day, allow at least one hour's travel time. The Port Authority of New York and New Jersey's Air Ride line (☎ (800) 247-7433) offers comprehensive information on ground transportation to and from all three airports.

No matter what airport you fly into, there are several advantages to ordering car service by phone for an airport journey. The cars are newer and larger than yellow cabs and you do not have to tip the driver. You can also order a pickup a day in advance and pay by credit card. If you ask for a 'price check' while ordering the taxi, the dispatcher can tell you the exact cost of the journey, which should run between $35 to $50, depending on your departure point and the airport destination. Some of the better services include:

Big Apple	(718) 232-1015
Citywide	(718) 405-9393
Communicar	(718) 457-3105
Dial	(718) 743-2877

JFK Carey Transportation buses (☎ (718) 632-0500) run to/from JFK at least every 30 minutes from 5 am to 1 am daily. Buses leave from 125 Park Ave, just a block south of Grand Central Terminal, and from the Port Authority Airport Bus Center near the 42nd St and Eighth Ave entrance, from 7:15 am to 11:15 pm each day. One-way fare to JFK is $13, with half-price tickets available for students. The journey takes at least one hour.

You can also take the subway to the Howard Beach–JFK station on the A line, which takes at least an hour, and then switch to a free yellow and blue bus at the long-term parking lot to the terminals, which takes another 15 minutes. (You have to haul your luggage up and over several flights of stairs at the Howard Beach terminal.)

Taxi fare from the airport is about $45. (In 1996, New York City introduced a pilot program mandating that taxis must offer a flat rate of $32 from JFK to any location in Manhattan. If the fare is still available when you arrive, there will be signs indicating the policy at the JFK taxi stands.)

The long-term parking lot at JFK costs $6 a day; short-term parking closer to the terminals costs $4 for four hours.

La Guardia Carey Transportation buses leave from Port Authority Airport Bus Center from 7:15 am to 12:45 am daily and from 125 Park Ave near Grand Central Terminal from 5 am to 1 am daily. Buses depart at least every 30 minutes and cost $10 one way; the trip takes 45 minutes to an hour. The Delta Water Shuttle (☎ (800) 221-1212) leaves frequently for La Guardia with two pickups: Pier 11 at South and Wall Sts and at E 34th St on the East River. Fare is $20 one way, $30 roundtrip.

La Guardia is also accessible via public transportation by taking the subway to the Roosevelt Ave–Jackson Heights and 74th St–Broadway stops in Queens (two linked

The Subway System

The city's subway system began in 1904 as a nine mile, privately-operated line along Broadway between City Hall and W 145th St. Over the next 30 years, this Interborough Rapid Transit (IRT) line expanded service to the Bronx, Queens and Brooklyn, including several elevated lines called 'els.' Competition also came from the rival Brooklyn-Manhattan Transit company (BMT), and the city-owned Independent Line (IND) on Eighth Ave. The private companies basically collapsed during the Depression, and the city wound up owning all three lines – designed to compete with rather than augment each other – by 1940.

That is why the New York City transit system must mix colors, letters and numbers to designate its 26 different subway trains. To this day, New Yorkers refer to the West Side 1, 2, 3 and 9 trains as the IRT line, and a few even use the designations BMT and IND for the rest of the system.

Visitors are best off ignoring all these confusing local distinctions and concentrating on how to get to specific destinations. The common mistake most visitors make is boarding an express train only to see it blow by the local stop they desired. Pay particular attention to the subway map – local stops are shown with solid lines, and express stops are circles.

The subway system benefited greatly from a huge infusion of federal, state and local funding during the '80s, and now trains are generally quieter, more reliable and free of graffiti. Almost every token booth offers bus and subway maps, and even pamphlets on such ludicrous subjects as 'Riding Escalators Safely.'

In 1995, the system began introducing magnetic strip Metrocards in certain stations, widely seen as a prelude to imposing a staged fare system. Unfortunately, the December 1995 25¢ boost in the subway fare – the biggest ever – was accompanied by huge reductions in the budgets for system maintenance and improvement. Some of the stations most in need of repair – Times Square and 72nd St–Broadway in particular – remain in atrocious states with confusing, badly-marked passageways, and are likely to stay that way in the near term. ∎

stations served by five lines). You then take the Q33 bus to the La Guardia main terminals or the Q47 bus to Delta Shuttle's Marine Air Terminal. Since this journey takes well over an hour and costs two tokens ($3), it is recommended only for those who absolutely can't afford the additional $7 for the direct Carey bus. In Upper Manhattan, pick up the M60 bus along the length of 125th St directly to La Guardia for a subway token, Metrocard or $1.50 in change.

Taxis to La Guardia from Midtown cost about $45.

Newark Olympia Trails (☎ (212) 964-6233) travels to Newark from a stop near Grand Central, at Park Ave and 41st St, from 5 am to 11 pm daily. Another bus departs to Newark from Lower Manhattan at One World Trade Center on West St from 6 am to 8 pm Monday to Friday and 7 am to 8 pm Saturday and Sunday. Both buses cost $7.

NJ Transit (☎ (201) 762-5100) runs a No 300 bus from Port Authority Airport Bus Center to Newark airport 24 hours a day; cost is $7 one way and $12 roundtrip.

A taxi to Newark will cost about $55.

Subway

It's noisy and confusing, and in the summer stations can feel like an inner circle of hell (though the subway cars are air-conditioned). But with a little attention to detail, you can figure out the 656 mile New York City subway system, used by 3.6 million people every day.

The subway is the fastest and most reliable way to travel, especially for trips totaling more than 20 blocks in north-south directions during the day. Taking a bus or a taxi guarantees that you'll hit traffic choke points at places like Times Square and wind up arriving at your destination only after a long and frustrating ride.

Most major Manhattan attractions –

especially those on the West Side and down-town – are easily accessible by several subway lines. Madison Square Garden, for example, is within walking distance (four blocks) of three subway stations on 34th St served by a total of 12 different lines. Throughout this chapter, the subway station, when listed for each site, is selected for being the closest to the destination or because it is served by the fastest and most reliable train.

Subway tokens, which allow you to ride the system for any distance, cost $1.50 and are available at booths near the turnstiles. MetroCards will also be accepted at all subway stations in mid-1997.

If you're buying tokens, it's a very good idea to buy enough for a day or week's travel in one shot – the tokens can be used on the blue-and-white city buses (which do not accept dollar bills or make change – but do accept MetroCard), and rush-hour lines at token booths can be wicked. Subway clerks sometimes appear irascible, since they barely slide the tokens through the booth slot and try to give you back as many singles as possible in change to avoid a big count-up at the end of their shift. But they are the single best source for information on how to get around.

As for safety, standing in the middle of the platform will bring you to the conduc-tor's car. The conductor can direct you through the system when he/she is not closing the doors of the train.

Of course, it's not a good idea to leave a wallet in your back pocket on a crowded subway, and all day-packs should be secured with a safety pin.

For subway information call ☎ (718) 330-1234.

PATH

New Jersey PATH trains (☎ (800) 234-7284) are part of a separate subway system that runs along Sixth Ave with stops at 34th St, 23rd St, 14th St, 9th St and Christopher St to Hoboken, Jersey City and Newark. A second line runs from northern New Jersey to the World Trade Center. These reliable trains run every 15 minutes and fare is $1 (machines take dollar bills).

Bus

City buses operate 24 hours a day, gener-ally along avenues in a south or north direc-tion, and cross-town along the major thoroughfares (including 34th, 42nd and 57th Sts). Buses that begin and end in a certain borough are prefixed accordingly: ie, M5 for Manhattan, B39 for Brooklyn, Q32 for Queens, Bx29 for Bronx.

You need exact change of $1.50, a MetroCard or a token to board the bus, and if you plan on switching to a connect-ing route, you must ask for a transfer slip upon boarding. Drivers will be happy to tell you if their bus stops near to a specific site, but don't engage them in a conversa-tion about directions unless you want to endure poisonous stares from the old-timers who prefer the bus to the subway.

Bus maps for each borough are available at subway and train stations, and each well-marked bus stop has 'Guide-a-Ride' maps showing the stops for each bus and nearby landmarks. Remember that some 'Limited Stop' buses along major routes pull over only every 10 blocks or so at major cross streets. 'Express' buses are generally for outer borough commuters and cost $4 and should not be used for short trips.

As a safety precaution, you can request to be left off at any location along a bus route from 10 pm to 5 am – even if it is not a designated bus stop.

Of course, you will discover the same woes found in every other major city during bad weather: after a 25 minute wait for a bus, three will come along in a row.

For bus information call ☎ (718) 927-7499.

Taxi

Is there a category of worker more maligned than the New York City cab driver? No, not all of them are thieves, incompetent or in desperate need of a shower. The most common tension between driver and pas-senger comes from arguments about the fastest route from one place to another. Most cabbies *will* attempt to ride down Broadway in bad traffic, or across town on crowded 59th St rather than use a faster

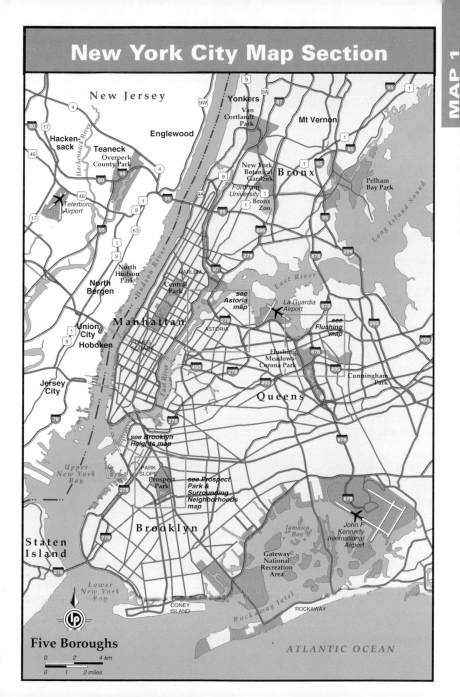

New York City Map Section

MAP 1

New Jersey

Yonkers
Van Cortlandt Park

Mt Vernon

Hackensack
Teaneck
Overpeck County Park

Englewood

New York Botanical Gardens

Bronx

Fordham University

Pelham Bay Park

Bronx Zoo

Teterboro Airport

North Hudson Park

Long Island Sound

North Bergen

HARLEM

Central Park

East River

La Guardia Airport

see Astoria map

see Flushing map

Union City
Hoboken

Manhattan

ASTORIA

Flushing Meadows-Corona Park

Cunningham Park

TIMES SQUARE

Jersey City

East River

Queens

see Brooklyn Heights map

Upper New York Bay

PARK SLOPE
Prospect Park

see Prospect Park & Surrounding Neighborhoods map

Jamaica Bay

John F Kennedy International Airport

Staten Island

Brooklyn

Gateway National Recreation Area

Lower New York Bay

CONEY ISLAND

Rockaway Inlet

ROCKAWAY

Five Boroughs

0   2   4 km
0   1   2 miles

ATLANTIC OCEAN

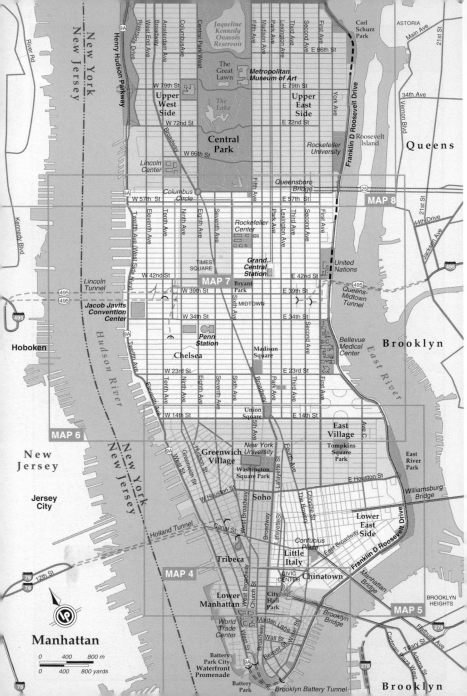

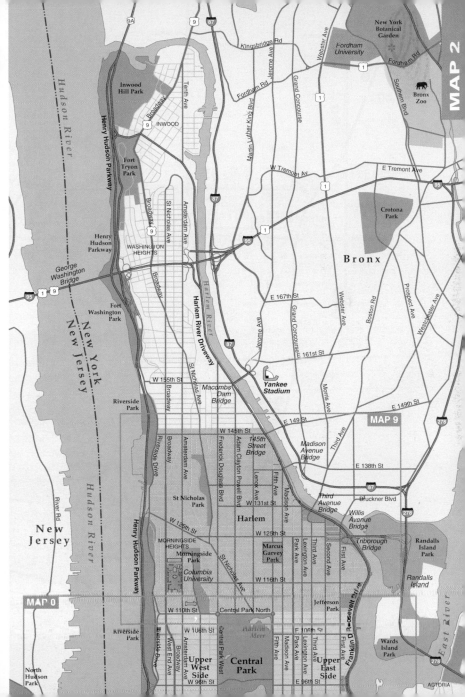

MAP 2

New York
Botanical
Garden

Fordham
University

Bronx
Zoo

Inwood
Hill Park

Kingsbridge Rd

Webster Ave

Fordham Rd

Southern Blvd

Fordham Rd

Tenth Ave

Broadway

INWOOD

Grand Concourse

Martin Luther King Blvd

Fort
Tryon
Park

Henry Hudson Parkway

W Tremont Av

E Tremont Ave

Broadway

St Nicholas Ave

Amsterdam Ave

Crotona
Park

Henry
Hudson
Parkway

WASHINGTON
HEIGHTS

Bronx

George
Washington
Bridge

Broadway

Harlem River

Harlem River Driveway

E 167th St

Webster Ave

Prospect Rd

Westchester Ave

New York
New Jersey

Fort
Washington
Park

Jerome Ave

Grand Concourse

E 161st St

River Rd

New
Jersey

Hudson River

W 155th St

St Nicholas Ave

Broadway

Macombs
Dam
Bridge

Yankee
Stadium

Morris Ave

E 149th St

Riverside
Park

E 149 St

MAP 9

Broadway

Amsterdam Ave

Frederick Douglass Blvd

Adam Clayton Powell Blvd

W 145th St

145th
Street
Bridge

Lenox Ave

Fifth Ave

Madison
Avenue
Bridge

Third Ave

E 138th St

River Rd

Hudson River

Riverside Drive

Henry Hudson Parkway

St Nicholas
Park

W 131st St

Harlem

Madison Ave

Bruckner Blvd

Third
Avenue
Bridge

Willis
Avenue
Bridge

Randalls
Island
Park

North
Hudson
Park

New
Jersey

Hudson River

W 126th St

MORNINGSIDE
HEIGHTS

Morningside
Park

Columbia
University

St Nicholas Ave

W 125th St

Marcus
Garvey
Park

W 116th St

Park Ave

Lexington Ave

Third Ave

Second Ave

First Ave

Triborough
Bridge

Randalls
Island

Riverside
Park

West End Ave

Broadway

W 110th St

Central Park North

Central Park West

Jefferson
Park

Franklin D Roosevelt Drive

Wards
Island Park

MAP 0

Riverside
Park

W 106th St

Amsterdam Ave

Broadway

Upper West
Side

West End Ave

W 96th St

Central Park West

Harlem
Meer

Central
Park

E 106th St

Fifth Ave

Madison Ave

Park Ave

Third Ave

Lexington Ave

First Ave

Upper
East
Side

E 96th St

East River

ASTORIA

KIM GRANT

MAP 3

Legend

Terminal **B**

Local Stop

Express Stop

Express and Local Stop

Normal Route Service

Rush Hour Service

Station Name

Brooklyn Bridge
4·5 **6**

Terminal for ❻ service

❹ and ❺ service continue

Subway service, 6AM-midnight:
- Bold Type: Full Time Service
- Light Type: Part Time Service
- Boxed Type: Terminal (Full or Part Time)

Local / Express

Free Transfers

For Travel Information call (718) 330-1234 (6AM-9PM)

215 Street 1

A

207 Street Inwood A

207 Street 9 rush hours, 1 other times 1

Fordham Rd C·D

Fordham Rd 4

Bronx Park East 2·5

BRONX ZOO

Dyckman St (200 St) A

Dyckman St 1

183 Street 4

182-183 Sts C·D

Fordham METRO NORTH FORDHAM

East 180 St 2·5

190 Street 1

191 Street 1·9

Burnside Av 4

175 Street A

181 Street A

181 Street 1·9

176 Street 4

HIGH BRIDGE PARK

WASHINGTON BRIDGE

Tremont Av C·D

METRO NORTH TREMONT

E Tremont Av (West Farms Sq) 2·5

174-175 Sts C·D

174 St 2·5

Tremont

2

5

METRO NORTH UNIVERSITY HTS

Mt Eden Av 4

176 Street C

170 Street 4

Highbridge

170 Street C·D

Freeman St 2·5

Morrisania

B **C** C TERMINATES HERE WEEKENDS ONLY

168 Street Washington Heights A B C 1·9

G. W. Bridge Bus Station

H A R L E M   R I V E R

167 Street 4

167 Street C·D

Simpson St 2·5

163 Street Amsterdam Av A·B·C

155 Street C·D

161 Street Yankee Stadium C·D·4

D

METRO NORTH MELROSE

Intervale Av 2·5

Prospect Av 2·5

157 Street 1

155 St A·B·C

3

Jackson Av 2·5

149 Street Grand Concourse 2·4·5

The Hub

BX55

Mott Haven

C

148 Street Lenox Terminal 3

145 Street 9 rush hours, 1 other times

145 Street A·B·C·D

EXIT FROM THE FIRST 4 CARS ONLY

145 St 4

2

3 Avenue 149 Street 2·5

6

137 Street City College 1·9

1

9

135 Street B·C

135 Street 2·3

Harlem

138 Street Grand Concourse 4·5

Cypress Av 6

5

6

Brook Av

125 Street 1·9

125 Street A·B·C·D

125 Street 2·3

METRO NORTH 125 ST

M60

125 Street 4·5·6

M60

TRIBOROUGH BRIDGE

RANDALLS ISLAND PARK

116 Street Columbia Univ 1·9

116 Street B·C

2

3

116 Street 2·3

116 Street 6

East Harlem

WARDS ISLAND PARK

Cathedral Parkway (110 Street) 1·9

Cathedral Pkwy (110 Street) B·C

Central Park N (110 Street) 2·3

110 Street 6

1

9

2

3

103 Street 1·9

103 Street B·C

103 Street 6

4

5

WARDS ISLAND PARK

96 Street 1·2·3·9

96 Street B·C

96 Street 6

Upper West Side

CENTRAL PARK WEST

LEXINGTON AV

M60

MANHATTAN

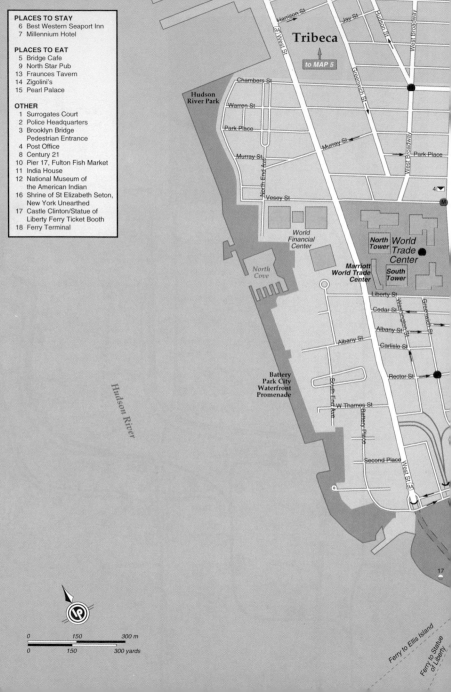

Tribeca

to MAP 5

Harrison St
Jay St
Hudson St
West Broadway
9A West St
Greenwich St

Hudson
River Park

Chambers St

Warren St

Park Place

Murray St

Murray St

West Broadway
Park Place

North End Ave

Vesey St

4

M

World
Financial
Center

North
Cove

North
Tower

World
Trade
Center

Marriott
World Trade
Center

South
Tower

Liberty St

Cedar St
West Thames St
Greenwich St

Albany St

Albany St

Carlisle St

Rector St

Battery
Park City
Waterfront
Promenade

South End Ave

W Thames St

Battery Place

Second Place

West St/9A

Hudson River

17

Ferry to Ellis Island

Ferry to Statue
of Liberty

LP

0   150   300 m
0   150   300 yards

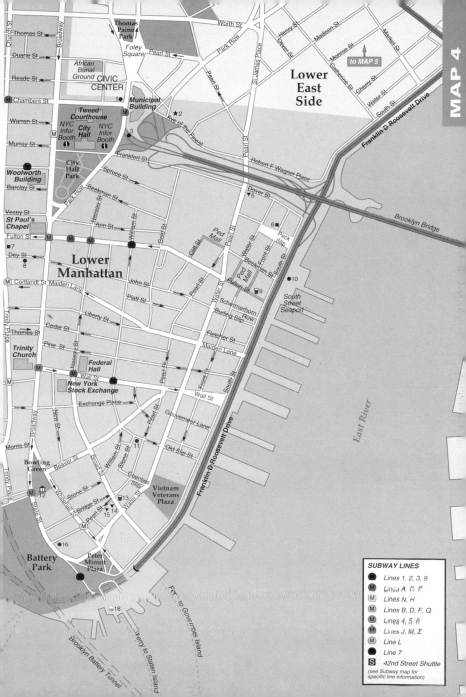

MAP 4

Thomas St
Duane St
Reade St
Chambers St
Warren St
Murray St

Broadway
Church St

Thomas Paine Park
Foley Square
Worth St
Park Row
Pearl St

African Burial Ground
CIVIC CENTER

Henry St
Oliver St
Madison St
Market St
Monroe St
Catherine St
Cherry St
Water St
South St
St James Place

to MAP 5

Lower East Side

Franklin D Roosevelt Drive

Municipal Building
★ 2
Ave of the Finest

1●

Tweed Courthouse
NYC Infor Booth
City Hall
NYC Infor Booth
3

Frankfort St
Robert F Wagner Place

Brooklyn Bridge

Woolworth Building
Barclay St
Vesey St
St Paul's Chapel
Fulton St

City Hall Park
Park Row
Spruce St
Beekman St
Ann St
William St
Nassau St

Dover St
5 ▼
6 ■
Peck Slip
Cliff St
Pearl St
Water St
Beekman St
Front St
South St

Lower Manhattan

Dey St
■7
8 ●
Cortlandt St Maiden Lane
John St
Platt St

Ped Mall
Ped Mall
Fulton St
9 ♨
10 ●

South Street Seaport

Schermerhorn Row
Burling Slip
Fletcher St
Maiden Lane

Trinity Place
Thames St
Cedar St
Pine St

Trinity Church
Liberty St
Nassau St
Pearl St
Water St
Front St
South St

Federal Hall
Wall St
New York Stock Exchange

Exchange Place
Broadway
New St
Broad St

Wall St

Gouverneur Lane
Old Slip St

East River

Morris St
Beaver St
Pearl St
William St
Stone St
Bridge St
11 ●

Franklin D Roosevelt Drive

Bowling Green
12 ♨
Whitehall St
Stone St
State St

Coenties Slip
Water St
13 ■
15 ▼ 14

Vietnam Veterans Plaza

16 ●

Peter Minuit Plaza

Battery Park

18

Ferry to Governors Island

Brooklyn Battery Tunnel
Ferry to Staten Island

to MAP 5

SUBWAY LINES

Ⓜ Lines 1, 2, 3, 9
Ⓜ Lines A, C, E
Ⓜ Lines N, H
Ⓜ Lines B, D, F, Q
Ⓜ Lines 4, 5, 6
Ⓜ Lines J, M, Z
Ⓜ Line L
● Line 7
Ⓢ 42nd Street Shuttle

(see Subway map for specific line information)

MAP 5

Stuyvesant
Square

Third Ave
E 15th St
to MAP 6
E 15th St
E 14th St
Second Ave
E 13th St
E 12th St
First Ave
Ave A
Ave B
Ave C
E 11th St
●104
105 ✝
E 10th St
▼106
▼107
▼110
109
▼108
E 9th St
▼111
▼112
East
Village
Tompkins
Square
Park
Franklin D Roosevelt Drive
East River
St Marks Place
●113
114
115
E 7th St
E 6th St
122 123 124
▼121
East
River
Park
119
E 5th St
120
E 4th St
118
125
First Ave
Second Ave
The Bowery
E 3rd St
E 2nd St
Ave A
Ave B
Ave C
Ave D
127
E 1st St
▼128
▼129
E Houston St
Williamsburg
Bridge
E Houston St
Sara D Roosevelt Parkway
303 ▼304
305
Ludlow St
Stanton St
Columbia St
302 ✝
Prince St
309
310
Rivington St
Allen St
Orchard St
Essex St
Suffolk St
Clinton St
Attorney St
Ridge St
Pitt St
The Bowery
Mott St
Mulberry St
Elizabeth St
306
Spring St
307
308
Chrystie St
Forsyth St
Eldridge St
313
314
Kenmare St
315
316
Delancey St
Lower
East
Side
Sheriff St
Columbia St
Jackson St
Cherry St
Broome St
317
▼318
319
320
Grand St
Little
Italy
322
Hester St
E Broadway
Henry St
Madison St
Montgomery St
Gouverneur St
Water St
Canal St
Eldridge St
Division St
Hester St
Chinatown
334
323
324
326
327
▼328
Bayard St
▼329
325
330▼ Pell St
333
331
332
Columbus
Park
Confucius
Plaza
East Broadway
▼335
Division St
Henry St
Rutgers St
Jefferson St
Clinton St
Montgomery St
Gouverneur St
Cherry St
South St
East River
Madison St
Monroe St
Catherine St
Pearl St
Chatham
Worth St Square
Park Row
Mott St
Oliver St
336
Water St
South St
Franklin C Roosevelt Dr
Manhattan Bridge
Pearl St
BROOKLYN
HEIGHTS
John St
Frankfort St
Water St
to MAP 4
Brooklyn
Bridge

Map 5 Neighborhood Keys

Greenwich Village Key	0's
East Village Key	100's

SoHo/Tribeca Key	200's
Little Italy/Chinatown/ Lower East Side Key	300's

Greenwich Village Key

PLACES TO STAY

1 Riverview Hotel
5 Incentra Village
18 Larchmont Hotel
27 Washington Square Hotel

PLACES TO EAT

2 Florent
3 El Faro
7 Benny's Burritos
10 'Original' Ray's Pizza
11 Sammy's Noodles
14 Bar Six
15 Jon Vie
16 French Roast
21 Picasso Cafe
23 Dix et Sept
28 Manatus
35 Grange Hall
37 Orbit
38 Mary's
39 Marinella
40 Universal Grill
42 Trattoria Spaghetto
43 Bleecker Street Pastry
44 Minetta Tavern
46 Le Figaro
47 Aggies
48 Cafe Lure
49 Rocco

BARS/CLUBS

4 Hudson Bar & Books
6 Corner Bistro
9 Village Vanguard
20 White Horse Tavern
22 Small's
25 Stonewall Inn
29 Sweet Basil
30 Washington Square Church
31 Blue Note
33 Bottom Line
34 Chumley's
36 Henrietta Hudson's
41 Bar d'O
45 Back Fence

OTHER

8 Gay & Lesbian Community Service Center
12 Patchin Place
13 Jefferson Market Library
17 Shoe and Leather Shops
19 Strand Bookstore
24 Stonewall Place
26 Northern Dispensary
32 Judson Memorial Church

East Village Key

PLACES TO STAY

115 St Marks Hotel

PLACES TO EAT

106 DeRobertis
107 Lanza's
108 Sharaku
109 Second Ave Deli
111 Hasaki
112 Veselka
121 Little Delhi
123 Roetelle AG
124 Benny's Burritos
126 Time Cafe
128 Lucky Cheng's
129 Princess Pamela's Southern Touch

BARS/CLUBS

101 System
104 Webster Hall
114 McSorley's
119 Scratcher
120 KGB
125 Swift Bar
127 CBGB

OTHER

102 Grace Church
103 Post Office
105 St Marks in-the-Bowery
110 10th St Baths
113 Cooper Union
116 Colonnade Row
117 Joseph Papp Public Theater
118 Old Merchant's House Museum
122 East Village Launderette

SoHo/Tribeca Key

PLACES TO DRINK & EAT

201 SOB's
203 Souen Restaurant
204 Helianthus Vegetarian Restaurant
213 Fanelli Cafe
218 Ear Inn
219 Lupe's East L.A. Kitchen
220 Cafe Noir
221 Gourmet Garage
222 Lucky Strike
224 Wetlands
225 Fast Folk Cafe
226 Walkers
227 Bubby's
228 Nobu
229 Riverrun Cafe
230 Chanterelle
232 Odeon

OTHER

202 Film Forum
205 Post Office
206 African Museum
207 New Museum of Contemporary Art
208 Guggenheim/SoHo
209 Alternative Museum
210 Leo Castelli Gallery
211 Howard Greenberg Gallery
212 Haas's Mural
214 Singer Bldg.
215 Fire Museum
216 St Nicholas Hotel
217 Haughwout Building
223 Post Office
231 Harrison Street Houses

Little Italy/Chinatown/ Lower East Side Key

PLACES TO STAY

307 Off SoHo Suites Hotel
315 Pioneer Hotel
322 World Hotel

PLACES TO DRINK & EAT

303 Bereket
304 Katz's Deli
306 Kitchen Club
311 Spring Street Natural
312 Cascabel Restaurant
313 Le Jardin Bistro
314 Lombardi's Pizza
318 Cafe Roma
319 Benito I Restaurant
321 N Bar
323 Nha Trang
324 New Pasteur
325 Thailand Restaurant
328 House of Vegetarian
329 Peking Duck House
330 Hay Wun Loy
332 Hong Ying Rice Shop
335 Nice Restaurant

OTHER

301 Puck Building
302 Old St Patrick's
305 Luna Lounge
308 First Roumanian-American Congregation
334 Eldridge St Synagogue
309 147 Ludlow Street
310 Schapiro's Wines
316 Lower East Side Tenement Museum
317 Old Police Headquarters
320 Bowery Savings Bank
326 Chinatown History Museum
327 Eastern States Buddhist Temple
331 Church of the Transfiguration
333 Post Office
336 First Shearith Cemetery

View of Lower Manhattan from Battery Park

Sidewalk antique sale, Greenwich Village

PLACES TO STAY
1 Westpark Hotel
4 St Moritz
5 Plaza Hotel
7 Sherry Netherland Hotel
9 Four Seasons
13 Ameritania Hotel
14 Woodward Hotel
17 Wellington Hotel
19 Salisbury Hotel
28 Peninsula
31 St Regis
35 Waldorf Astoria
36 Pickwick Arms
41 Algonquin
42 Royalton
43 Iroquois
45 Quality Hotel
46 Jolly Madison Towers
47 Morgan's
49 Hotel Metro
51 Herald Square Hotel
52 Wolcott Hotel
53 Grand Union
54 Chelsea Center Hostel
55 Senton Hotel
56 Gershwin Hotel
57 Madison Hotel
58 Howard Johnson
61 Colonial House Inn
62 Chelsea Hotel
63 Chelsea International Hostel
70 Gramercy Park Hotel
74 Chelsea Pines Hotel
85 Inn at Irving Place

PLACES TO EAT
2 Hard Rock Cafe
3 Jekyll & Hyde Club
10 Island Burgers & Shakes
11 Soup Kitchen International
15 Stage Deli
16 Carnegie Deli
18 Planet Hollywood
20 Motown Cafe
21 Harley-Davidson Cafe
22 Le Quercy
23 La Fondue
24 JP French Bakery
25 La Bonne Soupe
26 Aquavit
32 Vong
37 Mee Noodle Shop
38 Munson Diner
39 Mikes
59 Madras Mahal
60 Empire Diner
67 Cafe Bondi
68 Alva
69 Gramercy Tavern
71 18th & 8th
72 Food Bar
73 Candy Bar
75 Viceroy
76 Sam Chinita
79 America
81 Union Square Cafe
83 Old Town Bar & Grill
84 Pete's Tavern

OTHER
12 Gray Line Tours
40 Museum of Television
    & Radio
48 ICP Gallery Midtown
48 Pierpont Morgan Library
65 Limelight
66 Tramps
77 King
78 Splash

MAP 6

Upper East Side

to MAP 8

The Pond

E 61st St
E 60th St
E 59th St
E 58th St
E 57th St
E 56th St
E 55th St
E 54th St
E 53rd St
E 52nd St
E 51st St
E 50th St
E 49th St
E 48th St
E 47th St
E 46th St
E 45th St
E 44th St
E 43rd St
E 42nd St
E 41st St
E 40th St
E 39th St
E 38th St
E 37th St
E 36th St
E 35th St
E 34th St
E 33rd St
E 32nd St
E 31st St
E 30th St
E 29th St
E 28th St
E 27th St
E 26th St
E 25th St
E 24th St
E 23rd St
E 22nd St
E 21st St
E 20th St
E 19th St
E 18th St
E 17th St
E 16th St
E 15th St
E 14th St
E 13th St
E 12th St
E 11th St
E 10th St

Queensboro Bridge
To Astoria
25

PLACES TO SHOP
6   Bergdorf Goodman
8   Warner Brothers Store
27 Henri Bendel
29 Tiffany & Co
30 Trump Tower
34 Sak's Fifth Avenue
44 Brooks Brothers
50 Macy's
64 Different Light Bookstore
80 Paragon Athletic Goods
82 Barnes & Noble Superstore

Museum of Modern Art

Radio City Music Hall

St Patrick's Cathedral

Rockefeller Center

Midtown

Grand Central Station

Chrysler Building

Bryant Park

New York Public Library Main Branch

Herald Square

Empire State Building

LITTLE KOREA

FLATIRON DISTRICT

Madison Square

Cramercy Park

Union Square

Stuyvesant Square

Greenwich Village

East Village

United Nations

Roosevelt Island

Queens

Franklin D Roosevelt Drive

East River

Queens-Midtown Tunnel
495

To Flushing Meadows

Bellevue Medical Center

Ave C

Franklin D Roosevelt Drive

East River Park

SUBWAY LINES
Lines 1, 2, 3, 9
Lines A, C, E
Lines N, R
Lines B, D, F, Q
Lines 4, 5, 6
Lines J, M, Z
Line L
Line 7
42nd Street Shuttle
(see Subway map for specific line information)

to MAP 3

Hustle and bustle in Times Square

The Yellow River, Manhattan-style

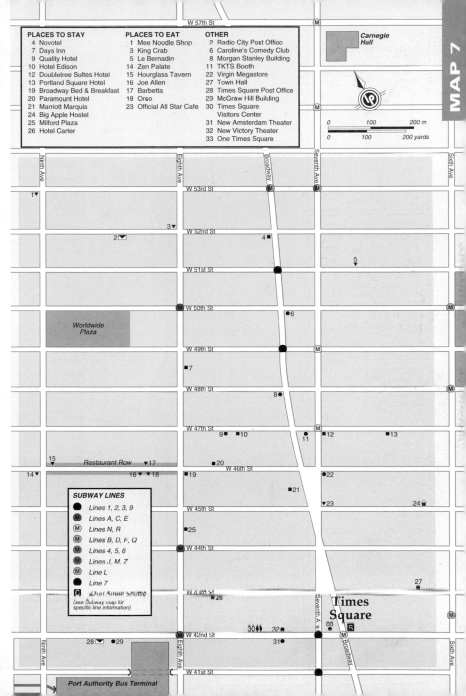

MAP 7

W 57th St

Carnegie Hall

PLACES TO STAY
4 Novotel
7 Days Inn
9 Quality Hotel
10 Hotel Edison
12 Doubletree Suites Hotel
13 Portland Square Hotel
19 Broadway Bed & Breakfast
20 Paramount Hotel
21 Marriott Marquis
24 Big Apple Hostel
25 Milford Plaza
26 Hotel Carter

PLACES TO EAT
1 Mee Noodle Shop
3 King Crab
5 Le Bernadin
14 Zen Palate
15 Hourglass Tavern
16 Joe Allen
17 Barbetta
18 Orso
23 Official All Star Cafe

OTHER
2 Radio City Post Office
6 Caroline's Comedy Club
8 Morgan Stanley Building
11 TKTS Booth
22 Virgin Megastore
27 Town Hall
28 Times Square Post Office
29 McGraw Hill Building
30 Times Square
   Visitors Center
31 New Amsterdam Theater
32 New Victory Theater
33 One Times Square

0   100   200 m
0   100   200 yards

North Ave
Eighth Ave
Broadway
Seventh Ave
Sixth Ave

W 53rd St

1▼

3▼   W 52nd St

2▼   4■   5▼

W 51st St

W 50th St   ●6

Worldwide
Plaza

W 49th St

■7   W 48th St

8●

W 47th St

9■ ■10   ●11 ■12   ■13

15▼ Restaurant Row ▼17   ■20 W 46th St

14▼   16▼ ▼18   ■19   ●22

                        ■21   ▼23   24⌂

SUBWAY LINES
● Lines 1, 2, 3, 9
Ⓜ Lines A, C, E   W 45th St
Ⓜ Lines N, R
Ⓜ Lines B, D, F, Q   ■25
Ⓜ Lines 4, 5, 6
Ⓜ Lines J, M, Z   W 44th St
Ⓜ Line L
● Line 7
Ⓢ 42nd Street Shuttle   27
(see Subway map for   ■
specific line information)

W 43rd St   Times
■26   Square

W 42nd St   30 32●   ●● Ⓢ

28▼ ●29   31●

Port Authority Bus Terminal   W 41st St

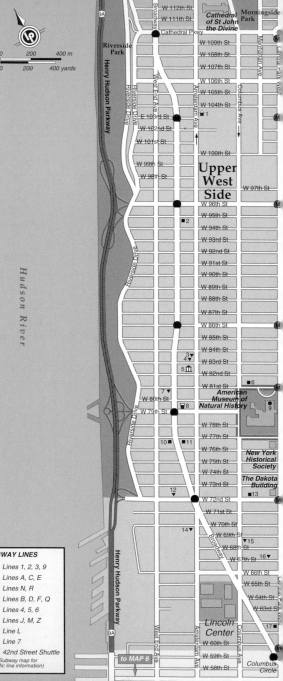

UPPER WEST SIDE
PLACES TO STAY
1 AYH Hostel
2 Newtown Hotel
6 Excelsior Hotel
10 Banana Bungalow
11 Broadway American Hotel
13 Olcott Hotel
17 Mayflower Hotel

PLACES TO DRINK & EAT
3 Tibet Shambala
4 Cafe Lalo
7 Zabar's
8 Dublin House
12 Empire Szechuan
14 Cafe Luxembourg
15 Empire Szechuan
16 Cafe des Artistes

OTHER
5 Children's Museum of Manhattan
9 Hayden Planetarium

CENTRAL PARK
PLACES TO DRINK & EAT
6 Boathouse Cafe
9 Tavern on the Green

OTHER
1 Science Center
2 Police Station
3 Cleopatra's Needle
4 Delacorte Theater
5 Belvedere Castle
7 Bethesda Fountain
8 Bandshell
10 Columbus Statue
11 Carousel
12 Park Visitor Information
13 The Dairy

UPPER EAST SIDE
PLACES TO STAY
3 Hotel Wales
8 Franklin
10 Gracie Inn
18 The Lowell
20 Pierre Hotel

PLACES TO DRINK & EAT
2 Kinsale Tavern
7 Manny's Carwash
9 Lexington Candy Shop
11 Bemelmans Bar
12 Voulez Vous
13 Cafe Greco
17 La Goulue
19 Arcadia
23 Madame Romaine de Lyon
24 Subway Inn
28 Favia Lite
29 British Open

OTHER
1 International Center
    of Photography
4 Cooper-Hewitt
5 National Academy
    of Design
6 East River Express
    Ferry Terminal
14 Frick Collection
15 Asia Society
16 Temple Emanuel
21 Barney's
22 Calvin Klein
25 Bloomingdale's
26 Antique Stores
27 Roosevelt Island Tram Station
30 Roosevelt Island Tram Station

SUBWAY LINES
⬤ Lines 1, 2, 3, 9
Ⓜ Lines A, C, E
Ⓜ Lines N, R
Ⓜ Lines B, D, F, Q
Ⓜ Lines 4, 5, 6
Ⓜ Lines J, M, Z
Ⓜ Line L
⬤ Line 7
Ⓢ 42nd Street Shuttle
(see Subway map for
specific line information)

0   200   400 m
0   200   400 yards

to MAP 6

Harlem

Central Park

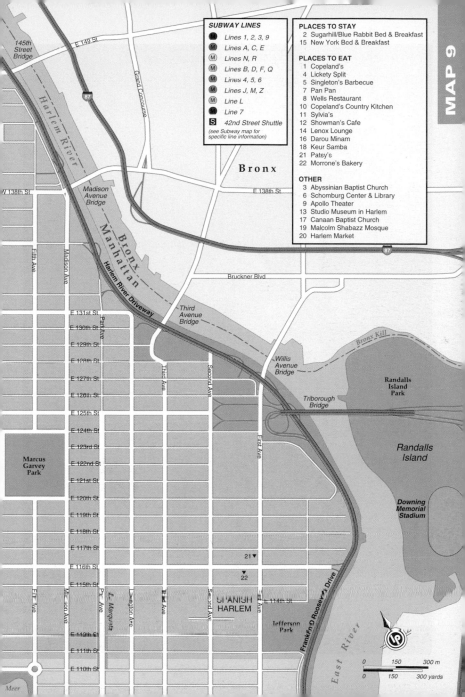

KIM GRANT

Dig the hat—it's not made of Styrofoam.

Central Park 'transverse' – they're making money on the metered trip.

Taxis cost $2 for the initial charge, with 30¢ for every additional quarter mile and 20¢ a minute while stuck in traffic. There's an additional 50¢ surcharge for rides after 8 pm. Tampered meters turn over every 20 seconds or so while the cab is stopped in traffic or at a light, and if you notice it happening, don't hesitate to ask if it is 'running too fast.' If the driver apologizes a bit too energetically you've probably busted him and can negotiate a lower fare than the meter. Tips are expected to run 10 to 15% with a minimum of 50¢. If you feel ripped off, ask for a receipt and note the driver's license number. The city's Taxi and Limousine Commission (☎ (212) 302-8294) is particularly aggressive and the threat of a complaint puts the fear of god into obnoxious cabbies.

For hauls that will last 50 blocks or more, it's a good idea to instruct the driver to take a road well away from Midtown traffic. Suggest the West Side Highway or Eleventh Ave if you hail a taxi west of Broadway; on the East Side, the best choice may be Second Ave (heading downtown) or First Ave (uptown), since you can hit a string of green lights in either direction.

One cab cliché does hold: only about two in every 10 cab drivers actually thank you for the tip, no matter how generous.

Car
It's nightmare to have a car in New York, especially because byzantine street cleaning rules require you to move your car several times a week. Parking garages in Midtown are usually operated by the Kinney Corporation, which has a hammer-lock on the industry and charges at least $30 during daylight hours. Cheaper lots can be found in Manhattan along West St in Chelsea, but even those $10 to $15 daily deals aren't a bargain after the phenomenal 18.25% parking tax is added. Using a hotel lot is no bargain – Midtown hotels can charge $40 a day, even for their guests.

Manhattan

For most visitors, Manhattan (population 1,487,536) *is* New York City. Even the residents of the outer boroughs refer to it as 'the city,' a tacit acknowledgment of the island's primacy. But it's important to remember that the Bronx, Brooklyn, Queens and Staten Island each have their own attractions. Only visitors who include at least one excursion out of Manhattan are truly taking advantage of what the entire city has to offer.

The following sections divide Manhattan into neighborhoods from the island's southern tip to the north. Remember that the most popular sites attract large crowds year round.

LOWER MANHATTAN
Walking Tour
It is essential to explore this area on a weekday, concentrated as it is on the activities of business, politics and the law. The best start-off point is **City Hall**, near the pedestrian approach to the Brooklyn Bridge. Behind City Hall stands the **Tweed Courthouse**, an inadvertent monument to late-19th century municipal corruption. Built in 1872, an estimated $10 million of the $14 million budget for this new city courthouse wound up embezzled by William Magear 'Boss' Tweed, the ruthless leader of the Democratic Party's Tammany Hall organization. The subsequent scandal toppled Tweed from power – but left an architecturally significant building with an impressive central hall.

Nearby at the intersection of Chambers and Centre Sts sits the former **Surrogate's Court**, a structure completed in 1914 with an interior that deliberately imitates the beaux arts style of Charles Garnier's Paris Opera House. The building is now home to New York City's official archival collection.

Strolling north on Centre St brings you to **Foley Square**, a complex of city, state and federal courthouses. The US Courthouse at

Bus Tour

Details on guided bus tours are available in the Organized Tours section. But a good cheap alternative to these tours is to take a self-guided loop of Manhattan on city buses. It's absolutely vital to start this tour in the morning, because traffic can be deadly in the afternoons. Items in bold text are covered in detail later in the guide.

Take the subway to the W 8th St station and catch the M5 bus on Sixth Ave north of Houston St going uptown (ask for a transfer).

The M5 travels first through **Chelsea**, past Ladies' Mile, where fashionable women shopped for millinery at the turn of the last century. Today the old ornate buildings between 14th St and 23rd St are being taken over by modern-day shopping malls. The bus continues past **Herald Square** and Macy's department store, and past **Bryant Park**, the broad lawn located behind the New York Public Library. You then travel the western edge of **Rockefeller Center**, past the GE building at 50th St and Radio City Music Hall.

Turning left at 59th, the bus skirts the southern end of Central Park before turning uptown at **Columbus Circle**. The monument, built in 1892, is the closest thing New York has to a grand avenue in the European tradition. Any chance of improving on the idea was destroyed by the construction in 1969 of the Gulf and Western Building, a huge, badly designed black and white office tower that has been remade into a muted brown glass luxury apartment building by Donald Trump.

Lincoln Center, the home of the Metropolitan Opera, the New York Philharmonic and the Julliard School of Music, appears on the left above 62nd St. Ten blocks later the bus moves over to Riverside Drive, bordered on its east side by blocks of well-kept apartment buildings, before passing **Grant's Tomb** at 122nd St, where Civil War hero and president Ulysses S Grant and his wife Julia are buried.

The M5 returns to Broadway at 135th St and 20 blocks later runs past **Audubon Terrace** on the west side of the street. Two under-appreciated museums are located at the former home of naturalist John James Audubon. The **American Numismatic Society** and the **Hispanic Society of America** are also here.

You can use the transfer on Broadway to take the M4 further uptown to **The Cloisters**. This granite copy of a monastery was built in the 1930s to house the Metropolitan Museum of Art's collection of medieval art. Nearby, on Broadway at 204th St, is **Dyckman House**. Built in 1783 and situated on what used to be a 28 acre farm, it is the last Dutch farmhouse to survive in Manhattan.

If you took time out to see anything so far, you'll want to return downtown via the A-train at 207th St–Inwood Station. To continue sightseeing from the bus, take the M4 which heads downtown along Broadway, east on Central Park North and continues south on Fifth Ave to Midtown. The bus will pass the **Museo del Barrio**, the **Museum of the City of New York**, the **Guggenheim Museum** and the **Metropolitan Museum of Art** – all part of 'Museum Mile.'

The M4 then passes by both Rockefeller Center's eastern edge and **St Patrick's Cathedral** at 50th St. By this time you are bound to be caught in traffic, so hop off the bus by the time it reaches the Empire State Building on 34th St and Fifth Ave. ■

40 Centre St, the familiar setting for organized crime trials, stands one block south of the New York County Courthouse, home to the state supreme court. Check out the lawyers holding noisy impromptu negotiations in its huge, bustling rotunda.

Turning left on Duane St brings you to the **African burial ground**, a cemetery for the city's early black residents unearthed in the late '80s and declared a national his-toric site. Many of the bodies discovered were of slaves wearing British uniforms – soldiers who were promised their freedom for fighting for the loyalists during the Revolutionary War.

Turning left onto Broadway brings you past the Sun Building at Chambers St. The newspaper – one of many located in this area during the early 20th century – no longer exists, but its clock remains, promising that the publication 'shines for all.'

The **Woolworth Building**, 233 Broadway, was the world's tallest (792 feet, 60 stories) when completed in 1913. Frank Woolworth, head of the famous discount store chain, reputedly paid the $15 million costs of the building with nickels and dimes. This so-called 'Cathedral of Commerce' includes a lobby gargoyle of Woolworth counting his change.

Carrying on down Broadway will bring you to **St Paul's Chapel**. Built in 1766, it is the oldest church in the city and the place where George Washington worshiped immediately after being sworn in as president. The building is quite undistinguished, but hosts noon-time music recitals every Monday and Thursday. The corridor from St Paul's past **Trinity Church** down Broadway includes a number of early monuments to capitalism, notably the old **Standard Oil Building** at 26 Broadway, a curved edifice built in 1922 by John D Rockefeller that houses the **Museum of American Financial History** (☎ (212) 908-4519). It's open Monday to Friday from 11:30 am to 2:30 pm.

The **Bank of New York Building** at 1 Wall St, which has an Art Deco lobby of blazing red and gold mosaic tiles, and the sleek and modern 1988 **Morgan Bank** headquarters at 60 Wall St symbolize their eras architecturally and stand as distinctive monuments to money.

Wall St, which begins across from Trinity Church, stands at the site where early Dutch settlers constructed a northern barrier to protect New Amsterdam from attacks by Native Americans and the British. Today it is the metaphorical home of US commerce. Walking along Wall St brings you to **Federal Hall**, also the starting point for four self-guided walking tours that go into the area's history in greater detail; a Heritage Trails map is given away free in the lobby. Across the street from Federal Hall stands the **New York Stock Exchange**, officially at 8 Broad St.

Continuing down Broad St and turning left on Pearl St will bring you to the histor-ical block at **Coenties Slip**, a Dutch docking station that became a street as the city extended further south. The archeological site of the old Dutch city hall is visible here, across the street from the **Fraunces Tavern Museum & Restaurant**. The current tavern is a 1907 renovation of the same place where Washington gave his farewell address to Continental Army officers in 1783.

Walking west on Bridge St brings you to **Battery Park**, where **Castle Clinton** stands, a fortification built in 1811 to protect Manhattan from the British. Ferries depart there for the Statue of Liberty and Ellis Island (see below for more information).

To the east of Battery Park is the **National Museum of the American Indian**, a division of the Smithsonian Institution. One block to the south of the museum near Pearl St and Broadway stands the **Shrine of St Elizabeth Seton** dedicated to America's first Roman Catholic saint. Tucked just behind this building is **New York Unearthed**, an interesting little exhibit of historical items discovered by archeologists and construction workers that's open Monday to Friday from noon until 6 pm.

From Battery Park you can head up West St to the **World Trade Center** to view the city from its 107th floor observatory. **The World Financial Center**, a complex built on landfill just next to the twin towers, has gallery spaces and shops that are perfect places to wait out bad weather.

If instead you wish to see Lower Manhattan's east tip, leave Battery Park at Pearl St. Detour one block south to **Peter Minuit Plaza**, reputedly the sight of the purchase of Manhattan for 60 guilders, before continuing up Pearl St. You will pass the **India House**, at 1 Hanover Square, a former bank building that's now an exclusive and somewhat secretive businessmen's club. Around the corner in a northerly direction on Beaver St (a name indicative of the trading activities of colonial New York) stands **Delmonico's**, part of the chain of famous restaurants that created the

American notion of 'dining out' in the 19th century. This 1891 structure includes a marble portico supposedly bought in Pompeii; the storied restaurant was closed for a while and is scheduled to reopen as a microbrewery and steak house.

Continuing up Pearl St to the intersection of Fulton St will bring you to the **Fulton Fish Market**, the city's wholesale seafood distribution point, and the **South Street Seaport**. Try to arrive as night falls to watch the lights come on the Brooklyn and Manhattan bridges. The sight is worth the extra money you'll pay for a drink at a South Street Seaport bar or cafe with a view.

Statue of Liberty

The most enduring symbol of New York City – and indeed, the USA – can trace its unlikely origins to a Parisian dinner party in 1865. There, a group of intellectuals opposed to the government of Napoleon III gathered in the house of political activist Edouard René Lefebvre de Laboulaye to discuss ways to promote French Republicanism. That notion of building a monument honoring the American conception of political freedom intrigued sculptor Frédéric-Auguste Bartholdi, a fellow dinner guest, who dedicated most of the next 20 years to turning the dream into a reality.

Laboulaye and Bartholdi decided that the structure should wind up in the US, and the latter traveled to New York in 1871 to choose a site for the work he had modeled on the Colossus of Rhodes. Soon afterward, the pair created a lottery to cover the $250,000 cost of construction of the statue, which included a metal skeleton by railway engineer Alexandre Gustave Eiffel, who later became world-famous for his eponymous Parisian tower.

On October 28, 1886, the 151, foot *Liberty Enlightening the World* was finally unveiled in New York harbor before President Grover Cleveland and a harbor full of tooting ships.

By the 1980s a restoration of the statue was in order, and more than $100 million was spent to shore up Liberty for its cen-

tennial. Substantial work was required for the rotting copper skin, and a new gold-plated torch, the third in the statue's history, was installed. The older stained-glass torch is now on display just inside the entrance to the staircase, near a fine museum describing the statue's history and its restoration. The exhibition also shows how the statue has always been exploited for commercial purposes.

The Statue of Liberty and Ellis Island (☎ (212) 363-7620) are a pleasant 15 minute ferry ride, and they each attract over two million visitors a year. Millions more take the boat ride just for the spectacular view of Manhattan but pass on taking the 354 steps to the statue's crown, the equivalent of climbing a 22 story building. (No one is allowed onto the statue's torch balcony.)

A trip taking in both the Statue of Liberty and Ellis Island is an all-day affair. In the summer you may wait up to an hour to embark on an 800 person ferry, only to be confronted by a three hour trek to the crown, followed by a bottleneck getting off both islands. If the statue is on your must-see list, get there at the very beginning of the day and make a beeline for the crown. And keep in mind, before waiting a hour or more to get to the top, that the view of Manhattan from the crown windows isn't any more or less spectacular than the one from ground level.

Though there is no charge to get off at Liberty Island, the ferries out of Manhattan (☎ (212) 269-5755) cost $7/3; seniors $5. They leave every 30 minutes from Battery Park (subway: South Ferry; Bowling Green) 9 am to 5 pm with extended hours during the summer. (Ferries also leave from Liberty State Park on the New Jersey side of the harbor; see the Northern New Jersey chapter.)

Ellis Island

Ferries to the Statue of Liberty make a second stop at Ellis Island, New York's main immigration station from 1892 to 1954. More than 15 million people passed through here before the island was abandoned. Barely visible further up the slip from the boat docks are the rotting remains

KIM GRANT

New York's ethnic mozaic is celebrated at the Immigration Museum.

of *Ellis Island*, a passenger ferry that sank in 1968 after years of neglect.

A $160 million restoration has turned the impressive red-brick main building into an **Immigration Museum** with a series of galleries on the history of the island. The exhibitions begin at the Baggage Room, and continue on to 2nd-story rooms where medical inspections took place and foreign currency was exchanged.

At all points, the exhibits emphasize that, contrary to popular myth, most of the ship-borne immigrants were processed within eight hours and that conditions were generally clean and safe. The 338 foot long Registry Room includes a beautiful vaulted tile ceiling made by immigrants from Spain. But walking though the registry today – described as 'light and airy' in museum literature – surely can't compare to days when the same room housed a queue of 5000 confused and tired people waiting to be interviewed by overworked immigration officers and inspected by doctors.

There is a 50 minute audio tour of the facility available for a additional charge ($3.50/2.50, seniors $3) that is a bit repetitive and padded with actor recreations of anonymous immigrant writings. Much more affecting are the recorded memories of real Ellis Island immigrants taped in the 1980s and available through phone banks in each display area.

A half hour film on the immigrant experience is worth checking out, as is the exhibition of how the influx of immigrants just before WWI changed the US. There's an interesting wall display of Tin Pan Alley sheet music that was aimed at this new foreign-born audience, including the songs *Yonkel the Cowboy Jew* and *Go On Good-a-Bye*, a 'characteristic Italian song' with words by one Joseph Murphy.

Castle Clinton

The ticket office for the Statue of Liberty boats is located in Castle Clinton, the fort built in 1811 to defend Manhattan from the British. Originally located 300 yards offshore before landfill engulfed it, Castle Clinton was converted to a theater in 1823, and has also served as an immigration station and aquarium. Today the castle is literally just a shell of its former self – there's no roof on the building anymore.

Trinity Church

This former Anglican parish (☎ (212) 602-0872), at the corner of Broadway and Wall St, was founded by King William III in 1697 and once had several constituent chapels, including the still-existent St Paul's Chapel at the corner of Fulton St and Broadway. Its huge land holdings in Lower Manhattan made it the wealthiest and most influential church throughout the 18th century.

The current Trinity Church is the third structure on the site and was built in 1846 by English architect Richard Upjohn. Its

280 foot bell tower made it the tallest building in New York City before the advent of skyscrapers. A pamphlet describing the parish's history is available for a 25¢ donation.

The long, dark interior of the church includes a beautiful stained glass window over the altar. Trinity, like other Anglican churches in America, became part of the Episcopal faith following US independence, but instinctive connections with Mother England are made painfully obvious by a pavement plaque near the entrance. It informs visitors that 'on this spot stood her Majesty Queen Elizabeth II on the occasion of her gracious visit 9 July 1976.' The notice goes on to generously note that 'His Royal Highness the Prince Philip stood nearby.'

It is open to visitors Monday through Friday from 9 am to 3:45 pm, Saturday from 10 am to 3:45 pm, and Sunday 1 to 3:45 pm, excluding lunchtime services.

Federal Hall

Distinguished by a huge statue of George Washington, Federal Hall (☎ (212) 767-0637), 26 Wall St, stands on the site where the first US Congress convened and where Washington later took the oath of office as the first US president. These events took place in the former city hall built by the British (replaced by the Greek Revival structure in 1842) which served as the US Customs House. Today there is a small museum dedicated to post-colonial New York open from 9 am to 5 pm weekdays. Guided tours of the building leave every hour on the half hour from 12:30 pm to 3:30 pm.

New York Stock Exchange

Though 'Wall Street' is the widely recognized metaphor for American capitalism, the world's best known stock exchange (NYSE; ☎ (212) 656-5167) is actually located around the corner at 8 Broad St, behind a portentous facade reminiscent of a Roman temple. A visitor's gallery overlooks the frenetic trading floor and includes an exhibit describing the exchange's history. The modern business of the exchange isn't explained very well, however, and not much is made of the famous 1929 stock market crash or even the 1987 debacle that led to restrictions on the computer-programmed stock dumping that triggered it off.

Free tickets to view the NYSE are distributed at a booth at 20 Broad St, Monday through Friday from 9:15 am to 4 pm. The tickets, which allow entrance to the visitors center in 45 minute time periods throughout the day, are usually snapped up by noon. While waiting in line, you'll see dozens of brokers wearing color-coordinated trading jackets popping out of the NYSE for a quick cigarette or hot dog.

National Museum of the American Indian

This museum (☎ (212) 668-6624), an affiliate of the Smithsonian Institution, abandoned its uptown spot at 155th St in 1994 and moved to the former US Customs House on Bowling Green. The Beaux Arts monument to commerce was built to collect federal duties imposed on foreign goods in the days before income tax; it is a grand but somewhat incongruous space for the US's leading museum on Native American art, established by oil heir George Gustav Heye in 1916. The facility's information center is found in the former collection office, with computer banks located next to old wrought-iron teller booths.

The galleries are on the 2nd floor, beyond a vast rotunda featuring statues of famous navigators and murals celebrating shipping history. This museum does little to explain the history of Native Americans, but instead concentrates its collection on Native American identity as reflected in its million-item collection of crafts and everyday objects. Computer touch-screens offer views on Native life and beliefs, and working artists are often available to explain their techniques. A gift shop offers Native American jewelry for sale.

The museum is open daily from 10 am to 5 pm, and admission is free.

South Street Seaport

This 11 block enclave of shops and historic sights (☎ (212) 732-7678) is visited each year by over 10 million people, and combines the best and worst in historic preservation. Pier 17, beyond the elevated FDR Drive, is a waterfront development project that's home to a number of shops (Benetton, The Gap) and overpriced restaurants. But the area also contains a number of genuinely significant buildings from the 18th and 19th centuries that once surrounded this old East River ferry port, which fell into disuse upon the building of the Brooklyn Bridge and the establishment of deepwater piers on the Hudson River.

Schermerhorn Row is a block of old warehouses bordered by Fulton, Front and South Sts that contains novelty shops, seafood restaurants and a pub. The **Fulton Market Building**, built across the street in 1983 to reflect the red-brick style of its older neighbors, is nothing more than a glorified fast-food hall and shopping arcade.

The **South Street Seaport Museum** (☎ (212) 748-8600) runs several interesting sights in the area, including three galleries, an antique printing shop, a children's center, a maritime crafts center and the historic ships. These are all open daily from 10 am to 5 pm and admission to the collection of buildings $6 for adults, $5 for seniors, $4 for students and $3 for children. You can also buy a combination ticket that includes a harbor cruise for an additional $10.

Just south of Pier 17 stand a group of tall-masted sailing vessels, including the *Peking*, the *Wavertree*, *The Pioneer* and the lightship *Ambrose*. All can be inspected with the price of admission to the museum. A booth on Pier 16 also sells tickets for an hour-long riverboat excursion from the Seaport Liberty Cruise Line (☎ (212) 630-8888) that highlights Manhattan's maritime history. Tours run at least three times each day from late March to the end of November and cost $12/6, $10 for seniors.

Pier 17 is also the site of the **Fulton Fish Market** (☎ (212) 669-9416), where most of the city's restaurants get their fresh seafood. The market is a perfect example of how this area maintains its old character while still catering to tourists. Management of the facility has long been thought to be controlled by the Genovese organized crime family and a recent crackdown on corruption led to months of labor unrest and a suspicious 1995 fire that destroyed a part of the market. Nevertheless, the nightly working of the market can be seen by visitors from midnight to 8 am, and guided tours (☎ (212) 664-9416) are available from April to October.

If you make the trek down to the Seaport, be sure to venture away from the crowd by taking Front St north a few blocks to Peck Slip, where you will see a few abandoned fish warehouses with their original signs intact.

City Hall

City Hall (☎ (212) 788-6865) has been home to New York's government since 1812. In an example of the half-baked civic planning that has often plagued big New York projects, officials neglected to finish the building's northern side in marble, betting that the city would not expand uptown! The mistake was finally rectified in 1954, completing a structure that architectural critic Ada Louise Huxtable has called a 'symbol of taste, excellence and quality not always matched by the policies inside.' On either side of the building stands 'The Key to City Hall,' an interactive video center with information on local landmarks and visitor services.

Walk to the 2nd floor to the spot at the top of the stairs where, in 1865, Abraham Lincoln's coffin was placed on its way from Washington, DC, to Springfield, IL. The Governor's Room, a reception area used by the mayor for important guests, contains 12 portraits of the founding fathers by John Trumbull, several examples of Federal furniture including George Washington's writing table, and the remnants of a flag flown at the first president's 1789 inaugural ceremony. Peeking into the City Council chambers may reveal the lawmakers deliberating the renaming of a city street in someone's honor, an activity which accounts for 40% of all the bills passed by the 51 member body.

City Hall's steps are a popular site for demonstrations and press conferences by grandstanding politicians and the lobby currently holds the World Championship trophy won by baseball's New York Yankees in 1996. Don't be discouraged by the grumpy security presence – the building is open to the public Monday to Friday from 10 am to 4 pm.

Brooklyn Bridge

This was the first steel suspension bridge ever built; the 1596 foot span between its two support towers was the longest ever when it opened in 1883. It is regarded by many to be the most beautiful bridge in the world and is a magnificent example of fine urban design.

Plans for an East River suspension bridge were drawn up by the Prussian-born engineer John Roebling (see also Niagara Falls, NY), who was knocked off a pier by a ferry in Fulton's Landing in June 1869, and died of tetanus poisoning before construction of the bridge began. His son Washington Roebling supervised construction of the bridge, which took 14 years and was plagued by budget overruns and the deaths of 20 workers. The younger Roebling himself was stricken by the bends while helping to excavate the riverbed for the bridge's western tower and remained bedridden for much of the project. There was one final tragedy to come in June of 1883, when the bridge opened to pedestrian traffic: someone in the crowd shouted,

KIM GRANT

perhaps as a joke, that the bridge was collapsing into the river, setting off a mad rush in which 12 people were trampled to death.

There's no fear of collapse today, as the bridge enters its second century following an extensive renovation in the early 1980s. The pedestrian walkway that begins just east of City Hall affords a wonderful view of Lower Manhattan, and you can stop at observation points under both stone support towers and view brass panorama histories of the waterfront at various points in New York's history. Once you reach the Brooklyn side (about a 20 minute walk) you can bear left to walk down to Cadman Plaza West to a park that will bring you to Middagh St, which runs east to west in the heart of Brooklyn Heights. Bearing right brings you to Brooklyn's downtown area, which includes the ornate Borough Hall and Fulton St pedestrian mall. (See the Outer Boroughs section of this chapter for more coverage.)

Fraunces Tavern Museum & Restaurant

Fraunces Tavern (☎ (212) 425-1778), 54 Pearl St, is on a block of historic structures that, along with nearby Stone St and the South Street Seaport, are the final examples of colonial-era New York that remain largely intact – the buildings here can be traced to the early 18th century.

On this site stood the Queen's Head Tavern, owned by Samuel Fraunces, who changed the name to Fraunces Tavern after American victory in the War for Independence. It was in the 2nd-floor dining room on December 4, 1783, that George Washington bade farewell to the officers of the Continental Army after the British relinquished control of New York City. In the 19th century, the tavern closed and the building fell into disuse. It was also damaged during several massive fires that swept through old downtown areas and destroyed most colonial buildings and nearly all structures built by the Dutch. In 1904, the building was bought by the Sons of the Revolution historical society and returned to an approximation of its colonial-era look – an act believed to be the first major attempt at historic preservation in the US.

The museum and restaurant are separate facilities, and eating a meal does not include entry to the museum, which is open Monday to Friday from 10 am to 4:45 pm and Saturday from noon to 4 pm. Admission is $2.50/1.

Just across the street from the tavern are the excavated remains of the old Dutch **Stadt Huys**, which served as New Amsterdam's administrative center, courthouse and jail from 1641 until the peaceful British takeover in 1664. This building, destroyed in 1699, was originally on the city's waterfront until landfill added a few more blocks to southern Manhattan.

World Trade Center

The massive twin towers of the World Trade Center (WTC; ☎ (212) 323-2340), which rise 1350 feet above the ground, are part of a complex that houses more than 350 different businesses employing 50,000 people. Built at a cost of $700 million from 1966-73, the sleek WTC has never stirred people's hearts in the same manner as the Empire State Building, though the project did change the city in a profound way: the one million cubic yards of rock and dirt unearthed for its foundation became the landfill on which the 24 acre Battery Park City development was built.

The twin towers have attracted two well-publicized daredevils: George Willig, who used mountain climbing equipment to scale the side of one building, and circus performer Philippe Petit, who claimed he was able to use a crossbow to run a tightrope across both buildings without anyone in authority stopping him before putting on a show a quarter-mile above the ground.

The WTC's array of federal and state government offices made it a tempting target for the terrorists who set off a truck bomb in the underground parking garage on February 26, 1993, killing six people.

The ticket booth for the WTC observation decks is open seven days a week from 9:30 am to 11:30 pm from June to September and 9:30 am to 9:30 pm the remainder of the year. Admission for adults/children is $7/3.50.

The **Commodities Exchange Center** (☎ (212) 938-2025) is located within the complex on the 9th floor of 4 World Trade Center. You can view the trading floor – home to a group of traders far more emotional than their Wall St brethren – from 9:30 am to 3 pm weekdays. Admission is free. The shopping plaza on the subway level underneath the buildings was the first indoor mall to open in New York City.

The **World Financial Center**, just across West St from the WTC, stands on the landfill created by the excavation for the WTC's foundation. This group of four office towers surrounds the **Winter Garden**, a glass atrium and ostentatious centerpiece that is the site of free concerts during the summer and exclusive black-tie events year round. During good weather it's pleasant to walk, run or bike down the mile-long esplanade running from the residential Battery Park City apartments from the north past the World Financial Center to the tip of Manhattan; when it's rainy you can pass an hour in the shopping area and art gallery located next to the Winter Garden. The Liberty St Gallery, 225 Liberty Place, has a number of worthwhile exhibitions and there's a museum-quality autograph store in the enclosed shopping plaza.

CHINATOWN & LITTLE ITALY

Chinatown and Little Italy are renowned as ethnic enclaves just north of the Civic Center and the financial district; Chinatown sprawls largely south of Canal St, while Little Italy is a narrow sliver extending north of the same thoroughfare.

The denizens of Chinatown now number about 100,000, many of whom live and work in a mini-society without using a word of English. This community, with its own rhythms and traditions, is catered to in many different ways: some banks along Canal St keep Sunday hours, and no fewer than seven Chinese newspapers are available on newsstands. Throughout the '90s, Chinatown has also been home to a growing community of Vietnamese immigrants, who have set up their own shops and incredibly cheap restaurants here.

In recent times, Chinatown has moved east and north, and you can find Chinese bakeries and shops in the area above Canal St. In effect, the area known as the 'Lower East Side' is breaking up into two distinct neighborhoods: south of Delancey St it's Chinese, north of Delancey is becoming absorbed as a hopping adjunct of the East Village. And these days, Grand St, which runs parallel to Canal St, is taking on a Chinese flavor, with busy fruit stands and fish stores open until 8 pm each night.

In contrast, Little Italy is confined largely to Mulberry St north of Canal St. This was once a very strong Italian neighborhood (film director Martin Scorsese grew up on Elizabeth St), and while many of the apartment buildings in this 10 block radius are still owned by former residents, there was an exodus from Little Italy in the mid-20th century to the Cobble Hill section of Brooklyn as well as the city's suburbs.

For that reason, there are few cultural sites and most people come to Little Italy specifically to eat, even though there are dozens of good restaurants serving Italian cuisine at all price levels elsewhere.

Off Mulberry St, on Elizabeth and Lafayette Sts, Little Italy begins to take on a more cosmopolitan character, as the overflow of SoHo-style shops, cafes and restaurants make their way into the area, taking over storefronts that once served as social clubs and stores for the old community. This neighborhood is being sold by realtors as having 'Montparnasse charm,' which means it's a hot area with overpriced, dumpy apartments. Take a stroll around Elizabeth and Lafayette – the area is literally changing from month to month.

Chinatown Walking Tour

For a tour of Chinatown, start on Canal St. West of Lafayette St, Canal St maintains a decidedly seedy character, with hardware and electrical supply stores co-existing with street vendors selling phony designer clothing and bootleg videos of films still playing in theaters. If you buy anything off a street-seller, make sure it's something you can wear or check out on the spot – a hat, a book or a leather jacket. The Chinese shopping district begins east of Baxter St, with several stands selling fresh fish and exotic produce, including guavas and durians, the infamously smelly fruit banned from the subways of Singapore.

Crossing Mott St brings you to most of the district's restaurants. The **Eastern States Buddhist Temple** (☎ (212) 966-4753), in a storefront at 64B Mott St, is a busy shrine with dozens of golden and porcelain Buddhas on display. You can buy a fortune for $1 and watch the devout make offerings.

The **Church of the Transfiguration**, 29 Mott St, began as an Episcopal church in 1801 and was purchased by the Roman Catholic Church 50 years later to meet the needs of what was then an Irish and Italian neighborhood. In the 1890s the ascendant and spiteful Irish church leaders forced Italian patrons to worship in the basement. The church got its first Chinese pastor in the 1970s and today holds services in Chinese.

Turning left on Pell St, an old road named for a butcher who plied his trade here in the colonial period, brings you to Doyers St. Chinatown began in this small enclave in the 1870s when Chinese railway workers, fed up with racial discrimination in the American West, moved to New York City in large numbers. During Chinese New Year celebrations in late January and early February, papier-mâché dragons snake their way around this corner to the sounds of firecrackers shooing away evil spirits.

Exiting Doyers St brings you toward two examples of the neighborhood's previous ethnic history. **Chatham Square** is where public auctions took place to sell the goods of Irish debtors in the early 19th century. Walking 150 yards south on St James Place brings you to **First Shearith Israel Graveyard**. This cemetery, which dates back to the 1680s, served early Portuguese and Spanish immigrants, and is the oldest

Jewish cemetery in the US. If you're a contrarian, seek out the restaurants on Catherine St or East Broadway, which are hardly ever patronized by tourists.

Turning around and heading north brings you up the Bowery and to the grand but pollution-marred entrance to the Manhattan Bridge. Heading four blocks west of Mulberry St on Canal St will bring you to **Cortlandt Alley** on the south side of the street, a perfectly preserved four block enclave of gloomy old factories and warehouses that are often featured in movies – it's worth a quick exploration.

Chinatown History Museum

The nonprofit Museum of Chinese in the Americas (☎ (212) 619-4785), 70 Mulberry St, is in a century-old former public school building which reopened in early 1996 after a year long renovation. The museum sponsors walking tours and crafts workshops on paper lantern-making and other creative endeavors. Recent exhibits include 80 works made in captivity by the survivors of the *Golden Venture*, a ship full of illegal immigrants from China that ran aground near New York harbor in 1993. Thirty-three of the Chinese who crossed over on the ship have been detained by the US immigration service for more than three years.

The museum is open Tuesday to Sunday from 10:30 am to 5 pm. Admission is $3/1; children under 12 are free.

Little Italy Sights

The **Old Police Headquarters** at 240 Centre St is an example of how public officials in New York often approved the construction of European-style monuments without providing proper setback space or park land to allow passers-by to fully appreciate their grandeur. This building overwhelmn its neighbors, just as it did upon its completion in 1909. It was converted into apartments in 1988.

The **Old St Patrick's Cathedral** at 263 Mulberry St appears bland and unimpressive because of a fire that destroyed much of its exterior. But the structure served as

---

The Stanford White Legacy

As you walk out of Chinatown, take note of the old Bowery Savings Bank building at 130 Bowery. The bank's Romanesque archway and vaulted, gold leaf interior are a quiet respite from the noisy fruit stands and traffic on the corner of Bowery and Grand St.

It was designed in 1894 by Stanford White, the most talented and colorful architect of the gilded age. His firm, McKim, Mead and White, created many of New York City's Beaux Arts masterpieces, including the original Pennsylvania Station, built in 1911 (and since razed). Widely considered to be White's greatest creation, Penn Station was demolished in 1965 for a newer facility, over the protests of many prominent public figures, including modernist architect Philip Johnson.

Once the elegant old train palace had been replaced by the ugly, inadequate and badly designed Penn Station/ Madison Square Garden complex that now stands in Midtown, public outcry forced the creation of the City's Landmarks Preservation Commission. Thanks to the laws protecting landmarks and increased public awareness of the city's architectural treasures, other works by White – including the Player's Club on Gramercy Park, the Washington Square Arch and the Brooklyn Museum of Art – will remain untouched by the wrecker's ball.

White himself met an ignominious end. A roué and spendthrift art collector, he was nearly bankrupt by 1905. He conducted a wild affair with the young married socialite Evelyn Nesbit, and they often met for trysts in his apartment located above an earlier version of Madison Square Garden. It was there on the roof garden restaurant that White was shot and killed by Nesbit's jealous husband Harry K Thaw. Subsequent revelations about the May-December romance during Thaw's trial permanently damaged White's reputation and led a jury to declare Thaw not guilty by reason of insanity. ■

the city's first Roman Catholic Cathedral from 1809-78, when its more famous successor was built uptown on Fifth Ave. The old cathedral and its damaged Georgian interior can be viewed only during weekend services, Saturday at 5 pm and Sunday at 9:30 am and 12:30 pm.

As you continue up Mulberry to Houston St, you will approach the back of the stunning red-brick **Puck Building**, the home of the turn-of-the-century American humor magazine. The building, with its two gold-leaf statues of the portly Puck, is a popular spot for wedding receptions and film shoots.

LOWER EAST SIDE

Architecturally, this storied old tenement area still retains its hardscrabble character, with block after block of crumbling buildings. You can still see why early 20th century residents, about half a million Jews from Eastern Europe who worked in factories in the area, lamented that 'the sun was embarrassed to shine' on their benighted neighborhood.

But like Little Italy, the Lower East Side has lost most of its traditional ethnic flavor. There is no Jewish community left here, though many businesses remain. The people living behind the crumbling doorways of the contemporary Lower East Side are more likely to be young people living in their first city apartment or long-term residents holding onto the good deal on a rent-controlled apartment. Also, a growing Latino community has spilled over on the Lower East Side's northern border, and the Chinese have been moving into the area south of Delancey St.

In recent years, more than a dozen no-name bars and late-night lounges have opened in the four-block area on and around Ludlow St, which runs south from Houston St. On Saturday nights, the streets are packed with grunge rockers, dance club addicts and underage drinkers. As the East Village, located just above this area north of Houston St, continues its swift gentrification, the Lower East Side seems on track to become the city's quin-

tessential outlaw neighborhood. And the opening of the Red Square building on E Houston St, with its $1300-per-bedroom rents, statue of Lenin and huge clock, seems a harbinger of the neighborhood's eventual transformation into a desirable place to live.

Orchard St

The 'Orchard St Bargain District' is the market area defined by Orchard, Ludlow and Essex Sts above Delancey St, which runs east to west. This is where Eastern European merchants set up pushcarts to sell their wares when this was still a largely Jewish neighborhood.

Today the 320 odd shops in this modern-day bazaar sell sporting goods, leather belts, hats and a wide array of off-brand 'designer fashions.' While the businesses are not exclusively owned by Orthodox Jews, they still close early on Friday afternoon and remain shuttered Saturday in observance of the Sabbath. There's an unspoken rule that shop owners should offer a discount to their first customer of the day – usually 10% – for good luck, so it helps to arrive at 10 am if you're serious about buying something. Offering to pay in cash may also attract a discount. If you hate haggling, pick up a set of discount coupons and a store directory at the Orchard St Bargain District offices (☎ (212) 995-8258), 261 Broome St.

There's not much for sale in the Lower East Side that you couldn't pick up elsewhere in the city, with the exception of **kosher food products**, such as the wines at Schapiro's (☎ (212) 674-4404), 126 Rivington St, which offers a short tour of its facilities on Sunday. You can pick up unleavened bread at Streit's Matzoh Company, 150 Rivington St; potato knishes at Yonah Shimmel Bakery, 137 E Houston St, and sweet and sour pickles directly out of the wooden barrels at Essex Pickles, 25 Essex St.

A free tour of the district leaves each Sunday at 11 am from Katz's Deli on the corner of Ludlow and Houston Sts.

Lower East Side Tenement Museum

The neighborhood's heartbreaking heritage is preserved at this museum. The gallery (☎ (212) 431-0233), 90 Orchard St, is open Tuesday through Sunday from 11 am to 5 pm, and offers a video on the difficult life endured by the people who once lived in the surrounding buildings, which often did not have running water or electricity.

Across the street, the museum has recreated a turn-of-the-century tenement owned by Lucas Glockner, a German-born tailor. This building, in which an estimated 10,000 people lived over 72 years, is accessible only by guided tour. The tours leave Tuesday through Friday at 1, 2 and 3 pm and every 45 minutes on the weekend from 11 am to 4:45 pm. Tickets to the museum, which include the tenement tour, are $7/6 for adults/children. From April to October the museum also sponsors a walking tour of the neighborhood. Call ahead for more information.

Synagogues

Nearby the tenement museum, near the corner of Rivington and Orchard Sts, is the **First Roumanian-American Congregation** (☎ (212) 673-2835), 89 Rivington St, one of the few remaining Orthodox synagogues in the Lower East Side (of the 400 that thrived in the neighborhood in the early 20th century). The building, currently under renovation, features a wonderfully ornate wooden sanctuary that can hold 1800 of the faithful, but membership in the *shul* has dwindled to under 50 people.

The landmark **Eldridge St Synagogue** (☎ (212) 219-0888), at 12 Eldridge St between Canal and Division Sts east of the Bowery (subway: Grand St), is another struggling place of worship in an area that is now completely part of Chinatown. The Moorish synagogue faces one of the oldest surviving blocks of tenements in New York City. These old and dirty buildings are now occupied by recent Chinese immigrants, who patronize the employment agencies in the ground floor offices of those tenements. The synagogue has a museum and offers tours on the hour from 11 am to 4 pm

Sunday, Tuesday, Wednesday and Thursday. Admission is $4/2.50.

SOHO

This neighborhood is not named after its London counterpart but is a geographic conceit for the rectangular area 'SOuth of HOuston St' extending as far down as Canal St. No one really knows for sure why Houston St is pronounced HOW-ston, though it is assumed that a man named William Houstoun who lived in the area pronounced his surname in that manner. (Somewhere along the line the second 'u' in the spelling of the street was dropped.)

SoHo is a paradigm of inadvertent modern urban renewal. The district is filled with block after block of cast-iron industrial buildings that date to the period just after the Civil War, when the area was the city's leading commercial district. These multi-story buildings housed linen, ribbon and clothing factories, and there were often showcase galleries located on the street level. But the area fell into disfavor as retail businesses relocated uptown and manufacturing concerns moved out of the city. By the 1950s the huge lofts and cheap rents attracted artists and other members of the avant-garde. Their political lobbying not only saved the neighborhood from destruction, but assured that a 26 block area was declared a legally protected historic district in 1973. Today, SoHo is the city's leading area for art galleries, clothing stores and boutiques selling oh-so-precious curios. Unadorned lofts sell for more than $300,000 and rental rates are simply impossible.

It's preferable to visit SoHo on a weekday morning, when the neighborhood is populated largely by the people who work in the galleries and assorted offices. True to the 'downtown' clichés, these office workers are dressed invariably in sleek black outfits and wear some of the most adventurous eyewear you'll see in the city. On Saturday and Sunday, West Broadway (a separate street from Broadway) becomes a sea of suede, and it and nearby Prince St are packed with tourists and street artists selling homemade jewelry and paintings in defiance of the laws requiring a city license to sell such wares. A few vendors have been arrested for this, and a democracy wall covered with handbills protesting the police crackdown is located on Prince St near the corner of Mercer St.

Walking Tour

You can begin your exploration of SoHo by taking the subway to the Broadway–Lafayette St station and walking south down Broadway.

On the very first block you will encounter four fine art museums described in detail further on: the Alternative Museum, the African Museum, the New Museum of Contemporary Art and the Guggenheim SoHo. Just past Prince St on the right, you will then pass the **Singer Building**, 561-563 Broadway, a very attractive iron and brick structure that was the main warehouse for the famous sewing machine company. At 521-523 Broadway, above the fabric store and gourmet food shop, you can view what's left of the marble-faced **St Nicholas Hotel**, the 1000 room luxury hotel that was *the* place to stay when it opened in 1854. The hotel, which closed by 1880, was the headquarters of Abraham Lincoln's War Department during the Civil War.

As you walk through SoHo, stop to look up at the buildings you're passing – many still have elaborate decorated flourishes that have been obscured or destroyed on the street level. A perfect example is the **Haughwout Building** which houses the Staples office

supply store at 488 Broadway. This was once the headquarters of the EV Haughwout crockery company. Built in 1857, it was the first building to use the exotic steam 'elevator' developed by Elisha Otis.

One block further south, at Grand St, you will encounter a parking lot that is the site of an **antique market** on Sunday. Turning right and walking west four blocks will bring you to West Broadway; near this corner you will find a half dozen late night restaurants and bars that are worth checking out for a drink.

Heading north up West Broadway will bring you past the gallery of art titan Leo Castelli (☎ (212) 431-5160), at No 420; Castelli represents many contemporary greats at this and two other SoHo locations. Ileana Sonnabend (☎ (212) 966-6160) is at the same address on the 3rd floor. There are a number of influential galleries on Wooster St, which parallels West Broadway immediately to the east, including Paula Cooper (☎ (212) 674-0766), 149-155 Wooster St; and the Howard Greenberg Gallery (☎ (212) 334-0010), 120 Wooster St, which specializes in photography. Other big galleries nearby include Edward Thorpe (☎ (212) 431-6880), 103 Prince St, and Jay Gorney (☎ (212) 966-4480), 100 Greene St.

On the southeast corner of the intersection of Prince and Greene Sts you will see a local landmark: artist Richard Haas' now fading mural of an apartment front painted on the bare brick wall of 112 Prince St.

Alternative Museum

At 594 Broadway, on the 4th floor of a building that houses several other art galleries, this is more of a pay-to-view gallery than a full-fledged museum. There's a suggested admission charge of $3. The museum (☎ (212) 966-4444) is open Tuesday through Saturday from 11 am to 6 pm.

Museum for African Art

This facility (☎ (212) 966-1313), 593 Broadway, is the city's only space dedicated solely to the works of African artists,

---

Looking Up at Buildings

If you're interested in making a fuller exploration of SoHo's physical makeup, pick up a copy of the *AIA Guide to New York City* ($24). This superb companion from the American Institute of Architects is perfect for anyone interested in the city's aesthetic history, though its larger-than-a-brick size makes it difficult to carry around all day. ■

and there's a heavy concentration on tribal crafts, musical instruments and depictions of spirituality. The interior was designed by Maya Lin, the young architect who first found fame for her stark and stunning Vietnam Memorial in Washington, DC.

The African Museum charges a $4/2 admission for adults/students and is open Tuesday to Friday from 10:30 am to 5:30 pm, and Saturday and Sunday from noon until 6 pm.

New Museum of Contemporary Art

This museum (☎ (212) 219-1222), 583 Broadway, is at the vanguard of the contemporary SoHo scene and offers exposure to art works that are less than 10 years old. That's probably why one of the museum's recent exhibits was called 'Temporarily Possessed: Works from the Semi-Permanent Collection.' Signage artist Jenny Holzer and sculptor Jeff Koons have had their work exhibited in this museum.

The museum is open Sunday and Wednesday through Friday from noon to 6 pm, and Saturdays from noon to 8 pm. It's closed Monday and Tuesday. Admission is $4 for adults, $3 for artists, students and seniors, and entry is free on Saturday evenings from 6 to 8 pm.

Guggenheim Museum SoHo

The Solomon R Guggenheim Museum's decision in 1992 to open a downtown branch (☎ (212) 423-3500), 575 Broadway, was part of its extensive renovation and expansion that tripled its showcase space. The SoHo branch also lent legitimacy to the neighborhood's claim to being the center of the US's arts scene. In addition to featuring works by living artists in mid-career such as sculptor Dan Flavin, the museum's two floors house overflow from the Guggenheim's permanent collection.

The Guggenheim SoHo is open Wednesday to Friday and Sunday from 11 am to 6 pm and Saturday from 11 am to 8 pm. Admission is $5/3 (kids under 12 free). If you plan on visiting both branches of the Guggenheim, it's a wise idea to buy a ticket

---

The Gallery Scene

In early 1996, art dealer Mary Boone shocked the New York City cultural elite by announcing that she was moving her gallery from SoHo to a new space at 745 Fifth Ave. Boone, a pioneer in mixing art and commerce in the '80s, who launched the careers of Julian Schnabel, David Salle and Jean-Michel Basquiat, claimed that the 'energy and focus of art has shifted uptown.' But skeptics believed that Boone's move was prompted by a class-driven distaste for the coffeehouses and shops that have opened in SoHo, which attract crowds interested in looking at – but certainly not buying – overpriced contemporary art. In any case, SoHo is still the place to go if you're looking for funky galleries, though a few have moved over to Chelsea; more mainstream spaces can be found on Madison Ave above 59th St.

You can pick up information on what's on display by picking up the free monthly *NY/SOHO* map, available in downtown galleries; or scan the Goings on about Town section in the *New Yorker* or the entertainment section of the Sunday *New York Times*. ∎

---

good for admission to both during a seven day period, which costs $10/6.

TRIBECA

This neighborhood of old warehouses, loft apartments and funky restaurants derives its name from its geographical location: the 'TRIangle BElow CAnal' St, an area roughly bordered by Broadway to the east and Chambers St to the south. Though not as touristy or architecturally significant as SoHo, its northern neighbor, Tribeca nonetheless has its attractions, including a fair share of the 'scene' restaurants and bars, along with actor Robert De Niro's Tribeca Films production company.

The warehouses – most of which still retain long truck loading platforms covered by metal awnings – make great apartment spaces. As such the neighborhood is not yet overrun with boutiques and chain stores, which have driven some art galleries and plenty of well-heeled residents out of SoHo. Tribeca is home to more than a handful of famous people, including actor Harvey Keitel and magazine publisher–professional hunk John F Kennedy Jr. In winter, it's not unusual to spot a star hanging out at a local restaurant or bar, though on summer weekends the place reverts back to its old character as a windswept industrial district when this same crowd flees the city for resort areas on Long Island and Cape Cod. Late afternoon summer light can be stunning in this neighborhood, and the desolation chic makes the area a favorite for fashion photographers.

The Franklin St subway station is located in the heart of Tribeca, or you can get to the neighborhood's northern border by taking the A, C or E train to Canal St and walking south on West Broadway.

Harrison St

The eight townhouses on the block of Harrison St immediately west of Greenwich St were all built between 1804 and 1828 and constitute the largest collection of Federal architecture left in the city. But they were not always neighbors: six of them once stood two blocks away on a stretch of Washington St that no longer exists. In the early 1970s, that area was the site of Washington Market, a wholesale center that was the fruit and vegetable equivalent of the Fulton Fish Market. A new home had to be found for the row houses when the market was relocated uptown to allow the development of the waterfront, including Manhattan Community College and the unattractive concrete apartment complex that now looms over the townhouses. Only the buildings at 31 and 33 Harrison St remain where they were originally constructed.

New York City Fire Museum

The Fire Museum (☎ (212) 691-1303), 278 Spring St, occupies a grand old firehouse dating back to 1904. There's an amazingly well-maintained collection of gleaming gold horse-drawn firefighting carriages along with modern-day fire engines. The development of the New York City fire-fighting system, which began with the 'bucket brigades,' is also explained along the way. All the colorful heavy equipment and the museum's particularly friendly staff make this a great place to bring children, even though they are not allowed to hop on any of the engines.

The museum is open Tuesday to Saturday from 10 am to 4 pm; suggested admission is $6 for adults, $4 for seniors and students, and $1 for children.

GREENWICH VILLAGE

This storied neighborhood is one of the city's most popular, and a symbol throughout the world for all things outlandish and bohemian. Generally defined by a northern border of 14th St and a southern demarcation of Houston St, Greenwich Village runs from Lafayette St all the way west to the Hudson River. The area just south of Washington Square Park (including Bleecker St running west all the way to Seventh Ave) is a lively and somewhat overcrowded collection of cafes, shops and restaurants; beyond Seventh Ave is the West Village, a pleasant neighborhood of winding streets and townhouses.

Greenwich Village began as a trading port for Native Americans, who liked the easy access to the shores of what is now Hoboken, NJ, just across the Hudson River. Dutch settlers established a number of tobacco plantations, and the peaceful wooded area was named Greenwich Village by their English successors. As the city began to develop a large servant class, Greenwich Village became New York's most prominent black neighborhood until many of those residents moved to Harlem just before the 1920s in search of better housing.

Its reputation as a creative enclave can be traced back to at least the early 1900s, when artists and writers moved in, and by the '40s the neighborhood was known as a gathering place for gays. The center of 'the Village' is dominated by New York University, which owns most of the property around Washington Square Park, and the brownstone buildings abandoned by blacks all those years ago are now some of the most fashionable and valuable properties in the city.

Central Village Walking Tour

The best place to start is the arch at **Washington Square Park**. Head south on Thompson St past a series of chess shops where Village denizens meet to play the game for $1.50 an hour. At the intersection of Thompson and Bleecker Sts (Bleecker being the main east-west thoroughfare in Greenwich Village), look up at the southwest corner and you will see the old sign for the legendary jazz club **Village Gate**, which has recently relocated to Midtown. Turn right on Bleecker and head east for two blocks, which will bring you to two old coffee-houses associated with New York's '50s beatnik culture: **Le Figaro**, which still has a worthwhile weekend jazz brunch, and **Caffe Borgia**. You're better off taking a look around Bleecker St and then taking a right on MacDougal St where you'll find a great cup of cappuccino at Caffe Reggio at No 119, which still retains some Old World character, thanks to its dark walls and massive trademark espresso machine. Double-back a half block to **Minetta Tavern**, an old Village hangout with a decent restaurant. It's a great place to stop for a beer to admire the old photos of '50s-era celebrities that used to hang out there. On the opposite corner is Cafe Wha? a legendary old club where Jimi Hendrix once played. (Its 'in' days are long past.) Head west down Minetta Lane, making a left onto Minetta St which brings you past a block of 18th century slums that have been preserved and improved into desirable row houses. The old Minetta Brook still runs under some of the houses.

Crossing Sixth Ave and walking west on Bleecker St brings you past a three block stretch of record stores, leather shops, restaurants and delicious Italian pastry shops. Turn right on Seventh Ave, noting the famous jazz club **Sweet Basil** on the left and head north up three blocks to Grove St, where a right turn will lead to **Stonewall Place**, site of the 1969 gay rebellion (see the Gay & Lesbian New York sidebar).

Heading east (right) on Waverly Place brings you to the oddly shaped **Northern Dispensary** at 165 Waverly Place. It was built in 1831 to combat a cholera epidemic that was then sweeping through this neighborhood and was New York's oldest public health facility until 1989, when it was shut down by city human rights officials after the dental clinic there refused to treat patients with HIV. The three sided Dispensary creates the strangest spot in New York City: the corner of Waverly Place and Waverly Place!

Back on Sixth Ave, you will want to turn left and examine the red-brick **Jefferson Market Courthouse**, now a public library, and the **Jefferson Market Gardens** which are open to the public. Just behind the building on W 10th St is **Patchin Place**, an enclosed courtyard block of flats that was home to both journalist John Reed and poet e.e. cummings.

Double-back to Sixth Ave and head up two blocks to W 11th St and head east. On the right you'll find the tiny **Second Cemetery of the Spanish and Portuguese Synagogue** which was used from 1805-29. Continue along W 11th St and you'll pass by a series of traditional row houses, including builder **Andrew Lockwood's House** at No 60, which was

---

Greenwich Village's Rock Landmarks

Rock fans interested in more contemporary landmarks will want to take note of 161 W 4th St, where Bob Dylan once lived and was inspired to write 'Positively 4th St.' He reputedly smoked his first joint at **The Kettle of Fish** bar, 100 W 3rd St, during its previous incarnation as the Folk City music club. Jimi Hendrix lived and recorded at the **Electric Lady Studios**, just a few steps east of Sixth Ave at 55 W 8th St (check for the Hendrix photo in a 2nd floor window). It was later used by the Rolling Stones. ∎

built in 1842 on a lot that was originally part of the larger Wouter Van Twiller Farm. Turn right when you reach Fifth Ave and you'll be heading directly back toward the arch in Washington Square Park.

Washington Square Park

Washington Square Park is purported to be, per inch, the most crowded recreational space in the world. A visitor from China or India might raise an eyebrow over that boast, but a stroll through the busy park on the weekend lends some credence to the claim.

The park, like many public spaces in the city, began as a 'potter's field' – a burial ground for the penniless. Its status as a cemetery protected it from development. It was also the site of public executions, including the hanging of several petty criminals to honor a visit to New York by the French statesman Marquis de Lafayette in 1824. The magnificent old tree near the northwestern corner of the park has a plaque stating it was the 'Hangman's Elm,' though no one is quite sure if it was actually used for executions.

Pay particular attention to the Stanford White **Arch**, originally designed in wood to celebrate the centennial of George Washington's inauguration in 1889. The arch proved so popular that it was replaced in stone six years later, and adorned with statues of the general in war and peace (the latter work is by A Stirling Calder, the father of artist Alexander Calder).

In 1916, artist Marcel Duchamp climbed to the top of the arch by its internal stairway with a few friends and declared the park the 'Free and Independent Republic of Washington Square.' These days the anarchy takes place on the ground level, as comedians and buskers use the park's permanently dry fountain as a performance space. The fountain was once used as terminus and turnaround for the Fifth Ave buses that ran under the arch. You'll probably notice that the park is also the site of the most brazenly open drug-dealing in the city, as hustlers conduct a brisk marijuana trade selling to students of nearby New

York University with the whispered come-on 'smoke, smoke?'

The **Judson Memorial Church** graces the park's south border. This yellow-brick Baptist church honors Adoniram Judson, an American missionary who served in Burma in the early 19th century. Designed by Stanford White, this national historic site features stained-glass windows by muralist John La Farge, who was born near the park, and marble frontage by Augustus Saint-Gaudens.

One block east of the park, at 245 Greene St, is the building where the Triangle Shirtwaist Fire took place on March 25, 1911. (A plaque declares it the 'site' of the fire, but it is the actual building.) This sweatshop had locked its doors to prevent the young seamstresses who toiled there from taking unauthorized breaks. The inferno killed 146 young women, many of whom had jumped to their deaths from the upper floors because the fire department's ladders did not extend to the top floors of the 10 story building. Every year, the New York Fire Department holds a solemn ceremony on the date in memory of the city's most deadly factory fire.

The row of townhouses at Washington Square North was the inspiration for *Washington Square*, Henry James' novel of late 19th century social morés, though James did not live here as is popularly assumed. A hundred yards up Fifth Ave to the right is the **Washington Square Mews**, a quiet, cobblestone street of stables that now house NYU offices.

West Village Walking Tour

After touring the central part of Greenwich Village, it's time to wander the less-crowded and charming West Village, roughly defined as the area west of Seventh Ave to the Hudson River. It's a confusing neighborhood to negotiate, since many of the ancient streets doubleback on each other (there is even a corner where W 10th St meets W 4th St just to the west of Seventh Ave). This neighborhood is loaded with buildings of architectural or historic importance – look for bronze landmark plaques explaining their significance.

Start on the southeast corner of Seventh Ave and Bleecker St. Head south down quiet Commerce St one block and turn right on Bedford St. You are already standing just a few yards from 75½ Bedford St, a quirky 9½ foot wide house that poet Edna St Vincent Millay lived in (1923-24) which has recently been restored. Right next door, at No 77, stands what is possibly the oldest house in the Village, a red-brick residence that was built in 1799.

Continuing west on Bedford just beyond the corner of Barrow St brings you to a spare wooden door at No 86 – this is **Chumley's Bar**, a former speakeasy run by Lee Chumley, a socialist who welcomed many writers to his place in the late 1920s. The bar's address is said to have inspired the slang phrase '86 it' – a shorthand imperative to get rid of something, which may have been whispered to warn Chumley's patrons to drain their beverages in anticipation of Prohibition-era police raids.

You might want to detour for a moment up Barrow St to check out the ivy-covered **Federal row houses** at Nos 49 and 51, and then have a look at the block of six perfectly preserved handsome red-brick residences on the west side of the street before continuing west on Bedford.

There's a wonderful 1894 horse stable at 95 Bedford St, and an early-19th century home called **Twin Peaks** at No 102, which got its name from the dual mock-Tudor tops that were added to it in the 1920s. Just before reaching the corner of Bedford and raucous **Christopher St**, the spiritual center of gay life in the Village, take a look at Grove St – that curved array of row houses has been featured in several movies, including *Annie Hall*. Other buildings in this neighborhood have detailed plaques on them noting who built them.

After a gander at the somewhat tacky leather shops on Christopher St, walk west to busy **Hudson St**, which will bring you to a fine and lively stretch of cafes, curio shops and bars. This is a very mixed neighborhood – some of the bars and book shops

cater to gays and lesbians (the desired clientele can be gleaned by the names of the businesses, such as 'Rubyfruit' and 'Henrietta Hudson's'), but there are plenty of straight-friendly cafes and restaurants.

Four blocks north of Christopher St on Hudson St is the storied **White Horse Tavern**, at No 567, which has a popular outdoor dining area. This is the place where poet Dylan Thomas is often said to have drunk himself to death in 1953. (He did spend his last night on the town there, but died a few days later in a hospital.)

Walking north two more blocks on Hudson St brings you to **Abington Square**, where Hudson St and Eighth Ave vector north. Stay to the left on Hudson and walk two more blocks north to Jane and Horatio Sts. Turning left on either street will lead you through a few more lovely blocks of old, stone row houses and toward the Hudson River running path.

Just one block north of Horatio St is the Gansevoort–Little W 12th St **meatpacking district**, still active and fetid on weekday mornings and, at night and on weekends, the site of several of the city's roughest gay bars. Since the early '90s, several bars and clubs have opened catering to the straight crowd.

Walking east back on 14th St will bring you to Eighth Ave, where you may choose to turn left (north) and walk straight into the heart of Chelsea's restaurant and bar district to have a meal or refreshment. Or you can choose to continue east five more blocks to **Union Square**.

EAST VILLAGE

This area of funky shops, bars and cafes, bordered by 14th St to the north and E Houston St to the south, and from Lafayette St to the East River, doesn't have much in common historically with Greenwich Village. The area was a series of rich and large farmland estates that were only overtaken by urban development in the late 19th century as New York became more industrial and moved northward from Lower Manhattan. By the early 20th century, this region was considered the northern section

Gay & Lesbian New York

San Francisco's reputation notwithstanding, New York City has long been the true center of gay culture in the USA. At the beginning of the 20th century, gays and lesbians were widely known to meet in hidden clubs around the Bowery. Later, men gathered in the theater district, while lesbians attended drag clubs in Harlem. After WWII, Greenwich Village, once the city's largest black neighborhood, became the city's prime gay enclave, though quiet clubs and bars could be found uptown.

Throughout the '50s, the police regularly arrested gays and lesbians on morals charges, leading to the establishment of The Mattachine Society, the country's largest gay political organization. At one time, it was illegal for women to dress in men's clothing, and lesbians in drag were often arrested and transported to Women's House of Detention on Sixth Ave and 8th St.

The signal moment of the modern gay rights movement occurred in New York on June 27, 1969. That night, the police launched a raid on the Stonewall Inn, a Christopher St men's bar. Its patrons were mourning the burial earlier that day of self-destructive singer Judy Garland, an icon for the gay community, and many angrily resisted the bust. Three nights of riots followed.

The Stonewall Rebellion and other protests led to the introduction in 1971 of the first bill designed to ban discrimination on the basis of sexual orientation. The controversial measure was finally passed by the city council in 1986, and seven years later gay couples won important legal protections when New York allowed the registration of 'domestic partnerships.' Mayor David Dinkins also declared the area where the original bar once stood as 'Stonewall Place' and unveiled statues of two gay couples in Sheridan Square by artist George Segal.

Today the gay character of Greenwich Village has even become something of a visitor attraction. Even local gay residents complain that the area around Hudson and Christopher Sts is being ruined by day-tripping partygoers and tourists intent on getting a glimpse of gay life. That helps explain why Chelsea is now the hottest gay neighborhood in the city, with clubs, cafes, gyms and restaurants that cater to the community. The leading zone for lesbian clubs and restaurants is the 10 blocks of Hudson St north of Houston St. There's also a thriving gay club scene in the East Village, along with a host of gay bars scattered uptown. For gay-friendly accommodations, eateries and night spots, see the sidebars in the related sections.

Information The Gay and Lesbian Switchboard (☎ (212) 777-1800) is the best all-around information on what's happening in town. This 24 hour service has a very extensive automated information system that offers descriptions of the newest club scenes and specific support services. The line is also staffed by volunteers from noon to midnight.

The Lesbian and Gay Community Services Center (☎ (212) 620-7310), 208 W 13th St, serves some 5000 people each week through its legal aid workshops and social events. They also provide assistance to travelers and hand out visitor information. A calendar of events at 'The Center' is available for those who stop in from 9 am to 11 pm.

Gay Men's Health Crisis (GMHC; ☎ (212) 807-6664) and the Community Health project (☎ (212) 675-3559) offer blood testing, health care for those with HIV and a wide range of counseling. The Anti-Violence Project hotline (☎ (212) 807-0197) is staffed 24 hours a day.

Organized Tours Gay-oriented tours and holidays are booked by many New York-based agencies, including One on One Travel (☎ (212) 213-3412) and RSVP travel (☎ (800) 328-7787).

Special Events There are several important annual events for New York's gay community. **Gay Pride Day**, held on the last Sunday in June, features a parade down Fifth Ave and special events all over town. The huge annual **Halloween** parade, traditionally followed by a promenade of drag queens down Christopher St, attracts hoards of tourists toting video cameras. **Dance marathons** that raise funds for AIDS research are held in the autumn and summer. ■

of the Lower East Side, a poorer cousin to Greenwich Village. But it has come into its own during the '90s, as the old tenements have been taken over by artists and restaurateurs in search of cheap rents.

The Ukrainian and Polish community established here more than 100 years ago is still very much in evidence, and senior citizens from this population hang out in **Tompkins Square Park** alongside punks, junkies, anarchists, drug-dealers and dog-walking yuppies. The police have clashed with protesters in the park and squatters in abandoned tenements.

The best way to explore the East Village is by simply walking up or down First Ave between 14th and Houston Sts. On this 15 minute walk you can see the neighborhood in lively transition – the four to six story buildings that line both sides of the avenue house a succession of laundries, bars, coffee shops, Eastern European meat stores, pharmacies and restaurants offering a virtual world tour of cuisines – there are places serving Italian, Polish, Indian, Lebanese, Japanese and Thai fare. The same array of gastronomic choices can be found along Second Ave, though the bars and cafes are a bit more upscale.

The few blocks around E 9th St has become adopted as a hot spot by Japanese expatriates and visitors, and there are shops, bars and very good sushi restaurants to be found there.

Boutiques selling all-natural products, antiques, furniture and clothing both new and used are springing up all over the East Village, but a good number of them can be found clustered on E 9th St just east of Second Ave. There are also a number of herbal medicine stores nearby, in keeping with the naturalistic character of the neighborhood.

You can get a nice slice of East Village life by having a late night drink in **7D**, a horseshoe-shaped bar at the south end of Tompkins Square Park. During the day, it's a quiet place for old men to hang out; at night it's nothing less than a grungey pickup joint fueled by malt liquor specials. The park is somewhat of an unofficial border

between gentrified East Village (to the west) and the more dangerous part of the neighborhood (to the east).

In recent years the East Village has seen tensions sparked by the gentrification that has pushed poorer residents further east toward the river into **Alphabet City**, which is marked by Aves A, B, C and D. City officials have tried to polish up the neighborhood's reputation by dubbing the district 'Loisaida,' a derivative of the Spanish phrase for 'Lower East Side,' and a *Carnaval* takes place here every Memorial Day weekend. Latino culture is certainly in strong evidence throughout the neighborhood, and wall murals and paintings on store gates along Ave B have a distinctly Latino character, as do the stores selling votive candles and other items of faith. But the hard fact remains that Alphabet City is one of the city's most open drug-dealing areas, mainly because some of the most cutting-edge (and sometimes illegal) dance clubs are located there. Ninth St between Ave A and First Ave is the site of heavy drug-dealing, which can also be found the further east you travel.

Astor Place

This square is named after the Astor family, who built an early New York fortune on beaver trading and lived on **Colonnade Row** just south of it at 429-434 Lafayette St. Four of the original nine marble-faced Greek Revival residences still exist, but they are entombed beneath a layer of black soot. Across the street, in the public library built by John Jacob Astor, stands the **Joseph Papp Public Theater**, one of the city's most important cultural centers and home to the New York Shakespeare Festival.

Astor Place itself is dominated by the large brownstone **Cooper Union**, the public college founded by glue millionaire Peter Cooper in 1859. Just after its completion, Abraham Lincoln gave his 'Right Makes Might' speech condemning slavery in the Union's Great Hall. The fringed lectern he used still exists, but the auditorium is only open to the public for special events.

Walking two blocks north and turning west on E 10th St brings you to **Grace Church** designed by James Renwick. This Gothic Revival Episcopal church was made of marble quarried by prisoners at Sing Sing, the state penitentiary in the upstate town of Ossining. After years of neglect, Grace Church has recently been cleaned up, and its floodlit white marble makes for a strangely elegant nighttime sight in this neighborhood of dance clubs, record stores and pizza parlors. The same architect is thought to have created **Renwick Triangle**, a movie-set-perfect group of brownstone Italianate houses one block to the east at 112-128 E 10th St.

Another significant church to note is **St Mark's-in-the-Bowery** at Second Ave and E 10th St, also an Episcopal place of worship that stands on the site of the farm, or *bouwerie*, owned by Dutch Governor Peter Stuyvesant, whose crypt is under the grounds. The church, damaged by fire in 1978, has been restored with abstract stained-glass windows and is open from 10 am to 6 pm Monday to Friday.

In this neighborhood, E 8th St is called **St Mark's Place**, once a nexus for the artistic fringe. Now the block east of Astor Place contains a community center where local punks and junkies hang out alongside stalls selling books, illegal concert tapes, and T-shirts. East of Second Ave on St Mark's there are a half dozen lively late-night cafes and bars.

Old Merchant's House

Not much remains of the neighborhood that existed here before the tenement boom, but this museum (☎ (212) 777-1089) in the 1831 house of drug importer Seabury Tredwell at 29 E 4th St is a remarkably well-preserved example of how the business class lived. Occupied by Tredwell's youngest daughter Gertrude until her death in 1933, its original furnishings were still intact when it began life as a museum three years later.

The forlorn and abandoned building just past the empty lot was also owned by the Tredwell family, but not much has been done with it.

The Old Merchant's House is open Sunday to Thursday from 1 to 4 pm. Admission is $4/2.

10th St Baths

The waning of Eastern European traditions on the Lower East Side led to the closure of many old bath houses in Manhattan, and the AIDS crisis prevented their continuation as gay gathering places. But these historic old steam baths (☎ (212) 674-9250) at 268 E 10th St still remain. Here you can get a Russian-style oak-leaf massage followed by a plunge in an ice-cold bath, provided your heart can stand the strain. There's also a small cafe on the premises.

The 10th St Baths are open seven days a week from 9 am to 10 pm. Both sexes are admitted on Monday, Tuesday, Friday and Saturday. Thursday and Sunday are for men only, and women have exclusive entry on Wednesday. General admission is $19, with massage rates starting at $42.

CHELSEA

In addition to being home to much of New York's gay and straight night life from Seventh Ave to the West Side piers, Chelsea is also the site of many 'districts' – areas where generally one type of business activity predominates. Roughly bordered by 14th St to the south running all the way up to 23rd St, west of Broadway, this neighborhood was the dry goods and retail area for the gilded age, and many of the emporia built to attract well-heeled shoppers are now office buildings. Closer to the Hudson River on Eighth and Ninth Aves, Chelsea is dominated by housing projects and warehouses. It's here that you'll find some of the city's most popular nightclubs, such as the Tunnel.

The prime site on noisy 23rd St is the **Chelsea Hotel**, the red-brick residential hotel with ornate iron balconies that is dominated at street level by no fewer than seven plaques declaring it a literary landmark. Even before Sid Vicious murdered his girlfriend there, the hotel was notorious for being a literary hangout for the likes of Mark Twain, Thomas Wolfe, Dylan Thomas and

Arthur Miller. Jack Kerouac is famous for typing *On the Road* on a single roll of tele-type paper during one marathon session at the Chelsea.

The **Chelsea Piers Complex**, on the Hudson River at the end of 23rd St, is a recent addition to the neighborhood. It is a large urban complex that caters to sporting types of all stripes – you can set out to hit a bucket of golf balls at the four level driving range, then change your mind and ice skate in the complex's indoor skating rink instead, or even rent in-line skates to cruise along the Hudson River waterfront down to the Battery. Though the Piers complex is somewhat cut off by busy West St, its wide array of attractions brings in the crowds. The Chelsea Studios are also located here, where the TV series *Law & Order* and *Spin City* are shot. See Activities later in this chapter for more details.

Union Square

This garden square on the convergence of 14th St and Broadway was one of New York City's first uptown business districts, and throughout the mid-19th century it was the site of many workers' rallies and polit-ical protests, the source of its name. By the 1960s, this was something of a depressed part of town, and the park in Union Square was one of the city's 'needle parks,' a hangout for junkies. It's been revived in recent years, and is home to the city's largest open-air produce market, the Green-market, which operates Wednesday, Friday and Saturday mornings year round.

The area north of Union Square running to Madison Square, just above 23rd St was once known as Ladies' Mile. In the late 19th century commercial establishments such as B Altman's and Lord & Taylor catered to women shoppers. Variances in modern day zoning laws have led to a return of large-scale retailing to Sixth Ave above 14th St to 23rd St.

The late-19th century building that once housed the Hugh O'Neill dry goods store at 655 Sixth Ave is one of the few cast-iron palaces that have yet to be taken over by a big store. But it has been cleaned up and its flood-lit Corinthian columns look quite dramatic at night. This is the building that was 'blown up' in the opening moments of the Bruce Willis thriller *Die Hard With a Vengeance*.

Flatiron District

This neighborhood is named after the **Flatiron Building** at the intersection of Broadway, Fifth Ave and 23rd St. Built in 1902, the Flatiron Building was famously featured in a haunting 1905 color-tinted photograph by Edward Steichen, and domi-nated this plaza when the neighborhood was the city's prime stretch of retail and enter-tainment establishments. The Flatiron was also renowned for being the world's tallest building until 1909, when it was overtaken by the nearby **Metropolitan Life Tower** at 24th St and Madison Ave, which has an impressive clock tower and golden top. For a 10 block radius the Flatiron District, loaded with loft buildings and boutiques, does a good imitation of SoHo without the European pretensions and crowds.

Just above the Flatiron Building is **Madison Square Park**, which defined the northern reaches of Manhattan until the city's population exploded just after the Civil War. The park contains several statues of war heros along with one dedicated to the man who may be the most obscure US president: former New York Governor Chester Allen Arthur, who became chief executive upon the assassination of James Garfield in 1881. On the site of the New York Life Building, at 51 Madison Ave, once stood the original Madison Square Garden, scene of various important public events and entertainment – sporting events, concerts and political conventions – from 1879 to the late 1920s.

GRAMERCY PARK

Gramercy Park is one of New York's loveli-est spaces, the kind of garden area com-monly found dotted throughout Paris and other French cities. Unfortunately, when the neighborhood was designed on the site of a marsh in 1830, admission to the park was restricted to residents. The tradition still holds, and mere mortals must peer through iron gates at the foliage.

Two other exclusive institutions are located here, worth noting for their architecture. The **National Arts Club** (☎ (212) 475-3424), 15 Gramercy Park South, was designed by Calvert Vaux, one of the men behind the creation of Central Park. It holds exhibitions that are sometimes open to the public. The club has a beautiful vaulted stained-glass ceiling above its wooden bar.

The **Players Club**, 16 Gramercy Park, is an actors' hangout created in 1888 by Shakespearean actor Edwin Booth (brother of Lincoln assassin John Wilkes Booth) and designed by Stanford White.

Fortunately, you can get inside **Pete's Tavern** (☎ (212) 473-7676), 124 E 18th St, the place patronized by short-story writer O Henry, who is said to have written his Christmas story *The Gift of the Magi* in a front booth. The author probably didn't eat the free popcorn at Pete's, but it tastes as if it was made in his day. You can get a decent burger and beer here or find the same fare by walking a block away to the equally popular Old Town Bar and Grill (☎ (212) 529-6732), 45 E 18th St, a wood-paneled 1892 pub.

MIDTOWN

You'll wind up spending a great deal of time in New York's teeming Midtown area, since it's the place where many of the city's most popular attractions are located. Very few people live in the center of Manhattan,

and most apartment houses are found east of Third Ave and west of Eighth Ave. Midtown isn't the most dangerous part of town, but as in any similar district in cities around the world, you should be particularly savvy about moving around there, since you'll meet up with some of the city's most aggressive panhandlers.

Herald Square

This crowded convergence of Broadway and Sixth Ave at 34th St is the location for **Macy's Department Store**, which for years has inaccurately claimed to be the world's largest department store. The busy square doesn't offer much in the way of cultural landmarks, with two indoor malls south of Macy's on Sixth Ave that offer a boring array of shops, and an HMV record store across the street.

Far more interesting is **Little Korea**, the small enclave of Korean-owned shops on 31st to 36th Sts between Broadway and Fifth Ave. Over the past few years this little neighborhood (particularly 32nd St) has seen an explosion of restaurants serving Korean fare.

The **Garment District**, where most of New York's fashion firms have their design offices, stands to the west of Herald Square on Seventh Ave from 34th St to Times Square. During workdays the side streets are packed with delivery trucks picking up racks of clothing. Broadway between 23rd St and Herald Square is called the **Accessories District** because of the many ribbon and button shops located there that serve the fashion industry. There are a number of stores on 36th and 37th Sts immediately west of Seventh Ave that sell so-called designer clothing at wholesale prices.

Empire State Building

New York's original skyline symbol (☎ (212) 736-3100) is a limestone classic built in just 410 days during the depths of the Depression at a cost of $41 million. Located on the site of the original Waldorf-Astoria Hotel, the 102 story, 1454 foot Empire State Building opened

KIM GRANT

50¢ tour guide

in 1931 and was immediately the most exclusive business address in the city. The famous antenna was originally to be a mooring mast for zeppelins, but the Hindenberg disaster put a stop to that plan. One airship accidentally met up with the building: a B25 crashed into the 79th floor on a foggy day in July 1945, killing 14 people.

Since 1976, the building's top 30 floors have been floodlit in seasonal and holiday colors (eg, green for St Patrick's Day, red and green for Christmas, pink for Gay Pride weekend). This tradition has been copied by many other skyscrapers, including those with ornate golden tops around Union Square, lending elegance to the night sky.

Looking down on the city from the building's 102nd floor means standing in line for an elevator on the concourse level and sometimes being confronted with another line at the top. Getting there very early or very late helps you avoid this. Don't bother with the other exhibits on the concourse, which thrive purely on their proximity to the ticket office.

The Empire State Building's observatories on the 86th and 102nd floors are open from 9:30 am to midnight daily, with the last tickets sold at 11:25 pm. Admission is $4.50/2.25.

Pierpont Morgan Library

The Pierpont Morgan Library (☎ (212) 685-0008), 29 E 36th St off Madison Ave, is part of the 45 room mansion owned by steel magnate JP Morgan. This formerly private collection features cold temperatures (the better for the Morgan's manuscripts, tapestries and books), a study filled with Italian renaissance art works, a marble rotunda and a three-tiered East Room main library. Morgan spared little expense in his pursuit of ancient works of knowledge or art: there are no fewer than three Gutenberg Bibles in residence here.

The Morgan Library has long had a stuffy reputation and its curator is trying to liven things up with a year-round program of lectures and concerts in the Garden Court. This lovely glass-enclosed space also contains an expensive cafe and book-store. The Morgan is open Tuesday to Friday from 10:30 am to 5 pm, Saturday from 1:30 am to 6 pm and Sunday from noon to 5 pm. Admission is $5/3.

Grand Central Terminal

When the New York Central Rail Road built this prestige terminal in 1913, the 'cut and cover' installation of tracks for its new electric trains leading to the north created the unusually wide expanse of Park Ave. Grand Central is no longer a romantic place to begin a cross-country journey – today it serves as a terminus for the Metro North commuter trains to the northern suburbs and Connecticut. It is also home to a large community of street people who live in the track areas under Park Ave.

The station is well worth seeking out because of its huge Romanesque south facade, marred a bit by an ugly car ramp, as well as the huge main concourse and its vaulted ceiling constellation. The starlight zodiac has been restored, as have the lower levels of the terminal, which include the **Oyster Bar**, a famous seafood restaurant that's quite noisy thanks to its vaulted tile ceiling. A nice bar on a balcony on the western side overlooks the concourse and its central clock and passenger information center.

The Municipal Art Society conducts free walks through Grand Central every Wednesday at 12:30 pm. During the hour long tour, you will cross a glass catwalk high above the concourse and learn that the ceiling constellation was mistakenly laid out in a 'god's eye view,' with the stars displayed from above rather than below.

Chrysler Building

Just across from Grand Central Terminal at Lexington Ave and 42nd St is the 1048 foot Chrysler Building, an Art Deco masterpiece designed by William Van Allen in 1930 that briefly reigned as the tallest structure in the world until superseded by the Empire State Building. The building, a celebration of the car culture, features gargoyles that resemble hood ornaments (barely visible from the ground) and a

200 foot steel spire that was constructed as one piece and placed at the top of the building as a distinctive crowning touch. Nestled at the top is the Cloud Club, a businessmen's spot that closed years ago, and a private apartment built for Walter Chrysler, head of the company.

You can walk through the lobby and admire the African marble anytime, but the building doesn't offer much in the way of interest for visitors – no top floor restaurant or observation deck. Until one exists, the Chrysler will be known primarily as the landmark most often mistaken by tourists for the Empire State Building.

United Nations

The UN (☎ (212) 963-7713), which has its visitors' entrance at First Ave and 46th St, is technically located on international territory overlooking the East River. Tours of the facility show you its **General Assembly**, where the annual autumn convocation of member nations takes place, the **Security Council** chamber, where crisis hearings are held year round, and the **Economic and Social Council** chamber. A park south of the complex includes Henry Moore's *Reclining Figure* and several other sculptures with a peace theme.

The UN was created in 1945 by an international conference in San Francisco, and met for two years in Flushing Meadows park in Queens before the Rockefeller family donated $8.5 million for the purchase of the land. The complex itself, appropriately enough, was designed by a large international committee of architects.

For years there have been complaints about the UN's spendthrift ways, but they are not much in evidence in the headquarters. The buildings have a dated, late-'50s feel to them, with a lot of Norwegian wood, and the carpeting is woefully worn.

It's open seven days a week, March to December from 9:15 am to 4:45 pm and maintains the same hours Monday to Friday in January and February. English-language tours of the complex leave every 45 minutes, and are available on a limited

basis in several other languages. Admission is $6.50 for adults, $4.50 for seniors and students. Children ages five to 17 are $3.50 and children under five are not admitted.

New York Public Library

The New York Public Library's Main Branch (☎ (212) 930-0800), at 42nd St and Fifth Ave, which recently celebrated its centennial, contains a massive 3rd-floor reading room for 500 people that still has its original lamps, more than 11 million books in its permanent collection, and display galleries of precious manuscripts by just about every author of note in the English language. The library's notable stone lions are adorned by Christmas wreaths each holiday season.

It's open Tuesday and Wednesday from 11 am to 6 pm, Monday and Thursday to Saturday from 10 am to 6 pm.

Located just behind the library, **Bryant Park** was once overrun by drug-dealers but has been impressively restored and is a pleasant place to sit if you can claim one of the park's marble benches or folding chairs. It's a popular midday sunbathing site and a free outdoor movie festival is held there on Mondays during the summer months.

Rockefeller Center

The 19 buildings of the 22 acre Rockefeller Center comprise the most coherent and best known public complex in the US, though some might find the '30s-era 'progress of man' theme of the architecture a little overbearing.

More than 200 small-scale dwellings were cleared away beginning in 1931 for Rockefeller Center, which took nine years to complete (one original holdout still survives: the building that houses Hurley's Bar at 49th St and Sixth Ave). The 70,000 construction workers on the project were watched constantly by 'sidewalk supervisors' – passers-by who peered through holes cut into the fence around the site. When the laborers set up a small Christmas tree on the site, a tradition began that continues to this day: the annual lighting of the

Rockefeller Center Christmas tree the week after Thanksgiving invariably attracts thousands of visitors to the area.

The completion of the center was tainted by a controversy over artwork. A mural painted by Mexican artist Diego Rivera in the lobby of the 70 story RCA (now GE) Building was rejected by the Rockefeller family because it featured the face of Lenin. The fresco was covered during the opening ceremony and was later destroyed. Its replacement features the more acceptable figure of Abraham Lincoln.

In 1989, controlling interest in Rockefeller Center was sold to a Japanese consortium, triggering off bitter lamentations in the press about the selling of American icons to foreigners, as if the buildings were in danger of being relocated to Tokyo. The Japanese holding company went broke when real estate values plummeted.

But the center's money travails have not seemed to result in a lack of exterior maintenance. Take special note of the tile work above the Sixth Ave entrance to the GE building, the three flood-lit cameos along the side of Radio City Music Hall, and the back-lit gilt and stained-glass entrance to the East River Savings Bank building at 41 Rockefeller Plaza, immediately to the north of the skating rink/outdoor garden cafe in the heart of the complex.

Radio City Music Hall This 6000 seat Art Deco movie palace (☎ (212) 247-4777) had its interior declared a protected landmark. Even the smoking rooms and toilets are elegant. Concerts here sell out quickly and tickets to the annual Christmas pageant featuring the hokey-but-enjoyable Rockettes dancers now run up to $65. But you can see the interior by taking a tour which leaves every half hour from 10 am to 5 pm Monday to Friday and 11 am to 5 pm Sunday. Admission is $12.50/9.

NBC Studios The NBC television network has its headquarters in the 70 story GE building that looms over Rockefeller Center, and the *Today* show broadcasts from 7 to 9 am seven days a week from a glass-enclosed street-level studio near the fountain area (an ice skating rink during the winter months).

Tours of the NBC studios leave from the lobby of the GE Building from Monday to Saturday from 9:30 am to 4:30 pm. Admission is $8.25, and children under six are not permitted.

St Patrick's Cathedral

St Patrick's Cathedral (☎ (212) 753-2261), just across from Rockefeller Center on 50th St and Fifth Ave, is the main place of worship for the 2.2 million Roman Catholics in the New York diocese headed by conservative John Cardinal O'Connor, a major player in New York City political life and favorite of Pope John Paul II. (The diocese of Brooklyn, a separate district, serves 1.7 million Catholics.)

The cathedral, built at a cost of nearly $2 million during the Civil War, originally didn't include the two front spires (added in 1888). The well lit St Patrick's isn't as gloomy as its Old World counterparts, and the new TV monitors in restricted view seats are testimony to the church's determination to have its place in the modern world.

Passing by the eight small shrines along the side of the cathedral brings you past the main altar to the quiet **Lady Chapel**, dedicated to the Virgin Mary. From here you can see the handsome stained-glass **Rose Window** above the 7000 pipe churchorgan. A basement crypt behind the altar contains all of O'Connor's predecessors.

Unfortunately, St Patrick's is not a place for restful contemplation during the day because of the constant buzz from visitors. It's also a regular site of protest by gays who feel excluded by the church hierarchy. The exclusion of Irish gays from the St Patrick's Day Parade since 1993 (an event not sponsored by the Catholic Church per se, but identified with Catholic traditionalists) has triggered protests near the cathedral every year in March.

It's open from 6 am to 9 pm daily. Masses are held frequently on the weekend, and the Cardinal presides over the service at 10:15 am Sunday.

Fifth Ave

Fifth Ave's reputation as a high-class area dates back to the early part of the 20th century, when its uptown portion was known as Millionaire's Row due to the series of mansions that extended all the way up to 130th St. Uptown addresses were then considered very desirable for their 'country' air and open spaces. Today it's a hodgepodge of retail and residences following the spectrum of the city's economy. At its start, Washington Square Park in Greenwich Village, there are a number of high rise apartment buildings that date back to the '30s, giving way to retail clothing stores and carpet wholesalers in the Flatiron District from 14th St to 42nd St.

In Midtown, the street is the site of airline offices and a few high-end shops and hotels, including the garish **Plaza** hotel at Grand Army Plaza overlooking the corner of Central Park and Fifth Ave. The huge institution really doesn't have much of a grand lobby, but it is worth a walk through just to say you've been there. The fountain in front of the hotel, which features a statue of the Roman goddess Diana and faces the southeastern entrance to **Central Park**, is a good spot for a rest and a bit of lunch – provided you're not downwind from the horse-drawn carriages that line 59th St during the summer months.

Most of the heirs of the millionaires that built mansions on Fifth Ave above 59th St either sold them for demolition or converted them to the cultural institutions that make up **Museum Mile** (see Upper East Side). The **Villard Houses**, actually located on Madison Ave behind St Patrick's Cathedral, are surviving examples of these grand homes. The six four-story townhouses were built by financier Henry Villard in 1881; they were eventually owned by the Catholic Church, and then sold to become part of the 1000 room New York Palace hotel. The Urban Center Bookstore (☎ (212) 935-3592), the city's leading shop for architectural works, is located in the north wing of the Villard Houses.

Most of the more exclusive boutiques are uptown on Madison Ave (see Things to Buy), but Gianni Versace, Liz Claiborne and Tiffany's are all still on Fifth Ave above 50th St. On 57th St nearby, you can shop at Burberry's, Hermès and Charivari, among several other designer boutiques. Here are a few Fifth Ave stores worth noting:

Saks Fifth Ave
  at 50th St (☎ (212) 753-4000)
Henri Bendel
  at 55th St (☎ (212) 247-1100)
Tiffany & Co
  at 57th St (☎ (212) 755-8000)
Bergdorf Goodman
  at 57th St (☎ (212) 753-7300)

Museum of Modern Art

The Museum of Modern Art (☎ (212) 708-9480), 11 W 53rd St, known as 'Moma' (pronounced with a long o), distinguishes itself by its manageable, three floor layout. Among the first-rate works in its sculpture and painting galleries are a number of works by Picasso, Van Gogh's *Starry Night* and Matisse's *Dance 1*. A quiet stand-alone gallery is dedicated solely to Monet's paneled *Water Lilies*, and the Abby Aldrich Rockefeller Sculpture Garden is the setting for a summer series of concerts during July and August. A few years back, saxophonist Sonny Rollins came to the garden to give his first solo concert in decades, playing against the noises of the traffic on Fifth Ave.

At least once a year, Moma puts on an important exhibit of a single major artist's work – recent retrospectives focused on the abstractionist Piet Mondrian, Picasso's portraiture and American painter Jasper Johns. The museum recently bought the Dorset Hotel and two brownstones behind it on 54th St and is undergoing a major expansion of space to be completed within the next seven years.

The museum places a special emphasis on photography and film, two areas of visual expression that get short shrift at the larger Metropolitan Museum of Art. There are daily film screenings in Moma's two basement theaters, and an Oscar, awarded to the museum's film department in 1978, is on permanent display along with an impressive collection of film posters.

If you're pressed for time or simply undecided where to go, it's a good idea to rent the $4 audio tour of the museum narrated by chief curator Kirk Varnedoe, which comes in a cell phone that you can program to get more information about specific works of interest.

The museum is one of the few major cultural institutions in New York City that is open on Monday, and instead closes on Wednesday. Hours are Saturday to Tuesday from 11 am to 6 pm, Thursday and Friday from noon to 8:30 pm. Admission is $8 for adults, $5 for seniors and students; children under 16 are free. The museum offers free admission to everyone on Thursday and Friday after 5:30 pm.

Museum of Television & Radio

This couch potato's paradise (☎ (212) 621-6800), at 25 W 52nd St, contains a collection of over 50,000 American TV and radio programs available with the click of a mouse from the museum's computer catalog. It's a great place to head when it's raining or when you're simply fed up with walking. Nearly everybody checks out their favorite childhood TV programs on the museum's 90 consoles, but the radio listening room is an unexpected pleasure. It's nice to remember – or discover – just how funny those old radio comedies really were.

It's open Tuesday to Sunday from noon to 6 pm, with additional hours to 8 pm on Thursday. Admission is $6 for adults, $4 for students and seniors, $3 for children under 12.

Intrepid Air & Space Museum

The Intrepid Air & Space Museum (☎ (212) 245-2533), on the waterfront at W 46th St, is located on an aircraft carrier that served in WWII and Vietnam. It's a triumph of shipbuilding as well as an advertisement for US military might. The carrier's flight deck features several fighter planes, and the pier area contains the Growler guided-missile submarine, an Apollo space capsule and Vietnam-era tanks.

The museum is open June to August daily from 10 am to 5 pm and the rest of the

year Wednesday to Sunday 10 am to 5 pm. Admission is $10 for adults, $7.50 seniors, veterans, students and persons 12 to 17, and $5 for children six to 11 years old.

TIMES SQUARE

Before TV, Times Square was the nation's largest space for glittery advertising directed at a mass audience. Dubbed the 'Great White Way' after its bright lights, it has long been celebrated as New York's crossroads. But Times Square fell into a deep decline in the 1960s, as once-proud movie palaces that previously showed first run films turned into 'triple X' porn theaters, and the square became known as a hangout for every colorful, crazy or dangerous character in Midtown.

For years the city tried change Times Square's gamey reputation, and it finally seems to be working, as companies have reinstalled colorful billboards above the street and built themed showcases, such as the Virgin Megastore and the neighboring Official All Star Cafe, smack in the middle of the square. The combination of color, zipping message boards and (at last count) four massive color TV screens make for quite a sight these days, and each year some 24 million people visit the square. Several media companies – among them German publisher Bertlesmann, Reuters and the US magazine group Condé Nast – have built headquarters in and around Times Square recently.

Up to a million people gather here every **New Year's Eve** (see Special Events) to see a brightly lit ball descend from the roof of One Times Square at midnight, an event that lasts just 90 seconds and leaves most of the revelers spending the first few hours of the new year wondering what to do with themselves.

Walking Tour

Strolling around Times Square gives you a good look at the city's many architectural styles, from the **McGraw Hill Building**, 330 W 42nd St, an Art Deco curiosity, the Greek Revival **Town Hall**, 113 W 43rd St, a concert venue and lecture space, and the more garish office blocks built in the last few years on Broadway itself, including the **Morgan Stanley** tower at No 1589, with its 24 hour stock market ticker, a more colorful variant on the 'zipper' news wire that runs along the bland white building at One Times Square.

The block of 42nd St between Times Square and Eighth Ave was for a long time a haven for porn shops, but aggressive zoning changes and tax breaks by the city government for 'legitimate' businesses led to their closure. This block is changing rapidly, with the restoration by architect Hugh Hardy of the neighborhood's oldest venue, the 1899 **New Victory Theater**, into a center for children's productions. Disney is updating the **New Amsterdam Theater**, built in 1904, as a permanent home for its theatrical versions of children's classics. Madame Tussauds waxworks palace and actor Dan Ayckroyd's House of Blues nightclub are also slated to move in within a year or two. (At the moment, the porn industry thrives on a small stretch of Eighth Ave from 42nd to 48th Sts – a desultory array of video shops, strip joints and book shops that seems doomed to be overrun within a few years as property values increase.)

A free two hour walking tour of the changing neighborhood is offered by the Times Square Business Improvement District every Friday at noon. It leaves from the Times Square Visitor's Center (☎ (212) 869-5453) at the Sewlyn Theater on the north side of W 42nd St between Broadway and Eighth Aves.

CENTRAL PARK

This 843 acre rectangular park in the middle of Manhattan was designed to be an oasis from the urban bustle, but on weekends it's packed with joggers, in-line skaters, musicians and tourists. Its quieter areas are found above 72nd St, where the crowds thin out and the landscaping becomes more apparent to the visitor. The park is currently in the midst of a restoration program that has led to the re-seeding of many open spaces.

A good stroll through the park begins on the west side at the Columbus Circle entrance, through the **Merchants' Gate** and up to **Sheep Meadow**, a wide expanse of green for sunbathers and Frisbee players. Turning right, a pathway (called a transverse) runs along the south side of the meadow to the Carousel, and then the Dairy building, where the park's visitor center is located not far from the Wollman skating rink.

Just north of the Dairy, past the statue of Christopher Columbus, is **The Mall**, enclosed on both sides by a group of 150 American elms. These trees, which have not suffered from the Dutch elm disease that destroyed most of the country's elms, are believed to be the largest surviving stand in the country. At the end of the mall is **Bethesda Fountain**, a hippie hangout in the '60s that has been restored. Continue on the path to the right to Bow Bridge. You can cross the bridge to the **Ramble**, a lush wooden expanse that was once a gay pickup area but is now a meeting place for dog owners of all sexual persuasions. It offers stunning scenery during the autumn months. The Ramble gives way to Belvedere Castle and the **Delacorte Theater**, where the Public Theater holds two free Shakespeare productions each summer. Immediately beyond is the **Great Lawn**, where the occasional free concert is held, along with annual open-air performances of the New York Philharmonic and Metropolitan Opera in June and July. The Great Lawn is undergoing a much needed re-seeding, temporarily moving the concerts to **North Meadow** above 97th St.

At the W 72nd St park entrance is **Strawberry Fields**, the three acre landscape dedicated to the memory of John Lennon that contains plants from more than 100 nations. This spot was frequently visited by Lennon, who lived in the massive Dakota apartment building across the street, where he was shot on December 8, 1980.

Park Activities

There are many activities in the park,

and more information on what's happening is available at the visitor center in the **Dairy** (☎ (212) 794-6564) in the middle of the park along the 65th St pathway. It's open Tuesday to Sunday from 11 am to 4 pm.

The Central Park roadway that loops around the park for six miles is closed to traffic in the evenings and on weekends, and is a popular track for runners, in-line skaters and bikers, though the wicked S-shaped curve near E 106th St and the Lasker Pool should be avoided by beginner skaters. A soft, 1.6 mile cinder path encircles the **Jacqueline Kennedy Onassis Reservoir**, named in 1994 in her honor as she regularly used the track. The **New York Road Runners Club** (☎ (212) 860-4455) sponsors regular runs through the park and operates an information booth near the reservoir entrance at E 90th St. (See also the information under Activities.)

The **Central Park Wildlife Center** (☎ (212) 861-6030) is a small zoo built in the 1930s that has been renovated for the comfort of the animals housed there. Zoo residents include a lazy polar bear and several seals, whose frequent feedings delight the children who visit. The zoo is open from April to October Monday to Friday from 10 am to 5 pm and Saturday and Sunday from 10:30 am to 5:30 pm. In the winter the zoo is open daily from 10 am to 4:30 pm. Admission is $2.50 for adults, $1.25 for seniors, 50¢ for children ages three to 12.

Without a doubt the most touristy thing to do in the park is to rent a **horse-drawn carriage** for a short spin along the smelly carriage paths. The carriages line up along 59th St (Central Park South) and cost $34 for 30 minutes and $10 for every 15 minutes thereafter. Drivers expect a generous tip on top of that charge.

UPPER WEST SIDE

The Upper West Side begins as Broadway emerges from Midtown at Columbus Circle. A number of middle to top-end hotels can be found along Central Park South, and many celebrities live in the massive apartment buildings that line Central Park West all the way up to 96th St.

Lincoln Center

Lincoln Center (☎ (212) 875-5400), at Columbus Ave and Broadway, is a complex of seven large performance spaces built in the 1960s, replacing a group of tenements that were the real-life inspiration for the musical *West Side Story*. There's a clean, if architecturally uninspired look to Lincoln Center during the day, but at night the chandeliered interiors look simply beautiful from across Columbus Ave. For more information on the performance companies, see the Entertainment section.

If you are at all interested in high culture, Lincoln Center is a must-see, since it contains the **Metropolitan Opera House**, adorned by two colorful lobby tapestries by Marc Chagall, the **New York State Theater**, home of the New York City Ballet, and the New York City Opera, the low-cost and more daring alternative to the Met. The New York Philharmonic holds its season in **Avery Fisher Hall**.

The Lincoln Center Theater group has its home at the 1000 seat **Vivian Beaumont Theater**, which also contains the smaller and more intimate, in-the-round **Mitzi Newhouse Theater**. To the right of the theaters stands the **New York Public Library for the Performing Arts**, containing the city's largest collection of recorded sound, video and books on film and theater.

The Julliard School of Music, attached to the complex by a walkway over W 65th St, contains **Alice Tully Hall**, home to the Chamber Music Society of Lincoln Center and the **Walter Reade Theater**, the city's most comfortable film revival space and the major screening site of the New York Film Festival, held every September.

Tours of the complex leave from the concourse level each day, and explore at least three of the theaters, though just which ones you see depends on production schedules. It's a good idea to call ahead for a space (☎ (212) 875-5350). Tours costs

$8.23 for adults, $7 for students and seniors, $4.50 for children six to 17.

New-York Historical Society

As the antiquated, hyphenated name implies, the New-York Historical Society (☎ (212) 873-2400), 2 W 77th St (subway: 81st St), is the city's oldest museum, founded in 1804 to preserve artifacts of history and culture. It was also New York's only public art museum until the founding of the Metropolitan Museum of Art in the late 19th century, and in this capacity obtained John James Audubon's original watercolors for his *Birds of America* survey, which are on display in a 2nd-floor gallery.

The museum is somewhat overshadowed by its neighbor, the American Museum of Natural History, and has suffered severe financial problems in recent years. But it is well worth a visit, since viewing its quirky permanent collection is like traipsing through New York City's attic: there's even an army cot that George Washington actually slept in.

It's open Wednesday to Sunday from noon to 5 pm.

American Museum of Natural History

The museum of natural history (☎ (212) 769-5100), with its entrance at Central Park West and 79th St (subway: 81st St), was founded in 1869; today it has over 30 million artifacts in its collection. It is no doubt most famous for its three large dinosaur halls, which reopened in June 1995 after a significant renovation, and present the latest knowledge on how these behemoths behaved and theories on why they disappeared. Knowledgeable guides roam the dinosaur halls ready to answer questions, and there are 'please touch' displays that allow you to handle, among other items, the skullcap of a pachycephulasaurus, a plant-eating dinosaur that roamed the earth 65 million years ago.

Perhaps to remind people that there's more to the museum than the dinos, an audio tour is available ($5/3) that directs you to 50 'treasures of the permanent col-

lection' among its four floors, including the scary-looking plaster blue whale that hangs from the ceiling above the Hall of Ocean Life. While some of the mammal halls still have a gloomy, Victorian era look to them, the museum is aggressively trying to update the entire facility.

The museum is open daily except on Thanksgiving and Christmas. Hours are Sunday to Thursday from 10 am to 5:45 pm and Friday and Saturday from 10 am to 8:45 pm. Admission is $7/4/5 for adults/children/seniors and students. A combination ticket for the museum, which includes entry to a Naturemax show or a Planetarium sky show, is $10/7. For Naturemax alone the charge is $7/4/5. Admission to the Planetarium alone costs $5/2.50/4.

Children's Museum of Manhattan

The children's museum (☎ (212) 721-1223), 212 W 83rd St (subway: 86th St), features discovery centers for toddlers and a postmodern Media Center for kids under 16. There, technologically savvy kids can work in a TV studio. The museum also runs crafts workshops on weekends.

There are two affiliated children's museums elsewhere in the city. The **Brooklyn Children's Museum** (☎ (718) 735-4400) emphasizes art and design. The **Staten Island Children's Museum** (☎ (718) 273-2060) specializes in science and nature.

The Children's Museum of Manhattan is open Monday, Wednesday and Thursday from 1:30 pm to 5:30 pm and Friday, Saturday and Sunday from 10 am to 5 pm. Admission is $5, $2.50 for seniors, children under two are free.

Columbia University

Columbia University (☎ (212) 854-1754) and the affiliated Barnard College are located on upper Broadway (subway: 116th St–Columbia) in a spot once far removed from the downtown bustle. Today, the city has definitely enveloped and moved beyond Columbia's gated campus. But the school's main courtyard,

The Chrysler Building, NYC

KIM GRANT

Rockefeller Center, NYC

KIM GRANT

Radio City Music Hall, NYC

MICHAEL CLARK

Central Park Lake, NYC

Guggenheim Museum, NYC

with its statue *Alma Mater* perched on the steps of the Low Library, is still a quiet place to enjoy the sun and read a book. Hamilton Hall, in the southeast corner of the main square, was the famous site of a student takeover in 1968, and since then is periodically a place for protests as well as pretty wild student parties. As you would expect, the surrounding neighborhood is filled with inexpensive restaurants, good bookstores, and cafes like the landmark **Hungarian Pastry Shop** (☎ (212) 866-4230), 1030 Amsterdam Ave, where you can eavesdrop on the crisis-driven student conversations while waiting for your espresso.

Cathedral of St John the Divine
The Cathedral of St John the Divine (☎ (212) 316-7540) dominates Amsterdam Ave just behind the Columbia University campus (subway: Cathedral Parkway or 116th St–Columbia University). It is the largest place of worship in the US, a massive and dark 601 foot long Episcopal cathedral that, upon completion, will be the third largest church in the world (after St Peter's Basilica in Rome and the newly built Our Lady at Yamoussoukro in the Ivory Coast).

But it's unlikely that St John, which had its cornerstone laid in 1892, will be finished in your lifetime. Work has yet to begin on the stone tower on the left side of the west front or the crossing tower above the pulpit. In 1978, the Episcopal Diocese of New York began training local young people in stone cutting, and their work can be seen in the courtyard to the south of the church behind the sundial during warm weather. Other features shown on the church's cutaway floor plan near the front entrance, such as a Greek amphitheater, are merely wistful visions of the distant future.

Still, the cathedral is a flourishing place of worship and community activity, the site of holiday concerts, lectures and memorial services for famous New Yorkers. There's even a Poet's Corner just to the left of the front entrance – though,

unlike at Westminster Abbey, no one is actually buried there.

The cathedral is open from 7 am to 5 pm Monday to Saturday and from 7 am to 8 pm on Sunday. Sermons at its Sunday High Mass at 11 am feature well-known intellectuals such as Prince Charles's guru Sir Laurens van der Post. (There is also a 9:30 mass in Spanish.)

General Grant National Memorial
Popularly known as Grant's Tomb (☎ (212) 666-1640), this landmark monument at Riverside Drive and W 122nd St (subway: 116th St–Columbia) is where Civil War hero and president Ulysses S Grant and his wife Julia are buried. Completed in 1897 – 12 years after Grant's death – the granite structure cost $600,000 and is the largest mausoleum in the country. The building was a graffiti-marred mess for years until the general's relatives threatened to move his body somewhere else and shamed the National Park Service into cleaning it up.

It's open Wednesday to Sunday from 9 am to 4:30 pm.

Riverside Church
Riverside Church (☎ (212) 222-5900), 490 Riverside Drive at 122nd St (subway: 116th St–Columbia), is a gothic marvel overlooking the Hudson River built by the Rockefeller family in 1930. The observation deck, 355 feet above the ground, is open to the public during good weather, and its 74 carillon bells, the largest grouping in the world, are rung every Sunday at noon and 3 pm.

It's open daily from 9 am to 4 pm, with inter-denominational services on Sunday at 10:45 am.

HARLEM
New York's most identifiable African American neighborhood is going through a bit of an identity crisis. Tourist dollars are certainly flowing in thanks to the many Japanese and European travelers eager to learn about Harlem's significant history. But the many bus tours that move through

its streets give off an unseemly vibe – much like an urban safari undertaken by people too fearful to move about on foot. Over the past decade, Harlem has also become home to a community of about 10,000 West Africans, who have brought their own distinct culture and cuisine into the neighborhood.

For the visitor, traveling to Harlem is not a cause for self-congratulation, but an exercise in smart exploration. Certainly, the run-down buildings and racial tensions between some blacks and 'outsider' shop owners (mostly Asian and Jewish) are signs that all is not perfect, or even very well, in Harlem. But you needn't exercise any more caution here than in any other neighborhood. Perhaps even less: the troubles have led the city to post police cars on 125th St at every other block or so. The city has also aggressively promoted Harlem to developers, and the plan seems to be working: by late 1998, a new 'Harlem USA' entertainment and retail complex is scheduled to open just a few steps away from the Apollo Theater, complete with a 12 screen cinema, a rooftop skating rink and a Disney store.

The best time to visit Harlem is on a Sunday morning, when people head to services at the dozens of small churches in the neighborhood. Wednesday is also good, since you can end the day at the Apollo Theater watching its famous amateur night. A selective listing of Harlem's jazz clubs is in the Entertainment section.

As you explore Harlem, you should note that the major avenues have been renamed in honor of prominent blacks, but that locals still call the streets by their original names, making getting around a little confusing. From west to east: Eighth Ave/Central Park West is Frederick Douglass Blvd. Seventh Ave is Adam Clayton Powell Jr Blvd, named for the controversial preacher who served in congress during the 1960s. Lenox Ave has been renamed for the Muslim activist Malcolm X. 125th St is also known as Martin Luther King Jr Blvd.

First time visitors will probably be surprised to discover that Harlem is but one express stop away from the Columbus Circle–59th St station downtown. The trip on the A and D trains takes just five minutes, and they deposit you one block from the Apollo Theater and two blocks from Lenox Ave, where many soul food restaurants are located. The 2 and 3 trains from the West Side stop on Lenox Ave at 116th St, site of the Harlem open-air market, and Lenox and 125th St.

Apollo Theater

The Apollo Theater (☎ (212) 749-5838) has been Harlem's leading space for political rallies and concerts since 1914. Virtually every major black artist of note in the '30s and '40s performed there, including Duke Ellington and Charlie Parker. After a brief desultory spell as a movie theater and several years of darkness, the Apollo was bought in 1983 by radio magnate Percy Sutton and revived as a live venue. It still holds its famous weekly amateur night – 'where stars are born and legends are made' – on Wednesdays at 7:30 pm. Watching the crowd call for the 'executioner' to yank hapless performers from the stage is often the most entertaining part of amateur night. On other nights the Apollo hosts performances by established R&B and hip hop artists.

Studio Museum in Harlem

The Studio Museum in Harlem (☎ (212) 864-4500), at 144 W 125th St, has given exposure to the crafts and culture of African Americans for nearly 30 years, and provides working spaces to promising young artists. Its photography collection includes works by James VanDerZee, the master photographer who chronicled the Harlem Renaissance of the '20s and '30s.

It's open Wednesday to Friday from 10 am to 5 pm and Saturday and Sunday from 1 to 5 pm. Admission is $5 for adults, $3 for seniors and students and $1 for children under 12.

Schomburg Center for Research in Black Culture

The nation's largest collection of documents, rare books and photographs is located at the Schomburg Center for Research in Black Culture (☎ (212) 491-2200) at 515 Lenox Ave. Arthur Schomburg, a man born in Puerto Rico of a white father and black mother, started gathering works on black history during the early 20th century while becoming active in the movements for civil rights and Puerto Rican independence. His collection was bought by the Carnegie Foundation and eventually expanded and stored in this branch of the New York Public Library. The Schomburg Center has a theater where lectures and concerts are regularly held.

It's open Monday to Wednesday from noon to 8 pm and Friday and Saturday from 10 am to 6 pm. The center's gallery spaces are also open Sunday from 1 to 5 pm.

Sunday Gospel Services
Some of the churches in Harlem have cut deals with bus operators, and their services are packed with visitors who attempt to take pictures during the services or even leave early. It's much better to go on your own to a place that welcomes visitors but not tour groups. Just show up respectfully well dressed – *sans* camera.

The **Abyssinian Baptist Church** (☎ (212) 862-7474), 132 W 138th St, was a downtown institution started by an Ethiopian businessman that moved north to Harlem in 1923, mirroring the migration of the city's black population. Its charismatic pastor, Calvin O Butts, is an important community activist whose support is sought by politicians of all parties. The church has a superb choir and holds services every Sunday at 9 am, 11 am and 3 pm.

The **Canaan Baptist Church** (☎ (212) 866-0301), 132 W 116th St, may be Harlem's friendliest church. It's a good idea to show up a bit early and introduce yourself to the parishioners before the Sunday 10:45 am service (10 am during the summer).

Harlem Market
Vendors at the Harlem market, at W 116th St and Lenox Ave, do a brisk business selling tribal masks, oils, traditional clothing and assorted African bric-a-brac. Most of the people at the market used to sell their wares from tables set up along 125th St, but were moved to the open-air site, amid great controversy, in 1995 after retailers complained about their presence. You can also get cheap clothing, leather goods, music cassettes and bootleg videos of films still in first run theaters. The market is operated by the **Malcolm Shabazz Mosque**, the former pulpit of Muslim orator Malcolm X, which stands across the street.

The market is open daily from about 10 am to 5 pm and is shut only in the coldest weather.

To Tour or Not to Tour
Harlem has become a very popular destination for foreign visitors who want to see the neighborhoods, but don't wish to walk its streets. As a consequence, bus companies have been doing a big business on guided tours to the neighborhood. But it's worth checking the true cost of the service. One operator offers a $70 trip to Amateur Night at the Apollo, with dinner at an unspecified soul food restaurant. Taking the subway yourself ($3 roundtrip), picking up a ticket at the Apollo box office (prices range from $7 to $20) and finding your own restaurant ($15 or less) represents a huge savings for those on a budget.

Harlem Spirituals (☎ (212) 757-0425) offers several three hour trips to Harlem that leave from in front of the Ed Sullivan Theater at Broadway and 53rd St. Prices for adults/children start at $32/23 and run much higher for nighttime excursions. Both Harlem Spirituals and Musical Fest of Harlem (☎ (212) 222-6059) run Sunday morning tours of Gospel services in local churches, with prices starting at $55/45 including lunch.

Big Onion Walking Tours (☎ (212) 439-1090) offers a very informative tour of historic Harlem for $9/7. ■

Spanish Harlem

Spanish Harlem is the name given to the area from Fifth Ave above 96th St east to the river, a formerly Italian neighborhood that now contains one of the biggest Latino communities in the city. There, you will find **La Marqueta**, a colorful, ad-hoc collection of produce stalls on Park Ave above 110th St that is a signature attraction in 'El Barrio.'

Several landmark remnants of **Italian East Harlem** remain in business: Rao's Restaurant (pronounced RAY-o's; ☎ (212) 722-6709), 455 E 114th St, a tiny 12 table restaurant closed weekends, and Patsy's Pizzeria (☎ (212) 534-9783), 2287 First Ave. And check out Morrone's Bakery (☎ (212) 722-2972), 324 E 116th St, for great peasant bread.

El Museo del Barrio El Museo del Barrio (☎ (212) 831-7272), 1230 Fifth Ave (subway: 103rd St–Lexington), located in an unprepossessing office block, began in 1969 as a celebration of Puerto Rican art and culture and has since expanded its brief holdings to include the folk art of Latin America and Spain. Its galleries now feature pre-Columbian artifacts and a collection of more than 300 *santos*, hand-carved wooden saints in the Spanish Catholic tradition. Temporary exhibits feature the work of local artists who live in Spanish Harlem.

El Museo del Barrio is the best starting point for any exploration of Spanish Harlem. It's open Wednesday to Sunday from 11 am to 5 pm, with extended summer hours on Thursday to 7 pm. Admission is $4 for adults, $2 for seniors and students, and children under 12 get in free.

Every January 5, the museum holds a **Three Kings Parade** in which thousands of schoolchildren, along with camels, donkeys and sheep, make their way up Fifth Ave to 116th St, the heart of the neighborhood.

WASHINGTON HEIGHTS

Near the northern tip of Manhattan, Washington Heights is named after the first US president, who set up a Continental Army fort there during the War for Independence. An isolated rural spot until the late 19th century, Washington Heights is today an unremarkable neighborhood of large apartment buildings. In the 1990s, the neighborhood welcomed the arrival of thousands of new immigrants from the Dominican Republic.

There's a lot of drug activity in Washington Heights, and big business is done selling to downtowners and suburbanites who drive into the city on the George Washington Bridge.

But there's no real need to fear a trip here – the area around the Cloisters, which includes **Fort Tryon Park**, is quite beautiful in warm weather and very safe.

And those who fear the druggy reputation of Washington Heights will be happy to know that the eight cultural institutions in the area offer a Sunday Uptown Treasures Tour, where free shuttle buses run between the museums from 11 am to 5 pm. (Call any one of the following places to find out the schedule.)

Audubon Terrace

Audubon Terrace, at Broadway between 153rd and 155th Sts (subway: 155th St–St Nicholas Ave), is the former home of naturalist John James Audubon, and currently the site of three little-known museums.

The **American Numismatic Society** (☎ (212) 234-3130) has a large permanent collection of coins, medals and paper money. It is open Tuesday to Saturday from 9 am to 4:30 pm and Sunday from 1 to 4 pm. Admission is free.

The **Hispanic Society of America** (☎ (212) 690-0743) has furniture and artifacts of Spanish and Portuguese culture, including significant artworks by El Greco. Few people make the journey up here – guards often outnumber visitors, and they'll have to come upstairs to turn on the lights so you can see the paintings. There are also some nice statues in the courtyard. It's open Tuesday to Saturday from 10 am to 4:30 pm and Sunday 1 to 4 pm; admission is free.

The **American Academy and Institute**

of Arts and Letters (☎ (212) 368-5900) opens its bronze doors to the public several times a year for temporary exhibitions; call ahead for the schedule. Admission is free.

Morris-Jumel Mansion
Built in 1765, the columned Morris-Jumel Mansion (☎ (212) 923-8008), 65 Jumel Terrace at 160th St east of St Nicholas Ave (subway: 163rd St–Amsterdam Ave), served as George Washington's Continental Army headquarters. After the war it returned to its former function as the summer residence of a wealthy local family. The mansion's interior is a designated landmark and contains many of the original furnishings, including a bed on the 2nd floor that reputedly belonged to Napoleon. The ghost of Eliza Jumel, the woman who lived here until her death in 1865, is said to still move about the place.

It's open Wednesday to Sunday from 10 am to 4 pm; admission is $3 for adults, $2 for seniors, students and children (under 10 are free).

The Cloisters
Built in the 1930s the Cloisters (☎ (212) 923-3700), in Fort Tryon Park (subway: 190th St), incorporates fragments of old French and Spanish monasteries and houses the Metropolitan Museum of Art's collection of medieval frescos, tapestries and paintings. In the summer, the best time to visit, concerts are held on the grounds, and more than 250 varieties of medieval flowers and herbs are on view. The museum and the surrounding gardens in Fort Tryon Park are very popular with European visitors, so get here early during the warm months.

It's open Tuesday to Sunday from 9:30 am to 4:45 pm. Admission is $7/3.50 (kids under 12 free).

Dyckman House Museum
The Dyckman House (☎ (212) 304-9422), 4881 Broadway, was built in 1783 on the site of a 28 acre 17th century farm and is the last remaining old Dutch farmhouse to survive in Manhattan. Excavations of the property have turned up valuable clues about colonial life. To get to the Dyckman House take the subway to the 207th St station and walk one block south – many people mistakenly get off one stop too soon at Dyckman St.

It's open Tuesday to Sunday from 11 am to 4 pm, and admission is free.

UPPER EAST SIDE
The Upper East Side is home to New York's greatest concentration of cultural centers, as Fifth Ave above 57th St is called **Museum Mile**. The neighborhood is filled with many of the city's most exclusive hotels and residential blocks. The side streets from Fifth Ave east to Third Ave from 57th to 86th Sts have some stunning townhouses and brownstones, and walking through this area at nightfall affords a voyeuristic opportunity to peer into the interiors and see the grand libraries and living rooms in these homes.

The East Side is served by just three subway lines running up and down Lexington Ave, and the stations listed for sites in this section are served by the 6 local train and the 4 and 5 express trains.

Frick Collection
The Frick Collection (☎ (212) 288-0700), 1 E 70th St (just off Fifth Ave), is located in a mansion built in 1914 by businessman Henry Clay Frick, one of the many such residences that made up 'millionaire's row.' Most of these mansions proved too expensive for succeeding generations and were eventually destroyed, but the wiley and very wealthy Frick, a Pittsburgh steel magnate, established a trust to open his private collection as a museum. (Frick's home in Pittsburgh is also a museum; see the Southwest Pennsylvania chapter.)

It's a shame that the 2nd floor of the residence is not available for viewing, though the 12 rooms on the ground floor are grand enough. The Frick's Oval Room is graced by Jean-Antoine Houdon's stunning figure *Diana the Huntress* and you'll find works by Titian, Vermeer, Bellini, and portraits by Gilbert Stuart, Sir Joshua Reynolds, Thomas Gainsborough and John Constable.

It's well worth picking up the small guide to the galleries ($1) to fully appreciate the significance of the works on display.

It's open Tuesday to Saturday from 10 am to 6 pm and Sunday from 1 to 6 pm. Admission is $5/3; children under 10 are not permitted.

Temple Emanu-El

Five blocks south of the Frick, at E 65th St and Fifth Ave, stands Temple Emanu-El (☎ (212) 744-1400), the world's largest reformed Jewish synagogue, which is significant for its Byzantine and Near-Eastern architecture. It's open to the general public daily from 10 am to 5 pm (it closes at 4 pm on Friday).

Whitney Museum of American Art

The Whitney Museum of American Art (☎ (212) 570-2676), 945 Madison Ave at 75th St (subway: 77th St), is part of Museum Mile in spirit if not exact location. It is housed in an extraordinarily ugly brutalist structure by Marcel Breuer that virtually defines the institution's mission to provoke.

The collection was established by Gertrude Vanderbilt Whitney in the 1930s, who began a Greenwich Village salon for prominent artists such as Edward Hopper. The Whitney specializes in 20th century and contemporary art, and is known for its biennial celebration that gathers more attention for the political statements made by the artists than for the quality of their works. Recent major exhibits included a retrospective on the photographer Robert Frank and an assessment of American Beatnik culture.

The Whitney is open Wednesday from 11 am to 6 pm, Thursday from 1 to 8 pm and Friday and Sunday from 11 am to 6 pm. Admission is $8 for adults $6 for seniors and students, children under 12 free. There is free admission for all ages Thursday from 6 to 8 pm.

KIM GRANT

The Whitney has smaller exhibits at its branch in the Philip Morris Building, 120 Park Ave, across the street from Grand Central Terminal; admission is free.

Metropolitan Museum of Art

The Metropolitan Museum of Art (☎ (212) 879-5500), at Fifth Ave and 82nd St, is New York's most popular single-site tourist attraction, and functions something like a self-contained cultural city-state with three million individual objects in its collection. As only one of its 4.9 million annual visitors, you must plan an assault on its collections, and arrive early or calculate the effects of the weather on museum attendance carefully. 'Met' crowds are impossible on rainy Sunday afternoons in the summer, but during horrible winter weather, you might find the 17 acre museum nearly deserted on a Friday evening.

Once inside the **Great Hall**, pick up a floor plan and head to the ticket booths, where you will find a list of exhibits closed for the day along with a line-up of special museum talks. The Met presents more than 30 special exhibitions and installations each year, and clearly marked floor plans show you how to get to those on offer. To the right of the hall, there is an information desk that offers guidance in several languages (these change depending on the volunteers) and $4 audio tours of the special exhibits.

It's best to target exactly what you want to see and head there first, before culture and crowd fatigue sets in (usually after 90 minutes). Then you can put the floor plan away and get lost trying to get back to the main hall. It's a virtual certainty that you will stumble across something interesting along the way.

Casual Walking Tour If you do not want to see anything in particular, then make a loop of the 1st floor before heading to the 2nd-floor painting galleries. Entering the Egyptian Art section in the north wing, you will pass the tomb of Pernebi (circa 2415 BC), several mummies and incredibly well-preserved wall paintings before seeing the **Temple of Dendur**. The temple, threatened with submersion during the building of the Aswan dam, found a home in New York under this glass enclosure – if you look closely at its walls you can see the graffiti etched by European visitors to the site in the 1820s. (The accompanying history makes plain that the temple was a gift to the US in exchange for building a permanent space for it.)

Exiting the gallery door behind the temple brings a culture shock as you see the Met's collection of **baseball cards**, including the rarest and most expensive card in existence: a 1909 Honus Wagner worth some $200,000. Carrying on to the left brings you to the **American Wing** of furniture and architecture, with a quiet, enclosed garden space that serves as a respite from Met hordes. Along the garden are several stained-glass works by Louis Comfort Tiffany, as well as an entire two story facade of the Branch Bank of the US, preserved when the building was destroyed downtown in the early 20th century.

You then pass through the dark galleries dedicated to **medieval art**. Turning right, you reach a pyramid-like addition that houses the Lehman collection of **impressionist and modern art**, which includes several works by Pierre August Renoir (including *Young Girl Bathing*), Georges Seurat and Pierre Bonnard. An unexpected bonus in this gallery is the rear terra-cotta facade of the original 1880 Met building, now completely encased by later additions and standing mutely on view as its own piece of architectural art.

Heading back toward Fifth Ave brings you through the Rockefeller collection of **Africa and Pacific Island** arts. At the museum cafe, turn left and wander through the **Greek and Roman** art section before winding up back at the south side of the Great Hall.

On the 2nd floor, you will see the Met's famous collection of **European paintings**, located in some of the museum's oldest gal-

Museum Madness

In recent years, attendance at New York's museums has exploded as tourists have discovered that they are low-cost family alternatives to Broadway shows (for which ticket prices begin at about $45) and the cinema (first-run films now cost $8.50). As a consequence, cultural centers have been brazenly boosting admission charges, and at the same time becoming unbelievably crowded. Though you wouldn't know it by the forbidding Checkpoint Charlie–like entrances, most museums' admission charges are voluntary. If you're on a budget, keep a keen eye out for the words 'suggested donation' at the entrance. You can also call ahead to find out whether a museum has weekly 'pay as you wish/free admission' times, or pick up a copy of *Museums New York*, available free at most museum entrances, which offers discount admission coupons.

It would take several days to see all the institutions along Museum Mile, so it's best to pick just one or two sites and explore them thoroughly. Details on the museums and more can be obtained by dialing ☎ (212) 777-2787/ARTS, the Department of Cultural Affairs' 24 hour hotline listing events and concerts at cultural institutions, or by picking up *The Culture of NYC*, a guide and series of maps available at major museums. ■

leries, with colonnaded entryways. Here you will see works by every artist of note, including self-portraits by Rembrandt and Van Gogh, *Portrait of Juan de Parej* by Velazquez, and a suite of rooms dedicated to impressionist and post-impressionist art.

The Met offers free guided walking tours of museum highlights and specific galleries every half hour from 10:15 am to 4 pm Tuesday to Friday. Check the calendar, given away free at the Great Hall information desk for the specific schedule.

The Met is open Tuesday to Thursday and Sunday from 9:30 am to 5:15 pm and Friday and Saturday from 9:30 am to 8:45 pm. Suggested admission is $7 for adults, $3 for seniors and students, children under 12 free.

Solomon R Guggenheim Museum

The Solomon R Guggenheim Museum (☎ (212) 423-3500), 1071 Fifth Ave, is the distinctive spiral art space designed by Frank Lloyd Wright to hold one of the 20th century's greatest private bequests. A 1993 renovation added a 10 story building behind Wright's structure that many complained made the museum resemble a commode, but it did add space for the 5000 work Guggenheim collection, including the major donation in 1976 of impressionist and modern works by Justin Thannhauser.

The museum is open Sunday to Wednesday from 10 am to 6 pm and Friday and Saturday from 10 am to 8 pm. Admission is $8/5, children under 12 free; pay-as-you-wish hours are Friday from 6 to 8 pm. A combination ticket that includes admission to the SoHo branch of the museum is $10/6.

National Academy of Design

The National Academy of Design (☎ (212) 369-4880), 1083 Fifth Ave, was founded by painter-inventor Samuel Morse and has a permanent collection of paintings and sculptures. The academy's works have been housed since 1940 in a grand mansion designed by Ogden Codman, who also designed the Breakers mansion in Newport, RI. The academy's house is notable for its marble foyer and spiral staircase.

It's open from Tuesday to Sunday from 11:30 am to 5:30 pm with late hours on Friday until 8 pm. Admission for adults/students is $5/3.50; for seniors and children under 16 it's free.

Cooper-Hewitt National Museum of Design

The Cooper-Hewitt National Museum of Design (☎ (212) 860-6868), 2 E 91st St, stands in the 64 room mansion that billionaire Andrew Carnegie built in 1901 in a spot then far away from the downtown bustle. Within 20 years, the country surroundings that Carnegie sought disappeared as other wealthy men followed his lead and built palaces around him.

The museum, a branch of the Smithsonian Institution, is a must for anyone interested in architecture, engineering, jewelry or textiles. The museum has also examined advertising campaigns and household item design. If you only have a passing interest in any of this, the place is still worth a visit for its garden.

It's open Tuesday from 10 am to 9 pm, Wednesday to Saturday from 10 am to 5 pm and Sunday from noon to 5 pm. Admission is $3 for adults, $1.50 for seniors and students, and children are free. There is no admission charge Tuesday from 5 to 9 pm.

Jewish Museum

The Jewish Museum (☎ (212) 423-3200), 1109 Fifth Ave, examines 4000 years of Jewish history, ceremony and art. A $25 million renovation of the building, a 1908 banker's mansion, greatly increased gallery space for its more than 30,000 items of Judaica and added a new gallery dedicated to teaching children about Jewish heritage. In 1996, the museum held the first comprehensive exhibition of 20th century Russian and Soviet Jewish artists.

It's open Sunday to Thursday from 11 am to 5:45 pm and Tuesday from 11 am to 8 pm. Admission is $7 for adults, $5 students and seniors, children under 12 are free; free admission is offered to everyone on Tuesday night from 5 to 8 pm.

International Center of Photography

The ICP (☎ (212) 860-1777), 1130 Fifth Ave (subway: 96th St–Lexington), is the city's most important showplace for exhibitions on the careers of major figures in photography, and has recently had retrospectives on fashion photographer and filmmaker William Klein and French photojournalist Henri Cartier-Bresson.

It's open from Wednesday to Sunday from 11 am to 6 pm and Tuesday from 11 am to 8 pm. Admission is $4 for adults, $2 for seniors and students, $1 for children under 12.

There is also an ICP gallery in Midtown (☎ (212) 768-4682), 1133 Sixth Ave (subway: 42nd St–Seventh Ave), which has the same opening hours and admission price.

Museum of the City of New York

The Museum of the City of New York (☎ (212) 534-1672), at Fifth Ave and 103rd St (subway: 103rd St–Lexington Ave), doesn't seem to have a coherent plan to its displays and somewhat duplicates the function of the older New-York Historical Society across town (see Upper West Side). Consequently, both institutions – overshadowed by their many world class neighbors – attract few visitors and have suffered financially since the '80s. Nevertheless, the Museum of the City of New York is forging ahead with an expansion, tracing the city from its beaver trading port days to the modern era. It has a notable 2nd-floor gallery with entire rooms from demolished homes of New York grandees, an excellent collection of antique doll houses, teddy bears and toys, along with and an exhibition dedicated to Broadway musicals.

It's open Wednesday to Saturday from 10 am to 5 pm and Sunday from 1 to 5 pm. Admission is $5/3 adults/children, or $8 for an entire family.

Roosevelt Island

New York's most planned neighborhood is located on a tiny island no wider than a football field in the East River between Manhattan and Queens. Once known as Blackwell's Island after the farming family that lived here, the island was purchased by the city in 1828 and became the location of several public hospitals and an insane asylum. In the 1970s New York State built apartments for 10,000 people along the island's only street. The planned area along the cobblestone roadway resembles an Olympic Village, or, as some less kindly put it, a college dorm complex.

Most visitors take the three minute aerial tramway over, admire the stunning view of the East Side of Manhattan framed by the 59th St Bridge and head straight back. But it's worth spending an hour or so on the island during good weather, if only to enjoy the quiet and the flat roadway and paths that circle it, making it a perfect spot for both running and picnicking. Roosevelt Island Tours (☎ (212) 223-0157) offers group excursions of the island and its six landmarks for $10 per person.

The Roosevelt Island tramway station (☎ (212) 832-4543) is located at 59th St and Second Ave. Trips leave every 15 minutes on the quarter hour from 6 am to 2:30 am daily. The tram is subject to closures for maintenance and bad weather but Roosevelt Island has its own subway station accessible from Manhattan via the Q train during the day and the B train on nights and weekends. Just make sure the train you get on (nearest stop: 63rd St–Lexington) lists '21st St–Queensbridge' as its final destination.

ACTIVITIES

Unless you're ambitious enough to head out to Staten Island to hike (see the section on Outer Boroughs), the city offers little respite from the urban bustle. There is one spot that offers a wide array of activities: the **Chelsea Piers Complex** (☎ (212) 336-6000) on the Hudson River and 23rd St. This huge complex has a four level driving range overlooking the river and an indoor ice-skating rink. A huge sports and fitness center there offers a running track, swimming pool, workout center, even sand volleyball and rock-climbing. A day pass costs $26. The complex is open

Monday to Friday from 6 am to 11 pm, Saturday from 7 am to 8 pm and Sunday from 8 am to 8 pm.

Gyms

Gyms all over the city offer day rates for about $15. Many advertise in the *Village Voice*. One well-located, no frills gym to keep in mind is the Prescriptive Fitness Gym (☎ (212) 307-7760) at 250 W 54th St. It offers $13 daily rates for its well-maintained machines, and there's no 'scene' at the club.

Running

There are three traffic-free spots to run in Manhattan: Central Park's six mile roadway loops around the park and is closed to cars each weekday from 10 am to 3 pm and all weekend. If you don't want to jockey for space with bladers and bikers, try the Jacqueline Kennedy Onassis Reservoir (subway: 86th St on either side of the park), which is encircled by a soft 1.6 mile path. West Side has a runner's pathway along the Hudson River from 23rd St all the way down to Battery Park City, which passes a very pleasant stretch of public park and offers great views of the Jersey shoreline and the Statue of Liberty. The Upper East Side boasts a path that runs along FDR Drive and the East River from 63rd St to about 115th St. If you're alone it's not advisable to run further north than 105th St, since the path isn't well lit beyond that point.

The New York Road Runner's Club (NYRRC; ☎ (212) 860-4455), 9 E 89th St, organizes weekend runs all over the city as well as the annual October **New York Marathon**. Information and assistance for runners can be found at the NYRRC booth at the Engineer's Gate entrance to Central Park at E 90th St.

Bicycling

If you hit the city's pockmarked streets, use a trail bike with wide wheels. Also wear a helmet and be alert so you don't get 'doored' by a passenger exiting a taxi. Transportation Alternatives (☎ (212) 475-4600), 92 St Marks Place, is a bike advocacy group that sponsors free or low-cost weekend trips to the outskirts of the city – their newsletter is available at major bike shops.

Many places rent bicycles for the day, including Metro Bicycle with seven stores (one at 6th St and Broadway; ☎ (212) 663-7531) and Sixth Ave Bicycles (☎ (212) 255-5100), 545 Sixth Ave. Frank's Bike Shop (☎ (212) 533-6332) is an out-of-the-way shop in the Lower East Side (subway: Grand St) that attracts many customers thanks to its helpful staff and very low prices.

ORGANIZED TOURS
Bus Tours

Gray Line (☎ (212) 397-2620) offers more than 29 different tours of the city from its main bus terminal at Eighth Ave and 54th St, including a hop-on, hop-off loop of Manhattan. The cheapest tours begin at $15/7.50 for adults/children and go as high as $50/37.50. There are downsides to these tours: you may get a non-native guide who knows far less about the city than some of the passengers.

New York Apple Tours (☎ (800) 876-9868) offers tours on rumbling old London double-decker buses that sometimes break down in mid-tour. Buses leave on a loop of Manhattan from the Plaza hotel and W 50th St and Eighth Ave; it costs $25/16 for two days of unlimited use of the buses.

Walking Tours

There are many companies and organizations that conduct urban treks, and their phone lines offer detailed information on the latest schedules. Big Onion Walking Tours (☎ (212) 439-1090), established in 1991 by two Columbia University history doctoral candidates, operates year round. They specialize in ethnic New York and run an annual Christmas Day tour of the Jewish Lower East Side. Their walks cost $9 for adults, $7 students and seniors. Howard Goldberg's Adventures on a Shoestring (☎ (212) 265-2663) has been charging the same $5 admission since 1963 for tours of historic houses and other places of interest.

Citywalks (☎ (212) 989-2456) has two-hour tours of specific neighborhoods from March to November at a cost of $12 per person. The Municipal Art Society (☎ (212) 439-1043) is famous for its free tours of Grand Central Terminal each Wednesday at 12:30 pm; other regularly scheduled tours cost $10 a person. Arthur Marks (☎ (212) 673-0477), a weekend fixture in Greenwich Village, leads more expensive $20 tours of the streets. He wears a floppy hat and is prone to rattle off a show tune or two to illustrate points of interest.

Perhaps the weirdest new tour available is one offered by Kenny Kramer, the real-life inspiration for the *Seinfeld* character of the same name. He offers weekend walks past major sites of the TV series for $27. Call ☎ (800) 572-6377 – that spells 'KRAMERS' – for information.

Boat Tours

More than one million people a year take the three hour, 35 mile Circle Line cruise around Manhattan (☎ (212) 563-3200), which leaves from Pier 83 at 42nd St on the Hudson River, from March to December. This is *the* tour to take, provided the weather is good and you can enjoy the waterside breezes on an outside deck. The quality of the narration depends on the enthusiasm of the guide; be sure to sit well away from the narrator to avoid the inevitable 'where are you from?' banter. Tickets for adults/children/seniors cost $18/9/16.

Circle Line also runs a 2½ hour Tuesday night Jazz Cruise from Pier 83 and a Thursday night Country Music Cruise during the summer. Tickets are $20; call for reservations.

World Yacht (☎ (212) 563-3347) has well-regarded culinary cruises around Manhattan year round that leave from Pier 81 at W 41st St. Reservations and proper dress are required, and tickets for adults/children range from $29/16 for a two hour lunch to $75 for a three hour dinner.

Helicopter Tours

Gray Line has three different helicopter tours of Manhattan that depart on the half hour from the heliport (☎ (212) 397-2600) at E 34th St and First Ave. Tours last up to four hours and cost $61/52.50 to $91/82.50 depending on the duration. Island Helicopter Sightseeing (☎ (212) 683-4575) has departures from the same site from 9 am to 9 pm daily; ticket costs range from $44 to $129, and they slap on an unconscionable $5 additional charge for tickets purchased on the day of departure.

SPECIAL EVENTS

Hardly a week goes by without a special event taking place in New York. In fact, there are some 50 officially recognized parades each year honoring certain causes or ethnic groups, along with several hundred street fairs. Most of New York's street fairs offer a rather unremarkable selection of fast food, house plants, athletic socks and cheap belts. You're bound to come across one as you stroll through town during the summer months.

Fifth Ave shuts down several times a year for the elaborate major parades, including the granddaddy of all ethnic celebrations, the St Patrick's Day Parade on March 17th. All events are generally celebrated in Manhattan unless otherwise specified.

January
  First Night, December 31–January 1 (see the sidebar on New Year's Eve)
  Chinese New Year, late January or early February
February
  Black History Month
March
  St Patrick's Day Parade
April
  Antiques Show
  Avignon-New York Film Festival
May
  Fleet Week, parade of naval ships
  Ninth Ave International Food Fair
June
  JVC Jazz Festival
  Toyota Comedy Festival
  Buskers Festival
  Puerto Rican Day Parade
  NY Shakespeare Festival, June to September
  Gay Pride Day
  Welcome Back to Brooklyn Celebration, Brooklyn

New Year's Eve

In addition to the annual festivities in Times Square, there's a five mile midnight run in Central Park and fireworks at the South Street Seaport. **First Night** is a day-long festival of alcohol-free family events that runs from 11 am on December 31 to 1 am New Year's Day, including ballroom dancing in Grand Central Station's main concourse. Tickets for adults/children are $20/5; call ☎ (212) 922-9393 for details. ∎

July
> *Independence Day Fireworks,* July 4
> *Lincoln Center Festival,* July to August, every other year, with the next festivals scheduled for 1998 and 2000
> *Mostly Mozart*
> *Central Park Summerstage,* July to August

August
> *Harlem Week*

September
> *New York is Book Country*
> *New York Film Festival*
> *Caribbean Day Parade,* Brooklyn
> *US Open Tennis Tournament,* Flushing Meadows, Queens
> *Queens Fall Festival,* September to November, Queens

October
> *Halloween Parade*
> *New York Marathon*

November
> *International Poster Fair*
> *Thanksgiving Day Parade*

December
> *Rockefeller Center Christmas Tree Lighting*
> *Singing Christmas Tree Celebration,* South Street Seaport

PLACES TO STAY

It's harsh but true: if you want to find a good, cheap place to stay in New York City, the best thing is to find a friend who lives there. Failing that, you must plan this part of your trip very carefully. Decent rooms under $100 a night have always been a rarity, and the low US dollar has brought in so many foreign visitors that hotels in all categories are experiencing astounding 90% occupancy rates. That makes the already limited bargain choices even harder

to book. Unlike most places to stay in other US cities, few Manhattan hotels offer parking, though they will be happy to tell you in advance if there is an overpriced lot in their immediate neighborhood. Bear in mind that parking in a Midtown lot for a week could cost more than $150.

But don't despair: you just need to keep in mind that two phone calls made before your arrival could turn out to be the smartest money spent on the vacation – one to make a reservation as far in advance as possible, the other confirming the booking just before you arrive.

If you do come to New York on the fly and with a limited budget, you might want to front load your costs by taking a night in a pricier hotel. After a shower and a good night's sleep, start making phone calls to cheaper places – or head to a select few, in person, well before the checkout time.

Hostels

New York International Hostel (☎ (212) 932-2300), 891 Amsterdam Ave (subway: 103rd St), is the HI-AYH facility in the city, and books up its 480 beds quickly during the summer. As it's open for check-in 24 hours a day, it's the place to head if you land in town at an odd time. A bed costs $20 for members, with a small $3 surcharge for non-members. The drug-dealing on Amsterdam Ave led the hostel to install computer card keys for the rooms a few years ago.

The *Chelsea International Hostel* (☎ (212) 627-0010), 251 W 20th St, has a party atmosphere and beds for $18, with a limited number of private rooms at $40. A few blocks up and to the west is the quieter *Chelsea Center Hostel* (☎ (212) 643-0214), 313 W 29th St; its 22 beds are $20.

There are a few alternatives to the HI-AYH facility further uptown: the *International Student Center* (☎ (212) 787-7706), 38 W 88th St, welcomes non-US residents under age 30 for $12 a night. The *Big Apple Hostel* (☎ (212) 302-2603), 119 W 45th St, is a spare facility just off Times Square that's open all day and has a laundry along with $20 beds. *Banana Bungalow* (☎ (212)

769-2441), 250 W 77th St, located in an old hotel, sleeps six in a room for $12 to $18 a night, but its dirty conditions have led to a number of second night departures. A renovation is underway, which may improve the place but also drive up the prices, so call ahead.

If you want to say you stayed in Harlem, call the *New York Bed and Breakfast* (☎ (212) 666-0559), 134 W 119th St, a house run by Giséle Allard, a colorful, talkative expatriate from Montreal. All five rooms cost $20 per person and share a bath. Giséle also runs a 30 bed hostel nearby at 239 Lenox Ave, and she is very proud of the clean new mattresses on offer for an incredible $12 a night.

Sugar Hill (☎ (212) 926-7030), 722 St Nicholas Ave, and the *Blue Rabbit* (☎ (212) 491-3892), 730 St Nicholas Ave, are sister hostels with 30 beds in each facility. Dorm beds are $14 and private rooms that sleep two are $16 per person per night.

Hotel Discounters

Hotel consolidators are copying the patterns of airline travel by serving as last-minute clearing houses for unsold rooms. The Hotel Reservations Network (☎ (800) 964-6835) books rooms in 20 US cities, and their service includes nearly 100 Manhattan hotels for as little as $70 a night. As with airline consolidators, you must pay in advance, though the room can be canceled on 24 hours' notice. Accommodations Express (☎ (800) 444-7666; 7 am to 11 pm EST) offer smaller discounts – around 15% – but deal with a larger number of rooms in every price category.

Quickbook (☎ (800) 789-9887) discounts moderate Midtown hotels; the office is open from 9 am to 5 pm. You can ask them about room availability in many of the hotels listed below.

B&Bs

The city does not have a single clearing house for B&B reservations, and so several rival companies vie for the business, many offering spots in 'outlaw' B&Bs not registered with the city or any organization.

Rooms tend to be the same price as at the cheapest hotels, about $75 to $120 a night, with two night minimum stays in the summer. To avoid disappointments and misunderstandings, reservation services should be prepared to describe the level of contact you will have with a host, and also provide a detailed description of the neighborhood and its nearest attractions. (Most services offer reduced rates for monthly rentals.)

Urban Adventures (☎ (212) 594-5650) has 600 rooms in its registry from $75 to $125 for double occupancy. New York Bed and Breakfast (☎ (800) 900-8134), has singles/doubles starting at $60/90, with a good selection of rooms in Greenwich Village. Manhattan Home-Run Bed and Breakfast (☎ (212) 879-4229) is a newer, smaller service with 250 rooms with private bath that range from $70 to $110 a night.

The Fund for the Borough of Brooklyn has information on Brooklyn B&Bs and mails out a list of locations; call ☎ (718) 855-7882, ext 51.

On City Island in the Bronx, there's *Le Refuge Inn* (☎ (718) 885-2478), 620 City Island Ave, a B&B run by transplanted French chef Pierre Saint-Denis. It's open year round and has eight rooms (four with shared bath) with rates of $73/85.

Suites & Long Stays

In addition to the B&B services, there's Manhattan East Side Suites Hotels (☎ (800) 637-8483), a group of nine East Side locations offering kitchen-equipped suites from $159 a night weekdays and $140 on weekends, with lower rates for extended stays. City Lights Bed and Breakfast (☎ (212) 737-7049) has a 'Live Like a Millionaire' service that offers entire private apartments in uptown locations for $170 to $245 a night.

Lower Manhattan

Most of the available hotels below Houston St cater to a business clientele, so most offer very good deals on weekends. The downside is that the neighborhood is quite dead once the office workers go home, and you'll even have to go uptown to eat, since the many Wall St area restaurants open only for lunch.

One middle range option, Best Western's *Seaport Inn* (☎ (212) 766-6600), 33 Peck Slip, sits in the shadow of the Brooklyn Bridge at the South Street Seaport. Rates for singles are $99 to $150.

The business-oriented *Millennium Hilton* (☎ (212) 693-2001), 55 Church St (subway: Cortlandt St), rises above the street like a black plinth but is still dwarfed by the World Trade Center across the street. It's good for free-spending travelers who want great views but care little about night life, which is reflected in the weekday prices – singles start at $245. On weekends, however, the rates drop to $139 and include buffet breakfast.

Chinatown
Budget If you're on a strict budget and have ever stayed in a Chinese-run hotel in Southeast Asia, you might try the *World Hotel* (☎ (212) 226-5522), 101 Bowery. This transient place is relatively clean, with 130 tiny rooms running $25/35 with shared bath, and a few closet-like spaces for $12. It's only for those with little pocket money and a strong sense of adventure. Even the most adventurous travelers should avoid the nearby *Grand Hotel* and *Hotel Paradise*, which both have the look (and odor) of flophouses and are run by suspicious and unhelpful staff.

Middle If you can ignore the garish interior design, the *Off SoHo Suites Hotel* (☎ (800) 633-7646), 11 Rivington St (two blocks south of E Houston St), has efficiencies starting at $85, though you may have to share a kitchen with another room. A party of four can book adjoining suites for a total of $139.

The *Pioneer Hotel* (☎ (212) 226-1482), 341 Broome St (subway: Grand St), is a nice find on the outskirts of Chinatown with singles/doubles for $33/57.

SoHo
Zoning laws kept hotels out of this neighborhood for years, but a savvy real estate magnate built the *SoHo Grand* (☎ (212) 965-3000), 310 West Broadway, just outside the restricted zone; it's a well-located spot near Canal St. Unfortunately the exterior of this 367 room facility looks like a college dorm. Inside you'll find a cast-iron staircase, a staff dressed in black (naturally) and models and assorted Eurotrash lounging in over-stuffed couches along the 2nd floor bar area. Singles range from $199 to $300, with doubles from $219 and up. Suites are available at $400 and up.

Greenwich Village
There are a number of hotels and inns downtown that cater to gay travelers; see the Gay & Lesbian Accommodations sidebar for more information.

Most downtown accommodations are bottom-end or middle values.

The *St Marks Hotel* (☎ (212) 674-2192), 2 St Marks Place, has a great location in the East Village but the block is noisy and you won't want to inquire about the activities of your neighbors. Singles/doubles are $45/65.

The *Incentra Village* (☎ (212) 206-0007), 32 Eighth Ave, is a charming 12 room inn that's gay and lesbian friendly and booked solid every weekend. This well-maintained, quiet place has a lovely parlor; rates are $100/129 for smaller rooms, and $130/170 for suites.

The best feature of the *Riverview Hotel* (☎ (212) 929-0060), 113 Jane St (subway: 14th St–Eighth Ave), is its location in the West Village overlooking the Hudson River just west of some of the neighborhood's most beautiful blocks. The hotel's 220 rooms are very spare, with closet-like singles for $30 a night and $150 a week with baths at the end of the hall. Doubles are $49/250 for a night/week. It's not a particularly friendly place for single women, but it's safe and cheap. A $5 key fee is refunded upon checkout.

With 160 rooms, *The Washington Square Hotel* (☎ (212) 777-9515), 103 Waverly Place (subway: W 4th St), has earned a good reputation for its location and price, but its popularity makes last-minute booking difficult. Singles/doubles cost $70/99.

A good, and as yet undiscovered, alternative is the nearby *Larchmont Hotel* (☎ (212) 989-9333), 27 W 11th St. Located on a quiet block just off Fifth Ave, the hotel's 52 rooms have sinks (baths and kitchens in the hallways) and cost $45/60.

Chelsea, Flatiron District & Gramercy Park

Bottom End The *Gershwin* (☎ (212) 545-8000), 3 E 27th St, is more a hostel than a hotel, and has aura of a performance space. Just four blocks north of the Flatiron Building, this increasingly popular spot features a funky lobby that's a shrine to Andy Warhol. Dorm beds are $20 per person; private rooms start at $65. In many ways, it's more bohemian in character than the far more famous (and pricey) Chelsea Hotel, and features an actual tin Campbell Soup can signed by Andy Warhol. The Gershwin's reputation and popularity make reservations a must, and it's becoming a popular hangout for young travelers who are staying in hostels and hotels elsewhere in the city.

Just a few steps away from the Gershwin is the gamier but cheap *Madison Hotel* (☎ (212) 532-7373), 21 E 27th St – a good alternative for those without reservations. Very spare rooms with private bath are provided for $60/80.

The *Senton Hotel* (☎ (212) 684-5800), 39-41 W 27th St, has a garish neon sign and looks a bit dicey from the outside, but rooms have TVs, are reasonably clean and cost $40 with shared bath and $60 private.

Middle The *Chelsea Hotel* (☎ (212) 243-3700), 222 W 23rd St, once a low-cost hangout, is now cashing in on its fame as a literary landmark. The rooms are uneven in quality and the front desk clerk will snicker if you ask for Sid Vicious' room (since remodeled and renumbered). Actor Ethan Hawke – as aspiring author – is currently the Chelsea's most famous

---

> ### Gay & Lesbian Accommodations
>
> Some hotels cater exclusively to gays and lesbians; ironically the laws designed to protect the gay community from discrimination also prevent them from specifically excluding straights, but the policy is quite clear. It's necessary to make reservations at least a month in advance.
>
> Jay Lesiger runs the popular *Chelsea Pines Inn* (☎ (212) 929-1023), 317 W 14th St, offering rooms from $55 to $89. The *Colonial House Inn* (☎ (212) 633-1612), 318 W 22nd St, is in the same price range. The *East Village B&B* (☎ (212) 260-1865), 252 E 7th St, welcomes lesbians.
>
> Gay-friendly hotels include the *Washington Square Hotel* (see Greenwich Village under Places to Stay), the *Grand Union* (☎ (212) 683-5890), 34 E 32nd St, and the *Gramercy Park Hotel* (see Chelsea & Gramercy Park). All have clean rooms for under $120 a night. ■

---

resident. There are some shared-bath rooms for $70 a night, but they're nearly always booked. Rooms with private baths have climbed in price in recent years and now start at $125.

The *Gramercy Park Hotel* (☎ (212) 475-4320), at the corner of E 21st St and Lexington Ave, advertises itself as a 1st class place, and though the location overlooking Gramercy Park is perfect, it's a bit dowdy and the service tends to be slow and inattentive. It does have a wonderfully dark lobby bar that's worth checking out if you're merely passing by. Singles start at $135 a night.

Top End The *Inn at Irving Place* (☎ (212) 533-4600), 56 Irving Place at E 17th St, is a charming and more expensive 12 room townhouse that has a reputation for romance. Rates begin at $250 and go as high as $325 depending on the season.

Midtown

Bottom End There are several good places just south of Herald Square. The *Wolcott Hotel* (☎ (212) 268-2900), 4 W 31st St, is a 280 room Beaux Arts hotel designed by

John Duncan, the architect of Grant's Tomb. Rates are $70/75.

The no-frills The Herald Square Hotel (☎ (212) 279-4017), 19 W 31st St, has held its rates for about five years, which run $45 for a small room with a shared bath, $55 for private bath. Double rooms begin at $75.

Middle The area of Park Ave south of Grand Central Terminal is an unremarkable but busy stretch between Midtown and the Flatiron District that has a number of reasonably priced and unfancy hotels. Howard Johnson on Park Ave (☎ (212) 532-4860), 429 Park Ave South, is a comfortable place with singles/doubles starting at $105/115.

The Hotel Metro (☎ (212) 947-2500), 45 E 35th St off Madison Ave, combines '30s Art Deco (its lobby walls feature movie posters from Hollywood's golden era) with the comfort of a gentlemen's club. It has an attractive lounge and library area. Upstairs you'll find rather plain rooms, but the price ($125 to $175) and location (near the Morgan Library and the Empire State Building) make this 160 room hotel a worthy choice.

The Jolly Madison Towers (☎ (212) 685-3700), 22 E 38th St just off Madison Ave, is very popular with Latin American tourists who hang out in its wonderfully tacky Whaler Bar. Rates start at $99.

Just around the corner from the main branch of the New York Public Library is the Quality Hotel (☎ (212) 447-1500), 3 E 40th St, a 186 room business hotel that cuts deeply into its $152/167 regular rates on weekends, when occupancy drops.

The Hotel Iroquois (☎ (212) 840-3080), 49 W 44th St, is a poorer version of the more famous Algonquin (which stands nearby), and charges $90 and up depending on the season.

Furnishings are a bit frayed at the 400 room Pickwick Arms Hotel (☎ (212) 355-0300), 250 E 51st St, but the place is popular with European travelers. Rates start at $65 and there's a decent restaurant on the premises serving a $5.95 buffet lunch.

The Ameritania Hotel (☎ (212) 247-5000), 1701 Broadway, next door to the Ed Sullivan Theater where the Late Show with David Letterman is televised, is popular with European bus tours. It's decorated like a futuristic disco, and the desk clerks usually knock off 10% from the $112/130 room rate if they are told you heard about the hotel in a guidebook.

The following middle-range hotels are located very near Central Park South.

The Woodward Hotel (☎ (212) 247-2000), 210 W 55th St, a quiet and efficient Best Western property, is located near Carnegie Hall and has singles/doubles from $115/135; there's access to a good local gym.

The Hotel Wellington (☎ (212) 247-3900), at the corner of Seventh Ave and 55th St, is just two blocks south of Carnegie Hall and has 700 unremarkable but reasonably priced rooms at $125/135. The Salisbury Hotel (☎ (212) 246-1300), 123 W 57th St, is virtually across the street from icons of both high and low culture: Carnegie Hall and Planet Hollywood. Rooms are $169, with suites available for $200.

Just south of Columbus Circle is the Westpark Hotel (☎ (212) 246-6440), 308 W 58th St. It's tough booking a room there in the summer because of its word-of-mouth popularity with European travelers. Singles/doubles start at $75/88, with two-room suites available for as low as $140.

Like all the hotels on Central Park South, the St Mortiz (☎ (212) 755-5800), 50 Central Park South, has a great location, but is well past its prime and the staff seems woefully overworked. That's probably why you can get room deals for as little as $125 overlooking the park.

Top End Most of the expensive Midtown hotels have rates starting at $160 that fluctuate greatly according to demand.

Morgan's (☎ (212) 686-0300), 237 Madison Ave, is a sleek and unmarked hotel still popular with the European gliterati. Rates are $200 and up for singles and $220 to $285 for doubles, with suites beginning at $395.

Publishing executives still love to lunch at the Royalton (☎ (212) 869-4400),

NEW YORK

44 W 44th St, keeping the hotel's restaurant an A-list must, but the hotel itself is easy to book. Rooms are $245 for singles and $275 and up for doubles.

Across the street, the *Algonquin* (☎ (212) 840-6800), 59 W 44th St, still attracts people thanks to its reputation as the site of the 1930s' Algonquin Round Table of writers, but the $200-plus rooms are often small and cramped. The old furniture was replaced during a 1991 renovation.

The legendary *Waldorf Astoria* (☎ (212) 355-3000), 301 Park Ave, is the place where members of the British Royal Family turn up for fundraising dinners; singles/doubles start at $225/250, though weekend specials bring the price down to about $180. The lobby is quietly elegant but surprisingly not as grand as you would expect; the restaurants and bars within are suitably expensive but not remarkable enough to justify the prices.

The *Peninsula* (☎ (212) 247-2200), 700 Fifth Ave at 55th St, once known as the Gotham Hotel, is one of the oldest surviving grand hotels in Midtown, dating back to 1904. It is totally renovated and has a world famous spa and athletic club that sprawls over three floors. Rates are $340 and up for doubles only.

Across the street the *St Regis* (☎ (212) 753-4500), Fifth Ave and 55th St, is well-known for its 1st class service and King Cole bar, which features a mural by Maxfield Parrish that was moved from the old Knickerbocker Hotel in Times Square. Its double rooms cost $425.

The *Plaza* (☎ (212) 759-3000), 768 Fifth Ave, has recently been bought by a hotel group that will presumably rein in the garish decorative excesses of the previous owner, New York developer Donald Trump. But even at $250 a night and above, you're not likely to get anything better than a postage-stamp sized view of Central Park unless you positively insist on one before checking in. The ground floor is always busy with nonresidents meeting for expensive drinks in the Oak Room or tea in the garden court. For about same amount of money, you're better off across the street at

the elegant *Sherry Netherland* (☎ (212) 355-2800), 781 Fifth Ave.

Rates at the elegant limestone *Four Seasons* (☎ (800) 332-3442), 57 E 57th St, begin at $420/470 and continue up to $800 for a suite.

Times Square

Middle The *Broadway Bed and Breakfast* (☎ (212) 997-9200), at 264 W 46th St, just across the street from Restaurant Row, is a former run-down Times Square area hotel that has been turned into a reasonably priced and well-located small inn with 42 neat rooms. Singles/doubles are $78/85 and come with continental breakfast. If you need a Midtown space on short notice, try the *Hotel Carter* (☎ (212) 944-6000), 250 W 43rd St, a 1000 room hotel with rates as low as $50 a night. Conditions in this huge hotel are not 1st class.

The *Milford Plaza* (☎ (212) 869-3600), 270 W 45th St, is a Ramada-owned 1300 room standard hotel that is a favorite for out of town bus tours and airline crews. Rooms are $75/100, with special three day weekend deals. *Days Inn Midtown* (☎ (800) 572-6232), at the corner of Eighth Ave and 48th St, and *Quality Hotel and Suites Midtown* (☎ (212) 768-3700), 157 W 47th St, are bland chain hotels with rates from $99 to $120.

The renovated and clean *Portland Square Hotel* (☎ (212) 382-0600), 132 W 47th St, is just steps away from the middle of Times Square and has $45 shared rooms; private rooms start at $70. The *Hotel Edison* (☎ (212) 840-5000), 228 W 47th St, was once a high-class spot for Broadway stars that caters to tourists now, though its colorful coffee shop is still a hangout for theater people. Rates are $95/105.

Top End Top-end hotels around Times Square charge upwards from $160 a night but don't really offer much distinction; they are charging for their location. All are rather loudly lit, and the lobbies are set back from the street to discourage outsiders. They include the *Marriott Marquis* (☎ (212) 398-1900), 1535 Broadway; the

Novotel (☎ (212) 315-0100), 226 W 52nd St; and the *Double Tree Suites* (☎ (212) 719-1600), 47th St and Seventh Ave.

For more character try the *Paramount* (☎ (212) 764-5500), 235 W 46th St. This was a hip place in the early '90s, but it's no longer difficult to get into the Whiskey Bar on the street level. Singles start at $125.

Upper West Side
The Broadway American Hotel (☎ (212) 362-1100), 2178 Broadway, attracts visitors with its $45 rooms with shared baths, but it's best to pay $89 for a private bath or go elsewhere because it's a renovated welfare hotel that still has more than 100 long-term residents.

The Excelsior (☎ (212) 362-9200), 45 W 81st St, is an old 169 room hotel that overlooks the Museum of Natural History. Rates run from $89 for a single and two-room suites begin at $129. The *Mayflower* (☎ (212) 265-0060), 15 Central Park West at W 61st St, though a bit stodgy, has over 500 rooms and often offers special deals for three-day weekends.

The 96 room *Newtown* (☎ (212) 678-6500), 2528 Broadway, is a smaller-sized alternative to the big West Side hotels. Rates are $65/75.

The *Hotel Olcott* (☎ (212) 877-4200), 27 W 72nd St, is an old residence hotel well-known as a bargain spot on the Upper West Side. The hotel is just steps away from the Dakota building and the 72nd St entrance to Central Park, and you'll have to book early to get its singles that start at $85.

Upper East Side
Middle The 12 room *Gracie Inn* (☎ (212) 628-1700), 502 E 81st St, is an undiscovered country-style inn near the East River run by Sandra Arcara with singles/doubles starting at $79/139. You get a good breakfast with the room.

The *Franklin* (☎ (212) 369-1000), 164 E 87th St, is a standard place with 53 rooms running from $115 to $125.

Top End Some of New York's most elegant and expensive hotels are located on

the Upper East Side. For around $275 or more a night you can enjoy the quiet elegance of the *Pierre* (☎ (212) 838-8000), at 61st St and Fifth Ave. Steps away from Madison Ave is the intimate and quiet 61 room *Lowell* (☎ (212) 838-1400), 28 E 63rd St, the of-the-moment place to stay for West Coast celebrities like Quentin Tarantino. Rates start at $295.

A slightly cheaper East Side alternative is the *Hotel Wales* (☎ (212) 876-6000), 1295 Madison Ave at 92nd St, a century-old hotel recently restored to its former glory. Its 100 rooms start at $160 a night and include a continental breakfast.

PLACES TO EAT
If you decide to eat in a different restaurant every night in New York City, 46 years would pass before you ran out of options. Only Paris offers a greater selection of elegant culinary experiences; but at the opposite end, absolutely no other city can beat New York's selection of reasonably priced restaurants. Of course, mixed among these 17,000 restaurants are more than a few mediocre places, usually serving fast-food versions of Chinese or other ethnic dishes. Travelers looking to spend a bit more on a 'bistro' experience rather than a fast-food place can get squeezed: dinner at a moderately priced but unremarkable restaurant can add up to $75 for two.

Don't be shy about asking about cost: most waiters, whatever the price level of a restaurant, neglect to tell you the cost of off-menu 'specials' or recommended wines. And if you're looking for a night of drinking, do it at a bar, not a restaurant; proprietors like to gouge on alcohol prices, especially for specialty drinks such as margaritas. The single best source for restaurants is the *Zagat Survey*, available at bookstores all over the city. Restaurant reviews also appear weekly in *Time Out* and *New York* magazine, and in the Friday section of the *New York Times*.

Groceries
New York City's food stores are uniformly small and over priced, but you can cobble

together a decent and healthful lunch from one of the fruit stands set up on major avenues all over the city, especially on Sixth Ave near the office buildings in Midtown and on Third Ave above 59th St near the large apartment blocks. There are numerous fruit stands on the Upper West Side along Broadway, where you can stock up on provisions for a Central Park picnic. (Remember that grapes and the like should be washed since they've been exposed to pollution all day.)

Gourmet Garage has two locations – in SoHo (☎ (212) 941-5850), 453 Broome St, and on the Upper East Side (☎ (212) 535-5889), 301 E 64th St just east of Second Ave – which offer a very good selection of fruit, breads and cheeses. The store also sells healthy portions of rice and beans for $4 and elaborate sandwiches like tandoori chicken for around $5. *Zabar's* (☎ (212) 787-2000), on the corner of Broadway and W 80th St, is perhaps the city's most popular emporium, with very good prices on items such as smoked salmon. A few blocks south, *Fairway Market* (☎ (212) 595-1888), 2127 Broadway at W 74th St, tends to have low prices on cheese and prepared salads. On the East Side, try the *Vinegar Factory* (☎ (212) 987-0885), 431 E 91st St, for a similar range of gourmet food choices.

Lower Manhattan

Pearl Palace (☎ (212) 482-0771), 60 Pearl St, is a no frills Indian restaurant open seven days a week, 24 hours a day, that fuels brokers and support staff from nearby Wall St firms. They offer a bargain all-you-can-eat buffet lunch ($6.99) Monday to Friday from 11 am to 2:30 pm that includes a salad bar. *Zigolini's* (☎ (212) 425-7171), 66 Pearl St, specializes in filling focaccia sandwiches, all for under $7.50. Some of the specials are named after customers who suggested them.

There are dozens of places to eat in South Street Seaport, few of them better than an average McDonald's. The *North Star Pub* (☎ (212) 509-6757), 93 South St, is a passable imitation of a British pub with traditional fare, like bangers and mash for $9.95. It's packed with office workers on weekdays.

Chinatown

Chinese Food Everyone in New York has their favorite restaurant in Chinatown. Former mayor Ed Koch is a proud patron of *Peking Duck House* (☎ (212) 227-1810), 22 Mott St. It was over the signature specialty that Koch helped then-Paris mayor Jacques Chirac lay plans to rid the French capital of dog droppings. (The meal was more successful than Chirac's subsequent program.) *Hay Wun Loy* (☎ (212) 285-8686), 28-30 Pell St, specializes in fresh fish right out of the tank and dim sum. *Hong Ying Rice Shop* (☎ (212) 349-6126), 11 Mott St, is a prototypical basement-level Chinatown eatery, serving dishes such as shrimp with black bean sauce for $8.95. Vegans should check out the *House of Vegetarian* (☎ (212) 226-6572), 68 Mott St. The barbecue 'pork' and 'duck' dishes for $6.95 taste so much like the real thing, you'll wonder if the entire menu is a put on.

New York's Sidewalk Vendor Cuisine

Even the healthiest eater may be tempted to try some fast food from one of the city's thousands of streetside stands, which now serve much more than the traditional New York hot dog with onions ($1.50). It's possible to find vendors offering up fruit, healthy soups, Middle Eastern fare such as falafel (crushed and spiced chickpeas fried and served in a toasted pita), chicken or breaded eggplant sandwiches, take-away Thai dishes and Italian sandwiches on focaccia bread. You'll find lots of vendors on side streets just off the main avenues in Midtown, and a filling meal and a soda will generally cost you between $3 and $8 – provided you don't buy lunch near a museum or a tourist site such as the Statue of Liberty, where prices tend to run $1 or $3 higher. Avoid the 'hot' pretzels though – they are almost invariably rock hard and at $2 are overpriced. ■

Just a bit further afield, on East Broadway running directly east from Chatham Square to the Manhattan Bridge, are a number of restaurants and food stands that cater to mostly locals since visitors tend to flock to Mott St. You'll find moderately priced Hong Kong-style food at the *Nice Restaurant* (☎ (212) 406-9779), 35 East Broadway. Its 2nd-floor banquet room is a popular spot for Chinese wedding receptions.

Vietnamese & Thai Food In recent years a number of Vietnamese restaurants have found a home in Chinatown. *Nha Trang* (☎ (212) 233-5948), 80 Baxter St, is often packed at lunch with jurors and lawyers from the nearby city courthouses, who eat at crowded tables with other strangers. A filling meal can be had for well under $10 if you stick with dishes such as the $3.50 barbecued beef on rice vermicelli and the $2.75 shrimp spring rolls. The super-rich, but delicious Vietnamese-style coffee with condensed milk is available for $1.50. A virtually identical menu is available next door at *New Pasteur* (☎ (212) 608-3656), 85 Baxter St.

The *Thailand Restaurant* (☎ (212) 349-3132), 106 Bayard St, serves up the most authentic Thai dishes outside of Bangkok. Particularly good is the $7.95 spicy vegetarian soup – it's the closest thing to a cure for the common cold.

Little Italy
A good rule of thumb while looking for a restaurant in Little Italy is to avoid any place where the manager hangs out in the street trying to drum up business. During summer months, the two blocks of Mulberry St north of Canal St are closed to traffic to allow the small restaurants more space for outdoor seating. Most of the places with al fresco dining offer entrees for $15 and under, and if you stick with pasta, you can't go far wrong.

Benito 1 (☎ (212) 226-9171), 174 Mulberry St, is one of the better known choices here. By far the best spot to sit down for a while is *Cafe Roma* (☎ (212) 226-8413),

385 Broome St, where you can have cannoli and espresso in a quiet setting after a Chinatown or SoHo meal.

SoHo
Once the center of nouveau dining, many of the restaurants in SoHo are growing tired, or are plagued by erratic food quality and inattentive service. Many restaurants don't accept reservations; and when you're told the wait is '20 minutes,' rest assured that's SoHo-speak for an hour.

Budget *Lupe's East LA Kitchen* (☎ (212) 966-1326), 110 Sixth Ave, is a reasonable Mexican restaurant that is popular among locals for lunch. It offers good burritos and enchiladas in the $6.50 range.

Moderate *Lucky Strike* (☎ (212) 941-0479), 59 Grand St, features French bistro fare, and the menu, painted on mirrors above the table, has remained unchanged for several years. It gets very crowded late on Fridays and Saturdays when a DJ plays the front room. *Fanelli's Cafe* (☎ (212) 226-9412), 94 Prince St, is the one of the grittier places in the neighborhood. It's a dark, smokey bar with a pressed tin ceiling and burgers for a reasonable $10.

Moderate – Vegetarian SoHo offers three notable restaurants. *Souen* (☎ (212) 807-7421), 219 Sixth Ave, has a wide selection of macrobiotic menu items, as well as less stringent vegetarian dishes. *Helianthus Vegetarian* (☎ (212) 598-0287), 48 MacDougal St, features Chinese and Japanese food and offers a lunch deal that includes a dumpling and rice with dishes like lemon mock chicken and sautéed udon for around $5.50. *Spring Street Natural* (☎ (212) 966-0290), 62 Spring St, is a louder and busier restaurant with a large menu that in addition to vegetarian selections includes healthy fish and chicken dishes for $15 and under.

Top End *Cascabel* (☎ (212) 431-7300), 218 Lafayette St, offers a dramatic eating experience with blood-red decor and adventurous menu. Everything is delicious – but costly (around $50 per person).

The *Kitchen Club* (☎ (212) 274-0025), 30 Prince St, is an intimate space where owner-chef Marja Samson works in full view of diners. She's a bit eccentric – if you spot a worm in your salad she will respond with a lecture on the wonders of organic foods. The mushroom dumplings, Japanese box dinners and pumpkin ice cream are sublime; credit cards are not accepted.

Tribeca
In recent years Tribeca has overtaken SoHo as the trendiest dining spot in the city, but there is still a healthy selection of moderately priced restaurants.

Moderate *Odeon* (☎ (212) 233-0507), 145 West Broadway, is an amazing phenomenon: a once-trendy '80s restaurant that has not only survived, but thrived in this decade. It serves bistro fare such as lamb sandwiches and steak frites for under $18 until 2 am every day.

Riverrun (☎ (212) 966-3894), 176 Franklin St (subway: Franklin St), features an unambitious menu, but decent food. The pints are $2.95 during happy hour and the juke box is the cheapest in the city at 10¢ per play. *Walker's* (☎ (212) 941-0142), 16 N Moore St, is a dark watering hole with three dining rooms and a very reasonable Sunday brunch. It serves straightforward fare – sliced turkey sandwiches and hamburgers for $6.95. Jazz combos play Sunday nights with no cover charge.

Bubby's (☎ (212) 219-0666), at 120 Hudson St, is always packed on weekends for their breakfast fare, with locals hoping to spot actor Harvey Keitel, who lives in the neighborhood. You may have to wait an hour for a table.

Top End Reservations are required weeks (and for Saturdays months) in advance at *Chanterelle* (☎ (212) 966-6960), 2 Harrison St, which offers a fixed-price dinner menu for around $80 per person. Its changing menu often features a heavenly seafood sausage, and the combined experience of service and cuisine in the spare dining room is world class.

Greenwich Village
Picking a restaurant around Bleecker St between Broadway and Seventh Ave is difficult – there are many choices, and more than a few are mediocre. Tread warily and consider these selections, or head to the cheaper choices on Second and Third Aves in the East Village (see section below). Most of the following are within walking distance of the W 4th St subway station.

Budget There are some two dozen cafes in Greenwich Village, and one of the best is *Bleecker Street Pastry* (☎ (212) 242-4959), 245 Bleecker St, where you can linger over a cappuccino and sweet Italian croissant for $4.00 among locals reading their morning papers. *Jon Vie* (☎ (212) 242-4440), 492 Sixth Ave, is a traditional French bakery where you can get a caloric pastry and a coffee for $1.95 before 11 am. *French Roast* (☎ (212) 533-2233), 78 W 11th St, is a 24 hour cafe serving light sandwiches and desserts at reasonable prices. It's a good place to peruse the New York newspapers.

Passers-by can watch the homemade

This Year's Model
Nobu (☎ (212) 219-0500), 105 Hudson St, the oh-so-trendy sushi restaurant, has taken chi-chi dining in Manhattan to a new level of insanity. In order to make a mere reservation, you must provide them with a credit card – they threaten to charge $25 per person if anyone neglects to show up. Its tasting menu, prepared by hot chef Nobuyuki Matsuhisa, begins at $60 a person, and while some say it's worth the price, the inattentive service makes the whole evening feel like a complete rip-off – you're better off going to the far cheaper restaurants in the East Village on E 9th St off Third Ave. For now Nobu is coasting on star power, but what will they do when Meryl Streep stops eating there? ∎

Gay Eats

Virtually all of the restaurants in Greenwich Village and Chelsea are gay-friendly. There are three popular restaurants on Eighth Ave within a few blocks of each other south of 23rd St that are better known for their scenes than the food: *The Viceroy* (☎ (212) 633-8484), *Candy Bar* (☎ (212) 229-9702) and *Food Bar* (☎ (212) 243-2020). *Eighteen and Eighth* (☎ (212) 242-5000), named after its location, has cheap lunches for under $6 and flirtatious male waiters.

You can pick up reduced admission club flyers at *Florent* (see Greenwich Village under Places to Eat) and *Manatus* (☎ (212) 989-7042), 340 Bleecker St, an all-night place.

Nearby on Bedford St are three restaurants with gay clientele: *Mary's* (☎ (212) 741-3387), at No 42, an old Italian restaurant; *Universal Grill* (☎ (212) 989-5621), at No 44; and *Orbit* (☎ (212) 463-8717), at No 46. Each is packed on weekends for dinner and brunch.

Aggie's (☎ (212) 673-8994), 146 W Houston St, is a coffee shop popular with lesbians – single females tend to receive better service than anyone else. ∎

noodles being prepared at *Sammy's Noodles* (☎ (212) 924-6688), 453-461 Sixth Ave, which sprawls over several storefronts. Lunch specials start at $4.50 and none of the noodle dishes are more expensive than $6.95.

Despite its trendiness and late-night scene, *Bar Six* (☎ (212) 645-2439), 502 Sixth Ave, is actually a reasonable place to stop for lunch. Grilled chicken or rockfish sandwiches cost just $6.95 and include soup or salad.

Picasso Cafe (☎ (212) 929-6232), 359 Bleecker St, is another good budget choice, serving light-crusted pizza and sandwiches for under $10 in a fine garden space right in the heart of the West Village.

Moderate *Dix et Sept* (☎ (212) 645-8023), is a mid-priced French bistro located, naturally enough, on the corner of Seventh Ave and 10th St. It accurately proclaims itself to be 'Paris without the attitude.' *Grange Hall* (☎ (212) 924-5246), 50 Commerce St, just off Barrow St a block from Sixth Ave, is a converted neighborhood tavern with a beautiful wooden bar that serves organic foods. It's very popular and the wait can be as long as an hour without a reservation, but the prices are reasonable – the $7.95 smoked trout salad appetizer is a meal in itself. *Caffe Lure* (☎ (212) 473-2642), 169 Sullivan St, is a cramped and popular French

bistro with a wood-burning oven. The individual pizzas, all under $11, are delicious, but the best thing on the menu is the $7 lobster and spinach salad appetizer (only cash accepted). Avoid the place on hot summer nights – the oven turns the restaurant into a sauna.

El Faro (☎ (212) 929-8210), 823 Greenwich St, is a classic old Spanish restaurant that's quiet during the week, and impossibly crowded on Friday and Saturday nights. The decor hasn't changed in 20 years, nor have the waiters. Main dishes like the spicy shrimp diablo may seem pricey at $16, but they're enough to feed two people.

In the heart of the meat-packing district sits *Florent* (☎ (212) 989-5799), 69 Gansevoort St (off Washington St), a 24 hour French-run bistro offering hanger steak, hamburgers and breakfast selections. On the weekend closest to July 14th, the restaurant takes over Gansevoort St for an open-air Bastille Day celebration featuring everything from drag queens to Frank Sinatra imitators. It's also a great place to pick up reduced admission flyers for downtown nightclubs.

Moderate – Italian There are many midrange Italian restaurants in Greenwich Village. Among the best is *Trattoria Spaghetto* (☎ (212) 255-6752), 232

Bleecker St at the corner of Carmine St, a converted old coffee shop with traditional red-checked vinyl tablecloths. Almost all the pasta dishes are $10.

Slightly more expensive, and certainly more colorful, is *Rocco* (☎ (212) 677-0590), 181 Thompson St just north of Houston, where the friendly and attentive wait staff will be happy to provide your favorite dish even if it's not on the menu. This gathering place for local Village eccentrics has been around for 60 years.

Marinella (☎ (212) 807-7472), 49 Carmine St, not only has a multi-paged menu, but displays extensive daily specials on a blackboard which is wheeled from table to table. The Northern Italian chicken, fish and veal entrees cost about $14.

East Village

In terms of price, pure choice and reliability, this area is the best in the city for travelers on a budget. It offers just about everything but fancy French dining.

Budget *Benny's Burritos* (☎ (212) 254-2054), 93 Ave A, decorated in '60s kitsch (lava lamps, pink walls and Formica tables) is a local pioneer in low-fat Cal-Mex food. The super-filling burritos and enchiladas are $7 and under, and include plenty of options for vegetarians. But watch out for the lethal margaritas. A larger and more crowded Benny's is located in the West Village at 113 Greenwich St (☎ (212) 727-0584).

Bereket (☎ (212) 475-7700), 187 E Houston St on the corner of Orchard (subway: Second Ave), is a 24 hour kebab eatery with a good selection of vegetarian dishes. It's a favorite with club hoppers heading to and from the newest no-name club on nearby Ludlow St.

South and to the east of the Union Square subway station are many delis and diners that will provide you with a filling meal at low prices. Some that stand out are: *Veselka* (☎ (212) 228-9682), 144 Second Ave, a Polish diner with a strong local following. It's decorated by murals by local artists, has great soups and grill chefs who treat making pancakes as a performance art. The late French-Italian actor Yves Montand's favorite hangout in New York was the *Second Ave Deli* (☎ (212) 677-0606), 156 Second Ave, a quintessential Jewish deli offering great fare (the matzo ball soup comes with sprigs of fresh dill). This restaurant offers much better bargains than the more touristy alternatives in Midtown: the Carnegie Deli and Stage Deli.

Moderate *Time Cafe* (☎ (212) 533-7000), 380 Lafayette St, is a pleasant surprise: a trendy nightspot, popular with models, that actually serves very good organic food, although the service can sometimes be inattentive. There's a good selection of pizzas at $10.95 and other entrees top out at about $18.00. *Roettelle AG* (☎ (212) 674-4140), 126 E 7th St, is a Swiss restaurant incongruously located on a block in the East Village that retains much of its Polish character. Strapping waitresses serve healthy portions of *sauerbraten* and *veau emincee* (sliced veal with mushrooms) for around $16 an entree.

The Pizza War

An odd little pizza war is taking place in New York among several unrelated pizzerias named Ray's. While all claim to be the 'original Ray's,' that distinction is generally thought to belong to the one located at Sixth Ave and 11th St. Oddly enough, though, no one seems sure what it was about this Ray's that prompted the good word of mouth. One decent Ray's claimant is located near the Puck Building on Prince St, but you're better off passing it by and patronizing *Lombardi's* (☎ (212) 941-7994), 32 Spring St, indisputably the oldest pizza restaurant in New York. Established in 1905, this brick oven pizzeria only serves pizza pies and huge calzones, delicious half-moon dough shells stuffed with ricotta cheese and herbs. The fresh mushroom pie is served with three different types of mushroom. ∎

Little Delhi

Sixth St between Second and First Aves has been dubbed 'Little Delhi' thanks to the 19 restaurants that have popped up on the block since the late '70s. All are crowded on weekend nights. (Don't bother asking the proprietors if all the restaurants share the same kitchen – it's a tired joke they've heard a million times before.) In general, the restaurants offering live Indian music and/or a wine list wind up being more expensive than their alcohol-free counterparts. Arrive at the dry places with your own store bought beer – there's an Indian market on the corner of First Ave and 6th St with a very good selection. ∎

With its pressed-tin ceilings and faded paintings, *Lanza's* (☎ (212) 674-7014), 168 First Ave (near E 10th St), is a throwback to an earlier time in the East Village. Its five-course Italian dinner (for just $11.95) includes a selection of delicious desserts. If you're not hungry but want a strong espresso and an Italian pastry, try the nearby *DeRobertis* pasticceria (☎ (212) 674-7137), 176 First Ave, which has been in business since 1904.

Lucky Cheng's (☎ (212) 473-0516), 24 First Ave, is a Thai restaurant featuring drag queen 'waitresses' that has been over-taken by curious out-of-towners. Reservations are often not respected – you can encounter an hour-long wait – and the food is as temperamental as the he/she server. If you're looking for a high concept food experience in the East Village, call *Princess Pamela's Southern Touch Restaurant* (☎ (212) 477-4460), 78 E 1st St, where you'll be treated to soul food, live entertainment most weekends, and often the Princess herself, who will be happy to sit down and share her opinions of the famous and the infamous who have eaten there – mention Idi Amin and you'll make an evening of it.

Japanese In recent years E 9th St has become something of a Little Tokyo with excellent sushi restaurants lining the street.

Hasaki (☎ (212) 472-3327), 210 E 9th St, has the best reputation. Try there first, but if you find you have a long wait ahead of you, then go next door to *Sharaku* (☎ (212) 598-0403), 8 Stuyvesant St, where there are plenty of tables and a large menu featuring many Japanese specialties aside from the sushi.

Chelsea

It could be argued that Chelsea has the best and most varied dining experiences in the city. But for some of its more popular (and expensive) restaurants, you'll need to make weekend reservations weeks in advance.

Budget One of New York's oddest hybrid cuisines is the cheap and filling fare developed by Chinese immigrants who once lived in Cuba and moved to the US following the revolution in the late '50s. The best of the Cuban-Chinese restaurants in Chelsea is *Sam Chinita* (☎ (212) 741-0240) on Eighth Ave and 17th St, with its diner atmosphere and items such as plantains and *ropa vieja*, well-cooked beef in a spicy sauce.

The 24 hour *Empire Diner* (☎ (212) 243-2736), 210 Tenth Ave, attracts many Chelsea club hoppers at night.

Moderate *America* (☎ (212) 505-2110), 9 E 18th St, is a huge, noisy place with a multi-page menu that's worth checking out for the elevated bar in the back that is covered by a skylight. Have a drink there and then head for the as-yet undiscovered *Cafe Bondi* (☎ (212) 691-8136), 7 W 20th St, an isolated spot with a back garden that specializes in Sicilian cooking.

Alva (☎ (212) 228-4399), 36 E 22nd, is a dark and sleek American bistro that has a light bulb motif in honor of the inventor Thomas Alva Edison. There is a reasonable wine list and fresh fish entrees for around $18.

Top End The two best places are the *Union Square Cafe* (☎ (212) 243-4020), 21 E 16th St, and the *Gramercy Tavern* (☎ (212) 477-0077), 42 E 20th St. These sister restaurants are renowned for providing five-star dining at three-star prices; as a consequence it's necessary to book weeks beforehand to eat on a weekend night. Gramercy Tavern serves a $57 fixed-price menu nightly.

Midtown

Budget *Madras Mahal* (☎ (212) 684-4010), 104 Lexington Ave, is but one of 10 Indian restaurants between 27th and 29th Sts, but this vegetarian Indian restaurant is the only one in the city that conforms to kosher rules of preparation. There's a lunch buffet available for $6.95.

Just off the northeast corner of W 55th St and Eighth Ave is the *Soup Kitchen International* stand (☎ (212) 757-7730), whose gruff owner, Al Yeganeh, was parodied in an episode of the hit TV series *Seinfeld* as the 'Soup Nazi.' This colorful character requires that you announce your selection within seven seconds (the better to move the line of patrons along), but his hot and cold soup selections are absolutely delicious and come in three sizes ($6/8/10), and come accompanied by a fresh piece of bread, salad and fruit. Be aware that the queue can last up to 40 minutes at lunchtime no matter what the weather, and that the proprietor tends to close his shop up for weeks at a time to take unannounced vacations.

La Fondue (☎ (212) 581-0820), 43 W 55th St, offers very reasonable lunches in a narrow dining space off Sixth Ave. Fondue for one costs $7.95, and daily lunch specials are available for $8.95 including a main course, salad and a glass of wine. Across the street, the slightly more expensive *La Bonne Soupe* (☎ (212) 586-7650), 48 W 55th St, has similar lunch specials with a French flavor.

There are more than two dozen delis, pubs and moderately priced restaurants on 55th and 56th Sts between Sixth and Fifth Aves serving Midtown office workers. It's also worth checking out the *JP French Bakery* (☎ (212) 765-7575), 54 W 55th St, which offers coffee, Gallic pastries and sandwiches on fresh *baguettes* for $7 and under.

Mike's (☎ 246-4115), 650 Tenth Ave, is a Cajun-influenced cheap bistro with ever-

changing decorative themes that have turned the place into a pinball machine and a Christmas shrine to Madonna (the singer, not the Virgin).

One of the most authentic restaurants in the city must be the *Munson Diner* (☎ (212) 246-0964), 600 W 49th St at Eleventh Ave, where cab drivers hang out before and after their shifts. The burgers are greasy, the waitress will call you 'Hon,' and the door to the women's bathroom is locked, in order to keep the street ladies from conducting their business on the premises.

Moderate *Le Quercy* (☎ (212) 265-8141), 52 W 55th St, is an unpretentious, but authentic French bistro where you can get a good glass of steely Sancerre. A three course lunch costs $19, with several options per course, including broiled monk fish and chicken *grandmere*.

Island Burgers and Shakes (☎ (212) 307-7934), 766 Ninth Ave, specializes in *churascos*, a juicy breast of chicken sandwich that comes in more than 50 different varieties for under $8.

Two popular delis are the *Carnegie Deli* (☎ (212) 757-2245), 854 Seventh Ave (at W 54th St), and *Stage Deli* (☎ (212) 245-7850), 834 Seventh Ave (at W 53rd St). The Carnegie is a tourist trap that nonetheless offers huge sandwiches for about $12, the latter is a pale imitation of the former.

Top End There are plenty of restaurants that rely on expense account executives in Midtown, but few have the quality to match their prices. One that certainly does is *Aquavit* (☎ (212) 307-7311), 13 W 54th St. The main dining room is in a stunning six story glass-enclosed atrium complete with a silent waterfall. The $55 fixed-price menu may seem steep, but it's worth every penny considering that the entrées, like venison with berry sauce, are sublime.

Vong (☎ (212) 486-9592), 200 E 54th St and Second Ave, offers pricey Asian fare to office workers in an elegant setting. It's best to go there for the lunch specials, all running around $20.

Theme Restaurants

There has been an explosion of tourist trap restaurants in the Midtown area around 57th St, transforming what was once one of the most exclusive shopping districts on earth. Some high end shops such as Burberry's and Chanel are still located there, but the region has become home to a growing number of logo-peddling theme palaces. Some are simply ludicrous (the unsuccessful Fashion Cafe, supposedly created by supermodels who are equally famous for not actually eating), or just plain fake (Hansen's 'olde style' Brewery).

The formula behind these places follows a plan mapped out by Robert Earl, the British businessman behind the Hard Rock Cafe and Planet Hollywood. These glittery places have celebrity 'owners,' usually movie or sports stars with a minor financial interest, who show up with their friends at the opening. Schwarzenegger, Stallone and Willis only show up for invitation-only parties for their latest films, but videos of the visitations are played forever, as the gullible line up for hours in the vain hope of seeing Sly chow down on a chili burger.

Needless to say, you have a better chance of seeing a celebrity walk by you on the street as you wait to get into the restaurant. (And wait you will – the theme joints keep you waiting for 20 minutes even if they're empty.) Moreover, it's impossible to judge the service and simple fare on offer at the restaurants, since their heavy volume increases the chance that you'll come across a badly-cooked meal or a waiter with an attitude. Expect, at any rate, to be steered if not pressured into buying merchandise: these places see a profit margin of 15% on the food, but realize a 50% gain on the T-shirts.

Hard Rock Cafe The granddaddy of all theme restaurants (☎ (212) 459-9320), 221 W 57th St, has been in New York since 1983 and offers glimpses of rock memorabilia of dubious provenance. Just how many times did Elvis really strum that guitar, anyway?

It's open Sunday to Thursday from 11:30 am to midnight and Friday and Saturday from 11 am to 2 am.

Harley-Davidson Cafe This shrine to the storied Milwaukee, WI, motorcycle company is at 1370 Sixth Ave and features gas tanks signed by celebrities and pictures of anyone

Times Square

The sidestreets off Times Square are filled with hamburger joints and a variety of middle range ethnic restaurants of varying quality. You'll do okay if you stick to unambitious food choices or patronize the following selections.

It may not look like much from the outside, but *King Crab* (☎ (212) 765-4393), 871 Eighth Ave, specializes in delicious and cheap seafood dinner specials for under $12, and is a good option before the theater. *Mee Noodle Shop* (☎ (212) 765-2929), 795 Ninth Ave, is part of the city's best chain of cheap Chinese restaurants, serving a hearty bowl of broth, noodles and meat for just $4.95. Mee serves the same menu at two other locations: 922 Second Ave at 49th St and 219 First Ave at 13th St.

An expensive option in Times Square is *Le Bernardin* (☎ (212) 489-1515), 155 W 51st St, which is renowned for its ultra-fresh fish offerings. The food lives up to its reputation, but the setting, in a bland block of office buildings, doesn't quite justify the $48 lunch menu tab.

Restaurant Row Restaurant Row is officially the block of W 46th St between Eighth and Ninth Aves, but locals use the name to refer to almost all the restaurants west of Times Square.

Some mediocre places – usually those serving glorified pub grub – survive thanks to their proximity to the theater district, but there are a few gems here too. *Joe Allen* (☎ (212) 581-6464), at No 326, serves entree salads, sandwiches and soup in a brick-walled room lined with the posters of who owned, rode on or even stood near a Harley-Davidson. It's so commercial the menu's available for sale at $10. Open from 11 am to 2 am daily.

Jekyll & Hyde Club The Jekyll & Hyde Club (☎ (212) 541-9505), 1409 Sixth Ave, is refreshingly free of celebrity connections and features waiters dressed as vampires and ghouls, along with a flashy show where a Frankenstein monster comes to life. Complain about the long wait to get in and your waiter will point to a skull and say, 'That guy was dying to get in.' If that's your idea of a funny line, this place is for you.

It's open Monday, Tuesday and Thursday from 11:30 am to 2 am, Wednesday and Sunday from 11 am to 2 am and Friday and Saturday from 11 am to 3 am.

Motown Cafe This place (☎ (212) 489-0097), 104 W 57th St, opened in 1995. The background music, as expected, is quite good (often accompanied by a karaoke-style show where dancers lip-synch to big Motown hits) and the food, displayed on a menu that resembles an old LP cover, is more than passable. The food is reasonably priced and has a Southern influence (collard greens, ribs and sweet-potato fries). It's open daily from 11:30 am to 2:30 pm.

Official All Star Cafe The cafe (☎ (212) 840-8326), 1540 Broadway at 45th St, is an enormous restaurant-cum-sports stadium in Times Square with sports memorabilia such as Andre Agassi's ponytail, a backboard smashed by Shaquille O'Neal, and Monica Seles' tennis racquets. It serves more than 50 types of hamburgers and features the Charlie Sheen Room, filled with the actor's autographed baseball collection. It's open daily from 11 am to 2 am.

Planet Hollywood This restaurant (☎ (212) 333-7827), 140 W 57th St, displays film artifacts and costumes in a noisy, flashing-light atmosphere that resembles a futuristic disco. No reservations are taken, and you stand in line outside for about 45 minutes just to get to another line inside. There are enough movie items visible through the window and on display in the gift shop next door to get enough of the experience without actually eating in the restaurant. It's open 11 am to 1 am every day. ■

famous Broadway flops. It's impossible to get into the place before the theater without a reservation but it clears out completely for walk-ins by the 8 pm curtain time. *Orso* (☎ 489-7212), right next door at No 322, is also run by Joe Allen and serves more expensive Tuscan food at about $17 to $20 per entree. It's popular with theater people and has a daily late night seating at 10:30 pm for those coming out of performances. *Barbetta* (☎ (212) 246-9171), at No 321, is in an old townhouse that may have once been a brothel. You can get a $25 fixed-price menu in its quiet garden. *Hourglass Tavern* (☎ (212) 265-2060), at No 373, is a tiny place with reasonably priced stews and fish dishes that was inaccurately described as an expensive restaurant in the John Grisham novel *The Firm*.

Just around the corner is *Zen Palate* (☎ (212) 582-1669), 663 Ninth Ave, which serves an exclusively vegetarian menu.

Upper West Side
Budget The Upper West Side has dozens of cheap Chinese restaurants, pubs and coffee shops. The most reliable Chinese selection is *Empire Szechuan* with seven city locations, including 251 W 72nd St (☎ (212) 496-8460), and 193 Columbus Ave above 68th St (☎ (212) 496-8778). These bustling places serve generally healthy fare, and offer lunch specials for around $7.

Tibet Shambala (☎ (212) 721-1270), 488 Amsterdam Ave, has a menu split evenly between meat and vegetarian dishes for $8.95 and under (salad and rice included).

Cafe Lalo (☎ (212) 496-6031), 201 W 83rd St, has a 14 page menu of slightly expensive pastries, but you can spend an entire rainy afternoon here reading the dozens of newspapers and magazines on offer.

Top End The neighborhood's moderate restaurants tend to have mediocre food and inattentive service. If you're in that price range, head a little further south on Ninth Ave to 40th St and pick a place with an interesting window-displayed menu. But if you're looking to splurge, try either of the neighborhood's well-known and expensive restaurants. *Cafe Luxembourg* (☎ (212) 873-7411), 200 W 70th St, is impossible to get into without a reservation before performances at Lincoln Center, when it offers a $19.95 special dinner.

The romantic *Cafe des Artistes* (☎ (212) 877-3500), 1 W 67th St, has seen countless marriage proposals over the years. The restaurant features a famous mural of naked nymphs prancing through Central Park, which almost obscures the generally high quality of the entrees in the $20 range. Men must wear jackets after 6 pm.

Tavern on the Green (☎ 873-3200), at W 67th St and Central Park West, is the most profitable restaurant in the US, pulling in an astounding $32 million annually from visitors who want to admire its flood-lit topiary statues in the back garden. The restaurant has improved its food quality from atrocious to not bad, but the wait staff is alternately patronizing or inattentive. If you must visit, absolutely insist on sitting outside or by a window and expect to pay about $50 a person, even for brunch.

Harlem
Harlem is justifiably famous for its soul food, but there's also a growing West African influence in the neighborhood. Vegetarians or those seeking low-fat choices will have a hard time. All the following restaurants are within walking distance of the 125th St subway stations. Most places serve big portions at incredibly cheap prices.

Soul Food By far the most famous restaurant in Harlem is *Sylvia's* (☎ (212) 996-0660), 328 Lenox Ave, which has a gospel brunch on Sunday afternoon (reservations required). *Copeland's* (☎ (212) 234-2357), 547 W 145th St, off Broadway, is famous for its $12.95 midweek nighttime buffet; eating à la carte (entrees run as high as $17) means a higher tab. *Copeland's Country Kitchen* is a sister restaurant at 203-205 W 125th St, just steps away from the Apollo Theater.

You can get the real deal at much better value at *Singleton's Barbecue* (☎ (212) 694-9442), 525 Lenox Ave, where the $5.50 lunch specials offer pigs feet, 'smother' chicken livers and other delicacies with a choice of two vegetables.

International *Pan Pan* (☎ (212) 926-4900), 500 Lenox Ave, offers spicy Jamaican meat patties for $1.25 and coffee-and-roll breakfasts for $1. Members of the Senegalese staff at *Darou Minam* (☎ (212) 864-9024), 1943 Powell Blvd, don't speak English very well, but the delicious West African dishes they serve transcend all language barriers. Their specialty is *mafe* – lamb prepared in a peanut sauce – for just $5. *Keur Samba* (☎ (212) 864-6161), 120-126 W 116th St just off Lenox Ave, is considered the best French African restaurant in the neighborhood for its spicy fish stews that start at $7.

Upper East Side
Budget *Favia Lite* (☎ (212) 223-9115), 1140 Second Ave, is a healthy Italian restaurant near the 59th St Bridge that serves surprisingly tasty pasta entrees, listing calories and fat content for every menu item. The large grilled chicken pizza costs $15; skimmed milk or soy mozzarella is available at no extra charge.

The *Lexington Candy Shop* (☎ (212) 288-0057), 1226 Lexington Ave at 83rd St, is a picture perfect lunch spot (complete with an old-fashioned soda fountain) that serves some of the most reasonable fare in one of the city's most expensive neighborhoods.

There are dozens of moderately priced restaurants on Second and Third Aves between 60th and 86th Sts that offer lunch specials for under $10. *Cafe Greco* (☎ (212) 737-4300), 1390 Second Ave, between 71st and 72nd Sts, is a typical example of the norm, serving continental dishes and a good weekend brunch.

Moderate Many small, wood-paneled restaurants with a French flavor line Madison Ave north of 60th St and several nearby side streets. Two fine places to find a bit of Paris (including slightly pricey entrees ranging from $17 to $24 and a well-dressed clientele) are *La Goulue* (☎ (212) 988-8169), 746 Madison Ave near 64th St, and *Madame Romaine de Lyon* (☎ (212) 759-5200), 132 E 61St (off Park Ave). It's possible to have a moderately priced and pleasant meal at either by sticking to the appetizer side of the menu or having lighter fare such as omelets.

The ambiance and food is *tres* French at *Voulez-Vous*, (☎ (212) 249-1776), 1462 First Ave at 76th St, but the wait staff is friendly and helpful, with prices running to about $30 per person with wine.

Top End *Arcadia* (☎ (212) 223-2900), 21 E 62nd St, is one of best dining experiences in the city – well worth every penny you spend (which can run to $80 per person). The food has a French American taste to it, you can't go wrong with anything on the menu, and the service is attentive, but unintrusive. It's an intimate space, adorned by a mural of the four seasons by Paul Davis, and it can be a little crowded if you're seated in the middle; when making reservations ask for a side banquet.

ENTERTAINMENT

No single source could possibly list everything that happens in the city, but *Time Out* tries hard and is the single best guide to night life. High culture events get big play in the Sunday and Friday *New York Times* and the *New Yorker*; dance clubs and smaller music venues take out numerous ads in the *Village Voice*. The free sheets *It*, *New York Press* and *New York Listings* all have roundups of cultural events.

NYC On Stage (☎ (212) 768-1818) is an information line listing music and dance events that is open 24 hours.

The Broadway Show Line (☎ (212) 563-BWAY/2929) provides descriptions of plays and musicals both on and off the Great White Way; you can use it to obtain information on ticket prices and make credit card purchases.

Ticketmaster

Ticketmaster (☎ (212) 307-7171 for concerts, 307-4100 for the performing arts) has a lock on sales for most major concerts and sporting events, despite the rock group Pearl Jam's valiant attempt to file an anti-trust complaint against the company's handling fees, which can add up to $7 to the ticket price.

You can order by phone or visit Ticketmaster outlets at Bloomingdale's, the HMV and Tower record stores, and the Sony Building at 550 Madison Ave.

Theater

While Times Square is ostensibly the center of New York's legitimate theater (the 'theater district'), the productions around Times Square are increasingly dominated by the holy trinity of overblown spectaculars: Andrew Lloyd Webber, Cameron MacIntosh and the Disney Company.

Though long running productions like *Cats*, *Miss Saigon* and *Beauty and the Beast* attract large audiences, storied old theaters better suited to drama (such as the Biltmore, Brooks Atkinson and Barrymore) sit empty for lack of serious content. The high costs and critical frustrations of Broadway led even Broadway giant Neil Simon – who has a theater named after him on 52nd St – to debut his *London Suite* in a Union Square theater in 1994.

All this movement has blurred the distinction of what is and what isn't a 'Broadway' show. But in general, Broadway productions are those that take place in the large theaters around Times Square – either plays featuring big stars or musical spectaculars – which attract more than nine million patrons each year.

'Off Broadway' usually refers to dramas that are performed in smaller (200 seats or fewer) spaces elsewhere in town, a big business in itself that now boasts annual attendance of 3.5 million people a year. Prominent spots for Off Broadway performances include: **PS 122** (☎ (212) 477-5288), 150 First Ave (near E 9th St; subway: Union Square), located in a converted public school; the **Circle in the Square Theater** (☎ (212) 307-2705), 1633 Broadway at 50th St; the **Samuel Beckett Theater** (☎ (212) 874-4126), 410 W 42nd St near Ninth Ave; and the **Performing Garage** (☎ (212) 966-3651), 33 Wooster St (subway: Spring St).

'Off-Off Broadway' events are readings, experimental performances and improvisations held in spaces with less than 100 seats with an as-yet unmeasured annual patronage.

Cinemas

New Yorkers take film very seriously, so going to the cinema can be a trying experience in the evening and on weekends. Though prices are now $8.50, most first-run films sell out a half hour early on Friday and Saturday nights. You're likely to have to stand in one line to buy a ticket and another to get into the theater. What's worse, movie chains publish semi-fictitious start times in order to leave about 20 minutes to sell you popcorn and soda. You

can at least avoid one queue by calling ☎ (212) 777-FILM/3456 and prepaying for the movie of your choice for an additional $1 per ticket charge; you get the ticket by swiping your credit card through a machine upon arrival.

Despite the attendant hassles, New York offers the cinéaste plenty of choices, and you can still duck into a movie house on a rainy or hot afternoon (though movie-mad New Yorkers under the age of 65 can't get admission discounts).

The 12 screen *Sony Theaters Lincoln Square*, at Broadway and 68th St, includes a 3D Imax theater and first-run features.

Sony (☎ (212) 336-5000) and Cineplex Odeon (☎ (212) 505-2463) have multiplexes throughout Manhattan. The *Angelika Film Center* (☎ (212) 995-2000), at the corner of Mercer and Houston Sts (subway: Broadway–Lafayette St) and *Angelika 57* (☎ (212) 586-1900), an uptown relative at 57th and Broadway; as well as the *Lincoln Plaza Cinemas* (☎ (212) 757-2280), opposite Lincoln Center at Broadway and 63rd St, specialize in foreign films and are always crowded on weekends.

Independent films and career retrospectives are held at the three screen *Film Forum* (☎ (212) 727-8110), 209 W Houston St (subway: Houston St), and Lincoln Center's *Walter Reade Theater* (☎ (212) 875-5600), which has very comfortable, screening-room quality seats.

Discount Theater Tickets

The TKTS booth in the middle of Times Square (☎ (212) 768-1818) sells same-day tickets to Broadway and Off-Broadway musicals and drama. Tickets sell at either half price or 75% off regular box office rates as determined by the producers, plus a $2.50 service charge per ticket. The booth accepts cash or traveler's checks only.

The booth has an electric marquee listing the available shows. On Wednesday and Saturday matinee tickets go on sale at 10 am, and on Sunday the windows open at noon for afternoon performances. Evening tickets go on sale every day at 3 pm, and a line begins to form up to an hour before the booth opens.

A good tip: wait until 7 pm to buy your tickets, when the best available house seats go on sale for many productions. Lines tend to be shorter on Wednesday evenings, because many visitors have already taken in an afternoon performance.

There is a smaller, less crowded TKTS outlet at 2 World Trade Center that maintains the same hours. ■

Far-out fringe works can be seen at *Anthology Film Archives* (☎ (212) 505-5181), 32 Second Ave (subway: Second Ave).

Classical Music & Opera

The *New York Philharmonic* (☎ (212) 721-6500) has been getting rave reviews under the direction of German-born conductor Kurt Masur, though the aging and conservative Philharmonic audience at **Avery Fisher Hall** in Lincoln Center still resists programs that deviate from the standard repertory. The audience is also pretty rude: nanoseconds after the final note, patrons go running up the aisles in order to beat the traffic home. Tickets range from $15 to $60.

Visiting philharmonics and the *New York Pops* orchestra perform at storied **Carnegie Hall** (☎ (212) 247-7800), 57th St and Seventh Ave. A schedule of monthly events is available in the lobby next to the box office, and you can usually get tickets as low as $12 for non-subscription events.

The *American Symphony Orchestra*, the *Chamber Music Society of Lincoln Center* and the *Little Orchestra Society* hold their seasons at **Alice Tully Hall** (☎ (212) 721-6500) at Lincoln Center.

More intimate venues for classical music include the **Merkin Concert Hall** (☎ (212) 362-8719), 129 W 67th St, **Symphony Space** (☎ (212) 864-5400), 2536 Broadway at 95th St, and **Town Hall** (☎ (212) 840-2824), 123 W 43rd St.

The *Metropolitan Opera* (☎ (212) 362-6000), holds its season from September to April in its namesake Lincoln Center theater. It's nearly impossible to get into the first few performances of operas that feature such big stars as Jessye Norman and Plácido Domingo, but once the B-team moves in, tickets become available. Aficionados have been complaining about a general drop in the vocal quality on stage, but the sets for classics like *Aida* are uniformly spectacular. Tickets for center orchestra seats start at $115, but you can get in the upper balcony for $16. Standing-room is also available on a limited basis.

The more daring and lower-cost *New York City Opera* (☎ (212) 870-5630) takes the stage at Philip Johnson's **New York State Theater** (☎ (212) 870-5570) next door at Lincoln Center, for a split season that runs for a few weeks in early autumn and picks up again in the late spring.

Dance & Ballet

New York is home to more than half a dozen world-famous dance companies. The *New York City Ballet*, established by Lincoln Kirstein and George Balanchine in 1948, performs at New York State Theater in Lincoln Center during the winter. During the spring, the *American Ballet Theater* (☎ (212) 477-3030) takes over at the Metropolitan Opera House for a short season.

City Center (☎ (212) 581-1212), a Moorish palace on W 55th St between Sixth and Seventh Aves, is home to the *Alvin Ailey American Dance Theater* every December and hosts engagements by the National Ballet of Spain and other foreign companies.

The most offbeat dance venue is the **Joyce Theater** (☎ (212) 242-0800), a renovated cinema in Chelsea at 175 Eighth Ave and 19th St. The season includes visits by such bold physical groups as the Erick Hawkins and Merce Cunningham dance companies.

Popular Music

When major singers and 'super groups' that regularly fill arenas play a smaller venue in New York, their record company usually buys up all the tickets and hands them out as freebies, so don't feel disappointed if you missed Bruce Springsteen's surprise club appearance. It's easier to get tickets to see lesser lights.

Major concerts are announced months in advance and are usually held at **Madison Square Garden** (☎ (212) 456-6000), **Radio City Music Hall** (☎ (212) 247-4777) or the **Beacon Theater** (☎ (212) 496-7070), 2124 Broadway (subway: 72nd St), a converted movie palace on the West Side.

The Concert Hotline (☎ (212) 249-8870) tells you who's playing in the clubs, but the narrator's rapid-fire delivery may be difficult to follow if English is not your native language.

Jazz The basement-level *Village Vanguard* (☎ (212) 255-4037), 178 Seventh Ave (subway: Christopher St), may be the world's most famous jazz club; it has hosted literally every major star of the past 50 years. The cover charge runs $15 to $20 with a two drink minimum.

Legendary trumpeter Doc Cheatham, now in his 90s, plays the Sunday jazz brunch at *Sweet Basil* (☎ (212) 242-1785), 88 Seventh Ave South, which hosts weeklong visits by other big stars. *Smalls* (☎ (212) 929-7565), 183 W 10th St, is a unique place without a liquor license that hosts an incredible $10, 10 hour jazz marathon every night from 10 pm to 8 am that attracts top talent coming off gigs in other mainstream joints.

Other intimate spaces are *Bradley's* (☎ (212) 228-6440), 70 University Place (subway: Union Square), and *Zinno* (☎ (212) 924-5182), 126 W 13th St.

By far the most expensive club is the *Blue Note* (☎ (212) 475-8592), 131 W 3rd St, featuring big stars playing short sets with music charges up to $60. You can hear acid jazz and other fringe music at the *Knitting Factory* (☎ (212) 219-3055), 74 Leonard St in Tribeca.

The wildly popular Mingus Big Band plays every Thursday at *Fez* (☎ (212) 533-2680), 380 Lafayette St (subway: Bleecker St), which hosts experimental music every other night of the week. *Iridium* (☎ (212) 956-4676), 44 W 63rd St, is trying to make a name for itself by breaking new jazz acts. See also the Harlem section, earlier in this chapter, for information on jazz clubs in that part of town.

Harlem's Cotton Club era is long gone, but there are still several places to hear jazz both modern and traditional. Because of declining patronage, most have performances only on weekend nights; call ahead to check times and possible cover charges. The old *Lenox Lounge* (☎ (212) 722-9566), at Lenox Ave and 125th St, is worth visiting

Tipping in Clubs
Nightclubs in New York are notorious for trying to obscure the fact that you are only obligated to tip on waiter service. At the end of a set, you're likely to be handed a credit card slip or bill that includes the music charge for each person in the total. This is standard procedure at expensive places like the *Blue Note* jazz club. Tip generously if you wish, but deduct the music charge before calculating it. ■

anytime for its remarkable Art Deco interior. *Showman's Cafe* (☎ (212) 864-8941), 2321 Frederick Douglass Blvd, features jazz combos and R&B vocalists. The same mix of styles, along with a late night menu, can be found at *Wells Restaurant* (☎ (212) 234-0700), 2247 Powell Blvd. *Lickety Split* (☎ (212) 283-9093), 2361 Powell Blvd, specializes in Caribbean bands.

Rock Well-known intimate concert spaces include the *Bottom Line* (☎ (212) 228-6300), 15 W 4th St in the Village, and *Tramps* (☎ (212) 727-7788), 51 W 21st St in Chelsea. The prototypical punk club *CBGB* (☎ (212) 982-4052), 315 Bowery, is still going strong after 20 years. Big names turn up at the small *Mercury Lounge* (☎ (212) 260-4700), 217 E Houston St, and *Irving Plaza* (☎ (212) 777-6800), 17 Irving Place (subway: Union Square).

New clubs turn up in the Lower East Side all the time – check out the flyers in the neighborhood's bars and restaurants.

Blues, Folk & World Music The *55 Bar* (☎ (212) 929-9883), 55 Christopher St, is an authentic smokey joint that never charges a cover. Visiting blues masters play at *Chicago Blues* (☎ (212) 924-9755), at 14th St and Eighth Ave, and the uptown *Manny's Car Wash* (☎ (212) 369-2583), 1558 Third Ave (subway: 86th St).

International artists are brought to New York by the World Music Institute (☎ (212) 545-7536) for concerts at the *Washington Square Church*, 135 W 4th St, and other

Antique dealer, Houston St, NYC

DAVID ELLIS

KIM GRANT
Street musician, Union Square, NYC

KIM GRANT
Fire escapes on the Lower East Side, NYC

KIM GRANT

Walking to work across the Brooklyn Bridge

DAVID ELLIS

Brownstones, Park Slope, Brooklyn

venues throughout the city. The Deadhead tradition lives on at *Wetlands* (☎ (212) 966-4225), 161 Hudson St (subway: 1/9 to Canal St). College radio favorites play *Far Side* (☎ (212) 673-9143), 269 E Houston St (subway: Second Ave) on the Lower East Side. The *Back Fence* (☎ (212) 475-9221), 155 Bleecker St, which never charges a cover, is the best folk venue among many in the center of Greenwich Village. The *Fast Folk Cafe* (☎ (212) 274-1636), 41 N Moore St (subway: Franklin St), is a new all-acoustic venue sponsored by *Fast Folk Magazine*.

SOB's (☎ (212) 243-4940), 204 Varick St (subway: Houston St), specializes in Afro-Cuban sounds, and is the home of salsa master Tito Puente. Uptown, the place to go is the *Latin Quarter* (☎ (212) 864-7600), at Broadway and 95th St.

Bars

A proper listing of New York City's better drinking places would take up most of an entire book; what follows is a highly selective list of places to find great beer and a good time. Most bars are open until 2 am, though some keep the beer flowing until 4 am on Friday and Saturday.

Lower Manhattan *The Greatest Bar on Earth* (☎ (212) 524-7011), at Windows on the World on the 107th floor of One World Trade Center, has an exceedingly silly name, but you can't beat the view and the beer is moderately priced ($5) for the setting.

SoHo & Tribeca *Ñ*, 33 Crosby St (subway: Grand St), is a dark and easy-to-miss tapas bar with a friendly staff. But don't go there hungry or you'll wind up spending more than you wanted to. *The Ear Inn*, 326 Spring St (subway: Spring St), is located in the old James Brown House (not the God father of Soul). This old place near the Hudson River attracts sanitation workers and office dwellers with its great shepherd's pie and inexpensive lunch choices. *Cafe Noir*, 32 Grand St (subway: Grand St), is a good place to munch on North

African appetizers while watching the passing SoHo parade from the open-air bar railing.

Greenwich Village *Chumley's*, 86 Barrow St (subway: Christopher St), is a hard-to-find, storied speakeasy serving decent pub grub (cash only). It was among the first places in the city to serve American microbrews exclusively. *The Corner Bistro*, 331 W 4th St (subway: Christopher St), is a famous West Village bar with carved wooden tables where you can eat charred hamburgers until 2 am.

East Village *The Scratcher*, 209 E Fifth St (subway: Astor Place), is popular with Irish people. It's a true Dublin-style pub, a quiet place to read the newspaper during the day over coffee, but crowded and raucous at night. *Swift*, 34 E 4th St just off the Bowery, is another wildly popular Irish bar with live bands and the best pint of Guinness in New York City. *KGB*, 85 E 4th St, is a 2nd-floor living room site for literary meetings.

McSorley's Old Ale House, 15 E 7th St, is the well-known subject of Joseph Mitchell's *New Yorker* stories. A cramped and stodgy old bar, it refused to admit women until the 1970s; these days it often has a long line of tourists and NYU undergraduates waiting to get in. Don't bother waiting unless you simply must get a whiff of 100 year's worth of stale beer that the sawdust on the floor hasn't absorbed (you're best off dropping by in the afternoon).

Upper West Side *Dublin House*, 225 W 79th St (subway: 79th St), shouldn't be remarkable, but it is, thanks to the odd combination of old men and Columbia University undergrads who patronize the place. Columbia's grad students tend to hang out at the *Night Cafe*, 938 Amsterdam Ave at 106th St. The bar has a pool table and an ornate pressed-tin ceiling, but the beer is available in bottles only.

Upper East Side *Kinsale Tavern*, 1672 Third Ave (subway: 96th St), is a gathering place with over 20 beers on tap that attracts European rugby and soccer fanatics with early-morning live satellite broadcasts of matches during the winter months. (Many bars on Second and Third Aves offer the same TV transmissions.) In a city packed with Irish pubs, *The British Open*, 320 E 59th St (subway: 59th St–Lexington Ave), in the shadow of the Queensboro Bridge, draws fans of golf and the Royal Family. *The Subway Inn*, 143 E 60th St, just above the 59th St–Lexington Ave subway station, is an old bar that looks like it hasn't changed in 40 years, right down to the barmen's white shirts and thin black ties.

Lounges

Throughout the '90s there has been a big growth in lounges catering to both gay and mixed crowds. Lounges are exclusively defined by their crowds – those downtown offering cigars and bourbon attract office workers; Chelsea lounges are almost exclusively gay. Patrons tend to be a bit better dressed in these places, with the significant exception of hole-in-the-wall joints in the East Village and the Lower East Side. Some of the lounges feature live music – places that charge admission to hear performers are listed in the Live Music section.

Gay Entertainment

On the whole, gay drinking places tend to cater only to men, but the more popular dance clubs welcome women, even though they are largely cruise joints; men entering lesbian bars and clubs are more likely to encounter open hostility.

Popular clubs in the Chelsea area include *Champs* (☎ (212) 633-1717), 17 W 19th St, a gathering place for the clean-cut crowd and *Splash* (☎ (212) 691-0073), 50 W 17th St, where well-toned boys put on a water show. There's an array of cruise joints here as well: *Rome* (☎ (212) 242-6969), 290 Eighth Ave, *Barracuda* (☎ (212) 645-8613), 275 W 22nd St, and *King* (☎ (212) 366-5464), 579 Sixth Ave, which has a male-only 3rd floor grope room.

For dancing, it's best to go to a gay night at a mainstream club (many of the following are listed under Dance Clubs). *Twilo* (☎ (212) 268-1600), 530 W 27th St, is a popular place with a $20 cover. The club is also the site of a Sunday afternoon tea dance. *Webster Hall* becomes Lavender Lounge on Wednesday. *Tunnel's* clientele gets gayer as the night grows longer – some set their alarms for dawn on Sunday and party at Tunnel well into Sunday afternoon.

The rough trade has traditionally met in forbidding bars along the West Side piers in Chelsea, but hangouts not already decimated by the AIDS pandemic are now closing because of increased property values. *The Spike* (☎ (212) 243-9688), 120 Eleventh Ave, and *The Eagle's Nest* (☎ (212) 691-8451), 142 Eleventh Ave, still survive, but *The Lure* (☎ (212) 741-3919), 409 W 13th St, is currently the most popular leather bar. None of these places welcome the curious.

The Christopher St area in Greenwich Village (subway: 1/9 to Christopher St) is the site of many popular restaurants and bars, including *The Monster* (☎ (212) 924-3558), 80 Grove St, and *Uncle Charlie's* (☎ (212) 255-8787), 56 Greenwich Ave, crowded places with large after-work clientele. *The Stonewall Inn* (☎ (212) 463-0950), 53 Christopher St, though not the bar of the famous rebellion, stands near the same site. Bars catering to older gays include *Julius* (☎ (212) 929-9672), 159 W 10th St, and *Marie's Crisis* (☎ (212) 243-9323), 59 Grove St, which features show tunes.

Henrietta Hudson (☎ (212) 924-3347), 438 Hudson St, is open until 4 am every night, and *Crazy Nanny's* (☎ (212) 366-6312), 21 Seventh Ave South, calls itself a 'place for gay women – biological or otherwise.' *The Clit Club* (☎ (212) 529-3300) meets Friday at The Bar Room, 432 W 14th St, and has been the leading hot spot for years. *Rubyfruit* (☎ (212) 929-3343), 531 Hudson St, is a favorite with older women. ■

Greenwich Village *Hudson Bar and Books*, 636 Hudson St, is a narrow faux library that has free jazz on weekend evenings. This place has two club-like uptown cousins: *Beekman Bar and Books*, 889 First Ave near the UN, and *Lexington Bar and Books*, 1020 Lexington Ave. The latter enforces a pretentious jackets-only policy. *Bar d'O*, 29 Bedford St (subway: W 4th St), is a sleek lounge with drag acts several nights a week. It attracts a chic crowd of gays and straights who arrive at about 11 pm to scene and be scene.

East Village It's easy to gain entry at the *10th St Lounge*, 212 E 10th St (subway: Union Square), so the place must no longer be 'in.' Still, it's a pleasantly austere place to have a drink. *147 Ludlow St* (subway: Delancey St), is a place so cool it doesn't have a name. A DJ plays from 7:30 pm to 4 am nightly.

Midtown At the Rainbow Room's *Promenade Lounge*, on the 65th floor of the GE Building, 30 Rockefeller Plaza, you must wear a jacket and decent clothing, but for the price of admission to visit the top of the Empire State Building, you get a stunning view that *includes* that landmark and a drink to go along with it.

Upper East Side *Bemelmans Bar*, 35 E 76th St (subway: 77th St), is an elegant space in the Carlyle Hotel where you'll feel uncomfortable without a jacket (there's a cover charge for evening performances). The lounge at *The Mark Hotel*, 22 E 77th St, is a quiet, green velvet space that epitomizes Upper East Side elegance.

Dance Clubs

If a club is around long enough to be listed here, it's by definition no longer hot. The monthly magazine *Paper* is the best source for clubs. You should also keep an eye out for club and band flyers on walls and billboards while walking through the East Village – it is often the only way to find out about some clubs that for legal reasons do not have phones or advertise. Most of the following are located below 14th St and attract a mixed gay and straight crowd.

It generally costs about $20 to get in to the clubs from Thursday to Saturday. Don't even think about going to any of these places before 11 pm, even on a weeknight; things don't truly pick up until 1 am or later. Some of the phone numbers listed are pretty useless since the clubs don't generally pick up.

Buddha Bar is an unremarkable space popular for its live salsa music nights and Juicy, the Sunday night lesbian lounge. 150 Varick St (subway: Houston St; ☎ (212) 255-4433)

Don Hill's is a transvestite favorite for its $10 Olivia Newton-John nights. 511 Greenwich St at Spring St (subway: Spring St; ☎ (212) 334-1390)

Limelight is, like other Limelights, a deconsecrated church; it's currently closed due to federal drug investigations (a patron OD'd on the premises) but it may reopen by the time you read this. 660 Sixth Ave (subway: 23rd St; ☎ (212) 807-7850)

Nell's is the original European velvet lounge; it attracts a rougher crowd now and there's a metal detector at the door. 246 W 14th St (subway: 14th St–Eighth Ave; ☎ (212) 675-1567)

Palladium is a former concert hall now almost exclusively dedicated to live hip hop and house music. It's in danger of being torn down for an NYU dorm. 126 E 14th St (subway: Union Square; ☎ (212) 473-7171)

Roxy is an old favorite featuring roller-skating that refuses to die. 515 W 18th St at Tenth Ave (subway: 14th St–Eighth Ave; ☎ (212) 645-5156)

Save the Robots is a hard core, very late night place that's now featuring Japanese pop. 25 Ave B (subway: Second Ave; ☎ (212) 995-0968)

System offers mostly house music in the old Cat Club performance space. 76 E 13th St (subway: Union Square; ☎ (212) 388-1060)

Tunnel is a massive three floor club featuring Junior Vasquez, the city's most popular DJ, on Saturday night. 220 Twelfth Ave at 27th St (subway: 23rd St–Eighth Ave; ☎ (212) 695-7292)

Webster Hall is a huge, five level club with midget go-go dancers; it's also famous for its Lavender Lounge gay nights and Psychedelic Thursdays. 125 E 11th St (subway: Union Square; ☎ (212) 353-1600)

Comedy Clubs

It's generally acknowledged that stand-up comedy has been in a pathetic state for several years with unfunny, amateurish comics playing to half-empty houses all over town. If you're looking for main-stream laughs, stick with the top-level comedians who play *Caroline's* (☎ (212) 757-4100), at 1626 Broadway in Times Square, or *Chicago City Limits* (☎ (212) 888-5233), 1105 First Ave. *Catch a Rising Star* (☎ (212) 244-3005), the legendary launching ground for many comedy stars of the '70s, has moved to nicer quarters at 253 W 28th St and offers decent pub fare and musical performers on some nights.

Those looking for more cutting edge comedy should head to the Lower East Side and try the nightly shows at *Surf Reality* (☎ (212) 673-4182), 172 Allen St between Stanton and Rivington Sts, and the *Luna Lounge* (☎ (212) 260-2323), 171 Ludlow St (subway: Second Ave).

SPECTATOR SPORTS
Baseball

Baseball's recent labor woes led to a serious decline in the sport's attendance nationwide, and you can usually get same-day tickets to any New York Mets (☎ (718) 507-8499) or New York Yankees (☎ (718) 293-6000) game, unless the teams are in a late-season pennant race. The 162 game season lasts from early April to early October, and when one team is on the road, the other is at home. The Mets play in windswept Shea Stadium in Flushing Meadows, Queens (subway: Willets Point–Shea Stadium); it's a 40 minute journey from Midtown. The Yanks play at their legendary namesake stadium in the South Bronx (subway: 161st St–Yankee Stadium), just 15 minutes from Midtown. Most games begin at 7:30 pm and tickets range from $6.50 to $20. In

1997, the two rival teams began playing a limited number of regular season inter-league games for the first time. (For more on the stadiums and their surrounding neighborhoods, see the Queens and Bronx sections.)

Basketball & Hockey

The NBA New York Knicks (☎ (212) 465-6741) and the NHL New York Rangers (☎ (212) 465-6741) play at 19,000 seat Madison Square Garden, Seventh Ave and 33rd St. Both teams sell huge amounts of season tickets, and so visitors must book generally bad seats through Ticketmaster or Madison Square Garden, or deal with the many scalpers who hover around the area on game nights. Scalpers try to get a premium on seats that already cost up to $75 (see the sidebar in the Facts for the Visitor chapter). When dealing with scalpers, the best strategy is to wait until after the 7:30 game time, when prices should drop.

THINGS TO BUY
Cameras

New York's camera prices are hard to beat, but some of the camera stores in Midtown have reputations for bait and switch tactics, so if you go in to buy a Canon lens and the salesman begins offering a cheaper no-name alternative that's supposedly 'better,' beware. And because the industry is domi-nated by shops owned and operated by Orthodox Jews, they usually close in obser-vation of the Sabbath early Friday and all day Saturday and are shuttered during all major Jewish holidays.

You won't meet with sleazy salesmen at the following places: B&H Photo-Video (☎ (800) 947-9979), 119 W 17th St, is New York's most popular camera store but suffers from zoo-like crowding and a pay-first, pick-up-second bureaucracy. It's open Monday and Tuesday 9 am to 6 pm, Wednesday and Thursday 9 am to 7:15 pm, Friday from 9 am to 1 pm and Sunday 10 am to 4:45 pm. Ken Hansen Photo (☎ (212) 317-0923), 509 Madison Ave, 18th floor (at 53rd St), specializes in Leicas and other top-end equipment. It's open Monday to Friday from 8:30 am to 5 pm.

Antiques

There are several antique furniture stores on 59th St between Third and Second Aves. More stores can be found in the area of Broadway just below Union Square and along E 12th St. Vendors selling lighting, rare books, prints and other items of interest can be found at The Metropolitan Art Auction (☎ (212) 463-0200), 110 W 19th St, and The Chelsea Antiques Building (☎ (212) 929-0909), 110 W 25th St.

Top-level auctions are held at Christie's (☎ (212) 546-1000), 502 Park Ave, which held a popular and bizarre sale in 1995 of items from Frank Sinatra's attic, and Sotheby's (☎ (212) 606-7000), 1334 York Ave. Friday's edition of the *New York Times* contains announcements of exhibitions.

Leathergoods & Shoes

Low-cost knockoffs of Coach bags and leather backpacks are available in numerous stores along Broadway just above Houston St, on Bleecker St and on W 4th St immediately off Sixth Ave. More than a dozen stores selling Doc Martens, hiking boots and other sturdy walkers can be found on W 8th St between Fifth and Sixth Aves – check ads in the *Village Voice* for specials.

Higher-priced shoe stores can be found in SoHo among the clothing boutiques. See also Where to Shop, below.

Jewelry

High-end jewelry shoppers should visit Cartier, Harry Winston and Tiffany and Co, all on Fifth Ave between 52nd and 57th Sts. If you're looking for diamonds and pearls at lower prices, you should visit the Diamond District on W 47th St off Fifth Ave (closed weekends). The vendors here are very skilled in looking pained while offering you the best deal possible – while still making a healthy profit. There's also a stretch of diamond shops on Canal St just north of Chinatown.

Cheap Clothing

Dozens of shops sell off-brand clothing at wholesale prices in the Garment District, mainly on W 37th St between Eighth and Ninth Aves. For jeans, many people head to Canal Jeans (☎ (212) 226-1130), 504 Broadway, and the nearby Urban Outfitters (☎ (212) 475-0009), 628 Broadway. But these stores now sell an array of accessories and are no longer the cheapest places in town. For true bargains on casual wear, go to Dave's Army and Navy (☎ (212) 989-6444), 779 Sixth Ave. It's packed on Saturday afternoons with foreign visitors stocking up on $25 pairs of Levi's.

Music

Tower Records (☎ (212) 505-1500), with its main branch at 692 Broadway, has the best selection of music, but you pay generally higher prices (about $15) there than at HMV, which has a downtown store in Herald Square and uptown branches on Lexington Ave and E 86th St and Broadway at 72 St. Both chains are being given a run for their money by the massive Virgin Megastore (☎ (212) 332-0400), at 45th and Broadway in Times Square.

Shops specializing in CDs for under $10 along with bootlegs and imported music are found on Bleecker St in the West Village. Triton, 247 Bleecker, and Route 66 Records, across the street at 258 Bleecker, are among the best in the city. Uptown, NYCD (☎ (212) 724-4466), 426 Amsterdam Ave, runs a permanent special where if you buy four CDs, you get the fifth one free. Other Music (☎ (212) 477-8150), 15 E 4th St, brazenly opened right across the street from a Tower Records outlet, and thrives thanks to its selection of offbeat CDs.

Traditionalists should head to Carmine St in Greenwich Village, where stores still sell old lps. Footlight Records, 113 E 12th St, has a magnificent collection of out-of-print albums and foreign movie soundtracks.

Where to Shop

If you can't get it in New York, it's not available. But it helps to know the places where you can get the best or the cheapest.

Bloomingdale's 'Bloomie's' (☎ (212) 705-2000), at 59th St and Lexington Ave, may think of itself as a New York version of Harrods, but this incredibly cramped, crowded and badly designed department store matches it in attitude and almost nothing else. It does not duplicate the famous London emporium's architectural splendor, magnificent food hall or grand selection of merchandise.

Still, it's worth visiting if there's a good advertised clothing sale and to see the designer shops. It's also entertaining in a weird way to walk through the bizarre first floor perfume section, where dozens of clerks try to spray you with the latest scent while repeating the sales pitch in an automaton-like fashion.

Bloomingdale's is open Monday to Friday from 10 am to 8:30 pm, Saturday from 10 am to 7 pm, and Sunday from 11 am to 7 pm.

Century 21 Located across the street from the World Trade Center, Century 21 (☎ (212) 227-9092), 25 Church St (subway: Cortlandt St), has big bargains on designer clothing, perfume, sportswear and kitchen products. It's one of the few discount places where the selection of men's wear is as extensive as the women's department. You never know exactly what's on offer, but you will be guaranteed to find marked down Armani shirts and Betsey Johnson dresses on the racks.

Shopping at the store – which doesn't advertise, opens early and stays closed on Sunday – is a ritual for downtown office workers and people waiting out their two weeks of jury duty at the nearby courthouses.

It's open Monday to Wednesday from 7:45 am to 7 pm, Thursday from 7:45 am to 8:30 pm, Friday from 7:45 am to 8 pm and Saturday from 10 am to 7 pm.

Kiehl's This quirky downtown pharmacy (☎ (212) 475-3400), 109 Third Ave, has a patient staff that has been selling organic skin-care products since 1851. This precursor to the Body Shop has a very loyal clientele, and celebrities such as Richard Gere can be spotted in the place buying products and admiring the late owner's eccentric collection of antique Harley-Davidson motorcycles.

Macy's Most New Yorkers have an affectionate regard for Macy's (☎ (212) 695-4400), one of the city's last surviving general interest retailers, in large part because of its sponsorship of a fireworks festival on the 4th of July and the annual Thanksgiving Day Parade. Though Macy's has experienced financial problems in recent years, the store's stock hasn't diminished and it continues to hold its famous Wednesday 'One Day Sales.'

Madison Ave The funkiest boutiques may be in SoHo, but more formal shopping can be found on Madison Ave above 42nd St. On the Upper East Side, Madison Ave is as close as New York comes to a *Place Vendome* Parisian experience, as designers try to outdo each other in their showplace stores. There are fewer crowds on Sunday, but you won't be able to drop in on any of the avenue's 1st-rate art galleries, which are closed that day. Walking north on Madison Ave from 42nd St, you will see the following shops:

Brooks Brothers – A legendary store selling conservative clothing and formal wear for men; includes a smaller women's department. No 346 (☎ (212) 682-8800)

Worth and Worth – The place for men's hats, custom-made umbrellas and scarves. No 331 (☎ (212) 867-6058)

Barney's – The flagship of the hip and haughty clothing chain store that's famous for treating potential customers as too fat, too poor, and, in the men's department, too straight. No 660 (☎ (212) 826-8900)

Calvin Klein – The media savvy designer opened this flagship store in early 1995. No 654 (☎ (212) 292-9000)

The Coach Store – The place for expensive leather bags, wallets and belts that never go on sale. No 710 (☎ (212) 319-1772)

Gruen Optika – The best store in the city for one-of-a-kind eyewear. No 740 (☎ (212) 988-5832)

Giorgio Armani – Not to be outdone by anyone, Armani opened up a massive flagship store at 65th St and Madison in 1996. No 815 (☎ (212) 988-9191)

Gianni Versace – The other high priest of Italian style has his own shop for fashion obsessed rockers. No 816 (☎ (212) 744-5572)

Missoni Boutique – The popular Italian designer's expensive knitwear is sold here. No 836 (☎ (212) 517-9339)

Yves St Laurent – Selections from the legendary master of French *couture* are sold here. No 855 (☎ (212) 472-5299)

Givenchy – The place for traditional French suits and accessories. No 954 (☎ (212) 772-1040)

Polo/Ralph Lauren – An old mansion makes an appropriate setting for Lauren's clothing aimed at aristocratic wannabes. Madison Ave and 72nd St (☎ (212) 606-2100)

Paragon Athletic Goods This sporting goods store (☎ (212) 255-8036), 867 Broadway (subway: Union Square), not only has the best selection of sports merchandise, but it regularly beats prices found at chain stores such as Herman's and Sports Authority. Particularly notable for its end-of-season sales on tennis racquets and running shoes, Paragon also has the best selection of in-line skates in the city and a helpful staff that will literally spend an hour helping you choose the best kind.

Warner Bros Studio Store The Warner Bros Studio Store (☎ (212) 754-0300), at the corner of E 57th St and Fifth Ave, is like a theme restaurant that dispenses with food and simply sells corporate identity. Whether or not you care for items like a Sylvester stapler or a Bugs Bunny coffee mug depends on your regard for the old Looney Toon cartoon characters. You can also buy authenticated animation cels for upwards of $2500. Plenty of people love this store, and have made it one of the most profitable retail outlets in New York City.

It's open Monday to Saturday from 10 am to 7 pm and Sunday from noon to 6 pm. In 1996, the **Walt Disney** company opened a similar theme store (☎ (212) 702-0702) just two blocks south at 711 Fifth Ave.

Outer Boroughs

THE BRONX

The Bronx – a geographic area that has a curious article before its name, like the Hague and the Yucatan – is named after the Bronck family, Dutch farmers who owned a huge tract of property in the area. They, in turn, gave their name to 'Bronck's River,' which led to the derivation used today.

The Bronx has dubious world renown as a metaphor for urban decay, even though the southwestern part of the borough – the area unofficially referred to as the South Bronx – doesn't quite live up to its reputation, thanks to a 10 year, billion dollar program to build low income housing.

The borough, once a forest-like respite from the rest of the city but now home to 1.2 million people, is definitely a study in contrasts. The Morrisania section of the lower Bronx is still riddled with abandoned buildings, while Fieldston, in the northern reaches of the borough, is a privately owned community of Tudor homes occupied by some of the city's richest residents. The Bronx also boasts the quiet and isolated fishing community of City Island as well as the 2764 acre Pelham Bay Park, the city's largest.

The Bronx Tourism Council (☎ (718) 590-3518) offers a visitor's guide to the borough and keeps track of community events. The Bronx County Historical Society (☎ (718) 881-8900) sponsors weekend walking tours of various sites.

Yankee Stadium

Many people might be tempted to pass up a visit to Yankee Stadium, baseball's mecca, because of its location in the South Bronx. The area is really not at all hazardous, though its reputation for being crime-ridden has been exploited by New York Yankee owner George Steinbrenner, who seems intent on hustling the city into constructing a grander facility downtown or moving the team to the New Jersey suburbs.

Steinbrenner will probably make good

on one of those threats just after the year 2000, when the Yankee Stadium lease expires. But for now you can still visit what the team calls 'the most famous stadium since the Roman Coliseum' in all its active glory on summer game days. Gates open 90 minutes before game time, and fans can visit the left field **Memorial Park** where plaques are dedicated to such baseball greats as Babe Ruth, Mickey Mantle and Joe DiMaggio. Across the street from the stadium stand several bustling memorabilia shops and restaurants. **Stan's Sports Bar** gets particularly raucous when the Yankees play the arch-rival Boston Red Sox.

Yankee Stadium is 15 minutes from downtown via the 4 and D subway trains.

New York Botanical Garden

The 250 acre New York Botanical Garden (☎ (718) 817-8705) has suffered financial woes in recent years, but it will be worth visiting once the Victorian **Enid A Haupt Conservatory**, a grand Victorian iron and glass edifice, is restored (sometime in 1997). There's also an outdoor **Rose Garden** just next to the conservatory, and a **Rock Garden** with a multi-tiered waterfall. The shop in the museum building sells plants along with 'zoo doo,' manure manufactured by the residents of the nearby Bronx Zoo.

It's open Tuesday to Sunday from 10 am to 6 pm, with the same hours on Monday and national holidays. Admission for adults/children is $3/1, with free entry all day Wednesday and Saturday from 10 am to noon.

You can reach the Botanical Gardens and Fordham by taking the D subway train to Bedford Park Blvd and walking east down the hill seven blocks to the gate. Metro North trains (☎ (212) 532-4900) leave hourly from Grand Central Terminal

---

The Bronx Bombers & the Sultan of Swat

The New York Yankees are the most successful team in the history of baseball. The 'Bronx Bombers' have been in the World Series 34 times and won it 23 times, including in 1996. The team's most famous player was left-handed slugger George Herman Ruth (1895-1948). Ruth – popularly known as 'Babe,' 'The Bambino,' and more formally as the 'Sultan of Swat' – was the sport's first superstar, an icon whose charisma on and off the field helped make baseball the National Pastime.

In 1920, Ruth, then recognized as one of the best pitchers in the game, was sold to the Yanks by the Boston Red Sox, creating for that team the 'Curse of the Great Bambino,' which dictates that the Sox never again win the World Series (they haven't), and instigating a rivalry between the two teams that remains heated to this day.

But the Yankees didn't want a pitcher – it was Ruth's bat they were interested in. With the Yankees, Ruth began playing the outfield permanently; he took the field every day and began to hit home runs in numbers the game had never seen before. In 1927 he hit 60 round-trippers, which remained a record for a single season until 1961. His career total of 714 home runs (659 for the Yankees) wasn't surpassed until 1974.

Ruth helped the Yankees win their first American League pennant in 1921 and their first World Series in 1923. During the 1926 World Series, he became the first player to hit three home runs in one game (a feat he repeated in his very last game in 1935 when he was playing for the Boston Braves).

Yankee Stadium was built in 1923 and renovated in 1976. It is still commonly referred to as 'The House that Ruth Built,' because it was partly designed to suit his hitting style and was made large enough to fit the many fans who came just to see him.

A year after his retirement from baseball Ruth was among the first players inducted to the National Baseball Hall of Fame (see Cooperstown, NY). After a brief coaching stint with the Brooklyn Dodgers he later starred as himself in the 1942 movie *Pride of the Yankees*, which was about his Yankee teammate, Lou Gehrig. Ruth himself was the subject of two later films, *The Babe Ruth Story* in 1948 and *The Babe* in 1991. ■

to the Botanical Garden stop; it costs $3.50 each way.

Bronx Zoo

The Bronx Zoo (☎ (718) 367-1010), which recently changed its official name to the more politically correct Bronx Wildlife Conservation Society (subway: Pelham Parkway), attracts more than two million visitors annually to its 265 acre site. Nearly 5000 animals are on exhibit, all in comfortable, naturalistic settings. It's best to visit the zoo in warm weather, since many of the outdoor rides are shuttered during the winter months and the animals retreat into shelter areas, and you're stuck touring the older buildings that are home to reptiles and birds.

The usual array of lions, tigers and bears is mostly observed along the Bengali Express Monorail (tickets: $2), which is open from May to October and offers a 25 minute narrated journey through the Wild Asia areas. The Jungle World indoor exhibit, open year round, is a 37,000 sq foot re-creation of the Asian tropics with 100 different species of animal and tropical plants. You'll either be delighted or terrified by the World of Darkness, where bats hover nearly unseen (but not unsmelled).

The zoo is open daily from 10 am to 4:30 pm during the winter, and closes an hour later during the summer months. Admission from November to March is $3/1.50; in the summer, when everything is open, it jumps to $6.75/3. Admission is free on Wednesdays year round.

Liberty Lines Express (☎ (718) 652-8400) runs buses to the Bronx Zoo that picks up passengers along Madison Ave (at 26th, 47th, 54th, 63rd, 69th, and 84th Sts) for $4. You can also reach the zoo via the 2 or 5 trains, or with a car by taking the Bronx River Parkway (parking: $5).

It's difficult – and also exhausting – to walk from the Botanical Garden to the zoo, but if you must, they are best linked by going down Southern Blvd and taking a left at Bronx Park South to the Boston Rd entrance to the zoo.

Arthur Ave

Just south of Fordham University is the Belmont section of the Bronx, the most authentic Italian neighborhood in the city. This is a neighborhood for pure gastronomic exploration (see Places to Eat, below), and a place to soak up true Italian American culture.

Belmont is the perfect place to stock up on Italian provisions, including live chickens at the Arthur Ave Poultry Market, No 2356, and Teitel Brothers Wholesalers (☎ (718) 733-9400), on the corner of 186th St and Arthur Ave. The **Arthur Ave Retail Market** contains indoor food stalls, including Mike & Sons, a cheese shop with heartbreakingly good aged parmesan and prosciutto. The Cosenza fresh fish store, No 2354, sells clams on the half shell to pedestrians from a small table on the street, while clerks at the Calabria Pork Store (☎ (718) 367-5145), No 2338, offer free samples of hot and sweet homemade sausages that age on racks along the ceiling.

The **Belmont Italian American Playhouse** (☎ (718) 364-4700), 2384 Arthur Ave, is the neighborhood's most lively performance spot. It's the site of a season of new theatrical works that runs from April to December, and a place where local authors and musicians perform year round – if you're lucky, you'll be in town for one of the rooftop doo-wop concerts (Dion and the Belmonts came from this neighborhood).

You can reach Arthur Ave by taking the Metro North trains from Grand Central to Fordham Rd or the 4 subway train to the stop of the same name and walking east 11 blocks, then turning right at Arthur Ave and continuing south down three blocks.

City Island

Surely the oddest and most unexpected neighborhood in the Bronx is City Island, a 1½ mile long fishing community 15 miles from Midtown. City Island has numerous boat slips, is home to three yacht clubs, and is the place to go if you're interested in diving, sailing or fishing in Long Island Sound. Perhaps the strangest thing about this self-contained little spot, cut off from the rest of the Bronx by Pelham Bay Park, is that there's hardly a trace of the New York accent found in conversation between the locals – in fact their inflections and accents betray a New England influence.

All of its shops and 20 odd seafood restaurants are located along City Island Ave, which runs the length of the island. The short side streets are filled with attractive clapboard houses that overlook the surrounding water, and the main marinas are found on the western side.

If you make the trip, have a seafood meal and check out the **Undersea Museum** (☎ (718) 885-0701), which contains a wealth of items obtained by local divers and a film about whaling. It's open in the summer Monday to Friday from 10 am to 5 pm and weekends from noon to 5 pm; admission is $4.50.

You can reach City Island by taking the 6 subway train to its terminus at Pelham Bay Park and getting on the Bx29 bus which runs directly to City Island Ave, or by taking an express bus from Madison Ave in Midtown directly to City Island ($4 each way).

Places to Eat

Arthur Ave-Belmont Some of the restaurants in this eight block neighborhood have been in business since just after WWI, including *Mario's* (☎ (718) 584-1188), 2342 Arthur Ave; and *Ann & Tony's* (☎ (718) 933-1469), 2407 Arthur Ave, a family-style Neapolitan restaurant with pasta specials for $12 and under. There are often lines outside of the more famous *Dominick's* (☎ (718) 733-2807), 2335 Arthur Ave, a cash-only place where the crusty waiters serve large portions at long tables for around $12 a dish. (There are no menu prices – the waiters present you with a final figure at the end of the meal.)

City Island Locals hang out at the *Rhodes Restaurant* (☎ (718) 885-1538), 288 City Island Ave, open every day until 2 am and

serving standard pub specials and burgers for around $8.

BROOKLYN

For years, a sign on the eastern side of the Brooklyn Bridge welcomed visitors to the 'fourth-largest city in the America.' The sign has been replaced by one with a less separatist sentiment, but Brooklyn's pride – and right to claim fourth-largest city status – still remains (it is home to 2.3 million people). The borough also makes the dubious claim that 'one out of every seven famous people' in the US was born in Brooklyn!

Brooklyn, officially called Kings County, derives its name from *breucklen*, the Dutch word for marshland. For most of its 350 year history, Brooklyn was a collection of farming villages, and its citizens joined greater New York City with great reluctance. Even after the 1898 consolidation, the borough remained independent in spirit: citizens enjoyed Prospect Park, Brooklyn's own version of Central Park, followed the fortunes of the Brooklyn Dodgers baseball team, and sun worshipped at the ritzy resort hotels on Coney Island. But much of Brooklyn's separate city pretensions were destroyed in the late '50s, when the Dodgers moved to the West Coast and many of the borough's residents began moving to the suburbs. Today Brooklyn's inner neighborhoods are home to newer immigrants from the Caribbean, Eastern Europe and the former Soviet Union. The old carriage houses and brownstones in neighborhoods along the eastern part of the borough have been snapped up by professionals looking for a nice space within commuting distance of Manhattan.

The Brooklyn Tourism and Festivals Project (☎ (718) 855-7882) issues a free calendar of events called *Meet Me in Brooklyn*. It's updated every three months and is available at all Brooklyn cultural institutions. *Brooklyn Bridge*, a $2.75 monthly magazine on sale in shops and newsstands throughout the borough, has a more extensive list of happenings.

Brooklyn Heights

This neighborhood of brownstones and mansions by the mouth of the East River developed as a ferry departure point for Lower Manhattan in the early 19th century. Walking along its promenade, you get a stunning view of Manhattan's skyscrapers framed at the bottom by the far less impressive metal storage warehouses along the waterfront.

You can begin a tour of 'The Heights' at the 1848 Beaux Arts **Brooklyn Borough Hall** (☎ (718) 875-4047), 209 Joralemon St (subway: Jay St–Borough Hall). If you are particularly energetic, you can get to Borough Hall from downtown Manhattan via a 20 minute walk across the Brooklyn Bridge and bearing right on the bridge's pedestrian walkway, which will bring you south along Adams St to the building. Borough Hall is open from Monday to Friday during business hours; a free tour of the facility is held every Tuesday at 1 pm. From behind the building, continue down Montague St, the main avenue for cafes and bars. One block north runs the parallel Pierrepont St (pronounced PIER-pont), site of the Brooklyn Historical Society (see below).

Montague St ends at Pierrepont Place and the waterfront promenade, and here you can turn right and continue north on Columbia Heights to **Fulton Landing**, the old ferry dock at the base of the Brooklyn Bridge. This was the main departure point for Manhattan-bound ferries before the bridge was completed in 1883. Now classical music concerts are held on a barge here and it's a perfect place to watch the sun set beyond Manhattan.

Heading back up the hill along Henry St, note the old wooden frame houses around Middagh St before returning to **Atlantic Ave**, the busy thoroughfare featuring several Middle Eastern spice shops and an array of restaurants. Sahadi Importing Co (☎ (718) 624-4550), 187-189 Atlantic Ave, wholesales its dried fruits and nuts all over the country, and it's worth stopping in to pick up some snacks or simply to enjoy the exotic atmosphere.

Brooklyn Historical Society

This research library (☎ (718) 624-0890), 128 Pierrepont St, also has a museum dedicated to borough history in a fine terra cotta auditorium that's a national landmark. Its digitized collection of 31,000 photographs and prints is on computers available for browsing in the 2nd-floor library when the museum is open. Unfortunately, the Brooklyn Historical Society and its museum are closed until 1998.

The New York Transit Museum

The transit museum (☎ (718) 243-8601), located in a decommissioned subway station from the 1930s at the corner of Boerum Place and Schermerhorn St, a block north of Atlantic Ave (subway: Jay St–Borough Hall), has a distinctly low tech look to it. Virtually unchanged since its opening in 1976, the museum does not have a video presentation, let alone any computer-driven exhibits. What it does have is an impressive collection of subway cars from the transit system's first 100 years on the platform of the old station; most have their original ads still intact. Keep an eye out for the silver car used in the 1995 film *Money Train*, along with the model R-1, the vintage that inspired Duke Ellington's *Take the A Train*. You will also see the 1947 R-11 model, which featured 'germicidal' lighting designed to sterilize tunnel air. The cars were discontinued amid fears that the lights would also sterilize subway conductors and trainmen.

The Transit Museum runs tours of the system in antique subway cars several times a year; call for a schedule. It's open Tuesday, Thursday and Friday from 10 am to 4 pm, Wednesday from 10 am to 6 pm and Saturday and Sunday from noon to 5 pm. Admission is $3/1.50.

Brooklyn Academy of Music

The Brooklyn Academy of Music (BAM; ☎ (718) 636-4100), 30 Lafayette Ave (subway: Atlantic Ave), the oldest concert center in the US, consists of the **Majestic Theater** and the **Brooklyn Opera House**. BAM hosts visiting opera companies from

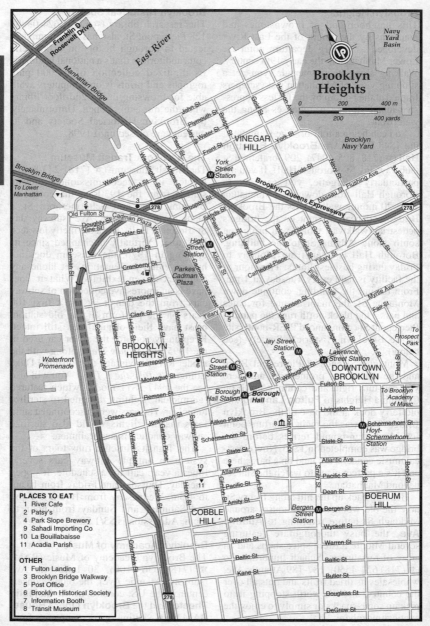

Brooklyn Heights

0   200   400 m
0   200   400 yards

PLACES TO EAT
1 River Cafe
2 Patsy's
4 Park Slope Brewery
9 Sahadi Importing Co
10 La Bouillabaisse
11 Acadia Parish

OTHER
1 Fulton Landing
3 Brooklyn Bridge Walkway
5 Post Office
6 Brooklyn Historical Society
7 Information Booth
8 Transit Museum

around the world in subtitled productions and is home to the Mark Morris dance troupe.

You can take public transportation to BAM or call to reserve a spot on the bus that leaves from the corner of 51st St and Lexington Ave in Manhattan an hour before the performance; it costs $10 roundtrip.

Prospect Park

Created in 1866, the 526 acre park (subway: Grand Army Plaza or Prospect Park) is considered the greatest achievement by Frederick Law Olmsted and Calvert Vaux, the same landscaping duo that designed Central Park. Though less crowded than its more famous Manhattan sister space, Prospect Park offers many of the same activities along its broad meadows, including **ice-skating** at the Kate Wollman Rink (☎ (718) 287-6431), which is open daily from October to early March. Admission costs $2.50/1, with skate rental for $3.50. There is also the **Lefferts Homestead Children's Museum** (☎ (718) 965-6505), open only on weekends, and a small **zoo** (☎ (718) 399-7339), open from 10 am to 4 pm with an admission charge of $2.50/50¢. Information on other activities, including park walks, carousel rides and art exhibitions, can be obtained by visiting the boathouse (subway: Prospect Park) or calling ☎ (718) 965-8999.

Grand Army Plaza stands at the northwest entrance to the park, marked by an 80 foot **Soldiers' and Sailors' Monument** constructed in 1898 to commemorate the Union Army's triumph during the Civil War. In the summer, you can visit a gallery in the arch that's dedicated to local artists as well as climb an observation deck just below the four horse bronze chariot. New York City's only structure honoring President John F Kennedy is located in a small fountain park just to the north of the Grand Army arch. The immense Art Deco **Brooklyn Public Library** faces the arch on its south side.

On Saturday and Sunday year round, a free hourly trolley service makes a loop from Prospect Park to points of interest around the museum, including the park zoo and ice rink, the botanical garden, and the Brooklyn library. Ask at the museum information desk for the time it passes by the entrance.

Park Slope

This rectangular-shaped residential neighborhood is located immediately west of Prospect Park, and most of its shops and restaurants are located along the 18 blocks of Seventh Ave bookended by two subway stations (subway: D, Q trains to Seventh Ave; F train to Seventh Ave–Park Slope). Novelist Paul Auster and essayist Ian Frazier live here, and there's a literary atmosphere to the area, with four book shops within easy walking distance, including Booklink (☎ (718) 965-9122), 320 Seventh Ave, which features the work of local writers. Park Slope is a pleasant place to have lunch or dinner, or just linger over coffee. Ozzie's (☎ (718) 398-6695), 57 Seventh Ave, is a coffee shop cum literary hangout patronized by Auster and actor John Turturro. There are several more cafes along the street.

Eastern Parkway

Named after the six lane boulevard that runs along the north end of Prospect Park,

---

Brooklyn Bar Culture

For an absolutely fascinating look at the Brooklyn beer-drinking culture, visit *Farrell's Bar & Grill* (☎ (718) 788-8779), 215 Prospect Park West (subway: 15th St–Prospect Park). The drinking begins before noon in this male-dominated local joint, and only Budweiser is on offer in either 75¢ glasses or 32 ounce Styrofoam cups (you can also quaff shots of bourbon or whiskey). The 60 year old Farrell's once banned chairs – the theory being that if you couldn't stand up, you could no longer be served. There are a few seats now, but most patrons still do their drinking leaning against the bar. ■

Prospect Park & Surrounding Neighborhoods

PROSPECT HEIGHTS

PARK SLOPE

WINDSOR TERRACE

Greenwood Cemetery

Prospect Park

Prospect Lake

Brooklyn Botanic Garden

Grand Army Plaza Station

To Brooklyn Heights, Manhattan Bridge

Atlantic Ave

0   300   600 m
0   300   600 yards
Not All Streets Shown

PLACES TO DRINK & EAT
1 Healthy Henrietta's
2 Lemongrass Grill
3 Ozzie's Coffee Shop
5 Tom's Restaurant
6 Wizard Restaurant
9 Park Slope Brewing Company
11 Farrell's Bar & Grill

OTHER
4 Soldiers' and Sailors' Monument
7 Public Library
8 Brooklyn Museum
10 Booklink Book Shop

this area was once one of the most exclusive neighborhoods in Brooklyn. The area cuts through Prospect Heights and Crown Heights, home to the Lubavitch sect of Orthodox Jews and a large Caribbean community. There have been major tensions between the two groups in recent years, but it is quite safe to explore shops and restaurants along Washington Ave, which runs in front of the Brooklyn Museum of Art.

Brooklyn Museum of Art Were it located anywhere else, the Brooklyn Museum of Art (☎ (718) 638-5000), 200 Eastern Parkway (subway: Eastern Parkway–Brooklyn Museum), would be considered a premier arts institution. Even though it is shadowed by the Met, this museum is very much worth a visit. It's never really crowded, even on Sunday, and you can take up an entire day exploring its collection and seeing the nearby Botanical Gardens and Brooklyn Children's Museum.

On the museum's first two floors are galleries dedicated to African, Islamic and Asian art. Particularly good are the modern 3rd-floor galleries containing colorful Egyptian cartonnages (mummy casings) and funerary figurines. The 4th floor, which overlooks a tiled court crowned by a skylight, has period rooms, including a reconstruction of the Jan Schenck House, a 17th century Dutch settlement in Brooklyn. The 5th floor has colonial portraiture, including a famous Gilbert Stuart painting of Washington in which the general looks particularly uncomfortable wearing his false teeth, along with a collection of 58 Auguste Rodin sculptures.

The Brooklyn Museum of Art is open Wednesday to Friday from 10 am to 5 pm, Saturday 11 am to 9 pm and Sunday 11 am to 6 pm.

Brooklyn Botanic Garden The 52 acre botanic garden (☎ (718) 622-4433), 1000 Washington Ave (subway: Eastern Parkway–Brooklyn Museum), has more than 12,000 different plants in its 15 gardens. There's a fanciful Celebrity Path with slate steps honoring famous Brooklynites, and a Fragrance Garden that makes for a wonderful walk. Unfortunately, someone recently made off with several of the Steinhardt Conservatory's Bonsai trees, a few of which were 250 years old or more.

The botanic garden is open Tuesday to Friday from 8 am to 6 pm and Saturday and Sunday from 8 am to 4:30 pm from April to September. Winter hours are Tuesday to Sunday from 10 am to 4:30 pm. Admission for adults/seniors/children is $3/1.50/50¢. Admission is free on Tuesday.

Coney Island

This former summer playground (subway: Coney Island) was where sweating city dwellers came to enjoy the fun house, minor games of chance and bumper-car rides in the Dreamland amusement park before WWI. It is a ghostly shadow of its former self, especially after Labor Day, when the storied Cyclone roller coaster closes for the season. But it's still worth the 60 minute trip from Manhattan, especially since it is also the site of the New York Aquarium (see below) and just a quarter-mile boardwalk stroll from Brighton Beach, the nation's largest grouping of Russian émigrés.

As you emerge from the colorfully decrepit subway station, you'll see a 24 hour coffee shop right in the middle of the station. Hardbitten patrons sit at a counter-top hunched over their meals and dozens of menu items are advertised on the bright yellow walls of the shop – meanwhile your nose is assaulted by the smell of sausages, hot dogs, home fries and other greasy delights. Then pass through the doors to Surf Ave, where Russian residents pick up odd tools and electronic equipment at **flea market** stalls along the street.

Not far from here is the **Coney Island Sideshow** (☎ (718) 372-5159), 1208 Surf Ave, a small museum and freak show where you can see snake charmers, tattooed ladies and sword swallowers for a $3/2 admission charge.

Nathan's, the city's prototypical fast-food stand, has been open at the same Surf Ave site for more than 75 years and still sells its famous hot dogs ($2) from 8 am to 4 am daily.

Along the Boardwalk you will see two relics of Coney Island's past glory: the bright red parachute jump, moved here from the 1939 World's Fair in Queens, and the ivy covered **Thunderbolt** roller coaster, which operated from 1925 to 1983; it's older than the more famous Cyclone in the Astroland Amusement Park just up the boardwalk.

New York Aquarium The New York Aquarium (☎ (718) 265-3400), along the Coney Island boardwalk (subway: W 8th St–NY Aquarium) may look thoroughly unattractive from the outside and lack the computerized gadgetry of newer facilities elsewhere, but its manageable scale makes it a perfect place for young children. There's a touch pool where kids can handle starfish and other small forms of sea life, and a small amphitheater with Sea World–style dolphin shows several times daily. Most kids love viewing whales and seals from the outside railing overlooking their tanks or from the observation windows that afford views of the animals' underwater habitats. You can spend the better part of a day at the aquarium viewing its 10,000 specimens of sea life.

It's open every day from 10 am to 5 pm, and admission is $6.75/3.

Brighton Beach

There's more than a little bit of Russia to be found in Brighton Beach (subway: Brighton Beach), just a five minute walk north on the boardwalk from the New York Aquarium. Russian shops, bakeries and restaurants line Brighton Beach Ave, which runs parallel to the boardwalk just one block from the beach.

Brighton Beach has been identified as the main money laundering spot in the US for the Russian *mafiya*. But there's no reason to worry about crime on the street – just about the only criminal behavior you'll observe are the *babushkas* selling illegal prescriptive medicine Moscow-style on the street corner. This community is so close-knit that a non-Russian speaker will stick out like a sore thumb. But the restaurants and shops are tolerant and friendly to outsiders, a category that includes Brooklynites in any other neighborhood.

Williamsburg

This neighborhood, located just over the namesake Williamsburg Bridge, is home to a large Orthodox Jewish community – a living embodiment of what Manhattan's Lower East Side once was in the early 20th century. But the windswept northern area of Williamsburg (subway: L to Bedford Ave), is much different and varied in character. The north has long been home to a large population of Central European immigrants, mostly from Poland. In recent years, this aging community has been augmented by many aspiring artists and writers who are taking advantage of the cheap rents and large loft spaces. The two distinct communities coexist quite peacefully. On sunny Sunday afternoons, you can see Polish senior citizens hanging out on just about every other doorstep, exchanging greetings in their native language after church services,

while paint-splattered younger folks gather in the local bars for brunch, beer and cigarettes.

Though the local press has noted Williamsburg's growing popularity with the cutting edge art crowd, there has yet to be an invasion of art galleries or Manhattan-level rents. A college campus atmosphere prevails along Bedford St, where locals looking for apartment shares post signs on mini 'democracy walls,' and musicians advertise for band mates.

For the moment, the local cafes and restaurants in Williamsburg serve as de facto galleries where artists hang out and display their work. To get into the rhythm of the place check out the L Cafe (☎ (718) 388-6792), 189 Bedford Ave, Plan-eat Thailand (☎ (718) 599-5758), just across the street at No 184, and Teddy's Bar (☎ (718) 384-9787), 96 Berry St (at N 8th St).

Though Williamsburg doesn't have much to offer culturally as yet, it's only a five minute subway trip from Manhattan's Union Square and worth seeing in good weather: you can grab a good meal here and admire the sunset view of Manhattan from Kent Ave along the waterfront.

Brooklyn Brewery Since 1988, the Brooklyn Brewery made its award-winning Brooklyn Lager under contract at breweries outside of the borough. But the beer 'came home' to Brooklyn in 1996 with the opening of a microbrewery in Williamsburg (☎ (718) 486-7422), at 79 N 11th St. Housed in a series of buildings that once made up the Hecla Ironworks factory (the firm that made the structural supports for the Waldorf-Astoria Hotel), the brewery offers free self-guided tours every Saturday from noon to 4 pm. Call ahead during summer to find out if the tours have been booked.

Special Events
Brooklyn hosts a few notable events throughout the year; contact the Brooklyn Tourism and Festivals project (☎ (718) 855-7882) and see the Special Events calendar that appears under Manhattan.

Places to Eat

Brooklyn Heights Brooklyn Heights has two excellent bring-your-own-bottle restaurants: *Acadia Parish* (☎ (718) 624-5154), 148 Atlantic Ave near Clinton St, serves filling Cajun fare. Nearby is *La Bouillabaisse* (☎ (718) 522-8275), 145 Atlantic Ave, where the signature dish and other French fare often attract lines out the door.

For those who don't want to bother with shopping around for something to drink with a meal, there's the newest outpost of the *Park Slope Brewing Co* (☎ (718) 522-4801), 62 Henry St, which serves a dozen local microbrews and sandwiches for $7 and under.

At Fulton Landing stands the famous *River Cafe* (☎ (718) 522-5200), 1 Water St, a romantic restaurant with delicately prepared American cuisine and a $65 fixed-price dinner menu – you'll need to make early reservations for a window seat. Just as good, but much cheaper, is *Patsy's* (☎ (718) 858-4300), 19 Old Fulton St, a shrine to Frank Sinatra disguised as a pizzeria that serves delicious big pies for $13.

Park Slope Vegetarians are served by *Healthy Henrietta's* (☎ (718) 622-2924), 787 Union St, with specialties such as scrambled tofu and vegetable burritos for under $8. The *Lemongrass Grill* (☎ (718) 399-7100), 61A Seventh Ave, has spicy and generous Thai dishes, including a wide selection of meatless choices, for $12 and under. The original *Park Slope Brewing Co* (☎ (718) 788-1756), 356 Sixth Ave at 5th St, serves hearty pub grub and local brews.

Eastern Parkway The streets near the Brooklyn Museum of Art have a number of West Indian restaurants, including the *Wizard* (☎ (718) 399-9141), 806 Washington Ave, which serves pumpkin soup and $2 meat patties. *Tom's Restaurant* (☎ (718) 636-9738), 782 Washington Ave, is a legendary, 60 year old place that is a must for its egg cream sodas and hearty breakfasts, all under $5. Gus, the friendly owner, seems to know everyone and serves favored

customers a free toasted corn muffin smothered in honey.

Coney Island Two blocks away from the boardwalk is *Totonno's* (☎ (718) 372-8606), 1524 Neptune Ave, one of the city's best brick-oven pizza restaurants. Totonno's is open only Thursday to Sunday from noon to whenever he runs out of fresh mozzarella cheese. *Gargiulos* (☎ (718) 266-4891), 2911 W 15th St, is a noisy family-style place once famous for its huge Styrofoam Octopus, reputedly stolen from the aquarium. The octopus is gone, but you can get filling Southern Italian dishes for about $15.

Brighton Beach Some of Brighton Beach's restaurants cater to regional sectors of the Soviet émigré population, such as *Cafe Pearl* (☎ (718) 891-4544), 303 Brighton Beach Ave, which serves Georgian specialties for about $12, or the *Winter Garden* (☎ (718) 934-6666), on the Boardwalk, which attracts Muscovites. The bakeries on Brighton Beach Ave sell fantastic dark Moscow bread for $1.50 a loaf. You can enjoy a sticky sweet cherry drink while watching videos of Russian variety programs at *Caffe Cappuccino* (☎ (718) 646-6207), 290 Brighton Beach Ave.

At night, two raucous nightclub-restaurants offer set menus and elaborate floor shows. The *National* (☎ (718) 646-1225), 273 Brighton Beach Ave, charges $55 per person on Friday, Saturday and Sunday nights for its eye-popping, completely over-the-top variety show and dinner, well-oiled by carafes of vodka. *Primorski* (☎ (718) 891-3111), 282 Brighton Beach Ave, has a cheaper set menu – $20 ($25 on weekends) – but if you lose track of the vodka consumption the bill is sure to be much larger.

Williamsburg Williamsburg is home to the renowned *Peter Luger's Steak House* (☎ (718) 387-7400), 178 Broadway (subway: Marcy Ave), an old warehouse of a restaurant that has the reputation of serving New York's best beef. This out-of-the-way place takes cash only and dinner with a drink costs about $45 per person.

In northern Williamsburg (subway: Bedford Ave) you can visit *Plan-eat Thailand* (☎ (718) 599-5758), 184 Bedford Ave, and enjoy Southeast Asian dishes for $8 to $10 while listening to live jazz and checking out the work of local artists on the walls. (This place was called Planet Thailand until bozo lawyers from Planet Hollywood threatened to sue them.) At *Oznot's Dish* (☎ (718) 599-6596), 79 Berry St, the Mediterranean-flavored menu offers dishes for under $10. *Bean* (☎ (718) 387-8222), 167 Bedford Ave, is a bustling and inexpensive vegetarian restaurant.

QUEENS

With a land area of 282 sq miles, Queens is the largest borough in New York City, and the residential neighborhoods near the East River have always attracted newer immigrants looking for affordable housing within easy commuting distance of Manhattan, and many settled near the traditionally industrial neighborhoods of Long Island City, Astoria and Maspeth.

However, a strange phenomenon has happened over the years – most of the newer immigrant groups have augmented, rather than replaced, those already in Queens. It's now the most ethnically diverse place in the city, and perhaps even the world – more than 100 minority groups live there, speaking over 120 different languages or dialects – and the borough's population approaches two million.

The Queens Council on the Arts has a 24 hour hotline (☎ (718) 291-2787) on community cultural events; in keeping with the multi-cultural demographics of the borough, it provides information in English, Spanish, Korean and Chinese.

Astoria

Home to the largest Greek community in the US, Astoria (subway: N to Broadway; R to Steinway St), a residential neighborhood, also has a smattering of Eastern European immigrants. Astoria was a mid-19th century ferry depot named after

millionaire fur merchant John Jacob Astor. It soon developed into a neighborhood of factories, including the Steinway piano company, which still operates there. The German and Italian craftsmen who lived in Astoria were replaced by Greek immigrants in the years following WWII.

Today, Astoria is proudly a working-class neighborhood of brick and concrete apartment blocks and two story wooden homes.

Craftsmen at Work You can view two very different examples of skilled craftsmanship in Astoria. The Byzantion Woodworking Company (☎ (718) 932-2960), 37-20 Astoria Blvd, doesn't offer tours, but you can drop by from Monday to Saturday to see artisans at work carving elaborate Greek Orthodox religious items for clients from around the US and Canada. The Steinway Piano Company (☎ (718) 721-2600, ext 164), at 19th Ave and 38th St (subway: Ditmar Blvd), offers free 2½-hour tours of its facility every Thursday; call ahead to reserve a place, since the tours are often booked by school groups months in advance.

American Museum of the Moving Image The American Museum of the Moving Image (☎ (718) 784-0077), at 35th Ave and 36th St (subway: Steinway St), stands in the middle of the Kaufman Astoria Studio complex, a 75 year old film production center that has been the shooting site of everything from the Marx Brothers' *Coconuts* to *Glengarry Glen Ross*. Unfortunately, the studios are not open to public tours, but this museum makes a good effort at showing the mastery behind filmmaking, with galleries showing the makeup and costumes from films like *The Exorcist* and movie sets from the 1987 *Glass Menagerie*, directed by Paul Newman. Film and TV serials are played in a small theater built by conceptual artist Red Grooms, inspired by the '30s Egyptian-themed movie palaces.

Those familiar with London's far more ambitious Museum of the Moving Image will no doubt be disappointed by the

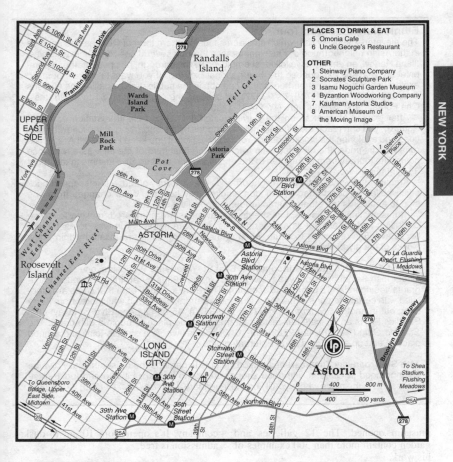

PLACES TO DRINK & EAT
5 Omonia Cafe
6 Uncle George's Restaurant

OTHER
1 Steinway Piano Company
2 Socrates Sculpture Park
3 Isamu Noguchi Garden Museum
4 Byzantion Woodworking Company
7 Kaufman Astoria Studios
8 American Museum of
   the Moving Image

smaller New York version. In early 1996, the museum spent several million dollars introducing interactive displays to its two floors of galleries. Now you can use computer screens to create your own video backdrop, listen to famous film soundtracks or re-dub dialogue from famous films.

The museum also holds interesting retrospectives on famous filmmakers year round. If you decide to make the short 15 minute subway ride out to Queens, go when there's an interesting film on offer – and end your day with a Greek meal on Broadway.

It's open from Tuesday to Friday from noon to 5 pm and Saturday and Sunday from noon to 6 pm. Admission for is $7/4 for adults/seniors, and $2.50 for children and students.

Isamu Noguchi Garden Museum Tucked away among the East River warehouses in Long Island City, the cinder-block Isamu Noguchi Garden Museum (☎ (718) 721-1932), 32-37 Vernon Blvd (subway: N to Broadway), stands on the site of a studio designed by the Japanese-American sculptor, who died in 1988, three years after the

Ethnic Neighborhood Tour

The elevated 7 subway line, which cuts across the northern third of Queens and ends up in the Asian neighborhood of Flushing, passes through several colorful ethnic enclaves. Illana Harlow, an enthusiastic folklorist employed by the borough, has put together a pamphlet on what she has dubbed the 'International Express.' If you want to make a detailed exploration of these neighborhoods, you can obtain the publication by calling the Queens Council on the Arts (☎ (718) 647-3377), or sending the organization $1 to its address: One Forest Park, Woodhaven, NY 11421-1166.

After leaving Manhattan on the 7 train (catch it at Grand Central Station or Times Square), you can reach the different neighborhoods by disembarking at the following stations and exploring the blocks nearby. You won't get lost if you keep Roosevelt Ave, which runs directly under the elevated train tracks for the final third of the line, as a reference point. The journey from Manhattan to the end of the line at Main St–Flushing takes about 35 minutes.

Architecturally, most of these neighborhoods are uniformly bland, a landscape of brick office buildings punctuated by wooden single-family houses. What changes from one stop to another is the ethnic character found around the subway.

In this section of Queens, the streets *and* avenues are numbered, making for some confusing addresses. But as a general guide, numbered streets run west to east; numbered avenues run north to south. Most of the following sites are located within a few blocks of the given subway stop.

46th St–Bliss St, 52nd St–Lincoln Ave, 61st St–Woodside Woodside, one of the city's oldest Irish neighborhoods was reinvigorated in the 1980s by an influx of young immigrants fleeing Ireland's depressed economy. There are so many bars that some are identified with certain regions of Ireland – Dubliners patronize one pub while folks from Kerry hang out in another. *Sidetracks* (☎ (718) 786-3570), 45-08 Queens Blvd (subway: 46th St–Bliss St), is an upscale bar-restaurant that's a good place to begin a pub crawl. The *Starting Gate* (☎ (718) 429-9269), 59-10 Woodside Ave, is a singles joint and a good place to end up at on Friday and Saturday nights.

74th St–Broadway The heart of Jackson Heights is perhaps the most ethnically diverse neighborhood in Queens, with food shops catering to Korean, Filipino and Indian residents. This is the place where you'll find the legendary *Jackson Diner* (☎ (718) 672-1232),

museum opened. The 12 galleries and garden contain more than 300 examples of his work.

It's open from April to November only on Wednesday, Saturday and Sunday from 11 am to 6 pm, and a tour of all the galleries takes place at 2 pm. Admission is $4/2.

Just two blocks north, where Broadway meets Vernon Blvd, is the **Socrates Sculpture Park** (☎ (718) 545-5707), a year-round, open-air public space with changing works by local artists on a former illegal waste dump overlooking the East River. The works on display, including the five windchimes along the shore line, have a stark industrial look to them, in keeping with its location right next to a steel

company. It's open from 10 am to dusk; admission is free.

Flushing Meadows Park

Flushing Meadows Park (subway: Willets Point–Shea Stadium) is the site of **Shea Stadium**, the ballpark of the New York Mets, and the **National Tennis Center**, home of the US Open. It was also the site of the spectacular 1939 and 1964 World's Fairs.

The center of the park is dominated by the distinctive, 380 ton **Unisphere** globe, built for the '64 fair by US Steel. A few of the old buildings constructed for the fair are still in use, though Philip Johnson's New York State Pavilion is an embarrassing

37-03 74th St, which many consider the city's best Southern Indian restaurant. Yes, this is a dingy converted coffee shop, but it's famous for its *masala dosa* appetizer, a massive crepe with potato, onion and peas, and the *seekh kabob*, a long sausage made of tender lamb. Jackson Heights is also known to have the largest gay population outside of Manhattan.

82nd St–Jackson Heights A strip of Argentine restaurants and shops can be found near this station, including *La Porteña* (☎ (718) 458-8111), 74-25 37th Ave, which serves Buenos Aires–style barbecue. There's also a large Colombian population served by such nightclubs as *Chibcha* (☎ (718) 429-9033), 79-05 Roosevelt Ave, with salsa and jazz shows on Friday and Saturday nights beginning at 11 pm.

Junction Blvd Several Latino subcultures exist side by side here. The *Broadway Sandwich Shop* (☎ (718) 898-4088), 96-01 Roosevelt Ave, serves garlicky toasted Cuban pork sandwiches for under $5 and steaming hot cups of strong *cafe con leche*. Nearby, *Quisqueya Restaurant* (☎ (718) 478-0704), 97-03 Roosevelt Ave, offers sweet plantain plates for $2 and Dominican specialties like young-goat stew for $7.50.

103rd St–Corona Plaza Corona, traditionally an Italian neighborhood, was also a place where well-known black jazz musicians bought comfortable houses in the '20s and '30s. Louis Armstrong lived at 34-56 107th St from 1929 until his death in '71, and the landmark is scheduled to be converted into a museum by 1998. Recently, Corona has seen an influx of Muslims from Pakistan and India, in addition to a large community of Mexicans. Tomas Gonzalez runs a mini-empire with his *La Espiga* (☎ (718) 779-7898), 42-13 102nd St, which is a combination bakery, restaurant and grocery store. People line up for the fresh tortillas which are made three times a day. The shop also sells Mexican embroidery.

Ben Faremo, The Lemon Ice King of Corona (☎ (718) 699-5133), 52-02 108th St, is open year round (winter closing: 6 pm) serving homemade ices – its signature ice has chunks of lemon and is the perfect refresher for a summer day. (The Lemon Ice King is about a mile from the subway. Walk south on 104th St to Corona Ave, turn left and walk two blocks to 52nd Ave; or take the Q23 bus to Forest Hills and get off on 108th St and 52nd Ave on the opposite corner from the shop.) ∎

mess; rusty, overgrown with weeds and closed to the public.

New York Hall of Science This former World's Fair pavilion (☎ (718) 699-0005), which resembles a Stalin-era concrete block, houses a children's museum dedicated to technology. It stands next to an outdoor park with a few early space-age rockets.

It's open Wednesday and Friday to Sunday from 10 am to 5 pm, Thursday from 2 pm to 5 pm. Admission for adults/children is $4.50/3; free on Wednesday.

Queens Museum of Art The former New York City building of the 1939 World's Fair has been completely renovated as a museum (☎ (718) 592-9700) and contains displays dedicated to both fairs held in the park. The building was also the site of the first sessions of the UN before the body moved into its permanent quarters on Manhattan's East Side (a gallery explains the history of those early peacemaking meetings).

The major attraction of the museum is the **Panorama of New York City**. This 9335 sq foot model of the metropolis debuted at the '64 fair and was a big hit with visitors who marveled at its details reproduced at a scale of 1:200.

In 1994 the panorama was cut up into 273 four-by-10-foot sections and updated to include all of the significant new additions to the local skyline. Today it's a stunning sight with more than 835,000 tiny buildings. A glass-bottomed observation deck encircles the panorama, and every 15 minutes there's a mock sunset, prompting thousands of tiny lights to flicker on across the diorama.

The Queens museum is open Wednesday to Friday from 10 am to 5 pm and Saturday and Sunday from noon to 5 pm; admission is $3/1.50.

Flushing

It's hard to imagine that this bustling neighborhood (subway: Main St–Flushing) was once secluded forest that in the mid-17th century served as a secret meeting place for Quakers determined to circumvent Dutch Governor Peter Stuyvesant's religious intolerance. The country village was also the site of the first commercial nursery in the US, visited by George Washington soon after his inauguration as president. Flushing eventually became an urban eyesore, the site of a huge commercial ash heap (mentioned in F Scott Fitzgerald's *The Great Gatsby*) and a series of junkyards often noted by travelers to Long Island. The area was reclaimed as park land for the

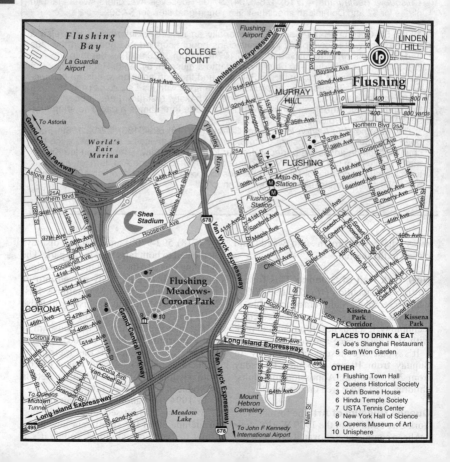

PLACES TO DRINK & EAT
4 Joe's Shanghai Restaurant
5 Sam Won Garden

OTHER
1 Flushing Town Hall
2 Queens Historical Society
3 John Bowne House
6 Hindu Temple Society
7 USTA Tennis Center
8 New York Hall of Science
9 Queens Museum of Art
10 Unisphere

World's Fair of 1939, and saw a huge influx of Korean and Chinese immigrants in the 1980s.

Packed as it is with discount shops, 24 hour coffee shops and municipal offices, Flushing is anything but architecturally charming. But at some spots, with the prevalent signage in Korean, you could possibly believe you're in a residential neighborhood in Seoul. While some of the older residents have resented the incursion of new Asian immigrants, Flushing has not suffered from any outward tensions between the various communities.

Flushing's center is located at the corner of Roosevelt Ave, which runs east-west, and Main St, which runs north-south – right at the subway exit.

Queens Historical Society The Queens Historical Society (☎ (718) 939-0647), 143-35 37th St, is in the Kingsland Homestead, a wooden 1765 estate house, just beyond Margaret Carmen Green.

You can get there by traveling two blocks east on Roosevelt Ave, turning left, and walking two more blocks north. The historical society offers maps of 'Freedom Mile,' listing 19 places of religious significance, and brochures published in English, Korean, Spanish and Chinese. The tour is a bit of a cheat, since some of the sites are really the locations of important places that no longer exist. But you can still see the 1661 **John Bowne House**, which stands today at 37-01 Bowne St, near the Kingsland Homestead. Quakers met in the house, which is the oldest residence in Queens.

A 10 minute walk south on Bowne St will bring you what must be Flushing's most exotic sight: the **Hindu Temple Society of North America** (☎ (718) 460-8484), 45-57 Bowne St. The temple, complete with carved elephant headed gods, was designed and built in India and reconstructed here in 1977. Taking your shoes off and entering the 2nd floor of the temple, you can observe devotees offering coconut milk to the deity Maha Vallabha Ganapati. There are daily services at the temple,

which is open from 8 am to 9 pm, and at the side of the building a cafe serves yogurt drinks and light fare.

In late August, the temple holds a **festival** to the god Ganesh that lasts nearly two weeks, which includes visiting performers from India and a parade through Flushing.

Leaving the temple, you should turn right on Holly Ave, then right again on Kissena Blvd, which will eventually bring you back to Main St.

Places to Eat
Many of Queens' international dining options are covered in the Ethnic Neighborhood Tour sidebar, earlier in this chapter.

Astoria You can have a cheap dinner at the 24 hour *Uncle George's* (☎ (718) 626-0593), 33-19 Broadway, which serves daily specials of barbecue pork and potatoes for $8 and red snapper for $12. The taste of the restaurant's *tzatziki*, the Greek dip made of yogurt, garlic and cucumber, will last in your mouth for hours. Just across the street is the smokey and sleek patisserie *Omonia* (☎ (718) 274-6650), 32-20 Broadway, where it's possible to linger over an espresso, close your eyes and hear nothing but Greek spoken around you.

Flushing It's hard to offer a comprehensive list of the best of Flushing's many restaurants, but *Joe's Shanghai* (☎ (718) 539-3838), 136-21 37th Ave, is known throughout the city for its steaming bowls of handmade dumplings and noodle dishes. *Sam Won Garden* (☎ (718) 321-0101), 136-17 38th Ave, across from the municipal parking lot, is open 24 hours and offers a menu of sushi and Korean barbecue. Two people can feast there for about $30.

STATEN ISLAND
Residents of the 'forgotten borough' of Staten Island have long entertained thoughts of succession from greater New York City. Its tiny population of 378,977 – largely white, middle class and

politically Republican – has historically had little clout in predominately Democratic New York City. Most politicians have made little secret of their disdain for this suburban tract of land close to the New Jersey shoreline – in fact, former Mayor David Dinkins made his very first trip to Staten Island when campaigning for office in 1989. What's worse, the borough is home to the city's largest garbage dump – a fact snickered about in Manhattan and deeply resented on Staten Island. (The dump is scheduled to be closed permanently by 2001.) The borough's image is not helped by the gray, dirty and unimpressive waterfront near the ferry terminal.

Staten Island grew when railway magnate Cornelius Vanderbilt established a ferry service between it and the port of New York in the early years of the 19th century. The island retained its character for verdant farmlands and large estates for the rich, and there was little development there until the 1960s, after the construction of the Verrazano Narrows Bridge finally forged a land link with the rest of New York City. Even still, most New Yorkers know the borough as the place to turn around after a pleasantly breezy ferry ride when the weather turns hellish in the summer, or simply as the starting point of the New York City Marathon. Of course, there's more to Staten Island that just that, and it's worth a day trip.

The Staten Island Chamber of Commerce (☎ (718) 727-1900) provides information on cultural events and attractions Monday to Friday from 9 am to 5 pm. The *Staten Island Advance* covers local news and events.

Eighteen bus routes converge on the St George Ferry Terminal in Staten Island; you can pick up buses from there to all the major sites. The buses leave within minutes of the ferry's arrival.

Staten Island Ferry
The ferry (☎ (212) 806-6940) is one of New York's enduring bargains, taking 70,000 passengers each day on the free 20

minute, six mile journey from Lower Manhattan (subway: South Ferry) to Staten Island (the return trip is 50¢). It operates on the half hour 24 hours a day, and only the most brutal weather keeps ferries in their slips. (Ferries carrying cars operate from early morning until 9:30 pm and charge $3 per vehicle)

This is the low-cost, hassle-free alternative to the crowded boat trips to the Statue of Liberty and Ellis Island. You'll pass within a half mile of both on the way out to Staten Island, and the view back at Manhattan and Brooklyn Heights is breathtaking. It's best to pack a lunch or snack before heading out to the ferry, since the food on the boat itself is dreadful and the South Ferry terminal, an outdated facility slated for replacement within a few years, doesn't have a decent restaurant. (See Places to Eat for restaurants clustered around the island's ferry terminal.)

Snug Harbor Cultural Center
The Snug Harbor Cultural Center (☎ (718) 448-2500), 1000 Richmond Terrace, is on the site of a retirement complex for about 1000 sailors built between 1831 and 1917. The group of five buildings just inside the north gate are some of the finest small scale Greek Revival structures left in the US. The Great Hall and the Veterans Memorial Chapel nearby have impressive interiors.

In 1976, the city took control of the rundown 83 acre site, which overlooks the oil tankers and container ships docking in New Jersey, and restored it as a complex for the borough's cultural institutions. You can easily spend a day exploring the **Botanical Garden** (☎ (718) 273-8200), the **Children's Museum** (☎ (718) 273-2060) and the **Newhouse Center for Contemporary Art** (no phone), open Wednesday to Sunday from noon to 5 pm. A free tour of the 28 landmark buildings on the site leaves from the visitors center every Saturday and Sunday at 2 pm.

You can get to the Snug Harbor Cultural Center by taking the S40 bus two miles west from the ferry terminal.

Jacques Marchais
Center of Tibetan Art

Home to the largest collection of Tibetan art outside of China, the Jacques Marchais Center (☎ (718) 987-3478), 338 Lighthouse Ave, was built by art dealer Edna Koblentz, who collected the works under an alias that did not betray her gender. It opened to the public in 1947, a year before her death, and includes a number of golden sculptures and religious objects made of human bone. Just about the only authentic thing missing from the home, built in the style of a Tibetan temple, is the smell of yak butter. The museum holds its annual weekend-long Tibetan cultural festival in the early part of October in the outdoor garden amongst the stone Buddhas.

There's a bonus in store for those who make the trek out to the museum: just across Lighthouse Ave from the museum, you can get a glimpse of the only private home designed by **Frank Lloyd Wright** ever built in New York City. It's the low-slung, cliff-side residence at 48 Manor Court, constructed in 1959.

The Marchais Center is open Wednesday to Sunday from 1 to 5 pm, with concerts and demonstrations each Sunday at 2 pm. Admission for adults/ children/seniors is $3/1/2.50.

You can get to the Marchais Center by taking the S74 bus along Richmond Rd for 25 minutes and asking the driver to let you off at Lighthouse Ave. The museum is located at the top of a hill.

Historic Richmond Town

The village of Richmond (☎ (718) 351-1611) was once the county seat of Staten Island, and 11 original buildings still stand in what is now a borough preservation project, including the 300 year old redwood **Voorlezer's House**, which is believed to be the oldest surviving school building in the country. In the 1960s, 11 other historic structures from around the island were moved here in an ambitious attempt to protect local history.

Historic Richmond Town is best seen in warm weather, when you can enjoy the surrounding landscape along Richmond Creek. During the summer season, volunteers dressed in period garb roam around the grounds ready to explain the ways of 17th century rural colonial life.

You can begin an exploration of the 100 acre site at the village courthouse, which serves as a visitors center. Every hour, a guide embarks from there on key tours of the 15 buildings open to the public. There's also a historical museum in the former country clerk's office.

Historic Richmond Town is open during the summer months Wednesday to Friday from 11 am to 5 pm and Saturday and Sunday from 1 to 5 pm. From September to June it's open Wednesday to Sunday from 1 to 5 pm; Admission is $4/2.50. You can reach the center by taking the S74 bus from the ferry to Richmond Ave and St Patrick's Place, a journey of about 35 minutes.

Greenbelt Nature Walks

The 2500 acre Greenbelt environmental preserve (☎ (718) 667-2165) in the middle of Staten Island encompasses several parks with five different ecosystems, including swamp areas and freshwater wetlands. It's one of New York City's unexplored nature treasures, offering some spectacular walks not far from the bustle of downtown Manhattan. Casual walkers and aggressive hikers are served by its 28 miles of trails. Birdwatchers should also head to the Greenbelt to track its 60 different species of birds.

The **High Rock Park** section of the Greenbelt offers six trails through hardwood forest and three gardens. You can get there by taking the S74 bus from the ferry to Rockland Ave, walking up Rockland and bearing right at Nevada Ave to the park entrance.

The **William T Davis Wildlife Refuge** once housed the wells that gave Staten Islanders their drinking water; today it is a sanctuary for migrating birds and the site of the Greenbelt Native Plant Center. You can reach the refuge walking trails by taking the S62 or S92 buses from the ferry along Victory Blvd to Travis Ave.

Places to Eat

There are a cluster of cheap restaurants near the ferry terminal. The *Sidestreet Saloon* (☎ (718) 448-6868), 11 Schuyler St, just a few minutes' walk from the ferry, is a popular lunch spot for workers from the borough court house across the street. The *Cargo Cafe* (☎ (718) 876-0539), at the corner of Slossen Terrace and Bay St three blocks east of the ferry terminal, has lunch specials like fish & chips for $4.25.

La Caleta (☎ (718) 447-0397), 75 Bay St, has Spanish seafood specials and

chicken dishes for $8 and under. Nearby, the *Clipper* (☎ (718) 273-5100), 38 Bay St, is a diner open from 6 am to midnight daily (open until 3 am Friday and Saturday), with most dishes under $10. *Gilly's Luncheonette* (☎ (718) 448-0579), located at 9 Hyatt St immediately behind Staten Island Borough Hall, has sandwiches for $4 and under.

RH Tug's (☎ (718) 447-6369), 1115 Richmond Terrace, is a nice spot for waterfront al fresco lunching just three minutes west of the Snug Harbor Cultural Center. Sandwiches run about $8.

Long Island

Long Island (population 2,609,212 in Nassau and Suffolk Counties), as the name implies, is the largest island in the US, 120 miles from end to end. It is a study in stark geographic and economic contrasts, beginning with crowded Brooklyn (Kings County) and Queens (Queens County) on the western shore. (For coverage of Brooklyn and Queens see the Outer Boroughs section of the New York City chapter.) The island then gives way to the suburban housing and strip malls in neighboring Nassau County.

The terrain becomes flatter and less crowded in rural Suffolk County, which comprises the eastern end of the island. Suffolk County itself contains two peninsulas – commonly called the north and south 'forks' – divided by Peconic Bay.

The island was first a series of whaling and fishing ports, as well as the exclusive outpost for the ultra-rich, who built estates along the secluded coves on the north shore. In the years following WWII, Nassau County became increasingly more populated, as thousands of middle-class families moved to the suburbs. One prime location was Levittown, built in 1947 in the center of Nassau County. It features thousands of look-alike, low-cost homes in huge tracts near major highways and railway lines leading into Manhattan. Named after the Levit & Sons company that developed it, the town attracted 55,000 residents became the model for hundreds of similar suburban communities across the US.

In Suffolk County, economic development patterns were geographically reversed. The North Fork is home to salaried workers and owners of small farms, while the South Fork is dominated by several villages (Hampton Bays, Southampton, Bridgehampton, East Hampton and Amagansett) known collectively as the Hamptons. It's the place where actors, writers and enter-

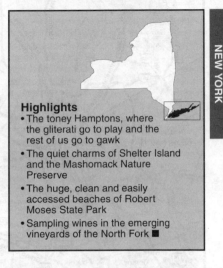

Highlights
- The toney Hamptons, where the gliterati go to play and the rest of us go to gawk
- The quiet charms of Shelter Island and the Mashomack Nature Preserve
- The huge, clean and easily accessed beaches of Robert Moses State Park
- Sampling wines in the emerging vineyards of the North Fork ■

tainment executives gather to schmooze away the summer season on private estates and in expensive restaurants.

For most visitors, a trip to Long Island means a trip to the beach, whether the destination is crowded Jones Beach, quiet Shelter Island or the more showy Hamptons enclaves. All are within easy reach via public transportation, which is the best option for summer weekends, when traffic jams are particularly hellish. However, if you're interested in exploring Long Island's historic mansions, or sampling wine in the vineyards of the North Fork, it's best to have a car.

ORIENTATION & INFORMATION
The Long Island Expressway (LIE, I-495) cuts through the center of the island, and ends by joining two smaller roads. The older Route 25 (also known as the Jericho Turnpike) runs roughly parallel to I-495, then continues to the end of the North Fork at Orient Point. Route 27 (also

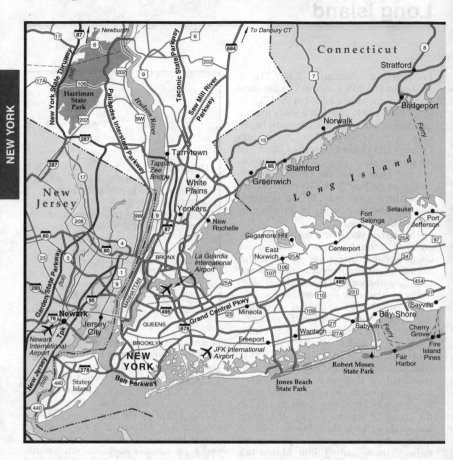

known as the Sunrise Highway) runs along the bottom of Long Island from the Brooklyn border and eventually becomes the Montauk Highway, and ends up at the end of the South Fork at Montauk Point. A trip to the end of Long Island takes at least three hours, but on weekends, traffic jams can turn it into a five hour ordeal.

Maps & Guidebooks The Streetwise series of pocket-sized maps are detailed and available at most major New York City bookstores. There's a very good one charting the major Long Island roads and rail network, as

well as having detailed maps of specific towns. Maps and local guidebooks are available at the well-stocked Bookhampton shops. There's one at 93 Main St in Southampton (☎ (516) 283-0270) and another at 20 Main St in East Hampton (☎ (516) 324-4939).

Tourist Offices The Long Island Convention and Visitors Bureau (☎ (800) 441-4601) publishes an annual free travel guide. You can obtain maps, restaurant listings and lodging guides from the local chambers of commerce by calling:

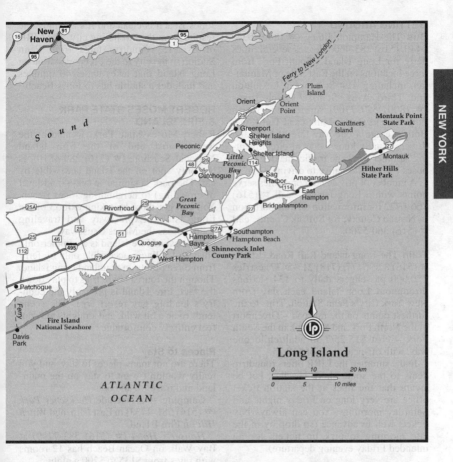

NEW YORK

| | Sound | | | | |

New Haven · 91 · 95 · 1

15 · 95 · 95A

S o u n d

ATLANTIC
OCEAN

Long Island

Orient
Plum Island
Orient Point
Gardiners Island
Montauk Point State Park
Greenport
Shelter Island Heights
Shelter Island
Peconic
Little Peconic Bay
Sag Harbor
Amagansett
Montauk
Hither Hills State Park
Cutchogue
East Hampton
Great Peconic Bay
Riverhead
Bridgehampton
Quogue
Hampton Bays
Southampton
Hampton Beach
Shinnecock Inlet County Park
West Hampton
Patchogue
Fire Island National Seashore
Davis Park

0   10   20 km
0   5   10 miles

Southampton	(516) 283-0402
East Hampton	(516) 324-0362
Shelter Island	(516) 749-0399
Montauk	(516) 668-2428
Greenport-Southold	(516) 477-1383

ACTIVITIES

It's possible to bike along Route 25 on the North Fork, and along the side roads in the Hamptons, especially along the seven mile Route 114 (the Sag Harbor Turnpike) from East Hampton to Sag Harbor.

There are excellent opportunities for guided walks in the Sunken Forest, located in the middle of the **Fire Island National**

Seashore (☎ (516) 597-6183). You can also enjoy strolls in the Mashomack Nature Preserve on **Shelter Island**. Off-season, it's possible to embark on long, uninterrupted walks along the shoreline from East Hampton to Montauk.

Surfers head to the Georgica Jetties, Montauk and Shinnecock Inlet. Directions and information on conditions can be obtained in season by calling ☎ (516) 283-SURF/7873.

Two hour kayak explorations of Peconic Bay are offered by Shelter Island Kayak Tours (☎ (516) 749-1990) for $45 per person.

GETTING AROUND

Bus The Hampton Jitney (☎ (800) 936-0440, (516) 283-4600) leaves several times daily for Long Island's South Fork from three locations on the East Side of Manhattan, including 41st St between Lexington and Third Aves. Sunrise Coach Lines (☎ (800) 527-7709) services the North Fork from its stop at 44th St and Third Ave. Both average a one-way fare of $15, and drivers usually know ways of circumventing summer weekend traffic, making these buses a good alternative to driving a car.

A number of private bus companies serve points within Long Island – call ☎ (516) 766-6722 for information on transportation in Nassau County; for Suffolk County, call ☎ (516) 360-5700.

Train The Long Island Rail Road (LIRR, ☎ (516) 822-5477, (718) 217-5477) carries 250,000 passengers daily to 134 stations throughout Long Island each day from New York City's Penn Station. Trips to the furthest points on the railroad – Greenport in the North Fork and Montauk in the South Fork – cost $15.25/7.50 adult/child one way, with off-peak rates of $10.25.

In the summer, the LIRR offers roundtrip deals to the south shore beaches, but be aware that the lines at the station ticket office are very long on Friday nights and Saturday mornings. You can always buy tickets well in advance (so drop by in the late morning to pick up tickets for an intended Friday evening departure).

JONES BEACH

Jones Beach (☎ (516) 785-1600) is without a doubt the *least* exclusive beach area on Long Island. Tens of thousands of people converge on its six mile stretch of ocean, and there's parking for nearly 25,000 cars in its lots. The boardwalk concessions and miniature golf course are often overrun with people on summer weekends, though in true New York style, entrepreneurs roam the beach (illegally) selling ice cream, soda and beer to thirsty sunbathers.

Though it's always mobbed, the sand at Jones Beach is clean and it's an enjoyable respite from the sweltering city. The LIRR offers $15 roundtrip fares from Penn Station in the city to the Freeport station on Long Island that takes under 40 minutes and includes a shuttle bus to Jones Beach.

ROBERT MOSES STATE PARK & FIRE ISLAND

Robert Moses State Park, located at the westernmost end of the Fire Island National Seashore (☎ (516) 289-4810), is the only spot on the island accessible by car. The park is similar in scale (and level of crowding) to neighboring Jones Beach. You can get there by taking exit 53 of the Long Island Expressway and traveling south across the Moses Causeway.

The rest of Fire Island is a summer-only cluster of villages accessible only by ferry from three points on mainland Long Island. Though the tourist board tries to play down the fact, Fire Island is probably the country's leading gay resort area. The scene tends to be a bit wild, and straights may not feel entirely comfortable.

Places to Stay

There are not many places to stay, and you really wouldn't want to stay on the mainland and travel in and out.

Camping spots include *Heckscher Park* (☎ (516) 581-4433) in East Islip, and *Watch Hill* on Fire Island.

Houser's Hotel (☎ (516) 583-7799) at Bay Walk on Ocean Beach has 12 rooms with rates from $135 to $200 a night.

The *Ocean Beach Hotel* (☎ (516) 583-9292) is a 21 unit facility open from May to September charging $65 to $185 per room.

Getting There & Away

The three ferry terminals are all close to the Bayshore, Sayville and Patchogue (pronounced PATCH-oag) LIRR stations. The ferry season runs from early May to November; trips take about 20 minutes and cost an average of $10/5 adults/kids roundtrip, with discount season passes available:

Fire Island Ferries (☎ (516) 665-3600) sail from Bayshore to Saltaire, Fair Harbor and Ocean Beach.

Sayville Ferry Service (☎ (516) 589-8980) runs from Sayville to Cherry Grove and the Pines.

Davis Park Ferry Company (☎ (516) 475-1665) travels from Patchogue to Davis Park and Watch Hill.

THE HAMPTONS

Prominent artists, musicians and writers have long been attracted to the beautiful beaches and rustic Cape Cod-style homes in the Hamptons, but the easy-money '80s brought an influx of showier summertime visitors who made their fortunes in the fashion industry and on Wall Street. In recent years, the Hamptons have become truly 'hot,' as West Coast entertainment moguls purchased large homes here, following in the footsteps of Steven Spielberg. Year-round residents seem annoyed and amused by the show in equal measures.

If you're celebrity obsessed, you're better off heading to the Hamptons instead of standing in line at Planet Hollywood in New York City. On Saturday morning you actually stand a very good chance of spotting Uma Thurman or Robert De Niro shopping at East Hampton's popular Red Horse Market.

Many of the attractions, restaurants and hotels in the Hamptons close the last week in October and remain shut until late April. B&B prices drop – and traffic jams along the Montauk Highway disappear – about two weeks after Labor Day.

Southampton

Southampton village doesn't have half the flash of its neighbors to the east, but it's a pleasant place to spend an afternoon in search of history and art. You can get maps and brochures about the town at the Chamber of Commerce office at 76 Main St, located among a group of high-priced craft shops and decent restaurants.

Just a few steps away from the tourist office is the **Halsey Homestead**, a saltbox house built in 1648, just eight years after the first European settlers arrived in the area. It's open to the public from June to September Tuesday to Saturday from 11 am to 4:30 pm and Sunday from 2 to 4:30 pm.

The **Parrish Art Museum** (☎ (516) 283-2111), 25 Jobs Lane, is just a short walk away from Main St. It has been open to the public since 1898, and its gallery features the work of major artists – a recent exhibition was dedicated to Roy Lichtenstein, who lives nearby. The museum is open Wednesday to Saturday from 11 am to 5 pm and Sunday from 1 to 5 pm. In the winter the museum is closed on Tuesday and Wednesday. Suggested admission is $3.

Sag Harbor

Sag Harbor, seven miles north from Bridgehampton on Route 27, is an old whaling town on Peconic Bay that's far less beach-oriented than the other Hampton towns. Its **Whaling Museum** (☎ (516) 725-0770) is just west of the shops on its Main St, and celebrates this history. It's open from May to October Monday to Saturday from 10 am to 5 pm and Sunday from 1 pm to 5 pm; admission is $3/1.

Sag Harbor's *American Hotel* (☎ (516) 725-3535), on Main St, has only eight rooms starting at $150 a night, but the ground floor restaurant and bar is a hangout for such weekending worthies as ABC newsman Peter Jennings.

East Hampton & Amagansett

The heart of trendy Long Island is East Hampton, where you can shop at the Coach leather store, catch readings and art exhibitions at the **Guild Hall** (☎ (516) 324-0806) and dine at the *Maidstone Arms* (☎ (516) 324-5006), 207 Main St, the most elegant and expensive restaurant in town.

Driving or biking down Main Beach along Ocean Ave will afford glimpses of the larger saltbox estates with water views. You can see some other grand (private) houses by turning right at **Lilly Pond Lane** and peeking through the breaks in the high shrubbery.

Amagansett is basically an extension of

East Hampton distinguished by the huge flagpole in the center of the Montauk Highway. The *Stephen Talkhouse* (☎ (516) 267-3117), 161 Main St, is a 20 year old concert venue (Elvis Costello has appeared here) that has an active bar scene on non-performance nights.

Montauk

Montauk is a long, flat 13 mile drive away from Amagansett along Route 27. If you're a biker looking for a challenge, peel off to the right and take the **Old Montauk Highway**, an undulating road overlooking the ocean that passes by several resorts, including the 175 room *Gurney's Inn* (☎ (516) 668-3203), a spa with rates starting at $260.

Montauk itself is more honky-tonk than the rest of the Hamptons, with more reasonable restaurants and a rougher bar scene. The LIRR train terminus is a long 10 minute walk to the center of town. **Montauk Downs State Park** (☎ (516) 668-3781), has a fine public golf course that charges $20 per person for a round; there are long waits for tee times in the summer.

If you drive out to **Montauk Point State Park**, stop in the scenic overlook and avoid the parking lot at the very end, which charges for a view that's not really worth the money, unless you intend to visit the unimpressive **Montauk Lighthouse Museum** for an additional fee of $2/1.

Places to Stay

There's camping at *Hither Hills State Park* (☎ (516) 668-2461).

In the Hamptons, there's virtually no price difference between places calling themselves B&Bs and smaller inns – most have rates well over $100 in high season.

The recently renovated *Mill House Inn* (☎ (516) 324-9766), 33 N Main St, East Hampton, run by Dan and Katherine Hartnett, has eight themed rooms starting at $100 a night off season and $185 in summer.

The Fariel family has run the *Sea Breeze Inn* (☎ (516) 267-3159) in Amagansett since 1957. It's located just a block away

from the LIRR station, and its 12 rooms are all clean (some with shared bath). Rates are $60 to $140, with weekly discounts available. Owner Rob Fariel hangs out with guests in the 1st floor bar and can proffer flawless advice on where to eat and what to see in the area.

The motels in more isolated Montauk run a bit cheaper during the summer – about $125 a night – but many are booked solid on a monthly basis by groups of students employed at the resorts and restaurants.

Places to Eat

It's easier to find reasonably priced places to eat than reasonably priced lodging, though that is not saying much in the Hamptons.

Budget There are a few cheap seafood stands on Route 27 near Napeague Beach (between Amagansett and Montauk) that serve fish sandwiches, fresh steamers and fried clams for $10 and under during the summer months. The most popular are the *Lobster Roll* (☎ (516) 267-3740), with its distinctive 'Lunch' sign, the *Clam Bar*, which also does a brisk business selling T-shirts to its BMW and Mercedes-driving clientele, and *Cyril's*, a restaurant presided over by an ex-Marine with a handlebar mustache, which serves an excellent sesame shrimp meal. In Montauk, the *Shagwong Restaurant* (☎ (516) 668-3050) on Main St serves good tavern-style meals year round.

Top End The *Laundry* (☎ (516) 324-3199), 31 Race Lane one block from the East Hampton train, was among the first celebrity-spotting restaurants to open in the Hamptons. There's less attitude here than in other places, and the food – generally fresh-fish entrees in the $18 range – is actually quite good.

SHELTER ISLAND

Nearly a third of quiet Shelter Island's land mass is dedicated to the **Mashomack Nature Preserve**, and there's an attractive town center in Shelter Island Heights, a cluster of Victorian buildings on the north side of the island. It's a perfect place to explore nature and a true respite from the crowds in the Hamptons.

There's bicycle rental on the island; see Bicycling in North Fork, below.

Places to Stay & Eat
Local B&Bs include the *Azalea House* (☎ (516) 749-4252), 1 Thomas Ave, which has five rooms with rates from $50 to $125. *Shelter Island B&B* (☎ (516) 749-0842), 7 St Mary's Rd, has four rooms (two with a private entrance) for $60 on weekends.

You can get very good off-season rates at the *Ram's Head Inn* (☎ (516) 749-0811), a large, columned place overlooking the water on Ram Island Dr on Shelter Island. It charges $70 for a private bath in midweek off peak; during the summer rates jump to $125 or more a room.

The dining choices on Shelter Island are very seasonal. The *Dory* (☎ (516) 749-8871), near the Shelter Island Heights Bridge, is a smoky bar that serves simple fare on a waterfront patio. *Shelter Island Pizza* (☎ (516) 749-0400), on Route 114, is just about the only place open every day year round.

Getting There & Away
The North Ferry Company (☎ (516) 749-0139) runs boats every 15 minutes from the North Fork terminal (near the LIRR station in Greenport) to Shelter Island from 6 am to 11:45 pm; a car and driver costs $6.50, additional passengers $1. The trip takes seven minutes.

South Ferry Inc (☎ (516) 749-1200) leaves from a dock three miles north from Sag Harbor from 6 am to 1:45 am; a car and driver is $7, passengers $1.

NORTH FORK
Greenport is the main town in the North Fork, where you can catch a ferry to/from Shelter Island. There's not a lot of social life here – the town held a big parade to celebrate the opening of a children's carousel – but it's a friendly place with cheaper lodging and food options than the South Fork villages.

The people in Greenport live there year round, and many are farmers or employees of the local Grumman aerospace company, one of the region's biggest employers (though layoffs have rocked the town recently).

Efforts to revive the slumping farming and manufacturing economy in the North Fork led to the establishment of several vineyards during the '80s. Now, Greenport is the perfect base to begin an exploration of the area wineries.

Wineries Tour
Today there are 16 vineyards in eastern Long Island, all but three of them located in the North Fork near Route 25. Just look for the distinctive green 'wine trail' road signs that crop up past Riverhead; nine of the vineyards are clustered within two miles of the town of Cutchogue (pronounced KUTCH-oag).

You can get more information on touring the wine trail by contacting the Long Island Wine Council at ☎ (516) 475-5492. Be aware that the vineyards get very crowded during summer weekends and most vineyards are open weekends only during the winter. In season, try to visit during the week – and have a hearty breakfast before quaffing a lot of wine, since you'll have to drive from one place to another.

Long Island seems to have perfected the art of making white wine, but its reds still need a bit of work. Judge for yourself by visiting a few – the wine makers are more than happy to pour out a few free glasses of their product. The largest facility is **Pindar Vineyards** (☎ (516) 734-6200) in Peconic, which offers frequent tours of the 250 acres of vines daily from 11 am to 6 pm. They also have evening wine festivals several times a year where light food is served for a small charge.

Both **Peconic Bay Vineyards** (☎ (516) 734-7361), which has a an array of tasty dry Chardonnays and dessert wines, and **Bedell Cellars** (☎ (516) 734-7537), a leader in the quest for a great Long Island red, also offer daily tastings.

Orient Point

The Cross Sound Ferry Company (☎ (516) 323-2525) takes passengers and autos from Orient Point, at the tip of the North Fork, to New London, CT; reservations are recommended. Autos cost $28, passengers $13 one way. The company also offers an auto-free hydrofoil shuttle from the terminal to the Foxwoods Casino and Resort in Connecticut.

Before you depart the area, however, make it a point to visit the tiny hamlet of **Orient**, about three miles in from the ferry terminal; follow the signs for the 'Orient Business District' at the Civil War monument at the side of Route 25. There's not much of a business district in this tiny 17th century hamlet, just an old wooden post office and a general store. But Orient is a remarkably well-preserved collection of white clapboard houses and former inns. It's everything a colonial town is supposed to be – quiet, manageable and very pretty. Further out of town, you can bike past the Oyster Ponds just east of Main St and also check out the beach at Orient Beach State Park.

Bicycling

The Greenport bike shop does not rent bikes and directs people to a campground several miles out of town. Visitors on foot should instead take the ferry to Shelter Island ($1) and walk toward the Shelter Island Heights Bridge to Piccozzi's Bike Shop (☎ (516) 749-0045) on Bridge St (about a five minute walk – call ahead in the summer to reserve). Bikes

can be rented for $18 a day, and are sturdy enough for a strenuous trek across Shelter Island or back to Greenport for a 20 mile exploration of the North Fork and Orient Point.

Places to Stay & Eat

The best place to stay in Greenport is the *White Lions Inn* (☎ (516) 477-8819), 433 Main St. This large old home has five rooms (two with shared baths), and is just a four block walk from the Shelter Island ferry dock and LIRR train station. Owner Pat Kulsziski is an enthusiastic host eager to have her guests try out her newest breakfast concoction. Rates are $65 to $110, with free parking at the back of the house.

The *Seafood Barge* (☎ (516) 765-3010), on Route 25 three miles from Greenport, is one of the best places in the area to taste the sweet Peconic Bay scallops, a local specialty that was devastated by brown tide in 1994. The restaurant, which overlooks the Port of Egypt Marina, charges $18 for dinner entrees, and offers a selection of lunch specials for $8.95.

In Greenport, restaurants are clustered around the marina. *Claudio's* (☎ (516) 477-0715), across from the ferry dock, is a landmark that gets quite noisy at the long wooden bar, but the food is considered to be expensive and mediocre by locals. A better option is *Aldo's* (☎ (516) 477-1699), 103-105 Front St, which is also expensive ($19 entrees like lamb loin), but serves sublime desserts and biscotti made in the small bakery next to the restaurant. Reservations are required on weekends.

Hudson Valley

Whether from the blurry view of an Amtrak train window or a considered examination from a Hudson River tour boat, it's easy to imagine a New York of another era, when New York City itself was – by today's measure – a relatively small port at the mouth of the Hudson River, dotted with tall buildings, some even reaching four or five stories. In fact, history is a major attraction along the Hudson's banks. Stone fences and Victorian cottages, along with the opulent and extravagant historic mansions, are rather common here.

Today New Yorkers who live in the upstate region closest to the Big Apple still boast of their active but bucolic environment. Small towns dot the river, river traffic is abundant and dairy farms, roadside produce stands and dirt roads adorn the landscape. This is the same landscape, by the way, that is captured in the luminous paintings by the famous artists of the Hudson River school and is on view in galleries from New York City to Albany (including the Olana mansion, near Hudson, and the art gallery at Vassar College in Poughkeepsie).

Pick-your-own farms, horseback-riding stables, hiking and biking trails and canoeing trails compliment the valley's historic landmarks, which range from Washington Irving's 19th century Sleepy Hollow haunts near Tarrytown to President Franklin and Eleanor Roosevelts' home, library and cottage in Hyde Park.

HISTORY

In 1609, Henry Hudson, sailing for the Dutch East India Company, sailed up a river known to the Indians of the upper Hudson as Muhheakunnuk ('great waters in motion') in search of a northern passage to the Pacific. Hudson's ship, *Half Moon*, got as far as present-day Albany. (Two years later, in the Canadian bay that bears his name, he was set adrift with eight others by his own crew and never seen again).

Highlights
- Washington Irving's cottage Sunnyside, south of Tarrytown
- Val-Kill, Eleanor Roosevelt's humble home near Hyde Park
- Olana, the Persianesque mansion of Hudson River school painter Frederick Church
- The Storm King Art Center, an outstanding outdoor sculpture park between Newburgh and West Point
- Pick-your-own apple orchards and berry farms in the Mid-Hudson Valley ■

The Native Americans that Hudson and subsequent Europeans encountered were Algonquian (Mohican) and the more powerful Iroquois, who controlled much of the fur trade that the Dutch, English and French all sought to profit from. The Iroquois, or Six Nations, Confederacy remained intact until the American Revolution.

During the Revolutionary War, General George Washington made his headquarters at Newburgh on the west bank of the river. In 1802, the US Military Academy – better known as West Point for its position on the river – was established a few miles below Newburgh. The river's strategic value soon turned commercial, and it contributed to the prosperous early days of the nation. When the Erie Canal was completed in 1825 between Albany and Buffalo, New York essentially became the port for the farms and factories of the nation's Midwest.

When Washington Irving moved to

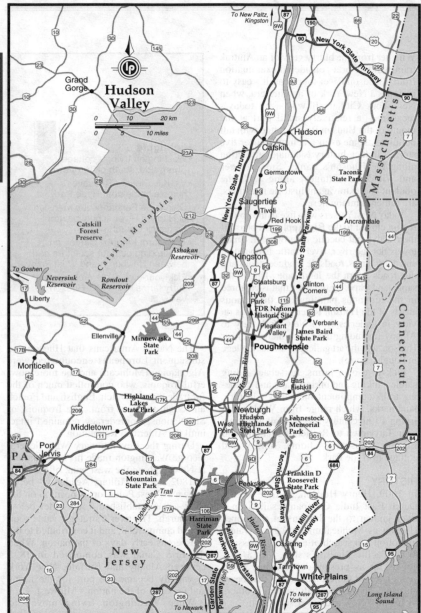

Sunnyside just south of Tarrytown, it was to combine the watery solitude of this Sleepy Hollow by the river with proximity to the bustling metropolis of New York City. Many residents of the valley today try to achieve the same balance. Many also have suffered some of the same disappointments: 10 years after building Sunnyside on a serene hillside, the railroad came up the river and would not be stopped even by America's most famous author. Irving cursed the coal-burning steam engine as it passed his home, shaking the ground. He made a compromise of sorts by finally using the train to venture into New York City.

ORIENTATION
The Hudson Valley generally refers to the area south of Albany that follows the Hudson River and lies between the Catskill Mountains to the west and the Taconic highlands and the Connecticut state border to the east. The river itself begins in the Adirondacks at Lake Tear-of-the-Cloud and flows south (over 300 miles) to New York Bay, where it forms an estuary so large that Dutch navigator Henry Hudson mistook the river for the object of his 17th century search: the northwest passage across the continent to the far east. The spot where the river begins and the inlet ends changes with the tides.

The Hudson Valley is often divided into the Lower, Mid and Upper sections of the valley; the bridges that cross the river help define each area to some degree.

Heading north from New York City, the Lower Hudson Valley stretches north and west from the Tappan Zee Bridge, connecting Nyack and Tarrytown to Cold Spring just below the Newburgh-Beacon Bridge. It also takes in West Point, Newburgh and Goshen.

The Mid Hudson Valley extends from the Newburgh-Beacon Bridge (and I-84), north to the area east of the Kingston-Rhinecliff Bridge, and includes Rhinebeck, Red Hook and Tivoli.

The Upper Hudson Valley extends roughly from the area east of the Kingston-

Rhinecliff Bridge, north to the area between Hudson and New Lebanon.

Communities along this stretch of the west bank of the Hudson, including the town of Kingston, will be found in New York's Catskills chapter. Below the Catskills, the area west of the Hudson River is included here, beginning in Nyack and extending north to Newburgh.

Note Just over New York's eastern border are Connecticut's Litchfield Hills, and further north are Massachusetts' Berkshire Hills. These are very popular tourist destinations, especially in the summer, when outdoor activities and festivals abound. The area is dotted with inns and B&Bs, and all of it is detailed in Lonely Planet's *New England – a travel survival kit*. However, most of the same variety of attractions and scenery can be found in New York in the Mid- and Upper Hudson Valley with fewer tourists to compete for space.

INFORMATION
Post offices, hospitals and banks or ATMs are easily found and widely available throughout the region, especially in the larger towns like Newburgh, Milbrook, Tarrytown and Poughkeepsie. Banks and post offices are quite obvious, usually on the main street; hospitals are seldom on the main street, but nearby.

Hudson Valley Tourism (☎ (800) 232-4782) has it's own free guide with information on regional special events. Or call for a free visitor's guide to Orange County (☎ (800) 762-8687), which includes West Point and the Storm King Art Center; Rockland County (☎ (800) 295-5723), which includes Harriman and Bear Mountain state parks; Westchester County (☎ (800) 833-9282), which includes Tarrytown and Peekskill.

There's a State Information Center at Harriman, exit 16 off I-87 (the New York State Thruway).

GETTING THERE & AROUND
If you fly or take the train into this region, be prepared to arrange for automobile

transportation to get around, especially in the smaller towns.

Air
The main airports in the region are La Guardia in New York City and the Albany airport to the north (see the Capital District & Mohawk Valley chapter). Newburgh's Stewart international airport is served by several carriers, including United Express, American, Delta, Midway and USAir.

Train
Amtrak (☎ (800) 872-7245) passenger trains run the length of the river and connect several of the communities along the eastern shore, from Penn Station in New York City north to Croton-on-Hudson, Poughkeepsie, Rhinecliff and Hudson.

Metro North (☎ (212) 532-4900, (800) 638-7646) runs frequent commuter trains from Grand Central Station in New York City on its Hudson Line, which stops at the Poughkeepsie terminal.

Car
To get around, a car is essential, especially to see the countryside and smallest towns.

Route 9, the principle scenic north-south road in the Hudson Valley, hugs the east side of the river for the most part; when it strays, Routes 9D near Cold Spring and 9G near Rhinebeck continue the scenic riverside drive. On the west side of the river it's Route 9W.

The area further east of the river is paralleled by the Taconic State Parkway, which connects the towns of Old Chatham, southeast of Albany, and East Fishkill, southeast of Poughkeepsie in Dutchess County. The Saw Mill River Parkway diagonally traverses the lower eastern valley from southwest to northeast. There it turns into I-684, which runs into I-84 as well as Route 22, an eastern north-south valley route straddling the Connecticut, Massachusetts and Vermont borders.

The Lower Hudson Valley further west of the river is traversed by east-west I-287, which runs into north-south I-87 (the New York State Thruway – often called the

'Northway'). I-87 continues north into the Catskills region. Also on the river's west side is the Palisades Interstate Parkway, which begins in Ft Lee, NJ, and runs north through Harriman State Park and ends at Route 9W in Bear Mountain State Park.

East-west routes include Routes 17 and 6 in the Lower Hudson Valley; I-84 in the Mid-Hudson and Routes 44, 199 and 308 in the Upper Hudson Valley.

Car Rental There are rental companies in towns like Poughkeepsie, but the best rates are from the larger towns with airports, in this case Albany, but not Newburgh, which is very expensive.

Bicycle
The country roads east of the Hudson River are perfect for biking. There are several well-traveled bike trails in the region and two in particular near Millbrook. A 39 mile tour connects the villages of Millbrook, Verbank, Pleasant Valley and Clinton Corners. A shorter 27 mile trip takes in Clinton Corners, Pleasant Valley and Schultzville.

For further information, find *Mountain Biking Destinations in the NY Metropolitan Area* by Joel Sendek (Urban Country Publications) or *25 Bicycle Tours in the Hudson Valley* by Peter Kick (Back Country Books).

LOWER HUDSON VALLEY: WEST OF THE RIVER
Nyack
Nyack sits on the west bank across the river from Tarrytown (see below) and the Tappan Zee Bridge. A ferry once connected both towns. Nyack has always been a sort of commuter village for New York City. It's still a pleasant place to walk, with several good eateries, shops and bookstores within a few blocks of the Main and Broadway intersection. Five times a year, the intersection is closed off to host a street fair.

Information The Nyack Chamber of Commerce (☎ (914) 353-2221), 92 Main St, near the corner of Cedar St, is in the Rock-

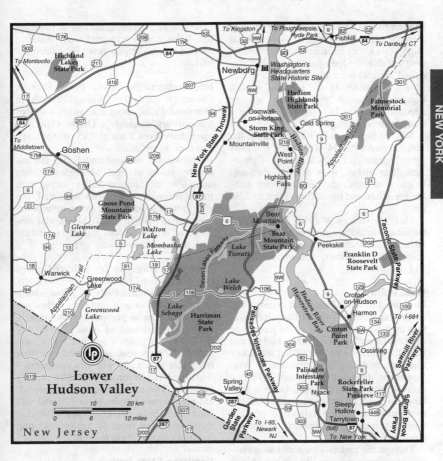

Lower
Hudson Valley

0   10   20 km

0   6   12 miles

New Jersey

land County Building and has walking tour maps of Nyack.

Bookstores include the Pickwick Bookshop (☎ (914) 358-9126), 8 Broadway, a browser's delight. There is a rumpled air to the place and a sprawling children's corner. You can easily lose track of time here, as the owner himself does. Official hours are daily from 10 am to 6 pm, but the store is often open later.

The Ben Franklin Bookshop (☎ (914) 358-0440), at 17 N Broadway, is another great place to browse, but the tidy opposite of nearby Pickwick's. There is a good selection of local history and literature, but the specialty is rare mystery and science fiction. Open daily from 11 am to 5:30 pm.

Places to Stay *Best Western Nyack* (☎ (914) 358-8100), 26 Route 59, is just off the I-87/I-287 New York State Thruway, at (northbound) exit 11. From town, it's at the top of Main St, walking distance to the main drag. Rooms are in the $70 to $80 range.

Super 8 Motel (☎ (914) 353-3880), 47 Main St (next door to McDonald's), is a bit cheaper with rooms from $50 to $60.

Places to Eat The *Runcible Spoon Bakery Cafe* (☎ (914) 358-9398), 37 Broadway at High St, is a very inviting place, roomy and comfortable. Open-faced sandwiches called 'Scans' are a big summer item and go for $3 to $5. In the fall and winter, homemade soups make their steamy appearance. Open daily from 7 am to 7 pm, until 5 pm on Sunday.

Next to Ben Franklin's Used Books, the *Vintage Deli* (☎ (914) 353-0609) is a low-priced diner serving authentic Cuban-American dishes, with chicken, rice and beans, pork stews and the like. Open daily for breakfast and lunch from 7 am to 2:30 pm.

Three Broadway (☎ (914) 358-2900), 3 Broadway near the corner of Main St, is an attractive and casual French-style bistro open daily for dinner, with entrees in the $11 to $16 range.

West Point

Dedicated to duty, honor and country, the castle-like turrets of the Military Reservation at West Point jut out of the landscape in irregular and imposing tiers, as if carved from the rocky shore. West Point was a key fortification during the Revolutionary War. Sometime between 1778 and 1780, a massive wrought-iron chain (with a log-boom to protect it) was stretched across the river to Constitution Island to prevent British ships from attempting to control river navigation.

Though the cadets – men and women – still live a strict military life, it's possible to visit and tour the sprawling complex at your own pace. You might even imagine the plight of a young Edgar Allen Poe, a cadet in 1830, who was dismissed for insubordination after only eight months of less than military endeavor.

The campus is impressive. Miles of pathways criss-cross a grand preserve of red brick and gray stone Gothic and Federal-style campus buildings, churches and temples, stadiums, a boat landing and panoramic views of the Hudson River. If at first you didn't know this was a military establishment, the landscaping might

offer a clue; anything hinting at disorder has been neatly trimmed. Just walking around can make you yearn for a needless haircut.

Information The West Point Visitors Center (☎ (914) 938-2638) is actually in Highland Falls, about 100 yards south of the military academy's Thayer Gate. It's open daily from 9 am to 4:45 pm for maps and tour information.

The village of Highland Falls, and the nearby town of Fort Montgomery, are unique to the Hudson Valley; rather than rustic colonial or renewed industrial, the atmosphere around West Point reflects the rather prim (shined shoes), blue-collar aesthetic of a professional military operation with a Midwestern touch.

Things to Buy The Toy Soldier Gallery (☎ (914) 446-6731, (800) 777-9904), 501 Main St, Highland Falls, is a fascinating store to browse and certainly helps put the entire area in perspective. A brightly colored assortment of mostly metal toy soldiers includes ancient Romans, modern Zulus and uniformed warriors from just about any war you can name – from the Civil War to several 20th century varieties. The toys are not cheap; individual pieces range from $5 to $20 and sets start at about $100. Open Tuesday through Friday from 10 am to 4:45 pm, Saturday from 10 am to 5 pm.

Harriman State Park

Harriman State Park is large (72 sq miles), close to New York City (40 miles) and a good place for a swim (three lakes with sandy beaches). Both Harriman and the adjacent Bear Mountain State Park (see below) lie between I-87 to the west and the Palisades Interstate Parkway to the east. I-287 runs south of the park system, and Route 6 marks the northern boundary, between the town of Harriman and the Bear Mountain Bridge, which crosses the Hudson River.

Both parks have several well-maintained hiking trails. The Appalachian Trail (see the Outdoor Activities chapter) also passes through both parks on its way from New Jersey to Connecticut. Admission to the parks is free, but parking is not; at Harriman beach parking is $5, other lots are $3.

Hiking and swimming are the most popular activities in Harriman. For free trail maps, visit the Harriman Park Visitor Center (☎ (914) 786-5003), open daily from mid-April to mid-October from 8 am to 6 pm, and to 5 pm during the winter.

The three lakes in Harriman are used for both boating and swimming. The good news for swimmers is that no gas motors are permitted; still, lots of rowboats plus a few electric motorboats are available for rent. Day parking is $5 at each lake.

Near the eastern edge of the park (exit 14 off the Palisade Parkway, near Willow Grove), **Lake Welch** has the only campground (see below) in either Harriman or Bear Mountain. Parking is included if you camp, but day-use parking is $5.

Lake Tiorati (☎ (914) 351-2568) is just below the Appalachian Trail and is another good spot for hiking, swimming, boating, picnicking and, in the winter, ice skating.

At **Lake Sebago** (☎ (914) 351-2583) there's a good swimming beach, hiking trails and row boats for rent, but only for those staying in the cabins (see below). Boats rent for $3 per hour.

Places to Stay Tent camping is at Lake Welch, and cabins are at Lake Sebago.

Lake Welch's *Beaver Pond Campground* (☎ (914) 947-2792) is open from mid-April to mid-October. Basic campsites are $13, and $14 gets you a 14 sq foot wooden platform with tent stakes. For reservations call the New York State Camp number (☎ (800) 456-2267).

Lake Sebago Cabins (☎ (914) 351-2360) are a great deal for families or groups of four to six. There are 38 rough cabins here, each with four cots (you can add two more for a fee). You must bring your own bedding and towels. The cabins are open from mid-April to mid-October, and the rates are $50 a night (two night minimum), or $200 for a week.

Bear Mountain State Park

Adjacent to the larger Harriman State Park, Bear Mountain State Park (☎ (914) 786-2701) borders the west bank of the Hudson and was once the designated spot for Sing Sing Prison until President Teddy Roosevelt intervened in 1910. The view from Bear Mountain peak (1305 feet) takes in the Manhattan skyline on a clear day, as well as the river and surrounding mountain greenery. Hiking, spring wildflower viewing, fall foliage viewing, pool swimming and fishing are the popular activities; in the winter, cross-country skiing, sledding and ice skating take over.

Bear Mountain is open year round, from 8 am until sunset. Admission to the park is free, but parking is $4.

The Bear Mountain **Trailside Museum & Zoo** (☎ (914) 786-2701) is across the road from the Bear Mountain Inn (see below) and has several exhibits on the geological and natural history of the area. The Appalachian Trail passes through the park here, along with the Bear Mountain Nature Trail. The zoo is a refuge of sorts for rescued and wayward animals of the region. Both the museum and zoo are open daily from 9 am to 4:30 pm, and admission is free.

The *Bear Mountain Inn* (☎ (914) 786-2731) is also in the park. (Campers must go to nearby Harriman State Park.) This mountain stone and timber inn has been around since the 1920s, and the giant stone fireplaces in the lobby area are worth a visit, even if you stay elsewhere. There are 15 rooms in the main building and four lodges down the road. Rooms (with one or two beds) are $90 on Friday and Saturday, $70 from Sunday through Thursday. The restaurant is open for dinner every night from about 5 to 9 pm.

Newburgh

Like its neighbors Poughkeepsie and Hudson, Newburgh was an important whaling village once upon a time. The small industrial city is mostly remembered these days as General George Washington's headquarters during the Revolutionary War.

Newburgh could serve as a textbook of American architecture from the Revolutionary War period to the present. Unfortunately, one chapter of the book would include the demise of such historical towns. The oldest of the town's remaining commercial and residential buildings are in disrepair, and the best views are looking east across the river. Nevertheless, there is distinct historic sense to Newburgh and nearby Downing Park is a good spot for a picnic by the pond.

Washington's Headquarters State Historic Site Washington's headquarters (☎ (914) 562-1195), 84 Liberty St, is the home of a small museum and **Hasbrouck House**, where Washington stayed in 1782-83 until the end of the war. The site features several galleries, period furniture and a 50 foot map that wraps around an entire room. Plan to spend about an hour here.

Both the museum and house are open from mid-April to late October, Wednesday through Saturday 10 am to 5 pm, and Sunday 1 to 5 pm. The site maintains weekday winter hours for families or small groups, but you must call ahead. Admission is $3 for adults; $1 for kids five to 13.

Driving Note If you're driving north from Newburgh, Route 9W (between the Newburgh-Beacon Bridge and the Mid-Hudson Bridge at Poughkeepsie) is not as scenic as you might expect. The infrequent river view is hardly worth the string of strip malls, light industry and local traffic you will encounter. Either jump onto the Northway (I-87) or cross the river and proceed north on Routes 9D and 9 to the Poughkeepsie area.

Across the river, views are more spectacular, but Washington's Headquarters is only 12 miles north of popular West Point; it's common to visit West Point, drive north to Newburgh, see George and Martha's place, then cross the river at the Newburgh-Beacon Bridge to the other side.

Places to Eat *26 Front Street* (☎ (914) 569-8035), at – yes – 26 Front St, is a handsomely converted warehouse on the waterfront with a wonderful river-and-valley view from the deck, where you can eat and dance in the evening until the wee hours. There's even a small dock, in case you'd prefer to arrive by boat. The restaurant opens at 11 am for lunch, and dinner is served until 9 pm. After that, there's a $5 cover, and the dancing goes until 4 am.

Storm King Art Center
This art center (☎ (914) 534-3115) is a beautiful outdoor walk-through sculpture park on the featuring some of the finest modern and contemporary sculpture in North America, including works by modern masters Calder, Moore and Noguchi. The setting matches the artwork, angle for angle. There is also a fine indoor museum with a gift and book shop. Several picnic areas are available, but the nicest is near Parking Lot B. On weekends only there is an open-air cafe that sells sandwiches and soft drinks.

Walking tours depart from the gift shop daily at 2 pm, and take about 50 minutes. On Saturday, a shuttle bus tour is also available. Tours are included with the admission price.

Storm King is open daily from April to mid-November, from 11 am to 5:30 pm. Admission is $7 for adults, $5 for seniors, $3 for students and kids and free for kids under five.

Storm King is in Mountainville, south and west of nearby Cornwall-on-Hudson and West Point. From I-84, I-87 or Route 9W, exit to Route 32, where blue and white signs will point you to Storm King Art Center on Old Pleasant Hill Rd.

Goshen
Goshen, about 17 miles west of Harriman State Park on Route 17, is among the more appealing towns of the lower Hudson region. The old Federal and Victorian structures are well maintained, and the town is perfect for walking. Except for the modern and rather grotesque County Building (early 'industrial park' style), Goshen's colonial roots seem intact. The gem of the

bunch, **Goshen Court House** (☎ (914) 294-6644), 101 Main St, has been in continuous use as a court of law since 1841; it's open to the public weekdays from 9 am to 4 pm.

Walking-tour maps are available from the Goshen Chamber of Commerce (☎ (914) 294-7741), Park Place, and the kiosk in the town square.

The **Goshen Historic Track** (☎ (914) 294-5357), Park Place, dates from 1854 and features trotter racing from the Fourth of July to Labor Day. There is no betting, and the $2 admission is all you'll lose here. Opening day (July 4) also features a big fair with bed-races, and a few jokes if it rains. The nearby **Trotting Horse Museum and Hall of Fame of the Trotter** (☎ (914) 294-6330), 240 Main St, is open daily.

Places to Stay *Dobbs Stagecoach Inn* (☎ (914) 294-5526), 268 Main St, is comfortable, full of English antiques and in the center of town (three short blocks from the free public tennis courts). The four rooms range from $65 to $130 per night. Kids are welcome, if you can maintain that they are at least 12 years old.

LOWER HUDSON VALLEY: EAST OF THE RIVER
Tarrytown & Sleepy Hollow
Washington Irving once stated that Tarrytown got its name from the Dutch farm wives who complained that their husbands tarried a bit too long at the village tavern after selling their farm produce at the nearby markets. The more likely, but less appealing, linguistic explanation finds it a variation of the Dutch *tarwe*, meaning wheat.

Peaceful, picturesque Tarrytown is the first of the historic Hudson River towns on the east bank of the river and makes a good base for visiting the many historic homes of the lower valley, all of which are within a few miles. A town landmark is the **Music Hall Theater** near the corner of Broadway and Main St, a classic old brick edifice with a bright marquee listing current theater and music events.

In December 1996, the village of North Tarrytown decided that it might do better to attract tourists if it changed its name to Sleepy Hollow – and so it did. Look out for old maps that might bear its former name.

Information The Sleepy Hollow Chamber of Commerce (☎ (914) 631-1705), 54 Main St, Sleepy Hollow, is open Monday to Friday, 9 am to 5 pm.

Historic Hudson Valley (☎ (914) 631-8200, (800) 448-4007) is a nonprofit organization based in Tarrytown that maintains five of the most historic sites in the Lower

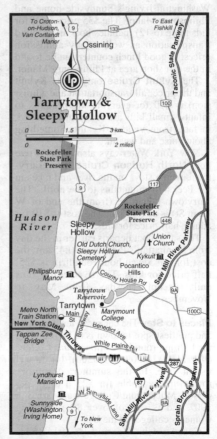

Hudson Valley: Sunnyside, Philipsburg Manor, Kykuit, Van Cortlandt Manor and the Union Church of Pocantico Hills.

River Cruises New York Waterway offers several tour packages as well as a transportation service between Tarrytown and New York City (see Getting There & Away, below). During the summer, boats make roundtrip cruises daily except Tuesday starting at 10:45 am. In late spring and from Labor Day to early November, cruises operate on Friday, Saturday and Sunday only.

The **Sleepy Hollow Cruise** visits both Washington Irving's Sunnyside home and Philipsburg Manor. The $35 price (half for kids three to 12) includes boat and ground transportation as well as any admission prices. A good lunch counter can be found in the gift shop area at Philipsburg Manor.

The **Kykuit Cruise** only visits Kykuit and the price (all transportation and admission) is $60 for everyone from adults to infants; small kids are really discouraged, in fact, from visiting Kykuit. Something about noise and wealth.

New York Waterways also offers a two hour **North Hudson Cruise** from Tarrytown, which stays on the river and takes in the Peekskill mountains to the north. The Tarrytown departure (from the end of W Main St) is at 1:15 pm. The cost is $10 for adults; half price for kids.

The same boat departs earlier in the day from Manhattan's Pier 78 at 10:45 am; the cost for this seven hour roundtrip is $35; half price for kids. The river cruise runs daily except Tuesday from May to November.

Places to Stay The cheapest, least touristy and prettiest spot in town is to be found on the hilltop grounds of *Marymount College* (☎ (914) 332-8209, 631-3200), 100 Marymount Ave. In the summer, dormitory rooms are available for $25 a night per person. Marymount College was started in 1907 and is one of over 80 remaining women's colleges in the US.

Courtyard by Marriott (☎ (914) 631-1122), 475 White Plains Blvd (Hwy 119), south of town, has rooms and several larger suites from $115 to $145.

The *Tarrytown Hilton Inn* (☎ (914) 631-5700), 455 S Broadway (Hwy 9), is one of the more attractive Hiltons to be found and seems to have acknowledged its historic locale; even the bar has a homey-antique touch. Rooms are pricier here, in the $115 to $175 range, and large suites are in the $200 to $400 range.

Places to Eat One of best diners in the valley is *Bella's Restaurant & Donut Shop* (☎ (914) 332-0444), 5 S Broadway near the corner of Main St. The donuts will tempt those who swore off donuts years ago. They are fresh, homemade and they go early. Bella's also serves goulash, pot roast, hearty soups and sandwiches. Prices are diner-reasonable. Open Monday to Saturday from 7 am to 9 pm, Sunday from 7 am to 3 pm.

For good homemade Greek food, try *Lefteri's Gyro Restaurant* (☎ (914) 524-9687), at 1 N Main, near the corner of Broadway. This small family-run business serves big pita sandwiches (chicken, beef or veggie), homemade Greek pastries and the 'small' Greek salad is a meal in itself. Most lunch items are under $6, and dinners are only slightly more. Open every day from 11 am to 10 pm.

The *Main Street Cafe* (☎ (914) 332-9834), 24 Main St, is a moderately upscale American bistro with interesting sandwiches (portobello mushrooms or London broil, for example) and half orders of seafood pasta, all in the $7 range. Broiled salmon and fresh pasta dinners are in the $13 range. In the summer, there are outside tables on the Main St sidewalk. Open Tuesday to Saturday for lunch from noon to 3 pm; for dinner from 5 to 10 pm, and Sunday from noon to 9 pm.

Entertainment If you start feeling depressed from visiting too many mansions, you can return to architectural Earth with a quick visit to the *Tarrytown Music Hall* (☎ (914) 631-3390) at 13 Main St.

The theater is an 1885 Queen Anne-style building and listed in the National Register of Historic Places. It is now a performing arts center with frequent jazz, classical and folk concerts, as well as dance, opera, musicals, dramas and children's theater. For concert schedules, call ☎ (914) 332-8495 or 332-8497.

Getting There & Away Tarrytown is just off the Tappan Zee Bridge at the junction of Route 9 and I-287. If you're coming across the bridge from the west (Nyack), take the first exit (exit 9) after the toll booth, and go to Route 9, which is the main north-south road in the area.

Metro North (☎ (212) 532-4900, (800) 638-7646), the Hudson Valley commuter train, also offers train and shuttle-bus packages to several historic sites in the area. The Tarrytown station is just south of the New York Waterways dock at the end of W Main St.

However there's a more interesting way to arrive if you're carless or want to be (you can walk to Sunnyside and around Tarrytown without a car). New York Waterway (☎ (800) 533-3779) operates one-way and roundtrip transportation from Pier 78 in Manhattan daily, except Tuesday, during the summer, and weekends only in May and October, weather permitting. Boats leave Manhattan at 10 am and Tarrytown at 4 pm; the trip takes about 90 minutes. One-way fares are $12.50 for adults; $6.50 for kids three to 12.

Historic Homes & Churches
Historic Hudson Valley (see Information under Tarrytown, above) maintains most of the historic sites in the Lower Hudson. Three other sites are included in the historic region as well: the Old Dutch Church, the Sleepy Hollow Cemetery and Lyndhurst.

All of the sites maintained by Historic Hudson Valley are open daily except Tuesday, and information for Kykuit has a separate number (☎ (914) 631-9491). Generally, all sites keep the same hours: from 11 am to 5 pm, Saturday from 10 am to 5 pm, Sunday from 2 to 5 pm; and charge

---

History & Manors
The aristocratic land system that came with the arrival of the Europeans certainly exacted its price from the general population, who had to make do with humble farmhouses and old stone churches. Nevertheless, the monuments of wealth and power are scattered up and down the Hudson River. They often lie deep within a manicured park, where even the gardeners seem to carry the authority of the past.

A word on the word 'manor:' In the 17th and 18th centuries, it carried a specific legal meaning similar to its medieval European use, complete with hereditary rights granted by royal charter. With few exceptions, most of these New World mansions are Gothic in mood and proportion – good settings for a scary fireside story. ■

---

the same admission: $7 for adults, $6 for seniors, $4 for kids six to 17. The sites below are listed from south to north.

Sunnyside This cottage (☎ (914) 591-8763), which Washington Irving described as 'made up of gable ends and full of angles and corners as an old cocked hat,' is three miles south of Tarrytown just off Route 9. Even today, it's easy to imagine Irving staring into the deep forests and ravines and envisioning the Headless Horseman of Sleepy Hollow chasing poor Ichabod Crane.

As the costumed tour guide will surely tell you, Irving's old Dutch cottage was 'cute, cozy, quiet and charming.' It's easy to see the age of Romanticism at work on the grounds, just as it worked on Irving's imagination. Like all romantics, he found a divine spirit in nature. The formal English hedges are gone, replaced by a carefully designed 'natural' look. The climbing wisteria that Irving planted over a century ago still clings to the house. The house tour reveals how people of leisure spent time at home, took advantage of the daylight hours and often gathered round the piano in the evening.

To see Irving's home, you must take the one-hour tour, which begins in the gift shop near the parking lot. Tours leave every half hour, beginning at 10:30 am; the last tour begins at 4 pm in the summer and 3 pm in the fall and spring (the combination of earlier sunsets and small windows make it too dark to see late in the day). Sunnyside operates daily except Tuesday from March through December from 10 am to 5 pm.

Lyndhurst This historic home (☎ (914) 631-4481), 635 S Broadway (Route 9), is a classic 19th century Gothic Revival mansion designed by the leading architect of the genre, Alexander Jackson Davis, in the 1830s. The home, which overlooks the Hudson, was built for the mayor of New York City, William Paulding. The landscaping is as spectacular as the building, particularly the rose garden. A small map identifying most of the flora is available for free at the entrance gate when you drive in.

Lyndhurst is open daily except Monday, from May through October from 10 am to 5 pm, and Saturday and Sunday from 10 am to 5 pm the rest of the year. Tours are conducted throughout the day. Admission is $9 for adults, $8 for seniors, $4 for kids seven to 16, six and under free.

Philipsburg Manor Two miles north of Tarrytown on N Broadway (Route 9), this manor (also called the Philipsburg Restoration, ☎ (914) 631-3992) dates from 1865 and is one of the most accessible of the lower valley mansions. Like many wealthy Europeans, the Dutchman Frederick Philipse was awarded a large tract of land here, on which he built a family home, a water-powered grist mill and a Dutch church. Visitors will see farm workers in period dress doing the chores of the day, from tending the garden to milking the cow. There is a museum shop and a good lunch counter cafe. Philipsburg is also the starting point for tours to Kykuit.

Old Dutch Church & Sleepy Hollow Cemetery Across the road from Philipsburg Manor, this 1865 church (☎ (914) 631-1123, 631-0081) was part of the original manor.

Adjacent to the church is the Sleepy Hollow Cemetery, formerly the Tarrytown Cemetery until Washington Irving petitioned to rename it to 'keep that beautiful and umbrageous neighborhood sacred from the anti-poetical and all-leveling axe' and 'to secure the patronage of all desirous of sleeping quietly in their graves.'

In fact, Washington Irving is buried here in a section called Beekman Mound; other section names include Poet's Mound and Sunnyside. The whole place is sort of mysterious. It's hilly, and the roads are narrow and curvy – it's easy to get lost for a moment.

Kykuit Home to several generations of Rockefellers, Kykuit (☎ (914) 631-9491) has only recently been open to public tours. The house is essentially a fine-art gallery with a kitchen, furniture and staff. Fine porcelain and famous paintings – including several by modern masters – adorn the interior. Outside, the exquisite garden overlooking the Hudson River (Kykuit means lookout) is home to modern sculptures by Henry Moore, Alexander Calder, Jacques Lipchitz, Giacometti, Picasso and others. And despite its expensive patina, it must be said of Kykuit that it avoids the ostentatiousness of many Hudson Valley mansions.

Reservations are essential to visit Kykuit; chances are slim that you will join a tour if you simply show up in a hopeful mood (though the steamy month of August is probably your best bet for a last-minute visit). If you do decide to trust your luck, go in the morning, get on the day's wait list, and wait around on the deck in back, or stroll across the bridge to the mill to get away from the mob scene in the gift shop.

All tours leave by shuttle bus from nearby Philipsburg Manor. The basic tour is $18 per person; seniors and students are $16, but there are no discounts for kids, a policy no doubt meant to blunt the natural attraction between small children and porcelain. The tour lasts about two hours and includes the house, galleries and garden. The hectic scene at the shuttle bus area improves dramatically once you reach Kykuit.

There is a good cafe inside the gift shop area, which is open daily from 9:30 am to 8 pm; you eat on a covered deck, or take away a picnic lunch for $6.

Union Church at Pocantico Hills This old stone church (☎ (914) 631-8200), on River Rd in Pocantico, must be seen from the inside out. It's home to several stained-glass windows by Henri Matisse and Marc Chagall; the modern art treasures were commissioned by the Rockefeller family and were completed between 1954 and 1965. Most of Chagall's nine windows are dedicated to Old Testament prophets. Matisse's rose window was his last completed work of art.

The church is open to visitors April through December, Wednesday to Friday from 1 to 4 pm; Sunday from 2 to 5 pm. To reach the church, go north from Tarrytown about two miles, and turn right (east) just before Philipsburg Manor onto Route 448. The church is about three miles away on your right.

Van Cortlandt Manor In Croton-on-Hudson, this manor (☎ (914) 271-8981), S Riverside Ave, is another Historic Hudson Valley property, built in 1748 by one of the most influential Dutch families of the day. The home and 200 year old gardens overlook both the Hudson and the Croton rivers. The furnishings are a major attraction; perhaps three quarters of the family's original possessions are on display, from Queen Anne and Chippendale furniture to the colonial kitchen – complete with pots and pans, jugs, mixing bowls and graters. Not a microwave in sight. There is even a Milk Room with a stone floor for cold storage.

For a telling sign of the politics of the day, notice the gun-slits built into the sides of several outer walls, a reminder of the failure to live peacefully with the native inhabitants of the area.

The manor is open daily except Tuesday from April through December, 10 am to 5 pm. Admission is $7.

Rockefeller State Park Preserve
Three miles north of Sleepy Hollow (North Tarrytown) is the Rockefeller Preserve (☎ (914) 631-1470), a peaceful and beautiful getaway from the hustle and bustle that historic touring can stir up. The preserve is a rolling, woodsy expanse of solitude and old fields and pastures marked by low stone walls. A free walking tour map is available at the small administrative building, and a large notice board tells some of the area's history, from the earliest Munsee-speaking Indian people, to the developers of the Neuwe Netherlands to the Rockefeller benefactors.

A short trail walk from the entrance will put you on the edge of small Swan Lake. The preserve is free, but it costs $4 to park in the adjacent lot. Open from 9 am to 6 pm, or sunset. The area is closed in the winter, usually from December to mid-April.

The preserve is just off Route 117, one mile east of Route 9, about a mile north of Philipsburg Manor.

Ossining
This is a handsome riverside village between Tarrytown and Peekskill on Route 9. The **Ossining Historical Museum** ☎ (914) 941-0001), 196 Croton Ave, houses Indian artifacts, antique dolls and items from nearby Sing Sing Prison. The museum is open weekdays from 1 to 5 pm. Sing Sing fans can see more prison items at the nearby **Ossining Urban Cultural Park** (☎ (914) 941-3189), 95 Broadway, including an old electric chair and life-size replicas of prison cells. The center is open Tuesday to Saturday, from 10 am to 4 pm.

Peekskill
Peekskill doesn't have the spiffy antique look of other riverside towns, but it does have an active arts scene, reasonable accommodations and eateries and a few very interesting shops.

One of the most interesting used book-

The Rockefeller Legacy

Perhaps no family has had a larger influence on 20th century American history than the Rockefellers, who have left their stamp not only on business but also domestic politics and international relations. Their works and deeds have a particular impact upon New York, New Jersey and Pennsylvania.

It all started when the wily Ohio-born patriarch John D Rockefeller (1839-1937) bought into an oil refinery in 1859 with three partners, including his brother William (1841-1922). In the years following the end of the Civil War, John successfully built an empire of oil refineries in the Midwest while William, a genius with money, organized the finances in New York (which included shady stock dealing). By the 1880s, Standard Oil Company had a hammer-lock on crude oil processing and sales in the US. (See Oil City in the Northern Pennsylvania chapter.)

The Rockefellers put their business interests in a trust, and for a time were so powerful they even forced the railroad companies to give them a 'rebate' on shipments of petroleum. But John D's ruthless behavior attracted the attention of state and federal officials who normally gave the corporate chieftain free rein on business matters. After the trust was declared illegal by the Ohio state supreme court, Rockefeller incorporated Standard Oil in New Jersey and continued to make millions as the internal combustion engine made automobile travel part of the American lifestyle.

By the time the Standard Oil monopoly was broken into 34 different companies by the US Supreme Court in 1911, John D Rockefeller had amassed a fortune worth more than $1 billion. (Standard Oil's constituent parts are now huge businesses in their own right and are common sights on US roadsides today, including Exxon, Mobil, Texaco, Amoco, British Petroleum, Shell, Chevron and Atlantic Richfield.) Rockefeller spent the rest of his days looking after the various charitable and educational institutions he founded, including the University of Chicago and a New York City-based medical research facility now known as Rockefeller University.

John D Rockefeller Jr (1874-1960) took over control of the family's fortune after his father retired and also left his mark on society, particularly on New York City. In the height of the Depression, the younger Rockefeller proposed the building of a new Metropolitan

stores in the Hudson Valley must be the Bruised Apple (☎ (914) 734-7000), 923 Central, featuring floor-to-high-ceiling stacks of used, rare and out-of-print books. There are good sections on local history, travel and exploration and art. Open Tuesday, Wednesday, Thursday from 10 am to 6 pm; Friday and Saturday from 10 am to 8 pm; and Sunday from noon to 6 pm.

The *Paramount Center for the Arts* (☎ (914) 739-2333), 1008 Brown St, shows excellent international and independent films, which generally change every two days. The theater is also the setting for occasional concerts and plays.

Places to Stay & Eat *Peekskill Inn* (☎ (914) 739-1500), 634 Main St, near the junction of Routes 9 and 6, is a large (over 50 rooms) motel/inn with a view of the river and rooms from $60 to $80.

Susan's (☎ (914) 737-6624), 12 N Division St, serves good American bistro-style food for lunch and dinner. Prices range from $5 to $10 for lunch; $10 to $16 for dinner. Susan's is open daily from noon to 9 pm, and 10 pm on weekends.

Cold Spring

When President Abraham Lincoln visited Cold Spring during the Civil War to inspect cannons made in the village, their inventor proudly demonstrated the cannons' power by firing a round at the facing cliffs across the river. According to the WPA *Guide to New York* (1940), Lincoln was unimpressed, remarking: 'I'm confident you can hit that mountain over there, so suppose we get something to eat. I'm hungry.'

Cold Spring, on Route 9D, is still a good place to find a meal, and its peaceful Main St is filled with old inns and several antique

Opera House on property occupied by hundreds of small brownstone apartment blocks. When that plan fell through, Rockefeller proceeded with a massive project that became known as Rockefeller Center, the limestone office and shop complex that changed the face of central Manhattan. He also built Riverside Church in upper Manhattan and donated valuable land on the East Side for the headquarters of the United Nations. (See the New York City chapter.)

John D Jr's six children all played prominent roles in public life. Among them were John D III (1906-1978), one of the founders of New York City's Lincoln Center; Winthrop (1912-1973), who settled in Arkansas and became that state's Republican governor from 1967 to 1970; and David (born 1925), the chairman of Chase Manhattan Bank and a recognized leader of the American business establishment.

But perhaps the most famous scion was Nelson Rockefeller (1908-1979). He served Presidents Roosevelt, Truman and Eisenhower in a variety of positions and helped establish the current site of the Museum of Modern Art in New York. He was also elected governor of New York state for four terms and built the massive Empire State Plaza complex (see Albany in the Capital District & Mohawk Valley chapter). Rockefeller was a socially liberal Republican who was so self-conscious of his wealth he used the phrase 'thanks a thousand' to express gratitude. A leading contender for the Republican presidential nomination in the 1960, 1964 and 1968 elections, Nelson was appointed by Gerald Ford to serve as vice president following Richard Nixon's resignation in 1974. Even today, the shrinking GOP left is known, derisively, as 'Rockefeller Republicans.'

Today the Rockefeller billions are spread among dozens of cousins, and the family name is not as prominent in the public eye. But John D IV, the great-grandson of the patriarch, continued the tradition of public service by moving to West Virginia to work with the poor in Appalachia. Known as 'Jay' Rockefeller, he served as Democratic governor of that state and is now a US senator, and is considered one of the most articulate liberal voices in the country. And the $2.5 billion, New York-based Rockefeller Foundation, created by John D Sr in 1913, continues to award over $100 million in grants every year to promote world-wide policy reforms in education, health and the environment.∎ – DE

---

shops. A **walking tour** (☎ (914) 265-2756) begins at 63 Chestnut St, from mid-May to mid-November, every Sunday at 2 pm. To inquire, call (☎ (914) 265-2756), or inquire at any of the antique shops on Main St.

Places to Stay & Eat There are several very nice, if pricey, B&Bs here, including the *Pig Hill B&B* (☎ (914) 265-9247), 73 Main St, a pink-brick Victorian in the middle of the village. Summer rates vary for rooms with private bath and fireplace ($150/125 on weekends/weekdays), to rooms with a shared bath ($130/100). Non-summer rates drop by about 20%, and start at $80.

The Depot (☎ (914) 265-5000), 1 Depot Rd, is right by the Amtrak tracks, as you'll definitely discover at some point during your stop here (it's a converted train lounge). In the summer, several umbrella-

shaded outdoor tables vibrate slightly as the train goes by. Inside, a lovely horseshoe bar also affords a quick glimpse of the passing trains. Food ranges from fish and chicken to burgers and pasta, mostly in the $6 to $18 range.

Karen's Kitchen (☎ (914) 265-1083), 55 Main St, is a popular local breakfast spot; try it for lunch and dinner, too, or for a weekend brunch. It's open daily.

The Vintage (☎ (914) 265-4726), 91 Main St, is an upscale woodsy dining spot, with a few outside garden tables in the summertime. The menu is something like nouvelle Italian with salmon, steak and pasta dishes, plus a fancy burger or two. Lunches range from $6 to $10, dinners from $12 to $20. Open daily from 10.30 am to 2:30 pm; and from 5 to 10:30 pm. The Sunday brunch is $11. There is also a bar here.

Henry's-on-the-Hudson (☎ (914) 265-3000), 184 Main St, is a small bistro-style restaurant with sandwiches, burgers, fish & chips, ribs, chops and the like. Lunches range from $6 to $10; dinners from $10 to $20. They are open Sunday to Thursday from noon to 10 pm, Friday and Saturday till midnight.

MID-HUDSON VALLEY
Poughkeepsie

Poughkeepsie (pooh-KIP-see, population 28,000), the largest town on the east bank of the Hudson, has suffered the same urban renewal fate as many towns in New York; as industry moved out, decay moved in. But like many of those same communities, there is an active effort to revitalize the town (the old historic districts are usually the first to feel the paint brush). One of the organizations most responsible for efforts to improve conditions in the valley is headquartered here. Scenic Hudson, Inc (☎ (914) 473-4440), at 9 Vassar St in the old downtown section, is a nonprofit group that has done much to slow the thoughtless development of the open rural spaces that for so long characterized the entire valley.

Information The Poughkeepsie Area Chamber of Commerce (☎ (914) 454-1700), 110 Main St, is open Monday through Friday, 8:30 am to 4 pm.

The Dutchess County Tourism Office (☎ (914) 463-4000, (800) 445-3131), 3 Neptune Rd, is open Monday through Friday, from 9 am to 5 pm, and has information about Poughkeepsie as well as the surrounding area.

Vassar College This well-respected liberal arts school (☎ (914) 437-7000), 4455 Raymond Ave at the corner of College Ave, was established as a private women's college in 1861 and remained so until 1969 (when it went co-ed). Tours of the campus are conducted daily during the summer months.

Vassar is home to a fine and recently refurbished art gallery, the **Francis Lehman Loeb Art Center** (☎ (914) 437-5632,

437-5237), which is home to several paintings from the Hudson River school (see the sidebar in this chapter). It's open daily except Monday from 10 am to 5 pm and 1 to 5 pm on Sunday.

Locust Grove This 1830 mansion (☎ (914) 454-4500), 370 South Rd (Route 9), about two miles south of the Mid-Hudson Bridge, is the former home of telegraph inventor Samuel B Morse. Built in the Italian Villa style popular in the mid-19th century, it's also home to a beautiful wildlife and bird sanctuary with easy hiking trails. In addition to the ornate mansion furnishings, some of Morse's old telegraph equipment is displayed.

Open from late May through September, from Wednesday to Sunday, and during October and early May on weekends only. The home is open from 10 am to 4 pm, but the grounds stay open until about 8 pm. Admission is $4 for adults, $3.50 for seniors and $1 for kids seven to 16.

Places to Stay There are a number of motel chains along Route 9 just south of the Mid-Hudson Bridge, including the *Econo Lodge* (☎ (914) 452-6600), 418 South Rd (Route 9), with rooms from $45 to $55. The *Holiday Inn Express* (☎ (914) 473-1151), 341 South Rd, has rooms from $80 to $95.

Fancier accommodations can be had just south of town at *Inn at the Falls* (☎ (914) 462-5770), 50 Red Oaks Mill Rd, overlooking the Wappinger Creek falls. The rooms, which range from $120 to $160, are lavish and done in several distinctly different styles, from quilted Victorian to black-tile modern; see your room before deciding!

Places to Eat There are several decent eateries, bakeries and pubs across from the Vassar campus on Raymond Ave.

The *Culinary Institute of America* (☎ (914) 471-6608) must bear the nickname of CIA, but this is the best student cooking you'll find, and the institute has a solid reputation in the region. There are four restaurants on the campus – the Italian *Caterina de Medici*, the French *Escoffier*, the *American Bounty* and *St Andrew's Cafe*, the least formal (and least expensive) of the bunch and where you have the best chance of getting a good meal without a reservation.

Entertainment *Bardavon Opera House* (☎ (914) 473-2072), 35 Market St, is one of the premier theaters in the Hudson Valley. Performances at the restored 1869 venue range from touring dance and opera companies to silent films with live Wurlitzer organ accompaniment.

Hyde Park

Hyde Park, a few miles north of Poughkeepsie, is forever associated with the Roosevelts – other than these main tourist sights, there's not much else for tourists here.

Museum of the Franklin D Roosevelt Library This library (☎ (914) 229-8114, (800) 337-8474), 511 Albany Post Rd, is the nation's first Presidential Library and the only one ever put to use by a sitting president.

Roosevelt came from a prominent and wealthy Hudson Valley family, but the former governor of New York made his mark with his promise of a New Deal to help bring the country out of the tailspin of the 1930s Great Depression. Several exhibits at the museum highlight these relief programs, along with exhibits about Pearl Harbor and America's entry into WWII.

The museum features old photos, FDR's voice on tape (from the fireside chats and several speeches), a special wing in memory of Eleanor Roosevelt and FDR's famous 1936 Ford Phaeton car, with special hand controls so he could drive – despite his restricted mobility because of polio. Roosevelt's White House Desk is also here, supposedly just as he left it on his last day at work in 1945, less than a year after he had been elected to a record fourth term as president.

The museum is open daily November through April, from 9 am to 5 pm; and from May through October, from 9 am to 6 pm. Admission is $5 for adults, $4 for seniors and free for kids under 16.

Eleanor Roosevelt National Historic Site Better known as **Val-Kill** (Dutch for valley stream; ☎ (914) 229-9115), this site is two miles east of Hyde Park. Eleanor herself used to make the drive frequently, but townspeople apparently pulled over to the curb quickly when she came by – not so much out of their respect and admiration for the popular First Lady, but rather due to their knowledge of her erratic driving habits.

Eleanor Roosevelt used Val-Kill as a retreat from the main house at Hyde Park, in part to pursue her own interests and maintain her own identity. The cottage, as she called it, was her own place – not FDR's, not his mother's. After the president's death, Eleanor made this her permanent home. The peaceful grounds are dotted with sugar maple and pine trees, and a dirt road leads to the cottage from the entrance off Route 9G.

The first impression of the cottage is how unpretentious it is. Unlike many of the famous residences up and down the

Hudson, Val-Kill was not meant to impress anyone; comfort was a priority, and you see it immediately in the comfortable and non-matching furniture, the everyday chinaware and the plain restaurant water glasses. This was the dinnerware she used to entertain statesmen, kings and queens and local students she invited home for dinner.

Eleanor was involved in human rights before the term was coined, and she helped establish the International Declaration of Human Rights, earning her the designation 'first lady of the world.' Instead of great works of art, the wood-paneled walls of the cottage are crammed with family photos.

Val-Kill is open daily from May through October and weekends only in April, November and December. Free admission.

Vanderbilt Mansion National Historic Site This mansion (☎ (914) 229-9115) is about two miles north of Hyde Park on Route 9, and another valley spectacle of wealth and lavish architecture of the Beaux Arts style – an eclectic mix of classical Greek, Roman and Baroque lines. Country palaces like the Vanderbilt Mansion are all the more amazing when you realize they were essentially weekend or seasonal getaways – even though they resemble old banks, post offices or libraries. The mansion is open year round, daily from 9 am to 5 pm from April until November; and closed Tuesday and Wednesday during the winter.

Mills Mansion About five miles north of Hyde Park on Albany Post Rd (Route 9) in Staatsburg, Mills Mansion (☎ (914) 889-8851) is an updated Greek Revival-style building with requisite white columns in front. It was built in 1832 and remodeled in 1896. This is no ordinary addition – it's ostentatious in the extreme. There are guided house tours every half hour (otherwise you'd get lost in amid the 65 rooms). The palatial grounds at Mills Mansion are open year round, but the mansion is open from May to early September, Wednesday through Saturday from 10 am to 5 pm, Sunday from noon to 5 pm; and again from early September to the end of October,

Wednesday to Sunday from noon to 5 pm. Admission is free.

Rhinebeck

Rhinebeck is one of the prettier villages along the Hudson and was once a well-known stagecoach stop. It's probably the only town in the valley to sport both a New-Age bookstore and a cigar shop on the same street.

The famous **Beekman Arms** inn is still in operation (see below) and has been expanded with succeeding generations. Rates have changed over the years, and a sign in the lobby recalls another era:

> Lodging 3 pence
> With breakfast, 4 pence
> Only 5 lodgers to a bed
> No boots can be worn in bed

The **Old Rhinebeck Aerodrome** (☎ (914) 758-8610), Stone Church Rd, between Rhinebeck and Red Hook, is a combination museum/air-show with vintage planes from WWI; you can even take a ride in an open cockpit plane for $25, but you have to provide your own scarf. Summer weekend airshow admission is $10 for adults; $5 for kids six to 10. Weekday (non-airshow) admission is $5 and $3.

Places to Stay & Eat The *Beekman Arms* (☎ (914) 876-7077), on Route 9 at the intersection of Route 308 in the middle of town, got its start in 1766, which makes it difficult to contest its claim as America's oldest continuously operating inn. Rates range from $90 to $110 for a room in the main building. The two adjacent suites go for $125 a night, but expect to pay about $10 more in fall foliage season, from the end of September till the end of October, or until all the leaves drop. From May through October, there is generally a two-night minimum stay.

The restaurant adjacent to the lobby is a very good and rather expensive dining spot. Their specialty is cedar plank salmon with garlic mashed potatoes. Entrees begin at $20. The atmosphere is friendly, dim and woodsy.

La Parmagiana (☎ (914) 876-3228), on Route 9, is an old Baptist church converted to an upscale brick-oven Italian trattoria with excellent food. Open Wednesday through Sunday for lunch and dinner, with most entrees in the $5 to $15 range.

See also nearby Red Hook, below.

Red Hook

Red Hook is a small community hidden among the winding roads and greens, about five miles north of Rhinebeck via Route 9, and just east of **Annandale-on-Hudson**, home of Bard College.

The *Grand Duchess B&B* (☎ (914) 758-5818) is a quiet and elegant spot with rooms for $85. Nearby, the *Santa Fe Restaurant* (☎ (914) 757-4100), west of Red Hook in the village of **Tivoli**, is a fabulous Cal-Mex place (and a genuine cut above the spaghetti-sauce diners with Mexican names that abound on the East Coast). Sante Fe is open for dinner nightly (except Monday) and most of the regional items are in the $6 to $12 range.

Millbrook

Millbrook lies east of the Hudson in the Taconic Region, midway between the river and the Connecticut border. The area has long been an upscale alternative to the Hamptons in Long Island, and there's a privileged old-money feel about the area. A maze of back-roads retreats, riding trails and genteel country homes seem to appear and disappear among the winding country roads.

Millbrook itself is as pretty a little town as you'll find, complete with a village green, shiny fire station and spiffy Main St diner. This is a town with a center, and it's an easy place to linger. The area counts among its more famous visitors one Timothy Leary, who spent some of his early LSD-experimenting days around Millbrook at the nearby Hitchcock estate. Some of the townsfolk were scandalized, but it's hard to tell these days if they're bragging or complaining.

Institute of Ecosystem Studies This

center for the study of ecology is between the Taconic State Parkway and the town of Millbrook, just off Route 44, where a sign will point the way. The institute is a combination gardening education center and wetland ecology center. Besides being a lovely spot to walk through, you can sign up for courses that last from one day (or afternoon) to a weekend, to a week, to six weeks. Courses include Natural Science Illustrating and Drawing in the Greenhouse. There are also eco-excursions, which range from $30 to $50 for half and full-day trips, including Wetland Ecology from a canoe, among others. Call for more information (☎ (914) 677-5343), or write for a brochure: Institute of Ecosystem Studies, Box R, Millbrook, NY 12545.

Innisfree Garden This garden (☎ (914) 677-8000), on Tyrell Rd, is one of the most beautiful in the valley – and there are many. When the great Irish poet William Yeats wrote 'The Lake Isle of Innisfree,' he described a spot in the imagination that is always alive. The 200 acre garden here was designed by Walter Beck, who designed a series of cup gardens, with terraces, streams and stones arranged in meticulous fashion, all of which comes to a delicate rest on the edge of Tyrell Lake – all reminiscent of Yeats' 1893 poem, part of which reads:

> And I shall have some peace there, for peace comes dropping
> slow, Dropping from the veils of the morning to where the
> cricket sings . . .

Innisfree is open from May through October, Wednesday to Friday from 10 am to 4 pm, and Saturday and Sunday from 11 am to 5 pm. Admission is $2, and is only collected on weekends. To find Innisfree from Millbrook, head west on Route 44 at the traffic light, turn left of Tyrell Rd, and follow the signs.

James Baird State Park This park (☎ (914) 452-1489), 122 Freedom Rd, off the Taconic State Parkway in **Pleasant Valley**, is about a 10-minute drive from the

Millbrook area, and a great day-use park (no camping). It's popular for short hiking, picnicking and biking in the summertime; a nature center is open Friday, Saturday and Sunday during July and August. From mid-June through October there is a popular farmers' market and concert series on Sunday from 1 to 5 pm. Winter activities include cross-country skiing (over the golf course) and getting warm by the fireplace at the *Restaurant in the Park* (☎ (914) 473-5520), open weekends from 9 am to 6 pm. Park admission is free.

Places to Stay The *Cottonwood Motel* (914) 677-3283), on Route 44 just outside town, is a sparkling white motel, set back from the road a comfortable distance, with rooms in the $60 range.

The *Mill at Bloomvale Falls B&B* (☎ (914) 266-4234), is three miles west of Millbrook at the junction of Routes 82 and 13. Look for a small wood sign announcing the Mill, an 18th-century stone cider mill that used the adjacent falls for power. At night, the only sound you hear is the rushing water; sleep comes quickly here. You can also borrow the house canoe to explore the stream. There are four rooms sharing two baths. Prices (including a fine breakfast, with apple muffins) range from $85 to $115. The Mill is open from the end of May through November, and there is a two night minimum on weekends.

Cat in Your Lap B&B (☎ (914) 677-3051) is the cutesy name for another fine B&B right in the village of Millbrook. It's an old Victorian with five rooms divided between the main house and the barn. Prices are similar to the Mill, $90 to $110.

Places to Eat For basic diner fare, try the handsome *Millbrook Diner* (☎ (914) 677-5319) near the village green, an occasional backdrop site for TV commercials. The diner's old wooden figurehead is a local landmark. The tables inside are adorned with jukebox units, and the food – especially breakfast – is just right. Open daily from 6 am to 9 pm.

For pricier and fancier fare, try *Allyn's*

Restaurant & Cafe (☎ (914) 677-5888) on Route 44, about four miles east of the village of Millbrook. Dinner entrees range from $15 to $22, and international is the theme. Allyn's is open Sunday, Monday, Wednesday and Thursday from 11:30 am to 9:30 pm; and Friday and Saturday from 11:30 am to 10:30 pm.

Mid-Valley Farms
The Hudson Valley has long been a rich agricultural area. Small farms are abundant, and gardening is a common activity. There are hundreds of local farms, produce stands and pick-your-own farms in the region, though the number of family-run farms is dwindling. Mid- to late summer is the time to visit, of course, but check on the harvest schedule; depending on the weather, rain and so forth, harvest times vary. Most farms are open daily during the summer.

Greig Farm This farm (☎ (914) 758-1234) occupies the whole of Pitcher Lane in Red Hook, between Routes 9 and 9G. It's a one-stop produce market with a bakery and education center. The pick-your-own system works like this: They give you a container (tray or basket), you pick what you want from the seasonal fruits and vegetables, then you weigh your pickings at the register and pay wholesale prices. There is also a cut-your-own flower garden, as well as a picnic area and a weekend snack bar.

Popular pickings in the mid- to late summer include asparagus, peas, strawberries, blueberries, blackberries, raspberries and a dozen varieties of apples (Empire, Jonathan, Rome, etc) and pumpkins – especially popular in the fall before Halloween.

The farm education program is very popular locally; the summer sessions for kids fill up by spring, and they don't advertise. If you're visiting the area for several days, you may want to ask about the kids' summer day-camp programs. A three day session for pre-school kids costs $60 per child; kids in grades 1 to 3 can do a five day program for $125; and kids in grades 4 to 6 can do five longer days for $165. Greig Farm is open daily April through December, from 9 am to 5 pm, though summer hours usually extend to 6 or 7 pm.

Ronnybrook Farm Dairy This farm (☎ (518) 398-6455) is in Ancramdale near the junction of Routes 82 and 199. Ronnybrook's glass bottles can be found in local stores here, not far from the Massachusetts and Connecticut borders. There are no tours as such, but a telephone call will usually produce an invitation to see a working dairy farm, especially if children are involved.

Fishkill Farms This is a very good produce market and pick-your-own farm (☎ (914) 897-4377), E Hook Cross Rd, just south of I-84 and a mile west of the Taconic Parkway. Apples, pumpkin, berries and more are available, but if you are after a certain fruit or vegetable, call ahead to be sure it's harvest time. Open year round, daily from 9 am to 6 pm; until 5 pm in the winter.

UPPER HUDSON VALLEY
Olana
Olana (☎ (518) 828-0135) was the home of painter Frederick Edwin Church (1826-1900). Church set out to create a three-dimensional landscape painting using the grounds around his home as a canvas. Church originally planned to build a French chateau on the land he bought in the mid-19th century. But after a two year trip to the Middle East, he changed his plans and commissioned Calvert Vaux to design a villa with influences of Moorish architecture; the Persianesque project was finished in the late 1870s.

Although some of the views are now spoiled by industrial eyesores along the Hudson's west bank, the house and grounds are still breathtaking and the view from the 'front porch' on a summer afternoon resembles some of the large canvases of the Hudson River school of landscape painters.

From mid-April to Labor Day, Olana is open only for guided tours beginning on the hour Wednesday to Sunday from 10 am to 4 pm, then until October 31 from noon to 4 pm. Call ahead; tickets ($3) sell out.

Olana is about five miles south of Hudson, across the Hudson River from the town of Catskill. Take the New York State Thruway (I-87) to exit 21, cross the Rip Van Winkle Bridge to Route 9G south. The entrance to Olana is on Route 9G one mile south of the bridge. Look for the sign on the left and go up the hill.

Montgomery Place
This estate (☎ (914) 758-5461), in **Annandale-on-Hudson**, is maintained by the Historic Hudson Valley (see Tarrytown Information). The 1805 Neo-Classical riverside villa is impressive, but the grounds are among the prettiest of any of the great estates. The estate also has a pick-your-own orchard. Open from April through October, daily (except Tuesday), from 10 am to 5 pm, and weekends only in November and December. Admission is $7/6/4 for adults/seniors/kids six-17. Montgomery Place is north of Rhinebeck, just west of Route 9G on River Rd, before the entrance to Bard College.

Clermont State Historic Site
This site (☎ (518) 537-4240), between Annandale-on-Hudson and **Germantown** off Route 9G, is the early-18th century home of the Robert Livingston family; part of the attraction here is the history of the home and its occupants. The original manor was burned to the ground by the British during the Revolutionary War, but rebuilt soon after. Born in Scotland, the Robert Livingstons made a fortune in the new nation, and a great grandson, Robert R Livingston, was a delegate to the Continental Congress, which produced the Declaration of Independence. He also negotiated the Louisiana Purchase of 1803 from Napoleon for Thomas Jefferson.

In Paris he also met and became partners with Robert Fulton, who was busy working on a contraption called a steamboat. In 1807, the first steamboat, *North River*,

Hudson River School of Landscape Painters

The Hudson River school is the name given to the group of landscape painters who made the rural Hudson Valley and the wilderness of the Catskill Mountains across the river an important American subject of art. The expansion and prosperity that came in the first decades of the 19th century – especially after the completion of the Erie Canal in 1825 – gave the country a strong national consciousness, and along with it, the freedom to begin exploring distinctly American (that is, non-European) themes. The new artists shunned popular historical themes along with formal portraiture in favor of scenes from everyday life – romanticized to be sure, but with a detailed realism that was new to the American art scene around New York. Like Washington Irving, author of 'The Legend of Sleepy Hollow,' the romantic impulse was at work.

Thomas Doughty was the self-taught founder of the school, but its leading spirit was Thomas Cole, whose detailed landscapes included such canvases as 'Catskill Mountain House' and 'Sunday Morning on the Hudson.' Cole was followed by Asher Durand, John Kensett and Frederick Church (see Olana, earlier). Both Cole and Church injected allegorical elements into their work, but most members of the school worked using a purely representational style, one which some critics found to be uninspired and tedious. By the end of the century, some members of the school seemed to agree, having dispersed to even more spectacular scenery in the American West – like Bierstadt and his Rocky Mountain landscapes. The school did succeed in elevating the status of landscape painting in the US, and in immortalizing the mountain slopes, valleys, streams and falls of the Catskill and Adirondack mountains. Even John James Audubon's famous *Birds of America* bears the influence of the school's detailed recording of nature.

Today, a bright day in the Hudson Valley is sure to bring out a few painters by a quiet river bank or budding hillside, with brush in hand and eye on the same landscapes that inspired their famous predecessors. ∎

---

made its appearance on the Hudson River. Later, it was called *Clermont*.

The house is Georgian in style, and original furnishings are on view. The grounds, which extend down to the river, offer a fine view of the Catskill Mountains across the river. The grounds are open daily year round from 8:30 am to sunset. The mansion and visitor center are open from mid-April through October, Wednesday to Sunday from 10 am to 5 pm. Admission is free.

Hudson

Hudson is a beautiful old town given over to antique shops – the light industry of the Hudson Valley. Hudson is another former whaling village, and the architecture is worth a trip through town. Warren St in particular is part of the classic-Americana downtown of small family-owned businesses selling everything from charming junk to the family jewels. Hudson's other claim to fame is its (former) red light district, said to be the oldest in the country.

There's a AAA travel services office (☎ (518) 828-4537) at 179 Healy Blvd, open from 9 am to 5 pm Monday through Friday with later hours (to 6:30 pm) on Thursday.

American Museum of Firefighting (☎ (914) 828-7695), 125 Harry Howard St, is a one-of-a-kind exhibit, with an antique fire apparatus dating from 1731, paintings, old photos, the works. The museum is open daily from 9 am to 4:30 pm, and admission is free.

Shaker Museum & Library

About 20 miles from the town of Hudson via Route 66, **Old Chatham** is home of the Shaker Museum & Library (☎ (518) 794-9100), Shaker Museum Rd. Its location, however, must be put in context: it's even closer to the border of Massachusetts, home of the Pilgrims and several early religious movements.

The Shakers were an early experimental communal group, one of many to follow the trail of New England religious migration. The original group of the United Society of Believers in Christ's Second Appearing came from England with Mother Ann Lee in 1774. In 1792, the first Shaker community was established in nearby New Lebanon (NY), near the Massachusetts state line.

The Shakers got their nickname from their love of music and dance, all in the name of religious ritual and harvest cele-bration. Singing and simple dance move-ments were an integral part of their religious services. The Shakers also had the unique ability to simultaneously entertain the notions of communal living and celibacy. Even though their numbers have accordingly dwindled over the years, their legacy is preserved in the fascinating museum in Old Chatham. It's open from May through October, daily except Tues-days, from 10 am to 5 pm. Admission is $6 for adults, $5 for seniors and $3 for kids eight to 17. In the communal tradition, a family rate is $14.

Catskills Region

The Catskills refers to both the mountains and an entire region of small towns, farms, resorts, streams and hiking trails north and west of the Hudson Valley, yet its far reaches are still within a day's drive from New York City. The name comes from the Dutch *Katsbergs*, meaning mountain cats; the original name evolved among the early Dutch immigrants to Catskills, *kill* being Dutch for stream. The original cats have since been exterminated.

The Catskill Mountains, which are part of the Appalachian Range, are older than the Adirondacks and worn, with few peaks over 3000 feet. These are located in the north where excellent downhill and cross-country ski opportunities attract visitors from throughout the northeastern states. The Catskill region, just 2½ hours north of New York City, includes towns, resorts and a network of hiking trails within the boundaries of the 1094 sq mile Catskill Forest Park, 40% of which is publicly owned and protected. Like the Adirondack Forest Preserve, the Catskill Forest Preserve was established in the late 19th century when the governor of New York signed a law that required these lands 'be forever kept as wild forest lands.' Over the years the parcels grew to their present sizes.

During the same period, developers built deluxe hotels in the southern Catskill Mountains, transforming the area into a popular destination for affluent city dwellers wanting to escape to the wilderness. Most of the hotels have since disappeared, but the site of the most famous one to have burned down – Catskill Mountain House – still attracts hikers. The southern Catskill foothills (which are actually outside the boundaries of the park) are also home to the remaining 'Borscht Belt' resorts. In their heyday in the 1950s and '60s, these huge resorts were packed with New York's Jewish families drawn here by the tightly-scheduled activities, sports,

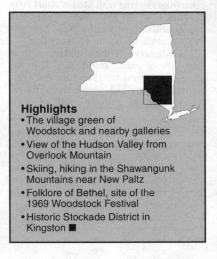

Highlights
- The village green of Woodstock and nearby galleries
- View of the Hudson Valley from Overlook Mountain
- Skiing, hiking in the Shawangunk Mountains near New Paltz
- Folklore of Bethel, site of the 1969 Woodstock Festival
- Historic Stockade District in Kingston ■

food and 'name' entertainment offered nearly around the clock. Wilderness this was not.

ORIENTATION

The Catskills region is bordered by the Hudson River on its eastern edge and by the Delaware River on its southwest border with Pennsylvania. The Catskill Mountains and the older Shawangunk Mountains are havens for hikers, and numerous trails criss-cross the region.

The Catskill Forest Preserve provides the region with its essential identity. Most of the towns in the preserved area retain the qualities of small villages, laid out along a single main street. The towns covered in this section form a loop of sorts, beginning at Woodstock, then proceeding west on Route 28 from I-87 through Boiceville, Mt Tremper, Phoenicia, Shandaken, Big Indian, Highmount, Fleischmanns and Arkville. From Arkville, Route 30 travels north to Margaretville and Roxbury. At Route 23A, you head east to Hunter,

Windham, Tannersville, Haines Falls, completing the loop in the town of Catskill. Restaurants and lodgings are scattered throughout the area.

The west bank of the Hudson River includes the towns of Catskill, Kingston and Saugerties, all along Route 9W; and the village of New Paltz in the foothills of the Shawangunk Mountains near the junction of I-87 and Route 299. Each lies outside the Catskill Forest Preserve.

The area between the Pennsylvania border and the preserve is home to the famous Catskill resorts, a New York insti-

tution once better known as the Borscht Belt; it's concentrated among the towns of Liberty, Monticello and Ellenville. Along the Delaware River, Narrowsburg and Barryville are popular spots for white-water rafting and hiking.

INFORMATION

The Ulster County Information Office (☎ (800) 344-5826) has information on Kingston, Woodstock, Saugerties, Boiceville, Mt Tremper, Phoenicia, Shandaken, Big Indian and Fleischmanns.

The Greene County Promotion and

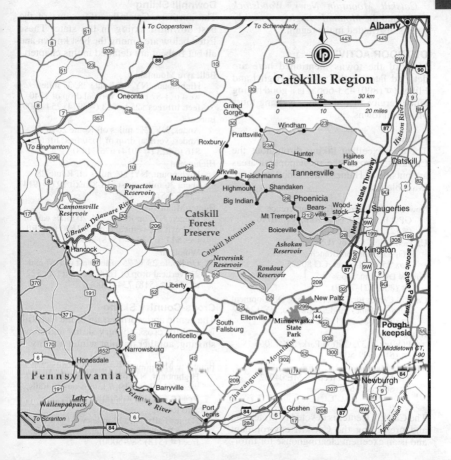

Tourism Dept (☎ (800) 542-2414) covers Hunter, Windham, Tannersville, Haines Falls and Catskill.

The Delaware County Tourism Board (☎ (800) 642-4443) handles Fleischmanns, Arkville, Margaretville and Roxbury.

The Sullivan County Info Center (☎ (800) 882-2287) has information on the large resorts in the southern Catskill foothills.

The New York State Department of Environmental Conservation (DEC; ☎ (518) 382-0680), 2176 Guilderland Ave, Schenectady, NY 12306, is an excellent source of information about the region's ecology.

Catskill Mountain News, *Woodstock Times* and the *Mountain Eagle* are weekly papers distributed in the region.

OUTDOOR ACTIVITIES

Most of the towns mentioned here are detailed later in this chapter. High Land Flings (☎ (800) 453-6665) is a good hiking guide service that also does walking tours of several towns.

Hiking

There is excellent hiking throughout the Catskills. Two of the most popular areas are outside of Haines Falls. Good maps are available from:

New York/New Jersey Trail Conference
    GPO Box 2250, New York, NY 10116
    (☎ (212) 685-9699)
US Geological Survey (USGS),
    Map Distribution Branch
    Box 25286, Denver, CO 80225
Timely Discount Topos
    (☎ (800) 821-7609)
Catskill Center for Conservation & Development
    (also publishes guides) Arkville, NY 12406
    (☎ (914) 586-2611, 586-3044)
Jimapco
    PO Box 1137, Clifton Park, NY 12065
    (☎ (518) 899-5091)
Delorme Mapping
    276 US Route 1, Freeport, ME 04032
    (☎ (800) 335-6763)

The Catskill Center is devoted to protecting and preserving the Catskill environment and is an excellent clearinghouse for information. Their Erph House in Arkville (see below) is also a center for cultural events. The center sells copies of the Catskill history book, *Kaaterskill: From the Catskill Mountain House to the Hudson River School*, published in 1993 by Black Dome Press Corp (☎ (518) 734-6357), RR1, Box 442, Hensonville, NY 12439.

Backcountry Publications (☎ (802) 457-1049), PO Box 175, Woodstock, VT 05901, and Purple Mountain Press (☎ (914) 254-4062), Main St, Fleischmanns, also publish detailed guides.

Downhill Skiing

The northern Catskills offer some of the best downhill skiing in the state. These listed below are among the best known and all but Bobcat are detailed in this chapter:

Belleayre Mountain
    Highmount, NY; off Route 28, 37 miles west of I-87 exit 19; vertical drop of 1340 feet; lift fees $25 to $33 (☎ (914) 254-5600)
Bobcat
    Andes, NY; 2½ miles off Route 28 in Andes; vertical drop of 1050 feet; lift fees $16 to $23 (☎ (914) 676-3143)
Highmount
    Highmount, NY; 1½ miles off Route 28 about 36 miles west of I-87 exit 19 (☎ (914) 254-5265)
Hunter Mountain
    Hunter, NY; on Route 23A 20 miles east of I-87 exit 20; vertical drop of 1600 feet; lift fees $17 to $39 (☎ (518) 263-4223)
Ski Windham
    On Route 23 W 25 miles west of I-87 exit 21; vertical drop of 1600 feet; lift fees $22 to $35 (☎ (518) 734-4300)

Cross-Country Skiing

The gentle and worn terrain of the Catskills is ideal for cross-country skiing and snowshoeing, another popular winter activity.

Belleayre Mountain
    Highmount, NY; off Route 28, 37 miles west of I-87 exit 19; 7 kilometers of trails; free (☎ (914) 254-5600)
Villagio Resort
    Haines Falls, NY; 12 miles west of I-87 exit 21 on Route 23A; 14 kilometers of trails; free (☎ (518) 589-5000)

White Birches
   Windham, NY; 25 miles west of I-87
   exit 21; 17 kilometers of trails; $8 to $10
   (☎ (518) 734-3266)

GETTING THERE & AROUND
Bus
Adirondack Trailways (☎ (800) 225-6815) offers daily service to many Catskill area towns, including Kingston, Saugerties, Catskill, Hunter and Woodstock. Ulster Country Rural Transportation (UCRT; ☎ (914) 340-3333) offers local bus transportation.

Train
Amtrak (☎ (800) 872-7245) runs north and south along the east bank of the Hudson River. Two stations are near the Catskills: Rhinecliff, across the river from Kingston, and Hudson, opposite the town of Catskill. Both locations offer bus service around the region via Adirondack Trailways.

Car
Part of the Catskills' charm is the clustering of small villages and towns, most easily accessible by car.

Eastern Catskills

From south to north, the towns of New Paltz, Kingston and Catskill are easily reached by car or motorcycle from I-87 (New York State Thruway).

NEW PALTZ
New Paltz (pop 11,000), nine miles west of the banks of the Hudson River, is a recreation center and home to SUNY-New Paltz. From I-87 exit 18, head west on Route 299.

Founded by French Huguenot religious refugees in 1677, New Paltz still shows off its original stone architecture on Huguenot St. The difference between Huguenot St and Main St is easy to spot: about 300 years separate the elegant old stone facades

from the usual roadside shops and franchises along Route 299's Main St.

New Paltz is also a center for outdoor recreation in the area, including rock climbing at nearby **Minnewaska State Park** and several farmers' markets

To get the flavor of the original village, visit the Huguenot Street Visitor Center (☎ (914) 255-1889, 255-1660), at 6 Broadhead Ave, which conducts tours of six preserved stone structures from June until early September, Wednesday through Sunday, from 9:30 am to 4 pm. A rather thorough two hour tour is conducted twice daily and costs $7/3.50 for grown-ups/kids; a one hour tour costs half that much.

KINGSTON
Like most Hudson River communities on the eastern edge of the Catskills, Kingston (population 23,000) is built on a fairly steep slope which ends at the waterfront, where a ubiquitous maritime theme dominates what was an early Dutch trading post. It was the state capital for a brief period in 1777 when New York's provincial congress was driven from New York City by the British.

Kingston is at exit 19 on I-87, about 90 miles north of New York City, a two hour drive. A gateway to the Catskills, the town is laid out along pleasant narrow streets with old stone homes.

The best source of information, including free walking tour brochures, is the Kingston Urban Cultural Park Visitor Center (☎ (914) 331-9508, (800) 331-1518) which has two locations: downtown, in the Rondout area, at 20 Broadway, and in the Stockade area, at 308 Clinton Ave. Both are open daily from May through October, 11 am to 5 pm.

Adirondack Trailways stops at Dietz Stadium Diner (☎ (914) 331-0744) at 400 Washington Ave.

Things to See & Do
At the southeastern end of town, at the end of Broadway, is the interesting **Rondout Historic District**. To get there, take Route 587 from I-87 to Route 32/28, which is

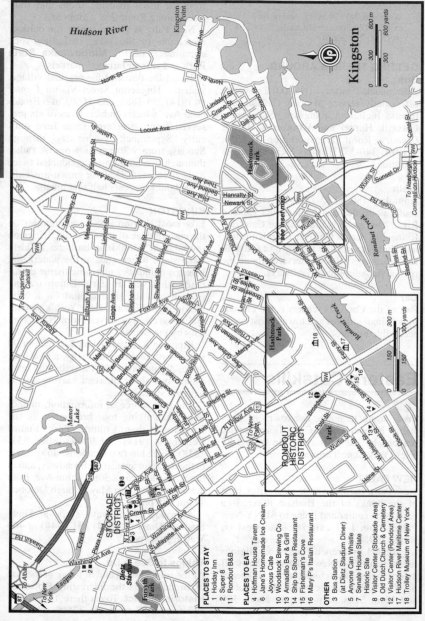

Hudson River

Kingston Point

Kingston

0   300   600 m
0   300   600 yards

see inset map

Hasbrouck Park

RONDOUT HISTORIC DISTRICT

Rondout Creek

0   150   300 m
0   150   300 yards

STOCKADE DISTRICT

Dietz Stadium

Forsyth Park

Manor Lake

PLACES TO STAY
1   Holiday Inn
2   Super 8
11 Rondout B&B

PLACES TO EAT
4   Hoffman House Tavern
6   Jane's Homemade Ice Cream,
    Joyous Cafe
10 Woodstock Brewing Co
13 Armadillo Bar & Grill
14 Ship to Shore Restaurant
15 Fisherman's Cove
16 Mary P's Italian Restaurant

OTHER
3   Bus Station
    (at Dietz Stadium Diner)
5   Anyone Can Whistle
7   Senate House State
    Historic Site
8   Visitor Center (Stockade Area)
9   Old Dutch Church & Cemetery
12 Visitor Center (Rondout Area)
17 Hudson River Maritime Center
18 Trolley Museum of New York

Broadway. Once a bustling 19th century terminal port of the Delaware and Hudson Canal, the Rondout today is a revived neighborhood and shopping area, boasting restaurants and exhibits.

The **Trolley Museum of New York** (☎ (914) 331-3399), 98 E Strand, offers rides on old trolleys for $3/1 for adults/kids. Across the street at 1 Rondout Landing, the **Hudson River Maritime Center** (☎ (914) 338-0071) celebrates the history of life on the river. The center is open daily from early May through October. The cost is $2/1.50 for adults/kids. River excursions operate daily from Rondout Landing during the summer.

Another historic Kingston neighborhood is the 17th century district called the **Stockade**, a fortification built by Peter Stuyvesant. The **Senate House State Historic Site** (☎ (914) 338-2786), 312 Fair St, an early senate house, is here, along with **Beavier House** and other historic homes. The **Old Dutch Church & Cemetery** (☎ (914)339-6759), on Main St, is free and open Monday to Friday from 9 am to 4 pm. To find the Stockade, take Washington Ave from the traffic circle after exiting I-87, drive south a few blocks, and then make a left on Main St.

Places to Stay & Eat

The *Holiday Inn* (☎ 914) 338-0400), 503 Washington Ave, just off I-87 at exit 19, has a large indoor atrium with a whirlpool that you may have to traverse to get to your room. Single/double rooms are $95/135 from late May to mid-October; rates are about 15% less during the winter.

Super 8 Motel (☎ (914) 338-3078, (800) 800-8000), 487 Washington Ave, is next to the Holiday Inn, with rooms in the $60 to $75 range.

The *Rondout B&B* (☎ (914) 331-8144), 88 W Chester St, is a classy Federal-style home with broad porches, two private rooms ($90 per night) and two rooms with shared bath ($75).

In the Stockade, check out *Jane's Homemade Ice Cream* (☎ (914) 338-815), 305 Wall St, and the *Joyous Cafe*, 307 Wall St.

Anthony's Uptown Restaurant (☎ (914) 339-2184), 33 Crown St at the corner of John, serves dinner Monday to Saturday, from 5 to 10 pm. The restaurant is housed in an 18th century stone structure, and has personality to spare; dinner is continental fare, and most entrees are in the $10 to $15 range.

In the Rondout, the *Armadillo Bar & Grill* (☎ (914) 339-1550), 97 Abeel St, has a good New York version of Tex-Mex food, and is open Tuesday through Sunday from 11:30 am to 11 pm.

The *Woodstock Brewing Co* (☎ (914) 331-2810) is not in Woodstock, but in Kingston at 20 St James St, in an 1830 brick structure. The brewery conducts free tours which include samples of freshly made beer.

Hoffman House Tavern (☎ 914) 338-2626), 94 N Front St, is in a sturdy 1711 stone building, now an official historic landmark. It has a full bar and serves good pub food.

Ship to Shore Restaurant (☎ (914) 331-7034), 15 W Strand in the Rondout, is a popular local eatery with fishnet decor; the food is good with burgers from $3 to $6, seafood salad for $4 and great fish & chips for $4. It's open daily from 11 am to 10 pm.

Mary P's Italian Restaurant (☎ (914) 338-0116), 1 Broadway, in the Rondout, serves northern Italian fare. Weather permitting, sit on the garden deck overlooking a small inlet of the Hudson River. Pasta, veal and seafood dishes are priced around $16; daily lunch menu around $10. It's open daily from 11 am to 10 pm.

Fisherman's Cove (☎ (914) 338-5056), 3 Broadway, is a good fast-food spot in the Rondout, with great gumbo and chowders for $3 and fish baskets for $9. Open daily from 11 am to 10 pm.

Things to Buy

Kingston touts its history, but its shops are up-to-date. One of the most unlikely is the Parent-Teacher Store (☎ 914) 339-1442), at 63 N Front St, which sells books, games and kits for the curious of science, music, art and history; open Monday to Thursday from 10 am to 6 pm, Friday from 10 am to 7 pm, and Saturday from 10 am to 5 pm. Outback Antiques (☎ (914) 331-4481), at 72 Hurley Ave, resembles a musty old barn on the outside but is really a charming vintage clothing store inside, complete with lace pillows. You may have to ring the doorbell to rouse the owners even during regular hours, 10 am to 5 pm daily, except Tuesday.

Anyone Can Whistle (☎ (914) 331-7728), 323 Wall St, near Jane's Ice Cream in the heart of the Stockade area, is a fascinating try-anything-you-want music and musical arts store. It's open weekdays from 10 am to 6 pm; Saturday till 5 pm.

CATSKILL

From Haines Falls and the North/South Lake area, you'll continue on Route 23A east of I-87 to the town of Catskill (population 4700), where Hudson River school painter Thomas Cole lived during the 19th century when the town and surrounding area were more scenic. You can visit the **Thomas Cole House** (☎ (518) 943-6533), 218 Spring St off Route 385, although the national historic landmark contains none of the painter's works. You may wish to bypass the town, proceeding on to Hudson, site of Olana, the home of Cole's student Frederick Church. (See the Hudson Valley chapter.)

There are several other tourist attractions geared especially for kids, west of town on Route 32. Take Routes 23A to 32 south and you'll come upon them, one after the other.

A Wild West re-creation, **Carson City & Indian Village** (☎ (518) 678-5518, (800) 622-2489) has gun shows, country music shows, Native American exhibits and train and stagecoach holdups. The adults/children's admission is $11/7.

Clyde Peeling's Reptileland is the home of pythons, crocs and cobras. Clyde's (☎ (518) 678-3557), Route 32, is open Memorial Day to Labor Day, from 10 am to 6 pm, and then on weekends to Columbus Day. Adult/children's admission into Reptileland is $6.50/4.25.

The **Catskill Game Farm** (☎ (518) 678-9595) on Route 32, two miles south of Clyde Peeling's Reptileland, is more zoological than carnival compared to its neighbors. It started in the 1930s as a conservation project to protect rare and endangered animals from around the world, both tame and wild. Today, the family-operated complex tends to approximately 2000 animals and runs a successful nursery which – among other success stories – breeds wild horses from Mongolia. The farm is open from May through October, daily from 9 am to 6 pm; from the end of May to the beginning of September, daily animal shows are part of the schedule. The cost is $12/8 for adults/kids four to 11. Several amusement rides for kids are also available at 90¢ each.

Northern Catskills

WOODSTOCK

Ten miles northwest of the Catskills' largest town of Kingston, Woodstock (population 6200) is best known for the 1960s event that actually never happened here. The Woodstock music festival actually took place more than 40 miles southwest near the town of Bethel, where today a simple roadside plaque marks the spot.

Woodstock today is not so simple. This attractive village is a charming cross between quaint and hip. You will still see a few tie-dyed locals who look as if they were in a 1960s time warp, and a handful of shops and businesses retain the names of a mythical time: Exodus, Sunflower, Pegasus, Pondecherry and Not Fade Away. But the town's reputation as a legitimate colony of the arts goes back to the early 1900s. Today, the town seems content with this bygone reputation: chain stores are virtually non-existent, and many quality one-of-a-kind shops line both sides of Tinker Rd and Mill Hill Rd.

You will also see a younger crowd in

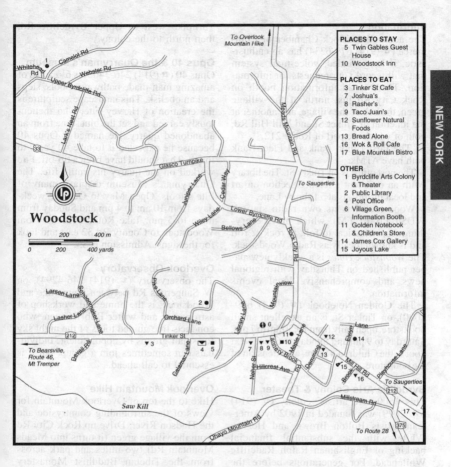

PLACES TO STAY
5 Twin Gables Guest House
10 Woodstock Inn

PLACES TO EAT
3 Tinker St Cafe
7 Joshua's
8 Rasher's
9 Taco Juan's
12 Sunflower Natural Foods
13 Bread Alone
16 Wok & Roll Cafe
17 Blue Mountain Bistro

OTHER
1 Byrdcliffe Arts Colony & Theater
2 Public Library
4 Post Office
6 Village Green, Information Booth
11 Golden Notebook & Children's Store
14 James Cox Gallery
15 Joyous Lake

Woodstock

0   200   400 m
0   200   400 yards

their 20s who would not look out of place in New York City's East Village. In fact, Woodstock is fast returning to its New England small-town roots and most of today's residents appear to be artists, musicians or well-heeled folks from downstate who own summer homes here. With art galleries, fashionable clothing stores, theatrical and musical productions, and a good selection of places to stay and eat, Woodstock should be at the top of your list of towns to visit in the region.

Seeing Woodstock means strolling about town, enjoying the friendly feel of the place, browsing through the galleries and crystal shops. It also means people watching. The small village green at the center of town offers the perfect vantage point from which to pursue the last of these activities. If you happen to be in town on Christmas Eve, you will be one of the first to know how Santa Claus arrives on the village green. This is the best-kept secret around, and it's never dull; recent arrivals have been by camel and hang-glider – on separate occasions, of course.

Information

The active Woodstock Chamber of Commerce (☎ (914) 679-6234) has an enthusiastic, if long-winded, voice-mail system that will record your requests for information. There is an information booth on Rock City Rd just north of the village green, the hub of the village, and another at the junction of Tinker St and Mill Hill Rd, both of which are part of Route 212.

The First Union Bank and Fleet Bank both have ATMs.

The post office is on Tinker St. The library (with an excellent reference section on art and local history) is at 5 Library Lane.

Woodstock has its own radio station, WDST (100.1 FM), which plays everything from classical to folk to rock & roll and is known locally as Radio Woodstock. The *Woodstock Times* is a weekly newspaper published on Thursday with regional news and comprehensive local events information.

The Golden Notebook (☎ (914) 679-8000), on Tinker St, is an excellent small bookstore, open daily from 10:30 am to 7 pm, Saturday to 9 pm and Sunday to 6 pm. Next door is the Children's Store, an extension of the bookstore.

Byrdcliffe Arts Colony & Theater

This 1500 acre artists' colony (☎ (914) 679-2079) was founded in 1902 by American artists Bolton Brown and Hervey White with the substantial financial backing of Englishman Ralph Radcliffe Whitehead. For generations before the 1969 Woodstock Festival, artists and concert goers traveled to Byrdcliffe to share their common vision of peace and justice. Their hopeful message was set to music by song writers and performers, including Pete Seeger, Peter, Paul and Mary and Louisiana bluesman Leadbelly. Today, there are still artists-in-residence, craft demonstrations, exhibitions and performances at the Byrdcliffe Theater. Performances are announced in the *New York Times* and the local *Woodstock Times*.

To get there, take Rock City Rd north from the village green to the Glasco Turnpike west to Upper Byrdcliffe Rd, then north to the colony.

Opus 40 & the Quarryman's Museum

Opus 40 (☎ (914) 246-3400) is 6½ acres of amazing man-made pathways, pools, steps and an obelisk. This landscape sculpture is the creation of Harvey Fite, who meticulously carved and set the bluestone from an abandoned quarry. He named it Opus 40 because he expected it to take 40 years to finish. That should have been a tip-off; Fite worked on the quarry his entire life. The Quarryman's Museum displays many of Fite's tools. Open May to October weekdays from 10 am to 4 pm and Sunday from noon to 5 pm. Take Route 212 east from Woodstock to County Rd 32 east and look for the signs. Admission is $5.

Overlook Observatory

The observatory (☎ (914) 246-4294), on W Saugerties Rd between Saugerties and Woodstock, is the home and workshop of astronomer and writer Bob Berman, who conducts free guided tours of the night sky for small groups by appointment. Individuals can sometimes join a group, but it is essential to call ahead.

Overlook Mountain Hike

Hike to the top of Overlook Mountain for views of the surrounding countryside and the Hudson River. Drive up Rock City Rd from the village green (it turns into Meads Mountain Rd) two miles and park across from the Tibetan Buddhist Monastery (☎ (914) 679-5906). Hike up the path from the parking lot 2.4 miles to the top, and see what the monks see.

Places to Stay

The *Saugerties-Woodstock KOA* (☎ (914) 246-4089) has 100 sites at about $20 each. It's open from April to November. From I-87 exit 20, take Route 212 west for 2¼ miles to the campground.

The *Rip Van Winkle Campground* (☎ (914) 246-8334) has 90 sites for $18 each and is open from early May to early October. Take Route 212 west two miles from I-87 exit 20 and then go half a mile north on County Rd 32 to Blue Mountain Rd.

Twin Gables Guest House (☎ (914) 679-9479), 73 Tinker St, is a good bet. The house is right in the middle of town, and the nine rooms are roomy, very nicely furnished and the price is fair. Single/ doubles with shared bath are $45/60. A double with private bath is $75.

The *Woodstock Inn* (☎ (914) 679-8211), 38 Tannery Brook Rd, a block behind Tinker St, is an attractive and quiet motel with weekday/weekend rooms for $69/110, which includes a continental breakfast.

Places to Eat

Tinker St, Woodstock's main street, has an abundance of good restaurants, cafes and bakeries. My favorite for breakfast and lunch is *Rasher's* (☎ (914) 679-5449), 13 Tinker St, which serves excellent soups, sandwiches, veggie chili, omelets and bargain lunch specials Monday to Friday from 8 am to 4 pm, and Saturday and Sunday to 9 pm.

On the same side of street, *Taco Juan's* has good knishes, enchiladas and burritos for under $5, and an arty 'psyche-deli' menu on the wall.

The *Tinker St Cafe* (☎ (914) 6789-2487), 59 Tinker St, is a bar/ restaurant and music club open daily for lunch and dinner. Burgers, sandwiches, veggie salads and specialties like jambalaya round out the menu.

Joshua's (☎ (914) 679-5533), 51 Tinker St, serves Middle Eastern and Israeli dishes, as well as bacon and cheese baguette sandwiches (hey, it's Woodstock). The hummus, babaganoush and tabouli are good, along with potato latkas, several pasta dishes and a mixed

---

The 1969 & 1994 Woodstock Festivals

About half a million people descended on Max Yasgur's farm in Bethel, NY (40 miles southeast of the town of Woodstock), from August 15 to 17, 1969, for a music festival billed as 'Three Days of Peace & Music.' The lineup of musicians for the Woodstock Festival – Joan Baez, Joe Cocker & the Grease Band, Country Joe & the Fish, Crosby Stills & Nash, Arlo Guthrie, Richie Havens, Jimi Hendrix, Santana, John Sebastian, Sha-Na-Na, Sly & the Family Stone, Ten Years After and The Who – has never been matched.

Festival promoters sold tickets for a remarkable $7 for one day and $18 for three. The entire event cost only $3 million to stage; unfortunately, less than one quarter of the half-million concertgoers paid for admission and the festival had trouble paying its bills.

Despite numerous setbacks ranging from broken toilets to a serious mud problem after a day of rain (earning it the 'Hog Farm' nickname), there were no riots and no violence. It was the most successful hippie gathering in the world. The most violent scene probably occurred when activist Abbie Hoffman ran on stage to make a speech, only to be greeted by The Who's Pete Townsend who promptly bashed him over the head with his electric guitar. Lucky he didn't run into Jimi Hendrix who often set his guitar on fire.

If anyone needed to be reminded that the '90s are not the '60s, the 1994 Woodstock II Festival did the job. Promoted as a 'commemoration concert' on an 840 acre dairy farm in the nearby town of Saugerties (where the 1969 festival planners had originally hoped to hold their concert), Woodstock II promised 'two more days of Peace and Music.' And it delivered; performers included Aerosmith, Crosby, Stills & Nash, Cypress Hill, Peter Gabriel, the Red Hot Chili Peppers and the Spin Doctors. The concert was broadcast on pay-per-view cable and tickets were $135. The 1994 concert cost $30 million and is still waiting to turn a profit with record sales. Hundreds of shuttlebuses brought folks to the field from parking lots throughout the Hudson Valley, but only 250,000 tickets were sold. Meanwhile, the original 'Woodstock Generation' was at home, waiting for the video. ■

---

meat grill of lamb, chicken, shrimp, beef and vegetable; generous portions of food cost from $5 to $20.

The *New World Home Cooking Co* (☎ (914) 679-2600), 424 Zena Rd at the corner of Sawkill Rd, is a hip country gourmet eatery specializing in a Caribbean-Thai-down home mix; Jamaican jerk chicken is a local favorite, along with *ropa vieja* (Cuban pot roast), and my personal favorite: Purple Haze shrimp. Big servings in deep dish plates are the order of the day. Open for lunch Monday to Friday from 11 am to 2 pm, and daily for dinner from 5 to 11 pm. On weekends, like much of Woodstock, it's best to call ahead for reservations. To find New World, take Route 212 east from the Route 375 junction 1½ miles, and turn right on Zena Rd; the restaurant is across the street from an elementary school house.

Bread Alone (☎ (914) 679-2108), 22 Mill Hill Rd, is a landmark for bread lovers. Knowing that most folks cannot live by bread alone, they also offer fine pastries, morning burritos and eggs (in the $2 to $4 range), and several gourmet deli items. Bread Alone is open Monday through Friday from 7:30 am to 5 pm, and to 7 pm on weekends.

For innovative Chinese and Japanese food, the *Wok & Roll Cafe* (☎ (914) 679-7760), 50 Mill Hill Rd, is all Woodstock. Besides good teriyaki and stir-fry dishes, plus a great take-out menu, you can brush up on your music history by watching either of two wall-mounted TVs: One plays a video of the original 1969 Woodstock Festival, and the other plays a video of the upstart 1994 Woodstock II. The cafe is open daily 11 am to 2 pm and 4 to 10 pm, and until 11 pm on Friday and Saturday.

Try *Sunflower Natural Foods* (☎ (914) 679-5361), in the small Bradley Meadows Shopping Center on Mill Hill Rd, for a decent selection of health food items, fresh juices and produce. Open daily from 9 am to 9 pm, Sunday from 10 am to 7 pm.

There are several excellent restaurants just a short drive from the village of Woodstock that are worth finding. Two miles west of the village green on Route 212 is the small town of Bearsville, where you'll find the *Bear Cafe* (☎ (914) 679-5555), serving American and French bistro fare in a rather serene brookside setting. The food is excellent, on the pricey side but affordable and popular with local and New York City celebrities. The adjacent *Little Bear* (☎ (914) 679-8899) shares the forest setting with the Bear Cafe and has a well-deserved reputation for serving the best Chinese food north of New York City.

Also a bit out of town, the *Blue Mountain Bistro* (☎ (914) 679-8519), at the junction of Routes 212 and 375, about a mile east of town at the Woodstock Golf Club, is a popular upscale cafe with Mediterranean cuisine, open for lunch and dinner Tuesday through Sunday.

Entertainment
Performing Arts & Concert Series
Woodstock and its environs support a concentration of performing arts programs and concert series, including *The Bearsville Theater/River Arts* (☎ (914) 679-2100) which puts on plays, concerts and stand-up comedy.

During the summer, the Byrdcliffe Arts Colony & Theater (see above) holds craft demonstrations, art exhibits and theatrical performances.

Maverick Concerts (☎ (914) 679-7558), Maverick Rd off Route 375, is the oldest chamber music series in the US (since 1916). Sunday concerts are presented at 3 pm from mid-June to early September with top performers. Concerts are listed in the Sunday *New York Times* during the summer; people often drive up from the city for this.

Clubs *Tinker Street Cafe* (☎ (914) 679-2487), 59 Tinker St, is a good blues and R&B club; Bob Dylan played here in the early '60s while hanging out at Big Pink with his musical buddies and members of The Band.

Joyous Lake (☎ (914) 679-1234), 42 Mill Hill Rd, is a popular restaurant and nightclub with dancing open nightly.

Getting There & Away
Adirondack Trailways (☎ (914) 679-2115,

(800) 225-6815) stops at Houst & Sons hardware store (☎ (914) 679-2115), 4 Mill Hill Rd.

By car, from I-87, take exit 19 to Route 28 west, then Route 375 north, or take exit 20 to Route 32 west to Route 212 to town. Coming from Mt Tremper, take Route 212 east past Bearsville to town.

ROUTE 28 TO ARKVILLE
The route from Woodstock to Arkville begins by dropping south on Route 375 (at the junction of Route 212 in Woodstock) which deadends at the Ashokan Reservoir and the junction of Route 28. Turn right, and you're on your way.

These towns are not very far apart – something to consider if you're planning lodging and dining in the area.

Mt Tremper & Boiceville
As you travel west on Route 28, you will pass several small towns. About 15 miles of the road follows the northern edge of the Ashokan Reservoir, which supplies New York City with drinking water. Route 28A loops around the more deserted southern side of the reservoir.

Continuing west past Boiceville (notable for its bakery, see below), Route 28 meets Route 212. Mt Tremper is less than a mile north on Route 212.

Zen Mountain Monastery The monastery
(☎ (914) 688-2228), Box 197 RB, S Plank Rd, is located on a 200 acre sanctuary. Guests and staff maintain the grounds, eat together and meditate. The discipline is fairly rigorous, but it is well worth the investment in time and effort. Retreats of various lengths are offered and can be as short as a weekend. To reach the sanctuary, take Route 212 north from Route 28 to the first four-way intersection and then go left on S Plank Rd and look for the monastery a block up on your right.

Places to Stay & Eat The *Kenneth L Wilson Camping Area* (☎ (914) 679-7020) is on County Rd 40 in the park of the same name

about four miles east of Mt Tremper. County Rd 40 crosses Route 28 a little over a mile west of Boiceville in the town of Beresford. The campground is open from mid-May to late October. Cost is $12 per night.

La Duchesse Anne (☎ (914) 688-5260), 4 Miller Rd, is one of several good French restaurants in the Catskills, set in an old house in a wooded setting. You can eat dinner here for $10 to $20; basic rooms are available for $40 to $60.

The *Mt Tremper Inn* (☎ (914) 688-5329), on Route 212 at Wittenberg Rd, is a plant-filled guest house that rents 10 rooms with shared baths and two with private bath for $60 to $75.

When you get to tiny Boiceville, pull off at *Bread Alone* (☎ (914) 657-3328) on the north side of Route 28. The best baked goods anywhere in the Catskills are served up at this bakery, which has another branch in Woodstock.

Catskill Rose (☎ (914) 688-7100), on Route 212, is one of the better-known restaurants in the area and a favorite among locals. The kitchen features a good selection of both vegetarian and meat dishes; the smoked duck receives rave reviews. Most dinners range from $10 to $17.

Phoenicia
Phoenicia, on the Esopus Creek west of Mt Tremper on Route 28, is the center of tubing in the Catskills. The American White-Water Affiliation (☎ (914) 688-5569), PO Box 85, Phoenicia, NY 12464, is a national organization that promotes white-water rafting.

It is also famous for Folkert's Brothers (☎ (914) 688-9936), a small sporting goods store on Main St that is known across the Catskills for fly-fishing supplies. Start up a conversation and you might find out how fly fishing got its start in the Catskills.

Adirondack Trailways stops in front of Folkert's Brothers (☎ (914) 688-9936) on Main St.

Esopus Creek Tubing Visitors can tube
on the Esopus Creek, which runs along

Route 28. The more exciting tubing starts five miles northwest of town where water is released from the Schoharie Reservoir and ends five miles downstream at the bridge in Phoenicia. The floating trip takes about two hours. There is also an easier course that runs southeast from Phoenicia and takes about 1¾ hours. Tubes can come with seats and handles, and outfitters rent paddles and life jackets. The outfitters will drive you to the put-in site.

FS Tube & Raft Rental (☎ (914) 688-7633), at 4 Church St behind the Phoenicia Inn, rents tubes with/without seats for $7 and $10/10 and $13; transportation to the site costs $3. They also rent rafts for $50.

The Town Tinker Tube Rental (☎ (914) 688-5553), on Bridge St half a block south of Main St, rents tubes with/without seats for $10/7. You can also rent life jackets, wet suits and helmets. Tube Taxi shuttle is $3 per trip. Bon voyage.

Places to Stay The *Hide-A-Way Campsite* (☎ (914) 688-5109) is open from mid-April to mid-October. From Route 28 take the Phoenicia/Woodland Valley detour, when you come to the railroad tracks, take a right onto High St (which is also Woodland Valley Rd here), and follow it for about 3½ miles to the campground.

Sleepy Hollow Campsite (☎ (914) 688-5471) is on Route 28 about a mile east of the Phoenicia Hotel. There's also the *Woodland Valley Campground* (☎ (914) 688-7647) six miles southwest of Phoenicia and *Uncle Pete's Campsite* (☎ (914) 688-5000).

The *Phoenicia Hotel* (☎ (914) 688-7500) on Main St is the place to stay in town. The large and popular bar downstairs and a patio area are great for hanging out. The 24 rooms (three with shared baths) are all air-conditioned with TV. The weekday/weekend rates are $45/60; weekly rates are available.

Places to Eat *Sweet Sue's* (☎ (914) 688-7852) on Main St is as famous throughout the Catskills for its pancakes as Folkert's is

for its fly-fishing equipment. Sue's creates more pancake combinations, around $5, than you could possibly dream up on a snowy week in the Catskills. French toast, burgers and standard lunch fare is also available.

Shandaken

The town (pronounced shan-DAY-ken) is located at the heart of an area (also called Shandaken) that runs along Route 28 and includes the towns of Phoenicia, Mt Tremper and Big Indian. Also known as the French Catskills, this area offers excellent hiking and fine dining at any of the area's several French restaurants and inns.

Among these, the most famous inn, *Auberge Des 4 Saisons* (☎ (914) 688-2223), provides what is perhaps the best dining experience in the northern Catskills. Located in a secluded setting on Route 42 about half a mile off Route 28, the restaurant features delicious appetizers including smoked salmon, pate and goat cheese on French beans for $5 to $7. The entrees are equally good: stand-outs include poached salmon with mustard sauce on spinach ($17), mussels with thyme ($15), roasted duck in three peppercorn sauce ($17) and rabbit with flageolets ($18). The restaurant also offers a good selection of wines. Rooms are available for $60 to $100 per person, including meals.

Big Indian

A stone's throw west of Shandaken on Route 28, *Rudi's Big Indian* (☎ (914) 254-4005) restaurant stands alone just outside of this tiny hamlet. It occupies a modern building with several distinct dining areas, including a deck with umbrellas, a fairly lavish Victorian dining room and another called the conservatory, though greenhouse comes to mind. Rudi's serves generously portioned chicken pot pies for lunch along with burgers and salads. Dinner selections of fresh fish, pasta and grilled meats are in the $14 to $18 range. Rudi's is open daily during the summer from noon to 9:30 pm, and Thursday to Monday during the winter and spring.

The nearby inn *Val D'Isere* (☎ (914) 254-4646) is furnished in an eclectic mix of modern and traditional – shag carpets and old oak furniture. Rooms with shared bath are $45. The restaurant is unpretentious and the menu includes frogs' legs ($14), lamb ($13) and duck ($13).

Highmount

Just before you enter Fleischmanns on Route 28, you'll pass through the village of Highmount. On a hill overlooking the road (you'll have to look up to see it) is the *Gateway Lodge* (☎ (914) 254-4084). It's a warmly furnished house with a wood-burning fireplace and a piano. There are four rooms with bath and five with a shared bath. Rooms are tastefully furnished. Singles/doubles with shared bath are $40/50, with private bath they are $50/60.

Fleischmanns

Fleischmanns is on Route 28 just before Route 30 enters from the north. Adirondack Trailways stops at Petry's Store (☎ (914) 254-4010) on Main St.

The town was originally known as Griffin Corners. Charles Fleischmann, a Hungarian immigrant, developed a bit of land here in the 1880s and assembled a band to greet family members as they arrived at the old train station. The Fleischmann family gave a park to the town and in 1913 the town changed its name to honor him. Baseball great Honus Wagner played ball here before going on to become one of the all-time great shortstops with the Pittsburgh Pirates.

The little town is also home to Purple Mountain Press on Main St, an excellent press that specializes in regional history and folklore.

Roberts' Auction (☎ (914) 254-4490) on Main St, auctions everything from nuts and bolts to antiques every Saturday night at 7 pm. You can find items here for as little as a dollar and for substantially more. Come early because seats fill up fast.

Places to Stay & Eat On Main St, *River Run* (☎ (914) 254-4884) is an unusual inn, in that host Larry Miller welcomes pets. The large, restored house has an inviting front porch complete with Adirondack chairs. There are four rooms on the 2nd floor with private baths and three on the top floor with shared bathrooms. Weekday/weekend rates are $25 to $70/35 to 85. The least expensive rate is for a single-bed, shared-bath room. The best deal here is the 'retro wing,' a space with a private bath, twin beds, shared kitchen and television for a very reasonable $45/60. River Run also has a two-bedroom apartment with a private entrance, kitchen and barbecue for $90 per night.

La Cabana (☎ (914) 254-4966) is a Mexican restaurant with several unusual menu items, like *pollo en Pipian* (chicken in chile-and-pumpkin-seed sauce); *huachinango a la Veracruzana* (red snapper with tomato, onion and pepper sauce) or loin of pork in wine.

Arkville

Arkville is home to the **Catskill Center for Conservation & Development** (☎ (914) 586-2611; see Hiking, above). Located in the Erph House, a white house perched on a hill, they can provide information on hiking and environmental preservation in the Catskills.

In warm weather, the **Delaware & Ulster Rail Ride** (☎ (914) 586-3877, (800) 225-4132) does a one hour roundtrip Catskill train ride for $7/4 for adults/kids.

The *Bavarian Fireside Restaurant* (☎ (914) 586-4465), on Route 28, offers an interesting dining setting. The building looks like a worn Alpine A-frame house liberally bedecked with antlers; inside are carpets piled on top of carpets, lanterns and plates, guns and steins, copper kettles and oil paintings. They serve all the wursts – knockwurst, weisswurst, bockwurst and bratwurst – as well as veal done all ways German. Lunch is around $5 and dinners are $8 to $12.

The Adirondack Trailways bus stops at the Delaware & Ulster Rail Ride.

MARGARETVILLE

Margaretville, at the junction of Route 28 and Route 30, is the major commercial town in the northern Catskills area and is a good place to stop for supplies. The former theater on Main St is now the **Margaretville Antique Center** (☎ (914) 586-242). The Adirondack Trailways bus stops at the Inn Between Rest Stop (☎ (914) 586-4265).

Places to Stay & Eat

The *Margaretville Mountain Inn* (☎ (914) 586-3933) is an 1886 slate-roofed home on top of the mountain overlooking the town. The 2nd-floor rooms have the best views and are more expensive. Weekday/weekend rates are $50 to $75, including a full breakfast. After entering Margaretville from Route 28 make a left at the first light and then the make the first right onto Walnut St. Drive up the hill for 1½ miles to the inn.

Merritt's Motel (☎ (914) 586-4464) on Route 28 has singles/doubles for $35/45. It's across the road from the East Branch of the Delaware River about a half mile east of Margaretville.

Buswell's Bakery & Restaurant (☎ (914) 586-3009) on Granary Lane serves great pies, muffins and other baked goods daily year round from 8 am to 8 pm. Breakfast and lunch selections include pancakes, omelets and sandwiches. Dinners are served beginning at 2 pm – hot turkey, roast beef and Reubens are some of the house specials. As you come across the green bridge into town from Route 28 west the first left is Granary Lane.

JOHN BURROUGHS MEMORIAL

Roxbury, a small town along Route 30 about 12 miles north from Margaretville, is the site of Boyhood Rock, a huge glacial boulder marking the John Burroughs Memorial. A plain bronze plaque, dedicated to the prolific naturalist writer, portrays Burroughs looking over the land he loved, with an inscription from his poem

'Waiting': 'I stand amid the eternal ways.' To find the modest memorial, go north from Roxbury to Hardscrabble Rd, then west for about a mile to Burroughs Memorial Rd, then 1½ miles to the memorial itself.

HUNTER

Hunter Mountain is, by far, the most popular ski resort in New York. The town itself (population 500), perched in the northern reaches of Hunter Forest Park, has little to recommend it, but the skiing and summer festivals with the accompanying party atmosphere make it an interesting place to stay. What little there is of Hunter is strung out along Route 23A.

From Route 30 north to Route 23 at Grand Gorge, turn right (south), and drive about six miles to Prattsville, where Route 23 branches off to Route 23A, which will bring you to Hunter.

Adirondack Trailways stops at Peter's Hunter Auto Repair (☎ (518) 263-4713) on Main St.

Hunter Mountain Ski Area

Hunter Mountain (☎ (518) 263-4223, (800) 467-7669) ski resort probably makes more snow than any other mountain in the US. The resort's 24-hour snowmaking capacity is almost as impressive as the skiing. Hunter has everything: 15 lifts, a network of 50 trails and restaurants featuring everything from sushi to burgers. During the summer, Hunter operates one chair lift that affords visitors great views of the Catskills' slopes and valleys. An interesting book, *The Sleeping Giant* by Paul E Pepe, traces the development of the mountain into a commercial sports area.

Hunter Mountain also sponsors a series of **summer festivals** (☎ (518) 263-3800) from July to early September every year, the biggest of which is the German Alps Festival in late August.

Places to Stay & Eat

Devil's Tombstone Campground (☎ (914) 688-7160) is on Route 214 four miles south of Hunter. The cost is $9 per night for a very basic site with toilets, but no showers, to six people. Open from mid-May to early September.

Atop a hill on Route 23A is the *Heartbreak Hotel* (☎ (518) 263-5050), a 150-room hotel with walls painted in colorful cartoon characters. This is a party hotel: you can squeeze as many people as you can into a room on weekdays/weekends for $50/80. There are also large bunkrooms that rent in their entirety for $75, or for $10 a head. The hotel also has its own large dance club, the War Zone (free for guests; $5 to $10 for everyone else), an all-night diner and a recording studio.

The *Forester Motor Lodge* (☎ (518) 263-4555) on Route 23A has a good view of the mountain. Large but basic rooms on weekdays/weekends during summer are $75/90; winter rates are $65/85.

The best place to stay in town, affording magnificent views of the mountain, is *Scribner Hollow* (☎ (518) 263-4211) on Route 23A. Each of the rooms is individually decorated in styles ranging from 17th century Spanish adobe to 21st century futuristic; all of the rooms have cathedral ceilings, some have fireplaces and many have bedroom lofts. 'Future world' has a fireplace and a tiered bathtub with a waterfall; the 'Hunting Lodge' has log-cabin walls and a bear carpet. Ask to see a few so you can pick one you like. Below the hotel is a grotto with an indoor heated pool, small waterfall and faux-stone columns. Weekday, weekend or peak rates for most basic single or double rooms range from $125 to $200. More elaborate rooms, suites and townhouses range from $200 to $400. Rates include breakfast and dinner, and all rates are cheaper in spring and summer.

Scribner Hollow's restaurant, *The Prospect* (☎ (518) 263-4211), overlooks Hunter Mountain. It features good American and Italian dishes, including roasted herbed chicken, duckling à l'orange and veal, all served with salad, potato and vegetable, in the $15 to $20 range.

Hunter Mountain Bagels (☎ (518) 263-5022) on 23A sells bagels and sandwiches.

It's a sit-down deli and a very good unofficial information center for the Hunter area, with maps and friendly advice.

Entertainment

Hunter is a town for partying. In addition to Heartbreak Hotel, there is the *Hunter Village Inn* (☎ (518) 263-4788) on Main St with music and happy hours, as well as *Tequilla's* (☎ (518) 263-4863) and *Pete's Place* (☎ (518) 589-9840). The bar in Scribner Hollow is a bit mellower than the rest.

WINDHAM

Ten miles up Route 296 from Hunter, you'll come to the more family-oriented ski resort town of Windham (population 1700). Adirondack Trailways stops at the Four Star Food Center (☎ (518) 734-4600) on Main St.

You'll find **Ski Windham** (☎ (518) 734-4300, (800) 729-4766) has a helpful staff and its modern facilities are open year round. In the winter, the resort operates a system of 33 trails and five lifts. Lift fees range from $22 to $35. In the summer, these same trails are used by mountain bikers. The resort is also the site of craft fairs and antique shows.

The **White Birch Cross-Country Ski Touring Center** (☎ 518) 734-3266) has everything you need for cross-country skiing, including lessons and equipment rentals.

Places to Stay & Eat

The *White Birches Campground* (☎ (518) 734-3266) has 130 sites open from mid-May to mid-October for $15. Take Route 23 one-tenth of a mile west of the junction with Route 296, then go north on Old Rd to Nauvoo Rd and follow the signs.

The *Hamilton Motel* (☎ (518) 734-3190) on Route 23 has weekday single/double rates for $50/60, add $5 for weekends.

The *Kopper Kettle Motel* (☎ (518) 734-3575), at the intersection of Route 23 and 296 (across the bridge), has singles/doubles for $45 to $55/50 to $60, slightly less during the summer.

The *Brooklyn Bridge Pub* (☎ (518) 734-5219) on Route 23 off Route 296 offers good burgers, and steak, chicken, or pork chop dinners for $10 to $12.

Tequila's Restaurant (☎ (518) 263-4863), in the middle of town, serves good Tex-Mex and Cajun dishes for lunch and dinner.

TANNERSVILLE

East of Hunter on 23A, Tannersville is so named for the leather tanning industry that once thrived here. Before the introduction of chemical substitutes, hemlock bark was required in the tanning process. The Catskills, whose hillsides were once covered with hemlocks, provided a convenient source of the raw material. However, the mountains were quickly stripped of hemlock in the early days of the industry,

---

The Late, Great Catskills Hotels

The area around Haines Falls was home to three of the biggest of the 19th century Catskill hotels, the most famous of which was the Catskill Mountain House. Built it the mid-19th century, this resort was the first of its kind: a deluxe hotel built in a remote wilderness on a cliff, with breathtaking views of North and South lakes and the Hudson Valley.

Part of the resort's attraction was its inaccessibility. After a long and difficult journey to the hotel by stage coach, guests were rewarded with spectacular scenery and elegant accommodations. However, the introduction of the automobile allowed vacationers to travel even greater distances from the cities in search of even more magnificent surroundings. By the 1920s, the Catskill Mountain House showed signs of disrepair and by 1943 it was closed permanently. In 1963, the state bought the abandoned hotel and burned it.

Two other deluxe hotels in the area, the 800 room Kaaterskill Hotel and the Laurel House, built at the top of Kaaterskill Falls, met with similar fates. The former burned accidentally in a fire in 1924; the abandoned remains of the latter were burned by New York State in 1966. ■

---

and now Tannersville and the surrounding areas are home instead to several exclusive residential developments. For visitors, the town offers a few good restaurants and bars for after-ski entertainment.

Adirondack Trailways stops at Warms Restaurant (☎ (518) 589-9871) on Main St.

Platte Clove Hike

For a pleasant hike along a stream punctuated by small waterfalls, try Platte Clove, a nature reserve run by the Catskill Center for Conservation & Development (☎ (914) 586-2611). The reserve gets few visitors, making it an ideal stop for those wanting a bit of solitude. Take County Rd 16 south from 23A near Tannersville (turn at Pete's Place) for about five miles. About one mile past Hutterian Brothers on the left you will see a tiny sign for Platte Clove.

Places to Stay & Eat

The *Sun View Motel* (☎ (518) 589-5217) has rooms for $48 during the week and $65 to $80 on weekends.

The *Eggery Inn* (☎ (518) 589-5363) is a large house with great views, a big dining room and a woodstove. At the Tannersville traffic light go south on County 16 for 1½ miles to the inn. Weekday/weekend rooms are $75 to $85/90 to $100.

As the name suggests, the *Last Chance Antiques & Cheez Cafe* (☎ (518) 589-6424), Main St, specializes in cheese dishes, including a fondue, nachos and chili with cheese. Most selections are under $6 for lunch. The restaurant also sells the antiques and collectibles that cover every inch of its wall space.

Maggie's Krooked Cafe (☎ (518) 589-6101), on Main St, has a funky atmosphere, small tables and good food. The breakfasts are great, including a local favorite, the 'SOB Omelet' ('south of the border'), made with grilled veggies and salsa.

HAINES FALLS

Haines Falls, five miles east of Tannersville on 23A, is most notable as the jumping off point for some of the most popular hiking destinations in the Catskills. It's usually just a day-trip, but there is a campground. *North-South Lake Campground* (☎ (518) 589-5058), three miles northeast of Route 23A from Haines Falls, is a large area with showers, boat rentals, play areas and trailheads. It's open from mid-May to late October for $16 per night; reservations are essential in the summer.

Kaaterskill Falls Hikes

The 260-foot falls are the highest in New York and a popular destination for hikers. The falls actually make two plunges on Spruce Creek. The Laurel House Hotel, which used to stand at the headwaters of the falls, dammed the creek and released the water over the falls periodically for groups of people who paid 25¢ to watch. The falls inspired generations of painters, including Thomas Cole – one of the Hudson River school painters – who immortalized the falls in his work *View of Kaaterskill Falls*.

To get there, drive one mile east of Haines Falls on Route 23; as the highway begins to dip there is a small parking area on the right. Park here and cross the highway and walk east along the north shoulder for a quarter mile to the trail head. The falls are a rocky and slightly steep half mile from the highway. Since this is a popular hike, arrive early on weekends.

To get to the top of the falls look for a sign in Haines Falls indicating the turnoff for North/South Lake. The trailhead is off Laurel House Rd on the way into North/South Lake.

North/South Lake Area

This is probably the most popular outdoor destination in the Catskills. There is a trail from the North/South Lake area up to the site of the Catskill Mountain House. Take the turnoff at the sign for North/South Lake in Haines Falls and follow the signs.

The *North/South Lake Campground* (☎ (518) 589-5058) has over 200 sites at $13 and is open from early May to early November. The campground and lakes are about three miles from Haines Falls. You can rent canoes and rowboats at the campground.

Southern & Western Catskills

In the southern foothills of the Catskill Mountains the famous **Catskill resorts** are grouped around Monticello and Liberty along Route 17, and north of Route 17 on Route 209 near **Minnewaska State Park** and **Ellenville**.

These resorts evolved from the boarding houses that sprang up here in the late 19th and early 20th centuries, when Jewish immigrants sought an escape from the poverty and crowded conditions of New York City. The area became known as the 'Borscht Belt,' and the small boarding houses grew into enormous (although not especially graceful) resorts, offering guests every imaginable kind of activity, from swimming in Olympic-size pools to skiing to golf. As the resorts grew, so did the program of activities. Whole families, from children and teenagers to parents and grandparents, were catered to. Two major components of the Borscht Belt experience were the food (and lots of it) and the comedians. Woody Allen captures some of this in scenes in *Annie Hall* and *Broadway Danny Rose*. The 1990 hit, *Dirty Dancing* was set at one of these resorts in their waning glory.

With the advent of jet travel, the resorts went into decline, and many closed as guests chose to travel to Florida, the Caribbean and Europe instead. More recently, Atlantic City has been drawing away a lot of their business. The surviving resorts have redefined themselves with big-name entertainment (from singers and bands like Tom Jones, Neil Sedaka and Frankie Valli & the Four Seasons, to such comedians as Jackie Mason, George Carlin and Brett Butler), special interest promotions (singles, golf, tennis, Mother's and Father's Day) and conference facilities. Gurumaya and her Siddhi Yoga organization have even bought up a former Borscht Belt hotel in South Fallsburg. The ones that remain, like the huge *Grossingers* in Liberty, prove the Darwinian maxim of survival of the fittest.

Others that survive are: *Concord* (☎ (800) 431-3850); *Kutsher's* (☎ (800) 431-1273); the *Nevele* (☎ (800) 647-6000); *New Brown's Hotel* (☎ (800) 327-6967); the *Pines Resort Hotel* (☎ (800) 367-4637); *Raleigh* (☎ (800) 446-4003); and the *Villa Roma* (☎ (800) 533-6767).

ALONG THE DELAWARE RIVER
The Delaware River divides New York State and Pennsylvania, and offers some of the best recreation in the region. For more coverage, see Delaware Water Gap in Northern Pennsylvania and Northern New Jersey chapters.

The town of **Narrowsburg** on Route 97 sits at a once-strategic bend in the Delaware River. Its 18th century stockade history is on display at the **Fort Delaware Museum of Colonial History** (☎ (914) 252-6660) daily during July and August, and weekends in June, from 10 am to 5:30 pm. Admission is $4/2.75 for adults/kids.

Narrowsburg is also one of several points along the river for **rafting** and **canoeing**. Lander's Delaware River Trips (☎ (800) 252-3925) runs raft and canoe trips from April to mid-October on a daily basis. Reservations are suggested. Trips range from three to six hours, cover five to 10 miles of river (depending on river and weather conditions) and cost $26/13 for adults/kids 12 and under.

Another summer river destination is **Barryville**, at the junction of Route 97 and Route 55, along an especially beautiful part of the Delaware River. Wild & Scenic River Tours (☎ (800) 836-0366) does rafting, canoeing and tubing daily from May to October, or whenever it gets too cold to coax people onto the water. The company provides shuttle transportation, and trips can range from two to six hours. Weekday rates are $21 per person, weekends $24. **Tubing** is a bargain at $12 per person. Kids 12 and under get a discount, according to the 'Pay What They Weigh' plan: 10¢ a pound when accompanied by two adults per raft.

Capital District & Mohawk Valley

Much of New York's history unfolds near the confluence of the Hudson and Mohawk rivers, only a few miles from the state's modern capital at Albany. Henry Hudson himself sailed far up the river in 1609, believing at first that he had discovered the fabled northwest passage to the Orient of Marco Polo legend. Later, waves of Dutch, English and French explorers, traders and settlers would battle each other as well as the Iroquois and other Indian groups for dominance in the region. When the Erie Canal was built in 1825, it connected Albany to Buffalo, utilizing the most navigable parts of the Mohawk River as it went. The pace of development of both the state and the nation's interior increased dramatically with the canal's completion.

Points of interest in the region include Saratoga Springs, a year-round retreat for the arts and the summer home of the US's oldest thoroughbred racetrack; Cooperstown, pristine home to the National Baseball Hall of Fame; and Binghamton, a sleepy college town to the southwest on the Susquehanna River near the Pennsylvania state border.

The primary east-west highway in the state, I-90, follows the Mohawk Valley from Oneida Lake – between Syracuse and Rome – and links the towns of Cazenovia, Utica, Herkimer, Canajoharie, Amsterdam and Rotterdam to Albany. From Albany I-90 dips south to join I-87 (for eight miles), then crosses the Hudson River and continues to the southeast into Massachusetts. I-88 is the other major east-west highway in the region, connecting Binghamton to Albany, 140 miles to the northeast.

I-87, also known as the Northway, runs north-south and connects Albany to Saratoga Springs, Glens Falls, Lake George and the Adirondacks. The other principle north-south route in the region is Route 28, which links Oneonta (at the

Highlights
- A day of spring water and spas or horseracing in Saratoga Springs
- National Baseball Hall of Fame in quaint Cooperstown
- The Albany Institute of History & Art, with a great gallery of Hudson River school landscape paintings ■

junction of I-88) to Cooperstown and the Adirondacks further north.

ALBANY

Located on the west bank of the Hudson River, Albany (population 100,000) is the state capital of New York and a city that has managed to retain, and retrieve, the historic charm of an old and vibrant northeastern city. Ornate state buildings and brownstone houses grace the downtown and the tree-lined streets of the neighborhoods. The marble and glass buildings of the enormous Empire State Plaza dominate downtown and stand in sharp contrast to the otherwise historic surroundings. Albany's character is largely defined by its role as the seat of the nation's second largest state government. Although it continues to be a manufacturing center, it is the city's service economy that has allowed Albany to escape the economic devastation that has accompanied the decline of basic manufacturing in other northeastern cities. In fact, the city enjoys a relatively healthy economy that supports excellent restaurants, revitalized neighborhoods, architectural gems and an array of amenities which make Albany worth a visit.

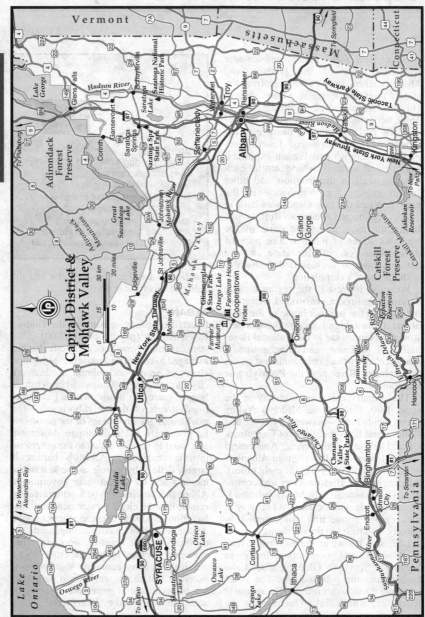

History

The Albany plateau was once the heart of the five Indian nations that included the Iroquois and Mohawk tribes. The plateau runs for 18 miles northwest to the Mohawk Valley. The first Europeans to arrive in the area in the 1500s were French trappers. In 1609, Henry Hudson sailed the *Half Moon* up the river that bears his name, opening the area to Dutch fur traders, who built a fort and developed a trading center. The first permanent settlement was established by a handful of Walloon families, French Protestants who fled the Spanish Netherlands looking for religious freedom and converts. They called their settlement Fort Orange. The town that grew up around the fort was known as Beverwyck (Beaver Town) and was controlled jointly – and with considerable contention – by the Dutch West India Company and a powerful diamond merchant, Kiliaen Van Rensselaer. In 1652, Peter Stuyvesant, who was – at that time – a director for the Dutch West India Company, declared Beverwyck an independent town. Twelve years later, Stuyvesant was forced to surrender the town and fort to the English, who once again renamed it, this time in honor of the Duke of York and Albany. Albany was officially granted a charter in 1686. The Dutch were allowed to keep their own language, religions and customs, all of which are still in evidence in Albany today.

Throughout the 17th and 18th centuries Albany remained an important link in the fur trade and its strategic location made it a logical meeting place for representatives from the various colonies. The British tried to capture it during the Revolutionary War, but failed. It became the state capital in 1797. With the opening of the Erie Canal between Buffalo and Albany in 1825, the city grew dramatically. Albany built a 4000 foot pier to service canal boats to transport people, wheat, salt, glass and other items. The railroad reached town in 1851 and the city soon became an important transportation crossroads and manufacturing center. The city's strategic location and its diverse economic base have helped it – in more recent times – to maintain a vibrant economy and to launch a preservation and renewal movement for much of the city.

Orientation

Albany is completely surrounded by interstate highways. The New York State Thruway, I-90, enters from the east and circles the city westward. I-87 comes in from the south and I-787 completes the circle to the east.

The 98 acre Nelson A Rockefeller Empire State Plaza sits at the center of the city. (For more on Rockefeller, see the sidebar in the Hudson Valley chapter.) Its white, gleaming marble buildings and sculpture gardens are bounded by Madison Ave to the west and State St to the east. Another major street, Washington Ave, runs northwest and soon forks into Western and Central Aves. State St divides many street addresses into north and south.

Within walking distance of downtown are several historic residential neighborhoods and the 84 acre Washington Park.

Albany is an easy town to get around in, by foot or by car. There's even free parking downtown.

Information

The Albany County Convention & Visitors Bureau (☎ (518) 434-1217, (800) 258-3582) is at 52 S Pearl St. You can also get information from the Albany Urban Cultural Park Visitors Center (☎ (518) 434-6311) in Quackenbush Square at the corner of Broadway and Clinton Ave.

The main post office (☎ (518) 462-1359) is at 445 Broadway in the Court Building. There are other post offices in Empire Plaza on the concourse level and in the capitol.

There are two good used bookstores in town: Dove & Hudson (☎ (518) 432-4518), 296 Hudson at the corner of Dove, and the Bryn Mawr Book Shop (☎ (518) 465-8126), at the corner of Spring and Dove Sts.

The Albany Public Library is on Washington Ave between Dove and Lark Sts. The *Times Union* is the daily newspaper, and *Metroland* is the giveaway 'alternative newsweekly.'

NEW YORK

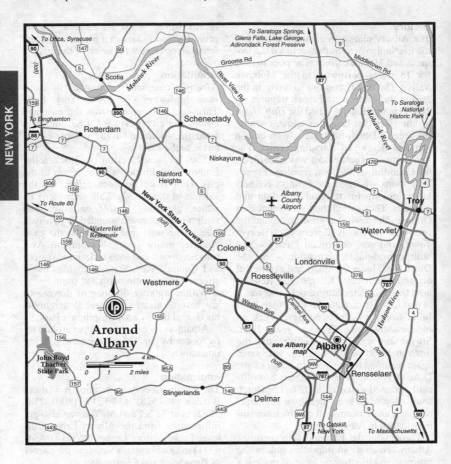

Empire State Plaza

Elevated slightly above the surrounding streets and buildings, the Empire State Plaza is 98 acres of brilliant white marble-and-glass buildings and sculpture gardens, which afford great views of the surrounding city and country. The plaza houses legislative offices, courtrooms, various state agencies, a collection of modern art and a performing arts center whose modern-curvy silhouette is called 'the Egg' by locals. Empire Plaza is bounded by Madison Ave and State St on the north and south and Eagle and

Swan Sts on the east and west. On weekends, when the plaza isn't crowded, people come here to rollerskate and play rollerhockey on the hundreds of feet of marble tiles.

For a quick orientation to the city and surrounding region, check out the view from the **observation deck** on the 42nd floor of the Corning Tower Building (☎ (518) 474-2418).

The collection of modern art (☎ (518) 473-7521) is on display along the concourse below the plaza and in the buildings surrounding the plaza.

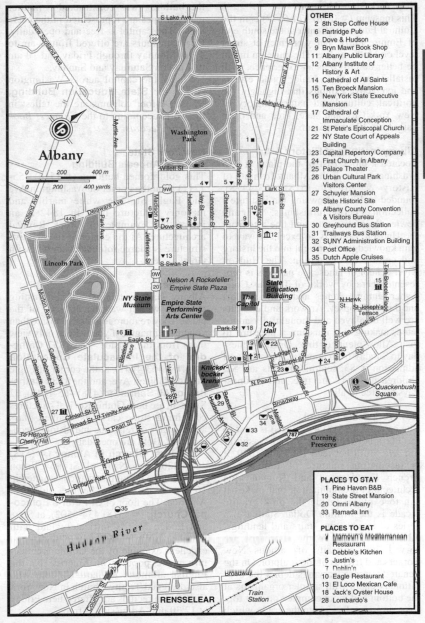

NEW YORK

Albany

0   200   400 m
0   200   400 yards

OTHER
2   8th Step Coffee House
6   Partridge Pub
8   Dove & Hudson
9   Bryn Mawr Book Shop
11 Albany Public Library
12 Albany Institute of
    History & Art
14 Cathedral of All Saints
15 Ten Broeck Mansion
16 New York State Executive
    Mansion
17 Cathedral of
    Immaculate Conception
21 St Peter's Episcopal Church
22 NY State Court of Appeals
    Building
23 Capital Repertory Company
24 First Church in Albany
25 Palace Theater
26 Urban Cultural Park
    Visitors Center
27 Schuyler Mansion
    State Historic Site
29 Albany County Convention
    & Visitors Bureau
30 Greyhound Bus Station
31 Trailways Bus Station
32 SUNY Administration Building
34 Post Office
35 Dutch Apple Cruises

PLACES TO STAY
1   Pine Haven B&B
19 State Street Mansion
20 Omni Albany
33 Ramada Inn

PLACES TO EAT
1   Mamoun's Mediterranean
    Restaurant
4   Debbie's Kitchen
5   Justin's
7   Doblin's
10 Eagle Restaurant
13 El Loco Mexican Cafe
18 Jack's Oyster House
28 Lombardo's

New York State Museum

This museum (☎ (518) 474-5877) is in the Cultural Education Center at the south end of Empire Plaza, but you enter at street level on Madison Ave. The museum might be better described as an experience, with installations built to scale, sound effects and interactive exhibits that highlight the political, cultural and natural history of New York City and state. Free and open daily from 10 am to 5 pm.

Albany Institute of History & Art

Located a block east of the plaza at 125 Washington Ave is the Albany Institute of History & Art (☎ (518) 463-4478), founded in 1791. Browsing the institute's collection of period furnishings, silver and pewter, decorative arts, and fine arts from the Hudson Valley is an excellent way to gain knowledge and insight into the history and culture of the region. The Hudson River school of landscape painters is represented here by works of Thomas Cole, Asher Durand, James and William Hart and Jasper Cropsey. Artwork and exhibits are well displayed and thoughtfully annotated, making this museum a pleasure to visit. Allow plenty of time. Open Wednesday to Sunday from noon to 5 pm. General admission is $3, seniors/students are $2; children under 12 are free, and Wednesdays are free to all.

New York State Capitol

The capitol (☎ (518) 474-2418) is next to the Plaza between State St and Washington Ave. Built between 1867 and 1899, it is fascinating mixture of Italian and French Renaissance and Romanesque architecture, a combination that makes it fun to explore. Inside the pink granite facade is the Million Dollar Staircase, a series of intersecting stairs and landings. Alongside of one of the staircases are carved 300 portraits of famous New Yorkers and friends of the sculptor. On the Senate Staircase, carvings depict the evolutionary chain with simpler organisms at the bottom and more complex ones at top. (Not surprisingly – given the era in which the building was constructed – neither man nor apes are represented in the carvings.) The capitol is free and open daily. One hour tours are offered from 9 am to 4 pm Monday through Friday and 10 am to 4 pm on Saturday and Sunday.

Facing the capitol across Washington Ave is the **State Education Building**, whose 90-foot columns are the tallest in the world according to the *Guinness Book of World Records*.

New York State
Court of Appeals Building

This gold-domed building (☎ (518) 455-7711) is on the corner of Washington Ave and Eagle St. The white marble and masonry structure built in 1842 is an interesting example of Greek Revival architecture. At the center of the massive structure is a large rotunda decorated with Greek orders.

Churches

Albany has a number of interesting churches within walking distance of the plaza. They're more impressive inside than you might imagine if you were to only view them from the outside. The 1852 **Cathedral of the Immaculate Conception** (☎ (418) 463-4447), at the corner of Eagle St and Madison Ave, and the 1884 **Cathedral of All Saints** (☎ (418) 465-1342), 62 Swan St, are both Gothic Revival structures containing stone carvings, stained glass and displays of religious and historic decorative art. Both are open daily.

The **First Church in Albany** (☎ (518) 463-0220), on N Pearl St at Clinton Square, has a pulpit that was constructed in 1656 and is said to be the oldest in America. The floor of **St Peter's Episcopal Church**, (☎ (518) 434-3502), at State and Lodge Sts, is intricately laid with mosaics. Built in 1859, the church is an excellent example of the Gothic architecture made popular in America by the English architect Richard Upjohn, who also designed Trinity Church in New York City. Organ recitals are offered here Friday at 12:30 pm. Admission is free.

Schuyler Mansion State Historic Site

The Schuyler Mansion (☎ (518) 434-0834), 32 Catherine St, was the home of Philip Schuyler (SKY-ler), a Revolutionary War general and senator. During the war, he commanded forces for the northern frontier from his home. As a result, the mansion was visited by many prominent political and military figures of the day, including Washington and Franklin. It was here that his daughter, Betsy, married Alexander Hamilton. British General John Burgoyne was held captive in the mansion after defeat by American forces at the Battle of Saratoga in 1777. The house was bought by the State of New York in 1912 and carefully restored. It contains excellent examples of colonial furnishings. Open mid-April through October, Wednesday to Saturday, from 10 am to 5 pm, and Sunday from 1 to 5 pm. Free, with a donations box.

Historic Houses

Begin at **Historic Cherry Hill** (☎ (518) 434-4791), S Pearl St between First and McCarty Aves, the home of the powerful Dutch diamond merchant Philip Van Rensselaer. Built in 1787, the home was once the center of a 900 acre farm. You can tour the grounds and the home, which contains an excellent collection of decorative arts, including silver, china and glassware, as well as colonial furnishings and paintings. Open Tuesday through Saturday from 10 am to 3 pm and Sunday from 1 to 3 pm, with guided tours on the hour. Admission is $3.50; students $2; children six to 17, $1.

Eight blocks from plaza is **Ten Broeck Mansion** (☎ (518) 436-9826) on Ten Broeck Place. The house was built in 1798 by Revolutionary War general Abraham Ten Broeck and currently houses the Albany County Historical Society.

The **New York State Executive Mansion** (☎ (518) 474 2418), 138 Eagle St, was the governor's home and is conveniently located adjacent to Empire Plaza on the west. This enormous red-brick Victorian was built in 1856 and altered many times, first by private owners and then by successive political administrations. It's open to the public by appointment on Thursday.

While you are in the area, stroll down **Bleeker Place**, which runs perpendicular to the entrance to the Executive Mansion. The street is lined by rows of wooden colonial houses built in the 1850s.

SUNY Administration Building

This two-winged neo-Gothic monster was once the offices of the Delaware & Hudson Railroad. On top of its central tower is a weathervane in the shape of Henry Hudson's ship, *Half Moon*. The six-by-nine-foot weathervane is the largest working one in the country and weighs a ton – 'and yet it spins,' as Galileo once said.

Lark St

Downtown, Lark St between Madison and Washington Aves is an interesting street of counter-culture establishments, restaurants and even an upscale tattoo parlor, all of which have helped it earn the saintly nickname of 'Greenwich Village North.'

Organized Tours

Walking Tours The Urban Cultural Park Visitors Center (☎ (518) 434-6311) does free 1½ hour walking tours June to September on Saturday. They also have a tape tour and trolley tours for $4 each.

Cruises Dutch Apple Cruises (☎ (518) 463-0220), 137 Broadway, conducts two hour narrated cruises along the Hudson River from May to October for $8.

Special Events

As the name suggests, the Annual Tulip Festival in early May is a three day celebration of the city's Dutch heritage held in Washington Park.

The Altamont Fair in mid-August is a week-long country fair at the nearby Altamont Fairgrounds.

Places to Stay

Bottom & Middle There are a number of independently owned motels along Central Ave within the first three miles west of the intersection with I-87 (exit 2). The rooms are very basic and generally clean, but a spot check of the bathrooms is advisable. Most rooms range from $25 to $35 a night.

Of these, a favorite is *Jack's Motel & Chinese Restaurant* (☎ (518) 456-5588), at 1881 Central Ave. Check in at the restaurant, the desk closes at 11 pm. Rooms are $26/28. Another motel within the same category is *Skylane Motel* (☎ (518) 456-1130), 1927 Central Ave. Rooms here are $30 to $35.

Next door to the Ramada Inn on Western Ave, three miles from downtown, is the *Capital Lodge* (☎ (518) 982-8989, (800) 489-4423, fax 489-8967), 1230 Western Ave. Smallish, typical motel rooms range from $40 to $50.

A nice downtown option is *Pine Haven B&B* (☎ (518) 482-1574), 531 Western Ave, where the rooms are furnished with antique dressers, iron bedframes, featherbeds and other Victorian amenities. Singles/doubles without bath are $50/65, with private bath $65/80. These rates include continental breakfast served in the dining room, which features a fireplace on cold mornings.

Also downtown, just east of Empire Plaza, is *State Street Mansion* (☎ (518) 462-6780, (800) 462-6780), 281 State St. This renovated guesthouse was formerly a seminary. Rooms have private or shared baths. Rates start at $50/85.

Top End Located across from the state university, the *Ramada Inn* (☎ (518) 489-2981, fax 489-8967), 1228 Western Ave, provides coffee makers and televisions in every room. Other amenities include an indoor pool, saunas and an exercise room. It's almost as comfortable as the pricier Omni, and at $69 to $89, including full breakfast in their restaurant, it's more reasonable.

The *Omni Albany* (☎ (518) 462-6611, fax 462-2901) is at the corner of State and Lodge Sts. Rates range from $120 to $150.

Places to Eat
Budget Several eateries are found on Madison Ave (Route 20), a pleasant part of

town, frequented by students from the College of St Rose and SUNY Albany.

Nepenthe (☎ (518) 436-0329), 154 Madison Ave, is a vegetarian restaurant where the menu changes daily. The restaurant offers an array of salads from $2 to $8 a pound. Good dishes (mostly vegan) include sesame noodles, Szechuan eggplant, cashew curry rice and a vegetarian Reuben in the $6 range.

Shalimar (☎ (518) 434-0890), 31 Central Ave, serves inexpensive Pakistani/Indian food in modest surroundings. Vegetable curries with rice are $5; several meat dishes are in the $5 range. *Mamoun's Mediterranean Restaurant* (☎ (518) 434-3901), 206 Washington Ave, near the corner of Lark St, serves tasty and authentic Middle Eastern food daily from 11:30 am to 10 pm.

Nature's Way (☎ (518) 462-0222), 277 Washington Ave, features vegetarian and meat dishes, including turkey burgers ($5), tofu tortellini ($7) and burritos ($6).

Dahlia's (☎ (518) 482-0931), 858 Madison Ave, serves kosher international vegetarian food. The food ranges from Moroccan stew to curries, moussaka, gado gado and falafel. Dahlia's also makes its own ice cream and cones. Closed from late November to late January.

Along Lark St between Madison and Washington Aves, you can choose from several inexpensive eateries, including *Debbie's Kitchen* (☎ (518) 463-3829), 290 Lark St, a popular take-out (or sit-in) spot, featuring excellent sandwiches from $4.50, deli salads and desserts.

A good coffeeshop/diner is the *Eagle Restaurant*, which is downstairs in a red brick building, opposite the library, on Washington Ave between Lark and Dove Sts.

El Loco Mexican Cafe (☎ (518) 436-1855), 465 Madison Ave, is a very popular and reasonably authentic Mexican restaurant serving lunch and dinner daily.

Moderate & Top End Several miles west of downtown, *Grandma's Country Restaurant* (☎ (518) 459-4585), 1273 Central Ave, serves American food with freshly prepared side dishes. Entrees include liver and onions, pot roast and chicken, all of which come with three side dishes: good food and huge portions for modest prices, ranging from $9 to $14. Leave room for the great pies baked on premises; big slices will run you $2.75 to $3.25.

Quintessence (☎ (518) 434-8186), 11 New Scotland Ave, is a trendy stainless-steel diner with a tuxedoed host and a bar where you might expect a counter. The food is upscale from the grill. Selections include burgers and teriyaki chicken and beef from around $6. The restaurant also has special theme menus, like 'Asian night' with dishes for $8 to $10. There's dancing Wednesday through Saturday and a band on Sunday. Make reservations for dinner; the place can be packed any night.

Lombardo's (☎ (518) 462-9180), 119 Madison Ave near S Pearl St, is an atmospheric neighborhood Italian place that's been here for years; unfortunately for Lombardo's the atmosphere of the neighborhood has enjoyed better days. The front room has a high, decorative tin ceiling with a long bar and wooden booths. Lombardo's serves traditional pastas with tomato sauce ($10) and special pastas like linguine with butter shrimp, fish and white beans ($14). There are also good fish, veal and chicken dinners. Open Monday to Saturday from 4 to 11 pm.

Justin's (☎ (518) 436-7008), 301 Lark St, has an upscale, creative menu and jazz brunches, very popular with the college crowd. You have a choice here of two menus. The reasonably priced cafe menu features grilled andouille sausage for $6.50 and beans and rice for $4. The more expensive restaurant menu includes basil pepper salmon ($18), Thai coconut shrimp ($15) and jerk chicken ($12).

For a taste of typical Albany, try *Jack's Oyster House* (☎ (518) 465-8854), 42 State St, The restaurant's namesake, Jack Rosenstein, opened his first oyster house in 1913 and the present one in 1937. The food is as good as the atmosphere, especially if you like clams and oysters, which are served on the half shell for $5 to $6 or in stews for $6.50. Jack's also serves seafood dishes, most in the $12 to $14 range. Pulitzer Prize-winning author William Kennedy *(Iron Weed)* immortalized Jack's in a 1985 *Esquire* article called 'Jack and the Oyster.'

Entertainment

Pauly's Hotel (☎ (518) 426-0828), 377 Central Ave at Quail St, is a convivial bar (but not a hotel) featuring local rock bands and dancing most nights.

The *8th Step Coffee House* (☎ (518) 434-1703), 14 Willet St, holds poetry readings, features local folk and acoustic performers, and has a weekly local mic night.

For late night jazz, check out *Justin's* restaurant (☎ (518) 436-7008), 301 Lark St, which has jazz on weekends from 10:30 pm on with a $3 cover and $7.50 minimum.

Bogie's (☎ (518) 482-4368), 297 Ontario St, near the corner of Madison Ave, is another good spot to hear local rock every night of the week. Cover prices average $5, depending on the act. There are pool tables and a nice people-watching, U-shaped bar.

The *Partridge Pub* (☎ (518) 482-9701), 869 Madison Ave, is another campus hangout with a DJ and dance music, open evenings until 2 am.

Theater and classical music happens at the Empire State Performing Arts Center (known as The Egg; ☎ (518) 473-1845), which has two theaters with dramatic, dance and music events.

Palace Theatre (☎ (518) 465-4663), 19 Clinton Ave, is the home of the Albany Symphony Orchestra, the Berkshire Ballet and Theatreworks USA. It's also a venue for visiting acts.

The *Capital Repertory Company* (☎ (518) 462-4534), 111 N Pearl St, does a six-play season.

Getting There & Away

Air Albany County airport (☎ (518) 869-9611) is served by American, Continental, Delta, Mohawk, Northwest, United and USAir. Approximate fares at press time range from $469 roundtrip to Chicago; $341 roundtrip to Washington, DC.

NEW YORK

Bus There are two bus terminals. Trailways (☎ (518) 436-9651), 380 Broadway, is across from the SUNY administrative building. Adirondack Trailways (☎ (800) 858-8555) is also here. They have service to/from New York City, Long Island, the Catskills, the Adirondacks and points west.

Bonanza Bus Lines runs from Albany to Connecticut and Massachusetts. You buy tickets through Adirondack Trailways.

The cleaner and nicer Greyhound terminal (☎ (518) 434-0121) is half a block away on the corner of Hamilton and Liberty Sts. Greyhound (☎ (800) 231-2222) runs regular buses to Atlantic City, Buffalo, New York City, Montreal and other places. Some one-way/roundtrip fares: Albany to New York City is $19/34; to Buffalo, $29/58; to Montreal, $49/98.

Train The Amtrak station (☎ (518) 462-5763, (800) 872-7245) is across the Hudson River in Rensselaer. Amtrak has daily service up and down the Hudson River Valley.

To get to the station from Albany, cross the Hudson on Routes 9 and 20 and follow the green train signs. To get to Albany from the station make a left out of the parking lot onto East St, take a left at the second light onto Partition St, then your next left onto Broadway, which takes you over the train tracks and to the intersection with Routes 9 and 20. Make a right and you cross the river to Albany.

Car Albany is accessible from I-90 from western New York or Massachusetts and I-87 from southern or northern New York.

Getting Around
The Capital District Transportation Authority (CDTA; ☎ (518) 482-8822) runs in Albany and in the immediate region to/from Schenectady, Troy and Saratoga Springs. It costs 75¢ plus zone charges of 20¢ or 30¢.

CDTA buses No 1 and 31 run to/from the airport and downtown. Taxis cost about $15 for the same route.

SARATOGA SPRINGS
Famous for its mineral springs and horseracing, Saratoga Springs (population 25,000) is a gracious town of Victorian architecture, manicured gardens, modern spas and classic pavilions, museums and a renowned program of concerts and dance performances.

Here you can 'take the cure,' as visitors have been doing for more than a century, which is to say that – even on a modest budget – you can pamper yourself with mineral baths, unwind in beautiful surroundings and check out the restorative powers of the spring water. In August, however, the atmosphere is far from relaxing, as the town is packed with boisterous race fans who travel long distances to enjoy some of the world's best thoroughbred horseracing. Just thirty miles north of Albany, Saratoga Springs is easily accessible and worth exploring.

History
Before the arrival of Europeans, the springs at Saratoga attracted wild animals, making this area a favorite hunting spot of the Mohawk and Oneida Indians, who called it *Saraghoha*, meaning 'fast water place.' Legend has it that Europeans were first introduced to the curative powers of the springs in 1767, when Mohawks brought Sir William Johnson, superintendent of Indian Affairs for the British, to recover here from a variety of war-related ailments. Johnson had been a trapper and, as the story goes, had developed a close relationship with several of the tribes of the Five Nations.

The commercial development of springs began only two decades later. Gideon Putnam arrived in the area in 1789 and bought the land around what later became known as Congress Spring (now in Congress Park). In 1802, he built the first hotel here. Horseracing and other commercial developments followed quickly.

During the Civil War, John Morrissey, a champion bare-knuckle heavyweight boxer and US congressman, took over a racetrack and built a casino (still standing in Congress

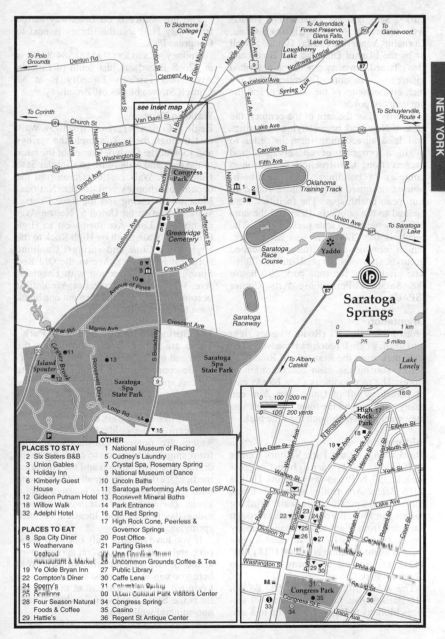

Saratoga Springs

0   .5   1 km

0   25   .5 miles

0   100   200 m

0   100   200 yards

PLACES TO STAY
2 Six Sisters B&B
3 Union Gables
4 Holiday Inn
6 Kimberly Guest
   House
12 Gideon Putnam Hotel
32 Willow Walk
32 Adelphi Hotel

PLACES TO EAT
8 Spa City Diner
15 Weathervane
   Seafood
   Restaurant & Market
19 Ye Olde Bryan Inn
22 Compton's Diner
24 Sperry's
25 Scallions
28 Four Season Natural
   Foods & Coffee
29 Hattie's

OTHER
1 National Museum of Racing
5 Cudney's Laundry
7 Crystal Spa, Rosemary Spring
9 National Museum of Dance
10 Lincoln Baths
11 Saratoga Performing Arts Center (SPAC)
13 Roosevelt Mineral Baths
14 Park Entrance
16 Old Red Spring
17 High Rock Cone, Peerless &
   Governor Springs
20 Post Office
21 Parting Glass
23 Van Gordon Street
26 Uncommon Grounds Coffee & Tea
27 Public Library
30 Caffe Lena
31 Columbian Spring
33 Urban Cultural Park Visitors Center
34 Congress Spring
35 Casino
36 Regent St Antique Center

Park). Saratoga had arrived. The resorts were visited by President Ulysses S Grant, Cornelius Vanderbilt and Jay Gould, as well as by the likes of Diamond Jim Brady and Boss Tweed. An early guidebook described visitors as a mixture of 'gentlemen of the turf, connoisseurs of the odd trick, and the amateurs of poker.'

Shortly after the turn of the century, the state of New York began buying the springs and land surrounding them in order to begin a program of conservation and preservation. Construction began on a complex of buildings, pools and bath-houses designed to rival those found in European health spas. The facilities were opened to the public in 1935 and the area officially became a state park in 1962. The result is the 2000 acre Spa State Park, which contains beautifully landscaped grounds, spas, outdoor pools and pavilions. The grounds of the state park also house the Saratoga Performing Arts Center (SPAC).

Orientation

From I-87, exit 13N (Route 9) goes right into town, where it becomes Broadway. The state park is on the west side of Broadway before you hit the main concentration of stores. The race course is a few blocks east of Broadway off of Union Ave. You can easily walk around the town, although you may want to drive through the state park.

Information

The Urban Cultural Park Visitors Center (☎ (518) 587-3241) is across from Congress Park at 297 N Broadway in Drink Hall, a 1916 Beaux Arts trolley station that was converted to a public spring-water drinking building in 1941. It's open Monday through Saturday from 9 am to 4 pm and Sunday from noon to 4 pm. During July and August there is an information booth (☎ (518) 584-4471) set up at the Broadway entrance to Congress Park.

The AAA office (☎ (518) 587-8449), 116 Ballson Ave, has maps and travel services Monday to Friday from 9 am to 5 am; there are extended hours on Thursday.

The post office is on Broadway across from City Hall and the library is next to Congress Park.

Cudney's Laundry (☎ (518) 584-8460) is at 126 S Broadway just south of Lincoln Ave. S&S Friendly Laundry is at 57 Church St, two blocks off Broadway.

Walking Tour

Begin at Congress Park on Broadway. Walk east through the park, sample the springs and look at the Casino. Come out the back of the park and walk south on Circular St to Union Ave. Walk east on Union past the decent old houses and to the National Museum of Racing and the Race Course. Walk back west on Union to Nelson Ave; go north to Lake Ave then west to High Rock Ave. Walk north on High Rock to the High Rock Cone and springs. Continue north on High Rock Ave to the Old Red Spring at the intersection with Excelsior Ave. Walk south on Excelsior Ave until it becomes Maple Ave and then cut one block west to return to Broadway.

The Springs/Saratoga Spa State Park

There are public springs throughout the town and in Congress Park, but the major-ity are concentrated in Saratoga Spa State Park. A spring even runs through the lobby of the information building. The park is open daily 8 am to dusk. Admission is $4 per car; free if you walk or bicycle in.

Except in the coldest weather, spring waters are pumped constantly, spilling from spigots into concrete catch basins or drains. The taste of each and the purported medicinal effects vary greatly. Carry a cup with you for tasting. There is also a helpful guide, *The Springs of Saratoga,* that pro-vides the history and location of each spring.

If you have time for only one stop in the park and wish to visit several springs, park at the Geyser area lot on Loop Rd. From here you can walk to most of the sights on Loop Rd. At the north end of the parking lot is the **State Seal** spring, which pumps non-mineral well water.

Across Loop Rd and about 50 feet southeast of the parking lot are the unmarked **Polaris Spring** and **Pump Well No 5**. These are also piped, but – because they bubble up very close to the ground – you may have to clear away questionable-looking vegetation to taste the water.

Across Loop Rd to the northwest of the parking lot is Geyser Brook. Running along the edge of the stream, you'll come across several springs, including **Hayes Well**, immediately across Loop Rd. The well is marked by a square cobblestone block about four feet high capped with a stone. A spring pours out of one side and on the other is a one-inch pipe from which you can inhale carbon dioxide, for that special feeling. Do not inhale deeply or your nasal passages will be burned.

Walk north a few feet and you'll find **Island Spouter**, a geyser next to the brook that spouts a continuous stream of water 10 to 20 feet into the air above a large mound of calcified minerals. If you walk north on the asphalt path above the west side of Geyser Brook, you will come to **Orenda Spring**. Its highly mineralized water contains so much radium that a sign has been posted, warning drinkers not to overindulge. If you walk along the dirt trail below the asphalt path on the west side of the creek, you will come to a mound of minerals created by the build up from the Orenda runoff as it heads into the brook.

Elsewhere in the park, **Coesa Spouter** is visible from the northwestern corner of the Coesa parking area. It spouts 10 feet up from a pipe in the middle of a small creek and its water is said to be valuable in curing 'ailments of the digestive tract.' **Hathorn No 3** is at the intersection of Route 50 and the park's east-west road. Like Coesa, the water is purported to be a laxative. Another freshwater spring is located at the north end of the park, south of Geyser Rd and next to the old bottling plant. **Charlie Spring** flows out of a wall near the SPAC (see Entertainment, below).

Besides the spring waters, the park features a full range of resort-like amenities, including two swimming pools, the Olympic-sized **Peerless Pool** and the

Victoria Pool. Even if you don't want a swim, check out Victoria's gracious surroundings and arched pavilions. You can spend an entire afternoon relaxing here for $6 (children six to 12, $3). The park also has walking trails, a golf course, tennis courts and picnic areas.

Congress Park
The small, formally landscaped Congress Park is located directly across from the visitors center, off Broadway. The park houses Morrissey's restored 1870 Victorian **Casino** which is now a museum and art gallery. Around the casino are Italian sculpture gardens and three springs, including **Congress Spring** which is inside a Greek Revival pavilion. The spring was 'improved' by Gideon Putnam in the late 1700s and its water bottled and sold in the 1820s. **Columbian Spring**, a freshwater spring, also runs through the park.

You can drive into the park from Broadway and park on the road right past the entrance gate.

Springs in High Rock Park
High Rock Park is a narrow park downtown two blocks east of Broadway. The park itself isn't particularly attractive and is bordered by a few modern townhouses. However, the park's springs are of historical interest. It was here, according to legend, that in 1767 the Mohawk Indians introduced Sir William Johnson to the restorative powers of the highly mineralized water, and – in doing so – opened the area to commercial development. Around 1800 Alexander Bryan built a public house of logs on the ridge above the springs and filled a water trough 'similar to those in use for feeding swine' for the use of his customers. Bryan's home is now a restaurant, Ye Olde Bryan Inn (see Places to Eat, below).

The **High Rock Cone** is a cone formed by the mineral deposits of the spring water pumped through it. The cone sits inside a semi-circular cement and cobblestone grotto with a pavilion roof. The water bubbles out very slowly from the top of the cone. **Governor Spring**, about 50 feet to the south of the cone, was drilled in 1908 and is named for New York Governor Charles Evans, who signed a bill protecting the springs. It has a strong mineral taste. Behind it is the very mild tasting **Peerless Spring**, which is actually pumped from across High Rock Rd.

Other Springs in Town

The **Old Red Spring** is at the northern end of High Rock Ave near the intersection with Excelsior Ave a few blocks from High Rock Park. In 1784, a bathhouse was built here. The spring, which has a high iron content, was called the 'beauty water spring' because it was said to be good for the complexion and as a cure for eye problems.

The **Rosemary Spring** is behind the Crystal Spa and in front of the Grand Union Motel at 92 S Broadway; although it looks as if it were on private motel property, it is open to the public.

Mineral Baths

The **Roosevelt Baths** (☎ (518) 584-2011) are located inside Saratoga Spa State Park. Although the baths are closed for renovation (as of this writing), the stately Georgian-style building is worth a look when you visit the park. For an old-fashioned mineral bath, people still go to the nearby Lincoln Baths (see below).

The **Lincoln Baths** (☎ (518) 583-2880), on S Broadway between the park entrance and the National Museum of Dance, are operating year-round until the renovation at Roosevelt Baths is completed. The Lincoln Baths started in 1911 in a remodeled gas company building and moved to their present home in 1935. In the Georgian-style building are men's and women's sections with semi-private soaking rooms. Each has a deep tub and a massage table. The customary treatment here is to sit in the bubbly water, which contains 16 minerals, for 20 minutes, then relax on a table for another 20 minutes. Moving around in the tub increases the amount of carbonation, just like shaking a bottle of soda. Some weekday/weekend rates: massage only,

$23/26; bath and massage, $35/40; bath only, $13/15.

The **Crystal Spa** (☎ (518) 584-2556), 92 S Broadway, is the only private bath facility in town. It pumps water from the publicly accessible Rosemary Spring, located behind the building. The facilities and treatments here are more luxurious than those in the public baths in spa park. The 15 soaking rooms have tile floors. A mineral bath, sauna and 30 minute massage costs $44. Other services include body wraps and seaweed treatments. The spa is closed on Wednesday and Thursday except during summer.

Saratoga Race Course

From late July through August, the town is transformed as horseracing fans flock to the Saratoga Race Course (☎ (518) 584-6200), the oldest active thoroughbred racetrack in the US. Hotel prices soar, the streets are jammed with fancy cars and the nights are long, as gamblers celebrate or commiserate over their wins and losses. You don't have to be a high-stakes gambler to enjoy the race track. Admission is only $2 ($5 for grandstand admission) and the minimum bet is $1. On the way in, pick up a copy of the *Post Parade*, which lists each horse's record by race and describes how to place bets. Once inside, you can walk right up to the fence and stand a few feet from the horses as they charge past. You can also stand near the winner's circle and watch the congratulations bestowed on jockey, owner and horse.

Even if you lose all your money, you can still rise to cheer as the horses race for the wire, take in the crowds and enjoy the great musical entertainment. Jazz and folk groups change on a daily basis and the house Dixieland band guarantees that there is never a lull in the fast-paced, spirited atmosphere.

The track is closed Tuesday with steeplechase on Wednesday and Thursday; post time is generally at 1 pm. Parking near the track will run you in the neighborhood of $3. There is free admission from 7 am to 9:30 am. This is the time to come and watch the horses' morning workouts and get a free tour of the stables.

There are plenty of outdoor food concessions at the track where you can buy typically overpriced food. Picnic tables are available in the grassy areas near the Victorian clubhouse, or you can sit under the grandstand and watch the races on television while you eat. As an alternative, you can eat at one of the several $15-minimum clubhouse dining rooms, but only if you are properly attired: 'collared shirts for men, no shorts or abbreviated wear.'

National Museum of Racing & Hall of Fame

This state-of-the-art museum (☎ (518) 584-0400), on Union Ave across from the track, contains exhibits on the history of horseracing in England and America, and on jockeys, thoroughbreds and breeding. In addition to paintings, sculptures and memorabilia, the museum has interactive exhibits built to scale, and a multimedia center where you can view an 18 minute film, *Race America*, or a video of a famous race of your choice in one of the video booths that line the walls. Open Monday to Saturday from 10 am to 4:30 pm and Sunday from noon to 4:30 pm, and from 9 am to 5 pm during racing season. Admission is $4.

National Museum of Dance

The museum (☎ (518) 584-2225) is on S Broadway next to the Lincoln Baths in the former Washington Baths building. The country's only museum dedicated to preserving the history and art of American dance, the building has a hall of fame and changing exhibits. A must for dance fans, it's open from the end of May to mid-June on weekends from 10 am to 6 pm, and from mid-June to early September from Tuesday to Sunday. Admission is $3/2 for adults/students and seniors.

Yaddo

Yaddo (☎ (518) 584-0746), on Union Ave east of the race course, is a private estate that has served as a retreat for writers, poets, artists and composers since the 1920s. The massive cut-stone mansion and lush grounds were built and developed by industrialist Spencer Trask and his wife. After their four children were killed in a smallpox epidemic, the Trasks converted the estate into a working community where they hoped artists might 'find the Sacred Fire and light their torches at its flames.' The mansion is still an artists' retreat and is, therefore, off limits to the public. However, the beautifully landscaped gardens – including a mysterious wooded area and formal rose garden – are open to visitors during the day.

Special Events

The Saratoga Polo Association (☎ (518) 584-3255) hosts polo events for about 15 days during August at a field two miles from town. Go north on Broadway, left on Church St for half a mile to Seward, right on Seward for one mile to the railroad overpass, and then turn right and look for the field on your left. Adult/senior admission is $5/3.

Places to Stay

Every August hotel prices double or even triple as the town fills up for the three to four week thoroughbred racing season. You need to book a year in advance to be sure of getting a room during this time. Rooms can also be scarce, and prices accordingly high, in May during commencement ceremonies at Skidmore College. Any other time of year – with the exception of the midwinter – is a good time to visit Saratoga.

Camping The nearest campground to Saratoga is *Cold Brook Campsites* (☎ (518) 584-8038), about 10 miles north in Gansevoort. Open May to early October, the campground has 272 sites, laundry facilities and hot showers. There's a $20 daily fee. Take I-87 to exit 16 and go north one mile on Gurn Springs Rd, or follow Route 50 north out of town.

Further north in Corinth is *Rustic Barn Campsites* (☎ (518) 654-6588). Open May through September, this is a small campground with 55 sites, providing hot showers and laundry facilities for $15 to $17 a day. Take Route 9N north from Corinth for 12 miles.

Middle The cheapest places to stay are the independently owned motels outside of town, along Route 9 (S Broadway) between exit 13N and town.

The *Kimberly Guest House* (☎ (518) 584-9006), 158 S Broadway at Lincoln Ave, rents eight rooms with kitchens and televisions. Some rooms share baths. During the winter, rooms are $35. As the summer approaches and the temperatures rise, so do the rates. In July, they're $55. By August, they've risen to $99.

Saratoga Motel (tel (518) 584-0920), 440 Church St two miles west of town, offers rooms ranging from $55/80 to $95 during racing season, making it one of the best deals in town during peak season.

The recently renovated *Holiday Inn* (☎ (518) 584-4550), Broadway at Circular St, is next to Congress Park. Rooms are spacious and rates vary from $52 to $75. During the racing season, expect to pay around $190.

Brunswick House (☎ (518) 584-6751), 143 Union Ave, is a rooming house that is transformed, during racing season, into a B&B. Weekly rates for rooms with shared/private bath are $65/80. In July and August, daily rates are almost as high as weekly rates are during the rest of the year. Rooms range from $70 to $80/85 to $95.

Top End *Willow Walk* (☎ (518) 584-4549), 120 High Rock Ave across from the High Rock Park springs, is one of the newest B&Bs in Saratoga. There are four rooms with private baths, and a living room with a wood-burning fireplace. Two of the bedrooms have twin beds and two rooms have queens. Off-season rates are $60 to $80; summer rates $85 to $95, and race season $135 to $145.

Union Gables (☎ (518) 584-1558, (800) 398-1158), 55 Union Ave, is one of the loveliest B&Bs in town. The restored turn-of-the-century Victorian has 10 spacious,

individually decorated rooms with private baths and refrigerators. Rates from November to April are $80; in September, October and May to July they're $90; in August, you can expect to pay about $200.

If you have transportation and like personal attention, try the *Saratoga B&B* (☎ (518) 584-0920), 434 Church St, two miles outside of town. There are actually two houses here, each with four rooms. One house was built in 1850 and has been lovingly restored. Each room is a suite with gas fireplace, television and phone. In the other house, the spacious rooms are decorated with period furnishings and handmade quilts. All rooms have private baths, and two have fireplaces. Rooms, with full breakfast, run $65 to $135. During race season, they're $95 to $195.

Six Sisters B&B (☎ (518) 583-1173), 149 Union Ave, has four rooms, several with porches. All rooms have refrigerators and are air-conditioned. Rates include a full breakfast. From November to March, rooms cost $60 to $89; from April to October they're $85 to $105; and in August, they go up from there.

Its location in the middle of Saratoga Spa State Park makes the *Gideon Putnam Hotel* (☎ (518) 584-3000, (800) 732-1560, fax 584-1354) the most famous hotel in town. Owned by the State of New York, the Georgian colonial hotel has recently been renovated in keeping with the vintage elegance of Saratoga. Guests approach the hotel – as one might expect – up a grand driveway. The lobby is expansive, with marble floors, potted palms and period furnishings. Rooms are extremely comfortable and the hotel has several restaurants and bars and easy access to all the recreational activities in the state park. The hotel is in a beautiful setting right off the Avenue of Pines. Rates May 1 to October 31 are $94 to $147; in August, they range from to $236 to $433.

The *Adelphi Hotel* (☎ (518) 587-4688), 365 Broadway, is old Saratoga personified – including its seasonal schedule (it's only open from May to October). The Adelphi was built in 1877 and is elegantly Victorian throughout. Rates vary from

$100 to $150 during the off season, but rise to $200 to $300 during June graduation at nearby Skidmore College and the August racing season.

Places to Eat

Budget The town diner is *Compton's* (☎ (518) 584-9632), 457 Broadway between Caroline St and Lake Ave. It's open Monday to Friday from 4 am to 2:45 pm and weekends from 3 am to 2:45 pm. Just a bit south of downtown is the *Spa City Diner* (☎ (518) 584-9833), 133 S Broadway, which has been around since 1948 and is open 24 hours.

The *Weathervane Seafood Restaurant & Market* (☎ (518) 584-8157), on S Broadway, a mile south of Congress Park, serves fresh and moderately priced seafood. Open daily for lunch and dinner.

Uncommon Grounds Coffee & Tea (☎ (518) 581-0646), 402 Broadway, is a convivial morning or late-night spot for good coffee, pastries or fresh bagels. Open daily from 7 am to 11 pm, and midnight on Friday and Saturday.

Moderate *Scallions* (☎ (518) 584-0192), 404 Broadway, serves very good sandwiches with fresh turkey breast, salmon, hummus etc, most for around $6.50. There are also several chicken dishes with sun-dried tomatoes, artichoke hearts, curry and other stuff for $11.

Hattie's (☎ (518) 584-4790), 45 Phila (fie-la) St, has been serving Southern cooking since 1938. The restaurant has recently regained its reputation as a Saratoga landmark and very good eatery. Southern fried chicken is $11, ribs are $13 and pork chops $12.

Four Seasons Natural Foods & Cafe (☎ (518) 584-4670), 33 Phila St, a short block east of Broadway, serves excellent buffet-style vegetarian fare, with home-made soups, deserts and cornbread. The cafe is open daily from 11 am to 8 pm.

Ye Olde Dryun Inn (☎ (518) 587-2990), 123 Maple Ave behind the Sheraton, is a popular place because of its 'rustic' look – stone walls, exposed beams and

fireplaces. The look would seem faux if it weren't in fact a 19th century building. There are more tables than the space warrants, but the atmosphere is pleasant and no one minds. Grilled sandwiches and hot and cold salads are around $7. Chicken, meat and fish entrees range from $12 to $17.

Sperry's (☎ (518) 584-9618), 30½ Caroline St, has excellent fish and meat dishes from $15 to $20 and a fine wine list. The food and service are quite good and the atmosphere very casual.

Cohan's-on-the-Lake (☎ (518) 583-1995), 700 Crescent Ave, is two miles from downtown Saratoga, overlooking Saratoga Lake. The Cohans consist of owner Bob and his three sons. The menu ranges from big sandwiches ($5) to pasta, beef tenderloin and shrimp scampi (around $15). Weekends feature live acoustic music on Saturday and a Sunday jazz breakfast. Drive east on Union Ave (Route 9P), over I-87, and turn right at Crescent Ave.

Entertainment

As if there weren't already enough to draw visitors to town, Saratoga Performing Arts Center (SPAC; ☎ (518) 587-3330) offers world-class entertainment. Located in Saratoga Spa State Park, SPAC is the summer home for both the New York City Ballet and the Philadelphia Orchestra. In addition, the outdoor amphitheater draws big-name entertainment ranging from Frank Sinatra to Twyla Tharp's Dance Company to the New York City Opera. Tickets range from $15 to $35, and you can often get lawn seats for $12.50 to $15.

Caffe Lena (☎ (518) 483-0022), 47 Phila St, is the 'oldest continuously operating coffee house in America.' Now run as a nonprofit, the cafe is a wonderful throwback to the '60s folk scene, and an authentic Saratoga original. It still books top acoustic musicians and provides a serious venue for young performers. The cafe is open Thursday, Friday, Saturday and Sunday.

One Caroline Street (☎ (518) 587-2026), 1 Caroline St, is a fine jazz and blues bistro (live jazz four nights a week). One Caroline also serves excellent food, including a Sunday brunch.

Parting Glass (☎ (518) 583-1916), 40-42 Lake Ave, is a block east of Broadway near the fire department, and in addition to the extensive beer selection, the big attractions is the traditional Irish music, a mainstay here. The club draws top performers from Ireland and the US.

Things to Buy
The Regent St Antique Center (☎ (518) 584-0107), 153 Regent St, a block east of Congress Park, houses 30 antique dealers in one building. This is a great place to hunt for regionally produced stoneware and crockery as well as silver, glassware, paintings and books. Open daily 10 am to 5 pm year round.

Other interesting antique shops, used clothing stores and music shops can be found off Broadway on Phila and Caroline Sts.

Getting There & Away
Bus Both Greyhound and Adirondack Trailways stop at the Spa City Diner (☎ (518) 584-0911), 133 S Broadway.

CDTA buses will run you around the immediate region – see Albany, earlier.

Train The Amtrak station (☎ (518) 587-8354), West Ave, is a couple of miles outside of town. Saratoga Springs is on the Montreal to New York City line, with one train going north and one south daily. At press time, fares from New York's Penn Station to Saratoga Springs were $34/68 one way/roundtrip, except Friday and Sunday, when it jumps to $56/112.

Car Saratoga is off I-87 at exit 13 N. The exit leads you along Route 9 past Saratoga Spa State Park and right onto Broadway.

Enterprise Rent-A-Car (☎ (518) 587-0687), 78 Church St; and Thrifty (☎ (518) 583-4601), 243 Union Ave, are national car-rental agencies with local agents.

Getting Around
The CDTA Saratoga Springs bus No 98 makes a big loop through town from Monday to Saturday. It costs 75¢.

During August racing season, Upstate Transit (☎ (518) 584-5252) runs a shuttle bus to/from the track and Broadway downtown for $1.

The Battle of Saratoga
For many Europeans, the American defeat of British General Burgoyne's army at Saratoga was proof that Americans could fight successfully against the British. The battle is often characterized as a turning point in the war because the American victory led to France's entry into the war on behalf of the US.

Burgoyne believed that the key to defeating the colonies was to control the Hudson River. He left St Johns (now St Jean) in Canada in mid-June 1777 with a 9000 man army of British, German, Canadian and Iroquois troops. Burgoyne's strategy involved acting in concert with other British forces, specifically those of colonel St Leger marching from Lake Ontario in the east and General Howe coming from New York City to the south. However, in early August, Colonel St Leger's forces, under fear of attack by a larger American force led by Benedict Arnold, retreated back to Canada after penetrating 50 miles east. Meanwhile, General Howe had moved his army against Philadelphia and hadn't left enough troops in New York City to aid Burgoyne in the north.

In spite of setbacks, Burgoyne pushed on to Saratoga (now Schuylerville) and decided to engage the Americans. The American troops were now commanded by General Horatio Gates, who was aided by Polish engineer Thaddeus Kosciuszko. In two battles on September 19 and October 7, Burgoyne's forces suffered heavy casualties and retreated to Saratoga. An American force that had grown to 20,000 men surrounded them there, and, on October 17, Burgoyne surrendered. ■

Safari, Inc, (☎ (518) 885-9260) runs carriage rides to/from the Gideon Putnam Hotel and points in Saratoga Spa State Park for $20.

AROUND SARATOGA SPRINGS
Saratoga National Historic Park
In October 1777, British forces were defeated at the Battle of Saratoga, a major turning point in the campaigns of the Revolutionary War. The battle is commemorated at various sites within the 2800 acre Saratoga National Historic Park (☎ (518) 664-9821), PO Box 648, Route 32, Stillwater, NY 12170, located 14 miles east of Saratoga Springs via Route 29. At the visitor's center, 2½ miles into the park, you can pick up a guide to key battle sites which you can visit along a nine mile driving tour. The route, which forms a loop, is open from early May to late November. There is a $4 vehicle fee; bicycles are also permitted on the route for $2. Or, you can hike the trails for $2. The park is open year round and is a popular spot for cycling, hiking, and cross-country skiing.

Seven miles north of the visitor's center – and still within the park boundaries – is **Schuylerville**, formerly the town of Saratoga. Located on Route 4 at the southern end of the town is the **Philip Schuyler House** (☎ (518) 695-3664). Schuyler was a Revolutionary War general who commanded the Northern frontier from his home in Albany. Schuylerville was the site of his summer house, which was burned by British General Burgoyne's retreating forces. The present house was rebuilt in 30 days on the same site. The house, which has been carefully restored with period furnishings, is open Memorial Day through Labor Day, Wednesday through Sunday from 9 am to 5 pm. From the day after Labor Day until the end of September, the house is open Saturday and Sunday, 9 am to 5 pm. Guided tours are available.

Also in Schuylerville is the **Saratoga Monument**, a 155 foot obelisk commemorating this decisive battle. Dedicated in 1912, the monument sits upon a 300 foot

hill which affords spectacular views of the surrounding countryside. The monument is currently closed for renovations.

COOPERSTOWN
With a population of only 2300, Cooperstown is the most popular small-town destination in the state. The draw, for most visitors, is the presence of three very different but equally interesting museums: the Fenimore House, the Farmers' Museum and the National Baseball Hall of Fame.

Don't let the commercialism associated with baseball deter you from stopping here as you travel upstate. The town has a great deal to recommend it, including the museums, it's location on the forested banks of Lake Otsego, its attractive 19th century architecture and excellent accommodations and restaurants.

Cooperstown was founded in 1786 by William Cooper, a wealthy land agent and the father of novelist James Fenimore Cooper, author of *The Last of the Mohicans* (1826) and The Leatherstocking series, *The Pathfinder* (1840) and *The Deerslayer* (1841). Cooper spent much of his childhood here as did another Cooperstown resident, Stephen Clark, a descendent of Edward Clark who made his money in Singer sewing machines. Stephen Clark was the force and fortune behind the creation of the three museums that have turned Cooperstown into a popular tourist spot.

An earlier local resident, General Abner Doubleday was falsely credited with inventing the game of baseball in 1839. Despite the historical inaccuracy, Cooperstown has been the home to the National Baseball Hall of Fame since its opening in 1939. This is the most popular sports museum in the US, attracting more than 400,000 devotees annually. In late July or early August, the town is even more crowded than usual as baseball fans make a pilgrimage here for the inductions into the Hall of Fame and the Hall-of-Fame Game.

Orientation & Information
The chamber of commerce (☎ (607) 547-9983) is in the Higgins Cottage located at

PLACES TO STAY
3 Otesaga Hotel
9 Baseballtown Motel
11 Ellsworth House
12 Lindsay House
14 Chestnut St Guest
   House
15 Bourdon Guest House

PLACES TO EAT
4 Cooperstown Diner
5 Sal's Pizzeria
6 Danny's Main
   Street Market
7 Clinton's Dam Sandwich

OTHER
1 Farmer's Museum
2 Fenimore House
8 Post Office
10 National Baseball
   Hall of Fame & Museum
13 Chamber of Commerce

Otsego Lake

Cooperstown

To Glimmerglass
State Park

Doubleday
Field

To Index,
I-88

31 Chestnut St on the way into town. They
have information on the town, and limited
accommodations details.

The post office is on Main St opposite the
National Baseball Hall of Fame. Willis
Monie (☎ (607) 547-8363, (800) 322-2995),
139 Main St, is a good used bookstore.

National Baseball Hall of Fame & Museum

The Hall of Fame (☎ (607) 547-7200),
baseball's national shrine, is what brings
most visitors to Cooperstown. Located on
Main St, the museum houses all the important baseball artifacts: famous players'

bats, gloves and uniforms and balls hit by
Babe Ruth, Willie Mays and Reggie
Jackson, just to name a few. Plaques honoring the players – and a handful of man-
agers, umpires and others – who have been
voted into the Hall are on display. In addition to the thousands of artifacts, the
museum has its own movie theater and
offers exhibits on every imaginable aspect
of baseball. There are many superb interactive statistical exhibits and, for the more
serious fans, a library. From May to September, the museum is open daily from
9 am to 9 pm. From October to April, the
doors close at 5 pm. Admission is $9.50.

If you intend to visit the Fenimore House Museum and the Farmer's Museum, you can buy a combination ticket and save from 20 to 25% off the price of single tickets.

Farmer's Museum & Village Crossroads

Along with the Fenimore House, the Farmer's Museum (☎ (607) 547-2533) and

NEW YORK

The Origin of Baseball

Although Cooperstown is popularly considered the birthplace of baseball, it almost certainly was not. In 1907, baseball's owners, attempting to establish the American origins of baseball, set up a commission to investigate the issue. The Mills Commission took their mission seriously and came up with a story establishing baseball as a truly 'American' game complete with a deceased military hero as inventor. The inconvenient fact that baseball had developed almost directly from the British game of 'rounders' was ignored.

The commission announced that baseball had been invented in Cooperstown in 1839 by Abner Doubleday (who was actually off studying at West Point that year). Doubleday had died in 1893 and so was unavailable to comment on the Mills Commission's findings.

Doubleday or not, baseball was being played in the 1840s in the urban areas of the northeast, with many organized baseball clubs. In 1876 the National League was formed and truly professional ball was born, in the sense that players were now openly paid for their services.

Baseball gained in popularity, and in 1902 the American League was formed, challenging the monopoly of the old National League. The first 'World Series' was played a couple of years later, and modern baseball was in full swing.

Although there were a handful of black players in the National League during the late 1800s, professional baseball became strictly segregated and remained so until after WWII. The major leagues (and their minor league 'farm teams') were reserved for whites only. Black players were relegated to the Negro Leagues, playing under harsh conditions and for little money. In 1947 Jackie Robinson signed with the Brooklyn Dodgers and became the first black player in modern baseball. He was quickly followed by other young players from the Negro Leagues, and baseball was integrated. However, many of the finest players of that era never had the chance to test their skills against 'all comers.'

Until relatively recently, players were at the mercy of the powerful and autocratic owners. The famous 'Black Sox' scandal of 1919 (subject of the 1988 film *Eight Men Out*) was triggered by the low salaries and poor treatment of the players. Big-time gamblers were able to bribe enough players on the Chicago White Sox to affect the outcome of the World Series that year. In reaction, the owners banned eight players from the game for life and set up a governing system with a strong Commissioner of Baseball. The commissioner system stayed in place until the last few years, while a committee of owners replaces the commissioner (temporarily, they say).

In the 1970s, Curt Flood, a star outfielder with the St Louis Cardinals, challenged baseball's 'reserve clause,' a contract clause which bound a player to one team in perpetuity. Although Flood won his case, leading to the free agency and vastly increased player salaries of today, he paid a heavy price – no one would hire him and he never played again.

Baseball has long been a game of tradition, with statistics and records playing an important part in the game's mythology and helping to build its popularity. Free agency, player strikes, lockouts, escalating salaries and astronomical profits have all affected the public perception of baseball in recent years, but perhaps TV is most responsible for baseball's recent travails. Baseball can be a slow game to watch and doesn't adapt to the small screen as well as other sports. But even though it may no longer be the most popular sport around, it still remains the National Pastime.

For an extensive overview of the sport, look for Ken Burns' *Baseball*, a PBS documentary series available on videotape. ■

adjacent 'Village Crossroads' are holdings of the New York State Historical Association. The museum is comprised of a dozen 19th century buildings built in the region and moved to Cooperstown on land donated by the Clark estate. The buildings – including a general store, blacksmith shop, printing office, barn and more – have been assembled to capture the atmosphere of rural life and to exhibit rural trades and skills. Demonstrations range from farming practices to baking bread to printing.

In the main barn is the **Cardiff Giant**, a 2990 pound carving that – in the 19th century – was passed off as the petrified, skeletal remains of a giant, dug up in nearby Cardiff. In fact, cigar maker George Hull had the giant sculpted out of gypsum. Even after the hoax was discovered, people continued to line up – as they do today – to see the 'petrified giant.'

From June 1 through Labor Day the museum is open daily from 9 am to 5 pm; during the month of May, and from early September to October 31, and for the week after Christmas, the museum is open daily from 10 am to 4 pm; in April and November it's open Tuesday through Sunday 10 am to 4 pm; and for the month of December until Christmas, Friday and Sunday 10 am to 4 pm. Admission is $9.

Fenimore House

Across from the Farmer's Museum is the stone Fenimore House (☎ (607) 547-2533) which was the home of Edward Clark, of Singer sewing-machine fame, the town benefactor. Heirs to his estate converted the home into a museum, which displays an outstanding collection of folk art, American Indian artifacts and paintings from the Hudson River school of landscape painters. Included here are Thomas Cole's *Last of the Mohicans* and Gilbert Stuart's *Joseph Brandt*.

The museum also houses memorabilia of James Fenimore Cooper. Ironically, Cooper's work is far more popular in other countries than in the US, where it came under sharp attack as early as the later part of the 19th century. American writers and poets of that time – most notably Twain and Whitman – were breaking with the British literary traditions and developing a truly authentic American voice in their writing. Cooper's romanticized characters, his unrealistic and contrived dialogue and his conservative views as expressed in his essays were harshly criticized, especially by the sharp-witted Twain.

More recently, however, Cooper's work gained some favor when his *Last of the Mohicans* was made into a popular movie. Whatever your views of the writer and his work, it's fascinating to view our country's history – as is done at the Fenimore House – through the lives of one of its literary figures. From July 15 to Labor Day the museum is open daily from 9 am to 5 pm. After Labor Day until October 31 and the week after Christmas, it is open daily from 10 am to 4 pm. From December 1 to 24, the museum in open Friday through Sunday. Admission is $9.

Places to Stay

Camping The nearest campground is the *Cooperstown Beaver Valley Campground* (☎ (800) 726-7314), Route 28 Box 704, about four miles south of Cooperstown near the town of Index. The campground has 100 sites and complete facilities, including laundry, hot showers and boat rentals. Sites are $21 and they offer a free shuttle bus to town on July and August weekends.

There's also *Cooperstown Famous Family Tent & Trailer Campground* (☎ (607) 293-7766), RD 3 Box 281, located four miles south of Cooperstown. From Route 28, take County Rd 11 west for four miles. Sites with laundry facilities and hot showers cost $18.

Located on the northeast side of Otsego Lake, *Glimmerglass State Park*, RR 2 Box 580, (☎ (607) 547-8662) offers campsites with hot showers and laundry facilities for $10.

Middle *Bourdon Guest House* (☎ (607) 547-9387), 60 Susquehanna Ave, offers the best bargain in town. There is a single, small, very clean, dormered room on the 2nd floor of this old Cooperstown home, with two beds, a television and fridge. The bathroom is in the room, but the shower is a short walk down some stairs and through the house. The single/double rate is $30/35 in the summer and $25/30 in the winter.

The *Ellsworth House* (☎ (607) 547-8367), 52 Chestnut St, is a three room B&B. Single/double rates with breakfast are $30/55. The *Lindsay House* (☎ (607) 547-5618), 56 Chestnut St, has three small studios with private entrances for $45 to $55.

Eight miles south of town is the *Brookside Motel*, offering inexpensive rooms with singles/doubles at $42/44.

The *Chestnut St Guest House* (☎ (607) 547-5624), 79 Chestnut St, has two rooms. One is decorated with baseball memorabilia and has a shared bath for $65, including continental breakfast. The other is a one bedroom suite with a kitchen and sleeping porch for $90. You cook for yourself if you rent the suite. The hosts, John and Pam Miller, are friendly and knowledgeable about the area.

The downtown *Baseballtown Motel* (☎ (607) 547-2161), 61-63 Main St, has unremarkable but large rooms with televisions for $45 to $59 for singles and $48 to $98 for doubles.

Top End Located right on Otsego Lake, the *Otesaga Hotel* (☎ (607) 547-9931), Lake St, PO Box 311, is a beautiful Georgian resort with manicured lawns, a golf course, tennis courts, pool and boat rental. Built in 1909, it has been very nicely maintained and is well worth visiting for a drink or a meal even if you don't choose to stay here. Open from late April to late October only, room rates are on a modified American plan only (with breakfast and dinner). Singles/doubles range from $160 to $190/230 to $260.

Places to Eat
The restaurants along Main St on the few blocks between Chestnut and Fair Sts generally serve inexpensive 'family style'

basic foods. The town diner, with good, solid diner fixtures is the *Cooperstown Diner* (☎ (607) 547-9201), 136½ Main St. A few doors down is *Sal's Pizzeria* (☎ (607) 547-5721), 110 Main St.

Danny's Main Street Market (☎ (607) 547-4053), 92 Main St, is a very good deli, with sandwiches made to order, fresh coffee and pastries.

Clinton's Dam Sandwich (☎ (607) 547-9044), on Hoffman Lane, just off Main St by the Baseball Hall of Fame, serves excellent sandwiches, most under $5, daily from 10 am to 4 pm.

Dining at the *Otesaga Hotel* (☎ (607) 547-9931) is a lovely experience and good value considering the elegant surroundings. They have a $12.50 lunch buffet, the set dinner is $27 including tax and gratuities and Sunday brunch is $15, served from 11 am to 2 pm. Jackets are required for men in the evening.

The *Fly Creek Cider Mill & Orchard* (☎ (607) 547-9692) on Route 28 about three miles northwest of town, is a water-powered cider press that uses original equipment to make great cider.

Entertainment
In addition to supporting three excellent museums, this tiny town is home to *The Glimmerglass Opera*, which stages performances at the Alice Busch Opera Theater (☎ (607) 547-2255) on Lake Otsego about eight miles north of Cooperstown on Route 80. The theater is partially open to the outdoors in the summer. The season is July and August.

A trio performs nightly throughout the season in the lounge at the *Otesaga Hotel* (see above).

Getting There & Away
Bus Pine Hills Trailways and Adirondack Trailways stop in front of the Chestnut St Deli (☎ (607) 547-5829), Chestnut St. The one-way/roundtrip fare from Cooperstown to Albany is $18/34.

Car By car from I-88, take exit 16 and then Route 28 north 18 miles to town. From I-90 (the New York Thruway), take exit 30 to Route 28 south 28 miles to town.

Getting Around
A trolley runs throughout town on weekends daily from June 27 through Labor Day. From Memorial Day weekend to June 27 and after Labor Day through Columbus Day, the trolley runs on weekends only. Service is from 8:30 am to 9 pm and costs $1.50 for the entire day.

BINGHAMTON
Binghamton (population 53,000) got its start as a river and canal town: When the Chenango Canal was completed in 1837, Binghamton became a busy link connecting the nearby Pennsylvania coal fields to the Erie Canal and ports beyond. SUNY-Binghamton (formerly Harper College) adds about 12,000 students to the area and provides an active theater and arts scene. The area is also known for several gold-domed Russian Orthodox and Ukranian Catholic churches.

Information
The Broome County Chamber of Commerce (☎ (607) 772-8860, (800) 836-6740), 49 Court St, has walking and driving tour maps of Binghamton and nearby Endicott and Johnson City – collectively known as the Triple Cities.

Things to See & Do
The Forum & Playwright Theater This theater (☎ (607) 778-2480), 236 Washington St, features a free 'Twilight Zone' exhibit about writer Rod Serling, who grew up in Binghamton.

Chenango Valley State Park A 20 minute drive northeast of town via I-88, this park (☎ (607) 648-5251) is a popular recreation spot for swimming, biking, nature-trail hiking and cross-country skiing.

Discovery Center of the Southern Tier This is a great kids' museum (☎ (607) 773-8661), 60 Morgan Rd, with several

hands-on exhibits, including a flight simulator. Open daily during July and August, and Tuesday through Sunday the rest of the year.

Roberson Museum & Science Center
This museum (☎ (607) 772-0660), 30 Front St, features displays of regional history and folk art, and has a kid-friendly science exhibit and planetarium. The museum is open daily, and admission is $4 and $3 for kids five to 17. The planetarium is another $1.

Carousel Museum This museum (☎ (607) 724-5461), at the Ross Park Zoo (☎ (607) 724-5454), 60 Morgan Rd, is home to a beautifully restored merry-go-round. There are five others in and around the town – all wood-carved and all working – but this is a good place to start. The carousels operate from the end of May until early September, weather permitting, and are free.

Places to Stay
Good rooms ranging from $45 to $75 can be found at *Super 8 Motel* (☎ (607) 775-3443), on Upper Court St, near Route 11.

Best Western Binghamton Regency Hotel (☎ (607) 722-7575), 225 Water St, is the newest big hotel in Binghamton and doubles as a conference center. It's downtown, has a pool and rates are reasonable in the $70 to $80 range.

Places to Eat
The *Spot Diner Restaurant* (☎ (607) 723-8149), 1062 Front St, is a Binghamton institution, tour-bus stop and reliable spot for breakfast, lunch and dinner every day of the year; it's open 24 hours.

A popular student hang-out, restaurant and late-night coffeehouse is the *Lost Dog Cafe* (☎ (607) 771-6063), 60 Main St, open Sunday through Thursday from 11 am to midnight; Friday and Saturday from 11 am until 2 am. The Lost Dog features a good Sunday brunch that's a bargain ($6 for Texas eggs). Other menu items include Greek chicken, pita pizzas, big salads and Italian sodas.

The Adirondack Region

The beautiful Adirondack region covers most of the northern triangle of New York state. When people refer to the 'Adirondacks,' they are speaking not only of the mountains, but also of the park and the region, all of which are inextricably woven together.

The Adirondack Park, established in 1892, is six million acres of private and public land covering 20% of the entire state. Inside the park are roads, towns and ski resorts – including Lake Placid, site of the 1932 and 1980 Winter Olympics – as well as mountain trails, jewel-like lakes and rivers. The Adirondack Forest Preserve is the 40% of the Adirondack Park that is owned by the state and protected from development by the designation 'forever wild' in the state Constitution. This is one of the least densely populated regions in the country. A five hour drive from New York City, the region offers visitors spectacular scenery and sublime solitude. Within the park, which is the largest outside of Alaska, are 46 mountains over 4000 feet high, including New York's tallest, Mt Marcy (5344 feet); 2800 lakes and ponds, 6000 miles of rivers, and many thousands more of streams. The Hudson River begins on Mt Marcy at Lake Tear-of-the-Clouds. There are only about 1300 miles of roadway in the park, but there are also over 2000 miles of hiking trails which attract both casual and avid hikers. When the park was first established, a blue line was used on an official map to designate the borders. Residents who live within the park's boundaries speak with understandable pride of living within the 'Blue Line.'

HISTORY

The Adirondack Mountains are not, as is popularly believed, part of the Appalachian chain. They're actually an outcropping of the Canadian Shield, a much older rock formation that lies mostly underneath Canada,

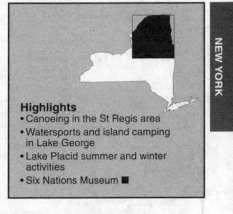

Highlights
- Canoeing in the St Regis area
- Watersports and island camping in Lake George
- Lake Placid summer and winter activities
- Six Nations Museum ■

but which surfaces in New York State as the Thousand Islands and the Adirondacks. The eastern Adirondacks, south of Lake Placid, are the most mountainous and the most spectacularly scenic. Looking at a map of the entire region, you'll note that many of the lakes and streams run in a northeast to southwest direction. This is because they were carved out by glaciers moving in this direction about 10,000 years ago. In the southwestern section of the park, many of the lakes are interconnected, providing over 100 miles of excellent canoeing.

The Adirondack region includes ecosystems that range from alpine to wetlands. Forest cover includes white pine, red spruce, maple, beech, birch and other species. Park fauna includes whitetail deer, black bear, raccoons and in a few places, moose. You can easily spot hawks and, of course, waterfowl. Fishing for trout, salmon, pike and other species is still considered excellent, despite the acid rain which has harmed these populations. Swarms of insects – in particular, the infamous black flies – can be a nuisance, especially during June and July, so bring

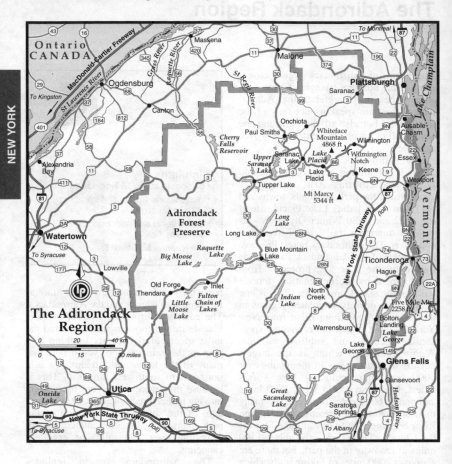

plenty of bug repellent, or 'bug dope,' as the locals say.

The origin of the name 'Adirondack' is unclear. A widely believed explanation is that the name is an Iroquois word – *ha-de-ron-de* or *rat-eh-ron-tak* – meaning 'bark eaters,' a term which the Iroquois used pejoratively to describe the poor hunting skills of the Algonquian Indians. A Williams College professor and surveyor, Ebenezer Emmons, mistook the word for a Huron term meaning 'they of the Rock Clan,' and thus christened the mountains while on an expedition, believing that he

was commemorating the Indians of the region. American Indians did, in fact, use the Adirondacks to hunt, fish and gather forest products, but moved south during the winter to escape the rugged terrain and harsh, sometimes violent, weather.

Over the years Europeans were led to the Adirondacks by Indians. Early Europeans and Americans were especially interested in exploiting the park for its natural resources, specifically beaver for fur and pine trees for ship masts. During the 1800s, the park was logged mercilessly. White pine was cleared for building, hemlock bark for leather tanning and spruce for making paper. The Adirondacks were denuded of much of their original timber by the early 1900s, but have since managed to recover. Today, logging – now referred to as 'managed-forestation' – is once again a big business in the region, and the source of an ongoing debate.

In the 19th century, during the period of the heaviest logging, the Adirondack region was also being exploited as a tourist destination for those seeking to escape to the wilderness. In the decades after the Civil War, entrepreneurs opened large hotels throughout the Adirondacks. At the same time, conservationists urged that the land be saved to protect the watershed. The region's remoteness and beauty attracted millionaires – among them, the Rockefellers, Morgans and Vanderbilts – who built luxurious estates running into the tens of thousands of acres. These vast complexes, arrogantly referred to by their owners as 'camps,' popularized the notion of the region as a playground for the rich.

The battle between developers and conservationists continues to this day. For many residents, development means sorely-needed jobs. For environmentalists and part-time residents fleeing New York City, development continues to threaten the pristine wilderness. The Adirondack Park Agency (APA) regulates land use, both public and private, within the park. It's hard to find a landowner who doesn't dislike the APA because of its restrictions or a conservationist who doesn't wish the agency would do more to preserve the region.

ORIENTATION

The Adirondack region described here extends beyond the Blue Line, and includes the area north and east of the park boundary. Occasionally, people will include Saratoga Springs (near the state capital of Albany) in the region, though most residents of that town would wonder why. Interstate 87 runs the length of the Adirondacks from the Lake George area north to Plattsburgh and the Canadian border 20 miles beyond. Together, Lake George and Lake Champlain form a contiguous border which separates the Adirondack region from neighboring Vermont to the east; several ferries connect the lakes' shores.

There are relatively few roads within the Adirondacks. In addition to I-87, the main north-south road is Route 30 which begins at the Canadian border with Quebec, and connects the towns of Malone, Saranac Lake, Tupper Lake and Blue Mountain Lake. The term 'north country' is a bit elusive (like 'upstate'), but tends to refer to the Blue Mountain Lake area northward; like the 'Blue Line' designation, north country residents are proud of the term, even if it does mean that they shovel more snow and ice during the long winters. (How long? In Lake Placid, July is the only 'killing frost-free' month!)

Route 22 is a particularly scenic route which skirts the west edge of Lake Champlain and connects the historic towns of Ticonderoga, Crown Point and Essex. Lake Placid of Winter Olympic fame is a year-round recreation center, and close to the rugged High Peaks region. Route 3 connects Plattsburgh and the Tupper Lake area, and continues westward to Lake Ontario. Route 28 is a mostly east-west route that runs through Blue Mountain Lake, and connects Old Forge in the southwestern portion of the park to Lake George in the southeast.

There are three primary drainages for the Adirondacks: the St Lawrence River, the Hudson River and Lake Champlain.

INFORMATION
Tourist Offices

There are two Visitors' Interpretive Centers which feature indoor and outdoor exhibits about the park. One is in the town of Paul Smiths (☎ (518) 327-3000) on Route 30, one mile north of Paul Smith's College. The other is the Newcomb Center (☎ (518) 582-2000), 14 miles east of the town of Long Lake on Route 28. Both are open daily year round, except Christmas and Thanksgiving, from 9 am to 5 pm (until 7 pm from May 1 to October 1). The centers also sponsor various educational programs and lectures.

NEW YORK

There are also local and regional tourist offices in just about every 'major' town.

Adirondack Mountain Club

Those who are interested in seriously exploring the park should contact the Adirondack Mountain Club (ADK). The club, which has been around since 1922, promotes conservation, hiking, canoeing and outdoor use of the Adirondacks. It also offers educational programs, guided hikes, senior getaways, nature courses (on birds, mushrooms, plants), photography, rock climbing, fly-tying, kayaking and more. ADK headquarters (☎ (518) 668-4447, (800) 395-8080), RR3, Box 3055, Lake George, NY 12845, is on Route 9 south of exit 21 off of I-87. There is also an Adirondack Loj & ADK High Peaks Information Center (☎ (518) 523-3441), Box 867, Lake Placid, NY 12946, in the northern Adirondacks. Take Route 73 south of Lake Placid for about two miles to Adirondack Loj Rd. Go down Loj Rd for five miles.

ADK members get a 10% discount on everything sponsored by the organization, including accommodations, and the *Adirondack* magazine every other month. Adult/senior/student membership costs $35/25/20.

Media

The *Adirondack Journal* and the *Chronicle* are free weeklies available in the Adirondack region. They contain news, community information and ads. The *Adirondack Daily Enterprise* is the only weekday daily published in the park. The paper is published in Saranac Lake and available in most towns.

OUTDOOR ACTIVITIES
Hiking

Whether you're interested in an easy day-hike or a far more adventurous wilderness backpacking experience, the Adirondacks offer the best hiking trails in New York, and some of the best in the New York/New Jersey/Pennsylvania region. The New York State Department of Environmental Conservation maintains the Adirondack trails with assistance from conservation groups. It's easy to find the trail heads, which are marked by brown wooden signs with yellow lettering. You can camp anywhere on state land as long as it isn't above 4000 feet or within 150 feet of water or within 100 feet of a trail. Much of the Adirondacks is privately owned and only a few owners allow public access, so look for the 'No Trespassing' signs.

Hiking Guidebooks   There are two excellent series of books on the Adirondack trail networks. One is put out by the Adirondack Mountain Club (ADK, see above); and the other is the *Discover the Adirondacks* series by Backcountry Publications (☎ (802) 457-1049), PO Box 175, Woodstock, VT 05901.

The ADK publishes guides that break up the region into seven parts. Each book includes a large removable, topographical map. The club also publishes guides on rock and ice climbing, natural history, literature about the Adirondacks and a good field guide.

The Discover series includes 11 books – one for each of 11 different parts of the region – which describe hiking, snowshoeing and cross-country skiing trails and include topographical maps.

Warning to Hikers

Be careful hiking in the Adirondacks. Although the mountains are deceptively gentle in appearance, the terrain is, in fact, difficult. Add to this the sheer size of the wilderness, and the result is the nearly annual tragedy, often involving an experienced, lone hiker who wanders from the established trails. In the summer of 1990, 38 year old David Boomhower got lost while on a solo 10 day hike along the popular 130 mile Northville-Lake Placid Trail. He left on June 5 and died in early August after trying to survive on insects, snails and plants. One of the final entries in his journal, found after his death, reads 'Just what happened? I didn't bring enough food, ran out, and also encountered a string of bad weather. Took (unreadable) trail . . . Somehow got lost off that . . . I'm surprised they haven't found me . . . ' ■

Maps The *Adirondack North Country Regional Map* shows all state-owned land as of 1986. It's available free or for $1.25 by mail from the Adirondack North Country Association (☎ (518) 891-6200), 183 Broadway, Saranac Lake, NY 12983.

The USGS Map Distribution Branch, Box 25286, Denver, CO 80225, publishes maps on different parts of the region. You'd need to buy quite a few to cover the entire park. USGS maps are also available from outdoor stores in New York City and the Adirondacks or from Timely Discount Topos (☎ (800) 821-7609).

Jimapco maps (☎ (518) 899-5091), Box 1137, Clifton Park, NY 12065 (north of Albany), is a good source of Adirondack hiking and boating maps.

The ADK also publishes maps which can be purchased separately from their guides.

Downhill Skiing

The weather, elevation and comfortable facilities combine to make much of the Adirondack Park prime ski country. Lake Placid was chosen twice to host the Winter Olympics and another bid is likely. Meanwhile, there's great skiing across the park, though the Lake Placid–Whiteface Mountain area is the most famous.

Big Tupper
     Tupper Lake, NY; three miles south of Tupper Lake on Route 30; vertical drop of 1150 feet; lift fees $18 to $20. (☎ (518) 359-7902)
Gore Mountain
     North Creek, NY; off Routes 8 and 28, 16 miles north of Warrensburg; 2100 feet; $24 to $33. (☎ (518) 251-2411)
Whiteface Mountain
     Wilmington, NY; on Route 86, 10 miles east of Lake Placid; 3200 feet; $28 to $34. (☎ (518) 523-1655)
Willard Mountain
     Greenwich, NY; on Route 40, six miles south of Greenwich, which is 10 miles east of Saratoga Springs on Route 29; 500 feet; $16 to $20. (☎ (518) 692-7337)

Cross-Country Skiing

Cross-country skiing is for experts and beginners alike. Ask about trail difficulty and weather conditions as novice Nordic skiers can roam far from any community before realizing their predicament. This is not the lift-and-lodge experience.

Adirondack Park Visitors Center
     Paul Smiths, NY; on Route 30, one mile north of 92; 17 kilometers of trails; free. (☎ (518) 327-3000)
Adirondack Loj
     Lake Placid, NY; off Route 73, eight miles southeast of Lake Placid; 20 kilometers; $6. (☎ (518) 523-3441)
Ausable Chasm Cross Country Ski Center
     Ausable Chasm, NY; exit 34 off I-87 on Route 373; 26 kilometers; $4. (☎ (518) 834-9990)
Bark Eater
     Keene, NY; 17 miles north of exit 30 off I-87, half mile off Route 73 on Alstead Hill Rd; 20 kilometers; $5 to $8. (☎ (518) 576-2221),
Cascade Ski Touring Center
     Lake Placid, NY; five miles south of Lake Placid on Route 73; 20 kilometers; $5 to $6. (☎ (518) 523-9605)
Cold River Ranch
     Tupper Lake, NY; 13 miles west of Saranac Lake on Route 3; 10 kilometers; free. (☎ (518) 359-7559)
Gore Mountain
     North Creek, NY; 16 miles north of Warrensburg on Route 28; 11 kilometers; $2 to $4. (☎ (518) 251-2411, (800) 342-1234)
Mt Van Hoevenberg
     Lake Placid, NY; off Route 73, seven miles south of Lake Placid; 50 kilometers; $4 to $8. (☎ (518) 523-2811, (800) 462-6236)
Whiteface Inn Nordic Ski Center
     Lake Placid, NY; off Route 86, 1½ miles west from Main St; 30 kilometers; $6 to $10. (☎ (518) 523-2551)

Canoeing

To a canoeist, the Adirondacks are heaven on water. The terrain is hilly, but the base is often gentle and level, and ideal for canoeing. Adirondack Park offers some of the best canoeing in the northeast. Canoe trips can vary from a dilettante afternoon to several days of canoeing, camping and portaging – or carrying – your canoe and supplies. There is a wealth of information, outfitters and guides to help.

Prices You can bring your own equipment, rent the equipment you need or sign on for a complete guided tour, including meals and shuttle service. Prices, of course, vary accordingly. Basically, there are four ways to go.

• Bring your own equipment, maps, food, experience and knowledge of the terrain. Instruction and paddling programs are available for adults and children.

• Rent the necessary equipment from a good canoe outfitter who will also help you plan a comfortable itinerary (canoes rent for $25 to $50 a day, depending on weight).

• Rent a complete (or partial) outfitting kit, including canoe, car racks, portage and camping/cooking gear, food, shuttle transportation and itinerary; prices range from $40 to $80 per person/per day; a four day family camp and canoe package for two adults and two kids runs about $500.

• Sign up for a guided trip which includes all of the above plus your own expert. Prices range from $80 to $100 per person for a one day excursion to about $200 a day for small groups on trips of more than a day.

Routes & Outfitters One of the most popular canoe routes runs from Old Forge on the Fulton Chain of Lakes in the Central/Southwestern section of the park through chains of lakes up to any one of a number of northern lake towns such as Tupper Lake, Saranac Lake or Paul Smiths. The New York State Department of Environmental Conservation (☎ (914) 255-5453, (518) 897-1309), in Albany, NY 12233, distributes a short pamphlet, *Adirondack Canoe Routes*, describing this and other routes. A more detailed map, like those from the USGS, is also advisable before setting off on such a trip, not to mention advice from local canoeists. Other popular trips include the St Regis area to Tupper Lake, a trip of three to four days.

For a more leisurely day trip, you can canoe down the North Branch of the Moose River, beginning at the North Street Bridge near Old Forge. The trip, which takes about four hours, is easy and scenic as the river twists its way along the gently curved banks of hardwood forests and grassy wetlands. Take along a picnic to enjoy on one of the many small, sandy beaches. There is one portage of about 300 yards along the route. For an even easier canoeing trip, you might try Nick's Lake, two miles from Old Forge.

If you arrive in the area without a boat, you can find one to rent at the marinas on most lakes, or try Tickner's Adirondack Canoe Outfitters (☎ (315) 369-6286), 1 Riverside Dr in Old Forge, or Adirondack Canoes and Kayaks (☎ (518) 359-

---

The Fifth Season: Blackflies, Head Nets & Bug Dope

Summer in the Adirondacks is a favorite time of year for bugs as well as humans. During the month of June in the Adirondacks, give or take a week, blackflies can change your life.

Blackflies are tiny, the size of a poppy seed, and they swarm. They definitely discourage summer recreation for the unprepared hiker, canoeist, swimmer. They can be fierce, and the only remedy is preparation – either chemical or fashion. Head nets are considered a must by local outfitters, especially if you want to do anything but dive into your tent cursing the day you expressed interest in the wilderness.

You can buy bug suits, hooded bug sweatshirts, or simple head nets in almost any sporting goods or general store in the Adirondacks.

An alternative is chemical lotions and sprays. Some contain DEET, which many people consider too strong for prolonged application. Candles with citronella also help at campsites.

With any of the chemical applications, take extreme care with children, who should not be allowed to apply such lotions or sprays; many can cause adverse reactions if swallowed or smeared in the eye. ■

2174), 96 Old Piercefield Rd and Route 3 in Tupper Lake.

Further north, the St Regis canoe area north of Upper Saranac Lake is prized by canoeists. There are 58 lakes and ponds in this area where you can canoe for weeks, or put in for a leisurely afternoon.

A good trip with small children begins and ends in the Fish Creek Ponds Loop near Upper Saranac Lake. This trip can take from one to three days, and begins and ends at Fish Creek public campground. The 10 mile loop connects Fish Creek Pond, Little Square Pond, Floodwood Pond, Rollins Pond, Whey Pond and Copperas Pond. There are only three portages, each less than a quarter mile.

Another modest 10 mile trip through the St Regis canoe area is between Saranac Inn and Paul Smiths College. Also known as the 'Seven Carries route,' the trip begins with a 1½ mile portage to Little Green Pond, and crosses Little Clear Pond, St Regis Pond, Green Pond, Little Long Pond, Bear Pond, Bog Pond, Upper St Regis Lake and Spitfire Lake. The average portage here is no more than a quarter mile.

You can rent canoes, arrange for a guide service or car shuttles at St Regis Canoe Outfitters (☎ (518) 891-1838) in Lake Clear, NY 12945, off Route 30. This is one of the most thorough of all Adirondack canoe outfitters.

GETTING THERE & AROUND

Air
USAir has regular service into Adirondack Airport (☎ (518) 891-4600) in Saranac Lake, 16 miles west of Lake Placid. Roundtrip from Albany to Saranac Lake is about $300; service is daily except Saturday. USAir also serves Plattsburgh, Watertown, Syracuse and Albany airports, mostly from their Pittsburgh, PA, hub.

Bus
Adirondack Trailways (☎ (800) 858-8555) runs throughout the region. The summer schedule is fairly extensive, but winter is more limited. Sample fares are included in coverage of Adirondack destinations.

Champ (☎ (518) 523-4431) is the Essex County public transportation system. It runs regular service to/from Lake Placid and Ray Brook, Saranac Lake, Wilmington and other places. You can also flag the bus down on any main route and it will stop. Rates are from $1.50 to $5.

Train
Amtrak stops at Westport (☎ (518) 523-4431), 37 miles east of Lake Placid on Route 22. Champ public transportation (☎ (518) 523-4431) runs to/from the train station if scheduled in advance. The one-way/roundtrip fare is $25/45 for one or $30/50 for two.

The train also stops in Plattsburgh, and in Saratoga Springs to the south (see the Capital District & Mohawk Valley chapter).

Car
I-87 runs north-south from New York City through the eastern portion of the Adirondacks and up into Canada. Almost every road through the park could be called a scenic route and most are only two lanes. Route 30 is an especially beautiful road that runs through the middle of the Adirondack Park for 160 miles from the Great Sacandaga Lake in the south to Malone above the northern edge. Routes 28 and 3 both enter from the west and intersect with Route 30 at about mid-park. The town of Blue Mountain Lake and the Adirondack Museum are at the intersection of Routes 30 and 28. Routes 73 and 86 from the east are also lovely byways.

Boat
Three ferries (☎ (802) 864-9804) cross Lake Champlain between Vermont and the low plain between the lake and the eastern side of the Adirondacks. The northernmost crosses between Grand Isle, VT, and Plattsburgh, NY. The 12 minute crossing is done year round from 5 am to 1 am. The one-way/roundtrip car and driver fare is $6.75/10.75; adult passengers are $1.75/2.50; kids six to 12 are 50/75¢. From Plattsburgh you can take Route 3 south through the northern

Adirondacks to Saranac Lake, a distance of about 50 miles.

The ferry between Burlington, VT, and Port Kent, NY, is 40 miles from Lake Placid. From Port Kent, which is inside the Blue Line of the park, take Route 373 west, which runs into Route 9N west and then Route 86 west into Lake Placid. The one hour crossing is done from mid-May to mid-October daily from 8 am to 5:30 pm, with slightly longer hours during the summer. The one-way/roundtrip car and driver fare is $12/21; adult passengers are $3/5.50; kids six to 12 are $1/1.50.

Another ferry crossing connects Charlotte, VT, and Essex, NY. Essex is on Route 22 which runs south along the western shore of Lake Champlain to Ticonderoga, a distance of about 40 miles. You can also head south 12 miles to Route 9N, which runs west into Route 73 and then to Lake Placid. The 20 minute crossing is done from April 1 to January 2. There are over 20 crossings each way from 6:30 am to 10 pm from mid-May to mid-October and fewer in spring and fall. The one-way/roundtrip car and driver fare is $6.75/10.75; adult passengers are $1.75/2.50; kids six to 12 are 50/75¢.

The Fort Ti Ferry (☎ (802) 897-7999) runs to/from Shoreham (Larabees Point), VT, and Ticonderoga, NY, from early May to late October. The ferry runs on demand and the crossing takes six minutes. In May, June, September and October it runs from 8 am to 6 pm; in July and August it runs from 7 am to 8 pm. The fare is $5 for a car and up to four passengers; bikes are $1; and pedestrians are 50¢ (the same as it was 150 years ago). The Fort Ti ferry is the oldest business in Vermont, and was originally a military crossing in use during the French & Indian War.

Today, on the Fort Ti side, some people are content to spend part of a summer afternoon by the small sandy parking lot just watching the ferry and its small assortment of people come and go. There is even a converted trailer-snack shop under a shady group of trees for refreshments while you wait.

LAKE GEORGE

Lake George, located at the southeastern entrance to the park, is the largest lake completely within the park boundaries. The 32 mile long lake – dotted with 365 islands – is often described as the 'Queen of America's Lakes,' in part for its deep-blue, crystal-clear water and wild shorelines. Called Lac du Sant Sacrement by Jesuit missionary Isaac Jacques when he was led here by Indian guides in 1646, the lake was of strategic importance during the French & Indian War. In 1755, British General William Johnson renamed the lake after King George. More recently, during the mid-20th century, the lake became the haunt of city-weary artists, among them the artist Georgia O'Keeffe and her husband, photographer Alfred Steiglitz, who managed to capture with his camera their quotidian existence along the lake's forested shores.

At the southern end of the lake is Lake George Village (population 900), a town crammed with motels and tacky souvenir shops, all of which stand in marked contrast to the otherwise scenic surroundings. Don't let Lake George Village discourage you from visiting the lake. As tourist towns go, it isn't that bad and, as a major tourist destination, it offers a variety of inexpensive places to stay, including a hostel.

Orientation

From I-87 (the Northway), exit 21 lets you off at the south end of town on Route 9, and exit 22 puts you at the north end.

Information

The Lake George Chamber of Commerce & Visitors Center (☎ (518) 668-5755) is on Route 9/Canada St at the south end of the village (opposite Prospect Mountain), on the east side of the street. They are open daily during the summer season from 9 am to 5 pm, and Monday to Friday the rest of the year. During July and August another office (☎ (518) 668-2846) is open on Route 9N right off of I-87 exit 22.

The post office (☎ (518) 668-3386) is on Canada St a block north of Beach Rd, right at the center of town.

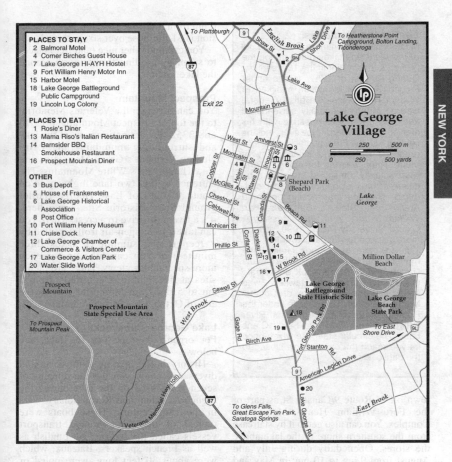

PLACES TO STAY
2 Balmoral Motel
4 Corner Birches Guest House
7 Lake George HI-AYH Hostel
9 Fort William Henry Motor Inn
15 Harbor Motel
18 Lake George Battleground
     Public Campground
19 Lincoln Log Colony

PLACES TO EAT
1 Rosie's Diner
13 Mama Riso's Italian Restaurant
14 Barnsider BBQ
     Smokehouse Restaurant
16 Prospect Mountain Diner

OTHER
3 Bus Depot
5 House of Frankenstein
6 Lake George Historical
     Association
8 Post Office
10 Fort William Henry Museum
11 Cruise Dock
12 Lake George Chamber of
     Commerce & Visitors Center
17 Lake George Action Park
20 Water Slide World

Parking is something neither the Indians nor the English of the 18th century had to deal with. Now they do, along with everyone else who comes to Lake George Village. A good place to park is the big lot across the street from the steamboat landing. It's metered parking, but – good news – you can feed the meter for 10 hours at a time, for 50¢ an hour. Bad news: The meters operate 24 hours a day, seven days a week. There is another lot nearby with an attendant where the standard charge is $5 a day (you get $2 back if you ride the steamboat).

Fort William Henry Museum

This fort (☎ (518) 668-5471) is a re-creation of the 'site of the *Last of the Mohicans*' as the banners and plaques tirelessly note. The fort was built in 1755 by the order of British General William Johnson. A victorious French and Indian force burned it to the ground in 1757. It was rebuilt by Americans seeking tourist dollars in 1953. Inside are reconstructed barracks and other rooms and artifacts. During July and August a 'living history' program includes cannon firing and musket ball making. The fort is at the center of

Last of the Mohicans

Much of James Fenimore Cooper's *Last of the Mohicans* takes place during the French & Indian War in the 18th century. During August of 1757, forces under French General Montcalm attacked Ft William Henry. Inside British General George Munro eventually surrendered and was given safe passage with his men to Fort Edward. However, Indians fighting with the French attacked the surrendered British and killed many of them. Their reasons for doing so and what actually transpired are quite a bit different from the popular image of blood-thirsty savages massacring unarmed Anglos. Ian Steele's *Betrayals: Fort William Henry and the 'Massacre'*, Oxford University Press, 1990, gives a more balanced portrayal of events.

In any case, in his book James Fenimore Cooper told the story of the Indians Uncas and Chingachgook and Anglo guide Natty Bumppo, or 'Hawkeye,' who safely hid the daughters of Colonel Munro in a cave. This cave is under the Route 9 bridge over the Hudson River between Glens Falls and South Glens Falls. The circular staircase which once let you reach the cave is now closed to the public. ■

town off of Route 9/Canada St as part of the Fort William Henry Motor Inn Complex. You can also get to it by staircase from the southern shore of the lake above the stores. Open daily during July and August from 9 am to 10 pm; in May and June and from Labor Day to Columbus Day, from 10 am to 5 pm. Admission is $8; over 60 and ages three to 11, $6.

Million Dollar Beach (Lake George Beach State Park)

This small, sandy beach (☎ (518) 668-3352) is a short walk south of Fort William Henry along the shore of the lake. The beach was originally developed (and so named) for the wealthy clientele of the bygone era of big resorts along the lake. There are picnic facilities here, a bathhouse and lifeguards on duty daily from 9 am to

6 pm from mid-June to Labor Day. Admission is $1 for those over six; parking is $3.

You can find other nice (and free) places to swim by heading further north around the lake.

Prospect Mountain

You can drive up the Veterans Memorial to the top of Prospect Mountain (☎ (518) 668-3352) for dramatic views of the lake and surrounding mountain ranges, including Vermont's Green Mountains and New Hampshire's White Mountains. The entrance to this two lane highway is on Route 9 south of Lake George Battleground State Historic Site. From here, it's a five mile drive to a crest, where you can take a free, open-air trolley pulled by a Jeep to the summit (it takes three minutes) or you can hike up for even more spectacular views. There are picnic sites at the summit. Open daily from 9 am to 5 pm from Memorial Day to the end of October for $5 per vehicle.

Lake George Shipwrecks

For organized cruises of the lake, see below.

History buffs, boating enthusiasts and divers will enjoy viewing the remains of seven boats used on the lake during the French & Indian and Revolutionary Wars in the 18th century. These boats were typical of the flat-bottomed transport vessels called the *bateaux* by English as well as French speakers. Bateaux, which were about 30 feet long, were poled or oared across the lake in order to transport troops and supplies. In the summer of 1758, after the British failed to take Fort Ticonderoga (Fort Carillon) from the French, British and American forces sunk over 200 boats to store them for retrieval after the winter. The troops returned in the spring of 1759 to retrieve the bateaux, but they missed many, including those on display.

The best-known group is referred to as the Wiawaka Bateau Cluster, which is on the state register of historic places. What's left of the seven boats is submerged in 25 to

40 feet of water about 150 feet northeast of the Camp Wiawaka boat house on the eastern side of Lake George off of Route 9L (East Shore Dr) near Lake George Village. Visitors are free to dive and look at what is left of the boats on the lake bottom, but not to touch them.

Scuba diving here is rather popular, but the old diving paradox remains: the colder the water the clearer the view. Lake George is 200 feet deep in parts, and old war-wrecks are the viewing prize. Call ☎ (518) 668-4644 for information.

For more information, contact the Lake George Historical Association (☎ (518) 668-5044), Bateaux Below, PO Box 2134, Wilton, NY 12866; or the Dept of Environmental Conservation, Region 5 (☎ (518) 891-1370), Route 86, Box 296, Ray Brook, NY 12977.

Other Things to See & Do

For more serious amusement-park type fun, you can head for **Lake George Action Park** (☎ (518) 668-5459), at West Brook Rd on Route 9, an 1890s theme park with rides and shows; and **Water Slide World** (☎ (518) 668-4407) which features a wave pool, 13 water slides and hot tubs, just south of town on Route 9. Both are open mid-June through Labor Day.

Before heading back to the wilderness, you can make one more stop along Route 9 and take in the attractions at New York's largest amusement park, **Great Escape Fun Park** (☎ (518) 798-1084, 792-3500) with raft rides, roller coasters, live shows and divers – and a nice Adirondack backdrop. Open Memorial Day to Labor Day daily from 9:30 am to 6 pm, later on weekends. Expect big crowds in the summer. Prices are $22 for adults, $18 for kids (age three to 11), and free for kids under two.

Lake George Cruises

A cruise, even one as short as an hour, is a good way to enjoy the lake and take in the scenery along its shores. Several tour boats (☎ (518) 668-4644) leave from Beach Road on the southern shore of the lake opposite Fort William Henry. From

late June to Labor Day, one hour sightseeing cruises leave daily about every hour, and from May 1 to the end of June and from Labor Day to October 31, four times daily. Basic sightseeing cruises cost $7; $6.50 for seniors and $3.50 for those three to 11. There are also less-frequent 2½-hour cruises.

From late June to Labor Day, dinner cruises leave daily at 6:30 pm. From May 1 to late June and Labor Day to October 31, they leave on Saturday at 6:30 pm. There is also a 10 pm entertainment cruise. The dinner cruise costs $27/17 for adults/children three to 11. The entertainment cruise is $7.75/5.

French & Indian War

The French & Indian War, which lasted from 1754 to 1763, is known in Europe as the Seven Years' War. In the early 1750s, fur traders and land speculators in the American colonies began to express interest in lands claimed by France east of the Appalachian Mountains. The French had built a line of forts from Lake Erie to western Pennsylvania from which they controlled their land. In 1754, the British colonial government sent young George Washington and 150 troops to dislodge the French. Washington failed, as did a force of 1500 men under British General Braddock (see Pittsburgh in the Southwestern Pennsylvania chapter).

The British and American troops fared poorly against the French and their Indian allies until 1757 when William Pitt became prime minister of England. Pitt borrowed heavily to pay for a vast infusion of troops and ships which helped change the course of the war. In 1759, the Anglo-American forces captured Fort Niagara on eastern Lake Erie, Fort Crown Point on southern Lake Champlain and Quebec. When British and American troops captured Montreal in July 1760, French resistance in the New World collapsed. In 1763 the Peace of Paris agreement gave Britain all of North America east of the Mississippi, as well as Florida and Canada. ∎

The Lake George Steamboat Co (☎ (518) 668-5777, (800) 553-2628) has cruises on their paddleboat *Minne-ha-ha*, and on the *Mohican* and dinner cruises on the *Lac de Saint Sacrement*. You can get on/off at Baldwin Landing in Ticonderoga on the north end of the lake if you just want to go one way. The 4½ hour cruise leaves from late June to Labor Day, daily at 9 pm. The roundtrip fare is $14.50/7.25. The one-way fare is $10.50/5.25.

From mid-May to Columbus Day in early October, lunch cruises leave daily at 11:30 am for $24.50/12.25. From late June to Labor Day, a dinner cruise leaves at 6:30 pm for $34.40/17.25. From July 3 to the end of August, moonlight cruises leave at 10 pm for $12.50/6.25.

Special Events
The **Lake George Opera Festival** (late July to mid-August; ☎ (518) 793-3858) is a professional opera company which stages performances at Queensburg High School on Aviation Rd in Glens Falls. Tickets range from $10 to $60.

The **Lake George Jazz Festival** draws national jazz artists on the second weekend in September in Shepard Park. Call the Lake George Arts Project (☎ (518) 668-2616) for schedule details.

Places to Stay
See also Bolton Landing, below, which has a luxury resort.

Camping The State of New York maintains campgrounds for visitors on 92 of the islands in Lake George. For information and reservations in any New York state park, call ☎ (800) 456-2267. In addition, Lake George Islands Public Campgrounds (☎ (518) 668-5441) are on three islands, each accessible by boat from nearby shore points. All the island campsites are open from mid-May to mid-September.

Long Island (☎ (518) 656-9426) is on the southern end of the lake, and has 90 sites at $11 per site. You get there by boat from Lake George Village. You can also get there from Cleverdale, Kattskill Bay and Pilot Knob on the eastern side of the lake, or from Diamond Point or Bolton Landing on the western side.

Glen Island (☎ (518) 644-9696) is in the narrows of Lake George (not to be confused with Narrow Island) and is accessible from Boltons Landing. It has 213 sites at $13 each. Glen Island also has a camp store. To get to Boltons' Landing drive north from Lake George Village on Route 9N about 10 miles.

Narrow Island (☎ (518) 499-1288) is in the Mother Bunch of Islands in the northern half of the lake. It has 96 sites for $13 each. You can get there from Silver Bay on the west side of the lake or Hulett's Landing on the east. To get to Silver Bay drive north from Lake George Village on Route 9N for 29 miles. To get to Hulett's Landing take Route 9 south five miles to Route 149. Take Route 149 north for 12 miles to Fort Ann where it turns into Route 22. Take 22 for about 20 miles to the turnoff for Route 6. Go west for five miles and you'll be in Hulett's Landing. This is a long ride, and unless you plan to be on the eastern side of the lake, you're better off getting to Narrow Island from Silver Bay.

There are a fair number of campgrounds around Lake George Village. The *Lake George Battleground Public Campground* (☎ (518) 668-3348) is at the south end of town on Route 9. It has 50 sites in a shady pine grove with showers and bathrooms. Rates are $10 to $15 plus $1.50 per day. Day use is $3 per car or $1 for walk-ins. It's a good place to shower at the day use rates. Open May 7 to October 11.

Adirondack Camping Village (☎ (518) 668-5226) is located on a shaded hill and has 150 sites and full amenities, including hot showers, camp store, recreation room and laundry. Sites cost $18 to $22. Go north on Route 9 for three-quarters of a mile from I-87 exit 22. Open mid-May to mid-September.

Heatherstone Point Campground (☎ (518) 668-5193) has 250 sites at $11 per site for up to six people (a bargain by camping standards). It is open from mid-May to mid-

September. Take Route 9N two miles north of Lake George Village.

Hostels The *Lake George HI-AYH Hostel* (☎ (518) 668-2634) is located in the basement of St James Episcopal Church on the corner of Iroquois and Montcalm Sts. This is basic dormitory-style accommodation with 10 beds to a room. When crowded there's a maximum three-night stay. The hostel is open from late May to Labor Day. The rate for members/non-members is $10/12. From the Trailways bus stop walk one block south on Canada St and then one block west on Montcalm.

B&Bs *Corner Birches Guest House* (☎ (518) 668-2837), 86 Montcalm St at Helen St, is the only B&B left in Lake George. Four comfortable and clean rooms share one bathroom, and you're free to watch TV in the living room. Year-round rates, including a breakfast of coffee, juice and toast, are $35 to $45.

Motels & Efficiencies Route 9/Canada St is lined with motels from one end of town to the other. Rates are highest from late June through Labor Day weekend. The *Balmoral Motel* (☎ (518) 668-2673), 444 Canada St, is at the north end of town in the middle of the Route 9/9N fork. There are 25 nicely furnished rooms; the management is friendly and the swimming pool – with an island in the middle – is the largest in town. Off/in-season rates are $35 to $54/55 to 85.

The *Harbor Motel* (☎ (518) 668-3124) is at the center of town on Route 9/Canada St. Rooms are functional, if a bit shabby. Rates are $35 to $65/45 to 95.

Lincoln Log Colony (☎ (518) 668-5326) is located at the south end of town on Route 9/Canada St, by the corner of Veterans Memorial Hwy (the road to Prospect Mountain). It has large clean efficiencies with funky motel furniture and paneled cabins with a nostalgic pine smell. There's also a pool. Rooms are $60/82. Cottages and apartments come in four sizes from $60 to $85/84 to 99.

The *Fort William Henry Motor Inn* (☎ (518) 668-3081, (800) 234-0267) is at the center of town in the Fort William Henry complex. There are wonderful views of the lake from the property, but not – unfortunately – from all of the rooms. Rooms here are not much better than those in other motels in town, but it has some resort-like accommodations, including terraces, indoor pool and miniature golf courses. There are several types of rooms, with rates for each, ranging (off/in-season) from $50 to $75/130 to 160.

Places to Eat

The food in Lake George Village doesn't compare with the scenery, but there are some fair choices. The village is walkable, and most places do not have street numbers.

The *Prospect Mountain Diner* (☎ (518) 668-4381) is at the south end of the village on the west side of Canada St, near the visitors center. This traditional chrome and vinyl diner offers typical diner fare and great pie for $1.50 a slice.

The *Barnsider BBQ Smokehouse Restaurant* (☎ (518) 668-5268) is on the east side of Canada St. Barbecued ribs and chicken are the featured dishes, along with burgers and a variety of sandwiches. Open daily for lunch and dinner.

Rosie's Diner (☎ (518) 668-2499) is at the north end of the village by the fork in the road for Routes 9 and 9N (Lake Shore Dr). Rosie's is open daily from 7 am to 10 pm, and very popular with local residents. It's also one of the last places where the ice cream list is happily limited to the basic three ice cream groups: chocolate, vanilla and strawberry.

The *Meeting Place Restaurant* (☎ (518) 792-9565), Route 9, is just in front of the Days Inn next to the sprawling outlet mall. This is a cut above coffee-shop food, and the restaurant serves breakfast, lunch and dinner daily from 7 am. Breakfast specials from $3 and dinner entrees from $9 to $15; the bargain, however, is brick oven pizzas from $4.

There are several Italian restaurants

along the Route 9 strip. *Mama Riso's Italian Restaurant* (☎ (518) 668-2550) is at the south end of town. The food is good, as the menu will remind you. Most dishes range from $12 to $15. Open daily for dinner from 4 pm.

Lox of Bagels & Moor (☎ (518) 793-8681) is south of Lake George in the Glens Falls area, just east of I-87 at exit 18, and a good spot for fresh bagels, fresh lox and a good deli. Open daily from 7 am.

Things to Buy

The 'Million $ Half Mile' (☎ (518) 793-2161) is a factory outlet strip at I-87 exit 20. There are actually four malls here open every day with 50 stores and counting.

Nearby, and somehow surviving the outlet mall phenomenon, is the quite unique Doll Shop (☎ (518) 792-0393) on Route 9 just east of the mall's fringe. The shop's sloping front lawn is remarkable for the array of large doll figures which adorn the green, and seem to watch you as you approach. Inside, the shop is small, cramped and charming and the owner (Peggy) can tell you about every item on display, which includes figurines to paper dolls. The shop is open year round, daily except Monday, from 10 am to 5 pm, but you may have to ring the doorbell to get in.

Getting There & Away

Adirondack Trailways (☎ (800) 858-8555) stops at the Mobil Station at the corner of Canada and Amherst Sts, but tickets must be purchased a block away at Capri Pizzeria (☎ (518) 668-5027), 221 Canada St. There are three buses north and three south daily during the summer. The bus stop is two blocks from the hostel. One-way/roundtrip tickets to Albany are $10/20; to Plattsburgh $33/64.

GLENS FALLS
Hyde Collection

The town of Glens Falls houses the Hyde Collection (☎ (518) 792-1761), 161 Warren St, a remarkable collection of art amassed with a thoughtful and expert eye by Char-

lotte Pryun Hyde, heiress to a local paper fortune. The collection is on display in her rambling Florentine Renaissance mansion. Here you can view works from European and American artists spanning five centuries, from Rembrandt and Reubens to Matisse and Eakins. Also on display from the permanent collection are tapestries, sculpture and period furnishings. A new educational wing serves as a space for temporary exhibits and lectures. From January to April, the museum is open Tuesday through Sunday, 10 am to 5 pm. During the rest of the year, it is open Wednesday through Sunday, noon to 5 pm. Admission is free. To get there take Route 9 to Glens Falls and go east on Warren St.

BOLTON LANDING

The largest and one of the most impressive of the Adirondack resorts, the Sagamore, is in the tiny village of Bolton Landing, 10 miles north of Lake George Village on the west shore of the lake.

The **Marcella Sembrich Memorial Studio** (☎ (518) 644-9839), home of the 20th-century opera singer, is also here. The studio contains mementos of the singer's career during the early part of the century. It's open to visitors from mid-June to mid-September. As you drive up Route 9N just before entering Bolton, you'll pass the iron gate of Sembrich's house on the east side of the road.

Places to Stay

Hilltop Cottage B&B (☎ (518) 644-2492) is on 9N opposite Carey's Lakeside Motel, about half a mile south of the first of two traffic lights in town; the address is 6883 Lakeshore Dr (Route 9N), but you won't see any address numbers. This B&B is the former caretaker's cottage for the Sembrich estate across the street. Anita and Charlie Richards rent out three rooms in the comfortable and well-maintained home and adjacent cabin. The rooms with shared bath are $50, one with a private bath is $65. The single cabin, which has a television, fridge and microwave, is $75.

The Sagamore Resort (☎ (518) 644-9400, (800) 358-3585), 110 Sagamore Rd, Bolton Landing, NY 12814, is on a private island, accessible by a bridge, east of town. The main building, with its dramatic approach up a sweeping driveway, is stunning. The white structure with green shutters was built as an inn in the 1920s, and has suffered two major fires during its history. It was completely renovated in 1985.

Everything about this resort speaks of luxury and opulence: the restaurants, indoor pool, tennis courts, ornate furnishings, professional service and breathtaking views of Lake George. The Sagamore's reputation as the most lavish resort in the Adirondacks is well-deserved. Not surprisingly, the price tag for such an experience is high. From July through August, there is a three-night minimum stay. Prices begin at $190 for a room without a view and rise to $390 for a suite overlooking the lake. The resort is open year round; room rates drop dramatically from early November until late December, and can be had for $90 to $100.

Places to Eat

Odds of getting a decent meal are better in Bolton Landing than the sprawling village scene down the road at Lake George.

The *Bolton Diner* (☎ (518) 644-3522), a blue-and-yellow diner at the center of town, is located on the site formerly occupied by the Bill Gates Diner which was taken apart and reassembled in the Adirondack Museum (see below). The diner serves comforting diner food, and the prices are reasonable; a breakfast special with three eggs, pancakes, meat, toast, homefries and coffee goes for $6. The diner is open daily in the summer for breakfast, lunch and dinner; in the winter, for breakfast and lunch only.

Pumpernickel's (☎ (518) 644-2106), on Lake Shore Dr, is adjacent to the Bolton Pines Motel, about eight miles north of Lake George Village. The menu tries to be international, with a pronounced German flavor. Entrees range from $12 to $20, and

includes a salad bar. Open daily for dinner from 5 to 9 pm.

There are five restaurants at the Sagamore Resort – six if you count the converted steamship/dinner cruise. *Mr Brown's Pub* has good bar food, including sandwiches, burgers and salads from $7 to $10, and is open from 11 am to midnight. The *Sagamore Dining Room* serves breakfast from 7 to 11 am, and offers standard dinners of steak, seafood and pasta, in the $15 to $25 range, from 5:30 to 9:30 pm. The changing menu at the *Trillium* is far more adventurous. Selections might include peppered mahi mahi, seared breast of duckling or a seafood ragout. Entrees are $20 and up, and formal attire is expected. A Sunday brunch (requiring reservations) happens from 10 am to 1 pm, and costs $26/13/4 for adults/kids six to 12/kids one to five.

Getting There & Away

Adirondack Trailways (☎ (800) 858-8555) stops at Neuffer's Citgo gas station (☎ (518) 644-2561) at the south end of town. There's one bus north and one south daily during the summer. One-way/roundtrip from Bolton Landing to New York City is $30/56; to Montreal, $38/74.

ROUTE 9N: LAKE GEORGE TO TICONDEROGA

The 39 mile drive along the western shore of Lake George from Lake George Village north is a pleasant one. There's a spectacular view of the lake at a scenic overlook after you drive over Five Mile Mountain.

After passing Bolton Landing, you drive through the small towns of **Silver Bay** and **Hague**. *Indian Kettles* restaurant (☎ (518) 543-6576) in Hague has a good view of the lake. The 'kettles' in the name refers to the depressions in the large rock surfaces of the surrounding mountains. The depressions were formed when smaller rocks tumbled about in a single spot, eventually eroding the surface to create a hole. You can eat lunch at the restaurant for under $10 and enjoy the view.

TICONDEROGA

The town of Ticonderoga is on the northern tip of Lake George. Visitors – particularly history buffs – stop here to visit Fort Ticonderoga. Other than the fort, there's little to recommend the town. Ferries to Larrabee's Point, VT, offer an additional possible excursion (see Lonely Planet's New England travel survival kit).

Some visitors might connect the name Ticonderoga to a long-familiar brand of yellow No 2 pencils, and – in fact – from the mid- to late-18th century, the town was an important graphite mining center.

Route 9N intersects Montcalm St at a traffic circle around the Liberty Monument, which depicts an Indian, a Green Mountain Boy, a French soldier, and a Royal Highlander (early multiculturalism). You can follow the signs from here through town to get to Fort Ticonderoga.

Fort Ticonderoga

The fort (☎ (518) 585-2821) is a mile northeast of town on Route 74. Originally named Fort Carillon, it was built by the French in 1755 to control the southern reaches of their conquests in America and was strategically located at the southern end of Lake Champlain and the northern end of Lake George. So critical was its location that the fort was attacked a record six times and nicknamed 'Key to the Continent.' In 1758, a French force of only 3500 – under the command of the Marquis de Montcalm – defended the fort against 15,000 British and American colonial troops. However, the following summer, British forces under General Jeffrey Amherst captured and renamed the fort.

Sixteen years later, in 1775, Ethan Allen and his Green Mountain Boys captured the fort for the Americans in a surprise attack. Two years after that, General John Burgoyne captured the fort for the British who abandoned the fortifications and burned the buildings. This historic fort would have been commemorated today with little more than an historical marker if it had not been for the family of William Ferris Pell who

bought the grounds in 1820 and began a complete restoration. Today, it is one the country's few major historical sites that is privately owned.

Inside the reconstructed buildings are collections of weapons, tools, uniforms and documents from the colonial and revolutionary periods. While the fort is open, there are weekly events, including fife and drum concerts, historical drills and craft demonstrations. Open from early May to mid-October daily from 9 am to 5 pm, until 6 pm during July and August. Admission for adults/kids seven to 12 is $8/6. Children under seven are free. *MV Carillon* (☎ (518) 585-2821) conducts short history cruises on the lake near the fort. Narrated tours leave the fort four times a day, weather permitting, on a replica of a 1920s cruise boat. Tickets are $7.50/4.50.

As a side trip on a clear day, you might drive up to **Mt Defiance** (☎ (518) 585-2821). It was at the summit that British General John Burgoyne mounted cannons and forced the American forces at Fort Ticonderoga to surrender in 1777. There are fine views from here of Lake Champlain, the valleys and Green Mountains. Open daily, mid-May to mid-October, 9 am to 5 pm. Admission is free.

Places to Stay

Most visitors to Fort Ticonderoga do not opt to stay over in the town. There is a campground outside of town and a few motels on the main road, Montcalm St.

Brookwood Park Campsites (☎ (518) 585-7113), situated in a shaded campground in the countryside, has 65 sites, laundry facilities and a small store. The sites are $15 each; open from early May to mid-October. The campground is south of Ticonderoga on Route 9N five miles south of the intersection of Route 74.

A *Super 8 Motel* (☎ (518) 585-2617), at the intersection of Route 9N and Route 74, is open year round, and has rooms $45 to $65.

Stone House Motor Lodge (☎ (518) 585-7394, 429 Montcalm St, has about 20 rooms located in two buildings, one a motel and the other a converted restaurant, now referred to as a 'lodge.' Rooms in the lodge are slightly nicer. Rooms run from $40 to $70. Closed in winter.

Circle Court Motel, 440 Montcalm St, like the Stone House Motor Lodge, is on the small traffic circle (with the arresting Liberty Monument sculpture in the middle), and open year round. Rates for single/double rooms range from $50 to $60, slightly lower in the winter.

Places to Eat
Your best bet, if you're staying over, is to check the menus in the lobby at either of the two motels near the traffic circle. There are fancier dinner spots in the area, but a very decent eatery is the *Hot Biscuit Diner* (☎ (518) 585-3483) two doors down from the Circle Court Motel, on Montcalm St.

Getting There & Away
Adirondack Trailways (☎ (800) 858-8555) stops at Hank's General Store (☎ (518) 585-6680), 112 Champlain Ave. There is one bus north, and one south daily during the summer. One-way/roundtrip fares from Ticonderoga to Plattsburgh are $26/50; to Albany, $18/33.

ESSEX
The village of Essex is between Ticonderoga and Plattsburgh along the very scenic Route 22 which drifts along the western shore of Lake Champlain, and is certainly one of the prettiest drives in all upstate New York; even the occasional satellite dish blends easily with the gentle terrain here.

The little hamlet of Essex is picturesque, starting with the mural on the fire station; this old fire house dates from the early 1800s, and is one of several 'village architecture' highlights.

The *Essex Inn* (☎ (518) 963 8821), on Main St, is an historic site, dating from about 1810; it's open year round, with a variety of rooms priced from $75 to $110.

Several good restaurants can be found here, including the *Old Dock House*

(☎ (518) 963-4232), located on the small marina, just down the alleyway between the firehouse and the ice cream shop. The Dock House is open daily from mid-May to mid-October from 11:30 am to 10 pm, and features fresh fish, pasta and grilled meats.

JJ's Terrace (☎ (518) 963-8842), is on Route 22, about 1½ miles south of town, and serves pizza and homey dishes like pot roast and pasta for about $6.

Hersey's Ice Cream Shop (☎ (518) 963-7951) on Main St is open daily, late May to mid-September, from 11 am to 9 pm.

BLUE MOUNTAIN LAKE
Blue Mountain Lake is a tiny village of 200 people in the geographic center of the Adirondacks. Despite its size, the town houses several important cultural attractions, including the Adirondack Museum and Adirondack Lake Center for the Arts. In addition, the town serves as a gateway to the Fulton Chain of Lakes in the southwestern Adirondacks (see Canoeing, above) and a network of excellent hiking trails, including the Blue Mountain Trail.

Adirondack Museum
One of the finest regional museums in the US, the Adirondack Museum (☎ (518) 352-7311), on Route 30 just north of the intersection with Route 28, is housed in a complex of 22 buildings overlooking Blue Mountain Lake. Each building focuses on different aspects of Adirondack life. You can wander through indoor and outdoor exhibits of rustic Adirondack furniture displayed in a restored Victorian cottage, a typical 19th century luxury resort hotel room, a hermits' camp, or the reassembled Bill Gates Diner (a former private railroad car – doubtfully related to the Microsoft billionaire) originally located in Bolton Landing. In addition, there are exhibits depicting the history and lore of the logging and mining industries of the region. Boating enthusiasts in particular will want to explore the popular exhibit on boat building which includes fine examples of watercraft, ranging from dugout

and birch-bark canoes to speedboats. The museum is open Memorial Day weekend to mid-October, daily from 9:30 am to 5:30 pm. Allow at least three hours. Admission for adults/seniors/children ages seven to 16 is $10/9/6.

Outfitters
Blue Mt Outfitters (☎ (518) 352-7306), PO Box 144, Blue Mountain Lake, NY 12812, is just north of the junction of Routes 28 and 30, and functions as a complete outfitters store, general store and information clearing house for the area. Ernie and Kim LaPrairie know the area well. They rent equipment, and provide guided canoe and kayak trips and canoe instruction. Camping and canoe trips are individually planned. Rates average $75 a day per person, including food. Family rates are slightly cheaper.

Special Events
The **No Octane Regatta** (☎ (518) 352-7311) is a gathering of human and wind-powered watercraft on Blue Mountain Lake in mid- to late June. There are races, canoe jousting, a clam bake and a parade. Call the Development Office (☎ (518) 352-7311) for exact dates.

Places to Stay
There are more places to stay in the area near Old Forge, see below.

LaPrairie's Lakeside Cottages (☎ (518) 352-7675) is an extension of Blue Mt Outfitters, about a quarter mile north of the junction of Routes 28 and 30. There is a private sandy beach, good for summer swimming. Rooms are in the $50 to $60 range. Like other motels in the area, LaPrairie's is a 'full housekeeping' cottage, meaning a full kitchen as close to home as you'll get.

Hemlock Hall B&B (☎ (518) 352-7706, winter 359-9065) is a large lodge with eight rooms in the main building, 10 cabins and four motel units located in a shaded pine forest overlooking the lake. The main lodge has an enormous stone fireplace and an inviting porch. Hemlock Hall has its own beach and canoes.

All room rates are double occupancy with breakfast and dinner, and you eat family-style at tables with other guests. Rooms are $80 to $110. Most of the cottages are on the hill right above the lake. These rent for $100 to $125 a night. It's open mid-May to mid-October. To get there take Route 30 north from the intersection with Route 28; in a quarter mile you should see the sign for the lodge and Maple Lodge Rd. If you get to the Adirondack Museum, you've gone too far.

The *Hedges* (☎ (518) 352-7325, winter 761-3115) is a hotel with a history. The main house was originally owned by retired Brigadier General Hiram Duryea who, for some unknown reason, preferred to be called 'Colonel.' The Colonel's son, who made his money in corn starch, shot his father after being told to do so – so he said – by the angels. Subsequently, the estate was auctioned off and converted into a hotel in 1921.

The main house has four rooms and the stone lodge has six more; there are also 14 cottages. The guest room furnishings are basic rustic camp style, but the tennis courts, the beach, the canoes and, most of all, the location on the lake are what attract guests. Double rates, including breakfast and dinner at your own table, are from $120 to $150. Open mid-June to mid-October. Take Route 28 west from the intersection with Route 30 for about one mile to the Hedges Rd, and turn on the north side of the road.

Places to Eat
There is a scarcity of restaurants and cafes in Blue Mountain Lake, which is another reason to stay at either Hemlock Hall or the Hedges where meals are included. There is a diner on the south side of Route 30 just before the intersection with Route 28. Look carefully, it's in a brown building off the road. Alternatively go west to Old Forge for more options; see below.

Potter's Restaurant (☎ (518) 352-7331), at the intersection of Routes 28 and 30, serves American food in a dining room full of artifacts from the Adirondacks. They are open during the summer daily except Tuesday from 8 am to 8 pm; they close from mid-September to mid-May.

The dining rooms of the *Hedges* and *Hemlock Hall* (see above) are open to the public, but you must call ahead for reservations.

Things to Buy
Cedarwood Gift Shop (☎ (518) 352-7675), PO Box 144, Blue Mountain Lake (in the post office building) is run by the LaPrairie family, and sells local Adirondack crafts, jewelry and baskets – some with antlers for handles. Open daily from the end of May through September, from 10 am to 5 pm.

Entertainment
Adirondack Lakes Center for the Arts (☎ (518) 352-7715), PO Box 205, Blue Mountain Lake, is a visual and performing arts center, near the junction of Routes 28 and 30. Evening performances include folk music, classical music and storytelling. During the day, the center runs a series of workshops – for kids and adults – which include canoe construction, wildlife photography and basket making. There is a gallery and gift shop. The center is open year round, Monday through Friday, from 9 am to 5 pm; during the summer season (late May to early September), they are open weekends from 10 am to 4 pm. Admission to the gallery is free.

LONG LAKE
Eleven miles north of Blue Mountain Lake on Route 30 sits the small town of Long Lake. If you drive through, stop at the *Adirondack Hotel* (☎ (518) 624-4700), by the small bridge north of the center of town. Look for the boulder out front with 'Adirondack Hotel' painted on it. There has been a hotel on this site since the 1800s, although most of the original one burned down in 1900.

The current owners keep it open year round. The hotel has white halls with pine floors and basic, clean rooms. Rooms with

shared/private bath are $35/45 to $50/60 for double occupancy. Rooms without bathrooms have sinks. There are two restaurants in the hotel, one serving sandwiches and burgers in the $5 to $7 range, and a slightly fancier and more expensive dining room.

The *Longlake Diner* (☎ (518) 624-3941) is just off Route 30 (by Hoss' Corner and Custard's Last Stand), and open daily from 6 am to 8:30 pm, year round. It's got good diner food, fresh salads, turkey and gravy and homemade soups.

OLD FORGE
Old Forge (and the neighboring village of Thendera) sits in the southwest corner of the Adirondacks, at the western edge of the Fulton Chain of Lakes (eight in all). The area is the snowmobiling capital of the region during the winter, and the summer attracts canoe and hiking buffs. Contact the Old Forge Tourist Information Center (☎ (315) 369-6983), PO Box 68, Old Forge, NY 13420, for seasonal events information, daily from 9 am to 5 pm. Most of the motels, B&Bs and restaurants in the area are also good sources of information on recreation spots, hiking trails and canoe trips through the chain of lakes.

Most shops and businesses are along Route 28 (Main St), including the post office, coin laundry and two banks with ATMs.

Adirondack Scenic Railroad
This scenic railroad (☎ (315) 369-6920) is a project of the Adirondacks Railway Preservation Society in nearby Thendara (just west of Old Forge), and operates vintage open-window coaches through some very pretty country between the old Thendara and Minnehaha stations, complete with fake, weekly train robberies. The twice-daily trips take about an hour, run from early May to late November, and cost $6 for adults, $4 for kids two to 12.

Canoe Outfitters
There are hundreds of canoe trails in the Adirondacks, but one of the best known

begins at Old Forge – the **Adirondack Canoe Route**, a 90 mile scenic journey that follows the Racquette River all the way up to the Saranac Lakes. Some portage is required.

For more information, contact the local tourist office in Old Forge (☎ (315) 369-6983), or

State DEC Office
    50 Wolf Rd, Albany, NY 12233
    (☎ (518) 457-7433)
Tickner's Adirondack Canoe Outfitters
    Riverside Drive, Old Forge, NY 13420
    (☎ (315) 369-6286)
Adirondack Mountain Club
    Box 3055, Luzerne Rd, Lake George,
    NY 12845 (☎ (518) 668-4447)
St Regis Canoe Outfitters
    PO Box 318, Lake Clear, NY 12945
    (☎ (518) 891-1838)

Places to Stay & Eat

There is no shortage of basic motels along Route 28 between Blue Mountain Lake and the Old Forge area. Restaurants aren't as common.

Camping The Inlet area between Old Forge and Blue Mt Lake has several good camp sites, including *Limekiln Lake Campground* (☎ (315) 357-4401), about three miles southeast of Inlet and Route 28. This is a big public campground, with room for RVs. It's open from May to November, weather permitting. Rates are $11 per site, and boat rentals are available.

A more interesting campsite is available for boaters only. *Alger Island Campground* (☎ (315) 369-3224) is about eight miles east of Old Forge, and open from late May until early September. Minimal facilities include toilets but no showers. Rates $12 per site (only 17 sites total).

Year-round camping is available at the *Old Forge KOA* (☎ (315) 369-6011), about a half mile north of Old Forge, off Route 28. This site has the usual array of KOA facilities, including several cabins, laundry, grocery store and playground. Rates from $20 for campsites, to $35 for cabins for two.

B&Bs, Inns & Restaurants *Cinnamon Bear B&B* (☎ (315) 357-6013) is a charming bargain in the village of Inlet on Route 28; just look for the circular sign. This refurbished old farm house has four upstairs rooms, larger than most B&Bs, with two semi-private shared baths between the rooms. The year-round rates are $65 for two people; add a few dollars extra for kids to cover breakfast.

Moose River House B&B (☎ (315 369-3104), at 12 Birch St, is in the village of Thendara. There are four rooms here, two with private bath. Year-round rates are $65 and $85.

Van Auken's Inne & Restaurant (315) 369-3033), Forge St, in Old Forge, is across the street from the Adirondack Scenic Railroad, and set in a beautiful old white Victorian building with a long front porch where you can have lunch or drinks in the evening. Grilled dinner entrees like pork tenderloin, duck and fresh fish range from $12 to $20. Van Auken's is open daily in the summer season from 11:30 am to 9 pm, and until 10 pm on weekends. The rest of year they close most Sundays.

Van Auken's is also an inn with 12 rooms, all with private bath, TV and telephone, ranging from $65 to $85 for singles or doubles.

Seventh Lake House Restaurant (☎ (315) 357-6028, just above the village of Inlet, at the west edge of Seventh Lake (part of the Fulton chain), at 479 Route 28, is one of the best diner spots west of Blue Mountain Lake. The fare is contemporary American, but the owners call it 'civilized dining in the wilderness.' Entrees range from $10 to $20. The restaurant is open daily from June through September from 5 to 9 pm for dinner; weekends only during the rest of year.

The *Farm Restaurant* (☎ (315) 369-6199) is on Route 28 in Thendera, next to Old Forge and across the street from the post office. This place has character written all over it, from the food to the antiques to Frank, the owner. The Farm is open daily for breakfast and lunch only, from 7 am to 2 pm.

LAKE PLACID
Lake Placid Village (population 2500) is actually situated on Mirror Lake. Lake Placid – the lake, not the town – is nearby. Lake Placid was the site of the 1932 and 1980 winter Olympics. Only two other towns – Innsbruck, Austria and St Moritz, Switzerland – have hosted two Winter Games. This little resort town isn't as swank as many other major winter sports destinations, but it has a great deal to offer in summer as well as winter. Sports enthusiasts come in the winter to ski the High Peaks region of the Adirondacks, for ice skating and other winter sports (see Outdoor Activities near the beginning of this chapter). In the summer, the region offers excellent cycling, mountain biking, hiking, golf and boating. You can also see Olympic athletes training in the various Olympic facilities. Lake Placid became an Olympic center because Dr Melville Dewey, of Dewey Decimal System fame, opened the Lake Placid Club as a resort here in 1895. The club began winter sports in 1904 and the resort mushroomed.

Orientation & Information
Lake Placid is in the middle of the High Peaks region on Routes 73 and 86. It's accessible from the north and south on Route 30, from the west on Route 3; and from the east on I-87 to Route 73.

The Lake Placid Visitors Bureau (☎ (518) 523-2445), 216 Main St, is in the large brownstone building connected to the new Olympic Center building at the south end of town. It's open Monday to Friday from 8 am to 5 pm; Saturday from 9 am to 5 pm; and Sunday from Christmas to mid-March from 9 am to 5 pm. You can pick up the helpful booklet that lists all the places to stay in Lake Placid and surrounding towns.

The post office is located in the fork between Main St and Parkside Dr downtown (☎ (518) 523-3071). The local weekly newspaper is the *Lake Placid News*.

Olympic Center & Olympic Sites
The Olympic Center (☎ (518) 523-1655,

(800) 462-6236), the large white building next to the visitors bureau on Main St, was used for the 1980 Olympics and houses four ice skating rinks. It was on the adjacent high school running track that speed skater Eric Heiden made history by winning five individual gold medals. You can watch athletes training here for free or take in an ice show or hockey game.

You can visit the following Olympic sites separately or all together on the Olympic Site Tour. The all-inclusive **Olympic Site Tour Package** costs $12/10 adults/kids and is available mid-June to mid-October.

The drive up **Whiteface Mountain Memorial Highway** will take you to Whiteface Mountain, the only Adirondack 'high peak' accessible by car. To get there, drive 17 miles north on Route 86 to Wilmington and then take Route 431 eight miles up the 4900 foot mountain. On clear days, you can view the surrounding peaks and mountain ranges as far off as Montreal and Vermont. The highway is open from late May to mid-October, 9 am to 4 pm; from mid-June to early September it's open from 8 am to 6 pm. The toll is $8 for each car and driver and an additional $4 for each passenger ($25 maximum).

You can also take a **chair lift** up another 3600 feet to the Whiteface Mountain summit. The chair lift entrance is on Route 86 before you get to Wilmington; it's open from mid-June to mid-October and costs $6/4/3.50 for adults/children/seniors.

The **Olympic Jumping Complex** (☎ (518) 523-1655, 523-2202) is the training facility for the US Olympic ski jump teams, located southeast of town on Route 73. Thanks to artificial surfaces, ski jumpers train here year round. When there is no snow, ski jumping takes place on a porcelain in-run and plastic-covered landing hill. You can take a chair lift followed by an elevator ride to the top of the 26 story viewing room. It's open daily year round from 9 am to 5 pm and costs $3/2 for adults/seniors and kids. Children under seven are free. Your admission also includes **Kodak Sports Park**, the

NEW YORK

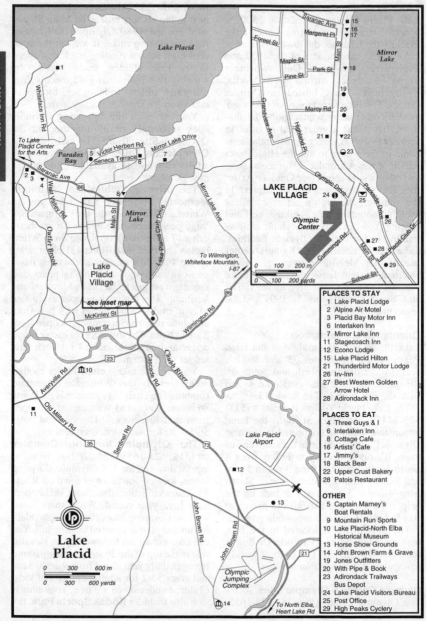

Lake Placid

PLACES TO STAY
1 Lake Placid Lodge
2 Alpine Air Motel
3 Placid Bay Motor Inn
6 Interlaken Inn
7 Mirror Lake Inn
11 Stagecoach Inn
12 Econo Lodge
15 Lake Placid Hilton
21 Thunderbird Motor Lodge
26 Irv-Inn
27 Best Western Golden
    Arrow Hotel
28 Adirondack Inn

PLACES TO EAT
4 Three Guys & I
6 Interlaken Inn
8 Cottage Cafe
16 Artists' Cafe
17 Jimmy's
18 Black Bear
22 Upper Crust Bakery
28 Patois Restaurant

OTHER
5 Captain Marney's
   Boat Rentals
9 Mountain Run Sports
10 Lake Placid-North Elba
    Historical Museum
13 Horse Show Grounds
14 John Brown Farm & Grave
19 Jones Outfitters
20 With Pipe & Book
23 Adirondack Trailways
    Bus Depot
24 Lake Placid Visitors Bureau
25 Post Office
29 High Peaks Cyclery

freestyle ski jump training center. Skiers jump, then flip and turn, into a 17 foot deep pool of water. It's right next to the Jumping Complex.

The **Olympic Sports Complex at Mt Van Hoevenberg** (☎ (518) 523-4436) is the site of bobsled, luge and cross-country skiing events. Visitors take a trolley up the mountain to view displays and videos of sledding sports. Tours of the bobsled and luge areas are also available. Open year round from 9 am to 4 pm, closed Monday from mid-December to mid-March. The trolley only runs from mid-June to mid-October. Admission for adults/seniors and kids five to 12 is $3/2. Mt Van Hoevenberg is a few miles east of the Jumping Complex on Route 73. For summer activities, see Bicycling, below.

From late December to late February, Tuesday to Sunday from 1 to 3 pm, visitors can take a bobsled ride on the course with a professional driver and brakeperson ($20 per person). You can also pilot yourself on the last five turns of the Olympic luge run on weekends from 1 to 3 pm.

John Brown Farm & Grave

The famous American abolitionist who was hanged for his part in the raid on the US Arsenal at Harpers Ferry, Virginia, in 1859 is buried outside of Lake Placid in North Elba. The historic site (☎ (518) 523-3900) includes Brown's farm and his gravestone, as well as those of two of his sons and nine other men killed at the raid on Harpers Ferry.

Brown was born in Connecticut in 1800 and lived in Ohio for a number of years; he moved to North Elba in 1849 to participate in a radical social experiment led by Gerrit Smith. The plan was to give land to any free black man who wished to farm it. Brown moved to North Elba to teach farming practices. It was here that he and his followers organized the raid, hoping to use the captured arms to launch a general rebellion. On October 16, 1859, Brown and a group of followers attacked the federal arsenal. They were captured on October 18, and hanged on December 2.

There is a self-guided tour of the farm building, the 244 acre farm and the graves. The house is open from late May to late October, Wednesday through Saturday from 10 am to 5 pm. You can walk around the grounds and look at the graves any time of year. Take Route 86 from town to Route 73 south. Drive 1.7 miles to the fork with a sign noting the 'John Brown Historic Site.' Drive half a mile down this road (John Brown Rd) to the farm.

ADK Adirondack Loj

The ADK High Peaks Information Center (☎ (518) 523-3441), Box 867, Lake Placid, NY 12946, is located on Heart Lake. Take Route 73 south of Lake Placid for about two miles to Adirondack Loj Rd (pronounced lahj, and also known as Heart Lake Rd). Drive on Adirondack Loj Rd for five miles and you're at the combination information center, campground and lodge (the Adirondack Loj), at the base of many of the region's tallest mountains and with immediate access to the lake and numerous trails.

The center has an information number (☎ (518) 523-3518) for daily weather and trail conditions in the north country.

The Loj is a large house situated on its own lake in addition to 20 kilometers of cross-country and snow-shoe trails that connect to hundreds of miles of state trails. Inside, you enter a common room with rocking chairs in front of a large fireplace, over which is hung a moose head; there's also a good library of books and magazines on the Adirondacks.

The year-round Loj has bunks and private rooms for guests, open to ADK members and non-members alike. There are also two cabins, 14 lean-tos and 36 campsites – see Places to Stay, below, for details.

Bicycling

The Lake Placid area is great bicycling country. Country-road and off-road trails are abundant, and road shoulders tend to be wide enough for cars to safely pass. Any of the several bike shops in town can provide you with maps and rentals. A half day of cycling, for example, could take you around the River Rd loop, a trip of about 12 miles.

Bike rental rates are competitive, and usually range from about $7 an hour, to $15 for half a day, to $20 for a full day. Each shop also rents helmets, car racks and kids' safety equipment.

Placid Planet Bicycles (☎ (518) 523-4128), 200 Saranac Ave (at the corner of Whiteface Inn Rd), does sales, repairs and rentals, and they'll help you with maps and suggestions for either off-road or country-road cycling.

High Peaks Cyclery (☎ (518) 523-3764), 331 Main St, rents bikes, in-line skates, rock climbing equipment and camping supplies (but not sleeping bags!).

Mountain Run Sports, 359 Main St, does anything connected with sports, from bikes to water skis to skateboards. They also rent tennis racquets and give water ski lessons.

In the summer, the cross-country ski trails at Mt Van Hoevenberg are open to mountain bikers, both experienced and novice. Trail fees are $4 and bikes and helmets are available to rent at the High Peaks Mountain Biking Center (☎ (518) 523-3764).

Other Things to See & Do
The **Lake Placid-North Elba Historical Museum** (☎ (518) 523-1608), on Averyville Rd two blocks from Route 73, is housed in a former railroad station. The former waiting room displays old farm implements, furnishings and photographs from the region, as well as memorabilia from the Olympics. Open from June to September, Tuesday through Sunday, noon to 4 pm. To get there, take Route 73 south to Averyville Rd, go right to the museum. It's free.

There is also a **nature trail** with interpretive signs identifying various plants and trees along Lake Placid. The trail starts behind the Howard Johnson's Restaurant off Route 86. Pick up a trail guide from the Lake Placid Visitors Center (☎ (518) 523-2445) in the Olympic Center on Main St before going.

Outfitters
Jones Outfitters (☎ (518) 523-3468), 37 Main St, rents canoes, paddleboats and kayaks. They also teach fly fishing and lead fishing and boating trips year round. In addition to the lake, which is just out the front door, they also go to the good fishing rivers, like the Ausable, the Chubb, the Saranac and the Bog. Half and full day trips range from about $100 to $150. Overnight canoe trips, complete with guide, equipment and food, are also available.

You'll understand how serious these folks are about fish with a quick glance at the chalk board outside the shop. In the summer, it lists the names of hatch flies that the fish are biting; poetic entries include Yellow Sallys, Red Quills, Olive Caddis and Stonefly Nymphs.

Captain Marney's Boat Rentals (☎ (518) 523-9746/1388), 3 Victor Herbert Rd, rents fishing boats, water-ski boats and canoes. Open May to October from 9 am until nightfall.

Organized Tours
Adirondack Adventure Tours (☎ (518) 523-1475), 126 Main St, gives daily tours of area Olympic and historic sites.

Lake Placid Sightseeing (☎ (518) 523-4431) offers a two hour tour of historic and Olympic sites in the area. Tours depart from all major hotels and motels in the area. For an even quicker orientation, Trolley Mini-Tours (☎ (518) 523-4431) in Hilton Plaza has a one hour 'Meet the Town' tour that picks people up at various points in town.

Tours are also given of the Olympic center, see above.

Airplane Flights The Adirondack Flying Service (☎ (518) 523-2473) offers 20 minute flights year round at $20 per person. Sail-plane rides are $45 for 20 minutes and $55 for 30 minutes.

Carriage Rides Lake Placid Carriage Rides (☎ (518) 523-2483), 1 Main St, takes folks on carriage rides around Mirror Lake from mid-June to Labor Day.

Special Events

Sporting events, particularly ice skating, hockey and skiing, take place all winter long in Lake Placid. The events and schedules change every year; the Olympic Regional Development Authority (☎ (518) 251-2411, (800) 462-6236) can send a schedule and answer questions. In June, the Lake Placid Horse Show is a main event.

Places to Stay

A note on seasons and prices: Lake Placid is a premier resort area, and the press of the Olympic stamp is everywhere. There are bargains to be had, but prices are the highest in the Adirondacks. The high season is generally the summer months from mid-June to early September, followed by the winter ski season from about a week before Christmas until March 15; weekends can be higher year round. Rates are lower, often considerably so, after mid-October and mid-March.

Wilmington, 15 miles east of Lake Placid, offers additional (and sometimes cheaper) accommodations.

ADK Camping, Cabins & Lojs The *ADK Adirondack Loj*'s (see above) rooms have wooden bunks, thick and firm mattresses and, if you're lucky enough to get a bunk facing the lake, great views. Private rooms have double beds.

It's your best choice in the bottom-end accommodations bracket – if not in any bracket – and it's open to members and non-members alike.

All room rates include breakfast; if you want dinner, it's $11 more. The food is good and served family-style at long tables. The menu is creative and different each night, but usually includes soup, salad, fish or chicken, pasta or rice and dessert.

My favorite detail of the Loj: there are 46 beds to match the 46 high peaks of the Adirondacks. Weekday/end rates for bunk rooms are $25/30 for the 18 bunk room or $32/30 for the six bunk room. Private rooms are $40/49. Cabins are $75/95 or $12/16 per person with a minimum of 10 people required. Lean-tos are $12/16 in

winter/summer for two people and $2.50 for each additional person. Campsites are $8/13 in winter/summer and $1.50 for each additional person. Breakfast is $5 for those in cabins, lean-tos and campsites.

About 3½ miles by foot from the Adirondack Loj is the John Brooks Loj (JBL). It has bunk rooms for $21/26 and $25/30 on the weekday/end. Breakfast is included and dinner is $11. JBL lean-tos are $7 for the first two and $1 for each extra person; breakfast/dinner is $5.50/11.50.

ADK also maintains two backcountry cabins, Grace Camp, which sleeps six, and Camp Peggy O'Brien, which sleeps 12. These camps are a 3¼ mile walk from the town of Keene Valley on Route 73 about 15 miles southeast of Lake Placid. They're open year round and have bunks, tables, firewood, cooking stoves (you bring the fuel) and cooking implements. There are also lean-tos around Camps Grace and O'Brien. Weekday/end rates for Grace Camp are $50/70; for O'Brien it's $85/110. Breakfast/dinner is $5.50/11.

ADK members get a 10% discount on everything; see the Adirondack Mountain Club entry under this chapter heading.

Other Camping The *Whispering Pines Campground* (☎ (518) 523-9322) has 80 sites ranging from $7.50 to $17.50 for two. You can choose between sites in the open or ones in the shade. Open from May 1 to the end of October. Take Route 73 six miles south of Lake Placid from the junction with Route 86.

Bottom End The *Irv-Inn* (☎ (518) 523-4359), 67 Parkside Ave, has three rooms with a shared bath on a residential block. The rooms are comfortable and small and you get to share a television room with homeowner Irvin. Rates are $35 and $40.

Most of the cheaper motels extend along Saranac Ave on the way into town from Route 86 on the west. Rooms facing the road can be noisy because of all the traffic, so get a back room if you need quiet. The *Alpine Air Motel* (☎ (518) 523-9261), 99 Saranac Ave, has rooms in several motel buildings spread out along the roadside property. There's a large pool in the middle of the complex, and the atmosphere is convivial. Rates are $34 to $46 from early May to mid-June and late October to early December. They're $45 to $65 during the rest of the year. Alpine Air also rents suites at $70/99.

The *Econo Lodge* (☎ (518) 523-2817) is on Cascade Rd (Route 73), about a mile south of the Olympic Center in town. In-season rates for singles/doubles range from $65/100; off-season ranges from $45/75.

Middle The *Thunderbird Motor Inn* (☎ (518) 523-2439, (800) 499-2668) is located on a hill across from the Best Western at 140 Main St. Standard rooms with psychedelic orange doors look out over nothing in back or across Main St to the lake in front. Rates are $48 to $85; they're cheapest from November to mid-December and from April through July.

The *Placid Bay Motor Inn* (☎ (518) 523-2001), 70 Saranac Ave, on Route 86 as you enter Lake Placid from the west, is open year round. The sky-blue building with carved birds on the facade makes it hard to miss. The decor here is a bit severe: shag carpeting, bright gold velour bed covers and low ceilings. But the rooms are neat and good sized, and there is a pool. Seasonal rates vary from $40 to $80 for a double.

The *Adirondack Inn* (☎ (518) 523-2424, (800) 556-2424), 217 Main St, is across the street from the Olympic Center, in the middle of town. The place is modern, clean and the rooms are large and each one has a small fridge. The inn has an indoor and outdoor pool, in addition to the small sandy beach facing Mirror Lake. Rooms range from $60 to $130, depending on the season.

Interlaken Inn (☎ (518) 523-3180, (800) 428-4369), 15 Interlaken Ave, is just north of Mirror Lake, and it's the closest thing to a Victorian country inn that you'll find in the area. There are only 12 rooms, all with private bath, and prices range from $50 to $110. Even if you stay elsewhere, the

restaurant is worth a trip; it's run by the highly regarded Culinary Institute of America (see Poughkeepsie in the Hudson Valley chapter).

The *Best Western Golden Arrow Hotel* (☎ (518) 523-3353), 150 Main St, is right on the lake and has a beach, heated pool, saunas, Jacuzzi and racquetball court. Rooms are furnished in upmarket motel style. Single or double rates for summer non-lakefront rooms range from $110 to $150. From January to late March, prices vary from $60 to $140. During the slow season (spring), you can expect to pay between $60 and $100.

Top End The *Stagecoach Inn* (☎ (518) 523-9474), 370 Old Military Rd just south of town, is the oldest hotel in Lake Placid. Originally a stagecoach stop, it was converted into a hotel in 1833, and later into a B&B. There's a great front porch, fireplaces, antique furniture, all in a beautiful country setting. A room with private bath and fireplace is $80 to $95; other private rooms are $70 to $85; and shared bath $60 to $70. A full breakfast is included. You reach the inn by traveling south from town on Route 73; make a right at the sign for the John Brown Historic Site, then another immediate right onto Old Military Rd (Essex County Route 35). Go 1.3 miles and the inn is on your left.

The *Mirror Lake Inn* (☎ (518) 523-2544), 5 Mirror Lake Dr, is just north of Swiss Rd. This is an Adirondack classic, and one of the most elegant retreats in upstate New York. Afternoon tea, private beach, canoeing, tennis, spa, lakeside dining and the list goes on. Prices range from a modest off-season $95 to the in-season high of $225.

Lake Placid Lodge (☎ (518) 523-2700), on Whiteface Inn Rd, is rustic, remote and expensive. The lodge overlooks the west end of Lake Placid, and offers everything from stone fireplaces and sunset cruises to swimming and snow shoeing. Rates range from $175 to $200 for rooms without fireplace to suites for $450.

The *Lake Placid Hilton* (☎ (518) 523-4411, (800) 755-5598), One Mirror Lake Dr (near the junction of Main St and Saranac Ave), is really a complex of several buildings. The best rooms – all of which have a view of Mirror Lake or the mountains – are in the tallest of these buildings, located on the hill at the corner of Main St and Saranac Ave. The hotel complex offers a vast number of amenities, including indoor and outdoor pools, a restaurant, lounge and game room. Rooms are big, nicely furnished and each has a balcony. Rooms in the main building are $96 to $148, but from July 1 to September 8, all rooms are $148. Rooms in the outer buildings range from $76 to $148 depending on the season and whether or not you have a view of Mirror Lake. Ask about ski packages that include lift tickets to Whiteface Mountain, and about late January and spring specials.

Places to Eat

Budget & Moderate At the *Upper Crust Bakery & Cafe* (☎ (518) 523-2269), 215 Main St, you can get breakfast for $4 or $5. They also sell take-out bakery items. Open for breakfast and lunch only, from 6 am to about 2:30 pm.

The Cottage Cafe (☎ (518) 523-9845), 5 Mirror Lake Rd, is a very popular local spot for lunch and dinner. The menu includes hot sandwiches, chicken burritos, feta salad and everything is under $8. Best value on the lake.

For the best deli sandwiches in Lake Placid, find *Three Guys & I* (☎ (518) 523-4897), 89 Saranac Ave, across the street from Howard Johnson's. A big, fresh-roasted turkey sandwich is $4, subs are about $5 and they sell fresh French bread. This is a good place to put together a picnic basket. Open daily from 8 am to 8 pm during July and August, and until 5 pm the rest of the year. They also deliver during the summer.

There are several places serving good American fare on Main St along Mirror Lake, including the *Black Bear* (☎ (518) 523-9886), 157 Main St, with a nicely varied menu that includes fish sandwiches and Reubens (about $5) and ribs, scampi

and pasta ($10 to $14). They also serve great pie. The tables at the rear of the restaurant look out over the lake. The restaurant is open from 6:30 to 10 pm weekdays, and around the clock on Friday and Saturday.

The *Artist's Cafe* (☎ (518) 523-9493) is a cozy place located down a long staircase at 1 Main St on the corner of Saranac Ave. Tables in the back of the dining area look directly over Mirror Lake. You can get a sandwich, omelet or burger here for $5 to $6. Dinner selections include scampi and New York strip steaks, ranging from $6 to $19, and they have an artsy kids menu to boot.

Jimmy's Restaurant (☎ (518) 523-2353), 21 Main St, also has unobstructed views of Mirror Lake from tables at the rear of the restaurant. They serve Italian-American dishes like pasta and calzones, as well as burgers, deli sandwiches and salads for $5 to $6, and dinner selections featuring veal, chicken and seafood for $13 to $15. There is a popular weekday happy hour from 4 to 6 pm.

Top End The *Interlaken Inn* (☎ (518) 523-3180), 15 Interlaken Ave, serves a five-course, fixed-price meal for $25, Thursday through Monday with seatings between 6 and 8 pm. There is also a full à la carte menu. The food here is excellent and entrees change daily. The inn is in an old Victorian house with appropriately dark walls and furnishings and has accommodations (see above). Expect to spend a minimum of $20 per person for dinner. Reservations are advised.

Patois Restaurant (☎ (518) 523-4573), 217 Main St, is in the Adirondack Inn, across from the Olympic Center. This is one of the newer fine dining spots in town, and boasts of its world cuisine with Thai nouean, portobello mushrooms and spicy West Indian dishes. Open for dinner only, from 5 to 10 pm nightly.

Entertainment

At the center of town, you'll find three bars all in a row at 137 Main St: *Roomers*

(☎ (518) 523-3611), *Tiffany's* and *Goldberrie's* (both ☎ (518) 523-1799).

The Lake Placid Center for the Arts (☎ (518) 523-2512), on Saranac Ave, is a year-round multi-purpose center that presents professional theatrical, music and dance performances, shows films and conducts workshops.

The *Lake Placid Sinfonetta* (☎ (518) 523-2051) is a summer orchestra of 19 professional musicians. They present a six-week season of concerts in July and August at a variety of locations including at the Lake Placid Center for the Arts.

The *Pendragon Theater* (☎ (518) 891-1854), 18 Park St, stages three plays by well-known playwrights (usually one by Shakespeare) every summer, as well as plays during the rest of the year. Tickets are $14/12 for adults/students.

Things to Buy
With Pipe & Book (☎ (518) 523-9096), 91 Main St, sells fine pipes and natural blended tobaccos. They also have a great selection of new, rare and used books, scenic prints and good hiking and driving maps of the Adirondack region. This is a great browsing store, with more rooms upstairs and downstairs. Open daily from 9:30 am to 6 pm, and Sunday from 10 am to 4 pm.

Getting There & Away
Air USAir has regular service into Adirondack Airport (☎ (518) 891-4600) in Saranac Lake, 16 miles west of Lake Placid. Champ public transport (see below) has regular runs to Lake Placid from the airport.

Bus Adirondack Trailways (☎ (800) 858-8555) stops at the 326 Main St Deli (☎ (518) 523-4309). There's one bus in and out each way daily. One-way/roundtrip from Lake Placid to Saratoga Springs costs $18/34; to Montreal, $54/108.

Champ (☎ (518) 523-4431) is the Essex County public transportation system. It runs regular service to/from Lake Placid and Ray Brook, Saranac Lake, Wilmington and other places. You can also flag the bus

down on any main route and it will stop. Rates are from $1.50 to $5.

Train Amtrak stops at Westport (☎ (518) 523-4431), 37 miles east of Lake Placid on Route 22. Champ public transportation (☎ (518) 523-4431) runs to/from the train station if scheduled in advance. The one-way/roundtrip fare is $25/45 for one or $30/50 for two.

WILMINGTON
About 15 miles east of Lake Placid is the small town of Wilmington (population 1000), home to Whiteface Mountain, the highest peak in the northeast. (For skiing information see Outdoor Activities near the beginning of this chapter.) The town is a good place to stop over if you plan to ski or hike on the mountain, or if you want to visit Lake Placid but not pay the higher prices to stay there.

Things to See & Do
Geology buffs will be particularly interested in a hike in **High Falls Gorge** (☎ (518) 946-2278), 4½ miles southwest of Wilmington on Route 86. The marked interpretive trail, which is privately owned and operated, is a deep ravine cut by ice, wind and the Ausable River at the base of Whiteface Mountain. Markers along the trail describe the geology, flora and fauna of the surrounding mountain area. Along the trail, you can enjoy waterfalls and the only remaining stand of virgin forest in the Adirondacks, the rest of the forest having been devastated by massive logging operations at the turn of the century. The trail is open from Memorial Day to mid-October, daily from 8:30 am to 4:30 pm. Admission for adults/over 62/children 12 to 17/four to 11 is $4.95/3.95/3/1.50.

The North Pole theme park, **Santa's Workshop** (☎ (518) 946-2211), is on Route 431, just 1½ miles west of Wilmington and 12 miles east of Lake Placid. Children can meet Santa Claus and his helpers, pet live reindeer and go on amusement park rides. This is billed as the oldest theme park in the US. It's open June 10 through

October 14, Monday through Sunday, from 9:30 am to 4:30 pm in July and August and reduced hours during other times. In July and August, admission is $11.95 for adults and $7.95 for children three to 17; under three are free. Rates are slightly cheaper at other times.

Places to Stay & Eat

The *Lake Placid-Whiteface KOA* (☎ (518) 946-2171) is an enormous campground open year round. There are 200 sites, a pool, laundry facilities, canoes, miniature golf, tennis and more. Sites are $18. From Route 86 take a right on Fox Farm Rd and you'll come to the campground in less than half a mile.

Twin Acres Campsites (☎ (518) 946-7207) has 40 sites on a quiet campground open from May 1 to October 15. Take 86 to Springfield Rd, then Springfield Rd 1½ miles to the campground.

High Peaks Base Camp (☎ (518) 946-2133) is less dramatic than the name implies, but is well located near downhill and cross-country slopes. The Base Camp sleeps 200 people in a complex of what appears to be hastily constructed bunk houses, some with private rooms. The bunks are crammed together closely, causing one visitor to remark that it reminded him of being in the army. Still, the rooms are clean and the beds comfortable. In addition, the weekday/weekend price of $15/18 including breakfast can't be beat. Tent sites are an amazing $3 and include access to showers and toilets.

To get there take Route 86 from Lake Placid to Fox Farm Rd in Wilmington. Go right on Fox Farm Rd for 0.8 miles. Make a right on Springfield Rd and go 2.6 miles to the Base Camp on the right.

Located behind the Base Camp is a trout pond filled with thousands of fat fish, waiting to be served for lunches and dinners at the *Wood Parlor* restaurant. A trout dinner runs $10. You can also get appetizers like chicken wings, zucchini sticks, and nachos for around $3. Spaghetti, crab cakes and salads are all under $7. High Peaks Base Camp also hosts a Saturday

night coffee house, the Frog Pond Theater (☎ (518) 946-2133) with local and regional musicians and singers.

Wilkommen Hof (☎ (518) 946-7669, (800) 541-9119) is on Route 86 south of the four-way stop in town. This B&B, run by Heike and Bert Yost, is a converted farmhouse with a German theme. It has a comfortable common area with fireplace and television, a sauna and a hot tub. There are nine rooms. During the winter the weekday/end rate for those with private bath is $70/80; during summer it's $60/70. For the rooms with shared bath the rates are from $50 to $63.50. The rates include a full breakfast. In the winter, the Yosts serve a German dinner for $15. In the summer, you can swim in the Ausable River, located directly across the road.

AUSABLE CHASM

Traveling east on Route 86/9N for 35 miles from Lake Placid, you'll come to the town of Ausable Chasm near I-87. The chasm (☎ (518) 834-7454, (800) 537-1211) is a gorge which was formed five million years ago as the Ausable River carved layers of sandstone, leaving cliffs, waterfalls and rapids. Today visitors walk through the chasm on a series of walkways, bridges and stone steps (which can be slippery). The walk is three-quarters of a mile, followed by a 10 minute boat ride through the grand flume. From late May to Late October, the chasm is open daily from 9:30 am to 5 pm. Admission for the walk and boat ride is $12.95 for adults, $10.95 for seniors and $7.95 for children.

SARANAC LAKE

Situated in the middle of a chain of lakes, including the Upper and Lower Saranac, the town of Saranac Lake (population 5400) is 10 miles northwest of Lake Placid on Routes 86 and 3. The town was settled early in the 19th century and became a major tuberculosis treatment center later in the century. With the recent, alarming resurgence of the disease in the US, it's of value to note that as late as 1930, tuberculosis – or consumption as it was more

NEW YORK

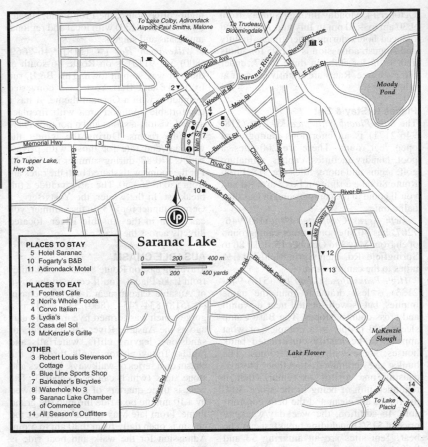

To Lake Colby, Adirondack
Airport, Paul Smiths, Malone

To Trudeau,
Bloomingdale

Margaret St

Stevenson Lane

86

3

Pine St

E Pine St

Broadway

Bloomingdale Ave

Saranac River

Moody
Pond

1

Olive St

2

Woodruff St

Main St

Helen St

Shepard Ave

Church St

Dorsey St

4

5

6

8 7

9

St Bernard St

River St

Memorial Hwy

3

S Hope St

To Tupper Lake,
Hwy 30

Lake St

Riverside Drive

86

River St

10

Kiwassa Rd

Riverside Drive

Lake Flower Ave

11

12

13

Saranac Lake

0   200   400 m

0   200   400 yards

McKenzie
Slough

Lake Flower

McKenzie
Slough

To Lake
Placid

Dupreys St

Edwards St

14

PLACES TO STAY
5 Hotel Saranac
10 Fogarty's B&B
11 Adirondack Motel

PLACES TO EAT
1 Footrest Cafe
2 Nori's Whole Foods
4 Corvo Italian
5 Lydia's
12 Casa del Sol
13 McKenzie's Grille

OTHER
3 Robert Louis Stevenson
   Cottage
6 Blue Line Sports Shop
7 Barkeater's Bicycles
8 Waterhole No 3
9 Saranac Lake Chamber
   of Commerce
14 All Season's Outfitters

commonly referred to then – killed more Americans than heart disease.

The first sanitarium for the treatment of tuberculosis was established here in 1884 by Dr Edward Livingston Trudeau, a young New York physician, who was diagnosed with tuberculosis at the beginning of his career. Instead of heading to the tuberculosis sanatoria of Europe, he decided to return to a place he had once visited for pleasure, the Adirondacks. After a great deal of hardship, he opened the Adirondack Cottage Sanitarium, located just northeast of the remote village of Saranac

Lake (in the 1880s the village was a 32 mile stagecoach ride from the nearest railroad station).

The sanitarium was located on the wooded slopes of Mt Pisgah with views of the Saranac River and Whiteface Mountain. By 1890, 25 patients had traveled here to take the cure, and by 1898 that number had quadrupled. Health-seekers were drawn here in the hopes that the same climate and landscape that invigorated pleasure seekers would prove as virtuous for them. Today, Trudeau's original sanitarium – known as Little Red – survives on the grounds of the Trudeau Institute on Algonquin Ave near Lower Saranac Lake.

The area around Saranac Lake continues to offer visitors – in a far more accessible manner – the pleasures of the wilderness: small lakes and ponds, ancient forests and wetlands. You can also wander along the village's winding streets to view cottages and treatment centers dating from the late 19th century.

Information

To enjoy the wilderness experience, contact the Saranac Lake Chamber of Commerce (☎ (518) 891-1990, (800) 347-1992), in the municipal building at 30 Main St. They publish booklets describing wilderness areas, as well as places to stay. It's open Monday to Friday from 8 am to 5 pm.

Several banks and ATMs are on Broadway, Church and Main Sts. The post office is at 60 Broadway. For laundry, try American Village (☎ (518) 891-2150), 28 Bloomingdale Ave. Adirondack Medical Center (☎ (518) 891-4141), Lake Colby Dr, is the major hospital in the region.

Robert Louis Stevenson Cottage

The house (☎ (518) 891-1990), which was Stevenson's home for the winter of 1887-88, contains the largest collection of Stevenson memorabilia in the US, including old photos, clothing, ice skates and a lock the author's hair. Stevenson wrote the essays *The Master of Ballantrae*, *The Wrong Box* and *A Christmas Sermon* here. Open from July 1 to September 15, Tuesday to Sunday from 9:30 am to noon and from 1 to 4:30 pm daily except Monday. Admission for adults/children is $1/50¢. Take Main St north to Bloomingdale Ave, turn south on Pine St to Stevenson Lane.

Horseback Riding

XTC Ranch (☎ (518) 891-5684), off Route 73, southeast of Saranac Lake and Lake Placid past the ski jump area, has hourly and half-day horseback trail rides, riding lessons and mini cattle-drives for city slickers. Rates are $25 per hour; rides begin at 10 am, noon, 1 pm and 3 pm daily during summer.

Bicycling

Barkeater Bicycles (☎ (518) 891-5207, (800) 254-5207), 49 Main St, sells, rents and repairs bikes, and is a good source of information about local bike trails. Free bike trail maps are available by the front door, from beginner to expert. Bikes rent for $15 a day to about $75 for a full week.

The Wilderness Cure

In 1882, one in every seven human deaths was from TB. The disease was thought to be hereditary until the 1882 discovery of the bacillus. Quickly, a public health question arose: should patients be confined to hospitals?

In the late 19th century, the choices for TB patients were simple:

- Pay $25 a week to stay at one of Saranac Lake's modest 'cure cottages'
- Go to a crowded hospital
- The last choice: go to a sanitarium where they don't want you to die on the premises. Hence the inevitable advice, 'seek a warmer climate,' ie, go home to die.

In 1939, a doctor told his patients: 'We never use the word 'cured.' When you leave here you are not even arrested (as in, the disease being under control). You are called 'quiescent' if we discharge you . . . If you continue to be alright for a couple of years you are arrested, but you are cured of TB only when you die of some other disease.'

Reminiscences of patient Eva Milbover in 1896 give a glimpse of life in the cottages: 'I obeyed regulations – up in the morning, to the main building to breakfast, back to Nathan Cottage, undressed and back to bed   Then up and dressed for the midday meal in the main building, back to the cottage, undressed, to bed; up and dressed for dinner in the main building, a short social hour, back to bed in the cottage – while I did that, others were doing all sorts of hanky-panky.' ■

Barkeater's is open Monday through Saturday from 10 am to 5 pm.

Outfitters

All Seasons Outfitting (☎ (518) 891-6159), (800) 236-5217), 168 Lake Flower Ave (Route 86), on the south end of town across from Pizza Hut, has a retail store and gives guided tours and has equipment rentals for canoeing, kayaking, skiing, hiking and camping. Open daily year round in summer and in winter peak seasons.

Blue Line Sport Shop (☎ (518) 891-4680), 82 Main St, has hiking and camping supplies, footwear and bugsuits, area maps and everything and anything to do with fishing. It's open Monday to Saturday from 8:30 am to 5:30 pm, Sunday from 9 am to 3 pm.

Special Events

The **Great International Steamboat Regatta** in June invites steamboats from the US and Canada to chug around on Lake Flower and the Lower and Middle Saranac Lakes. The **Adirondack Guideboat Show** in July displays classic Adirondack boats. The **Can-Am Rugby Tournament** in August has over 100 Canadian and American teams playing in the largest North American tournament.

Places to Stay

Fogarty's B&B (☎ (518) 891-3755, (800) 525-3755), 37 Riverside Dr, has five rooms, some of which overlook Flower Lake. The single/double rate is $40/50.

Adirondack Motel (☎ (518) 891-2116), 23 Lake Flower Ave (Route 86), is a clean and quiet spot on the lake with a dozen rooms, some with kitchenettes. Rates in the late fall and spring go from $40 to $60 for doubles and efficiencies; in the summer and peak winter season they're $60 to $85.

Sunday Ponds B&B (☎ (518) 891-1531), on Route 30 in Saranac Inn, is a 10 to 15 minute drive southwest of Saranac Lake, opposite the St Regis Wilderness Canoe Area (which has excellent cross-country ski trails). Sunday Ponds is clean and rustic with old quilts, antiques and a screened-in porch. There are four rooms, two with private bath. It's open year round and rates are $50 to $60 double, plus $15 per extra person.

The *Hotel Saranac* (☎ (518) 891-2200, (800) 937-0211), 101 Main St, is a large red-brick hotel run by hospitality management students of Paul Smiths College. The hotel is spotless and the service good, if somewhat over anxious. There are 92 modestly furnished and comfortable rooms. The ones on higher floors have good lake views. Rates are reasonable; a single/ double costs $45 to $60/51 to 68. B&B and modified American plans are also available.

Poetry of the Woods

The pastoral poetry of many famous American poets, including Walt Whitman and Henry Wadsworth Longfellow, was inspired by the rugged and wild country of the northeast. It often evokes the mystery Americans found in the thick woods and Native American ways; below is a portion of *The Adirondacks*, a poem written in 1858 by Ralph Waldo Emerson (1803-82).

. . . we swept with oars the Saranac,
With Skies of benediction, to Round Lake,
Where all the sacred mountains drew around us,
Tahawus, Seaward, MacIntyre, Baldhead,
And other Titans without muse or name.
Please with these grand companions, we glide on . . .
Through gold-moth-haunted beds of pickerel-flower,
Through scented banks of lilies white and gold,
Where the deer feeds at night, the teal by day . . .
The wood was sovran with centennial trees –
Oak, cedar, maple, poplar, beech and fir,
Linden and spruce. In strict society
Three conifers, white, pitch and Norway pine.
Five-leaved, three-leaved, and two-leaved, grew thereby . . .
'Welcome!' the wood gods murmured through the leaves –
'Welcome, though late, unknowing, yet known to me' . . . ∎

Places to Eat

Nori's Whole Foods (☎ (518) 891-6079), 70 Broadway, is a good, friendly, neighborhood health food store for self-catering. They also sell some prepared items you can eat at the one table up front. Nori's is open Monday to Friday from 9 am to 7 pm and Saturday from 10 am to 5 pm year round.

Up the block from Nori's is the *Footrest Cafe* (☎ (518) 891-6867), 138 Broadway, a very casual place with bookshelves inside and a deck outside. People often kick back here with a cappuccino or espresso and read. The Footrest serves its soups in bowls made of bread ($2.50) and has a good chicken breast sandwich on homemade bread for $4.25, also nachos ($3) and other wholesome foods. The deck fills up in the summer.

Inside the Hotel Saranac at 101 Main St is *Lydia's* (☎ (518) 891-2200), a restaurant run by chefs and hospitality folk from Paul Smiths College. Lydia's has a Sunday buffet brunch with waffles, omelets, eggs, meat, salad and desserts for $10. Kids under 12 eat for $5. Lydia's also serves American lunches, like grilled swordfish ($6.50), strip steak sandwich ($7.50), and Reubens, tuna melts and other sandwiches for $4.25. Dinners include a mixed meat grill of lamb, venison sausage and bacon for $14, Thai-style duck for $13.50, and Adirondack trout for $13. The food is good as is the service.

Corvo Italian Restaurant (☎ (518) 891-0510), 94 Main St across from the Hotel Saranac, is clean and attractive. Lunches are a bargain with pasta dishes and sandwiches under $5, dinners from $10 to $15. It's open daily from 11 am to 10 pm, Sunday from 2 to 9 pm.

Casa del Sol (☎ (518) 891-0977), 154 Lake Flower Ave, on Route 86 just outside of town as you arrive from Lake Placid, is the best Mexican food for many miles around. All the selections – burritos, tostadas, flautas, chimichangas – are good. Portions are large and prices a reasonable $5.50. But forego the salsa, which is really a bland tomato topping.

Nearby, *McKenzie's Grille* (☎ (518) 891-9920), 148 Lake Flower Ave, serves family-style fare, including pasta, barbecue, fresh fish and salads. Open daily from 7 am to 10 pm.

Entertainment

Waterhole No 3 (☎ (518) 895-9502), 43 Main St, is upstairs and across the street from the town hall. The Waterhole features good local music from rock to folk. Admission ranges from $3 to $10.

Getting There & Away

Adirondack Trailways (☎ (800) 858-8555) stops at the Hotel Saranac (☎ (518) 891-3300), 101 Main St.

Champ (☎ (518) 523-4431) public transportation runs regular service to/from Saranac Lake, Ray Brook, Lake Placid, Wilmington and other places. You can also flag the bus down on any main route (Routes 3, 73, 86) and it will stop. Rates are from $1.50 to $5.

AROUND SARANAC LAKE
Six Nations Indian Museum

The museum (☎ (518) 891-2299), 14 miles north of Saranac Lake Village and one mile from Onchiota on County Rd 30, is dedicated to preserving the culture of the Iroquois Confederation, originally comprised of the Mohawk, Seneca, Onondaga, Oneida and Cayuga tribes, and later, the Tuscaroras. On display in the four rooms of the museum are artifacts, historic documents and models of typical Iroquois villages, as well as contemporary Iroquois crafts. The museum stands as a reminder to visitors that the Native American culture and history long pre-dates their contact with Europeans.

This small, excellent museum has been carefully managed by four generations of the Fadden family; John Fadden will most likely greet you and if you show the least bit of curiosity, he is happy to discuss the museum's extensive collection. There are four rooms, all in a row in longhouse style, and each one is rich with artifacts, clothing, artwork and historic scenes, quotations and photos. Several cartoons by local Indian artists are on display, including one showing two Indian guides, with a couple of tourists nearby. One Indian guide tells his Indian buddy that 'We're about three miles from Crow's Landing, but tell them it's a heap many moon to land of Black Devil Bird.'

Other displays are more serious, like this excerpt from 1940 speech by Chief Joseph Hill (Big White Owl) to the First Inter-American Congress which was held at Patxcuaro, Michoacan, Mexico:

When we are unable to relate the heroic deeds of our great nobles, chieftain sages, prophets and warriors; when the Indian mother cannot lull her children affectionately in her arms and against her breast, then the white man shall have definitely strangled us and we will no longer be deserving of the designation 'American Indian.'

The Six Nations Museum is open from July to Labor Day, daily except Monday, from 10 am to 6 pm, and by appointment in May, June, September and October. Admission for adults/children is $2/1. The family used to allow dogs inside, until one went after a pelt on the wall.

Thousand Islands & St Lawrence Seaway

The lower part of the St Lawrence River, at the outflow of Lake Ontario, is dotted with 1700 small islands known as the Thousand Islands. Some of these islands are so small, they appear as only specks on a map. Appearances, in this case, are not deceiving: most of the islands are home to a few solitary trees, a jumble of rocks, or a single – albeit magnificent – vacation house. A few islands are large enough to support small towns, summer camps, state parks and dense growths of pines, birches and oaks. All of the islands are surrounded by the St Lawrence's deep blue waters.

There are competing legends as to how the region came to be known as the Thousand Islands. An Iroquois legend has it that the Great Spirit, or Master of Life, created a bountiful and beautiful land for the Indian nations who had agreed not to fight each other. When the nations broke their promise, the Great Spirit sent messengers to retrieve the paradise in a huge blanket. As the land was being lifted into the sky, it fell out of the blanket and broke into thousands of pieces creating the Thousand Islands. Modern geologic legend suggests that the islands are part of a granite mass which was crushed, twisted and pushed above the surface over time.

The islands straddle both sides of the US/Canadian border. The greatest concentration of islands is at the mouth of the river, particularly between the summer resort-towns of Clayton and Alexandria Bay, NY. These waterfront towns offer visitors a few interesting sights and activities, but the big draw here is fishing for muskie, northern pike and largemouth bass, or camping at one of the region's many state parks. Some of the best camping is on the Canadian side of the river in St Lawrence Islands National Park. Running through the center of the river is the Thousand Islands Seaway, a major transit line for huge oil, grain and ore transports traveling from the

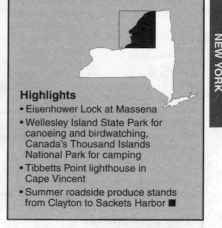

Highlights
- Eisenhower Lock at Massena
- Wellesley Island State Park for canoeing and birdwatching, Canada's Thousand Islands National Park for camping
- Tibbetts Point lighthouse in Cape Vincent
- Summer roadside produce stands from Clayton to Sackets Harbor ■

Atlantic through the Great Lakes. Residents and visitors alike enjoy watching the ships as they pass by at night, their lights twinkling in the darkness.

Alexandria Bay, at the turn of the century, was a bustling resort town boasting several large resort hotels. Today these grand hotels are gone, but many of the estates – built during the same time on privately owned islands – remain. The largest of these estates is George Boldt's Rhineland-inspired castle on Heart Island, located near the town of Alexandria Bay.

To truly enjoy the islands and the sense of escape they afford, you need to travel the St Lawrence by boat. You can rent a houseboat, take car-ferries between the islands or take one of the boat tours that leave frequently from Alexandria Bay. You can also drive, bike and camp along the river's shore.

INFORMATION
The 1000 Islands International Council (☎ (315) 482-2520, (800) 847-5263), PO Box 400, Collins Landing (under the

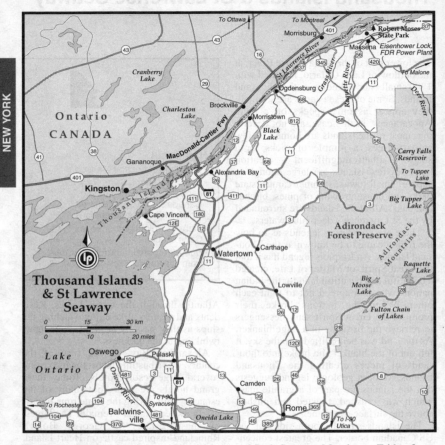

Thousand Islands & St Lawrence Seaway

Thousand Islands Bridge), Alexandria Bay, NY 13067, promotes tourism along the St Lawrence River in both New York and Ontario (Canada). The visitors center is open daily from 8 am to 5 pm, and is a source of materials on fishing, camping and attractions for the entire region. Another very helpful information source is the 1000 Islands-Gananoque Chamber of Commerce (☎ (800) 561-1595) in Gananoque, Ontario.

There is a regional AAA office (☎ (315) 393-4280, (800) 244-4280 toll-free in the region) in Ogdensburg, at Route 37

and Park St, open Monday to Friday from 8:30 am to 5 pm.

For information on Canadian and America currency see Money in the Facts for the Visitor chapter. For information on getting into Canada see the Crossing International Borders sidebar in the Western New York chapter.

FISHING
For information on license fees, contact the local office of the NY State Dept of Environmental Conservation (☎ (315) 785-2262) at 317 Washington St, Watertown,

NY 13601. In Canada, contact the Ministry of Natural Resources (☎ (613) 342-8524), PO Box 605, Oxford Ave, Brockville, Ontario K6V 5Y8.

The chambers of commerce in local towns can give you lists of licensed fishing guides: Alex Bay (☎ (315) 482-9531, (800) 541-2110); Cape Vincent (☎ (315) 654-2481) and Clayton (☎ (315) 686-3771, (800) 252-9806).

The 1000 Islands International Council (see above) is an excellent source for fishing guides.

GETTING THERE & AROUND

Air The region has limited commercial airline service. USAir has daily routes between Pittsburgh and Watertown. United, American and Delta serve Syracuse – 45 miles south of Watertown via I-81.

Bus Both Greyhound and Trailways serve parts of the Thousand Islands region. One-way/roundtrip fares from Watertown to Syracuse is $12/24; Massena to Plattsburg is $16/30.

During the summer, Thousand Islands Bus Line (☎ (315) 788-8146) runs buses from Watertown to several Thousand Islands towns including Alexandria Bay and Clayton.

Train Syracuse, 45 miles south of Watertown, has the nearest Amtrak terminal to the region.

Car A car is almost essential to explore much of the Thousand Islands region. I-81 is the main north-south road in the region and connects Syracuse to Watertown and the St Lawrence Seaway at the international border between Canada and the US via the Thousand Islands International Bridge. From I-81, the primary road heading northwest is Route 12/37, which connects Alexandria Bay, Ogdensburg and Massena. Route 11 is another southwest-northeast road connecting Watertown to Malone in the northern Adirondacks.

Thousand Islands

ALEXANDRIA BAY & AROUND

Locals call it Alex Bay or just Alex. This attractive summer resort town of 1200 is ideally located near the Thousand Islands Bridge, four miles north of I-81 on the St Lawrence River. Boldt Castle is nearby on Heart Island. At the turn of the century, Alex Bay was home to several luxurious resort hotels. These are gone, and the resorts that remain are really just glorified motels and hotels.

The town, however, is still pleasant enough, with tree-lined streets, old buildings and a welcome arch on Church St. Even the commercial strip of James St – lined with tour-boat companies, sandwich shops and souvenir stores – while unquestionably tacky, is only four blocks long and relatively low-key.

Alex Bay does get crowded with tourists from mid-June to August. But its location makes it a good base from which to explore the region. If you have a limited amount of time, you can take a boat tour from here. If time is not a factor, rent a boat and meander the waterways.

Information

The Alexandria Bay Chamber of Commerce (☎ (315) 482-9531, (800) 541-2110), on the east side of Market St off James St, is open from mid-May to early October, daily from 9 am to 5 pm and the rest of the year on weekdays from 9 am to 5 pm.

The post office is on Bethune St. The local weekly newspaper is the *Thousand Islands Sun*.

There is a 24 hour laundry at the intersection of Route 12 and Church St.

Boldt Castle

This 120 room, Rhineland-inspired stone castle (☎ (315) 482-2501) on Heart Island across from Alex Bay, is billed as the site of the 'saddest true love story

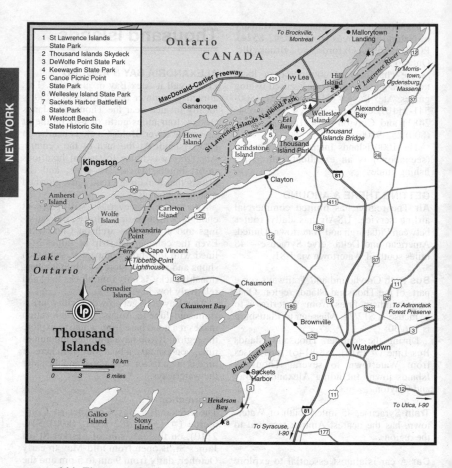

1 St Lawrence Islands
  State Park
2 Thousand Islands Skydeck
3 DeWolfe Point State Park
4 Keewaydin State Park
5 Canoe Picnic Point
  State Park
6 Wellesley Island State Park
7 Sackets Harbor Battlefield
  State Park
8 Westcott Beach
  State Historic Site

Thousand Islands

ever told.' The story begins in 1900 when George Boldt, who had worked his way up from the kitchen to ownership of New York City's Waldorf-Astoria Hotel, decided to have a castle built for his wife, Louise. He bought Heart Island and had it reshaped into a heart. In 1904, as the castle was nearing completion, and with 2.5 million dollars invested, Louise died. Boldt stopped all work on the estate, and the building and grounds were left to decay until 1977 when the Thousand Islands Bridge Authority took

over the castle and began the slow process of renovation.

The castle, with its numerous towers, is quite dramatic from the outside. However, during its long period of abandonment, much of the interior was stripped of its marble and exotic wood detailing, leaving only bare walls. The castle and its grounds – including a five story playhouse and a boathouse – still make an interesting visit. From late May to mid-October it's open daily from 10 am to 6 pm. Admission for adults/children six to 12 is

$3.25/1.75. Uncle Sam Boat Tours has a ferry that is the only way to get to the island, see Organized Tours below.

Thousand Islands Skydeck in Canada

This 395 foot observation tower (☎ (613) 659-2335) is located on Hill Island, Canada, which you reach by way of the Thousand Islands Bridge. It offers excellent views of the islands and the river. Open from June 1 to Labor Day daily from 8:30 am to 9 pm; May 8:30 am to dusk; and after Labor Day to October 31 from

9 am to 6 pm. Admission for adults/kids six to 12 is C$6/4.

Thousand Island Park & Wellesley Island

The town of Thousand Island Park is located on Wellesley Island, a large American island which can be reached from both the US and Canadian mainlands by the Thousand Islands Bridge. The town was originally a Methodist camp meeting ground. Today it's home to summer residents who carefully maintain elaborate

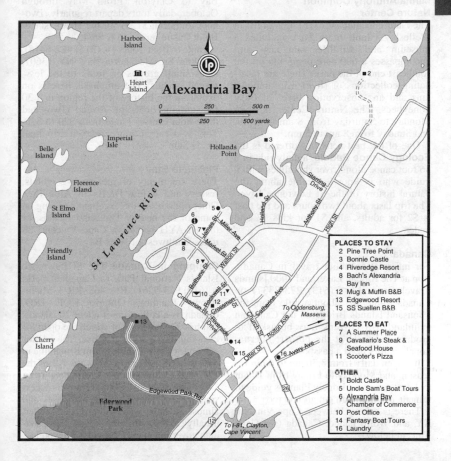

Alexandria Bay

PLACES TO STAY
2 Pine Tree Point
3 Bonnie Castle
4 Riveredge Resort
8 Bach's Alexandria Bay Inn
12 Mug & Muffin B&B
13 Edgewood Resort
15 SS Suellen B&B

PLACES TO EAT
7 A Summer Place
9 Cavallario's Steak & Seafood House
11 Scooter's Pizza

OTHER
1 Boldt Castle
5 Uncle Sam's Boat Tours
6 Alexandria Bay Chamber of Commerce
10 Post Office
14 Fantasy Boat Tours
16 Laundry

19th century Victorian homes. Visitors enjoy driving through the town and admiring the architecture. Residents, however, seem to find the experience less than enjoyable.

To get to Wellesley Island, take I-81 to the Thousand Islands Bridge (a $2 toll going northbound, free southbound). For Thousand Island Park, take exit 51 (the first exit after the bridge) and follow the signs to 'Thousand Island Park Resort Community.'

Minna Anthony Common Nature Center

The Nature Center (☎ (315) 482-2479) in Wellesley Island State Park includes a museum and wildlife sanctuary and encompasses a 600 acre peninsula on the southeast end of the park. There are fascinating collections of (live) fish, amphibians and an 'observation hive' of busy honeybees. The Nature Center is open Monday to Saturday from 8 am to 8 pm, and Sunday from 8 am to 5 pm.

One of the best activities offered is the **Ecology Canoe Paddle**, a daily ride in a 36 foot canoe along river shorelines with a guide who is knowledgeable about the natural history of the St Lawrence River. The trip lasts about two hours and the cost is $2 for adults, and $1 for kids 13 and under.

Canada

For information about travel in Canada, stop at The Rideau Lakes and 1000 Islands Travel Council (☎ (613) 273-7337) on Canada Route 401 about a mile from the Thousand Islands Bridge on the Canadian mainland. US citizens may be asked to produce valid ID at the border; international visitors need a passport.

It's open daily from 8:30 am to 6 pm in-season, and Monday to Friday from 10 am to 3 pm otherwise. Lonely Planet's guide to Canada can help you get around too.

There is a ferry between Cape Vincent, NY, and Wolfe Island, Canada (see Cape Vincent below).

Organized Tours

For those who wish to view the islands from the air rather than by water, 1000 Island Helicopter Tours (☎ (315) 482-5722, 782-6642), Route 12, will take you up in a chopper on weekends in May and October and daily from mid-June to mid-September. It's closed Wednesdays.

Uncle Sam Boat Tours (☎ (315) 482-2611, (800) 253-9229), 2 James St, cruises the island region on triple-deck paddle wheelers. Like their competitor, they offer a variety of tours and cruises from Alex Bay to Clayton. From May through October, daily tours depart regularly. Two-hour tours run $12/6.50; the Heart Island/ Boldt Castle ferry trip is $6/4.

Fantasy Boat Tours (☎ (315) 482-6415), 24 Otter St, Alexandria Bay, NY 13607, takes small groups on tours to the less-visited islands. The emphasis here is on exploring the history of the region in a 30 foot antique boat, the *Joshua*. Two- and three-hour cruises range from $20 to $30. This is a rather more relaxed trip than Uncle Sam's.

Places to Stay

There are plenty of inexpensive motels, resorts and a few B&Bs in Alex Bay. Other options are the excellent camping on some of the nearby Thousand Islands, or the HI-AYH hostel in Cape Vincent, 28 miles southwest of Alex Bay.

Camping in Canada The St Lawrence Islands National Park (a Canadian park; ☎ (613) 923-5261), Box 468, RR 3, Mallorytown Landing, Ontario KOE 1RO, Canada, is a collection of about 20 islands, and has 21 sites – 15 of which are open for camping, the rest for day use. The islands extend for some 45 miles from Brockville in the east to Kingston in the west. All of the sites are easily accessible by boat from either side of the river, but only one is accessible by car. They all have outhouses and almost all have water pumps and shelter, usually cabins with camp stoves. The Canadian government even provides firewood.

The one car-accessible site is at Mallory-town Landing at the park headquarters. This site has flush toilets, running water and a boat launch for getting to nearby Grenadier Island. It is 15 miles north of the Thousand Islands Bridge on the Canadian mainland. Take Canada Route 401 north and look carefully for the sign for Mallory-town Landing, which is easy to miss. You'll see a parking area and boat launch on your right along the river. The park headquarters is hidden behind the greenery on the side of the road opposite the parking area.

As for the other island camping sites, moving up the St Lawrence River, you'll find one off the coast of the Canadian city of Brockville *(Stovin)*; five on or near Grenadier Island *(East, West, North and Centre Grenadier, and Adelaide)*; one between Hill Island and the Canadian mainland near the Canadian town of Ivy Lea *(Georgina)*; one between Wellesley Island and Canada *(Mulcaster)*; three between Grindstone Island, offshore from Clayton, NY, and the Canadian city of Gananoque *(Camelot, Endymion and Gordon)*; five more in this same area, between the Canadian town of Gananoque and Grindstone Island *(Thwartway, Mermaid, Aubrey, Beaurivage, McDonald)*; and two off the shore of the Canadian town of Kingston *(Milton and Cedar)*.

There is no reservation system for camping in the park. On summer weekends many sites fill up by Friday, so you may want to think about arriving on Thursday night. All payments are done on a self-registration system. You calculate camping and mooring fees and put them in an envelope and deposit it in a slot at the site.

Camping fees are C$10 at Mallorytown and C$7 at Grenadier Island because they both have running water and flush toilets. Camping on the other islands is C$6. Day/overnight mooring fees are C$3 to $9/6 to 18 depending on the size of your boat. A seasonal mooring pass is C$17 per meter. Firewood is included in overnight camping fees or is otherwise C$3. Parking at Mallorytown Landing costs C$3 per day; launch and leave also costs C$3. Fees are in effect and firewood is provided from late May to the Canadian Thanksgiving, but the campgrounds are open year round.

There is a ferry from Mallorytown Landing to Grenadier Island (see Getting Around).

Camping in the US For general information about camping in US parks in the Thousand Islands area, call ☎ (315) 482-2593.

The largest US campground in the area is at *Wellesley Island State Park* (☎ (315) 482-2722). The park has 430 sites, including 10 cabins. The land used to be a working farm run by Edison Bradley, who also owned Old Grand Dad distillery. The park is spread over 2600 acres and the campground extends from the St Lawrence River to Eel Bay. Park amenities include hot showers, miniature golf, a nine hole golf course, a marina, a beach and hiking trails. Fees are collected from April 24 to October 12; $13 per campsite for up to six people. Follow the signs after crossing the Thousand Islands Bridge onto Wellesley Island. The campground is two miles west of exit 51 on I-81.

Other campsites include *Canoe Picnic Point State Park* (☎ (315) 654-2522), 3½ miles southwest of Wellesley Island and accessible by boat only. The 30 sites are open from May 16 to September 14 and cost $10.

DeWolf Point State Park (☎ (315) 482-2012) is on Wellesley Island, four miles north of the Thousand Islands Bridge. There are 13 sites for $13 each. Open from mid-May to Labor Day.

Keewaydin State Park (☎ (315) 482-3331) is half a mile west of Alex Bay on Route 12, and one of the prettiest parks in the region, with several old gazebos. There are 41 sites at $13 each, open from late May to early September.

B&Bs *Mug & Muffin B&B* (☎ (315) 482-2188), 18 Crossmon St, is a clean and renovated Cape Cod home with three rooms (one with private bath), ranging from $50 to $75. Open from May to mid-October.

The *SS Suellen B&B* (☎ (315) 482-2137), 26 Otter St, is a renovated and compact suburban-style house. Accommodations include three bedrooms with private baths, heated pool and dock access. July and August rates, including continental breakfast, are $75/85 on weekdays/ends. Subtract about $20 from those rates during off-season (October to May).

Top End Inns & Resorts *Bach's Alexandria Bay Inn* (☎ (315) 482-9697), 2 Church St, is just off the downtown area, across from the St Lawrence River. This is a lovely pale lavender Italianate Victorian (with purple trim). There are several handsomely furnished rooms with private bath. The year-round rates range from $70 to $130, depending on the number of guests, and day of the week.

Of the four major resorts in or around town, the nicest is *Riveredge* (☎ (315) 482-9917, (800) 365-6987), 17 Holland St, which was rebuilt in the late 1980s after a devastating fire. The 129 rooms all have views of the river. Rooms have been named to describe particular views, including 'castleview,' 'bayview,' and 'channel view.' Of these, the channel view rooms open up to the most spectacular scenery. Rooms have private balconies, are furnished with armoires and double beds and are decorated with paintings by local artists. There are two restaurants, indoor and outdoor pools, an exercise room and boat dock. In-season (July through August) rates range from $125 to $200 on weekdays, and $175 to $250 on weekends. Off-season rates drop to $95 to $165 weekdays, and $130 to $220 weekends. Rates vary according to views.

The *Edgewood Resort* (☎ (315) 482-9922, (888) 334-3966), Edgewood Park Rd, is located just west of downtown on the river. The grounds are beautifully landscaped. A wonderful old hotel stands unused in the middle of the grounds, and the resorts' 160 rooms are in motel buildings. The decor here is contemporary, if unexceptional. There is a restaurant and

bar, outdoor pool, beach and dock. Rates are $29 to $99 for rooms away from the river and $49 to $159 on the river. The highest rates apply from late June to early September.

Bonnie Castle (☎ (315) 482-4511, (800) 955-4511), Holland St, is the most expansive of these motel-like 'resorts.' Rooms come with wet bars, tiled bathrooms and free cable TV. Resort amenities abound, including tennis courts, indoor and outdoor pools and a restaurant. The landscaped grounds are spread out over several acres, with parking lots in between. In-season rooms range from $85 to $150.

Pine Tree Point (☎ (315) 482-9911), at the end of Anthony St, offers a variety of accommodations ranging from cabins to suites, all set on tree-covered grounds. There are 95 guest rooms, a restaurant, pool and picnic area. The rate schedule is relatively complicated. Waterfront rates range from $105 to $170; off-water rooms range from $55 to $115.

Places to Eat
Many visitors to Alex Bay dine in the restaurants located in the Riveredge or Bonnie Castle resorts. There are a few informal dining choices located in the downtown area, and a string of fast-food spots.

A Summer Place (☎ (315) 482-9805), located downtown at 24 James St, is a tavern that serves salads, burgers and sandwiches ranging from $3 to $5. They also offer a few Mexican dishes such as deep-fried jalapeños for $5 and fajitas for $8.

Scooter's Pizza (☎ (315) 482-4821), 62 Church St, is good for pizza and buffalo wings.

If you want to spend a bit more money, try *Cavallario's Steak & Seafood House* (☎ (315) 482-9867) on Church St half a block south of James St. The facade here has been made to look like a castle and the interior is decorated in a red-velvet 'knight' motif, including armor and weapons. The pricey dinner selections are standard knights-in-armor fare, steak and seafood in the $16 to $22 range. Open for dinner from 4 to 10 pm.

Getting There & Away

Bus During the summer, Thousand Islands Bus Line (☎ (315) 788-8146) runs buses from Watertown to several Thousand Islands towns including Alex Bay and Clayton.

Car Take I-81 to just before its northern terminus at the Thousand Islands Bridge and exit at Route 12. Alex Bay is four miles to the east. From the northeast, take Route 37 along the St Lawrence Seaway to Alex Bay.

Getting Around

There is a ferry (☎ (613) 923-5261) from Mallorytown Landing to Grenadier Island that runs four times a day each way in season. The roundtrip rate for adults/children seven to 14 is C$8/6.

CLAYTON

Just 11 miles southwest of Alex Bay on the St Lawrence River is the quieter town of Clayton. This town of 2100 people was once a shipbuilding and lumbering port. Today, the town mostly provides services for summer island residents and fishermen. There are a few interesting attractions here, but the big draw is fishing, and the town is home to the Muskie Hall of Fame which contains fishing paraphernalia and a replica of the world record, 69 pound, 15 ounce muskellunge.

Antique Boat Museum

This museum (☎ (315) 686-4104), 750 Mary St, houses 150 freshwater boats, ranging from Native American dugout and birch-bark canoes to examples of the St Lawrence Skiff to the thickly varnished Kris-Kraft pleasure boats that once belonged to the region's millionaire summer residents. Open from mid-May to mid-October, daily from 9 am to 4 pm. Admission for adults is $6, $2 for kids five to 17.

Places to Stay & Eat

Try *Bertrands Motel* (☎ (315) 686-3641),

229 James St, a two story motel in the middle of town with basic rooms for $60 in-season and $50 or less off-season. Across the street is the *Koffee Kove* (☎ (315) 686-2472), a sandwich shop/diner where you can get a sandwich for under $4.

A bit fancier is the *Thousand Island Inn* (☎ (315) 686-3030), 335 Riverside Dr, an old brick hotel with large rooms in the $60 to $80 range. The hotel's restaurant is open daily for breakfast, lunch and dinner. The inn operates seasonally only, from May through September.

The Clipper Inn (☎ (315) 686-3842), on Route 12 in town, is one of the fine dining spots in the region. It's certainly worth the drive from Alex Bay. Daily specials generally feature fresh seafood, prime rib and pasta, all in the $14 to $18 range. Open from April through December, from 4 to 10 pm.

CAPE VINCENT

Cape Vincent is a lovely village (population 700) on the cape where the St Lawrence River meets Lake Ontario. The town was named for Vincent LeRay de Chaumount, who came here seeking asylum for the failing Napoleonic government. Napoleon's brother and sister lived here briefly before returning to France. The village celebrates its French heritage at the Annual French Festival. Cape Vincent is on Hwy 12E, 28 miles southwest of Alex Bay.

There aren't many attractions in Cape Vincent, but the town's main street, Broadway, is lined with towering trees and big old houses, and there is a very nice playground at the end of James St. The only auto ferry across the river leaves from Cape Vincent; you can travel from here to the historic city of Kingston in Ontario by ferrying to Wolfe Island's Point Alexandria, driving across the island, then ferrying to Kingston. If you have a car, you can also stay at the HI-AYH hostel on the grounds of the lighthouse and drive to Alex Bay.

For information about Cape Vincent, contact the visitors center at the Tibbetts Point Lighthouse (☎ (315) 654-2700), open from May to October from 10 am to 4 pm, and also from 6 to 8 pm for the often dazzling sunset.

River Rams Wool Farm
The wool farm and shop (☎ (315) 654-3673) is 1½ miles east of downtown on River Rd (Route 12E). The owners raise sheep, llama and Komondor dogs. It's best to call before stopping by. The shop sells sweaters and other products made from the wool produced on the farm, as well as wool for knitting, sheepskin hides, moccasins, mittens and hats.

Places to Stay
Cape Vincent has one of the most picturesquely located HI-AYH hostels in the country (☎ (315) 654-3450). It's on the grounds of the 1854 Tibbetts Point Lighthouse, right on the lake – about three miles west of town. The dorm rooms are in two white houses that used to be the lighthouse keepers' quarters. It's friendly and quiet. The hostel is open from mid-May to late October, following the Wolfe Island ferry schedule that runs from town. Beds in dorm rooms for members/non-members are $10/13. Check-in is from 5 to 9:30 pm with a 10 pm curfew. The hostel is closed from 9:30 am to 5 pm.

To get there, take Route 12E west from Clayton into Cape Vincent. Where 12E turns south in the middle of town keep going west on Broadway, which becomes Lighthouse Rd and leads you to the lighthouse/hostel.

The *Buccaneer Motel* (☎ (315) 654-2975), at Point St on the river, has 10 rooms which extend along a single corridor in a motel building located a few steps from the water. There are four more rooms in the main house, with a shared bath. The main floor of the house has large floor-to-ceiling windows. Motel rooms are $60 to $80; the rooms in the main house go for $120 and include a big breakfast.

Places to Eat
As in Alex Bay, there are several taverns and cafes that serve burgers, salads and sandwiches. The *Anchor Inn* (☎ (315) 654-3566), 790 E Broadway and *Aubrey's Inn* (☎ (315) 654-3754), 126 St James St, are good diners serving breakfast, lunch and dinner.

The *Roxie Hotel* (☎ (315) 654-2456), 111 E Broadway, is open year round from 7 am to 10 pm and has a good Friday-night fish fry.

Wolfe Island Ferries
A ferry (☎ (315) 783-0638) makes 11 trips daily each way between Cape Vincent, NY, and Wolfe Island, Canada, from early May to late October. The schedule may change slightly each year. The crossing takes 10 minutes and costs $6 for a car and driver or $1 for a walk-on.

You can then drive seven miles across Wolfe Island and take another ferry (☎ (613) 544-2231) to Kingston, Canada. The crossing here takes 25 minutes, and runs year round. Currently, the ferry is free, but it may cost C$3 to C$4 in the future. The ferry makes about 15 trips each way a day in summer, fewer in winter.

SACKETS HARBOR
Sackets Harbor is a picturesque lakeside village with a strong sense of history. A key naval battle was won by the Americans here at the expense of the British in the War of 1812.

Information
The Sackets Harbor Chamber of Commerce (☎ (315) 646-1700) and the Sackets Harbor Visitors Center (☎ (315) 646-2321) share the same location on Broad St overlooking the harbor. Both operate daily in the summer, and this far north summer is only from July to Labor Day, from 10 am to 4 pm. During the month of June and from Labor Day until mid-October, the information center is open from Wednesday through Saturday, 10 am to 4 pm.

Sackets Harbor Battlefield Historic Site

This site (☎ (315) 646-3634), 505 W Washington St, is in the village. A small house-museum tour takes you through the commandant's 1850s four story residence, as well as a hands-on exhibit of the naval battles during the War of 1812 – kids can pretend to shoot at the British boats. The tours operate daily from 10 am to 4:30 pm. The cost is $3 for adults, $2 for seniors, and $1 for kids five to 12.

The **Madison Barracks** (☎ (315) 646-3374) is both historical and contemporary – that is, it's a residential community with about 200 year-round residents who make their homes in the renovated Army barracks. The small visitor's center at 85 Worth Rd is open daily from June through September from 8 am to 8 pm during the week; 10 am to 5 pm on Saturday; and 11 am to 4 pm on Sunday. They have free walking-tour maps of the area.

Places to Stay & Eat

Cheaper accommodations are available in nearby Watertown. But in town, *Ontario Place* (☎ (315) 646-8000), 103 General Smith Dr, is a classy old waterfront hotel, with very nice rooms in the $60 to $75 range.

The Barracks Inn Restaurant (☎ (315) 646-2376) is part of the old Madison Barracks, though separate from the inn. The feeling is historic here – the barracks date from the War of 1812 – but the food is fresh. Seafood and steak entrees with an Italian flavor dominate. There is also a nice outside dining area overlooking the lake and harbor. Dinners are in the $14 to $18 range; lunches in the $6 to $12 range. Like many establishments in the area, the restaurant is only open from June until Labor Day weekend in early September. Open daily for lunch and dinner from 11 am to 10 pm.

Tin Pan Galley (☎ (315) 646-3812), 110 Main St, is a great spot for breakfast, lunch and dinner, and less formal and expensive than its upstairs partner, *One Ten Main Street*, owned by the same folks.

St Lawrence Seaway

The seaway, which officially opened in 1959, is jointly operated by the US and Canada. A system of 15 locks allows large cargo vessels to travel 2350 miles from the Atlantic Ocean to Duluth, Minnesota, on Lake Superior. Along the way, the water level rises 602 feet. The channel is extremely narrow in some places, notably off of Alexandria Bay, where a disastrous 1976 oil spill wreaked havoc on the ecosystem. The area has never fully recovered. Of the 15 locks, two belong to the US, including the Dwight D Eisenhower Lock near Massena, NY. From here, you can watch ships passing through the lock and learn how the system works at the visitor center (☎ (315) 764-3200), open May to October. For information on when ships are passing through, call ☎ (315) 769-2422.

SEAWAY TRAIL

The New York State 'Seaway Trail' is a 450 mile driving and bicycling route on a series of highways following the seaway through New York (and Northern Pennsylvania) along the St Lawrence River, Lake Ontario and Lake Erie. The well-marked trail includes Routes 104, 3, 12E, 12 and 37 (from Oswego to Massena) and provides an interesting alternative to super-highways. Green and white 'Seaway Trail' signs help guide you along the historic and scenic route, which leisurely makes its way through small towns and villages. There are also 42 brown and white interpretive signs along the trail marking events that took place here during the War of 1812.

MASSENA

Before the engineering marvel of the St Lawrence Seaway and Eisenhower Locks, Massena was a small industrial town dominated by an aluminum plant. In 1900, Henry Warren led a canal-digging enterprise between the Grasse River and the St Lawrence River. The water in the new

SLSDC

A ship passes through a
St Lawrence Seaway lock.

canal dropped 45 feet in about three miles, creating a power source that spurred the town's growth.

In 1959, the St Lawrence Seaway opened – the long-sought joint effort of the Canadian and US governments to create a deepwater channel between the Atlantic Ocean and the Great Lakes.

The Canadians actually led the effort, and the US joined in when it became apparent that the canal might be built without its involvement – or benefit.

Watching Ships Go By

To see a 700 foot ocean-going ship (or 'laker') passing through the narrow canal at Massena is stunning. The best place to see it happen is the **Eisenhower Lock Visitor Center** (☎ (315) 769-2049), just off Route 37 (follow the signs). There are two viewing decks, one above the other, and the cost is 25¢ per person. The center is open daily during the summer from 8 am to 9 pm, but you can see the ships easily from the adjacent parking lot any time.

To make sure you get to see a ship passing through, call **Seaway Eisenhower** (☎ (315) 769-2422) to hear a 24 hour recorded message giving the estimated arrival times (and ship names) of both upbound and downbound ships.

St Lawrence-Franklin D Roosevelt Power Project

The Power Project Visitors Center (☎ (315) 764-0226) is hard to miss. It sits atop the

3200 foot dam than spans the St Lawrence River between the US and Canada (look for the different colors of brick used by each country's builders). The power project is part of the same scheme that delivered the Eisenhower Lock and Robert Moses State Park in the mid-1950s.

There are several highlights here. The 5th floor glass-enclosed observation deck offers a four-way view of the entire region, including the seaway's shipping channel. There are also several energy-related exhibits, including several of the hands-on variety. On the 3rd floor, you can stand in front of a large picture window to view the **control room and power plant**. There are also two large murals by American painter Thomas Hart Benton depicting 17th century French explorer Jacques Cartier's early voyages and meetings with members of the Mohawk tribes.

Admission and parking are free, and the visitors center is open from late May to early September, daily from 9:30 am to 6 pm; until 4:30 pm from September to mid-October; and Monday through Friday, 9 am to 4:30 pm the rest of the year.

Places to Stay

Camping *Robert Moses State Park* (☎ (315) 769-8663) is one of the prettiest parks in the northeast, situated on both the mainland and Barnhart Island. The park is reached via a tunnel which passes under the Eisenhower Lock. The park is spacious and serene. Whitetail deer, beaver, shy (they say) bobcat and coyote live here, along with several song birds, waterfowl and birds of prey.

The park is open for camping from mid-May to mid-October. Campsites are $13 per day. There are also about a dozen cabins available by the week only for $265 (reservations required for the cabins). There is a visitor's center, a nature interpretive center with wildlife and natural history, and environmental displays. The park (and beach) is open year round, and entrance is $5 per car. Robert Moses State Park is one of several 'carry in – carry out' parks in New York State. Trash barrels have been removed from day use areas, with faith in the visitors to hang on to their own garbage.

Motels *Super 8 Motel* (☎ (315) 764-1065) is at Route 37 and Grove St, about three blocks from downtown Massena. The motel is decent enough, and rates are relatively low: $42 to $52.

EconoLodge Motor Inn (☎ (315) 764-0264) is on Route 37W about 2½ miles west of the downtown area. This is a relatively upscale EconoLodge, and is not part of a motel strip. Rooms range from $60 to $85 year round. There is also a good German restaurant on the premises.

Places to Eat

The *Oak Tree Cafe* (☎ (315) 769-0473) in the St Lawrence Center Mall, is just off Route 37 (across from the bridge to Canada), and is open Monday to Saturday from 10 am to 9 pm; Sunday 10 am to 6 pm.

Baurenstraube Restaurant (☎ (315) 764-0246), located in the EconoLodge on Route 37W (see above), is one of the nicest motel eateries you'll find, and specializes in German fare. The Friday and Saturday all-you-can-eat dinner buffet is the best deal around at $10. Open daily for breakfast from 6 to 10 am, and daily for dinner from 5 to 10 pm; and Sunday from 6 am to 3 pm.

FREDERIC REMINGTON MUSEUM

The Remington Museum (☎ (315) 393-2425), 303 Washington St, in the artist's nearby boyhood home town of Ogdensburg, NY, is 30 miles west of Massena, and about mid-way to Alexandria Bay. The museum houses the largest collection of Remington's bronze sculptures, oil paintings and pen-and-ink sketches, as well as many of the artist's personal effects. Born in 1861, Remington is best known as a chronicler of the American Western experience. He left Yale at 19 and moved West where he spent five years capturing what he saw – including frontiersmen and cowboys riding on horseback, soldiers fighting and Native Americans hunting – in photographs, illustrations for newspapers and sketches which would later serve as the basis for his work in bronze and on canvas.

Remington died in 1909 at his home in Connecticut. After his death, his widow returned to Ogdensburg and rented a home which, shortly after her death in 1923, opened as a museum. Admission for adults/seniors and 'youths' is $3/2. Open May 1 to October 31 Monday to Saturday from 10 am to 5 pm; Sunday from 1 to 5 pm. From November 1 to April 30 Tuesday to Saturday from 10 am to 5 pm.

Finger Lakes Region

The Finger Lakes region is one of New York's most scenic and rural destinations. The name is derived from the 11 long, slender, finger-like bodies of water running north-south in the western part of the state. Named for several of the tribes of the Six Nations of the Iroquois Confederacy, the largest lakes are the Cayuga, Seneca and Keuka at 39, 35 and 19 miles long, respectively. These are among the deepest glacial lakes on the continent as well; Seneca Lake is the deepest at 650 feet. Boating, fishing, swimming, cycling and winter cross-country skiing are among the many recreational offerings to be found. What's more, the area produces most of New York's wine, and numerous wineries, often in restored farm buildings, dot the rolling countryside.

The Finger Lakes region is often divided into the Northern Tier – including the towns of Canandaigua, Geneva and Seneca Falls – and the Southern Tier – including Ithaca, Corning and Watkins Glen. Stretching north and south between the tiers are the lakes and 'wine trails' along the roads leading to dozens of wineries on the hills above the lakes. The gorges and waterfalls in Watkins Glen State Park and in the state parks around Ithaca are among the most spectacular natural sites in the region. Taughannock Falls, at 215 feet, is the highest waterfall around, even higher than its better known counterpart in Niagara. Ithaca, home of Cornell University, is one of the most admired towns, and Seneca Falls is the birthplace of America's organized women's rights movement and the site of Elizabeth Cady Stanton's 19th century home.

Rochester is home to a lively arts and photography scene, anchored by Eastman House and the Kodak International Center of Photography. Syracuse is a city with history on display, from the Erie Canal Museum to the Salt Museum, honoring the

Highlights

- Grape Festival, Naples, south of Canandaigua Lake, late September
- Winery hopping on the shores of Seneca and Keuka lakes
- Charming, lush Ithaca, home to Cornell University
- Excellent state parks and camping, including Watkins Glen State Park ■

humble and ubiquitous seasoning discovered in a local spring by the Iroquois.

HISTORY

Before it was settled by Europeans, the Finger Lakes region was home to much of the Iroquois Confederacy, a political union of Cayuga, Mohawk, Onondaga, Oneida, Seneca and later Tuscarora, Indian nations. During the Revolutionary War, many of the Iroquois allied themselves with the British. Though not the first group in history to pick the wrong side, the Iroquois paid a far worse price than the average lottery loser. In addition to military defeats, disease and continuing encroachment by European settlers, the Iroquois communities around the Finger Lakes were devastated for good in 1779 when General George Washington sent a heavily armed expedition to punish the Indians for their isolated and brutal attack on a Scotch and Irish community near Lake Otsego. Entire communities were wiped out, and much of the land was deeded to Revolutionary War veterans as payment for service.

With the completion of the Erie Canal in 1825, the economy of the region changed dramatically. From Albany to Buffalo, towns and cities prospered along with the canal's economic promise (see the Erie Canal Museum entry in Syracuse). Today, parts of the canal attract recreational boaters, and visitors to several historic cobblestone buildings. The roads south of the old canal now weave through family farms, orchards and vineyards scattered among the low hills and long valleys of the Finger Lakes.

ORIENTATION

The towns of the region are described beginning with the Southern Tier at Ithaca and moving counterclockwise around the lakes to the Northern Tier. Towns with the most notable historical architecture, particularly Greek Revival mansions, tend to be in the Northern Tier. The allure of the Southern Tier towns is reflected in their proximity to the lakes, their village greens and rural pace.

The northern Finger Lakes region is defined for drivers by east-west Route 20

NEW YORK

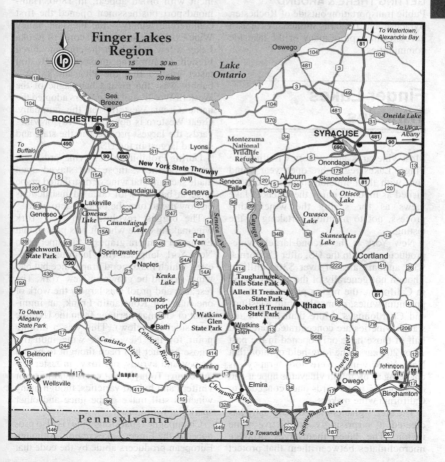

which skirts the northern fringe of most of the lakes, and I-90 which links Rochester and Syracuse. Route 17 marks the southern edge, and connects the towns of Bath, Corning, Elmira and Owego. The western edge is marked by I-390 which drops south from Rochester, and the eastern edge by I-81 which connects Syracuse to Cortland. The primary north-south routes within the region are Routes 21, 14 and 89, which parallel the western shores of Canandaigua, Seneca and Cayuga lakes.

GETTING THERE & AROUND

Public transportation outside of Rochester, Syracuse and Ithaca is limited. A car is a necessity to explore many of the lakeside communities.

Finger Lakes Wineries

Most vineyards and wineries dotting the Finger Lakes region are open year round and, with their hillside locations, can be visited as much to enjoy the splendid lake views as for seeing the winemaking process, not to mention partaking in the tasting.

New York is the second-largest wine-producing state in the US, after California, with annual sales of over $300 million. Though not generally of the quality found in California, the region produces several premium wines, primarily white Rieslings and Chardonnays. More than half of the state's wineries are concentrated here, and half of those have only opened in the past 10 or 20 years. The long-held opinion that New York wines were too 'grapey' is changing as premium vineyards appear and occasionally win awards once conceded to California wine makers.

The area's glacier-carved geography has created a surprisingly productive wine region. The lakes themselves produce microclimates between them that protect the vines. In fall and winter, the lake water stores heat, which mitigates extreme temperatures and protects the vines against frosts. The water's cooler temperatures through spring and summer prevent damage from high temperatures. Sloping hills and glacial soils surrounding the lakes provide drainage terrain ideal for grape growing.

History

During the 1820s, a Hammondsport minister began making sacramental wine in the Finger Lakes. Apparently, this was a sacrament with broad appeal; in 1860, Hammondsport businessmen opened the first commercial winery – the Pleasant Valley Wine Company – near the shores of Keuka Lake. A few years later the company hired French Champagne makers. A Boston taster gushed that the Pleasant Valley's bubbly was 'the great Champagne of the Western World' and the owners adopted the name Great Western for the company. Great Western is now part of Taylor Vineyards, the largest producer in the state and second largest in the US.

During Prohibition many vineyards went out of business; those that stayed open made sacramental wine or distributed grape juice in barrels with detailed instructions on how *not* to turn the product into wine.

The biggest revolution in New York winemaking came when it was proven that European vinifera grapes – far superior to New York labrusca (not lambrusca) varieties, which make good grape juice but bad wine – could be grown in New York. The research and proof was largely the work of one man, Dr Konstantin Frank, an immigrant of German heritage from the Ukraine (see sidebar, below). This was a turning point for the New York wine industry, whose product had been thought to be too grapey and syrupy, or 'foxy' in taster terminology. Today's vineyards tend to favor vinifera and hybrid varieties, though many wineries still make grape juice and other sparkling fruit juices.

Champagne (sparkling wine) is also produced in the Finger Lakes region. Although European producers abide by the code that

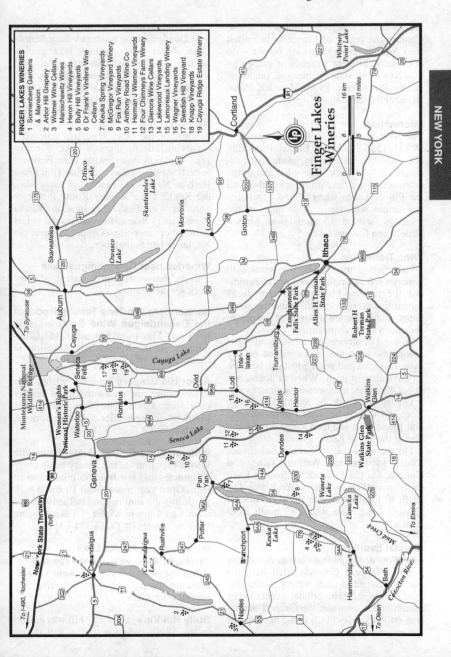

NEW YORK

FINGER LAKES WINERIES
1 Sonnenberg Gardens & Mansion
2 Arbor Hill Grapery
3 Widmer Wine Cellars, Manischewitz Wines
4 Heron Hill Vineyards
5 Bully Hill Vineyards
6 Dr Frank's Vinifera Wine Cellars
7 Keuka Spring Vineyards
8 McGregor Vineyard Winery
9 Fox Run Vineyards
10 Anthony Road Wine Co
11 Herman J Wiemer Vineyards
12 Four Chimneys Farm Winery
13 Glenora Wine Cellars
14 Lakewood Vineyards
15 Lamoreaux Landing Winery
16 Swedish Hill Vineyard
17 Wagner Vineyards
18 Knapp Vineyards
19 Cayuga Ridge Estate Winery

allows only Champagne produced in the Champagne region of France to be called so, US producers – surprising no one – do not. Many different varieties of grapes go into New York state champagne, predominantly Pinot Noir, Pinot Meunier, Pinot Blanc and Chardonnay. Cheers.

Information

The New York Wine & Grape Foundation (☎ (315) 536-7442), 350 Elm St, Penn Yan, NY 14527, is an industry group that promotes all New York State wine and grape producers. They have information about all the Finger Lakes wineries and brochures for various wine trails, as do many of the wineries around Canandaigua, Keuka, Seneca and Cayuga lakes.

Wine Trails

'Wine trails' – usually lakeside roads with wineries left and right – are found throughout the region. Most trails have signs directing drivers to specific wineries; some signs simply picture a bunch of grapes to indicate a nearby vineyard.

A word of advice: roads and road signs among the lakes have not changed greatly over the years, and getting lost can become an adventure in itself. When in doubt, ask about distances, intersection landmarks etc.

On the west side of Keuka Lake, take Route 54A north between Hammondsport and Branchport and then Route 54 to Penn Yan at the top of Keuka Lake.

On the west side of Seneca Lake, take Route 14 between Watkins Glen and Geneva. On the east side of Seneca Lake (also from Watkins Glen) take Route 414 north to Route 96A. On the west side of Cayuga Lake, take Route 89 north from Ithaca.

Special Events

The Wine & Grape Foundation distributes a *Wine Country Calendar* that lists the events planned at each winery during the year. There are promotional events every month in the summer; the Grape Foundation (☎ (315) 536-7442) is the best source for information.

Glenora Winery (☎ (607) 243-5511), near Dundee on the western side of Seneca Lake, hosts two summer jazz performances, on the third Sunday in July and again in August. Across the lake to the east, the Hector Jazz Festival goes into full Dixieland mode the last weekend of August, in the town of Hector, near Finger Lakes National Forest.

Some of the other regularly scheduled events include the Seneca Lake Wineries Frühling Wein Fest (Spring Wine Festival) in early April, the Cayuga Wine Trail Fresh Herb & New Wine Festival in early May, the Keuka Lake Winery Route Picnic & Summer Wine Festival in June, the Keuka Lake Winery Route Harvest Festival in late September and the Grape Festival in Naples in late September.

Wineries near Canandaigua Lake

This is the westernmost extent of New York's wine country.

Sonnenberg Gardens Tasting Room of the Canandaigua Wine Co Open daily from mid-May to mid-October. 151 Charlotte St, at the Sonnenberg Mansion in Canandaigua (☎ (716) 394-7680)

Arbor Hill Grapery Open daily from May to December, and on Saturday and Sunday only from January through April. 6461 Route 64, in the hamlet of Bristol Springs, near Naples (☎ (716) 374-2870)

Widmer Wine Cellars & Manischewitz Wines Free tours of the winery begin every 45 minutes and last from 45 minutes to an hour. Open year round from 10 am to 4:30 pm during the summer and fall seasons and from 1 to 4 pm in winter. 1 Lake Niagara Lane, in Naples (☎ (716) 374-6311)

Wineries near Keuka Lake

Several of the area's oldest vineyards are along the western side of Keuka Lake. Most are open to the public for tasting, and several offer tours.

Bully Hill Vineyards The hill was named in the 1700s, when a 'bully' hill meant one that was easily conquerable. The site of Bully Hill is actually the original site of the Taylor wine company, whose owner, Walter S Taylor, is a fourth generation descendent of the Taylor wine family. Walter Taylor isn't allowed to tell you this because in 1977 Coca-Cola, which had bought the newer and larger Taylor Wine Co in nearby Pleasant Valley, sued to prevent him from using his name or the paintings of any ancestors on his wine labels. Walter responded by putting paintings of his goat on many labels and proclaiming: 'They have my name and heritage but they didn't get my goat.' RD 2, in Hammondsport, 1½ miles up County Rd 76 from Route 54A (☎ (607) 868-3610).

The *Bully Hill Restaurant* (☎ (607) 868-3490/4814) is open from May 1 to November 1 from 11:30 am to 3:30 pm on the grounds of Bully Hill Vineyards, offering sandwiches, grape leaves and pasta dishes – all designed to go well with wine.

Dr Frank's Vinifera Wine Cellars & Chateau Frank This is the home of the vinifera revolution in Finger Lakes winemaking, and is run by Dr Konstantin Frank's son and grandchildren. The winery is known for its Johannesburg Riesling, Pinot Noir and champagne. Open Monday to Saturday from 9 am to 5 pm; Sunday from noon to 5 pm. 9749 Middle Rd, on Route 76 between Hammondsport and the Route 54 junction (☎ (607) 868-4884)

Heron Hill Vineyards This is a small, family-owned vineyard specializing in vintage varietals and specialty wines, including late harvest wine. Open daily from May through November. RD 1, Middle Rd, three miles north of Hammondsport on Route 76 (☎ (607) 868-4241)

Keuka Spring Vineyards Open in May and June on weekends from 11 am to 5 pm; in July and August daily from

11 am to 5 pm; and in the harvest season of September and October Friday through Monday from 11 am to 5 pm. 273 E Lake Rd on Route 54, in Penn Yan at the northeast tip of the lake (☎ (716) 621-4850)

McGregor Vineyard Winery This winery offers a clear view of Bluff Point above the lake and is open year round. 5503 Dutch St, on Route 54 between Hammondsport and Penn Yan on the east side of Keuka Lake (☎ (607) 292-3999)

Wineries near Seneca Lake

The largest number of quality wineries in the Finger Lakes are to be found on the western and eastern shores of Seneca Lake. Most wineries in the area are open from mid-morning until about 5 pm. Heading

---

Konstantin Frank

New York is famous for its native labrusca grapes – Delaware, Concord, Catawba and Niagara – which make great jam but mediocre wine. For years New York winemakers used labrusca grapes because they believed that European vinifera grapes could not survive in the state. Enter Dr Konstantin Frank, born of German parents in the Ukraine in 1899. Frank held a doctorate in plant sciences and had been director of a large state-owned vineyard in the Ukraine. In 1953, he came to the US speaking many languages – though not English – and went to Geneva near Seneca Lake to ask for work at the New York State Experimental Station. He was allowed to hoe blueberries and work as a janitor.

A few years later Charles Mourner, who was working at the Urbana Wine Co, which later became Gold Seal, hired Frank. Frank and Fournier experimented with grafting native American rootstock to European vinifera buds to prove the latter could grow in New York. Dr Frank's successful experiments led to the growth of the state's huge wine industry. He later opened his own winery – Dr Frank's Vinifera Wine Cellars – although it wasn't until his son Willy Frank took over in the 1980s that the business expanded beyond experimentation to the production of fine wines. ∎

south from Geneva on Route 14, the wineries come in bunches on the west shore on Seneca Lake, including the following.

Fox Run Vineyards Occupying a restored 19th century dairy barn on the western shore of Seneca Lake, Fox Run boasts a turn-of-the-century grape crusher. Open on weekends only in May and daily from June to October. 670 Route 14, Penn Yan (☎ (315) 536-4616)

Anthony Road Wine Co This winery is housed in an unassuming farm building and is known for good buys in Rieslings and Chardonnays, as well as a late-harvest dessert wine. Open daily from April through December and by appointment from January to March. 1225 Anthony Rd, near Penn Yan (☎ (315) 536-2182)

Four Chimneys Farm Winery Four Chimneys is a small organic winery, but important as organically produced wines are catching the attention of larger wine makers interested in sustaining their vineyards. Open daily from May through November for tastings. RD 1, Hall Rd, in the village of Himrod (☎ (607) 243-7502)

Herman J Wiemer Vineyards Operated by a winemaking family from the Mosel region of Germany, it's known for excellent Riesling wines. Open daily April through November, Monday to Saturday from 10 am to 5 pm, Sunday from 11 am to 5 pm; from December to April, Monday through Friday only. Route 14 in Dundee (☎ (607) 243-7971)

Glenora Wine Cellars This is the largest producer of vinifera wines in the eastern US, and is well known for excellent sparkling wines and Rieslings. Glenora, one of the first wineries on Seneca Lake, has one of its most commanding views. The winery shows an interesting 12 minute video which follows the journey from vine to glass. Open year round, and its Wine Garden Cafe is open from May through

October. 5435 Route 14, in Dundee (☎ (607) 243-5511)

Lakewood Vineyards Lakewood has a good view of the lake and surrounding countryside; it's known for, among others, an 'ice wine' made from frozen grapes, and a fruity mead. Open daily May through December from 10 am to 5:30 pm, Sunday from noon to 6 pm. From January to April, they open on Friday, Saturday and Sunday. 4024 Route 14, north of Watkins Glen (☎ (607) 535-9252)

Wagner Vineyards & Ginny Lee Cafe Open year round daily from 10 am to 5 pm. 9322 Route 414, in Lodi on the eastern shore of Seneca Lake (☎ (607) 582-6450)

Lamoreaux Landing Winery This winery is on the southeast shore of Seneca Lake, and is one of the most recent to appear in the region; it already has a reputation as a premium producer. The view of the lake below is splendid, as are the vinifera wines. Open year round, Monday through Saturday from 10 am to 5 pm, Sunday from noon to 5 pm. County Rd 137 in Valois (☎ (607) 582-6164)

Wineries near Cayuga Lake

There are several vineyards and wineries on the western shore of Cayuga Lake between Seneca Falls and Ithaca – these consist of a section of the Cayuga wine trail (see Ithaca, below).

Swedish Hill Vineyard Swedish Hill makes several good white wines as well as a popular red. Open year round, January to April daily from 10 am to 5 pm; May to December daily from 9 am to 6 pm. 4565 Route 414, in Romulus (☎ (315) 549-8326)

Knapp Vineyards & Restaurant This winery produces among the best white wines in the region. Open April to December, Monday through Saturday from 10 am to 5 pm, Sunday from noon to 5 pm; January to March, weekdays from 10 am to 4 pm. The restaurant is open from April until mid-December. 2770 County Rd 128, in Romulus (☎ (607) 869-9271)

Cayuga Ridge Estate Winery This winery gives hands-on seminars in grape growing and winemaking in addition to the usual tastings. Open mid-May to December daily from noon to 5 pm. 6800 Route 89, Ovid (☎ (607) 869-5158)

Finger Lakes – Southern Tier

ITHACA

Like its ancient Greek namesake, Ithaca recalls a somewhat bygone time. This handsome college town of 30,000 people is dominated by distinguished Cornell University which overlooks it and Cayuga Lake. Cornell is an integral part of Ithaca; the hilltop Ivy League campus is adjacent to the downtown area, flanked by Cascadilla Gorge to the south and Fall Creek Gorge to the north, both of which wind their way to Cayuga Lake. The local population nearly doubles when combined with Cornell's student body of 18,000 and the 6000 students at nearby Ithaca College, a music conservatory and fine arts school.

Though small, it's culturally rich, the quintessential college town; bookstores and eateries are abundant, and foot traffic is ample on the small streets and arcades. Ithaca's idea of a shopping mall, for example, is the DeWitt Mall – a converted turn-of-the-century schoolhouse without a single national franchise. Not that Ithaca lacks for modern conveniences; the roads are paved, the traffic lights work and dogs must be on leashes.

Ithaca sparkles like few other upstate New York communities its size; it's a recreational hub and gateway to the Finger Lakes region. Residential and business districts share the space with creeks, waterfalls and gorges and several town and lakeside parks, museums and theaters. Fall afternoons by the lake may be highlighted by university rowing shells sliding through the calm water at the south end of Cayuga Lake. Ithaca Falls, Buttermilk Falls and Taughannock Falls are close by.

Ithaca marks the beginning of the Cayuga Wine Trail (see Wineries near Cayuga Lake, above). The surrounding countryside also provides ample offerings at the town's farmers' market.

Orientation & Information

Ithaca sits at the southern tip of Cayuga Lake, at the crossroads of Routes 13 and 96. Binghamton is 53 miles to the southeast, Syracuse 57 miles to the northeast.

Tourist Information The Ithaca/Tompkins County Convention & Visitors Bureau (☎ (607) 272-1313, (800) 284-8422, fax 272-7617), at 904 E Shore Dr, is open Monday through Friday from 9 am to 5 pm; additionally, from mid-May until November, the office is open on weekends from 10 am to 5 pm, and offers information on Ithaca and Cayuga Lake.

There's a AAA office (☎ (607) 273-6727), 303 W Lincoln St, that has maps (free for members), auto club and travel services.

Post The downtown post office (☎ (607) 272-5455) is at the corner of Buffalo and Tioga Sts.

Bookstores Two of the best bookstores in town are The Bookery I and The Bookery II (☎ (607) 273-5055), in the DeWitt Mall, 215 N Cayuga St. Bookery I is the more esoteric of the two; used, rare and out-of-print books are its specialty.

Bookery I is open Monday through Saturday from 10 am to 6 pm. Bookery II offers a rambling collection of contemporary prose, poetry, travel and children's books. Bookery II is open Monday through Saturday from 9:30 am to 9:30 pm, Sunday from 11 am to 6 pm.

Borealis Bookstore (☎ (607) 272-7752), 111 N Aurora St, specializes in literature, mystery, philosophy and New Age titles; it

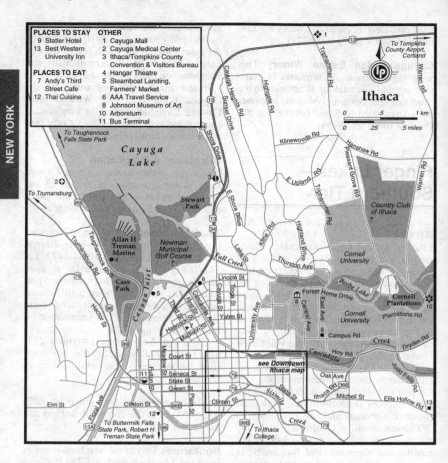

PLACES TO STAY
9   Statler Hotel
13 Best Western
    University Inn

PLACES TO EAT
7   Andy's Third
    Street Cafe
12 Thai Cuisine

OTHER
1   Cayuga Mall
2   Cayuga Medical Center
3   Ithaca/Tompkins County
    Convention & Visitors Bureau
4   Hangar Theatre
5   Steamboat Landing,
    Farmers' Market
6   AAA Travel Service
8   Johnson Museum of Art
10 Arboretum
11 Bus Terminal

is open Monday through Saturday from 10 am to 6 pm, Sunday from noon to 5 pm.

For a large selection of discounted and remaindered books set in a 160 year old building complete with tin ceiling, try the Corner Bookstore (☎ (607) 273-6001), 115 S Cayuga St, open Monday through Saturday from 9:30 am to 9 pm, Sunday from noon to 5 pm.

Library The Tompkins County Public Library (☎ (607) 272-4555), 312 N Cayuga St at the corner of Court St, is open Monday through Thursday from 10 am to 9 pm, Friday and Saturday from 10 am to 5 pm.

Media WICB, at 91.7 FM, is the Ithaca College station and carries NPR. For news and weather, try WHCU 870 AM.

The *Cornell Daily Sun* is an independent and reliable student-run morning newspaper featuring international as well as campus news. The *Ithaca Journal* is the regular town paper, published daily except Sunday. The *Ithaca Times* is a free weekly arts and entertainment guide.

Laundry The ABC Laundromat (no ☎), 308 Stewart Ave, is adjacent to the ABC Cafe and is open daily from 8 am to midnight. A more complete service is the Cayuga Mall Laundromat & Cleaners (☎ (607) 257-4922), on the north side of Ithaca near the intersection of Route 13 and Triphammer Rd, offering self-service and drop-off service, and open daily from 7 am to 11 pm.

Medical Services Cayuga Medical Center at Ithaca (formerly Tompkins Community Hospital; ☎ (607) 274-4011), 101 Dates Dr, is near Cayuga Lake in the northwest corner of town. Cornell University's Gannett Health Center (☎ (607) 255-5155) is on the campus' Central Ave.

Cornell University

Founded in 1865, Cornell boasts of several notable departments, from the Colleges of Agriculture, Architecture, and Human Ecology to the Schools of Hotel Administration and Industrial & Labor Relations. A particle accelerator is located beneath the school's football field, a juxtaposition that

some regard with irony. Call the **Wilson Synchrotron Lab** (☎ (607) 255-3480) for tour information.

Cornell is a lovely and inviting campus; the mixture of old and new architecture, shaded arcadian walkways and the panoramic view of Cayuga Lake make it a common destination for tourists.

One of the best views of the lake and beyond is from the 5th floor of the **Johnson Museum of Art** (☎ (607) 255-6464), which houses a major Asian collection, as well as pre-Columbian, American and European exhibits. The museum is at the corner of University and Central Aves on the western edge of campus, and metered parking is available near the entrance. This striking modern structure, designed by acclaimed architect IM Pei, is known on campus as 'the sewing-machine building.' See for yourself. The museum is open Tuesday through Sunday from 10 am to 5 pm. Admission is free.

Cornell's classic Ivy League landscaping is punctuated by the **Cornell University Plantations** (☎ (607) 255-3020), near the eastern end of campus, on Plantations

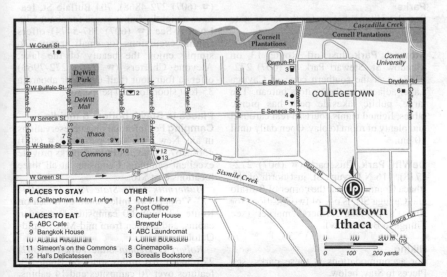

PLACES TO STAY
6 Collegetown Motor Lodge

PLACES TO EAT
5 ABC Cafe
9 Bangkok House
10 Acadia Restaurant
11 Simeon's on the Commons
12 Hal's Delicatessen

OTHER
1 Public Library
2 Post Office
3 Chapter House Brewpub
4 ABC Laundromat
7 Corner Bookstore
8 Cinemapolis
13 Borealis Bookstore

Downtown Ithaca

Rd. This is not a large green house in a far campus corner, but an elaborate and diverse complex which includes an Arboretum, a botanical garden that houses an array of poisonous plants and the Weed Garden, my favorite. The Plantations contains miles of nature trails, which include Cascadilla and Fall Creek gorges. The complex is open from daily from sunrise to sunset, and admission is free.

Ithaca Commons

This pedestrian mall occupies two blocks of State St in the heart of downtown Ithaca, between Cayuga and Aurora Sts. The Commons is attractive and people-friendly, in keeping with Ithaca's genteel charm, and is home to several restaurants, galleries, crafts shops and clothing stores. During the summer, the Commons sports a free Thursday-evening music series, ranging from jazz to country. Parking is available on adjacent streets, and it's an easy stroll to nearby Cascadilla Creek. (Note: Some addresses on the Commons are found listed as State St, others as The Commons.)

Parks

See also Hiking, below, for the larger state parks.

Stewart Park Just off Route 13 on Meadow St, Stewart Park (☎ (607) 272-1718) is at the southern edge of Cayuga Lake, adjacent to the visitors bureau. The large, public lakeside park has picnic tables, lighted tennis courts, a real carousel and plenty of room to play. Open daily until 10 pm.

DeWitt Park This park (☎ (607) 272-1718), 116 N Cayuga St, just north of the Ithaca Commons near the corner of Buffalo and Cayuga Sts, is one of two locations for Ithaca's popular farmers' market (see Things to Buy, below).

Hiking

For accommodations at these parks, see Places to Stay, below.

Buttermilk Falls State Park (☎ (607) 273-5761) offers five hilly woodland and deep gorge trails; adjacent to the park is the Larch Meadows Trail, a one mile wetlands trail. **Taughannock Falls State Park** (☎ (607) 387-6739) contains two major trails, one following the streambed to the falls, the other following the ridge and crossing over the falls. The 215 foot high Taughannock Falls drops down a steep gorge, and can be viewed from the two lookout points. **Robert H Treman State Park** (☎ (607) 273-3440), on Route 13 south of the city, features a three mile winding gorge trail which passes 12 cascades, including Devil's Kitchen and Lucifer Falls. This trail is part of the **Finger Lakes Trail** (☎ (716) 288-7161), which joins the Appalachian Trail with Canada's Bruce Trail. The entire 776 mile footpath, bordered by waterfalls, glens and glacial lakes, is off-limits to motor vehicles.

Cayuga Lake Cruises

Several luxury and charter boat companies offer Cayuga Lake day trips, dinner and moonlight cruises, generally from May through October. The *MV Manhattan* (☎ (607) 272-4868), 704 Buffalo St, features a nightly dinner cruise for about $30. Loon-A-Sea (☎ (607) 387-5474) offers fishing excursions for small groups. To simply enjoy the beauty of the lake, Alcyone Charters (☎ (607) 272-7963) offers a four hour (half-day) tour aboard a 35-foot sloop for $30 per person.

Places to Stay – bottom & middle

Camping For information and reservations in any New York state park, call ☎ (800) 456-2267. Three nearby state parks provide excellent camping. Campsites at all three locations cost $10.

Buttermilk Falls State Park (☎ (607) 273-5761) is two miles south of Ithaca on Route 13, with 60 campsites and seven cabins, and is open from mid-May to mid-October.

Robert H Treman State Park (☎ (607) 273-3440), five miles south on Route 13, features over 70 campsites and 14 cabins, and is open from mid-May through November.

Taughannock Falls State Park (☎ (607) 387-6739), eight miles north on Route 89, is one of the state's most popular parks. There are 76 campsites, 16 cabins, boat facilities, fishing, a small swimming beach and picnic areas with fire pits. Camping is available from late March to mid-October.

Motels *Collegetown Motor Lodge* (☎ (607) 273-3542, (800) 745-3542), 312 College Ave, is one block from the Cornell University campus in the heart of Ithaca's Collegetown district. This is a very decent motel in a bustling area, and the rooms are nicer and quieter than the exterior lets on; nevertheless, request a back room for more privacy. The front desk operates around the clock, and rooms feature coffee makers and modem jacks for laptop computers. Rooms range from $50 for a single to $75 for a double in the winter, and $70 to $100 from May to November.

Best Western University Inn (☎ (607) 272-6100), 1020 Ellis Hollow Rd, is at the far end of the East Hills Plaza, near the junction of Judd Falls Rd and Mitchell St, and walking distance to Cornell. Single or double rooms range from $60 to $100; they're slightly cheaper from December to March. Services at this attractive motel include continental breakfast, swimming pool and room refrigerators. A restaurant is open from 7 am to 9 pm daily, and Sunday from 7 am until 2 pm.

B&Bs There are quite a few B&Bs around Ithaca; the visitors bureau can help you find one.

Hanshaw House Inn (☎ (607) 257-1437, (800) 257-1437), 15 Sapsucker Woods Rd, is a few miles out of town in northeast Ithaca, just off Route 13. This remodeled 1830s farmhouse, complete with antique furnishings and private bath, has four rooms from $60 to $110. Its proximity to Cornell's Sapsucker Woods Bird Sanctuary is a peaceful plus.

The Archway Bed & Breakfast (☎ (607) 387-6175, (800) 387-6175), 7020 Sears-

burg Rd in Trumansburg, 10 miles north of Ithaca via Route 96 on the west side of Cayuga Lake, is an 1861 Greek Revival home with a hammock on the porch overlooking the garden. This historic home is adjacent to the Trumansburg Golf Course, and welcomes children. Room prices range from $60 to $85.

Places to Stay – top end

The Statler Hotel (☎ (607) 257-2500, (800) 541-2501), on Campus Rd, is Cornell University's hotel management training school, and it matches the campus in quality, not to mention price. Amenities include three restaurants, big banquet rooms, a 93 seat amphitheater, rooms with VCRs and computer modem hookups and free transportation from the airport. Rooms range from $100 for a single to $150 for a double room with a view of Cayuga Lake.

La Tourelle Country Inn (☎ (607) 273-2734, (800) 765-1492), 1150 Danby Rd (two miles south of town on Route 96B), is very comfortable, unpretentious, inviting and convenient. The inn sits on a hill with great views of Cayuga Lake, and walking trails are nearby. A year-round tennis court, known as the 'bubble,' is on the premises. Room rates range from $75 for a weekday reservation with a queen bed, to $115 for a weekend stay with two king beds.

Places to Eat

Ithaca might have the best variety of restaurants in all upstate New York, and you can even get a late dinner on a weeknight. Fresh and seasonal ingredients are the norm in many restaurants, and international, gourmet and vegetarian fare is offered for every budget.

The Ithaca Farmers' Market is a great place to look for prepared or self-catering options. See Things to Buy, below.

For great omelets, open-faced sandwiches and meatball dinners, try *Andy's Third Street Cafe* (☎ (607) 277-0007), 425 Third St, open daily for breakfast, lunch and dinner. The *ABC Cafe* (☎ (607) 277-4770), 308 Stewart, is a popular vegetarian restaurant in the Collegetown area with fresh pastries, daily international specials for the hip at heart and live weekend music. ABC is open Tuesday through Sunday from 11 am until about midnight.

Hal's Delicatessen (☎ (607) 273-7765), 115 S Aurora St, is a good New York deli with big sandwiches and reasonable prices, open daily from 6:30 am until 8 pm. Around the corner you'll find *Simeon's on the Commons* (☎ (607) 272-2212), 224 W State St, featuring an elegant long bar in a Victorian setting, excellent sandwiches, soups and a good people-watching view of the Commons. Lunch and dinner is served daily from 11 am until 11 pm.

Also in the Commons is *Acadia Restaurant* (☎ (607) 272-5708), 111 State St, serving excellent New Orleans-style Cajun and Creole lunches, including gumbo, red beans and rice, jambalaya and huge 'po-boy' sandwiches with sweet potato fries. Prices are in the $7 to $10 range, and there is a non-spicy kiddie menu.

The *Cafe DeWitt* (☎ (607) 273-3473), 215 N Cayuga St at the corner of Buffalo and Cayuga, is one of several eateries in the DeWitt Mall. The cafe spreads across the old schoolhouse walkway, adjacent to the eclectic shops. Always busy, it's open for breakfast and lunch Monday through Saturday from 8:30 am to 2:30 pm; from October through May, Sunday brunch is served from 11 am to 2 pm.

Around the corner from the Cafe DeWitt is *Oasis Natural Grocery* (☎ (607) 273-8213), open daily, offering fresh produce, vitamins, juices and a deli case of prepared foods.

Also in the DeWitt Mall, find the *Moosewood Restaurant* (☎ (607) 273-9610), at 215 N Cayuga St. This is the restaurant that (with ample help from the popular Moosewood cookbooks) rightly takes some credit for elevating vegetarian cooking to a loftier plane. Despite its vegetarian roots, Moosewood offers a fresh fish entree Thursday through Sunday, and several spicier ethnic dishes on Sunday only. Moosewood is open Monday through Saturday for lunch from 11 am to 2 pm, and daily for dinner from 5:30 to 8:30 pm.

Summer hours are slightly longer, and outdoor seating is available. Dinners range from $10 to $14, and there is usually a line to get in, made less tiresome by reading the flyers on the long bulletin board by the inside entrance.

John Thomas Steakhouse (formerly Auberge du Cochon Rouge; ☎ (607) 273-3464), 1152 Danby Rd adjacent to La Tourelle Country Inn, is set in a 150 year old restored country farmhouse and features 'dry-aged' beef, as well as lamb, seafood and chicken, from $18 to $30 – expensive, but a bargain when matched with comparable restaurants downstate. This is one of Ithaca's best; everything is prepared fresh on the premises, and dinners are served from 5:30 to 10:30 pm.

Thai Cuisine (☎ (607) 273-2031), 501 S Meadow St, serves authentic, if upscale, Thai dishes, with an additional vegetarian menu. Thai Cuisine is open daily for dinner from 5 to 9:30 pm, and on Saturday and Sunday for lunch from 11 am until 2 pm. Entrees range from $10 to $18, and weekend reservations are suggested. *Bangkok House* (☎ (607) 272-2426), at 216 The Commons, isn't as fancy as its Thai Cuisine cousin, but it's a good value nevertheless. Dinners, including vegetarian fare, range from $9 to $15, with duck, lamb and fish the house specialties. It's open for lunch and dinner Monday through Thursday from 11 am to 10 pm, Friday and Saturday from 11 am to 11 pm, and Sunday from 5 to 10 pm.

Entertainment
Theater The *Hangar Theatre* (☎ (607) 273-7890) is home to a popular summer theater series, is just off Route 89 in Cass Park, west of the Inlet to Cayuga Lake. Just look for the bright red building in the park. Call the box office (☎ (607) 273-4497) for more information.

Cinemas *Cinemapolis* (☎ (607) 277-6115), 17 E State St in the Commons, has two small theaters that generally feature foreign and independent films. *Fall Creek Pictures* (☎ (607) 272-1256), is at 1201 N

MICHAEL CLARK

Peaceful majesty of upstate New York

MICHAEL CLARK

Route 28 in the Mohawk Valley near Cooperstown, NY

MICHAEL CLARK
Congress Park in Saratoga Springs, NY

MICHAEL CLARK
Lake George, NY

RICK GERHARTER
Eleanor Roosevelt's home, Val Kill, in New York's Hudson Valley

Tioga St at the corner of Lincoln, and features specialty and Hollywood films after they complete their mall runs. The *State Theater* (☎ (607) 273-2781), at 109 W State St, is a renovated old-style movie house just west of the Commons, featuring both first-run and classic films. *Hoyt's Theater* (☎ (607) 257-2700), at the Pyramid Mall on the north end of town, has seven screens showing the best first-run commercial releases. The *Cornell Cinema* (☎ (607) 255-3522), on campus at 104 Willard Straight Hall, does a different double feature every night, often with independent and foreign films.

Brewpubs The *Chapter House Brewpub* (☎ (607) 277-9782), 400 Stewart at the corner of Osmun, is a popular town brewpub, open from 4 pm until midnight.

Music *The Nines* (☎ (607) 272-1888), 311 College Ave in the Collegetown district, is a popular rock club featuring the best local and touring bands.

Things to Buy
Ithaca Farmers' Market The Ithaca Farmers' Market is a outdoor market for fresh, organic produce and dairy, as well as a local arts and crafts showcase featuring painters, quilters, jewelers and musicians. Everything is made within a 30 mile radius of town.

The market is a great place to sample summer berries, autumn apples, Finger Lakes wines, bread and cookies just out of the oven and hot paper-plate meals from Mexican to macrobiotic. The market is also a 'moveable feast,' with two locations, each with its own schedule.

The Steamboat Landing site (with a covered pavilion) is at the Cayuga Inlet near Route 13 and Third St, and operates from April through December on Saturday from 9 am to 2 pm; and from May through December on Sunday from 10 am to 2 pm.

DeWitt Park is the other location, and handles the mid-week demand, open mid-May until November on Tuesdays from 9 am to 2 pm.

Farms & Food Ithaca and much of the surrounding countryside is well known for a variety of quality farms and orchards, roadside markets and stands and 'pick-your-own' farms; several offer tours. The state even issues a fruit and vegetable harvest calendar: *New York State Guide to Farm Fresh Food (Central Region)* is available from the state's agriculture department. See Tourist Offices in the state introduction to request one.

Just north of Ithaca is **Ludgate Farms** (☎ (607) 257-1765) at 1552 Hanshaw Rd, about one mile east of Route 13. Fresh fruits and vegetables, cider, honey and chestnuts fill the shelves, but the Hollywood Restaurant Pasta Sauce wins the name-of-the-week prize. It's open daily year round from 9 am to 9 pm.

CRS Growers (☎ (607) 257-2195), 2622 Triphammer Rd, is 1½ miles north of Route 13, with a view of Cayuga Lake. CRS is open from May through October.

Getting There & Away
Air Tompkins County regional airport (☎ (607) 257-0456) is five miles northeast of Ithaca via Route 13. This regional airport has daily flights by Continental and USAir to/from Newark, Pittsburgh, Syracuse, Philadelphia, La Guardia, Boston and White Plains.

Bus The bus terminal (☎ (607) 277-8800), 710 W State St at the corner of N Fulton St, serves Capitol Trailways of Pennsylvania, Empire Trailways, Greyhound, Hudson Transit and Vermont Transit. A one-way trip from Ithaca to New York City takes about five hours and costs around $32.

Train The nearest Amtrak terminal (☎ (800) 872-7245) is 60 miles north in Syracuse. (Service between Syracuse and Ithaca is provided by Greyhound.)

Car From the south, take I-88 west to Route 17; take exit 64 north on Route 96 to 96B, and into Ithaca. From I-81 to the east, take exit 11 or exit 12 to Route 13 west. From the west and the Watkins Glen area, take Route 14 south to Route 224 east to Route 13 which brings you to the north of town.

Getting Around

Ithaca Transit, TomTran and Cornell University (CU) Transit (☎ (607) 277-7433) all offer regular town bus service, from 30¢ to 60¢. Transfers are available between Ithaca Transit and all TomTran routes.

Taxi service is available 24 hours a day from Cayuga Taxi (☎ (607) 277-8294).

Ithaca and the surrounding countryside is great bicycling territory, for both mountain and road biking. Rentals (and bike route advice) is available from Cayuga Mountain Bike Shop (☎ (607) 277-6821), 138 W State St, a block below the Commons. It's open daily and evenings.

TRUMANSBURG

Trumansburg is a small town about 15 miles north of Ithaca on Route 96 on the west side of Cayuga Lake. Come here to stay at the Podunk Home Hostel (see below) and enjoy the sauna. TomTran (☎ (607) 274-5370) bus No 41 serves the route from Ithaca to Trumansburg. The trip takes about half an hour and costs 60¢.

Places to Stay & Ski

Definitely consider a stay at the *Podunk Home Hostel* (☎ /fax (607) 387-9277), 6383 Podunk Rd. The hostel is in a barn on a Finnish homestead and is operated by Oz, a very friendly Finn. There are nine beds on the 2nd floor of a barn along with a kitchen and wood-burning stove. Outside the hostel is a freestanding wooden and wood-fed sauna that operates in cold weather (because the hostel is only open from April 1 to October 30, you may only get to use it in October or if you come to cross-country ski later). Beds are $9.

In winter the hostel doubles as the reasonably priced Podunk Ski Touring Center and Ski Shop. The upstairs of the barn is converted into a post-ski relaxation area. The hostel/ski shop sits on many cross-country trails. Rentals, including trail fee, are $11 for the day or $18 for the weekend.

They also give lessons for $6 an hour for a group of four or $18 for an individual. And guests can use the sauna and then roll in the snow.

From Ithaca, you can take TomTran Bus No 41 to Trumansburg and call the hostel. If you're driving from Ithaca, take Route 96 north past Jacksonville and then make a left on Cold Springs Rd and a left on Podunk Rd to the hostel. From the north take Route 96 south to Trumansburg, then South St to the end then left on Podunk Rd and the hostel is about a quarter mile up, look for the sign.

Places to Eat

One-street Trumansburg is home to the *Rongovian Embassy to the USA*, a restaurant with an insane wall map, a bar and pizza for $10. Other food includes things like sautéed catfish. Kids under 12 eat free on Thursday nights; timing is everything.

Three doors down from the Rongovian Embassy is *Rondon's* (☎ (607) 387-5622), open from 5 am to midnight serving breakfast and burgers. You have to look hard to find anything over $3.50 on the menu.

WATKINS GLEN

The modest town of Watkins Glen is situated on the southern tip of Seneca Lake. Although once known for its salt wells, today Watkins Glen is famous for the unlikely duo of international auto-racing and a spectacular natural gorge with waterfalls. Both of these sights attract tourists to the area, but the town itself offers little to see. Route 14 becomes Franklin St as it runs through the commercial center of town. Route 414 from Corning runs into Franklin St at 15th St.

Information

The Schuyler County Chamber of Commerce (☎ (607) 535-4300), 1000 N Franklin St, is open May through October daily from 9 am to 9 pm, and during winter Monday through Friday from 9 am to 5 pm.

Watkins Glen International

The Watkins Glen International car-racing

track (☎ (607) 535-2481) is located three miles outside of town. Cars used to race on a 6.6 mile course through town streets, but saner minds built a 2.3 mile course in its present location in 1956. Since then the track has gone through some ups and downs, but today it hosts major NASCAR and Grand Prix races, including the **Winston Cup Race** in August.

The season runs from June to September and most tickets are from $10 to $50 depending on the race and how close you want to be to cars trying to break the sound barrier. You can also bring your RV and park next to the track during some races for $110. Take Route 414 north through town to County Rd 16 and then follow the signs three miles to the track.

Watkins Glen State Park

Watkins Glen State Park (☎ (607) 535-4511) was operated as a private tourist attraction until the state bought it in 1906. The glen has 19 waterfalls, grottos and lots of summer tourists, who walk along a dazzling self-guided 1½-mile gorge trail with 832 stone steps. The entrance to the park is on Franklin St between 10th and 11th Sts. There is camping here too, see below.

Timespell (☎ (607) 535-4960) is a narrated sound-and-light show projected on Watkins Glen gorge twice a night during the summer season. The show describes the natural and human history of Watkins Glen gorge over 45 million years recreating volcanic eruptions, crackling ice formations and other special effects of the planet earth. Timespell runs from mid-May to mid-October; the cost is $6.

The park is open from May until the first snow, which is usually some time in October or November.

Captain Bill's Seneca Lake Cruises

Captain Bill's (☎ (607) 535-4541/4680), at the foot of Franklin St, takes people by the boatload onto the lake from mid-May to mid-October. A one hour, 10 mile roundtrip tour costs $7/3 for adults/children two to 12. More expensive brunch, lunch and dinner cruises are also offered. Cruises run

on the hour from 10 am to 8 pm daily from mid-May to mid-October.

Places to Stay

On big race weekends during the summer the town is booked and prices jump up; if you're not planning on a race weekend visit, you'll have more choices.

Camping *Watkins Glen State Park* (☎ (607) 535-4511) has 300 sites at $10 each. It's open from mid-May until the park closes at the first snowfall. The sites are near the entrance at Franklin between 10th and 11th Sts.

The *Watkins Glen KOA* (☎ (607) 535-7404), has over 100 sites on 90 acres at $20 each. It's amenity-filled with laundry, pool, rental boats, cabins and a camp store. The KOA is open from late April to late October. Take Route 414 about 4½ miles south of the junction with Route 14.

Motels & B&Bs The *Seneca Lodge* (☎ (607) 535-2014) is in Watkins Glen State Park in a pine forest. It has small, inexpensive duplex-style cabins and basic motel rooms with two beds, a table and a TV. The dining room resembles a giant log cabin with place settings. Seneca Lodge is open from late April through November. Single/double cabins are $28/34, motel rooms are $50, and two/three bedroom A-frame rentals are $80/90.

The *Queen Catherine Motel* (☎ (607) 535-2517), in town at 436 S Franklin St, is open year round and has 15 rooms in a holiday-green building with red trim. The rooms have TVs, shag carpeting and no phones. Summer rates are $45/55; winter prices come down to around $35.

Clarke House B&B (☎ (607) 535-7965), 102 Durand Place at Franklin St, has four rooms sharing two bathrooms in a Tudor home. Rates are from $50 to $60, including a full breakfast in the dining room.

Places to Eat

There are several delis and fast-food outlets along Franklin St.

The *Wildflower Cafe* (☎ (607) 535-9797),

at 301 N Franklin St, features light American cuisine, often with fresh local ingredients, and is open daily for lunch and dinner.

A more traditional and upscale American restaurant is the *Town House* (☎ (607) 535-4619), at 108 N Franklin St, serving various grilled meats and seafood.

The Chinese *House of Hong* (☎ (607) 535-7024), at the corner of 4th and Franklin Sts, serves lunch specials from $4.

CORNING

Corning is at the intersection of Route 414 and Route 17 about 20 miles southwest of Watkins Glen. The town is named after Erastus Corning of Albany, who bought land here to build a railroad for the transport of Pennsylvanian anthracite to the nearby Chemung Canal. The town is better known as the home of the Corning Glass Works, a company that moved here from Brooklyn after the Civil War. Corning is still the largest employer in the town and surrounding area; most tourists just stop for the day.

After the Chemung River flooded downtown Corning in 1972, the Market St area was carefully restored to resemble its 19th century origins. The downtown cobblestone and brick arcade sets the tone for this old company town; the official street name sums it up: 'Historical Market St.'

Corning Glass Center

The Glass Center (☎ (607) 974-8271) is about a quarter mile west of Route 17 on Cedar St. This major tourist attraction houses a series of exhibits related to glass and its fascinating history. The first is the **Corning Museum of Glass**, which houses glass objects from 1400 BC to the present. There are 26,000 items in the collection, including a Baccarat table and the largest piece of glass in the world – a 20 ton yellow honeycomb monstrosity cast for the telescope at the Mt Palomar Observatory.

A major attraction is the **Hall of Science and Industry** with working glass welders and plenty of hands-on exhibits to explain such technology as fiber optics and binary coding. Another is the **Steuben Glass Factory**, an actual working factory where you can observe a small team of glass blowers transforming molten glass to finished object – one of the few places in the age of automation where art glass is still handcrafted. Steuben crystal is often used for gifts of state.

The center is open daily from 9 am to 5 pm. Admission for adults/seniors/children six to 17 is $6/5/4.

Rockwell Museum

The Rockwell (☎ (607) 937-5386), 111 Cedar St at Route 17 (in the Market St historic area), is primarily a museum of American Western art, early examples of Steuben glass and antique toys. The displays by Frederic Remington, Charles M Russell and 1830s landscapes by the 'explorer artists' are especially noteworthy. Open Monday to Saturday from 9 am to 5 pm and Sunday from noon to 5 pm. Admission is $4, $2 for kids six to 17.

Places to Stay

There are a few inexpensive motels in and around town. *Lando's Hotel* (☎ (607) 936-3612), at the corner of William and Bridge Sts, has singles/doubles for $35/45. The *Gatehouse Motel* (☎ (607) 936-4131), 145 E Corning Rd, goes for $38/52.

The *1865 White Birch B&B* (☎ (607) 962-6355), 69 E First St, has four good-sized rooms, each with queen beds, pine floors and white walls. Rooms with a private bath are $50 to $65; those with shared bath are $45 to $60.

Places to Eat

Most of Corning's eateries are in the downtown historic area, a block west of Route 17.

Medleys (☎ (607) 936-1685), 61 E Market St, is a bakery and restaurant serving good vegetarian chili, tabouli and pasta salads. Medleys is open from 7 am to 5:30 pm, with later hours one day a week for poetry readings.

The *Upstate Tuna Co* (☎ (607) 936-8862), 73 E Market St, lets customers cook for themselves. You buy your favorite chicken teriyaki or fish kabobs for about

$10 and start cooking on a grill with your fellow diners. The restaurant is open daily for dinner from 5 to 10 pm, and a bar which features dozens of imported and domestic beers is open until 1 am.

Getting There & Away

Corning is near the intersection of Routes 17 and 15 south of Seneca Lake and Watkins Glen. It's served by Capitol Trailways of Pennsylvania, Chenango Valley, Empire Trailways and Hudson Transit (for phone numbers see the Getting Around chapter). Some one-way/roundtrip fares are from Corning to Rochester, $17/32; to Syracuse, $16/31; to Ithaca, $9/18.

HAMMONDSPORT

Hammondsport is on the southern tip of Keuka Lake on Route 54A just off Route 54. It's a good town from which to explore nearby wineries, the largest – Taylor – and the most interesting – Bully Hill – are nearby (see the Finger Lakes Wineries section, above). The town itself has a pleasant village square. There's a laundry one block south of the square on Sheather St, and the post office is on Sheather St on the square.

Wine Museum of Greyton H Taylor

The museum (☎ (607) 868-4814), is on the grounds of Bully Hill Vineyard on County Rd 76 north of town. It is in one of the original Taylor Winery buildings and features old wine-making equipment and label artwork by Walter S Taylor, the owner of Bully Hill. Admission is $1.

Glenn H Curtiss Museum

This museum (☎ (607) 569-2160), half a mile south of town on Route 54, displays airplanes, motorcycles and engines. Open May to October, Monday to Saturday from 9 am to 5 pm, Sunday from 11 am to 5 pm; November to April, Monday to Saturday from 10 am to 4 pm, Sunday from noon to 5 pm. Admission is $4.

Keuka Lake Cruises

The *Keuka Maid* (☎ (607) 569-2628/3631) sails from Hammondsport along Keuka Lake from May to October. Fares are from $10 to $20.

Places to Stay

Camping *Hill 'N' Hollow Campsites* (☎ (607) 569-2711) has 40 shaded, grassy sites at $15 each. It's open from May 15 to October 15. From Route 17, take exit 38, go 1½ miles north on Route 54 then 6⅕ miles east on County Rd 113.

Motels & B&Bs There are some cheap chain motels around the Route 17 exit at Bath eight miles south of Hammondsport. The *Budget Inn* (☎ (607) 776-7536), 330 W Morris St, is a bit battered and some rooms are being used for storage, but those for rent are functional enough at $26/33 in winter and $33/44 in summer. You get coffee and a Danish in the morning. The more expensive but superior *Days Inn* (☎ (607) 776-7650) is next door.

Another Tyme (☎ (607) 569-2747), at 7 Church St, has three immaculate rooms named after times in the owner's life – the Douglas Room for her deceased husband; Mimi's Room for her mother-in-law; and the Kamakwie Room for her time in the Peace Corps in Africa. It's a couple of blocks from the town square. Rates are around $50 and include breakfast.

The *JS Hubbs B&B* (☎ (607) 569-2440/3629), 17 Sheather St, is in a big green house built in 1840 half a block north of the square. It has four large rooms all with private bath, but some of the toilets were installed in closets, which makes them a little cramped. There is parking, two very large common rooms with a TV and piano and a small greenhouse. Rooms are $60 to $70 with full breakfast.

Places to Eat

The *Crooked Lake Ice Cream Co*, at 35 Sheather St on the town square, has breakfast, lunch and great ice cream in an old-fashioned setting.

In town the *Village Tavern* (☎ (607) 569-2528), 30 Mechanic St on the square, has a good tavern atmosphere and tavern fare. Entrees are about $10.

Finger Lakes – Northern Tier

Route 20 runs along the northern tip of the Finger Lakes touching the tops of most of them and going through Canandaigua, Geneva, Seneca Falls and other towns.

PENN YAN

Penn Yan is on Route 54 on the northern tip of Keuka Lake in between the Northern and Southern Tiers and is ideally situated for winery visiting. The town's name is an amalgamation of 'Pennsylvania' and 'Yankee' because most of the early settlers came from Pennsylvania and New England. Today it's the world's largest producer of buckwheat and home of a large summer buckwheat festival.

Eileen O'Reilly's Belknap Hill Books (☎ (315) 536-1186), 106 Main St, is one of the better used bookstores in the region.

Windmill Farmers' Market

This is an indoor-outdoor farmers' market (☎ (315) 536-3032) on Route 54, six miles south of the Elm St /Route 54 intersection downtown. Mennonites (see Pennsylvania Dutch Country chapter), who still use horse and buggy to get around, come from the surrounding area to sell good produce, jams, molasses and baked goods. Open every Saturday, May to December from 8 am to 4:30 pm, and on Memorial Day, 4th of July and Labor Day.

Special Events

The **Buckwheat Harvest Festival** (☎ (315) 536-7434) is the fourth weekend in September. The National Buckwheat Institute serves buckwheat ice cream, buckwheat pizza, buckwheat shortcake and other buckwheat delights. There's also amusement games, arts & crafts and a parade.

Places to Stay

Camping *Keuka Lake State Park* (☎ (315) 536-3666) has 150 sites on 620 acres. It's

open from May 15 to mid-November. Take Hwy 54A south from town for six miles. The campground is on Pepper Rd near the town of Bluff Point.

Motels & B&Bs The *Towne Motel* (☎ (315) 536-4474), 206 Elm St, is a low-end motel in town. It's worn, but not dirty or unpleasant. Rooms have phones and air-con. Single/double rates are $28 to $37/47.

The *Colonial Motel* (☎ (315) 536-3056, (800) 724-3008), 175 W Lake Rd, has unremarkable rooms, but it's nicer than the Towne Motel and is across from the lake. Take 14A south to W Lake Dr, then go 1.4 miles to get there.

On the Beach (☎ (315) 536-4646), 191 W Lake Rd, is a chalet-like house on Keuka Lake across from the Colonial Motel. It's in a row of other houses off the road. Inside there are two basic rooms at parking level, the nicer part of the house is down some steps to the living and dining rooms, which overlook the lake. Rates are $50 to $60 with full breakfast. Follow directions to the Colonial Motel.

In town the *Wagner Estate B&B* (☎ (315) 536-4591), 351 Elm St, is on a large piece of property opposite the Wine & Grape Foundation. There's a common living room and the bedrooms have large, fluffy mattresses and about six down pillows each. Rates include a several course full breakfast. The single/double rate with private bath is $60/70; with shared bath $50/60.

The *Fox Inn* (☎ (315) 536-3101), 158 Main St, has four rooms with private baths, a two bedroom suite and the ghosts of two former inhabitants, according to the 19th century diary of a Penn Yan dentist. William Morris Oliver, one of the original Penn Yan residents, built the house. You can't miss its yellow facade and two story white columns. Double rooms from May 1 to November 1 are $75 or $85; $10 less for a single. The suite is $125. Rooms include a full breakfast; there is a huge garden out back and parking.

Places to Eat

Lloyd's Ltd (☎ (315) 536-9029), 3 Main St, sells pub food like hamburgers, onion rings ($2.50), sandwiches (under $4) and pizza ($4 to 15). They also have a vast selection of imported bottled beer.

CANANDAIGUA

Canandaigua is on the northern tip of Canandaigua Lake at the intersection of Routes 5 and 20. This late Victorian-looking town, oddly enough, gets more interesting the further north you go from the lake. There are particularly nice houses along Main St and on the side streets around the Sonnenberg Mansion, a handsome country estate and Canandaigua's chief tourist attraction (see Places to Stay).

Canandaigua comes from the Seneca 'kanandarque,' which means 'chosen spot,' and the site was the main village in the Seneca nation. In the 19th century this was where Susan B Anthony was tried for voting, found guilty and fined $100. She refused to pay and the authorities didn't have the nerve to imprison her. When the Susan B Anthony dollar coin was issued in the 1980s the Canandaigua National Bank paid her fine with 100 of the new coins. This dollar coin never has caught on with the American public.

The Chamber of Commerce (☎ (716) 394-4400) is on the south side of Route 20 east of town in an A-frame building.

Sonnenberg Gardens & Mansion

This 50 acre estate (☎ (716) 394-4922), 151 Charlotte St, with nine formal gardens, an arboretum and an 1887 stone mansion, is regarded as one of the finest Victorian gardens in the US. The site is open from mid-May to mid-October daily from 9:30 am to 5:30 pm. Admission for adults/seniors/children six to 16 is $5/4/2.

Granger Homestead & Carriage Museum

This is a magnificent 1816 Federal-style house and collection of carriages (☎ (716) 394-1472) at 295 N Main St. Open May to

October, Tuesday to Saturday from 10 am to 5 pm, Sunday from 1 pm to 5 pm.

Places to Stay & Eat

East of town about 10 miles is the *Cobblestones B&B* (☎ (315) 675-8638/8323) on Route 20 one mile west of the State Rds. 14A and 245 junction. A traveler reported $15 to $20 rooms, but they're not always open.

The Route 20 commercial strip east of town has a string of cheap and uninteresting motels. Try the *Budget Lodge* (☎ (716) 394-2800), which has doubles with one/two beds for $39/49.

A farmers' market is open from late June to late October on Fridays from 3 to 7 pm along Main St. For good pizza, wings, subs and pasta, try *Pudgie's Pizza* (☎ (716) 394-6720), 520 N Main St, open daily from 11 am to 11 pm. Route 20 as it passes by town has the usual complement of fast-food places.

GENEVA

Geneva is on Route 20 and Route 14 at the northern tip of Seneca Lake. It's the home of Hobart & William Smith College, which sits on a low bluff overlooking the lake. Convenient as a place to stay if passing through, the town offers little to see. There are two cinemas showing decent movies – one on Exchange St and one on Seneca St – downtown near the college.

Places to Stay

Cheerful Valley Campground (☎ 315) 781-1222) has 160 sites near the river for $18 each. Services include a coin laundry and pool. The campground is seven miles north of town on Route 14 less than one mile north of exit 42 from I-90.

Geneva is known for the *Belhurst Castle* (☎ (315) 781-0201), on Route 14 south of town. Belhurst is a large, red 1889 Medina stone castle on the lake. It was originally built for Carrie Harron Collins, a descendent of Henry Clay. There are 13 rooms complete with polished woodwork, stone and plaster walls, solid oak doors and gas fireplaces. Guests get a continental breakfast in the winter, but nothing during summer. There's a restaurant on the main floor. Off/in season rates are $85 to $225/125 to $295.

Places to Eat

The Geneva Area Farmers' Market is set up at the Geneva Recreation Complex, 666 S Exchange St. It has a good selection of local produce and baked goods. Open late June to mid-October on Thursdays from 7:30 to 11:30 am.

Belhurst Castle (☎ (315) 781-0201) serves lunch-time sandwiches and pasta from $5 to $7 and fish for about $10. Dinners are lavish, like the lakeside surroundings, and range from $15 to $25.

SENECA FALLS

Seneca Falls is on Route 20 three miles west of Cayuga Lake. It would be an unexciting town to visit except that it's the birthplace of the organized women's movement in the USA, thanks to Elizabeth Cady Stanton, who moved to Seneca Falls from Boston in 1847. While her husband Henry was away, Cady Stanton managed her family and home. On July 9, 1848, Cady Stanton expressed discontent about the confinement of women to 'the women's sphere' to a group of friends. A couple of days later the group met at Mary Ann M'Clintock's home and drafted a *Declaration of Sentiments* modeled on the *Declaration of Independence*. The declaration called for the right to vote and said that 'all men and women are created equal.' On July 19 and 20, 1848, over 300 women and men gathered at Wesleyan Chapel on Fall St for the first Women's Rights Convention and 68 women and 32 men signed the declaration.

Women's Rights National Historical Park

The 'park' is actually a complex composed of a visitors center (☎ (315) 568-2991) at 136 Fall St; what's left of the Wesleyan Chapel, site of the 1848 Women's Rights Convention; the M'Clintock House in nearby Waterloo and the Elizabeth Cady Stanton House in Seneca Falls.

The **Cady Stanton House**, 32 Washington St, has been restored in the spirit of historical accuracy. The original wallpaper has been copied and replaced, and the few pieces of original furniture that could be located, including her writing desk, have been placed in the house, but it is quite empty and appears to be missing a wing. A ranger gives a lecture tour on the hour. Free and open daily from 9 am to 5 pm.

National Women's Hall of Fame

The Hall of Fame (☎ (315) 568-2703), 76 Fall St, is a small private museum with large wall plaques describing the achievements of an expanding number of women in the arts, athletics, humanitarianism etc – everyone from Elizabeth Bailey and 'Mother' Seton to Jane Adams, Marian Anderson, Sojourner Truth and Emily Dickinson. It's a good place to come if you like a quiet, reflective museum experience. The museum is open from May to October, daily from 9:30 am to 5 pm; November to April, Wednesday to Saturday from 10 am to 4 pm. Admission is free.

Places to Stay & Eat

Cayuga Lake State Park (☎ (315) 568-5163) has almost 300 sites at $10 each, seven miles outside of town. Open May to November. Take Lake Rd east for three miles, then go four miles south on Route 89.

Venice Pizzeria (☎ (315) 568-9218) is a couple of doors down from the Women's Rights Information Center on Fall St. They sell subs in half/whole sizes for $2 to $5. Pizzas come in four sizes from $7 to $19 and slices are $1.25.

MONTEZUMA NATIONAL WILDLIFE REFUGE

The refuge (☎ (315) 568-5987) is traversed by I-90 and Routes 89 and 20 at the north end of Cayuga Lake about three miles east of Seneca Falls. The refuge is a major stopover point for waterfowl on the way south from Canada. It used to be part of a broad marsh system around the Finger Lakes that has largely been drained. Because the refuge is in the middle of a busy flyway, it gets a lot of birds. From mid-September until its ponds freeze, Canada geese and ducks stop by. The peak viewing times are generally in November. From mid-August to mid-October, with a mid-September peak, shorebirds like herons, egrets and sandpipers come through. From late February to April, Canada and snow geese and some ducks come back. Mid-May is peak warbler season.

SYRACUSE

Syracuse (population 165,000) is laid out around the southern end of Onondaga Lake and stands in sharp contrast to the more pastoral portions of the Finger Lakes region. Syracuse is a working-class town at heart, and appropriately owes much of its origin to the discovery of salt. With the completion of the Erie Canal in 1825, Syracuse's image as an industrial center took hold.

The town is enlivened by the presence of Syracuse University's student body, but commerce and industry still dominate the town's image. Railroads and highways criss-cross each other. A pre-Civil War National Guard Armory lends its name to the fashionable Armory Square area. A symbol of Syracuse's transformation, the old armory now houses the Rubenstein Museum of Science and Technology.

The downtown skyline is really more of a 'brickline,' with striking examples of Victorian Gothic, art deco and limestone Romanesque. There's no mistaking Syracuse for suburbia, as any resident will proclaim.

History

The Onondaga Indians chose Syracuse as the site of the capital of the Iroquois Confederacy in 1570. French Jesuits came into the region in the mid-1600s and established a mission called Fort Sainte Marie de Gannentaha in 1656, which they abandoned two years later after repeated conflicts with the Onondaga.

Indian guides showed French Father

Simon LeMoyne a local spring that they believed was occupied by an unfriendly spirit. Lemoyne saw the spirit of an untapped resource after tasting the briny water. Commercial salt production began in the last decade 18th century, when newcomers settled around Onondaga Lake. In 1797, the state administered (and taxed) the salt fields and leased them out to producers who made salt by boiling or evaporation. Today you can visit the Salt Museum, which describes the process as it took place in 'Salt City.'

Syracuse was chosen as a name for the city in 1805 when the city's first postmaster noted that the Greek city of the same name in Sicily had been founded around salt springs. In the mid-19th century, spurred by the success of the Erie Canal, Syracuse became a manufacturing and transportation center. In the 1960s and '70s, however, it suffered the same fate as many of its Rust Belt neighbors; employers and workers discovered the suburbs and the downtown decayed. Today, the Armory Square neighborhood, a collection of trendy shops and cafes, represents the downtown's revival.

Orientation & Information

Salina (sa-LIE-na) St divides Syracuse into east and west and Erie Blvd into north and south sections. I-81 and I-690 pass right through town, to the dismay of many.

The Syracuse Convention & Visitors Bureau (☎ (315) 470-1907, (800) 234-4797), at 572 S Salina St, is open Monday to Friday from 8:30 am to 5 pm and provides walking tour maps of the old downtown. There's a Tourist Information Center at Carousel Center, a big shopping mall.

In addition to numerous banks and ATMs in the downtown area, the major malls (Carousel Center; Shopping Town) also have ATMs.

There are three AAA offices in Syracuse, but the main office is at 3175 E Genesee St (☎ (315) 446-3134, (800) 765-4222). It's open Monday to Friday from 9 am to 5:30 pm (later on Thursday) and 9 am to 1 pm on Saturday.

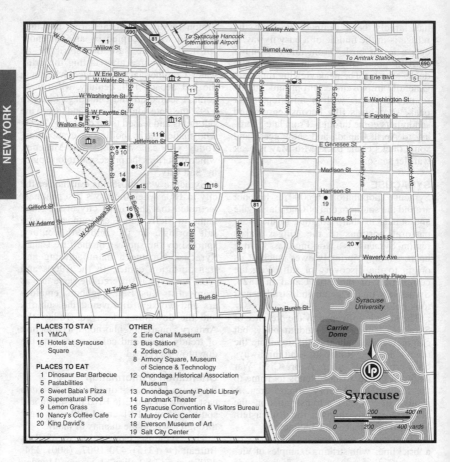

PLACES TO STAY
11 YMCA
15 Hotels at Syracuse
    Square

PLACES TO EAT
1 Dinosaur Bar Barbecue
5 Pastabilities
6 Sweet Baba's Pizza
9 Supernatural Food
9 Lemon Grass
10 Nancy's Coffee Cafe
20 King David's

OTHER
2 Erie Canal Museum
3 Bus Station
4 Zodiac Club
8 Armory Square, Museum
   of Science & Technology
12 Onondaga Historical Association
    Museum
13 Onondaga County Public Library
14 Landmark Theater
16 Syracuse Convention & Visitors Bureau
17 Mulroy Civic Center
18 Everson Museum of Art
19 Salt City Center

The main post office (☎ (315) 452-3401) is at 5640 E Taft Rd.

The Onondaga County Public Library (☎ (315) 448-4637) is at 441 S Salina St.

The *Syracuse New Times* and *The Guide* are two local free arts and entertainment guides. The *Pink Paper* is a free bi-monthly newsletter with articles and information of interest to the gay and lesbian community.

The *Post-Standard* and the *Herald-Journal* are the local dailies; on Sunday it's called the *Herald American*.

Erie Canal Museum

The museum (☎ (315) 471-0593), at 318 E Erie Blvd, is housed in the 1850 Weighlock Building at the corner of Montgomery St. Canal boats were towed along the water (now Erie Blvd) into the building; locks at the front and rear were closed and the water drained out. Each boat then lay on a huge wooden cradle and scale, which weighed it and determined the tax. The museum features a 12-minute video on the canal's history. There is also a restored 65-

foot canal boat on display that can be boarded and explored. The museum is open daily from 10 am to 5 pm, and admission is free.

Onondaga Historical Association Museum

This excellent small museum (☎ (315) 428-1864), 321 Montgomery St, is just a short walk from the Erie Canal Museum, and history buffs should make time for both. 19th century fashion, old photos, Iroquois culture and antique typewriters are among the featured displays. The museum is open Tuesday through Friday from noon to 4 pm, and Saturday from 11 am to 4 pm. Admission is free.

Everson Museum of Art

The museum (☎ (315) 474-6064), 401 Harrison St, has a fine collection of ceramics and American art. Noted modern architect IM Pei designed the striking and austere 1968 building, which is open Tuesday through Friday and Sunday, from noon to 5 pm, and Saturday from 10 am to 5 pm.

Sainte Marie among the Iroquois

This living history museum (☎ (315) 453-6767) of an early Jesuit mission, in Onondaga Lake Park on the northeastern side of Onondaga Lake, recreates the 'fateful meeting' of the Iroquois Nation and the French in the 17th century. The living-history exhibit features costumed interpreters who portray missionaries, blacksmiths, cooks and other workers of the time; visitors can talk to any of them in French or English about their work – from converting the local Indians to Christianity to hammering horseshoes. It's popular with kids, if a bit bizarre. The Ste Marie complex is open Tuesday to Sunday, 10 am to 5 pm from May 1 to December 31; and Wednesday to Sunday from January 1 to April 30. Take I-81 north to exit 24 (Onondaga Lake Pkwy/ Route 370 West). Go about 1½ miles to the entrance on the right. Admission for adults/kids five to 14 is $3.50/1.50.

Salt Museum

Opposite Ste Marie's, the Salt Museum (☎ (315) 453-6767), is built on the site of former salt works in Onondaga Lake Park. The small wooden building displays the salt-making process, in which brine was pumped up and into masses of boiling kettles or evaporation pans through wooden pipes, which wouldn't rust. The museum is open daily May to October from 1 pm to 5 pm; Sunday from noon to 5 pm. Admission is 50¢.

Milton J Rubenstein Museum of Science & Technology

Housed in the old armory in Armory Square at the corner of Franklin and W Jefferson Sts, the museum (☎ (315) 425-9068) has several exhibits designed for children, including a five-and-under planetarium sky show on weekends. The museum is open daily from 10 am to 5 pm, and admission is $4.50, and $3.50 for seniors and kids under age 12.

Special Events

The **New York State Fair**, with lots of food and music (and salt), is held at the State Fair Grounds in Syracuse, just west of I-690, for 13 days through the Labor Day weekend in September.

Places to Stay

Bottom End The *Downing HI-AYH Hostel* (☎ (315) 472-5788), 535 Oak St, is a mile northeast of downtown. It's a big house with 31 beds in several male and female dorm rooms, a large basement kitchen and a small library. There are a couple of private rooms as well. There's a 9 am to 5 pm lockout and an 11 pm curfew. The cost is $9.

The *YMCA* (☎ (315) 474-6851), 340 Montgomery St, is $86 a week or $30 a night; it's clean, if a bit run down. Rooms share a bath.

Middle There are a few moderately priced motels at Carrier Circle. Take I-690 east about 2½ miles to Thompson Rd north. Go about a mile to the circle. The *John Milton*

NEW YORK

Inn (☎ (315) 463-8555), Carrier Circle, has about 50 standard rooms at single/double rates of $35 to $60/40 to 60. The *Red Roof Inn* (☎ (315) 437-3309, (800) 843-7663) has rooms from $35 to $55. There are similarly priced places along Thompson Rd.

The *Bed & Breakfast Wellington* (☎ (315) 471-2433, (800) 724-5006), 707 Danforth St, is in a 1914 Tudor home designed by Ward Wellington Ward. It's a sturdy wood-and-stucco house on a quiet residential street with fireplace, four porches and sodas and juices stocked in the fridge. There are four rooms, each with private bath. Room prices range from $55 to $95, including a full breakfast.

Top End Downtown the 'Hotels at Syracuse Square' include the *Hilton Tower* (☎ (315) 471-7300, (800) 255-3892) and the *Hotel Syracuse* (☎ (315) 422-5121), 500 S Warren St, due to be remodeled soon. These are large luxury hotels with rooms in the $80 to $140 category.

The *Syracuse Marriott* (☎ (315) 432-0200, (800) 782-9847) is the luxury hotel out at Carrier Circle (see directions above). It has a heated indoor-outdoor pool, sauna, whirlpool, tanning salon and more. Weekday single/double rooms are $130/170; weekend rates are slightly cheaper.

Places to Eat

The regional farmers' market is a great place for food (see Things to Buy, below).

Without question, Syracuse's most unique eatery is the funky *Dinosaur Bar Barbecue* (☎ (315) 476-4937), 246 W Willow at the corner of Franklin St. This is a blues bar and restaurant frequented by a unique mix of bikers, tattooed waitresses and students and anyone else who likes to eat ribs while gazing at the walls crowded with old signs, car parts and bumper stickers ('No Feeding the Cooks'). Most dishes are under $8, including racks of ribs (pork or beef), chili, red beans and sausage, chicken sandwiches and homemade desserts. The Dinosaur is crowded at night with live blues and recorded music.

The Armory Square area has become a trendy restaurant row, with several cafes and restaurants within a few blocks of each other.

Supernatural Food (☎ (315) 424-2545), at 142 Walton St, is a health-food store and deli with good fresh soups, salads and sandwiches under $5. They are open Monday through Friday, 8 am to 6 pm, and Saturday, 9 am to 5 pm.

Pastabilities (☎ (315) 474-1153), 311 S Franklin St, makes a wide variety of its own pastas in unusual flavors, like paprika lasagna. The dining area is a crisply designed narrow room lined with booths and a bar; music in a garden courtyard adds to the summertime atmosphere. Lunch and dinner are served Monday through Saturday.

For good coffee, espresso drinks, homemade gourmet desserts and a good view of the people coming and going around Armory Square, try *Nancy's Coffee Cafe* (☎ (315) 476-6550), at 290 W Jefferson St. Nancy's is open Monday through Thursday from 10 am to 9 pm, Friday and Saturday until midnight.

For excellent (and expensive) Thai cuisine, try *Lemon Grass* (☎ (315) 475-1111), 238 W Jefferson St near the Armory, open for lunch and dinner Monday through Saturday, and for dinner only on Sunday.

Sweet Baba's Pizza (☎ (315) 472-2227), 218 Walton St, offers up excellent wood-fired pizza, ranging from the traditional to smoked salmon with brie, for $5 to $8, in addition to a good in-house dessert menu. Sweet Baba's is open Monday through Thursday from 11 am to 10 pm, Friday and Saturday from 11 am to midnight and Sunday from 3 to 9 pm.

If you like it hot, try *The Hot Shoppe* (☎ (315) 424-1010), 142 Walton St in Armory Square, a Cajun-Caribbean-Southwestern deli with spicy concoctions from around the world. Open daily from 8 am to 6 pm, Friday and Saturday till 9 pm.

The Syracuse University campus area, particularly Marshall St, has dozens of mostly fast-food outlets. One of the more interesting eateries here is *King David's*

(☎ (315) 471-5000), 129 Marshall St, for good Middle Eastern dishes, including steak shawarma, stuffed cabbage, grape leaves and baba ghanoush.

Things to Buy
The hungry and the curious alike should take a look at the **Central New York Regional Farmers' Market** (☎ (315) 422-8647). The market is a WPA construction dating from 1938, one of many mounted during the Great Depression. It's still one of the largest and oldest regional markets in the country, with over 300 stalls selling agricultural products from the US and abroad. The May to October period is the busiest. The market is open Saturdays year round, 7 am to 2 pm; and from May to October on Thursdays from 11 am to 7 pm. There are baked goods, jams, cheeses, a huge selection of New York state apples, all types of produce, a restaurant and more. Take I-81 to exit 23 (Hiawatha Blvd) and exit at the market.

Entertainment
Music The *Syracuse Symphony* (☎ (315) 424-8200) and the *Syracuse Opera* (☎ (315) 475-5915) perform at the John H Mulroy Civic Center (☎ (315) 435-3155), 411 Montgomery St.

The *Landmark Theater* (☎ (315) 475-7979), at 362 S Salina St, is a flourishing 1928 architectural leftover from Hollywood's make-believe tropical-vaudeville movie-palace days. The Landmark showcases everything from touring stage shows to rock & roll.

Theater In addition to the Landmark Theater (see Music), the *Salt City Center for the Performing Arts* (☎ (315) 474-1122), 601 S Crouse Ave, presents musicals, dramas and comedies year round.

Clubs *Zodiac* (☎ (315) 472-2665) is a dance club inside a warehouse across from the Pastabilities restaurant in Armory Square. It has music from thrash metal to jazz and blues Tuesday to Saturday 9 pm to 2 am, and live music on Wednesday and

Thursday. During the summer a courtyard barbecue pit adds to the atmosphere

Dinosaur Bar Barbecue (see Places to Eat) is a Syracuse landmark for live blues and all-around honky-tonk surroundings.

Getting There & Away
Syracuse is a transport hub. Two major highways cross it: I-81 and I-90 (the NY State Thruway).

Note: A new regional transportation hub under construction will house both train and bus terminals, beginning sometime in 1997, on the north side of town, near the farmers' market (see Things to Buy, above). Instead of 15 to 20 minutes by cab, it will be a short (five to 10 minute) drive to the downtown hub, with far more frequent bus service as well.

Air Hancock international airport (☎ (315) 454-4330; ground transportation ☎ 455-6351) is at exit 27 off of I-81. The airport has daily service by American, Continental, Delta, Mohawk, Northwest, TW Express, United and USAir. Fares vary from $99 roundtrip weekend specials for Syracuse to/from Philadelphia, and Syracuse to/from Chicago ($168 roundtrip), to $400 roundtrip for the same destinations with seven day notice.

Bus The bus station is on E Erie Blvd at Forman Ave. It's served by Greyhound (☎ (315) 471-7171) and Trailways (☎ (315) 471-7709).

Train The Amtrak station (☎ (315) 463-1135) is on Manlius Center Rd in East Syracuse. A taxi from the station to downtown costs about $12. You can also take the bus into town, but service is infrequent.

Getting Around
The Centro bus system (☎ (315) 442-3400) runs all over the city with a central stopping point at the downtown 'four corners' intersection of Fayette and Salina Sts, where an information booth is open Monday through Friday from 7 am to 6 pm, Saturday from

8 am to 4:30 pm. The base fare is $1, and transfers are free.

If you need a taxi anywhere in the Syracuse area, call Dependable Taxi (☎ (315) 475-0030). It costs about $14 to get from the airport to downtown.

TURNING STONE CASINO
Turning Stone (☎ (315) 361-7711) is in Verona, 35 miles east of Syracuse. It was the first legalized gambling casino in New York State and is owned and operated by the Oneida Indian Nation. Take I-90 (the NY State Thruway) exit 33 at Verona, and follow the bright signs to the nearby casino.

ERIE CANAL SIGHTS
Syracuse and New York State maintain several canal exhibits, parks and centers, all dedicated to maintaining the canal's place in history, as well as offering recreational possibilities.

West of Syracuse, the **Erie Canal Parkway** (☎ (315) 689-3278) in Jordon, 15 miles west from downtown, is a seven mile stretch of land and towpath along the original canal route. Three miles west of the parkway, the 300-acre **Camillus Erie Canal Park** (☎ (315) 672-5110) maintains another seven miles of navigable canal.

Heading east from Syracuse, The **Old Erie Canal State Park** (☎ (315) 687-7821) includes 36 miles of enlarged canal stretching from the **DeWitt Canal Center** (☎ 315) 471-0593), 10 miles east of Syracuse, to the **Erie Canal Village** (☎ (315) 337-3999), 30 miles east of Syracuse in Rome, an outdoor living museum situated on an original portion of the canal. The village is open May to September. In between, you'll find The **Chittenango Landing Canal Boat Museum** (☎ (315) 687-3801), about 12 miles east of Syracuse, the site of a dry-dock where canal boat construction and repair took place. The museum (and interpretive center) is open from April to June, weekends from 1 pm to 4 pm; July to September, daily from 10 am to 4 pm; October to March, the first Saturday of the month from 1 to 4 pm.

Canal Cruises
Mid-Lakes Navigation Co (☎ (315) 685-8500, (800) 545-4318) offers a variety of canal cruises during the season from mid-April to early November, depending on the famous weather. The shortest excursions are the lunch and champagne dinner cruises, for $18/34 per adult; a Sunday brunch cruise costs $29. A better value might be the four-hour cruise for $29 ($20 for kids), which includes a buffet meal.

For the more adventurous, two and three-day overnight cruises are available, and range from about $250 to $350 per person, and include all meals and transportation to and from area hotels. Two-day cruises, in particular, sell out early; advanced reservations are necessary during the busy summer season.

Cruises depart from Dutchman's Landing, about seven miles northwest of Syracuse via Route 370. From Syracuse, take I-81 to the I-90 exit heading west to exit 38 (Route 57), turn left to reach Route 370, then right at River Road, and right at Hillsdale Rd.

ROCHESTER
Rochester (population 230,000) is built across and around the Genesee River in western New York a few miles south of Lake Ontario. The city has a small, modern (but somewhat deserted at night) downtown encircled by an expressway and a number of neighborhoods with old homes and mansions from its industrial glory days. Rochester is home to Eastman Kodak, Xerox, Bausch & Lomb and the Eastman School of Music. There are several fine museums in town, including Kodak's International Center of Photography.

History
The Seneca Indians called the Genesee River *Casconchiagon*, 'river of many falls.' It was the power of the river and its 96 foot downtown waterfall that fueled the city's early industries. But Rochester grew slowly from 1789, when the first European settlers arrived, until the 1824 arrival of the Erie Canal, which passed through what is now Broad St. The canal turned Rochester into a

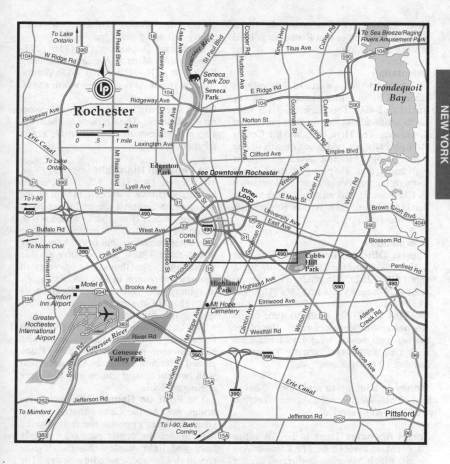

booming mill town. So many flour mills sprang up along the Genesee River in the early 19th century that the town was called 'Flour City.' Flower nurseries and horticulture supplanted flour mills as the major Rochester industry by mid-century; the city's impressive garden and park system dates to those early efforts.

Rochester happily bills itself as the 'world's image center,' with some justification. In 1853, John Bausch and Henry Lomb opened a small optical shop that grew to global dimensions. In the 1880s, a curious bank clerk named George Eastman

experimented with photographic techniques in his mother's kitchen; the Eastman Kodak Company followed. Even Xerox Corporation got its start in Rochester, as the Haloid Company in 1906.

Frederick Douglass published his abolitionist *North Star* newspaper here beginning in 1847, and Susan B Anthony was arrested for voting here in 1872. The prosperity of Kodak and others benefited Rochester throughout most of the latter 19th and 20th centuries. Beginning in the 1960s, however, Rochester experienced the hard economic times of many industrial cities, earning its place along the 'Rust Belt,' another image that Rochester is hard at work to transform.

Orientation

The central downtown area of Rochester is encircled by the 'Inner Loop,' a highway linked to I-490. The Genesee River runs north-south across the western portion of downtown. The High Falls and the Center at High Falls are two blocks north of the Inner Loop. Monroe Ave, a popular restaurant and shopping district, runs through the eastern portion of downtown as Chestnut St and emerges southeast of the Inner Loop. East Ave is Rochester's 'mansion row.'

Information

Tourist Offices The Greater Rochester Visitors Association (☎ (716) 546-3070, (800) 677-7282), 126 Andrews St, maintains a 24-hour events line (☎ (716) 546-6810) and an arts information line (☎ (716) 427-7777), a clue to some of old Rochester's modern priorities; the office is open year round, weekdays from 8 am to 6 pm, Saturday 9 am to 5 pm and Sunday 10 am to 3 pm.

Money In addition to a number of banks and ATMs, Wegmanns, a supermarket, has a 24 hour ATM service.

Travel Agencies There is a AAA office (☎ (716) 461-4660) at 777 Clinton Ave South, which has maps and travel agency services. Pierre Travel (☎ (716) 461-5220), 880 Winton Rd, is a full-service travel agency.

Post The main post office (☎ (716) 272-5952) is at 1335 Jefferson Rd; another post office is downtown at the Midtown Plaza off Clinton Ave.

Bookstores World Wide News (☎ (716) 546-7140), 100 St Paul St, has a large selection of domestic and foreign newspapers. Village Green Books (☎ (716) 461-5380), 766 Monroe Ave, is a very roomy

old bookshop with an extensive newsstand, a tasty deli and a snack bar.

Brownbag Bookshop (☎ (716) 271-3494), at 678 Monroe Ave, and Gutenberg Books (☎ (716) 442-4620), 675 Monroe Ave, are two used bookstores worth a visit.

Media The daily newspaper is the *Democrat & Chronicle*. The *Artvoice Rochester* is a local freebie with comprehensive entertainment listings.

The Center at High Falls

The Center (☎ (716) 325-2030), as its known, 60 Brown's Race St, is built on the site of a 19th century industrial water diversion, or 'race,' from the Genesee River. Inside are interactive 3-D exhibits that trace Rochester's development from its founding in the early 1800s. A computer-graphic video telegraphs thousands of years of geology and natural history into a minute's imaginary taxi ride through Rochester's past. Most of the exhibits are especially suitable for children.

The Center overlooks the 96-foot **High Falls**, over which Sam Patch jumped with his reluctant pet bear in 1829. Patch gained attention earlier in the same year with two successful jumps into the gorge at Niagara Falls.

The **Pont de Rennes** is a pedestrian bridge next to the Center that spans the Genesee River opposite the falls. During the summer the center puts on a nightly laser and light display that dazzles the chasm walls and cascading water. The event is free and can be enjoyed from May until early September.

George Eastman House & International Museum of Photography

The house that Kodak built, at 900 East Ave, is a 1905 colonial revival mansion. Daily docent tours begin at 10:30 am and 2 pm, but you can easily explore the exhibits on your own with a self-guided map; or tag along on one of the tours for a few minutes.

The museum (☎ (716) 271-3361), connected to the house by a long corridor filled with photos and history, has the world's

NEW YORK

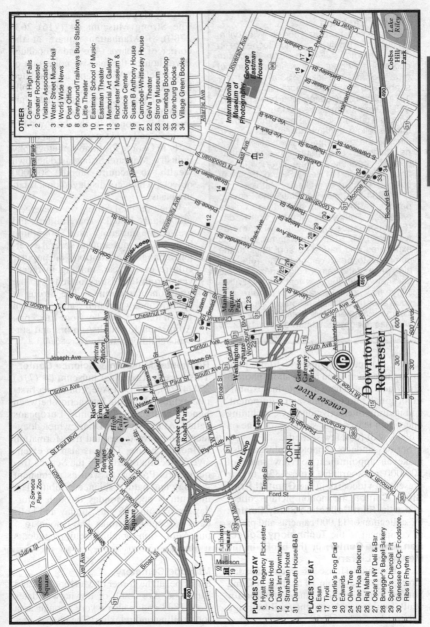

OTHER
1 Center at High Falls
2 Greater Rochester Visitors Association
3 Water Street Music Hall
4 World Wide News
6 Post Office
8 Greyhound/Trailways Bus Station
9 Litte Theater
10 Eastman School of Music
11 Eastman Theater
13 Memorial Art Gallery
15 Rochester Museum & Science Center
19 Susan B Anthony House
21 Cambell-Whittlesey House
22 GeVa Theater
23 Strong Museum
32 Browbag Bookshop
33 Gurenburg Books
34 Village Green Books

PLACES TO STAY
5 Hyatt Regency Rochester
7 Cadillac Hotel
12 Days Inn Downtown
14 Strathallan Hotel
31 Dartmouth House B&B

PLACES TO EAT
16 Esan
17 Tivoli
18 Charlie's Frog Pond
20 Edwards
24 Olive Tree
25 Dac Hoa Barbecue
26 Raj Mahal
27 Oscar's NY Deli & Bar
28 Brueger's Bagel Bakery
29 Spiro's Charcoal Pit
30 Genessee Co-Op Foodstore, Ribs in Rhythm

George Eastman

Eastman was born in 1854 in Waterville, NY, and his family moved to Rochester in 1860. Eastman's version of an American success story began when he dropped out of school at 14 to take a $3-a-week messenger job to help support his family. In 1874 he began working as a bank clerk at $15 a week. Three years later Eastman bought a cumbersome camera and, being a curious fellow, began to investigate ways to simplify the development process. In 1880 he invented and patented a dry-plate coating machine. A year later, with the financial support of Henry Strong, Eastman opened a factory to make dry plates.

In 1884 Eastman Dry Plate and Film Co patented a rollable film alternative to glass negatives. Four years later the first Kodak (Eastman made up the name) cameras were sold for $125. They came with 100 exposures and had to be sent back to the company to be developed. The relatively high price of the camera didn't deter people fascinated with the new technology. Within 10 years Eastman was a millionaire and soon after that, a multimillionaire. During his lifetime, Eastman gave over $100 million to charities. George Eastman died in 1932. ■

Strong Museum

The Strong Museum (☎ (716) 263-2700), 1 Manhattan Square at the corner of Monroe Ave and Woodbury Blvd, houses the massive collection of middle-class Americana accumulated by Margaret Woodbury Strong – dolls and doll houses, toys, household furnishings and furniture. Strong's father made his money in the buggy-whip business and then smartly invested very early in George Eastman's photography industry. Margaret Strong used her own wealth to acquire about 500,000 objects, which are displayed on a rotating basis.

When she died, Strong was the largest individual Kodak shareholder and created the museum with a $60 million bequest. The museum has several excellent changing exhibitions on popular culture every year, ranging in recent years from the history of Jell-O to the tradition of mourning. The Strong is open Monday through Saturday from 10 am to 5 pm, Sunday from 1 to 5 pm. Admission for adults/seniors and students/children three to 16 is $5/4/3.

largest collection of historic films, photographs, cameras and books about photography and film. There are rotating exhibits of original photographs and equipment, and inviting interactive displays, including one which leaves your shadowy outline on a blank wall for a few seconds.

Serious students of photography can also make an appointment to view some of 500,000 photographs from 1839 to the present on videodisk in the **Gannett Print Study Center**; the motion picture collection at the **Film Collection Study Center**; the collection of 11,000 cameras and pieces of equipment in the **Technology Collection Study Center**; or the books in the **Menschel Library**.

Eastman House is open Tuesday through Saturday from 10 am to 5 pm, and Sunday from 1 pm to 5 pm. Admission for adults/seniors and students/children age five to 12 is $6.50/5/2.50.

Rochester Museum & Science Center

This excellent regional museum (☎ (716) 271-4320), 657 East Ave, contains a first-rate exhibit about the interaction between Seneca Indians and colonial Europeans called 'At the Western Door,' which documents the devastation and transformation of Indian culture. There is also an extensive collection of art from the Seneca Iroquois Arts Project, as well as permanent geology and natural science exhibits. The museum is open Monday through Saturday from 9 am to 5 pm, Sunday and holidays (except Christmas Day) noon to 5 pm. Admission for adults/seniors/students is $6/5/3.

Mt Hope Cemetery

Mt Hope, at the corner of Mt Hope Ave and Elmwood Ave south of downtown, dates from 1838 and is also a very popular area for strolling and relaxing. The chapel, crematorium and other buildings represent neo-Gothic, Moorish Revival and Italianate styles, and the rolling expanse of 196 acres is used for walking, cycling or just enjoying the sun. Mt Hope is also the final resting place of Frederick Douglass, Susan B Anthony, Buffalo Bill's children and George Washington's drummer boy, among other luminaries. The Friends of Mt. Hope Cemetery (☎ (716) 461-3494) provide one hour tours of the grounds and buildings on Sunday at 2 and 3 pm. You can also get a pocket guide to the grave sites from the Rochester Visitors Association (☎ (716) 546-3070).

Other Things to See & Do
The **Susan B Anthony House** (☎ (716) 235-6124, 381-6202), 17 Madison St, was Anthony's home from 1866 to 1906. She was arrested here for voting in 1872 and helped write the *History of Woman Suffrage* in her attic. The historic home is open Thursday to Saturday from 1 to 4 pm.

The Corn Hill neighborhood was once known as the 'ruffled shirt district,' after its 19th century residents who built many of Rochester's largest homes near the Genessee River. One of the most notable of these structures is the 1835 **Campbell-Whittlesey House** (☎ (716) 546-7029) at 123 S Fitzhugh St.

The **Seneca Park Zoo** (☎ (716) 342-2744), 2222 St Paul Blvd, is open daily from 10 am to 5 pm, until 7 pm on summer weekends and holidays. Admission for adults/children is $2/1.50.

The **Charlotte-Genesee Lighthouse** (☎ (716) 621-6179) is north of Rochester on Lighthouse St off of Latta Rd east of Lake Ave, and open weekends from mid-May to mid-October from 1 to 5 pm.

The **Sea Breeze/Raging Rivers Amusement Park** (☎ (716) 323-1900), on Lake Ontario just north of Rochester in Irondequoit, has an old wooden roller coaster and a 1915 carousel as well as a modern water park. The wet complex is open mid-June to Labor Day at an adult/under-44-inches-tall fee of $11.50/8. Take

Jell-O
Jell-O, the trademark for a gelatin desert and metaphor for the weak of knee, was invented southwest of Rochester in the town of LeRoy in 1897 by Paul B Wait, a carpenter. Orator Woodward bought the rights for Jell-O for $450 in 1899, and in 1925 the Woodward family sold them for $60 million. ■

I-490 east through Rochester to Route 590 north to the lake, about 10 miles total.

Twenty minutes west of Rochester is the **Victorian Doll Museum and Chili Doll Hospital** (☎ (716) 247-0130), 4332 Buffalo Rd in North Chili (chai-lai), open Tuesday to Saturday from 10 am to 4:30 pm, Sunday from 1 to 4:30 pm; closed in January.

The **Genesee Country Museum** (☎ (716) 538-6822), Flint Hill Rd in Mumford, 20 miles west of Rochester, is a living history collection of 57 buildings representing most of the 19th century. Admission for adults/seniors/youth 13 to 17/children six to 12 is $10/8.50/6/5.

Cruises
Riverview Cruise Lines (☎ (716) 865-4930), 18 Petten St Extension, one block south of the intersection of Lake Ave and Stutson St, and The Spirit of Rochester (☎ (716) 865-4930) run cruises along the Genesee River into Lake Ontario during warmer months.

Colonial Cruise Lines (☎ (716) 586-3800), 10 Schoen Place in Pittsford south of Rochester, does two hour Erie Canal cruises at noon, 3 pm and 6 pm for $10 each. There are also lunch/dinner cruises for $21/32.

Special Events
The **Lilac Festival** (mid-May for one week) celebrates 20 acres of lilacs and other spring flowers with a parade, an arts and crafts fair and daily entertainment. Call ☎ (716) 256-4960 for more information.

The **Corn Hill Arts Festival** (first weekend after July 4) is an arts & crafts, music and entertainment festival in the historic Corn Hill neighborhood (see above).

Places to Stay

The *Cadillac Hotel* (☎ (716) 454-4340), 45 Chestnut St, is a nicely rundown hotel near the Trailways-Greyhound bus station. It's an eight story brick structure, with yellowed hallways leading to rooms with thick shag carpeting, old furniture and decent views of the city. Single/double rates are $29/34.

The *Days Inn Downtown* (☎ (716) 325-5010), 384 East Ave, has rooms for $65/75, including a complimentary continental breakfast. It's within walking distance of several restaurants, museums and galleries.

Decent, and usually cheaper, motels are outside of town near the highways.

Near the airport, take I-390 to exit 18 west (Brooks Ave/Airport exit). Go one block to Buell Rd and turn right. There are several discount motel chains along the first block of Buell, including *Motel 6* (☎ (716) 436-2170), at 155 Buell Rd, with rooms for $40/50. The nearby *Comfort Inn Airport* (☎ (716) 436-4400), 395 Buell Rd, has rooms from $50 to $65, with slightly cheaper rates from November to May.

B&Bs *Dartmouth House B&B* (☎ (716) 271-7872), 215 Dartmouth St, is an ideally located B&B in a 1905 English Tudor home between Monroe and East Aves, within walking distance of several restaurants and museums. There are four rooms, two with shared bath and two with private bath, with rates ranging from $60 to $110, including a generous candlelit breakfast.

Hotels The *Hyatt Regency Rochester* (☎ (716) 546-1234), 125 E Main St, is connected to the convention center by an enclosed skyway. The Hyatt was built in 1992 and is the best large hotel in town by far, with excellent service, a pool/health club and three restaurants. Weekday rooms range from $115 to $190; weekends are a better value, ranging from $95 to $115. The *Strathallan* (☎ (716) 461-5010,

(800) 678-7284), 550 East Ave, is a 150 room hotel set among several mansions, and boasts of service to match the neighborhood. All the rooms have balconies, fridges and most have small kitchenettes as well. Rates range from $110 to $165 and include a full breakfast buffet.

Places to Eat
Budget & Moderate – Monroe Ave

There are several good, inexpensive eateries along Monroe Ave, a popular restaurant-row destination southeast of the Inner Loop between Union and Alexander Sts. Monroe Ave is a popular street to stroll, with its variety of restaurants, herb shops and used clothing and antique stores.

Dac Hoa Barbecue (☎ (716) 232-6038), 230 Monroe Ave, has excellent Vietnamese noodle soups (pho) and dry noodle dishes (bun) from $5, Chinese barbecue dishes of duck and pork and several spicier Szechwan plates. Dac Hoa is open daily for lunch and dinner. The atmosphere is early florescent and the place is usually crowded.

Raj Mahal (☎ (716) 546-2315), 324 Monroe Ave at the corner of Alexander St, has excellent and mostly North Indian food (tandooris etc) and several vegetarian dishes, most from $10 to $15; it is open daily for lunch and dinner.

Oscar's NY Deli & Bar (☎ (716) 244-7077), 470 Monroe Ave, is a black-and-white deli that features overstuffed sandwiches that have famous Hollywood names – 'Cluck Gable' is chicken salad, for example. The food is good, so if you don't mind ordering a 'Pita Sellers' instead of saying 'roast beef and Swiss on a pita,' eat here. All basic sandwiches are priced between $5 and $6.

Bruegger's Bagel Bakery (☎ (716) 256-2420), 548 Monroe Ave, has a variety of good deli and bagel items.

Spiro's Charcoal Pit (☎ (716) 271-8690), 630 Monroe Ave, is a Greek diner. Try the $6 Greek combination plate of dolmas (grape leaves), spanakopita (spinach pie), tiropita (cheese pastry), a gyro, olives, fresh tomato and feta cheese.

The *Olive Tree* (☎ (716) 454-3510), 165 Monroe Ave, is a fancier Greek spot with a summer garden, housed in a restored 1864 brick storefront and featuring 'nouvelle' Greek cuisine, including the ever-popular retsina wine. The Olive Tree is open for lunch on weekdays, and for dinner Monday through Saturday from 5 to 9 pm.

The *Genesee Co-Op Foodstore* (☎ (716) 244-3900), 713 Monroe Ave, sells an assortment of natural foods. If the co-op doesn't fill you up, head next door to *Ribs in Rhythm* (☎ (716) 244-7427), 727 Monroe Ave, which serves ribs cooked over hardwood charcoal with Southern, Carolina or Jamaican barbecue sauce, from about $6.

Moderate – Park Ave Less than a mile from Monroe Ave is a rather recent addition to the restaurant scene in Rochester. Several interesting eateries and shops near the corner of Park and Berkeley St are worth a look, including *Esan* (☎ (716) 271-2030), 696 Park Ave, a very good northeast Thai cafe, open Tuesday through Sunday from 11 am to 10 pm. *Pasta Tivoli* (☎ (716) 271-7570), 690 Park Ave, has entrees from $6 to $10, open daily from 11 am to 10pm. *Charlie's Frog Pond* (☎ (716) 271-1970), 652 Park Ave, is an upscale diner, open daily for breakfast, lunch and dinner.

Top End The Society of Rochester Landmark Restaurants is a group of seven more expensive area restaurants all in restored historic buildings. Of these, *Edwards* (☎ (716) 423-0140), 13 S Fitzhugh St, in the 1873 Academy Building is among the most popular. The inside is a mix of mirrors and marble, but the food is creative, with meat and seafood entrees ranging from $12 to $20.

Richardson's Canal House (☎ (716) 248-5000), 1474 Marsh Rd, has a fixed-price dinner of appetizer, salad, an entree choice like duckling, sport fish or lamb and dessert for $32. The menu changes seasonally. Richardson's is near the Victor Rd exit, off I-490.

Entertainment

Theater The Genesee Valley Arts Association (GeVa; ☎ (716) 232-4382), 75 Woodbury Blvd at the corner of Clinton Ave South, hosts a number of plays at the GeVa Theater.

Cinema The *Little Theatre* (☎ (716) 232-4699, 240 East Ave, shows revivals and new independent movies.

The *Curtiss and Dryden Theatres* (☎ (716) 271-4090) at the Eastman House, 900 East Ave, show classic films at $4 for adults and $3 for children.

Music The Eastman School of Music (☎ (716) 274-1100/1110), 26 Gibbs St between Main and Scio Sts, has regularly scheduled jazz and classical concerts by students and visitors.

The *Rochester Philharmonic Orchestra* also plays at the Eastman Theater. Call ☎ (716) 222-5000 for schedule information.

Clubs The *Bamboo Club and Cafe* (☎ (716) 454-6895), 40-46 St Paul St, has a rotating schedule of jazz, R&B, oldies and modern music.

The *Horizontal Boogie Bar* (☎ (716) 2-BOOGIE/226-6443), 204 N Water St, and *Club Zei* (☎ (716) 232-1600), 171 St Paul St, serve up rock and alternative music.

Getting There & Away

Air The Greater Rochester international airport (☎ (716) 464-6000) is on Brooks Rd at exit 18 off of I-390. Most major carriers serve Rochester, including American, Delta, United, Continental and Canadian Pacific. Some roundrip fares are: Rochester to/from Chicago, $198; to/from New York City, $178; to/from Philadelphia, $258.

Bus The bus terminal (☎ (716) 346-3415) is at 187 Midtown Plaza (corner of Broad and Chestnut Sts). Trailways buses go to Buffalo, Syracuse, Niagara Falls and points further east like Albany and New York. Greyhound also runs similar connections.

NEW YORK

Daily service from Rochester to Buffalo (one-way/roundtrip) is $11/17; to Syracuse, $10/20; to New York City, $41/82.

Train The Amtrak station (☎ (716) 454-2894) is at 320 Central Ave. Trains run east through Syracuse and other cities all the way to New York City; west to Buffalo and other points. Fares from Rochester to Buffalo (one-way/roundtrip) are $15/30; to New York City (Penn Station), $60/120.

Car Rochester is about 10 miles north of I-90 (the NY State Thruway) by I-390 (Genesee Expressway) or I-490.

Getting Around

Bus The Regional Transit Service (RTS; ☎ (716) 288-1700) will take you anywhere you want to go in town. You can ride for free within the small area enclosed by the Inner Loop highways. Otherwise the base rate is $1.

Skyway The Skyway system is an enclosed network of walkways that connects downtown buildings. The Skyway runs from Main St near the Genesee River three blocks east to Elm St and then three blocks south to a parking garage on Woodbury Blvd.

Western New York

Western New York boasts the state's most famous tourist destination after New York City – Niagara Falls. Just a 15 mile drive from the falls is the city of Buffalo, the second largest city in the state. Most of the 10 million annual visitors to Niagara Falls bypass Buffalo, which may be a good reason in and of itself to visit this still-vital city. From here, you can continue south for 65 miles to the Chautauqua Institution on Chautauqua Lake which hosts a large and well-known nine week lecture, music and art event every summer.

GETTING THERE & AWAY

Air The major airport in the region is Greater Buffalo international airport (see Buffalo, below). Rochester international airport (see the Finger Lakes chapter) is also conveniently located.

Train Several Amtrak trains make daily runs between Buffalo and Rochester to the east, Buffalo and Niagara Falls and Toronto, Canada, to the north; and between Buffalo and Erie, PA, to the southwest.

Car I-90 stretches from New York's southwest corner to Buffalo, then runs east toward Rochester. The other major east-west road is Route 17 near the Pennsylvania border; Route 417, which branches off Route 17 just east of Allegany State Park is certainly one of the prettiest drives in all of New York. Other east-west roads are Route 20, which heads east from Buffalo to the Finger Lakes; and Route 104, from Niagara Falls to Rochester.

NIAGARA FALLS, NY
History

The Seneca, largest of the confederated Iroquois tribes, were the first people to populate the area around Niagara Falls. Among the Iroquois, the Seneca were known as 'the keepers of the western door' because

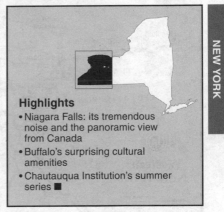

Highlights
- Niagara Falls: its tremendous noise and the panoramic view from Canada
- Buffalo's surprising cultural amenities
- Chautauqua Institution's summer series ■

they controlled the western-most regions of the Iroquois nation, which extended from the shores of Lake Erie east to the Hudson Valley. It was through the Seneca tribal territories that Iroquois warriors and hunters passed to attack and later exploit the western and southern nations. In 1678 Seneca guides led Father Louis Hennepin, a French priest serving under explorer Robert LaSalle, to the falls. Hennepin was, perhaps, the first to call attention to the cataracts as a natural wonder. In his account of his travels, which were widely read in Europe, he made reference to the falls, observing that 'the universe does not afford its parallel.'

For early Europeans, control of the portage around the falls was vital since they were the only break in the St Lawrence River to the Great Lakes waterway. The French were the first to build a fort in 1687 at the nexus of the Niagara River and Lake Ontario. In 1726, they built Fort Niagara north of the present-day falls. Throughout the French & Indian War of the 18th century, the French and British fought for control of the portage and the surrounding region. Finally, in

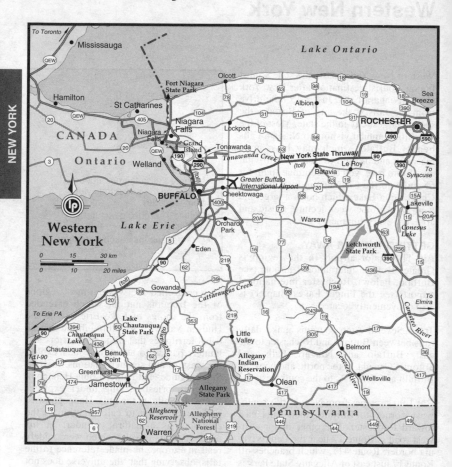

Western New York

0   15   30 km

0   10   20 miles

1759, the British took Fort Niagara and held it until 1796.

During this period, farming settlements sprang up on both sides of the Niagara River, only to be burned and looted during the War of 1812. After the war the region rebounded, particularly after the arrival of the Erie Canal in 1825. In 1855 the Roebling family (who later designed the Brooklyn Bridge in New York City) and backers built the Roebling Suspension Bridge across the Niagara Gorge. The two level bridge supported trains below and carriages above.

In the mid-19th century, the area around the falls became increasingly commercialized. Private owners went so far as to block off views of the falls with fences and then charged frustrated visitors to view the magnificent cataracts through small holes in the fences. Angered by such blatant exploitation of a natural resource, the Free Niagara Movement arose in 1869. Led by men like Frederick Law Olmsted, the group launched a well-organized campaign to force the state government to buy back land around the falls and create a public park. Finally, in 1885 the NY State Legislature

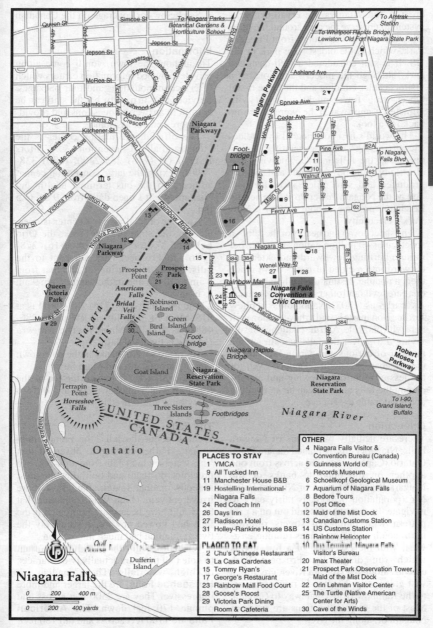

NEW YORK

Niagara Falls

| 0 | 200 | 400 m |
| 0 | 200 | 400 yards |

PLACES TO STAY
1 YMCA
9 All Tucked Inn
11 Manchester House B&B
19 Hostelling International-
   Niagara Falls
24 Red Coach Inn
26 Days Inn
27 Radisson Hotel
31 Holley-Rankine House B&B

PLACES TO EAT
2 Chu's Chinese Restaurant
3 La Casa Cardenas
15 Tommy Ryan's
17 George's Restaurant
23 Rainbow Mall Food Court
28 Goose's Roost
29 Victoria Park Dining
   Room & Cafeteria

OTHER
4 Niagara Falls Visitor &
   Convention Bureau (Canada)
5 Guinness World of
   Records Museum
6 Schoellkopf Geological Museum
7 Aquarium of Niagara Falls
8 Bedore Tours
10 Post Office
12 Maid of the Mist Dock
13 Canadian Customs Station
14 US Customs Station
16 Rainbow Helicopter
18 Bus Terminal, Niagara Falls
   Visitor's Bureau
20 Imax Theater
21 Prospect Park Observation Tower,
   Maid of the Mist Dock
22 Orin Lehman Visitor Center
25 The Turtle (Native American
   Center for Arts)
30 Cave of the Winds

created the Niagara Reservation parks system to preserve the area around the falls. Olmsted designed the gorge-front Prospect Park, which is the oldest state park in the US. It is still considered a well-designed park, although the modern additions of a visitors center building and the large metal Observation Tower might not meet with Olmsted's approval if he were to come back for a look.

The world's first commercial hydroelectric alternating current-generating facility opened at the falls in 1895, proving that electricity could be reasonably and cheaply produced and sent miles away for use. Today, the Niagara Power Project in nearby Lewiston produces about 17% of New York's electricity.

The sheer power and beauty of the falls – a spectacular 40 million gallons of water per minute hurtling downward and extending outward into a cloud of mist – have made them a popular destination for honeymooners, daredevils and other seekers of romance. As early as 1803, Napoleon's nephew Jerome Bonaparte is said to have made a visit here with his bride. And the challenge of surviving a trip over the falls has attracted a number of curious and daring individuals (see sidebar later in this chapter). Even for the less adventurous, viewing and experiencing the falls up close can be an exciting and memorable experience.

Orientation
There are actually two towns of Niagara Falls: Niagara Falls, NY, and Niagara Falls, Ontario (Canada), situated across from one another on the opposite banks of the Niagara River. The town of Niagara Falls, NY (population 62,000), is fairly easy to navigate. Its downtown is laid out on a grid pattern with numbered streets running north-south and named ones running east-west, with the exception of a few streets which run diagonally. Prospect Park extends along the Niagara River, creating a vast green strip. Niagara St runs east-west to the Rainbow Bridge gateway to Canada. Most of the major attractions are south of Niagara St, along the river.

See below for coverage on the Canadian side.

Information
Throughout the town, you'll come along privately-owned information centers which offer accommodations and tour packages. Services vary in quality, but the staff can be helpful in answering questions and providing more general assistance.

The official information center is the Niagara Falls Convention & Visitors Bureau (☎ (716) 285-2400, (800) 338-7890), next to the large convention center, adjacent to the bus terminal at 4th and Niagara Sts. It's open daily from 9 am to 5 pm.

Another official visitor's center is operated by the state of New York, the Orin Lehman Visitor Center (☎ (716) 278-1796), in Prospect Park adjacent to the falls. Open daily during the summer from 8 am to 10 pm and in the winter from 9 am to 6 pm.

The post office (☎ (716) 285-7561) is at 615 Main St. The library (☎ (716) 286-4881) is at 1425 Main St. The *Niagara Gazette* is the local daily paper.

There are several banks in the downtown vicinity around 4th and Main Sts.

You can park for free in the lot of the Rainbow Mall right downtown and walk to everything you'll need to see.

The Falls
Writing about the falls, the French missionary, Father Hennepin, observed that 'the waters which fall from this horrible precipice do foam and boil after the most hideous manner imaginable.' In a more irreverent vein, Oscar Wilde remarked that he would have been more impressed if the falls had flowed upward. It's unlikely the two gentlemen had much in common.

When describing the falls, it is important to note that there are actually two cataracts, or high waterfalls. The Canadian, or **Horseshoe Falls**, are the larger and more impressive. They are 2500 feet across and plunge 170 feet down. The **American Falls** are 1100 feet across and fall 180 feet.

Sometimes referred to as a separate cataract, **Bridal Veil Falls** actually forms the western portion of the American Falls. The parkland called Goat Island sits in the middle of the Niagara River. The middle of the river marks the international border between Canada and the US, the longest unprotected border in the world.

Originally about 200,000 cubic feet per second (or 5.5 billion gallons per hour) of water flowed over the falls, but today between a half and three-quarters of the water is diverted to run power turbines in the US and Canada. About 10% of the water flows over the American Falls and 90% over the Canadian Horseshoe.

The falls were formed about 12,000 years ago as glaciers melted releasing water from the Great Lakes along what became the Niagara River. The 37 mile long Niagara River connects Lake Erie and Lake Ontario. As it flows through the city of Niagara Falls, the river is actually flowing northward. The water cut through the rock over time creating a waterfall. When they were formed, the falls were seven miles downstream from their present location. The edge of the falls continues to erode upstream at the rate of about one inch every year. Note the piles of boulders at the base of the falls.

In 1969 the American Falls were actually shut off for a period of time. A dam was built across the river, and the flow diverted to the Horseshoe Falls because the Army Corps of Engineers wanted to study how to prevent further erosion. Gleeful tourists walked along the dry river bed and among the things found were 12 buckets of coins and two bodies.

The falls are illuminated at night throughout the year on a changing monthly schedule, but roughly according the sunset times. The **Festival of Lights** refers to the lighting of all the trees in the parks adjacent to the falls, and runs from late November to the first week in January.

Viewing the Falls

'Both sides' is the answer to the most often asked question – 'which is the best side for viewing?' For the best panoramic view, cross over to the Canadian side. Views from the American side are considered less satisfactory because you are generally standing too close for comfort, or at an angle which makes viewing difficult. One exception is the view from Prospect Observation Tower (see below) which was erected to improve the view from the American side, thus revealing an insecurity deeper than the river gorge itself. On the other hand, the American side allows you (you have no choice) to feel the immense power of the falls. You can easily walk or drive across Rainbow Bridge to Canada. (If you drive, prepare to pay about C$8 to park – see below.)

If you plan to visit a number of attractions in Niagara Falls, consider buying a **Master Pass**, which covers entry to the Cave of the Winds, *Maid of the Mist*, Prospect Park Observation Tower, the Viewmobile Tour, the Prospect Park Visitors Center film and the Schoellkopf Geological Museum. It costs $15 and is available at visitor's centers, Viewmobile stops and some sights.

Goat Island Goat Island is a half mile long island connected to the US mainland by free pedestrian and car bridges. From the island you can walk to **Three Sisters Islands**, a series of rapids approaching Horseshoe Falls. You can also walk down to **Terrapin Point**, the closest viewing point to Horseshoe Falls. From this spit of land you can imagine 17 year old Deanne Woodward being rescued from shooting over the brink after her boat capsized (see the Niagara Falls Daredevils sidebar).

To experience the falls up close, take an elevator down from Goat Island to the **Cave of the Winds** (☎ (716) 278-1730), where you'll walk along wooden walkways within 25 feet from the cataracts. You'll be provided with a yellow rain coat to protect you from the heavy mist. Admission is $4/3 for adults/kids. Open Memorial Day to Labor Day daily from 10 am to 7 pm; from Labor Day until early October, from 10 am to 6 pm.

Niagara Falls Daredevils

Since early in the 19th century, stuntsters have been attracted to the falls, challenging the raging waters on tightropes, in barrels, kayaks and rubber inner tubes. Some not-so-daring visitors have even gone over the falls unintentionally. In recent years, police have been fining daredevils for attempting to perform a stunt without a license.

In 1829, Sam Patch leaped twice from a platform about 100 feet above the gorge at the foot of the falls.

The first recorded woman plunger was Mrs Annie Edson Taylor, a teacher who, at 63, decided the way to fame was to go over the falls in a barrel. On October 24, 1901, friends strapped her into a barrel, towed it out in the stream and cast it loose. Taylor and her barrel went over. Less than 20 minutes later, the barrel was pulled to shore and Taylor got the fame she had sought.

The next person to challenge the falls was Englishman Bobby Leach, who went over in a steel barrel on July 25, 1911. He was so battered and bruised that he needed six months in the hospital to recuperate. Fifteen years later, while on a lecture tour in New Zealand, Leach slipped and fell on an orange peel, broke his leg and died from ensuing complications.

Another Brit, Charles Stephens, tried the falls in an oak barrel on July 11, 1920. Unfortunately, when his barrel hit the water, Stephens was catapulted out its bottom. Only his arm was recovered.

Jean Lussier of Quebec designed an innovative vehicle with a steel frame and 32 inner tubes and went over the top on July 4, 1928. He emerged an hour later in perfect health. For years afterwards Lussier sold small pieces of his inner tubes for 50¢ apiece. Twenty-three years later, Nathan T Boya duplicated Lussier's rubber ball and also made the drop successfully.

George Stathakis, a Buffalo chef, built a 2000 pound, wood-and-steel contraption and made the plunge on July 4, 1930. He lived through the drop but suffocated when his vehicle was trapped behind the falls for 22 hours.

Red Hill, Jr, built a shoddy craft christened 'The Thing' out of 13 inner tubes, fish net and canvas straps and launched it and himself into the rapids on August 5, 1951. The Thing began to fall apart even before it reached the brink. What was left of it floated to the surface soon after it hit the bottom. Hill's body was fished out the next day.

There is free parking at the eastern end of Goat Island close to Three Sisters Islands, or a $3 parking lot near Terrapin Point on the western side of the island.

Prospect Park Observation Tower As if craning its neck to get a better view, the green metal platform of the Prospect Park Observation Tower stands out as a reminder of the inferior views of the falls afforded visitors from the American side. The platform does provide excellent views of both the river canyon and falls and is well worth the modest 50¢ admission. You can take an elevator to the base of the falls or up to the top of the observation tower. You can also walk out on the observation deck at town level. The *Maid of the Mist* also leaves from here at the river level.

At the base of the falls, visitors can climb up a rickety cement and stone staircase and along a path which takes you reasonably close to the north side of the American Falls, at least close enough to get wet from the mist and spray. The view from the top is also spectacular; open daily from mid-May to mid-September, from 8 am to 11 pm, otherwise from 8:30 am to 4:30 pm.

Rainbow Bridge Travelers can drive across this bridge for 75¢ or walk across for 25¢. You'll get a magnificent, straight-on view of the falls from the Canadian side.

The Turtle (Native American Center for the Living Arts)

The center (☎ (716) 284-2427), 25 Rainbow Blvd South, serves as an exhibit

Only two people are recorded to have gone over the falls unintentionally. On July 9, 1960, Jim Honeycutt took 17 year old Deanne Woodward and her seven year old brother, Roger, out for a boat ride on the upper Niagara above the falls. To give the children a thrill, Honeycutt maneuvered the boat close to the falls, but when he turned it around, the engine failed. The boat wallowed and then flipped, hurtling all three into the waters which were rushing towards the edge of the falls. Deanne was pulled out at Terrapin Point on Goat Island very close to the brink. Honeycutt and Roger Woodward went over. Amazingly, Roger survived and was picked up by the *Maid of the Mist* tour boat, but Honeycutt died.

Canadian Karl Soucek made the plunge in a red barrel on July 3, 1984, and emerged with bruises, a hurt arm and a chipped tooth. Less than a year later, Soucek dropped 180 feet from the top of the Houston Astrodome in a specially designed barrel heading for a 10 foot deep pool of water. The barrel hit the edge of the tank and Soucek died of his injuries.

Steve Trotter survived the falls in a homemade rubber barrel on August 19, 1985. David Munday is the only person to have gone over twice and survived, in 1985 and 1993. Peter DeBernardi and Jeffrey Petkovich, from Niagara Falls and Ottawa, respectively, went over head to head in the same barrel on September 27, 1989. Both lived.

The most daring – and, perhaps, the most stupid (though the competition is stiff) – attempt of all was that of Tennessee's Jessie W Sharp, who shot the falls in a 12½ foot polyethylene kayak on June 5, 1990. Sharp had planned to ride the rapids beyond the falls to Lewiston, NY, where he had made dinner reservations. He skipped wearing a helmet so his face would be recognizable on film. It was, but his body was never found.

Tightrope walkers have also challenged the falls. The most famous, Jean François Gravelet – known as 'Blondin' – walked across many times beginning in the summer of 1859. Each time, Blondin would vary his routine, so as to continue to attract attention. On some attempts, he might somersault on the rope, ride a bicycle, push a wheelbarrow, cook an omelet or pull up a bottle of champagne from the *Maid of the Mist* to refresh himself. He even once carried his trusting manager across on his back.

In case you have ideas of your own, the current maximum fine for performing a stunt without a license (they don't grant licenses anyway) is $10,000. Payable if you survive. ■

space for American Indian arts and crafts, as well as an educational and performance center featuring craft demonstrations, lectures, Native American dance and storytelling. The large, steel and glass geodesic dome is named 'the Turtle' because the shape brings to mind the Iroquois belief that the earth was created on a turtle's back.

The center is open May through September daily from 9 am to 6 pm; otherwise Tuesday to Friday from 9 am to 5 pm and weekends from noon to 5 pm. Admission for adults/seniors/students is $4/3/2.

Other Things to See & Do

The **Schoellkopf Geological Museum** (☎ (716) 278-1780), in Niagara Reservation State Park, overlooks the Niagara gorge and houses exhibits and nature trails explaining the geology of the region. You can take a free guided tour along the rim or descend to the base of the falls. Walks vary in length and difficulty, but all are designed to be both informative and fun. Open daily from late May to early September; Monday to Wednesday during winter. Admission is 50¢.

The **Aquarium of Niagara Falls** (☎ (716) 285-3575), 701 Whirlpool St, is open daily from 9 am to 5 pm and until 7 pm during the summer. Admission is $6.25/4.25 for adults/kids four to 12. (A footbridge connects the aquarium and the geological museum.)

The **Niagara Power Authority** (☎ (716) 285-3211, ext 6660) is located at 5777 Lewiston Rd in the attractive village of

Lewiston, NY, north of the falls. The power project is one of the largest in the world. You'll find a visitors center and a good view of the Niagara gorge. The power complex is open daily in July and August from 9 am to 6 pm; and 10 am to 5 pm the rest of the year. Free admission.

Organized Tours
Although you can view the falls by walking or by a combination of driving and walking, many visitors prefer to take in the sights on a narrated bus tour. Typically, organized tours include stops on both sides of the border. On the US side, the major sights generally include a boat ride on the *Maid of the Mist*, a visit to the Prospect Park Observation Tower and Goat Island. On the Canadian side, you visit the tunnels behind the falls, the Minolta Observation Tower and also take a ride on *Maid of the Mist*. Check to see what the current tour stops are and compare the package rate with the costs for admission to the individual sights (don't forget the Master Pass detailed above) and the time you'd need to get there on your own.

From May to November, Aquatic Fantaseas/Niagara River Drift Dives (☎ (716) 635-8035, 283-3483) takes people out for scuba dives on the upper Niagara River above the falls. They provide the tanks; you bring everything else, including your faith in the current. The cost is $40 and includes a barbecue.

Bedore Tours (☎ (716) 285-5261, (800) 538-8433) offers tours with stops at the major attractions on the Canadian and/or American sides of the falls for $35 to $40.

You can arrange to fly over the falls by contacting Rainbow Helicopters (☎ (716) 284-2800), 454 Main St, near the Howard Johnson and Bedore Tours. The cost is $40 per person.

For informal and inexpensive sightseeing, hop on The Viewmobile (☎ (716) 282-0028), an open trolley that drives around town in a loop, stopping at various sights. Riders can get on and off at any stop and pick up the next tram. The cost is $3.50.

Maid of the Mist Tours Since 1846, Niagara Falls' biggest tourist attraction has been a boat ride on the *Maid of the Mist* (☎ (716) 284-8897), Canada (905) 358-5781) which leaves from the base of the Prospect Park Observation Tower. You'll be supplied with a raincoat before heading for the base of the American Falls and Horseshoe Falls where you can best experience the power and the fury of the water hurtling over the cliffs above. The trip lasts half an hour and costs $8.25/4.75 for adults/children. In season – from mid-June to late October – boats leave every 15 minutes from 10 am until early evening.

Maid of the Mist also leaves from the dock at Clifton Hill St and River Rd in Canada.

Places to Stay
Camping There are several campsites on Grand Island, five to seven miles south of Niagara Falls; take I-190. The *Niagara Falls KOA Campground* (☎ (716) 773-7583), 2570 Grand Island Blvd, is on Grand Island next to Fantasy Island amusement park; take exit N-19 from I-190 on Grand Island. The campground has a pool, laundry facilities, camp store, miniature golf and more. Open from April to mid-November; sites are $18 to $25. *Cinderella Campsite* (☎ (716) 773-4095) offers sites for $18 year round.

Niagara Falls Campground (☎ (716) 731-3434, (800) 525-8505), 2405 Niagara Falls Blvd (Route 62), is about seven miles east of Niagara Falls. Sites run from $16 to $21.

Hostels *Hostelling International – Niagara Falls* (☎ (716) 282-3700), 1101 Ferry Ave, has dormitory rooms with four, six or eight bunks to a room (a total of 44 beds). There is a large living room and the friendly owners will pick up visitors at the Buffalo airport for around $12. They also run a shuttle to the train ($2) and bus stations ($1). The hostel has laundry and kitchen facilities, and there's a Tops food store just three blocks away.

If you're staying at the hostel, bring a sleep sack or rent one for $1.50. During the summer, there is a $4 sunset van tour along the Niagara River. Guests also receive discount coupons for the *Maid of the Mist* boat tours and other attractions. You can also rent a bike here for $10 a day. There is a 9:30 am to 5 pm lockout and an 11:30 pm curfew. Guests are invited to help out by doing a small chore. The cost is $11. It's closed from December 16 to January 4.

The *YMCA* (☎ (716) 285-8491), Portage Rd and Main St, has rooms for men only. The rooms, which are minimally furnished with a single bed, a florescent light and a small desk, rent by the day/week for $25/50. Both men and women can rent floor space for $10 in an exercise room covered with mats. You share a clean bath and have free use of the gym. If you stay in the mat room during the summer, you have to get up early because the room is in use for activities beginning at about 7 am and continuing until 7 pm. There is a lock-up for personal belongings, and you can come and go throughout the day, unlike the hostel, which has a lockout.

Middle Route 62 (Niagara Falls Blvd), as it nears Niagara Falls, is lined with cheap motels. Off-season rates range from $25 to $40, and in-season during the summer from $40 to $50. The *Red Carpet Inn* (☎ (716) 283-2010), 6625 Niagara Falls Blvd, has off-season single/double/triple rates of $30/39/59; in-season rates are $45/55/79.

All Tucked Inn (☎ (716) 282-0919), 574 3rd St, has 10 clean rooms with basic furnishings. Two rooms have private baths and the others have sinks and share three clean bathrooms. There are no phones or televisions, and there is generally a 1 am curfew. From May 16 to September 14 the rates are $38 to $58; off-season they're $28 to $48.

Manchester House B&B (☎ (716) 285-5717), 653 Main St, is a private home built in 1903. There are four rooms which share two baths. This is a pleasant place, and the owners know the area well. You can also take advantage of the sitting room with its gas fireplace, television and music. Single/double rates from Memorial Day to Labor Day are $60 to $70, a bit less in the winter.

The old Niagara Hotel, built in 1924, is now the *Days Inn* (☎ (716) 285-9321), 201 Rainbow Blvd. Even the redecorated guest rooms can't restore the hotel to its former charm. The grand lobby is a dim reminder of better days. There is a cocktail lounge and restaurant. Rates November to March are $39 to $69; during the summer they're $79 to $129.

Top End The *Holley Rankine House B&B* (☎ (716) 285-4790, (800) 845-6649), 525 Riverside Dr, is a large stone house located across from the Niagara River. The long, comfortable living room with fireplace looks out over the river. There's also a nice stone terrace. The two rooms with private baths are $100 each and include a full breakfast.

Red Coach Inn (☎ (716) 282-1459), 2 Buffalo Ave near the bridge to Goat Island, offers one and two-bedroom suites furnished with European antique reproductions. The Inn is located above the Red Coach restaurant in a 1920's Tudor-style building. The suites, located at the front of the inn, have views of the street and river; rooms in the back of the building have a view of the parking lot. Rates from November 1 to April 30 for rooms/one/two-bedroom suites are $75/95/150. From May 1 to October 31, they're $95/125/175

The *Radisson Hotel* (☎ (716) 285-3361, fax 285-3900), 3rd St near the Rainbow Mall, has over 400 rooms in a new brown, brick building adjacent to the convention center. It's the newest and nicest of the full-service hotels. Rates mid-May to mid-September are $80 to $110; otherwise from $120 to $175.

Places to Eat

Food is not the main attraction in Niagara Falls. Choices are few. The downtown *Rainbow Mall Food Court* has a number of fast food concessions which sell stuffed potatoes, pizza, Chinese food, hot dogs and salads. You can sit at a table in the mall while eating or take food out to the adjacent Wintergarden structure, a giant 107 foot tall tree-filled atrium whose otherwise peaceful ambience is marred by pumped-in radio music.

George's Restaurant (☎ (716) 284-5766), 420 Niagara St, is a simple neighborhood restaurant with $3.50 breakfast specials, sandwiches for under $4, and dinners with selections like meatloaf with mashed potatoes for $4.50. You can't miss George's: it's the color of a bright pumpkin.

La Casa Cardenas (☎ (716) 282-0231), 921 Main St, is a Mexican restaurant located in a red house with green trim and turrets on Main St near the armory. The food here is unexceptional, but it provides a respite from diner food. Fajitas are $9, and a slew of chicken dishes are $8.50; burritos, enchiladas and tacos are $5.50.

Chu's Chinese Restaurant (☎ (716) 285-7278), 1019 Main St, is quite good and serves both Szechwan and Mandarin dishes. Open daily from 11 am to 11 pm.

Tommy Ryan's (☎ (716) 282-5025), 1 Prospect Point, is a '50s-style diner, with very decent diner food. Open from 11 am to 10 pm daily.

The *Goose's Roost* (☎ (716) 282-6255), 343 4th St, is next to the Convention Center. The food is quite good, somewhat on the Italian side with most dinners under $10. Open daily from 7 am to 11 pm.

More expensive is the *Red Coach Inn* (☎ (716) 282-1459), 2 Buffalo Ave. The dining room is decorated with faux wood beams and chandeliers, and diners are seated in comfortable captains chairs at oak tables. Lunch selections include sandwiches, salads, fish & chips and salads for $5 to $9. Dinners feature London broil, pork chops, veal and fish ranging from $12 to $18.

Getting There & Away

Air Buffalo's airport is the nearest. You can take bus No 24 from the airport to the Buffalo Transportation Center and then bus No 40 to Niagara Falls. The total cost will be around $3.

Alternately, the ITA Buffalo Airport Shuttle (☎ (800) 551-9369) runs three times a day between Niagara Falls and the Buffalo airport for $18/31 one way/roundtrip. ITA runs an extended schedule during the summer.

Bus The Niagara Frontier Transportation Authority bus system (NFTA; ☎ (716) 285-7211, 285-9319) runs bus No 40 between Niagara Falls and Buffalo every day all day long.

Express bus No 60 runs between Niagara Falls and Buffalo five times a day from Monday to Friday. Two express buses leave Niagara Falls for Buffalo before 7 am and three buses leave Buffalo for Niagara Falls roughly between 4:30 and 5 pm.

The fare for both buses is $1.70. The bus terminal is next to the visitors center at 4th and Niagara Sts.

For buses further afield you must take either Greyhound or Trailways from Buffalo.

Train Amtrak (☎ (716) 285-4224) stops at Lockport Rd and 27th St, one block east of Hyde Park Blvd. There is daily service to Buffalo (one way/roundtrip for $6/12) and to Toronto ($17/32).

Car You can get to Niagara Falls by I-190 from the south, a toll road from Buffalo, or by Route 62, a commercial strip that extends all the way from Buffalo to the falls. From Canada, the QEW highway leads to the Rainbow Bridge which dumps cars right downtown next to the American Falls.

Getting Around

Bus The NFTA (see above) runs buses through the town. The base fare is $1.10 and you add 20¢ for each extra zone crossed or for a transfer.

Bicycle The tourist information center distributes a *Bicycle Route Guide* of the Buffalo-Niagara Falls area. You can rent bikes at the hostel (see above) or try the yellow pages for a rental place near your accommodations.

TONY WHEELER

American Falls, Niagara Falls, NY

TONY WHEELER

The Cave of Winds, Niagara Falls, NY

Snowy day at the Syracuse Museum of Art, Syracuse, NY

Princeton University campus, NJ

Cape May, NJ

OLD FORT NIAGARA STATE PARK

The Old Fort Niagara is about 15 miles north of the town of Niagara Falls, within this state park (☎ (716) 745-7611). The fort was built by the French in 1726, but was captured by the British during the French & Indian War in 1759. The US took over in 1796, after the British retreated across the river to Fort George in Canada. The fully restored fort is open year round from 9 am to 7 pm. Admission is $6.25/4.00 for adults/kids six to 12.

NIAGARA FALLS, CANADA

It's not surprising that two cities in two countries share one name to describe their proximity to the falls. Both towns are essentially dedicated to serving the needs of the millions of annual visitors. Queen Victoria Park affords the best view of the falls from either side of the river, and it's a short drive, or short walk, across the bridge. In fact, weather permitting, pedestrians often arrive sooner than drivers due to the long line of cars at the international border.

In addition to the views (including nightly illumination of the falls) other notable attractions include Lundy's Lane Historical Museum and the Niagara Falls Museum. Summer Friday evenings also feature the 'Friday Fireworks' display, and the **Winter Festival of Lights** takes place every winter from late November until the first week of January.

History

Following the established presence of the Seneca peoples who originally settled the area, many British settlers took up residence around the falls – especially those who had opposed the American Revolution and were obliged to move on. The War of 1812 between the US and England didn't improve matters, and in July 1814, one of the bloodiest battles of the war was fought along the Niagara River at Lundy's Lane. In the early part of the 19th century, in fact, the battlefields were a major tourist attraction.

Information

Tourist Offices The Niagara Falls Visitor & Convention Bureau (☎ (905) 356-6061, (800) 563-2557), 5433 Victoria Ave, has restaurant and lodging information, and suggestions for enjoying the falls and other parts of the region. Ontario Travel & Tourist Information (☎ (905) 358-3221) also provides travel advice.

The Niagara Parks Commission (NPC; ☎ (905) 356-2241) maintains over 3000 acres of parkland from Lake Erie to Lake Ontario.

Entering Canada From the US side of Rainbow Bridge, it's a quick walk into Canada; the toll is light: 25¢ per person. If you take a car over, you may pay up to C$8 to park at Queen Victoria Park. Walkers can enjoy the advantage of riding on the **People Mover**. From the People Mover station, you can take a 19 mile roundtrip from the falls to Queenston Park. You can get on and off the vehicles,

Crossing International Borders

Despite its casual appearance and heavy tourist traffic, the US/Canadian border is a proper international boundary, and the normal rules apply.

Most Americans and Canadians will encounter little trouble as they cross from one side to the other. Nevertheless, you should have proof of citizenship with you. A driver's license is not always enough; passports, birth certificates, voter registration cards and 'green cards' may be requested by border guards. Citizens of other countries, of course, should possess proper documents, visas, etc. If you're renting a car in the US and are considering crossing the border, ask the rental agency if you'll need any additional documents.

Just because you are going over the bridge to get a better view, or a better photo, doesn't mean you won't be stopped, questioned or even searched – either upon entering Canada or upon re-entering the US. ■

and take your time exploring. The fare is $4/2 for adults/kids.

Currency Prices in Canada are routinely given in Canadian dollars, but most businesses accept US currency. Exchange rates vary widely, however, and banks – believe it or not – give the best rates. Credit-card exchange rates are also fair. See Money in the Facts for the Visitor chapter for more information.

Queen Victoria Park
While the American side can boast of offering the most thrilling proximity to the falls, the Canadians can rightly claim the best panorama. The long perspective across the river is magnificent and perhaps easier to take in, like a long leisurely breath – as opposed to the powerful gasp of the roaring water at the American vantage point.

In addition to the various tours (like *Maid of the Mist*, among others), the *Victoria Park Dining Room & Cafeteria* (☎ (905) 356-2217), affords a great view of the falls, and the cafeteria food is very good and reasonably priced.

Scenic Drive
The Canadian government has developed a beautiful scenic parkway (the Niagara Parkway) along the Niagara River north to Lake Ontario, and it is well worth the time.

Again, if you are driving a rental car from the US to Canada, mention this to the rental company which may provide you with additional documents for the car.

Other Things to See & Do
Close to the river, Niagara Falls itself is lined with fast food spots and hotels; traffic signals and neon lights are a sharp contrast to the falls. Nevertheless, the town can be inviting and the people helpful.

Lundy's Lane Historical Museum (☎ (905) 358-5082), 5810 Ferry St, takes its name from one of the bloodier battles of the War of 1812; the 1814 battle is remembered here, along with military exhibits and Seneca artifacts. The museum is open daily from May through November from 9 am to

4 pm, and Monday through Friday from noon to 4 pm the rest of the year.

The **Imax Theater** (☎ (905) 374-4629), 6170 Buchanan Ave, is home to the spectacular giant screen (six stories tall), which – among other things – dramatizes (and occasionally eulogizes) the daredevils, tightrope walkers and others of questionable decision-making powers, who have pitted their wits and bodies against the power and splendor of the falls. Imax is open daily July and August from 10 am to 9 pm; daily in March, May, September and October from 11 am to 8 pm; and daily with limited hours the rest of the year. Admission is $8/7/6 for adults/seniors and kids 12 to 18/kids five to 11).

The **Niagara Parks Botanical Gardens & Horticulture School** (☎ (905) 356-8554) is five miles north of the town of Niagara Falls on the Niagara Parkway, and operated by the Niagara Parks Commission year round from dawn to dusk. Free admission.

The **Guinness World of Records Museum** (☎ (905) 356-2299), 4943 Clifton Hill, is like walking through the book; you can stand face to face with the tallest, fastest and most ridiculous. Open year round and daily from 9 am to midnight during the summer; slightly shorter hours other months. Admission is $7/6/4 for adults/seniors and students/kids six to 12.

Getting There & Away
See Niagara Falls, NY, for information.

BUFFALO
New York state's second largest city, Buffalo (population 328,000), is not a major tourist destination, but it is a city of uncommon historical interest and magnificent architecture. This famous port city is located on Lake Erie in the far northwestern corner of the state, 20 miles from Niagara Falls and a few minutes from Canada by the Peace Bridge. It is Buffalo's proximity to Canada that is partly responsible for the recent boom to the city's economy. With the passage of the North American Free Trade Agreement (NAFTA), tariffs between the US and

Canada are being phased out, and Buffalo is once again becoming a major trading center. In addition, the city continues to be a manufacturing center, producing glass, rubber, auto parts, machinery and medical instruments. The economic boom is helping to fund a major renovation of the city's downtown and neighborhoods. The city recently added a second visitors' bureau, in fact, to help newcomers get around.

Historic buildings – from early skyscrapers to 19th-century residences – are perhaps Buffalo's greatest treasure. Only Chicago boasts a larger collection of build-

ings by American's foremost architects, Frank Lloyd Wright, Louis Sullivan and Henry Hobson Richardson. (Coincidentally perhaps, Buffalo is closer to Chicago than to New York City.) In addition, Buffalo's park system – the first of its kind in the US – was designed by the renowned landscape architect, Frederick Law Olmsted.

Buffalo is an interesting town to explore, and its moderately priced accommodations and accessibility to Niagara Falls make it a good stopping over place in western New York. Of course, if you're stopping over in the winter, be prepared for not only the

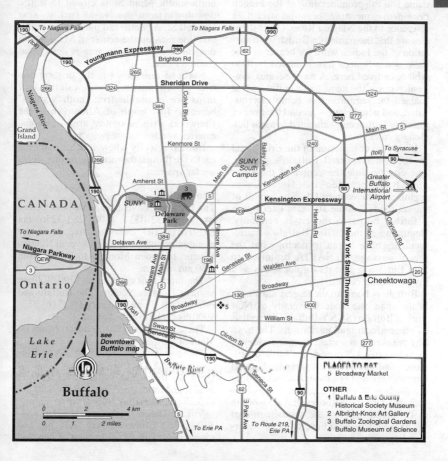

PLACES TO EAT
5   Broadway Market

OTHER
1   Buffalo & Erie County
    Historical Society Museum
2   Albright-Knox Art Gallery
3   Buffalo Zoological Gardens
4   Buffalo Museum of Science

snow, but the inevitable conversation it generates – especially how much heavier it is over in Syracuse.

History

The town of Buffalo was originally a French settlement, established in 1758. In 1800, the Holland Land Co purchased the land and made plans for a town to be called New Amsterdam. The settlers, however, demanded that the town be called Buffalo.

The derivation of the name is unclear. The most romantic explanation is that the name is a mispronunciation of the French *beau fleuve,* meaning 'beautiful stream,' a reference to the Niagara River. Other theories are that the name is a British mistranslation of the Indian word for beaver or that there was a Seneca Indian named Buffalo who once lived here. A more serious suggestion traces the name to the buffaloes that roamed the region before being exterminated, and which were – around the time of the early settlement – attracted to a salt lick along a creek.

It was the completion of the Erie Canal in 1825 that spurred Buffalo's growth. The city became the center of the shipping trade between the Great Lakes region and the eastern US. The arrival of the railroads – some 10 years later – was a further boost to the city's economy. Beginning in the 1970s, Buffalo's manufacturing base began to decline, but the recent passage of NAFTA promises to help Buffalo regain its former status as a major trading center.

Buffalo is home to the largest university in the state, the State University of New York at Buffalo (SUNY-Buffalo), as well as 17 other educational institutions. The town boasts several important former residents, including two US presidents, Millard Fillmore and Grover Cleveland. Samuel Clemens resided briefly in Buffalo, editing the *Buffalo Morning Express.* It was also here that Theodore Roosevelt was sworn in as US president after the assassination of William McKinley at the city's Pan-American Exposition in 1901.

Orientation

Buffalo's major streets radiate outward from its downtown business district. Because Lake Erie forms the city's western and southern borders, most of the city's major streets begin in the downtown area and run to the north and the east. Niagara Square serves as a point of orientation in the downtown. The visitors bureau and city hall are located nearby.

From Niagara Square, Niagara St branches out to the northwest and Delaware Ave to the north. Main St is three blocks east of Delaware Ave and runs north-south. Main St is closed to traffic downtown from the Naval Park to near Goodell St. A Metro rail public transportation line runs up the center of Main St and this car-free pedestrian area is designated Buffalo Place.

North of downtown is the historic district of Allentown. Good walking tour maps are available from both visitors' bureaus. Just north of Allentown is the Elmwood strip, a trendy area of shops, eateries and bookstores.

Buffalo is a city where it helps to have a car to see things; the most interesting sights are far apart.

Information

The Buffalo Convention & Visitors Center (☎ (716) 852-0511, (800) 283-3256, fax 852-0131), 107 Delaware Ave, is on the ground floor of the Statler Tower at Niagara Square. It's open Monday to Friday from 8:30 am to 5 pm.

The main post office is at 1200 William St, near Niagara Square. The Buffalo and Erie County Public Library (☎ (716) 858-8900) is on Lafayette Square.

There are at least half a dozen banks on Main St, downtown.

There is a AAA office (☎ (716) 634-7900) at 976 Delaware Ave just south of Utica St. It has maps and travel services available Monday to Friday from 8:30 am to 5:30 pm, Saturday from 9 am to 1 pm.

Village Green Bookstore (☎ (716) 884-1200), 765 Elmwood Ave, is a big and roomy spot with an assortment of new and

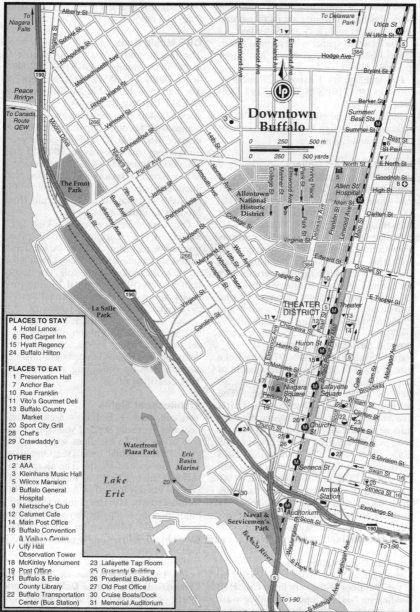

Downtown Buffalo

0   250   500 m
0   250   500 yards

PLACES TO STAY
4 Hotel Lenox
6 Red Carpet Inn
15 Hyatt Regency
24 Buffalo Hilton

PLACES TO EAT
1 Preservation Hall
7 Anchor Bar
10 Rue Franklin
11 Vito's Gourmet Deli
13 Buffalo Country
    Market
20 Sport City Grill
28 Chef's
29 Crawdaddy's

OTHER
2 AAA
3 Kleinhans Music Hall
5 Wilcox Mansion
8 Buffalo General
   Hospital
9 Nietzsche's Club
12 Calumet Cafe
14 Main Post Office
16 Buffalo Convention
    & Visitors Center
17 City Hall
    Observation Tower
18 McKinley Monument
19 Post Office
21 Buffalo & Erie
    County Library
22 Buffalo Transportation
    Center (Bus Station)

23 Lafayette Tap Room
25 Guaranty Building
26 Prudential Building
27 Old Post Office
30 Cruise Boats/Dock
31 Memorial Auditorium

used books, a good newsstand and long hours; open daily from 7 am to 11 pm and until midnight on Friday and Saturday.

The local newspaper is the *Buffalo News*; *Metro Weekend* is the giveaway arts paper in town.

For laundry, try Kenmore Cleaners & Coin-Op (☎ (716) 875-8270), 3197 Delaware Ave.

Buffalo General Hospital (☎ (716) 859-5600) is at 100 High St near the corner of Goodrich and Ellicott Sts.

Albright-Knox Art Gallery

Housed in a wonderful Greek Revival building adjacent to the site of the 1901 Pan-American Expo, the gallery (☎ (716) 882-8700), 1285 Elmwood Ave, is best known for its collection of 20th century art including works from all the major currents from abstract expressionism to pop art. The collection also contains paintings and sculpture from other historic periods. It's open from Tuesday to Saturday from 11 am to 5 pm; Sunday from noon to 5 pm. Admission is $4/3 for adults/seniors and children. Metered parking is available.

Naval & Servicemen's Park

Naval Park (☎ (716) 847-1773) on Lake Erie at Main St, displays scale models of ships, airplanes and armored vehicles, as well as some of the real things. The destroyer USS *The Sullivans*, named after five brothers who went down with their ship near Guadalcanal during WWII, is here, as are the guided missile cruiser USS *Little Rock* and the submarine USS *Croaker*. Everything is docked on a small inlet off of Lake Erie just south of I-190, where you'll also find a small museum. Open daily from April 1 to October 31 from 10 am to 6 pm; in November it's weekends only. Admission for adults/kids six to 16 is $6/3.50.

City Hall Observation Tower

Visitors are welcome to take an elevator up to the 28th floor of the very large City Hall building on Niagara Square and then walk three flights to the observation tower

(☎ (716) 851-5991). It's free and open from 9 am to 3 pm.

QRS Music Rolls

The largest and oldest player-piano roll maker in the country is QRS (☎ (716) 885-4600, (800) 247-6557), 1026 Niagara St. The factory is located in the historic 1885 Buffalo Electric Railway Co generating station building. In the 1920s, when player pianos were far more popular than they are today, QRS made 10 million rolls a year. Today they make between 200,000 and 300,000 rolls annually. Guests are welcome to tour the small factory and watch the production process. Tours are limited to 15, and take place at 10 am and 2 pm from Monday to Friday and cost $2.

On the premises is a one-of-a-kind 1912 Melville-Clark marking piano, a piano used as a recording device. A musician would play a tune on the piano, causing the music to be marked on the roll. The American Society of Mechanical Engineering designated the machine a national historical mechanical engineering landmark.

One-song piano rolls are on sale for $7.25. QRS also sells player pianos, which are priced at about $6500 new, but better deals for used pianos in need of refinishing are available by consulting western New York classified ads.

Architectural Sights

You can explore Buffalo's architectural treasures in greater depth if you take advantage of one of the excellent self-guided or guided architectural tours (see Organized Tours) sponsored by the Theodore Roosevelt Inaugural National Historic Site. If you are already versed in American architecture and would prefer going it alone, you might pick up a copy of Reyner Banham's book *Buffalo Architecture: A Guide* published by MIT Press and available in many local bookstores.

Buffalo has the largest concentration of Frank Lloyd Wright homes outside of Chicago, all located near **Delaware Park** (north of the downtown area) which was designed by landscape architect Frederick

Law Olmsted. Most of these residences are privately owned except the **Darwin Martin House**, 125 Jewett Pkwy at the corner of Summit, which is owned by SUNY Buffalo (☎ (716) 831-3485). The others include the William Heath House, 76 Soldiers Place at the corner of Bird Ave; the George Barton House, 118 Summit; Gardiner's Cottage, 285 Woodward Ave; and the Walter Davidson House, 57 Tillinghast Place. The homes can be distinguished from others in the neighborhood by their sleek and strong horizontal lines.

Frank Lloyd Wright's mentor, architect Louis Sullivan, and his partner Dankmar Adler, designed the **Prudential Building** on Church St. Sullivan is generally regarded as the father of the skyscraper. One of the finest examples of early skyscraper design is Sullivan's **Guaranty Building** at 28 Church St near Pearl. Built in 1895, the building was beautifully restored in 1983. Tours are available.

There are a number of other interesting buildings downtown, such as the art-deco **City Hall** on Niagara Square, the **Old Post Office** on Ellicott and Swan Sts, and the former **Buffalo Savings Bank** building at Main and Huron Sts. Henry Hobson Richardson designed nine of the buildings at the **Buffalo State Psychiatric Hospital**, 400 Forest Ave. These red sandstone buildings are excellent examples of the Romanesque revival that Richardson championed in the latter half of the 19th century. The **McKinley Monument**, designed by Carrère and Hastings and sculpted by A Phimister Proctor, is in the middle of Niagara Square.

The beautiful residential neighborhood of **Allentown** is located south of the intersection of Delaware and North Sts. The streets of this national historic district are lined with restored 19th century homes, galleries and restaurants. Walk past the 1869 **Dorsheimer Mansion** at 434 Delaware, which was designed by Henry Hobson Richardson, and the 1899 **Butler Mansion**, at 672 Delaware, designed by Stanford White.

The Finnish architects Eliel and Eero Saarinen designed the modernist **Kleinhans Music Hall** (☎ (716) 883-3560) on Symphony Circle. The building is famous for its modern curving lines and acoustical excellence.

F Scott Fitzgerald's childhood home is 29 Irving St. Mark Twain lived at 472 Delaware Ave while working for the *Buffalo Morning Express*. The **Wilcox Mansion** (☎ (716) 884-0095), 641 Delaware Ave, now a national historic site and museum, was the site of Teddy Roosevelt's inauguration following President William McKinley's assassination. Admission is $3/2/1 for adults/seniors/kids.

Other Things to See & Do

The **Buffalo Zoological Gardens** (☎ (716) 837-3900), 300 Parkside Ave, is located in Delaware Park and was part of Frederick Law Olmsted's original design for the park in 1875, making it the third oldest zoo in the country. The 23 acre site is home to a white tiger, rare Indian rhinoceros and, of course, bison. There is also a Lowland gorilla exhibit, a children's zoo and exhibits in the World of Wildlife Building. The zoo is open year round daily from 10 am to 5:30 pm. Admission $5.25/3.15.

The **Buffalo Museum of Science** (☎ (716) 896-5200), 1020 Humboldt Parkway, contains natural science exhibits and activities that allow visitors to investigate the natural world of dinosaurs and insects or unravel the principles of action and reaction. Open Tuesday through Sunday, 10 am to 5 pm. Admission is $5.25/3.25.

The **Buffalo & Erie County Historical Society** (☎ (716) 873-9644), 25 Nottingham Court, is in the building that once served as the New York State Pavilion at the 1901 Pan-American Exposition. Permanent and changing exhibits trace the history of Buffalo and explore the city's diverse cultures and traditions. It's open Tuesday through Saturday from 10 am to 5 pm; $3.50/1.50 for adults/kids seven to 15.

The **Burgwardt Bicycle Museum** (☎ (716) 662-3853/7882), 3943 N Buffalo Rd in nearby Orchard Park, is the only museum in the country devoted exclusively to bicycles. There are 300 bikes and other related paraphernalia on display, as well as exhibits tracing the history of bicycling. From mid-May to mid-September, it's open daily 11 am to 5 pm. The rest of the year it's open Monday, Friday and Saturday from 11 am to 5 pm and on Sunday from 1:30 to 5 pm.

The **Original American Kazoo Factory** (☎ (716) 992-3960) is about 30 minutes south of town in Eden, at 8703 S Main St. It's the only metal kazoo factory in the world. This is a one-of-a-kind place, a combination factory, museum and gift shop. It is open year round, Monday through Saturday from 10 am to 5 pm and Sunday from 12 to 5 pm. The admission is free.

Organized Tours

If you're without a car, you might want to consider a tour, especially if you want to get a glimpse of nearby Niagara Falls.

Gray Line (☎ (716) 625-9214) gives tours of Buffalo and Niagara Falls on both sides of the border from May 1 to mid-October. A five hour daytime tour that goes quickly around Buffalo and then up to Niagara Falls is $41, and a four hour evening tour is $34.

Trolley Tours of Buffalo (☎ (716) 885-8825) offers a 1½ to two hour tour of Buffalo sites from mid-April to mid-October for $12.50.

The Theodore Roosevelt Inaugural National Historic Site (☎ (716) 884-0095), 641 Delaware Ave in the Wilcox Mansion, offers **architectural walking tours** of the downtown and of the historic Allentown residential neighborhood. Tours leave from the Wilcox Mansion and range from hour-long, self-guided cassette tours offered year round, to guided tours for a minimum of six people, offered April to October. All tours cost $5.

You can also see Buffalo from Lake Erie or the Niagara River on a **cruise** boat. *Miss Buffalo* and *Niagara Clipper* (☎ (716) 856-6696) depart from 79 Marine Dr, adjacent to Naval & Servicemen's Park. *Miss*

Buffalo runs narrated sightseeing tours through the canal, taking in the sights around Lake Erie; *Niagara Clipper* sails on the upper Niagara River and around Grand Island. From May to September cruises depart throughout the afternoon and evening. A two hour tour costs $7.50; music, lunch, dinner and murder mystery cruises run from $14.50 to $41.

Special Events

The Western New York Snow Sculpting Competition (☎ (716) 856-3150) takes place in February. Shakespeare in the Park (☎ (716) 829-3742) has free, fully staged Shakespeare performed every night except Wednesday from July to August.

Places to Stay – bottom & middle

There are a few cheap motels on Main St above the downtown area. The *Red Carpet Inn* (☎ (716) 882-3491), 1159 Main St at Best St, is near the Anchor Bar in what some people consider a marginal neighborhood, especially late at night. Single/double rooms range from $35/50. There is also a shared kitchen.

Near the airport, there are several places to stay, including an *EconoLodge* (☎ (716) 634-1500, (800) 932-0291), 7200 Transit Rd. Single weekday/end rates are $42/48; double rates are $46/54. The *Microtel-Lancaster Hotel* (☎ (716) 633-6200), (800) 648-9880), 50 Freeman Rd, has a roomy lobby, good parking and clean rooms. Summer/winter rates range from $36 to $52 for singles or doubles.

The *Hotel Lenox* (☎ (716) 884-1700, (800) 825-3666), 140 North St, is an old classic in the city's historic Allentown district. The good-sized rooms are furnished with mismatched, but sturdy furniture. There is a student rate of $49 for up to four people in a room. Otherwise singles/doubles are $59/69; fancier suites go for $80/90 with kitchenette.

Places to Stay – top end

The *Hyatt Regency* (☎ (716) 856-1234), 2 Fountain Plaza, is truly a luxurious place located in the theater district on the Buffalo

Place pedestrian mall along Main St. The brick and stone building was originally an office tower that was converted into a hotel in 1984. Even if you don't stay here, it's a fun place to explore. The lobby is a plant-filled atrium. There are three restaurants, a bar, indoor pool and sun garden. Rooms are equally luxurious and run from about $89 to $155.

The *Buffalo Hilton* (☎ (716) 845-5100), 120 Church St at the corner of Lower Terrace, is a luxurious complex overlooking Lake Erie and the entire downtown. Year round rates range from $90 to $170; ask about discounts and weekend specials.

Places to Eat
In culinary terms, Buffalo is best known for its 'Buffalo-style' chicken wings and 'beef on weck.' Buffalo wings are covered in a spicy red chili sauce (unlike the honey-mustard sauce of lesser-known Rochester wings) and are served with creamy blue cheese dressing and celery sticks. Beef on weck is sliced roast beef on *kummelweck*, a hard roll impregnated with salt and sometimes caraway seeds. While both items are featured on menus throughout the city, there is a particular restaurant associated with each of these culinary inventions.

Budget & Moderate The *Anchor Bar* (☎ (716) 886-8920), 1047 Main St at E North St, claims to have invented Buffalo chicken wings. Located in a marginal neighborhood, the bar still packs in the crowds on the weekends. (Oscillating video cameras scan the parking lot and nervous bar patrons watch their cars on indoor video screens.)

Inside the red-brick building is a tin-ceilinged bar backed with a hundred baseball caps and other memorabilia. You can also dine in one of the two modern – but less imaginative – dining rooms. Wings come in single and double orders ($5/7). For lunch, the restaurant serves – in addition to Buffalo chicken wings – sandwiches and Italian specialties, including pizza, spaghetti, meatballs and vegetarian lasagna, all ranging from $4 to $6. Dinners

include homemade ravioli, chicken and fish selections, barbecued ribs and – of course – Buffalo chicken wings. Dinner will run you from $4 to $14.

On Thursday from June to September you can stop by the *Buffalo Country Market* (☎ (716) 856-3150) between 8 am and 2:30 pm to pick up fresh produce and baked goods. The market is on Buffalo Place in the theater district, just off Main St between Chippewa and Tupper Sts.

Broadway Market (☎ (716) 893-0705) is in the heart of the city's Polish neighborhood, 999 Broadway at Fillmore St. In this indoor market, small concessions serve an array of ethnic specialties.

Vito's Gourmet Deli (☎ (716) 852-5650), 206 S Elmwood Ave at the corner of Chippewa, sells 33 different combination sandwiches for $3.50 to $5.50. Choices of fillings include eggplant, salami, asiago cheese and artichoke spread, or sopresatta, provolone, roasted peppers and romaine lettuce. You can choose from one of their combinations or design your own sandwich. The deli is open Monday to Thursday from 10 am to 9 pm; Friday from 10 am to midnight; Saturday from 10 am to 3 pm.

Chef's (☎ (716) 856-9170), 291 Seneca St at Michigan St, is an Italian restaurant located a few blocks east of Main St in an industrial neighborhood. This is another Buffalo institution (like the Anchor Bar). The main building is an unpretentious three-story brownstone connected to two one-story additions. The decor is simple; the food is good. Dishes (most with tomato sauce) are offered in small/large portions ranging from $5 and $8. Typical dishes are spaghetti with meatballs or sausages, or ravioli stuffed with meatballs, mushrooms or sausages. Open Monday through Saturday, from 11:45 am to 9 pm.

The *Sport City Grill* (☎ (716) 849-1200) is located in a tall building at the corner of Church and Main Sts. Owned by former Buffalo Bills football quarterback Jim Kelly, it's a high-ceilinged bar/restaurant decorated with plastic cases filled with sports memorabilia and artifacts. At the center of it all is a big square bar with several televisions topped with a larger-than-life football. Sport City also sports good bar food. You can eat potatoes stuffed with shrimp, steak or chicken for $6 to $8. The pizzas baked in a hickory-fired oven run $6 to $8, steaks are $13, barbecue sandwiches $5 and ribs in three sizes, 6/12/24, are $7.45/13/25.

Preservation Hall (☎ (716) 884-4242), 532 Elmwood Ave, on the Elmwood strip, is a great vegetarian cafe and bakery, small and homey. Dishes range from pita sandwiches to Thai veggies over rice to spicy chili, all in the $4 to $7 range. They also serve an afternoon tea weekdays from 3 to 5 pm. Open daily from 10 am to 9 pm; weekends from 9 am.

Top End *Crawdaddy's* (☎ (716) 856-9191) is on the water near Navy Park at 2 Templeton Terrace. You'll recognize the typical waterfront decor: wooden exterior and roomy wood-beamed interior. There are several bars, an outdoor patio and a DJ Thursday to Saturday nights. Lunch includes Cobb salad ($6.45), seafood Caesar salad ($9), Jamaican seafood salad ($9) or blackened chicken sandwich ($6). Dinner selections include larger versions of the same salads for $13 to $15, as well as pasta with lobster, shrimp and scallops for $14 to $19 and other seafood dishes from $15 to $20.

If you want to splurge and enjoy excellent French cuisine, try *Rue Franklin* (☎ (716) 852-4416), 341 Franklin St, a bit north of downtown. Appetizers like rabbit galantine or fois gras terrine are around $7; entrees include trout with leeks, veal provençal and lamb shanks, and prices range from $16 to $21. Open Tuesday through Saturday for dinner only from 5:30 to 10 pm.

Entertainment

Theater Buffalo's theater district extends along Main St between Tupper and Chippewa Sts. A few theaters are located to the west, on Franklin and Delaware Sts.

You can make reservations from most hotels/motels, as well as through Ticketmaster (☎ (716) 852-2000).

The *Alleyway Theatre* (☎ (716) 852-2600), 1 Curtain Up Alley, is a small, intimate theater company that showcases new plays.

The *Buffalo Ensemble Theatre* (☎ (716) 855-2225), 220 Delaware Ave, is a small professional theater. Their repertory includes both new and classic works.

The *Paul Robeson Theater* (☎ (716) 884-2013), 350 Masten Ave, is in the African American Cultural Center, between Utica and Ferry Sts, east of the downtown area.

The *Theater of Youth* (☎ (716) 856-4410) at the Franklin St Theatre, 282 Franklin St, has staged plays for children and young adults for 20 years.

The *Ujima Theater Co*, in the Theater Loft (☎ (716) 883-0380), 545 Elmwood Ave, is a professional company dedicated to performing works by black and other playwrights.

Shea's Performing Arts Center (☎ (716) 847-0850, fax 847-1644), 646 Main St, is an enormous, classic theater where the best-of-Broadway concerts, opera and dance performances are staged.

Other theaters include the *Katharine Cornell Theatre* (☎ (716) 645-2038) at the Ellicott Complex of SUNY ('Buff State').

The *Studio Arena Theatre* (☎ (716) 856-5650), 710 Main St, performs modern and contemporary works.

Classical Music The *Buffalo Philharmonic Orchestra* (☎ (716) 885-5000) performs at the Saarinen-designed Kleinhans Music Hall (☎ (716) 883-3560), Symphony Circle. Kleinhans is one of five acoustically perfect concert halls in the country.

The *Lancaster Opera House* (☎ (716) 683-1776), 21 Central Ave, is a restored 350 seat, turn-of-the-century theater that hosts plays, musicals and concerts.

The *Greater Buffalo Opera Company* (☎ (716) 852-2073, fax 852-2075) is a local opera company that stages performances at Shea's Performing Arts Center (see above).

Dance The *Empire State Ballet* (☎ (716) 856-8311), 745 Main St, is a nationally-recognized touring company.

Clubs *Calumet Cafe* (☎ (716) 855-2220), 54 W Chippewa St, in the theater district, features top jazz performers in a classic bistro atmosphere. They also serve dinner on Thursday, Friday and Saturday nights.

Nietzsche's (☎ (716) 886-8539), 248 Allen St, showcases popular rock and blues bands and has a good little dance floor. Cover ranges from a free open-mike night (usually Monday) to about $5, depending on the act.

Lafayette Tap Room (☎ (716) 885-8800), 391 Washington Ave, is a good jazz and blues club.

Spectator Sports

Buffalo is a sports town. Get tickets either from Ticketmaster (☎ (716) 852-5000) or from the stadiums.

The Buffalo Bills football team (☎ (716) 649-0015) plays at Rich Stadium in Orchard Park from September to December, barring yet another trip to the Superbowl. This team is well known for playing great games until the national championship comes along.

Memorial Auditorium (☎ (716) 856-7300), 140 Main St, hosts NHL hockey's Buffalo Sabres (October to April), the Buffalo Bandits lacrosse team (January to March) and the Buffalo Blizzard soccer team (November to March).

The Buffalo Bisons minor league baseball team (☎ (716) 852-4700) plays at downtown Pilot Field, Washington and Seneca Sts, throughout the spring and summer.

Getting There & Away

Air The Greater Buffalo international airport (☎ (716) 632-3115), Genesee St, Cheektowaga, is served by American, Business Express, Continental, Delta, Mohawk, Northwest, TW Express, United and US Air.

Some average roundtrip fares are from Buffalo to Philadelphia, $228; to New York City (JFK), $238; to Chicago, $204.

Bus The Buffalo Transportation Center, 181 Ellicott St at the corner of Church St, is served by Empire Trailways (☎ (716) 852-1750) and Greyhound (☎ (716) 855-7533).

The Niagara Frontier Transportation Authority bus system (NFTA; ☎ (716) 285-7211, 285-9319) runs bus No 40 between Niagara Falls and Buffalo every day. Express bus No 60 runs between Niagara Falls and Buffalo five times a day from Monday to Friday. Two express buses leave Niagara Falls for Buffalo before 7 am and three buses leave Buffalo for Niagara Falls roughly between 4:30 and 5 pm. The fare for both buses is $1.70.

Train Amtrak stops at the downtown Buffalo Exchange Station (☎ (716) 683-8440), Exchange and Oak Sts; and at the Depew Station (☎ (716) 856-2075), 55 Dick Rd in nearby Cheektowaga, near the airport (about 16 miles from downtown).

A cab from Depew Station to downtown Buffalo is about $20 (see Getting Around, below).

Car Buffalo is reached by I-90 from the east and south and by I-190 from Niagara Falls to the north. The QEW in Canada to the west leads to the Peace Bridge over the Niagara River.

Several major car rental companies are at the airport, including Hertz, Alamo, National and Avis.

Getting Around

To/From the Airport Bus No 24 runs from the airport to the Buffalo Transportation Center.

The ITA Buffalo Airport Shuttle (☎ (800) 551-9369) runs between Buffalo airport and major hotels and the bus terminal for $11/18 one way/roundtrip. Buses leave the airport every hour on the hour.

A taxi is about $22.

Bus & Light Rail The Metro bus and rail system (☎ (716) 855-7211) has the same fare structure. The basic fare is $1.10 in exact change and you add 20¢ for each zone crossed beyond the basic zone. On the bus, you pay when boarding, but on the rail line you buy a ticket from a self-serve machine before boarding. If you're caught by roving inspectors without a ticket on the rail line, you get fined $20. The rail is free to/from the six southernmost above-ground stops on the line, from the theater district to the last stop south on Main St, almost at Lake Erie. North of the theater district stop, continuing to the SUNY Buffalo campus, the train goes underground and riders start paying. Buffalo's buses run from about 5 am to midnight; light rail runs from 6:30 am to 11:30 pm.

Taxi Taxi companies include:

Affordable Taxi	(716) 834-0007
Airport Taxi Service	(716) 633-8318
	(800) 649-8166
City Service Taxi	(716) 852-4000
	(800) 439-7006
Liberty Cab	(716) 877-7111
	(800) 464-7111

CHAUTAUQUA

The town of Chautauqua (pronounced sha-TAW-kwah) is 65 miles southwest of Buffalo on Lake Chautauqua in western New York's bucolic wine and farm country. This small town of 4600 is best known for its Chautauqua Institution, which hosts lectures, concerts, workshops, dance and theater for approximately 180,000 visitors each summer. The institution occupies 856 acres and has been designated a National Historic District because of its small winding streets illuminated by gas lights, its beautifully maintained Victorian buildings and gardens, and because the attendant, tranquil atmosphere is a throwback to a bygone era. Between attending lectures, taking music classes or swimming, visitors loll about on front porches and garden benches. Cars are banned (except for loading and emergencies), as is alcohol. Life here is as unstructured as you wish to make it. The psychologist William James, brother to Henry James, referred to Chautauqua – in a less than complimentary

tone – as a 'middle-class paradise, without a sin, without a victim, without a blot, without a tear.'

The institution does attempt to appeal to a broad audience through its diverse course offerings, ranging from writing to puppetry, from personal interaction and adjustment to archery. Lectures and entertainment are also geared to attract people of different ages and backgrounds.

You can visit the town in one day, but most visitors arrange for longer stays of a weekend, a week or longer. In fact, many visitors return year after year, bringing with them children and grandchildren. To receive information about the upcoming summer session, a schedule of entertainment and the various packages offered by the institution, write or call them at the Chautauqua Institution (☎ (716) 357-6200, (800) 836-2737), Chautauqua, NY 14722.

History

Chautauqua was founded in 1874 by Lewis Miller, an Ohio inventor and manufacturer and John Heyl Vincent, a Pennsylvania Methodist minister, as a vacation school for Sunday-school teachers. The institution quickly became a place for the public discussion of a wide range of contemporary issues. Traveling tent 'chautauquas,' not actually connected to the institution, toured the country in the early 20th century presenting lectures, concerts and sermons. William Jennings Bryan appeared on the chautauqua circuit many times to give his *Cross of Gold* speech. The Chautauqua Institution grew and eventually adopted its present mission: to encourage and present discussions of religious, social and political issues in a community environment.

Orientation

The town is situated between Route 394 and Chautauqua Lake. There are five gates to the institution, but visitors must enter through the main gate. At the center of the community is Bestor Plaza. Around the plaza are the Colonnade, a building housing the institution's offices, the post office, the library and a few restaurants.

Brick Walk extends along the north side of the plaza. One block east of the plaza is the amphitheater. Going around the lake, little Jamestown (population 34,000) seems to be an urban center compared to most of the hamlets facing the lake, such as Bemus Point, a recreation and boating hub.

Information
The institution's business offices (☎ (716) 357-6200, (800) 836-2787) are in the Colonnade building. There is an information desk in the Colonnade lobby (☎ (716) 357-6257) and at the main gate (☎ (716) 357-6263) on the way in.

The post office (☎ (716) 357-3275) on Bestor Plaza is open in-season from 9 am to 5 pm weekdays and 9 am to noon on Saturday with reduced hours off-season. Throughout the summer, the *Chautauquan Daily* newspaper is published out of the post office building. The institution bookstore is downstairs from the post office.

The Smith Memorial Library (☎ (716) 357-6296) on the plaza is open year round. Summer hours are Monday to Saturday from 9 am to 5 pm and Sunday from 2 to 4 pm. There are exhibits on Chautauqua's past in the library and Chautauqua historian Alfreda L Irwin has her offices there. Her book *Three Taps of the Gavel: Pledge to the Future, the Chautauqua Story* (Chautauqua Institution, 1987) is the institution's definitive history.

The use of cars on the grounds is restricted. Parking lots near the entrance gates charge $3.50 a day and long-term parking is available at the main gate parking office (☎ (716) 357-6225).

Activities & Entertainment
Everyone over 13 who enters the institution, including residents, must buy a gate ticket at the main gate. The ticket entitles its bearer to attend every event with the exception of operas, plays and special study courses. These require an additional ticket or fee.

Tickets are free on Sunday, in keeping with Chautauqua's Christian roots. Otherwise prices for adults/children 13 to 17 are as follows during their season from mid-June through August:

a day from 8 am to 8 pm	. . . $9
an evening after 5 pm	. . . . . $18
a day and evening	. . . . $26
a weekend	. . . . $38/17.50
one week	. . . . $140/56
two weeks	. . . . $260/67
three weeks	. . . . $390/75
four weeks	. . . . $515/85
five weeks	. . . . $640/92
six weeks to	. . . . $760/101
nine weeks (full season)	. . . $760/125

Admission to large events in the amphitheater is first-come, first-served and popular performances and lectures fill up quickly. The amphitheater is a 5000 seat, roofed outdoor structure that houses an enormous pipe organ.

Lectures The lecture series at Chautauqua enjoys national renown. President Franklin Delano Roosevelt gave his *I Hate War* speech at the Chautauqua Amphitheater in 1936. Nine other US presidents, from Ulysses S Grant to Bill Clinton, have lectured here, as have Leo Tolstoy and William Jennings Bryan. Today, every weekday morning during the nine week season a different lecture is given in the amphitheater. Lectures are organized around broad weekly topic headings, such as racism and ethnicity, emerging democracies, science and technology and ethics and public life. The lectures are followed by question-and-answer sessions. In addition, the Chautauqua Literary & Scientific Circle invites authors to speak on their work, as does the School of Art.

Chautauqua Literary & Scientific Circle
Founded in 1878, the Circle is a four year home-study program. In its early years, the Circle served as correspondence courses do today. In particular, they reached out to men and women from small rural towns who had little access to formal advanced study. The Circle also played an important role in the creation of adult education

programs in the US. Today, each graduating class comes to the **Hall of Philosophy**, an open-air plaza, for a graduation ceremony. On the floor of the Hall are tile plaques representing many Circle classes of the past.

Music The *Chautauqua Symphony Orchestra* is comprised of American and international musicians and is conducted by Uriel Siegel, as well as guest conductors. The institution also presents a nine-concert chamber music series, guest recitals and student recitals.

Larger concerts and performances take place in the amphitheater. Past performers include Glenn Miller, Peter, Paul & Mary, 10,000 Maniacs and Natalie Cole.

The *Chautauqua Opera* stages four operas each season. Tickets are $12.50 to $28 or all four for $72 to $97.

Dance Jean-Pierre Bonnedoux, a former dancer with the New York City Ballet and the Paris Opera, is the artistic director of the *Chautauqua Dance Co*. Each season they put on performances of modern dance and ballet.

Theater The *Chautauqua Conservatory Theater Co* presents four plays each season in Normal Hall. Tickets are available at the Opera/Theater Ticket Office at the Main Gate (☎ (716) 357-6250) and cost $8.

Religion There are morning Christian services most days of the week. On Sunday, sermons are given by visiting theologians. Throughout the season, lectures and discussions on religion and spirituality are far more ecumenical. Past speakers have included Norman Vincent Peale, Jesse Jackson, Elie Wiesel and Coretta Scott King.

Summer Schools The institution houses four schools of fine and performing arts: for art, dance, music and drama. Auditions are required and competition is rigorous. There are also over 200 **Special Studies**

courses (☎ (716) 357-6234/6255) which do not require participants to audition. These one-week courses include studies in literature, languages, art, dance and music. They cost $40 to $60.

Parents who bring their children to Chautauqua can enroll them in a variety of programs geared to kids of different ages and interests. There are day care, children's school, boys' and girls' clubs and youth activities. Contact the Chautauqua Institution business office (☎ (716) 357-6200) for current listings.

Recreation The Sports Club (☎ (716) 357-6281) on the lake rents sailboats and canoes, and there is also dock space for those who bring their own boats (☎ (716) 357-6288). The club also fields a number of softball, volleyball and basketball teams in the Chautauqua leagues.

The Chautauqua Yacht Club (☎ (716) 357-4001) has weekly races during the summer and teaches sailing through the Special Studies program (☎ (716) 357-6355).

There are four public swimming beaches (☎ (716) 357-6277/6309) on the lake within the grounds of the institution and eight tennis courts near the main gate.

Bike Rent (☎ (716) 357-5444) does just that on Massey Ave Monday to Saturday from 9 am to 6 pm and Sunday from 11 am to 6 pm.

Palestine Park
The park, which is reflective of the institution's religious beginnings, is a replica of the Holy Land complete with the Sea of Galilee, Dead Sea and other topographical features.

Organized Tours
Narrated bus tours of the institution (☎ (716) 357-6263) cost $3/1 for adults/children.

Places to Stay
The Chautauqua Accommodations Referral Service (☎ (716) 357-6204) can assist you in finding housing for your stay at the

institution. Or, you can drop by the information office in the Colonnade and pick up a copy of the *Accommodations Directory* that is updated before each season. The best budget options are generally rooms in houses or guest houses. At the upper end are the hotels and condos, some of which offer vacation packages ranging from one weekend to one week. The packages include accommodations, a gate ticket and tickets for a selected events. These cost from $125 to $600 depending on length of time and kind of accommodation.

Bottom End *Grace Cottage* (☎ (716) 357-2802, off-season (815) 235-7267), 10 Ames Ave, rents rooms by the day/week for $15 to $30/104 to 400. Guests may use the kitchen.

Rates at *27 Scott* (☎ (716) 357-3011, off-season 484-1438) are $28 to $40 a day. Rooms at *9 Whitfield* (☎ (716) 357-3925, off-season (309) 828-6874) have lake views and run $22 to $45/88 to 190.

If you're a student planning to stay the entire season, check out *CLSC-Alumni Hall* (☎ (716) 357-3105, off-season (814) 432-4474) at the corner of Cookman and Wyeth Sts. Rooms here are only $55 to $65 a week.

Middle The *Gleason* (☎ (716) 357-2595), 12 N Lake Dr, is a large lake-front house with a porch. Daily/weekly rates are $45 to $65/225 to 375.

The *Rose Cottage* (☎ (716) 357-5375), 2 Roberts, is an 1877 cottage located just one house from the amphitheater in the middle of town. Daily rates are $32 to $36.

Lakeside Cottages (☎ (716) 386-2535), 50 Lakeside Dr, has 20 cottages, one row of white, one row of green. The rooms are clean and attractive and are available by the day or week. Daily rates range from $80/100 (for two to four people). Weekly rates range from $450 to $500. There is also a B&B with single/double rooms for $40/50. Open April through October; sometimes longer for the B&B.

Sheldon Hall B&B (☎ (716) 664-4691)

on Main St in the hamlet of Greenhurst five miles west of Route 17 at the Jamestown exit, is a restored turn-of-the-century summer home, once favored by boat captains who dropped in from Lake Erie. Sheldon Hall has a 50 foot boathouse and an upstairs ballroom. There are 10 guest rooms, most with private bath; all include a full breakfast. Prices range from $60 to $100 a night. Open summer only, from Memorial Day to Labor Day.

Top End The *Atheneum Hotel* (pronounced A-thu-NEE-um; ☎ (716) 357-4444, (800) 821-1881) is, for many, a hotel which helps define the Chautauqua experience. The large white-and-green Victorian building overlooks the lake. Originally built in 1881, the hotel was renovated in 1983. The rooms all have high ceilings, and are comfortably furnished in Victorian period reproductions. Room rates include three meals a day (at dinner the hotel suggests 'ladies are to be dressed in their loveliest and gentlemen, neckties and jackets, please'). Single/double rates are $120 to $158/180 to 282. The more expensive rooms have lake views. The hotel offers discounts for longer stays.

Places to Eat

During the summer session, you can pick up fresh produce and baked goods at the farmers' market every Monday through Saturday from 7 to 11 am. The market is located at the main gate building.

The *Festival Market & Deli* (☎ (716) 357-5245) at the corner of Pratt and Ramble next to the Colonnade is open year round. You can buy reasonably priced soup and deli sandwiches here.

Chautauqua Courtyard restaurant next to the post office allows customers to cook food on a hot rock at the table. You can eat here for $10 to $15. You can also sit out front and eat ice cream.

The *Atheneum Hotel* (see above) serves a fixed-price breakfast/lunch/dinner for $13/16/30, and is rather formal. The tradition is to get two desserts with every meal.

The *Italian Fisherman* (☎ (716) 386-7000), on Lakeside Dr, on the lake, has two menus. Inside is a northern Italian fine dining area, with dinners in the $12 to $18 range. More casual and cheaper is the waterfront deck patio with a 'steak-on-the-lake' menu which sports an open grill with sandwiches, chops, burgers and big salads, mostly in the $6 to $10 range. The restaurant is open from mid-April to mid-September, daily from 11:30 am to 10 pm.

Getting There & Around

The Chautauqua Institution is located in the middle of the town of Chautauqua about 65 miles south of Buffalo. Take I-90 to the Westfield exit and then Route 394 to the entrance. From the south it's 16 miles north of Jamestown on Route 394.

There is a free shuttle bus and tram service running around the grounds from 8:20 am to 8:20 pm and after amphitheater and Norton Hall events.

Facts about New Jersey

Alas, New Jersey's unfortunate geographical position next to huge, assured New York City has diminished its place in the wider public consciousness. *Any* state would pale in comparison to the megacity, but the problem is exacerbated by the fact that travelers who pass through efficient Newark airport are exposed to New Jersey's least attractive side. The oil refineries, shipping docks and dirty marshland along the New Jersey Turnpike leading into New York certainly qualifies as the ugliest industrial landscape outside of the Midwestern 'rustbelt' states.

This is the New Jersey of punchlines and snickering asides. But in recent years, the state government has made great and largely successful efforts to emphasize the area's varied pleasures – 127 miles of beaches, thousands of acres of preserved parkland, and many historic sites tied to the nation's colonial history. When New Jersey was rocked in the late '80s by 'brown tide' (pollution-created bacteria) and medical wastes that turned up on beaches, the state swiftly moved to pass some of the nation's toughest laws against off-shore dumping. Those moves, along with winter programs to stem beach erosion, go a long way towards guaranteeing the continued health of the tourism trade, which brings in more than $20 billion a year. On the down side, the gambling mecca of Atlantic City is now getting competition from the Foxwoods casino in Connecticut, and state revenues from gaming are threatened by other planned casinos in upstate New York.

While it's true that New Jersey is both the most densely populated and the most urbanized state in the US, with about 1040 people per sq mile, this statistic is misleading because about two-thirds of the population lives in northern New Jersey within 30 miles of New York City. (Another large population nexus is in the Trenton-Camden area opposite Philadelphia.) In fact, almost a quarter of the state's 7419 sq mile land area is farm and another 40% is forest.

Just 15 miles directly west of the troubled city of Newark, there are pretty suburban towns such as Morristown and large mansion communities like Bedminster, where former First Lady Jacqueline Kennedy Onassis and one-time presidential candidate Steve Forbes purchased large tracts of verdant land. This horse country gives way to sparsely populated land as you head further west toward Pennsylvania. On the Jersey Shore – an area that begins at Atlantic Highlands in the middle of the state and runs south to its tip at Cape May – the population is concentrated within five miles of the ocean, with suburbs and farmland becoming more prevalent as you move further west. Those who explore New Jersey off the beaten track will have little problem agreeing that it really does deserve its nickname, the 'Garden State.'

HISTORY
Original Peoples
New Jersey's original residents were Algonquian people called the Lenni Lenape ('original settlers'), but the European colonists dubbed them the 'Delaware,' after the river where their communities were located. There were probably less than 20,000 Lenni Lenape living in New Jersey when European settlers first arrived in the mid-17th century. By 1758 the remaining Indians had been placed in the Brotherton reservation in Burlington County, one of the first reservations in the New World. In 1802 the Indians on the Brotherton reservation moved to New York State and then 20 years later to Wisconsin.

European Arrival & Colonialism
New Jersey's early colonial history is indistinguishable from New York's. New York Harbor and northern New Jersey was first

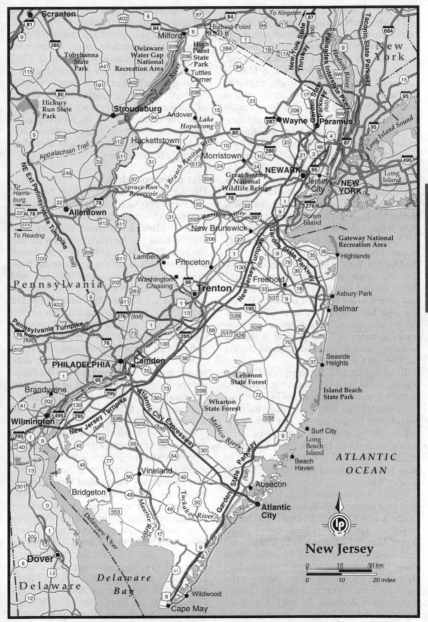

NEW JERSEY

explored by Giovanni da Verrazano in 1524, who anchored off of Sandy Hook. In 1609 Henry Hudson arrived to examine and chart Raritan and Newark Bays and the rocky Palisades west of Manhattan island. Cornelius Mey, for whom Cape May is somewhat inaccurately named, explored the Delaware River in 1614. Dutch settlers built a trading post at Bergen (now Jersey City) circa 1618 and another one at Camden in 1623. Indians also maintained trading posts along the Hudson at Hoboken.

Swedish and Finnish traders followed and established New Sweden along the Delaware River in 1638, but the Dutch of New Netherlands annexed the colony in 1655. In 1664 the English peacefully took over New Netherlands, which included much of New Jersey (see Facts about New York).

Charles II of England subsequently bequeathed New Amsterdam to his brother, the Duke of York, who in turn separated the territory south of New York between the Delaware and Hudson rivers from his land and gave it to his friends Lord John Berkeley and Sir George Carteret. This new colony was named *Nova Caesarea* or New Jersey in honor of Carteret's use of the Isle of Jersey as a Royalist stronghold during the English Civil War.

To attract settlers, Berkeley and Carteret offered fairly generous terms for colonists, including some representation in a territorial assembly. At the same time, Richard Nicolls, the British governor of New York, began recognizing land titles in New Jersey, unaware of Berkeley and Carteret's similar moves. As a result, land disputes in New Jersey continued through the Revolutionary War.

Within a few years Berkeley sold his land to a group of Quakers. In 1676 these Quakers and Carteret divided New Jersey into East Jersey and West Jersey. East Jersey, Carteret's portion, was actually the land *north* of a line drawn southeast from about Delaware Water Gap to Little Egg Harbor on the coast. West Jersey (the *southern* portion) became the first Quaker settlement in America. In 1681, Carteret's widow sold East Jersey to another group

of Quakers led by William Penn. The two Jerseys maintained freedom of religion, a liberal land policy and representative government, which attracted many settlers who brought African slaves with them. In 1702 the Quaker-run regions were united under a royal governor when their respective proprietors surrendered rights to the crown of England. (Nonetheless, each part of New Jersey maintained its own capital – Burlington and Perth Amboy – from 1703 to 1775, and the assembly was forced to alternate between them.)

War of Independence

During the Revolutionary War, New Jersey's residents were divided on the issue of separation from England. In spite of significant anti-British sentiment, loyalists were able to raise six battalions of men during the war. In 1774, a group of New Jersey residents, following the example of Bostonian rebels, dressed as Indians and burned a British tea ship in the Delaware River, an act dubbed the 'Greenwich Tea Party.' Once the war started, undecided residents were swayed to the rebel cause by the conduct of England's Hessian mercenaries, who pillaged the countryside.

Many Revolutionary War battles were fought in New Jersey and George Washington spent significant amounts of time there. He established the Continental Army's headquarters at Morristown during the winters of 1776-77 and 1779-80.

Because of its relatively small size, New Jersey fought aggressively for the political representation of the less populated states at the Constitutional Convention of 1787. The New Jersey Plan called for a national legislature with a single house of equal representation for each state, regardless of population. This countered the Virginia Plan, which proposed proportional representation. Under the so-called 'Great Compromise,' the US Senate, with equal representation for each state, was created along with the proportional House of Representatives. New Jersey adopted the US Constitution on December 18, 1787, the third state to do so. Three years later,

Trenton became the state's capital. New Jersey laws passed in 1790 and 1797 gave women the right to vote. But in 1807 women were disenfranchised by a law that was called 'highly necessary to the safety, quiet, good order and dignity of the State.'

Early Independence to Civil War

During the early independence years New Jersey upgraded its transportation system, improving roads and canals to link the state to New York and Philadelphia. Its population grew from about 15,000 in 1700 to more than 185,000 by 1795. With the population explosion came increasing industrial success. Federalist Alexander Hamilton founded his Society for Useful Manufactures in 1791 and chose the Passaic River Falls as the site of the city of Paterson – the first planned manufacturing town in US history. (Hamilton, who went on to serve as George Washington's secretary of the treasury, was shot and killed by Aaron Burr in a famous duel fought in Weehawken Heights, NJ, in 1804.)

Many New Jersey Quakers were active in the Underground Railroad in the years before the Civil War, but the general population of the state was divided about supporting the Union. Those who sold goods to the South feared the loss of southern markets, though they made up for the loss by supplying the Union Army.

Industrialization & 20th Century

After the Civil War the process of industrialization picked up, especially in the densely populated areas outside of New York City. As its economy expanded, a reform movement grew to limit the power of corporations and to give employees better working conditions. One of the leaders of the reform movement was Democratic Governor Woodrow Wilson, the former president of Princeton University who later served as US president from 1913 to '21. On the political side, New Jersey's large cities were controlled by Democratic 'machines' which controlled public works jobs and stifled opposition well into

the '60s, when the middle class moved to the suburbs and robbed these organizations of their base of support.

Meanwhile, Thomas Edison was almost single-handedly moving the industrial northern part of the state into a research-oriented scientific development as he perfected the electric light, phonograph and motion picture camera at his laboratories in Menlo Park, NJ. Thanks largely to his innovations, narrative motion pictures became possible, and Fort Lee was the world's first major film production center until around 1915, when the industry began moving to the West Coast. During WWI and WWII the state's industrial machine supplied chemicals, munitions and ships for the war effort.

As the US experienced a boom in suburban population after WWII, New Jersey's northern cities suffered job and population losses similar to those in other urban areas in the northeastern states, and the cities of Newark and Jersey City began repopulation by recent immigrants from Portugal, Cuba and India. By the mid-'80s, Monmouth and Ocean counties, which line the Jersey Shore, were among the fastest growing areas in the entire US. Even the formerly placid areas of Princeton and Morristown have experienced explosive growth in population in recent years.

GEOGRAPHY & GEOLOGY

New Jersey is on the Atlantic seaboard bordered by the Hudson and Delaware Rivers. The state is actually a peninsula, since its only land border is shared with New York to the north. To the west the Delaware River separates 100 miles of New Jersey from Pennsylvania and a few remaining miles from its southern neighbor of Delaware. Jersey's east coast is defined by the Hudson River and 127 miles of Atlantic Ocean beaches, which include a narrow strip of land – a narrow peninsula, barely connected to the mainland, that leads to several islands – from Bay Head to Wildwood Crest. This odd land mass actually gives that part of the state both an Atlantic Ocean coast and an inlet coast.

New Jersey is the 47th largest state – that is, one of the smallest. The state is 166 by 65 miles at its greatest dimensions. Its highest point is 1803 feet at High Point in the Kittatinny Mountains, which run along the northwest part of the state from the New York border into the Delaware Water Gap, a national recreational area on the Pennsylvania border.

The ugly industrial zones near Newark and Hackensack are actually marshes called the Meadowlands that have long been abused by the dumping of toxic wastes and garbage. New Jersey has more sites listed under the federal Environmental Protection Agency's 'Superfund' cleanup program than any other, and cleanup work on many dumps has been halted due to budget slashing in Washington.

The coastal plain covers the southern 60% of the state from Perth Amboy on the northeastern coast to Trenton on the Delaware River. In the interior of the state are low-lying marshes and coastal bays. The southern third of the state is largely a spare tract of protected land with sandy soil. Nearly all of the state is at or very near sea level, with the exception of the mountainous areas of the Piedmont Plateau in the northern part of the state.

New Jersey's chief rivers are the Delaware, Hackensack, Raritan and Passaic. Water flows from the Appalachian Ridge and Valley to the Hudson and Delaware river systems.

Mineral deposits found in New Jersey include zinc and iron ore, along with sand and gravel: the basic ingredients for construction projects.

CLIMATE

Although New Jersey faces the Atlantic on its eastern side, the ocean has only a minor effect on temperatures in the state – though the salt air leads to lower snowfall rates along the shoreline. Hurricanes from the south often lose their power as they make their way up the eastern seaboard, though the state can suffer severe damage every few years in an unexpectedly strong storm.

The main weather patterns are influenced by the winds coming off the mass of land to the west, and, in winter, the Arctic blasts from Canada that often plunge the entire northeast into freezing temperatures for weeks at a time. Generally, the northern Appalachian and Highland areas have the coldest winters, and the shore the hottest summers. New Jersey gets 40 inches of precipitation in the south annually, with slightly increasing totals to the north to over 50 inches.

Average temperatures in the state are 33°F in January; 51°F in April; 74°F in July; 55°F in October.

For a five day projection of weather conditions on land and a maritime forecast, call the National Weather Service Forecast Line (☎ (201) 624-8118), which is updated every five hours.

STATE PARKS & FORESTS

New Jersey is a transitional zone for plants and animals. Many northern species end their range in the state and many southern ones begin here. The coastal plain is the most important area for the mixing of flora and fauna.

About 40% of New Jersey is forested, with oak, beech, birch and hickory found in the northern part of the state, while the Pine Barrens, in the southern portion of the state, are dominated by pine and oak trees. The Pine Barrens also have over 30 species of orchid, and plants like turkeybeard, pixie moss, bladderwort and ferns. In slightly less temperate climates violets, dogwood, azalea and mountain laurel are found.

White-tailed deer are all over the state and pose a danger to drivers on back roads at night. In more mountainous areas, you can still find black bears, bobcats and coyotes. Much more common are smaller animals like squirrels, raccoons, skunks and opossum.

Fresh and saltwater fish abound in the waters of New Jersey. The ocean offers striped bass, bluefish, weakfish and mackerel. The Delaware River is a fertile spot to fish for shad, walleye, small-mouth bass and catfish.

New Jersey is on the Atlantic flyway and ducks, osprey and other migratory waterfowl along with hawks and other raptors are frequently seen. Common songbirds include orioles, bluebirds, cardinals and goldfinches.

Many of New Jersey's state parks are located along the shoreline or offer watersport opportunities. The most prominent of these attractions include Lake Hopatcong, the state's largest lake, and the Gateway NRA in Atlantic Highlands. Camping, canoeing and hiking can be found at the Delaware Water Gap NRA off Route 80 in the northwestern region of the state, and the Pine Barrens near Atlantic City offer more than a million acres of protected wilderness.

GOVERNMENT & POLITICS
New Jersey is governed by a bicameral legislature which is composed of a 40 member state senate (with four year terms) and an 80 member General Assembly (popularly elected to two year terms). Under the local constitution, the governor is one of the most powerful state executives in the nation and serves a four year term, to which he/she can be re-elected once.

In presidential politics, New Jersey is considered a bellwether state, tending to back the ultimate winner. State voters supported Ronald Reagan in 1980 and 1984, George Bush in 1988, and Bill Clinton in 1992 and 1996. For statewide offices, New Jerseyans divide their choices fairly evenly between the Democratic and Republican parties, with voter turnout about 52% of the qualified population.

New Jersey has 15 electoral votes, a reflection of its congressional representation of two US senators and 13 US representatives. The current governor, Republican Christine Todd Whitman, was a political neophyte from northern New Jersey who first won fame running on an anti-tax platform for US senate in 1990, and narrowly lost to incumbent Bill Bradley. Whitman opposed then-governor Jim Florio's highly controversial plan to increase taxes to better fund education in depressed areas of New Jersey and balance the state budget. Three years later, Whitman beat Florio promising to roll back taxes 30% during her first term. She kept that promise in part by borrowing against the state employee pension funds to balance the budget, a gambit that critics claim will eventually lead to disaster after she leaves office. Nevertheless, Whitman, who at press time seems poised to face Florio in a rematch in 1997, is seen as a popular pro-choice Republican moderate with a bright future, perhaps as a vice presidential running-mate for a more famous national figure in 2000 or even as a presidential candidate in her own right.

ECONOMY
New Jersey's per capita income of $18,700 is among the highest in the US. The state benefits from its location between two of the busiest container ports in the world – the Port of New York and New Jersey (the largest container port in the country) and the Delaware River Ports.

New Jersey had early industrial successes with leather making in Newark and Orange; glass making and iron works began the era of heavy industrialization in the latter part of the 18th century. Today, a high proportion of New Jersey's labor force is engaged in high-tech industries and research, and several Japanese companies have set up shop along Route 3 in the northern part of the state. New Jersey is also a national leader in pharmaceutical research and development, with industry leaders Johnson & Johnson, Merck and Carter Wallace headquartered in the state.

There are currently some four million people in New Jersey's labor force. The service sector employs 23%. Other major employment sectors are wholesale and retail (20%); trade (18%); manufacturing (17%); and government (14%).

Tourism is an important part of the state's economy, and several regions (including the Jersey Shore, Atlantic City and the Skylands area in the northwest) cater largely to weekenders and summer visitors. Tourism currently brings nearly

$20 billion to the state and is responsible in part for over 300,000 jobs.

Only about 1% of New Jersey residents work in agriculture, though the state is renowned for its peaches, blueberries and tomatoes. New Jersey corn is known for being among the sweetest available in the northeast. Over 25% of farm income comes from greenhouses or plant nurseries growing flowers and trees, and a similar amount comes from poultry, livestock, milk and eggs.

POPULATION & PEOPLE

The first big wave of European immigrants in the post-colonial period came in the 1840s, when large groups of Irish immigrants came to the area to escape the famine. They were followed by Germans, Italians and Poles, most of whom settled in the big cities along New York Harbor.

Of New Jersey's current population of 7.7 million people, about 79% is white. Blacks account for 13%. Hispanics are the third largest group, at about 8% of the population. There are statistically small but culturally significant communities (30,000 people or more) of Koreans, Indian Asians and Filipinos.

Almost 90% of state residents live in urban areas. Newark is New Jersey's largest city with 275,000 people, followed by Jersey City with 230,000.

MEDIA

New Jersey, situated as it is between the large markets of New York City and Philadelphia, does not have its own television or radio industry, though cable super station WWOR/Channel 9 has its studios in Secaucus, and New York public television station WNET is officially licensed out of Newark.

New Jersey's first weekly newspaper, the *New Jersey Gazette*, started in Burlington in 1777. Its first daily was the *Newark Daily Advertiser*, begun in 1832. Today there are over 20 daily and 175 weekly newspapers in the state. The leading ones are the *Newark Star-Ledger*, the *Record* of Hackensack, the *Asbury Park Press*,

Central Jersey's largest newspaper, and the *Trentonian*, a colorful tabloid based in the state capital.

ARTS & EVENTS
Music

Ever since Thomas Edison perfected the phonograph in 1878, New Jersey has played a big role in popular music. Frank Sinatra, the patron saint of all Jersey musicians, was born in Hoboken more than 80 years ago. Jazz great Count Basie hailed from Red Bank, and the 1500 seat theater in the town's Monmouth Arts Center is named in his honor. Singers Frankie Valli and Whitney Houston both hail from Newark.

Of course, Ocean Township native Bruce Springsteen will be forever associated with the Jersey Shore, even though he now spends most of his time in Los Angeles. His E Street Band was named after a road in the shore community of Belmar. The region also spawned rocker Jon Bon Jovi and the metal band Twisted Sister.

Most of these local artists have returned to play at the Garden State Arts center, an open-air venue located in Telegraph State Park at exit 116 on the Garden State Parkway. It's also the site for ethnic festivals from May to October.

The Bruce Blunder

Back in 1984, when every politician from Ronald Reagan on down was cynically trying to associate themselves with Bruce Springsteen's hit album *Born in the USA,* a group of New Jersey legislators got the bright idea to try and designate 'Born to Run,' the singer's signature tune, as the state song. It didn't take long for cooler heads to point out that a song calling the place 'a rat trap – a suicide rap' and advising kids to 'get out while they're young' wasn't exactly an ideal state anthem. The embarrassed lawmakers – undoubtedly not rock fans – hastily named 'Born to Run' an 'unofficial' state song. To this day, New Jersey is still looking for a more upbeat official musical theme. ∎

The New Jersey Symphony Orchestra (☎ (800) 255-3476) is a well-regarded group based in Newark that plays a winter pops concert series and a full array of summertime events throughout the state. The New Jersey State Opera (☎ (201) 623-5757) shares space with the orchestra at Newark's Symphony Hall.

New Jersey's major annual music event is the Waterloo Festival of the Arts, which takes place at Waterloo Village in Stanhope from June to August and features concerts by well-known jazz and rock bands along with a program of classical concerts.

Theater & Film
Millburn's Paper Mill Playhouse is a non-profit institution that is the official state theater of New Jersey. It offers a program of six plays and musicals each year. The McCarter Theater Center in Princeton won a 1994 Tony Award as the best regional theater in the US. It also hosts performances from internationally-known dance companies and soloists like pianist Alicia De Larrocha and violinist Nadja Salerno-Sonnenberg. Foreign companies like the Bolshoi Ballet also make visits to the State Theater in New Brunswick, a recently restored 1921 vaudeville palace. It's also the performance site of the Crossroads Theater Company, the state's best-known black acting ensemble.

New Jersey is featured in many films, including those of local filmmaker John Sayles: *The Return of the Secaucus Seven* and *City of Hope*. The Woody Allen film *Stardust Memories* was filmed largely in Ocean Grove, with the town's huge auditorium standing in for the Hotel Stardust. Perhaps the most famous film made in New Jersey was *On the Waterfront*, made entirely in Hoboken. One of the first films with a distinguishable narrative, Edwin S Porter's *The Great Train Robbery*, was filmed in 1903 in the woods of northern New Jersey.

Visual Arts
It's hard to compete with New York's array of visual arts, but the Newark Museum has

nearly 70 galleries of ancient and modern art and the country's largest collection of Tibetan crafts.

Crafts shows take place throughout the state, notably in Margate, Allaire State Park and Waterloo Village. The Antiques Show at the Atlantic City Convention Hall, which takes place each March, is the largest such event in the world. In Flemington, near Princeton, you can see glass craftsmen at work at the Flemington Cut Glass Company, and view old kilns built when the town was dominated by the pottery industry.

RELIGION
Although New Jersey was the first Quaker settlement in America, today 46% of New Jersey's citizens identify themselves as Roman Catholic, and there is a strong conservative Catholic presence in the suburbs. Other major religious groups include Baptists (10%), Methodists (7%) and Jews (4%). A few small towns in the south of the state are home to Orthodox Jewish sects. There are also small numbers of Moslems, Hindus and Buddhists concentrated in the northern cities.

INFORMATION
Tourist Offices
For information, you can call or write to the New Jersey Division of Travel & Tourism (☎ (800) 537-7397), CN 820, Trenton, NJ 08625-0820.

Other state visitors centers are:

Atlantic City Expressway
    Farley Plaza, on the Expressway
    (☎ (609) 965-6316)
Deepwater
    I-295 north, two miles north of the
    Delaware Memorial Bridge
    (☎ (609) 299-5272)
Knowlton
    I-80 east, five miles from Delaware Water Gap
    (☎ (908) 496-4994)
Liberty State Park
    exit 14B off the NJ Turnpike near Jersey City
    (☎ (908) 915-3400)
Liberty Village
    1 Church St, Flemington
    (☎ (908) 788-5279)

NEW JERSEY

Montvale
exit 172 off the Garden State Parkway
(☎ (201) 391-5737/7951)
Ocean View
off the Garden State Parkway, Seaville
(☎ (609) 624-0918)
Trenton
115 W State St, Trenton
(☎ (609) 695-0640)

Taxes

New Jersey state sales tax is 6%, but clothes are not subject to the tariff, which is why many New Yorkers patronize outlet stores to avoid their state's hefty 8.25% sales tax. There's a reduced 3% state sales tax in designated economic development areas in downtown Trenton and Newark, as well as the Meadowlands near Hackensack where the massive Ikea houseware store and Secaucus factory outlets are located.

Gasoline

New Jersey is one of just three states that have outlawed self-serve gas stations. Moreover, you won't pay a lot for the full-service experience: at many places along the Jersey Shore, the price of a gallon of regular gasoline is often as low as $1.35. The downside: long lines at the service stations in the heat of summer.

Fishing

You have to get a license to fish, and they are available at local sporting goods stores, Kmarts and other stores around the Delaware Water Gap National Recreation Area (though not at information offices). New Jersey and Pennsylvania offer reciprocal privileges for fishing from either side of the Delaware River, so you need only buy one state's license; but you will need a state license if you plan to fish in local streams and lakes.

There are no fewer than 22 types of freshwater fishing licenses. Generally speaking, you'll pay $25 (plus a possible $5 trout stamp) for out-of-state seasonal licenses, but the prices change. Up-to-date fee information is available from the New Jersey Fish, Game and Wildlife Commission (☎ (609) 292-2965) and the Penn-sylvania Fish Commission (☎ (717) 657-4518). Recreational fisherman using ocean charter boats do not need to obtain a license, but there are 'bag limits' on the amount of fish you can catch, depending on the type of fish being pursued.

Call the New Jersey Fish, Game and Wildlife Commission for full license and seasonal updates, along with information on the 160 charter boats offering scenic trips and fishing expeditions throughout the state.

ACCOMMODATIONS

The New Jersey Hotel & Motel Association (☎ (800) 365-6965) has a statewide reservation service.

Hostels & Camping There is a hostel in Layton (☎ (201) 948-6750), near Delaware Water Gap.

The are many campgrounds in New Jersey, and a listing of state and privately run facilities is available from the Department of Environmental Protection's Division of Parks and Forestry (☎ (609) 984-0370, (800) 843-6420). Information on campgrounds is also found through the New Jersey chapter of the American Camping Association (☎ (609) 852-0145) and the Cape May County Campground Association (☎ (800) 441-2267). You can also contact the private Campground Owners Association (☎ (609) 465-8444) for listings and advice.

B&Bs The Bed & Breakfast Innkeepers Association of New Jersey can be reached at ☎ (908) 449-3535. Bed & Breakfast Adventures can be contacted at ☎ (800) 992-2632.

Other services specializing in New Jersey are Amanda's B&B Reservation Service (☎ (908) 249-4944), 21 S Woodland Ave, East Brunswick, NJ 08816; New Jersey B&B Adventures (☎ (609) 522-4000), 103 Godwin Ave, Suite 132, Midland Park, NJ 07432; and Plain & Fancy B&B Reservation Service (☎ (800) 374-7829), 1905 Breckenridge Place, Toms River, NJ 08753.

GETTING THERE & AWAY

Air

Newark's international airport is at exits 13A and 14 on the NJ Turnpike. It is served by many national and international airlines and is the hub of Continental Airlines. Its new international arrival terminal and proximity to Manhattan make it a worthwhile choice for air travelers. See Getting There & Away under New York City for details.

The Atlantic City international airport (☎ (609) 645-7895) is off Tilton Rd in Pomona and is visited by small airlines servicing the city's casino industry.

Bus & Train

New Jersey Transit runs trains to the western New Jersey suburbs, which stop at Hoboken, and trains from New York City's Penn Station to the Jersey shore as far as Bay Head. The state agency operates buses all over the state and to New York City and points in Philadelphia.

The telephone numbers for NJ Transit bus and rail services vary depending on the location of the caller (it's free if you're already in state). This is a 24 hour recorded line.

Northern New Jersey	(800) 772-2222
Southern New Jersey	(800) 582-5946
Pennsylvania	(215) 569-3752
elsewhere	(201) 762-5100

Amtrak (☎ (800) 872-7245) runs up the northeastern corridor, with stops in Princeton Junction and Philadelphia on the way to Washington, DC. Amtrak trains that stop at Princeton Junction tend to be more expensive than the NJ Transit trains which make a few more local stops.

The PATH train (☎ (201) 963-2558, (800) 234-7284) runs from Newark's Penn Station, Hoboken and Jersey City to Manhattan's World Trade Center, with a separate line that runs under Sixth Ave terminating at 34th St (see also New York City's Getting Around section). The fare is $1 each way. It's cheapest and easiest to take PATH between these cities.

Car

Two of New Jersey's major highways are north-south toll roads. The NJ Turnpike (part of I-95) extends from New York City to the Delaware Memorial Bridge; it is well traveled by trucks and badly pockmarked. In contrast, the Garden State Parkway is one of the best-maintained roads in the US, and runs from the top of the state to Cape May with exits all along the shore. To obtain recorded information on conditions along the Garden State Parkway, call ☎ (908) 727-5929.

The Atlantic City Expressway runs from Camden/Philadelphia to Atlantic City.

I-80 and I-78 run from east to west, connecting the northern part of the state with rural Pennsylvania and the midwestern US.

New Jersey is connected to New York City by the George Washington Bridge, the Goethals Bridge and the Lincoln and Holland Tunnels. It is connected to Delaware by the Delaware Memorial Bridge and there are numerous crossings into Pennsylvania across the Delaware River.

Jersey Shore

NEW JERSEY

The New Jersey coast stretches 127 miles from Sandy Hook in the north to Cape May in the south. Thanks to its beaches and the casinos of Atlantic City it's the most-visited area of the state, accounting for a large portion of New Jersey's 178 million tourists. (For coverage of Atlantic City and Cape May see the Southern New Jersey chapter.) Along the way are towns that run from seedy to beautiful. Along the Jersey Shore, which stretches along the central part of the state from Sandy Hook to Island Beach State Park, it's possible to visit the dry religious Methodist village of Ocean Grove and the massive Six Flags Great Adventure theme park on the same day.

Towns are listed from north to south from New York City; the population figures given are deceptive since they only reflect the year-round population. During the summer all towns have massive influxes of summer residents, who boost the populations 10 or 20 fold and create big traffic jams.

ORIENTATION & INFORMATION

The Shore Regional Tourist Board is in Point Pleasant Beach at ☎ (908) 899-6686.

Look for the *Coast Star*, a 25¢ weekly local newspaper covering the coast from Long Branch to Avon, and *Sunny Day*, a yearly summer guide to the shore distributed free for basic beach information and advertisements.

BEACHES

The Jersey Shore beaches are beautiful, although narrow, particularly the further north you go. The shore suffers from frequent battering by storm and erosion, which washes the sand out to sea or further south. As it moves south, the sand is naturally cleansed and becomes noticeably whiter. In recent years the shore area has used generous federal funds to offset the damage done by winter storms and insure

Highlights
- Fishing for 'blues' and other ocean catches off charter boats from Belmar and Point Pleasant
- The charming B&Bs of Spring Lake, once known as the 'Irish Riviera'
- Six Flags Great Adventure's Safari Park and tacky (but thrilling) amusement rides
- Partying hard in the clubs of the Jersey Shore ■

that the beaches, and by extension the revenues they bring in, do not disappear.

Almost all towns impose a fee to use the beaches. Day rates are under $8 per person, but rates go down if you pay by the week, month or season. Badges that can be pinned on your suit are sold at the beaches and in town halls, and are almost invariably checked by retirees guarding beach entrances. The beaches are usually free before 9 am or after 5 pm, when lifeguards are not on duty.

ACCOMMODATIONS

When booking a room, remember to ask if the hotel or inn provides air-conditioning. Many simply have fans, and despite the proximity to the Atlantic Ocean, the shore can get uncomfortably muggy during August and September.

GETTING THERE & AROUND
Bus & Train

Beaches from Long Branch to Bay Head are served by NJ Transit North Jersey Coast train service; points further south to Cape May are served by bus. (See the Facts about New Jersey chapter for details on NJ

Transit.) NJ Transit buses serve these cities and towns:

- New York City and Jersey City to Seaside Heights
- New York, Philadelphia and Camden to Wildwood and Cape May
- Philadelphia to Ocean City
- New York City, Jersey City, Newark, Philadelphia and Camden to Atlantic City

NJ Transit has increased summer train service from New York City (Penn Station), Hoboken and Newark to shore points including Long Branch, Asbury Park, Bradley Beach, Belmar, Spring Lake, Manasquan, Point Pleasant and Bay Head with shuttle buses running from some stations to the beach, which is usually about a half mile away. A combination roundtrip train ticket and one-day beach pass to these points costs $12 from Hoboken or Newark and $15 from New York.

Local buses run along Main St from Asbury Park to Point Pleasant Beach.

Car

If you're in a hurry, it's best to take the Garden State Parkway, which runs from near New York City along the entire length of the shore a few miles inland from the beaches and towns. There are exits from the Garden State Parkway for most shore points.

If you have more time, driving along the coast or near to it on local roads can be pleasant, although Route 71, which runs along the shore points about two miles in from the ocean, gets crowded in summer. Be aware that local police are particularly aggressive about issuing speeding tickets, and, at night, pulling over drivers on suspicion of drunken driving.

HIGHLANDS
Twin Lights Historic Site
(Navesink Light Station)

The brownstone dual lighthouses (☎ (908) 872-1814) are connected by a museum that was the former keeper's home. A lighthouse has been on this site since 1756, and the first twin towers were built in 1828 (the

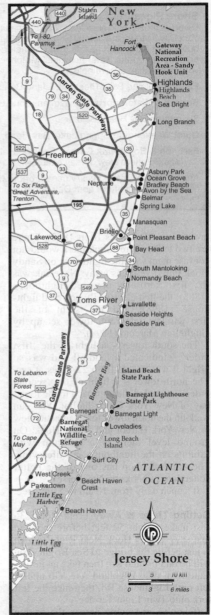

NEW JERSEY

Shore Pleasures

Given its proximity to New York City (90 minutes or less) and direct accessibility from New York City by train, the Jersey Shore is a perfect place for a quick trip away from the urban bustle. But each town has its own character – from sleepy to wild – and they offer different kinds of on-the-water activities. Match your interests to the following list, and select your destination accordingly:

Fishing Belmar, Point Pleasant, Island Beach State Park

Surfing & Watersports Manasquan, Long Branch

Swimming Bay Head, Belmar

Quiet Weekending Spring Lake, Bay Head, Ocean Grove

Partying & Boardwalk Games Seaside Heights, Wildwood
(see Southern New Jersey chapter)

And remember, almost every oceanfront town in New Jersey shuts down for the season about two weeks after Labor Day and remains dead until the following May. ■

---

present structure dates from 1862). There are two towers here so mariners would not confuse them with the lighthouse on Sandy Hook only five miles away. Navesink was the first kerosene powered lighthouse (1883); the first electrically powered lighthouse (1898); and the sight of the first wireless telegraph tower set up by Guglielmo Marconi (1899).

The south tower – a light of the 'first order' – indicated a landfall and was so bright it was visible from 22 miles at sea. The north tower – a light of the 'second order' – signaled the approach to the lower bay of New York City's harbor. You can walk up the north tower for a fantastic view of New York Harbor and Sandy Hook. On ground level there is a museum with exhibits on the lighthouse and lifesaving. The museum shop has one of the better collections of books on New Jersey.

It's open daily from 10 am to 5 pm; free.

Getting There & Away From Route 36 east make a right 50 feet before the sign that says 'Sandy Hook Next Right' which is just before the bridge to Sea Bright. You will be on Portland Rd; then take an immediate right onto Highland Ave. Go uphill, left onto Lighthouse Rd, then take the left fork onto Twin Light Terrace.

If you've just come across the bridge

onto Route 36 west take the exit marked 'Highlands Business Center.' Make a circle going under the bridge and then come up onto Portland Rd and continue as above.

Fishing

Schupp's Landing (☎ (908) 872-1479), 12 Bay Ave, rents boats for fishing, which cost $55 per day for a fiberglass four seater and $50 for a wood three seater. They also sell bait, tackle, ice and food. It's open April to November, Monday to Friday from 5:30 am; weekends from 5 am. Boats must be returned by 5 pm.

Places to Stay & Eat

Conners Hotel (☎ (908) 872-1500), 326 Shore Dr, is a 20 room hotel with its own pool on the bay. The rooms are small and clean, with no phone or TV. There is a restaurant (dishes $15 to $20) and bar in the hotel. Singles/doubles are $42/47; the two rooms with kitchens are $67/77. Open only from Memorial Day to Labor Day.

Moby's, at the very end of Bay Ave past Schupp's boat rentals, has fish ($6) and clam ($4.25) sandwiches; platters ($8 to $9); and lobster (around $10). The food is to-go but they have some seating. *Bahr's* (☎ (908) 872-1245), 2 Bay Ave, is across from Moby's. They have seafood at slightly higher prices. The *Clam Hut* (☎ (908) 872-0909) is on Atlantic St on the water with similar food to Bahr's.

Getting There & Away

Car There are two exits from Route 36 to Highlands. Coming east on Route 36 from Atlantic Highlands, the exit leads north and intersects with the western end of Bay Ave, Highlands' main street. Coming west on Route 36 the exit takes you almost immediately to the eastern end of Bay Ave near Moby's restaurant.

Boat Highlands is also served by TNT Hydrolines (☎ (908) 872-2628) to/from Manhattan and Brooklyn, which docks in Highlands behind Conner's Hotel. There are scheduled commuter hydrofoils leaving in either direction Monday to Friday and extra boats during the summer.

SANDY HOOK-GATEWAY NATIONAL RECREATION AREA

Sandy Hook is a 1650 acre peninsula with beaches, marshes, dunes, hiking, a fort and lighthouse controlled by the NPS.

Visitor Center & Lifesaving Museum

The visitor center (☎ (908) 872-0115) is on the right about two miles past the toll plaza at 2 Spermaceti Cove. It's staffed by park rangers and has pamphlets, maps and some books.

It also has a one room exhibit on the US Lifesaving Service. The Service began in 1848 on Sandy Hook at Spermaceti Cove and was formally established by the federal government in 1878. Several times during the summer a shipwreck rescue with original equipment is reenacted from the beach behind the visitor center.

There is an admission charge of $4 per car weekdays and $5 weekends from Memorial Day to Labor Day.

Fort Hancock & Sandy Hook Museum

Because ships sailing into New York harbor have to pass close to Sandy Hook, the tip of the peninsula has been an important location for forts since the Revolutionary War. Various gun emplacements were built over the years, particularly from 1890 to 1904. The Army designated the collection of emplacements Fort Hancock in 1895. Its original building went up in 1898 and 1899.

The Sandy Hook Museum was built as a jail in 1899. Inside, the jail cells are still intact and there are also photographs and information on the Sandy Hook Lighthouse, the oldest lighthouse still operating in the US in its original state (closed to the public). It's open July and August Monday to Friday from 1 to 5 pm; weekends from 10 am to 5 pm. Other months it is only open weekends from 1 to 5 pm; free.

Beaches

There are seven miles of ocean beaches each with their own parking areas. Areas C, D, E, G (Gunnison) and I (North Beach)

NEW JERSEY

Fighting Mother Nature

Throughout the last decade, New Jersey's oceanfront communities have worked hard to prevent erosion of the shoreline by monitoring tides, planting sand grass and rebuilding seawalls during the off season. Many environmentalists think these efforts are too costly and ultimately fruitless, but given the importance of the beachfronts to the local economy, the efforts will continue.

Federally backed replenishments *are* successful in the short term, but the winter of 1990 and its two major blizzards brought unexpected devastation to the area. Atlantic City (see the Southern New Jersey chapter) lost more than three feet of beach despite the presence of dozens of 'geotubes' – 12 foot tall artificial sand dunes made of plastic. The geotubes may not have kept the sand from shifting, but they did keep the roiling waters from damaging beachfront casinos. Still, the cost of replenishing the damaged beach in Atlantic City alone could run as high as $7 million. ■

have food and beach supplies from April to October. The food is burgers, hot dogs and fries with most things under $5. Chairs and umbrellas are $4/7 per day weekday/end. Area F is reserved exclusively for fishing. Windsurfing is best on Sandy Hook Bay opposite Area C.

Special Events
There are free summer concerts on beach Area D from late June through early August. The NPS schedules about eight concerts per summer in a wide variety of styles, including blues, jazz, country and swing.

Places to Stay & Eat
There is no place to stay on Sandy Hook. The nearest place is the *Fairbanks Motel & Marina* (☎ (908) 842-8450) at 344 Ocean Ave in Sea Bright, the first town across the Highlands Bridge south of Sandy Hook. The rooms are smallish with refrigerators and TVs but no phones. From May to late September singles/doubles are $65/80 weekdays and $80/90 weekends. In winter prices drop to $50/65.

Sea Gull's Nest at Beach Area D has an upstairs bar and restaurant that serves seafood salad and tuna salad on a roll. The restaurant is open from May to October depending on the weather. The *Mirasol* (☎ (908) 741-7522), a Portuguese and Spanish restaurant, is next to the Fairbanks. Lunch dishes are about $8.

Getting There & Away
The turnoffs from Route 36 for Sandy Hook are clearly marked just before or after, depending on your direction, the Highlands Bridge.

LONG BRANCH
Long Branch (population 28,658) was supposedly founded following a wrestling match held here in 1688 to settle a dispute between Lenni Lenape Indians and European settlers. The Europeans won and began building, and by the mid-19th century Long Branch was a major seaside town featuring gambling and wide beaches.

Seven American presidents – including Ulysses S Grant, William McKinley and Woodrow Wilson – vacationed in the town. When President James Garfield was shot on July 2, 1881, just four months into his term, he was brought to Long Branch to recover from his wounds, but he died of complications two months later.

When gambling ended in the 1890s, Long Branch became a middle-class resort. Today it's something even less than that, since the tides along its two mile beach tend to be too rough for good swimming – it attracts more aggressive surfers these days. In general, the strip of oceanfront stretching from Long Branch to Asbury Park has become depressed and eroded in recent years, and those looking for a day in the sun should head further south.

Places to Stay & Eat
The *Fountains Motel* (☎ (908) 222-7200) is at 160 Ocean Ave on the corner of Morris Ave. It has 116 rooms and efficiencies with TVs and phones. The rooms are a reasonable $33/36 for singles/doubles, a reflection of the town's diminishing popularity.

The fortress-like *Ocean Place Hilton Resort & Spa* (☎ (908) 571-1400, fax 571-8974), 1 Ocean Blvd, is a world away from the Fountains. The rooms are large, with new furniture. While most rooms have a great ocean view, note that there is no convenient beach access from the side of the hotel facing the beach. Guests are clearly meant to spend their time inside the hotel, not in Long Branch. Single rooms vary from $88 to $145; for ocean view from $98 to $175; and for oceanfront from $138 to $195. Add $20 for doubles. There is no charge for children of any age.

The spa offers packages (from $163 to $599) or à la carte treatments (from $42 to $110), including aroma therapy, Moor mud facials, massage and personal training.

There are several places serving hot dogs, hamburgers and fries on the small commercial strip on the boardwalk including *Max's*, which has been serving hot dogs to daytrippers for years.

Nunzio's is at 220 Westwood near Morris

Ave near the train station, and has inexpensive submarine sandwiches for under $8.

Entertainment

Club Paradise (☎ (908) 870-9292) is at 160 Ocean Ave next to the Fountains Motel. It's a disco with five bars, a dance floor, and a DJ. The crowd is generally in their 20s. Open year round from Thursday to Saturday from 9 pm to 2 am.

Cafe Bar (☎ (908) 222-9729) is on the small commercial boardwalk strip opposite Franklin Terrace right on the water. It has seven bars, pool tables, a dance floor and live music from Thursday to Sunday for a generally under-30 crowd; open year round daily from noon to 2 am.

Getting There & Away

Bus & Train NJ Transit trains and buses stop at the station on 3rd Ave between N Bath Ave and Morris Ave. The one-way/roundtrip fare from New York is $9.15/13.50. The M27 bus runs between Long Branch and Asbury Park.

Car If you're driving along the coast, Long Branch is right off Ocean Ave/Ocean Blvd. Blue signs direct you to turn for the boardwalk. Long Branch is exit 105 on the Garden State Parkway.

MONMOUTH PARK

Monmouth Park (☎ (908) 222-5100) is two miles inland from Long Branch on Route 36. Thoroughbreds have raced on this site in three different structures on and off since 1870. President Ulysses S Grant had a box at the first track. Monmouth is considered one of the best-run tracks in the northeast, and its picnic area is usually solidly booked throughout the summer; call ahead for picnic information. Monmouth Park is a far more pleasant place to visit than the two New York racetracks, and easily accessible by train. If you want to spend a day with the horses, head here.

The racing season is from Memorial Day to Labor Day. There are 10 races a day on Tuesday, Wednesday and Friday to Sunday, with the first post time at 1:05 pm.

Admission is $1.50 for grandstand, $4 or $2 for the weather proof. Parking is $2.

Getting There & Away

Bus Academy (☎ (908) 291-1300) and Monmouth (☎ (908) 774-7780) bus lines run to the park from New York and surrounding towns.

Train The NJ Transit *Pony Express* (☎ (800) 772-2222) runs from Manhattan directly to the track with stops in New Jersey along the way. It takes about two hours from New York. Cost from New York, including admission, is $8.91/13 one way/roundtrip.

Car Take Route 36 west from Long Branch for two miles into Oceanport. Make a right at the large sign for Monmouth Park.

Boat Express Transportation (☎ (800) 262-8743) runs hydrofoil ferries on Tuesday, Saturday, Sunday and holidays from Pier 11 in Manhattan and the 69th St Pier in Brooklyn to Highlands. From there the ferry provides buses. The cost is $23 roundtrip and includes admission and a program.

ASBURY PARK

Asbury Park (population 16,800) was founded in 1871 and named after Francis Asbury, the man who established American Methodism. It's always been known as a dowdy resort for the middle class, famous in the '20s for its summer 'Baby Parade' of costumed kids. Cole Porter puckishly played on its reputation with a single line in his song 'At Long Last Love': 'Is that Grenada I see, or only Asbury Park?'

Asbury Park had a minor resurgence in the 1970s, when Bruce Springsteen exploded on the national scene after making a name for himself at the local Stone Pony club. But in the '80s, Asbury Park let its amusement area fall into decline, and pinned hopes on becoming a full-service summer resort area of high-rise condos and beach clubs with a planned $500 million development. But the scheme never found a well-heeled backer, despite rampant rumors that various famous artists – Johnny Cash, Willie Nelson, the Jackson family – were interested in buying land for a theme park. Today a bankrupt and unfinished high rise condo complex sits on Ocean Ave, a concrete monument to the town's failure to revive.

Meanwhile, all the town's amusement areas have closed, the famous carousel sold, and the old Convention Hall was condemned. Things hit rock bottom in January 1994, when the young mayor of Asbury Park and his wife were arrested for purchasing cocaine in a bar across the street from city hall. Since there's a big crack and prostitution problem in town, beach area motels should be avoided.

The Stone Pony is just about the only thing that endures, and still attracts top acts like the Pretenders. Every once in a while, Bruce drops by to play for old time's sake. Just about the only reason to visit Asbury Park and its honky-tonk desolation is the fact that it is the train stop for Ocean Grove, a quirky small town that is popular with young families (see below). But there is some stirring in the old town these days – Convention Hall opened recently after being shuttered for years, and hosted a homecoming concert by Springsteen. And there are plans to try to imitate Ocean Grove's success with families by encouraging artists to take over the abandoned shop fronts downtown.

Things to See & Do

Asbury Park has a fair beach and a wide wooden boardwalk dotted with a few abandoned attractions and a dusty scale model of the development plan. Badges for the beach (☎ (908) 775-0900) are $3 per day during the week and $4 on weekends; a season's pass is $20; for seniors and children 12 to 17 it costs $10.

Inside the Casino, where the carousel once stood on the southern end of the boardwalk separating Asbury Park from Ocean Grove, there are some dealers selling second-hand stuff. Saturday evenings during the summer there is an antique auction here from about 6 pm.

Places to Stay & Eat

There is one very comfortable B&B six blocks back from the shore in an attractive residential neighborhood. *Daisy's Place* (☎ (908) 775-1238), 605 Sunset Ave, has four rooms, each decorated for a different season. All rooms have sinks, TVs and refrigerators, and room rates include a full breakfast. Singles/doubles are $40/60 year round.

The *Berkeley Carteret Hotel* (☎ (908) 776-6700), on Ocean Ave in the northern part of town, is a former luxury facility and local landmark that has been open and closed several times in the past decade. It's best to call ahead to find out whether they are still serving the public.

Getting away from boardwalk grub, a good Caribbean restaurant, the *Islander II* (☎ (908) 988-3637), is west of the train station in the row of stores at the corner of Bangs Ave and Memorial Dr (behind the sign for 'Big Bill's Liquors'). They have curry goat for $6.50 and curry chicken for $5.75. Meals come with rice and beans and sweet plantains.

Entertainment

Just about the only place left hopping in town is the renowned *Stone Pony* night club (☎ (908) 775-4446), at the corner of 2nd and Ocean Aves.

Getting There & Away

Bus & Train The NJ Transit train and bus station is at the Transportation Center on Cookman Ave and Main St almost on the border of Asbury Park and Ocean Grove. The one-way/roundtrip train fare from New York is $9.15/13.50. NJ Transit local bus M20 runs along the coast stopping at many points between the Asbury Park and Point Pleasant Beach.

Car Asbury Park is off exit 100-A or 100-B from the Garden State Parkway.

OCEAN GROVE

For about a hundred years, Ocean Grove (population 8000) was run by a Methodist group that held summertime revival meetings in this square-mile community. Driving a car was not allowed on Sunday (unless it was the newspaper delivery truck), and crusty 'Peace Officers' strictly enforced the ban on Sabbath swimming. All that ended in 1979 when the Supreme Court ruled that the town charter was unconstitutional.

The town was founded in 1869 by the Ocean Grove Camp Meeting Association. According to its head, Dr William Osborn, it had the highest beach, best grove of trees and no mosquitoes. The town touts itself as a 'Victorian Experience' and there is indeed a lot of Victorian architecture (although not nearly so much as Cape May to the south). The contrast with decrepit Asbury Park, from which it is separated by narrow Wesley Lake, is striking. You can still see the cottage-backed tents lined up around the Great Auditorium in which the original founders used to stay when coming for summers.

Orientation & Information

Ocean Grove is laid out on a grid pattern, and you enter the town through one of several gates along Main St to the west. Gates are on Stockton Ave, Broadway and

Main Ave, which run east to west to Ocean Ave along the boardwalk and a half mile of coast. The most pleasant of the east-west streets running from the ocean is Pilgrim's Pathway, actually two parallel streets separated by a narrow park.

The tourist office (☎ (908) 774-4736) is at 64 Main Ave in the offices of the *Times*, the local weekly newspaper. It's open during the summer only Monday to Friday from 10 am to 4 pm. Off season, contact the Chamber of Commerce (☎ (800) 388-4768). During the summer season a tourist information booth is set up near the Great Auditorium.

The post office is on Main Ave just south of Pilgrim Pathway. The New Jersey National Bank (☎ (908) 988-3585), at the northwest corner of Main Ave and Pilgrim Pathway, changes foreign currency for a $10 fee; it's open Monday to Friday from 9 am to 2:30 pm, Saturday from 9 am to noon. The Mid Atlantic National Bank at the northeast corner changes travelers checks and has an ATM. It's open Monday to Friday from 9 am to 3 pm, Saturday from 9 am to noon.

There are two laundries, the Ocean Grove Launderette, at 53 Olin Ave, and

NEW JERSEY

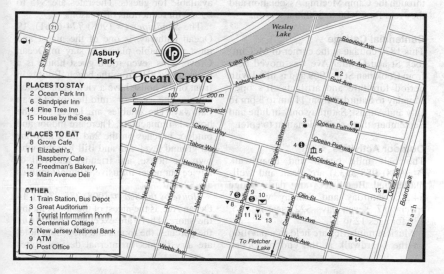

PLACES TO STAY
2 Ocean Park Inn
6 Sandpiper Inn
14 Pine Tree Inn
15 House by the Sea

PLACES TO EAT
8 Grove Cafe
11 Elizabeth's, Raspberry Cafe
12 Freedman's Bakery,
13 Main Avenue Deli

OTHER
1 Train Station, Bus Depot
3 Great Auditorium
4 Tourist Information Booth
5 Centennial Cottage
7 New Jersey National Bank
9 ATM
10 Post Office

the Main Avenue Launderette on Main Ave right near the intersection with Central Ave.

The Great Auditorium

The 6500 seat wood auditorium (for tickets call ☎ (908) 988-0645) stands at the center of town at the western end of Ocean Pathway. It was built to house the crowds that used to throng here (and still do in reduced numbers) to hear Sunday sermons by visiting ministers and for occasional mainstream music concerts by touring troupes such as the Preservation Hall Jazz Band. The Auditorium, built in 1894 in just 92 days, also played a role as the Hotel Stardust in the 1980 Woody Allen film *Stardust Memories*.

Tent City

Nineteenth century visitors to Ocean Grove set up hundreds of tents around the Great Auditorium and 114 of them are still clustered here. The uniform structures are actually tents at the front with small cabins at the back containing a kitchen and bathroom. The tent canvas and furniture are stored in the cabins during the off season. There is a 15 year waiting list to get a tent through the Camp Meeting Association and they rent for $2500 to $3000 a season.

Centennial Cottage

This 1874 cottage at the corner of McClintock St and Central Ave was moved here from Cookman St in 1969 and is filled with period furniture and artifacts. It's open Monday to Saturday from 11 am to 3 pm in July and August; Saturday only in June and September; there's a $1 donation to enter.

Outdoor Activities

The half mile beach and boardwalk (☎ (908) 988-5533) are clean and well-maintained. Beach fees are: daily badge $4.50; Saturday and Sunday weekend special $7; seven days $22; season $55, $30 for ages 12 to 17.

Musical ministries are held in a pavilion on the boardwalk at the end of Ocean Pathway. Seasonal beach activities include a sand sculpture contest, a volleyball tournament, a lifeguard tournament and various races.

Sunset Water Sports (☎ (908) 776-5293) in the Shark Island Yacht Club at 1601 Route 35 in neighboring Neptune, rents jet skis on the inlet.

Places to Stay

There are many places to stay in Ocean Grove, and most offer reductions for long stays. The following places are open only in season, unless otherwise noted.

The *Ocean Park Inn* (☎ (908) 988-5283, winter (201) 842-5516), 38 Surf Ave, is an immaculate B&B run by the friendly Ron and Terry Ens. There is a common kitchen with a microwave and surfboards and chairs for beach use. Room rates include continental breakfast with a different home-baked item daily. Rates are $30/55.

The *Pine Tree Inn* (☎ (908) 775-3264), 10 Main Ave half a block from the beach, is the quintessential Victorian B&B. All of the furniture is tasteful and antique. All rooms have sinks, some private baths and porches; it's very clean, and bicycles are available for guests. The rates are $45 to $95, with reductions off season.

The *Sandpiper* (☎ (908) 774-6261), 19 Ocean Pathway, is one of the nicest and most reasonable places to stay in Ocean Grove. This seven room guest house is a block and a half from the beach. Rooms in front of the house have a view of the beach across the grassy middle of Ocean Pathway. The doubles are large, and the house is immaculate. There are indoor and outdoor porches on the 2nd floor and one on ground level. Jan and Bill Knight, who own the house, are friendly and full of advice but never intrusive. Singles/doubles are $25/50.

House by the Sea (☎ (908) 775-2847), 14 Ocean Ave, is the nicest of the hotels facing the shore. There are excellent views from the porches, the rooms and the whole hotel are airy thanks to internal design. Rates depend on a combination of view and bath and include continental breakfast. Single and double rates are the same: $42 to $58 from Sunday to Thursday and $52 to $68 on Friday and Saturday.

Places to Eat

The majority of the restaurants are on Main Ave between Central Ave and Pilgrims Pathway.

The *Raspberry Cafe* (☎ (908) 988-0833), 60 Main Ave, is the place with the best breakfast food in town for under $10.

Main Avenue Deli (☎ (908) 502-0400), 54 Main Ave, sells pizza and calzones and hot Italian heros for $4.

Elizabeth's (☎ (908) 502-0306), 60½ Main Ave, has breakfast specials for $2 to $3, and sandwiches, hot dogs and burgers all for under $5.

Freedman's Bakery (☎ (908) 774-8235), 55 Main Ave, specializes in morning baked goods and coffee.

The *Grove Cafe* (☎ (908) 774-2444), at 68 Main Ave, serves crepes, burgers and sandwiches.

Getting There & Away

By train, take NJ Transit to Asbury Park and walk through the Ocean Grove gateways two blocks away.

Ocean Grove is on exit 100A on the Garden State Parkway.

AVON BY THE SEA

Residents pronounce the name of this quiet, family oriented town (population 2165) as AH-von, as if having their tonsils examined, and drop the precious 'by the Sea.'

Outdoor Activities

The beach (☎ (908) 502-4510) costs $3.50 daily; $40 for the season, $20 for seniors. The boardwalk is actually an asphalt walk – a sign of a '92 storm that ruined many beach communities. Avon doesn't have the small arcades and amusement halls you find in Belmar and Point Pleasant Beach. It's all quiet sun worship here.

Places to Stay & Eat

Sands of Avon (☎ (908) 776-8386), 42 Sylvania Ave, has been run for 33 years by Ann and Joseph Suchecki. Rates are $45/75 and include breakfast; open summers only. The *Victoria Hotel* (☎ (908) 988-9798), 105 Woodland Ave, has 14 rooms. There is a shared refrigerator, microwave, barbecue, telephone and TV. In-season weekday/weekend rooms are $55/80; off season $25/35.

The *Ocean Mist Inn* (☎ (908) 775-9625) is at 28 Woodland Ave across from the Atlantic View. The hosts, Joyce and Noel Winkleberry, are very friendly. In-season double rates, including continental breakfast, are $65 to $95 with shared bath. *Castlemara* (☎ (908) 776-8727, (800) 821-2976), 22 Lakeside Ave, is at the northern end of town half a block back from the shore and faces a small lake. Its 13 rooms all have heavy dark wood furniture and private bath. Rates are $70 to $90 for doubles and include breakfast; subtract $10 for singles.

Summer House (☎ (908) 775-3992), 101 Sylvania Ave, has rooms in pink, yellow and blue pastels. Rates ($60/130) include continental breakfast during the week and full breakfast on weekends.

The *Columns* (☎ (908) 988-3213), 601 Ocean Ave facing the beach, is Avon's ritziest restaurant, a place where families take their graduating high schoolers for a special meal. Tom Cruise, who grew up in the area, was once spotted dining here. You can sit on the large porch overlooking the ocean or drink at one of four bars inside. Burgers run $8, and full entrees are $15. There's live music from Wednesday to Sunday with a $2 to $5 cover.

Getting There & Away

Avon can be reached by exits 98 and 100A on the Garden State Parkway. The nearest NJ Transit train stations are at Bradley Beach to the north and Belmar to the south. The M20 bus stops at Main St and Sylvania Ave.

BELMAR
Belmar (population 5900) is a gathering place for people in their 20s, but following a riot after an MTV-sponsored beach party a few years ago, the town has tried to curtail its Fort Lauderdale image. A new law closes down all bars at midnight, and the police are pretty aggressive about cracking down on loud parties and drinking in public. Belmar's beach is popular with gays, who gather on the northern end of the beach at 2nd Ave near the border with Avon. But as yet, there are no discernible gay gathering places in town.

Belmar's local chamber of commerce (☎ (908) 681-1176) has information on events and activities.

Outdoor Activities
Besides the beach ($4 daily; $40 for the season, $10 for seniors), there's a small amusement area with a rooftop miniature golf course on Ocean Ave between 14th and 15th Aves. It's open until about 11 pm

and costs $5 per person. The Skate Rental (☎ (908) 681-7767) store in the Mayfair Hotel rents in-line skates and bicycles for $20 a day. They also rent boogie boards for $12 a day. Iron City Gym (☎ (908) 681-8098), on Ocean Ave between 9th and 8th Aves, has day passes for $8 per day; open year round.

Fishing   Boats leave the busy Belmar Marina (☎ (908) 681-2266) seven days a week, year round, from 7 am to 7:30 pm. The cost is generally from $21 to $33 to join a regularly scheduled departure. Captain Paul Hepler (☎ 908) 928-4519) runs charters from the marina, and the Fisherman's Den tackle shop (☎ (908) 681-6677) rents small motor boats for $25 per day from 6 am.

Places to Stay
Most of the places in town have the crowded and casual look and feel of rooming houses. *Carol's Guest House*

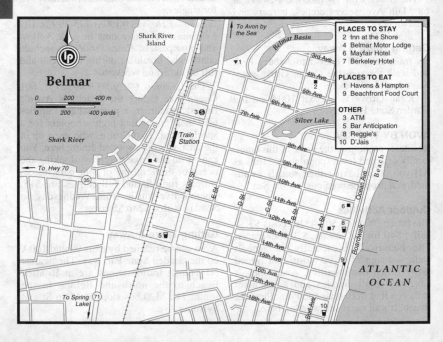

PLACES TO STAY
2 Inn at the Shore
4 Belmar Motor Lodge
6 Mayfair Hotel
7 Berkeley Hotel

PLACES TO EAT
1 Havens & Hampton
9 Beachfront Food Court

OTHER
3 ATM
5 Bar Anticipation
8 Reggie's
10 D'Jais

Belmar

0   200   400 m
0   200   400 yards

Shark River Island

Shark River

Train Station

← To Hwy 70

35

To Spring Lake 71

Belmar Basin

To Avon by the Sea

3rd Ave
4th Ave
5th Ave
6th Ave
7th Ave
8th Ave
9th Ave
10th Ave
11th Ave
12th Ave
13th Ave
14th Ave
15th Ave
16th Ave
17th Ave
18th Ave

Silver Lake

Main St
E St
D St
C St
A St
Surf St

Ocean Ave

Boardwalk

Beach

ATLANTIC OCEAN

The Jersey Dress Code

Belmar bars – and many other places along the shore – tend to require 'collared' shirts, so you'll be turned away from the door for wearing a $60 Armani black tee, but welcomed if wearing a $10 polo shirt. They also 'proof' just about everyone to ensure customers are of legal drinking age (21), so bring along ID. But Jersey shore bouncers (whose forearms are bigger than their necks) are shameless when it comes to bending the rules for women. If you're ambulatory and female, it doesn't matter what your age is or how you're dressed. Well, actually, the skimpier the better . . . ■

(☎ (908) 681-4422), 201 11th Ave, is the cheapest place in town at $25 per person, per night, including continental breakfast, with lower weekly rates. Rooms are very basic.

The year-round *Mayfair Hotel* (☎ (908) 681-2620), 1000 Ocean Ave on the corner of 10th Ave, has a big lobby, a kitchen and a pool. Rooms with private/shared bath are $85/75 Friday and Saturday; $45 other days.

The *Berkeley Hotel* (☎ (908) 681-9617), 107 12th Ave, is a very casual place half a block from the beach. Rooms are basic and run $55/75; open May to September.

The *Inn at the Shore* (☎ (908) 681-3762), 301 4th Ave, is three blocks back from the beach on the northern end of town, away from the crowds. Rates are from $45 to $85 and include continental breakfast.

If you want to stay across from the marina, the *Belmar Motor Lodge* (☎ (908) 681-6600, fax 681-6604) is at Route 35 and 10th Ave. A standard modern motel, rooms have TV, phone, and air-con. Rates are from $53 to $88.

Places to Eat

There is a food court serving pizza, burgers and Chinese food at the corner of Ocean and 14th Aves, and a McDonald's on the beach opposite 13th Ave.

Wingz R Way & Clam Bar is a unique place on Ocean Ave between 16th and 17th Ave, and features different styles of chicken wings, plus raw clams. Open till about 11 pm weekdays and 3 am weekends.

Havens & Hampton (☎ (908) 681-1231), 5th and Main Sts, features dining in a room overlooking the Shark River inlet. Fresh seafood dishes start at $12 and there are lobster specials with prices depending on the catch. *Ollie Klein's* (☎ (908) 681-1177), 708 River Rd, has a similar menu on the south side of the Main St bridge.

The *Circus Drive-In* (☎ (908) 449-2650) near Belmar on Route 35 is an old-fashioned '50s style drive-in where the waiter serves food to patrons still sitting in their cars. It's open only in summer.

Entertainment

Bar Anticipation (☎ (908) 681-7422), 703 16th Ave, is a massive, mostly outdoor bar complex. 'Bar A' is Belmar's pick up place, with 10 bars, live music and swimsuit competitions. The bouncers are burly and surly.

D'Jais (☎ (908) 681-5855) is a large dance club at the corner of Ocean and 18th Ave. It's open seven days a week from May to September.

Reggie's on Ocean Ave between 11th and 12th Aves, attracts a slightly older singles crowd; open from May to October with live music on weekends.

Getting There & Away

Bus & Train The local M20 bus stops at Main St (also known as F St) and 10th Ave. The train station is at 10th Ave and Belmar Plaza, between 9th and 10th Aves behind Belmar Mall one block east of Route 35. The one-way/roundtrip fare from New York is $9.45/14. Belmar is also part of NJ Transit's Summer Beach Package.

Car Belmar is exit 98 on the Garden State Parkway to Route 138 east.

SPRING LAKE

Spring Lake (population 5341) was developed as a 19th century resort around the lake that gives the town its name. It is one of the wealthier shore communities – and known locally as the 'Irish Riviera' for its

NEW JERSEY

expensive and elegant B&Bs and hotels. Locals, who tend to hang out on the town's quiet and charming Main St, would prefer less tourism.

Spring Lake used to have a number of huge ocean-front hotels that became too expensive to run by the '70s. The last remaining resort, the Essex and Sussex hotel, has been shut for years as its owners try to convert it to a condominium complex. Immediately south of the 'E&S' was the equally huge Monmouth, which was torn down to make way for the tract of new beachfront housing that extends for several blocks from the beach.

Information

Maps and information are available from the chamber of commerce (☎ (908) 449-0577), PO Box 694, Spring Lake, NJ 07762. The post office is at 1410 3rd Ave. The Bank of New York (☎ (908) 449-0888), at 3rd and Washington Aves, exchanges foreign currency. First Union

(☎ (908) 449-5500), at 3rd and Morris Aves, has an ATM. Fireside Bookshop (☎ (908) 449-1991), 1100 3rd Ave, sells local maps and tour books.

Outdoor Activities

The beach (☎ (908) 449-8005) costs $3.50 daily and $43 for the season; children 11 and under go free. On each end of the boardwalk are salt-water pools for resident use only.

Places to Stay

Spring Lake's hotels and B&Bs tend to be among the most expensive on the Jersey Shore, with daily rates over $100.

B&Bs *Victoria House* (☎ (908) 974-1882), 214 Monmouth Ave, has 10 well-appointed rooms, most at $120 a night with a two night minimum in summer.

The *Johnson House* (☎ (609) 449-1860), 25 Tuttle Ave, has singles/doubles from $90/110 and shared bathroom from $65, along with free parking.

NEW JERSEY

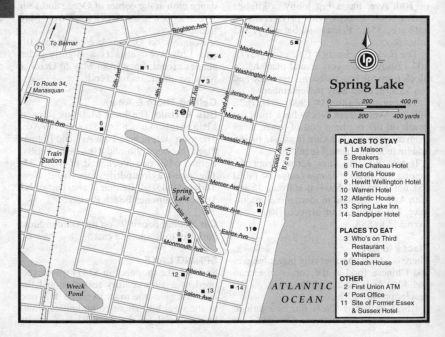

Spring Lake

0   200   400 m
0   200   400 yards

PLACES TO STAY
1 La Maison
5 Breakers
6 The Chateau Hotel
8 Victoria House
9 Hewitt Wellington Hotel
10 Warren Hotel
12 Atlantic House
13 Spring Lake Inn
14 Sandpiper Hotel

PLACES TO EAT
3 Who's on Third Restaurant
9 Whispers
10 Beach House

OTHER
2 First Union ATM
4 Post Office
11 Site of Former Essex & Sussex Hotel

ATLANTIC OCEAN

High Tech Boardwalk

After storms destroyed Spring Lake's two mile boardwalk, town officials decided to replace it with a gray-colored material that looks like wood plank but is actually a composite of recycled plastic bags and wood-pallet chips. This springy surface lasts longer, and better yet, doesn't give you splinters. ■

A Victorian-era house, the *Spring Lake Inn* (☎ (609) 449-2010), 104 Salem Ave, features an 80 foot wrap-around porch. It's your best bet if you're on a budget and want to stay in Spring Lake. It's only open from July 4 to Labor Day, but is large, airy and clean. Doubles with bath and air-con are $65 to $95; some rooms have shared bath from $35 to $65.

La Maison (☎ (908) 449-0969), at 404 Jersey Ave on a residential block, is an opulent, eight room B&B. Rates are $95 to $159; an efficiency cottage is available for weekly stays.

Hotels The *Atlantic House* (☎ (908) 449-8500), 305 2nd Ave, is the cheapest place in town and looks it. It is a large, musty place with long, wide, dark hallways, but the management is friendly and there's a large porch. Rates include continental breakfast on weekdays and full breakfast weekends. Singles are $32 to $45, doubles $58 to $68; open May to September.

The deck of the *Sandpiper Hotel* (☎ (908) 449-6060), 7 Atlantic Ave, looks over the ocean but most of its rooms do not. The hotel has a heated pool, and rates are $65 to $145 depending on demand. *The Chateau* (☎ (908) 974-2000), 500 Warren Ave, overlooks the north end of Spring Lake. Rooms come complete with TV and VCR, refrigerator, telephone, air-con and private bath. There is a multi-tier rate schedule from $52 to $185.

The *Hewitt Wellington Hotel* (☎ (908) 974-1212, fax 974-2338) is at 200 Monmouth Ave overlooking the lake. It's a large, white, wood structure with wrap-around porch and small pool and restaurant. Doubles off season/in season start at $70/110. Open April to October.

The *Breakers* (☎ (908) 449-7700, fax 449-0161), 1507 Ocean Ave, is one of the more upscale establishments with rooms from $150 to $270. The large white-and-brown chateau-style *Warren Hotel* (☎ (908) 449-8800, fax 449-7216), 901 Ocean Ave, is set half a block back from the beach with standard rooms starting at $139/194 in season and $110 off season.

Great Adventure Theme Park

The massive Six Flags Great Adventure theme park (☎ (908) 928-1821) is located in Jackson Township west of the Jersey Shore towns, and features a 350 acre drive-through safari with 1500 animals from seven continents, along with over 100 rides, shows and attractions. In the early '80s, the park had a reputation for attracting out of control teenagers, but then it was bought by Time Warner, which invested $100 million and touted its image as 'bigger than Disney World and a whole lot closer.'

The company recently sold Great Adventure to private investors, but you'll still get the sense that its one big advertisement for the Warner Bros studio, with the 'Lethal Weapon' water ride and Looney Tunes characters such as Bugs Bunny roaming the grounds. There's a very popular log flume and several harrowing roller coasters.

On summer weekends, Great Adventure has very long lines at its most popular rides, so it's important to go early or on a weekday. Throughout the season concerts by rock, country and jazz artists are included in the admission price.

The amusement area is open from April to October from 10 am to midnight, with the Wild Safari Park open from 9 am to 4 pm. Admission is $28 for both the rides and safari park; children under 54 inches tall pay $19. Adult season tickets are $59.95, and $199 for a family of four. Six Flags is located off exit 7A on the NJ Turnpike or exit 98 to I-195 on the Garden State Parkway. ■

NEW JERSEY

Places to Eat

The *Who's on Third* deli (☎ (609) 449-4233), 1300 3rd Ave, is the best place in town for burgers and other quick bites.

The *Beach House* (☎ (908) 449-9646) facing the sea at 901 Ocean Ave, is a place to quaff specialty drinks on the porch. Lunch burgers, sandwiches and pizza are around $6; dinner entrees are from $13 to $20. It's open May to October.

Whispers (☎ (908) 449-3330), in the Hewitt Wellington Hotel, serves pasta, chicken, veal and seafood dishes for about $17 to $22.

The restaurant in the *Sandpiper Hotel* (☎ (908) 449-6060), 7 Atlantic Ave, serves a large Sunday seafood brunch buffet ($14).

Getting There & Away

Train The train station is at Railroad Plaza and Warren Ave, one block east of Route 71. Check out the elaborate weather vane on top of the old structure. The NJ Transit fare from New York is $9.45/14.

Car To get to Spring Lake, take exit 98 on the Garden State Parkway which will bring you to Route 138 west; follow that to Route 71 south.

MANASQUAN

Located about 65 miles from both New York City to the north and Philadelphia to the southwest, Manasquan (population 5400) is one of the nicest towns on the Jersey Shore, with a rowdy beachfront area separated from the main town by a small canal. The 1½ mile beach front and the surrounding blocks to the west are filled with two-story cottages that stand empty after Labor Day. Near the intersection of Main St and 1st Ave there are a few popular bars and along the jetty at the southern end of town is considered one of the best surfing beaches in the state. Manasquan has a very nice downtown area, with a movie theater that has been turned into an arts center. Unfortunately, its lovingly restored train station was destroyed by an electrical fire in the winter of 1996.

Orientation & Information

Manasquan's town center is along Main St immediately west of Route 71, one block from the train station.

Call the Manasquan Chamber of Commerce at ☎ (908) 223-8303. There's an ATM a few doors away from the movie theater, and a post office in the parking lot immediately south of Main St.

On Route 71 between Manasquan and Point Pleasant Beach, and officially in the town of Brielle, is Escargot Books (☎ (908) 528-5955), 503 Route 71, which features 20,000 used books.

Outdoor Activities

The beach (☎ (609) 223-0544) costs $4 per day; $38 for the season, and $16 for seniors. It has an asphalt pathway and is populated by teens. There are three small amusement areas on the beach and a few stands selling hats and T-shirts.

Surfing The Manasquan Inlet Beach, immediately north of the jetty marking the northern side of the Manasquan River inlet, is rated highly by shore surfers. It's possible to get onto this beach along the jetty without a beach badge (though you are officially required to have one).

Places to Stay & Eat

O'Neill's Guesthouse (☎ (908) 528-5666), 390 E Main St, four blocks from the train station, is a newly renovated hotel with 20 guest rooms, most with private baths. Rates are $95 to $105 depending on whether you stay in the suite or a single room. Off season the rate drops to a flat $40. A slightly noisy bar & grill is on the premises. *Cooper House* (☎ (908) 223-1443), 324 E Main St, is a more traditional B&B with rates in the $75 range.

Carlson's Corner restaurant is on Riverside Dr at the beach serving burgers, fries, pork rolls and candy to surfers year round.

The *Squan Tavern* (☎ (908) 223-3324), 15 Broad St just off Main St, has been serving pizzas and heros to locals for 30 years. Most entrees run under $12. *Edgar's* (☎ (908) 449-4422), on the corner of Sea

Girt Ave and Route 71, is a bar serving cheap sandwich lunch specials for $8.95.

Entertainment
The *Osprey Hotel* (☎ (908) 528-1800), at Main St and 1st Ave, has live music in its eight bars Friday to Sunday with a $5 cover. At other times the disc jockey plays rock, house and even techno music to the under 30 crowd. It's open from Tuesday to Sunday, from 5 pm to 2 am, April to late September.

Leggett's (☎ (908) 223-3951) is a few doors south of the Osprey Hotel on 1st Ave. It's a year-round, seven-day-a-week bar with no cover. The music is generally conservative rock and the patrons are usually 35 and under.

Getting There & Away
Bus & Train The train station is on E Main St and Colby Ave about 500 feet east of Route 71, and the bus stops on Main St. The NJ Transit one-way/roundtrip fare from New York is $9.45/14.

Car Take exit 98 off the Garden State Parkway to Route 34, following signs to the Manasquan beach area (Route 71 north to Main St, turning east to the shore).

POINT PLEASANT BEACH
Point Pleasant Beach (population 5600) is the northernmost community on the Barnegat Peninsula, a narrow 22 mile barrier strip between the Atlantic and Barnegat Bay. European fishermen and farmers first settled along the bay in the early 19th century, and though some farms took in boarders who wanted to be near the shore, it wasn't until 1878 that lawyers from Trenton made the town of Point Pleasant into a resort.

They created the Point Pleasant Land Company and bought 250 acres on the peninsula, naming it Point Pleasant City. In 1875 the first bridge was built linking Brielle and Point Pleasant; the railroad and further development followed in 1880. Even today, the idea of private enterprise holds in Point Pleasant, since

the beach is dominated by two companies that have a hammer-lock on beachfront business in town.

Information
The chamber of commerce (☎ (908) 899-2424), 517-A Arnold Ave, has general information, and there's an ATM next door.

The post office is at 410 Arnold Ave, within sight of the train station. The Beach Laundromat is on Ocean Ave opposite the intersection with Homestead Ave. It's open from 7 am to 8 pm.

The streets near the boardwalk fill up with cars so you may have to park a block or two back from the beach. There are parking lots on Arnold and Ocean Aves with day-long spots for $3 to $5.

Outdoor Activities
Beaches The first Point Pleasant Beach boardwalk was built in 1885. Today the boardwalk has the usual collection of beach food – pizza, burgers, clams – plus a couple of huge bars stretching out over the water, and an amusement park with rides mostly for kids.

There are two privately owned beaches along the Point Pleasant boardwalk. Both are wide, white-sand beaches very crowded on weekends.

There's **Risden's Beach** (☎ (908) 892-8410), which goes from the southern end of the boardwalk to a point just north of Trenton Ave. Its weekday/weekend cost is $3.50/4.50; children four to seven are 50¢; and the seasonal pass is $50. Risden's also provides two large bath houses (☎ (908) 892-9743, 892-9580) along their section of the beach. For $5 during the week and $6 on weekends, you get a beach pass, unlimited access to a small, clean, locking wooden cubicle and a shower. The lockers tend to sell out early on weekends. It's open from about 9 am to 5 pm.

And there's also **Jenkinson's Beach** (☎ (908) 892-3274), which runs from Trenton Ave north to the Manasquan River inlet and includes an amusement park and a small aquarium. The beach costs $4/5 for weekdays/weekends; kids five to 11 are $1.

Jenkinson's has two small bath houses. The first is behind the gift shop almost at the northern end of the boardwalk. The bath houses cost $2.50 for adults and $1.50 for children ages five to 11, but do not provide lockers.

Fishing Many party and charter boats are run out of Ken's Landing (☎ (908) 892-9787, 899-5491), 30 Broadway, and departure times and costs are posted there. A half-day trip usually runs between $18 and $25. Some boats also run 90 minute nighttime cruises along the shore for $8/5 for adults/children. Clark's Landing (☎ (908) 223-6546) also has charter boats.

Scuba Diving The Inlet Dive Center (☎ (908) 899-4545), 318 Broadway, and Underwater Discovery (☎ (908) 295-5800), 201 Broadway, offer rentals and lessons.

Jenkinson's Pavilion & Aquarium
Rebuilt after a devastating fire a few years back, Jenkinson's Pavilion (☎ (908) 892-0844) on the boardwalk near the intersection with Arnold Ave, offers 50 rides. Tickets are 50¢ each and rides cost from

two to six tickets. Open April to October (indoor arcades open year round).

The aquarium (☎ (908) 899-1212) is open year round and displays seals, sharks, penguins and alligators. There are also touch tanks for children. Admission is $5.50/3.50.

Places to Stay
Motels are predominantly located on Broadway between Chicago and Boston Aves and on the southern end of Ocean Ave. There are also a few guest houses. Most places are seasonal – and on the Jersey Shore that means an almost complete shut-down at Labor Day.

Guest Houses *Century House* (☎ (908) 899-8208), 18 Forman Ave, is half a block from the boardwalk. The house has a pool, porch, grill, refrigerators, TV, and parking. Rooms are $50 per night Sunday to Thursday, $45 for two night (or more) stays. Weekends they are $65 for a single and $55 for two.

Kieffer's (☎ (908) 892-2292), 17 Arnold, is half a block to the beach. They have eight clean rooms with TVs. Singles/doubles

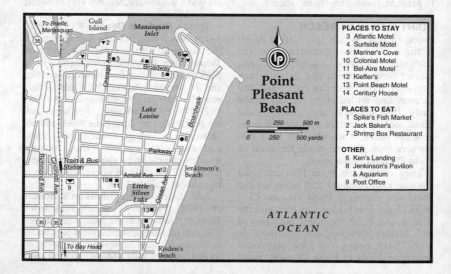

PLACES TO STAY
3 Atlantic Motel
4 Surfside Motel
5 Mariner's Cove
10 Colonial Motel
11 Bel-Aire Motel
12 Kieffer's
13 Point Beach Motel
14 Century House

PLACES TO EAT
1 Spike's Fish Market
2 Jack Baker's
7 Shrimp Box Restaurant

OTHER
6 Ken's Landing
8 Jenkinson's Pavilion & Aquarium
9 Post Office

Point Pleasant Beach

are $65/70 during the week and $5 more on weekends.

Motels There are a number of places on Broadway. It's fairly noisy due to traffic and the motels there face the street around small pools. They all come with bland but fairly new furniture, air-con, TV, parking and they usually have refrigerators. All rates assume double occupancy, and a few hotels offer off-season rates at a 50% discount.

Atlantic Motel (☎ (908) 899-7711, fax 899-4342), 215 Broadway, costs $65/99 weekdays/weekends and its rooms face away from the road so they're less noisy. *Mariner's Cove* (☎ (908) 899-0060), 50 Broadway, costs $89/109 weekdays/weekends; $10 for each additional person in the room. *Surfside Motel* (☎ (908) 899-1109), 101 Broadway, is $88 during the week and higher weekends.

The motels on Arnold Ave tend to be quieter than those on Broadway. The *Colonial Motel* (☎ (908) 899-2394), 210 Arnold, has rooms for $79 daily and efficiencies for $95. The *Bel-Aire Motel* (☎ (908) 892-2248), 202 Arnold, has weekday doubles for $89; $125 on Friday; $110 Saturday or Sunday. If you stay all three nights Friday to Sunday, you pay $99 per night.

A few motels are on the southern end of Ocean Ave, far enough from the honky-tonk areas of the boardwalk. The *White Sands/Ebb Tide* complex (☎ (908) 899-3370), 1106 Ocean Ave, is an amalgamation of three hotels to create an 'oceanfront resort.' It has 72 rooms, a 350 foot private beach, two pools and an oceanfront snack bar. In-season rates are from $90 to $135, which isn't bad given the location. Open April to November.

The *Point Beach Motel* (☎ (908) 892-5100), at Ocean and Trenton Aves. recently opened and is the cleanest place around. Weekday/weekend in-season rates are $105/115.

Places to Eat
The boardwalk has the usual pizza, burger and clam fast food places and there are a few delis and breakfast places along Ocean Ave behind the boardwalk.

Spike's Fish Market & Restaurant (☎ (908) 295-9400), 415 Broadway, cooks the fresh seafood they sell. A large tin bucket of steamers runs $10; open year round.

The *Shrimp Box* (☎ (908) 899-1637) is at Ken's Landing Marina on Broadway a few blocks west of Ocean Ave. Tables look over a small inlet named Lake Louise, where the fishing boats have their slips. Seafood appetizers are $5 to $6; fish entrees $13 to $17. Avoid the pasta.

The nicest place to eat is *Jack Baker's* (☎ (908) 892-9100), 101 Channel Dr Point. Its booths overlook Manasquan Inlet. It serves reasonably priced seafood for $15 and under, with numerous lunch specials (book ahead on summer weekends).

Entertainment
Martell's (☎ (908) 892-0131), on the boardwalk, has music seven days, with touring acts visiting on Monday. Cover is generally $5 or under when there is one. Open from April to November.

Things to Buy
The Point Pleasant Antique Emporium (☎ (908) 892-2222, (800) 322-8002) has 100 dealers under one roof at the corner of Bay and Trenton Aves.

Getting There & Away
Bus & Train The train and bus station is at Route 35 north and Arnold Ave. The one-way/roundtrip fare from New York is $9.45/14. The local M20 bus terminates here as well.

Car You get to Point Pleasant Beach by taking exit 98 on the Garden State Parkway, then Route 34 south to the traffic circle to the town.

BAY HEAD
Bay Head (population 1226) is the final town reached by the North Jersey Coast train line. The land was bought in 1876 by Princeton banker David Mount, who

purchased it from a retired sea captain. A few years later Mount and two other investors created the Bay Head Land Company to develop the town.

Bay Head remains a proper and quiet community with private Cape Cod-style homes along the beach. Although there is public access to the ocean, there's no boardwalk and it's very peaceful and quiet even in high season.

There is a very small permanent population along Route 35, but traveling here in the winter you'll see the area is ghostly, save for a few bars and coffee shops.

Information

The post office is at 82 Bridge Ave, one block away from the train terminus. Bay Head Book House, 89 Bridge Ave, has a small selection of books.

Beaches

The beach, just about the only activity here, was only opened to non-residents after the state sued the town. It has clean white sand and very few people, so it's worth coming to even if you're staying in another town. Beach passes are available from the Bay Head Improvement Association (☎ (908) 892-4179) on the western end of Mount St, though the address is 532 Lake Ave. The cost is $4.25 per day or $50/35 for full and half season, but you have to buy season tickets in pairs. Children under 11 are free.

Places to Stay

The *Bentley Inn* (☎ (908) 892-9589), 694 Main Ave, is the most casual place in Bay Head. The common areas have some wicker furniture, a couch or two and a TV. There is a wrap-around porch, a fireplace and parking. Seasonal rates are $49 to $89.

Nearby is *Conover's Bay Head Inn* (☎ (908) 892-4664), 646 Main Ave, which has a huge backyard and garden and a grill and refrigerator for guests. Room furniture in the 'bedchambers' are made of tasteful dark wood, and all have bathrooms. Rates including breakfast are $70 to $115/105 to 165 weekday/weekends.

Kaptain's Haven (☎ (908) 892-4479),

548 Main Ave, rents two room apartments and efficiencies for $300 to $550 a week.

The *Bay Head Sands* (☎ (908) 899-7016), 2 Twilight Rd, has very clean rooms, some with private baths. Rates, including breakfast and beach badges, are $70 to $110 weekdays and $85 to $140 weekends. *Bay Head Gables* (☎ (908) 892-9844), 200 Main Ave, is a nicely decorated place where all rooms have air-con and private baths, some with porches. The house itself has a 150 foot wrap-around porch. Weekday rates are $95 to $125, and $115 to $160 on weekends in season. Off-season rates are from $85 to $125; open year round.

The *Greenville Hotel & Restaurant* (☎ (908) 892-3100) is a year-round Victorian hotel at 345 Main Ave. Its 31 rooms all come with TV, telephone and private bath. Rates include continental breakfast and beach badges. In-season rates are from $77 to $102 during the week and from $132 to $202 weekends.

Bluff's Hotel & Restaurant (☎ (908) 892-1114) is right on the beach at 575 East Ave. Air-con rooms are $145 to $200 in season; a basic annex has rooms with fans from $90 to $130.

Places to Eat

Some of the hotels have decent restaurants. The *Bentley Inn*, 694 Main Ave, has a New American menu put together by Mike Cacirnes that includes items like marinated free-range chicken with grilled peaches ($14), salmon over corn with beans and zucchini ($16), as well as penne, tuna and steak. Open Tuesday to Saturday in season.

The restaurant in the *Grenville Hotel*, 345 Main Ave, serves beef, seafood and duck entrees for $17 to $22. *Bluff's Restaurant*, 575 East Ave right on the ocean, has lunch sandwiches from $6 and steak, chicken and seafood entrees for around $18.

Entertainment

Bluff's Bar (☎ (908) 892-1719) is a windowless two room structure underneath the main hotel, one of the 'preppiest' bars on the Shore – with locals wearing the uniform of brightly colored Izod shirts and chinos. There's live music on Tuesday and Thursday, and the younger crowd gathers in the whitewashed back room.

Getting There & Away

Train Bay Head is the terminus of NJ Transit service. The station is at Osborne Ave and Twilight Rd two blocks west of Route 35. The one-way/roundtrip fare from New York is $9.45/14.

Car From the north, exit the Garden State Parkway at exit 98 and take Route 34 to the junction with Route 35 and you'll come to Bay Head after Point Pleasant Beach. If you're driving south inland from the coast along Route 35, you'll drive right into Bay Head after Point Pleasant Beach.

From the south, you can take Garden State Parkway exit 90 and drive seven miles to the coast on Route 88. Bay Head is at the eastern end of the highway.

SEASIDE HEIGHTS

This town (population 2400) and its sister Seaside Park feature lots of motels, a mile-long boardwalk with two amusement piers, several bars and a good white-sand beach, although it is not as wide as Point Pleasant's and drops off sharply into the surf. This is a major destination for people 21 and over during the summer, particularly the bars and clubs.

Orientation & Information

Most of the town's bars and restaurants are along Atlantic Blvd, called 'Boulevard' by the locals even though there's more than one boulevard in town.

Town information and special events can be obtained by calling ☎ (908) 793-1510.

The post office is at 55 Sumner Ave. The nearest bookstore is Pyramid Books (☎ (908) 793-8300), at 1403 Grand Central Ave in Lavallette.

Note that Kearney St is pronounced 'CAR-nee.'

The best place to find parking is on Central Ave, which is immediately west of

(and parallel to) Atlantic Blvd. Central Ave has a wide median where many people park and walk the few blocks to the beach to save themselves time searching for an elusive parking space. Streets closest to the ocean tend to get very crowded, and most side streets run one way in the summer.

Moreover, the town has greedily set up meters on every available piece of open street. You must use them 24 hours a day, seven days a week. They cost 25¢ per half hour. There are all-day parking lots along Ocean Ave and the streets off it. Most charge $8 per day.

Outdoor Activities

The beach (☎ (908) 793-9100) is wide and free on Tuesday and Thursday. Other times, badges are $3.50; seasonal passes are $15 before May 14 and $20 afterwards. The boardwalk has the usual food items, two amusement piers, a lot of carnival games and a chair lift like those you find at ski resorts.

The Blaine Lockers are in a shop at the corner of Blaine and Ocean Terrace. For $4 you get the use of a small locker and showers from 8 am to 10 pm during the summer.

The **Funtown Pier** (☎ (908) 830-0191) is the southern pier with a log flume ($3), go-carts ($4), a Ferris wheel and a number of kiddie rides. Tickets are 50¢ each and rides cost from two to six tickets each.

The **Casino Pier** (☎ (908) 793-6488) is the northern former fishing pier now packed with more rides than Funtown. The highlight is a carousel (☎ (908) 830-4183) dating from about 1910, with some of its carved animals from the 1890s, and music is provided by a 1923 Wurlitzer organ. Tickets for Casino Pier's rides are also 50¢ each with rides costing two to six tickets. It's open from April to September.

Jet Skis Get Wet Watersports (☎ (908) 830-6424), at the Bayside Marina on Route 35 south just past the A&P, has jet skis for half hour/hour rental at $35/60. WaveRunner 500 Series are $35/60; and WaveRunner 650 Series are slightly more.

NEW JERSEY

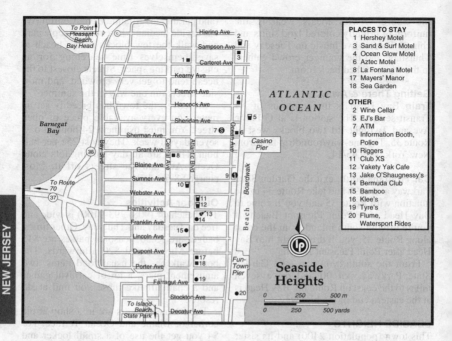

PLACES TO STAY
1 Hershey Motel
3 Sand & Surf Motel
4 Ocean Glow Motel
6 Aztec Motel
8 La Fontana Motel
17 Mayers' Manor
18 Sea Garden

OTHER
2 Wine Cellar
5 EJ's Bar
7 ATM
9 Information Booth,
   Police
10 Riggers
11 Club XS
12 Yakety Yak Cafe
13 Jake O'Shaugnessy's
14 Bermuda Club
15 Bamboo
16 Klee's
19 Tyre's
20 Flume,
   Watersport Rides

ATLANTIC OCEAN

Barnegat Bay

Casino Pier

Boardwalk

Beach

Fun-Town Pier

Seaside Heights

0   250   500 m
0   250   500 yards

To Point Pleasant Beach, Bay Head

To Route 70

To Island Beach State Park

Open from 9 am to 7 pm from two weeks before Memorial Day to two weeks after Labor Day.

The place to go for the largest WaveRunners, the 750 Series, is Island Pleasures (☎ (908) 830-2546, 270-9107) on Route 35 south in South Mantoloking, about seven miles north of Seaside Heights. The laid-back and knowledgeable owners, Terry and Chris, have been in business for 15 years and can tell you everything you want to know. Rates are half hour/hourly. They have Jet Ski 550s at $35/65, 650s at $45/85. WaveRunner 500 Series are $35/65, 650 Series $45/85, and 750 Series $55/105. Rates for two people on one jet ski run $15 extra. They also winterize and service jet skis for owners and rent pontoon boats.

Waterslides The biggest and best is Waterworks (☎ (908) 793-6495) at Sherman Ave and Ocean Terrace. It costs

$10 for two hours, but if you come at 9 am or 7 pm, you get three hours. Open from 9 am to 10 pm.

In-Line Skating Skates can be rented at the Big Top Arcade at 1020 Boardwalk; two hours for $10, four hours for $15, all day for $20. It's open Monday to Friday from 10 am to 8 pm, weekends from 7 am to 6 pm.

Bicycling Tyre's (☎ (908) 830-2050), 1900 Atlantic Blvd at the corner of Farragut, rents bicycles for hourly/daily/ weekly rates of $5/18/45.

Treasure Hunting Hobbysport (☎ (908) 240-5758) rents and sells metal detectors to search for lost coins and jewelry.

Places to Stay

Seaside Heights has a number of standard motels. In general, the closer you are to Ocean Ave and the beach, the cleaner they are.

Mayers' Manor (☎ (908) 793-6606), 57 Dupont Ave, may have the cheapest rooms in town at $35/65 daily and $125/165 weekly.

One of the best places is the *La Fontana Motel* (☎ (908) 793-0804/0669), at Grant and Central Aves, run by Guy and Edna Mazzanti and offering bungalow efficiencies from $45 to $75. *Proud Mary's Motel* (☎ (908) 830-0032), 1502 Atlantic Blvd, is named after the mother of the owners, not John Fogerty's famous song. There is a lot of traffic noise but rooms cost $65/85; no phone.

The *Belmont Motel* (☎ 908) 793-8519), located at 120 Sheridan Ave, has phones and clean, new furniture. Singles/doubles are $60 to $80/75 to 90.

The *Aquarius Arms Motel* (☎ (908) 793-0011), at the corner of Kearney and Central Aves costs $75/85. The block-long, block-wide *Hershey Motel* (☎ (908) 793-5000), 1415 Atlantic Blvd, has doubles in the $80s in season.

Seaside Park There are five motels just south of the Funtown Pier on Ocean Avenue, which are officially in the town of Seaside Park, but only by a few blocks. These places all have motel standards and are good choices because they face an empty beach instead of the noisy boardwalk. The *Holiday Motel* (☎ (908) 793-1488), 1505 N Ocean Ave, between Lafayette Ave and O St, has in season weekday/weekend doubles at $83/88; add $5 for an ocean view.

The *Charlroy Motel* (☎ (908) 793-0712), 1601 N Ocean Ave, between Decatur and Lafayette Aves, has rates at $69/89; no phone.

The *Sea Gull Motel* (☎ (908) 793-0815), 1401 N Ocean Ave, between O and N Sts, has the best rates at $55/75. The *Seascape Motel* (☎ (908) 793-8770), 1315 N Ocean Ave, between N and M Sts, has rooms for $75/85, off season for $50/60. Open to early October.

Luna-Mar (☎ (908) 793-7955), at N Ocean Ave and L St, charges $70/80.

On the Boardwalk *Sand & Surf Motel* (☎ (908) 793-7311), 1201 Ocean Terrace, near Fremont St, has dormitory-style rooms for one or two people at $40/69 weekday/weekend. The rooms are just small motel rooms in the basement, you don't actually share them. The *Ocean Glow Motel* (☎ (908) 793-1300) is at Hancock and Boardwalk. Rooms are a reasonable $66/80 in season and around $45 off season.

The bright yellow *Aztec Motel* (☎ (908) 793-3000) is at 901 Boardwalk, between Sherman and Sheridan Sts. Rooms overlook the ocean and Casino Pier. Rates are from $71 to $130/96 to 145 weekday/weekends, with a three day minimum stay during the summer.

The *Island Beach Motor Lodge* (☎ (908) 793-5400) is at 24th and Central Aves in South Seaside Park just before the entrance to Island Beach State Park. The motel has its own beach and heated pool. Basic room rates are $80 in season with a two-night minimum, and $25 to $50 off season. In/off season efficiencies are $100 to $120/25 to 80. It's a good place to stay if you're winter fishing at Island Beach State Park.

Places to Eat
The boardwalk is full of fabulously unhealthful fast-food stands, including vendors selling fresh-cut French fries from unskinned potatoes and orange ice cream, available at the *Kohr's* stands along the beach.

The *Berkeley Seafood Restaurant* (☎ (908) 793-0400), on 24th and Central Ave, is a seafood market with an upstairs restaurant. The fresh fish is served with cole slaw, salad, potato and bread for $9 to $15; they have no liquor license.

Bum Rogers Tavern (☎ (908) 830-2770), on Central Ave between 22nd and 23rd Aves, is a dark bar/restaurant that serves excellent Cajun garlic crabs for $10. Avoid the pasta or menu items that need special cooking attention. Monday to Wednesday they offer two-for-one dinner specials.

Entertainment

Most bars and clubs are on Boulevard between Sumner and Dupont St, or are right on the boardwalk.

Boardwalk *EJ's* (☎ (908) 793-4622), at Sheridan Ave and the boardwalk, is open 365 days a year and has one very long bar and six pool tables. Earlier in the day it gets an older local crowd. Open from 10 am to 2 am.

The *Wine Cellar* (☎ (908) 793-4245), a restaurant at Sampson and the boardwalk, also has live and DJ music several nights a week. Sunday from 2 pm to 5 pm they have laser karaoke 'matinee' parties; Monday is surf music night; Tuesday is grunge/metal night.

The *Aztec Motel* has a lounge (☎ (908) 793-1010) at Sherman and the boardwalk, with local live music from Friday to Sunday and a lot of drink specials.

Atlantic Blvd *Klee's* (☎ (908) 830-1996) is on Dupont and Atlantic Blvd. It's got live music from Tuesday to Sunday during the summer and on weekends in the winter. The music is light and mainstream, and so is the crowd.

Rigger's (☎ (908) 830-9600), at 519 Atlantic Blvd, is a year-round neighborhood bar populated by fishermen, which is why it's open from 7 am to 2 am daily.

The *Yakety Yak Cafe* (☎ (908) 830-1999) and *Club XS* (☎ (908) 830-3036) are next to each other at 406 and 408 Atlantic Blvd. Yakety Yak features '50s dance music on weekends, reggae on Thursday and comedy on Wednesday. Club XS has an alcohol-free teen night (ages 13 to 17) on Wednesday. Other nights it's a regular dance club.

The other large and popular nightspots nearby are *Bamboo* (☎ (908) 830-3660), corner of Lincoln Ave and Atlantic Blvd; and *Bermuda Club* (☎ (908) 793-7567), 302 Atlantic Blvd.

Jake O'Shaughnessy's (☎ (908) 830-6068), Atlantic Blvd at the corner of Hamilton, is a restaurant and bar for locals with live music from Sunday to Wednesday.

Getting There & Away

Bus NJ Transit runs long-distance buses from New York City to Seaside Heights (Bus Shore Service Route 137) one-way/roundtrip for $15/27. Jersey City to Seaside Heights (Route 67) costs $10.50/19.

Car Seaside Heights is exit 82 off the Garden State Parkway. You exit onto Route 37 east, which goes right into Seaside after eight miles. You can also drive down the Barnegat Peninsula on Route 35 south from Point Pleasant Beach and Bay Head.

ISLAND BEACH STATE PARK

This 3000 acre state park (☎ (908) 793-0506) takes up the southern third of the Barnegat Peninsula. The preserve is a combination of shore and marsh that stretches about nine miles from the end of Seaside Park to the inlet separating the peninsula from Long Beach Island. The land was bought in 1926 by Henry Phipps, a Pittsburgh steel millionaire, for development as a resort, but the stock market crash put a stop to the scheme. The tract of land remained untouched until the state bought it in 1953 and opened the park six years later, one of New Jersey's first efforts at preservation.

Because there is no public transportation to Long Beach Island, you'll need a car to get there – which is unfortunate because the traffic tends to be brutal in July and August.

Orientation & Information

The park is divided into a Northern Natural Area, a Recreational Zone, and a Southern Natural Area. Fires are allowed in the Southern Area. In-season weekday/weekend admission per car is $6/7; off-season costs $4. During the summer, the park charges an extra dollar to enter the Southern Natural Area, but limits the number of cars to about 300 – the number of parking spaces. The fees are high, but if you come to swim with several people, it is much cheaper than buying a beach badge per person as required elsewhere.

The park is open year round from 8 am to dusk.

Outdoor Activities

Beaches The sand is at its whitest and purest in the park, and it's a great place for swimming. The one mile strip of beach on the Atlantic is called the **Recreational Zone** and has lifeguards.

Fishing There is excellent surf fishing in the park, particularly for bluefish and striped bass. In summer you can haul in flounder, weakfish and kingfish. Surf-fishers may remain in the park overnight, but they must be 'actively engaged in fishing activities' from midnight to 4 am. Those caught sleeping are kicked out.

A limited number of Mobile Sport Fishing Vehicle (MSFV) permits are issued for those who want to drive onto the beach at the southern end of the island and fish. Permits are $25 for three days, $125 for the season. Fishing without a vehicle is free.

Birdwatching A 10 minute walk from the road in the Southern Zone is a well-marked bird blind with log seats overlooks an osprey nest on a pole nearby. Depending on the season, you'll also be able to see egrets, herons, ibises, ducks and other migratory birds.

Places to Eat

In-season there is a concession stand with mediocre beach food, so whenever possible bring your own. You can cook freshly caught fish in the southern zone.

LONG BEACH ISLAND

Long Beach Island is an 18 mile long barrier island with a series of small towns. Barnegat Light is in the north, Surf City and Ship Bottom at the center, and Beach Haven stands almost at the southern tip. The island is connected to the mainland by a causeway at its halfway point of the town of Ship Bottom.

This is the place to head if you want to immerse yourself in New Jersey's wide array of oceanfront activities. While the things to see and do are spread out along its length, the main points of interests are at Beach Haven and Barnegat Light.

Orientation & Information

Strict zoning bans the construction of high rises, but the entire land surface is crossed by streets dotted with summer season motels and cottages. Vegetation is sparse, and during severe storms parts of the island are cut off from the mainland.

Long Beach Blvd is the main – in some spots the only – street running from Barnegat Light on south, though it gives way to Bay Blvd as you approach Beach Haven. Bay Blvd is often referred to by locals simply as 'the Boulevard.'

The Chamber of Commerce for Southern Ocean County and Long Beach Island (☎ (609) 494-7211) is at 265 W 9th St in Ship Bottom. The causeway from the mainland, Route 72, puts you on 9th St. The chamber offices are on your left two blocks in from the causeway. You can pick up information on lodging and activities there.

TLC Shipping (☎ (609) 492-0060, fax 492-3939) in the Acme Surf Building, 1301 N Bay Ave, Beach Haven, NJ 08008, runs a message and fax service. This is useful if you're staying at a place without a phone. They charge $2 to register, then $3 to deliver each message. The domestic fax service is $4 for the first page, $1 for each extra.

The *Beach Haven Times* is the weekly newspaper for the island. If you want information about entertainment, restaurants, discount coupons, etc, pick up a copies of the *Summer Times Islander* and the *Beachcomber*, the free weeklies distributed in most stores.

Barnegat Lighthouse

The lighthouse (☎ (609) 494-2016), is on the northern tip of Long Beach Island on a 31 acre state park at the end of Broadway in the town of Barnegat Light. A lighthouse was first built here along 'Barendegat,' or

'Breakers Inlet' in Dutch, in 1834. Three years later, the land around the original lighthouse eroded, and it collapsed into the sea. A new lighthouse was opened in 1859 and until 1927 was used by mariners going to and coming from New York to change course and avoid the treacherous Jersey-coast shoals.

'Old Barney' was originally 900 feet from the shore and has had to be rescued several times from being undermined by erosion. The structure is made of internal and external circular walls 10 feet apart at the base and 18 inches apart at the top. The outer wall is 4½ feet thick at the base, tapering to 1½ feet at the top. The original light itself was a five-wick lamp burning sperm-whale oil, and a 10,000 pound Fresnel lens (now in the Barnegat Light Museum) magnified the beam so it could be seen for 30 miles. The light was set on brass rollers, and a wind-up weight device similar to those found in grandfather clocks rotated the light once every four minutes. If you climb the tower's 217 steps, you'll get a fantastic view of the mainland, Long Beach and the Barnegat Peninsula.

The lighthouse is open daily from 10 am to 4:30 pm from Memorial Day to Labor Day and weekends in May, September and October. Admission is $1, with free parking.

Barnegat Light Museum
The museum (☎ (609) 494-2096), is at the corner of 5th St and Long Beach Blvd in Barnegat Light in a turn-of-the-century one room schoolhouse. It's dedicated to the shipping industry of the 19th century, with whale vertebrae, a stingray tail, bottles and photos amongst other things. The Fresnel lens from the lighthouse is also on display here; it's 10 feet tall and has over 1000 thick glass prisms.

It's open daily July and August from 2 to 5 pm; in June and September weekends only from 2 to 5 pm; free.

Fantasy Island & Thundering Surf
Fantasy Island (☎ (609) 492-4000), 320 W 7th St in Beach Haven, is an old Victorian-style amusement park that has children's rides and various clown shows during the day. Ride tokens cost 50¢ each, and rides require three to five tokens. It's open from Memorial Day to Labor Day, and the indoor arcade is open year round.

Thundering Surf (☎ (609) 492-0869) is a large water slide next door to Fantasy Island with a half hour/hourly charge of $6/8. If you come at 9 or 10 am or 7 pm, you can get a full hour for $6.

Long Beach Island Foundation of the Arts & Sciences
The foundation (☎ (609) 494-1241), 120 Long Beach Blvd in Loveladies, offers courses in ceramics, jewelry, basketry, Chinese calligraphy, silk painting and other arts. They also have exhibits, shows, lectures and special children's programs during the summer only.

Outdoor Activities
The beaches are wide at the northern end of the island in Barnegat Light where reclamation has put about half a mile of sand and dune between houses that used to be beachfront. This is primarily the result of jetties built to protect Barnegat Lighthouse from being eroded into the bay. Beaches elsewhere are a short walk from the end of the street to the water.

Beach Badges There are six separate entities issuing badges among the 21 communities on Long Beach Island. Seniors are free everywhere.

Long Beach Township (☎ (609) 494-7606) sells a single badge good for all the communities not listed below. But not all of the Long Beach Township communities are next to each other and you might not be staying in any of them. Badges are $2/5/9 before June 15 and $2/5/12 after.

The prices that follow are quoted on daily/weekly/seasonal basis. Seasonal passes are generally $2 or $3 less if you buy them in May and in some places early in June. It's a bit confusing, so pick a single beach and stick with it.

NEW JERSEY

Beach & Tel	Badge Cost
Barnegat Light (609) 494-9196	$2/7/15
Beach Haven (609) 492-0111	$2/4/12
Harvey Cedars (609) 494-2843	$2/6/12
Ship Bottom (609) 494-2171	$2/7/12
Surf City (609) 494-3064	$2/8/16

Bath House Water's Edge (☎ (609) 494-4620) runs a bath house at 20th St and the ocean in Ship Bottom. Shower, bathroom, lockers and a beach badge are $4.75 for the day.

Beach Equipment Faria's has four locations on the island and a wide selection of items for rent, including beach equipment, bicycles, in-line skates, things for the home (fans, high chairs, TVs, tables), and sports equipment for volleyball, tennis, etc.

It rents items by the day/week, including umbrellas at $8/16, chairs $5/10, body boards $6/16, wet suits $12/30 and waterskis $8/20. Locations are 5th St and Long Beach Blvd, Surf City (☎ (609) 494-8616); 28th and Long Beach Blvd, Ship Bottom (☎ (609) 494-7368); on Center St, Beach Haven (☎ (609) 492-7484); and on Central Ave (Long Beach Blvd), Barnegat Light (☎ (609) 494-8533). Open from May to September.

The Acme Surf Company (☎ (609) 492-1024), 13th and Long Beach Blvd, Beach Haven, rents out body boards for $10/29, surfboards for $15/60 and wetsuits for $15/60 on a daily/weekly basis.

Ron Jon (☎ (609) 494-8844), at 9th St and Central Ave in Ship Bottom, has rentals for half a day/day/week. Surfboards, wakeboards and kneeboards are $10/15/50; wetsuits are $5/8/25; boogie boards are $3/5/18 for foam and $3/8/30 for slick. Ron Jon also rents umbrellas and chairs at $5 a day.

Sailing The Todt Sailing Center (☎ (609) 492-8550), at 25th and Atlantic Blvd in Spray Beach, rents sailing equipment. All rates are by the hour/two hours/additional hours. Sailboards are $17/28/14; Sunfish, which hold two, are $19/29/15.

Day boats come in three sizes. The 14

footer, which holds three, is $32/52/27. The 15 to 17 footer, which holds five, is $35/59/29. The 19 to 20 footer, for seven people, is $45/75/38.

Todt also has catamarans for rent: a 14 footer for two people is $31/52/26; 16 foot for three is $38/66/33; 18 foot for four is $48/86.

Lessons are available in packages from $70 to $210, depending on the item. It's open April to September from 9 am to 5 pm.

Bicycles Briggs Bicycles (☎ (609) 492-1143), 8401 Long Beach Blvd, Brighton Beach, rents bicycles. The rates are one hour for $4, four hours for $8; all day for $15; two days for $21. Tandems are $6 an hour and kid's bikes $25 a week.

In-Line Skates Island Skates (☎ (609) 492-6522), 13th and Long Beach Blvd, Beach Haven, rents in-line skates at $9 for two hours, $15 a half day and $18 a day.

Scuba Diving Triton Divers (☎ (609) 494-5599), 819 Barnegat Ave at the Causeway in Ship Bottom, breaks up the cost for a certification into several parts. Assume about $450 for a week's rental of equipment. Triton also runs trips for certified divers.

Fishing & Boating Charter boats may be rented out of the Barnegat Light Yacht Basin at the end of 18th St and the bay in Barnegat Light. The captains and boats are:

Ralph Brewster, *Fleet King*
  (609) 693-3321
Dick Clineman, *Lady Caroline II*
  (609) 693-3181
Wayne Eble, *Searcher*
  (609) 494-2369
Fred Ecker, *Connie Claire*
  (609) 494-6787
Lou Lichtman, *Pirate King II*
  (609) 494-0823, 667-2762
Hasl Tyson, *Frances*
  (609) 494-8956, 494-5090
Rocky Vendetti, *Roc-Lo*
  (609) 275-9150, 494-4825
Dave Wentling, *Sun Bird*
  (609) 494-0006, (215) 257-6661

NEW JERSEY

Cruises to Atlantic City or on the bay, and half-day fishing trips are run on the *Black Whale II* (☎ (609) 492-0333, 492-0202), which is docked at the Beach Haven Fishing Centre at Centre St and the bay in Beach Haven. Roundtrip to Trump's Castle in Atlantic City costs $30 and you get $15 in coins back for the slot machines.

Places to Stay
The liveliest town is Beach Haven, where there is the greatest concentration of bars and restaurants. A quieter time can be found in the small community of Barnegat Light at the northern end of the island. Generally speaking, the cheapest places to stay are outside of these two communities, and you can find motels up and down Long Beach Blvd from Surf City on south.

Camping There is no camping actually on Long Beach Island. The nearest campgrounds are on Route 9 south of the intersection with Route 72, which takes you onto the island. If you don't mind commuting 10 miles, *Sea Pirate Campground* (☎ (609) 296-7400) is on Route 9 in West Creek. Daily/weekly tent sites are $16.50/ 104. They have a pool and all the amenities needed for RV drivers. Open from late April to late September.

Baker's Acres (☎ (609) 296-2664), 230 Willets Ave, in Parkertown, is a mile or so south of West Creek on Route 9. The daily/ weekly tent site charge is $15.50/93.

Hotels & Motels – Barnegat Light
The casual *Inlet of Breakers Hotel* (☎ (609) 494-4848), 10 W 5th St, between Broadway and Central (Long Beach Blvd), is an 11 room red-and-white shingle house that dates to the 1890s and was originally known as 'The Social.' In its history, the house has served as a speakeasy and a brothel. You can stay in one of the brothel rooms upstairs – ceiling fans and shared bath – or one of the air-con rooms with private bathrooms downstairs.

Owner Ann Stavish Licciardello is friendly and can tell you anything you need to know about Long Beach Island. Upstairs rooms are $60 to $75 weekdays, $70 to $95 weekends. First-floor rooms are $75 to $100 and $95 to $140. The hotel offers 25% discounts for Sunday to Thursday stays.

The *White Whale Motel* (☎ (609) 494-3020), 20 W 7th St, has eight clean rooms, three efficiencies and a two bedroom apartment. The kitchens have a hot plate and toaster oven but no stove, though there's a grill in the back yard. Rooms run about $95; it's open April to October.

Ella's Motel (☎ (609) 494-3200), 18th and Long Beach Blvd, is a traditional motel open year round. In-season weekday/ weekend rates are $90/100; off-season rates may be as low as $45.

Guest House & Hotel – Surf City
C Sharp's Guest House (☎ (609) 494-6981), 1216 Long Beach Blvd at the corner of 13th St, has four rooms with shared baths. Rates are $50/85.

The *Surf City Hotel* (☎ (609) 494-7281), at 8th St and Long Beach Blvd, is a two story place with a bar and restaurant. Rates are $55 for shared bath to $85 for a private bath and TV.

Motels – Ship Bottom
The *Sandpiper Motel* (☎ (609) 494-6909) is at 10th and Long Beach Blvd, immediately on your right as you come off the causeway and start south on the island. It offers standard, clean rooms (microwaves available) and a pool; rates are just $55.

The *Admiral Motel* (☎ (609) 494-0410), 102 E 16th St, has moderate rooms at $75 and efficiencies for $90, but no phones.

Hotels – Brant Beach
Wida's Hotel (☎ (609) 494-7051) is a large, old beach hotel with 16 rooms that cost from $45 to $55. Open from Easter to late November.

B&Bs – Beach Haven
Almost all of the B&Bs are packed in an area six blocks long by one block wide within one block of the beach – from 3rd St in the north to Coral St in the south and between Atlantic and

Beach Aves. Most are top-end B&Bs with a Victorian theme.

The *Green Gables Inn & Restaurant* (☎ (609) 492-3553), 212 Centre St, has nicely decorated rooms and an excellent restaurant. Rates include a buffet breakfast and the owners speak French and Italian. Weekday/weekend rates are $75 to $95/85 to 105. Add $20 for a private bath.

Pierrot by-the-Sea (☎ (609) 492-4424), 101 Centre St, is right across from the beach. The nine bedrooms feature good wooden furniture and the common areas include a porch. The shared shower stalls, however, are in rather desperate need of repair. Doubles are from $90/150 and include a hearty breakfast.

Motels & Hotels – Beach Haven The *St Rita Hotel* (☎ (609) 492-9192/1704), 127 Engleside Ave, is the last surviving old hotel in Beach Haven, though it does not have much charm. Rooms with shared bath are $80/$105. A room for four ($145 in season) or six ($185) turns out to be a bargain. It's open mid-April to October.

The *Engleside Inn* (☎ (609) 492-1251), 30 Engleside Ave, has standard motel rooms right on the beach with a pool and the *Sand Bar*, an outdoor bar/restaurant. There's a small health club. Rates are $121 for a standard room, $137 for an efficiency, with oceanfront rooms $165. It's open year round, with off-season rates as low as $65.

The *Sea Shell Motel & Club* (☎ (609) 492-4611), 10 S Atlantic Ave at the corner of Centre St, is on the oceanfront. Standard motel rooms range from $130 to $160.

The *Mussel Beach Club* (☎ (609) 492-9644, winter 492-6130), 310 S Atlantic Ave, is actually a hotel, despite its name. All rooms are efficiencies and run $100 to $125.

Hotels – Beach Haven Inlet The cheapest place on the island is probably *Lorry's Island End Motel* (☎ (609) 492-6363), 23 Washington Ave, in Beach Haven Inlet at the very southern end of Long Beach. The nine rooms have TVs, full-size refrigerators and microwaves. The management is very laid back and welcomes large

numbers of young travelers. Weekdays/ weekend rates are $59/89 in the middle of the season. They accept cash only.

Garrison's Motel (☎ (609) 492-2266), is at 4804 S Long Beach Blvd, between Jacqueline and Joan Rds. It's a standard motel charging $70/80 on weekdays/ends.

Places to Eat
As you drive along Long Beach Blvd, you'll pass delis, a few pizza places, and a lot of seafood restaurants. Most of the seafood places serve fresh but uninspiring fare for about $15 per entree.

Barnegat Light The restaurants in Barnegat Light get very crowded at breakfast and dinner, and you may face an hour long wait for a table.

The best choice for breakfast is *Mustache Bill's Diner* at 8th and Broadway. Omelets, grits, toast and coffee are served for under $4. Bill's is open from 5 am to 3 pm and you'll have to wait for a table in the later morning during the summer. The *Inlet Delicatessen* at 33 West 4th St has reasonable sandwiches and basic food supplies. *Frank's Produce*, at 18th and Bayview next to the Viking Village shops, has a good selection of Jersey fruit and vegetables during the summer.

Kubel's (☎ (609) 494-8592), 7th St and Bayview Ave, is a year-round institution that is another reputed former brothel. Its bar is a fisherman's hangout and the restaurant is crowded in season. Seafood dishes cost around $17.

Surf City *Better Choice Healthy Foods Market* (☎ (609) 494-7050), 8 Long Beach Blvd, has takeout vegetarian sandwiches, and vitamins, herbs and groceries. *Panzone's* pizzeria, at 11th and Bay Ave and also at 22nd St and Long Beach Blvd, serves Italian specialties.

Beach Haven Terrace *Jose's by the Sea* (☎ (609) 492-1001), at 130th St and Long Beach Blvd, serves quesadillas, chili and burritos for about $8.

M&M Steam Bar (☎ (609) 492-9106), at

Delaware Ave and Long Beach Blvd, is a local institution with slow service and the motto: 'If it swims, we've got it; if it smells we've had it too long.' Don't worry – everything is fresh at this take-out place and most items are under $10.

Beach Haven There are three highly regarded seafood restaurants in Beach Haven near each other along the bay at the end of Dock St.

Morrison's (☎ (609) 492-5111), 2nd St and the Bay, has broiled or fried seafood platters, and buckets of fried shrimp, clams and chicken at tables overlooking the bay.

The *Boat House* (☎ (609) 492-1066), Dock Rd and West Ave, has a more adventurous menu including a $20 bouillabaisse. There's a sunny deck out back that opens at 5 pm daily for dinner.

The most expensive place on the island is the Victorian *Green Gables Inn* (☎ (609) 492-3553), 212 Centre St, which offers a different five course fixed-price dinner every day. Reservations are required for the meal, which will run about $50 per person.

Entertainment
Check the free *Summer Times Islander* and *Beachcomber* for listings of club appearances and concerts.

Beach Haven *The Tide* (☎ (609) 492-2121), 9th St and Bay Ave in the Bay Village shops, has alternative reggae music blasting its two bars. Weekend cover charges are $3 to $8; open May to September.

Tuckers (☎ (609) 492-2300), at Engleside Ave and the Bay, features top 40 music Friday, Saturday and Sunday year round and attracts a more middle-aged crowd.

Touche (☎ (609) 492-3366), 2 South Bay Ave, is the most adventurous music place with hip hop and progressive selections.

The bar gets very crowded during the daily happy hour from 4 to 6 pm.

The Sea Shell Club (☎ (609) 492-4611) is in the hotel at 10 S Atlantic, Beach Haven, with live music and dancing several nights a week.

Ship Bottom *Joe Pops Shore Bar* (☎ (609) 494-0558), 2002 Long Beach Blvd, Ship Bottom, has live music and open-mike nights.

The Quarter Deck (☎ (609) 494-3334), 351 W 9th St in Ship Bottom, has karaoke, bikini and Mr Long Beach Island contests as well as music.

Things to Buy
Bay Village and Schooner's Wharf are shopping complexes on opposite sides of 9th St in Beach Haven, selling beachwear, overpriced gift items and food.

Historic Viking Village is a string of fishermen's shacks that have been renovated into shops at 19th St and the bay in Barnegat Light. Each shop is independently run, selling wood carvings, jewelry and gourmet food items.

Phyllis Lo Duca of the Hodge Podge Shop (☎ (609) 361-9338, 597-0271) is also a reputed local psychic who does metaphysical counseling and karma and past-life readings.

The Kite Store (☎ (609) 361-0014), at 3rd St and Long Beach Blvd in Surf City, sells kites and sponsors a once-a-week kite fly on the beach.

For things Victorian, visit Cinnamon & Spice (☎ (609) 494-5413), 7th St and Broadway in Barnegat Light.

Getting There & Away
The island is exit 63 off the Garden State Parkway, which takes you along Route 73 west across the causeway. There is no public transport to Long Beach Island.

Northern New Jersey

The northern part of New Jersey is jam-packed with history and people. Along the shore of the Hudson River, you can find the satellite cities of Hoboken and Jersey City, old industrial towns with large ethnic populations. Nearby is West Orange, home of the Thomas Edison Historic Site.

The terrain changes dramatically in the northwestern part of the state, which is the northeastern gateway to the Poconos and Northern Pennsylvania. This rural respite from urban bustle is known as the Skylands region, and includes the Great Swamp National Wildlife Refuge and the Delaware Water Gap NRA, ideal places for hiking, birdwatching and fishing. If you're into skiing or watersports, you'll want to visit the Vernon Valley Great Gorge area to take advantage of what it can offer, depending on the season.

GETTING THERE & AROUND

Newark, Jersey City and Hoboken are all easily reached via the PATH trains from Manhattan. Short Line buses travel to selected suburban points, but to explore most of northern New Jersey you'll need a car. The top half of the state is transversed by I-80, which runs from the George Washington Bridge to Stroudsburg, PA (in the Poconos), and points west, and I-78, which runs just west of Jersey City to Allentown, PA, and points west.

Urban New Jersey

HOBOKEN

Hoboken (population 33,397) is a New Jersey version of Brooklyn Heights — a gentrified community of well-preserved brownstones and apartment blocks within easy commuting distance of Manhattan. Socially, the town is pretty evenly split between long-time residents and young

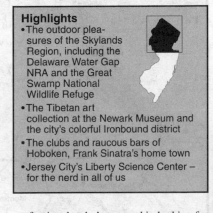

Highlights
- The outdoor pleasures of the Skylands Region, including the Delaware Water Gap NRA and the Great Swamp National Wildlife Refuge
- The Tibetan art collection at the Newark Museum and the city's colorful Ironbound district
- The clubs and raucous bars of Hoboken, Frank Sinatra's home town
- Jersey City's Liberty Science Center – for the nerd in all of us

professionals who've moved in looking for cheap rent. On Friday nights, the younger folks get a bit rowdy as they wind-down from the work week at local taverns' happy hours. Because Hoboken has a reputation as a weekend party town, the police have become rather aggressive about cracking down on drinking in public, so beware if you're out for a night of it in Hoboken.

The city has an important place in US popular culture. The first organized baseball game is generally agreed to have been played on a plain overlooking Manhattan in 1846. There's a memorial at the corner of Washington St and 11th St. 'The Chairman of the Board,' Frank Sinatra, was born in Hoboken in 1915 and got his start in local clubs; and the film classic *On the Waterfront* was shot on the city's docks in 1954.

History

This area, originally a tidal swamp, was called Hoboghan Hackingh or 'Land of the Tobacco Pipe' by the local Indians. The Dutch settled here after buying the land for a few blankets and beads. Virtually cut off from the rest of New Jersey by the rocky cliffs of the Palisades and the railway yards, Hoboken was a popular place for

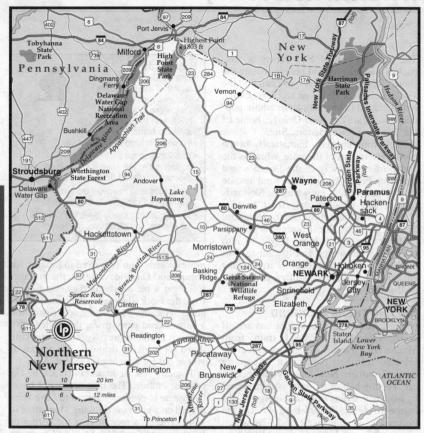

wealthy New Yorkers to visit by rowboat and stroll in the tree-shaded park called Elysian Fields.

In 1784, Colonel John Stevens bought the square mile of land for $90,000. He went on to build the country's first steam locomotive in 1825. In 1870 his family founded the Stevens Institute of Technology, an academy dedicated engineering and science. Thanks to its location directly across the Hudson from New York City, Hoboken grew to become a major railroad terminal and seaport. However, its fortunes went into decline when local industries started to relocate in the 1950s and '60s.

The empty warehouses and factories were slowly converted into commercial and artists' lofts and residential spaces as an artistic community developed. These days, with higher property prices, Hoboken is becoming too expensive for such a community.

Orientation & Information

Occupying little more than a square mile, the city is easily explored on foot, and a grid system makes getting around quite easy. Most of Hoboken's shops and restaurants are located within a few blocks of the ornate old Erie Lackawanna Train

Terminal, where the PATH trains stop, or along Washington Ave.

The city has no tourist office, but you can pick up a copy of the free weekly *Hudson Current*, which covers local arts and special events, at bars and shops all around town.

ATMs are found all along Washington St. The main post office is on River St between Newark and 1st Sts.

Hoboken Books (☎ 201-963-7781) is a good bookstore at 626 Washington St between 6th and 7th Aves.

Parking in Hoboken can be a headache, especially at night and on weekends. With the parking police aggressively checking for offenders, you should consider paying for parking rather than risk getting a ticket.

Hoboken City Hall & Historical Museum

Built in 1881, City Hall (☎ (201) 420-2026), at 1st and Washington Sts, is another registered State and National Historic Landmark. Inside, the Hoboken Historical Museum has display cases of local history and sells mementos of favorite son Frank Sinatra. It's open Monday to Friday from 9 am to 4 pm.

Places to Eat

Budget *Schnackenberg's Luncheonette* (☎ (201) 659-9834), 1110 Washington St between 11th and 12th Sts, is a wonderful place dating from the 1940s with prices from the '70s: most items are under $5, including burgers, sandwiches and milkshakes. It's open Monday to Saturday from 7:30 am to 6 pm.

Vito's Italian Deli (☎ (201) 792-4944), 806 Washington St between 8th and 9th Sts, makes great mozzarella sandwiches and other large heros. *City Hall Bake Shop* (☎ (201) 659-3671), on Washington St between Newark and 1st Sts, serves baked goods and coffee. *Piccolo's* (☎ (201) 653-0561), 92 Clinton St between Newark and 1st Sts, has been serving delicious cheesesteak sandwiches at the same location since 1955.

Moderate & Top End *Clam Broth House* (☎ (201) 659-6767), 38 Newark St, was established in 1899 and is still serving Italian and seafood dishes. It's decorated with photos of celebrities who've visited, including Frank Sinatra, Liza Minnelli and the ubiquitous Brooke Shields.

Helmer's (☎ (201) 963-3333), 1036 Washington St at the corner of 11th, is a traditional German bar-restaurant established in 1936. It's open from Monday to Thursday from noon till 10 pm (11 pm on Friday and Saturday), and is closed Sunday. It features an authentic menu of German cuisine with an impressively large beer selection. There are $5.50 lunch specials like knockwurst sandwiches with sauerkraut.

Leo's Grandevous Restaurant (☎ (201) 659-9467), 200 Grand St at the corner of 2nd St, is another classic. In the neighborhood where Frank Sinatra grew up, it is decorated with pictures of the singer and still attracts Frank's old neighbors with its standard Italian dishes from $20 to $30.

Established in 1985, *Cafe Louis* (☎ (201) 659-9542), 505 Washington St between 5th and 6th, is one of Hoboken's first gay-friendly establishments. The style of cuisine varies: one week it can be French, another Cajun or Spanish. With consistently good food in a pleasant room, prices range from $10 to $20. It's a nice place for Sunday brunch; open daily from 11 am to 3 pm.

Ali Ba Ba's (☎ (201) 653-5319), 912 Washington St between 9th and 10th, serves middle eastern food from $12 to $20.

Entertainment

Bars An old Hoboken bar from the turn of the century, *Maxwell's* (☎ (201) 798-4064), 1039 Washington St at 11th, is for many people the best reason to visit Hoboken. Maxwell's has a small back room that has been featuring the best up-and-coming rock acts since 1978 from Thursday to Saturday nights. Notable bands who played here prior to making it big include REM, Sonic Youth and Nirvana. Bruce Springsteen filmed his 'Glory Days' video (directed by Hoboken resident John Sayles)

NEW JERSEY

Hoboken

0   150   300 m
0   150   300 yards

PLACES TO EAT
1 Schnackenberg's Luncheonette
3 Helmer's
7 Ali Ba Ba's
8 Vito's Italian Deli
13 Leo's Grandevous Restaurant
14 Piccolo's
20 Clam Broth House

OTHER
2 Baseball Memorial
4 Maxwell's
5 Cafe Elysian
6 Excalibur
9 Hoboken Books
10 United Decorating Co
11 Cheap Maggie
12 Louise & Jerry's
15 Brass Rail
16 City Hall & Historical Museum
17 ATM
18 Scotland Yard
19 Piers Platters Records
21 Post Office
22 Santa Fe Yacht Club
23 Widow McShane's
24 Texas/Arizona
25 PATH Terminal
26 Ferry Terminal

at Maxwell's. There's usually $10 cover charge with burgers and pasta dishes on offer for around $10, as well as a popular weekend brunch. Maxwell's recently changed hands and the new owner plans to install a microbrewery on the premises, so some loyalists are worried that the place might be going too upscale.

Built in 1896, the *Cafe Elysian* (☎ (201) 659-9110), 1001 Washington St at 10th, has a beautiful old bar that became a beauty parlor and an ice cream parlor to survive the Prohibition years. Some of the regulars – many of whom park their motorcycles out front – look like extras in the

movie *On the Waterfront*, for which some scenes filmed here.

Louise & Jerry's (☎ (201) 656-9698), 329 Washington St between 3rd and 4th Sts, is a classic basement-level hangout with a coin-operated pool table and happy hour specials. The *Brass Rail* (☎ (201) 659-7074), 135 Washington St at 2nd, features a 2nd-floor restaurant serving decent French food, with live jazz Thursday to Saturday nights.

The bars across from the PATH station attract large crowds of young professional patrons. *Texas/Arizona* (☎ (201) 420-0304), on River Rd on the corner of Hudson Place, and *Santa Fe Yacht Club* (☎ (201) 420-8317), 44 Hudson Place, both serve Mexican specials and a broad range of beers. Between them, the raucous *Widow McShane's* (☎ (201) 659-9690) offers a more traditional pub setting, as does *Scotland Yard* (☎ (201) 222-9273), 72 Hudson St, which features an old London telephone box and Fullers, Bass and Double Diamond on tap.

Discos *Excalibur* (☎ (201) 795-1161), 1000 Jefferson between 9th and 10th, is a gay disco.

One 50 Nine (☎ (201) 963-5019), 159 1st St between Bloomfield and Garden Sts, plays modern rock. *Shooters* (☎ (201) 656-3889), 92 River Rd at the corner of Newark St, plays house music.

Things to Buy
Piers Platters Records, 56 Newark St between Washington and Hudson, is an independent store renowned for its alternative collection including vinyl and rare collectors' seven-inch records – mostly from the past seven years. Hand Mād (☎ (201) 653-7276), 116 Washington St, is an eclectic gift store offering 'folk, funk and fine art.' United Decorating Co (☎ (201) 659-1922), 421 Washington St, has vintage postcards, novelties, collectibles and other Americana.

Cheap Maggie (☎ (201) 795-3770), 314 Washington St, is a local version of the Gap with inexpensive jeans and other casual clothing.

Getting There & Away
Train The PATH train from Manhattan stops at the Erie Lackawanna Train Terminal in Hoboken.

Car From Manhattan take either the Holland or Lincoln Tunnels.

From the NJ Turnpike take exit 14C (Holland Tunnel exit), go to the bottom of the ramp and take a left at the first light, bear right under the overpass onto Observer Hwy with the town's main streets to your left. Or take exit 16E (Lincoln Tunnel exit),

bear right at the Hoboken exit and continue through the first light to the bottom of the ramp, turn right onto Park Ave, then left onto 14th St, then drive three blocks and turn right onto Washington St.

Ferry New York Waterway ferries (☎ (800) 533-3779) operate between Hoboken (near the Erie Lackawanna Train Terminal) and the World Financial Center in Lower Manhattan. Ferries leave every 20 minutes at peak times. The trip takes eight minutes and costs $2 each way.

JERSEY CITY
The area that is now Jersey City (population 228,537) was established by the Dutch in 1630, and the port town eventually became a strategic transportation link between New York and cities to the west and south.

Today most people, even many residents, would question whether Jersey City is worth a detour. It has earned dubious fame throughout the state for having an ineffective local government and a school system so bad that state officials seized control of the board of education. The city also has the dubious distinction of being the home of the terrorists who bombed New York City's World Trade Center in 1993.

Yet things are looking up, as more families move into Jersey City and prompt change. It's the gateway to Liberty State Park and the Liberty Science Museum, which overlook the Statue of Liberty from the west side of New York Harbor.

Manhattan Skyline Viewpoint
Located immediately outside the Exchange Place PATH station, the small **Grundy Park** offers a superb vantage point for views across the Hudson River to downtown Manhattan. It's a great place to watch the sunset or, if you're lucky, to see one of the remaining ocean liners gliding past the skyscrapers.

Facing Manhattan, to your right on the Jersey City side, stands the landmark **Colgate Clock** at 105 Hudson St. It's said to be the world's largest, with a dial 50 feet

Courting Miss Liberty

Just about everyone associates the Statue of Liberty with New York City. But a small group of enthusiastic historians and New Jersey officeholders think that Jersey City, not the Big Apple, is the territorial home of Liberty and Ellis Islands.

New Jersey's case is based on a 160 year old treaty that made Ellis Island, then three acres in size, part of New York. New Jersey claims that the 24½ acres of landfill that make up the modern-day Ellis Island should be under its jurisdiction under a clause that gives it the rights over any land underwater at the time of the agreement.

Other factors serve to encourage them in their campaign: About 80% of the immigrants who came through Ellis Island made their way to Jersey City en route to points west and south, and both islands are in their territorial waters. Moreover, Jersey City supplies both islands with their electricity and water.

In 1986, New Jersey sued in the state superior court to overturn the original treaty, but the judge ruled against them and his decision was upheld by the US Supreme Court in 1987. Now the state has decided to focus on claiming only the rights to the 24 acres of landfill added to Ellis Island since 1890. What's really at stake is the ability to collect $400,000 in sales taxes on items sold on Ellis Island, as well as the $1.2 million in potential income taxes paid by employees who work there. The state would also like to have the right to build a pedestrian bridge to the statue from Liberty State Park, freeing visitors of the need to take a boat ride to the island. Even still, it's unlikely New Jersey will ever prevail: after all, Miss Liberty has literally turned her back on the place from day one. ∎

in diameter; the minute hand alone weighs 2200 pounds.

Liberty State Park

This 1114 acre park (☎ (201) 915-3400) faces the Statue of Liberty and also offers spectacular views of Manhattan. Ferries depart from here for Ellis and Liberty Islands and are always far less crowded than their counterparts operating from Battery Park (see New York City chapter for information on the islands). With its combination of views, access to the islands, two terrific museums, picnic area, paths for walking, jogging, cycling and horse riding, children's playground, boating, swimming, fishing and summer concerts, Liberty State Park is well worth a visit.

Entering the park, you drive down State Flag Row (with the flags arranged in order of induction into the union) and some 1750 feet ahead of you stands the Statue of Liberty. Beyond, you can also see the Brooklyn Bridge, and to the right the Verrazano-Narrows Bridge linking Staten Island to Brooklyn. Check out the **Liberation Monument**. 'Dedicated to America's role of preserving freedom and rescuing the oppressed,' this statue features a US

soldier carrying a WWII concentration camp survivor.

The visitors center is open daily May to November from 6 am to 6 pm and during the winter from 8 am to 4 pm, with information on the park's facilities and special events.

Central Railroad of New Jersey Museum

This beautiful Victorian building was the departure point for 20 trains and the ferry slip to the immigration center on Ellis Island, and handled tens of thousands of people daily. The facility went into decline with the development of road transportation, and 30 years ago this whole park area was a wasteland with rotting docks and undeveloped marshlands.

In 1964 the state park was established and a clean up was completed in time for the 1976 US Bicentennial, with more improvements made for the Statue of Liberty's centennial in 1986. At the now deserted platforms, some of the old train names, routes and schedules are still posted, and displays highlight the history of the terminal and the people who passed through. It's open daily from 10 am to 5 pm.

Liberty Science Center

Also located in the state park is this spectacular modern museum (☎ (201) 451-0006), which bills itself as a family learning center for science, technology and nature. It features permanent exhibitions with three of the four floors dedicated to the theme of invention. Health-themed exhibits include the Touch Tunnel, Bodies in Motion and Illusion Labyrinth. Environmentally-themed exhibits include Microscope Stage, Sky Stage, City Deck and the Green House.

There are interactive exhibits, theater shows and presentations throughout the museum. On the entrance floor you can learn how to see in 3-D through live demonstrations and a 3-D slide show. Alternating shows feature the 'Superstars of Science,' and you can participate in the action by transmitting sound through a laser beam and watch a million watts of electricity flow through a coil to create lightning bolts.

The museum's shop, Tools & Toys, sells science-related products, books and toys. The *Laser Lights Cafe* has terrific views across the Hudson to the Statue of Liberty and the Manhattan skyline, but you'll probably go mad from the noise of the school kids.

Schedules vary daily so check if you are interested in any specific exhibits or presentations. Tickets for the exhibit areas, the Kodak Omni Theater and the 3-D show are sold separately or as a combination at a reduced rate. For the exhibits only: adults/seniors/children $9/8/6; Kodak Omni Theater: $7/6/5; combination exhibit and theater: $13/11/9. Children under two are admitted free to the exhibits (there is a $5 charge for the theater and $1.50 fee for the 3-D show). Parking costs $4.

It's open from April to September daily from 9:30 am to 5:30 pm and during the winter Tuesday to Sunday from 9:30 am to 5:30 pm.

Getting There & Away

By car, take exit 14B off the NJ Turnpike extension. Connecting NJ Transit bus service is available from the Exchange Place PATH station for $1.25.

NEWARK

With its rapidly growing international airport and a location across the Hudson River from New York City, Newark (population 314,000) is known by many tourists as the start or finish point to a visit to the mid-Atlantic region.

Newark began as a small village established by Puritan settlers in 1666, but soon grew larger thanks to the colonial leather-making industry. Ironworks and other heavy industries came to Newark in the late 18th and early 19th centuries, and the city was a leading supplier of the Union Army during the Civil War. The development of commercial businesses followed the end of the war, with both the Prudential and Mutual Benefit insurance companies being founded in Newark.

New Jersey's largest city lost population and jobs during the lean years following WWII. Today, Newark is known to domestic and foreign travelers alike for its airport. But the city is also home to a lively enclave of Portuguese immigrants and has one of the country's most beautiful museums. Though not a popular tourist destination, Newark does justifies a quick day-trip from Manhattan if you're in the area for more than a week.

Orientation & Information

Most of the city's attractions are centered around or within walking distance of Newark Penn Station, a busy terminal that is often confused with New York's Penn Station. The area east of the train station is called the **Ironbound district**, a vibrant, multi-ethnic community that was once surrounded by the major railroad lines. It has long been a home for European immigrants, and since the 1960s has been home to a large block of new arrivals from Portugal who have established their own restaurants, shops and fresh food markets on and around Ferry St.

There is no conventional tourist office in Newark, but a map and a guide to the city can be obtained by contacting the City Hall Public Information Office (☎ (201) 733-8165), 920 Broad St, Room 214, Newark,

NJ 07102. The office is open weekdays from 9 am to 5 pm and welcomes drop-ins.

The post office is on Franklin St east of Broad St. There is an ATM on Ferry St near Van Buren in the Ironbound district.

Newark Museum

Founded in 1909, the Newark Museum (☎ (201) 596-6550), 49 Washington St, features permanent galleries with frequently changing exhibits. In 1989 the museum opened 60,000 sq feet of new exhibition space designed by the architect Michael Graves (who makes his home in

Princeton). In all, the museum features 66 galleries covering all aspects and eras. It's a first class – though it should be noted, not world class – cultural facility.

The museum is especially proud of its world-renowned **Tibetan Collection** featuring a Buddhist altar, consecrated in 1990 by the Dalai Lama. There are also significant objects from Japan, Korea, China, India and other Himalayan areas. It is the largest and most comprehensive selection of Tibetan art in the US.

Among many other galleries you'll find **American Painting & Sculpture** from the

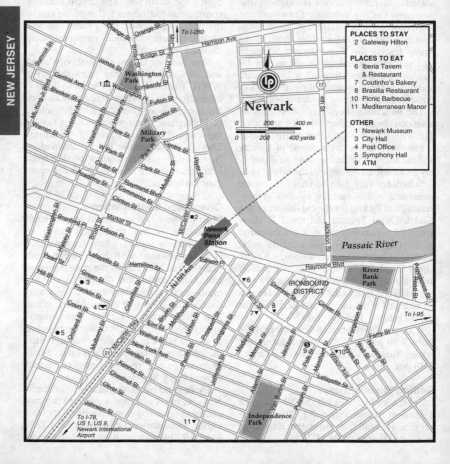

18th to 20th centuries, and the **Decorative Arts** collection features glass, ceramics and textiles from the Renaissance to the present. There are also well-known pieces of American silver, furniture and pottery, along with important objects from the Victorian era.

Permanent galleries feature selections from Africa, the Americas and the Pacific ranging from the pre-Columbian era to the present. Temporary exhibitions highlight various aspects of these diverse cultures.

Classical Art displayed at the museum includes works representing life in early Mediterranean societies – Egyptian, Greek, Etruscan, Roman – along with a permanent exhibit of Coptic art. There is also the highly regarded Eugene Schaeffer Collection of Ancient Glass.

The **Natural Science** collection includes a planetarium and a mini zoo with more than a hundred animals housed in naturalistic habitats.

In the museum's garden is a 1794 schoolhouse, the Newark Fire Museum and a collection of contemporary sculpture.

It's open Wednesday to Sunday from noon to 5 pm; free. The museum is located on Washington St at Central Ave in the University Heights section of downtown Newark. You can walk to the museum or take bus Nos 44 or 72 from Penn Station. Parking is available; be sure to have your parking ticket stamped at the museum's information desk.

Places to Stay

Newark's accommodations revolve around the needs of business travelers using the airport. There's really no need to stay here, unless you're looking for motel-style airport accommodations at a slight discount from New York City rates. *Days Inn-Newark Airport* (☎ (201) 242-0900) and *Hampton Inn-Newark Airport* (☎ (908) 355-0500), feature typical chain-motel amenities.

The only recommended downtown hotel is the *Gateway Hilton* (☎ (201) 622-5000, (800) 345-6565), on Raymond Blvd directly across the street from the train

station. Rooms begin at around $160 a night with weekend discounts available.

Places to Eat

The best places to dine are the Portuguese and Spanish eateries in the Ironbound district surrounding Penn Station. With the good value, authentic decor and swift, efficient service, you really feel like you have been transported to Lisbon. Lunch-time is the real bargain, when you can enjoy excellent specials for $5 to $10. In the evening, prices change to about $18 to $25 per person. Seafood (shrimp, clams, octopus), fish and barbecued meat dishes dominate the menus. Portions are large and it's taken for granted that you'll leave with leftovers.

The oldest restaurant here, *Iberia Tavern & Restaurant* (☎ (201) 344-7603), 82-84 Ferry St, is spotlessly clean with seats at the bar and tables. Across the street, their newer branch, *Iberian Peninsula Restaurant* (☎ (201) 344-5611), 67-69 Ferry St, features the same menu plus barbecued dishes. A little more formal (waiters wear tuxedo jackets instead of just crisp white shirts) is *Spain* (☎ (201) 344-0994), 419 Market St.

You can have a hearty *riodizio de churrasco*, or all-you-can-eat Brazilian barbecue, for just $15 at *Brasilia Restaurant* (☎ (201) 465-1227), 132 Ferry St, between Madison and Monroe Sts. *Mediterranean Manor* (☎ (201) 465-1966), 255 Jefferson St, features live Portuguese *fado* music.

If you just want a quick bite to eat or prefer to spend less try *Picnic Barbecue* (☎ (201) 589-4630), 232 Ferry St, between Wilson Ave and Alyea St.

There are a couple of Portuguese bakeries serving up snacks like *bolo de arroz*, sweet rice pudding cakes, including *Coutinho's Bakery* (☎ (201) 344-7384), 121 Ferry St.

Getting There & Away

For information on Newark's international airport, see the Getting There & Away section of the New York City chapter.

You should visit Newark via Amtrak, PATH train or NJ Transit, since most of the city's attractions are centered around or within walking distance of Newark Penn Station (not to be confused with New York's Penn Station). The cheapest choice – the $1 PATH train – is also the most convenient. For a daytrip from New York City, driving makes little sense, especially since the city achieved notoriety in the 1990s as one of the worst places in the country for car theft.

HACKENSACK
Meadowlands Sports Complex
Opened in 1976, this 750-acre complex (☎ (201) 935-8500) includes Giants Stadium, Meadowlands Race Track and Continental Airlines Arena.

Originally the whole Meadowlands area was 30 sq miles of swamp and landfill until it was drained in the 1970s for the new 76,000-seat home of the NFL Giants, who left Yankee Stadium for New Jersey. They were soon joined at Giants Stadium by the homeless (and hapless) New York Jets, who abandoned New York City's Shea Stadium without first cutting a deal for their own namesake place. Giants Stadium is also the area's outdoor rock concert venue, and virtually every major tour has scheduled stops there.

Continental Airlines Arena is home to the New Jersey Nets of the NBA, and the New Jersey Devils of the NHL, winners of the 1995 Stanley Cup. The Meadowlands Race Track has harness racing from late December to August and thoroughbred racing from Labor Day to early December.

Secaucus Outlet Center
This collection of brand-name discount outlets (☎ (201) 348-4780) is located in three industrial park areas in the Meadowlands. The best strategy is to head for the Harmon Cove Outlet center, pick up a map, and begin exploring its 55 shops and the dozens of surrounding outlet centers. You'll find, to name a few, Liz Claiborne and Calvin Klein clothing, Mikasa china, Church's Shoes, Door Store design center and the Passport International Food Hall. This is a place for shopaholics only, and it's

best to have a car, taking Route 3 from the NJ Turnpike and following the signs for the outlets.

Getting There & Away
Bus You can get to the Meadowlands by the No 129 bus, which leaves Port Authority Bus Terminal every half hour Monday to Friday from 6 am to 3:30 pm; fare is $1.90 each way. But getting from one far-flung outlet store to another is difficult by public transportation.

Other buses leave Port Authority in New York City on days there are events at the Meadowlands complex.

Car Traveling west out of New York from the Lincoln Tunnel, take Route 3 west to the Meadowlands Parkway. Follow the signs for the Harmon Cove Outlets for the shopping district.

EDISON NATIONAL HISTORIC SITE
Sadly, few people today fully know the impact on modern society made by America's greatest inventor, Thomas Alva Edison. His labs (☎ (201) 736-0550), at Main St and Lakeside Ave in West Orange, are open to the public as a national landmark.

Edison (1847-1931) perfected the electric light bulb, phonograph and movie camera, and had 1093 US patents issued to him, more than any other single person. This thoroughly ordinary man was not eccentric in any discernible way, although he was partial to afternoon naps on his workbenches at the lab. But he had a genius for applied science that literally changed the world – and at one time 7000 people worked for him at the lab and machine shop. Near his laboratory is a replica of the Black Maria, one of the first motion picture studios – it was built on a railway turn-around to catch the afternoon sun in the days before artificial floodlights. Also at the site is Glenmont, his 22 room mansion, which is now a museum.

It's open daily from 9 am to 5 pm; tours of the labs begin at 9:30 am and continue to 3:30 pm. Admission is $2.

Nearby the Edison site in West Orange is the **Turtle Back Zoo** (☎ (201) 731-5800), 560 Northfield Ave, a 16 acre park dedicated to endangered species that has a petting zoo and train ride perfect for small children.

Getting There & Away You can reach the Edison site by taking the NJ Turnpike out of New York to I-280 west (exit 15W). From I-280, take exit 10 at West Orange and make the first right onto Main St and follow the signs.

Skylands Region

Some 25 miles directly west of New York City, you'll find the rural Skylands recreation area. Located in the underpopulated northwest portion of the state, it is New Jersey's most concentrated area of outdoor activity – there are hot-air balloon flights, outdoor festivals and several state parks, including the Great Swamp National Wildlife Refuge. Made up officially of Warren, Sussex, Hunterdon and Somerset counties, the hill and forest region is completely different in character from the northeastern urbanized industrial belt, and is best reached and toured by car. Hunterdon County, with its rich farmland, offers scenic drives along Routes 519 and 12 and is particularly beautiful in the autumn. There are many scenic drives through Skylands, especially Route 515, which winds its way through some rich forested valleys.

The top half of the state is transversed by I-80 and I-78. Route 206 heads north-south off Route 78 or 80. Routes 15 or 23 take you into the countryside north of I-80.

The Skylands Regional Tourism Council (☎ (201) 366-6889) in Denville offers maps, information on activities and lodging listings.

GREAT SWAMP
NATIONAL WILDLIFE REFUGE
The Great Swamp National Wildlife Refuge (☎ (201) 425-1222) is a 7200 acre

site with 10 miles of trails through a habitat that's home to over 220 birds, along with permanent populations of muskrat, fox and fish. Two boardwalks wind along marshland, hardwood ridges, cattail marsh and water, brush, pasture and cropland. The swamp also contains many large old oak and beech trees, stands of mountain laurel and species of other plants of both northern and southern botanical zones.

History
The creation of the Great Swamp began when the Wisconsin glacier reached its furthest point south here, roughly 25,000 years ago. As the melting glacier withdrew northward, it left behind a barren landscape of sand and gravel ridges. These blocked the outlet of an ancient river basin and when the water that had melted from the glacier flowed into the basin, this natural dam formed a giant lake, 30 miles long and 10 miles wide. The lake eventually drained away, leaving extensive marshes and swamps.

In 1708 the Delaware Indians deeded a 30,000 acre tract, that included the Great Swamp, to British settlers for a barrel of rum, 15 kettles, four pistols, four cutlasses, some other goods and £30. Settlements slowly began to appear in the area, using wood from the Great Swamp for construction. By 1844, farms were established on the uplands. They drained the marshlands and hay became a major crop.

These small farms were uneconomical and eventually disappeared, and much of the uplands reverted to woods, the lower flatlands to swamp. An airport plan was scuttled in the early '60s by local residents who wanted the land saved as a preserve. The ensuing establishment of the Great Swamp National Wildlife Refuge was one of first such conservation attempts in the state of New Jersey.

Orientation
The Great Swamp entrance is off I-287's exit 30A. Signs lead you to the refuge headquarters (where you can pick up brochures) and the Wildlife Observation

Center on Long Hill Rd, the site of two boardwalk trails and an information kiosk.

Information

The Wildlife Observation Center, off Long Hill Rd, is particularly good for observation and photography. It has an unstaffed information booth, interpretive displays, rest rooms and two blinds for observing wildlife and trails.

The Refuge Headquarters (☎ (201) 425-1222), off Pleasant Plains Rd, is open Monday to Friday from 8 am to 4:30 pm. Volunteer staff are on hand on Sunday during spring and fall.

The Outdoor Education Center (☎ (201) 635-6629), located on Southern Blvd, is a starting point for canoe trips and bird-watching.

Walking Trails

The trails are open daily from dawn to dusk. Early morning and late afternoon are the best times to observe wildlife. Waterproof footwear or old sneakers are recommended for most of the year. From May to September insect repellent is a good idea with the threat of bites from numerous mosquitoes, ticks and deer flies.

Raptor Trust

This is a nonprofit organization (☎ (908) 647-2353) dedicated to the preservation and well-being of birds of prey. They operate a rehabilitation center where hundreds of distressed wild birds are given medical care, diet and housing each year. Orphaned birds are raised using techniques to avoid dependence on humans. The trust's goal is to always return healthy, self-sufficient birds back to their natural environment.

There is an outdoor area where several hawks and owls are kept. This gives you a rare opportunity to see these amazing creatures at close range. Open daily from 8:30 am to 4:30 pm; admission is free, but donations are requested.

Places to Stay

There are no accommodations in the Great Swamp, but the nearby *Olde Mill Inn*

(☎ (908) 221-1100), 225 Route 202, Basking Ridge, is a recently renovated colonial-style facility with singles/doubles from $125/135. In Morristown, you can stay at the *Best Western Morristown Inn* (☎ (201) 540-1700), 270 South St at exit 31 off I-287; rates range from $85 to $105.

Getting There & Away

The Great Swamp is approximately one hour from both New York City and Philadelphia, providing there is little traffic leading out of either city. By car from New York, take I-80 west to I-287 (south) to exit 30A for Basking Ridge. Follow the signs along Maple Ave for the Great Swamp and Lord Stirling Rd.

ACTION PARK– VERNON VALLEY GREAT GORGE

This 1200 acre complex five miles north of Vernon on Route 94 is a popular amusement area and water sport center from April to Thanksgiving. In the winter, it becomes the state's top ski resort. Call ☎ (201) 827-2000 for general information. Call ☎ (201) 827-2222 for information on special events, lodging and restaurants within the resort.

Action Park

Action Park boasts over 75 attractions such as spectacular water slides and a tidal wave pool, racing cars, bungee jumping, speedboats, a brewery and more. All inclusive admission is $26.95; tickets for children under 49 inches tall are $18.95.

Vernon Valley Great Gorge

New Jersey's ski capital has 52 slopes on three mountains. The vertical drop exceeds 1000 feet and runs are graded for difficulty. There is a lodge, ski rentals, ski school and restaurant. If there is not enough snow, the resort has the 'world's largest snowmaking system' capable of laying eight miles of three foot deep snow overnight. All-day lift tickets, which start at 9 am and include lighted night slopes, are $45/32 adult/child, or $38/27 for access to slopes from 9 am to 6 pm. Complete ski rentals are $23/18, and a learn to ski day package is available for $49/40.

DELAWARE WATER GAP NATIONAL RECREATION AREA

The Delaware Water Gap is a park scattered over 37 miles along both sides of the Delaware River, which defines the border of northwestern New Jersey and Pennsylvania. The 'gap' is a chasm made by the river as it cuts though the Kittatinny Ridge at the southern end of the park. The Appalachian Trail passes through the park. It also includes 200 miles of internal roads – it's best to get here and around by car.

Orientation & Information

Taking I-80 west from New York City brings you the Delaware River in about 90 minutes. The Delaware Water Gap consists of not only federally protected lands but also many New Jersey and Pennsylvania state parks. For more information on Pennsylvania's portion of this area see the Poconos section in the Northern Pennsylvania chapter.

General information is available from the NPS (☎ (717) 588-2435), Delaware Water Gap National Recreation Area, Bushkill, PA 18324.

The Kittatinny Point Visitor Center (☎ (908) 496-4458), off I-80 on the New Jersey side, is open daily from 9 am to 5 pm April to October. During July and August the center is open Friday and Sunday until

7 pm; October to March it's open weekends only from 9 am to 4:30 pm.

The Dingmans Falls Visitor Center (☎ (717) 828-7802) is off Route 209 near Dingmans Ferry, PA. It's open April to October daily from 9 am to 5 pm; November to March it is open weekends only from 9 am to 4:30 pm.

High Point State Park

This is one of the many state reserves here, and a good destination within the very large region.

You can reach High Point State Park (☎ (201) 875-4800) by turning north from I-80 onto Route 206 at Lake Hopatcong, then taking Route 521. The park, within the Delaware Water Gap 'zone,' offers hiking, swimming and camping, along with the 1803 foot High Point Peak – the highest elevation in New Jersey.

Hiking

The best hiking in the park is along 25 miles of the Appalachian Trail that traverses the park from its southern end and continues north, close to the eastern park boundary. Hikers on trips lasting at least two days are allowed to camp within 100 feet of the **Appalachian Trail**. There are also several other shorter trails throughout the park. The visitors centers have trail maps.

Beaches

The Delaware River is safe for swimming at most calm points. There are beaches at

NEW JERSEY

Airsports in the Skylands

Visitors who aren't satisfied with ground-level pleasures will love the Skylands region, which is the northeast's airsports center. In July, the state's **Festival of Ballooning** (☎ (201) 529-0464) is held at Solberg airport in Readington.

Up, Up and Away (☎ (908) 735-0870), 405 Airport Rd, Pittstown in Hunterdon County, a ballooning outfit, holds its very own hot-air balloon festival on the first weekend in August.

Among the many places offering ballooning trips or weekend skydiving courses are:

Festival Flights – 16 Lamington Rd, Bedminster ☎ (800) 116 8047

Skydive East – PO Box 84, Pittstown ☎ (908) 996-6262

Hunterdon Ballooning – PO Box 2116, Flemington ☎ (908) 788-5415. ■

Milford and Smithfield with lifeguards and bathhouses from mid-June to Labor Day.

Canoeing
Park visitors centers offer a list of canoe rental businesses and white-water raft outfitters. Among them: Kittatinny Canoes (☎ (717) 828-2338, (800) 356-2852) at the center of the park in Dingmans Ferry; Pack Shack Adventures (☎ (717) 424-8533) at the southern end of the park in Delaware Water Gap, PA; and River Beach Campsites (☎ (717) 296-7421) at the northern end of the park in Milford, PA.

Fishing
The lakes and ponds in the park support bass and pickerel and the streams have rainbow, brook and brown trout. In the Delaware River it's possible to catch shad, smallmouth bass, walleye, eels and catfish. See the Facts about New Jersey chapter for information on obtaining a license, which is required.

Birdwatching
The park is a good place to see hawks and turkey vultures and is also one of the few places in the east where bald eagles can be found during the winter. The best time for eagle spotting is mid-morning or late afternoon in January and February.

Places to Stay
Camping There are many campgrounds within driving distance of the park; the visitors centers and the NPS have a list of all facilities within a 40 mile radius of the park.

Dingmans Campground (☎ (717) 828-2266) is in the park at Dingmans Ferry, PA.

Campgrounds in Pennsylvania on the river include *River Beach Campsites* (☎ (717) 296-7241) and *Tri-State Canoe/Campground* (☎ (800) 562-2663). For other accommodations options in Pennsylvania see the Northern Pennsylvania chapter.

In New Jersey, camps along the Delaware River include *Cedar Ridge Campground* (☎ (201) 293-3512); the *Delaware River Campground* (☎ (908) 475-4517); and the *Worthington State Forest Campground* (☎ (908) 841-9575).

Hostels The HI-AYH *Delaware Water Gap Hostel* (☎ (201) 948-6750) is in the park on the river. There are 12 beds for $10 each. It has a kitchen, a common room and separate dormitories for men and women. Lock-out is from 9:30 am to 5:30 pm. The hostel is open year round but you should make reservations on weekends.

From New Jersey or New York City take I-80 west to exit 34B. Go north on Route 15 for 18 miles until it becomes Route 206 at Ross Corner. Take Route 206 north to Route 560 west and then go 2½ miles to Layton. Make a right at the Layton General Store and go 2½ miles to Old Mine Rd. Make a sharp right on Old Mine Rd and go two miles more to the hostel.

From Milford, PA, take Route 209 south across the Milford Bridge into New Jersey. Take the first right turn onto Old Mine Rd and drive 4½ miles south to the hostel.

Central New Jersey

The beltway between urban northern New Jersey and mid-Pennsylvania is packed with colonial history sites, including those in the state capital of Trenton.

PRINCETON

Princeton (population 12,016) is known throughout the world for its Ivy League university, which educates 6000 students on its attractive, wall-enclosed campus. In addition to the beautiful campus, the town has some lovely architecture, interesting historic sites and a nice array of shops and restaurants along Nassau St.

Princeton is particularly sleepy on Monday, when many of the places of interest are closed, and you should avoid the town in late May and June, since hotels are booked solid months in advance for graduation. During the summer there are very few students around; there's peace and quiet, but it's often accompanied by hot and humid temperatures. Spring and fall are probably better times to visit – what is a university town without students?

History

Settled in the late 17th century, Princeton was named Prince Town in honor of Prince William of Orange and Nassau. Nearby place names include Kingston, Queenston and Princessville. In 1756 Princeton became the home of the College of New Jersey – now Princeton University – with the entire college housed in Nassau Hall, the largest academic building in the colonies.

The Battle of Princeton, fought in a nearby field in January 1777, proved to be a decisive victory for General Washington and his troops during the War of Independence. Two of Princeton's leading citizens signed the Declaration of Independence, and during the summer of 1783 the town served as the young republic's capital when the Continental Congress met in Nassau Hall for four months.

Highlights
- The prototypical university town of Princeton, with its lush campus and impressive art collection
- The state capital of Trenton, chock full of colonial heritage
- The impressive New Jersey State Aquarium, a diamond in troubled Camden ■

NEW JERSEY

Located halfway between New York and Philadelphia, Princeton was the overnight stagecoach stop on the Trenton-New Brunswick line until the mid-19th century. In the 1830s the construction of a nearby canal and railroad spurred further commerce, real estate development and prosperity.

With its long-held status as a cultural center, Princeton has been home to world-renowned scholars, scientists, writers and statesmen including two US presidents, Woodrow Wilson and Grover Cleveland. In 1930, the Institute for Advanced Study was founded here, becoming the country's major residential institute for scholars, including Albert Einstein and TS Eliot.

There has continued to be an influx of scholars, research personnel, and also corporations from all parts of the world. Paul Robeson grew up in Princeton, and artisans from Italy, Scotland and Ireland emigrated here and contributed to the town's rich architectural and cultural history. F Scott Fitzgerald's first novel, *This Side of Paradise*, was modeled on his Princeton college days in the early '20s. Contemporary writers living in Princeton include John McPhee, Richard Preston, Peter Benchley and Joyce Carol Oates. It's not unusual to see a literary figures nursing a coffee in a cafe on Nassau St.

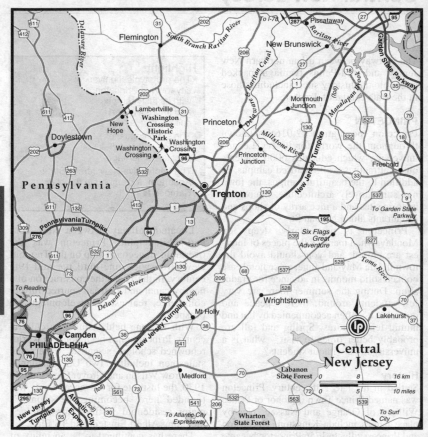

NEW JERSEY

Orientation & Information
Nassau St is the town's main street, with
the university on the south side and the
restaurants, shops, parking and hotels along
the north side, with Palmer Square the
central gathering spot.

The Princeton Convention and Visitors
Bureau (☎ (609) 683-1760), 20 Nassau St,
offers maps and brochures for those planning a trip to Princeton, but it doesn't
provide much helpful information for
those already in town – the phone line is
almost never answered by a live person.
But two other groups can assist you in

town: Historical Society of Princeton
(☎ (609) 921-6748) and, for university
information, the Orange Key Guide
Service & Campus Information Office in
MacLean House (☎ (609) 452-6303).

ATMs can be found along Nassau St; the
post office is in the middle of Palmer Square.

Micawber Books (☎ (609) 921-8454),
112 Nassau St, is open Monday to Saturday
from 9 am to 8 pm, Sunday from 11 am to
5 pm. The store often has readings for visiting authors and local writers.

Princeton Public Library (☎ (609) 924-
9529) is at 65 Witherspoon St and is open

Monday to Thursday from 9 am to 9 pm, Friday and Saturday from 9 am to 5:30 pm and Sunday from 1 to 5:30 pm.

A map of literary Princeton that immortalizes the homes and hangouts of local writers can be bought for $10 at the town's bookstores; profits benefit high school writing contests organized by the Humanities Council.

Princeton University

Free tours of the campus are offered by Orange Key Tours (☎ (609) 258-3603). Their office is in MacLean House, which is not well sign-posted – it's the light-mustard colored building adjacent to the gate across from Palmer Square. The office is open Monday to Saturday from 9 am to 5 pm and on Sunday from 1 to 5 pm; tours operate Monday to Saturday at 10 and 11 am, 1:30 and 3:30 pm, on Sunday at 1:30 and 3:30 pm. This is a volunteer organization staffed by students and the tours include a history of the university along with some information for any prospective students about academic and social life on the campus. Reservations are not necessary but notification is appreciated.

A collection of 20th century sculpture that includes works by Henry Moore, Jacques Lipchitz and Picasso is scattered throughout the campus.

Art Museum Located in McCormick Hall (☎ (609) 452-3787) on the campus, this museum is well worth a visit. Exhibits include paintings and sculpture from ancient times through to contemporary periods. Of special note are Chinese paintings and bronzes, examples of pre-Columbian and African art and some modern art, including works by Picasso and Warhol. Admission is free. Open Tuesday to Saturday from 10 am to 5 pm, Sunday from 1 to 5 pm. There is a free guided tour at 2 pm on Saturdays.

Historic Houses

Bainbridge House This Georgian-style house (☎ (609) 921-6748), 158 Nassau St, was built in 1766 for local tanner Job Stockton, and was the birthplace of Commodore William Bainbridge, commander of the USS *Constitution*. Now the location of the Historical Society of Princeton, it offers a museum, library and a shop where you can pick up free information literature and self-guided walking tour maps plus various books and other souvenirs of Princeton.

Morven This mansion (☎ (609) 683-4495), 55 Stockton St, is a bright yellow estate built in 1750 for the Declaration of Independence signer Richard Stockton. It was later the residence of Robert Wood Johnson (the founder of Johnson & Johnson) and from 1953 to 1981 served as the official residence of New Jersey governors.

It's open Wednesday 11 am to 2 pm or by appointment.

Drumthwacket This historic home (☎ (609) 683-0057), on Route 206, was built in 1835 by Charles Olden, a Civil War governor, and refurbished by the New Jersey Historical Society. Today it is the residence of Governor Christine Todd Whitman. Free tours are offered of the 1st-floor public rooms on Wednesdays from noon to 2 pm. Be sure to call ahead as these tours are not always operating. There is no admission fee; donations are welcomed.

Einstein's House Physicist Albert Einstein lived at 112 Mercer St, but is not open to the public. It is currently owned by a member of the Institute for Advanced Studies where Einstein studied. Einstein used a 2nd-floor room at the back of the house for a study with views of some pine and oak trees.

Thomas Clark House This house (☎ (609) 921-0074), on the road into Princeton Battlefield State Park, was built in 1770 by Thomas Clarke, a Quaker farmer. During the Battle of Princeton, General Hugh Mercer received severe bayonet wounds and was brought to the house (along with other wounded soldiers from both sides) where he died nine days

NEW JERSEY

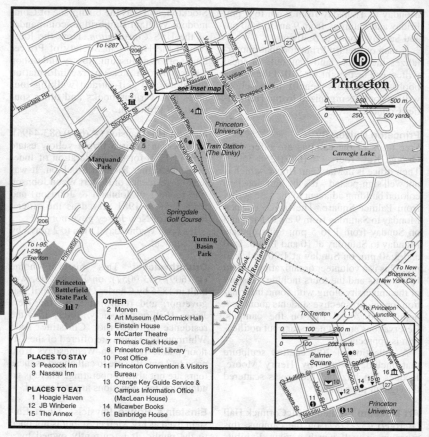

Princeton

PLACES TO STAY
3 Peacock Inn
9 Nassau Inn

PLACES TO EAT
1 Hoagie Haven
12 JB Winberie
15 The Annex

OTHER
2 Morven
4 Art Museum (McCormick Hall)
5 Einstein House
6 McCarter Theatre
7 Thomas Clark House
8 Princeton Public Library
10 Post Office
11 Princeton Convention & Visitors Bureau
13 Orange Key Guide Service & Campus Information Office (MacLean House)
14 Micawber Books
16 Bainbridge House

later. The house is furnished as it would have been at the time of the Revolution. There are occasional period demonstrations of domestic chores like cooking, textile production and other daily tasks.

It's open Wednesday to Saturday from 10 am to noon and 1 to 4 pm, and Sunday from 1 to 4 pm.

Princeton Battlefield State Park

Located at 500 Mercer St about a mile southwest of 'downtown,' Princeton Battlefield State Park commemorates the historic battle of Princeton. Fought on January 3,

1777, the battle was a decisive victory for George Washington and a major turning point in the American Revolution.

This is one of the few battlefields of the Revolution to remain virtually unchanged. An illustrated plan stands next to the flagpole, and graves of soldiers killed during the battle are to the north of the memorial columns. It's interesting to note that because Princeton was a Loyalist town, it was looted after the battle by the victorious rebel troops.

The park is open daily from dawn to dusk (free). Be sure to get a copy of the free leaflet describing the battle from Bainbridge House.

Outdoor Activities

Tennis Princeton Racquet Club (☎ (609) 329-6200), Raymond Rd, has five indoor courts open from September until May, with five outdoor courts open from May until September.

Golf Bunker Hill Golf Course (☎ (609) 359-6335), Bunker Hill Rd, and Princeton Country Club (☎ (609) 452-9382), Wheeler Way, off Route 1, are open to the public.

Places to Stay

Bottom End There are no budget places to stay in Princeton. The motels along Route 1 are the closest, making it awkward to stay inexpensively overnight here without a car.

Middle Heading towards Princeton from New York on Route 1 south are the following motel choices: The moderate *Red Roof* (☎ (908) 821-8800), 208 New Road, Monmouth Junction off Route 1 south, with singles/doubles from $42 to $60; *Days Inn* (☎ (908) 329-4555), $48/68; and the *Ramada Hotel* (☎ (609) 452-2400), $72/89.

Driving along Route 1 north from Trenton is the *McIntosh Inn of Princeton* (☎ (609) 896-2544), adjacent to Quaker Bridge Mall about five miles south of Princeton. Rates begin at $50. About a mile south of town on Route 1, the *Best Western Palmer Inn* (☎ (609) 452-2500) has rooms $75 to $102.

Top End Dating to 1775, the *Peacock Inn* (☎ (609) 924-1707), 20 Bayard Lane, has 17 comfortable rooms; rates are $90 with shared bath, $105 to $125 with private bath, including continental breakfast. Offering more atmosphere than the other expensive choices, the inn has the comfortable feel of an informal wealthy home.

Nassau Inn (☎ (609) 921-7500), Palmer Square, is a 1756 home with extensions, and is Princeton's other downtown hotel. Weekday rates start at $155 with special

corporate/AAA rates available on request; rates are $99 on weekends. Famous visitors to the inn include Fidel Castro, Indira Ghandi, J Edgar Hoover, Grace Kelly and Golda Meir.

The *Hyatt Regency Princeton* (☎ (609) 987-2584), 102 Carnegie Center off Route 1 north, has single/double rates at $161/186 weekdays, and around $85 weekends. The *Marriott Residence Inn* (☎ (908) 389-8100), Route 1 south, has weekday rates at $139/159, weekends $89/99.

Places to Eat

Budget *Hoagie Haven* (☎ (609) 921-7723), at 242 Nassau St, is open daily from 9 am to 1 am and serves excellent hot and cold sandwiches under $8.

The Annex (☎ (609) 921-7555), 128 Nassau St, has pub grub for under $10. *The Whole Earth Center* (☎ (609) 924-7429), 360 Nassau St, is a deli offering vegetarian and natural food choices.

JB Winberie (☎ (609) 921-0700), One Palmer Square, is a restaurant and bar with entrees under $12, a daily happy hour and an all-you-can-eat Sunday brunch buffet for $11.95.

Top End Both of the following restaurants require that men wear jackets at dinner:

Lahiere's (☎ (609) 921-2798), 11 Witherspoon St, is probably the best place in town, serving French-continental cuisine for lunch and dinner. It's closed Sunday. Lunch is from $25 to $40 per person; fixed-price dinner is $38.

Le Plumet Royal (☎ (609) 924-1707) at the Peacock Inn, 20 Bayard Lane, has a special $25 menu, with à la carte selections running from $40 to $60. Open daily for lunch and dinner and for Sunday brunch.

Entertainment & Spectator Sports

Check the *Princeton Weekly Bulletin* for the latest calendar of events.

Princeton University's McCarter Theatre (☎ (609) 683-8000) stages plays, musicals, concerts and various other events.

For information on the university sporting events, call ☎ (609) 258-3545.

Getting There & Away

Bus Suburban Transit buses (☎ (609) 249-1100) leave from New York City's Port Authority to Palmer Square, Princeton.

Train NJ Transit and Amtrak offer several daily trains to Princeton Junction. Passengers must then cross over to a smaller train (known to locals as 'the dinky') to make the five minute trip to Princeton itself. That train stops right next to the university campus.

Car From New York and northern New Jersey, take the NJ Turnpike to exit 9; follow Route 1 south to Princeton and take the Washington Rd exit (Route 571) to Nassau St. You can also take Route 1 all the way instead of the NJ Turnpike.

From Philadelphia, take I-95 north to Route 1 north; from there follow the directions given above. You can also take Route 206 north from I-95 all the way to Princeton.

Getting Around

Princeton is small enough for you to walk around. However, if arriving via public transport, note that the only hotels within walking distance are expensive, the rest are miles away on Route 1.

Associated Taxi (☎ (609) 924-1222), can help if you're in a hurry.

If you have a car, it's best to leave the car at the lot on Hulfish St if you're in for a day-trip.

TRENTON

New Jersey's state capital (population 88,675) is often ignored by travelers, and that's a pity, since its packed with colonial history. Its land plan was devised in the early part of the 18th century by William Trent, and residents called the place 'Trent's Town' – later shortened to the name used today. The Continental Congress met here briefly in 1784, but the town soon lost its status as the young republic's capital moved to New York City and then the District of Columbia. The town became state capital in 1790.

Trenton gained a reputation for building, becoming one of the most important industrial towns in the US during the 19th century. The Roebling Wire Rope Company manufactured the suspension cables used on the Brooklyn Bridge and other engineering feats, and the Lenox China Company was established in 1889 to rival the fine work produced by older European manufacturers.

Trenton has had several periods of recession, though the city has always been anchored by the state government, which has a number of office buildings downtown. Interestingly enough, the governor is based in Princeton, lending an emphasis to the state's clear division between the powerful executive branch and the legislature.

Trenton's sights can be taken in during a single day, making it a good stopover point between New York City and Philadelphia, or a place to visit while staying in Princeton – there's no real need to stay overnight here.

Orientation & Information

The Trenton Convention and Visitors Bureau (☎ (609) 777-1771) is at the corner of Lafayette and Barrack Sts. The Mercer County Chamber of Commerce (☎ (609) 393-4143), 214 W State St, provides a map and brochure of historic sites.

Most of the attractions in Trenton are along Broad St, which runs north-south through town, and State St, which crosses Broad.

State House

The New Jersey State House (☎ (609) 633-2709) was built in 1792 and remodeled and expanded extensively after an 1885 fire to become the large building that lords over W State St in downtown Trenton. Free tours of the building – which has recently undergone a $43 million refurbishing – embark from the grand rotunda on Tuesday, Wednesday, Friday and Saturday, and are keyed to the schedules of the many school groups that visit – it's best to call ahead to get a schedule and secure a spot. The hour-long tour brings you to the senate and assembly chambers, senate majority conference rooms and the governor's reception area.

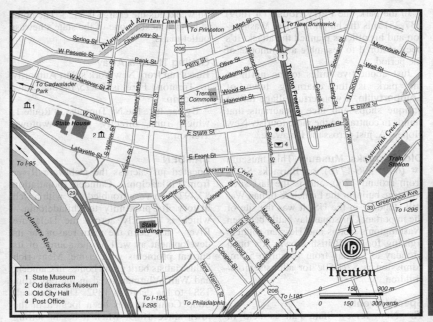

1 State Museum
2 Old Barracks Museum
3 Old City Hall
4 Post Office

Trenton

New Jersey State Museum

Right next to the State House is the New Jersey State Museum (☎ (609) 292-6308), 205 W State St, which has a decent collection of 19th and 20th century American art, dinosaur fossils, displays on Indian history and a collection of porcelain made in Trenton. It's worth a visit – there's no admission charge and shows in the 200 seat planetarium cost $1.

It's open Tuesday to Saturday from 9 am to 4:45 pm and Sunday from noon to 5 pm.

Colonial History

There are a number of colonial historic sites in and around Trenton.

Ellarsie This is an 1850 Italianate villa once owned by businessman Henry McCxall, and is the site of the **Trenton City Museum** (☎ (609) 989-3632), at Cadwalader Park just a mile west of the State House. The museum's 1st floor is a gallery

space for local artists, and its 2nd floor houses artifacts of city history. It's open Tuesday to Saturday from 11 am to 3 pm and Sunday from 2 pm to 4 pm; free.

Washington Crossing State Park This park (☎ (609) 737-0623), eight miles north of Trenton in Titusville on Route 29, is where the general made his Christmas night trip from Pennsylvania in 1776 to surprise the sleeping Hessian soldiers and retake a British-held village. The move halted the Revolutionary Army's winter retreat and led to decisive victories in Trenton and Princeton. The crossing is re-enacted every year on Christmas, and the park is a lovely spot for picnicking and biking during the summer. (It is at a secret spot somewhere near the park that Major League Baseball gets the rich, red mud umpires use to take the shine off new baseballs.) The park's open daily year round from 8 am to 8 pm.

In the park, the **Ferry House** (☎ (609) 737-2515) is the building where Washington and his officers planned the attack. It's been restored to resemble a farmhouse of the period.

Just about five miles to the north of the park is the charming town of **Lambertville**, a wonderful village full of antique shops and nice restaurants that stands in contrast to the more touristy New Hope, PA, just across the Delaware.

Old Barracks Museum This museum (☎ (609) 396-1776), on Barracks St, is from around 1760, and is the last such structure built for the French & Indian War still standing in the US. It was the site of the important Christmas day battle between Washington's troops and Hessian soldiers fighting for the British crown. It's open Monday to Sunday from 10 am to 5 pm; admission is $2/1/50¢ for adults/seniors/children.

Special Events
The New Jersey State Fair is held in Garden State Park the first week in August; call ☎ (609) 646-3340 for information. Trenton Heritage Days (☎ (609) 393-8998) are held on the Commons on the first weekend in June, featuring local arts and crafts stands.

Places to Stay
Trenton isn't particularly dangerous, though it has some dicey neighborhoods away from the town center. Like many government-dominated downtown areas, the area is quite dead at night, so you're better off looking for accommodations around Princeton to the north.

A good B&B choice is the *Inn to the Woods* (☎ (609) 493-1974), 150 Glenwood Dr in Washington Crossing.

The *McIntosh Inn* (☎ (609) 896-3700), on Route 1 in Lawrenceville, has budget accommodations in its 116 rooms for $48/60 midweek. The *Marriott* (☎ (609) 452-7900), at Forrestal Village, about 25 minutes north on Route 1, has a good weekend deal of $79 for a single or double;

on weekends the charge is $125. The hotel is located next to one of the state's newest outlet malls.

Getting There & Away
Buses run from New York's Port Authority to Trenton. Fare is $9.75/14 one way/roundtrip.

By car, take the NJ Turnpike to Route 1, which runs directly into downtown Trenton.

CAMDEN
Located just across the Delaware River from Philadelphia, Camden (population 87,492) is a very troubled city with a rich history. Its proximity to Philadelphia – which is directly across the Delaware River – has been the main reason for its development as well as the source of its current problems with crime. Many rich industrialists built grand homes in Camden, and Walt Whitman lived in the city from 1884 to his death in 1892. The Campbell Soup Company has been located in the town since 1869, when it began selling canned tomatoes and peas and about 20 years later, its famous soup.

Despite great efforts by the state to develop the waterfront near the Ben Franklin Bridge, which has included the construction of a new aquarium, Camden is an outpost for Philadelphia drug dealers, and violent crime is out of control. The city saw a record 60 homicides in 1995, overwhelming the local police force of 338 officers, and New Jersey has assigned state troopers to patrol the streets.

In mid-1996, the state seized control of the city's finances in an attempt to stem years of corruption and mismanagement, and the Campbell Museum, a quirky collection of fine-dining implements and utensils, closed because of a low number of visitors.

For the moment, Camden is not a place to spend the night – or even park a car on a quiet side street. But there's no need to shun the city entirely if you're on your way to or from Philadelphia. Camden's aquarium can be visited on a day-trip.

New Jersey State Aquarium

This massive new facility (☎ (609) 365-3300) opened in 1990 on a former ferry terminal as a sign of the state's commitment to the redevelopment of Camden. Unfortunately, this noble idea suffered from a bit of flawed execution, since the 760,000-gallon open tank held 60 species of fish native to the nearby ocean waters. Visitors were bored by these fish, and the aquarium scrambled to find way to offer a more interesting mix of sea life. In mid-1995, the aquarium was redubbed the 'totally new' Ocean Base Atlantic Center and introduced eight new attractions that accentuated the exotic, including a coral station of colorful Caribbean fish, a shark tank and an archway where you pass under schools of darting fish. The new displays are infinitely more exciting, and as a result the aquarium gets quite crowded on weekends. It's open daily from 10 am to 5 pm; admission is $9.95/8.45/6.95.

Getting There & Away

Camden is on the NJ Turnpike just before the Ben Franklin Bridge. Greyhound (☎ (212) 971-6300, (800) 231-2222) has buses to Camden from Port Authority in New York City, but do this only if you have accommodations lined up in Philadelphia, which is accessible by ferries from the aquarium directly to Penn's Landing.

NEW JERSEY

Southern New Jersey

The state's southern coastline is far less populated than the area covered in the Jersey Shore chapter, and the terrain is noticeably undeveloped, especially along the Atlantic City Expressway, where pine trees dominate the sides of the road. The area is dominated by three distinctly different summer resorts: the ever-troubled gambling town of Atlantic City, the noisy and fun seaside amusement area of Wildwood, and the quaint, southernmost Victorian-era resort of Cape May, home to the most pristine beach in the state.

ATLANTIC CITY

Since casino gambling came to Atlantic City (population 38,000) in 1977, the town has become the most popular tourist destination in the USA, with 37 million annual visitors spending some $4 billion at its 13 casinos and restaurants. Proximity accounts for much of that popularity, since nearly one third of the population of the US lives within 300 miles of Atlantic City.

While the casino industry has created 45,000 jobs and experienced record profits since 1993, little of this money has benefited the town, despite the many promises of prosperity made 20 years ago. Unemployment still stands at 15%, homelessness is still a big problem and the four block stretch of town from the end of the Atlantic City Expressway to the beachfront casinos is still a depressing collection of empty lots, rough looking bars and abandoned warehouses. The boardwalk itself is an odd collection of fortress-like casinos punctuated by the odd T-shirt shop and gyro stand. Since the self-contained casinos have their own restaurants, bars and nightclubs (the better to keep players entertained and spending in one place), there is no walking culture in the city.

The bottom line is that for non-gamblers, there is no reason to visit Atlantic City unless you're on your way to the Cape May

Highlights

- The gaudy gaming and over-the-top entertainment in Atlantic City
- The million acres of pristine wilderness and historic sites that make up the Pine Barrens preserve
- The Victorian beauty and white sand beach of Cape May, New Jersey's oldest seaside resort – and don't miss the Cape May County Zoo
- Lucy, the Margate elephant, a perfect folly of an attraction
- The colorful motels in Wildwood Crest, a garish neon reminder of the Eisenhower era ■

resort area or Philadelphia. For one thing, casino security people do not look kindly upon those simply wandering through the gaming areas without any intention of playing – which is probably just as well, since watching other people spend their money on noisy 25¢ slot machines gets old very quickly. But if you want to gamble, you can beat Atlantic City's selection of 700 blackjack tables and nearly 30,000 slot machines. If you visit, plan on trying your luck at something – even if you wish to spend only $10 or $15 – and remember that it's no sin to walk away if you're ahead of the game. Few people ever do.

History

Established in 1793, the town that today is Atlantic City was the first settlement of Absecon Island, along with its neighboring municipalities of Ventnor, Margate and Longport. Some 50 years later, a group of businessmen, led by Dr Jonathan Pitney, decided to develop a bathing village and health resort on the island. A charter was obtained to operate a railroad between

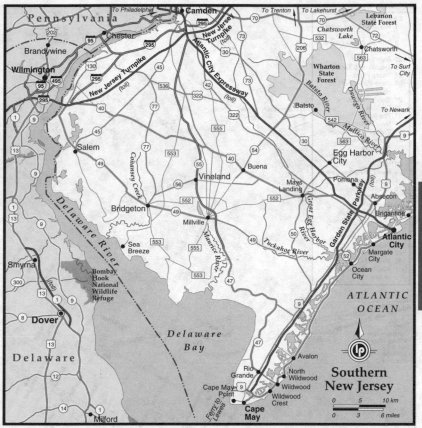

Southern
New Jersey

booming Camden and the site, and by 1854 an engineer named Richard Osborne had designed and named Atlantic City, which was incorporated that year.

The city's proximity to large population centers and inexpensive rail transportation made it possible for thousands of city dwellers to escape the summer heat and enjoy the seaside. The Boardwalk was built in 1870 and in time the amusement piers were added.

The resort was a playground for the rich and famous in the 1920s, and also became a stop on the pre-Broadway theater circuit. In 1921 the first Miss America pageant was

held, scheduled for September as a way of extending the season beyond Labor Day. By the 1930s, Atlantic City's population reached an all-time high of 66,000, and its nightclubs attracted the top talent of the day on the Steel Pier, which was dubbed 'the showplace of the nation.'

Decline set in after WWII, when jet travel and prosperity made it easier to travel to vacation spots in Florida, the Caribbean and Europe. Until the middle '70s, Atlantic City suffered from severe economic problems with a drop in tourism, rampant drug use and crime. The 1964 Democratic Convention that nominated Lyndon B Johnson for

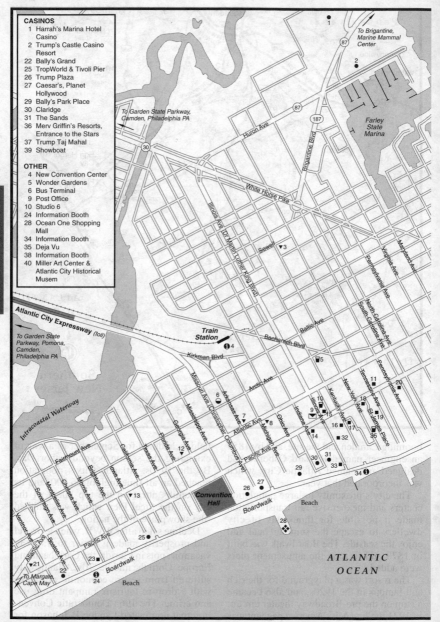

NEW JERSEY

CASINOS
1 Harrah's Marina Hotel Casino
2 Trump's Castle Casino Resort
22 Bally's Grand
25 TropWorld & Tivoli Pier
26 Trump Plaza
27 Caesar's, Planet Hollywood
29 Bally's Park Place
30 Claridge
31 The Sands
36 Merv Griffin's Resorts, Entrance to the Stars
37 Trump Taj Mahal
39 Showboat

OTHER
4 New Convention Center
5 Wonder Gardens
6 Bus Terminal
9 Post Office
10 Studio 6
24 Information Booth
28 Ocean One Shopping Mall
34 Information Booth
35 Deja Vu
38 Information Booth
40 Miller Art Center & Atlantic City Historical Musem

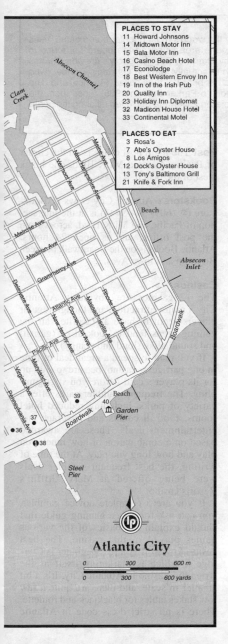

PLACES TO STAY
11 Howard Johnsons
14 Midtown Motor Inn
15 Bala Motor Inn
16 Casino Beach Hotel
17 Econolodge
18 Best Western Envoy Inn
19 Inn of the Irish Pub
20 Quality Inn
23 Holiday Inn Diplomat
32 Madieon House Hotel
33 Continental Motel

PLACES TO EAT
3   Rosa's
7   Abe's Oyster House
8   Los Amigos
12 Dock's Oyster House
13 Tony's Baltimore Grill
21 Knife & Fork Inn

Atlantic City

| 0 | 300 | 600 m |
| 0 | 300 | 600 yards |

NEW JERSEY

the presidency highlighted the city's woes – there was such a shortage of support services for the delegates that it was obvious that Atlantic City could no longer handle such a major event.

After a five year PR campaign to convince state voters, casino gambling was approved as a means of revitalizing the city, and the Resorts International casino opened in May 1978, attracting long lines at its slot machines and blackjack tables. By the '80s, gambling was a 24 hour a day affair, and a rail service was resumed connecting the town to Philadelphia.

Atlantic City still has a long way to go to return as a family resort. A bit belatedly, and with no small sense of shame, local officials have begun to push for non-gambling related attractions for the town. The state legislature has rewritten the casino law to try and ensure that more of the money made by the casinos is used in the city.

In 1997, a new $300 million convention center opened above the train station and houses a non-casino hotel, shops, theaters and restaurants. (The project is being developed by the same company responsible for New York's successful South Street Seaport complex and Baltimore's Inner Harbor.)

The old Convention Hall (site of the Miss America pageant) is to be refurbished as part of a $225 million project to restore the Columbus Blvd approach to the boardwalk, and Las Vegas casino giant Mirage Resorts is planning to build a high tech $2 billion complex of four new casinos (linked by people-moving walkways) which will open by 1998, bringing the total number of gambling palaces to 17 by the turn of the century (though the casinos will probably say there are 18 in town, since no casino will want to be known as the 13th to open, just as there are few 13th floors in the hotels). Critics worry that these moves are being made too late to prepare Atlantic City for competition from new East Coast casinos in Connecticut and upstate New York, which are likely to siphon some of the day-trip traffic to the town.

Monopoly

Many people know that Monopoly, arguably the world's most popular board game, uses the names of Atlantic City properties. The one area listed on the board not found in Atlantic City – Marvin Gardens – is in nearby Margate. But Monopoly's creator, Charles Darrow, actually misspelled the spot, which is actually Marven Gardens. Darrow (who reputedly 'borrowed' ideas freely from two other board games called 'Finance' and 'The Landlord's Game') sold the right to Monopoly to Parker Bros in 1935. Since then, the company has sold more than 160 million copies in 25 languages, often tailoring the board to reflect famous sites in local markets. ■

Orientation

Absecon Island is 10 miles long from north to south, with Atlantic City occupying four miles. Atlantic City is on a grid, each block is 100 numbers. From the Boardwalk, the principal parallel northeast-southwest avenues are named Pacific, Atlantic, Arctic and Baltic. The cross-streets perpendicular to the Boardwalk are mostly avenues named after states. What can be confusing is that they are not in any logical order, some states are not represented and some state capitals make an appearance. As well, Missouri Ave was recently renamed Christopher Columbus Blvd (Columbus Blvd), and Illinois Ave was renamed Dr Martin Luther King Blvd (MLK Blvd), and the names are used interchangeably.

Information

Tourist Offices & Publications The Visitors Information Center (☎ (609) 344-8338) is at 1716 Pacific Ave (between Indiana Ave and MLK Blvd). Five information booths stand along the Boardwalk between the Taj Mahal to the north and the Grand Casino to the south. There is also a desk inside the old Convention Center providing many brochures for local hotels open daily from 10 am to 7 pm.

The best of many free guides to the area are the monthly *AC Shoreline* and the weeklies *Whoot* and *At the Shore*.

Guides explaining the rules of all available games of chance are free at all casinos.

Money You will find banks and ATMs off the gaming areas of all the casinos.

Post The main post office is on the corner of Pacific Ave and MLK Blvd, one block west of the beach.

Bookstores Atlantic City News & Bookstore (☎ (609) 344-9444) is at the intersection of Pacific and MLK Blvd, across from the post office, and is open 24 hours. Atlantic Books is on the Boardwalk between Brighton and Iowa Aves.

Casinos

The 12 casinos are obviously Atlantic City's major attraction, and though regular players seem to have a 'favorite,' all the gaming areas tend to look alike (garish) and sound alike (loud and clangy).

If you plan to spend a great deal of time in one particular casino, be sure to sign up for its player's card before you start gambling. The frequent gambler cards offer a variety of perks, including reduced hotel rooms, food discounts and beverage and entertainment deals. These are awarded based on a combination of how much you play and how long you play. At the time of writing, the best frequent gambler deals were being offered at Merv Griffin's Resorts casino.

If you are a complete novice gambler, you can ask for a free gaming guide that should explain the basics of the various games played in that casino. The best casino to visit if you're a beginner is Claridge's, which is marketing itself as the 'friendly' casino in Atlantic City. It's a bit smaller in scale, and there are quite a few low stakes tables for blackjack and roulette. There is no strict dress code in Atlantic

City's casinos; shorts and T-shirts can be worn at any time.

It's worth checking out the tour of the Taj Mahal, which meets Monday to Friday at 2 pm, at the concierge desk in the bustling lobby. You'll be bombarded with facts about the casino business and Atlantic City, and the $5 tour fee is donated to a local charity for children with AIDS.

Note You must be at least 21 years old to gamble or be on the gambling floor.

The Boardwalk

Florence Valore Miller Art Center & Atlantic City Historical Museum On the site of the restored Garden Pier, at Connecticut Ave and the Boardwalk, this new complex (☎ (609) 347-5839) opened in 1994 and provides a look at the city's colorful past. Visitors to the museum will be reminded that Atlantic City, in its heyday, had a lot more going for it as a tourist attraction than it now does. Atlantic City was a place where such stars as Benny Goodman, Frank Sinatra and Duke Ellington headlined. The arts center, which occupies the building on the north of the pier, has changing exhibits of regional and local art. It's open daily from 10 am to 4 pm.

Steel Pier This amusement pier, directly in front of the Taj Mahal casino, is a part of Donald Trump's empire and was the site of the famous diving horse that plunged into the Atlantic before crowds of spectators.

The Boardwalk

Atlantic City's famous Boardwalk was the first in the world, built in 1870 by local business owners who wanted to cut down on the sand being tracked into hotel lobbies by guests returning from the beach. A man named Alexander Boardman came up with the idea, and the long stretch of planks became known as Boardman's Walk – later shortened to 'Boardwalk.' ■

Today it's just a collection of small amusement rides and candy stands.

Entrance to the Stars At the Boardwalk entrance to Atlantic City's very first casino (Merv Griffin's Resorts, called simply 'Resorts') stands the 'Entrance of the Stars,' dedicated by Frank Sinatra in 1978. It features celebrities' hand prints and signatures in concrete, including Milton Berle, Johnny Carson, Cher, Bill Cosby, Lena Horne, Tom Jones, Liberace, Dean Martin, Steve Martin, Luciano Pavarotti, Joan Rivers and Stevie Wonder – all of whom have headlined in the casino.

Convention Hall The site of the Miss America pageant (see Special Events, below) was the largest auditorium in the world without interior roof posts or pillars when it opened in 1929. If there is not an event in progress, see if you can take a look at the superb interior of the main hall, and the world's largest pipe organ. Every year, Miss America contestants line up for publicity shots amid the columns by the Convention Hall's entrance .

College basketball tournaments and various antique and flower shows take place at Convention Hall (☎ (609) 355-7155) during the winter months.

Tivoli Pier This two acre family amusement center (☎ (609) 340-4020) is inside the TropWorld Casino complex (at Iowa Ave), with Victorian era rides and musical shows. Admission is $11.10 for unlimited access to all the rides, or $5.60 for general admission plus Magic Walk ride and the show, plus $1.45 for each additional ride or attraction. Open all year.

Outdoor Activities

Golf Blue Heron Pines Golf Club (☎ (609) 965-1800), a public course in nearby Pomona, can be reached by exit 14 eastbound on the Atlantic City Expressway.

Bicycling Cycling is allowed along the Boardwalk from 6 to 10 am only. Bikes can be rented on the Boardwalk, in front of the Trump Taj Mahal, and by the ramps leading up to the Boardwalk at Resorts Casino and at Indiana Ave (between Sands and Claridge casinos). On weekends you can rent bikes at Ocean One (☎ (609) 344-8008) on the Boardwalk. ID or a deposit is required.

Special Events

During **Miss America Pageant Week** three nights of preliminary competition are held every September before the Saturday-night televised final of the famous beauty contest. There is also the Miss America Parade when the 50 contestants cruise along the Boardwalk in the back of convertibles. The day after Miss America is crowned, she appears on the beach to frolic in the surf, regardless of the weather. Call ☎ (609) 347-7571 for a complete schedule of events.

Cruises

The *Jetboat* (☎ (609) 348-0800) departs from the marina next to Trump's Castle for an hour-long cruise along Absecon Bay and a guided tour of the city from the water for $10.

If you plan to gamble and want a good middle-range hotel, book a package deal through a casino hotel or travel agent. The AmeriRoom Reservations hotline (☎ (800) 888-5825) specializes in these packages, which usually include meals, show tickets and complimentary chips. The city offers reservations service at ☎ (800) 447-6667, with rooms at all price levels and package deals.

If you just want a clean, basic room, try for a non-casino motel in Atlantic City or nearby Absecon on the mainland.

Places to Stay

Atlantic City's room rates vary considerably depending on the season. In the winter, it's possible to stay in a top hotel such as Merv Griffin's Resorts for as little as $50 a night. In summer the rates run much higher, especially during the week of Miss America festivities.

Bottom End Shoestring travelers are not well-served in Atlantic City, since motels and bars a few blocks off the boardwalk are known to be pickup spots for prostitutes.

The *Inn of the Irish Pub* (☎ (609) 344-9063), 164 St James Place, is right off the Boardwalk but on one of the city's gamiest blocks. Singles/doubles are $25 to $60 with shared bath, and from $75 with private facilities. Just next door is the *Brunswick* (☎ (609) 344-8098), which has similar rates.

Middle The following motels charge something along the following pattern for singles/doubles: winter midweek from $25 to $30, winter weekends from $50 to $80; summer midweek from $35 to $45, summer weekends from $60 to $100. Holiday weekends range from $60 to $200:

Bala Motor Inn
   MLK Blvd and Pacific Ave,
      ☎ (609) 348-3031
Midtown Motor Inn
   Indiana and Pacific Aves, ☎ (609) 348-3031
Miami Hotel
   Kentucky Ave between Boardwalk and
   Pacific Ave, ☎ (609) 344-2077
Economy Motel
   Pacific and Hartford Aves,
      ☎ (609) 348-9111
Casino Beach Hotel
   154 Kentucky Ave between Boardwalk
   and Pacific, ☎ (609) 348-4000
Continental Motel
   Boardwalk at MLK Blvd,
      ☎ (609) 345-5141
Quality Inn
   S Carolina and Pacific Aves,
      ☎ (609) 345-7070
Econo Lodge
   117 S Kentucky Ave between
   Boardwalk and Pacific,
      ☎ (609) 344-9093, ☎ (800) 323-6410
Madison House Hotel
   123 Illinois (MLK Blvd) near the Sands
   Casino, ☎ (609) 345-1400
Holiday Inn – Diplomat
   Boardwalk and Chelsea Ave,
      ☎ (609) 348-2200
Best Western Envoy Inn
   Pacific and New York Aves,
      ☎ (609) 344-7117

Days Inn
   Boardwalk and Morris Ave,
   ☎ (609) 344-6101
Howard Johnson Inn
   Tennessee and Pacific Aves,
   ☎ (609) 344-4193

Top End Atlantic City's casino hotels dominate the expensive choices. Rates run from $90 to $370 depending on the season and day of the week, usually with meals, shows, free use of health spa and casino chips. In the winter, rates can be as low as $50 – the trick is to walk up to the reception desk and act uncertain if you plan to stay the night. You will most likely be offered a room at a deep discount, provided you look well-dressed enough to spend money in the casino.

Showboat – a riverboat theme interior dominates the 700 rooms. Delaware Ave and Boardwalk (☎ (609) 343-4000)
Trump Taj Mahal – by far the most extravagant property in Atlantic City, and the second largest casino is the world (behind the MGM Grand in Las Vegas). Nine two-ton limestone elephants welcome visitors, and 70 bright minarets crown the rooftops. The German-crystal chandeliers in the casino and lobby alone cost $14 million, and despite the garish nature of the interior, the room rates are similar to those found in more modest facilities; it's also the site of the Hard Rock Cafe. 1000 Boardwalk (☎ (609) 449-1000)
Merv Griffin's Resorts – a 670 room Victorian hotel that served as a hospital during WWII and the center of 'Camp Boardwalk.' N Carolina Ave and the Boardwalk (☎ (609) 340-6000)
Sands Hotel, Casino & Country Club – a black glass box that was originally named the Brighton Hotel when it opened. Brighton Park and Indiana Ave (☎ (609) 441-4000)
Claridge Casino Hotel – one block west of the Boardwalk, accessible by a moving walkway that operates in one direction only – into the casino, not out; there are 500 rooms and a three floor, claustrophobic casino area. Indiana Ave and Boardwalk (☎ (609) 340-3400)
Bally's Park Place Casino Hotel & Tower – this 1200 room casino occupies the site of the 1860 Dennis Hotel, which is incorporated into the newer facility; it's the site of many heavyweight boxing matches. Park Place and Boardwalk (☎ (609) 340-2000)
Caesar's Atlantic City Hotel Casino – this 1000 room hotel is also the site of Atlantic City's Planet Hollywood theme-restaurant, which is just off the gaming area. Arkansas Ave and Boardwalk (☎ (609) 348-4411)
Trump Plaza Casino Hotel – this modern tower next to the Convention Center has a Warner Bros Studio Store overlooking the Boardwalk and 560 rooms. Mississippi Ave and Boardwalk (☎ (609) 441-6700)
TropWorld Casino & Entertainment Resort – one of the biggest places in own, with its own indoor theme park (Tivoli Pier), a 90,000 sq foot casino and 1020 rooms. Iowa Ave and Boardwalk (☎ (609) 340-4000)
Bally's Grand – the southernmost casino, formerly known as the Golden Nugget, has just over 500 rooms. Boardwalk between Boston and Pacific Aves (☎ (609) 347-7111)

Away from the Boardwalk, two casino hotels offer a more relaxed setting. The 725 room *Trump's Castle Casino Resort* (☎ (609) 441-7000), Huron Ave and Brigantine Blvd, overlooks the Farley State Marina and has an Art Deco theme.

   Harrah's Marina Hotel Casino (☎ (609) 441-5000), Brigantine Blvd, has 760 rooms in its two towers.

   The *Ramada Renaissance Suites* (☎ (609) 344-1200), is on the Boardwalk at New York Ave.

Places to Eat
Budget If you're hungry, some of the best bargains can be found at the various buffet restaurants offered by the casinos to keep patrons inside. Bally's Grand offers the *Cornucopia* $5.99 lunch/dinner, while the popular *Sultan's Feast* at the Taj Mahal, charges $4.99 for breakfast and lunch, $9.99 for a raw-bar dinner. Caesar's, which has a Planet Hollywood on the premises, charges $9.95 for lunch and dinner at the *Boardwalk Cafe*. TropWorld's *Pasta Pavilion* has a $6.95 dinner, including salad. *Pickles*, in Bally's Park Place Casino and *New Delhi Deli* in the Taj Mahal are moderately priced delis with à la carte selections.

   Tony's Baltimore Grill (☎ (609) 345-5766), 2800 Atlantic at Iowa, and *Angelo's*

Fairmount Tavern (☎ (609) 344-2439), Mississippi and Fairmount, are two popular economical Italian restaurants with entrees from $15 to $30.

Los Amigos (☎ (609) 344-2293), 1926 Atlantic Ave, at the corner of Ohio, is a good Mexican restaurant and bar with specials from $12 to $20.

Moderate *Rosa's* (☎ (609) 348-8889), New York and Sewell eight blocks from the Boardwalk, has terrific soul food with live jazz Friday nights. It's closed Sunday and Monday.

Top End In Venice Park, away from all the casinos, stands the *Old Waterway Inn* (☎ (609) 347-1793), 1700 Riverside Dr, highly recommended for its deck overlooking the water. It sports a casual atmosphere and excellent food with seafood dishes from $30 to $50. Atlantic City's two top seafood restaurants are *Docks Oyster House* (☎ (609) 345-0092), 2405 Atlantic Ave, and *Abe's Oyster House* (☎ (609) 344-7701), at Atlantic and Arkansas, with entrees from $30. The *Knife & Fork Inn* (☎ (609) 344-1133), at the junction of Atlantic and Pacific Aves near Albany Ave, is an institution since 1927 serving seafood and steaks for $45 and up; closed Sunday.

Entertainment
Casinos Each of the casinos offers a full schedule of entertainment, ranging from ragtime and jazz bands in hotel lobbies to top-name entertainers in the casino auditoriums. Ticket prices range from $15 to $100, with the smaller lounges providing free entertainment.

Check the *Whoot* flyer and the monthly *AC Shorecast* for current concerts. The *Comedy Stop* (☎ (609) 340-4000) in the TropWorld Casino is Atlantic City's leading comedy club, with admission prices from $12 to $14.

Music *Wonder Gardens* (☎ (609) 347-1466), corner of Arctic and Kentucky, is a long-established jazz club, a reminder of the busy strip of black night spots (like the defunct Harlem Club) that used to line Kentucky Ave.

Discos *Studio 6* (☎ (609) 348-3310), Mount Vernon between Pacific and Atlantic, is a club with a mixed gay-straight crowd. *Deja Vu* (☎ (609) 348-4313), on New York just off the Boardwalk, is a pickup bar. The funkier *Club Mirage* is in front of Trump Plaza on the Boardwalk by Mississippi Ave.

Things to Buy
There's not much on offer along the Boardwalk except the usual array of T-shirt shops and postcard stores. Fralinger's salt water taffy can be bought in several shops near the casinos.

Gordon's Alley (☎ (609) 344-5000), New Jersey's first pedestrian shopping mall, has some 30 stores covering a two block area between Atlantic, Pacific, Virginia and Pennsylvania Aves.

Ocean One, Atlantic City's major shopping center (☎ (609) 344-8008), is on a pier shaped like an ocean liner, on the Boardwalk between Arkansas Ave and Missouri Ave (Columbus Blvd). An annoying loudspeaker hectors pedestrians to come on in and check out what's on sale, but it's pretty standard stuff.

Getting There & Away
Air Atlantic City international airport (☎ (609) 645-7895) is off Tilton Rd in Pomona and is visited by airlines servicing the city's casino industry: Spirit Airlines (☎ (800) 772-7117); USAir Express and Continental Airlines.

The Philadelphia airport also has a (bus) shuttle service (see below).

Bus NJ Transit also runs buses from New York City to the depot on Arctic Ave between Columbus Blvd and Arkansas Ave. The one-way/roundtrip fare is $21.45/23. One-way/roundtrip buses from Philadelphia cost $10/18.

For a better deal, check out the casino buses from New York and Philadelphia, which run about $22 roundtrip but include food vouchers and quarters for the slots.

From New York's Port Authority, contact Academy (☎ (212) 971-9054) or Greyhound (☎ (800) 231-2222). Fares are cheaper Monday to Thursday. Gray Line (☎ (212) 397-2620) operates from 900 8th Ave, between 53rd and 54th Sts.

From Philadelphia, contact Leisure (☎ (800) 257-7510). Roundtrip tickets are normally valid for just 72 hours.

The Philadelphia Airport Shuttle (☎ (610) 521-1854, (800) 774-8885) also serves this route for $25 one way or $45 roundtrip. The shuttle runs four times a day. You can arrange for on-demand service, though it's only a good value if you have three or more people in your party.

Train NJ Transit runs trains from Philadelphia to Atlantic City; the trip takes about an hour and costs $9.

Car Atlantic City is exit 38 on the Garden State Parkway. The Atlantic City Expressway runs directly from Philadelphia to Atlantic City.

Getting Around
To/From the Airport Shuttle buses to downtown cost one way/roundtrip $8/15. By taxi, it costs around $25 to get to/from the casinos and the airport, about 10 miles away.

Jitney These mini-buses operate 24 hours with stops located on every corner throughout Atlantic City. Every sign has a color-coded number located by each casino stop, telling you which jitney to take (the jitneys have a color coded number on their hoods).

Tram A cheaper alternative to the rolling chairs (see below) are the Blue Trams that run up and down the Boardwalk. It costs $2 one way and $5 for an all-day pass.

Rolling Chair An Atlantic City tradition, the wicker rolling chairs are a sort of rickshaw which is pushed rather than towed along the Boardwalk. Rates are clearly posted inside each chair: up to five blocks

$5, six to 15 blocks $10, 16 to 23 blocks $15, 24 to 30 blocks $20. This experience can feel a bit creepy, especially on a hot day when your rolling chair operator is sweating in the sun.

Taxi For a cab, call Atlantic City Yellow Cabs (☎ (609) 344-1221).

AROUND ATLANTIC CITY
Marine Mammal Center
This nonprofit organization (☎ (609) 266-0538) has rescued over 1000 stranded whales, dolphins, seals and sea turtles that have washed ashore on local beaches since its establishment in 1978. The creatures are brought to the center for rehabilitation and eventual release. The museum features life-size replicas of marine mammals, turtles and game fish, and educational displays on ocean pollution and efforts to eradicate it.

It's open daily during the summer from 11 am to 5 pm, and from October to June on Saturday and Sunday from noon to 4 pm; donations requested.

To get here from Atlantic City, take the Brigantine Bridge (between Harrah's and Trump's Castle) into Brigantine. The center is on the left, two miles from the top of the bridge and 100 yards before Lighthouse Circle.

Historic Smithville
The Town of Historic Smithville began with the Smithville Inn, built in 1787. It was originally just one room on a busy stagecoach route but soon expanded to six rooms. Abandoned by 1900, the inn was restored and reopened in 1952 as a restaurant. The success of the venture triggered off the development of Historic Smithville, with buildings from the region's past brought here and restored. It's a worthy daytrip from Atlantic City or a rest stop when passing through the area since there are several interesting shops, a colorful carousel, miniature railway and water amusements on a lake.

The *Smithville Inn* (☎ (609) 652-0001) at press time was undergoing renovations, but the bakery at this national historic site was

JANE LEET

Luckily, Lucy isn't the only attraction in Margate.

still open for business. Call ahead for restaurant availability.

Historic Smithville is 12 miles north from Atlantic City on Route 9, or exit 48 on the Garden State Expressway.

Renault Winery

This 130 year old vineyard (☎ (609) 965-2111), at 72 N Bremen Ave in Egg Harbor City, is the oldest continuously operating winery in the country. It offers a guided tour, tastings and a museum featuring a priceless collection of champagne glasses and wine goblets, some dating back to the Middle Ages.

You get there by taking Route 30 west from Atlantic City for 16 miles to Bremen Ave, turn right and continue for 2½ miles to the winery.

MARGATE

A pleasant town just five miles south of Atlantic City on Absecon Island, Margate (population 8431) is best known for its gaudy motels and famous landmark – Lucy the Elephant. It also has a great beach and several popular bars that draw a young crowd from miles around.

Lucy the Elephant

This 65 foot 'folly' (☎ (609) 823-6473) was built in 1881 to attract prospective buyers to the new summer homes built by a local real estate developer named James V

Lafferty. The six story elephant is constructed of nearly a million pieces of wood covered with a gray tin 'skin.' Lafferty sold Lucy in 1887 and she became a tourist attraction, a tavern, a summer home for an English physician and his family and a centerpiece for a hotel (although Lucy was never a hotel herself). Visitors who have enjoyed the view from the top of Lucy include Henry Ford and Woodrow Wilson.

But after WWII Lucy fell into neglect and was closed to the public in the 1960s. The quirky landmark was saved by a committee of concerned locals, who moved her to her current location and raised sufficient funds to restore her exterior – and now Lucy is sporting a new $60,000 howdah.

Lucy is open to the public from May to October, before Memorial Day and after Labor Day the hours are Saturday and Sunday only from 10 am to 5 pm; in summer hours are daily from 10 am to 9 pm. Admission is $2/1.

Places to Stay

A Margate alternative for Atlantic City visitors are the *White Sands Condos* (☎ (609) 822-7141, fax 822-2650), 9010 Atlantic Ave, just north of Lucy. There is a choice of studios sleeping two to four at $800 a

---

The Jersey Devil

For years, parents in southern New Jersey have scared naughty children with tales of the local folklore character called the Jersey Devil. This demonic figure, who is said to haunt the Pine Barrens, has red eyes, bat wings and a forked tail. Alternately known as the 'Leed's Devil,' he is said to have been the 13th child born to a Mrs Leeds in 1735 in what is today Leeds Point near Smithville. One version of the story is that he escaped into the wilds after devouring the entire Leeds family. Whatever his misdeeds, a priest performed an exorcism in 1740 to banish his spirit, which may or may not have worked. At any rate, his legend led to the name of the state's NHL hockey team, winners of the 1995 Stanley Cup. ∎

week, efficiencies for $850 to $950, and larger apartments from $1100 for a week.

Places to Eat & Entertainment

Several bar-restaurants are clustered near Lucy the Elephant, including *Ventura's Greenhouse* (☎ (609) 822-0140) right in the elephant's shadow. The menu features appetizers and salads from $5 to $10. *Red's Club* (☎ (609) 822-1539) on the corner of Ventnor and Atlantic Ave, has live bands during the summer months. *Maloney's Tavern* (☎ (609) 823-3546), 23 S Washington St, is the rowdiest of Margate's bars.

Omar's (☎ (609) 822-6627), at the corner of Washington and Amherst Sts, serves inexpensive Mexican food and sandwiches. Right across the street is *Polo Bay* (☎ (609) 487-9189) and *Maynard's* (☎ (609) 822-8423).

Getting There & Away

Margate is on exit 36 on the Garden State Parkway. From the west, via the Atlantic City Expressway, take exit 2.

PINE BARRENS

This unpopulated part of New Jersey is made up of some one million protected acres of pine forest, which is a haven for birders and wildlife enthusiasts. The Pine Barrens aren't really a self-contained park but rather a regional preserve that includes sites such as Batsto Village and the Wharton State Forest. You can call the Pine Barrens information office at (☎ (609) 894-9342) for seasonal information on activities in the area, which includes camping, horseback riding and hiking.

Historic Batsto Village

This well-restored 19th century settlement (☎ (609) 561-3262) is a former iron and glass-making center that served as a major ammunition source for the Continental Army during the War for Independence. Its name is derived from the Swedish word 'Batstu' which means 'bathing place.' The grounds reflect life in the area at that time with guided tours of the Italianate Batsto Mansion and various outhouses. Sights

include a charcoal kiln, ice and milk houses, woodhouse, carriage house, stable, threshing barn, piggery, blacksmith and wheelwright shops, general store and post office and church.

It's open daily from 9 am to 4:30 pm. The mansion tour costs $2 and there is a parking fee on weekends and holidays from Memorial Day through Labor Day. To get here, take Route 542 off Route 9.

Outdoor Activities

Bel Haven (☎ (609) 965-2205), on Route 2 in Egg Harbor, rents canoes, kayaks, inner-tubes and rafts for some terrific trips around the Pine Barrens. Trips can last from two hours to two days. Canoe rentals run from $29 to $38 with reductions for the second day. Rafting trips vary from 2½ hours to six hours; $12 per person. Small rafts carry three or four people, larger rafts four to six.

Places to Stay

Wharton State Forest (☎ (609) 561-3262, 561-0024) has overnight cabin facilities in the Pines; $28 per night for four, and $56 for eight (plus reservation fee). The facilities include kitchen, bath and shower; you need to supply cooking/eating utensils, bedding, linens and food.

WILDWOOD

The 'Wildwoods' (population 4500) consist of three towns – North Wildwood, Wildwood and Wildwood Crest – on the southernmost island off mainland New Jersey. The majority of the boardwalk and its shops are in the noisy Wildwood, which is a big hangout for local teens and a favorite for European college students, mainly from Ireland, who spend the summers working at the amusement areas.

It's worth taking a drive out to Wildwood Crest, the southernmost town, during summer nights to look at the many perfectly preserved '50s motels with their garish neon signs. Even if you're not interested in joining the summer hoards of teenagers that stay in Wildwood, the local tourist office sponsors tours of the

NEW JERSEY

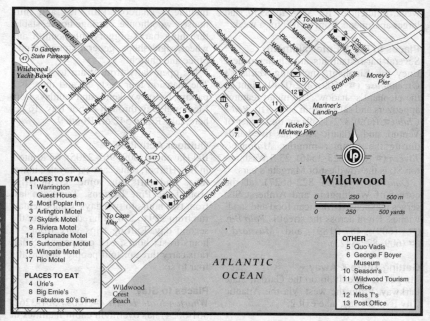

PLACES TO STAY
1 Warrington
   Guest House
2 Most Poplar Inn
3 Arlington Motel
7 Skylark Motel
9 Riviera Motel
14 Esplanade Motel
15 Surfcomber Motel
16 Wingate Motel
17 Rio Motel

PLACES TO EAT
4 Urie's
8 Big Ernie's
   Fabulous 50's Diner

OTHER
5 Quo Vadis
6 George F Boyer
   Museum
10 Season's
11 Wildwood Tourism
   Office
12 Miss T's
13 Post Office

Wildwood

*ATLANTIC
OCEAN*

Wildwood
Crest
Beach

---

town's Eisenhower era motels and diners during the high season. They are worth inquiring about if you're visiting nearby Cape May.

Information

The Wildwood Tourism Office (☎ (609) 522-1407, 800-992-9732) is right at the midpoint of the boardwalk at Schellinger Ave. It's open daily from 9 am to 10 pm in season; and from 9 am to 4 pm after Labor Day.

The post office is at 3311 Atlantic Ave between Wildwood Ave and Oak Ave.

The city has set up parking meters with the clumsiest design you will probably ever encounter. You have to lift a tiny metal hatch, maneuver a quarter into a hole, and spin a flimsy knob. Meters must be fed daily from 8 am to 3 pm; 25¢ gets you only 20 minutes, so consider a parking lot.

Outdoor Activities

Because of the southern migration of sand,

Wildwood's free beach is over a half mile wide at some points and growing. The beach angles very softly into the sea, without a sharp drop off as you find at some northern shore beaches, and the sand is fine and white.

The boardwalk is lined with cheap T-shirt and knick-knack shops, usually selling items for under $1.

There are also **amusement piers** off the boardwalk. Running from north to south are Morey's Pier (☎ (609) 522-5477) at 25th St; Mariner's Landing (☎ (609) 729-0586) and Nickel's Midway Pier (☎ (609) 522-9124) are both on Schellinger Ave. All three piers are open from April through the end of September and sell ride passes for $14.50. For $26 you can get access to two piers and three hours access to the Raging Waters water slide.

Fishing & Boat Rental There are boat rental places and party boats along the bay on Park Blvd between Columbine and Astor

Rds in Wildwood Crest. Try Starlight/Twilight Fishing (☎ (609) 729-7776) at Blake's Dock, 6200 Park Blvd; and the boats at Captain Royles Dock (☎ (609) 522-1395), 6100 Park Blvd. In North Wildwood try Aqua Boat Rentals (☎ (609) 522-5778), 5th and New York Aves.

Whale-Watching Captain Schumann's (☎ (609) 522-2919, (800) 246-9425), 4500 Park Blvd at Burk Ave in Wildwood, claims whale or dolphin sightings on 75% of his trips. The boats leave at 10:30 am, 2 pm and 7 pm daily and cost $8 per person.

Captain Sinn's (☎ (609) 522-3934), 6006 Park Blvd, North Wildwood, also runs three trips daily during the summer. The cost is $12 for whale-watching, $10 for dolphins. Sinn's also has trips on a replica of John F Kennedy's PT-109 at $12 per person.

Parasailing Atlantic Parasail (☎ (609) 522-1869), at Two Mile Landing Crab House Restaurant & Marina on Ocean Dr near the Cape May Inlet Bridge in Wildwood Crest, charges $35 for 300 feet of line and $45 for 600 feet. The trip in the air lasts about 10 minutes.

Jet Skis Ocean Water Sports (☎ (609) 729-4774) in front of Fun Pier on the Ocean in Wildwood, rents WaveRunner 500s half hour/hourly at $35/60; and 650s at $45/70.

Ocean Watersafaris (☎ (609) 522-3017), at the Wildwood Yacht Basin on Rio Grande Blvd just before the bridge, rents WaveRunner 500s at $35/50 and Jetski and WaveRunner 650s at $40/70. They also rent a waterski boat that holds five people and all equipment for $40/70 and $55 for each additional hour.

Places to Stay
Your choices are cheap rooming houses, a few guest houses, or one of the over 250 motels that fill up with teens looking for a good time.

Camping While there are no camping sites in Wildwood, there are a few within five miles of both Wildwood and Cape May. *North Wildwood Camping Resort* (☎ (609) 465-4440), 527-L Shellbay Rd, Cape May Courthouse, NJ, is off exit 9 (Shellbay Rd) from the Garden State Parkway. Sites without/with water and electric are $23.50/25.50 daily or $163/177 weekly.

Holly Shores Holiday Trav-L-Park (☎ (609) 886-1234), 491 Route 9, Cape May, has sites without/with hookups for $19/22. Open from April to October.

Beachcomber Camping Resort (☎ (609) 886-6035, (800) 233-0150), 462-G Seashore Rd, Cape May, NJ 08204, has sites with/without hookups for $16.50/18.50. Take the Garden State Parkway to exit 4A; go to the third light, make a left onto Seashore Rd (also called Railroad Ave). The campground is two miles ahead on the right.

Bottom End The cheapest places are generally in the quadrant bordered to the north and south by New Jersey and Atlantic Aves and to the east and west by Poplar and Pine Aves. Almost all shut soon after Labor Day.

The *Most Poplar Inn* (☎ (609) 729-9238), 305 E Poplar Ave, has clean, basic rooms with refrigerators, TV and shared baths. The per person rate is $20, which is a great deal. Weekly rates are $100. Owner Ted Skocki runs a tight ship and frowns on overly boisterous behavior. Open year round.

The *Arlington Hotel* (☎ (609) 522-2374), 325 E Magnolia Ave, is a five story building and singles/doubles with bath are $90/120 a week.

Also with clean and basic furnishings is the *Tess Sea Inn* (☎ (609) 522-5731), 107 E Magnolia Ave. Rooms with shared bath, sinks and fans are rented for the season at a weekly rate of $100 to $250. A few are kept for daily rental at $20 per person, per night.

The well-worn *Warrington Guest House* (☎ (609) 522-2340), 118 E Maple Ave, has 16 rooms with sinks, air-con and refrigerators with double rates at $35.

Middle & Top End There are dozens of midrange motels in Wildwood lining

Ocean and Atlantic Aves stretching into Wildwood Crest. Price is essentially determined by proximity to the boardwalk.

The *Riviera Motel* (☎ (609) 522-5353) is west of the Sun-N-Sea at Spicer and Ocean Aves. Rates are $80 to $95. The *Skylark Motel* (☎ (609) 522-5082), 3917 Atlantic Ave at the corner of Spencer Ave, is a basic motel with doubles from $36 to $74.

Another clean motel is the *Esplanade Motel* (☎ (609) 522-7890, fax 522-7204), 230 E Taylor Ave, between Atlantic and Pacific Aves. There are standard motel furnishings, a pool and a laundry. Double/efficiency rates are $30 to $55, or $36 to $85 at peak weeks.

Other decent motels include the *Wingate Motel* (☎ (609) 522-7412), at Atlantic and Rio Grande Aves, the *Surfcomber Motel* (☎ (609) 522-2267), 4800 Atlantic Ave near Taylor Ave, and the *Rio Motel* (☎ (609) 522-1461), 4800 Ocean Ave, at the end of Rio Grande Ave, with 115 rooms. All three have rooms from $55 to $100.

Places to Eat

Expect to spend a lot of time eating the fast food on the boardwalk. Wildwood restaurants specialize in all-you-can-eat buffets.

Big Ernie's Fabulous 50s Diner (☎ (609) 522-8288), 3801 Atlantic Ave at Garfield, is open 24 hours and features old 45s, posters and hubcaps on the walls. Burgers, sandwiches and eggs are served for $4 to $10.

There's a buffet at *Grand Smorgasbord* (☎ (609) 522-6742), at 16th Ave and the Boardwalk in North Wildwood, with breakfast for $4. Dinner is $8 for adults, $7 for seniors and children cost 50¢.

Urie's has a beef restaurant, a seafood restaurant and a bar on the waterfront at the Wildwood Yacht Basin on Rio Grande Ave just before the bridge to the mainland. The seafood buffet dinner is $14; kids under 12 can get kid's dinners, but not buffets, for $2. The buffet includes a loud and tacky 'Hawaiian show' on weekend afternoons, and Monday, Wednesday and Friday at 8 pm.

Entertainment

Look at copies of *Free Time* and *Shout*'s 'Nite Club Scene' section to find out what is happening at each club.

Miss T's (☎ (609) 522-7771), at Oak Ave and the Boardwalk, is open from noon to 5 am with a daily happy hour and bikini contests on Friday.

Season's (☎ (609) 522-4400), 222 E Schellinger, has music – mostly top 40 and oldies. It's open year round every day and never charges a cover. On Friday there's a free buffet during happy hour.

Quo Vadis (☎ (609) 522-4949), 4200 Pacific Ave, is a large dance club with disco colored lights that features bikini contests, ladies' night, and wet T-shirt contests. Open until 5 am.

Kitty's (☎ (609) 522-5071), at the corner of Walnut and Olde New Jersey Aves in North Wildwood, gets an older crowd for its live music shows.

Getting There & Away

Bus The bus stop (☎ (609) 522-2491) is at 3400 Oak Ave at New Jersey Ave. NJ Transit runs buses from New York City; fare is $25.45/45.75 one way/roundtrip. From Philadelphia the cost is $22.25/12.40.

At press time, the bus stop was in the process of being relocated from its old spot on the corner of Oak and New Jersey Aves. If you take the bus, it will leave you on New Jersey Ave somewhere near Rio Grande Ave, the main east-west street in Wildwood.

Car Take exit 4 on the Garden State Parkway to Rio Grande Ave, which runs east, right to the beachfront Ocean Dr in Wildwood. Exit 6 on the Garden State Parkway leads to Route 147, which enters North Wildwood as Ocean Dr and then becomes New Jersey Ave.

Getting Around

The Sightseer Tram (☎ (609) 522-6700) runs up and down the boardwalk from 10 am to 1 am during the summer. Pick it up at one of the shelters that look like bus stops; fare is $1.50.

The Wildwood trolley (☎ (609) 884-0450) runs back and forth on Ocean and Atlantic Aves from Schellinger Ave in Wildwood to Jefferson Ave in Wildwood Crest in season; it's $1.25.

CAPE MAY

Cape May (population 4700), which stands at the southern tip of New Jersey, is one of the oldest seashore resorts in the USA. A quiet collection of more than 600 gingerbread Victorian homes, the entire town was designated a national historic landmark in 1976. In addition to its attractive architecture, accommodations and eating places, Cape May boasts a lovely beach, a famous lighthouse, crafts shops and birdwatching. It's the only place in New Jersey where you can watch the sun both rise and set over the water.

History

Cape May is named after Dutch sea captain Cornelius Mey, who claimed the land for Holland in 1621. By 1660, the region was in British hands, and became a whaling

center by the 18th century. The town really flourished as a resort over the next 100 years and by 1853 the Mount Vernon Hotel, the world's largest vacation facility with a capacity for 3000 guests, opened in Cape May. (It burned down just three years later.) A massive fire wiped out most of the town center in 1878, and much of the Victorian architecture that exists today can be dated back to the rebuilding process in the late 19th century.

The town was in danger of becoming an overdeveloped, motel-ridden carbon copy of Wildwood following a hurricane in 1962. But several residents, including Bruce Minnix, who served as the town's mayor from 1972 to '76, successfully fought to have the area designated a national historic landmark.

Incidentally, Cape May is far enough south that it's below the Mason-Dixon line, the tradition demarcation between the 'Northern' and 'Southern' states.

Orientation & Information

Cape May is divided into Cape May City, where you find the hotels, main beach and boardwalk, and Cape May Point State Park,

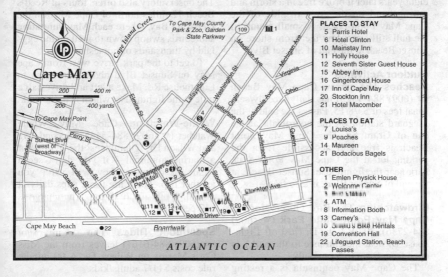

PLACES TO STAY
5 Parris Hotel
6 Hotel Clinton
10 Mainstay Inn
11 Holly House
12 Seventh Sister Guest House
15 Abbey Inn
16 Gingerbread House
17 Inn of Cape May
20 Stockton Inn
21 Hotel Macomber

PLACES TO EAT
7 Louisa's
9 Peaches
14 Maureen
21 Bodacious Bagels

OTHER
1 Emlen Physick House
2 Welcome Center
3 Bus Station
4 ATM
8 Information Booth
13 Carney's
18 Shield's Bike Rentals
19 Convention Hall
22 Lifeguard Station, Beach Passes

with the lighthouse, Sunset Beach and a bird refuge.

The Welcome Center (☎ (609) 884-9562) is at 405 Lafayette St. *This Week*, a publication of the Mid-Atlantic Center for the Arts, lists all activities in town.

The post office is at 700 Washington St.

Emlen Physick House

This 18 room mansion (☎ (609) 884-5404), 1048 Washington St, was designed in 1879 and is now the home for the Mid-Atlantic Center for the Arts. It's open year round with tours several times daily in July and August. Admission is $5/2.50.

Cape May Lighthouse

The 157 foot lighthouse (☎ (609) 884-2159) was built in 1859 and is still in operation, its light visible 25 miles out to sea. It's open daily from 10 am to 5 pm; admission is $3.50.

The Concrete Ship

Twelve experimental concrete ships were built during WWI due to a shortage of steel. The *Atlantis*, with a five-inch concrete aggregate hull, was built in 1918, but eight years later it broke free in a storm and ran aground on the western side of the Cape May Point coast. A small chunk of the hull still sits a few feet from shore on Sunset Beach at the end of Sunset Blvd.

Outdoor Activities

Beaches The narrow Cape May Beach (☎ (609) 884-9525) has daily/weekly/seasonal fees of $3/8/15. Passes are sold at the lifeguard station on the boardwalk at the end of Grant St. The Cape May Point Beach is free and accessible from the parking lot at the Cape May Point State Park near the lighthouse. Sunset Beach, at the end of Sunset Blvd, is also free.

Birdwatching The Bird Observatory at **Cape May Point State Park** (☎ (609) 884-2736), 707 E Lake Dr (just off Lighthouse Dr near the entrance to the park), is open from 9 am to 5 pm daily.

The Cape May peninsula is a resting

Cape May County Park & Zoo

One of this area's nicest discoveries is the Cape May County Park and Zoo, located a few miles north of town just off exit 11 of the Garden State Parkway (easily accessible to those with a car). The zoo is a beautifully maintained 200 acre facility with some 250 different species of animals, many of whom wander freely across a recreated African savanna and other natural habitats while humans observe the action from a discreet distance along the elevated boardwalk. There are also buildings where you can observe birds, reptiles and aquatic life from closer quarters.

The park, which is busy but not crowded even in summer, also offers nature and bike trails, a children's playground and a fishing pond. Best of all, access to the entire park is free, though they do encourage donations from visitors as they enter the parking lot. ∎

---

place for millions of migratory birds each year, and the hotline (☎ (609) 884-2626) offers information on the latest sightings. The observatory also offers tours of Reed's Beach 12 miles north of Cape May on the Delaware Bay, where each May, migrating shorebirds swoop down to feed on the eggs laid by thousands of horseshoe crabs.

To get to the park, drive west from Cape May on Sunset Blvd about two miles to Lighthouse Rd. Make a left and drive half a mile to the lighthouse, which is in the park.

Whale-Watching Cape May Whale Watcher (☎ (609) 884-5445), Second Ave and Wilson Dr, 'guarantees' the sighting of a marine mammal – if you don't see a whale or dolphin, they will offer you another trip. There are three trips daily at 10 am, 1 pm and 6:30 pm. The charge is $12 per person.

Speedboat Rides The *Shore Shot* (☎ (609) 884-6161) leaves from the Miss Chris Marina on Wilson Dr. A 90 minute ride costs $11/7 adults/kids.

Cape May Diamonds

Keep an eye out for 'Cape May diamonds' along Sunset Beach. That's what locals call the small pieces of quartz washed 200 miles downstream from the Delaware River that take on a smooth translucent look on their southward journey. The best time to look for the stones, and an occasional shark tooth or arrowhead, is right after a storm. ■

Fishing Party Boats leave daily from the Miss Chris Marina (☎ (609) 884-3939) at Third Ave and Wilson Dr.

Sailing The 80 foot wooden *Schooner Yankee* (☎ (609) 884-1919) sails from the Ocean Highway Dock at the foot of Two Mile Bridge near Cape May (PO Box 98, Cape May). Three-hour trips cost $23.50 and are available from May to September.

Bicycling Bikes may be rented for $17 a day at Shield's (☎ (609) 884-1818) at 11 Gurney just near the beach. It's open daily from 7 am to 7 pm.

Organized Tours

The Mid-Atlantic Center for the Arts (☎ (609) 884-5404), 1048 Washington St, offers a range of walking, trolley and boat tours. You can buy tickets at the ticket booth on the western end of the Washington St Mall, just before Decatur St. Prices are for adults/children.

Cape May Historic Districts Walking Tour
  year round; $4/1
Champagne Brunch Tour   a walking tour
  followed by brunch at the Mad Batter.
  Easter to Thanksgiving; $15/7.50
Gourmet Brunch Tour – a walking tour followed
  by a Southern breakfast at the Chalfonte
  Hotel. Easter to Thanksgiving; $15/7.50
Ocean Walk – a walk along the beach to discuss
  ecology. Memorial Day to Labor Day; $3/1
Mansions by Gaslight – tour of the Emlen
  Physick House (1879), the Abbey (1869),
  the Mainstay (1872) and the Humphrey
  Hughes House (1901). Wednesdays during
  the summer; $12/6

INNteriors Tour & Tea – tours of different inns
  and guest houses. Weekends from February
  to November; $12/6
Trolley Tours – three different drives: around the
  East End, the West End, and Beachfront
  (year round; $4/1). There are also children's
  trolley tours at the same price and moonlight
  trolley tours (June to September; $3.50).
Cape May by Boat – the boat leaves from Wildwood and circles Cape May; summer; $8

Special Events

The Cape May Music Festival (May to June) is a series of concerts from Renaissance to classical to jazz.

Victorian Week (October) is a 10 day string of events including house tours, a Victorian fashion show, lectures and workshops on Victorian desserts, glassware, crafts, etc.

The Victorian Holmes Weekend (November) is a suspense-mystery weekend with a Sherlock Holmes impersonator, tour and dining.

Christmas in Cape May (late November to early January) features house tours by gaslight and candlelight, wassail (punch made with wine or ale, spices and apples), and the town is beautifully lit up.

Places to Stay

Cape May is packed with expensive B&Bs and inns, and you can't walk 50 feet in the center of town without passing one.

Bottom End The best budget place in town is the *Hotel Clinton* (☎ (609) 884-3993, off-season (516) 799-8889), 202 Perry St near the intersection with Lafayette, run by Ezio and Linda Pradelli. Singles/doubles are $25 to $30/35 to 40.

Next door is the *Parris Hotel* (☎ (609) 884-8015/6363), 204 Perry St, a very distant second in the bottom-end category. Most rooms have private baths and some TVs, but they are cluttered and could be cleaner. Single rates are $35 to $55 with doubles running $10 more.

Middle Former mayor Bruce Minnix and his wife Corinne own *Holly House* (☎ (609) 884-7365), 20 Jackson St. This

1890 cottage is one of the 'Seven Sisters' – seven identical homes; five are along Jackson St. There are six non-ostentatious corner rooms, each with three windows and a shared bath. Weekday/end rates are $60/65.

The *Seventh Sister Guest House* (☎ (609) 884-2280), 10 Jackson St, is a few doors down from Holly House. The house is decorated with the artwork of co-owner JoAnne Myers, who welcomes other artists. Rooms are $65 to $80.

The *Hotel Macomber* (☎ (609) 884-3020), 727 Beach Dr on the corner of Howard St, has the cheapest rooms near the ocean. The hotel has modern renovations: shared bath doubles are $65, those with private bath are $95.

Top End The *Gingerbread House* (☎ (609) 884-0211) is a six room B&B at 28 Gurney St run by Fred and Joan Echevarria, and is a friendly and casual place to stay. Rates, including breakfast and afternoon tea, are $85 to $150.

The *Stockton Inn* (☎ (609) 884-4036, (800) 524-4283), 809 Beach Dr, is a motel and a 'manor house.' The motel has standard motel furnishings and a pool with rooms from $45 to $90. The manor is a converted Victorian house with 10 rooms and three suites, all with private bath. Rooms are $50 to $130. Suites are rented weekly at $500 to $1025.

The *Inn of Cape May* (☎ (800) 257-0432), at the corner of Beach Dr and Ocean Ave, is the sprawling white wooden structure with lavender trim. Rooms come in a wide variety of sizes, generally have high ceilings and white wicker furniture and run $50 to $200.

The *Mainstay Inn* (☎ (609) 884-8690), 635 Columbia Ave, was built in 1872 as a men's gambling club. Rooms are furnished in opulent dark woods with large beds and all have private baths. The building is so impressive that the owners give tours four times a week ($5). Off-season rooms are $95, but the in-season rates go up to $170. Rates include breakfast and afternoon tea. Closed January to March.

The *Abbey* (☎ (609) 884-4506), 34 Gurney St at the corner of Columbia Ave, is one of the most opulent places in town. Like the Mainstay, it is packed with antique furniture, has high ceilings and offers a tour with tea ($5). Rooms in the main building have refrigerators and in the cottage they all have private baths. Rates, including breakfast, are from $80 to $175.

Angel of the Sea (☎ (609) 884-3369, (800) 848-3369), 5-7 Trenton Ave, is probably the priciest place in town and renowned for its service. All rooms have baths and ceiling fans and access to wrap-around porches. Weekday/weekend room rates, including breakfast, are $150 to $250.

Places to Eat

Budget *Akroteria* is a collection of small fast-food shacks on Beach Dr between Jackson and Perry Sts, serving pita bread sandwiches, fruit salad, seafood, funnel cakes, ice cream and cheesesteaks all for around $5.

Bodacious Bagels (☎ (609) 884-3031), at Beach Dr and Howard St on the 1st floor of the Hotel Macomber serves bagel sandwiches ($6) and omelets ($6).

The *Sunset Beach Grill* is at the end of Sunset Blvd on Sunset Beach overlooking the sunken *Atlantis* and the ocean. It's a great place to order a sandwich and watch the waves.

Moderate *Louisa's* (☎ (609) 884-5882), 104 Jackson St, is an excellent small restaurant serving only dinner Tuesday to Saturday from 5 pm. The menu changes but appetizers include things like ginger-sesame or chili-orange noodles for $5.

Huntington House (☎ (609) 884-5868), on Grant and North Sts, has an all-you-can-eat buffet that costs $14 for adults and $5 for kids.

Top End *Maureen* (☎ (609) 884-3774) is on Beach Dr and Decatur St. This is a good place to splurge on appetizers like salmon and crab crepe ($8), entrees like scallops with mango ($17.50), bouillabaisse ($21), or veal or beef ($19 to $24).

Peaches, at two locations, 322 Carpenter's Lane (☎ (609) 884-0202), and 1 Sunset Blvd (☎ (609) 898-0100), serves more usual fare.

Entertainment
The Cape May Stage (☎ (609) 884-1341) is an excellent regional theater with a March to December season of plays.

Carney's (☎ (609) 884-4424), 401 Beach Dr between Decatur and Jackson Sts, has two bars and a weird decor of wagon-wheel lights, carved fish, fake plants, fake beams and fake brick. It is, however, a popular and unpretentious place to drink and hear music.

The *Shire* (☎ (609) 884-4700), 315 Washington Mall, has live music daily during the summer with small cover charges.

Things to Buy
The pedestrian mall along Washington St is crammed with shops and tourists. There are also 11 antique stores all over town; the visitors center offers a map noting all of them.

Getting There & Away
Bus NJ Transit (☎ (201) 762-5100, (800) 772-2222) runs buses from New York City to Cape May for $26.75/48.74 one-way/roundtrip and from Philadelphia for $12.40/22.25. The bus station is next to the chamber of commerce building near the corner of Lafayette and Elmira Sts.

Car Cape May is at the southern end of the Garden State Parkway, which leads right into town.

Ferry A ferry runs daily between North Cape May and the Delaware coastal town of Lewes (pronounced LOO-is, ☎ (800) 643-3779 for recorded information, (800) 717-7245 for reservations, which should be made a day in advance in high season).

The 17 mile trip across the Delaware Bay takes about 70 minutes and is a popular way for residents of Delaware and Maryland to visit the southern Jersey shore. It also saves New Jersey-based travelers heading south some time if they're leaving Cape May for a visit to Washington, DC, and points south (see Lonely Planet's *Washington, DC & the Capital Region*).

Ferries leave North Cape May between 6:20 am and 7:40 pm and Lewes between 8 am and 9:20 pm. There are at least five trips a day in winter with additional trips in summer. The one-way fare for vehicle and driver is $18; for foot passengers it's $4.50, for children six to 12 it's $2.25.

The ferry terminal is in North Cape May on Route 9 west of the Garden State Parkway. For additional details and directions you can call the Lewes, DE, terminal (☎ (302) 645-6346) or the North Cape May terminal (☎ (609) 886-9699).

Facts about Pennsylvania

'America Starts Here' is Pennsylvania's proud slogan (seen on license plates and in tourist literature), alluding to the historical events before, during and after the American Revolution that helped form the USA. Today, Pennsylvania's wealth of historical sites and beautiful scenery are rightly a major draw for visitors.

Philadelphia, sometimes overlooked by visitors short on time and rushing between New York and Washington, DC, is enjoying a well-deserved renaissance with its rich blend of history, architecture, cultural attractions, city parks, shops and wealth of eating and entertainment places. Nearby are the Brandywine Valley to the southwest and Bucks County to the north with picturesque scenery and historical sites, and to the west Valley Forge National Historic Park.

Pennsylvania Dutch Country, only some 90 minutes' drive west of Philadelphia, is a major attraction with its Amish community, who live by mixing Biblical precepts and the modern world. A bit further west is Gettysburg, where visitors can follow the course of the bloodiest battle in the Civil War in the National Military Park. Other popular destinations are Hershey, home of the chocolate company, and York, home of the Harley-Davidson motorcycle.

In the southwest, the state's other big city, Pittsburgh, used to be called 'Smokey City' because extensive mining emitted coal dust into the air. Today, like Philadelphia, it is being reborn and is a beautiful city well worth visiting. Southeast of Pittsburgh are the scenic Laurel Highlands, a center for white-water rafting and where Frank Lloyd Wright built the architectural masterpiece Fallingwater.

Northwest Pennsylvania saw the start of the US oil industry, whose remains are still visible, in stark contrast to the natural beauty of the surrounding Allegheny National Forest. The forests of the north are particularly beautiful in the fall. The city of Erie gives Pennsylvania access to the Great Lakes and played an important part in the War of 1812 with Britain. Route 6, also called the Grand Army of the Republic Hwy, offers a picturesque journey through the north of the state. The Poconos, in the northeast, is a resort region famous as a honeymoon destination, which also offers a wealth of outdoor activities year round.

HISTORY
War of Independence
Owing to its economic strength and the size of its population, Pennsylvania contributed heavily in men, material and financial support to the Revolutionary War. Philadelphia was made the capital of the new nation and British troops marched into Pennsylvania in September 1777, where they defeated Washington's forces at the Battle of Brandywine Creek. On September 26, the British captured and occupied Philadelphia. Washington tried to retake the city on October 4, but failed and withdrew to Valley Forge, where his forces spent the harsh winter being retrained.

In the meantime the capital was moved to York where an American congress approved the Articles of Confederation, later to become the country's first constitution. Benjamin Franklin (see the Philadelphia chapter for a biographical sidebar) helped negotiate an alliance with France; news of this led the British to withdraw to New York from Philadelphia in June 1778. Apart from some loyalist and Indian attacks on settlements, for the rest of the war the main campaigns took place in other states.

Early Independence
After the war it was felt that the Articles of Confederation were no longer adequate to keep the newly independent states together and in 1787 a federal constitutional convention was held in Philadelphia. On

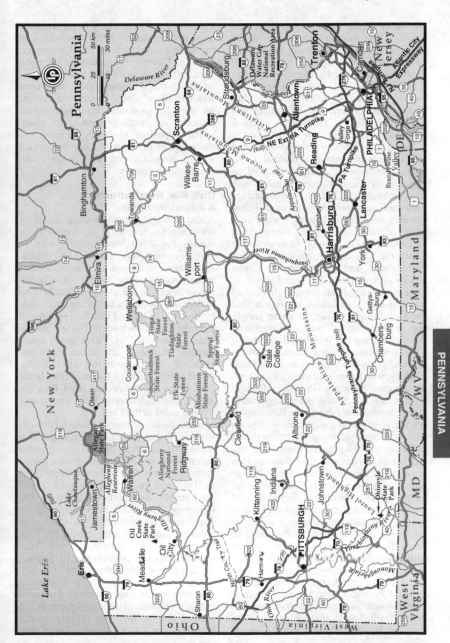

December 12, the Pennsylvania delegates, among whom were four signatories of the Declaration of Independence, ratified the new federal constitution. Then in 1790 Pennsylvania adopted a new state constitution. New York City had been made the capital of the US after the war, but Philadelphia became the national capital again from 1790 to 1800, from where it moved finally to Washington, DC.

The postwar years saw Pennsylvania invest energy and money in internal development, including the construction of an extensive system of canals, turnpikes and, later, railroads. As a result, the population expanded westward and northward. Pennsylvania became the country's main supplier of coal, iron and timber, but agriculture was also important in areas like Lancaster County. At the same time Philadelphia and Pittsburgh developed rapidly as manufacturing centers.

Just as merchants and others had opposed excessive British taxation before the Revolutionary War, so some people opposed excessive US federal taxation after the war. During the Whiskey Rebellion of 1794, western Pennsylvania farmers rebelled against taxes on homemade whiskey, which they sold to offset the costs of transporting grain. President George Washington had to call out a larger army than he commanded during the Revolutionary War to suppress the farmers. Five years later residents of eastern Pennsylvania objected to being taxed based on the number of windows in their houses. This revolt was known as the Hot Water Rebellion because homeowners threw hot water on assessors. Taxation issues subsided when Thomas Jefferson was elected president in 1800 and reduced taxes.

Slavery was not deeply entrenched in Pennsylvania because the state's Quakers had always been opposed to it. The state's first antislavery society had begun meeting in 1775 and the legislature passed the Gradual Emancipation Act on March 1, 1780, which said that no child born in Pennsylvania after that date could be enslaved. By 1850 all black people living in the state were free. Many Pennsylvanians also opposed slavery in the other states. In the state's south, towns like Gettysburg, York and Chambersburg near the Maryland border (the notorious Mason-Dixon Line, which separated northern 'free' states from southern 'slave' states) became main points on the 'Underground Railroad,' which helped slaves escape to freedom in Canada.

This opposition to slavery led many into the ranks of the Republican party, which was to dominate state politics until well into the 20th century.

Civil War, Reconstruction & Industrialization

About 350,000 Pennsylvanians, including 8600 blacks, served in the Union army during the Civil War, second only in number to New York. The state's industries, agriculture and natural resources contributed vitally to the North's war effort. It was in Pennsylvania, along the Cumberland Valley, that Southern forces tried to invade the North. The biggest invasion, by General Robert E Lee and a force of 75,000 Confederates, was halted by Union forces under General Meade at the bloody three-day battle of Gettysburg in July 1863. It produced more casualties than any other battle (and more American casualties than the whole of the Vietnam War) and was a turning point in the Civil War.

In the post-war years, although Pennsylvania's influence on national politics waned, its industrial production expanded enormously and business magnates gained immense power. Out of the discovery of oil in Titusville in 1859 grew such giants as John D Rockefeller's Standard Oil Company. Henry Clay Frick bought up the state's coal reserves and expanded the coke industry. Andrew Carnegie built his huge Carnegie Steel Company, which later became the main component of US Steel, the first billion-dollar corporation in the US.

The workforce for these expanding industries came from waves of European immigrants and as industry grew in the second half of the 19th century so did Pennsylvania's labor unions. Local iron molders formed a union in 1859 that eventually grew into the National Labor Union. Coal miners joined the Molly Maguires (a secret group that worked initially for miners of Irish descent) and later the United Mine Workers' Union. Railroad workers joined the Trainsmen's Union. The three largest nationwide organizations of workers were all founded in the state' – the Knights of Labor in 1869, the American Federation of Labor in 1888 and the Congress of Industrial Organizations in 1938.

Pittsburgh was the scene of several major labor strikes during this period: there was the Great Railroad Strike of 1877; in the steel industry at Homestead (a suburb of Pittsburgh) in 1892; and in the greater Pittsburgh region in 1919.

20th Century

During the two world wars, Pennsylvania again played a vital role in supplying materials for the war effort. In WWI over 300,000 men served in the armed forces and during WWII, official state histories say, incredibly, that one out of every seven members of the US armed forces was a Pennsylvanian.

Although Pennsylvania's economy was boosted by the world wars, the massive production efforts lasted only a few years after the end of each conflict. Eventually some of the state's natural resources like oil became exhausted or more difficult and more expensive to extract; there was a decline in the demand for coal, the textile industry departed and there was strong out-of-state and international competition for iron and steel. In response, Pennsylvania moved from heavy industry to service industries, high technology and tourism. A number of corporate giants have made their headquarters in the state and agriculture continues to be an important part of the economy.

From the 1930s, Republican dominance of state politics was gradually eroded by Democrat President Franklin D Roosevelt's New Deal (a response to the hopelessness of the Depression), as well as the influence of organized labor and the urbanization of the state. Philadelphia and Pittsburgh became important Democratic centers. Since the 1930s political control of the state has alternated regularly between the two parties. In 1986 and 1990, Democrat Robert Casey of Scranton was elected governor; in 1992 Democrats held majorities in both houses of the assembly. In 1994 Republican Tom Ridge was elected governor.

As was common with many US cities, Pennsylvania's major urban centers saw their downtown areas decline during the 1950s, '60s and early '70s as automobiles increased people's mobility and many middle-class people took to the suburbs. Since the mid-'70s, however, a number of these downtown areas, most notably in Philadelphia and Pittsburgh, have undergone a slow but significant revival.

GEOGRAPHY & GEOLOGY

Pennsylvania is roughly rectangular, occupying 44,820 sq miles; its share of Lake Erie measures another 735 sq miles. At its widest points, Pennsylvania stretches 310 miles west to east and 180 miles north to south. The Delaware River in the east separates the state from New Jersey and New York while its western border abuts Ohio and West Virginia. To the north is New York State and in the northwest a 40 mile stretch of shoreline along Lake Erie; to the south are West Virginia, Maryland and Delaware. Its highest elevation is 3213 feet on Mt Davis in the southwest and its lowest is sea level on the Delaware River.

Seven geographical regions run diagonally across the state from southwest to northeast.

In the northwestern corner is a narrow strip of the Central Lowland called the Erie Lowland, that runs along Lake Erie and is excellent for grape growing. It's separated from the Appalachian Plateau (which, in Pennsylvania, is often referred to as the Allegheny Plateau) by an escarpment. The Appalachian Plateau is a large area of low mountains, including the Poconos and the Alleghenies, and deep but narrow valleys separated by smaller plateaus, that occupies over half the state including all of western and most of northern Pennsylvania. The horizontal rock layers make it easy to mine bituminous (soft) coal in the southwest of the plateau.

Another escarpment, the Allegheny Front, separates the Appalachian Plateau from the next region to the south and east, the Appalachian Ridge & Valley. This is a 50 mile wide strip of low ridges separated by valleys which sweep and curve northeastward through central Pennsylvania. It includes the Blue, Tuscarora and Bald Eagle mountains, and the Lebanon, Lehigh and Cumberland valleys. Most of the nation's anthracite (hard) coal comes from here.

Two small regions divide part of the Appalachian Ridge & Valley from the Piedmont Plateau to the south. One, to the southwest, is the northern extension of the Blue Ridge Mountains known as South Mountain, which includes Gettysburg; the other, to the northeast, is the Reading Prong (part of the New England Upland), which juts out from the Delaware River. The Piedmont Plateau consists of fertile limestone lowlands along the southeastern segment of the state on which lies the Pennsylvania Dutch region with some of the richest soils in the country between the Allegheny River and Philadelphia.

Southeast of the Piedmont Plateau is a tiny strip of the Atlantic Coastal Plain that is now mostly covered by Philadelphia.

Pennsylvania has three major river systems – the Delaware in the east, the Susquehanna in the middle, and the Ohio in the west. Pittsburgh sits at the juncture of the Allegheny, Monongahela and Ohio rivers. Philadelphia is on the Delaware River, which carries more cargo than any other in the US except the Mississippi, and its tributary the Schuylkill River.

The standard work on Pennsylvania's geology is Bradford B van Diver's *Roadside Geology of Pennsylvania* available from Mountain Press, PO Box 2399, Missoula, MT 59806. Tim Palmer's *Rivers of Pennsylvania* (Penn State University Press, 1980) is also good.

Ned Smith's *Gone for the Day* (Pennsylvania Game Commission, 1971) is an entertaining collection of monthly columns written about the Pennsylvania mountains, rivers and animals. You can usually find it at the USFS office in Warren.

CLIMATE

Pennsylvania has a humid continental climate but some small climatic variations occur within the state, mainly because of elevation. In the southeast around Philadelphia and Pennsylvania Dutch Country, in the area near Lake Erie and along the Ohio and Monongahela river valleys the frost-free (or growing) period is longest – around six months. On the Appalachian Plateau the summers are shorter and the winters more severe.

Pennsylvania generally gets between 32 and 40 inches of precipitation a year, but snowfall in the colder regions can be well over 60 inches a year. See the Philadelphia and Pittsburgh climate charts in the Facts for the Visitor chapter.

ECOLOGY & ENVIRONMENT

Pennsylvania has been mining and burning coal for a long time and its use at one time led Pittsburgh to be given the nickname 'Smokey City.' In recent years the state government has imposed stringent environmental regulations on its production and use; the federal government's 1990 Clean Air Act has also meant that mining companies and electrical utilities have had to improve their technologies to make them less polluting.

About 35% of the state's electricity is produced by nuclear power. Since the nuclear accident at Three Mile Island, near Harrisburg, in 1979, when one of the reactors partially melted, the nuclear industry has improved its technology and safety procedures. Many people, however, remain unconvinced that nuclear power can ever be safe and there is strong opposition to its use.

The Pennsylvania chapter (☎ (215) 963-4300) of the Nature Conservancy is at 1211 Chestnut St, 12th Floor, Philadelphia, PA 19107. The Western Pennsylvania

Conservancy (☎ (412) 288-2777), Department OG, 316 Fourth Ave, Pittsburgh, PA 15222, is an independent organization that preserves natural lands in the west for public use. The two organizations are separate though they do cooperate on joint projects.

STATE PARKS & FORESTS

Pennsylvania has 114 state parks, the third-largest system in the US, which offer a wide range of activities from hiking, bicycling, swimming, boating, fishing and white-water rafting in the warmer months to downhill and cross-country skiing in winter. Many of the parks have visitor centers which, as well as providing information, offer interpretive programs on nature and environmental issues. For more details contact the Bureau of State Parks (☎ (717) 675-1121, (800) 637-2757), PO Box 8551, Harrisburg, PA 17105-8551.

There are over 3125 sq miles of state forests with 2500 miles of trails for hiking, bicycling, horseback-riding, cross-country skiing and snowmobiling, and include 280 sq miles of natural and wilderness areas for wildlife viewing. Information and maps are available from the Bureau of Forestry (☎ (717) 783-7941), PO Box 8552, Harrisburg, PA 17105-8552.

The more than 2000 sq miles of state game lands also have hiking and cycling trails. For information and maps contact the Pennsylvania Game Commission (☎ (717) 783-7507), Department MS, 2001 Elmerton Ave, Harrisburg, PA 17110-9797.

GOVERNMENT & POLITICS

Pennsylvania, like Kentucky, Massachusetts and Virginia, is officially designated a 'commonwealth,' which comes from 'common weal,' meaning the general well-being of the population. Pennsylvania is governed by a bicameral legislature, or general assembly, consisting of a 50 member senate (elected every four years) and a 203 member house of representatives (elected every two years).

Since the 1950s, Democrat and Republican membership of the general assembly has been split fairly equally. Moderate Republican, Tom Ridge, is currently state governor. The governor serves a four year term and may be elected to a maximum of two terms. The basic conservatism of the state is reflected in the Washington, DC, joke that Pennsylvania consists of Philadelphia and Pittsburgh with Alabama in the middle.

The judiciary is headed by a supreme court comprising a chief justice and six associate justices who are all elected for 10-year terms. At the local level, Pennsylvania is made up of 66 counties each run by a three member board of commissioners; Philadelphia is also classified as a county but is administered by a mayor and council.

ECONOMY

Pennsylvania is second only to West Virginia in bituminous (soft) coal production, and it produces almost all the anthracite (hard) coal in the US, of which it has large reserves. It is also a center for stone, limestone, slate, clay and sand. The petroleum industry had its peak year of production in 1891, but northwestern Pennsylvania still has oil (and natural gas) and the Quaker State Company is headquartered in Oil City, where the company's McClintock Well has been operating continuously since 1861.

Manufacturing has always been an important part of the state's economy. Pittsburgh still leads the US in iron and steel production and, although the industry has declined greatly since its 19th century heyday, it is still strong enough that demand outstrips production. Other leading manufactured products are food (including carbonated drinks, chocolate, meats, ice cream and pretzels), chemicals, building materials such as cement, industrial machinery, electronic equipment, precision instruments, paper and glass.

Over 30% of the state is classified as farmland, about 70% of which is used for poultry and dairy farming. Hay and corn (maize) are the main crops grown but the most valuable, believe it or not, is mushrooms. Pennsylvania leads the nation in the production of apples, peaches and cherries but grapes and berries are also important as are trees for the Christmas market.

Pennsylvania earns more than $9 billion a year from tourism.

There are six million people in Pennsylvania's labor force. The service sector employs 23%. Other jobs are in wholesale and retail sales (21%), manufacturing (20%), trade (18%) and government (12%). Less than 2% of Pennsylvania's residents work in agriculture. The per capita income is $14,000.

POPULATION & PEOPLE

Pennsylvania is the country's fifth most populous state, with nearly 12 million people, more than half of whom live in and around Philadelphia or Pittsburgh. Most of Northern Pennsylvania is sparsely populated. The two largest ethnic groups are whites (88.5%) and blacks (9.2%); other important ethnic groups are Hispanics 232,300, Chinese 29,500, East Indians 28,400, Koreans 26,800, Vietnamese 15,900, Native Americans 14,200, Filipinos 12,160 and Japanese 6610.

Native peoples occupying what is now Pennsylvania were the Lenni Lenape (or Delaware), Susquehannock, Shawnee and Iroquois.

William Penn's liberal and tolerant ideals attracted immigrants from all over Europe as well as from other colonies in the early years. The first to come were English and Welsh Quakers. German Mennonites arrived beginning in 1683 and founded Germantown near Philadelphia. Other small German sects included the Amish, Mennonites and Brethren, also known as 'Plain People,' and Moravians.

After the first quarter of the 18th century came Scotch and Scotch-Irish immigrants, as did Germans from the larger Lutheran and Reform churches. Many Irish came in the mid-19th century following a series of famines in their homeland. The latter 19th century pattern of immigration switched to southern and eastern Europe, and the descendants of these people – Slavs, Italians, Poles – form the largest group of Pennsylvania's population. Black immigration increased in the 20th century and since the 1960s the Hispanic and Asian populations have grown.

EDUCATION

Tinicum was the site of Pennsylvania's first school, which was established by Swedish settlers in the 1640s. William Penn's 1682 Frame of Government called for the education of all children in the colony, and attempts at this were first made by religious groups. In 1689, Quakers founded the Friends' Public School in Philadelphia, Pennsylvania's first public school. The Free School Act of 1834 provided for free elementary education and later laws expanded schooling to high schools.

There are now over 3200 public schools and more than 270 institutions of tertiary education. Rural Pennsylvania has many Catholic colleges. Pennsylvania State University ('Penn State') is the state university with 21 campuses; the main one is in the middle of Pennsylvania in a town called State College. Other major tertiary institutions are the University of Pennsylvania ('Penn,' an Ivy League school) and Temple University in Philadelphia, the University of Pittsburgh and Carnegie-Mellon University in Pittsburgh. There are many others.

INFORMATION
Tourist Offices

The main state authority is the Office of Travel Marketing (☎ (717) 787-5453, (800) 237-4363), 453 Forum Building, Harrisburg, PA 17120, which oversees the state's regional, county and local tourist offices. Many of these operate as an arm of or in conjunction with local chambers of commerce and are listed in the text under the destination heading's Information section. For a copy of the free annual *Pennsylvania Visitors Guide* write to the above address or call ☎ (800) 847-4872.

Welcome Centers Pennsylvania has 11 tourist offices known as 'Welcome Centers' at key locations on the state's highways. For more information, contact the Welcome

Center Division (☎ (717) 787-4433), Department of Transportation, 1211 Transportation & Safety Building, Harrisburg, PA 17120. All are open from 8:30 am to 5 pm daily.

I-70 West – one mile north of the Pennsylvania/ Maryland border

I-78 West – one mile west of the Pennsylvania/ New Jersey border

I-79 South – one mile south of the Edinboro exit

I-80 East – half a mile east of the Pennsylvania/ Ohio border

I-81 North – one mile north of the Pennsylvania/ Maryland border

I-81 South – four miles south of exit 64 for Lenox

I-83 North – half a mile north of the Pennsylvania/ Maryland border

I-95 North – half a mile north of the Pennsylvania/ Delaware border

Neshaminy – on the Pennsylvania Turnpike mile marker 351, seven miles west of the Pennsylvania/New Jersey border

Sideling Hill – on the Pennsylvania Turnpike mile marker 172, 10 miles east of the Breezewood exit

Zelienople, on the Pennsylvania Turnpike at mile marker 21, 21 miles east of the Pennsylvania/Ohio border

Accommodations

The Private Campground Owners Association (☎ (610) 767-5026), PO Box 5, New Tripoli, PA 18066, publishes the annual *Pennsylvania Campground Directory*, listing almost 200 campgrounds in Pennsylvania. The Pennsylvania Travel Council (☎ (717) 232-8880), Department 931, 902 N 2nd St, Harrisburg, PA 17102, distributes the annual *Pennsylvania B&B Directory* with about 175 listings.

Taxes

The statewide sales tax is 6% except for clothing which is exempt. Accommodation taxes in Pittsburgh and Philadelphia are 9% and 12% respectively.

Alcohol

Pennsylvania has government-run liquor stores, called Wine & Spirits Shoppes, throughout the state. Alcohol can only be sold at these package outlets and in restaurants and bars. Grocery stores, supermarkets and delis aren't allowed to sell liquor. Call ☎ (800) 272-7522 for information.

Philadelphia & Around

Philadelphia

Best known for its historical sites like the Liberty Bell and Independence Hall – and for its cheesesteaks and hoagies – Philadelphia (population 1,585,580) has been the butt of jokes by WC Fields and lesser-known detractors who dismissed the city as dirty and always closed. These days, nothing could be further from the truth. The 1976 Bicentennial celebrations inspired the city to renovate its historical buildings and cultural institutions and has only recently enjoyed a considerable renaissance.

Philly, as it's often called, now receives recognition as a major cultural center with world-class museums, performing arts centers and some stunning architecture. Fairmount Park, which is said to be the world's largest city park, and the tree-lined squares that help form the city's nucleus contrast beautifully with their urban surroundings. Philly's culinary scene has expanded from its renowned cheesesteaks and Italian food to hundreds of terrific restaurants serving a variety of domestic and international cuisine at all budget levels. Along with the numerous bars, coffeehouses, concerts, galleries and shopping options, Philadelphia is no longer a place to leave before dark.

The city does have its share of crime, urban decay and homeless problems, though these are mainly outside the downtown tourist area. The steady decline in the city's population since the 1950s is partly a response to these problems. However, Philadelphia has been ranked by the FBI as the safest of the nation's 12 largest metropolitan areas and in 1994 *Condé Nast Traveler* magazine ranked Philadelphia as the country's friendliest city.

Around the Old City you'll see tourists (mostly American) riding in horse-drawn

Highlights

- For anyone interested in the birth of the US, a trip to Independence Hall and the Liberty Bell (though the latter is now housed in a nondescript building) is a must
- Along Benjamin Franklin Pkwy are some great museums culminating in the magnificent Philadelphia Museum of Art on the edge of Fairmount Park
- Italian Market, a large outdoor market in South Philadelphia, has street stalls and specialty stores
- City Hall is the country's largest municipal building and an architectural delight; it has great views of the city from the observation deck
- The Civil War Library & Museum is a must for students of the war
- The renowned Museum of Archaeology & Anthropology in University City contains archaeological treasures from around the world
- Eating is a definite highlight – from the street food carts, to the Italian and Reading Terminal markets to the finest dining at some of the country's best restaurants
- Easy access to Pennsylvania's rolling, green countryside ■

carriages, lining up to visit Independence Hall or the Liberty Bell, being led by tour guides around the sights or just resting their feet in the parks. Market St, east of City Hall, is where Philadelphians of every description go to do their shopping. West of

City Hall are the office workers, some of whom cluster in small groups outside their office buildings puffing on a much-needed cigarette. University City, in West Philadelphia, is where college campuses and students dominate.

So ignore the disparaging remarks you may sometimes hear – the 'biggest small town in America' is well worth a visit.

HISTORY

William Penn made Philadelphia his capital in 1682, naming it after the Greek for 'brotherly love.' A survivor of London's Great Fire of 1666, Penn oversaw the plans for the city that included a grid system with wide streets, not the narrow, winding maze that caused so much havoc in England's capital. This format was the inspiration for most American cities.

Philadelphia quickly grew to become the second largest city (after London) in the British Empire, before ceding that title to New York City. Opposition to British policy in the colonies became focused here, and colonial leaders met to plan their course of action. The end result was the Declaration of Independence, and in 1790 the city became the temporary capital of the new United States before Washington, DC, got the job in 1800. The US Constitution was drawn up and first read here in 1786. Often led by the amazingly talented Benjamin Franklin, Philadelphia became a center of exciting new developments in the world of arts and science.

Between 1793 and 1820 Philadelphia suffered five yellow-fever epidemics, which killed thousands but led to the construction of the US's first city water system.

Philadelphia's fortunes declined in the 1800s as New York took over as the nation's cultural, commercial and industrial center. Philly never regained its initial status, despite the continuation of cultural and educational innovation, commerce and shipbuilding. In the mid-20th century, like many American cities, it suffered an exodus of middle-class people to the suburbs. In the 1970s, lavish celebrations for the nation's bicentennial inspired a massive clean up and renovation campaign for a Philadelphia that had become notoriously neglected. That renovation and restoration continues today.

ORIENTATION

Philadelphia sits on the west bank of the Delaware River in southeastern Pennsylvania. Most of the central area lies between the Delaware River in the east and the Schuylkill River, a tributary, in the west.

Philadelphia is easy to get around. It's laid out in a grid and most of the major sights and accommodations are within walking distance or a short bus ride or drive from each other. East-west streets are given names; north-south streets are mostly numbered, except for Broad St, the main north-south street (and the equivalent of 14th St), and Front St (the equivalent of 1st St). Market St is the main east-west route and divides the city's center between north and south.

Neighborhoods

Most of your time will probably be spent in Historic Philadelphia and Center City, a total of 26 blocks east to west. This part of

Philly is laid out around public squares, with City Hall more or less at the center in Penn (formerly Center) Square. The other squares, whose names have also been changed over the years, are: Washington (formerly Southeast) Square, near Society Hill; Rittenhouse (Southwest) Square, west of Broad St; Franklin (Northeast) Square, near Independence Hall; and Logan (Northwest) Square (with Logan Circle in the center), at the southeast end of Benjamin Franklin Pkwy.

The other central areas of interest are University City (in West Philadelphia), Fairmount Park (northwest of downtown) and South Philadelphia.

Historic Philadelphia This area includes Independence National Historic Park and Old City, with Front and 8th Sts marking its east-west borders, Vine St its northern and South St its southern border. Here you'll find major sights such as the Liberty Bell Pavilion, Independence Hall and Congress Hall. Also here are the quiet residential streets of Society Hill and the crowded South St area, Philadelphia's 'Greenwich Village.'

Penn's Landing, beside the Delaware River, where William Penn's boat docked after arriving from England, has several attractions. Christopher Columbus Blvd (formerly Delaware Ave) on the waterfront alongside the Delaware River has a number of nightclubs, especially north of the Benjamin Franklin Bridge.

This area has two hostels, a B&B and some hotels, along with numerous eating and drinking places.

Center City This part of downtown, from west of the historic district to the Schuylkill River, consists of a mixture of commercial, business and residential neighborhoods. Among the places of interest are City Hall, Antique Row, Chinatown, Reading Terminal Market plus numerous hotels, restaurants and shops.

South Philadelphia Bordered by South St to the north and by the Delaware and Schuylkill rivers to the east, south and west, this area has been the destination of many of the city's successive waves of immigrants. The colorful Italian Market is the main draw, along with the many popular restaurants, bars and food shops; a Vietnamese enclave has developed around S 8th St. In the far south are the Veterans and CoreStates Spectrum sports stadiums.

University City West over the Schuylkill River, this area is so-called because it's home to the University of Pennsylvania and Drexel University. One of the main attractions is the Museum of Archaeology & Anthropology; also here are the main post office and Amtrak's 30th St Station.

Other Districts Well worth a visit if time permits are the genteel Northwest Philadelphia suburbs of Chestnut Hill, Manayunk and Germantown four to six miles northwest of downtown.

More central, Northern Liberties, to the north of Old City between Vine St and Gerard Ave, is the city's oldest neighborhood and where William Penn actually lived. These days, with a few exceptions, it's rundown and has little to see or do.

See also Around Philadelphia later for day-trips to other suburbs and nearby attractions.

Maps
The maps in the *Philadelphia Official Visitors Guide* (available free from the Philadelphia Visitors Center in JFK Plaza) are good for most purposes but don't include some of the smaller streets. *Streetwise Philadelphia* is a laminated folding map of downtown and University City and also contains maps of the SEPTA rail system and the bus network. The Gousha Travel Publications map has details of Greater Philadelphia and includes a street index and a list of places of interest. If you'll be spending some time in and around Philadelphia, it might be worth getting the large-format street atlas *Metro Philadelphia* by ADC The Map People.

See also AAA, which provides maps to members, under Travel Agencies, below.

INFORMATION
Tourist Offices
The Philadelphia Convention & Visitors Bureau (☎ (215) 636-1666, (800) 537-7676), produces the free *Philadelphia Official Visitors Guide* as well as various special-interest brochures. You can obtain these and other information from the Philadelphia Visitors Center in JFK Plaza at 16th St and JFK Blvd. It's open daily from 9 am to 5 pm (to 6 pm from Memorial Day to Labor Day). There are also city visitor information desks at the NPS Visitors Center (see Independence National Historic Park, later) and in the baggage-claim area of Terminal A at Philadelphia international airport.

Money
The basic banking hours in the city are Monday to Friday from 9 am to 3 pm, though there are some variations with certain branches opening earlier and closing later, especially on Friday, and some opening on Saturday. Automatic teller machines (ATMs), known as money access centers (MACs), are readily available around the city; many of them accept Cirrus, MasterCard, Visa, Honor, Plus System, Express Cash and Discover.

Downtown banks with foreign-exchange facilities include:

Continental Bank
    1201 Chestnut (☎ (215) 564-7188)
First Fidelity Bank
    Broad St at Walnut St (☎ (215) 985-7068)
Mellon PSFS Bank
    Broad and Chestnut Sts (☎ (215) 553-3549)
PNC Bank
    Broad and Chestnut Sts (☎ (215) 585-5000)

Thomas Cook has two branches – at 1800 JFK Blvd (☎ (215) 563-5544) and 3728 Spruce St (☎ (215) 573-3400) which are open Monday to Friday from 9 am to 5 pm. Opposite the Philadelphia Visitors Center is American Express (☎ (215) 587-2300), 2 Penn Center Plaza at N 16th St and JFK Blvd, which is open Monday to Friday from 9 am to 5 pm.

Foreign Consulates

The following countries have consulates in or near Philadelphia:

Austria
3 Benjamin Franklin Pkwy,
20th Floor,
Philadelphia, PA 19102
(☎ (215) 665-7200)

Belgium
Curtis Center, Suite 1150,
Independence Square at
6th and Walnut Sts,
Philadelphia, PA 19102
(☎ (215) 238-8729)

Canada
GSB Building, Belmont &
City Line Ave, Suite 611,
Bala Cynwynd, PA 19004
(☎ (610) 667-8210)

Chile
Public Ledger Building,
at 6th and Chestnut Sts,
Suite 1030,
Philadelphia, PA 19106
(☎ (215) 829-9520)

Denmark
Public Ledger Building,
at 6th and Chestnut Sts,
Suite 956,
Philadelphia, PA 19106
(☎ (215) 625-0185)

France
4000 Bell Atlantic Tower,
1717 Arch St, Philadelphia,
PA 19103-2793
(☎ (215) 994-2175)

Germany
1101 CoreStates Plaza,
at 5th and Market Sts,
45th Floor, Suite 1695,
Philadelphia, PA 19106
(☎ (215) 922-2175)

Israel
230 S 15th St, 8th Floor,
Philadelphia, PA 19102
(☎ (215) 546-5556)

Italy
Public Ledger Building,
at 6th and Chestnut Sts,
Suite 1026,
Philadelphia, PA 19106
(☎ (215) 592-1218)

Japan
Mellon Bank Center,
1735 Market St, Room 731,
Philadelphia, PA 19101
(☎ (215) 553-2170)

Mexico
Philadelphia Bourse
Building, 21 S 5th St,
Suite 101,
Philadelphia, PA 19106
(☎ (215) 922-4262)

Netherlands
45 Brennan Dr,
PO Box 8047,
Bryn Mawr, PA 19101-8047
(☎ (215) 520-9591)

Norway
112-24 Christian St,
Philadelphia, PA 19147
(☎ (215) 462-2502)

Portugal
2001 Welsh Rd,
Philadelphia, PA 19115
(☎ (215) 925-3222)

Spain
3410 Warden Dr,
Philadelphia, PA 19129
(☎ (215) 848-6180)

Sweden
112-24 Christian St,
Philadelphia, PA 19147
(☎ (215) 465-5565)

Switzerland
Public Ledger Building,
at 6th and Chestnut Sts,
Suite 635,
Philadelphia, PA 19106
(☎ (215) 922-2215)

UK
Mather & Company,
226 Walnut St,
Philadelphia, PA 19106
(☎ (215) 925-0118) ■

PENNSYLVANIA

Terminal A at Philadelphia international airport has a foreign-exchange counter (open for most flight arrivals) in the 1st-floor baggage-claim area and another on the 2nd floor operated by Thomas Cook. Some hotels and restaurants (like Dickens Inn, ☎ (215) 928-9307, Head House Square, S 2nd St) also change money.

Post

The main post office (☎ (215) 596-5577), 2970 Market St opposite Amtrak's 30th St Station in University City, is open 24 hours daily. It has photocopiers and an information desk; general delivery is at the window with the sign '24 hour Box Caller.' The zip code is 19104.

A more central branch (☎ (215) 592-9610), 900 Market St at 9th St, is open Monday to Friday from 8:30 am to 6 pm, Saturday from 9 am to 4 pm. The B Free Franklin Post Office (☎ (215) 592-1289), 316 Market St, is a working post office with postal workers sometimes dressed in period costume (but charging modern prices), open daily from 9 am to 5 pm.

Travel Agencies

HI-AYH Travel Center (☎ (215) 925-6004), 624 S 3rd St near South St, sells discounted airline tickets. Council Travel (☎ (215) 382-0343), 3606A Chestnut St, and STA Travel (☎ (215) 382-2928), 3730 Walnut St, both in University City, offer competitive discount rates. So too does Travel Agents International (☎ (215) 563-4400), 126 S 19th St. American Express and Thomas Cook (see Money, above) also provide travel services.

If you're traveling the region by car, AAA (☎ (215) 864-5000), 2040 Market St, is a regular travel agency and specializes in auto-travel maps and services. It's open Monday to Friday from 8 am to 6 pm.

Also, check the classified ads in the Sunday edition of the *Philadelphia Inquirer* or the current issue of the free weekly *City Paper*.

Bookstores

The excellent Borders (☎ (215) 568-7400), 1727 Walnut St near Rittenhouse Square, has a wide selection of titles on most subjects. It runs a regular program of author readings and has a children's hour on Saturday, music on Friday night and a busy cafe upstairs. It's open Monday to Friday from 8 am to 10 pm, Saturday 9 am to 10 pm and Sunday 10 am to 7 pm.

Hibberd's Books (☎ (215) 546-8811), 1310 Walnut St, is a good used bookstore with a knowledgeable staff.

The Book Trader (☎ (215) 925-0219), at S 4th and South Sts, is a large used bookstore that also exchanges and sells LP records and CDs.

Tower Books (☎ (215) 925-9909), 425 South St, carries a wide variety of titles.

Open daily, Giovanni's Room (☎ (215) 923-9260), 345 S 12th St at Pine St, specializes in lesbian and gay titles.

Rand McNally Map & Travel Bookstore (☎ (215) 563-1101), 1650 Market St, has a good selection of maps and travel guides as well as travel gear; the staff is friendly and helpful. Traveler's Emporium (☎ (215) 546-2021) 210 S 17th St, is another store with a range of travel guides. Both carry Lonely Planet titles.

Libraries

The Free Library of Philadelphia (☎ (215) 686-5322), Logan Square (at 19th and Vine Sts), the country's first lending library, houses over six million books, magazines,

newspapers, recordings and other materials. Feature films, concerts, lectures and children's programs take place on Sunday afternoons. It's open Monday to Wednesday from 9 am to 9 pm; Thursday and Friday from 9 am to 6 pm; Saturday from 9 am to 5 pm; Sunday from 1 to 5 pm (it's closed on Sunday between June and August). It also has a cafeteria and a used bookstore. Bus No 76 passes by.

See also Library Hall, the Civil War Library & Museum and Rosenbach Museum & Library, later.

Laundry

Self-serve laundry facilities are available in hostels and budget hotels, while the more-expensive hotels will do your laundry for you. Downtown, at U-Do-It Laundry (☎ (215) 735-1255), 1513 Spruce St at S 15th St, open daily from 7 am to 11 pm, you can do your own dry cleaning as well as laundry. In South Philadelphia, Tenth St Cleaners (☎ (215) 463-3100), 1141-43 S 10th St at Ellsworth St near the Italian Market, is open daily from 7 am to 10 pm.

Medical Services

Philadelphia has many hospitals including the country's first, founded by Ben Franklin, Pennsylvania Hospital (☎ (215) 829-3000), 800 Spruce St at S 8th St. Also in the city's center, the Thomas Jefferson Hospital (☎ (215) 955-6000) is at Walnut and S 11th Sts. In University City is the Hospital of the University of Pennsylvania (☎ (215) 662-4000), 3400 Spruce St. Call the Philadelphia County Medical Society (☎ (215) 563-5343) if you need a doctor to visit you.

Emergency

For police or in fire and medical emergencies call ☎ 911. Other important emergency telephone numbers are:

Accidental Poisoning	(215) 386-2100
	386-2010
Dentist	(215) 925-6050
Lesbian & Gay Task Force, Violence & Discrimination Hotline	(215) 772-2005

PENNSYLVANIA

Suicide & Crisis Intervention Center
                        (215) 686-4420
Travelers' Aid Society   (215) 546-0571
Women Organized Against Rape (WOAR)
                        (215) 985-3333

Dangers & Annoyances

Like any major city, avoid the bad neighborhoods, especially West Philadelphia to the west of University City, and North Philadelphia. Downtown, the area around Walnut and S 13th Sts gets a bit sleazy at night, particularly on weekends when you may see a few police around.

Stay alert, avoid the subway at night unless you're going to a sports event in South Philly with thousands of others; watch your wallet and pocketbooks; don't wear expensive watches and jewelry; keep car doors locked when driving as well as when parked; and avoid quiet, poorly lit streets at night.

Penn Center Suburban Station, near City Hall and the Philadelphia Visitors Center, is one of the main mugging spots after dark.

There's a lot of traffic going to/from and between the nightclubs on the waterfront along Christopher Columbus Blvd (Delaware Ave) north of the Benjamin Franklin Bridge, Friday and Saturday nights. Pedestrians should be very careful.

WALKING TOUR

Much of downtown Philadelphia is best explored on foot. The following suggested walking tour covers Independence National Historic Park and takes in sections of Old City and Center City – you can follow the tour on our Historic District & Waterfront map. Most sites have additional information under their own headings, below.

Start at the **NPS Visitors Center**, on S 3rd St, where you can pick up information on the historic park. Outside the visitors center is the **Bicentennial Bell**, donated to the US by Britain in 1976. As you turn left, on the other side of the road you'll see the Neoclassic **First Bank of the US** (1797), which served as the country's bank until 1811. Further south, at S

3rd and Walnut Sts, is the Greek Revival **Philadelphia Exchange** (1834) designed by William Strickland. Only the exterior of these two buildings have been restored and they're not open to the public.

Turning right on Walnut St you come to a group of 18th century Georgian buildings, the first of which is **Bishop White House**, home of Reverend William White, first Episcopal bishop of Pennsylvania, from 1787 to 1836. At the other end is the headquarters of the **Pennsylvania Horticultural Society**. Continuing west, you'll see **Todd House**, at S 4th and Walnut Sts, occupied 1791-93 by lawyer John Todd, before he died of yellow fever.

Turn left (south) on S 4th St to Willing's Alley, then left (east) again to **St Joseph's Church** (1838). The church that pre-dated the current one was the first Roman Catholic church in the city.

Returning to S 4th St head north to **Carpenters' Hall** (1770) where the First Continental Congress met in 1744. North of the hall you pass the **Marine Corps Memorial Museum** with exhibitions on the founding of the US Marine Corps in 1775 and its role in the American Revolution. Diagonally across from here is the **Army-Navy Museum** which has exhibits dating from 1775 to 1800.

You're now on Chestnut St. Turn left and cross over S 4th St to the Greek Revival **Second Bank of the US**, home of the National Portrait Gallery. Beside the bank but set further back is **Library Hall**, containing the library of the American Philosophical Society, on the site of the country's first subscription library (1789).

Crossing over S 5th St brings you to several of the most important historical buildings in Philadelphia. The first is **Old City Hall** (1791), which served as the US Supreme Court from 1791 to 1800. Behind it is **Philosophical Hall** (1789), owned by the American Philosophical Society. In the center, **Independence Hall** (1756), a World Heritage Site, is where the Declaration of Independence was adopted and the US Constitution drafted. Beside Independence Hall, at the corner of S 6th St is

Congress Hall, where the US Congress met between 1790 and 1800 when Philadelphia was the nation's capital.

Turn left (south) on S 6th St and walk to Walnut St. As you do so, on your left you pass **Independence Square**, where the Declaration of Independence was read publicly for the first time on July 8, 1776.

Turn right (west) on Walnut St. On the corner of S 6th St is the **Norman Rockwell Museum** in the building where the celebrated artist delivered his paintings for the cover of the *Saturday Evening Post*. Opposite is **Washington Square**, one of the city's original squares. Continue along Walnut St to S 7th St then turn right (north).

As you head toward Market St, you pass Sansom St or **Jewelers' Row**, the center of the local jewelry trade. Just north of Ranstead St is the **Balch Institute for Ethnic Studies** and opposite is **Atwater Kent Museum** which documents the history of the city. At the corner of S 7th and Market Sts is **Declaration House**, also called Graff House, a reconstruction of the house where Thomas Jefferson wrote the Declaration of Independence.

Turning right (east) on Market St and crossing over 6th St brings you to the **Liberty Bell Pavilion**, housing the much-visited symbol of American independence. If you continue east along Market St past S 5th and S 4th Sts, you come to a group of 18th century Georgian buildings, among which is the **B Free Franklin Post Office**; behind them is **Franklin Court**, site of Ben Franklin's home and workplace.

Head back westward and turn right (north) on N 5th St to Arch St. On the corner is the **Free Quaker Meeting House** (1783), unlike other Quakers, the Free Quakers supported and fought in the Revolutionary War. On the other side of the street is **Christ Church Cemetery**, with the graves of Benjamin and Deborah Franklin. On the north side of Arch

St is the **US Mint**. East along Arch St you come first to **Arch St Friends Meeting House** (1804) then **Betsy Ross House** (1740); Betsy Ross is believed to have made the first US flag (see below).

Continue east to N 2nd St, turn left (north) then right (east) into **Elfreth's Alley**, a residential thoroughfare with houses dating from the 18th and early 19th centuries. On N 2nd St just north of the alley is **Fireman's Hall** (1876), originally a firehouse but now a museum.

Back south over Arch St you come to **Christ Church** (1754), once used by many of the city's early dignitaries. Carry on south over Market and Chestnut Sts; just past the entrance to the parking lot is **Thomas Bond House**, former home of the co-founder of the Pennsylvania

Independence Hall, where the Declaration of Independence was adopted, is in Independence National Historic Park

PENNSYLVANIA

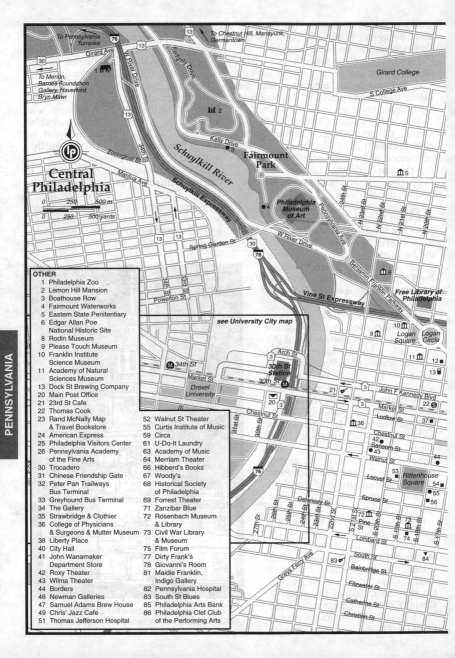

To Pennsylvania
Turnpike

To Chestnut Hill, Manayunk,
Germantown

To Merion,
Barnes Foundation
Gallery, Haverford,
Bryn Mawr

Girard College

S College Ave

Girard Ave

W River Drive

Sedgett Drive

Kelly Drive

**Central
Philadelphia**

Zoological Dr

34th St

Mantua Ave

Schuylkill River

Fairmount
Park

Schuylkill Expressway

0   250   500 m
0   250   500 yards

Philadelphia
Museum
of Art

Pennsylvania Ave

N 24th St

N 23rd St

N 22nd St

N 21st St

Spring Garden St

W River Drive

Benjamin Franklin Parkway

Vine St Expressway

Free Library of
Philadelphia

Powelton St

34th St

33rd St

see University City map

Arch St

30th St
Station

Logan
Square

Logan
Circle

M 34th St

Market St

Drexel
University

30th St

John F Kennedy Blvd

Market St

Ludlow St

Chestnut St

Chestnut St

Sansom St

Walnut St

Locust St

Rittenhouse
Square

31st St

30th St

29th St

28th St

27th St

26th St

25th St

24th St

23rd St

22nd St

21st St

20th St

19th St

18th St

17th St

16th St

Spruce St

Delancey St

Pine St

Pine
St

Lombard St

South St

Bainbridge St

Fitzwater St

Catharine St

Christian St

Gray's Ferry Ave

OTHER
1   Philadelphia Zoo
2   Lemon Hill Mansion
3   Boathouse Row
4   Fairmount Waterworks
5   Eastern State Penitentiary
6   Edgar Allan Poe
     National Historic Site
8   Rodin Museum
9   Please Touch Museum
10 Franklin Institute
     Science Museum
11 Academy of Natural
     Sciences Museum
13 Dock St Brewing Company
20 Main Post Office
21 23rd St Cafe
22 Thomas Cook
23 Rand McNally Map
     & Travel Bookstore
24 American Express
25 Philadelphia Visitors Center
26 Pennsylvania Academy
     of the Fine Arts
30 Trocadero
31 Chinese Friendship Gate
32 Peter Pan Trailways
     Bus Terminal
33 Greyhound Bus Terminal
34 The Gallery
35 Strawbridge & Clothier
36 College of Physicians
     & Surgeons & Mutter Museum
38 Liberty Place
40 City Hall
41 John Wanamaker
     Department Store
42 Roxy Theater
43 Wilma Theater
44 Borders
46 Newman Galleries
47 Samuel Adams Brew House
49 Chris' Jazz Cafe
51 Thomas Jefferson Hospital

52 Walnut St Theater
55 Curtis Institute of Music
59 Circa
61 U-Do-It Laundry
63 Academy of Music
64 Merriam Theater
66 Hibberd's Books
67 Woody's
68 Historical Society
     of Philadelphia
69 Forrest Theater
71 Zanzibar Blue
72 Rosenbach Museum
     & Library
73 Civil War Library
     & Museum
75 Film Forum
77 Dirty Frank's
78 Giovanni's Room
81 Maidie Franklin,
     Indigo Gallery
82 Pennsylvania Hospital
83 South St Blues
85 Philadelphia Arts Bank
86 Philadelphia Clef Club
     of the Performing Arts

PENNSYLVANIA

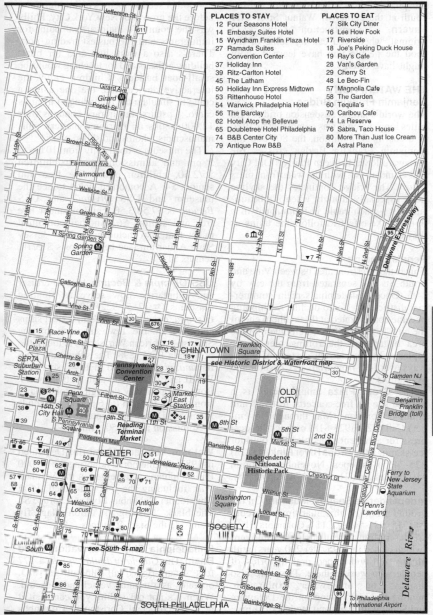

PLACES TO STAY
12 Four Seasons Hotel
14 Embassy Suites Hotel
15 Wyndham Franklin Plaza Hotel
27 Ramada Suites
   Convention Center
37 Holiday Inn
39 Ritz-Carlton Hotel
45 The Latham
50 Holiday Inn Express Midtown
53 Rittenhouse Hotel
54 Warwick Philadelphia Hotel
56 The Barclay
62 Hotel Atop the Bellevue
65 Doubletree Hotel Philadelphia
74 B&B Center City
79 Antique Row B&B

PLACES TO EAT
7 Silk City Diner
16 Lee How Fook
17 Riverside
18 Joe's Peking Duck House
19 Ray's Cafe
28 Van's Garden
29 Cherry St
48 Le Bec-Fin
57 Magnolia Cafe
58 The Garden
60 Tequila's
70 Caribou Cafe
74 La Reserve
76 Sabra, Taco House
80 More Than Just Ice Cream
84 Astral Plane

PENNSYLVANIA

Hospital and now a B&B. A little further south at the corner of Walnut St is **City Tavern**, a reconstruction of the 1773 original, where you can try some of the food the people you have learned about might have eaten.

THE WATERFRONT
Benjamin Franklin Bridge
The world's largest suspension bridge (1.8 miles long) when it was completed in 1926 at a cost of $37 million, the 800,000 ton Benjamin Franklin Bridge crosses the Delaware River between Philly's Old City and Camden, NJ, with the waterfront piers below. The bridge dominates the skyline here, especially at night when it's beautifully lit – each cable is illuminated in a domino-like effect to follow the trains as they cross.

Penn's Landing
This is the riverfront area between Vine and South Sts and separated from the city by I-95. Once Philadelphia's main commercial district, it fell into decline as shipping became concentrated at the southern end of the city. In the 1960s redevelopment of the area began and the rotting piers were replaced by the current system of walkways over I-95 from Market, Chestnut and Walnut Sts.

The **Great Plaza** amphitheater is a popular site for free concerts, festivals and ethnic celebrations (May through November). Call ☎ (215) 923-8181 or check the local press for a current schedule. The outdoor ice-skating **Blue Cross River Rink** (☎ (215) 925-7465) is open November through March. Bus Nos 21, 42 and 76 stop nearby.

Independence Seaport Museum On the ground floor of this maritime museum (☎ (215) 925-5439), 211 S Columbia Blvd, are descriptions of Philadelphia's shipyard (which closed in 1995 after 200 years) with photos and audiotaped oral histories of people who worked there. There are also displays on underwater exploration, hunting, fishing, rowing on the Delaware and Schuylkill rivers and models of ships.

Another section focuses on immigration; before the growth of New York City, Philly was the country's main arrival point for immigrants and the busiest trading port. There's also a workshop area for boat-building artisans and for teaching would-be small-boat builders. Children enjoy the interactive devices like the one using a crane to simulate the unloading of a ship's cargo. Upstairs, the library contains over 12,000 books on maritime matters, plus manuscripts, photos and ships' plans.

The museum is open daily from 10 am to 5 pm and admission is adults/children $5/2.50, children under five free and seniors $4. A combined ticket to see the museum and USS *Olympia* and USS *Becuna* is $7.50/3.50, children under five free and seniors $6. Another combined ticket that also includes the New Jersey State Aquarium (see below) costs $15/10, seniors $12.

USS *Olympia* & *Becuna* A naval cruiser and submarine now serve as floating museums (☎ (215) 922-1898). The USS *Olympia*, one of America's first steel ships and one of the few survivors of the Spanish-American War, served at the Battle of Manila Bay, 1898. The submarine USS *Becuna*, commissioned in 1944, served in WWII and the Korean and Vietnam wars. Both are open May through October daily from 10 am to 5 pm (to 6 pm on weekends Memorial Day to late September).

Admission is $5/2.50, seniors $4.

Vietnam Veterans Memorial Dedicated in 1987, this memorial honoring the 80,000 Philadelphians who served in the Vietnam War, including the 642 who died, is at Christopher Columbus Blvd and Spruce St. The black 'Missing in Action' flags fly alongside the Stars & Stripes.

Philadelphia Ship Preservation Guild Basin The *Gazela of Philadelphia*, a 177 foot, square-rigged tall ship built in 1883, operates as a training vessel and museum. When it's not out sailing you can visit it near the corner of Christopher Columbus

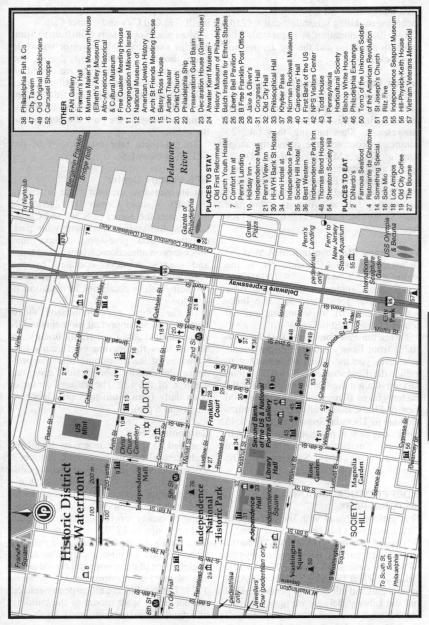

Historic District & Waterfront

PENNSYLVANIA

OTHER
3 FAN Gallery
5 Fireman's Hall
6 Mantua Maker's Museum House (Elfreth's Alley Museum)
8 Afro-American Historical & Cultural Museum
9 Free Quaker Meeting House
11 Congregation Mikveh Israel
12 National Museum of American Jewish History
13 Arch St Friends Meeting House
15 Betsy Ross House
17 Arden Theater
20 Christ Church
22 Philadelphia Ship Preservation Guild Basin
23 Decoration Museum (Graff House)
24 Atwater Kent Museum – History Museum of Philadelphia
25 Balch Institute for Ethnic Studies
26 Liberty Bell Pavilion
28 B Free Franklin Post Office
29 Jake & Oliver's
31 Congress Hall
32 Old City Hall
33 Philosophical Hall
37 Khyber Pass
39 Norman Rockwell Museum
40 Carpenters' Hall
41 First Bank of the US
42 NPS Visitors Center
43 Todd House
44 Pennsylvania Horticultural Society
45 Bishop White House
46 Philadelphia Exchange
50 Tomb of the Unknown Soldier of the American Revolution
51 St Joseph's Church
53 Ritz Five
55 Independence Seaport Museum
56 Hill-Physick-Keith House
57 Vietnam Veterans Memorial
38 Philadelphia Fish & Co
47 City Tavern
49 Old Original Bookbinders
52 Carousel Shoppe

PLACES TO STAY
1 Old First Reformed Church Youth Hostel
7 Comfort Inn at Penn's Landing
10 Holiday Inn –
30 Penn's View Inn
30 HI-AYH Bank St Hostel
34 Omni Hotel at Independence Park
35 Independence Park Inn
36 Best Western Independence Park
48 Thomas Bond House
54 Sheraton Society Hill

PLACES TO EAT
2 DiNardo's
4 Famous Seafood
4 Ristorante de Ghiottone
14 Something Special
16 Solo Mio
18 Los Amigos
19 Old City Coffee
27 The Bourse

Blvd and Market St. Opening hours vary according to sailing schedules: call ☎ (215) 923-9030. A donation is requested. The lightship *Barnegat* and the tug *Jupiter* are also docked here.

Penn's Landing Trolley Restored early 20th century trolleys operate on the waterfront along Christopher Columbus Blvd between Benjamin Franklin Bridge and Fitzwater St. Slow moving, they take 25 minutes to complete the roundtrip, stopping at Race, Market, Walnut, Dock, Spruce and Lombard Sts. The service operates on weekends Easter to late November, also Thursday and Friday from 11 am to dusk during July and August. A day pass costs $1.50/75¢. Call ☎ (215) 627-0807 for details.

New Jersey State Aquarium Across the Delaware River in Camden, NJ, is the region's largest aquarium (☎ (609) 365-3300). See Camden in the Central New Jersey chapter for details. See also Independence Seaport Museum, earlier, for details of combined tickets.

Taking the *Riverbus* ferry (☎ (800) 634-4027) from Penn's Landing to the aquarium saves you the hassle of dealing with traffic, the Benjamin Franklin Bridge and parking. Called the 'Delawhale' by locals, the ferry takes 10 minutes and offers a good view of Philly. Boats run every 30 minutes Monday to Thursday from 8:15 am to 5:45 pm, Friday to 8:45 pm, Saturday 9:15 am to 11:45 pm, Sunday to 5:45 pm (to 8:45 pm early July to early September). The roundtrip fare is $4/3.

INDEPENDENCE NATIONAL HISTORIC PARK
This park, combined with the rest of Old City, forms what has been dubbed 'America's most historic square mile.' The L-shaped city park is administered by the NPS and covers 45 acres west of the Delaware River between Walnut and Arch Sts and 2nd and 6th Sts. Independence Hall and the Liberty Bell are on most visitors' lists of 'must sees,' but other sights are well

worth seeing too. Several sights lie outside the 'L,' in Old City and Center City.

Most places open daily from 9 am to 5 pm, but this can vary by an hour or so, while some hours are extended during the summer and some buildings are closed on Monday. Admission to the visitors center and the park's buildings are free, as are the walking tours and other activities. Some buildings in the park are not open to the public.

To get there take bus No 76 or the SEPTA subway line.

NPS Visitors Center
For an overview, the best place to start is the NPS Visitors Center (☎ (215) 597-8974), near the corner of S 3rd and Chestnut Sts; the staff can answer your park questions and give you a map and brochures on attractions, free walking tours and events. A desk operated by the Philadelphia Convention & Visitors Bureau for help with general city information is here too.

In the lobby a computerized video display outlines important moments in US constitutional and civil-rights history. In the upstairs theater are continuous free showings of the 28 minute film *Independence* (directed by John Huston) about the creation of the US. The visitors center is open daily from 9 am to 5 pm (July and August to 6 pm).

Carpenters' Hall
Founded in 1724 to teach its members architectural skills, the Carpenter's Company, America's oldest trade guild, had much influence on Philadelphia's development, advising on building techniques and its members working as architects on many projects. This Georgian building built in 1770, still owned by the Carpenter's Company, was designed by Robert Smith (a master carpenter and a leading light of the group) and served as the site of the First Continental Congress in 1774. The exhibits are all carpentry-related and include a scale model of the building during its construction, early tools and

some Windsor chairs used by Congress delegates. It's closed Monday.

Second Bank of the US

Modeled after the Greek Parthenon, this 1824 marble-faced Greek Revival masterpiece was home to the world's most powerful financial institution until its charter was dissolved by President Andrew Jackson in 1836 – he didn't approve of the bank's conservative policies. The building then became the Philadelphia Customs House till 1935 and was restored in 1974. Try to visit the beautiful main banking room.

The bank is now home to the **National Portrait Gallery** with several pieces by Charles Willson Peale, America's top portraitist at the time of the American Revolution and whose subjects were among the most prominent men of the day. (See Art in the Facts about the Region chapter.) Other exhibits include a copy of the first edition of the Declaration of Independence (the original is in Washington, DC) and early prints of Philadelphia when it was the nation's capital.

Library Hall

Worth a visit to see a copy of the Declaration of Independence handwritten by Thomas Jefferson, first editions of Darwin's *Origins of Species* and Lewis and Clark's field notes, this is the research library and offices of the American Philosophical Society. The site on which the library sits was originally home to the first subscription library in the USA. The Library Company of Philadelphia, a forerunner of the Library of Congress, was later founded here in 1789, remaining until 1888 when the building was demolished. The present building, at 105 S 5th St, was constructed in 1959 and its facade is an exact reproduction of the original.

Independence Hall

Called the birthplace of American government, Independence Hall, on Chestnut St, was built between 1732 and 1756 as Pennsylvania State House, the colony's headquarters. At that time, it was on the outskirts of the city. The Second Continental Congress later met here from 1775 to 1783. The Assembly Room is where the delegates from the 13 colonies met to approve the Declaration of Independence (July 4, 1776) and where the design of the US flag was agreed upon (1777), the Articles of the Confederation were drafted (1781) and the Constitutional Convention was held (1787), producing the US Constitution. The assassinated body of President Abraham Lincoln lay in state here on April 22, 1865.

One of the country's best examples of Georgian architecture, the hall's simple, understated lines show the Quaker influence of Philadelphia's early days. British troops used the furniture in the 1st floor's two rooms and the large central hallway for firewood when they occupied the city in 1777-78 – what you see today are examples from the period. The **Supreme Court Chamber** is to your right as you enter. The Pennsylvania coat of arms, dating from 1785, hangs over the judge's chair. It replaced King George III's coat of arms, which was publicly burned outside in Independence Square after the Declaration of Independence was read in public for the first time.

The **Assembly Room**, across the hall, is where the events mentioned above took place and you can see original fixtures, including the chair George Washington used during the Constitutional Convention. The 2nd floor features the **Governor's Council Chamber**, where royal governors conducted affairs of state; the **Long Gallery**, where American patriots were imprisoned by the British during the revolution; and the **Committee of the Assembly's Chamber**, with a display of weapons used during the war.

The only way to see the building is to join one of the free tours that run about every 15 minutes. Lasting from 15 to 30 minutes, these tours can be crowded and rushed. Try to visit early or later in the day during the peak seasons – May through June and late September through October.

Congress Hall When Philadelphia was the nation's capital, this Federal-style west

wing of Independence Hall, originally the Philadelphia County Courthouse, is where the US Congress met. Here, the Bill of Rights and the first 10 amendments were added to the Constitution, the US Mint was established, George Washington was inaugurated for his second term and Vermont, Kentucky and Tennessee were admitted to the Union. Beautifully restored and still with some of its original furnishings, the hall is at S 6th and Chestnut Sts.

Old City Hall Built in 1791, Old City Hall, at S 5th and Chestnut Sts, was home to the US Supreme Court until 1800, while Philadelphia was the nation's capital. It became City Hall when the federal government moved to Washington, DC. In 1901, the local government moved over to Center Square. Today the hall contains exhibits on the early Supreme Court and the daily life of Philadelphia's late-18th century citizens.

Philosophical Hall Behind Old City Hall is Philosophical Hall (☎ (215) 440-3400), home of the American Philosophical Society, founded in 1743 by Benjamin Franklin and the USA's oldest learned society. Past members have included Thomas Jefferson, Marie Curie, Thomas Edison, Charles Darwin and Albert Einstein.

The society is still active in many fields, including medicine, computers, literary studies and quantum physics. You can only visit by appointment.

Independence Square This pleasant park, behind the Independence Hall complex, is where the Declaration of Independence was first read in public on July 8, 1776. Today, it makes a great spot to sit and relax and is an attractive shortcut between Walnut and Chestnut, S 5th and 6th Sts.

Liberty Bell Pavilion

Philadelphia's top tourist attraction, the famous bell is housed in an unattractive glass-and-brick pavilion on Market St (between S 5th and 6th Sts).

Commissioned to commemorate the 50th anniversary of the Charter of Privileges (Pennsylvania's constitution enacted in 1701 by William Penn) this 2080 pound bronze bell was made in London's East End by the Whitechapel Bell Foundry. The bell's inscription, from Leviticus 25:10 reads: 'Proclaim liberty through all the land, to all the inhabitants thereof.' The bell was secured in the belfry of the Pennsylvania State House (later called Independence Hall) and was tolled on important occasions, most notably the first public reading of the Declaration of Independence in Independence Square. The bell became badly cracked during the 19th century; despite initial repairs it eventually became unusable in 1846 after tolling for George Washington's birthday.

The bell only became famous after it was adopted by abolitionists of slavery in the mid-19th century, who were inspired by its Biblical inscription, which they took to symbolize liberty. In 1976 the bell was moved from Independence Hall for the country's Bicentennial celebrations as the large number of visitors couldn't be accommodated there. Visitors are admitted to the pavilion in groups and a park ranger gives a rundown of its history. The bell is floodlit after dark, and when the pavilion is closed you can listen to a recorded commentary outside.

Benjamin Franklin

A visit to Philadelphia should give you a deep appreciation for the talents and achievements of this newspaperman, scientist, inventor, philosopher, politician and diplomat. Born in Boston, the son of a soap maker, Franklin (1707-90) joined the workforce at the age of 12 as an apprentice at his brother's printshop.

He moved to Philadelphia in 1723 and founded the *Pennsylvania Gazette* which soon became the colonies' top newspaper. He became involved in local politics by helping to launch public-works projects to pave, clean and light Philadelphia's streets. He founded America's first circulating library, the American Philosophical Society and an academy that became the University of Pennsylvania. In 1743, a heat-efficient stove to warm houses was one of the first of a series of inventions. In 1748 he retired from the newspaper business to study electricity. In a famous experiment, he verified the identity of electricity in lightning by using a kite.

By now a political leader in Pennsylvania, Franklin sailed to Britain in 1757 to represent the colony in its quarrel with William Penn's descendants. He became an agent for several other colonies and the de facto ambassador for all 13. He had supported a united empire, but was disillusioned by the corrupt ways of the British political and aristocratic scene. He gradually became opposed to British taxes on the colonies and when he returned to America in 1775 he caused a stir by declaring his support for independence.

Franklin worked with Thomas Jefferson to draft the Declaration of Independence, served in the Continental Congress then sailed to France in 1776 to become ambassador to the court of Louis XVI. Dressed in simple Quaker clothes, he made quite an impression in his extravagant surroundings as a great speaker. His popularity helped him persuade the French king to stand by the 1778 Treaty of Alliance, saving the struggling American Revolution from certain bankruptcy. Franklin remained in France for five years, playing a pivotal role in the important European side of the struggle.

Returning to America in 1784, he was involved in the final draft of the US Constitution in 1787. Shortly before his death at the age of 84, his final public act was to sign a memorial to Congress urging the abolition of slavery.

Among the other public enterprises Franklin either launched or helped to create were the first fire-fighting company in America, the first fire-insurance company, street lighting and paving, the reorganization of the town watch, a local militia, the post office and the country's first hospital. ■

Franklin Court

This complex is a tribute to Benjamin Franklin, built on the site where he lived and worked. On Market St, he rented out a row of tenements that have been restored with exhibits illustrating some of his work. An archway leads to the courtyard where his house used to stand, now marked by a steel frame in the shape of the house. An **Underground Museum** displaying Franklin's various inventions reveals just how much this genius managed to achieve in a lifetime that spanned most of the 18th century. There's also a short biographical film and a phone bank where actors give voice to comments made about him by his contemporaries.

Franklin was the nation's first postmaster and **B Free Franklin Post Office** (☎ (215) 592-1289), 316 Market St, is a working post office with period furniture. Upstairs the **US Postal Service Museum** illustrates US postal history, with exhibits that include pony express pouches and originals of Franklin's *Pennsylvania Gazette*; it's open from 9 am to 4:30 pm.

Inspired by the Great Fire of London, Franklin designed the fire-proof structure next door at 318 Market St. His **printing office and bindery** at 320 Market St has working demonstrations of his equipment. At 322 Market St is a replica of an office of the *Aurora & General Advertiser*, a newspaper published by Franklin's grandson.

Christ Church

This beautiful Episcopal church (☎ (215) 922-1695), at Church and N 2nd Sts, was built in 1744. Its white steeple, added in 1754, dominated the city skyline in those early days. George Washington, Benjamin Franklin and Betsy Ross worshiped here, and the signers of the Declaration of Independence prayed here on July 5, 1776. It's open daily from 9 am to 5 pm (after services on Sunday) and a donation is requested. Three blocks west on N 5th St is **Christ Church Cemetery**, containing the graves of Benjamin and Deborah Franklin and other dignitaries.

Declaration House

Thomas Jefferson drafted the Declaration of Independence in rented rooms on this site at Market and S 7th Sts. The 18th century house was demolished in 1883 and reconstructed in 1975 for the Bicentennial. It's also known as Graff House after the original owner, Jacob Graff. There's an exhibition of Jefferson memorabilia, an eight minute documentary film, *The Extraordinary Citizen* and replications of his two upstairs rooms with period furnishings and reproductions of the chair and desk he used to write the declaration.

Todd House

Lawyer John Todd lived here from 1791-93 before dying of yellow fever during an epidemic that hit the city. His widow, Dolley Payne Todd (1768-1849), later became Dolley Madison, wife of James Madison, the nation's fourth president. The Georgian red-brick house, at S 4th and Walnut Sts, is typical of a middle-class home in the late 18th century. You can only visit as part of one of the popular park service tours. To be sure of a spot, sign up at the visitors center early in the morning.

Bishop William White House

This house, 309 Walnut St, is the restored home of Reverend William White, first bishop of the Episcopal Diocese of Pennsylvania. Built in 1787, the house's eight levels reflect 18th century, upper-class Philadelphia life and are furnished with period pieces. Again, to visit you have to join one of the park service tours. Sign up early at the visitors center.

Old St Joseph's Church

This is the site of the city's first Roman Catholic church, built in 1733 when Catholic services were strictly banned in Britain. William Penn tolerated all faiths in his colony, but the church was purposely hidden from view by an alley and courtyard. Its pastor dressed as a Quaker when traveling around the city. Irish and German craftsmen and domestic staff dominated the original congregation. The current church, built in 1838, is at 321 Willing's Alley. Check at the rectory (☎ (215) 923-1733) about visiting the church when services aren't being held.

Philadelphia Exchange

Another beautiful piece of architecture, this Greek Revival building, at S 3rd and Walnut Sts, stands out from its Federal and Georgian brick neighbors with its semicircular Corinthian portico and lantern tower. Designed in the 1830s by William Strickland, who was also responsible for the nearby Second Bank of the US, the country's first stock exchange opened here in 1834 and operated until the Civil War. It's closed to the public.

OLD CITY

Along with Society Hill, Old City – the area within Walnut and Vine Sts and Front and 6th Sts – *was* Philadelphia in the city's early days. As the city developed, the neighborhood's proximity to the Delaware River inspired the construction of warehouses, factories, banks and stores. When the city's manufacturing center relocated further west, the neighborhood declined and it wasn't until the gentrification of Society Hill in the 1970s that people started to look at Old City's dilapidated warehouses as suitable for conversion into apartments, galleries and other small businesses. The area has some great old buildings, especially Georgian ones, which have been revitalized though there are a few that remain rundown.

Elfreth's Alley

Believed to be America's oldest residential street, the alley connects N Front St with N 2nd St. The privately owned 33 houses date from 1728 to 1836. The small **Mantua Maker's Museum House** (☎ (215) 574-0560), at No 126 and also called Elfreth's Alley Museum, has period furniture and changing exhibits. It's open Tuesday to Saturday from 10 am to 4 pm, Sunday noon to 4 pm; in January and February it's only open Saturday from 10 am to 4 pm, Sunday noon to 4 pm. Admission is $1/50¢.

Fireman's Hall

North of Elfreth's Alley, this restored 1876 firehouse, 147 N 2nd St, is now a museum (☎ (215) 923-1438). With its terrific collection of firefighting memorabilia, graphics, photographs, film and restored early models of pumpers and rolling stock, it portrays the history of firefighting in America. The 1st floor deals with the early days, showing bucket brigades and the rise of an organized volunteer department led by Ben Franklin. The 2nd floor deals with the inception of the paid department, with models of early equipment and firefighting

First Friday

If you're in Philly between October and June, be sure to enjoy First Friday. On the first Friday of each month, the 30-plus Old City galleries, showrooms and co-operatives stay open until 8 pm. Young artists, students and other onlookers hang out and enjoy the exhibits. Things get going around 5 pm. ■

techniques. Brass name plaques list those who have died in the line of duty.

Other exhibits include a fireboat wheelhouse and a recreation of the typical living quarters of early professional firefighters. The museum is open Tuesday to Saturday from 9 am to 5 pm. A donation is requested.

Betsy Ross House

Some uncertainty surrounds Betsy Griscom Ross (1752-1836), an 18th century upholsterer and seamstress. Although it's now known that she didn't design the American flag, she may or may not have sewn the first US flag for the early federal government. This is either the house where she lived or it's next to the site where her house once stood. Though sparsely furnished, inside the restored two story house (☎ (215) 627-5343), 239 Arch St, built in 1740, you can see Betsy's sewing machine and other tools. It's open Tuesday to Sunday from 10 am to 5 pm; a donation is requested.

Arch St Meeting House

Built in 1804 on land donated by William Penn, at N 4th and Arch Sts, this is the country's largest Quaker meeting house. It's a good place to learn more about the Quakers, who still meet here twice a week. A receptionist answers questions and there's a small exhibition on Quakerism and a 14 minute slide show about William Penn. It's open Monday to Saturday from 10 am to 4 pm and a donation is requested.

US Mint

The US Mint (☎ (215) 597-7350), on Arch St opposite Christ Church Cemetery, is the world's largest. There are self-guided

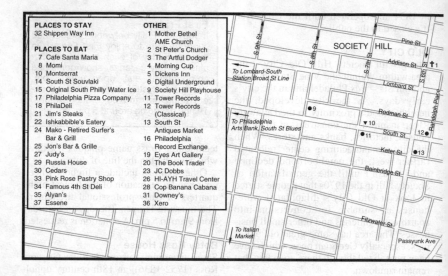

PLACES TO STAY
32 Shippen Way Inn

PLACES TO EAT
7 Cafe Santa Maria
8 Momi
10 Montserrat
14 South St Souvlaki
15 Original South Philly Water Ice
17 Philadelphia Pizza Company
18 PhilaDeli
21 Jim's Steaks
22 Ishkabbible's Eatery
24 Mako - Retired Surfer's Bar & Grill
25 Jon's Bar & Grille
27 Judy's
29 Russia House
30 Cedars
33 Pink Rose Pastry Shop
34 Famous 4th St Deli
35 Alyan's
37 Essene

OTHER
1 Mother Bethel AME Church
2 St Peter's Church
3 The Artful Dodger
4 Morning Cup
5 Dickens Inn
6 Digital Underground
9 Society Hill Playhouse
11 Tower Records
12 Tower Records (Classical)
13 South St Antiques Market
16 Philadelphia Record Exchange
19 Eyes Art Gallery
20 The Book Trader
23 JC Dobbs
26 HI-AYH Travel Center
28 Cop Banana Cabana
31 Downey's
36 Xero

audiovisual tours and you can watch the coinage operation from a glass-enclosed gallery. It's open July and August daily from 9 am to 4:30 pm; May and June, Monday to Saturday; September to April, Monday to Friday. Admission is free.

Congregation Mikveh Israel

Congregation Mikveh Israel (☎ (215) 922-5446), 44 N 4th St, was founded in 1740 and is the second oldest congregation in the country. It's one of only four synagogues in the world that uses the Sephardic (Spanish/Portuguese) Rite. There are services Friday evening, Saturday at 9 am and on Jewish holidays. Among the artifacts is a letter from George Washington to the congregation, thanking them for their congratulations to him on his becoming president.

National Museum of American Jewish History

Also on N 4th St, this is the country's only museum (☎ (215) 923-3811) devoted to the role of Jews in American history. The American Jewish Experience is a permanent exhibition and there are other smaller changing exhibits. The museum is open Monday to Thursday from 10 am to 5 pm, Friday 10 am to 3 pm and Sunday noon to 5 pm. Admission is $2.50/1.75.

Afro-American Historical & Cultural Museum

The museum (☎ (215) 574-0380), at N 7th and Arch Sts, contains one of the country's best collections concerning black history and culture. It has exhibits on African heritage through slavery, emancipation, the civil rights movement and beyond. There's also a renowned giftshop selling craftwork. The museum is open Tuesday to Saturday from 10 am to 5 pm, Sunday noon to 6 pm. Admission is $4/2.

Balch Institute for Ethnic Studies

The institute (☎ (215) 925-8090), 18 S 7th St, whose purpose is to promote greater understanding between different ethnic groups, has a small museum that documents Philadelphia's and other cities' migrant experience. It also has changing exhibitions, workshops, film screenings and lectures. In the lobby, a computer tells

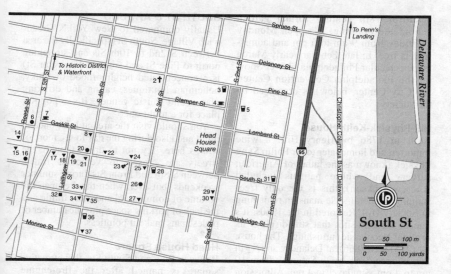

you which city organizations cater to which ethnic group. The institute is open Tuesday to Saturday from 10 am to 4 pm. A donation is requested.

Atwater Kent Museum – History Museum of Philadelphia

Over 300 years of the city's social history and local culture are represented at the museum (☎ (215) 922-3031), 15 S 7th St. Its collection of more than 75,000 artifacts, including military uniforms, dolls, model ships, radios etc, are used to depict ordinary daily life in Philadelphia's past. It's open Tuesday to Saturday from 10 am to 4 pm. Admission is $2/1.

SOCIETY HILL

Society Hill stands between S 6th and S Front Sts and Walnut and Lombard Sts, straddling Independence National Historic Park. A lovely residential neighborhood dominated by 18th and 19th century architecture, the area underwent major restoration during the 1960s and '70s. It's a pleasant place to stroll through – in particular, Delancey, American, Cypress and Philip Sts, narrow side streets lined with an attractive mix of colonial and contemporary homes, renovated warehouses converted into art galleries and high-end apartments.

Washington Square

On the northwest edge of Society Hill, this square is one of those in William Penn's original city plan, and its shaded benches offer a peaceful respite from a day's sightseeing. The **Tomb of the Unknown Soldier** is the country's only monument to the unknown American and British dead of the Revolutionary War. Once an upper-class residential district, in the 19th century Philadelphia's publishing industry became concentrated in the offices surrounding the square. These days, there's a mix of apartments as well as various offices and small businesses.

Pennsylvania Horticultural Society

The society's headquarters (☎ (215) 625-8250), 325 Walnut St, offer a soothing escape from the streets. There's a 1st floor exhibition of flower-related artwork and a beautiful 18th century formal garden behind the building. It's open Monday to Friday from 9 am to 5 pm and admission is free. In late February/early March the spectacular Philadelphia Flower Show (at the Philadelphia Convention Center, see City Center, below) is organized by the society.

Hill-Physick-Keith House

Built in 1786 by Henry Hill, a wine importer, and home later to Dr Philip Syng Physick (known as the father of American surgery and whose patients included Andrew Jackson), this is the only free-standing, Federal-style mansion remaining in Society Hill. Restored in the 1960s, it's one of the few sites that still displays its original Neoclassic furnishings. The house (☎ (215) 925-7866), at Delancey and S 4th Sts, is open Tuesday to Saturday from 10 am to 4 pm, Sunday 1 to 4 pm. Admission is $4/2.

SOUTH ST & AROUND

Usually compared to New York's Greenwich Village, South St (specifically the area between S 2nd to 10th Sts and stretching north to Pine St and south to Fitzwater St) is a concentrated neighborhood of funky, bohemian boutiques, eating and drinking places and music venues. It's a popular place for a night out.

You should visit the area at least once at night and also during the day to see more of what's here. Try not to drive, though: the streets are closed to vehicular traffic between S 8th and Front Sts during summer weekends, but even when they're open the volume of commercial and other traffic and the lack of parking space plus the number of pedestrians make it pointless.

Head House Square

Between Pine and South Sts, this attractive square is named after the fire-engine houses, called 'head houses,' built in the

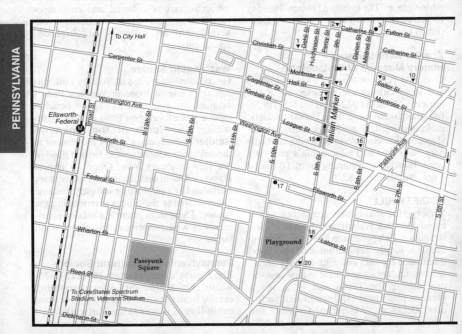

early 19th century. With cupolas, alarm bells and a fire officers' social club upstairs, the 'head house' at Second and Pine Sts escaped demolition and was restored. The shed between Lombard and Pine Sts was one of several built in 1745 for street trading; also restored, on summer weekends it's home to an open-air craft market.

Mother Bethel AME Church
Founded by two local freed slaves in 1787, this is the South St area's major historic building and is regarded as the birthplace of the African Methodist Episcopal (AME) Order. As a stop on the 'Underground Railroad,' this church and its pastor, Richard Allen, hid hundreds of fugitive slaves prior to the Civil War.

The present church (☎ (215) 925-0616), 419 S 6th St, is the fourth one built on this site; it dates from 1890 and was restored in 1987. Most of the congregation now live in West Philadelphia, but still worship here

despite attempts by some members to move the church. It's open Tuesday, Wednesday, Friday and Saturday from 10 am to 3 pm, Sunday 2 to 4 pm.

St Peter's Church
This was built in 1761 by Robert Smith (who also built Christ Church and Carpenters' Hall), when Christ Church was unable to cater to the growing Anglican congregation. Apart from the mid-19th century steeple, the beautiful church (☎ (215) 925-5968), at Pine and S 3rd Sts, looks much as it did when George Washington and his family worshipped here. It's open Tuesday to Saturday from 9 am to noon, Sunday 1 to 4 pm, with tours Saturday from 10 am to noon, Sunday 1 to 3 pm.

SOUTH PHILADELPHIA
South Philadelphia has been settled by succeeding waves of immigrants, from the Dutch and Swedish settlers of the 17th

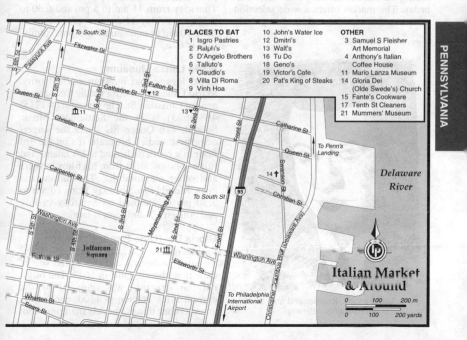

PLACES TO EAT	
1	Isgro Pastries
2	Ralph's
5	D'Angelo Brothers
6	Talluto's
7	Claudio's
8	Villa Di Roma
9	Vinh Hoa
10	John's Water Ice
12	Dmitri's
13	Walt's
16	Tu Do
18	Geno's
19	Victor's Cafe
20	Pat's King of Steaks

OTHER	
3	Samuel S Fleisher Art Memorial
4	Anthony's Italian Coffee House
11	Mario Lanza Museum
14	Gloria Dei (Olde Swede's) Church
15	Fante's Cookware
17	Tenth St Cleaners
21	Mummers' Museum

Italian Market & Around

PENNSYLVANIA

century, through the Jewish and many Italian arrivals in the 19th and early 20th centuries, to the black, Hispanic and Asian, particularly Vietnamese, settlers of more recent years. The Italian Market is the main attraction and, though still largely Italian, vendors and customers alike reflect this ethnic diversity. South Philadelphia also has several interesting museums, lots of restaurants and two major sporting venues. The area is served by SEPTA's Broad St Line and by bus Nos 2, 5, 17, 23, 47 and 50 from downtown.

Italian Market

A highlight of a visit to the city, the Italian Market, on S 9th St (between Christian St and Washington Ave) is the country's largest outdoor market. The stalls and specialty stores offer sights, sounds and smells rarely found in this age of supermarkets and gourmet stores. Closed on Sunday and Monday, the market's pace builds up during the week to the busy Friday and Saturday. The market offers a wide selection of items at low prices and locals regularly

Mario Lanza, local legend and international celebrity

travel miles to shop here. Easter and Christmas are especially good times to visit.

As well as the street stalls and the many butchers on S 9th St, look out for D'Angelo Brothers, specializing in sausages and paté; Claudio's with its cheese and olive selection; Talluto's, a traditional Italian deli; and Fante's Cookware (see Places to Eat and Things to Buy, below).

Nearby, the Vietnamese community has established shops and restaurants on and around S 8th St between Christian St and Washington Ave.

Samuel S Fleisher Art Memorial

This is a free art school (☎ (215) 922-3456), 709-21 Catharine St, founded by a wealthy woolens manufacturer in 1898, now housed in a former church. Administered today by the Philadelphia Museum of Art, it has a good art museum open to the public. In addition to the regular exhibits, four highly regarded art shows are held here during the year. It's open Monday to Thursday from 11 am to 5 pm and 6:30 to 9:30 pm, Friday 11 am to 5 pm, Saturday from 10 am to noon and 1 to 3 pm. Admission is free.

Mario Lanza Museum

Local legend and international celebrity, Mario Lanza was born Freddie Cocozza on nearby Christian St. The museum (☎ (215) 468-3623) is in the Settlement Music School, 416 Queen St, where the singer/actor first studied his craft. It's on the 3rd floor in a room dedicated to his talents and full of photos, stills from his films, posters and other memorabilia. The museum is open Monday to Saturday from 10 am to 3:30 pm (it's closed on Saturday in July and August). Admission is free.

Gloria Dei (Olde Swedes') Church

Philadelphia's original settlers were Swedish Lutherans and this is the site of their first church, built in 1643. The original log structure was replaced by the current brick version in 1700, containing, among other things, models (hanging from the ceiling) of the two ships that brought the first Swedish settlers. The church (☎ (215) 389-1513), 916 S Swanson St between I-95 and Christopher Columbus Blvd, is surrounded by a graveyard and several other 18th century buildings. It's open daily April to October from 9 am to 5 pm and by appointment at other times. A donation is requested.

Mummers' Museum

At this museum (☎ (215) 336-3050), 100 S 2nd St at Washington Ave, learn about the historic tradition of Philadelphia's Mummers and their annual New Year's Day parade. A 'mummer' is one who disguises or masquerades. Exhibits include some of their extravagant costumes, photographs, videos of the parades and a digital clock that counts down the days to the next January 1. It's open Tuesday to Saturday from 9:30 am to 5 pm, Sunday noon to 5 pm (but closed on Sunday in July and August). May to September there are free outdoor string-band concerts. Admission is $2.50/2.

CENTER CITY

Rittenhouse Square

The best known, and most popular and prestigious of the city's squares laid out by William Penn is named after the local 18th century astronomer, mathematician and clockmaker, David Rittenhouse. Surrounded by fancy apartment buildings, the square features a fine collection of statues as well as a children's wading pool and wooden benches. It's popular with city workers and tourists alike who come here in fine weather to rest under the shade of the trees, to enjoy a sandwich and a drink or to feed the squirrels.

Mutter Museum

Housed in the College of Physicians & Surgeons (☎ (215) 563-3737), 19 S 22nd St, this collection of pathological and anatomical specimens and medical artifacts was started in the late 19th century to educate medical students; it features a fascinating, but often gruesome collection of exhibits. These include the double liver shared by 19th century Siamese twins

Mummers' Parade

Said to be the country's oldest continual folk festival, it isn't known for sure how it started. It may have originated from a Swedish and Finnish custom of celebrating a 'Second Christmas' with wandering minstrels, or from the English Mummery Play, a kind of burlesque with harlequins dressed in silk and satin. Philadelphia's first Mummers appeared in the 1700s parading in the Washington Ave area, and the bands grew in size until in 1901 an official site was ordained for the parade: Broad St from South Philadelphia to City Hall.

Staged each New Year's Day, participants number over 25,000, mostly heterosexual men wearing sequins, feathers, makeup and outrageous costumes. They strut their way along Broad St, accompanied by bands that are traditionally limited to accordions, saxophones, drums, violins, banjos, bass fiddles, glockenspiels and clarinets.

Like Mardi Gras, the extravagant costumes are the highlight of the show. The Mummers are members of clubs that represent different city neighborhoods. They spend all year (and a lot of money) designing and creating their costumes, not to mention practising the music and choreographing their routines. Each year features different themes, such as fairy tales or Broadway shows.

The parade starts at 7 am and can last as long as 12 hours. Despite the low temperatures, there's always a large, enthusiastic and often heavy-drinking turnout. If you miss the parade, you can catch the Mummers' bands performing at the Mummers' Museum or during the summer at the Great Plaza at Penn's Landing, and at other special performances. To catch them in all their glory, though, you really need to see them on New Year's Day. ■

Chang and Eng Bunker, the tumor removed from President Cleveland's cancerous jawbone and numerous skeletons. Another display features various items swallowed by patients. The museum is open Tuesday to Friday from 10 am to 4 pm and admission is $2/1.

Liberty Place

This modern Art Deco, 60 story complex at 1650 Market St, can be seen from most parts of the city. It's notable not only for its distinctive blue-glass facade, but also for being the first building built higher than the William Penn statue on City Hall. Its construction inspired more high-rises, changing the city skyline completely. The complex has a 58 story twin, 2 Liberty Place, and is home to the Ritz-Carlton Hotel, offices and various shops.

City Hall

Probably Philadelphia's primary architectural highlight, the restored City Hall (☎ (215) 686-9074), at the intersection of Broad and Market Sts, is the country's largest municipal building. Completed in 1901, it took 30 years to build. The elaborately designed building was constructed without a steel framework so that the 22-foot-thick granite walls at the base support the central tower. It was the city's tallest building until the completion of Liberty Place in 1987. The 548 foot high City Hall is crowned by a 27 ton, 37 foot high bronze statue of William Penn. Before Liberty Place, a 'gentlemen's agreement' had limited the height of Philadelphia's buildings to the hat on Penn's statue. Now City Hall no longer dominates the Philadelphia skyline.

City Hall is open Monday to Friday from 9:30 am to 4:30 pm with free tours of the interior available. You can also visit the observation deck of the tower for a magnificent view of the city from 40 floors up. Take the elevator to the 7th floor, from where you follow a red line to a waiting area; another elevator takes you to the deck. Entry is free, but donations are requested. Note that the hours between 10 am and noon are often reserved for school groups.

Masonic Temple

This temple (☎ (215) 988-1917), 1 N Broad St, is the headquarters of the Grand Lodge of Free & Accepted Masons of Pennsylvania. Some of the Founding Fathers, including George Washington, were members and the temple library and museum contain letters and books from the period. The seven lodge halls are designed in different architectural styles: Corinthian, Egyptian, Gothic, Ionic, Norman, Oriental and Renaissance. Free 45 minute guided tours take place Monday to Friday between 10 am and 3 pm, Saturday at 10 and 11 am. It's closed on Saturday in July and August.

John Wanamaker Department Store

This restored, landmark store (☎ (215) 422-2000) is on Market St between Juniper and S 13th Sts. The main shopping area features a large bronze eagle and a 30,000 pipe organ (reputedly the world's largest); you can enjoy free performances twice daily, Monday to Saturday at 11:15 am and 5:15 pm. Wanamakers' Christmas light-and-music show should also be seen in November and December. The store is open daily from 10 am to 7 pm.

Pennsylvania Academy of the Fine Arts

Housed in a beautiful Victorian Gothic-style building, the academy (☎ (215) 972-7600), 118 N Broad St, was founded in 1805 (in another location). It boasts a prestigious – and the country's oldest – art school and museum. On display are the works of such noted early American painters as Charles Willson Peale (1741-1827), Gilbert Stuart (1755-1828) and Thomas Eakins (1844-1916). The museum is open Tuesday to Saturday from 10 am to 5 pm, Sunday 11 am to 5 pm. Guided tours are available Tuesday to Sunday at 12:30 and 2 pm and are included in the admission fee of $5.95/4.95.

Historical Society of Philadelphia

On display is an interesting exhibition on 300 years of local history, 'Finding Philadelphia's Past.' The museum contains important historical documents including many of William Penn's political papers and letters. Other exhibits include George Washington's desk and a painting of Ben Franklin by Norman Willson Peale, plus videos in the small theater.

The museum (☎ (215) 732-6201), 1300 Locust St, is open Tuesday and Thursday to Saturday from 10 am to 5 pm; Wednesday 1 to 9 pm. Admission is $2.50/1.50. Plan on spending about 1½ hours here, depending on your interest.

Reading Terminal Market

The large, indoor Reading Terminal Market (☎ (215) 922-2317) started in 1893 down by the Delaware River when the old markets spread along High St (renamed Market St in their honor) to here, under the Philadelphia & Reading Railroad's train shed. The farmers' market was renovated as part of the Convention Center development.

You'll find some of the city's best pretzels, hoagies and high-quality groceries here, though you won't find the bargains of the Italian Market in South Philly (see above). It's a terrific place to come for breakfast, lunch or a snack with a selection of good-value, top-quality food stalls. Another attraction in their own right are the Amish families who have a section where they sell their produce Wednesday to Saturday.

Most food stalls close by 3 pm and maps of the market can be found at various points around the complex. See Places to Eat, below, for suggestions.

Philadelphia Convention Center

A new city landmark, the Convention Center, 1101 Arch St, between N 11th and N 13th Sts, was built at a cost of $522 million; it covers a huge area and incorporates the Reading Terminal's former train shed and head house which now make up part of the main exhibition hall on the 2nd floor. The 1200 room Marriott Hotel is also part of the complex. The center is the site of a few special events, and is open to the public by free guided tour on Tuesday and

'Make It a Night'

To encourage people to stay downtown mid-week, 'Make It a Night' promotes Wednesday evening with free metered parking after 5 pm (after 6:30 pm in restricted zones), free outdoor entertainment, reduced prices at cinemas, late hours in museums and other special events. Call the 'Make It a Night' hotline at ☎ (215) 592-8282 or check the local press. ■

Thursday at 11:30 am, 12:30, 1:30 and 2:15 pm; meet at 12th and Arch Sts or call ☎ (215) 418-4700.

Chinatown

Philadelphia's eight block Chinatown, between N 8th and N 11th Sts and Vine and Arch Sts, lacks the ambience of its New York and San Francisco counterparts. Nor does it have much in the way of landmarks or sights – except for the colorful **Chinese Friendship Gate**, at N 10th St (between Arch and Cherry Sts), a decorative arch, built in 1984 as a joint project between Philadelphia and its Chinese sister city, Tianjin. Nonetheless, the neighborhood does offer a good selection of Chinese, Vietnamese, Thai and vegetarian eating places, many of which are inexpensive.

Pennsylvania Hospital

Founded in 1751 by Benjamin Franklin and Dr Thomas Bond, Pennsylvania Hospital (☎ (215) 829-3971), 800 Spruce St, was the country's first hospital. A booklet offering a self-guided walking tour is available on the 2nd floor of the Pine Building (the entrance is on Spruce St); this part of the hospital has been in use since 1755. Other places of interest include the **History of Nursing Museum**, the **Historic Library of Pennsylvania Hospital** (containing important collections on the history of medicine), North America's oldest surgical amphitheater for medical students and the 18th century medicinal **herb garden** on Pine St. The hospital is open Monday to Friday from 9 am to 4:30 pm. Admission is free.

Civil War Library & Museum

Highly recommended for Civil War buffs and founded in 1888, the three story museum (☎ (215) 735-8196), 1805 Pine St, boasts some unique artifacts, including items that belonged to generals Grant, Sherman, Meade and Mulholland. A gallery of changing exhibitions has dealt with such subjects as the role of women in the war, black soldiers and British contributions to the war. With over 12,000 volumes, plus manuscripts and other archival material, this is one of the country's most comprehensive Civil War libraries and museums. It's open Monday to Saturday from 11 am to 4 pm. Admission is $3/2.

Rosenbach Museum & Library

Housed in a superb 19th century townhouse on one of the city's loveliest streets, this small museum (☎ (215) 732-1600), 2010 Delancey St, contains a top collection of rare books and manuscripts. The original manuscript of James Joyce's *Ulysses* is on permanent display, as are the first four pages of Bram Stoker's *Dracula* and most of Joseph Conrad's manuscripts. The museum and library are open Tuesday to Sunday with 75-minute guided tours between 11 am and 4 pm (the last tour starts at 2:45 pm). Admission is $3.50/2.50.

Norman Rockwell Museum

Norman Rockwell (1894-1978) was an illustrator famous for his covers of the magazine *Saturday Evening Post* depicting many of the ordinary aspects of American life. The museum (☎ (215) 922-4345), 601 Walnut St, in the Curtis Publishing Company building in which the magazine was published, contains exhibits of the artist's life and work. These include his *Saturday Evening Post* covers, a short biographical video and photos of him painting portraits of celebrities. It's open Monday to Saturday from 10 am to 4 pm, Sunday 11 am to 4 pm. Admission is $2/1.50.

Edgar Allan Poe National Historic Site

Poe, America's noted 19th century horror-story writer, wrote 'The Black Cat' while he lived in the modest brick house on this site from 1843-44. Next door is a museum about the man and his work. Operated by the NPS, the site (☎ (215) 597-8780), 532 N 7th St, is open Tuesday to Saturday from 9 am to 5 pm; admission is free. It's somewhat north of the city center, but bus No 47 runs past. Plan about 1½ hours to see it.

Eastern State Penitentiary

Once home to Al Capone and used as part of the set of Terry Gilliam's sci-fi film *12 Monkeys*, this Gothic Revival building (☎ (215) 236 7326), on Fairmount Ave between N 20th and N 22nd Sts, ceased being a prison in 1970. Tours are available on weekends from 10 am to 7 pm and admission is $7/4. Children under seven aren't admitted. Starting in the Old Visitor's Room where you're issued with a hard hat, you stroll through the cell blocks, prison greenhouse and death row. Take a bus to Benjamin Franklin Pkwy (see below) and walk north on N 22nd St.

BENJAMIN FRANKLIN PARKWAY

Benjamin Franklin Pkwy is the focus for a superb collection of museums and other landmarks. Designed by French architects, Jacques Greber and Paul Cret, the 250-foot-wide parkway extends from Logan Circle northwest to Eskins Oval in front of the Philadelphia Museum of Art. Built in 1924 and modeled on the Champs-Élysées in Paris, it's a multi-lane thoroughfare lined with trees, flags from around the world, statues and fountains. Philly's version, however, is dominated more by traffic than cafes and promenading pedestrians. The parkway is served by bus Nos 32, 38, 48 and 76 from downtown.

Academy of Natural Sciences Museum

This, the country's oldest natural history museum, was founded in 1812, though the building itself dates from 1868. It has a terrific permanent dinosaur display, complete with computer videos and reconstructed skeletons. The museum (☎ (215) 299-1000), 1900 Benjamin Franklin Pkwy, also features such exhibits as 'Outside In,' a hands-on nature center for kids, and 'What on Earth,' a geology and gem exhibition. On weekends you can even go on a 'dig' for fossils in a simulated field station.

It's open Monday to Friday from 10 am to 4:30 pm, weekends and holidays from 10 am to 5 pm. Admission is $6.50/5.50.

Please Touch Museum
Popular with young children and their parents, the highly regarded Please Touch Museum (☎ (215) 963-0667), 210 N 21st St, emphasizes learning through playing. It features obstacle courses, a real city bus to play in (with steering wheel, horn and all), miniature trains, computers, a mock TV station with a working camera and a miniature supermarket. It's open July 1 to Labor Day daily from 9 am to 6 pm, to 4:30 pm the rest of the year. Admission is $6.95, adult or child.

Franklin Institute Science Museum
Founded in 1824, the world-class Franklin Institute Science Museum (☎ (215) 448-1200), at N 20th St and Benjamin Franklin Pkwy, moved into this four story, Greek Revival building in 1934. The museum pioneered the hands-on science concept so widespread nowadays.

Among the **Science Center's** features are a four ton, two story papier-mâché replica of a heart that you walk through; working devices that demonstrate aspects of physics; train-related exhibits (including a ride on a steam train) that are especially popular with children; a computer center; and a giant pinball machine. Downstairs, the **Fels Planetarium** has a computer-driven look at constellations, plus laser shows and astronomy exhibits. Housed in a four story dome, the **Tuttleman Omniverse Theater** features a 79 foot screen that surrounds the audience and uses an eight track sound system.

In the **Mandell Futures Center**, a 1990s addition to the museum, you can see the development of computers, telecommunications and space travel and environmental concerns of the next century.

The museum is open Monday to Saturday from 9:30 to 5 pm, Sunday to 6 pm; the Mandell Futures Center is open Monday to Wednesday from 9:30 to 5 pm, Thursday to Saturday to 9 pm, Sunday to 6 pm. Admission to the museum and futures center is $10.50/8.50; to these two plus the Tuttleman Omniverse Theater *or* Fels Planetarium it's $12.50/10.50; to everything it's $14.50/12.50.

Rodin Museum
A must see for many, this noteworthy museum (☎ (215) 763-8100), on Callowhill St near the corner of N 22nd St and Benjamin Franklin Pkwy, is home to the largest collection outside Paris of Auguste Rodin's sculptures. These include his famous *The Thinker, The Burghers of Calais* and *Gates of Hell*. It's open Tuesday to Sunday from 10 am to 5 pm and a donation is requested.

FAIRMOUNT PARK
Said to be the world's largest urban park, Fairmount Park (☎ (215) 685-0000) covers nearly 14 sq miles – 10% of the city's land. The southern section, roughly the shape of South America, stretches some four miles northwest from the Philadelphia Museum of Art to the Falls Bridge, near the East Falls neighborhood. Most of it is divided by the Schuylkill River into East and West Fairmount Park. Northwest from East Falls the park stretches along Wissahickon Creek (a tributary of the Schuylkill River) past Chestnut Hill.

The park is popular with city residents and is a great place for a picnic or a stroll (see Activities, below). In summer there are free classical concerts. It also has a fine group of authentic early American houses, which are open to the public. Sadly, litter in some parts of the park is a real problem.

Bus Nos 38 and 76 takes you to the Philadelphia Museum of Art and the zoo, but, if you don't have a car, to see all the sights it's worth considering taking Old Town Trolley Tours (☎ (215) 928-8687); see Organized Tours, later.

PENNSYLVANIA

Philadelphia Museum of Art

With over 300,000 paintings, sculptures, drawings, prints, decorative arts and period rooms this is the country's third largest art museum. Many of the 20th century's major artists are represented in its collection of mostly European and Asian art, with some masterpieces from the USA. Architecturally, the museum consists of three Greek-style 'temples' and the roof is covered by blue tiles with bronze griffins.

In the Great Stair Hall, just past the 1st floor entrance, stands the 1892 statue of the nude huntress *Diana* by Augustus St Gaudens; it was brought here from New York in 1932 after being saved from the demolished Madison Square Garden.

Highlights include the 19th century European & Impressionist Galleries, featuring the work of Renoir, Manet and Van Gogh. There are galleries for special exhibitions and other permanent exhibition galleries include American Art, Early 20th Century Art, Contemporary Art, Japanese & Chinese Art, Near Eastern & Asian Art, Medieval & European Art, Arms & Armor, European Art 1500-1700, English Period Rooms, European Art 1700-1850 and American Period Rooms. The museum also features complete buildings, including an Indian Hindu temple and a Japanese Buddhist temple from Nara. It also has a good bookstore and cafe.

The museum (☎ (215) 763-8100) is open Tuesday and Thursday to Sunday from 10 am to 5 pm; Wednesday to 8:45 pm. Normal admission is $7/4, seniors $6.50,

Rocky Was Here

Yes, the steps in front of the Philadelphia Museum of Art are the ones that Sylvester Stallone's character Rocky Balboa ascended in the original *Rocky* movie. The film won an Oscar for best picture. In the early 1980s, a bronze statue of the enduring character was erected outside the museum for the filming of *Rocky III*. Although it appeared again in *Rocky V* it was eventually deemed inappropriate for permanent residency here and moved to the front of the CoreStates Spectrum stadium. Nevertheless, you can enjoy Rocky's terrific view of the city from the top of the steps looking back along Benjamin Franklin Pkwy toward City Hall. ∎

but on Sunday before 1 pm it's free. 'Wednesday Nights at the Art Museum' are worthwhile, with live music, films, entertainment, food and drink, art history courses and other events.

Fairmount Waterworks

A National Historic Engineering Landmark, the beautiful Greek-style complex was built in 1815, and was designed to pump four million gallons of water daily from the Schuylkill River to a reservoir on the site now occupied by the Philadelphia Museum of Art. It was closed in 1909 due to pollution, but has been partially restored. Tours are offered on Saturday and Sunday afternoons from mid-June to mid-October; call park information for details.

The Philadelphia Museum of Art

Schuylkill River

Its name is Dutch for 'hidden river,' and it stretches for 100 miles from its source in Schuylkill County to the Delaware River in South Philadelphia. The Schuylkill River (pronounced SKOO-kill) was a major factor in the city's growth in the 18th and 19th centuries. Today, it provides Philadelphia with recreational benefits, particularly in Fairmount Park. Scullers are a familiar year-round sight, and people love to jog or stroll along the riverside.

Boathouse Row

Another major Philly landmark, this is home to the 'Schuylkill Navy,' a collection of rowing clubs renowned for their distinctive Victorian buildings on the east bank of the river. Built in the late 19th and early 20th centuries, these buildings are a lovely enough sight during the day, but after dark are illuminated to marvelous effect.

Early American Houses

The 19th century **Lemon Hill Mansion** (☎ (215) 232-4337), Poplar Dr, was owned by financier Robert Morris and is furnished with period artifacts. It closes from mid-December to mid-February.

Described by John Adams as 'the most elegant seat in Pennsylvania,' Georgian-style **Mt Pleasant** (☎ (215) 763-8100), Mt Pleasant Dr, was built in 1762 by a wealthy Scottish privateer and owned for a time by Benedict Arnold. It contains ornate woodwork and Chippendale furniture.

The Federal-style **Rockland** (☎ (215) 482-8644), near East Park Reservoir, was built in 1810 and its most distinguishing features are the curved staircase and decorative plaster ceilings. It's open Wednesday to Sunday from 10 am to 4 pm. Nearby, **Woodford** (☎ (215) 229-6115), a Georgian mansion dating back to 1756, has a collection of Colonial furniture and decorative art. Dr Philip Syng Physick once owned **Laurel Hill** (☎ (215) 235-1776), E Edgely Dr, built in the 1760s.

The largest house in the park, **Strawberry Mansion** (☎ (215) 228-8364), Strawberry Mansion Dr, features a Federal-style main section built in the 1790s, while the Greek Revival wings were added on in the 1820s. The owner's son was a strawberry grower. Today, an antique-toy exhibit, the mixture of Empire, Federal and Regency furniture and Tucker porcelain are the main attractions.

The houses are open Wednesday to Sunday from 10 am to 4 pm though the hours sometimes vary. Admission is $2.50/1.25 per house.

Japanese House & Gardens

A gift of the American-Japan Society of Tokyo, the authentic 16th-century-style Japanese teahouse (☎ (215) 878-5097), in West Fairmount Park, provides a peaceful retreat from the city. Set in beautiful Japanese gardens by a stream, it's open for guided or self-guided tours May to September, Tuesday to Sunday from 11 am to 4 pm; October to April weekends only 11:30 am to 4 pm. Admission is $2.50. During the spring and summer months you can enjoy tea ceremonies and origami demonstrations here. The house and gardens are part of the 22 acre **Horticultural Center** (☎ (215) 685-0096), which you enter via Horticultural Dr off Belmont Ave and which is open daily from 9 am to 5 pm.

Philadelphia Zoo

The 42 acre Philadelphia Zoo (☎ (215) 243-1100), at Girard Ave and N 34th St in West Fairmount Park, is the country's oldest zoo, having opened in 1874. It houses over 1700 mammals, birds, reptiles and amphibians. Despite its age and Victorian touches, the zoo has been modernized and features natural habitats for many of its 'stars,' not just cages. It's open daily from 9:30 am to 5:45 pm and admission is $8.50/6. Set aside at least three hours to see the zoo.

Scenic Drives

A great Philadelphia experience is to enjoy the views from the winding roads that run along the Schuylkill River. Kelly Dr, formerly E River Dr, is named after John B Kelly, father of Princess Grace. West River

Dr runs along the opposite bank. Belmont Plateau off Belmont Mansion Dr in West Fairmount Park offers spectacular views of Philadelphia especially at night. From Center City, take the Schuylkill Expressway or the W River Dr to Montgomery Dr and make a right at Belmont Mansion Dr.

Take special care when driving: the roads have sharp curves and accidents are common due to gawking drivers not paying attention to the road.

UNIVERSITY CITY

Philadelphia is a temporary home to over 30,000 students, and University City, in West Philadelphia, is the area west of the Schuylkill River and south of Market St stretching to about 42nd St where college campuses and students dominate.

The Philadelphia area is host to numerous colleges. The two largest here are the University of Pennsylvania (known as Penn), an Ivy League school, and Drexel University. For the visitor, University City's main attractions are the architecture of 30th St Station and Penn's campus and Penn's University Museum of Archaeology & Anthropology.

The area can be reached from downtown on the Market-Frankford and Subway-Surface subway lines or by bus Nos 21 and 42.

30th St Station

Worth a visit even if you're not catching a train, the Neoclassic station's main concourse is one of Philly's most romantic public spaces. The grand exterior, with its Corinthian columns, can be seen across the river from JFK Blvd and Market St Bridge – at night it's beautifully floodlit. The station's south side is a pleasant place for a quick snack.

University of Pennsylvania

Founded in 1740 as a charity school by William Penn, it was combined with Benjamin Franklin's Public Academy of Philadelphia in 1750. This academy became the nation's first university in 1779 and moved to this 260 acre campus from

east of the river in the 1870s. It has several architectural highlights.

On Locust Walk between S 34th and S 36th Sts, **College Hall** was the first building and is a classic example of the 'collegiate Gothic' style. The **Anne & Jerome Fisher Fine Arts Building**, on S 34th St between Walnut and Spruce Sts and facing the College Green, is generally referred to as the Furness Building, designed as it was by renowned local architect Frank Furness. Also designed by Furness is the nearby **Arthur Ross Gallery** (☎ (215) 898-4401), 220 S 34th St, a free art gallery with changing exhibitions. **The Quadrangle**, on Spruce St between S 36th and S 38th Sts, features collegiate Gothic-style dorms.

Museum of Archaeology & Anthropology

This world-renowned museum (☎ (215) 898-4000), 3260 South St, opened in 1887 and is a magical place with interesting permanent exhibits and a wide range of changing exhibitions. Its archaeological treasures hail from ancient Egypt, Mesopotamia, the Mayan peninsula, Asia, Greece, Rome, Africa, Polynesia and North America. Highlights include one of the world's largest crystal balls (this 55 pounder may have belonged to the Empress Dowager of China); samples of the oldest writing ever found, from Sumeria; bronzes from Benin in Nigeria; and a 12 ton granite Sphinx of Ramesses II, circa 1293-1185 BC.

The museum is open Tuesday to Saturday from 10 am to 4:30 pm, Sunday from 1 to 5 pm. Admission is $5/2.50.

BARNES FOUNDATION GALLERY

The Barnes Foundation Gallery (☎ (610) 664-4026), 300 N Latches Lane, Merion, about six miles northwest of downtown, reopened in late 1995 after being closed for 2½ years for renovations. (Previously, the museum was only open to students and scholars – the reopening represents the first time the public has been invited to view the collection in its own home.)

The gallery houses the world's largest

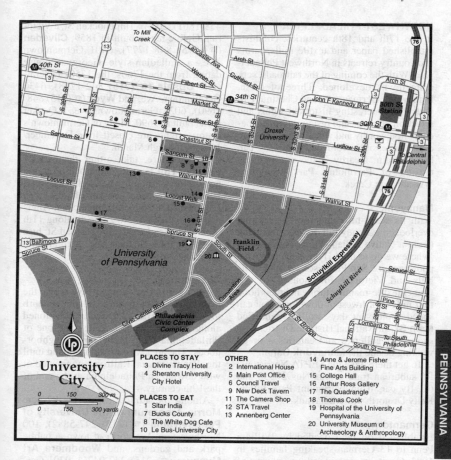

PLACES TO STAY
3 Divine Tracy Hotel
4 Sheraton University
   City Hotel

PLACES TO EAT
1 Sitar India
7 Bucks County
8 The White Dog Cafe
10 Le Bus-University City

OTHER
2 International House
5 Main Post Office
6 Council Travel
9 New Deck Tavern
11 The Camera Shop
12 STA Travel
13 Annenberg Center

14 Anne & Jerome Fisher
    Fine Arts Building
15 College Hall
16 Arthur Ross Gallery
17 The Quadrangle
18 Thomas Cook
19 Hospital of the University of
    Pennsylvania
20 University Museum of
    Archaeology & Anthropology

PENNSYLVANIA

private collection of impressionist, post-impressionist and early French modern paintings. It contains works by Cezanne (more than in all the galleries of France), Degas, Matisse, Manet, Monet, Modigliani, Picasso, Renoir, Rousseau, Seurat and van Gogh. As well as these, there is art and craftwork from around the world including antique furniture, ceramics, hand-wrought iron and Native American jewelry. The Barnes Foundation Gallery also provides an educational program on the world's different artistic traditions. It's open Thursday 12:30 to 5 pm

and Friday to Sunday 9:30 am to 5 pm; admission is $5.

The gallery is in a 13 acre property that is maintained as an **arboretum** and contains a wide diversity of plants. The arboretum school here teaches students botany, horticulture and landscaping.

To get to the gallery and arboretum take SEPTA's R5 train to Merion or bus No 44 from downtown; if you're driving, follow the Schuylkill Expressway northwest then turn left at the City Ave turn-off. Follow City Ave then turn right onto Lancaster Rd; Latches Lane is the fourth turn on the left.

NORTHWEST PHILADELPHIA

In the 17th and 18th centuries, colonists established paper and textile mills, farms and country retreats in Northwest Philadelphia. With the coming of the railroads, separate towns developed. Three of these, Manayunk, Germantown and Chestnut Hill with their interesting historical sights and selection of shops and restaurants are especially noteworthy and worth a visit. They're easily accessible from downtown by car, bus or train. Nearby is the northern extension of Fairmount Park straddling Wissahickon Creek.

Manayunk

With its steep hills and row houses that overlook the Schuylkill River, Manayunk (from a Native Indian expression meaning 'where we go to drink') has been dubbed a poor-person's San Francisco because of its hills and Victorian row houses. In this former textile-manufacturing neighborhood four miles northwest of downtown you can spend a pleasant day strolling gentrified **Main St** – a National Historic District with shops, art galleries and eateries – or go walking beside the **Manayunk Canal**.

To get there, take the SEPTA Norristown R6 suburban train or bus Nos 27, 32 and 61. By car, from Fairmount Park follow Kelly Dr north into Manayunk.

Germantown

Established on land deeded by William Penn to 13 German-speaking families in 1683, Germantown, six miles northwest of downtown, first became a papermaking, printing and publishing center. In the 19th century textile manufacturing spurred its growth. With the Depression in the 1930s it went into decline and in the 1950s a number of its wealthier and middle-class residents moved to the suburbs. Areas of urban decay remain, but nowadays Germantown has some superb restored Georgian, Victorian and early American residential architecture especially along and around **Germantown Ave**.

Some of the gems open to the public are **Ebenezer Maxwell Mansion** (☎ (215) 438-1861), 200 W Tulpehocken St, a Victorian Gothic house built in 1859; **Cliveden** (☎ (215) 848-1777), 6401 Germantown Ave, a Palladian-style Georgian house dating from the 1760s; the 1750s Federal-style **Upsala** (☎ (215) 842-1798), 6430 Germantown Ave; and **Wyck** (☎ (215) 848-1690), 6026 Germantown Ave, a Quaker home built in 1690. Many of Germantown's historic sights are closed from December/January through March.

To get there, take either the SEPTA Chestnut Hill East R7 suburban train and get off at Germantown, or the Chestnut Hill West R8 train and get off at Queen Lane, Chelten Ave or Tulpehocken. Alternatively, catch bus No 23 north along 11th St. By car, head north along Broad St, turn left onto Pike St then take a right onto Germantown Ave.

Chestnut Hill

Further north, Germantown Ave is also the main street of the posh residential suburb of Chestnut Hill, scenically positioned along the Wissahickon Valley and one of Philadelphia's most exclusive neighborhoods. The area was mostly farmland until the Pennsylvania Railroad connected it with downtown Philadelphia at the end of the 19th century.

Among the attractions are the 92 acre **Morris Arboretum of the University of Pennsylvania** (☎ (215) 247-5882), 100 Northwestern Ave north of town, a public park and gardens, and **Woodmere Art Museum** (☎ (215) 247-0476), 9201 Germantown Ave. Along **Germantown Ave** and its cobblestoned side streets you'll find fashionable shops and places to eat.

Take the SEPTA Chestnut Hill East R7 or Chestnut Hill West R8 suburban train or catch bus No 23 north along 11th St. By car, head north along Broad St, turn left onto Pike St then right onto Germantown Ave, which takes you through Germantown and Mt Airy onto Chestnut Hill.

ACTIVITIES

The huge Fairmount Park is the city's main center for outdoor activities. With around

100 miles of jogging, cycling and bridle paths and the Schuylkill River and Wissahickon Creek within its borders, the park is popular with city residents. For details of what's available in the park call Fairmount Park Information (☎ (215) 685-0000).

For **walking**, **jogging** and **bicycling** a paved 8.2 mile loop from the Philadelphia Museum of Art heads along Kelly Dr on the east bank of the Schuylkill River to the Falls Bridge then returns to the museum on West River Dr. Further north, Forbidden Dr is a 5.5 mile traffic-free gravel path on the west bank of Wissahickon Creek with some spectacular scenery.

In town, Bike Line (☎ (215) 735-1503), 1234 Locust St at S 13th St, rents mountain bikes for $15 a day plus deposit.

Rowing and **canoeing** are popular on the Schuylkill River. Fairmount Park also has 115 **tennis** courts open free to the public and five outdoor **swimming** pools. Call Fairmount Park Information for details. There are six 18 hole public **golf** courses too; for information call ☎ (215) 877-8813/8707. Weekends tend to be fully booked.

November through March you can go **ice skating** on Penn's Landing at the outdoor Blue Cross River Rink (☎ (215) 925-7465 for $5.

You can hire **in-line skates** from City Stores (☎ (215) 569-9900), 1845 Walnut St, for $5 per day plus deposit.

ORGANIZED TOURS

A variety of tours exist to help you explore the city. They can be booked directly with the operators, through your hotel front desk, at the Philadelphia Visitors Center (see Tourist Offices under Information, above) or with a travel agent.

Trolley Bus Tours

A good way to get a comfortable overview of the city is with Old Town Trolley Tours (☎ (215) 928-8687), 60 Laurel St, whose popular motorized 'trolley' buses give you a two hour tour of the city and Fairmount Park. You can get off and reboard as often as you like within one full loop. Trolleys leave daily about every 30 minutes. The tour costs $15/7, including admission to one of the Fairmont Park houses.

Philadelphia Trolley Tours (☎ (215) 923-8522) provides a similar tour of the city which takes 1½ hours and costs $10/5. Trolley buses also operate along Penn's Landing; see that section earlier.

Bus Tours

Gray Line (☎ (215) 569-3666), 3101 Orthodox St, has several bus tours in and around Philadelphia, which leave from 30th St Station and pick up from the major hotels. It operates a twice daily, three hour tour of Independence National Historic Park, Old City, Center City and South Philadelphia for $16/10. A three hour, night-time tour visits Manayunk, the Philadelphia Museum of Art and South St for $20/12. Gray Line also has tours to Valley Forge National Historic Park and Pennsylvania Dutch Country.

Walking Tours

Free walking tours are offered by the park rangers at the Independence National Historical Park; check with the NPS Visitors Center for the current schedule.

May to October, Centipede Tours (☎ (215) 735-3123), 1315 Walnut St, has walking tours of Society Hill every Friday and Saturday evening at 6:30 pm for $5/4. The tours leave from Thomas Bond House, 129 S 2nd St, and the guides dress in period costume.

The Preservation Coalition of Greater Philadelphia (☎ (215) 568-8225), 1 Penn Center at Suburban Station, 1617 JFK Blvd, has guided theme tours of the city's architectural heritage, including ones of City Hall and Chestnut Hill. Call for a schedule. The tour is $10/15 for members/non-members.

Carriage Tours

On Chestnut St opposite Independence Hall you can pick up a horse and carriage with a driver/commentator. A 20 minute tour of Independence National Historic Park costs $15 for four people; and each additional person costs $3 extra. Longer tours take in Society Hill and Old City.

Cruises

From Penn's Landing the *Spirit of Philadelphia* (☎ (215) 923-1419) offers popular two hour lunch ($26), three hour dinner ($44) and two hour 'moonlight' ($20; leaving at midnight) cruises along the Delaware River.

For $10/6, narrated 1½ hour boat rides are available three to four times daily on the *Holiday* (☎ (215) 629-8687) from the waterfront two blocks north of the Benjamin Franklin Bridge. Good views of the river and city are also possible on the Riverbus that goes to the New Jersey State Aquarium (see above).

SPECIAL EVENTS

Highlights of the Philadelphia calendar include:

January
  Mummers Parade – January 1, a New Year's Day parade along Broad St of 30,000 spectacularly dressed Mummers (See the earlier sidebar.)
February
  Black History Month – many special events, exhibitions, screenings, concerts etc at the Afro-American Historical & Cultural Museum and other venues
February/March
  Philadelphia Flower Show – the spectacular week-long, indoor flower show in the Convention Center is the world's largest
March/April
  The Cook & The Book – this five day festival brings together cookbook authors, food critics, chefs and restaurateurs to prepare special meals in many city restaurants
April
  Philadelphia Antique Show & Sale – the premier show of its kind in the country, at 103 Engineer's Armory, N 33rd St, West Philadelphia
  Penn Relays – one of the world's oldest, largest and best amateur athletic carnivals; held for over 100 years on Franklin Field at the University of Pennsylvania
May
  Africamericas Festival – 12 days of arts events and parades around the city celebrating black-American culture

  Jambalaya Jam – a three day celebration of Creole and Cajun food and New Orleans music at Penn's Landing
  Philadelphia Festival of World Cinema – a 12 day festival featuring some of the best international independent films
July
  Philadelphia Freedom Festival – Independence Day celebrations with parades, concerts and fireworks take place during the first week of the month
August
  Philadelphia Folk Festival – three days of international music held at Old Poole Farm in Schwenksville
September
  Super Sunday – organized by the Academy of Natural Sciences on the second Sunday of the month and aimed mainly at kids, with activities around town and a parade along Benjamin Franklin Pkwy
October
  Columbus Day Parade – held on the second Monday along S Broad St
November
  Fairmount Park Marathon – usually held on the second or third Sunday of the month
  Thanksgiving Day Parade – the country's oldest Thanksgiving parade with floats and bands along Market St and Benjamin Franklin Pkwy
  John Wanamaker's Light Show – a spectacular display in the Grand Court of Philadelphia's landmark department store that begins in November and ends after Christmas
December
  Christmas Tours of Historic Houses – features some of the historic houses in Fairmount Park and Germantown
  Kwanzaa Parade – a traditional parade celebrating black renewal, organized by the Afro-American Historical & Cultural Museum

PLACES TO STAY

Philadelphia has a wide range of accommodation possibilities, but finding a bed may be difficult at times – booking your room in advance will make life easier. Try to avoid visiting Philadelphia during school graduation week in late May when many B&Bs and hotel rooms are booked months ahead by proud families and friends. The Philadelphia Convention Center, which brings many visitors to the city, has put pressure on accommodations availability. Most hotels offer attractively priced weekend packages so rooms can be hard to find then.

If you're driving, you may need to factor in the cost of parking the car overnight, though some hotels offer free parking; check when booking.

You may see some of the cheaper downtown hotels advertised around town (at the Greyhound bus station for example) offering 'cheap accommodation and friendly service' – these aren't recommended.

Places to Stay – bottom end
Camping *Timberlane Campground* (☎ (609) 423-6677), 117 Timber Lane, Clarksboro, NJ 08020, 15 miles southwest across the Delaware River, is the closest. It has full facilities, accepts pets, is open year round (though only the hardiest campers might consider staying in the winter months) and has sites for $17, or $20 with hookup. From downtown, cross the Benjamin Franklin Bridge, take I-676 then I-76 south to I-295 south; at exit 18A, turn onto Cohawkin Rd for about 800 yards then turn right onto Friendship Rd; one block north turn right onto Timber Lane. Alternatively, from West Philadelphia follow I-76 to I-295 south and follow the directions as above.

Southwest of Philadelphia, *West Chester KOA* (☎ (610) 486-0447), PO Box 920P, Unionville 19375, is three miles north of Unionville on Route 162 beside the Brandywine River. It has 110 sites and is closed November through March. Riverside tent sites are $22.

Hostels The HI-AYH *Bank St Hostel* (☎ (215) 922 0222, (800) 392-4678), at 2 S Bank St, is a terrific, clean, comfortable hostel in Old City. In separate men's and women's dormitories, a bed costs $15. It has a large, well-equipped kitchen and dining area with free tea/coffee, a pool table, washer/dryer facilities and TV lounge. It's closed between 10 am and 4:30 pm, but you can drop off your bags during this time. There's a midnight

curfew Sunday to Thursday, 1 am on Friday and Saturday. It's a few minutes' walk from 2nd St Station (on the Market-Frankford subway line).

Also central, *Old First Reformed Church Youth Hostel* (☎ (215) 922-9663/4566), at N 4th and Race Sts, only opens July to early September. It costs $11 for a foam bed on the floor and includes a small breakfast. It has shower and laundry facilities and an 11 pm curfew; check in between 5 and 10 pm.

The 48 bed HI-AYH *Chamounix Mansion Hostel* (☎ (215) 878-3676, (800) 379-0017), Chamounix Dr, West Fairmount Park, is in a 19th century mansion in an attractive park setting, but a fair distance from downtown. Dorm beds are $11/14 for members/non-members; if the hostel isn't busy, a smaller dorm can be used as a private room for couples or families. There's a kitchen, vending machines serving snacks and drinks, TV lounge and free parking. It's closed between 11 am and 4:30 pm with a midnight curfew. It's also closed December 15 to January 15. To avoid a wasted trip, especially July through September, call ahead.

It's 30 minutes on bus No 38 from Market St to the corner of Ford and Cranston Rds in West Fairmount Park; from there walk one mile on Ford Rd to the stop sign; take a left on Chamounix Dr and continue to the hostel at the end of the road.

Hotels *Divine Tracy Hotel* (☎ (215) 382-4310), 20 S 36th St in University City, is a Christian-run, clean, 100 room hotel that doesn't accept credit cards. It has singles at $28 to $30 with shared bathroom, $33 to $40 with private bathroom; doubles are $40/50 with shared/private bathroom. Some rooms are available for low weekly rates of $75/95 for singles with shared/private bathroom, $110/130 for doubles but you'll need to book ahead. The hotel has strict rules: no smoking, no alcohol, no swearing, separate floors for men and women and a modest public dress code. There's no curfew; check in between 7 am and 11 pm.

Places to Stay – middle

B&Bs The city has some great central B&Bs offering superb value with friendly hosts, pleasant surroundings, lovely rooms and facilities – and good breakfasts. Most B&Bs only have a few rooms, so try to book ahead, especially for weekends. Most cost from $40 to $125 and accept major credit cards or personal checks. Some reservation agencies offering a selection of accommodations in and around Philadelphia are:

All About Town – B&B in Philadelphia
  PO Box 562, Valley Forge, PA 19481
  (☎ (215) 783-7838, (800) 344-0123)
B&B Center City
  1804 Pine St, Philadelphia, PA 19103
  (☎ (215) 735-1137/0582, (800) 354-8401)
B&B Connections
  PO Box 21, Devon, PA 19333
  (☎ (610) 687-3565, (800) 448-3619)
B&B of Philadelphia
  1530 Locust St, Suite K, Philadelphia, PA
  19102 (☎ (215) 735-1917, (800) 220-1917)

Antique Row B&B (☎ (215) 592-7802, fax 592-9692), 341 S 12th St off Pine St, is in a lovely, comfortable house. Prices range from $40/50 a single/double with a shared bathroom, to $80 for a suite with bathroom and kitchen. All rooms have telephone (local calls are free) and most have cable TV. A good, substantial breakfast is served in the dining room/lounge. Barbara Pope is a friendly host – if she has no vacancies, she'll help you book rooms elsewhere.

La Reserve (☎ (215) 735-1137/0582, (800) 354-8401), 1804 Pine St, in a beautiful, elegant 140 year old townhouse (the same address as the B&B), has eight large rooms from $45/50 with shared bathroom to $80/85 with private bathroom. Bill Buchanan, your host (who also operates B&B Center City; see the list, above) can book rooms elsewhere if it's full. Breakfast is served in the large chandeliered dining room. Check in between 3 and 7:30 pm unless you arrange otherwise when booking your room.

The friendly *Shippen Way Inn* (☎ (215) 627-7266), 416-418 Bainbridge St one block south of South St, is a lovely, restored circa 1750 B&B. Family owned and operated, its nine rooms each have private bath, phone and air-con. Prices range from $70 to $105 according to size and location. Breakfast features home baked breads and fresh fruits.

Thomas Bond House (☎ (215) 923-8523, (800) 845-2663), 129 S 2nd St, is a beautifully restored colonial house on the National Register of Historic Places. It has 12 period-furnished rooms, all with private bath. The rates vary, according to room size, from $80 to $125. A continental breakfast is served weekdays, a full breakfast at the weekend. Wine and cheese are served in the evening.

Hotels – Historic Philadelphia Choosing to stay in this location puts you within a few minutes' walk of 'America's most historic square mile.'

On the waterfront, *Comfort Inn at Penn's Landing* (☎ (215) 627-7900, (800) 228-5150), 100 N Christopher Columbus Blvd near the corner of Race St, has singles/doubles for $75/85, including continental breakfast, gym and free parking. *Penn's View Inn* (☎ (215) 922-7600, (800) 331-7634), at Front and Market Sts, overlooks the Delaware River. Some of the 27 rooms in this boutique property have fireplaces and Jacuzzis. Singles or doubles cost $89 to $165, including continental breakfast. It also has a renowned Italian restaurant and extensive wine bar.

Best Western Independence Park Inn (☎ (215) 922-4443, (800) 624-2988), 235 Chestnut St, has 36 designer-decorated rooms in a 19th century building. Singles or doubles with king-size beds cost $140; the price includes continental breakfast and afternoon tea.

Society Hill Hotel (☎ (215) 925-1919), 301 Chestnut St, has 12 rooms from $85 to $150 above a popular bar. The rooms are small and the breakfast (included in the price) is OK, but the cheerfully decorated rooms are quiet with fresh flowers and brass beds. The European atmosphere, friendly staff and location make this a good choice.

Hotels – Center City *Ramada Suites Convention Center* (☎ (215) 922-1730, (800) 228-2828), 1010 Race St, has 96 suites, a complimentary breakfast buffet and free validated parking. With a Chinatown location and close to the Convention Center, the hotel's larger-than-average rooms are attractively priced from $80/90.

Just off Rittenhouse Square, the grand *Warwick Philadelphia* (☎ (215) 735-6000), 1701 Locust St, features 200 spacious rooms furnished with old-world decor. Rooms are $145/160.

The popular *Doubletree Hotel Philadelphia* (☎ (215) 893-1600, (800) 222-8733), at Broad and Locust Sts, is a modern 25 story tower in a commercially and culturally active area. Facilities include an indoor swimming pool and health club. Singles or doubles cost from $135 to $155.

Embassy Suites Hotel (☎ (215) 561-1776, (800) 362-2779), 1776 Benjamin Franklin Pkwy, is near the parkway museums and other local sights. Featuring 288 complete suites with living room, kitchen area, wet bar, microwave, coffeemaker and separate bedroom, each suite has a balcony with city views. A cooked-to-order breakfast is included in the rates of $169/184.

Holiday Inn (☎ (215) 561-2556, (800) 465-4329), 1800 Market St, is within walking distance of the Convention Center, historic sights and stores. Its 445 rooms are often full. Singles/doubles are $140/150. The *Holiday Inn Express Midtown* (☎ (215) 735-9300, (800) 643-8696), 1305 Walnut St, is also near the Convention Center and business district with rooms starting from $135.

Hotels – University City *Sheraton University City Hotel* (☎ (215) 387-8000, (800) 325-3535), at S 36th and Chestnut Sts, is near the universities and four blocks from the Civic Center. It has 375 rooms with coffee service and there's an outdoor pool. Singles/doubles cost $89/99 to $125/135.

Places to Stay – top end
Historic Philadelphia The renovated *Holiday Inn – Independence Mall* (☎ (215) 923-8660, (800) 843-2355), 400 Arch St, is a modern eight story structure with singles or doubles from $150.

A luxury property featuring a health club with pool, Jacuzzi and sauna, the *Omni Hotel at Independence Park* (tel (215) 925-0000, (800) 843-6664), 401 Chestnut St, has 150 rooms with singles or doubles from $170. The large *Sheraton Society Hill* (☎ (215) 238-6000, (800) 325-3535), 1 Dock St, has 365 rooms, a four story atrium lobby, indoor pool and health club. Singles/doubles cost from $165/190.

Center City For old-world style on one of the city's most fashionable squares, try *The Barclay* (☎ (215) 545-0300, (800) 421-6662), 237 S 18th St, Rittenhouse Square East. Singles or doubles range from $155 to $185 during the week, but weekend rates are only $75, which must be one of the city's best deals. The intimate, European-style *Latham Hotel* (☎ (215) 563-7474, (800) 528-4261), 135 S 17th St, has 139 rooms, health club and pool, and is walking distance to shops and attractions. Rooms cost from $140.

Wyndham Franklin Plaza Hotel (☎ (215) 448-2000, (800) 996-3426), 2 Franklin Plaza at N 17th and Race Sts, is a massive complex offering health and sports facilities. It's 15 minutes' walk from the Convention Center or the shops on Walnut and Chestnut Sts and is close to the parkway museums. Singles/doubles are $155/175 to $195/215.

Hotel Atop the Bellevue (☎ (215) 893-1776, (800) 221-0833), 1415 Chancellor Court at S Broad St, occupies the top seven floors of the Bellevue Building, renowned for its French Renaissance facade. The beautifully refurbished, luxury, old-style rooms have good views and cost from $215 single or double.

Philadelphia boasts three deluxe properties. *Rittenhouse Hotel* (☎ (215) 546-9000, (800) 635-1042), 210 Rittenhouse Square West, occupies the first nine floors of this attractive building. The rooms feature floor-to-ceiling windows with city or square views. Singles/doubles cost $230/255.

The *Ritz-Carlton Hotel* (☎ (215) 563-1600, (800) 241-3333), at Chestnut and S 17th Sts, is part of the modern Liberty Place complex, but the interior has an elegant atmosphere of bygone days. Singles or doubles, with lower rates on lower floors, cost from $205 to $245. Possibly the city's best hotel, the *Four Seasons Hotel* (☎ (215) 963-1500, (800) 332-3442), 1 Logan Square near the Philadelphia Museum of Art, opened in 1983, but also has the feel of a much older place. Singles/doubles start from $240/300.

PLACES TO EAT

Eating is a definite highlight of a visit to Philadelphia. The city surprised a few people when its restaurants topped *Condé Nast Traveler* magazine's readers' poll of the country's finest. The city isn't only a winner in fine dining though.

Budget travelers can cook for themselves at a hostel or buy cheap food from one of the many street carts and there's terrific grocery shopping at South Philly's Italian Market and Center City's Reading Terminal Market. There are good restaurants where you spend $10 to $15, and many more great places to eat for under $25. (See also Coffeehouses under Entertainment, later.)

Philadelphia is famous for its cheesesteak sandwiches and hoagies, and the best places for these are mentioned below. Soft pretzels are another specialty – locals say that you should buy them from the Amish at Reading Terminal Market, they should be stuck together and rectangular or they're not the real thing, and you should eat them with mustard.

The Hoagie Sandwich
The hoagie got its name from the city's Hog Island Shipyard. The workers there used to call their lunch-time staple 'hoggies' before today's name stuck. ■

Historic Philadelphia & Around

Budget This is the heart of the tourist area so there aren't many budget places. *The Bourse*, on S 5th St beside the Liberty Bell Pavilion, has a large, elegant food court with counters selling Italian, Greek and Chinese food, cheesesteaks etc all in the $3 to $5 range. *Carousel Shoppe*, on S 3rd St near Walnut St, is a small luncheonette with a pretty storefront that serves a $1.35 breakfast, sandwiches for $2.85 and freshly squeezed lemonade.

Something Special, 114 N 3rd St, is a deli-restaurant serving roast chicken with rice or spaghetti for $4.95. To coincide with Monday night football games in the fall and winter, which you can watch here on TV, there's a $5.95 all-you-can-eat buffet.

In the Northern Liberties neighborhood to the north of the historic district, *Silk City Diner* (☎ (215) 592-8833), at Spring Garden and N 5th St, is a great 1940s diner. With a jukebox and tasty food, it's open from 7 am to midnight, Friday till 3 am, Saturday 24 hours. A cheesesteak or vegetable burger is $4.50, meatloaf with soup, mashed potatoes and gravy $7.50.

Moderate *Solo Mio* (☎ (215) 625-9820), 232 Arch St, decorated with local artists' work, is a tiny Italian restaurant serving tasty, reasonably priced specials for lunch and dinner. Spinach salad is $3.95 and mains like ravioli are around $14.95. The popular *Ristorante de Ghiottone*, 130 N 3rd St, has a range of pastas for less than $10 and sidewalk tables; it's a good idea to book for dinner.

For decent Mexican food or just a drink at the bar, try *Los Amigos* (☎ (215) 922-7061), 50 N 2nd St. It serves Mexican pizza from $4.25 and burritos for $11.

Popular with families, *DiNardo's Famous Seafood* (☎ (215) 925-5115), 312 Race St, is a branch of a Wilmington, DE, restaurant. Baltimore-style steamed crabs are the specialty, but the fish is also good. It's open Monday to Saturday for lunch and dinner, dinner only on Sunday. Main courses are between $10 and $20. Another good seafood place to try is *Philadelphia Fish & Co*

(☎ (215) 625-8605), 207 Chestnut St, with soups from $2.25 and roasted cod for $16.

Top End *City Tavern* (☎ (215) 413-1443), at S 2nd and Walnut Sts, is where Paul Revere arrived on horseback in 1774 with news of the British Parliament's closure of Boston Harbor. Today's building is a reconstruction of the original 1773 tavern popular with the political elite of the day. Presenting food that the Founding Fathers – and Mothers – would have eaten but 'adapted to modern tastes,' it's open daily. At lunch time wild mushroom bisque is $3.75, colonial turkey pie $8.75 with other mains that run up to $14.95; dinner mains are between $20 and $30. Reservations are recommended.

Old Original Bookbinders (☎ (215) 925-7027), 125 Walnut St at S 2nd opposite City Tavern, is a long-established Philadelphia landmark serving traditional seafood favorites like lobster and broiled fish. It's open for lunch and dinner Monday to Saturday, dinner only on Sunday. Expect to spend around $40 minimum; reservations are required.

South St & Around
Budget *Momi* (☎ (215) 625-0370), 526 S 4th St, is a clean diner serving tasty, inexpensive dishes – sandwiches $3 to $4, pizzas and spaghetti dishes $6.50. The menu lists a few of Momi's rules – 'keep your elbows off the table, chew your food, only order what you can eat' etc. It's closed Tuesday.

Mako – Retired Surfer's Bar & Grill (☎ (215) 625-3820), 301 South St, serves two dozen mussels for $5.95 and chicken wings from $4. It has a second bar upstairs. The small *Ishkabbible's Eatery* (☎ (215) 923-4337), 337 South St, is open for breakfast, lunch and dinner, serving savory, inexpensive dishes like chicken cheesesteak ($5.65) and vegetable cheeseburger ($4.75) and cookies baked on the premises. A top contender for Philadelphia's best cheesesteak honor is *Jim's Steaks* (☎ (215) 928-1911), 400 South St, where they cost from $4.15.

South St Souvlaki (☎ (215) 925-3026), 509 South St, is a terrific Greek taverna serving classic versions of gyros and souvlaki for $4.95, grilled fish ($10.95) and kebabs ($5). It has live Greek entertainment on Sunday nights. *Original South Philly Water Ice* (☎ (215) 629-1555), 506 South St, serves good-quality water ice, a local tradition. Burgers, hot dogs and sandwiches are also available.

Philadelphia Pizza Company (☎ (215) 627-3339), 418 South St, serves some of the city's best slices from $5.25 as well as pastas, hoagies, burgers and salads. *PhilaDeli* (☎ (215) 923-1986), 410 South St, is good for diner-type food, especially its all-day breakfast, hoagie sandwiches ($4.95), vegetable burgers ($4.95) and desserts.

A popular weekend brunch spot, *Montserrat* (☎ (215) 627-4224), 623 South St, is an established South St favorite for its varied menu offering items like potato and leek soup for $3.25, sautéed flounder $6.95 and meatloaf $8.95.

The *Pink Rose Pastry Shop* (☎ (215) 592-0565), 630 S 4th St at Bainbridge St, is great for carrot cake, muffins, cookies and coffee. It's closed Monday. The *Famous 4th St Deli* (☎ (215) 922-3274), at S 4th and Bainbridge Sts, is a long-established Jewish deli serving classic pastrami sandwiches and bagels for $5.95 and delicious homemade cookies (75¢ each). It's open for breakfast and lunch. *Alyan's* (☎ (215) 922-3553), 603 S 4th St, is an inexpensive Middle Eastern restaurant serving great hummus, falafel and delicious French fries.

Moderate Health-food restaurant *Essene* (☎ (215) 922-1146), 719 S 4th St, serves organically grown produce for lunch and dinner. Hummus is $4.95 and stir-fried tofu and vegetables $10.50. Entry is on Monroe St. *Cedars* (☎ (215) 925 4950), 616 S 2nd St, serves appetizing Lebanese favorites like falafel for $3.95, tabbouleh salad $4.95 and baked fish $10.95. *Russia House* (☎ (215) 629-4888), at No 614, is a tiny family-run restaurant serving Russian, Georgian and Ukrainian dishes. It's closed Sunday.

On the site of the birthplace of Larry Fine, one of the legendary Three Stooges comedy trio, *Jon's Bar & Grille* (☎ (215) 592-1390), 606 S 3rd at South St, has a pleasant outside dining area and a generally good, eclectic menu. A Mexican chili burger is $5.75, grilled chicken kebab $11.95.

Open for dinner only, *Judy's* (☎ (215) 928-1968), at S 3rd and Bainbridge Sts, is another Philly institution, serving terrific fish specials, spinach salad for $6.50, linguini $12 and classic American fare like roast pork chop for $12.50.

Top End To step out, try *Cafe NOLA* (☎ (215) 627-2590), 603 S 3rd St between South St and Bainbridge St, which serves delicious and acclaimed Creole specialties – the bananas Foster dessert is a dream.

Center City
Budget Pine St's Antique Row is home to some good-value options. *More Than Just Ice Cream* (☎ (215) 574-0586), 1141 Pine St, has good ice-cream sundaes for $3.75; apple pie, though a little pricey at $4.50, is good too. It's also a pleasant place for a meal, with huge portions. Further along, *Taco House* (☎ (215) 735-2240), 1218 Pine St, is a tiny Mexican shop serving quesadillas for $3.50 and enchiladas from $3.90. The food is always fresh at *Sabra* (☎ (215) 735-4424), 1240 Pine St, which offers tasty Middle Eastern dishes, with many priced around $5.

Caribou Cafe (☎ (215) 625-9535), 1126 Walnut St, is a French-style cafe with marble-topped tables and serving great croissants and muffins for breakfast. Lunch and dinner feature bistro-style fare – including vegetable lasagna ($8) and croque monsieur (a sandwich of French bread, ham and melted cheese) for $6.

The casual, Cajun *Magnolia Cafe* (☎ (215) 546-4180), 1602 Locust St, is in a pleasant townhouse setting; fried catfish is $8.50 and shrimp Creole $7.95. It has live jazz on Tuesday.

Reading Terminal Market This colorful indoor food market is one of your best bets for either groceries or delicious good-value eateries. Grab a free map and check out the selection. The market is open Monday to Saturday from 8 am to 6 pm, although many foodstalls start to close at 3 pm.

The Amish section is open Wednesday to Saturday only. *Fisher's Soft Pretzels & Ice Cream* (☎ (215) 592-8510) serves ice cream from $1.20 and perhaps the city's best pretzels.

Other popular choices include *Le Bus Bakery* (☎ (215) 592-0422), with great breads from $2 and pastries, muffins and other delights for $1.50; and *12th St Cantina* (☎ (215) 625-0321), with its homemade Mexican food, burritos for $3.05 and tacos for $1.20. Try *Olivieri's Prince of Steaks* (☎ (215) 625-9369) for terrific cheesesteaks at $3.60. *The Basic 4 Vegetarian Snack Bar* (☎ (215) 440-0991), serves vegetarian, natural foods and baked goods, including spinach pie for $2.80. *Bassett's Ice Cream* (☎ (215) 925-4315), extremely popular with the locals – despite, or because of, its ice-cream's high butterfat content – has single cones for $1.75.

There are many other good options, including Greek, Chinese, Japanese and Middle Eastern foodstalls.

Chinatown Chinatown has plenty of restaurants; there are some good choices for Vietnamese and vegetarian food as well as Chinese. The greatest concentration of restaurants is near the corner of Race and N 10th Sts.

The Vietnamese *Van's Garden* (☎ (215) 923-2438), 121 N 11th St at Cherry St, serves fried spring rolls for $3.25, shredded pork and rice ($6.25) and shrimp salad ($6.95). For vegetarian Chinese (certified kosher by the city's rabbis) *Cherry St* (☎ (215) 923-3663), 1010 Cherry St, has mock fish (a combination of taro root and wheat flour) in brown sauce for $8.95 or sautéed mixed vegetables $6.95. It also does seafood.

A good choice for Chinese non-vegetarian dishes is *Lee How Fook* (☎ (215) 925-7266), 219 N 11th St, with its sea bass and lemon chicken. It's closed Monday.

Another is the hole-in-the-wall *Joe's Peking Duck House* (☎ (215) 922-3277), 925 Race St; hot-and-sour soup of mushrooms and bean curd is $2.45 and noodles with seafood $7.50. *Riverside* (☎ (215) 923-4410), 234 N 9th St, is good for dim sum, like steamed stuffed bean curd for $6.95, fried wonton $2.75 and steamed dumpling $3.75.

Nothing special to look at, *Ray's Cafe* (☎ (215) 922-5122), 141 N 9th St, serves delicious Taiwanese food and an upscale gourmet coffee list. A lot of attention is paid to the coffee roasting, brewing process and presentation, using some of the world's finest beans. A cup costs $3.50 to $5 for most choices.

Moderate One of the city's best Mexican restaurants is *Tequila's* (☎ (215) 546-0181), 1511 Locust St; expect to pay about $30 for a three course meal.

Open for lunch and dinner in one of Philly's nicest residential neighborhoods, *Astral Plane* (☎ (215) 546-6230), 1708 Lombard St, features a varied menu in a casually decorated townhouse. At dinner, blue cheese and apple salad is $6.50, stuffed eggplant with vegetables and feta cheese $10.50.

Top End *The Garden* (☎ (215) 546-4455), 1617 Spruce St, serves superb European cuisine in an 1870 townhouse originally built for the Philadelphia Musical Academy. Beautifully decorated, it's one of the city's top restaurants and reservations are recommended. Mains are $15 to $25. It's closed on Sunday.

The elegant, good value *Ciboulette* (☎ (215) 790-1210), upstairs in the Bellevue complex at 200 S Broad St at Walnut St, features French Provincial cuisine. Main courses are $15 or less; smoked Atlantic salmon is $13, beef with wild mushrooms $14. Try to get a table with a Broad St view.

Le Bec-Fin (☎ (215) 567-1000), 1523 Walnut St, is, for many, reason enough to travel miles to the city. Rated by *Condé Nast Traveler* magazine readers as the country's top restaurant, classic French cuisine is served in its formal setting. It has a prix-fixe dinner menu of $95. The same food is served for a bit less in *Le Bar Lyonnais* downstairs. Book your table well in advance.

Earning almost as much praise, the Four Seasons Hotel's *The Fountain* (☎ (215) 963-1500), serves American/European cuisine. In addition, there's *Susanna Foo* (☎ (215) 545-2666), 1512 Walnut, a consistently top-rated restaurant serving Chinese specialties with New American inspiration.

South Philadelphia

Budget Visit the Italian Market, on S 9th St between Christian St and Washington Ave, and the area around it for the best prices for groceries, classic Philadelphia cheesesteaks, traditional Italian restaurants and some Vietnamese newcomers.

If you're buying groceries try *Isgro Pastries*, 1009 Christian St near the corner of 10th St, which has been here since 1904, for cakes and pastas; *D'Angelo Brothers*, 909 S 9th St for meat; *Claudio's*, 924-26 S 9th St, for cheese, salami and other Italian goods; and *Talluto's*, at S 9th St near Carpenter St, for varieties of pasta.

Two of Philadelphia's most popular cheesesteaks places are open 24 hours at the intersection of S 9th St and Passyunk Ave: *Geno's* (☎ (215) 389-1455) and *Pat's King of Steaks* (☎ (215) 468-1564). Both have cheesesteaks for $4.75 as well as other items like hot dogs and hoagies.

Villa Di Roma (☎ (215) 592-1295), 936 S 9th St, is plain looking, but serves good pasta with mains around $8.

At Christian and S 7th Sts, tasty water ice – called lemonhead regardless of its flavor – can be found at *John's Water Ice*, which has been serving the neighborhood since 1945. A cup of either lemon, cherry, chocolate or pineapple costs from 70¢. It's closed Tuesday.

Tu Do (☎ (215) 829-9122), 1030 S 8th St at League St near Washington Ave, serves good Vietnamese food in plain surroundings. Beef and rice-noodle soup is $2.85 and shrimp, beef and vegetables with rice is

$7.50. For Vietnamese and Chinese, try *Vinh Hoa* (☎ (215) 925-0307), around the corner at 746 Christian St (at S 8th St) which has beef and rice soup for $2.50 and chicken with black bean sauce for $6.25. Both serve lunch and dinner, have vegetarian options and close on Tuesday.

Moderate *Ralph's* (☎ (215) 627-6011), 760 S 9th St, is a decent Italian restaurant open for lunch and dinner. Ask for a table upstairs in the huge hall with traditional murals. Main courses like baked lasagna are in the $10 to $15 range.

The *Melrose Diner* (☎ (215) 467-6644), 1501 Snyder Ave, is a family-owned restaurant that's been serving American comfort food since 1935. According to some, it 'has its own culture' with vintage '70s interiors and an exciting history of mob-boss clientele.

Offering terrific value for the money, the popular, award-winning *Dmitri's* (☎ (215) 625-0556), 795 S 3rd St (at Catharine St), serves seafood fettucine ($12) and fried calamari ($12) and other Greek and Middle Eastern-style dishes for dinner. It has only 25 tables and doesn't take reservations, so be prepared to wait. Bring your own wine.

Walt's (☎ (215) 627-7701), 804 S 2nd St (at Catharine St), is a plain old seafood restaurant specializing in crabs for $20 – you walk through the bar to get to it at the back.

A South Philly classic, *Victor's Cafe* (☎ (215) 468-3040), 1303 Dickinson St near S 13th St, is renowned both for its Italian cuisine and opera-singing waitstaff. They are often students from the nearby Curtis School of Music or moonlighting professionals and regularly burst into song, performing operas and arias. Reservations are recommended. Mains are $13 to $20.

University City
Budget This student area has several inexpensive options. One of the bargain delights of Philadelphia are the numerous food carts lining the streets. Although there are some in Center City, the biggest concentration is in University City. Some places where you'll find lots of them are on the corners of S 36th and Walnut Sts, S 34th and Walnut Sts, S 32nd and Market Sts and along Market St between S 36th and S 34th Sts. Cheesesteaks are about $3, roast beef sandwiches $2.75, Chinese and Thai dishes $3.50.

The food court on the Market St side of 30th St Station offers a surprisingly good choice of eateries including Thai, Middle Eastern and Italian food. *Moishe's Bakery* has coffee and pastries ($1.50), and *Salumeria*, an Italian deli, has sandwiches for $2.25 and hoagies for $3.50.

Popular with students, *Le Bus* (☎ (215) 387-3800), 3402 Sansom St, is a bohemian cafeteria near the Penn campus, that once operated out of an actual bus. The basic, wholesome breakfasts, homemade soups, sandwiches, corn bread, muffins and pastries are delicious. A bowl of vegetarian chili soup is $3.45 and chicken salad $5.25.

Open daily, *American Diner* (☎ (215) 387 1451), 4201 Chestnut St, is a classic 1940s diner serving breakfast and decent omelets ($3.75), burgers ($4) and sandwiches ($4.50). It also has a great jukebox.

If you'd like something spicy, *Sitar India* (☎ (215) 662-0818), 60 S 38th St near Chestnut St, has an all-you-can-eat, daily lunch-time buffet for $5.95.

Moderate *White Dog Cafe* (☎ (215) 386-9224), 3420 Sansom St, in addition to being a good restaurant with a pleasant bar, is where owner Judy Wicks stages lectures and seminars on political issues. It serves New American food – which includes salmon burger for $9.50, tuna salad $9 and lemon sorbet with apricot sauce $5. It's open Monday to Saturday for lunch and dinner and has a popular Sunday brunch.

The *Palladium* (☎ 387-3463), 3601 Locust Walk, is in the middle of Penn's campus. Serving American cuisine, it's perhaps as well known for its cozy bar area, with a fireplace and couches.

ENTERTAINMENT

Philadelphia has something for everyone. With its rich arts program, Broad St south of City Hall has been transformed into Philly's premier cultural destination and called the Avenue of the Arts. South St is popular at night for a drink, a bite to eat, window shopping, listening to a band or people watching. Penn's Landing often has free plays or concerts. There are a number of popular night clubs on the waterfront along Christopher Columbus Blvd (Delaware Ave) north of the Benjamin Franklin Bridge – between midnight and 2 am on Friday and Saturday traffic jams are common.

For current events, check the *Weekend* section of Friday's *Philadelphia Inquirer* and the *Philadelphia Daily News* and the free weeklies *City Paper* and *Philadelphia Weekly*. Call the Performing Arts Hotline (☎ (215) 573-2787) for the latest schedule in theater, music and dance. Look for coupons for the free orchestral concerts in Fairmount Park. Also check Tower Records (open from 9 am to midnight daily) on South St for the latest music and dance-club happenings.

You can buy tickets for most entertainment from Ticketmaster (☎ (215) 336-2000), a computerized ticket service with locations around the city, or from Upstages at Philadelphia Arts Bank (☎ (215) 893-1145), 601 S Broad St. Upstages has another branch on the 2nd floor at Liberty Place, on S 16th and Chestnut Sts, where you can buy tickets for half-price on the day of the performance.

See also the Buying Tickets sidebar in the Facts for the Visitor chapter.

Theater

Philadelphia has a rich and varied theater scene. Productions range from Broadway shows in the major theaters to experimental drama in student repertory and community theaters. Prices for tickets run from as little as $5 to $10 in the smaller neighborhood theaters to between $15 and $60 or more for bigger productions in one of the main downtown theaters.

TONY WHEELER
Detail on the Philadelphia Museum of Art

Walnut St Theater (☎ (215) 574-3550), 825 Walnut St at 9th St, established in 1809, and *Merriam Theater* (☎ (215) 732-5446), 250 S Broad St, part of the Avenue of the Arts, stage mostly mainstream drama, dance and musical productions by local and touring companies. *Forrest Theater* (☎ (215) 923-1515), 1114 Walnut St, usually puts on big Broadway musical hits.

Philadelphia Arts Bank (☎ (215) 545-0590), 601 S Broad St, run by the University of the Arts, has a 230 seat theater with performances by local theater companies. The *Arden Theater Company* (☎ (215) 922-8900), presents works by both established and first-time playwrights in a new arts complex at N 2nd and Arch Sts.

Wilma Theater (☎ (215) 963-0345), 2030 Sansom St, provides good avant-garde drama and comedy. *Society Hill Playhouse* (☎ (215) 923-0210), 507 S 8th St, features contemporary drama, comedy and musicals. *Actors Center Theater* (☎ (215) 893-1145), 21 S 5th St at the Bourse, includes children's drama in its repertoire.

The *Annenberg Center* (☎ (215) 898-6791), 3680 Walnut St in University City, hosts performances by national and international artists as well as local companies. *Freedom Theater* (☎ (215) 765-2793),

1346 N Broad St, stages potent dramas drawing on the black-American experience.

Dance

If you're a ballet lover, the acclaimed Pennsylvania Ballet (☎ (215) 551-7224), 1101 S Broad St, is a must see. The company performs at the *Academy of Music* and *Merriam Theater* from September through June, including its popular annual production of Tchaikovsky's *Nutcracker* over Christmas. A subsidiary of the company is Off-Center Ballet, which experiments with new works.

The *Philadelphia Dance Company* (☎ (215) 483-8482), also known as Philadanco, explores the black experience through modern dance and ballet at the Annenberg Center and other venues. The company at the small *Koresh Dance Center* (☎ (215) 751-0959), 104 S 20th St, also puts on a range of performances from ballet to jazz.

Cinema

Philadelphia has a large selection of cinemas showing mainstream movies. Downtown, try the four-screen *Sameric* (☎ (215) 567-0604), 1908 Chestnut St. *Ritz Five* (☎ (215) 925-7900), 214 Walnut St in Society Hill, and *Ritz at the Bourse* (☎ (215) 440-1181), at S 4th and Ranstead Sts, show a mix of mainstream, limited-release and foreign films. Admission is $6.50 at both.

The 'arthouses,' *Film Forum* (☎ (215) 732-7704), 509 S Broad St at Lombard St, and *Roxy Theater* (☎ (215) 563-9088), 2021 Sansom St, show classic cult US and foreign films. *International House* (☎ (215) 855-6542), 3701 Chestnut St in University City, puts on first-run US films plus movies and documentaries from around the world; admission is $6.

Music

Penn's Landing features free summer concerts with various performances including blues, Latin, rock, jazz and big bands and the work of classical composers; call ☎ (215) 923-4992 for a current listing. You can also listen to recorded music in the music section of the Free Library of Philadelphia.

Classical & Opera The world-class Philadelphia Orchestra performs September through May at the *Academy of Music* (☎ (215) 893-1999), on S Broad St at Locust St; tickets cost from $12 to $78. It also does free evening concerts in a six week summer season at the *Mann Music Center* (☎ (215) 567-0707), George's Hill Dr near N 52nd St and Parkside Ave, in Fairmount Park.

Still in Fairmount Park, you can listen to chamber music at *Laurel Hill Mansion* (☎ (215) 235-1776), E Edgely Dr. After each recital there's a 'collation' – concert-goers gather to drink fruit punch and eat cakes.

Concerto Soloists of Philadelphia performs a series of evening concerts of chamber music at the *Walnut St Theater* (☎ (215) 574-3550), 825 Walnut St. Many of the city's musicians receive their training at the *Curtis Institute of Music* (☎ (215) 893-5261), 1726 Locust St, which has among its public offerings free student recitals during the academic year at 8 pm on Monday, Wednesday and Friday.

November to April, the Opera Company of Philadelphia (☎ (215) 928-2100), 30 S 15th St, puts on large-scale operas with international stars at the *Academy of Music*. The Pennsylvania Opera Theater (☎ (215) 731-1212) is a company that performs in English at the *Merriam Theater* (☎ (215) 732-5446), 250 S Broad St. Another company, The Academy of Vocal Arts Opera Theater (☎ (215) 735-1685), performs at various venues in and around Philadelphia.

Jazz & Blues Philadelphia has a strong jazz and blues tradition, its own sound and some terrific venues. The *Philadelphia Clef Club of the Performing Arts* (☎ (215) 893-9912), at S Broad and Fitzwater Sts, is part of the Avenue of the Arts. It promotes jazz by hosting public performances, keeping records of its history and training musicians. Jazz, blues and gospel programs are also organized by the Mill Creek Jazz & Cultural Society at the *The Loft at Milk Creek* (☎ (215) 473-4273), Mill Creek Community Center, 4624 Lancaster Ave in

West Philadelphia. Pick up the society's *Jazz Philadelphia* and *Gospel Philadelphia*, available free at the Philadelphia Visitors Center in JFK Plaza.

Some of the best jazz is at the upmarket *Zanzibar Blue* (☎ (215) 829-0300), 301 S 11th St. There are two jazz rooms and a dining room serving international cuisine. You don't have to eat, but there's a two drink minimum per set and sometimes a cover charge of around $10.

More down to earth, *Ortleib's Jazz Haus* (☎ (215) 922-1035), 847 N 3rd St, is in an old brewery in a rundown neighborhood. It serves Cajun and American food and there's no cover charge; parking is free. Tuesday night is a popular jam session when audience members join in. *23rd St Cafe* (☎ (215) 561-2488), 23 N 23rd St, also has a jam session on Tuesday night for local musicians. *Chris' Jazz Cafe* (☎ (215) 568-3131), 1421 Sansom St, has live sessions upstairs every night with no cover charge.

You can enjoy free jazz at *Reading Terminal Market* on Fridays from noon to 2 pm.

South St Blues (☎ (215) 546-9009), 2100 South St, is a bar that's been around a long time with live traditional blues nightly. A relative newcomer, *Warmdaddy's* (☎ (215) 627-2500), 4 S Front St, is a popular, upscale blues club-*cum*-restaurant serving Southern-style food with live music Wednesday to Sunday; closed Monday.

Gospel Philadelphia has a strong tradition in Gospel singing and regular concerts are organized by the Mill Creek Jazz & Cultural Society at the *The Loft at Milk Creek* (☎ (215) 473-4273), Mill Creek Community Center, 4624 Lancaster Ave in West Philadelphia. Singing also takes place in churches around the city and a list of these is given in *Gospel Philadelphia*, available free from the Philadelphia Visitors Center in JFK Plaza.

Rock *Khyber Pass* (☎ (215) 440-9683), 56 S 2nd St, is a small venue popular with college students, where you can see unsigned bands for a cover charge of around $5. Bigger-name acts perform at the *Trocadero* (see Dance Clubs, below) with a $10 to $15 cover charge. Part of the Silk City Diner, *Silk City Lounge* (☎ (215) 592-8838), Spring Garden and N 5th Sts, is a bar-lounge featuring live bands or DJs. It has something happening most nights; there's no cover during the week, but cover is about $5 Friday and Saturday nights.

In summer, the waterfront north of Benjamin Franklin Bridge is the center of Philadelphia nightlife. Some clubs are seasonal, so call ahead. *Maui* (☎ (215) 423-8116), Pier 53, 1143 N Christopher Columbus Blvd, is one of the biggest with alternative live music nightly. Centered around an old ferryboat, *Katmandu* (☎ (215) 629-1101), at No 417, has classic rock in a Caribbean atmosphere. A water taxi takes people between the clubs and is safer than negotiating Christopher Columbus Blvd on foot.

Mann Music Center (☎ (215) 567-0707), George's Hill Dr near N 52nd St and Parkside Ave, Fairmount Park, is the city's top outdoor venue. Major acts perform there during the summer, while the biggest of them play Veterans Stadium (see below, ☎ (215) 686-1776) or CoreStates Spectrum Stadium (see below, ☎ (215) 336-3600) both in South Philadelphia.

Check the current schedule at *Fels Planetarium*, in the Franklin Institute Science Museum (☎ (215) 448-1200), where laser shows feature the recorded music of bands like Pink Floyd, Aerosmith and U2.

Dance Clubs

In a former warehouse, *Milkbar Bar & Dancehall* (☎ (215) 928-6455), 417 N 8th St, is a trendy nightspot popular with the under-30s, featuring local and interstate techno and jazz artists. *Circa* (☎ (215) 545-6800), 1518 Walnut St, is possibly Center City's hottest nightspot; on Friday and Saturday night after a reasonably priced meal you can strut to '70s music. There's a $5 cover charge after 10 pm.

In Chinatown, *Trocadero* (☎ (215) 923-7625), 1003 Arch St, has dancing to the latest rock bands with admission from $6. In University City, *Chestnut Cabaret*

☎ (215) 382-1201), 3801 Chestnut St, offers a variety of dancing options from reggae to rock. *Woody's* (☎ (215) 545-1893), 202 S 13th St, is a popular gay bar and dance club.

Bars
Most of Philly's bars stay open till 2 am. See also Brewpubs. In Old City, *Jake & Oliver's* (☎ (215) 627-4825), 22 S 3rd St, is a trendy, cavernous pub selling 60 microbrews ($3 per pint) on tap, serving food and offering live blues music on Sunday afternoons. Towards South St in Head House Square are *The Artful Dodger*, 400-402 S 2nd St, and the *Dickens Inn*, at No 421. Both pubs serve British-style food and imported ales.

Downey's (☎ (215) 625-9500), 526 Front St at South St, is a beautiful Irish place with furnishings imported from the old country. It serves decent food and has a rooftop deck and balcony overlooking the Delaware River. *JC Dobbs* (☎ (215) 928-1943), 304 South St, a popular live-music bar, features rock and blues with a cover charge of around $5. Other options include *Cop Banana Cabana*, at S 4th and South Sts; *Mako – Retired Surfer's Bar & Grill* (☎ (215) 625-3820), 301 South St; and *Xero* (☎ (215) 629-0565), 613 S 4th St.

On Antique Row, at Pine and S 13th Sts, *Dirty Frank's* (☎ (215) 732-5010) is a real dive, with boarded up windows and no sign (look for the plain gray door), but it's a local institution. It has the cheapest booze in town and an interesting mix of patrons, including writers and artists.

In University City *New Deck Tavern* (☎ (215) 386-4600), 3408 Sansom St just up from Le Bus, is a popular student hangout. Try also *Murphy's Tavern* (☎ 349-8400), on Spruce St at 44th St, a dive bar attracting an entertaining mix of students and local residents.

Brewpubs
Philly has two microbreweries. *Samuel Adams Brew House* (☎ (215) 563-2326), 1516 Sansom St, is 'Philadelphia's first brewery since Prohibition.' With a bar and

restaurant upstairs, it also has rock/blues live music. A pint of one of the house brews costs $3.75. It's closed on Sunday. *Dock St Brewing Company* (☎ (215) 496-0413), 2 Logan Square, (at N 18th and Cherry Sts), offers a contemporary setting and jazz or Latin American music on weekends.

Coffeehouses
Old City Coffee, 221 Church St in Old City, is an attractive place to stop for good brewed coffee, cookies or a salad. In the South St area, *Cafe Santa Maria*, 517 S 5th St at Gaskill St, serves homemade biscotti and has books and magazines to peruse. The *Morning Cup*, 422 S 2nd St on Head House Square, is another good source.

In South Philadelphia, *Anthony's Italian Coffee House*, 903 S 9th St, is a small cafe serving good cakes and coffee. It has live music on weekends, small art exhibitions and poetry readings.

Bucks County (☎ (215) 387-6722), 3430 Sansom St in University City, has good coffee and pastries.

SPECTATOR SPORTS
Philadelphia's professional and college sports teams enjoy an enthusiastic following. The two major venues, Veterans Stadium and the indoor CoreStates Spectrum, are at the southern end of South Philadelphia on S Broad St. Tickets can be bought from Ticketmaster (☎ (215) 336-2000). Admission to baseball and hockey games varies from $5 to $20, and to football and basketball games from $15 to $50.

The sports complex is easily reached by subway on the SEPTA Broad St Line to Pattison Ave station which is within walking distance, or by bus C along Broad St. By car take exit 14 off I-95 or the Broad St southbound exit off I-76.

Veterans Stadium
With a 60,000 capacity, this is home to the Philadelphia Phillies National League baseball team, the Philadelphia Eagles, members of the National Football League, and the Temple University Owls football team. The annual Army-Navy football

game is played here and major rock concerts are sometimes staged here, too. Tickets for the Phillies' games are difficult to get (fans are not just fair-weather friends) and the best seats for Eagles' games are taken by season-ticket holders. The Phillies box office (☎ (215) 463-1000), open Monday to Friday from 9 am to 8 pm, and the Eagles box office (☎ (215) 463-5500), open Monday to Friday from 9 am to 5 pm, are both at 3501 S Broad St.

CoreStates Spectrum Stadium

This indoor arena seats 18,000 and is home to the NBA's Philadelphia 76ers (the 'Sixers') and the NHL's Philadelphia Flyers. Other big events are held here, too, including the US Pro Indoor Tennis Championships and concerts. Unless the home team is in with a chance of reaching the play-offs, you can usually buy a ticket on the day of the game. The box office (☎ (215) 336-3600), at Pattison Ave and S Broad St, is open Monday to Friday from 9 am to 6 pm, weekends from 10 am to 4:30 pm

A new stadium seating 20,000, Spectrum II, is being built and will connect to the CoreStates Spectrum by a tunnel; it'll be the new home for the Flyers and Sixers.

Franklin Field

In University City at Walnut and S 33rd Sts, Franklin Field is part of the University of Pennsylvania's sports facilities. It hosts the Penn Relays world-class amateur athletic meet each April as well as Penn's football games and other sporting events.

THINGS TO BUY

Philadelphia's main shopping districts are along Market, Walnut and Chestnut Sts east of Broad St, but South St, Reading Terminal Market and Italian Market are also worth visiting. Check the *Weekend* section of Friday's *Philadelphia Inquirer* for listings of antique fairs and art galleries.

Antique Row, along Pine St between S 9th and S 12th Sts, offers some wonderful items in its many antique stores. Additionally, several stores sell handcrafted and estate jewelry, collectibles, books and various items from around the world. Indigo Gallery, 1102 Pine St, has ethnic art, jewelry and household items from Asia, Africa and the Americas. Maidie Franklin Designs, 1106 Pine St, sells handmade Edwardian, Victorian and contemporary jewelry. Both are closed on Monday.

Walnut St in Center City has several commercial art galleries. Newman Galleries (☎ (215) 563-1779), 1625 Walnut St, is one of the oldest in Philadelphia, displaying works of local and national artists. Old City's galleries are concentrated on N 3rd St around Cherry and Race Sts. The FAN Gallery (☎ (215) 922-5155), 311 Cherry St, has regular exhibitions of contemporary artists.

The main center for jewelry is Jewelers' Row, on and around Sansom St between S 7th and S 8th Sts, where you'll find dozens of craftspeople, wholesalers and retailers. Some substantial discounts are available on metal jewelry and precious stones.

The South St area has a variety of interesting shopping. For music, Tower Records has two stores: one branch (☎ (215) 574-9888) is at No 610 while the other (☎ (215) 925-0422) selling classical music is over the road at No 537; both are open till midnight. Philadelphia Record Exchange (☎ (215) 925-7892), 608 S 5th St, is a long-established source of alternative rock with old 45s and LPs as well as CDs; Digital Underground (☎ (215) 925-5324), 526 S 5th St, specializes in new and used CDs, with an emphasis on independent artists; both are open daily.

South St Antiques Market (☎ (215) 592-0256), 615 S 6th St, in a former synagogue, houses a selection of vintage clothing, jewelry, furniture and other items. It's open Wednesday to Thursday and Sunday from noon to 7 pm, Friday and Saturday noon to 8 pm. Eyes Art Gallery (☎ (215) 925-0193), 402 South St, in a gift shop carrying a selection of exotic jewelry and handicrafts from third world sources.

Philadelphia's two most notable department stores are John Wanamaker (☎ (215) 422-2000), on Market St between Juniper and S 13th Sts, and Strawbridge & Clothier

(☎ (215) 629-6000), on Market St between N 8th and N 9th Sts. Strawbridge & Clothier is connected to The Gallery at Market East, a large shopping mall housing two more department stores, JC Penney (☎ (215) 238-9100) and Clover (☎ (215) 928-9544), other shops and a good food court. Two other large shopping malls are the modern Shops at Liberty Place (☎ (215) 851-9055), 2 Liberty Place, at S 16th and Market Sts, and the elegant Shops at The Bellevue (☎ (215) 875-8350), at S Broad and Walnut Sts.

Family-run, nationally renowned Fante's Cookware (☎ (215) 878-5557), 1006 S 9th St in the Italian Market, has operated since 1906 and sells everything for the cook from wooden spoons to copper utensils.

GETTING THERE & AWAY
Air
Philadelphia international airport (☎ (215) 492-3181) is served by direct flights from Europe, the Caribbean and Canada, and offers connections to Asia, Africa and South America. Domestically, it has flights to over 100 destinations in the USA. (See also the introductory Getting There & Away and Getting Around chapters.)

The following airlines have offices in the Philadelphia area:

Air Jamaica
  210 Goddard Blvd, King of Prussia
  (☎ (610) 265-7605, (800) 523-5585)
Alitalia
  2 Penn Center Plaza (☎ (215) 569-1245)
Atlantic Air
  Philadelphia International Airport
  (☎ (215) 365-7270)
British Airways
  1617 JFK Blvd (☎ (800) 247-9297)
Continental Airlines
  Philadelphia International Airport
  (☎ (215) 592-8005)
Delta Air Lines
  1617 JFK Blvd (☎ (215) 928-1700)
  1 Penn Center Plaza (☎ (215) 928-1700)
Korean Air
  2 Penn Center Plaza (☎ (215) 665-9080)
Midway Airlines
  Philadelphia International Airport
  (☎ (215) 492-4200)

Spirit Airlines
  Philadelphia International Airport
  (☎ (215) 563-7799)
Swissair
  Philadelphia International Airport
  (☎ (215) 492-3988)
USAir
  123 S Broad St (☎ (215) 563-8055)
  1617 JFK Blvd (☎ (215) 563-8055)
United Airlines
  123 S Broad St (☎ (800) 241-6522)
  1617 JFK Blvd (☎ (800) 241-6522)

Other airlines that fly to Philadelphia are Midwest Express (☎ (800) 452-2022), America West (☎ (800) 235-9292) and Northwest Airlines (☎ (800) 225-2525 domestic; (800) 447-4747 international) and TWA (☎ (800) 221-2000 domestic, (800) 892-4141 international).

The airport has five terminals labeled A through E. All international flights arrive at Terminal A, but USAir international departures leave from Terminal C. Terminals B and C are used by USAir for domestic departures and arrivals, while Terminals D and E are used by other domestic carriers.

There's an information desk and an ATM (MAC) in every terminal, while Terminals A, B and C each have a currency-exchange office. Terminals A and C also have a self-service postal counter for domestic mail. In Terminal A beside the ground-transportation desk there's a bank of TV monitors listing the type of local transport available, airport contact number, destination and approximate cost.

The standard roundtrip airfare to Pittsburgh starts from $118, New York City $158 and Atlantic City $138. See also the Getting Around chapter.

Bus
Philadelphia has two inter-city bus terminals close to each other in Center City. Greyhound bus terminal (☎ (800) 231-2222) is at 1001 Filbert St at N 10th St; NJ Transit (☎ (215) 569-3752, (800) 228-8246) also has a desk here. Left-luggage lockers cost $2 for up to six hours.

The Peter Pan Trailways terminal (☎ (800) 343-9999) is at N 11th St; Capitol Trailways (☎ (800) 444-2877) buses also stop here.

The one-way fare to New York City is $13 (2½ hours), to Atlantic City $10 (1½ hours), to Washington, DC $15 (three hours), to San Francisco $139 (27½ hours). There's no inter-city bus to Jersey City, but you can catch one to Newark then take NJ Transit. See also the Getting There & Away chapter.

Train

Amtrak (☎ (800) 872-7245) trains stop at 30th St Station on Market St beside the Schuylkill River in University City. Philadelphia is on Amtrak's Northeast Corridor route which runs between Richmond, VA, and Boston, MA, via Washington, DC, and New York City; there are also trains west to Lancaster, Harrisburg, Altoona, Pittsburgh and Chicago and south to Florida.

The ticket office is open Monday to Friday from 5:10 am to 10:45 pm, weekends 6:10 am to 10:45 pm. Baggage storage is available for $1.50 per item per day. There's a Travelers' Aid Society desk in case of emergency – call ☎ (215) 546-0571 if no one's there.

To New York City (2½ hours) the unreserved one-way fare is $30 while the one-way Metroliner fare is $65; to Washington, DC, (2¼ hours) it's $28 and $68 respectively. There are numerous fares to Pittsburgh depending on the day and time you travel – the roundtrip fare ranges from $74 to $134.

A cheaper but slightly longer way to get to New York City is to take the SEPTA suburban train to Trenton ($6) in New Jersey, where you connect with NJ Transit to Newark's Penn Station and continue on NJ Transit to New York City's Penn Station.

NJ Transit (☎ (215) 569-3752, (800) 228-8246) has a frequent rail service between Philadelphia and Atlantic City (about 1½ hours) for $6 one way.

Subway

The Port Authority Transit Corporation (PAT, ☎ (215) 922-4600) has frequent Hi-Speedline subway trains to Camden, NJ, for 75¢. City stops are: 15th-16th St Station, 11th-12th St Station and 9th-10th St Station along Locust St, and 8th St Station at Market St. Then it's a scenic ride across the Benjamin Franklin Bridge to Camden.

Car & Motorcycle

Several highways lead through and around Philadelphia. From the north and south, I-95 (Delaware Expressway) follows the eastern edge of the city beside the Delaware River, with several exits for midtown.

The Pennsylvania Turnpike (I-276) runs east across the north of the city and over the river to connect with the New Jersey Turnpike.

From the west, I-76 (Schuylkill Expressway) branches off the Pennsylvania Turnpike to follow the Schuylkill River to South Philadelphia and over the Walt Whitman Bridge into New Jersey. Just north of downtown I-676 (Vine St Expressway) heads east over the Benjamin Franklin Bridge into Camden, NJ. If you're coming from the east, take I-295 or the New Jersey Turnpike, which connects to I-676 over the Benjamin Franklin Bridge into downtown.

Like any big city, Philadelphia traffic 'enjoys' morning and evening peak hours. To avoid the worst of these use I-676, which leads under the busier city streets to Old City.

Boat

A ferry service operates across the Delaware River from Penn's Landing (see that section earlier) to the New Jersey State Aquarium in Camden.

GETTING AROUND
To/From the Airport

Philadelphia international airport (☎ (215) 492-3181), eight miles southwest of Center City, is easily accessed on SEPTA's (☎ (215) 580-7800) R1 airport rail line, which operates daily every 30 minutes from 5:25 am to midnight and takes about 20 minutes. The R1 can be boarded at Market East, Suburban, 30th St or University City stations; the one-way fare is $5, but there's a $2 surcharge if you buy a ticket on the train.

Shuttle-bus and limousine services also operate between the airport and the city. The cheaper ones cost only a few dollars more than the train and take you door to door. A shuttle to Center City costs about $8 to $12, to University City $8 to $10. Some to try are Lady Liberty Airport Shuttle (☎ (215) 222-8888), Airport Express (☎ (215) 745-8519), Philadelphia Airport Shuttle (☎ (215) 969-1818) or Airport-Limelight Limousine (☎ (215) 342-5557).

Taxis to Center City cost about $20 to $25, to University City $15 to $17, and take about 20 to 25 minutes.

Bus

The Southeastern Pennsylvania Transportation System (SEPTA) provides comprehensive transportation service in the city and suburbs. SEPTA's information line (☎ (215) 580-7800) is open daily from 6 am to midnight. The one-way fare on most routes is $1.60 for which you'll need the exact change or a token. SEPTA's DayPass gives you a day's unlimited riding on all city transit vehicles plus a one-way trip on the R1 airport rail line. It costs $6 and is available at regional rail stations, SEPTA sales outlets or the Philadelphia Visitors Center at 16th St and JFK Blvd. Transit maps can be bought at the visitors center for $3.95.

The bus No 76 route (punningly known as the 'Ben FrankLine') runs from Penn's Landing, through the Society Hill/South St area, along Market St to City Hall and the Benjamin Franklin Pkwy to the Philadelphia Museum of Art, Fairmount Park and the zoo. For only 50¢ you get to see many of the major sights and it leaves every 10 minutes Monday to Friday, every 20 minutes on weekends. Bus No 42 is another useful service that connects Old City with

the Civic Center and University City in West Philadelphia.

PHLASH (☎ (215) 474-5274) is a bus-shuttle that does a loop through downtown from Spring Garden St in the north to South St, and from Christopher Columbus Blvd (Delaware Ave) in the east to Logan Square in the west. It operates daily from 10 am to midnight. The normal one-way fare is $1.50 but on Wednesday it's $1; a day pass is $3.

Trolley Bus

Motorized trolley buses are a pleasant way to visit many of the sights. See Penn's Landing and Organized Tours, earlier.

Train

Philadelphia's rail network is run by SEPTA (☎ (215) 580-7800) and connects downtown with the suburbs and surrounding counties. Seven major routes are divided into six fare zones radiating from the city. One-way fares range from $3 to $6 during peak periods; off-peak fares are 50¢ to 75¢ cheaper. The main downtown stations are 30th St Station in University City, Penn Center Suburban Station at JFK Blvd and N 16th St, and Market East Station at Market and N 10th Sts beneath The Gallery shopping complex.

Useful routes are R7 to Germantown and Chestnut Hill East, R8 to Chestnut Hill West and R1 to the airport.

Subway

SEPTA operates three subway lines in Philadelphia. The Market-Frankford line runs east-west along Market St from 69th St in West Philadelphia to Front St from where it heads north to Frankford. The Broad St line runs north-south from Fern Rock in North Philadelphia to Pattison Ave in South Philadelphia near the Veterans and CoreStates Spectrum sports stadiums. The Subway-Surface line heads east-west along Market St from 13th St Station near City Hall to 33rd St, from where it forks to the northwest and southwest.

TONY WHEELER

Benjamin Franklin Parkway seen from the Philadelphia Museum of Art

TOM SMALLMAN

City Hall, Philadelphia

TOM SMALLMAN

Fountain, Logan Circle, Philadelphia

Old City, Philadelphia

Chinese Friendship Gate, Chinatown, Philly

Elfreth's Alley, Old City, Philadelphia

The PATCO (☎ (215) 922-4600) subway line to Camden, NJ, is a convenient, cheap way of getting across downtown (75¢).

Car & Motorcycle

Driving isn't recommended in central Philadelphia; parking is difficult and regulations are strictly enforced. Anyway, downtown distances are short enough to let you see most places on foot, and a bus or taxi can get you to places further out relatively easily. Park your car in a guarded lot and save it for trips out of the city or for evening trips; when booking a room with a hotel ask about its parking facilities.

If you want to cross downtown east-west, remember that the Vine St Expressway runs under the city streets and will save you a lot of time. Most downtown streets have alternate one-way traffic. The exceptions are Broad St with three lanes in both directions, Vine St, Benjamin Franklin Pkwy and Market St between City Hall and Front St and west of 20th St (between 20th and 15th Sts it's one way eastbound). Chestnut St is closed to traffic between 8th and 18th Sts.

Avoid South St on the weekend and every evening as the traffic jams are notorious; also avoid Christopher Columbus Blvd (Delaware Ave) north of the Benjamin Franklin Bridge on weekend evenings.

Car Rental The main rental companies have desks at the airport (in addition to the offices listed below). Typical weekday rental rates for a compact car are $50 per day plus $9 insurance with unlimited mileage; weekend rates are cheaper, as are week-long rates. Some of the main rental companies in Philadelphia are:

Avis
    200 Arch St (☎ (800) 831-2847)
    30th St Station (☎ (800) 831-2847)
Budget
    Corner of 21st and Market Sts
    (☎ (215) 492-9400)
Dollar
    Philadelphia International Airport
    (☎ (215) 365-2700)

Express
    4100 Presidential Blvd (☎ (215) 871-4227)
Hertz
    31 S 19th St (☎ (800) 654-3131)
    30th St Station (☎ (800) 654-3131)

There are many other local and specialist rental companies, which are listed in the yellow pages under 'Automobile Renting;' some offer competitive rates compared to the national companies.

Taxi

Philadelphia's cabs are carefully regulated. Downtown and in University City you can hail a cab easily enough during the day especially at 30th St Station, other train stations and around the major hotels. At night and in the suburbs you're better of phoning for one.

Get a free copy of *Taxi Talk* from the Philadelphia Visitors Center or your cab driver; it lists standard fares to hotels and restaurants, along with other useful information about the city. Some cabs accept credit cards. Fares are $1.80 for the first one-sixth of a mile, then 30¢ for each subsequent one-sixth plus 20¢ for every minute of waiting time. The fare from University City to Penn's Landing is about $7.

Some cab companies to try are:

Academy Cab
    8125 Frankford Ave (☎ (215) 333-3333)
Olde City Taxi
    6958 Torresdale Ave (☎ (215) 338-0838)
United Cab Association
    444 N 4th St (☎ (215) 238-9500)

Bicycle

Philadelphia isn't a bad place to get around by bicycle as it's reasonably flat, but there are few cycle lanes. Fairmount Park, however, has popular recreational-cycling paths. See the Activities section, earlier, for more details and for information about bike rentals. If you'd like to bicycle outside the city, you can take your bike on off-peak SEPTA and PATCO trains with a valid permit, available from ticket offices.

Around Philadelphia

VALLEY FORGE
NATIONAL HISTORIC PARK

This 5½ sq mile park, 20 miles northwest of downtown Philadelphia at N Gulph Rd and Route 23, was the site of the Continental army's renowned winter encampment from December 19, 1777, to June 19, 1778, while the British occupied Philadelphia. Not a battlefield, the site is held as a symbol of bravery and endurance – 2000 of George Washington's 12,000 troops perished because of freezing temperatures, hunger and disease. Despite such losses, the army was reorganized and emerged to eventually defeat the British.

For a travel brochure on Valley Forge and Montgomery County, contact the Valley Forge Convention & Visitors Bureau (☎ (610) 834-1550, (800) 345-8112), 600 W Germantown Pike, Plymouth Meeting, PA 19462; it also operates a 24 hour Funline (☎ (610) 834-8844) with a recorded message that details upcoming special events.

The visitors center (☎ (610) 783-1077) contains exhibits and an information desk with maps and brochures highlighting the park's major points of interest and the area's other attractions. There's also a 15 minute film, *Valley Forge: A Winter Encampment*. Costumed reenactments of the Continental army's training procedures are staged occasionally during warmer weather. If you have a car, you can get a map from the visitors center and take a 10 mile self-guided tour of the park. There are also organized bus tours from the visitors center.

The park is open daily from 8:30 am to 5 pm and admission to the site and visitors center is free.

Things to See

Important sights include the **National Memorial Arch** to the soldiers who endured that winter and the **Monument to Patriots of African Descent**, a bronze statue honoring the 5000 blacks who died in the war. **Isaac Potts House**, built in 1774, was used as Washington's headquarters and is furnished with period reproductions. It's open daily from 9:30 am to 5 pm; the $2/1 admission includes a short tour. The **Valley Forge Historical Society Museum** (☎ (610) 783-0535), Route 23, houses items that belonged to George and Martha Washington, as well as other artifacts from the encampment. It's open Monday to Saturday from 9:30 am to 4 pm, Sunday 1 to 4:30 pm. Admission is $2/1. The **Washington Memorial Chapel** built in 1903 is nearby.

Getting There & Away

From Philadelphia you can board SEPTA bus No 125 at the corner of N 16th St and JFK Blvd or at 30th St Station. On Saturday it only goes as far as King of Prussia Plaza, from where you catch bus No 99. Alternatively, you can catch bus No 45 from town to King of Prussia Plaza, then take bus No 99. The trip takes about 40 minutes and costs $6. There's no bus to the park on Sunday.

By car take the I-76 (Schuylkill Expressway) west to exit 25, then follow Route 363 to N Gulph Rd and follow the signs. Following the Pennsylvania Turnpike (I-276) west across the north of the city, take exit 24 to Route 363.

WASHINGTON CROSSING
HISTORIC PARK

This park (☎ (215) 493-4076), PO Box 103, Washington Crossing, PA 18977, is in **Bucks County**, northeast of Philadelphia. It marks the site where George Washington's army crossed the Delaware River into New Jersey on Christmas night, 1776, to surprise and defeat an encampment of Hessian mercenaries of the British army at Trenton. It was a turning point in the war. A reenactment of the crossing takes place every Christmas.

The park is divided into two parts, separated by the Delaware River – the eastern half is in New Jersey (see the Central New

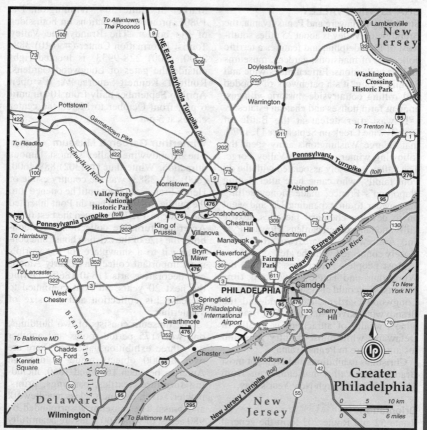

Jersey chapter). The visitors center, in the lower park, has a short film on the events. Nearby, **McConkey Ferry Inn** is where Washington dined before the crossing. In the upper park the 110 foot **Bowman's Hill Tower** affords a great view of the Delaware Valley. Washington had used the hill as a lookout. Admission to the tower is $2.50/2. To the north of the tower is a **wildflower preserve** (☎ (215) 493-4076) housing numerous species of plants native to Pennsylvania.

Admission to the grounds and visitors center is free. A 45 minute tour of the historic

buildings is $2.50/1, seniors $2. The park is open daily from 9 am to sunset, the buildings are open Monday to Saturday from 9 am to 5 pm and Sunday noon to 5 pm.

About seven miles north of the park, the historic town of **New Hope** is home to many artists and craftspeople.

Getting There & Away

There's no public transportation to the park, but the SEPTA R3 train stops at Yardley about five miles south. By car, take I-95 north from Philadelphia to exit 31 and follow Route 32 north for three miles.

BRANDYWINE VALLEY

Straddling Delaware and Pennsylvania, the Brandywine Valley is about 25 miles southwest of Philadelphia, and features a terrific collection of mansions, gardens, museums and art collections. Fifteen miles wide and 35 miles long, it's a patchwork of wooded and rolling countryside, historic villages, ancient farm houses and chateau estates.

It was after defeat at the Battle of Brandywine Creek on September 11, 1777, that George Washington's army spent the following winter camped at Valley Forge. The valley is closely associated with the du Pont family, who came here after fleeing Napoleon's France, made money selling gunpowder to an expanding US and went on to develop chemical factories, textile mills and landscaped gardens. Howard Pyle and Andrew Wyeth are two artists also closely connected with the area.

Most people's 'must sees' include the Winterthur and Hagley estates; if time permits, you could also stop in at Nemours, Longwood Gardens, Rockwood and the Brandywine River Museum. The Brandywine's wealth of attractions is mostly in Delaware, while most country inns and restaurants are in Pennsylvania.

Christmas exhibitions and events at most Brandywine Valley museums run from Thanksgiving through New Year's Day.

Orientation

Route 52 and Route 202 form the general eastern and western borders of the Brandywine Valley, which is accessible from Wilmington, DE; from Philadelphia, Route 1 heads southwest to Chadds Ford, Brandywine Battlefield Park and Longwood Gardens. I-95 goes to Wilmington. Route 52 connects Route 1 and I-95.

There's no public transportation from Philadelphia to the area, but Greyhound and Amtrak have frequent daily departures to nearby Wilmington in Delaware. You'll need your own transport to get around.

Information

The Greater Wilmington Convention & Visitors Bureau (☎ (302) 652-4088, 1300 Market St, Suite 504, Wilmington, DE 19801, promotes attractions on both sides of the border. The Brandywine Valley Tourist Information Center (☎ (610) 388-2900, (800) 228-9933) is located right outside the gates of Longwood Gardens, Route 1, Kennett Square, PA. It's open April to September daily from 10 am until 6 pm; from October to March the center closes at 5 pm.

Winterthur Garden & Museum

The Brandywine Valley's most famous attraction, Winterthur (☎ (302) 888-4600, (800) 448-3883) was the country estate of Henry Francis du Pont until he opened it to the public in 1951. When du Pont inherited the estate in 1927, he moved the best of his American furniture collection here, doubling the size of the existing house and converting it to a showplace for the world's most important collection of early American decorative arts (1640-1860). During the next 20 years, du Pont continued to increase his collection and the size of Winterthur.

The museum consists of two buildings, one with 175 period rooms and another with three exhibition galleries. There are over 89,000 objects made or used in America between 1640 and 1860, including furniture, textiles, paintings, prints, pewter, silver, ceramics, glass, needlework and brass. The museum is surrounded by 980 acres, of which 60 acres are beautifully planted with native and exotic plants.

Unless you join a special tour, you're free to stroll the galleries, explore the grounds or ride the year-round tram (space permitting) at your leisure. General admission is $8 adults, $4 children, $6 seniors and students. For an additional fee, excellent guided tours are available (reservations required). These are: Introduction to Winterthur, add $5; Garden Walks, available seasonally, add $5; Decorative Arts Tours, one/two hours, add $9/13. Call ahead because the tours are popular and fill quickly.

Hours are Tuesday to Saturday from 9 am to 5 pm; Sunday from noon to 5 pm, with

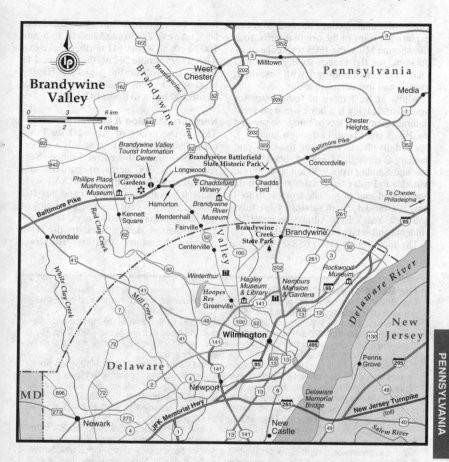

the garden open till dusk and the last tickets sold at 3:45 pm. It's closed Monday, New Year's Day, July 4, Thanksgiving, Christmas and December 26.

You can have continental breakfast, lunch, Sunday brunch and afternoon tea in the pleasant Visitors Pavilion (☎ (302) 888-4826); it's a good idea to make reservations for tea and brunch. In November, there's an Antiques Show here.

Winterthur is six miles northwest of Wilmington, DE, on Route 52, 10 minutes off I-95 via exit 7 (Delaware Ave, Route 52 north). If you're coming from Chadds Ford,

PA, drive west three miles on Route 1 to Route 52 south; from Longwood Gardens, Route 52 south is one mile east on Route 1.

Hagley Museum & Library

Beautifully situated on the banks of the Brandywine River, Hagley – like Winterthur – should be a must-see for visitors to the area. This 240 acre outdoor museum on the site of the birthplace of the Du Pont company tells the story of the du Ponts as part of the broader history of America's Industrial Revolution.

Du Pont started operations here as a

gunpowder manufacturer in 1802. You can explore the ruins of the original mills, tour Eleutherian Mills, the 1803 residence of EI du Pont, see the French-style garden and visit restored buildings with exhibits, models and live demonstrations.

Allow at least three to four hours for your visit. Hagley is a large site with great natural beauty and lots of things to see and do. Hours are: March 15 through January 1, open daily from 9:30 am to 4:30 pm; January 2 through March 14, open Saturday and Sunday from 9:30 am to 4:30 pm; Monday to Friday ticket sales at 1 pm with one guided tour of the site from 1:30 to 4 pm. It's closed Thanksgiving, Christmas and New Year's Eve. Admission is $9.75; students and senior citizens $7.50.

The museum (☎ (302) 658-2400) is on Route 141 north of Wilmington, DE. From I-95, take exit 7 to Route 52 north, to Route 100 North, to Route 141 north; or take exit 8 from I-95 (Route 202 north) to Route 141 south, and follow the signs to Hagley Museum. Or from Chadds Ford, PA, take Route 100 south to Route 141 north.

Nemours Mansion & Gardens

This is the estate of Alfred I du Pont, named after the site of the family's ancestral home in north central France. Surrounded by 300 acres of gardens and natural woodlands, the Louis XVI-style chateau was built in 1909-10 and has 102 rooms. Today it contains fine examples of antique furniture, oriental rugs, tapestries and paintings dating back to the 15th century. Nemours' exhibits illustrate

---

The Battle of Brandywine Creek

The British army nearly ended the American Revolution when it attacked and overwhelmed the American forces at Brandywine Creek on September 11, 1777.

In August, George Washington learned that 13,000 British and 5000 Hessian mercenaries under General William Howe had landed at the head of the Chesapeake Bay. They had been advancing slowly through Delaware, gathering intelligence and securing supply lines for an attack on Philadelphia, the new national capital.

In defense of Philadelphia, Washington moved 11,000 troops to the Wilmington area. Realizing that the Brandywine Valley presented a geographical obstacle to Howe, Washington and his French supporter, the Marquis de Lafayette, set up the bulk of their defenses along the high ground east of the creek at Chadds Ford, the most likely place for the British to cross. In addition, American troops covered two other fords on the Brandywine in hopes of forcing Howe to fight at Chadds Ford.

Howe anticipated Washington's plans and, using intelligence from local British sympathizers, on September 11 sent the bulk of his troops on a long march to the north around Washington's right flank under the cover of darkness and fog. Back at Chadds Ford, when the fog lifted Howe's generals made a decoy attack and marched a few columns back and forth among the hills to give Washington's scouts the impression that the main British force was gathering at Chadds Ford for a charge. Preoccupied there, Washington didn't realize until mid-afternoon that Howe with 11,000 Redcoats had nearly encircled his army. After brutal fighting, the remains of the American force escaped to Chester, PA. British troops suffered 600 dead and wounded; the Americans had 900 casualties and lost 400 men as prisoners of war.

Fifteen days later, Howe's troops marched into Philadelphia unopposed. Although Washington had been defeated, the battle helped persuade the French to make a formal alliance with the Americans, an alliance that would prove crucial to the final outcome of the revolution. In the meantime, Washington was able to regroup to fight again. As he reported to Congress following the battle: 'Notwithstanding the misfortune of the day, I am happy to find the troops in good spirits; and I hope another time we shall compensate for the losses now sustained.' ■

the du Ponts' lavish lifestyle, including vintage cars, a billiards room and bowling alley. The French gardens, stretching almost one third of a mile along the main vista from the mansion, are generally considered to be among the finest of their kind in America.

Located on Rockland Rd at Route 202 (in Wilmington, DE) Nemours (☎ (302) 651-6912) is open from May through November with the following guided tour schedule: Tuesday through Saturday at 9 am, 11 am, 1 pm and 3 pm; Sunday at 11 am, 1 pm and 3 pm. Admission is $8. Nobody under 16 is admitted. Tours take a minimum of two hours and include the mansion followed by a bus tour through the gardens. Visitors need to arrive at reception a good 15 minutes before the start of the tour. Reservations are recommended; the office is open Monday to Friday from 8:30 am to 4:30 pm.

Longwood Gardens
The superb 1050 acre gardens (☎ (610) 388-1000), Route 1, Kennett Square, PA, was established by Samuel du Pont at the beginning of this century. The gardens have beautifully maintained grounds and several large heated conservatories. There are 11,000 different kinds of plants, roses and orchids in bloom year round. In addition, there's an indoor children's garden with a maze, the historic Pierce du Pont House and one of the world's mightiest pipe organs. Night-time displays of illuminated fountains (summer), and festive lights at Christmas are breathtaking. Opening hours are April to October daily from 9 am to 6 pm, November to March daily 9 am to 5 pm. Admission is $10/2, youths 16 to 20 years of age $6; on Tuesday adults are charged $6. There are many well-publicized seasonal events here.

Rockwood Museum
This 1851 Gothic country estate, which was built by the merchant banker Joseph Shipley, stands on 72 of its original 300 acres. The museum consists of the porter's

lodge, gardener's cottage, barn and sundry outbuildings. A collection of British, Continental and American decorative arts from the 17th to 19th centuries is exhibited in the manor house, while the grounds contain six acres of exotic foliage. The Rockwood Museum (☎ (302) 761-4340), 610 Shipley Rd, is south of I-95 in Wilmington, DE. It's open Tuesday to Saturday from 11 am to 3 pm. Admission is $5, children $1, seniors $4. Guided tours run every 30 minutes, and you can walk around the grounds on your own.

Brandywine River Museum
A renowned showcase of American art, this museum is famous for its collection of works by three generations of the Wyeth family. Housed in a 19th century grist mill (☎ (610) 388-2700), Routes 1 and 100, Chadds Ford, PA, the galleries also feature other American artists like Howard Pyle, Maxfield Parrish, William Trost Richards and Horace Pippin, amongst hundreds of others. Seasonal events include an Antiques Show in May, and the Harvest Market & Christmas Shops from September through December. The museum is open daily from 9:30 am to 4:30 pm. Admission $5; senior citizens and students $2.50.

Phillips Place Mushroom Museum
This museum (☎ (610) 388-6082) is half a mile south of Longwood Gardens on Route 1, Kennett Square, PA. It houses a unique collection of exhibits explaining the history, lore and mystique of mushrooms (mushroom farming is a local tradition and the state's main money-making crop), featuring films, slides and nutritional charts. It's open daily from 10 am to 6 pm. Admission $1.25.

Chaddsford Winery
Operating from a renovated 18th century barn, this boutique winery (☎ (610) 388-6221) is on Route 1, five miles south of Route 202, Chadds Ford, PA. Producing small lots of varietal wines with grapes imported from the surrounding area,

PENNSYLVANIA

Chaddsford offers free guided and self-guided tours to see the grapes being crushed, fermented, barrel-aged and bottled. For $5 you can taste seven or eight of the wines. There are picnic tables around the barn. It's open Monday to Saturday from 10 am to 5:30 pm and Sunday noon to 5 pm.

John Chadds House

This former home of a ferryman, farmer and tavern keeper was built around 1725. The house (☎ (610) 388-7376), Route 100, Chadds Ford, PA, is open May to September, Saturday and Sunday noon to 6 pm. Admission is $2.

Barns-Brinton House

This house (☎ (610) 388-7376), Route 1, Chadds Ford, PA, was originally built as a tavern in 1714 and has been restored to its original appearance by the Chadds Ford Historical Society. It's open May to September, Saturday and Sunday noon to 6 pm. Admission is $2.

Brandywine Battlefield Park

The park (☎ (610) 459-3342) lies on the north side of Route 1 east of the Chadds Ford Bridge. At the visitors center, which has an audiovisual display on the battle and exhibits, you can pick up pamphlets on the battle, which took place on farms north of the park. You can also visit the restored farmhouses, which served as headquarters of the Revolutionary generals, George Washington and his French comrade the Marquis de Lafayette, who came close to losing their bid for American independence at Brandywine.

Revolutionary Times at Brandywine is a two day reenactment of the Battle of Brandywine Creek in mid-September; there are crafts and food then, too.

The park is open Tuesday to Saturday from 9 am to 5 pm, Sunday noon to 5 pm; admission to the park is free but to the buildings it's $3.50/1.50, seniors $2.50, and includes a guided tour.

Places to Stay

Accommodations in Wilmington, New Castle and Philadelphia are within easy reach of the Brandywine Valley. However, there are also options, a few very charming, that are closer. Route 202 (Concord Pike) has a larger selection of accommodations, with only one on Route 52 (Kennett Pike). Most motels and hotels offer good value packages (especially on weekends) which include room and admission to Brandywine Valley museums. Most accommodations are in the middle range.

On Route 202, the *Best Western Brandywine Valley Inn* (☎ (800) 537-7772), is at 1807 Concord Pike, one mile north of exit 8 on I-95, with singles/doubles from $69. In the same area and similarly priced is the *Holiday Inn of Wilmington – North* (☎ (302) 478-2222), at 4000 Concord Pike. Further north, the *Radisson Hotel Wilmington* (☎ (302) 478-6000), 4727 Concord Pike, has singles/doubles ranging from $60 to $90/85 to 109. Just south of the Pennsylvania border, the cheaper *Tally-Ho Motor Lodge* (☎ (302) 478-0300), 5209 Concord Pike, has singles/doubles for $45/60.

In Pennsylvania there is a selection of country-style inns and B&Bs. The 1987-built *Brandywine River Hotel* (☎ (610) 388-1200), Route 1 and Route 100, Chadds Ford, has 40 rooms with doubles from $109, suites $130. This hotel is not a piece of antiquity, but it is nicely designed to blend in with the surroundings, and it has a colonial-style interior.

Pace One (☎ (610) 459-3702), Thornton and Glen Mills Rds, is a combination restaurant (see Places to Eat) and B&B in a 250 year old restored barn. Doubles are $65/85. All seven rooms are decorated in different colors, with Lancaster oak queen beds, original watercolors of local scenes and private bath/shower. From the intersection of Route 52 and Route 1 near Chadds Ford, head east on Route 1 and then left on Thornton Rd. The inn is on your right.

The luxurious, top-end *Fairville Inn* (☎ (610) 388-5900), on Route 52 in Mendenhall, is a delightful establishment, run by Ole and Patricia Retlev. The main house was built in 1826, and there is a rear carriage house and barn. Seven of the 15 rooms have fireplaces and the entire place is beautifully decorated. Prices range from $100 to $150, with two suites for $180. A substantial continental breakfast and light but delicious afternoon tea are included. From Route 1 west of Chadds Ford, take Route 52 south to Mendenhall; Fairville is almost a mile past Mendenhall on the left side.

Places to Eat

At Greenville, DE, on Route 52 and convenient for many of the Brandywine attractions, there are a couple of nice places in the Powder Mill Square shopping complex. *Brew ha ha!* (☎ (302) 658-6336) is an espresso cafe serving soup, sandwiches and salads along with the coffee. *Cromwell's* (☎ (302) 571-0561) is an upscale tavern serving such specialties as crab cakes, chicken winglets and daily specials. Open daily from 11 to 1 am (10 pm Sunday).

Buckley's Tavern (☎ (302) 656-9776), 5812 Kennett Pike, Route 52, Centreville, DE, is one of the region's most popular drinking spots. There is a small pub with a dining room and garden room at the back. Everyone from gentry to farmers are regulars here, and the place is usually packed. There is a small menu featuring good food, dishes ranging from $5 to $1; open daily.

Chadds Ford Inn (☎ (610) 388-7361), Routes 1 and 100, dates back to the 1700s. The house was built by Francis Chadsey, an English Quaker who had bought the land from William Penn's commissioner of land grants. In 1736, his eldest son turned the house into a tavern, which through the centuries has evolved into a popular restaurant, furnished with colonial antiques. The international cuisine served is up to date, though, with lunch/dinner costing $10 to $15/25 to 40. Open daily.

Another popular historic restaurant is *Dilworthtown Inn* (☎ (610) 399-1390), Old Wilmington Pike at Brinton Bridge Rd, Dilworthtown, PA. Open daily for dinner ($30 to $50), this wood, stone and brick structure with fireplaces and gas lamps dates back to 1758 and serves French cuisine. To find the inn, head north on Route 1 from the junction with Route 202. After a mile and a half, turn left at the second traffic light and continue for another mile and a half. Go straight across at the stop sign and the restaurant is the second on your right.

Pace One (see Places to Stay) has a restaurant that is open daily (no lunch Saturday, extensive brunch on Sunday). Lunch/dinner costs about $15/30. Artwork and vases of fresh flowers decorate a dimly lit interior room with stucco walls, bare floors and a low ceiling. There is also a brighter porch-like outer room.

Pennsylvania Dutch Country

Pennsylvania Dutch Country is home to a community of Amish (AH-mish), Mennonites and Brethren collectively known as 'Plain People.' The Old Order Amish in particular, with their distinctive clothing, have become a major tourist attraction – the area is one of the most visited in Pennsylvania. It must be odd for people whose forbears emigrated to the New World to escape the attention and persecution of others to find themselves the objects of intense curiosity by camera-toting tourists. To maintain their privacy some have moved to farm other, less-developed parts of the state.

Most Pennsylvania Dutch live on carefully manicured farms, but because of a rising population, urbanization and other outside pressures, many now work in small-scale industries, producing quilts, furniture and crafts, which are sold to tourists from outlets along highways. Others work in family-style restaurants, sell produce at farmers' markets or offer buggy rides to tourists. There are tourist traps, but you can escape some of the commercialism by staying on a farm or one of the more-remote tourist homes or by visiting the back roads, where you'll see Amish people doing their daily farm work.

It's more correct to say Pennsylvania German since the use of 'Dutch' is a corruption of 'Deutsch,' meaning German; many of the early settlers came from German-speaking parts of Europe. Also, the Amish refer to anyone outside their community as 'English,' wherever they might be from.

You shouldn't take photographs of the Amish; they prefer that no one makes what they consider graven images of them. Don't even ask if they mind; they do, and will be uncomfortable about being approached.

The core of the Pennsylvania Dutch region is a string of towns, farms and sights spread out over an area of perhaps 20 by 15 miles. These lie to the east of Lancaster, the

Highlights
- A guided visit to an Amish or Mennonite community or home, away from the commercial areas
- The farmers' markets where you can buy baked goods, jams, meat, fruit, vegetables and crafts
- Locally made pretzels ■

area's main city and more or less its western boundary. Lancaster has a popular farmers' market and pretzel bakery and some historic sights, including the home of President Buchanan.

East of Lancaster, the most visited road is Route 340 (Old Philadelphia Pike), with the towns of Bird-in-Hand and Intercourse. South of this and also running east-west is Route 30 (Lincoln Hwy), which has many of the dairy farms and farm guesthouses and more sights. Route 896 (Hartman Bridge Rd) runs north-south between Routes 30 and 340, meeting Strasburg to the south at the junction with Route 741. To get off the beaten track, take any one of the side roads between Routes 30 and 340.

To the north of this core is the town of Lititz, home of the country's first commercial pretzel bakery, and to the northeast Ephrata, where the Ephrata Cloister is the site of a former ascetic religious community.

Though really separate, Reading, to the northeast of the true Pennsylvania Dutch region, is usually discussed as part of it. Most visitors to Reading go there to shop for factory-outlet bargains, but the Daniel

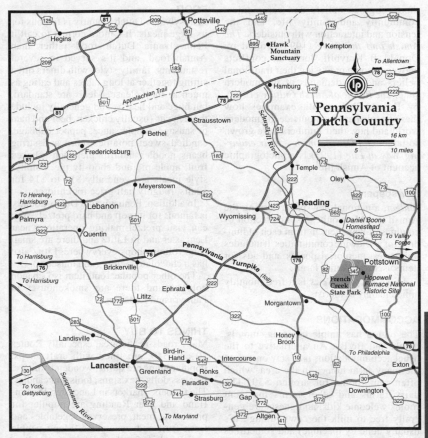

Pennsylvania Dutch Country

0   8   16 km
0   5   10 miles

Boone Homestead to the east and the Hawk Mountain Sanctuary to the north are well worth visiting. The towns of Palmyra and Lebanon, west of Reading, are also included in the region (see Food, later).

INFORMATION
Books

A wide selection of books on the people and the region are available locally. Many are published by Good Books in Intercourse. Several paperbacks that will answer most of your questions are *The Puzzles of Amish Life* by Donald B Kraybill; Merle &

Phyllis Good's *The 20 Most Asked Questions about the Amish and Mennonites*; and Merle Good's *Who Are the Amish?* (1985), which has lots of photographs.

For a more in-depth study, try Stephen M Nolt's *A History of the Amish – from the Reformation to Today*, Daniel & Kathryn McCauley's *Decorative Arts of the Amish of Lancaster County* is aimed specifically at crafts.

A number of books have been published by Johns Hopkins University Press. *Amish Society* (4th edition, 1993) by John Hostatler, examines Amish culture, explains their religious beliefs and ceremonies, community and family life, and the tension and interaction with outsiders. *The Amish and the State* (1993), edited by Donald B Kraybill, looks at conflicts between people practising their traditional beliefs and the demands of the modern state. *The Riddle of Amish Culture* (1989), by Donald B Kraybill, examines how these people have kept outside the modern world and how their numbers have grown so large. *Old Order Amish – their enduring Way of Life* (1993) is a photographic account of Amish life.

Newspapers

Budget, a national newspaper serving the Amish and Mennonites, is a collection of columns of news sent in from each of hundreds of worldwide communities. It includes obituaries, memorial poems, and ads for items useful on Amish farms.

Amish Country News is a free monthly aimed mainly at tourists.

ACCOMMODATIONS

The region has ample camping, motels, hotels and B&Bs. An alternative to the usual accommodations is to stay on one of the many farm homes in the area, which often rent rooms for around $30. The dairy farms and other farms that rent rooms welcome kids, and guests are generally free to milk the cows (though it's usually done by machine) and sometimes to feed the calves if they want to get close to nature. Some are listed here and the names of more are available from the visitors centers.

At the time of writing the HI-AYH Bowmansville Hostel (☎ (215) 445-4831), PO Box 157, Bowmansville, PA 17507, was being renovated; it may have reopened by the time you read this. It's at the junction of Route 625 and Maple Grove Rd off the Pennsylvania Turnpike northeast of Lancaster. For further information contact HI-AYH Delaware Valley Council (☎ (215) 925-6004), 624 S 3rd St, Philadelphia, PA 19147-2302.

FOOD

Pennsylvania Dutch Country is famous for its large meals. It's more correct to call it Pennsylvania Dutch food rather than Amish food, and it's served in several restaurants 'family style' with diners often sitting together at long tables and eating as much as they please. Meals are standard, but huge and hearty, and generally include three meats (usually chicken, beef and ham or sausage), apple sauce, pepper cabbage, candied sweet potatoes, corn and string beans, noodles and fruit pies such as baked fruit, apple pie and shoo-fly pie. Family-style meals are generally $11 to $14 for adults, roughly half price for children.

In addition, Pennsylvania Dutch Country is famous for its soft and hard pretzels. You can visit pretzel-making operations near Lancaster and in Lititz and there are small hand-rolling shops everywhere. Lititz also has a chocolate factory (and museum).

The other popular food item is Lebanon bologna and there are smokehouses in Palmyra and Lebanon.

THINGS TO BUY

Many roads in the area, especially Routes 30 and 340, are lined with craft shops. Popular items are quilts, wooden furniture, faceless dolls, hex signs, tools and candles. The farmers' markets in Lancaster, Bird-in-Hand and near Reading are popular for pies, jams, meat, preserved vegetables and fresh fruit and vegetables. Many people visit Reading for the bargains in clothing etc available from the factory outlets.

ORGANIZED TOURS
Air

Glick Aviation at Smoketown airport (☎ (717) 394-6750), Airport Dr, a mile west of Bird-in-Hand, does a 15 minute flyover of Lancaster County for $30/40 (plus tax) for two/three passengers. It's open Monday to Saturday from 9 am to 5 pm, Sunday 1 to 5 pm.

Bus

Amish Country Tours (☎ (717) 392-8622, 768-3600; write to them at PO Box 414,

Amish, Mennonites & Brethren

The Old Order Amish are the most distinctive of the 'Plain People' in Lancaster County, but the Amish are one of three major groups, including Mennonites and Brethren, that are themselves further divided into various smaller churches and groups with differing beliefs.

The Amish, Mennonites and Brethren all trace their origins to 16th century Switzerland. A religious sect calling itself the Brethren began in Zurich in 1524 with the belief that a church should be made up of a group of individuals baptized as adults. Because of this belief they were called Anabaptists and were persecuted. Some Anabaptists became known as Mennonites after Menno Simons, a former Catholic priest and early leader. In 1693 a Swiss Mennonite bishop named Jacob Ammon split from the Anabaptists and his followers eventually became known as the Amish. The first large groups of Amish arrived in Pennsylvania in the 1720s and '30s.

Amish, Mennonites and Brethren are unified on the issues of separation of church and state, a Bible-centered life, voluntary adult membership and a 'forgiving love' that translates into conscientious objection to war. Where they differ is in dress, use of technology, some Biblical interpretation and language.

Most of Lancaster's Brethren and Mennonites are indistinguishable from the rest of the county's worldly folk in dress. The distinctive Old Order Amish and Old Order Mennonite dress similarly (but not the same) and have certain prohibitions on the use of technology. But then there are other groups of Mennonites, Brethren and even Amish – the Amish Mennonites or 'Beachy Amish' – who wear distinctive clothing but use 'worldly' items.

To oversimplify, the Old Order Amish generally travel by horse and buggy, wear distinctive clothing and prohibit certain technology. Decisions about technology are made by Amish bishops based on whether they are too 'worldly' and whether their use may result in the disintegration of the closely knit community. And any prohibitions are constantly under reinterpretation.

Men wear dark suits without lapels, suspenders, solid-colored shirts, black socks and shoes and broad-brimmed hats. Women wear dresses of solid fabric that cover their arms and go beneath the knees. These dresses are covered by a cape and apron. Hair is worn in a bun on the back of the head. Single women wear black prayer coverings for church services and white after marriage. Single men wait to grow beards (but never mustaches) until after they are married.

While many Amish won't drive a car, they'll ride with friends or hire vehicles to take them somewhere, and bus travel is acceptable. This brings us to the wheel. Bicycles, which encourage young people to go far from their homes, aren't used. Rubber wheels are permitted on wagons, tricycles and scooters but not on large farm equipment. The most obvious example is the tractor, which must have steel wheels. Tractors are permitted around the barn and to power machinery, but not in the fields. The tractor speeds up farming and eliminates the need for labor, which is considered beneficial.

Power is acceptable if it comes from batteries and some fuel generators; gas lanterns are fine. Phones are allowed outside homes but not inside.

Children attend one room Amish schoolhouses until the eighth grade. They're exempt from the usual compulsory US school attendance to age 16. In their late teens Amish youngsters have a choice to stay or leave the community – about 87% choose to stay. The Amish speak Pennsylvania Dutch (a German dialect), High German at worship services and English. The community is divided into church districts of 150 to 200 people. They have no central church – the district members gather at a different home every second Sunday for a three hour service of hymn singing (without music) and scripture reading.

Lancaster County's 20,000 strong Amish community is the second largest in the country and the population is doubling every 20 years. ■

Bird-in-Hand, PA 17505) is the largest bus-tour operator in the area and runs several narrated bus tours from the Plain 'N' Fancy Farm, on Route 340 midway between Bird-in-Hand and Intercourse. The 2½ hour minitour takes the back roads past farmlands and homes, visits an Amish dairy farm to sample ice cream and stops at an Amish shop. It leaves three times daily Monday to Saturday, once on Sunday and costs adults/children $14.95/9.95.

The 4½ hour Amish Farmlands tour visits farms, a reconstructed Amish house, the Old Order Amish House at the Amish Country Homestead, a one room Amish school, a wine tasting and two seasonal roadside stops (which may include a bakery, furniture factory or crafts sale) once daily, Monday to Saturday. The price is $24.95/14.95.

Combined tours of Pennsylvania Dutch Country and Hershey are run by Shope's Tours (☎ (717) 569-0535, (800) 899-0535), PO Box 43, Intercourse, PA 17534, daily from 9 am for $20/7.

Gray Line (☎ (215) 569-3666) has tours to Pennsylvania Dutch Country from Philadelphia.

Bicycle

Lancaster Bike Touring (☎ (717) 396-0456), 41 Greenfield Rd, Lancaster, PA 17602, does two and three day guided tours for $210/315, including stays in a local B&B. An unguided two day tour (you get a map and the B&B stay) is $130. It also rents bikes for $5/20 per hour/day.

Personal Guide

A personal guide sits in your car while you drive, and directs you to communities away from the commercial areas. The Mennonite Information Center (☎ (717) 299-0954), 2209 Millstream Rd, Lancaster, PA 17602, provides visitors with a personal guide for $23 for two hours. The friendly Old Order Amish Tours (☎ (717) 299-6535), 63 E Brook Rd, off Route 896 near Ronks, takes individuals or small groups on private tours of Amish farms and homes. The rate for a two hour tour is $24 for two people, $28 for three and $32 for four.

Red Rose Excursions (☎ (717) 397-3175), 255 Butler Ave, Lancaster, PA 17601, is owned and operated by Plain People – in this case, Old Order River Brethren – and charges $30 for two hours, then $12 for each additional hour.

GETTING THERE & AROUND

Pennsylvania Dutch Country is about 90 minutes' drive west of Philadelphia on Route 30. If you're coming from further north, take the Pennsylvania Turnpike (I-76) to Route 222 south, which runs directly into Lancaster. Route 422 north off the Pennsylvania Turnpike near Valley Forge will take you to Reading. You can reach Lancaster and Reading by bus (see Getting There & Away in those cities), but to explore the region adequately, you'll need a car, motorcycle or bicycle.

Note The Amish use their horses and buggies as a means of transportation, so if you're driving, at times you'll need to slow down considerably and travel at their pace for a while.

LANCASTER

Lancaster (population 60,000) is a pleasant town 57 miles west of Philadelphia. Originally settled by Swiss Mennonites around 1700, it was named in the mid-18th century after the birthplace in Lancashire, England, of Lancaster County's first commissioner, John Wright. Lancaster is noted for being the capital of the US for a day, September 27, 1777, when Congress, after fleeing Philadelphia following George Washington's defeat by the British at the Battle of Brandywine, stopped here overnight. It was also the home of James Buchanan (1791-1868), 15th president of the USA. Today it's known for its farmers' market, some historic buildings and its outlet stores.

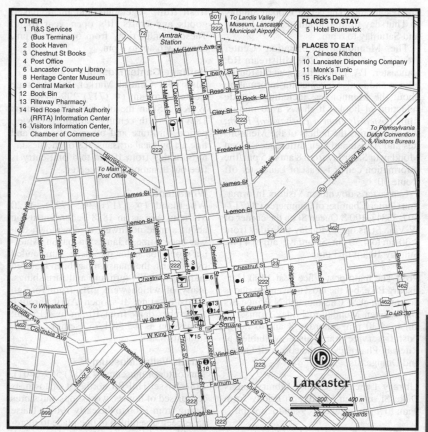

OTHER
1 R&S Services
   (Bus Terminal)
2 Book Haven
3 Chestnut St Books
4 Post Office
6 Lancaster County Library
8 Heritage Center Museum
9 Central Market
12 Book Bin
13 Riteway Pharmacy
14 Red Rose Transit Authority
   (RRTA) Information Center
16 Visitors Information Center,
   Chamber of Commerce

PLACES TO STAY
5 Hotel Brunswick

PLACES TO EAT
7 Chinese Kitchen
10 Lancaster Dispensing Company
11 Monk's Tunic
15 Rick's Deli

Orientation

King St between Water and Duke Sts, and
Queen St between Orange and Vine Sts
mark the main downtown commercial area.
Queen St divides the city between east and
west, Orange St divides it between north
and south. Penn Square, with its Soldiers &
Sailors monument, is the town's central
point. A one-way system operates downtown: Route 222 runs north along Lime St
and south along Prince St; Route 462 runs
east along King St, west along Walnut St;
Route 23 runs east along Chestnut St, west
along Walnut St.

Information

Tourist Offices The Pennsylvania Dutch
Convention & Visitors Bureau (π (717)
299-8901), 501 Greenfield Rd, Lancaster,
PA, 17601, is the tourist office for the
region. It's on the northeast side of Lancaster city off Route 30 at the Greenfield
Rd exit. It has a 15 minute audiovisual
display about the region, *There is a Season*,
that gives a basic overview but isn't worth
the $2 charge. Get a copy of the free *Penn-
sylvania Dutch Country/Lancaster County
Map & Visitors Guide*; it contains discount
coupons to attractions, accommodations

and restaurants. The center is open Sunday to Thursday from 8:30 am to 5 pm, Friday and Saturday to 6 pm.

The Mennonite Information Center (☎ (717) 299-0954), 2209 Millstream Rd, Lancaster, PA 17602, has general tourist advice and is also a center for information about the Mennonites, including a wide selection of books. It shows a 20 minute film, *Postcards from a Heritage of Faith*, which explains the beliefs of the Mennonites and Amish and their differences. Open Monday to Saturday from 8 am to 5 pm, the information center is east of Lancaster off Route 30.

Lancaster's downtown Visitors Information Center/Chamber of Commerce (☎ (717) 397-3531), 100 S Queen St on the corner of W Vine St, is open Monday to Friday from 8:30 am to 4:50 pm, Saturday 9 am to 4 pm, Sunday 10 am to 3 pm.

Post The main post office is at 1400 Harrisburg Pike, but the most convenient one is downtown at W Chestnut and N Prince Sts and is open Monday to Friday from 7:30 am to 4:30 pm, Saturday 8 am to noon. Postal services are also available at Riteway Pharmacy on the corner of Queen and Orange Sts.

Library Lancaster County Library, on N Duke St, is open Monday to Friday from 9 am to 9 pm, weekends 9 am to 5:30 pm.

Bookstores Several good used bookstores are near Central Market. Book Bin (☎ (717) 392-6434), 14 W Orange St, has a wide selection of used books. Book Haven (☎ (717) 393-0920), 146 N Prince St, and Chestnut St Books (☎ (717) 393-3773), 11 W Chestnut St, have old and rare books, maps and prints.

Central Market

Though very touristed, Central Market (☎ (717) 291-4739), on the northwest corner of Penn Square, is worth visiting. One of the oldest covered markets in the US and the country's oldest publicly owned farmers' market, it has a good selection of fresh fruit, vegetables and meat, baked goods and crafts. It's open year round Tuesday and Friday from 6 am to 4 pm, Saturday 6 am to 2 pm.

Heritage Center Museum

Also near Central Market, the Heritage Center Museum (☎ (717) 299-6440), 13 W King St in the old city hall, contains 18th and 19th century paintings, pewter, period furniture and other craftwork and fine art by local artisans. It's open Tuesday to Saturday from 10 am to 4 pm; entry is free but donations are accepted.

Wheatland

Wheatland (☎ (717) 392-8721), 1120 Marietta Ave, is an 1828 Federal mansion about a mile northwest of downtown that was once home to James Buchanan, America's only bachelor president. Surrounded by gardens, the mansion has been restored and features his furniture and furnishings, many of which were gifts from foreign heads of state. It's open April through November daily from 10 am to 4:15 pm; admission is $5.50/1.75, seniors $4.50, students $3.50.

Landis Valley Museum

This outdoor museum (☎ (717) 569-0401), 2451 Kissel Hill Rd northeast of town, is comprised of homes, workshops and stores dating from 1760 to the early 1900s. These have been assembled in one place to recreate the rural life and work of that period. You can see presentations of craftmaking, including blacksmithing, leather working, spinning, basket weaving, tin smithing, lace-making and chair caning. The museum is open April through October, Tuesday to Saturday from 9 am to 5 pm, Sunday noon to 5 pm; admission is $7/5, seniors $6.

From downtown take Lime St (Route 222) north to the exit for Route 272; turn right and follow Route 272 to the traffic lights just past the Quality Inn; turn left at the lights onto Kissel Hill Rd and the entrance to the museum is about 300 yards on the right.

Anderson Pretzel Bakery

This large pretzel bakery (☎ (717) 299-1616), 2060 Old Philadelphia Pike, is two miles east of town on Route 340. Guided tours of the bakery along an overhead catwalk are free Monday to Friday from 8:30 am to 4 pm. The factory store is open year round Monday to Thursday from 8:30 am to 5 pm, Friday 7 am to 5 pm; between April and December it also opens on Saturday 8:30 am to 3 pm.

Organized Tours

Historic Lancaster Walking Tour (☎ (717) 392-1776), 100 S Queen St in the downtown visitors center/chamber of commerce, does daily walking tours April through October, Monday to Saturday at 10 am and 1:30 pm and on Sunday at 1:30 pm. It costs $5/2, seniors $4.

Places to Stay

You can't stay in town cheaply, but if you go southeast on Route 462/30 there's a commercial strip with hotels and motels and, further out into Pennsylvania Dutch Country, campgrounds and farm houses. (See Places to Stay in Bird-in-Hand, Intercourse and Strasburg, below.)

B&Bs *O'Flaherty's Dingeldein House* (☎ (717) 293-1723, (800) 779-7765), 1105 E King St (Route 462), is two miles east of town before the intersection with Route 30. It's a small, comfortable B&B with four rooms, two with shared bath and two with private bath. The common areas have gas fireplaces and there's parking at the rear. Single rooms with shared/private bath are $60/70, doubles $70/80.

Nearby, *King's Cottage* (☎ (717) 397-1017, (800) 747-8717), 1049 E King St, is a large, airy place with a library, fireplace and afternoon tea. Its eight rooms have private baths, wooden floors, good carpet, big beds and antique furniture. Rates are $80 to $120.

Hotels & Motels *Garden Spot Motel* (☎ (717) 394-4736), five miles east of Lancaster at 2291 Route 30, is a good value.

It has 18 clean, well-lit rooms and a coffee shop on the premises. Rooms are $43/47 a single/double. If you want to stay downtown it'll have to be at the 225 room *Hotel Brunswick* (☎ (717) 397-4801, (800) 233-0182), at E Chestnut and N Queen Sts. The exterior is an unattractive mix of concrete and brick and the standard rooms cost $60/65. It has free parking.

Places to Eat

In addition to Central Market's fresh food, you can buy prepared Middle Eastern food from *Saife's* in the market; spinach or meat pies are $1.25, as is the vegetarian *kibbe* (made of bulgar wheat, potato, parsley and peas).

The *Chinese Kitchen* (☎ (717) 295-9890), 113 W King St, has lunch specials for $2.95, with most mains, like sweet and sour pork, in the $3 to $4 range. It's closed on Monday. *Rick's Deli* (☎ (717) 299-7295), 50 W King St, specializes in salads, like Nantucket (shrimp, olives, tomato and egg) for $4.50 or Marseille (tuna, pasta, olives, tomato and eggs) for $4, and sandwiches for $3 to $5. It's closed on Sunday.

The *Monk's Tunic*, on W Orange St between S Prince and S Queen Sts, has daily mains of falafel, pasta, calzones, spinach pies and quesadillas for around $5, sandwiches for $4.25. It also prepares its own blends of coffee and presents live poetry and music on Tuesday evenings.

Lancaster Dispensing Company (☎ (717) 299-4602), 33-35 N Market St, is a pub with a varied menu of sandwiches, seafood and pasta salads, and a good vegetarian and Mexican selection; mains are in the $5 to $7 range. It's open Monday to Saturday from 11 am to 2 am, and on Sunday 4 to 11 pm.

Getting There & Away

Air Lancaster municipal airport (☎ (717) 569-1221) is eight miles north of town on Route 501. USAir (☎ (800) 428-4322) has five daily flights to Philadelphia and Pittsburgh, two to Reading. Roundtrip fares to Philadelphia start from $178.

PENNSYLVANIA

Bus The Capitol Trailways/Greyhound terminal is at R&S Services (☎ (717) 397-4861), 22 W Clay St, just west of N Queen St less than a mile north of downtown. There are three buses daily to Philadelphia ($12.35, two hours) and to Pittsburgh ($34.80, five hours).

Train The Amtrak train station (☎ (717) 291-5080) is at 53 McGovern Ave, about a mile north of downtown. There's a daily train to Philadelphia ($9 one way, 80 minutes) and Pittsburgh ($67 one way, five hours).

Car The quickest way to Lancaster from Philadelphia is via the Pennsylvania Turnpike (I-76); at exit 21 take Route 222 south into town. Northward, Route 222 leads to Reading, southeast of town it leads to Maryland. Another option from Philadelphia is to take Route 30 west, which passes through the heart of Pennsylvania Dutch Country. From Lancaster, Route 30 continues southwest to York and Gettysburg. Route 283 leads northwest from Lancaster to Harrisburg, Route 501 heads north to I-78.

Getting Around

Red Rose Transit Authority (RRTA; ☎ (717) 397-4246) is the Lancaster County bus service; it has an information center at 47 N Queen St where you can also buy tickets. Lancaster County is divided into five fare zones with the city of Lancaster as the central or base zone. One-way fares range from $1 to $2.

Cars can be rented from Payless Rent-a-Car (☎ (717) 396-0000), 625 E Orange St.

INTERCOURSE & AROUND

Yes, Intercourse is the real name of this small town along Route 340 (Old Philadelphia Pike), eight miles east of Lancaster. Founded in 1754 and originally called Cross Keys, no one knows for sure how it obtained its current name. The reason usually given is that it's because the town stands at the intersection of the old King's Hwy (Route 340) and the old Newport Rd (Route 772). Another possible explanation is that the name evolved from a sign, which read 'Enter Course,' at the entrance to an old racing track on King's Hwy. Intercourse became the town's official name in 1814.

Almost everything in Intercourse is along Route 340.

Information

The Intercourse Tourist Information Center (☎ (717) 768-3882), on Route 340 in the Cross Keys Village Center, is a good resource for the town and the region. It's open Monday to Saturday from 10 am to 5 pm. A small post office, opposite Kitchen Kettle Village, is open Monday to Friday from 8:30 am to noon and 1 to 4:30 pm, Saturday 8:30 to 11 am.

People's Place

The People's Place (☎ (717) 768-7171), 3513 Old Philadelphia Pike, is a cultural center that gives visitors a sensitive introduction to Amish and Mennonite life; it's very informative with parts more geared to children than adults. It shows *Who Are the Amish?*, a 30 minute film about Amish life from birth to death for $3.50/1.75; it also has the **Amish World Museum**, with exhibits on clothing, buggies and religious practices, for the same price. You can see both for $6.50/3.25. *Hazel's People* is a film about the Mennonite community narrated by Geraldine Page shown in July and August for $5. There's also a bookstore with a wide selection of books on Amish and Mennonite life.

The People's Place is open Monday to Saturday from 9:30 am to 5 pm.

Amish Experience Theater & Country Homestead

These are at the Plain 'N' Fancy Farm (☎ (717) 768-8400) restaurant and shopping area on Route 340 between Intercourse and Bird-in-Hand. The theater shows the film *Jacob's Choice*, dealing with a young Amish man's dilemma – whether to stay and follow the traditional way of life or enter the world of the 'English.' Next door, the Country Homestead is a replica of an Amish home.

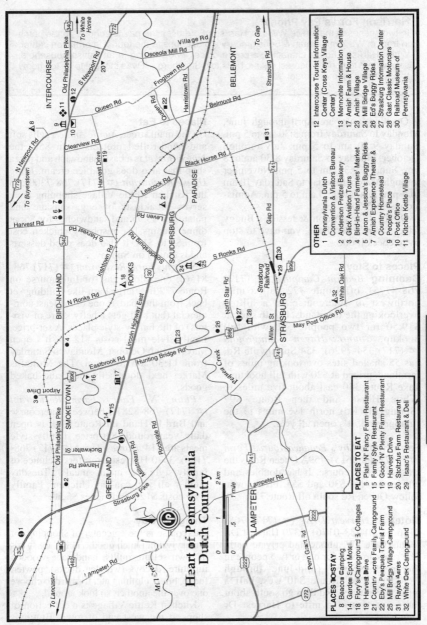

Heart of Pennsylvania Dutch Country

INTERCOURSE

BIRD-IN-HAND

SMOKETOWN

RONKS

STRASBURG

BELLEMONT

PARADISE

SOUDERSBURG

LAMPETER

GREENLAND

To Lancaster

To White Horse

To Gap

To Buyerstown

PLACES TO STAY
8 Beacon Camping
14 Garden Spot Motel
18 Flory's Campground & Cottages
19 Harvest Drive
21 Country Acres Family Campground
22 Eby's Pequea Tourist Farm
25 Mill Bridge Village Campground
31 Rayba Acres
32 White Oak Campground

PLACES TO EAT
5 Plain N' Fancy Farm Restaurant
15 Family Style Restaurant
16 Good N' Plenty Farm Restaurant
19 Harvest Drive
20 Stoltzfus Farm Restaurant
29 Isaac's Restaurant & Deli

OTHER
1 Pennsylvania Dutch
  Convention & Visitors Bureau
2 Anderson Pretzel Bakery
3 Glick Aviation Tours
4 Bird-in-Hand Farmers' Market
5 Aaron & Jessica's Buggy Rides
6 Amish Experience Theater &
  Country Homestead
7 People's Place
9 Gast Classic Motorcars
10 Post Office
11 Kitchen Kettle Village
12 Intercourse Tourist Information
  Center (Cross Keys Village
  Center)
13 Mennonite Information Center
17 Amish Farm & House
23 Amish Village
24 Mill Bridge Village
26 Ed's Buggy Rides
27 Strasburg Information Center
28 Gast Classic Motorcars
30 Railroad Museum of
  Pennsylvania

PENNSYLVANIA

Harrison Ford's Pay Phone

In two scenes in the movie *Witness*, Harrison Ford uses the pay telephone on the porch in front of WL Zimmerman & Sons grocery store, opposite the tourist information center. When Harrison Ford's character, a police officer who's hiding in an Amish household, asks where to find the nearest phone, he is told Strasburg – it was thought to be too goofy to say it was in Intercourse! ■

Opening hours are April through June, Monday to Saturday from 8:30 am to 5 pm, Sunday 9:30 am to 5 pm; July through October, Monday to Saturday 8:30 am to 8 pm, Sunday 9:30 am to 5 pm; November through March, Monday to Saturday 10 am to 5 pm, Sunday 9:30 am to 5 pm. Admission is $6/3.50.

On the site is Aaron & Jessica's Buggy Rides; there's no phone, you have to stop by to check it out.

Places to Stay

Camping *Beacon Camping* (☎ (717) 768-8775), off Route 772 half a mile northwest of Intercourse on a hilltop overlooking the farmlands, has 46 sites at $19.50 for two people, $20 with full hookup. *Country Haven Campground* (☎ (717) 354-7926), 354 Springville Rd, has 55 shaded sites overlooking miles of farmland, priced at $20 with full hookups. Take Route 340 east about five miles to White Horse and then Route 897 (Springville Rd) north 1½ miles to the campground. It's open all year.

Farm Home *Eby's Peaquea Tourist Farm* (☎ (717) 768-3615), 459A Queen Rd, is the closest to Intercourse. It has doubles and efficiencies for $30 and $55. From town, follow Queen Rd south off Route 772.

Motel At *Harvest Drive* (☎ (717) 768-7186, (800) 233-0176), 3370 Harvest Dr, rooms have TV, phone and private bath. The rates are $67 for one or two people in the peak season (mid-June through October). Take Route 340 west half a mile to Clearview Rd then go south about three-quarters of a mile to Harvest Dr then west.

Places to Eat

On the main street, *Auntie Annie's* sells soft and hand-rolled pretzels from 85¢; the *Lunch Basket* is a basic sandwich and pizza shop that also does good ice cream. *Kling House Restaurant* (☎ (717) 768-7300), in the Kitchen Kettle Village shopping area, serves breakfasts of egg, sausage and potato for $3.95 and sandwiches for $5; at dinner, mains like raspberry chicken cost from $9 to $14. It also does good desserts and is closed on Sunday.

Stoltzfus Farm Restaurant (☎ (717) 768-8156), one block east of Intercourse on Route 772 in a large barn-like building set back from the road, is one of the least commercial (but still gets a hefty share of visitors) of the family-style places. A set-price, family-style meal costs $12.25. It's open May through October, Monday to Saturday from 11:30 am to 8 pm. The Stoltzfus Market next door sells meat and baked goods.

Plain 'N' Fancy Farm Restaurant (☎ (717) 768-8281), between Intercourse and Bird-In-Hand on Route 340, is open daily year round. Set-price, family-style meals are $14. *Harvest Drive* (☎ (717) 768-7186), 3370 Harvest Dr, offers a choice of family-style or menu meals. Tuesday there's all-you-can-eat chicken. Family style costs $12, sandwiches $5.50.

Things to Buy

Intercourse is the epicenter of shopping for Pennsylvania Dutch goods. There are stores in town selling quilts, handmade wooden furniture, decoys (wooden ducks), pewter, fudge, brass, clothing etc. It's hard to choose one over the another, so look around.

Kitchen Kettle Village is a collection of shops at the west end of town. Bratton's

Woodcraft (☎ (717) 768-3214) in the 'village' sells good wooden furniture. At the Old Candle Barn (☎ (717) 768-8926), at the intersection of Routes 340 and 772, you can watch candle-making downstairs. For quilts, try Nancy's Corner of Quilts (☎ (717) 768-8790) on the main street.

On Route 772 for several miles north-west of Intercourse there are a number of places selling wooden furniture, quilts and secondhand wares.

Getting There & Away
RRTA (☎ 397-4246) bus No 13 from Duke St in Lancaster stops several times daily in Intercourse. By car from Lancaster follow King St (Route 462) east out of the city then take the left fork onto Route 340. If you're coming from Philadelphia, Route 772 connects Route 222 and Route 30 with Intercourse.

BIRD-IN-HAND & AROUND
A few miles east of Lancaster on Route 340, Bird-in-Hand (population 700) was given its name in 1734; the name may have been taken from the sign at the town's then-main hotel. Today, the small town has many stores and restaurants.

Bird-in-Hand Farmers' Market
The farmers' market (☎ (717) 393-9674), on the main street, has fewer 'gourmet' items than Lancaster's Central Market, but has more Amish homemade jams, pies and other foods. The market is open year round Friday and Saturday from 8:30 am to 5:30 pm; April through November on Wednes-day; and July through September on Thurs-day. Skip the gifts from the giftshop outside the market; you're better off shopping in Intercourse. See also Things to Buy, below.

Amish Farm & House
This is a reconstruction of an Old Order Amish farm (☎ (717) 394-6185), 2395 Route 30 East, with animals and buildings on 25 acres. It's open daily from 8:30 am to 5 pm; admission is $5/3, seniors $4.50. The ticket gets you a guided tour of the house with a description of the Amish culture and

way of life; after the tour you can wander round the farm by yourself. From Bird-in-Hand take Route 340 west to Route 896; turn south to Route 30 then head west for just under a mile.

Horse & Buggy
Abe's Buggy Rides (☎ (717) 392-1794), on Route 340 half a mile west of Bird-in-Hand does a two mile tour year round, Monday to Saturday from 8 am to dusk for $10/5.

Places to Stay
Flory's Campground & Cottages (☎ (717) 687-6670), on N Ronks Rd between Routes 30 and 340 a mile south of Bird-in-Hand, has 71 sites priced from $19. It also rents four rooms in a guesthouse for $50/60 a single/double and has bicycle rentals. It's open year round. *Country Acres Family Campground* (☎ (717) 687-8014), 20 Leven Rd, has 60 sites at $15 to $20 each. Take N Ronks Rd south to Route 30 then go east to Leven Rd.

Places to Eat
Good 'N' Plenty Farm Restaurant (☎ (717) 394-7111), Eastbrook Rd (Route 896), is a large family-style restaurant open Monday to Saturday from 11:30 am to 8 pm. It's closed in December and January. The set-price meals are $14 ($6 for children aged four to 10). Take Route 340 west to Route 896 then head south to the restaurant.

The *Family Style Restaurant* (☎ (717) 393-2323), serves an all-you-can-eat buffet and family-style meals. The breakfast buffet is $5, lunch $7 and dinner $14. It usually has specials for young children (age two to 12). It's open daily April through November, weekends the rest of the year. Take Route 340 west to Route 896; head south to Route 30 then west to the restaurant.

Things to Buy
Country Barn Quilts & Crafts (no phone), just east of Bird-in-Hand on Route 340, is an Amish-owned store operated in a con-verted tobacco barn on an Amish farm. It has a good selection of carpets, quilts, wall

PENNSYLVANIA

hangings, pillows and carvings. It's open Monday to Saturday from 9 am to 5 pm.

Three discount factory-outlet malls are south of town on Route 30 near the intersection with Route 896. They are Millstream Designer Factory Shops (☎ (717) 392-7202), Rockvale Square Outlets (☎ (717) 293-9595) and Quality Center (☎ (717) 299-1949).

Getting There & Away

RRTA (☎ (717) 397-4246) bus No 13 from Duke St in Lancaster stops several times daily in Bird-in-Hand. By car from Lancaster follow King St (Route 462) east out of the city then take the left fork onto Route 340. If you're coming from Philadelphia, Route 772 connects Route 222 and Route 30 with Route 340.

STRASBURG & AROUND

Strasburg, at the less-visited southern end of Pennsylvania Dutch Country on Route 741, makes for a pleasant visit. It's the most picturesque and least commercialized of the regional towns and has some interesting attractions for car and train buffs.

The Strasburg Information Center (☎ (717) 687-7922), off Route 896, is north of town in the Historic Strasburg Inn near Gast Classic Motorcars. It's open Wednesday to Sunday from 8 am to 3 pm.

Mill Bridge Village

The most elaborate of the replicas, Mill Bridge Village (☎ (717) 687-8181), two miles south of Ronks on S Ronks Rd, is a recreated colonial 'village' that includes an Amish house, school, covered bridge, blacksmith, log cabin, broommaker, mill, barnyard and zoo. Often, people are working in each building who can tell you how things were done in the 18th century. Admission is $10/5, seniors $8, which includes a buggy tour. If you camp here (see Places to Stay & Eat), you get free admission to the village.

Amish Village

This recreated Amish village (☎ (717) 687-8511) of about six major buildings, includ-

ing an Old Order Amish house, blacksmith shop, schoolhouse, animals and store, is on Route 896 two miles north of Strasburg. Admission is $5.50/1.75, which includes a tour of an Amish home. The village is open daily from 9 am to 5 pm.

Gast Classic Motorcars

Housing a varied collection of fully operational cars, Gast Classic Motorcars (☎ (717) 687-9500) is on Route 896 about half a mile north of town. Among others on display are a 1957 three wheeled Messerschmidt Kabinenroller; a 1957 BMW Isetta 300 that opens in front to let the driver in; a 1948 Tucker (less than 100 were made); and a 1967 Amphi-Car that does 75 mph on land and 12 mph in water. The museum also has some Harley-Davidsons in the foyer and lined up outside.

It's open Sunday to Thursday from 9 am to 6 pm, Friday and Saturday 9 am to 8 pm. Admission is $6/3.50.

Strasburg Railroad

From the Strasburg Railroad station (☎ (717) 687-7522), on Route 741 a mile east of town, a steam train does a 45 minute, nine mile, scenic roundtrip tour through the countryside to the village of Paradise. The train runs six times daily April through November, weekends only December through March. The regular fare is $7/4, the open-air observation car is $8/5; an all-day ticket with unlimited travel costs $14.

Railroad Museum of Pennsylvania

Opposite the Strasburg Railroad station is the Railroad Museum of Pennsylvania (☎ (717) 687-8628). Spanning 150 years of Pennsylvania railroads, it features a collection of steam locomotives and railcars as well as artifacts like uniforms and engineers' tools. It's open Monday to Saturday from 9 am to 5 pm, Sunday noon to 5 pm; admission is $6/4, seniors $5.

Horse & Buggy

Ed's Buggy Rides (☎ (717) 687-0360), on Route 896 a mile north of Strasburg, provides leisurely three mile rides through the county. It's not Amish, but the buggy-ride experience is the same. A half-hour ride costs $6.50/3.50. Ed's also does sleigh rides in the winter.

Places to Stay & Eat

White Oak Campground (☎ (717) 687-6207), White Oak Rd, has 180 year-round sites in the woods or on the grass at $15, or $17 with power, for two adults and two children; each extra person is $2. Take May Post Office Rd south for about four miles then turn east on White Oak Rd a quarter mile. *Mill Bridge Village Campground* (☎ (717) 687-8181) has fishing, free buggy rides and free admission to Mil! Bridge Village. Camping rates are $22; power and water is another $4.

Rayba Acres (☎ (717) 687-6729), 183 Black Horse Rd about three miles east of Strasburg off Route 741, is a dairy farm that's been in the family for over 100 years. Rooms are available in the old and new houses. The old house has six large carpeted rooms, two with private bathroom; the rates are $30/43 per person without/with bath. The new house has rooms with bath for $48 per person.

Sycamore Haven Farm Home (☎ (717) 442-4901), 35 S Kinzers Rd, is a farm next to a large sycamore tree. Double rooms are $30, plus $5 for each additional person and $1.50 for a continental breakfast. Take Route 741 east for about six miles then turn left on S Kinzers Rd for about half a mile.

Isaac's Restaurant & Deli is part of a small shopping mall on Route 741 just east of Strasburg. Fitted out like an old railroad carriage it serves mostly sandwiches for around $5. It has a good vegetarian selection.

Getting There & Away

Strasburg is at the intersection of Routes 741 and 896 about three miles south of Route 30. There's no public transportation from Lancaster, though RRTA bus No 14 stops at Rockvale Square about three miles to the north at the intersection of Routes 896 and 30.

LITITZ

A pretty town with many 18th and 19th century red-brick buildings, Lititz was founded in 1756 by Moravians who had fled religious persecution in Europe. Lititz is home to the **Sturgis Pretzel House** (☎ (717) 626-4354, (800) 227-9342), 219 E Main St, the first commercial pretzel bakery in the US, which was established by Julius Sturgis in 1861. You can tour the bakery and make your own pretzels for $1.50. It's open April through December, Monday to Saturday from 9:30 am to 4:30 pm; and January and February on Saturday only 9:30 am to 4:40 pm.

Around the corner is the **Wilbur Candy Americana Museum** (☎ (717) 626-1131), 45 N Broad St beside the railroad line. Though fairly small, it's probably more interesting for adults than Hershey's Chocolate World. A video explains how chocolate is made and a two room display of old chocolate-making equipment, including molds for Easter eggs, is beside a chocolate shop. The museum and shop are open Monday to Saturday from 10 am to 5 pm. Admission is free.

RRTA (☎ (717) 397-4246) bus No 10 from Lancaster stops several times daily in Lititz. Lititz is about 12 miles north of Lancaster on Route 501.

EPHRATA

Ephrata (EH-fra-ta, population 12,130), on Route 322 about midway between Lancaster and Reading is home to the **Ephrata Cloister** (☎ (717) 733-6600), 632 W Main St. Ephrata was founded in 1732 by Conrad Beissel, a Pietist (Pietism was a reform movement in the German Lutheran church in the 18th and 19th centuries). It was a communal society made up of religious celibates and ascetics of both sexes and affiliated married householders; at its peak it had about 300 people and its last cellibate member died in 1813. The word Ephrata means 'fruitful' or 'plentiful.'

The striking collection of medieval-style buildings – tall, steep-roofed, wood-and-shingle structures – are in their original locations. The doors were made low to force most people to bend 'in humility.' Members of the community lived and worked under a rigorous schedule and ate little food. Note the bed made of a 15 inch wide plank with a wooden block for a pillow.

The cloister printed many books, including a translation of the Mennonites' *Martyrs Mirror*. Ephrata is also known for its *Frakturschriften* ('broken writing'), each letter a combination of strokes, and the beautiful a capella singing. It's open Monday to Saturday from 9 am to 5 pm and Sunday noon to 5 pm. Admission is $5/3, seniors $4, which includes a slide show and guided tour.

RRTA (☎ (717) 397-4246) bus No 11 runs between Lancaster and Ephrata. By car, take Route 222 north from Lancaster or south from Reading to Route 322 west.

READING

Reading (RED-ding, population 78,400) straddles the Schuylkill River about 45 miles northwest of Philadelphia. The area was originally settled by the Lenni-Lanape people who fished the river. The Dutch set up a trading post in 1663 and European settlers began arriving toward the end of the century. The town was laid out in the 1740s by the sons of William Penn, Thomas and Richard, and named after Penn's county seat in Berkshire, England. During the 19th century it became an important manufacturing and industrial center, a position it maintains today.

Reading itself doesn't have the attractions of the rest of Pennsylvania Dutch Country though there are a few sights outside town, including Daniel Boone's birthplace. Reading is more noted for its huge collection of factory-outlet stores and modestly promotes itself as 'the outlet capital of the world.' The town gets busy from mid-September – when visitors combine a trip to see Pennsylvania's fall colors with some early Christmas shopping – and stays busy until after Christmas.

Orientation

Downtown Reading is on the east bank of the Schuylkill River. Business Route 422 becomes Penn St, the main street in town, which leads west over the river to the suburbs of West Reading and Wyomissing and the factory outlets. Penn St divides the town between north and south. The north-south Business Route 222 becomes 6th St in town.

Information

Not surprisingly, the Reading & Berks County Visitors Information Center (☎ (610) 375-4085, (800) 443-6610), in the VF Outlet Village complex at Park Rd and Hill Ave, has lots of information about the factory outlets but can also help you with other attractions. It's open Monday to Friday from 9 am to 7 pm, Saturday 10 am to 3 pm and Sunday 10 am to 2 pm.

The main post office, on N 5th St between Court and Washington Sts, is open Monday to Friday from 8 am to 5 pm, Saturday 8 am to 3 pm. The library, at Franklin and S 5th Sts, is open Monday to Wednesday from 8:15 am to 9 pm, Thursday and Friday 8:15 am to 5:30 pm and Saturday 8:45 am to 5 pm.

Things to See

The main sight in town is the **pagoda** (☎ (610) 372-0553). It's odd to see one in the middle of Pennsylvania, but there it is, red-and-gold, neon-lit at night and several stories high. Sitting on a hill in Mt Penn Reserve with good views across Reading, it's open daily from 11 am to 5 pm; admission is free. Take Duryea Dr up through the reserve to get there.

The **farmers' market** at the Shillington Restaurant (see Places to Eat) is also worth visiting.

Places to Stay

Reading is busiest from mid-September till after Christmas, so it's best to book ahead. During that time, room rates at the hotels and motels go up by as much as 40% to 50%.

Camping The nearest private campground is 10 miles southwest in Adamstown. *Sill's Family Campground* (☎ (610) 484-4806)

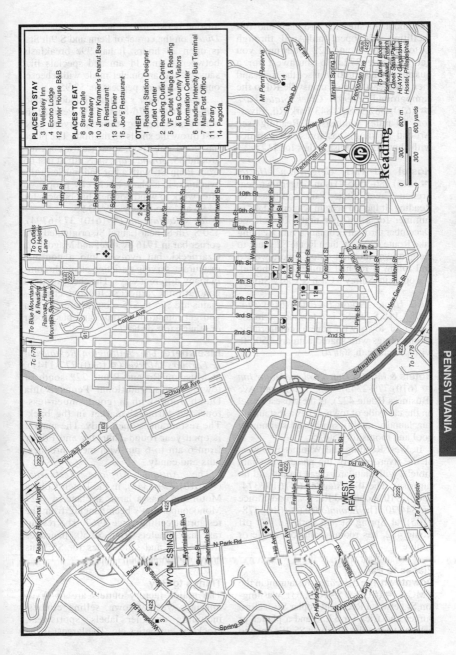

PLACES TO STAY
3   Wellesley Inn
4   Econo Lodge
12 Hunter House B&B

PLACES TO EAT
8   Strand Cafe
9   Athleatery
10 Jimmy Kramer's Peanut Bar
    & Restaurant
13 Penn Diner
15 Joe's Restaurant

OTHER
1   Reading Station Designer
    Outlet Center
2   Reading Outlet Center
5   VF Outlet Village & Reading
    & Berks County Visitors
    Information Center
6   Reading Intercity Bus Terminal
7   Main Post Office
11 Library
14 Pagoda

has about 90 sites for $16 each and full facilities. It's open mid-April through October. Take Route 222 south until you get to Route 272. Go southwest for a quarter of a mile until you see the signs and then southeast on Bowmansville Rd to the campground. *French Creek State Park* (☎ (610) 582-9680), 843 Park Rd, Elverson, 14 miles southeast of Reading (see Around Reading), has forested campsites with showers and flush toilets for $12.

Hostel HI-AYH *Geigertown Hostel* (☎ (215) 286-9535/7) is in Geigertown near French Creek State Park southeast of Reading. It has 20 beds in winter and 48 in summer for $8.50 per night. It's closed December through February. From Reading take Route 422 east, then Route 82 south to Geigertown; turn left onto Geigertown Rd and follow it for half a mile to the hostel. It's opposite Shirey's Cash & Carry Store.

B&B *Hunter House B&B* (☎ (610) 374-6608), 118 S 5th St, is a townhouse in the center of town with several comfortable rooms. Rates with shared bath are $50/60; with private bath $60/70.

Hotels & Motels *Dutch Colony Motor Inn* (☎ (610) 779-2345), 4635 Perkiomen Ave (Business Route 422), is the closest motel on the east side of town. It has a restaurant, bar, laundry facilities, a heated swimming pool and rooms for $50/55.

In West Reading and Wyomissing, west of the river, most of the places are chain motels, with standard, clean rooms and no surprises. The *Wellesley Inn* (☎ (610) 374-1500), 910 Woodland Rd, is a good choice for $44/70. The *Econolodge* (☎ (610) 378-5105), at Spring St and Park Rd just off Route 422, has rooms from $50 single or double.

Places to Eat
Downtown The *Athleatery* restaurant in the YMCA (☎ (610) 375-4700), 631 Washington St between Reed and Poplar Sts, sells a burger and fries for $3.50 and a platter of fish and vegetables for about $5. It's open to anyone between 6:30 am and 3 pm. *Penn Diner*, on the corner of Penn and S 9th Sts, is open 24 hours. It has 99¢ breakfasts between 6 and 11 am and specials like sausage and an omelet made with cheese, onions and green peppers for $2.95.

Jimmy Kramer's Peanut Bar & Restaurant (☎ (610) 376-8500), 332 Penn St, is named after the free peanuts everyone gets. Just throw the shells on the floor. The place has good pub food; most sandwiches are around $5. *Strand Cafe*, on N 6th St just up from Penn St, with a bar and music in the evenings, is a place where city people go after work to wind down. It has burgers for $4.95 and sandwiches for $3.95.

Joe's Restaurant (☎ (610) 373-6794), 450 S 7th St near Laurel St, originated as a corner bar in 1916 by Jozef and Magdalena Czarnecki, but evolved into a gourmet restaurant serving varieties of mushrooms in many different ways. The chefs are third generation Czarneki's. It's not cheap – mains are $25 to $35 – but where else can you get mushroom strudel and black bear or other game dishes?

Elsewhere The *Shillington Restaurant & Farmers' Market* (☎ (610) 777-1141), at Museum Rd and Route 222 south of town, serves traditional Pennsylvania Dutch food with a good, much-less-touristed farmers' market in the back. The restaurant is open daily. The market is open year round Thursday and Friday from 6 am to 6 pm with meat, produce, nuts and candy.

The *Antique Airplane Restaurant* (☎ (610) 779-2345), in the Dutch Colony Motor Inn, has a large airplane, a 1927 Monocoupe, that's been hanging from the restaurant ceiling since 1967. The restaurant has omelets from $2.50, pancakes from $2.25 and sandwiches for $5, plus homemade bread and soup.

Things to Buy
The major factory outlets are in Wyomissing, west of town, selling clothes, including designer labels, sportswear, crockery, cosmetics etc. The largest is the

VF Factory Outlet (☎ (610) 378-0408) in the VF Outlet Village at Park Rd and Hill Ave. Among the others spread around town are: Reading Outlet Center (☎ (610) 373-5495), 801 N 9th St; Outlets on Hiester's Lane (☎ (610) (602) 921-9394), 755 Hiester's Lane; and Reading Station Designer Outlet Center (☎ (610) 478-700), 951 N 6th St.

Getting There & Away
Air Reading regional airport (☎ (610) 372-4666) is two miles northwest on Route 183. USAir (☎ (800) 428-4322) has nine daily flights to Philadelphia, six to Pittsburgh and two to Lancaster. Roundtrip fares to Philadelphia cost $178.

Bus The Reading inter-city bus terminal (☎ (610) 374-3182), at N 3rd and Court Sts, is served by Bieber Trailways (☎ (610) 683-5384) and Capitol Trailways (☎ (717) 233-7716, (800) 444-2877). Bieber Trailways has a one-way fare to New York City for $17.40 (two hours). With Capitol Trailways the one-way fare to Philadelphia is $8.90 (1¼ hours), to Pittsburgh $46 (5¾ hours).

Car From Philadelphia take I-76 (Schuylkill Expressway) north to the Pennsylvania Turnpike, then head west to exit 22; take I-176 north to Route 422 and follow it west into downtown. From Harrisburg you can either take the Pennsylvania Turnpike east to exit 21, then Route 222 northeast, or take Route 322 then Route 422 east into Reading.

Getting Around
The Berks Area Reading Transportation Authority (BARTA; ☎ (610) 921-0601) is the county bus line. Most fares around town are $1.

AROUND READING
Daniel Boone Homestead
The famous outdoorsman was born in a log house on the site of the present homestead (☎ (610) 582-4900) on Daniel Boone Rd in Birdsboro, nine miles east of Reading. The reconstructed house includes the original foundation, portions of 18th and 19th century building material, period German and English furnishings and a spring in the basement. Inside the visitors center is a video of a fellow in

---

Daniel Boone
Daniel Boone (1734-1820) is one of America's most famous 'frontiersmen.' Boone owes much of his fame to John Filson, who added an appendix concerning 'The Adventures of Col Daniel Boone' to his book *The Discovery, Settlement, and Present State of Kentucke*. He was also the model for James Fenimore Cooper's *Leatherstocking* character and is even mentioned in Byron's *Don Juan*.

Boone was born the sixth of 11 children to a Quaker family in southeastern Pennsylvania. He had little schooling, although he did have some early experience as a farmer, weaver and blacksmith. When Daniel was 16, his family moved to northwestern North Carolina.

The Boone family home in North Carolina was on the American frontier, and although Daniel married Rebecca Bryan and had 10 children, he spent much of his life on expeditions around the country. One of his earliest was accompanying British General Braddock in his expedition to Fort Duquesne (today's Pittsburgh) in 1755.

Boone is famous for his travels in Kentucky and fighting against Native Americans there, beginning in 1767. He loved the 'dark and bloody ground' so much that he decided to build Boonesboro in Kentucky in 1774. From 1775 to 1783 Boone was a major force in expanding settlement in Kentucky and defending settlements from Native Americans. Boone himself was captured and escaped several times.

Boone was a good fighter but a lousy businessman. In 1799, after losing his Kentucky lands, he went to Missouri and stayed there until his death 21 years later. ■

old garb talking as though he knew Boone. Admission is $4/2, seniors $3, which includes a guided tour. Around the homestead are 600 acres of land with hiking and biking trails. The opening hours are Tuesday to Saturday from 9 am to 5 pm and Sunday noon to 5 pm.

Take Route 422 east to the intersection with Route 82; continue straight through the traffic lights and after the sign for the homestead turn left onto Daniel Boone Rd. The entrance to the property is about a mile from the turning.

Blue Mountain & Reading Railroad

The railroad (☎ (610) 562-2101/4083) does a 90 minute scenic steam-train ride along the Schuylkill River valley from Temple in north Reading for $7/5. Take Route 222 north for about five miles until you see the Temple Family Restaurant then make a left onto Tuckerton Rd. Drive across the tracks to the station house.

Hawk Mountain Sanctuary

The sanctuary (☎ (610) 756-6961), Rural Route 2, Kempton, 28 miles north of Reading, was originally established in the 1930s to protect migrating hawks from hunters, but it's also a preserve for bald eagles, ospreys and other migrating birds. Spring and fall bring over 24,000 of them to the sanctuary. A four mile walking trail connects with the Appalachian Trail. You can rent binoculars at the visitors center, open daily December through August from 9 am to 5 pm, September through November from 8 am. It gets busy on weekends. Admission is $4/2, seniors $3. Take Route 61 north then Rural Route 2 east.

French Creek State Park

The 11.5 sq mile French Creek State Park (☎ (610) 582-9680), 843 Park Rd, Elverson, about 14 miles southeast of Reading off Route 422, has camping facilities and 32 miles of hiking trails. Fishing and boating are available on Scotts Run and Hopewell lakes. Memorial Day to Labor Day there's swimming daily from 11 am to 7 pm in a pool beside Hopewell Lake.

You can see deer, squirrels and, in the spring and fall, many migratory birds.

From Route 422 take Route 82 south, Route 724 east then Route 345 south into the park. Surrounded on three sides by the park is **Hopewell Furnace National Historic Site** (☎ (610) 582-8773), 2 Mark Bird Lane, a restored early-19th century village with a cold-blast ironmaking furnace. Call for special events.

LEBANON & AROUND

In Lebanon (population 25,000), Weaver & Baum's (☎ (717) 274-6100), at 15th Ave and Weavertown Rd, is a competitor to the larger Seltzer's (see Palmyra, following) in the production of Lebanon bologna. There's no tour but you can have a look at the smokehouses. It's open Monday to Saturday from 9 am to 4 pm.

If you head east on Route 422 you'll come to **Willow Spring Park** (☎ (717) 866-5801), with a small lake open for swimming from Memorial Day to Labor Day, Monday to Thursday from 10 am to 6 pm, Friday to Sunday 10 am to 6 pm. It costs $5/3 on weekends, $3/2.50 weekdays. July through September there's also scuba diving daily from 8 am to 6 pm for $10; the rest of the year diving is by appointment only on weekends. The Jolly Roger Dive Shop (☎ (717) 866-5535) opposite the entrance to Willow Springs has swimming and scuba-diving equipment and tests oxygen tanks. From Lebanon head for the traffic lights two miles east of the junction with Route 501; turn right at the lights onto Tulpehocken Rd and the park is a quarter of a mile on the left.

Getting There & Away

Lebanon is on Route 422 eight miles east of Palmyra, 87 miles west of Reading. Capitol Trailways stops at Great Vacations Travel Agency (☎ (717) 272-0161), 515 Great Cumberland St; the office is in what looks like the entrance to a former cinema and is open Monday, Tuesday, Thursday, Friday from 9 am to 6:30 pm, Wednesday 8 am to 6:30 pm, Saturday 9 am to 1 pm.

Up to six buses leave daily for Harrisburg, four for Reading; the one-way fare for both is $5.25.

Getting Around

The County of Lebanon Transit office (COLT; ☎ (717) 274-3664) is at 200 Willow St; the main bus stop is at Willow and N 7th Sts.

PALMYRA

Palmyra is the home of Seltzer's (☎ (800) 282-6336), 230 N College St, the largest producer of Lebanon bologna in the USA. The US government classifies the bologna officially as 'semi-dry fermented sausage.' Whatever it's called, they make tons of it every day.

According to the company: The meat arrives and is aged, cured, ground and smoked before being put through a metal detector and cut into appropriate sizes. It's not actually cooked, so much as fermented, a combination of lowering the pH balance, salting and smoking to protect it.

There's a free tour of the small plant and the smokehouses Monday to Friday from 8:45 to 11:45 am and 12:30 to 3:15 pm. The sales outlet is open Monday to Friday from 7 am to 5 pm, Saturday 7 am to 1 pm. Seltzer's is signposted off Main St (Route 422), but not too clearly – turn at the crossroads with Turkey Hill Minit Mart and Cinderella Shoppe on opposite corners.

Palmyra is a couple of miles east of Hershey on Route 422. The Capitol Trailways bus stops at Lauck's Brothers store (☎ (717) 838-9652), 30 E Main St.

South Central Pennsylvania

The terrain of South Central Pennsylvania tends to be flat and fairly monotonous. The area's major river is the Susquehanna, which flows through Harrisburg, the state capital, southeastward between Lancaster and York into Maryland and the Chesapeake Bay. Gettysburg, with its Civil War battleground, is clearly the most interesting place to visit. The town of Hershey too is hard to resist, although for many it's something of a let down except for those young enough to enjoy the chocolate-world fantasy.

Other notable places are the Harley-Davidson factory in York and the Three Mile Island nuclear plant near Harrisburg.

GETTYSBURG

Gettysburg (population 7000) is about 55 miles southwest of Lancaster and 30 miles southwest of Harrisburg. Its position at the junction of several roads and its proximity to the Mason-Dixon line helped to make it the site of a battle that would be the bloodiest in US history. The battle proved to be a turning point in the Civil War and helped inspire Lincoln's Gettysburg Address.

It also helped inspire today's busy tourist industry capitalizing on both the battle and the war. Nevertheless, Gettysburg National Military Park is certainly worth visiting to see where the Union and Confederate armies fought each other. The former home of President Eisenhower is another attraction nearby. Most of the rest of the tourist attractions can be skipped, unless you have a particular interest. Gettysburg, the town, with its many fine historic buildings is small enough to walk around.

Orientation

The approximately 1½ sq mile of Gettysburg is laid out around Lincoln Square. Several large roads converge on the town. Route 30 (York and Chambersburg Sts in town) and Route 116 (Hanover, York

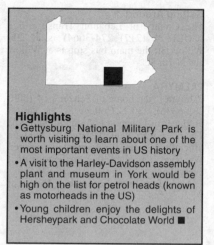

Highlights
- Gettysburg National Military Park is worth visiting to learn about one of the most important events in US history
- A visit to the Harley-Davidson assembly plant and museum in York would be high on the list for petrol heads (known as motorheads in the US)
- Young children enjoy the delights of Hersheypark and Chocolate World ■

and W Middle Sts) cross east-west. Route 97 enters from the south (Baltimore St) and leaves from the north as Route 34 (Carlisle St). Business Route 15 enters town as Steinwehr Ave from the southwest and exits in the northeast as Harrisburg Rd. Finally, Route 134 enters from the south as Taneytown Rd and ends in town as Washington St.

Gettysburg National Military Park surrounds the town and still has homes and stores in it, as the area did at the time of the battle.

Information

The town tourist office is the Gettysburg Travel Council (☎ (717) 334-6274), 35 Carlisle St, open daily from 9 am to 7 pm. The First Federal Savings Bank, on Chambersburg St, is open Saturday from 8:30 am to noon. The national military park also has a visitors center; see below.

The main post office (☎ (717) 337-3781), 155 Buford Ave, is open Monday

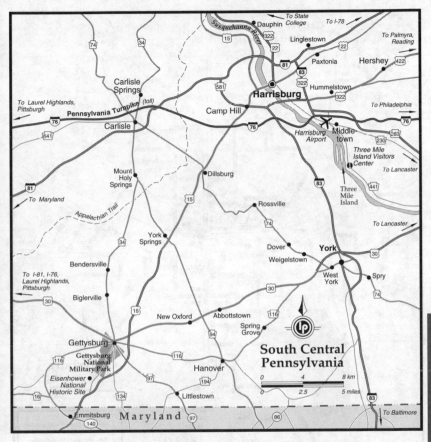

to Friday from 8 am to 4:30 pm, Saturday 9 am to noon.

Adams County Library, on High St between Baltimore and S Stratton Sts, is open Monday to Thursday from 9 am to 8:30 pm, Friday and Saturday 9 am to 5 pm, Sunday 1 to 5 pm.

Walking Tour

Start at the Gettysburg Travel Council on Carlisle St one block north of Lincoln Square and walk south toward the square. On the first day of battle Union soldiers streamed into town from the north and west across Lincoln Square in retreat south toward Cemetery Hill. As they retreated, they dragged cannons and stopped periodically to fire north along the streets toward the pursuing Confederate troops.

Continue west (right) on Chambersburg St to **Christ Lutheran Church** on your left. A Union chaplain who had been tending the wounded inside was killed here by advancing Confederate troops because he didn't identify himself as a man of the cloth on being challenged.

Continue west for three blocks then go left (south) for one block on West St and

PENNSYLVANIA

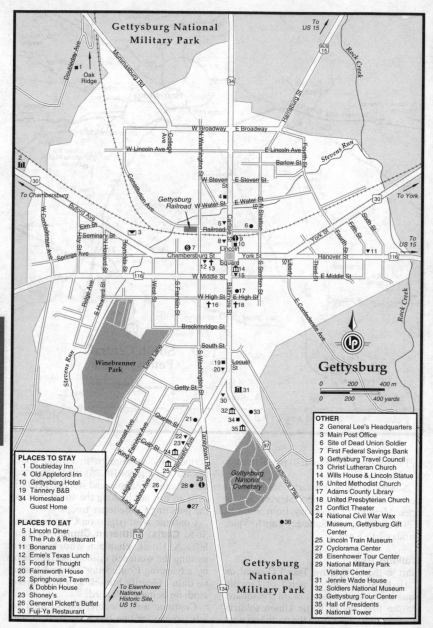

Gettysburg

| 0 | 200 | 400 m |
| 0 | 200 | 400 yards |

PLACES TO STAY
1 Doubleday Inn
4 Old Appleford Inn
10 Gettysburg Hotel
19 Tannery B&B
34 Homestead
    Guest Home

PLACES TO EAT
5 Lincoln Diner
8 The Pub & Restaurant
11 Bonanza
12 Ernie's Texas Lunch
15 Food for Thought
20 Springhouse Tavern
22 Springhouse Tavern
    & Dobbin House
23 Shoney's
26 General Pickett's Buffet
30 Fuji-Ya Restaurant

OTHER
2 General Lee's Headquarters
3 Main Post Office
6 Site of Dead Union Soldier
7 First Federal Savings Bank
9 Gettysburg Travel Council
13 Christ Lutheran Church
14 Wills House & Lincoln Statue
16 United Methodist Church
17 Adams County Library
18 United Presbyterian Church
21 Conflict Theater
24 National Civil War Wax
    Museum, Gettysburg Gift
    Center
25 Lincoln Train Museum
27 Cyclorama Center
28 Eisenhower Tour Center
29 National Military Park
    Visitors Center
31 Jennie Wade House
32 Soldiers National Museum
33 Gettysburg Tour Center
35 Hall of Presidents
36 National Tower

Herr's Mill in Intercourse, PA

Battlefield in Gettysburg National Military Park, PA

TOM SMALLMAN
Cathedral of Learning, Oakland
suburb of Pittsburgh, PA

TOM SMALLMAN
Pennsylvania Capitol in Harrisburg

TOM SMALLMAN
Northern Pennsylvania's fall foliage

TOM SMALLMAN
Presque Isle State Park, Erie, PA

then turn right (east) onto W Middle St, which, during the second and third days of the battle, was part of the Confederate line. Go two blocks and turn right (south) onto S Washington St, then walk one block and turn east (right) onto W High St. Here on the site of the **United Methodist Church** (built after the war) was an earlier church in which the wounded were treated. Two trenches were dug in front of this church to bury the dead, wrapped in blankets and packed next to each other.

Nearby, Lincoln sat in the pew of the **United Presbyterian Church** on the corner of Baltimore St, and the retired President Eisenhower worshipped here as well. Lincoln paraded south along Baltimore St on his way to give his address at the National Cemetery.

Turn north (left) on S Stratton St; go two blocks to the intersection with York St. Before turning west (left) on York St look north to the southeastern corner of N Stratton St and the railroad tracks; there, after the battle, an unidentified Union soldier was found dead holding a photo of his three children. The photo was reproduced all over the country until his wife in upstate New York identified the man as Sergeant Amos Humiston.

Continue west on York St to Lincoln Square; note **Wills House** (and the Lincoln Statue in front), in which Lincoln wrote the final draft of the Gettysburg Address.

Gettysburg National Military Park

Established on February 11, 1895, the eight sq mile park encompasses almost the entire area of the three day battle. In essence, the park is a huge shrine attracting thousands of visitors each year. The battlefield contains more than 1600 monuments, statues, cannons and plaques set up all over the place in dedication to the people who fought here. All were erected in good faith, but with so many the effect is a somewhat cluttered one.

Information The National Military Park Visitors Center (☎ (717) 334-1124), less than a mile south of Lincoln Square in the park off Taneytown Rd, is open daily from 8 am to 5 pm. There you can pick up the *Official Map & Guide*. The map takes you along a route past markers (signs with a single large white star on them) with descriptions of the action at the important points. A self-guided driving tour using the map takes two to three hours. The visitors center has a large selection of books about the battle and the Civil War.

Licensed battlefield guides charge $25 per carload of up to five people for a two hour tour that is well worth it. Guides are available on a first-come, first-served basis and you need to get there early, except in winter. There are also guided walks with park rangers of the National Cemetery and High Water Mark.

Things to See & Do The visitors center has a good, small, free **museum** with Civil War uniforms, guns, implements and other artifacts that are just enough to satisfy the moderately curious. Also in the visitors center is the **electric map**. You sit in tiered seats around a large diorama illuminated with colored lights on the floor in the middle of the room; a park service employee narrates the progress of the three day battle. Admission is adults $2, children under 15 free. The museum and the electric map are open the same hours as the visitors center.

The most famous part of the battlefield is probably the part of **Cemetery Ridge** against which Confederate General Pickett hurled his cavalry – Pickett's Charge – resulting in 80% casualties. This is less than half a mile south of the visitors center, and you can walk to it on the **High Water Mark Trail**. There are other longer hikes. The one mile **Big Round Top Loop Trail** goes through a forest and past breastworks built by both troops. The nine mile **Billy Yank Trail** and 3½ mile **Johnny Reb Trail** are other options. Another interesting part of the battlefield, liked by kids as well as adults, is the **Devil's Den**, a mass of boulders used as a hideout by Confederate snipers.

In the **Cyclorama Center** is a large 360° circular painting of the battle displayed around the audience. A guide describes the

The Battle of Gettysburg

Gettysburg is the most famous battle of the Civil War. War buffs spend their lives studying the battle or only one day of it. At Gettysburg, from July 1 to 3, 1863, the 75,000 men of Robert E Lee's Confederate army met the 97,000 men of Union General George G Meade. The battle resulted from a chance sighting by a group of Confederate troops, sent to get supplies, of some of Meade's cavalry.

It began on July 1 with Confederate troops attacking Union troops on McPherson Ridge, west of Gettysburg. The Union troops held their position until the afternoon, when they were beaten back in a rout through town. Thousands were captured before they could regroup on Cemetery Hill south of town. The first day of battle ended with the Union troops, who had retreated, fortifying their positions while the bulk of Meade's army arrived to reinforce them.

By dawn of the second day the Confederate troops were laid out along an arc running through the middle of Gettysburg and along Seminary Hill. Facing them a mile away to the east was a smaller arc of Union troops on Cemetery Ridge. Lee ordered attacks against both flanks of the Union line. Confederate James Longstreet's attack smashed through the Union left flank at a peach orchard south of town and overran the Union position on Little Round Top. On the other flank though, RS Ewell's attack didn't succeed in dislodging the Union troops and, ultimately, Longstreet's success couldn't be exploited successfully by the Confederates.

On the third day, Lee's artillery bombarded Union positions on Cemetery Ridge and Cemetery Hill; the Union artillery responded. The sickening high point came when Confederate General George Pickett led a massive charge of 12,000 men across an open field toward the Union line at Cemetery Ridge. In less than an hour 10,000 of Pickett's men were dead or wounded and the expression 'Pickett's Charge' entered the lexicon as a brave but futile attempt to defeat an enemy.

After the battle, there were 51,000 dead, wounded and missing troops, and 5000 dead horses. Lee's invasion of the North had been stymied and he would never again attempt an operation of this size. Union General Meade 'won' the battle, but was too cautious (or too afraid) to pursue the Confederate army.

The dead were buried all over the battlefield in hasty graves and some weren't buried at all until Pennsylvania Governor Andrew Curtin ordered that land be purchased for a cemetery. This became the Gettysburg National Cemetery and on November 19, 1863, the cemetery was dedicated; near the end of the ceremonies Abraham Lincoln gave his now-famous Gettysburg Address. ■

battle and illuminates different parts of the painting in a 20 minute show. Think of it as early TV. This one was finished in 1884 by Paul Philippoteaux, who was already known for his cycloramas on the Battle of Waterloo and the Crucifixion of Jesus. He did three other versions of Gettysburg. The cyclorama is open from 9 am to 5 pm; admission is $2/free, seniors $1.50.

The **Gettysburg National Cemetery** contains the graves of more than 6000 US servicemen, including 3582 Union soldiers killed in the Civil War. Nearly half of the Civil War burials were unknown soldiers. You can view the battlefield from the 307 foot high **National Tower**, southeast of the visitors center. It's open daily from 9 am to 7:30 pm in summer, to 5:30 pm the rest of the year. Admission is $4.90/2.65, seniors $4.35.

Eisenhower National Historic Site

The farm house, west of the national park, that was the home of President Dwight D Eisenhower (Ike) and his wife, Mamie, is administered by the NPS as a historic site. You can only visit it by shuttle bus from the Eisenhower Tour Center (☎ (717) 334-1124) behind the visitors center in the National Military Park. The bus leaves every 30 minutes between 9 am and 4 pm; admission to the house is $3.75, children aged 13 to 16 are $1.75, children six to 12 are $1.15. The Eisenhower Tour Center, open daily from 8:30 am to 4:15 pm, runs a biographical video which you can watch while waiting for the shuttle; there are also photographs and some WWII military artifacts.

General Lee's Headquarters

One of the few old homes open to the public, this house (☎ (717) 334-3141) on Buford Ave (Route 30), was Lee's head-quarters during the battle on July 1, 1863, and has a collection of memorabilia from the period. It's open daily March through November from 9 am to 9 pm, December through February to 5 pm; admission is $1.50/free.

Wills House & Lincoln Room Museum

The house (☎ (717) 334-8188), 12 Lincoln Square, in which Lincoln revised the Get-tysburg Address, has some Lincoln arti-facts in a room on the 2nd floor. Contrary to popular belief, Lincoln didn't write his most famous speech on the back of an envelope while on the way to Gettysburg. He actually wrote a draft in Washington and revised it here in Gettysburg before delivering it at the National Cemetery on November 19, 1863. The house is open Sunday to Thursday from 9 am to 5 pm, Friday and Saturday 9 am to 7 pm; the admission is $3/1.50.

The Conflict Theater

The Conflict Theater (☎ (717) 334-8003), 213 Steinwehr Ave, shows three audiovi-sual programs – narrated stories told against a backdrop of slides, photos and period music. The programs are 'Three Days at Gettysburg' (the story of the battle), 'The War Within' (the story of the Civil War) and 'Adventure at Gettysburg' (a fictional story of a young boy who gets involved in the battle, aimed at kids). The programs are 50 minutes each. During the summer on Satur-day the theater shows 'The Conflict,' a four part Civil War series from 1 to 5 pm. The theater is open weekdays (except Wednes-day) from noon to 6 pm, Saturday 10 am to 7 pm; Sunday 1 to 5 pm. Admission is $5/4.

Jennie Wade House

Jennie Wade, shot by a stray bullet while making bread in her house, is said to be the only civilian killed in the battle. The house (☎ (717) 334-4100), on Baltimore Pike, was actually hit by 200 bullets. Although many Gettysburg residents prefer not to discuss it, the Wade house is one of those locally believed to be haunted; there have allegedly been incidents of 'positive move-ment' of items in the cellar, including a swinging chain. It's open daily from 9 am to 7 pm; admission is $5.25/3.25.

Gettysburg Railroad

April through October, the Gettysburg Railroad (☎ (717) 334-6932), 106 N Wash-ington St, runs a 1½ hour, 16 mile steam train ride to Biglerville; the roundtrip fare is $7.50/3.50, seniors $7.

Other Sights

The **National Civil War Wax Museum** (☎ (717) 334-6245), 297 Steinwehr Ave, is one of those tacky tourist sights that's actu-ally worth a visit although it doesn't have any horror figures. Inside is the **Battle-room Auditorium**, a show of electroni-cally controlled, life-sized mannequins reenacting Pickett's Charge and the giving of the Gettysburg Address. It's open daily from 9 am to 5 pm, and admission is adult $4.50, youth 13 to 17 $2.50, children six to 12, $1.75.

The **Hall of Presidents** (☎ (717) 334-5717, (800) 447-8788), on Baltimore St near the main entrance to the National Cemetery, features portraits and wax sculptures of

Old Glory Trivia

The grave of Jennie Wade and the white-brick Gettysburg College 'Old Dorm' building, used as an observation post and hospital at the time of the battle, are two of only 20 places in the USA at which the American flag can legally be flown 24 hours a day. Nor-mally, the flag must be taken down at night. ■

presidents and their first ladies. It's open daily from 9 am to 5 pm in spring and fall, until 9 pm during the summer. Admission is $5.25/3.75, seniors $4.50.

A huge collection of uniforms, guns, detailed dioramas of Civil War scenes and other memorabilia are housed in the **Soldiers National Museum** (☎ (717) 334-4890) on Baltimore St. It's open daily from 9 am to 7 pm and admission is $5.25/3.25. As well as toy trains and dioramas, the **Lincoln Train Museum** (☎ (717) 334-6296), 200 Steinwehr Ave, has a simulated a train ride with Lincoln on board – as exciting as it sounds. It's open daily from 9 am to 7 pm and admission is $5.25/3.25.

Organized Tours

Gettysburg Tour Center (☎ (717) 334-6296), 778 Baltimore St, has two packages. Package Plan I does a 23 mile bus tour of the battlefield and visits the Hall of Presidents *or* Soldiers National Museum; the Lincoln Train Museum *or* Gettysburg Battle Theater; Jennie Wade House *or* National Tower; and the National Wax Museum *or* Lincoln Tower Museum. It costs $26.75/16.95. Package Plan II does the battlefield, National Tower, National Wax Museum, Soldier's National Museum, Lincoln's Train, Battle Theater, Lincoln Room, Hall of Presidents and Jennie Wade House for $38.95/24.75. It also sells an audio-tape tour that takes about two hours for $12.95.

The Ghost of Gettysburg Candlelight Walking Tours (☎ (717) 337-0445), takes you on a one mile, 1½ hour tour of sites where ghostly happenings are said to have occurred. Tours leave from Lincoln Square daily at 8 and 9:45 pm and cost $6; you need to book ahead.

Special Events

May
> *Gettysburg Spring Bluegrass Festival* – two days of concerts usually on the first weekend of the month (☎ (717) 642-8749)

June/July
> *Gettysburg Civil War Heritage Days* – commemoration of the Battle of Gettysburg, with an encampment, concerts and battle

re-enactments during the last weekend in June and first week in July (☎ (717) 334-6274); coincides with Civil War Institute lectures by Civil War scholars at Gettysburg College (☎ (717) 337-6590); the Civil War Collectors Show (☎ (717) 334-6274), with displays of Civil War artifacts; and the Civil War Book Fair

August
> *Gettysburg Fall Bluegrass Festival* – four days of concerts over the third weekend of the month (☎ (717) 642-8749)

November
> *Anniversary of Lincoln's Gettysburg Address* – commemoration with memorial services at the National Cemetery on November 19 (☎ (717) 334-6274)

Places to Stay

There are a fair amount of accommodations available in the town of Gettysburg as well as in the surrounding area, but it gets crowded in summer, especially on weekends and during the Gettysburg Civil War Heritage Days (see above). The cheaper places are generally a few miles out of town; check out Business Route 15 south or Route 34 north.

Camping Gettysburg has a number of large campgrounds within three or four miles of town; all of them have major facilities like swimming pool, laundry, store, propane gas and anything else you might need.

Battlefield Camp Resort (☎ (717) 334-1577), three miles southwest on Business Route 15 (Steinwehr Ave) has 250 sites for $16 for two people, $18.50 with electricity. It's open May 1 to October 15. *Artillery Ridge Camping Resort* (☎ (717) 334-1288), three miles south at 610 Taneytown Rd, has sites for $12.50 for two people or $17 with water and electricity; each extra person is $3. It offers fishing, rents bicycles and organizes trail rides. One mile further south *Round Top Campground* (☎ (717) 334-9565), 180 Knight Rd off Taneytown Rd, has tent sites for $12.50, RV sites for $18.75.

Drummer Boy Camping Resort (☎ (800) 336-3269), 1300 Hanover Rd, has sites for $17, or $20.50 with water and electricity.

Rates are an extra $2 on weekends, or $4 on public-holiday weekends. It's open April through October, organizes entertainment and activities on weekends and rents bicycles. From town take Route 116 east for 1½ miles to just past the junction with Route 15 then turn left onto Hanover Rd.

Gettysburg Campground (☎ (717) 334-3304), 2030 Fairfield Rd, has sites for $16.50 each, $20.50 on weekends. It's open April 1 to November 30. From town take Route 116 (which becomes Fairfield Rd) west for three miles. A further three miles west is *Granite Hill Campground* (☎ (717) 642-8749), 3340 Fairfield Rd. It has sites for $18, with water and electricity $21, and is open year round.

Guesthouse A real bargain, the *Homestead Guest Home* (☎ (717) 334-2037), 785 Baltimore St, is in the building that was the former Soldiers' Orphans Homestead, built for the orphans of men killed at Gettysburg. It's a friendly place run by Mrs Mary Collins and Mrs Louise O'Connor, the sisters were raised in the house and Mary will happily tell you about its history. Rooms cost $25/30 without/with a private bathroom.

Motels The *Criterion Motor Lodge* (☎ (717) 334-6268), 337 Carlisle St, has rooms for $40 to $55. In a quiet location, the *Blue Sky Motel* (☎ (717) 677-7736), 2585 Biglerville Rd (Route 34), is a small place with 16 rooms, a small picnic area and a heated pool. Rooms are $36/39. Take Route 34 north for 4½ miles.

The *Perfect Rest Motel* (☎ (717) 334-1345), 4½ miles south on Business Route 15, has 25 rooms and a swimming pool. Singles/doubles are $40/45.

B&Bs The *Tannery B&B* (☎ (717) 334-2454), 449 Baltimore St, is a Gothic house decorated with Civil War memorabilia and there's a porch out the front with rocking chairs. Rates, including continental breakfast, are $65/75.

The *Old Appleford Inn* (☎ (717) 337-1711, (800) 275-3373), 218 Carlisle St, is a large, beautiful Victorian house that has 11 rooms all with private baths. The house is nicely furnished, with high ceilings, a library, five wood-burning fireplaces, wooden floors and a large sun room. Rooms (named after Union and Confederate generals) are from $78/88.

Hotels & Inns The *Gettysburg Hotel* (☎ (717) 337-2000, (800) 528-1234), 1 Lincoln Square in the center of town, was built in 1797 and has been fully renovated. Rooms are $86/115 to $115/135. The *Doubleday Inn* (☎ (717) 334-9119), 104 Doubleday Ave (at Oak Ridge, near stop No 3 on the self-guided driving tour of the battlefield) is a large, white house that overlooks a quiet part of the battlefield and Gettysburg College. There are nine rooms, five of which have private baths with clawfoot tubs. Every Saturday a historian from the National Military Park Visitors Center comes to the house to speak and answer questions. Rooms are $74/84 without private bath, $94/104 with.

Places to Eat
Budget Opposite the entrance to the park on Steinwehr Ave is a conglomeration of fast-food places, including *Pizza Hut, KFC, Hardee's* and *McDonald's*.

Food For Thought (☎ (717) 337-2221), 48 Baltimore St, is a student hangout with a laid-back atmosphere and natural food. It has books and magazines for browsing and on weekends some students play improvised music. For breakfast there's yogurt with fruit and granola for $2; lunch dishes like pita bread with turkey, hummus and salad are $4.25, vegetarian quesadilla $3.75.

Ernie's Texas Lunch, 58 Chambersburg St, is a Formica-boothed neighborhood place that serves burgers or Texas hot dogs with mustard, onion and chili for $1.22. Sandwiches cost $1.15 to $3.65 and hoagies from $3.65. It's closed Sunday. The *Lincoln Diner* (☎ (717) 334-3900), 32 Carlisle St next to the railroad tracks, is a good diner popular around lunch and open 24 hours a day. Sandwiches are $1.75, hamburgers $2.15, roast beef $5.95.

Moderate If you like to gorge, *General Pickett's Buffet* (☎ (717) 334-7580), 571 Steinwehr Ave, has an all-you-can-eat lunch buffet for $6 and one at dinner for $10. Soup, salad and dessert buffet are $5 at either lunch or dinner. Kids under 10 accompanied by an adult eat for $2. There are also all-you-can-eat buffets at *Shoney's* (☎ (717) 334-7618), 259 Steinwehr Ave, and *Bonanza* (☎ (717) 334-0470), 39 N Fifth St.

Fuji-Ya Restaurant (☎ (717) 3334-7274), 44 Steinwehr Ave, serves Japanese, spicy Korean and Chinese dishes. Bulgogi (marinated beef) is $7, chicken teriyaki $6.50, shrimp with broccoli $7. It's open for lunch and dinner Tuesday to Saturday, dinner only on Sunday and Monday.

The *Springhouse Tavern* in Dobbin House (☎ (717) 334-2100), 89 Steinwehr Ave, is an old tavern with a bar built in the early 19th century by the great-great-great grandfather of the present owner. Salmagundi (a salad of garden greens with ham, turkey, eggs and cheese) costs $6.25, sandwiches with two meats of your choice plus salad are $5.75. Dinner mains of marinated chicken breast are $10.25, ribs $15.95.

The *Pub & Restaurant*, on the corner of Lincoln Square, is a popular eatery whose large windows afford good views of the square. You can also dine outside on the sidewalk. It serves pasta dishes for $9 to $15 and a variety of sandwiches for $5.50; it also offers seafood and steaks and a wide selection of beer and wine.

Top End *Farnsworth House* (☎ (717) 334-8838), 401 Baltimore St, is a restaurant in an 1810 brick-and-wood home with most of the original walls, floors and rafters intact. Dinner is served by staff dressed in period outfits and the cuisine is early American. Most main dishes are $10 to $19; grilled chicken is $12.95 and walnut apple cake $3.25. It's open for dinner only daily from 5 to 9 pm.

Dobbin House (☎ (717) 334-2100), 89 Steinwehr Ave above the Springhouse Tavern, has dishes like roast duck for $16.75 and is open daily for dinner only from 5 to 9 pm.

Entertainment
The *Majestic Cinema*, just north of Lincoln Square on Baltimore St, shows movies for $5.75 (matinees $3.75). For a beer try the *Pub & Restaurant* on Lincoln Square.

Things to Buy
Gettysburg is full of shops selling Civil War trinkets and antiques, most of which appear comparable in quality and price, but you'll have to wade through a lot to find anything of quality. Innumerable items are emblazoned with the word 'Gettysburg' or some Blue (Union) or Gray (Confederate) icon. The Gettysburg Gift Center (☎ (717) 334-6245), part of the Civil War Wax Museum at 297 Steinwehr Ave, is as good a place as any for trinkets, but other shops advertise antiques and you might find them worth a look.

Getting There & Away
Incredibly, there is no public transportation of any kind to or around Gettysburg. By car, it's accessible on Route 30 from Philadelphia, Lancaster or York, from Harrisburg on Route 15 and from Maryland on Routes 15 and 97. From Philadelphia you can also take the Pennsylvania Turnpike (I-76) west to exit 17 and follow Route 15 south.

HARRISBURG
Harrisburg (population 52,000), the state capital, is a small picturesque city lying on the shores of the Susquehanna River. Originally a ferryboat station known as Harris's Ferry, it was renamed Harrisburg in 1785 when John Harris, son of one of the first European settlers here, refused a state-government order to name it Louisburg in honor of France's Louis XVI. It became the state capital in 1812 and was incorporated as a city in 1860. It still retains a small-town feel, though, and has managed to preserve many of its 18th and 19th century buildings, especially in the residential streets near the center and along Front St. It's not heavily touristed and is somewhat overshadowed as a place to visit by the nearby Hershey and Three Mile Island nuclear power plant.

Orientation & Information

Market St divides the city north and south; 2nd St, between State and Market Sts, is a busy shopping area. The Chamber of Commerce (☎ (717) 232-1377), 114 Walnut St, isn't a tourist office as such but does have brochures on the town and region; you may need to ask the person on reception for a map if none is on display. It's open Monday to Friday from 9 am to 5 pm. The main post office, 813 King Blvd, is open Monday to Friday from 7 am to 6 pm, Saturday 8 am to 2 pm; another more central post office is in the Federal Building at Third and Walnut Sts.

State Capitol

Italian Renaissance in style, the impressive, 651 room State Capitol (☎ (717) 787-6810), on N 3rd St between North and Walnut Sts, has a 272 foot bronze dome modeled on St Peter's Basilica in Rome, a red-and-gold rotunda, bronze doors, paintings, sculptures and stained glass. The marble staircase and surrounding balconies are modeled on the one at the Opera House in Paris. On the 4th floor is a viewing area from which visitors can watch the action in the senate chamber. There are free guided tours Monday to Friday from 8:30 am to 4:30 pm, weekends 9 am to 4 pm.

State Museum of Pennsylvania

This museum (☎ (717) 787-4978), at N 3rd and North Sts beside the State Capitol, houses many Civil War artifacts as well as the huge *Battle of Gettysburg* painting. Also on view are exhibits on archeology, geology and industry; a small planetarium operates on weekends. The museum is open Tuesday to Saturday from 9 am to 5 pm, Sunday noon to 5 pm, and is free.

Museum of Scientific Discovery

More interesting for children with its interactive displays is the Museum of Scientific Discovery (☎ (717) 233-7969), on the 3rd floor of the Strawberry Square Shopping Center at N 3rd and Walnut Sts. There's a flight simulator like the ones used by pilots in training and an exhibition on dinosaurs. The museum is open Tuesday to Friday from 9 am to 5 pm, Saturday 10 am to 5 pm, Sunday noon to 5 pm. Admission is $5/4.

City Island

City Island is an island park in the Susquehanna River which can be reached from downtown on foot across the Walnut St footbridge or by car across Market St Bridge. It has a bathing beach, nature trails and jogging tracks.

Places to Stay

There are few accommodations in the center of town. Opposite the entrance to the Harrisburg Transportation Center, the basic *Alva Restaurant & Hotel* (☎ (717) 238-7553), 19 S 4th St, has functional singles/doubles from $28/35.

Most accommodations are in motels to the north of town near I-81 and I-83 along N Front St. *Super 8 Motel* (☎ (717) 233-5891), 4125 N Front St (at the I-81 Front St exit), is the closest with standard, clean rooms for $47/55.

Places to Eat

The *Strawberry Square Shopping Center* has a food court on the 2nd floor – it's centrally located. *Bangkok Wok*, at N 3rd and Liberty Sts opposite the main staircase of the State Capitol, has Thai food with most dishes about $5.50, but it's open for lunch only. Nearby, *Esquire Deli*, N 3rd St, has omelets from $2 and soup for $1.50. There are several places along N 2nd St, the pick of which is the popular *Zephyr Express* (☎ (717) 257-1328), at No 402; it serves pasta for $5.25 and pizza $4.50. It has a good vegetarian selection and is open daily from 11 am.

Getting There & Away

Air Harrisburg airport (☎ (717) 948-3913) is 15 minutes' drive southeast of Harrisburg in Middletown near the river. USAir (☎ (800) 428-4322) has six daily flights to Philadelphia and Pittsburgh. Roundtrip fares to Philadelphia cost from $208.

Bus & Train The bus and train stations are in the refurbished Harrisburg Transportation Center (☎ (717) 232-4251), 411 Market St at S 4th St The center has a cobbled forecourt and its train section has an elegant, wood-paneled interior. There's a daily Amtrak train to Philadelphia ($14 one way, 55 minutes) and Pittsburgh ($65 one way, 5¾ hours). The Greyhound bus station is below the train station; Capitol Trailways also stops here. There are five buses daily to Philadelphia ($13 one way, 2½ hours).

Car Harrisburg is at the intersection of a number of major highways. The east-west Pennsylvania Turnpike (I-76) passes through Harrisburg between Philadelphia and Pittsburgh. I-83 and I-81 pass through town connecting it with Maryland to the south; I-83 also connects with York 25 miles to the south. Route 230 joins

Harrisburg with Lancaster 43 miles to the southeast.

Getting Around
Capitol Area Transit (CAT; ☎ (717) 238-8304), 901 Cameron St, operates the city's buses. The CAT Transfer Center, in Market Square at Market St and S 2nd St, is the main downtown bus stop and has a customer-service kiosk where you can obtain route maps, schedule details and bus passes. The one-way fare around town is $1.10. CAT also runs motorized trolley buses between the State Capitol, Strawberry Square Shopping Center and City Island for 50¢.

THREE MILE ISLAND
Three Mile Island, in the Susquehanna River off Route 441 about 10 miles south of Harrisburg, is America's most famous nuclear plant because of its partial melt-

---

Nuclear Accident at Three Mile Island
On March 28, 1979 the core of the Unit 2 nuclear reactor, which had only been operating for about three months, overheated and partially melted. In the process the plant released significant amounts of radioactive gases.

The essential problem was that a valve became stuck open and allowed water that normally cooled the core to flow out. Reactor operators failed to notice the stuck valve for over two hours because of inadequate training. When it finally closed, operators, after noticing that water had been lost, added water to cool the reactor; this colder water caused many of the very hot fuel rods to shatter. Pennsylvania's governor ordered pregnant women in the Harrisburg area to be evacuated and many others left as well.

Subsequent reports found that there were no 'significant' health effects caused by the meltdown. The cleanup cost about $1 billion and included evaporating 2.3 million gallons of 'slightly radioactive' water into the atmosphere (don't breathe too deeply).

It can be argued that the Three Mile Island accident was profoundly helpful to the US anti-nuclear movement. Afterwards, opponents had a clear-cut example of a near-disaster, and massive demonstrations against nuclear power followed in the 1980s. The industry has been under intense scrutiny since the accident and no new nuclear plants have been planned although those under construction were completed.

The accident also provided a salutary lesson to the nuclear industry, which thereafter sought to improve training and safety procedures and to design more user-friendly operating equipment. ■

down in 1979. The plant consists of two units, imaginatively named Unit 1 and Unit 2. It cost about $1.1 billion to build, but today would cost five times that much, making nuclear power (surprise!) vastly unprofitable. Unit 2, in which the accident occurred, is permanently shut down, but Unit 1, which was shut down after Unit 2's accident, was reactivated in 1985 and is expected to run until about 2014. The steam coming out of the tower is warm water vapor from the cooling process.

The Three Mile Island Visitors Center (☎ (717) 948-8829) is outside the nuclear-power plant on Route 441 and is open June 1 to August 31, Thursday to Sunday from noon to 4:30 pm; Thursday to Saturday the rest of the year. The center has an exhibition area showing how the plant operates. Tours of the nuclear plant are available, but are mostly for educational groups. Individuals can go on a group tour, but they need to book about three to four weeks ahead; these tours are usually on the first Saturday of the month. The tour and admission to the visitors center are free. You can take photographs of the plant from the 2nd-floor observation deck in the visitors center, but not when you're touring the island.

There's no public transportation to here though CAT bus No 7 from Harrisburg goes as far as Middletown a few miles to the north.

HERSHEY

Twelve miles east of Harrisburg, the home of the Hershey chocolate empire, Hershey (population 8000) is a rather ordinary place that nevertheless attracts millions of visitors with its amusement park and chocolate-town theme. Milton S Hershey, a Mennonite, was born in 1857 in Derry Church and his career as a confectioner began at the age of 19 when he opened a candy store in Philadelphia. But success only came after he started the Lancaster Caramel Company 10 years later. Eventually, in 1903, with money from that enterprise he bought some land back in Derry Church to build a chocolate factory, and

the small town, whose name was later changed to Hershey, expanded around it.

Orientation & Information

In town Route 422 becomes Chocolate Ave, the main thoroughfare; most of the attractions are to the north of Chocolate Ave. Visitor information (☎ (717) 534-4900) is available inside the main entrance to Hershey's Chocolate World in Hersheypark. The post office, off Chocolate Ave West behind the Good Year store, is open Monday to Friday from 6:30 am to 4:30 pm, Saturday 9 am to noon.

Try to avoid Hershey at weekends, when it gets really busy.

Hersheypark

Hersheypark (☎ (717) 534-3005, (800) 437-7439) is a 90 acre landscaped park that Milton Hershey originally established in 1906 as a recreation area for his workers. The **amusement park** has over 50 rides and, surprisingly, no chocolate theme. The admission price of $24.95/15.95 entitles you to use all the rides and entry to the nearby ZooAmerica. The opening hours are fairly complicated, but Hersheypark is open Memorial Day to Labor Day daily from 10 am to generally 10 pm; it's also open some weekends in May and September.

ZooAmerica (☎ (717) 534-3860), is a wildlife park beside Hersheypark, featuring animals of North America. It's open mid-June to August daily from 10 am to 8 pm, September through mid-June daily 10 am to 5 pm. Entry to the zoo only is $4.75/3.50, seniors $4.25.

Visitors were once able to tour the actual chocolate factory, but due to health regulations the tour is no more. In its place is a free tour through **Chocolate World** (☎ (717) 534-4900), a mock factory where visitors sit in little plastic cars, which move along a conveyor past exhibits telling the story of the making of chocolate. At the end you get a free chocolate sample – a Hershey's 'kiss.' Young kids love it, but others might be disappointed by the tackiness. You exit through a candy store selling

Hershey products, and a food court. Chocolate World opens daily year round at 9 am but closing hours vary quite a bit: May through September it closes mostly at 8 pm, at 5 pm the rest of the year.

Hershey Museum

The small museum (☎ (717) 534-3439), 170 W Hershey Park Dr, has a collection of American Indian and Inuit art, Hershey chocolate-making machinery, an exhibition on the life of Milton S Hershey and a collection of Pennsylvania Dutch artifacts. It's not really worth the admission price of $4.25/2, seniors $3.75. It's open daily from 10 am to 5 pm, and an hour later in the summer.

Hershey Gardens

The 23-acre botanical gardens (☎ (717) 534-3492), on Hotel Rd north off Hershey Park Dr, began life in 1937 as a rose garden and have grown to include various other flowers, shrubs and specimen trees such as European beech and Japanese maple. The gardens are open mid-May through October daily from 9 am to 5 pm. Admission is $4.25/2, seniors $3.75.

Places to Stay

Rooms rates are higher in the summer months when kids are on vacation, and the hotels and motels can fill up quickly on weekends. Most of the budget and mid-range places are along Chocolate Ave.

Campground *Highmeadow Campground* (☎ (717) 566-0902) is fully equipped with showers, laundry, a grocery store and two swimming pools. A site for up to a family of four is $24.50, or $30 with full hookup. To get there follow Chocolate Ave west to the junction with Hershey Park Dr (Route 39), turn right for about 500 yards then left onto Matlack Rd.

B&Bs Reservations for B&Bs can be made by contacting the Hershey B&B Reservation Service (☎ (717) 533-2928), PO Box 208, Hershey, PA 17033.

Hotels & Motels *Hershey Travel Motel* (☎ (717) 533-7950), 905 E Chocolate Ave, has modest but clean rooms with cable TV and attached bathroom for $30/45. About 1½ miles south of Chocolate Ave, the *Cocoa Motel* (☎ (717) 534-1243), 914 Cocoa Ave, at the intersection with Route 322, has fine rooms for $48/58.

The *Simmons Motel* (☎ (717) 533-9177), 355 W Chocolate Ave, is a good-value place close to most attractions and amenities; it has rooms from $55/65. The neat, two story *White Rose Motel* (☎ (717) 533-9876), 1060 E Chocolate Ave, is surrounded by flowers and has rooms for $85/95.

Set on a 90 acre hilltop, the luxurious, Mediterranean-style *Hotel Hershey* (☎ (717) 533-2171), (800) 533-3131; fax 534-8887), north of Hersheypark is the premier place to stay in town. Facilities include indoor and outdoor pools, tennis courts, golf, horseback riding and croquet. Rates start at $200/215.

Places to Eat

In Hershey's Chocolate World is a food court selling sandwiches and ice cream. Most of the town's eateries are on Chocolate Ave. *Hardee's*, on W Chocolate Ave, is a fast-food place. *Breads 'N' Cheeses Coffee House* (☎ (717) 533-4546), 243 W Chocolate Ave, has delicious pastries from 95¢ and slices of cake like lemon torte for $1.75. It also sells a variety of breads from $1.50, cheeses from around the world and 20 kinds of coffee. *Lucy's Cafe* (☎ (717) 533-1045), at No 267, is an Italian-style bar and restaurant serving ravioli for $9.95 and lasagna for $10.75. It's closed on Sunday.

Spinner's Restaurant (☎ (717) 533-9050), 845 E Chocolate Ave, has been here for over 40 years and specializes in pasta, seafood and beef. Pasta mains are $11, seafood and beef from $17 to $24. It's open for dinner only from Tuesday to Saturday. At the top end, Hotel Hershey's *Circular Dining Room* (☎ (717) 533-2171) is dominated by stained-glass windows and overlooks the formal gardens. Men must wear jackets. A four course meal at dinner costs $43.

Getting There & Away

Bus Capitol Trailways (☎ (800) 444-2877) buses stop outside the Mobil service station on W Chocolate Ave, just to the west of Lucy's Cafe. You can buy tickets on the bus. There are two buses daily to Lancaster ($8.15 one way, 2½ hours) and Reading ($7.25 one way, 1½ hours).

Car From Philadelphia take the Pennsylvania Turnpike (I-76) to exit 20; take Route 72 north, then follow Route 322 west to Route 422. From Pittsburgh take the turnpike east to exit 19, then Route 283 north and Route 322 east. East from Harrisburg follow Route 322 then Route 422 into town.

YORK

York (population 42,000), about 20 miles southeast of Harrisburg and 25 miles southwest of Lancaster, was Pennsylvania's first settlement west of the Susquehanna River. Established in 1741, it was the capital of the US between September 30, 1777, and June 27, 1778, when Congress fled Philadelphia following the British victory at the Battle of Brandywine. During that period Congress met at the York County Colonial Courthouse where the Articles of Confederation, later to become the country's first constitution, were drafted and adopted.

Today, York is the home of the Harley-Davidson motorcycle assembly plant (though the company is headquarted in Milwaukee, WI). The downtown area has suffered the fate of many US cities; people have fled to the suburbs to live and the city center has an abandoned feel about it.

Information

The York Visitor Information Center (☎ (717) 848-4000, (800) 673-2429), is at 222 Arsenal Rd beside the Days Inn Motel, at the intersection of I-83 and Route 30; take exit 9E off I-83 and follow the signs. It's open daily from 9 am to 5 pm and the staff are friendly and helpful. The post office (☎ (717) 848-2381) is at 200 S George St.

Harley-Davidson Company

Many visitors come to Harley-Davidson (☎ (717) 848-1177), 1425 Eden Rd, to see where America's legendary motorcycles are manufactured. A guided tour starts with the Rodney Gott Antique Motorcycle Museum, which displays a bike from every production year from 1906. You then enter the assembly plant to see workers making parts and building the motorcycles. In the entrance area you can see a good film about the history of the company and there's a gift shop selling all kinds of Harley-Davidson merchandise.

Tours of the plant and museum are given Monday to Friday at 10 am and 1:30 pm and last 1½ hours; tours of the museum only are run Monday to Friday at 12:30 pm and Saturday at 10, 11 am, 1 and 2 pm and last 30 minutes. Take exit 9E off I-83 onto Route 30 east; at the third set of traffic lights turn left into Eden Rd.

York County Colonial Courthouse

The court house, 205 W Market St at N Pershing Ave, is a facsimile of the original, where Congress met while York was the national capital. You can visit it along with several other historical buildings on a guided tour ($4) organized by the local historical society (☎ (717) 848-1587). In the courthouse there's an audiovisual presentation and copies of the Articles of Confederation and Declaration of Independence on display. It's open Monday to Saturday from 10 am to 4 pm.

Harley Hogs

They say that the reason Harley-Davidsons are called 'hogs' is because years ago a young motorcycle racer used to parade around with a small pig on his gas tank after winning a race. Others followed his lead and the 'hog' became inseparable from the motorcycle. ■

Getting There & Away

Bus York is served by Greyhound and Capitol Trailways. The bus terminal (☎ (717) 845-9611) is at 315 N George St, beside the railroad track in a run-down part of the city. The terminal is open weekdays from 6:15 am to 7:45 pm, Saturday 6:15 am to 5:30 pm, Sunday 8:15 to 5:30 pm. There are up to five buses daily to Harrisburg ($4 one way, 40 minutes) and three to Lancaster ($5.35 one way, 45 minutes).

Car You can reach York south from Harrisburg on I-83, northeast from Gettysburg on Route 30 and southwest from Lancaster also on Route 30.

Southwestern Pennsylvania

Southwestern Pennsylvania is dominated by Pittsburgh, a city that was built on iron and steel and is now in the process of reinventing itself. Many work-weary Pittsburghers head for the Laurel Highlands to the southeast, a popular outdoor playground, especially noted for its white-water rafting in the Youghiogheny River. The highlands are also the location of Fallingwater, Frank Lloyd Wright's architectural masterpiece. The Johnstown area, to the northeast of the highlands, has been the site of a series of devastating floods, the most horrific of which occurred in 1889.

Around Pittsburgh are several state parks – Raccoon Creek to the west, Moraine and McConnell's Mill to the north – that are popular outdoor recreation areas. Also to the north is the small town of Harmony, site of a 19th century celibate commune.

PITTSBURGH

Pittsburgh (population 370,000) once had a reputation as the most polluted city in the US – the daytime air was so blackened by coal smoke that the town was called 'Smokey City.' Fortunately, those days are long gone with Pittsburgh having undergone a remarkable transformation.

Today it's a diverse and attractive corporate, financial and educational city. It has been listed several times among the US's top five most liveable cities in the *Places Rater Almanac* and is certainly well worth a visit. The Andy Warhol Museum is reason enough for many people to make the trip, but outside the downtown glass and steel there is the student district of Oakland and some picturesque, old neighborhoods like Troy Hill on the North Side.

History

Pittsburgh's strategic location at the point where the Ohio River meets the Monongahela and the Allegheny rivers has made it a

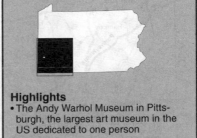

Highlights
- The Andy Warhol Museum in Pittsburgh, the largest art museum in the US dedicated to one person
- The ride up one of the inclined planes to Mt Washington and the view of Pittsburgh from the top
- White-water rafting and canoeing on the Youghiogheny River in the Laurel Highlands
- Fallingwater, Frank Lloyd Wright's architectural masterpiece ■

natural commercial and transportation center since the 18th century. At that time the area became a flashpoint in French and British rivalry over the Ohio River Valley.

In 1753, before the start of the French & Indian War (1754-63), a 22-year-old George Washington was sent to establish a British presence in the region. He chose the point near the tip of today's Golden Triangle, at the fork of the three rivers, to build a fortification. Sources disagree: some say the French took the spot and built Fort Duquesne *before* Washington built his fort, others say it was taken from him. In any case, this ideal location allowed the French to control the upper Ohio River Valley. But after a few defeats (see the sidebar on the Battle of Fort Necessity, later), the British returned in 1758, ejected the French and built Fort Pitt, named after prime minister William Pitt the Elder. From this, Pittsburgh is named.

During the 19th century Pittsburgh became famous for iron and steel production

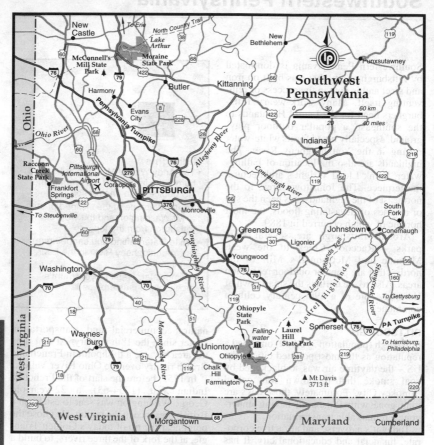

as it helped fulfill the needs of the country's westward expansion. The Civil War, by the end of which Pittsburgh was producing 50% of the country's iron and steel, gave its industries further stimulus. Then Andrew Carnegie, a Scottish-born immigrant, modernized and expanded steel production, becoming the world's richest man in the process. The growth was not without its conflict and there were violent strikes at Homestead in 1892 and throughout greater Pittsburgh in 1919.

Despite a downturn during the Depression of the 1930s, the mass-production of the automobile and the advent of WWII stimulated demand for steel once more. During the 1960s and '70s the industry declined, but since the 1980s Pittsburgh has re-emerged as a high-technology, finance and service-oriented center. An urban renewal program has seen the downtown area transformed, but not without a price: many architecturally important buildings were razed to make way for glass skyscrapers. Fortunately, many, like the Allegheny County Courthouse remain, and some of Pittsburgh's traditional character can be seen in the older residential neighborhoods.

The people are generally friendly and helpful, and in this regard are very typical of American towns or cities.

Although a strong blue-collar element remains, the shift in employment to the service and high-technology industries means there is now a large and growing white-collar workforce. The city's ethnic diversity is reflected in the different architectural flavors of its neighborhoods and symbolized by the University of Pittsburgh Nationality Rooms. The North Side has many touches of its German heritage, including Penn Brewery (originally called Eberhardt & Ober Brewery). On the South Side, Eastern European influences can be seen in the Ukrainian, Serbian and Lithuanian churches. Many Eastern European Jews settled in Squirrel Hill in the 1920s.

Bloomfield has a strong Italian heritage while nearby Lawrenceville and Polish Hill have a mix of Irish, Italian and Polish communities. Blacks have also settled in the city, but, in terms of numbers, their presence isn't as evident as in Philadelphia. There are also people from the Middle East, most notably Lebanese and Syrian.

Orientation

Pittsburgh is a fairly confusing city to navigate because of its shape – a triangle of land (downtown and Oakland) separated from the city's northern and southern parts by rivers. There's no consistent street pattern, although major thoroughfares in the city often run parallel to the rivers. Fifth Ave and Liberty Ave are the major downtown streets.

The approach to Pittsburgh from the south is spectacular. You enter through Fort Pitt Tunnel then cross Fort Pitt Bridge into the heart of the **Golden Triangle**, the westernmost portion of the city center (basically 'downtown') bounded to the north by the Allegheny River, to the south by the Monongahela River and to the east by I-579 (Crosstown Blvd).

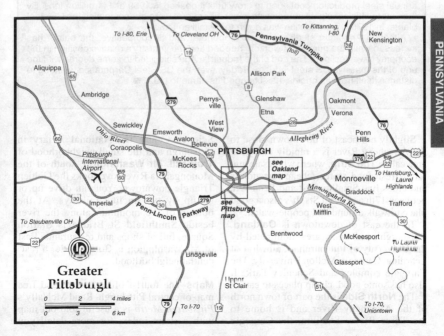

The US Iron & Steel Industry

Pittsburgh was one of the main centers of the American iron and steel industry. Soon after they arrived in the 17th century colonial settlers collected iron from bogs and then mines. By the 18th century, American iron production had increased so much that Britain passed the 1750 Iron Act, which forbade the building of mills in the colony, but allowed pig iron (crude unfinished iron) to be sent to Britain for manufacturing.

With the expansion of the US railroad industry beginning in the 1830s, the demand for iron increased. A leading producer of iron for years, Pennsylvania also had huge deposits of anthracite coal, which, it was discovered in the mid-19th century, could be substituted for charcoal in the smelting of iron. The combination of Pennsylvania coal, Great Lakes iron ore and cheap water transportation ensured that the Midwest would be the center of the US iron industry.

The true boom came when a cheap way to manufacture steel – a hard metal formed by combining iron and carbon – was discovered. In 1856 Englishman Henry Bessemer created the Bessemer process for making steel, in which hot air was blasted through molten iron to burn out its impurities. By 1872, 2% of US pig iron was being converted to steel; 20 years later it was up to 50%. By the second decade of the 20th century it was over 90%, with the US producing almost 25 million tons a year, more than any other country.

Huge new steel factories also created whole new labor conditions. Steel mills required thousands of workers and many more specialists than in iron production. Each worker had to be competent at an individual job, but at the same time was given less autonomy by management. Steel workers were some of the first to establish strong unions to battle management control of working conditions and hours.

In 1901 the US Steel Corporation, formed partly from Pittsburgh industrialist Andrew Carnegie's steel company, became the single largest industrial operation on earth. US annual steel production continued to grow until it peaked in 1969 at 141 million tons. By then more efficient plants abroad with lower labor costs were out-competing the US steel plants. In 1975 US production was down to 89 million tons.

Although American steel has since rebounded and is competitive, the output has increased while the number of workers needed and the industry's relative position in the economy have declined. The end of the Industrial Age coincided to some degree with the end of the massive US steel industry. Today, even the US Steel Corporation, wanting to distance itself from its origins, has changed its name to USX. ■

Slightly northeast of downtown close to the Allegheny River is a rapidly changing area called **The Strip**, where wholesale and retail fresh-food stores, cheap restaurants and clubs line Smallman St and Penn Ave between 17th and 22nd Sts. It's also a good place to walk around and people-watch.

To the east of downtown is **Oakland**, Pittsburgh's university area, dominated by the University of Pittsburgh's Cathedral of Learning, Carnegie-Mellon University, The Carnegie complex and Schenley Park. It also has some good, cheap places to eat.

The **North Side** is the part of town north of the Allegheny River and is home to the Three Rivers Stadium, the Carnegie Science Center the National Aviary in Pittsburgh and the small neighborhood of **Troy Hill**. **Mt Washington**, south of the Monongahela River, overlooks the Golden Triangle downtown. You can drive up or go up by two incline railways. At the bottom of the mountain along the river beside Smithfield St Bridge is Station Square, full of shops and restaurants. East of Mt Washington is **South Side**, a residential neighborhood.

Maps The tourist office has a good free map of central Pittsburgh. Rand McNally's *Pittsburgh Metro* is a useful fold-out map with a street index; for more detail you could try its *Pittsburgh & Vicinity* city atlas, part of the StreetFinder series.

Information

Tourist Offices The office of the Greater Pittsburgh Convention & Visitors Bureau (☎ (412) 281-7711, (800) 366-0093), on the 18th floor at 4 Gateway Center, is open Monday to Friday from 9 am to 5 pm. The bureau has a recorded 24 hour number (☎ (412) 391-6840), with the latest on what's happening around town. There are three other visitors centers in the city and one at the airport.

The downtown visitors center branch (☎ (412) 281-9222), on Liberty Ave in front of 4 Gateway Center, is open Monday to Friday from 9:30 am to 5 pm and weekends until 3 pm; it's closed on Sunday in January and February. In Oakland, the visitors center (☎ (412) 624-4600), in a log cabin on Forbes Ave next to the Stephen Foster Memorial Theater, is open Tuesday to Sunday from 10 am to 4 pm. In Mt Washington, the visitors center (☎ (412) 381-5134), in the lower level of the Carnegie Library, 315 Grandview Ave, is open Wednesday, Friday and Saturday from 10 am to 5 pm, Tuesday and Thursday 1 to 5 pm.

Finally, the visitors center has a desk (☎ (412) 472-0868), open daily from 8 am to 8 pm, on the lower level of the Landside terminal, at Pittsburgh airport.

Foreign Consulates The following countries have consulates in Pittsburgh:

Belgium
    700 N Bell Ave, Suite 290,
    Pittsburgh, PA 15106 (☎ (412) 681-5548)
Canada
    South Wing, Gateway II, 9th Floor,
    Pittsburgh, PA 15222 (☎ (412) 392-2308)
Denmark
    1300 Oliver Building
    Pittsburgh, PA 15222 (☎ (412) 355-6438)
France
    800 Presque Isle Dr,
    Pittsburgh, PA 15329 (☎ (412) 327-2911)
Germany
    1 Mellon Center, 500 Grant St,
    Pittsburgh, PA 15219 (☎ (412) 394-5568)

Money The Mellon Bank (☎ (412) 234-5000), on Mellon Square, and the PNC Bank (☎ (412) 762-2510), at 5th Ave and Wood St, have currency-exchange counters; there is also a Mutual of Omaha (☎ (412) 472-5151) currency-exchange office at the airport.

Post The main post office (☎ (412) 642-4478), at 7th Ave and Grant St downtown, is open Monday to Friday from 7 am to 6 pm, Saturday 7 am to 2:30 pm. There is also a post office at the airport; one in Oakland in the Carnegie Library, open Monday to Friday from 9 am to 5 pm; and another on Shiloh St at the top of the Monongahela Incline in Mt Washington, open Monday to Friday from 8:30 am to 5 pm, Saturday 8:30 am to noon.

Travel Agencies Council Travel (☎ (412) 683-1881) has its office in Oakland at 118 Meyran Ave, Pittsburgh, PA 15123.

Bookstores A branch of B Dalton (☎ (412) 261-4680) is in Station Square, and Barnes & Noble (☎ (412) 642-4324), 339 6th Ave, is open Monday to Friday from 7 am to 9 pm, Saturday 9 am to 9 pm, Sunday 11 am to 6 pm.

There are three good used bookstores close together in Oakland. The best of them is Caliban Book Shop (☎ (412) 681-9111), 416 S Craig St, run by John Schulman and Emily Hetzel. There are also two off S Craig St, the Bryn Mawr-Vassar Book Store (☎ (412) 687-3433), 4612 Winthrop St, and Townsend Booksellers (☎ (412) 682-8030), 4612 Henry St.

Libraries Part of The Carnegie complex, the Carnegie Library (☎ (412) 622-3102), 4400 Forbes Ave in Oakland, is one of the best in the US. It's open Monday to Wednesday and Friday from 9 am to 9 pm, Thursday and Saturday 10 am to 5 pm; Sunday 1 to 5 pm (it's closed on Sunday during the summer).

Useful Organizations For information on hosteling in western Pennsylvania contact

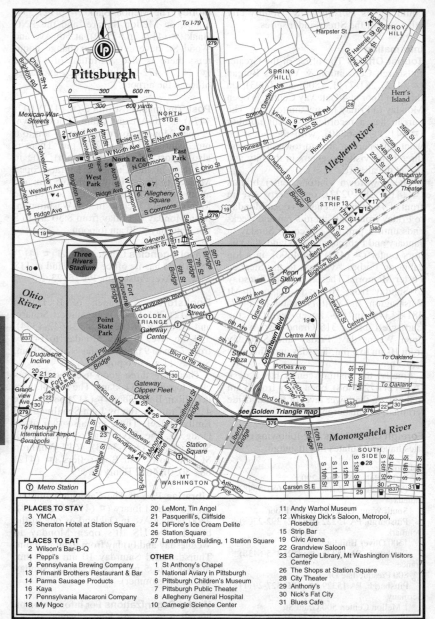

PLACES TO STAY
3 YMCA
25 Sheraton Hotel at Station Square

PLACES TO EAT
2 Wilson's Bar-B-Q
4 Peppi's
9 Pennsylvania Brewing Company
13 Primanti Brothers Restaurant & Bar
14 Parma Sausage Products
16 Kaya
17 Pennsylvania Macaroni Company
18 My Ngoc

20 LeMont, Tin Angel
21 Pasquerilli's, Cliffside
24 DiFiore's Ice Cream Delite
26 Station Square
27 Landmarks Building, 1 Station Square

OTHER
1 St Anthony's Chapel
5 National Aviary in Pittsburgh
6 Pittsburgh Children's Museum
7 Pittsburgh Public Theater
8 Allegheny General Hospital
10 Carnegie Science Center

11 Andy Warhol Museum
12 Whiskey Dick's Saloon, Metropol,
   Rosebud
15 Strip Bar
19 Civic Arena
22 Grandview Saloon
23 Carnegie Library, Mt Washington Visitors
   Center
26 The Shops at Station Square
28 City Theater
29 Anthony's
30 Nick's Fat City
31 Blues Cafe

the HI-AYH Pittsburgh Council (☎ (412) 422-2282), Room 202, Wightman School, Community Building, 5604 Solway St, Pittsburgh, PA 15217, east of Oakland. The Western Pennsylvania Conservancy (☎ (412) 288-2777), Department OG, 316 4th Ave, Pittsburgh, PA 15222, is an independent organization that preserves and administers natural lands in the west for public use.

Medical Services Pittsburgh has many hospitals, including a number of teaching hospitals that offer routine patient care. Montefiore University Hospital (☎ (412) 648-6000), 3459 5th Ave in Oakland, is part of the University of Pittsburgh Medical Center. The Allegheny General Hospital (☎ (412) 359-3131) is at 320 E North Ave on the North Side. For women only there is the Womancare Magee-Women's Hospital (☎ (412) 641-1000), 300 Halket St in Oakland.

For doctor referral in the Pittsburgh area call ☎ (412) 321-5810.

Emergency In the case of fire and medical emergencies or for police call ☎ 911. Other important emergency telephone numbers are:

Dentist	☎ (412) 321-5810
Pittsburgh Council for	
International Visitors	☎ (412) 624-7800
Rape Action Hotline	☎ (412) 765-2731
Travelers' Aid Society	☎ (412) 281-5474

Point State Park

The green park with the huge spouting fountain at the meeting of the three rivers is a small oasis downtown and isn't as crowded as other city parks. In the park, **Fort Pitt Museum** (☎ (412) 281-9284), 101 Commonwealth Place, has Native American artifacts, muskets and displays on the history of the three forts at the point and the French-British conflicts. Its portrayals of Native Americans are not flattering. The museum is open Wednesday to Saturday from 9 am to 5 pm, Sunday noon to 5 pm; admission is $4/2, seniors $3.

Nearby, the free sandstone-and-brick

Fort Pitt Blockhouse, is the only portion left of the original Fort Pitt. It's open Wednesday to Saturday from 10 am to 4:30 pm and Sunday noon to 4:30 pm. During summer it's also open Tuesday.

Allegheny County Courthouse

The magnificent 19th century courthouse (☎ (412) 355-5410), on the corner of Forbes Ave and Grant St, is a Romanesque stone building designed by architect Henry Hobson Richardson. It's open Monday to Friday from 8:30 am to 4:30 pm and entry is free.

Andy Warhol Museum

Choosing Pittsburgh as the home of this museum (☎ (412) 237-8300), 117 Sandusky St on the North Side over the 7th St Bridge, raised many an eyebrow, especially in New York. Some devotees felt that Manhattan, where Andy Warhol (1928-87) achieved fame for his innovative and often confronting artwork, would have been more appropriate. But he was born and raised in Pittsburgh and so it came here. Administered by The Carnegie (see that section, later), the museum opened in 1994 and most reviews have been favorable – even many New Yorkers have said it's worth the trip west to see it.

As well as depicting the story of his life, the museum's seven floors display Warhol's now-classic reproductions of Campbell soup cans and celebrity portraits, along with less-well-known items, like his time capsules, drawings, prints, sculptures and films. The opening hours are Sunday and Wednesday from 11 am to 6 pm and Thursday to Saturday from 11 am to 8 pm. Admission is $5/3, seniors $4. Quite a few buses take you there, including bus Nos 13A, 13B and 13C. For more on Warhol's life see the sidebar under Arts in the Facts about the Region chapter.

Carnegie Science Center

The Carnegie Science Center (☎ (412) 237-3400), 1 Allegheny Ave at North Shore Dr near Three Rivers Stadium, is good for kids, but adults may find it less interesting.

PENNSYLVANIA

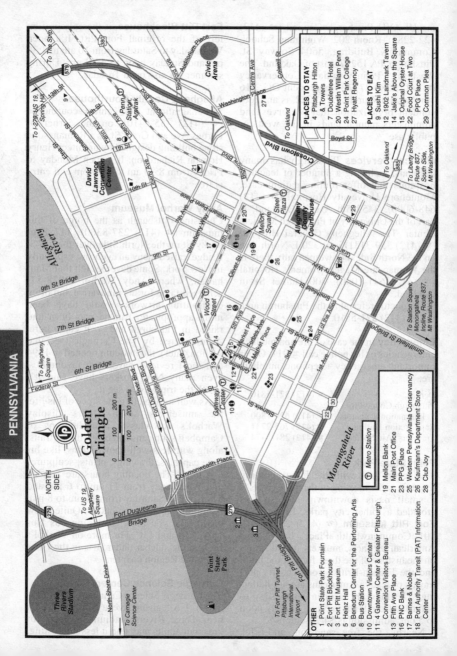

PENNSYLVANIA

Three Rivers Stadium

To Carnegie Science Center

North Shore Drive

Golden Triangle

NORTH SIDE

To US 19,
Allegheny
Square

Allegheny River

To Allegheny Square

9th St Bridge

7th St Bridge

6th St Bridge

Federal St

To I-279–US 19,
Spring Hill

9

579

13th St
12th St
11th St

Penn Ave

Penn Station,
Amtrak

Bigelow Blvd

10th St

David Lawrence Convention Center

Liberty Ave

8
7

11th St

10th St

Liberty Ave

9th St

William Penn Place

Strawberry Way

8th St

7th St

6

7th Ave

6th Ave

6th St

5th Ave

Wood Street

16

Market Place

5th Ave

Forbes Ave

14

15
13
12

Market Square

11
10

Gateway Center

Stanwix St

Penn Ave

River Blvd

Fort Duquesne Blvd

Commonwealth Place

Point State Park

1

279

Fort Duquesne
Bridge

To Fort Pitt Tunnel,
Pittsburgh
International
Airport

Fort Pitt Bridge

2
3

Monongahela River

279

22
30

Smithfield St Bridge

To Station Square,
Monongahela
Incline, Route 837,
Mt Washington

To Liberty Bridge,
Route 837,
South Side,
Mt Washington

385

To Oakland

Crosstown Blvd

Boyd St

Steel Plaza

Mellon Square

Allegheny County Courthouse

Grant St

Ross St

William Penn Place

Smithfield St

Oliver St

3rd Ave
4th Ave
Wood St
Blvd of the Allies
1st Ave

25
24
23

26

28

29

27

Washington Place

Bedford Ave
Auditorium Place

Colwell St

Washington Centre Ave

Civic Arena

To The Strip

380

To Oakland

579

0   100   200 m
0   100   200 yards

It has lots of hands-on exhibits plus an aquarium, the Henry Buhl Junior Planetarium, a giant Omnimax theater and the USS *Requin*, a WWII submarine.

The center is open Monday to Thursday from 10 am to 5 pm, Friday to Sunday 10 am to 6 pm. The Omnimax shows are on Friday and Saturday at 7 and 8 pm. Admission prices are quite complicated: to see the exhibits only costs $5.75/4.25, the Omnimax Theater only is $5.75/4.25, admission to both is $10/6.50; to the exhibits and planetarium is $10/6.50; to all three it's $12/8.50; and to the submarine only is $3.50/2.50. Parking costs extra – there isn't any other parking around, so you have to pay. Alternatively, catch bus No 16A, 16D, 16U or 18E from downtown.

National Aviary in Pittsburgh

The highly rated national aviary (☎ (412) 323-7235), on Arch St west of Allegheny Square, is one of the few in the US where visitors are welcome to wander through simulated habitats while birds fly freely around (though some are caged). The more than 400 species from around the world include a pair of bluewinged kookaburras, rare Micronesian kingfishers and Mickey the talking crow. The aviary is open daily from 9 am to 5 pm (though the last admission is at 4:30 pm). Admission is $4/2.50, seniors $3. Take bus No 16B, 16C, 16D or 16U.

Pittsburgh Children's Museum

The museum (☎ (412) 322-5058), 10 Children's Way in the Old Post Office Building in Allegheny Square, has interactive exhibits (including a two story climbing maze) and live performances with an emphasis on the different cultures that go to make up Pittsburgh. It's open Tuesday to Saturday from 10 am to 5 pm, Sunday noon to 5 pm. Admission is $4, seniors $3; on Tuesday there's a single admission price of $2. Take bus Nos 16B, 16C, 16D or 16U.

Mexican War Streets

North of the national aviary, these are a series of streets off North Ave, built after the Mexican War (1846-48), some of which are named after battles in the war. Buildings on these streets – especially Taylor Ave and Monterey, Resaca and Palo Alto Sts – are examples of attractively redone homes (mostly Greek Revival and Victorian). A few on North Ave itself are waiting to be restored. Bus Nos 16B and 16C pass by.

St Anthony's Chapel

Off the main tourist route, this church (☎ (412) 323-9504), 1704 Harpster St above the city in Troy Hill, has over 5000 religious relics contained in elaborately carved and decorated reliquaries. The main attraction is one reliquary, in the left transept, that holds over 700 items, including (reputedly) a thorn from Jesus's crown of thorns, a splinter from his cross and a piece of stone from the Holy Sepulcher. The interior of the church is beautifully ornate and the walls are dominated by a near-life-size depiction of the Stations of the Cross. Viewing hours are Tuesday, Thursday and Saturday from 1 to 4 pm and Sunday 11 am to 4 pm.

Getting There & Away Bus No 6A goes up Troy Hill Rd to Lowrie St. By car, take North Ave to the second traffic light after I-279, which is Vinial St. Go right on Vinial St then left on Troy Hill Rd; follow this road to the top of the hill and make a right on Lowrie St; turn left on Froman St and left again onto Harpster St.

Incline Railroads

The Monongahela Incline (☎ (412) 442-2000) and Duquesne (doo-KANE) Incline (☎ (412) 381-1665) are two single-car trains that run up and down steep-sided Mt Washington. They're all that remain of 15 incline railroads that opened up the mountain to development in the 19th century and allowed easier access to the city. These are the original 19th century cars with hand-carved cherry and maple interiors and amber glass transoms; the Monongahela Incline has been spruced up, possibly because of its proximity to Station Square,

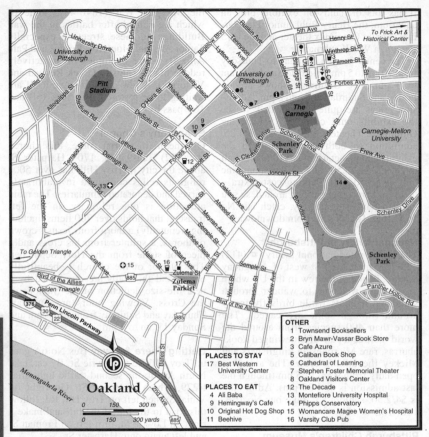

PLACES TO STAY
17 Best Western
     University Center

PLACES TO EAT
4   Ali Baba
9   Hemingway's Cafe
10 Original Hot Dog Shop
11 Beehive

OTHER
1   Townsend Booksellers
2   Bryn Mawr-Vassar Book Store
3   Cafe Azure
5   Caliban Book Shop
6   Cathedral of Learning
7   Stephen Foster Memorial Theater
8   Oakland Visitors Center
12 The Decade
13 Montefiore University Hospital
14 Phipps Conservatory
15 Womancare Magee Women's Hospital
16 Varsity Club Pub

but the Duquesne Incline is in need of a facelift. The views of Pittsburgh from the top are great.

The fare is $1 each way and takes about two to three minutes. The inclines run Monday to Saturday from 5:30 am to 12:45 am, Sunday 7 am to 12:45 am.

For an interesting trip, go to Station Square and walk across W Carson St to the Monongahela Incline entrance. Ride up the Monongahela Incline, walk west along Grandview Ave/Mt Washington Overlook to the Duquesne Incline. Then ride down, walk over the footbridge and

back east to Station Square (the last part of the walk is less interesting as it's mostly past parking lots).

Station Square
Station Square (☎ (412) 261-9911) is a group of shops and restaurants in a renovated former railroad warehouse complex south across the Smithfield St Bridge at W Carson St at the base of Mt Washington. The Landmarks Building, 1 Station Square, is the former terminal of the Pittsburgh & Lake Erie Railroad.

The Station Square stop on the light-rail

and subway system is east of the complex and south of the bridge and Carson St. Bus Nos 41A to 41E, 41G, 46A to 46D, 46F to 46H, 46K, 51A and 51C pass by.

Phipps Conservatory

Phipps Conservatory (☎ (412) 622-6914), Curto Dr, is in the 456 acre **Schenley Park** in Oakland. Given to the city by Andrew Carnegie's partner Andrew Phipps in 1893, the conservatory is an excellent collection of iron-and-glass greenhouses connected by high, wide passageways also of iron and glass. It contains tropical plants, orchids, bonsai and giant topiary and is open Tuesday to Sunday from 9 am to 5 pm. Normal admission is $4/2, seniors $3, but this goes up slightly for seasonal flower shows.

Bus No 84B runs nearby and bus Nos 53F, 53H, 53K, 56U and 67H run through the park.

The Carnegie

The Carnegie (☎ (412) 622-3131), 4400 Forbes Ave, Oakland, is the commonly abbreviated name for the building complex containing the **Carnegie Museum of Art**, the **Carnegie Museum of Natural History**, the **Carnegie Library of Pittsburgh** and the **Carnegie Music Hall**. The museum of natural history has a great dinosaur collection, including a complete Tyrannosaurus rex skeleton; the museum of art has an extensive display of impressionist, post-impressionist and modern American and European art.

Andrew Carnegie

Pittsburgh industrialist Andrew Carnegie (1835-1919) is one of the most interesting and certainly the best remembered of America's 19th century industrial barons. He amassed a fortune by driving his steel workers hard, often brutally, and then retired and gave much of his fortune away, claiming it was the duty of the wealthy to do so.

Growing up in impoverished surroundings in Scotland, Carnegie emigrated to the US at the age of 12 with his parents. While working as a telegrapher, he caught the eye of Thomas Scott, a Pennsylvania Railroad official. Scott ensured that Carnegie, by the age of 24, was promoted to superintendent of the western division of the railroad; he lent Carnegie money and gave him financial advice so that by his 30s the young Scotsman was a wealthy investor.

When the depression of the 1870s came, Carnegie put all of his assets and efforts into the emerging steel industry. He built plants, held down wages and reinvested profits in capital improvements. Soon the Carnegie Steel Company was the dominant force in the industry. Carnegie believed firmly in 'vertical integration' and his corporation owned everything from the raw materials to the final product. In 1901 he sold his Carnegie Steel Company to the US Steel Corporation for the then-astronomical price of $250 million.

Interestingly, Carnegie had mixed feelings about the rights of labor and the duties of capitalists. His most famous ideas on the subject were published in the 1889 article 'Wealth.' Carnegie wrote that it was the duty of the wealthy to return 'their surplus wealth to the mass of their fellows in the forms best calculated to do them lasting good.' In his latter years, Carnegie lived up to his words, endowing an amazing number of libraries, cultural institutions, universities and other noble causes throughout the US. ■

The Carnegie is open Tuesday to Saturday from 10 am to 5 pm and Sunday 1 to 5 pm. Admission to all museums is $5/3, seniors $4. There are free tours of the library Tuesday, Thursday and Saturday at 11 am and 2 pm; you meet at the library entrance.

To get there take bus No 54C, 61A, 61B, 61C, 67A, 67C, 67E, 67F or 67J along Forbes Ave.

Cathedral of Learning

The Cathedral of Learning is the name given to the imposing Gothic 42 story University of Pittsburgh building (☎ (412) 624-6000), at Bigelow Blvd and 5th Ave, built in 1937. Inside are the interesting **Nationality Classrooms**. Each of the mostly functioning 23 classrooms is designed and decorated in a particular ethnic style and historic period. The Irish one, for example, represents a 6th century church oratory. Some, like the Syria-Lebanon room (which was actually brought over from Damascus), can only be seen with guides.

Monday to Saturday from 9 am to 4:30 pm and Sunday from 11 am to 4:30 pm you can enter the building and look at the rooms – there are 18 on the 1st floor and five on the 3rd. Guided 1½ hour tours are given daily for $2/50¢, seniors $1, call the information number above for tour details. On the 1st floor also check out the students' **Commons Room** with its vaulted ceilings supported by 50-foot columns.

Take bus No 54C, 61A, 61B, 61C, 67A, 67C, 67E, 67F or 67J along Forbes Ave.

Frick Art & Historical Center

This complex (☎ (412) 371-0600), 7227 Reynolds St in Point Breeze east of Oakland, includes Clayton, the former home of famous Pittsburgh industrialist and Carnegie partner Henry Clay Frick, the Frick Art Museum, the Carriage Museum, a greenhouse and a children's playhouse.

Clayton (☎ (412) 371-0606), completed in 1872 then subsequently remodeled and expanded, was a modest residence for a 19th century multimillionaire. Frick entertained Teddy Roosevelt here in 1902. It has

been expertly restored to its original state and contains the world's only player organ (it plays on command from music rolls like a player piano). The house can only be seen by guided tour, which must be booked in advance. Tours are Wednesday to Saturday from 10 am to 5:30 pm, Sunday noon to 6 pm, and cost $5. The **Frick Art Museum** displays Flemish, French and Italian paintings and decorative arts and is free (see the sidebar).

The center is open Tuesday to Saturday from 10 am to 5:30 pm and Sunday noon to 6 pm. Admission is free.

Getting There & Away Bus Nos 67A, 67C, 67E, 67F, 71C and 74A take you there from downtown.

By car, take Parkway East (Route 376) to the Edgewood/Swissvale exit. At the exit ramp follow the signs to Edgewood, then turn right on Braddock Ave. Go 1.3 miles and then left on Penn Ave. At the second traffic light turn left on S Homewood Ave. Go one block to Reynolds St then take a left turn again. The parking lot is on the left.

From Oakland take 5th Ave to Penn Ave and make a right; go about eight blocks to make a right on S Homewood Ave and follow the directions as above.

Pittsburgh Zoo

The 75 acre Pittsburgh Zoo (☎ (412) 665-3640), 1 Hill Rd in Highland Park northeast of downtown, has over 5000 animals in recreated habitats, including a number of endangered species like the white rhino and silverback gorilla. Memorial Day to Labor Day it's open daily from 10 am to 5 pm; the rest of the year 9 am to 4 pm. Admission is $6/4; parking costs $2.50.

From downtown take bus No 71A or 71B from 5th Ave; by car take Route 28 north to exit 5 over Highland Park Bridge then follow the signs.

Organized Tours

Gray Line (☎ (412) 741-2720, 761-7000) does a two hour 'historic' tour of downtown, Mt Washington (with a ride on the

Henry Clay Frick

Pittsburgh's second best known industrialist, Henry Clay Frick (1849-1919) was the son of a modest farmer who maneuvered his way to becoming a millionaire by the age of 30. Despite only a few years of schoolroom education, Frick was always good with numbers. While still in his teens, he began working for his maternal grandfather, who owned the Overholt Distillery. By 19 he was the firm's bookkeeper.

At age 20 Frick saw the value of coal for the burgeoning US steel industry and bought as much land containing coal reserves (then at low prices because of the 1870s depression) as he could. Early in his career, he obtained a $10,000 bank loan to expand his coke ovens, which converted coal to useful fuel.

Frick fortuitously met steel magnate Andrew Carnegie while in New York City on a wedding trip in 1881. Carnegie proposed a merger between the Frick Coke Company and Carnegie Steel Company and, wisely, Frick accepted..The union joined Carnegie's steel mills with the masses of coal they needed for fuel.

Although Frick and Carnegie were business partners and industrialists, they had somewhat different views on the responsibility of the wealthy and the rights of workers. Nothing symbolized their clash more than Frick's handling of a strike at Carnegie's Homestead steel plant. Carnegie wanted the union broken but believed that Frick went too far in calling in hundreds of armed Pinkerton strikebreakers to attack them. For his brutality in breaking the strike, Frick was stabbed and shot by New York anarchist Alexander Berkman in 1892. Frick recovered, but in 1900 he and Carnegie parted ways.

Frick became head of the new US Steel Corporation, which arose from the sale of the Carnegie Steel Company. He soon resigned with tens of millions of dollars in assets. He moved to New York City and eventually built a home at 70th St and Fifth Ave, which is now the Frick Collection Museum. ■

Duquesne Incline) and the North Side for $14/7. A 'cultural' tour of downtown and Oakland includes a visit to the Nationality Classrooms in the Cathedral of Learning; it costs $17/8.50. Gray Line also combines the historic tour with a river cruise on one of the boats of the Gateway Clipper Fleet for $22/11.

The Gateway Clipper Fleet (☎ (412) 355-7980) leaves from the dock next to the Sheraton Hotel in the Station Square complex. A narrated 2¼ hour cruise of the three rivers leaves Monday to Saturday at noon; a two hour evening cruise leaves Tuesday and Thursday at 7:30 pm. Both cost $7/4.

Special Events

Following are some of the highlights of the Pittsburgh calendar:

May
  Pittsburgh Folk Festival – celebrates the city's ethnic diversity in Monroeville (☎ (412) 373-0123)

May to July
  Three Rivers Shakespeare Festival – plays are put on at the Stephen Foster Memorial Theater in Oakland (☎ (412) 624-6805)
June
  Three Rivers Arts Festival – arts, crafts, food and performances for three weeks at Gateway Plaza and Point State Park (☎ (412) 481-7040)
July
  South Side Summer Street Spectacular – the town's largest neighborhood festival, on E Carson St in mid-July (☎ (412) 481-0651)
August
  Pittsburgh Three Rivers Regatta – world's largest inland regatta (☎ (412) 261-7055)
  Harambee Black Arts Festival – artists, performers and food (☎ (412) 243-5259)
September
  A Fair in the Park – arts & crafts show sponsored by the Craftsmen's Guild of Pittsburgh in Shadyside (☎ (412) 431-6270)

Places to Stay

Pittsburgh suffers in general from not having a large number of places to stay, and what is available is generally expensive.

Even if you can afford it, you may not be able to find a room in town on peak weekends, especially when the hotels offer cheaper weekend packages. Most midrange places are northwest of town near the airport and require a car to be reached.

In the center, budget choices are very limited. If ever a town were in need of a budget travelers' hostel, Pittsburgh is it. Fortunately, the HI-AYH has plans to open one in the near future; for details contact the local HI-AYH Council (see Useful Organizations under Information, earlier).

Places to Stay – bottom end

The nearest campground is in *Raccoon Creek State Park* (☎ (412) 899-2200), 25 miles northwest of town. It has all conveniences, 176 sites for $12 and is open mid-April to mid-December. Take Routes 22/30 west to Route 18 north, which passes through the park. The campground is about two miles north of Frankfort Springs.

Downtown, *Point Park College* (☎ (412) 392-3824), 201 Wood St at Blvd of the Allies, rents two person dormitory rooms with separate baths for $15 per person from June to mid-August. Bring your own sheets and towels. In North Side is a *YMCA* (☎ (412) 321-8594), at W North Ave and Monterey St, with rooms for $26.70 per person per night or $63.25 a week; prices go down for longer stays. The rooms are simple with bed, lamp, dresser and shared bath and you also get use of the gym. Bus Nos 16B and 16C stop here.

Places to Stay – middle

The majority of the mid-range places are about 15 miles northwest of town toward the airport in the suburb of Coraopolis along Beers School Rd, which is lined with independent and chain motels. Take Route 60 to exit 3, then follow Business Route 60 north a couple of miles to the Beers School Rd exit. The independent ones are sometimes cheaper and the chains sometimes nicer.

The cheapest is *Glass Tower Motor Inn* (☎ (412) 264-6101), 1457 Beers School

Rd, with singles/doubles for $34/39; it also has a restaurant and bar. The *Red Roof Inn* (☎ (412) 264-5678), at No 1454, is a good choice among the chains with clean, comfortable rooms for $40/51 and a courtesy van to the airport. The *Pittsburgh Plaza Hotel* (☎ (412) 264-7900), at No 1500, has rooms at similar rates but includes a continental breakfast in the price. At No 1420 *Hampton Inn Airport* (☎ (412) 264-0020) is another that includes a free continental breakfast and is one of the more elegant of the chain motels; it has rooms for $55/60.

If you want to be close to town, the *Best Western University Center* (☎ (412) 683-6100; fax 682-6115), 3401 Blvd of the Allies at Halket St in Oakland, has rooms for $65/75. There's a diner and pub next door.

Places to Stay – top end

In Oakland *Shadyside B&B* (☎ (412) 683-6501), 5516 Maple Heights Court (off 5th Ave between Graham and Ivy Sts), is a large Jacobean stone mansion with a library/sitting room, a billiards room, and a balcony and kitchen. There are nine rooms, five with a private bath. Rates are $90 to $135 single or double.

Downtown, *Westin William Penn* (☎ (412) 281-7100), (800) 228-3000; fax 553-5239), 530 William Penn Place in Mellon Square, is a renovated national historic landmark built by Henry Clay Frick in 1916. The plush bedrooms are decorated in French provincial, Italian or American colonial styles. The rates are $130 to $200 single or double, depending on the style of the room.

The *Hyatt Regency* (☎ (412) 471-1234, (800) 233-1234, fax 281-4797), 112 Washington Place, near the Civic Arena, is a renovated brick-and-glass tower with good views of the city. It has an indoor heated pool and health club. Rooms are $155 single or double during the week, $89 on weekends. The 700 room *Pittsburgh Hilton & Towers* (☎ (412) 391-4600, (800) 445-8667; fax 594-5161), 600 Commonwealth Place at Gateway Center, has views across the Allegheny River, a health club and several restaurants. Rates are $164 single or double. In the Station Square complex the *Sheraton Hotel at Station Square* (☎ (412) 261-2000) has standard doubles for $164, but offers various discounts, so ask.

The *Doubletree Hotel* (☎ (412) 281-3700, (800) 445-8667; fax 281-2652), 1000 Penn Ave, is connected by walkway to the David Lawrence Convention Center next door. Single/doubles are $160/180 and rooms are decorated with prints by Pittsburgh artists.

Places to Eat – budget & moderate

Downtown The food court below street level in *Two PPG Place*, the smaller of the Gothic black-glass buildings on Market Square, has stalls selling burgers and Chinese, Greek and Italian dishes. The court is busy at lunch time and most meals are between $4 and $7.

The *Original Oyster House* (☎ (412) 566-7925), on Market Square diagonally opposite the PPG food court, is a seafood restaurant with a long marble bar where you stand and eat raw shellfish at market prices. Large platters of fried fish and fries cost $4.25. The *1902 Landmark Tavern* (☎ (412) 471-1902), 24 Market Square, is a modern lunch place with pressed-tin ceilings, wooden booths and a long bar. Prices are higher than the Oyster House and the atmosphere is less casual. It sells a mixture of seafood and other dishes; oysters are $9 and chicken Dijon $13.95.

Kaufmann's department store (☎ (412) 232-2320), 400 5th Ave, has several eateries; the *Tic Toc Restaurant* on the 1st floor has sandwiches for $3 to $6. Daily specials include baked meatloaf with mashed potatoes for $5.25 or a roast beef sandwich for $4.50.

Sushi Kim (☎ (412) 281-9956), 1241 Penn Ave near 13th St and the train station, serves Korean and Japanese food. Large meat dishes like bulgogi (marinated beef) are grilled at your table and cost $11.30. Spicy Korean soup-casseroles of ox leg, cod fish or tofu cost between $7 and $9. It's closed Monday.

The Strip If you're buying food to cook, try the *Pennsylvania Macaroni Company*, a delicatessen, and the *Parma Sausage Products* store on Penn Ave in The Strip just to the northeast of downtown. The Strip also has a lots of choices for food service from *My Ngoc*, on Penn Ave, serving Vietnamese, Thai and Chinese dishes for $5 to $8 to *Primanti Brothers Restaurant & Bar*, at Smallman and 18th Sts, for Italian submarine sandwiches served 24 hours.

Kaya (☎ (412) 261-6565), 2000 Smallman St at 20th St, serves Caribbean and Spanish food daily from 11 am till late and has a wide selection of microbrew beers, wines and spirits. It has soup and salad for $4 to $6 and mains such as rice and chicken or vegetarian paella for $7.

Oakland As befitting a student neighborhood, Oakland is full of cheap places to eat, including fast-food outlets, most of them along Forbes Ave between Bouquet St and Meyran Ave. S Craig St between Forbes and 5th Aves is another restaurant area.

Roy Rogers Tuck Shop, in the Cathedral of Learning, is a cheap cafeteria selling burgers from $2 and chicken meals for $3.

The *Original Hot Dog Shop* (☎ (412) 687-8327), 3901 Forbes Ave at Bouquet St, known as 'The O,' has a U-shaped counter, two street entrances and tables. Not surprisingly, it sells hot dogs, from $2.50, but has branched out into things like spaghetti for $3 and 16 inch pizza for $4. The busy *Hemingway's Cafe* (☎ (412) 621-4100), 3911 Forbes Ave, has Cajun salad for $5.75 and seafood pasta for $8.75; it also does steak, pizza and chicken dishes. It serves cocktails at the bar and has poetry readings on Tuesday evenings.

Ali Baba (☎ (412) 682-2829), 404 S Craig St, is a Middle Eastern place that serves a student special of rice, salad, string beans and lamb for $4. Lunch prices are good, with hummus dishes from $2.65 and falafel for $3.25. At dinner most mains are under $8.

North Side *Wilson's Bar-B-Q* (☎ (412) 322-7427), 700 N Taylor Ave, has a few tables, an old counter and good barbecues. Smell the wood smoke and order from the simple menu: a 'whole slab of ribs' for $17.25, plates from $6 to $9 and sandwiches for $3.50. It's closed Sunday. *Peppi's* (☎ (412) 231-9009), 925 Western Ave, has good sandwiches (all under $5), wooden floors and benches and a pressed-tin ceiling. You order at the counter then wait for your name to be called.

The landmark *Pennsylvania Brewing Company* (☎ (412) 237-9402), at Troy Hill Rd and Vinial St, is a red-brick German brewery and pub-restaurant. The owner is a descendant of Franz Daniel Pastorius who founded Germantown in Philadelphia in 1683 and drank beer with William Penn at Penn's own brewhouse. Authentically German, diners can view the brewery's spotless copper brewing tanks from the dining area. Bratwurst on a baguette is $3.50, salads around $5 and hot meals like Wiener schnitzel $9. The brewery makes 10 authentic naturally brewed German beers from $2.25. It's open Monday to Thursday from 11 am to 10 pm, till midnight on Friday, Saturday and Sunday.

Mt Washington Station Square, at the foot of the Monongahela Incline, has a mix of food choices. Budget options include *Jimbo's Food & Drinks* for sandwiches, subs and tacos, and *Coffee Express* for coffee and pastries. Mid-range choices include the *Sesame Inn* (☎ (412) 281-8282), a Chinese restaurant serving wonton soup for $1.50, shrimp mains for $9.95 and good vegetarian dishes such as Buddhist Delight (stir-fried vegetables) for $6.95. The *Italian Oven* (☎ (412) 261-2111) has pizzas from $8.25 and pastas from $5.25. The *Cheese Cellar* (☎ (412) 471-3355) serves a mix of Mexican and Cajun dishes; beef burritos are $3.75 and Cajun chicken $8.95.

At the top of the Monongahela Incline, you'll find *DiFiore's Ice Cream Delite* (☎ (412) 381-4640), 120 Shiloh St, selling burgers ($2) and hoagies in half and whole sizes ($2.50 to $7) as well as ice cream.

Places to Eat – top end

Downtown The *Common Plea* (☎ (412) 281-5140), located at 308 Ross St near the Allegheny Courthouse, has dark wooden walls and antique pictures. The menus are printed as summonses and feature a mix of seafood, beef and veal with mains from $18 to $27. *The Harvest* (☎ (412) 281-3700), 1000 Penn Ave in the Doubletree Hotel, has an Edwardian look with mirrors, wooden paneling and furniture, and brass fittings. It features a changing seasonal menu of meats, fish, poultry, vegetables and fruit. Lunch mains are $10 to $16 and dinner up to $26.

Specializing in North Italian and regional American cuisine, *Jake's Above the Square* (☎ (412) 338-0900), 430 Market St near Gateway Center, has gotten rave reviews for the food, which is served in a modern place with large windows overlooking Market Square. Dinner mains are $18 to $30, lunch $8 to $18.

Mt Washington The Landmarks Building, 1 Station Square, houses the *Grand Concourse Restaurant* (☎ (412) 261-1717), part of which overlooks the river. Set in the magnificent main hall of the former railroad terminal it specializes in seafood like baked Boston cod for $15.25 and lobster for $22.

A row of restaurants with great views of the Golden Triangle line Grandview Ave at the top of the Duquesne Incline; most serve Italian or American cuisine in the $18 to $40 range. *LeMont* (☎ (412) 431-3100), 1114 Grandview Ave, is decorated with a dark ceiling, large chandeliers, brass and mirrors. Appetizers are under $10; veal, beef and seafood mains are around $20. Other restaurants nearby are *Tin Angel* (☎ (412) 381-1919), at No 1200, *Pasquerilli's* (☎ (412) 431-1660), at No 1204, and *Cliffside* (☎ (412) 431-6996), at No 1208.

Entertainment
The free weeklies *City Paper* and *In Pittsburgh* have detailed listings of current events and schedules. You can also check

the entertainment sections of the daily newspapers, the *Pittsburgh Post-Gazette* and the *Pittsburgh Tribune-Review*, or call the 24 hour Activities Hot Line (☎ (412) 391-6840).

Theater The *Pittsburgh Public Theater* (☎ (412) 321-9800), Allegheny Square in North Side, puts on six productions a season (October through June) from contemporary musicals to classic dramas. Tickets are between $25 and $35. Downtown, the *Benedum Center for the Performing Arts* (☎ (412) 456-6666), 719 Liberty Ave (Penn Ave at 7th St), has many Broadway shows. *Station Square Playhouse* (☎ (412) 279 3881) is a small theater by the river; tickets are available from TIX in Heinz Healey's store in the Station Square shopping area.

City Theater (☎ (412) 431-4400), 57 S 13th St in South Side, is noted for its innovative performances. In Oakland there's the *University of Pittsburgh Theater* (☎ (412) 624-0933) in the Cathedral of Learning, and the *Stephen Foster Memorial Theater* (☎ (412) 648-7547), Forbes Ave at Bigelow Blvd, home of the annual Three Rivers Shakespeare Festival.

Classical Performance The Pittsburgh Symphony Orchestra plays October through May at the elaborately designed *Heinz Hall* (☎ (412) 392-4800), 600 Penn Ave, and in summer at Point State Park. The *Benedum Center for the Performing Arts* (☎ (412) 456-6666), Penn Ave at 7th St, is the venue for performances by the Pittsburgh Dance Council, Pittsburgh Ballet Theater Company, Pittsburgh Opera and Civic Light Opera. The *Pittsburgh Ballet Theater* (☎ (412) 281-0360) is at 2900 Liberty Ave.

Cinema The *Beehive* (☎ (412) 687-9428), 3807 Forbes Ave, Oakland, is an arthouse movie theater showing US and foreign cult and classic films. It has an excellent coffee shop. Also in Oakland, the *Pittsburgh Playhouse* (☎ (412) 471-9700), 222 Craft Ave, puts on first-run non-mainstream movies.

The *Rex Theatre* (☎ (412) 381-2200), 1602 E Carson St, South Side, features first-release films for $7; all day Wednesday and matinees during the rest of the week it costs only $3.50.

Live Music Oakland and South Side have a number of venues for rock music and R&B. *Electric Banana* (☎ (412) 682-8296), 3887 Bigelow Blvd in Oakland, offers the latest in contemporary alternative rock music by mostly local musicians. The cover charge is about $4 to $8. *The Decade* (☎ (412) 682-1211), 223 Atwood St in Oakland, has been here for more than two decades, and has music by local and national bands nightly with a cover charge up to $6. *Cafe Azure* (☎ (412) 681-3533), 317 S Craig St, Oakland, has live jazz Friday and Saturday nights.

In South Side, E Carson St is the place to go for rock and R&B. At No 1601 *Nick's Fat City* (☎ (412) 481-6881), hosts local R&B and rock bands Tuesday to Sunday; *Anthony's* (☎ (412) 431-8960), at No 1306, has music nightly with no cover charge. The *Blues Cafe* (☎ (412) 431-7080), at E Carson and 19th Sts, has blues and jazz Wednesday to Saturday nights with a cover charge of about $3; it also has jazz sessions on weekend afternoons.

Dance Clubs In The Strip, the *Metropol* (☎ (412) 261-4512), 1600 Smallman St, in a former warehouse, and the *Rosebud* (☎ (412) 261-2221), at No 1650, have dancing to live rock bands. *Cloud 9* (☎ (412) 281-8277), at Smallman and 21st Sts, has dancing to DJs nightly with a cover charge of $2 to $3.

Downtown, *Club Joy* (☎ (412) 232-0188), 520-522 3rd Ave, also has dancing to DJs Wednesday to Saturday. *Upstage* (☎ (412) 681-9777), 3609 Forbes Ave in Oakland, has dancing nightly to alternative music; the cover charge is $2.

Bars *Whiskey Dick's Saloon* (☎ (412) 471-9555), next to the Metropol on Smallman St in The Strip, is an inexpensive, down-to-earth but noisy bar. In Mt Washington the

Grandview Saloon (☎ (412) 431-1400), 1212 Grandview Ave, is a trendy bar with loud music and great views of downtown from the outdoor balconies.

Next to the Grand Concourse Restaurant in the Landmarks Building, Station Square, is the elegant *Gandy Dancer* (☎ (412) 261-1717), with good food and a piano player in the evenings.

In Oakland the *Varsity Club Pub* (☎ (412) 681-8756), 3401 Blvd of the Allies, is next to the Best Western University Center hotel.

Brewpubs & Coffeehouses The *Pennsylvania Brewing Company* (☎ (412) 237-9402) is at Troy Hill Rd and Vinial St in North Side (see Places to Eat).

The *Beehive* coffee shop (☎ (412) 687-9428), 3807 Forbes Ave, is in the lobby of a still-functioning arthouse movie theater, selling a variety of international coffees and teas as well as cakes and pastries. You can take your drink into the theater at the back of which are some tables and chairs. The *Strip Bar* (☎ (412) 471-1043), 1814 Penn Ave in The Strip, has music all night and is open till 4 am on weekends. *Starbucks* has a number of coffee houses around town, including one in the Barnes & Noble bookstore on Smithfield St.

Spectator Sports
The Three Rivers Stadium (☎ (412) 321-0650) is at 400 Stadium Circle by the river on the North Side. The Pittsburgh Pirates National League baseball team plays here April through October while the Pittsburgh Steelers football team uses it August through December. The Pittsburgh Penguins NHL (ice-hockey) team plays at the Civic Arena (☎ (412) 333-7328), at Washington Place and Center Ave east of downtown, October through April.

The Pittsburgh Marathon takes place in May and the finishing line is in Point State Park.

Things to Buy
Downtown, Kaufmann's (☎ (412) 232-2320), 400 5th Ave, is a long-established

department store. Two modern shopping centers are PPG Place (☎ (412) 434-1900), in the black-glass Gothic tower at Market Square and Arcade Shops at Fifth Ave Place (☎ (412) 456-7800), 120 5th Ave. Station Square (☎ (412) 261-9911), at W Carson St near Smithfield St Bridge in Mt Washington, has nearly 70 shops in the former railroad warehouse complex.

Getting There & Away
Air Pittsburgh international airport (☎ (412) 472-3525/5525), 16 miles from downtown, is the headquarters of USAir (☎ (412) 922-7500) and has connections to Europe, Canada and Japan and all major centers in the US. USAir has offices downtown at 4 Gateway Center and 525 Grant St.

Other airlines with city offices are:

American Airlines
   Westin William Penn Hotel,
    530 William Penn Place (☎ (800) 433-7300)
British Airways
   535 Grant St (☎ (800) 247-9297)
Delta Air Lines
   1 Mellon Bank Center, Suite 2420
    (☎ (412) 456-2240, (800) 221-1212)

The airport has two terminals – Landside, where you check in and pick up baggage, and Airside, where the flight boarding gates are located; the terminals are connected by the 'People Mover,' an underground rail shuttle. Non-passengers can visit the Airside terminal but must go through a security check.

The Landside terminal has a Pittsburgh Visitor Information Center (☎ (412) 472-0868), open daily from 8 am to 8 pm; a Travelers' Aid Society desk (☎ (412) 472-3599) for answers to questions on transportation and to rent car seats for children; Mutual of Omaha (☎ (412) 472-5151), which changes money and provides business services; a post office open Monday to Friday from 8:30 am to 4 pm; and car rental services. Both terminals have an airport information desk.

Some examples of standard economy fares are: to New York's JFK airport $150 one way and Los Angeles $727/746 one way/roundtrip; the roundtrip fare to Philadelphia starts from $118.

Bus The Greyhound bus station (☎ (412) 392-6513), at 11th St and Liberty Ave, is near the Amtrak station. It has left-luggage lockers ($4 per day) and a Travelers' Aid Society office (☎ (412) 281-5474), with information on local transportation. The one-way fare to Philadelphia is $29 (seven hours) and New York City $59 (10½ hours).

Train Amtrak (☎ (412) 471-8752) operates from Penn Central Station, 1100 Liberty Ave at Grant St. The original railroad station is a magnificent stone building with a domed forecourt and marble flooring in the huge hall now occupied by offices. The more prosaic modern Amtrak station is at the rear. There are daily trains to Philadelphia ($70 one way, eight hours), Harrisburg ($65, 5¾ hours) and New York City ($97, 10 hours).

Car Pittsburgh is amply served by the interstate system. I-79 passes through western Pittsburgh connecting it with Virginia to the south and Lake Erie to the north. From I-79, I-279 leads into town. The Pennsylvania Turnpike (I-76) passes through the north and east of Pittsburgh; from the east take exit 6 onto I-376 into town; from the north take I-79/279.

Getting Around
To/From the Airport The Airline Transportation Company (☎ (412) 471-8900) runs buses every 30 minutes to/from downtown for $12/20 one way/roundtrip, to Oakland $12.50/21. A cab to downtown costs about $28, to Oakland about $33. To get to the airport by car from downtown follow Route 60 (Airport Expressway) north to exit 6.

Bus & the 'T' The Port Authority Transit (PAT, ☎ (412) 442-2000) operates the city's local transport system and has a downtown information center (☎ (412) 255-1356), 534 Smithfield St, open Monday to Friday

from 7:30 am to 5 pm. Buses are free within downtown's Golden Triangle until 7 pm, after which the one way fare is 75¢.

PAT also runs a 22.5 mile light-rail system called the 'T,' between downtown and Mt Washington/South Side. Three of the five downtown stations are underground – Gateway Center, Wood St and Steel Plaza; the other two are Penn Park and Station Square.

Most bus and T-fares around the city are $1.25; transfers cost 25¢. Bus Nos 61A to 61C and 71A to 71D along 5th Ave, connect downtown with Oakland.

Taxi If you're arriving by bus or train be aware that some taxis at the stations may be operating uninsured or are otherwise unsafe, especially if they're unmarked. Approved companies include Yellow Cab (☎ (412) 665-8100), People's Cab (☎ (412) 681-3131), Colonial Transit (☎ (412) 833-3200) and UJSP Taxi (☎ (412) 322-5486). Rates are $1.80 for the first one-seventh of a mile and 20¢ for each additional one-seventh. A ride between downtown and Oakland costs about $7.

Car & Motorcycle The highways and roads are fairly confusing and crowded on approaches to the many bridges across the Allegheny and Monongahela rivers. The approaches are not always marked and when driving you may find yourself suddenly on a bridge approach with no turnoff; then suddenly you're out of downtown on the North or South Sides.

The two main thoroughfares connecting the North and South Sides via downtown are I-279 and I-579. Penn Lincoln Parkway (I-376) runs eastward beside the Monongahela River. Most downtown streets have alternate one way traffic systems and parking can be difficult; a tourist map of the city, available from the Travelers' Aid Society, indicates public parking lots.

The main **car rental** companies have desks at the airport. Typical weekday rental rates with Enterprise for a compact car are $31 per day, with the first 150 miles free, then 25¢ for every additional mile. Some of

PENNSYLVANIA

the main rental companies with offices downtown are:

Avis
625 Stanwyx St
(☎ (412) 261-0540, (800) 831-2847)
Budget
700 5th Ave (☎ (800) 435-7751)
Enterprise
231 3rd Ave (☎ (412) 391-7766)
Thrifty
875 Greentree Rd (☎ (412) 921-8200)

AROUND PITTSBURGH
Raccoon Creek State Park
The 11.4 sq mile Raccoon Creek State Park (☎ (412) 899-2200), 25 miles west of town on Route 18, offers opportunities for outdoor recreation throughout the year. There's swimming and fishing in, and boating on, Raccoon Creek Lake. The park has six short walking trails and 10 miles of bridle trails. In winter there's ice fishing, ice skating and, on designated trails and roads, cross-country skiing and snowmobiling.

Wildlife includes deer, rabbit and squirrel, and there are scores of bird species. In the southeast of the park is a wildflower reserve which is seen at its best in the second week of May. The park has camping from mid-April through mid-December. Take Route 60 north from Pittsburgh to exit 9 then follow the signs. There is also camping here; see Pittsburgh Places to Stay.

Harmony
Harmony, west of I-79 about 25 miles north of Pittsburgh on Route 19, was the home of the Harmony Society, a communal group founded in 1804. Possessions were owned collectively and within a few years, the Harmonists had planted thousands of acres of farms and orchards and constructed over 100 buildings. In 1807 the members made the self-extinguishing decision to adopt celibacy. In 1814 the Harmonists moved to Indiana, then Ohio, before dissolving in 1905. The town of Harmony was bought by Mennonite Abraham Zeigler, whose descendants still live here.

Several of the original buildings remain, including one which is now the **Harmony Museum** (☎ (412) 452-7341), 218 Mercer St, where Harmonist and early Mennonite exhibits are displayed; it's open daily June through September from 1 to 4 pm; in other months Sunday, Monday, Wednesday and Friday also from 1 to 4 pm. Admission is $3.50. From Pittsburgh take I-79 north to exit 27 onto Route 19.

Moraine State Park
About 10 miles north of Harmony, Moraine State Park (☎ (412) 368-8811), east of I-79 and off Route 442, is named after the moraine (fragments of rock) left by receding glaciers after the last Ice Age. In the more recent past it was heavily mined and drilled for coal and oil, but the area was so well restored that little evidence of those days remains.

The five sq mile **Lake Arthur** is a 1960s re-creation of a glacial lake that existed here thousands of years ago. It was produced by damming the tributaries of Muddy Creek and has formed a series of habitats that now support a wide variety of bird species. Sailing, windsurfing and fishing take place on the lake and there are a couple of beaches where you can go swimming. Along the northern shore is a paved seven mile bike trail; rentals are available.

McConnell's Mill State Park
Nearby, west of I-79 off Route 422 and Route 19, the four sq mile McConnell's Mill State Park (☎ (412) 368-8091), gets its name from the 19th century grist mill (now being restored) that operated here beside Slippery Creek till 1928. Memorial Day to Labor Day there are free guided tours of the mill daily from 10 am to 6 pm.

The main attraction, however, is the 400 foot deep **Slippery Rock Gorge**, carved by a receding glacier some 20,000 years ago. Experienced rock climbers hone their skills on **Breakneck Ridge**, while novice climbers practice on **Rim Road**, opposite the mill. Slippery Creek, which runs through the gorge, is popular for kayaking and white-water canoeing, but there are no rentals in the park. There are several hiking trails in the park, including a section of the **North Country National Scenic Trail** (see Hiking & Backpacking in the Outdoor Activities chapter for more on the scenic trail).

LAUREL HIGHLANDS

The Laurel Highlands (regional population 857,000) is a wooded, hilly region which broadly speaking runs from east of Uniontown, about 50 miles southeast of Pittsburgh, near the West Virginia/Maryland border, northeastward to near Johnstown, 56 miles almost due east of Pittsburgh. The most interesting area of the highlands is in its lower section, particularly Ohiopyle State Park with the Youghiogheny River running through it, Frank Lloyd Wright's Fallingwater, Bear Run Nature Reserve and a 30 mile scenic stretch along Route 40. The Pennsylvania Turnpike (I-70/76) and Route 30 cross the region east-west; north-south Route 381 crosses from Route 30 southwest to Route 40 and traverses the heart of this region.

The Laurel Highlands tourism promotion agency (☎ (412) 238-5661) is at 120 E Main St, Ligonier, on Route 30 about 40 miles east of Pittsburgh, 10 miles east of Latrobe. You'll need a car to fully explore the area – it's probably cheapest to get one in Pittsburgh.

Ohiopyle State Park

This 29½ sq mile park is bisected by the Youghiogheny (YOCK-a-GAY-nee, generally just called 'the Yock') River Gorge and surrounds the village of Ohiopyle (oh-HI-oh-pile), a center for white-water rafting. The park is crowded during the summer especially on weekends; the best times to visit are May and September.

In the village, just off the main street near the river and bridge, is a Laurel Highlands visitor information center (☎ (412) 329-1127), open May through October, while the park office (☎ (412) 329-8591) is about a half mile south of Ohiopyle off Route 381.

The Ferncliff Peninsula, immediately east of Ohiopyle across the river, a four acre teardrop of land formed by a loop in the river, is covered in wildflowers in season.

White-Water Rafting Rafting trips are run on the Youghiogheny River in Pennsylvania and Maryland and on nearby rivers in West Virginia. The Youghiogheny is generally divided into 'Middle Yough' (nine miles of easy rapids, classes I and II), 'Lower Yough' (seven miles of moderate rapids, classes III and IV) and 'Upper Yough' (11 miles of moderate to challenging rapids, class IV and V). The Middle and Lower Yough are in Ohiopyle State Park and the Upper Yough is in Maryland, about an hour away.

On weekends, if you rent or bring your own gear, you have to get a launch permit for $2.50 per person from the park office; there are a limited number of permits so reserve in advance. Monday to Friday you don't need a permit.

The offices of the rafting companies are in the village on or near Route 381. Rates are lower during the week and vary according to the season. Laurel Highlands River Tours (☎ (412) 329-8531, (800) 472-3846) does guided trips on the Middle Yough from $20 to $29 per person, the Lower Yough for $28.50 to $54.50 and the Upper Yough for $105.50 to $135.50. All trips include lunch. Other companies offering guided trips are Wilderness Voyageurs (☎ (800) 272-4141), Mountain Streams (☎ (800) 723-8669) and White Water Adventurers (☎ (412) 329-1488, (800) 992-7238).

Ohiopyle Trading Post (☎ (412) 329-1450) and Youghiogheny Outfitters (☎ (412) 329-4549) rent tents and other gear – they rent only.

Other Activities White-water **canoeing** and **kayaking** are also popular on the river, and the rafting companies offer courses. A one day clinic with Laurel Highland Tours costs from $65 to $75. Boat rental is $40 for two people.

The park has 27 miles of **cycling** trails along the river, an off-road mountain-bike trail and 41 miles of **hiking** trails. You can

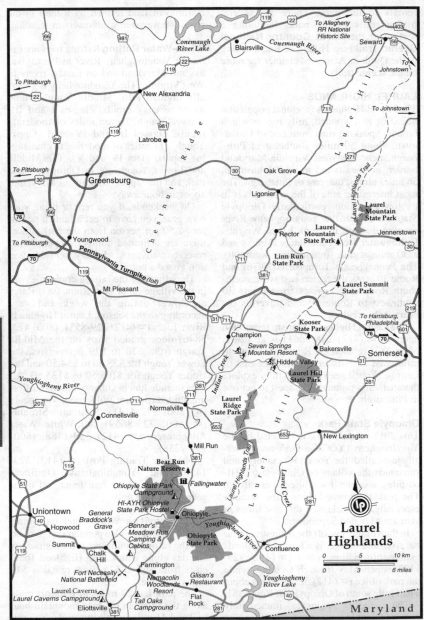

Laurel
Highlands

hike or drive to overlooks above the river at Baughman Rock, Tharp Knob and the Kentuck Scenic Overlook. Bicycle rental is available around the village; a mountain bike costs $4/14 per hour/day. In winter there's **cross-country skiing** and 19 miles of trails for **snowmobiling**.

Places to Stay & Eat The *park campground* (☎ (412) 329-8591) has 223 sites, with hot showers and toilets for $12 per site, and is open year round. The 25 bed HI-AYH *Ohiopyle State Park Hostel* (☎ (412) 329-4476), to the north of the village by the river, is a large white house with a kitchen, dining room, living room, day lockers and showers. The hostel is open year round and rates are $9/11 for members/nonmembers; family rooms are available. Up past the visitors center on the right is the *Ohiopyle Guest House* (☎ (800) 472-3846) with four rooms for $35 per person for the first night, $25 each additional night; the rate includes a continental breakfast.

Falls Market Inn & Restaurant (☎ (412) 329-4973) on the main street (Route 381) rents basic singles/doubles upstairs for $25/40 with laundry and shared bath. It's the only place in the village to buy groceries, and the small restaurant (open daily from 7:30 am to 6:30 pm) has hoagies for $1.65, sandwiches from 90¢. *Fox's Pizza* (☎ (412) 329-1111) in the community center has pizzas from $4.

Getting There & Away There's no public transportation to Ohiopyle, though there are buses from Pittsburgh to Uniontown, 20 miles to the west. Route 381, which passes through the park, connects with the Pennsylvania Turnpike (I-70/76) to the north and Route 40 to the south which runs northwest to Uniontown and southeast into Maryland.

Fallingwater
Three miles north of Ohiopyle on Route 381, beside the Youghiogheny River, is Fallingwater (☎ (412) 329-8501) designed by Frank Lloyd Wright. It's an impressive

Frank Lloyd Wright's masterpiece, Fallingwater

house made of concrete and sandstone quarried on the site and is designed as a series of levels cantilevered over a stream leading to a waterfall. The house is in the Zen artistic tradition of a viewer being one with artwork – more precisely here, the resident being one with the waterfall. The home was completed in 1939 for the Kaufmann family, which donated it to the Western Pennsylvania Conservancy (see Useful Organizations under Pittsburgh). Its furnishings and fittings are intact, as Wright designed them.

Guided tours are given April 1 to mid-November Tuesday to Sunday from 10 am to 4 pm. Mid-November to March tours are on weekends, weather permitting. The 45 minute tour is $8/5 Tuesday to Friday, $12 on weekends and holidays. The two hour tour leaves at 8:30 am and costs a steep $30 weekdays, $35 weekends. If the tours are full, you can walk around the grounds, which are open from 8:30 am, for $3. Children under nine years old can't go on a tour, but supervised care is available for them.

PENNSYLVANIA

Bear Run Nature Reserve
Half a mile north of Fallingwater on the
western slope of Laurel Ridge, the eight
sq mile Bear Run Nature Reserve, Route
381, Mill Run, PA 15464, is administered
by the Western Pennsylvania Conservancy (☎ (412) 329-8501). The reserve
has 20 miles of trails through oak and
hemlock forests beside the Youghiogheny
River Gorge. There's cross-country skiing
in winter. The reserve provides a habitat
for field mice, white-tailed deer, bobcats
and black bears; more than 130 bird
species have been observed here. The
reserve has six camping areas where
rough camping is allowed. You must
bring your own water.

The nearest town for supplies and tent
rental is Ohiopyle.

Skiing
The ski season runs roughly from mid-
December to early April and there are
resorts in the highlands offering downhill
and cross-country skiing (see Bear Run,
above). Rentals are available at the resorts;
call for fees and details of lesson packages.

Seven miles east of Route 381, **Seven
Springs Mountain Resort** (☎ (814) 352-
7777, (800) 452-2223), Champion, PA
15622, has a vertical drop of 750 feet and
lift fees from $30 to $38; for a snow report
call ☎ (800) 523-7777.

Hidden Valley (☎ (814) 443-2600,
(800) 443-7544); Hidden Valley, PA 15502,
south of the Pennsylvania Turnpike (I-70/
76) on Route 31, has a vertical drop of 610
feet and lift fees from $20 to $34; for a
snow report call ☎ (800) 443-7544.

Laurel Highlands Hiking Trail
The 70 mile trail runs northeast from
Ohiopyle State Park through Laurel Ridge,
Laurel Summit and Laurel Mountain state
parks to near Seward on Route 56, northwest of Johnstown. Some parts are rough,
particularly in the south. In winter it's suitable for cross-country skiing and snowshoeing. There are eight camping areas
with toilets and water; campsites must be
booked in advance. For more information

contact Laurel Highlands Hiking Trail
(☎ (412) 455-3744), RD 3, PO Box 246,
Rockwood, PA 15557.

Along Route 40
Route 40 was the first federal public-works
project in the nation and helped to open the
Ohio River Valley to settlement by Europeans. Begun in 1811 in Cumberland, MD,
it pushed on to Wheeling, WV, in 1818,
then to Vandalia, IL, in 1830. The National
Road, as it was called, was the primary
route from the East Coast to the western
frontier until the 1850s. Today's Route 40
follows essentially the same direction.
There are a number of places to stay along
the road, but bring camping gear with you
if you plan to camp.

Fort Necessity National Battlefield The
battlefield (☎ (412) 329-5512), 11 miles
southeast of Uniontown, commemorates
the battle that began the French & Indian
War on July 3, 1754. It contains a replica of
the original fort – actually just a one room
log building encircled by a low wooden
palisade. The visitors center has an audiovisual display on French-British rivalry in
North America, George Washington and
the Battle of Fort Necessity. The battlefield
also encompasses the nearby, but unrelated
Mt Washington Tavern, built in 1828 for
travelers on the National Road, and the
grave of General Braddock (a mile west
on Route 40), whose body was moved to
the roadside in 1804, though he was killed
50 years earlier.

The battlefield is open daily from 8 am to
sunset, the visitors center and Mt Washington Tavern from 8 am to 5 pm. Admission
is $2/free.

Laurel Caverns Laurel Caverns (☎ (412)
438-3003), about 12 miles southeast of
Uniontown off Route 381, are Pennsylvani-
a's largest with 2.3 miles of passageways
and a depth of 450 feet. You enter via the
Norman E Cales Visitors Center. The temperature inside is a constant 52°F. There's a
guided tour of the lighted, developed
section which takes a short foray into the

The Battle of Fort Necessity

Britain began the French & Indian War in 1754 by sending George Washington, then in the colonial army, with a group of Virginian troops to establish a British presence among the French in the Ohio River Valley. In late 1753 Washington first went to present-day Pittsburgh on a diplomatic mission to persuade the French to leave, but this failed. A military force was set up and Washington arrived here in a meadow that he called a 'charming field for an encounter.'

Washington's troops attacked and killed some French troops in May and the French sent reinforcements from Fort Duquesne (Pittsburgh). Washington built a 'fort of necessity' and surrounded it with trenches. A combined French and Algonquian force of about 700 attacked Washington's 400 men on July 3 and after a day of fighting Washington surrendered. He and his men were allowed to walk home and the French burned the fort.

A year later Washington returned to the area as an aide to British General Edward Braddock. In a poorly planned attack, Braddock was killed near Fort Duquesne (and eventually interned next to Route 40) as were over 900 Redcoats. The British continued to lose the war until William Pitt the Elder, the British prime minister, dedicated more of Britain's resources to it. By 1760 the British had gained virtual control of North America, a fact which was later ratified by the 1763 Treaty of Paris. ■

undeveloped part; self-guided explorations are possible but you'll need to bring a flashlight. The caverns are open May through October daily from 9 am to 5 pm; weekends only March, April and November. Admission is $8/5, seniors $7.

Places to Stay – camping *Laurel Caverns Campground* (☎ (412) 438-3003) has 50 sites near the caverns (see above) from $8 for two people tenting to $12 for RVs; it's open May through October.

Benner's Meadow Run Camping & Cabins (☎ (412) 329-4097), on Nelson Rd 2½ miles north of Route 40, is a huge site with laundry, playground, store and swimming pool. There are 250 sites for $15 each, plus $3 with full hookup. It's open mid-April through mid-November. The secluded *Tall Oaks Campground* (☎ (412) 329-4777), one mile south of Farmington on Route 381, has a pool and over 100 sites open year round (though tent camping in winter is a bit rough) for $6.50 per person.

Places to Stay – hotels & motels *Laurel Highlands Motel* (☎ (412) 438-4500), on Route 40 three miles west of the junction with Route 381, is behind an outdoor museum of farm equipment, stoves and

other items. The motel has small rooms with a double bed and TV and rates at $30/50 a single/double. The nearby *Lodge at Chalk Hill* (☎ (412) 438-8880, (800) 833-4283), set back from the road, has a few low wooden buildings with balconies overlooking a small lake. The comfortable rooms cost $54/65.

The *Nemacolin Woodlands Resort* (☎ (412) 329-8555, (800) 422-2736), on Route 40 just east of Farmington, is one of Pennsylvania's best places to stay. It has 200 rooms in different sizes – the larger ones have whirlpools, king-size beds and balconies. Rates start at $240/290. The resort has a large, well-equipped spa, polo field, small ski slope, two golf courses, a rose garden, seven restaurants and a 12,000 bottle wine cellar!

Places to Eat In Chalk Hill there's a *Subway* sandwich shop with most subs around $2.50 and *Zeb's Pizza* serving small pizzas from $2 and hoagies for $3. Occasional diners and neighborhood places line Route 40. One of the best is *Glisan's Restaurant* (☎ (412) 329-4636), a mile west of Flat Rock, that has CD juke boxes at the table. Large, standard dinner specials with rolls, ham, potato, vegetable and soup cost $3.75.

PENNSYLVANIA

Specializing in seafood, the more upmarket *Watering Trough* (☎ (412) 438-9716), on Route 40 at Summit west of Chalk Hill, can only be entered from the eastbound lane. It has a bar, a large fireplace and wood stove and opens daily at 5 pm for dinner only. A main meal of shrimp costs $14.95, pasta $11.

JOHNSTOWN

Johnstown (population 28,000), 70 miles east of Pittsburgh at the fork of the Little Conemaugh and Stoney Creek rivers, is named after Joseph Schantz, a Swiss Mennonite immigrant who changed his surname to Johns and founded the town at the start of the 19th century. The town has been flooded often, but the most devastating took place in 1889 – the worst flood in US history.

Information

The visitors center (☎ (814) 536-5107), 111 Market St at Washington St, is open Monday to Friday from 9 am to 4:30 pm; and June to August on weekends 9 am to 1 pm. The post office, on Washington St, has a philatelic counter and is open Monday to Friday from 8 am to 5 pm, Saturday 8 am to noon. The Cambria County Library (☎ (814) 536-5131), 238 Main St at Walnut St, is open Monday to Thursday from 9 am to 9 pm, Friday and Saturday 9 am to 5 pm.

Johnstown Flood Museum

The museum (☎ (814) 539-1889), 304 Washington St, has flood debris, models and 3-D photographs of the damage done by the flood. In the theater on the 2nd floor an excellent 30 minute documentary describes the cause of the 1889 flood and its aftermath. Ironically, the building (originally a library) was built with money given by Andrew Carnegie after the flood which was caused by the dam that burst at his private club. The museum is open November through April daily from 10 am to 5 pm; May through October on Friday and Saturday it stays open till 7 pm. Admission is $4/2.50, seniors $3.25.

Inclined Plane

The Inclined Plane (☎ (814) 536-1816) is a cable car that rises 896 feet up Yoder Hill at a 71.9% gradient from Johns St (Route 56) in central Johnstown to Edgehill Dr in Westmont, a residential suburb. It was opened in 1891 to provide fast passage to higher ground and is said to be the steepest in the world. The cable car has enough space for two automobiles. At the top is a visitors center, where you can see the drum turning the cable, and a platform with views of Johnstown and the river valleys.

The Inclined Plane runs four times an hour and is open weekdays from 6:30 am to 10 pm; Saturday 7:30 am to 10 pm, Sunday 9 am to 10 pm. The one-way fare for a foot passenger is $1.25; for a vehicle and driver $3.

Other Attractions

The **Alma Hall**, 440 Main St, housed 300 people on its top floors during the flood. People were pulled in by ropes, an attorney was swept into his own office in the building by the water and two women gave birth – but no one died. **Grandview Cemetery**, in Westmont, has 777 unknown flood victims buried in an 'Unknown Plot.' Take Menoher Blvd or Millcreek Rd from town to the cemetery; or take Route 56 east, then Route 403 south to Route 271 south and follow the signs. A 3200 foot row of **American elms** runs along Luzerne St at the end of Millcreek Rd near the cemetery. Johnstown, and more specifically the borough of Weston where the trees are located, have lost trees to Dutch elm disease in the past, but the borough council and the local residents keep constant vigilance for any early tell-tale signs of the disease.

Places to Stay

Camping The nearest campground, *Woodland Park* (☎ (814) 472-9857), 220 Campground Rd, near Ebensburg, about 18 miles north of town, has shaded tent sites for $12, RV sites for $14. It's open from mid-April to mid-October. Take Route 56 east to Route 219 north; then

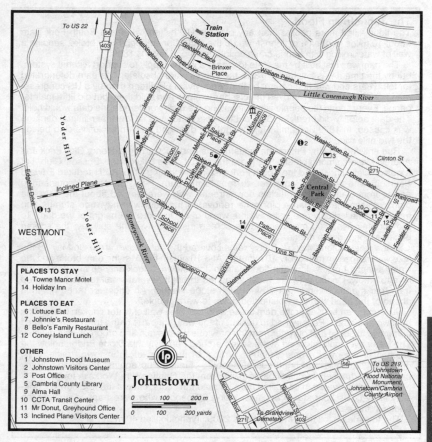

PLACES TO STAY
4 Towne Manor Motel
14 Holiday Inn

PLACES TO EAT
6 Lottuce Eat
7 Johnnie's Restaurant
8 Bello's Family Restaurant
12 Coney Island Lunch

OTHER
1 Johnstown Flood Museum
2 Johnstown Visitors Center
3 Post Office
5 Cambria County Library
9 Alma Hall
10 CCTA Transit Center
11 Mr Donut, Greyhound Office
13 Inclined Plane Visitors Center

Johnstown

take Route 22 west for 3¾ miles to Campground Rd and follow it one mile north to the campground.

Hotels & Motels *Towne Manor Motel* (☎ (814) 536-8771), 155 John St, is actually better than its exterior appearance suggests. It has large rooms at $30/36 and complimentary morning coffee but no towels in the bathroom. The *Holiday Inn* (☎ (814) 535-7777, (800) 446-4656), 250 Market St, is the best place in town with rooms for $72 single or double.

About five miles south of town at the junction of Routes 56 and 219 is a commercial strip with motels and fast-food outlets. Here, the *Super 8 Motel* (☎ (814) 266-8789), 1440 Scalp Ave, has rooms for $45/49.

Places to Eat
There isn't a great deal of choice. Main St has a *McDonald's*, *KFC* and *Burger King*. *Bello's Family Restaurant* (☎ (814) 535-3722), 421 Main St, an Italian restaurant, makes a good calzone for $3.25. It's closed weekends. Nearby, *Johnnie's Restaurant*, probably the best of the

PENNSYLVANIA

The Johnstown Flood

The flood killed more people than any other in US history when the South Fork Dam about 10 miles northeast of Johnstown up the Little Conemaugh River broke, sending a wall of water roiling with debris crashing into town on May 31, 1889.

The dam was first built by the state to create a water supply to support a canal system, but by the time it was finished in 1853, the canals were obsolete. The dam deteriorated for four years and was first bought by the Pennsylvania Railroad then by a US congressman from Altoona, who removed the discharge pipes and sold them but did little maintenance. Every spring the people who lived along the river wondered if the dam would hold. The dam actually did break in 1862, but the lake water was so low that minimal damage was caused. In 1879 Benjamin Ruff bought the dam and built an exclusive club beside the two mile wide lake.

Ruff enlisted wealthy Pittsburgh industrialists Andrew Carnegie, Henry Clay Frick and Andrew Mellon, among others, to finance the club. Locals called it the 'Bosses' Club,' but it was officially christened the South Fork Fishing & Hunting Club. Ruff recruited Edward Pearson, who wasn't an engineer, to rebuild the dam. Pearson refused engineering advice from Cambria Iron officials downstream, who were worried about the dam. He didn't replace the discharge pipes; he renovated the dam with hay, tree stumps and manure, installed only one spillway and, worst of all, lowered the height of the dam. To protect their fish, club members had a screen installed over the spillway; the screen became clogged with debris.

In the week before May 31, heavy rains covered the Johnstown area. On May 30 the lake waters rose an inch every 10 minutes. At 3:10 pm on the 31st the dam broke and the water swept 14 miles along the floodplain to Johnstown. It took only 45 minutes for the lake to empty. On the way, the water smashed through several small towns, tearing up train tracks and obliterating a 75 foot high stone viaduct. An engineer raced his train ahead of the flood with the whistle tied down to warn people.

Just under an hour after the dam broke a 35 foot high wall of water choked with debris hit town at 40 mph. People tried to get out of the way, but parts of the town were already under two to seven feet of water from the previous week's rain and progress was difficult. The water eventually stopped at the seven-arched Pennsylvania Stone Bridge below the junction of the rivers. Tons of debris – most of the town of Johnstown, trains, logs, machinery, animals and hundreds of people – jammed up against the bridge. Many people were trapped in rolls of barbed wire from the Gautier Wire Works in town.

The debris, covered in oil spilled from railroad tank cars, caught fire and burned, possibly lit by coals from steam engines, killing 80 people who were trapped against the bridge in the water.

The total death toll from the flood was 2209. Typhoid killed 40 more. ■

cheapies, has steak mains for around $6 and Greek salad for $3.95.

The friendly *Lettuce Eat* (☎ (814) 536-1172), 130 Market St, serves chef salad ($3.30), soups ($1.80) and sandwiches ($2). It's open daily from 7 am to 4 pm. *Coney Island Lunch* (☎ (814) 535-2885), 127 Clinton St, has a hot dogs (90¢), hamburgers (from 90¢), breakfast all day – and a sign saying 'Please no Tips'!

The *Incline Station Restaurant & Pub*, in the Inclined Plane's visitors center has burgers for $5 and sandwiches for $4.75 plus good views of Johnstown.

Getting There & Away

Air Johnstown/Cambria County airport (☎ (814) 536-0002) outside town is served by USAir. Take Route 56 east to Route 219 north then the first exit to the airport.

Bus Greyhound (☎ (814) 536-4714) has a desk inside the Mr Donut cafe, 139 Clinton St at Locust St. The desk is staffed Monday to Friday from 10 am to 3:30 pm, Saturday 1 to 3 pm; at other times you can get tickets from the person serving behind the food counter. There's one bus daily to Harrisburg ($25, five hours) and Philadelphia

($42, eight hours), and two to Pittsburgh ($15, four hours).

Train From the Amtrak station (☎ (814) 535-3313), 47 Walnut St at Johns St, there are two trains daily to Harrisburg ($48, three hours), Philadelphia ($70, 4¼ hours) and Pittsburgh ($22, 1½ hours).

Getting Around
Cambria Country Transit Authority (CCTA; ☎ (814) 535-5526, (800) 252-3889) provides the local bus service. Timetables are available from the 'Bus Stop' general store in the Transit Center, where local buses arrive and depart. Fares are between $1 and $1.40. For a taxi call Yellow Cab (☎ (814) 535-4584) or Friendly Cab (☎ (814) 467-5587).

AROUND JOHNSTOWN
Johnstown Flood National Memorial
The memorial (☎ (814) 495-4643) is about 10 miles northeast of Johnstown at the site of the former South Fork Dam where the flood began. A short trail leads from the visitors center to the site of what is left of the dam. The visitors center has similar exhibits to the Johnstown Flood Museum and a gripping, dramatized 35 minute film entitled *Black Friday*, which tells the story of the flood with horror-movie music and clips from fictional flood movies. The memorial and center are free and open daily Memorial Day to Labor Day from 9 am to 6 pm, to 5 pm the rest of the year.

From Johnstown take Route 56 south to Route 219 north and follow it to the St Michael/Sidman exit. Take Route 869 east for 1½ miles then make a left onto Lake Rd at the sign for the memorial. Follow Lake Rd for 1½ miles to the visitors center.

Allegheny Railroad Portage
When the Allegheny Railroad Portage opened in 1834 it reduced traveling time between Pittsburgh and Philadelphia from three weeks to four days and helped open up the west. A feat of engineering, the portage consisted of a series of inclined planes over the Allegheny Mountains. The 2.3 sq mile national historic site (☎ (814) 884-6150) about 25 miles northeast of Johnstown off Route 22, provides interpretive programs and guided hikes. It's free and is open daily mid-June to Labor Day from 9 am to 6 pm, to 5 pm during the rest of the year.

Blue Knob State Park
You can go downhill skiing at **Blue Knob Ski Resort** (☎ (814) 239-5111, (800) 458-3403), on Blue Knob Mountain (3146 feet) within the state park, about 20 miles east of Johnstown on Route 869 east of Route 219. Lift fees are from $22 to $32. The park (☎ (814) 276-3576) has eight miles of snowmobiling trails and in summer 17 miles of hiking trails; it also has primitive campsites. For a snow report call ☎ (800) 822-3045 in Pennsylvania, ☎ (800) 458-3403 from outside the state.

PENNSYLVANIA

Northern Pennsylvania

More remote, more forested and less populated than the south of the state, Northern Pennsylvania stretches along New York state's southern border from Lake Erie in the west to the Delaware River in the east. In late September and early October the fall colors make it particularly beautiful.

The Allegheny National Forest is a mighty presence in the west and the region south of Erie is where the world's commercial oil industry began in the mid-19th century, especially around Oil City, Titusville and Oil Creek. Northern Pennsylvania is dotted with many state forests suitable for outdoor activities and also has its own Grand Canyon near Wellsboro. In Scranton to the east lies more evidence of the state's industrial past. The Pocono

Mountains to the south and east of Scranton, close to Pennsylvania's eastern border with New York and New Jersey, are immensely popular for outdoor recreational activities.

I-80 cuts east-west across the state, but further north Route 6, also called the Grand Army of the Republic Hwy, is more scenic and connects with the many attractions of Northern Pennsylvania.

WILLIAMSPORT

Williamsport is on Route 15 off I-180 about 16 miles north of I-80 along the west branch of the Susquehanna River. The Lycoming County Tourist Promotion Agency (☎ (800) 358-9900) is in a 19th century building at 848 W 4th St.

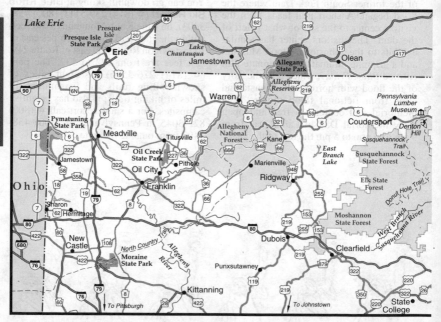

The town was first settled in the late 18th century. It became the main northern river port in the valleys of the Susquehanna and the center of a huge lumber industry that brought immense wealth to the region. This wealth produced quite a few millionaires who, towards the end of the 19th century, built grand mansions along W 4th St, which today is known as **Millionaires' Row**. A number of these houses are open to the public.

Annually, in the third week of August, young baseball teams from around the world compete in the **Little League World Series**. During the rest of the year you can visit the stadium and international headquarters (☎ (717) 326-1921) of Little League baseball about a mile south of town on Route 15.

There's also the **Little League Museum** (☎ (717) 326-3607) on Route 15. It tells the story of the development of Little

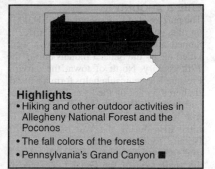

Highlights
• Hiking and other outdoor activities in Allegheny National Forest and the Poconos
• The fall colors of the forests
• Pennsylvania's Grand Canyon ∎

League baseball from its humble beginnings in Williamsport in 1939. It's open Memorial Day to Labor Day, Monday to Saturday 9 am to 7 pm, Sunday noon to 7 pm; the rest of the year it's open Monday to Saturday 9 am to 5 pm, Sunday noon to 5 pm. Entry is $4/1.

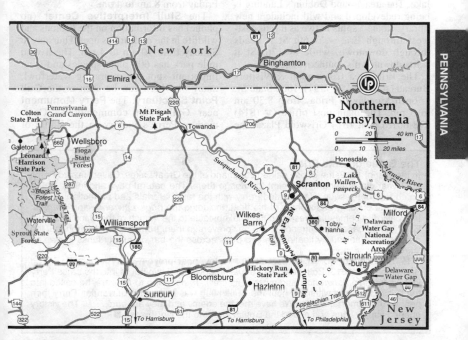

ERIE & AROUND

The port town of Erie (population 109,000), on the southern shore of Lake Erie, is named after the Eriez Indians who were killed off by the Seneca Indians during the 17th century. North of town, the curving Presque Isle peninsula helps form a natural, sheltered harbor on the lake. The town was laid out in 1795 and played an important role in America's victory in the Battle of Lake Erie during the War of 1812 with Britain. Today Erie is an important industrial and manufacturing center. Lake Erie is the shallowest of the Great Lakes and is especially vulnerable to pollution, which in the 1970s had wiped out much of the lake's marine life. A combined community effort reversed this and the fish have returned.

Orientation & Information

Peach and State Sts are the main north-south streets. State St leads north to the public dock at Dobbin's Landing on the lake. The area around Dobbin's Landing is being redeveloped and will include a new library. Route 5 splits in two as it runs east-west through Erie – as 6th St it heads through downtown, while as 12th St it skirts downtown's southern edge.

The Erie Area Convention & Visitors Bureau (☎ (814) 454-7191), 1006 State St, is open Monday to Friday from 8:30 am to 5 pm. The main post office (☎ (814) 878-0018) is at 1314 Griswold Plaza; the downtown post office, in the Federal Building & US Courthouse at State St and S Park Row, is open Monday to Friday from 9 am to 4 pm. Given its size it has adequate banking facilities, including ATMs.

Mid-City Laundry, at E 4th and State Sts, is open Monday to Friday from 8 am to 10 pm, weekends 10 am to 6 pm, and charges $1.25 per wash.

Presque Isle State Park

Presque Isle (the name means 'almost an island') is a peninsula one mile across at its widest point and 6½ miles long that's attached to the mainland about four miles west of Erie. The peninsula is actually getting longer – there's continual loss of sand from the main body, but growth at Gull Point at the eastern end. The peninsula forms and protects Presque Isle Bay, considered to be one of the finest natural harbors on the Great Lakes. The park office (☎ (814) 833-7424) is open Monday to Friday from 8 am to 4 pm.

The **Stull Interpretive Center** (no phone) has information on the habitats and wildlife in the park and is open Thursday to Sunday from 10 am to 4 pm. The five sq mile park has 600 plant species and is an important spot for migrating waterfowl, many of which can be seen at the **Gull Point Sanctuary**. The **Perry Monument** near Gull Point commemorates Commodore Perry's victory in the Battle of

---

The Battle of Lake Erie

In the War of 1812, the British gained command of the Great Lakes. Oliver Hazard Perry, a 27 year old lieutenant, was sent to engage them. The natural bays and inlets on the south side of Presque Isle provided Perry with the raw materials and protection needed during the building of six ships of his fleet, including the brigs *Lawrence* and *Niagara*. Ironically, the peninsula presented the final obstacle to the launch of the ships into Lake Erie. A sand bar at the entrance to the bay prevented them from moving through, but the problem was solved by floating the two brigs across the bar on empty tanks known as 'camels.'

Perry engaged the British fleet at Put-in-Bay, near present-day Sandusky, OH, on September 10, 1813. Both fleets had equal firepower and two hours into the battle Perry lost his flagship, *Lawrence*, and most of its crew. Transferring to *Niagara*, he sailed into the British fleet and within an hour the British flag was lowered in surrender. Perry then penned the immortal words: 'We have met the enemy and they are ours . . . . ' The victory opened supply lines and ended the British threat to the Northwest. ■

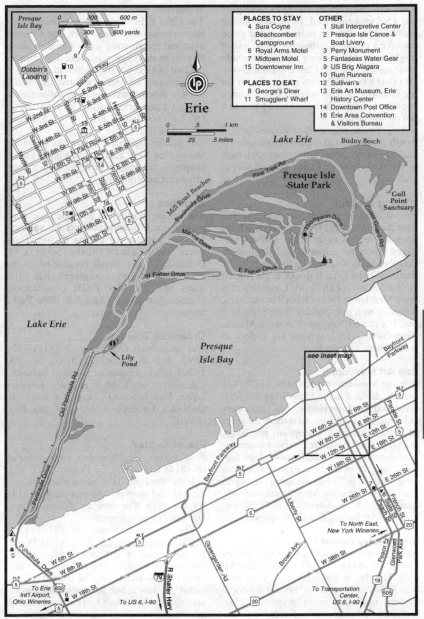

PENNSYLVANIA

Lake Erie, September 10, 1813. The park has a 5.8 mile bike trail, 10 miles of hiking trails and beaches for swimming, but given the lake's pollution problems of the past it might be worth checking whether it is safe to do so. Presque Isle Canoe & Boat Livery (☎ (814) 838-3938) rents canoes for $6 for the first hour, $20 for seven hours. It's open Monday to Friday from 10 am to 5 pm, to 6 pm on weekends.

To get there take I-79 or Routes 19 or 5 to 6th St, then head west to Peninsula Dr and turn north. A bus from downtown runs to the park June to Labor Day on weekends only.

US Brig *Niagara*

Pennsylvania's official flagship, the US Brig *Niagara* (☎ (814) 452-2744) is a fully operable replica (with a few timbers salvaged from the original) of Commodore Perry's sailing ship, which took part in the Battle of Lake Erie. It docks at the foot of Holland St east of Dobbin's Landing and is open Monday to Friday from 9 am to 5 pm, Saturday to 6 pm, Sunday from noon to 5 pm. It's closed November through March. Admission is $4/2, seniors $3. Expect to spend about an hour here.

Erie Art Museum

Erie Art Museum (☎ (814) 459-5477), 411 State St, housed in the 1839 Greek Revival-style Old Custom House, has temporary exhibitions as well as permanent displays of American and European paintings, drawings and sculptures. Also on permanent display is a sculpted scene depicting local people in an Erie diner (which no longer exists). The museum is open Tuesday to Saturday from 11 am to 5 pm, Sunday 1 to 5 pm. Admission is $1.50/50¢, seniors 75¢, but it's free on Wednesday.

Erie History Center

Near the art museum is the Erie History Center (☎ (814) 454-1813), 417 State St, open Tuesday to Saturday from 9 am to 5 pm. It has an extensive library on local history, including many maps and photographs. A donation is requested.

Wineries

The Lake Erie shore line stretching from Pennsylvania into New York and Ohio is excellent for growing wine. The best place to visit in this region is about 12 miles to the east of Erie where you'll find a number of vineyards clustered around the small town of **North East**. For more information contact Lake Erie Quality Wine Alliance (☎ (800) 600-9463), PO Box 10755, Erie, PA 16514-0755.

If you're especially interested in wine-tasting, see New York state's Finger Lakes chapter – the region is about a 2½ hour drive east on Route 17.

Activities

The strong winds on Presque Isle Bay make it good for **windsurfing** and **sailing**. It's also popular for **scuba diving**. Fantaseas Water Gear (☎ (814) 835-3483), 44 Peninsula Dr just outside Presque Isle State Park, rents diving equipment, has dive tours and provides PADI certification courses. See also Presque Isle State Park, above.

Organized Tours

The small boat *Little Toot* (☎ (814) 455-5892, 866-2830), 4712 Cherry St, PA 16509, offers 45-minute narrated sightseeing cruises on Lake Erie daily June to Labor Day for $6/3. There's a booth at Dobbin's Landing where you can buy tickets.

Places to Stay

Sara Coyne Beachcomber Campground (☎ (814) 833-4560), 50 Peninsula Dr just outside Presque Isle State Park, has a laundry and showers and tent sites for $12, RV sites $16. The sites are close together, but there's a beach nearby.

The *Midtown Motel* (☎ (814) 455-7529), a gray building at 26th and Peach Sts just south of downtown, has singles/doubles for $34/38. The *Downtowner Inn* (☎ (814) 456-6251), 205 W 10th St at Sassafras St, has a bar and swimming pool and rooms for $40/45. There are many motels west of town near the intersection of Route 5 and Peninsula Dr (Route 832). Here the *Royal Arms Motel* (☎ (814) 833-9855), 1015 Peninsula Dr, has large rooms for $39/44.

Places to Eat

Chain restaurants and fast-food outlets line Peach St south of 26th St and to the west at the intersection of Route 5 and Peninsula Dr (Route 832).

In town, the friendly *George's Diner* (☎ (814) 455-0860), near the intersection of State and 26th Sts, has fish & chips for $4.25 and sandwiches from $2; it doesn't accept credit cards. At Dobbin's Landing the mid-range *Smugglers' Wharf* (☎ (814) 459-4273), 3 State St, has a bar and views of Presque Isle Bay. It serves clam chowder for $2.75, Caesar salad for $5.50 and seafood fettuccini for $13.95.

Entertainment

Rum Runners, a bar at Dobbin's Landing about 200 yards east of Smugglers' Wharf restaurant, looks out over Presque Isle Bay. *Sullivan's*, at French and E 3rd Sts, one block east of State St, is an old Irish pub with music at weekends.

Getting There & Away

Greyhound buses leave from the Transportation Center (☎ (814) 864-5949), 5759 Peach St two blocks north of Kuntz Rd about three miles south of downtown, open daily from 8:30 am to 10:30 pm. There are four buses daily to Pittsburgh ($19 one way, 2¼ hours). From Pittsburgh I-79 takes you directly to Erie. I-90 heads west to Ohio and east to New York along the shores of the lake.

Erie international airport (☎ (814) 833-4258) is southwest of town at 4411 W 12th St. Erie Airways (☎ (814) 833-1188), 1603 Asbury Rd, is the local airline. It's also served by USAir.

Getting Around

Erie Metro Transit Authority (EMTA; ☎ (814) 459-4287), 127 E 14th St, operates the local bus service. The one-way fare is $1. Some routes don't operate on Sunday or holidays. For a taxi call Erie Yellow Cab (☎ (814) 455-4441), 1619 State St.

PYMATUNING STATE PARK

About 45 miles southwest of Erie and just north of Jamestown near the Ohio border, Pymatuning State Park (☎ (412) 932-3141) contains the 21½ sq mile Pymatuning Reservoir, the largest artificial lake in the state. The land around the reservoir provides habitat for a wide variety of bird species. The **Pymatuning Wildlife Management Area** contains the state's only nesting bald eagles as well as other raptors and waterfowl, and the visitors center (☎ (814) 683-5545) on Ford Island has exhibits on local flora and fauna.

There's cross-country skiing in winter and fishing is popular on the lake. The park has three campgrounds with sites for $10 and $12, and it's accessible on Routes 6 or 322 west of I-79. Food and other supplies can be found in Jamestown.

TITUSVILLE

Titusville (population 6450), about 42 miles southeast of Erie on the banks of Oil Creek, was founded in 1796 and named after Jonathan Titus, one of the early surveyors of the area. Lumber became the main industry until Edwin Drake drilled the world's first oil well. It's a small working town though it's trying to develop its tourism around oil history. It's worth a stop on the way through to see the world's first oil well.

Titusville is at the intersection of Routes 8 and 27 about 15 miles north of Oil City, about 40 minutes drive east of I-79 and about 40 minutes north of I-80.

Drake Well Memorial Park

The memorial park (☎ (814) 827-2797) commemorates the spot where oil was first drilled by Edwin Drake of the Seneca Oil Company in August 1859. A museum contains artifacts, books, documents and photographs, and shows a 27 minute film about the construction of the well, starring Vincent Price as Edwin Drake. In the park are some old oil pumps, a couple of

The World's First Oil Well

Today, when we think of oil we usually think of the Middle East, Texas or the North Sea, but it all began in Titusville, PA, in the mid-19th century.

Petroleum had been used for thousands of years by Native Americans in medicine and paint. It was collected from springs or along the tops of creeks where it appeared naturally. In the 19th century, European Americans used it in its natural, foul-smelling state as a medicine, to grease wagon wheels and to burn for light. By the early 1850s whale oil was becoming scarce and people began refining petroleum into kerosene.

In 1859, the Seneca Oil Company was leasing a natural oil spring in the Oil Creek Valley near Titusville; wanting to increase production, it sent Edwin Drake to improve output. Drake first dug for oil, then decided to drill and recruited William ('Uncle Billy') Smith, a salt-well driller from near Pittsburgh, to build the well.

Smith built a derrick, engine house and steam engine. Drilling began in June, but was unsuccessful until Drake drove a cast-iron pipe down into the rock first then drilled inside it. On August 26, the drill bit hit a cavity; the drilling material was pulled out and work was stopped for the day, but next morning when Uncle Billy checked the well, he found it full of oil. When a pump was attached, the well yielded 20 barrels a day, double that of any other production method at the time.

Oil speculators soon followed Drake and many wells were dug in the area along Oil Creek. By 1862 thousands of barrels of oil were being produced daily, driving the price of oil so low that Drake's well proved unprofitable and was shut down. ■

carriages and a replica of the original derrick and steam-driven drill.

The park is open Tuesday to Saturday from 9 am to 5 pm, Sunday noon to 5 pm. Admission is $4/2, seniors $3. Take Route 8 southeast from town for 1¼ miles, then go east on Bloss St to the park just past the bridge.

Places to Stay & Eat

Oil Creek Camping Resort (☎ (814) 827-1023), four miles south off Route 8, just outside Oil Creek State Park, has large sites for two people at $13 or $17 with full hookup. In town, *Colonel Drake Hotel* (☎ (814) 827-2267), 102 N Franklin St at Central Ave, has been here since 1865, although in different incarnations. The simple hotel has 15 rooms at $30/35 a single/double. Downstairs there's a bar and restaurant which serves sandwiches for $4.75 and spaghetti for $6.95. The town also has a several fast-food places on Franklin St and Central Ave.

OIL CITY & AROUND

The aptly named Oil City (population 12,000), straddling the Allegheny River and its tributary Oil Creek, was the center

of the 19th century oil industry in the region. Oil magnate John D Rockefeller raised his first million dollars here. (See the sidebar in New York's Hudson Valley chapter.)

The countryside is littered with remnants from that time, but the streams and much of the wilderness of the Allegheny foothills seem to have recovered from that early industrial onslaught. Oil City, a fairly unattractive industrial town, is still involved in the refining of oil and the manufacture of related machinery. Oil City is also the headquarters of the Quaker State Corporation, one of the first companies to produce motor oil.

Orientation & Information

Downtown, centered on Seneca and Center Sts, is bounded to the south by the Allegheny River and to the west and north by Oil Creek; south of the Allegheny River over the State St Bridge is another small commercial center. Route 8 becomes Seneca St in town. The chamber of commerce (☎ (814) 676-8521), 102 Center St, open Monday to Friday from 8:30 am to 4:30 pm, is where you can get some tourist information. The post office, on Seneca St opposite the Venango Museum, is open Monday to Friday from 8:30 am to 1 pm and 2 to 4 pm.

With the exception of the Venango Museum, the things to see are outside Oil City proper.

Venango Museum

Venango Museum (☎ (814) 676-2007), 270 Seneca St in a former post office building, has changing exhibits on the region and its people such as Jeannie Seely, the country singer, who was born in Titusville. The museum is open Tuesday to Saturday from 10 am to 4 pm, Sunday 1 to 4 pm. The admission is $2/1.

McClintock Well

The McClintock Well, the oldest continuously operating oil well in the US (it has been pumping since 1861) is an interesting piece of history but not much to look at.

As you head north out of town on Route 8 turn left onto Waitz Rd at the blue building marked 'bmi' by the bridge. Walk about 80 yards west between two fences and continue across some railroad tracks; look to your right and you'll see the small well, which is quietly pumping oil into green Quaker State Corporation tanks.

Oil Creek & Titusville Railroad

This restored train runs along an old scenic rail line for 13½ miles from Perry St Station in Titusville, with stops at the Drake Well Museum and Petroleum Center in Oil Creek State Park (a flag stop only), to Rynd Farm Station, four miles north of Oil City just off Route 8. The train has a working postal service and runs mid-June to the end of October, Wednesday to Sunday. The fare is $9/5, seniors $8. Bicycles can go on the trains for $1. For more information contact Oil Creek & Titus Railroad (☎ (814) 676-1733), PO Box 68, Elm St, Oil City, PA 16301.

Oil Creek State Park

Entry to the 11 sq mile park is just north of Rynd Farm Station, over the bridge. The visitors center (☎ (814) 676-5915) is at Petroleum Center, an oil-industry hub during the 1860s boom, though you'd hardly know it today with the area's restored natural beauty.

The park has over 52 miles of hiking trails, including the 32 mile **Oil Creek Hiking Trail**, which follows the Oil Creek Valley from Drakes Well in the north to Rynd Farm in the south. There's also a 9.5 mile paved **cycling** trail, and you can rent bikes form Oil Creek Outfitters (☎ (814) 677-4684) in Petroleum Center for $3 for the first hour, $2.50 for each succeeding hour. The trails provide access to remote parts of the park that are good for **birdwatching**. The creek also offers conditions for beginner-level **canoeing**. In winter there's **cross-country skiing**.

Pithole

There isn't much left of Pithole – a ghost town off Route 227 six miles east of Oil Creek State Park – just cellar holes on a hillside. The discovery of oil in January 1865 attracted many people and the town was laid out in May. By September, Pithole had 15,000 people, 57 hotels, a daily paper and the third-busiest post office in the state. When the oil ran out, so did the people. By the following year the population had rapidly reduced to 2000 and in 1870 to only 281.

The visitors center (☎ (814) 827-2797) here has a small exhibit on Pithole's history and there's more information at the Drake Well Memorial Park museum.

Crude Oil

Crude oil is found under the western slopes of the Appalachian Mountains in western Pennsylvania, southwestern New York, eastern Ohio and West Virginia. It's renowned for its paraffin base (from the Latin *para linum* – 'little affinity' – meaning little affinity for chemical change, ie it is very stable) It also has a high natural lubricity and viscosity and is relatively free of impurities like sulfur, tar or asphalt. ■

Punxsutawney Phil

Punxsutawney, a town about 90 miles northwest of Pittsburgh on Route 36 near Route 119, is home to the famous 'weather forecaster' Punxsutawney Phil, a groundhog. According to legend, if he casts a shadow on Groundhog Day (February 2) winter will last six more weeks. The elaborate ceremony takes place at Gobbler's Knob, a hill just outside town, but most of the year Phil lives in the children's library in Mahoning East Civic Center in town. In June there's also the Groundhog Festival, when Phil is given a 'magic potion' to ensure that he lives a long time. Punxsutawney Phil was made even more famous by the film *Groundhog Day*, starring Andie MacDowell and Bill Murray. ∎

Places to Stay

The *Corbett Inn* (☎ (814) 676-8521), 370 Seneca St north of downtown close to the industrial sprawl, is a no-frills place but the rooms are large and clean. The rates are $39/44 a single/double. *Flower Cottage B&B* (☎ (814) 677-3786), 515 W 6th St, is on a quiet suburban street southwest of downtown. It has two rooms that share a bath for $45 each, a family TV room and a backyard packed with flowers in season. *Holiday Inn* (☎ (814) 677-1221), 1 Seneca St, has rooms overlooking the Allegheny River; rates are $66/76.

Places to Eat

There are fast-food places along Seneca St. South over the bridge, *Yuen's Chinese Restaurant* (☎ (814) 677-0818), 11 E 1st St, is mostly a take-out place but you can eat at the tables; it has chow mein for $5.50 and pork with broccoli for $6.95. *Famoore's* (☎ (814) 676-4789), opposite Yuen's at No 18, is a popular family restaurant serving standard food at reasonable rates, with corned beef hash, egg and toast for $3.95, pancake, sausage and two eggs, $3.30. *Kate's* in the Holiday Inn has a bar and serves onion soup for $2.75 and pasta for $8.50. The busy *Hoss's Steak & Sea House* (☎ (814) 677-3002), 520 N Seneca St, has a lunch-time all-you-can-eat soup-and-salad bar for $4.

Getting There & Away

Buses leave from outside McNerneny's store (☎ (814) 677-1307), 245 Seneca St; you can purchase tickets inside. There's a daily bus to Pittsburgh ($30.45 one way, 5¼ hours) at 5:15 pm. Route 62 heads west to I-79, Route 8 runs south to I-80.

Getting Around

Venango Bus Public Transport (☎ (814) 677-0818) operates the local bus service Monday to Saturday. Fares within Oil City are 75¢, to the nearby towns of Franklin and Cranberry they're $1.50.

HERMITAGE & SHARON

Hermitage and its neighbor town of Sharon, near the Ohio border, are home to a collection of 'world's largests.' There's no reason to stay here, but if you're in the area they might be worth a quick look. Hermitage has no real center other than the commercial strip, but Sharon (population 17,500), on the Shenango River, is much older, and there are some fine old red-brick buildings on State St, the main street downtown. To get there, from I-80 take Route 18 north to Sharon; Route 62 from I-79 runs west to Hermitage and Sharon. Mercer County Tourist Promotion Agency (☎ (412) 981-5880) is at 1 W State St, Sharon.

Things to See

In Hermitage, **Kraynak's Santa's Christmasland** (☎ (412) 347-4511), on Route 62 half a mile east of the intersection with Route 18, is said to be the largest Christmas store in the world. True or not, it does have a huge collection of artificial trees, trains, stuffed animals, toys, candy and animated figures. It's open Monday to Saturday from 9 am to 9 pm, Sunday 10 am to 6 pm.

The **Avenue of 444 Flags**, the 'world's

PENNSYLVANIA

largest display of American flags,' lines the entrance road to Hillcrest Memorial Cemetery next to Kraynak's. There's one flag for every day that US citizens from the US Embassy in Iran were held hostage in 1979-81.

Locals claim that Daffin's Candies (☎ (412) 342-7502), 496 E State St (Route 62) in Sharon, has the 'world's largest display area for chocolate,' but it doesn't seem *that* large; at the back in a small room are some large chocolate figures on permanent display. Daffin's is open Monday to Saturday from 9 am to 9 pm, Sunday 11 am to 5 pm. **Reyers** (☎ (412) 981-1100/2200), claims to be the 'world's largest shoe store.' It has a store on W State St and a factory outlet on E State St.

Places to Stay & Eat

Route 62 has many motels. The *Royal Motel* (☎ (412) 347-5546), 301 S Hermitage Rd, near the junction of Routes 18 and 62, has rooms with TV and phone for $35/39 a single/double.

In Sharon *Quaker Steak & Lube* (☎ (412) 981-7221), 110 Connelly Blvd, is a former gas station converted into a restaurant that sells about 30,000 chicken wings a week, in a number of sauces from mild to atomic, starting at $4. It also operates the nearby *Hot Rod Cafe* selling similar food and housing a car used by Sylvester Stallone in *Rambo III*.

ALLEGHENY NATIONAL FOREST

The 797 sq mile Allegheny National Forest in northwestern Pennsylvania along the New York border is bounded to the west by the Allegheny River and crossed by numerous streams and trails. The forest, consisting mostly of hardwoods of hemlock, maple, white ash, yellow poplar and black cherry, is on the Allegheny Plateau; much of the land is between 1000 and 2300 feet in elevation.

When the national forest was first proclaimed people called it the 'Allegheny Brushpatch' because it had been stripped of most its timber in the late 19th and early 20th century – thousands of acres of old-

growth forests were cut for the shipbuilding and construction industries. The timber has since grown back, but parts of the forest continue to be harvested and Allegheny black cherry is one of the most valuable woods in the world.

The forest is full of wildlife, including black bear, elk, deer, raccoon, fox, beaver, muskrat, turkey and grouse. Black bears are usually not harmful unless you come between a mother and her cubs; generally they can be scared off by yelling, waving and clapping. Don't bring food to your tent; bears have a keen sense of smell – keep it in a car or out of bear reach hanging from a line 10 feet above the ground between two trees.

The US Army Corps of Engineers administers a series of lakes and dams in the region as part of a system of flood-control projects in the Allegheny and upper Ohio River valleys. The forest also encompasses several state parks.

Orientation

The major landmark, the Allegheny Reservoir to the north, crosses the state border into New York. The southern end of the reservoir forks to form two bodies of water: to the east Kinzua Bay stretches eight miles into the forest; to the west the Allegheny River flows west, then south, marking the western boundary of the forest. The Clarion River forms much of the southern border.

Warren, west of the reservoir, is the main town in the region and is the best place to pick up supplies. There's a large supermarket in town and if people want a taste of civilization after (or before) roughing it in the forest, it has some restaurants and motels.

The town of Kane, southeast of Kinzua Bay, is a major town to the east. The other principal settlements are Ridgway in the southeastern corner of the forest and Marienville, which is south-central. At the center of the forest is the village of Sheffield.

Route 6 crosses the forest from Warren through Sheffield then runs southeast to

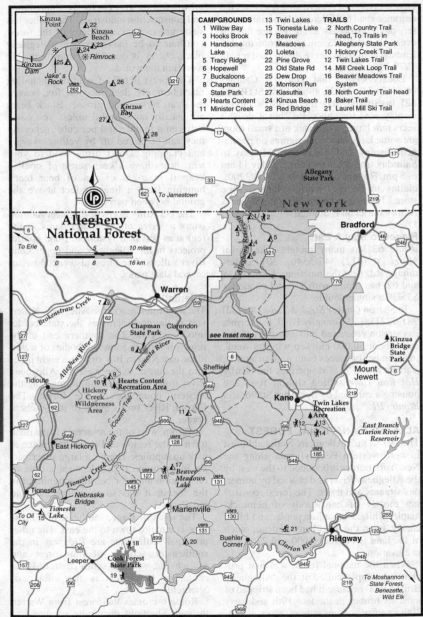

CAMPGROUNDS
1 Willow Bay
3 Hooks Brook
4 Handsome
   Lake
5 Tracy Ridge
6 Hopewell
7 Buckaloons
8 Chapman
   State Park
9 Hearts Content
11 Minister Creek
13 Twin Lakes
15 Tionesta Lake
17 Beaver
   Meadows
20 Loleta
22 Pine Grove
23 Old State Rd
25 Dew Drop
26 Morrison Run
27 Kiasutha
24 Kinzua Beach
28 Red Bridge

TRAILS
2 North Country Trail
   head, To Trails in
   Allegheny State Park
10 Hickory Creek Trail
12 Twin Lakes Trail
14 Mill Creek Loop Trail
16 Beaver Meadows Trail
   System
18 North Country Trail head
19 Baker Trail
21 Laurel Mill Ski Trail

Kane. Route 66 runs southwest from Kane to Marienville and Cook Forest State Park. From I-80, Route 8 north to Route 62 at Oil City will follow the forest's western border north to Route 6.

Information

The USFS (☎ (814) 723-5150), 222 Liberty St in Warren, is open Monday to Friday from 8 am to 4:30 pm. The staff is friendly and helpful and can provide lots of information on activities and camping in the forest; they sell topographical maps of the region too. The USFS has an office at the Kinzua Point Information Center (☎ (814) 726-1290), at the intersection of Routes 59 and 262 at the fork of the Allegheny Reservoir, nine miles east of Warren. It's open Memorial Day to Labor Day, Monday to Friday from 8 am to 4:30 pm.

The USFS also has four ranger stations where you can get information: Bradford (☎ (814) 362-4613) at the junction of Routes 321 and 59 west of town; Ridgway (☎ (814) 776-6172), on Route 948 north of town; Marienville (☎ (814) 927-6628), on Route 66 north of town; and Sheffield (☎ (814) 968-3232), on Route 6 east of the village.

Also in Warren is the regional tourist office, Allegheny National Forest Vacation Region (☎ (814) 726-1222, (800) 624-7802; the toll-free number only works in 15 eastern US states), downstairs at 315 2nd Ave at Pennsylvania Ave.

Camping is the main form of accommodation, but there are motels in Warren and Kane. If you are camping bring some insect repellent. In Warren, the O-So White Coin Laundry is at Thorne's Market Place east of downtown along Pennsylvania Ave.

Things to See

The **Allegheny Reservoir** is a 18¾ sq mile lake held back by the **Kinzua Dam** (built in 1966), which inundated much of the land granted to Chief Cornplanter (son of a Seneca woman and a Dutchman) in 1791. His descendants were removed from the land and sent to New York in the 19th century. The Kinzua Dam Visitors Center

---

Kinzua Railroad Bridge

From the mid-1800s rapid industrial growth around Buffalo, NY, produced high demand for coal. The railroads carried the coal that fueled the fires of industry, heated homes and also powered the trains. But between Pennsylvania's coal and the awaiting industry to the north lay an obstacle – the Kinzua Valley.

When the Kinzua Railroad Bridge was first built in 1882 to allow a branch of the Erie Railroad to ship coal north across the valley, it was the world's highest viaduct and longest rail viaduct. Completely rebuilt in 1900 to carry heavier loads, it was in service till 1959. ∎

(☎ (814) 726-0661), operated by the US Army Corps of Engineers, is open Monday to Friday from 9 am to 3:30 pm, weekends 9 am to 4:30 pm; October through March it only opens weekends 10 am to 4 pm. There are great views from **Jake's Rock** near the Kinzua Dam and at **Rimrock** across Kinzua Bay on Route 59.

To the east, outside the forest, the 301 foot high **Kinzua Railroad Bridge** in Kinzua Bridge State Park stretches 2053 feet across the Kinzua Creek Valley. The second highest railroad viaduct in the US and the fourth highest in the world, it's fairly spectacular. The Knox, Kane, Kinzua Railroad (☎ (814) 927-6621) runs steam trains from Kane and Marienville across the bridge from June through October. The roundtrip fare from Marienville for adults/children is $20/13; from Kane it's $14/8. To get to the bridge by road take Route 6 northeast of Kane until just past the town of Mt Jewett, then take the first road north (left) to the park.

The 13½ sq mile **Hickory Creek** area east of Tidioute, has been designated as 'wilderness' and can be reached from the **Hearts Content Recreation Area**, which itself contains stands of old-growth hemlock and white pine forest.

The **Tionesta Lake** area is in the southwest corner of the forest about 15 miles northeast of Oil City. The natural lake, fed by the Allegheny River and Tionesta Creek, is surrounded by 2000 acres of old-growth forest. The visitors center (☎ (814) 755-3524) here, open Memorial Day to early December, Tuesday to Saturday from 8 am to 4:30 pm, has information on the lake and hiking trails. At the eastern end of the lake near the Nebraska Bridge is a usually submerged **ghost town**. You can only see it when the water is particularly low; the bridge itself is sometimes even underwater.

The **Allegheny Islands Wilderness** consists of seven islands on the Allegheny River between Kinzua Dam and Tionesta.

In **Cook Forest State Park** (☎ (814) 744-8407) to the south is the Forest Cathedral Natural Area containing one of the largest old-growth forests of white pine and hemlock in Pennsylvania. Many now exceed three feet in diameter and approach 200 feet in height.

Southeast of the forest one of only two herds of **wild elk** left in the eastern US roams east of the town of Benezette (ask for directions in Ridgway). The elk number over 255 and the best time to see them is in the early morning or late afternoon.

Hiking & Backpacking

There are hundreds of miles of hiking trails throughout the forest, and you can camp along most of them (see Camping, below). The USFS office in Warren and the ranger stations (see Information earlier) have trail maps, topographical maps and information on conditions. For guidebooks, check out *The Allegheny National Forest Hiking Guide* by Bruce Sundquist et al, available from Sierra Club, Allegheny Group, PO Box 8214, Pittsburgh, PA 15217; or *Fifty Hikes in Western Pennsylvania* (Backcountry Publications, VT, 1995) by Tom Thwaites.

The 86.8 mile section of the **North Country National Scenic Trail** in the Allegheny National Forest connects with Baker Trail in Cook Forest to the south and to trails in Allegany State Park in New York

to the north. The trail enters the national forest west of Marienville and runs north to the New York border. For a trail guide write to the North Country Trail Association, PO Box 311, White Cloud, MI 49349.

Other good trails include the 16.7 mile **Mill Creek Loop Trail** south of the Twin Lakes recreation area near Kane; the **Beaver Meadows Trail System** near the Beaver Meadows recreation area north of Marienville, a 7.1 mile system of five interconnecting trails; the 11.6 mile **Hickory Creek Trail**, which starts near Hearts Content campground and loops through the wilderness between Middle Hickory and East Hickory creeks; and the 14.7 mile **Twin Lakes Trail** between the Twin Lakes recreation area and the North Country Trail.

Canoeing

April through October the reservoirs, lakes, rivers and creeks of the Allegheny National Forest offer opportunities for novice and experienced paddlers. There are plenty of boat-launching sites, campgrounds and outfitters renting canoes and equipment.

A few outfitters are listed below. Just to give an idea of cost, the Kinzua-Wolf Run Marina rents canoes for $5.50/20 per hour/day. Two-day guided trips that include camping on Allegheny River islands are run by Outback Adventures (☎ (814) 589-7359) on Route 62 at the Tionesta Bridge. They cost from $40 to $50 per canoe, including paddles, jackets and taxes. Call for reservations.

Allegheny Outfitters
  Market St Plaza in Warren
    (☎ (814) 723-1203)
Bob's Trading Post
  in Kane (☎ (814) 945-6223)
Eagle Rock Motel & Campground
  in Tionesta (☎ (814) 755-4444)
Indian Valley Campground & Canoe Livery
  in West Hickory (☎ (814) 755-3578)
Kinzua-Wolf Run Marina
  on Route 59 four miles east of Kinzua Dam
    (☎ (814) 726-1650)
Loves Canoe Rental
  in Ridgway (☎ (814) 776-6285)

The **Allegheny Reservoir** has 91 miles of shoreline and there are free boat ramps at Kiasutha, Willow Bay and Dewdrop campgrounds, and at Elijah and Roper Hollow launch sites. A pleasant 45 mile float on the **Allegheny River** goes from the Kinzua Dam at the reservoir to Tionesta, where the river curves westward away from the forest. The **Tionesta Creek** runs 45 miles through scenic country from Chapman State Park (five miles south of Warren) to Tionesta Dam near Tionesta. The water level from Sheffield to the dam is too low to paddle after mid-May or early June. The creek partially follows Route 6, then Route 666.

The **Clarion River** can be canoed for 60 miles from Ridgway to its confluence with the Allegheny River. The first 19 miles of the float (from Ridgway to Hallton) are faster water and have four rapid areas that the park service classify as 'intermediate' until mid-May. The first rapid is six miles south of Ridgway near a railroad trestle, beware of the underwater pipe beneath the trestle. The other rapids are at the 15, 15.5 and 16 mile points. These three rapids are known as 'X,' 'Y' and 'Z.'

For 12 miles **Brokenstraw Creek**, between Spring Creek (about 15 miles west of Warren) to the Allegheny River near Buckaloons campground, has some of the best fast-water canoeing. **Beaver Meadows Lake**, a small lake in the Beaver Meadows recreation area five miles southwest of Clarendon is good for waterfowl watching and has a campground.

Chapman State Park (☎ (814) 723-5030), five miles southwest of Clarendon, has a small lake where the Tionesta Creek begins; it isn't managed by the USFS, for information contact the park office.

Cross-Country Skiing

The national forest has over 70 miles of ski trails. **Laurel Mill Trail** (10.3 miles) near Ridgway is the longest within the forest and the only one that's groomed. Check with the USFS office in Warren for information. Outside the forest, the **Quehanna**

Trail, southeast past Benezette in Moshannon State Forest (☎ (814) 765-3741) is much longer at 75 miles.

Birdwatching

The national forest provides a variety of habitats for birds, from the commonly seen red-winged blackbird to the rare bald eagle. Migrating raptors and waterfowl arrive in early March and songbirds in mid-April. A comprehensive checklist indicating the seasonal presence of bird types is available from the USFS. Some good viewing spots are along the Allegheny and Clarion rivers, the North Country Trail and at the Allegheny Reservoir.

Fishing

The forest has some of the best fishing in the country's northeast, combining as it does the Allegheny Reservoir, many small lakes and the Allegheny River and its tributaries. Fish vary from walleye and muskellunge in the Kinzua Dam to brook and brown trout in the mountain streams. For information check with the USFS office in Warren and the ranger stations or call the 24 hour fishing hotline (☎ (814) 726-0164). Licenses are available from campgrounds, bait shops and gas stations around the forest.

Camping

Camping is allowed anywhere on national forest land, including along hiking trails, except within 1500 feet of the Allegheny Reservoir.

Campgrounds are rated from grade 1 where campgrounds are walk-in only, have no water or toilets and usually involve no fee, to grade 5 where campgrounds are accessed by paved roads, have electricity, hot showers, interpretive programs and sites for RVs. Fees at most designated camping areas vary from $6 to $13 depending on facilities. You can make reservations through the National Recreation Reservation System (☎ (800) 280-2267), which charges a reservation fee. If you're looking for a last-minute site, call the Kinzua Point

Information Center (☎ (814) 726-1290). Most of the higher-grade campgrounds are open mid-April to mid-December while the lower-level ones are open year round.

Many of the designated, maintained campgrounds are near the Allegheny Reservoir; *Tracy Ridge* and *Willow Bay*, close to the New York border, are accessible by car, five others only by boat or on foot – *Hooks Brook, Handsome Lake, Hopewell, Pine Grove* and *Old State Rd.* Near Kinzua Bay on the southeastern fork of the reservoir that stretches toward Kane there are developed campgrounds at *Kinzua Beach, Dew Drop, Kiasutha*, and *Red Bridge*, but *Morrison Run* is only accessible by boat or on foot.

Near the Allegheny River there are campgrounds at *Buckaloons* and *Hearts Content*. Other campgrounds are at *Twin Lakes*, south of Kane; *Beaver Meadows*, five miles north of Marienville; *Loleta*, six miles south of Marienville; *Minister Creek*, in the center of the forest off Route 666; *Chapman State Park* (☎ (814) 723-5030), operated by the state; and *Tionesta Lake*, near the town of Tionesta.

There are also many privately operated campgrounds in the region. Contact the Allegheny National Forest Vacation Region tourist office in Warren (see Information, above) for help.

Getting There & Away

The nearest inter-city buses stop at Oil City and Erie, and at Jamestown, NY. You'll need a car to get around.

Route 6 runs east of I-79 to Warren and through the forest. From Erie take Route 19 south to Route 6 east, or take I-90 north to Route 17 east to Jamestown, NY, where it hooks up with Route 60/62 south to Warren. Route 62 runs northeast from Oil City along the western perimeter of the forest to Warren and connects Warren with New York state. North off I-80, Route 219 heads north to Ridgway, and Route 36 runs northwest to Tionesta. Northeast off Route 36, Route 949 leads to Ridgway, while Route 899 heads north to Marienville. From Pittsburgh take Route 28 north to I-80 at Brookville, where it meets Route 36.

ROUTE 6: ALLEGHENY NATIONAL FOREST TO SCRANTON

Route 6, otherwise known as the Grand Army of the Republic Hwy in honor of the Civil War fallen, has been designated a National Recreational Trail. It traverses some of the most beautiful scenery in the state and is lined with lots of motels and campgrounds.

Susquehannock Trail System About 60 miles east of Kane this 85 mile system heads south off Route 6. It's a series of old railroad grades and logging and fire trails that loop through the 412 sq mile Susquehannock State Forest and connects with the **Black Forest** and **Donut Hole** trails further south. A map and information are available from the state's District Forester (☎ (814) 274-8474), PO Box 673, Coudersport, PA 16915.

Pennsylvania Lumber Museum A few miles further east on Route 6, this museum (☎ (814) 435-2652) shows the history of logging in the region and includes a logging camp, steam-powered sawmill and nature trail. The visitors center also has an information desk on the region. The museum is open daily from 9 am to 5 pm, though the logging camp closes at 4:15 pm. Entry is $3.50/1.50.

Denton Hill Ski Area Opposite the museum is the entrance to the Denton Hill downhill and cross-country skiing area (☎ (814) 435-2115) which has night skiing and some of the steepest slopes in the northeast. Lifts cost $25 for eight hours.

Pennsylvania Grand Canyon The most striking natural feature in the area is the Pennsylvania Grand Canyon, a 47 mile long valley cut by Pine Creek, that reaches a depth of 1450 feet at Waterville to the south near Willamsport. Off Route 6 you can reach the canyon south from Ansonia or by taking Route 660 west from

Wellsboro. The canyon passes through **Leonard Harrison State Park** and **Colton Point State Park**, both of which offer camping and there's canoeing in spring on Pine Creek when the water is high enough. The state parks also have short hiking and horseback-riding trails. Call ☎ (717) 724-3061 for information. From Ansonia the **West Rim Trail** follows the canyon south to meet the **Mid-State Trail** just north of Blackwell.

Wellsboro Ten miles east of the canyon, Wellsboro is the main town in the area and the seat of Tioga County. It's a picturesque place, with a tree-lined Main St lit at night by electric 'gaslights.' The tourist office (☎ (717) 724-0635) is at 114 Main St. There are several places offering accommodations. The *Penn Wells Hotel & Lodge* (☎ (717) 724-2111), 62 Main St, is an old-world hotel with rooms from $39/49, a bar and an elegant dining room serving chicken for $8.95. *Wellsboro Diner*, at Main and Queen Sts, is fast and efficient with breakfast specials of two eggs, ham and sausage for $3 and sandwiches from $1.50.

Mt Pisgah State Park About 45 miles east of Wellsboro and two miles north of Route 6, this state park (☎ (717) 297-2734), consists of 1302 acres along Mill Creek at the foot of Mt Pisgah (2260 feet). It has a series of short hiking trails; some of them become cross-country ski trails in winter. There's fishing and boating on Stephen Foster Lake and swimming in a nearby pool.

SCRANTON

First settled in 1771 and then known as Slocum Hollow, Scranton (population 82,000) is an industrial city in the Lackawanna Valley; it's named after Seldon Scranton, who created the Delaware, Lackawanna & Western (DL&W) Railroad in 1853.

The city lies at the center of the anthracite coal-mining area that fueled northeast Pennsylvania's iron and steel industries in the 19th century and the railroads that transported the region's prod-

ucts. Coal's heyday lasted till around 1950 when increasing road haulage and the introduction of diesel locomotives reduced demand for it. Since then Scranton has successfully developed alternative industries in printing and electronics.

Information is available from the Greater Scranton Chamber of Commerce (☎ (717) 342-7711), 222 Mulberry St. The post office, 235 N Washington Ave at Linden St, is open Monday to Friday from 7:30 am to 5:15 pm, Saturday 9 am to noon.

Not surprisingly, the town's main attractions relate to its industrial past.

Steamtown National Historic Site

The history of the railroads both locally and nationally can be seen at the Steamtown National Historic Site (☎ (717) 340-5200), 150 S Washington Ave, in the former DL&W railyard, and is managed by the NPS. In the visitors center a museum has exhibits, audio and videotapes of people who worked for the railroads and a film called *Steel & Steam* about the history of steam trains in Pennsylvania.

Outside is a working roundhouse (where steam trains were stored and repaired) and several operating steam locomotives. Opening hours are from 9 am to 5 pm daily and entry is $6/2, seniors $5. Plan on spending about two or three hours here.

Other Attractions

You can learn more about the fossil fuel and the people who mined it by visiting the **Pennsylvania Anthracite Heritage Museum** (☎ (717) 963-4804). It's open Monday to Saturday from 9 am to 5 pm, Sunday noon to 5 pm; admission is $3.50/1.50, seniors $2.50. Next door, a tour is available 300 feet down the former **Lackawanna Coal Mine** (☎ (717) 963-6463), open April through November daily from 10 am to 4:20 pm; tours cost $5/3.50. Both are at McDade Park (☎ (717) 963-6764), Bald Mountain Rd, west of town; take exit 57B off I-81 or exit 38 off the Pennsylvania Turnpike (Northeast Extension) and follow the signs.

In town, a block south of Steamtown are

the **Scranton Iron Furnaces** (☎ (717) 963-3208), 159 Cedar Ave, which consist of four blast furnaces built between 1848 and 1857. At their peak in the 1880s they were the second highest producer of iron in the US. They're open daily from 8 am to dusk and admission is free.

Getting There & Away

Martz Trailways bus terminal (☎ (717) 342-0146) is at 23 Lackawanna Ave opposite the Steamtown Mall; Capitol Trailways (☎ (800) 444-2877) and Greyhound (☎ (800) 231-2222) also stop here. There are regular daily buses to New York City ($24.75 one way, 2½ hours) and Philadelphia ($17 one way, three hours).

The northeast extension of the Pennsylvania Turnpike runs directly to Scranton from Philadelphia. I-81 north and I-84/Route 6 east connect the city with New York state.

THE POCONOS

To the east and south of Scranton, and running northeast from Bucks County, are the Pocono Mountains, 2400 sq miles of mountains, streams, waterfalls, lakes and an abundance of forests that are home to over a 100 varieties of trees and many rare species of plants and animals. Pocono comes from 'pocohanne,' a Lanape Native American word meaning 'stream between the mountains.' The mountain region contains one state forest and nine state parks.

A natural 'four-season' choice for nature, sports and outdoor enthusiasts, it's a heavily touristed area especially on weekends and in the fall when visitors come to see the changing colors of the hardwood trees. Many people stay at the expensive resorts offering guidance and a program of abundant activities (as well as heart-shaped beds). However, the Poconos can be seen for a reasonably modest price if you're willing to do a little of your own research.

The Nature Conservancy (☎ (717) 643-7922), PO Box 211, Blakeslee, PA 18610, a private, nonprofit conservation organization, has named the Poconos as one of the '40 Last Great Places' in the world because

of the range of ecosystems found here. However, the rise in pollution has reduced the number of trees, making the remaining natural areas even more important.

Orientation & Information The Poconos occupy the northeast corner of Pennsylvania, bordering New York and New Jersey. I-80, I-84 and Route 6 head east-west; Route 191 runs north-south through most of the length of the region and the northeast extension of the Pennsylvania Turnpike, Route 9, cuts through the southeastern corner.

Stroudsburg, at the intersection of several highways, including I-80, is the main commercial center for the Poconos. The Pocono Mountains Vacation Bureau (☎ (717) 421-5791), Box 4M, 1004 Main St, Stroudsburg, PA 18360 operates 10 information centers throughout the region. Call ☎ (800) 722-6667 for brochures or call ☎ (717) 424-6050 for current information. The *Poconos Vacation Guide* has a comprehensive listing of services.

If you come to see the fall colors you can call the 24 hour Pocono Fall Foliage Hotline (☎ (717) 421-5565) mid-September to mid-November to find out where the best viewing is.

Jim Thorpe

The small town of Jim Thorpe (population 5000) set in the hillside rising above the Lehigh River, is one of the prettiest in Pennsylvania, with many of its early buildings still intact. Originally settled in 1815 as Mauch Chunk ('Bear Mountain'), in 1954 it combined with the neighboring town of East Mauch Chunk and changed its name to Jim Thorpe, in honor of the great Native American athlete (see the sidebar).

The visitor information office (☎ (717) 325-3673), in a former railroad station at Lehigh Ave and Broadway, is open Monday to Friday from 9 am to 4:30 pm, weekends 10 am to 5 pm.

On Race St is **Stone Row**, a collection of original row houses built by Asa Packer (1805-79), a wealthy industrialist who founded the Lehigh Valley Railroad. You

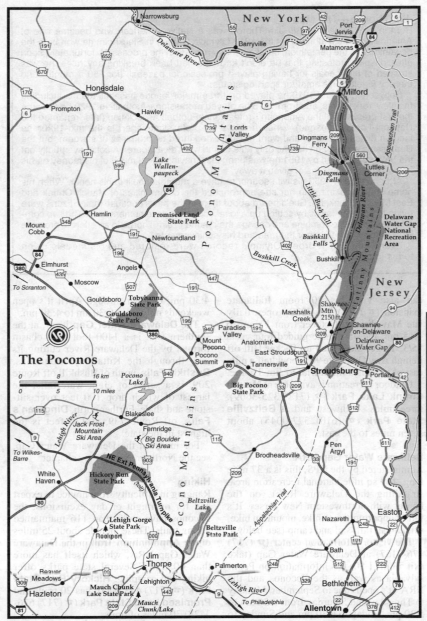

The Poconos

0   8   16 km
0   5   10 miles

Jim Thorpe – The Man

Born in Oklahoma in 1888, Jim Thorpe was a Native American who became one of America's greatest athletes. At the 1912 Olympic Games in Stockholm he won both the decathlon and the pentathlon, breaking many records in the process. Unfortunately, soon after, despite protesting that he didn't know he had been breaking any rules, he was stripped of his medals for having played professional baseball (for $60 a month) and thereby forfeiting his amateur sporting status.

Between 1913 and 1919 he played on three major league baseball teams, including the New York Giants, and from 1915 he played professional football. In 1920 he became the first president of the American Professional Football Association (later renamed the National Football League). When he gave up professional sport in the mid-1920s he found it difficult to adjust and went to Hollywood lured by promises of stardom, but the Depression arrived and he was only able to find work as a laborer. Alcohol eventually got the better of him and by 1951 he was penniless, having spent much of his money on his fellow Native Americans or given it away.

After he died in 1953 his wife sought to have a memorial built in his honor. When his home state wouldn't help her she approached the communities of Mauch Chunk and East Mauch Chunk, PA. She'd heard about them in the news because their citizens were trying to save the towns by setting up a local economic development fund. The two communities agreed to combine and change their name to Jim Thorpe in an effort to promote local tourism and to honor the man and his achievements..

Eventually, Jim Thorpe's Olympic records were restored and his medals given to his family. ■

can also visit his 20 room Italianate mansion (☎ (717) 325-3229), open daily late May through October from 11 am to 4:15 pm; the 45 minute guided tour costs $5/3. To get there head up Packer Hill off Lehigh Ave. On Route 903 about half a mile east of town is a **memorial** to Jim Thorpe.

Outdoor recreation is available at **Mauch Chunk Lake Park** (☎ (717) 325-3669), three miles southwest, and at **Beltzville State Park** (☎ (610) 377-0045) about seven miles to the east.

Delaware Water Gap NRA

Administered by the NPS, this is a 37 mile long, 109 sq mile national recreation area, straddling the Delaware River, on the border with northwestern New Jersey. It's full of opportunities to hike, mountain bike, ski, canoe, raft, sail and camp (see below).

The visitor information center (☎ (717) 476-0167) at Delaware Water Gap (take exit 53 off I-80) has information on Pennsylvania as well as the Poconos and the NRA. It's open June to September, Monday to Thursday and Saturday from 9:30 am to 5:30 pm, Friday to 6:30 pm and Sunday to

4:30 pm; October through April it's open weekends only from 9:30 am to 4:30 pm.

The **Delaware Water Gap** itself, at the southern end, is a 1400 foot high chasm formed by the Delaware River cutting its way through the Kittatinny Mountains. **Bushkill Falls**, north of Bushkill off Route 209, is a series of eight waterfalls, the largest of which drop 100 feet over siltstone and shale. Further north, **Dingman's Falls**, off Route 739, at 130 feet is the highest in the state.

For more on the Delaware Water Gap, see the Northern New Jersey chapter.

Hiking

Ranging in difficulty from novice to expert and for overnight or day excursions, the Poconos have more than 116 maintained hiking trails. These include about 25 miles of the **Appalachian Trail** in the Delaware Water Gap NRA, which itself has more than 60 trails. Several state parks offer hiking and camping. **Hickory Run State Park** (☎ (717) 443-0400) has 20 trails and **Promised Land State Park** (☎ (717) 676-3428) 30 miles of trails.

Mountain Biking

The Poconos have a variety of mountain biking facilities and many Pocono resorts offer bicycle riding (check in the *Poconos Vacation Guide*). Biking trails range from forest paths to canal towpaths and abandoned railroad beds. The **Switchback Gravity Railroad Trail**, an abandoned railroad bed in Lehigh Gorge State Park (☎ (717) 427-5000), is the longest rail-to-trail conversion in Pennsylvania.

Bicyclists can traverse more than 30 miles of gentle grades along the Lehigh River through the Lehigh Gorge near Jim Thorpe. In Jim Thorpe, Blue Mountain Sports & Wear (☎ (717) 325-4421), at Race and Susquehanna Sts, rents bikes for $25 per day.

Skiing

The Poconos have a number of large ski resorts.

Camelback (☎ (717) 629-1661, (800) 233-8100), PO Box 168, Tannersville, PA 18372, in Big Pocono State Park, has a vertical drop of 800 feet and snowboarding facilities; for a snow report call ☎ (800) 233-8100.

Shawnee Mountain (☎ (717) 421-7231, (800) 233-4218); PO Box 339, Shawnee-on-Delaware, PA 18356, has a vertical drop of 700 feet; for a snow report call ☎ (800) 233-4216.

Close to each other are Big Boulder Ski Area (☎ (717) 722-0101, (800) 468-2442), PO Box 702, Blakeslee, PA 18610; and Jack Frost Mountain Ski Area (☎ (717) 443-8425), PO Box 216, Blakeslee, PA 18610. The vertical drop at Big Boulder is 475 feet, at Jack Frost Mountain 600 feet; for a snow report to either call ☎ (800) 475-7669.

Cross-country ski trails can be found in the resorts, and many hiking trails in state parks and forests become cross-country ski trails in winter.

Watersports

Mauch Chunk Lake and Lake Wallenpaupeck are two of the many lakes offering opportunities for **sailing** and **canoeing**. For the more adventurous there's white-water canoeing and **rafting** on the Lehigh River through the Lehigh Gorge and on the Delaware River. A number of companies provide rentals and guided trips. Kittatinny Canoes (☎ (800) 356-2852), at Dingman's Ferry, has guided canoeing and rafting trips from $20 to $25 per person. Jim Thorpe River Adventures (☎ (717) 325-2570/4960, (800) 424-7238), 1 Adventure Lane, Jim Thorpe, has guided raft trips for four hours or longer from $36 to $45.

Adventure Sports (☎ (800) 487-2628), PO Box 175, Marshalls Creek, PA 18335, rents rafts and canoes for $23 per person (minimum of two in a canoe, four in a raft). Lehigh Rafting Rentals (☎ (717) 443-4441), PO Box 296, White Haven, PA 18661, rents canoes and rafts at similar rates.

For information on fishing see the Delaware Water Gap coverage in the Northern New Jersey chapter.

Places to Stay

Accommodations range from luxury resorts (including the 'couples resorts' with their heart-shaped pools and beds for honeymooners) and family resorts offering room-and-recreational packages to hotels, motels, B&Bs, housekeeping cottages, small country inns, an HI-AYH hostel and campgrounds. The *Poconos Vacation Guide*, available from the Pocono Mountains Vacation Bureau (see Orientation & Information, above) has a listing of accommodations and you can reserve a room by calling ☎ (800) 722-6667. Prices sometimes rise on weekends and public holidays.

Camping You can backpack along the Appalachian Trail and in the Delaware Water Gap NRA; see Hiking in the Outdoor Activities chapter.

Several state parks offer camping. *Hickory Run State Park* (☎ (717) 443-0400), south of the junction of I-80 and the northeast extension of the Pennsylvania Turnpike, and *Promised Land State Park* (☎ (717) 676-3428), off I-84, have campgrounds with toilets and showers as well as more primitive sites. *Tobyhanna State Park* (☎ (717) 894-8336), off Route 423, has 140 sites but no flush toilets or running water. Rates are $10 to $12.

There are also many private campgrounds. *Hemlock Campground* (☎ (717) 894-4388), 362 Hemlock Dr, Tobyhanna, PA 18466, has full facilities and well-spaced sites for $16. The secluded *Mt Pocono Campground* (☎ (717) 839-7573), PO Box 65, Mt Pocono, PA 18344, is off Route 196. It has a grocery store, hot showers and sites for $18.

Hostel The HI-AYH *La Anna Hostel* (☎ (717) 676-9076), RR 2, PO Box 1026, Cresco, PA 18326, is on La Anna Rd which runs between Routes 191 and 423 north of the village of La Anna. It has a kitchen, wood stove and 40 beds for $12; private rooms are available.

B&Bs Jim Thorpe has some beautiful old B&Bs. *Cozy Corner* (☎ (717) 325-2961), 504 North St, is in a Victorian house replete with antiques. It's open year round and has singles or doubles from $55/65 without/ with private bathroom. The *Alpine Inn* (☎ (717) 325-9484), 80 Broadway, is very central and has rooms with continental breakfast for $60. *Priscilla's* (☎ (717) 325-2617), 14 Race St opposite St Mark's Church, is a Federal-style house with rooms including private bath for $70.

Hotels & Motels In Jim Thorpe, the ornate, Victorian *Inn at Jim Thorpe* (☎ (717) 325-2599), 24 Broadway, has a restaurant and bar and rooms from $65/90.

In Stroudsburg, *Days Inn* (☎ (717) 424-1771), 100 Park Ave off Main St, has singles/doubles from $58/99. The *Best Western Pocono Inn* (☎ (717) 421-2200), 700 Main St, has rooms for $89 single or double. Business Route 209 south of town has more hotels.

Places to Eat

If you're self-catering, Stroudsburg and Jim Thorpe offer the best options to pick up supplies.

In Jim Thorpe, *Cafe on Broadway* is a small cafe good for soups and sandwiches and open from 9 am to midnight. The *Black Bread Cafe* (☎ (717) 325-8957), 47 Race St, serves soup (from $1.95) and a wide range of sandwiches, including a BLT for $4.25 and hoagies for $4.95; it also has vegetarian options. It's open for lunch daily and for dinner on weekends.

In Stroudsburg the restaurant in the *Best Western Pocono Inn*, 700 Main St, does standard food and is popular at breakfast time. A breakfast special or pancakes costs $3, oatmeal $1.25. Nearby, *Marita's*, also on Main St, is a brightly decorated Mexican restaurant open for lunch and dinner, with combinations of burrito and a taco of your choice for $6.95.

Getting There & Away

Bus Greyhound (☎ (800) 231-2222) runs through Jim Thorpe, between Philadelphia and Scranton, picking up and dropping people off at Susquehanna St and Broadway opposite the visitors center. Martz Trailways stops at Martz Express (☎ (717) 839-76110) in Mt Pocono and at Stroudsburg Travel Service (☎ (717) 421-3040) in Stroudsburg; it has regular services to Philadelphia, New York, Scranton and Wilkes-Barre.

Car & Motorcycle From Philadelphia the northeast extension of the Pennsylvania Turnpike leads directly into the Poconos, as does I-80 from New Jersey and I-84 from New York. I-81 south from New York state (Binghamton) skirts Scranton to join I-380 which connects with both I-84 and I-80.

Index

671

LONELY PLANET JOURNEYS

FULL CIRCLE: A South American Journey *by Luis Sepúlveda (translated by Chris Andrews)*
Full Circle invites us to accompany Chilean writer Luis Sepúlveda on `a journey without a fixed itinerary'. Extravagant characters and extraordinary situations are memorably evoked: gauchos organizing a tournament of lies, a scheming heiress on the lookout for a husband, a pilot with a corpse on board his plane . . . Part auto-biography, part travel memoir, *Full Circle* brings us the distinctive voice of one of South America's most compelling writers.

THE GATES OF DAMASCUS *by Lieve Joris (translated by Sam Garrett)*
This best-selling book is a beautifully drawn portrait of contemporary Syria. Through her intimate contact with local people, Lieve Joris explores women's lives and family relationships – the hidden world that lies behind the gates of Damascus.

IN RAJASTHAN *by Royina Grewal*
Indian travel writer Royina Grewal takes us behind the exotic facade of this fabled destination: here is an insider's perceptive account of India's most colorful state. *In Rajasthan* discusses folk music and architecture, feudal traditions and regional cuisine . . . Most of all, it focuses on people – from maharajahs to itinerant snake charmers – to convey the excitement and challenges of a region in transition.

ISLANDS IN THE CLOUDS: Travels in the Highlands of New Guinea *by Isabella Tree*
This is the fascinating account of a journey to the remote and beautiful Highlands of Papua New Guinea and Irian Jaya. The author travels with a PNG Highlander who introduces her to his intriguing and complex world. *Islands in the Clouds* is a thoughtful, moving book, full of insights into a region that is rarely noticed by the rest of the world.

KINGDOM OF THE FILM STARS: Journey into Jordan *by Annie Caulfield*
With honesty and humour, Annie Caulfield writes of travelling in Jordan and falling in love with a Bedouin. Her book offers fascinating insights into the country and unpicks some of the tight-woven Western myths about the Arab world within the intimate framework of a compelling love story.

LOST JAPAN *by Alex Kerr*
Lost Japan draws on the author's personal experiences of Japan over a period of 30 years. Alex Kerr takes his readers on a backstage tour: friendships with Kabuki actors, buying and selling art, studying calligraphy, exploring rarely visited temples and shrines . . . The Japanese edition of this book was awarded the 1994 Shincho Gakugei Literature Prize for the best work of non-fiction.

SEAN & DAVID'S LONG DRIVE *by Sean Condon*
Sean and David are young townies who have rarely strayed beyond city limits. One day, for no good reason, they set out to discover their homeland, and what follows is a wildly entertaining adventure that covers half of Australia. Sean Condon has written a hilarious, offbeat road book that mixes sharp insights with deadpan humour and outright lies.

SHOPPING FOR BUDDHAS *by Jeff Greenwald*
Shopping for Buddhas is Jeff Greenwald's story of his obsessive search for the perfect Buddha statue. In the backstreets of Kathmandu, he discovers more than he bargained for . . . and his souvenir-hunting turns into an ironic metaphor for the clash between spiritual riches and material greed. Politics, religion and serious shopping collide in this witty account of an enlightening visit to Nepal.

LONELY PLANET TRAVEL ATLASES

Lonely Planet has long been famous for the number and quality of its guidebook maps. Now we've gone one step further and in conjunction with Steinhart Katzir Publishers produced a handy companion series: Lonely Planet travel atlases–maps of a country produced in book form.

Unlike other maps, which look good but lead travelers astray, our travel atlases have been researched on the road by Lonely Planet's experienced team of writers. All details are carefully checked to ensure the atlas corresponds with the equivalent Lonely Planet guidebook.

The handy atlas format means no holes, wrinkles, torn sections or constant folding and unfolding. These atlases can survive long periods on the road, unlike cumbersome fold-out maps. The comprehensive index ensures easy reference.

* full-color throughout
* maps researched and checked by Lonely Planet authors
* place names correspond with Lonely Planet guidebooks
  –no confusing spelling differences
* legend and traveling information in English, French, German, Japanese and Spanish
* size: 230 x 160 mm

Available now:

Thailand; India & Bangladesh; Vietnam; Zimbabwe, Botswana and Namibia

Coming soon:

Chile; Egypt; Israel; Laos; Turkey

LONELY PLANET TV SERIES & VIDEOS

Lonely Planet travel guides have been brought to life on television screens around the world. Like our guides, the programs are based on the joy of independent travel, and look honestly at some of the most exciting, picturesque and frustrating places in the world. Each show is presented by one of three travelers from Australia, England or the USA and combines an innovative mixture of video, Super-8 film, atmospheric soundscapes and original music.

Videos of each episode–containing additional footage not shown on television–are available from good book and video shops, but the availability of individual videos varies with regional screening schedules.

Video destinations include: Alaska; Australia (Southeast); Brazil; Ecuador & the Galápagos Islands; Indonesia; Israel & the Sinai Desert; Japan; La Ruta Maya (Yucatán, Guatemala & Belize); Morocco; North India (Varanasi to the Himalaya); Pacific Islands; Vietnam; Zimbabwe, Botswana & Namibia.

Coming soon: The Arctic (Norway & Finland); Baja California; Chile & Easter Island; China (Southeast); Costa Rica; East Africa (Tanzania & Zanzibar); Great Barrier Reef (Australia); Jamaica; Papua New Guinea; the Rockies (USA); Syria & Jordan; Turkey.

The Lonely Planet TV series is produced by:
Pilot Productions
Duke of Sussex Studios
44 Uxbridge St
London W8 7TG UK

Lonely Planet videos are distributed by:
IVN Communications Inc
2246 Camino Ramon
California 94583, USA

107 Power Road, Chiswick
London W4 5PL UK

Music from the TV series is available on CD & cassette.
For ordering information contact your nearest Lonely Planet office.

LONELY PLANET PRODUCTS

Lonely Planet is known worldwide for publishing practical, reliable and no-nonsense travel information in our guides and on our web site. The Lonely Planet list covers just about every accessible part of the world. Currently there are eight series: *travel guides, shoestring guides, walking guides, city guides, phrasebooks, audio packs, travel atlases* and *Journeys*—a unique collection of travelers' tales.

EUROPE

Amsterdam • Austria • Baltic States & Kaliningrad • Baltic States phrasebook • Britain • Central Europe on a shoestring • Central Europe phrasebook • Czech & Slovak Republics • Denmark • Dublin city guide • Eastern Europe on a shoestring • Eastern Europe phrasebook • Finland • France • Greece • Greek phrasebook • Hungary • Iceland, Greenland & the Faroe Islands • Ireland • Italy • Mediterranean Europe on a shoestring • Mediterranean Europe phrasebook • Paris city guide • Poland • Portugal • Portugal travel atlas • Prague city guide • Russia, Ukraine & Belarus • Russian phrasebook • Scandinavian & Baltic Europe on a shoestring • Scandinavian Europe phrasebook • Slovenia • Spain • St Petersburg city guide • Switzerland • Trekking in Greece • Trekking in Spain • Ukrainian phrasebook • Vienna city guide • Walking in Britain • Walking in Switzerland • Western Europe on a shoestring • Western Europe phrasebook

NORTH AMERICA

Alaska • Backpacking in Alaska • Baja California • California & Nevada • Canada • Florida • Hawaii • Honolulu city guide • Los Angeles city guide • Mexico • Miami city guide • New England • New Orleans city guide • New York, New Jersey & Pennsylvania • Pacific Northwest USA • Rocky Mountain States USA • San Francisco city guide • Southwest USA • USA phrasebook • Washington, DC & The Capital Region

CENTRAL AMERICA & THE CARIBBEAN

Bermuda • Central America on a shoestring • Costa Rica • Cuba • Eastern Caribbean • Guatemala, Belize & Yucatán: La Ruta Maya • Jamaica

SOUTH AMERICA

Argentina, Uruguay & Paraguay • Bolivia • Brazil • Brazilian phrasebook • Buenos Aires city guide • Chile & Easter Island • Chile travel atlas • Colombia • Ecuador & the Galápagos Islands • Latin American Spanish phrasebook • Peru • Quechua phrasebook • Rio de Janeiro city guide • South America on a shoestring • Trekking in the Patagonian Andes • Venezuela

Travel Literature: Full Circle: A South American Journey

AFRICA

Arabic (Moroccan) phrasebook • Africa on a shoestring • Africa The South • Cape Town city guide • Central Africa • East Africa • Egypt & the Sudan • Egypt travel atlas • Ethiopian (Amharic) phrasebook • Kenya • Kenya travel atlas • Malawi • Morocco • North Africa • South Africa, Lesotho & Swaziland • South Africa travel atlas • Swahili phrasebook • Trekking in East Africa • West Africa • Zimbabwe, Botswana & Namibia • Zimbabwe, Botswana & Namibia travel atlas

ISLANDS OF THE INDIAN OCEAN

Madagascar & Comoros • Maldives & Islands of the East Indian Ocean • Mauritius, Réunion & Seychelles

Also Available: Antarctica • Travel with Children • Traveller's Tales

MAIL ORDER

Lonely Planet products are distributed worldwide. They are also available by mail order from Lonely Planet, so if you have difficulty finding a title please write to us. North American and South American residents should write to Embarcadero West, 155 Filbert St, Suite 251, Oakland CA 94607, USA; European and African residents should write to 10 Barley Mow Passage, Chiswick, London W4 4PH; and residents of other countries to PO Box 617, Hawthorn, Victoria 3122, Australia.

NORTH-EAST ASIA

Beijing city guide • Cantonese phrasebook • China • Hong Kong city guide • Hong Kong, Macau & Canton • Japan • Japanese phrasebook • Japanese audio pack • Korea • Korean phrasebook • Mandarin phrasebook • Mongolia • Mongolian phrasebook • North-East Asia on a shoestring • Seoul city guide • Taiwan • Tibet • Tibet phrasebook • Tokyo city guide

Travel Literature: Lost Japan

MIDDLE EAST & CENTRAL ASIA

Arab Gulf States • Arabic (Egyptian) phrasebook • Central Asia • Iran • Israel & the Palestinian Territories • Israel & the Palestinian Territories travel atlas • Istanbul city guide • Jerusalem city guide • Jordan & Syria • Jordan, Syria & Lebanon travel atlas • Middle East • Turkey • Turkey travel atlas • Turkish phrasebook • Trekking in Turkey • Yemen

Travel Literature: The Gates of Damascus

INDIAN SUBCONTINENT

Bengali phrasebook • Bangladesh • Delhi city guide • Hindi/Urdu phrasebook • India • India & Bangladesh travel atlas • Indian Himalaya • Karakoram Highway • Nepal • Nepali phrasebook • Pakistan • Rajasthan • Sri Lanka • Sri Lanka phrasebook • Trekking in the Indian Himalaya • Trekking in the Karakoram & Hindukush • Trekking in the Nepal Himalaya

Travel Literature: Shopping for Buddhas

SOUTH-EAST ASIA

Bali & Lombok • Bangkok city guide • Burmese phrasebook • Cambodia • Ho Chi Minh city guide • Indonesia • Indonesian phrasebook • Indonesian audio pack • Jakarta city guide • Java • Laos • Lao phrasebook • Laos travel atlas • Malay phrasebook • Malaysia, Singapore & Brunei • Myanmar (Burma) • Philippines • Pilipino phrasebook • Singapore city guide • South-East Asia on a shoestring • Thailand • Thai phrasebook • Thailand travel atlas • Thai audio pack • Thai Hill Tribes phrasebook • Vietnam • Vietnamese phrasebook • Vietnam travel atlas

AUSTRALIA & THE PACIFIC

Australia • Australian phrasebook • Bushwalking in Australia • Bushwalking in Papua New Guinea • Fiji • Fijian phrasebook • Islands of Australia's Great Barrier Reef • Melbourne city guide • Micronesia • New Caledonia • New South Wales & the ACT • New Zealand • Northern Territory • Outback Australia • Papua New Guinea • Papua New Guinea phrasebook • Queensland • Rarotonga & the Cook Islands • Samoa • Solomon Islands • South Australia • Sydney city guide • Tahiti & French Polynesia • Tasmania • Tonga • Tramping in New Zealand • Vanuatu • Victoria • Western Australia

Travel Literature: Islands in the Clouds • Sean & David's Long Drive

THE LONELY PLANET STORY

Lonely Planet published its first book in 1973 in response to the numerous 'How did you do it?' questions Maureen and Tony Wheeler were asked after driving, bussing, hitching, sailing and railing their way from England to Australia.

Written at a kitchen table and hand collated, trimmed and stapled, Across Asia on the Cheap became an instant local best seller, inspiring thoughts of another book.

Eighteen months in South-East Asia resulted in their second guide, South-East Asia on a shoestring, which they put together in a backstreet Chinese hotel in Singapore in 1975. The 'yellow bible', as it quickly became known to backpackers around the world, soon became the guide to the region. It has sold well over half a million copies and is now in its 8th edition, still retaining its familiar yellow cover.

Today there are 200 titles, including travel guides, walking guides, language kits & phrasebooks, travel atlases and travel literature. The company is one of the largest travel publishers in the world. Although Lonely Planet initially specialized in guides to Asia, we now cover most regions of the world, including the Pacific, North America, South America, Africa, the Middle East and Europe.

The emphasis continues to be on travel for independent travelers. Tony and Maureen still travel for several months of each year and play an active part in the writing, updating and quality control of Lonely Planet's guides.

They have been joined by over 50 authors and 155 staff at our offices in Melbourne (Australia), Oakland (USA), London (UK) and Paris (France). Travelers themselves also make a valuable contribution to the guides through the feedback we receive in thousands of letters each year.

The people at Lonely Planet strongly believe that travelers can make a positive contribution to the countries they visit, both through their appreciation of the countries' culture, wildlife and natural features, and through the money they spend. In addition, the company makes a direct contribution to the countries and regions it covers. Since 1986 a percentage of the income from each book has been donated to ventures such as famine relief in Africa; aid projects in India; agricultural projects in Central America; Greenpeace's efforts to halt French nuclear testing in the Pacific; and Amnesty International.

'I hope we send the people out with the right attitude about travel. You realize when you travel that there are so many different perspectives about the world, so we hope these books will make people more interested in what they see. These are guidebooks, but you can't really guide people. All you can do is point them in the right direction.'

– **Tony Wheeler**

LONELY PLANET PUBLICATIONS

Australia
PO Box 617, Hawthorn 3122, Victoria
☎ (03) 9819 1877 fax (03) 9819 6459
e-mail talk2us@lonelyplanet.com.au

USA
Embarcadero West, 155 Filbert St, Suite 251
Oakland, California 94607
☎ (510) 893 8555, TOLL FREE (800) 275 8555
fax (510) 893 8563
e-mail info@lonelyplanet.com

UK
10 Barley Mow Passage, Chiswick,
London W4 4PH
☎ (0181) 742 3161 fax (0181) 742 2772
e-mail 100413.3551@compuserve.com

France
71 bis rue du Cardinal Lemoine, 75005 Paris
☎ 1 44 32 06 20 fax 1 46 34 72 55
e-mail 100560.415@compuserve.com

World Wide Web: www.lonelyplanet.com